AF726177

TRADE IN KNOWLEDGE

Technological change has transformed the ways knowledge is developed and shared internationally. Accordingly, in the quarter-century since the WTO was established, and since its Agreement on Trade-Related Aspects of Intellectual Property Rights came into force, both the knowledge dimension of trade and the functioning of the IP system have been radically transformed. The need to understand and respond to this change has placed knowledge at the centre of policy debates about economic and social development. Recognizing the need for modern analytical tools to support policymakers and analysts, this publication draws together contributions from a diverse range of scholars and analysts. Together, they offer a fresh understanding of what it means to trade in knowledge in today's technological and commercial environment. The publication offers insights into the prospects for knowledge-based development and ideas for updated systems of governance that promote the creation and sharing of the benefits of knowledge.

ANTONY TAUBMAN is Director of the Intellectual Property, Government Procurement and Competition Division of the WTO Secretariat.

JAYASHREE WATAL is a former senior officer in the Intellectual Property, Government Procurement and Competition Division of the WTO Secretariat.

TRADE IN KNOWLEDGE

Intellectual Property, Trade and Development in a Transformed Global Economy

Edited by

ANTONY TAUBMAN

JAYASHREE WATAL

CAMBRIDGE
UNIVERSITY PRESS

CAMBRIDGE
UNIVERSITY PRESS

Shaftesbury Road, Cambridge CB2 8EA, United Kingdom

One Liberty Plaza, 20th Floor, New York, NY 10006, USA

477 Williamstown Road, Port Melbourne, VIC 3207, Australia

314–321, 3rd Floor, Plot 3, Splendor Forum, Jasola District Centre, New Delhi – 110025, India

103 Penang Road, #05–06/07, Visioncrest Commercial, Singapore 238467

Cambridge University Press is part of Cambridge University Press & Assessment, a department of the University of Cambridge.

We share the University's mission to contribute to society through the pursuit of education, learning and research at the highest international levels of excellence.

www.cambridge.org
Information on this title: www.cambridge.org/9781108490429

DOI: 10.1017/9781108780919

© 2022 The World Trade Organization

This publication is in copyright. Subject to statutory exception and to the provisions of relevant collective licensing agreements, no reproduction of any part may take place without the written permission of Cambridge University Press & Assessment.

First published 2022

A catalogue record for this publication is available from the British Library

ISBN 978-1-108-49042-9 Hardback
ISBN 978-1-108-74847-6 Paperback

Cambridge University Press & Assessment has no responsibility for the persistence or accuracy of URLs for external or third-party internet websites referred to in this publication and does not guarantee that any content on such websites is, or will remain, accurate or appropriate.

CONTENTS

FIGURES

TABLES

CONTRIBUTORS*

VITO AMENDOLAGINE is an Assistant Professor in Political Economy at the University of Bari. His research is focused on international trade and development economics. He has an MSc in Economics and Econometrics from the University of Essex, a PhD in Economics from the University of Bari and a PhD in Economics from the University of Glasgow. He has working experience with UNIDO, the London School of Economics and the University of Pavia.

LEE BRANSTETTER is a Professor of Economics and Public Policy at Carnegie Mellon University, where he directs the Future of Work initiative at the Block Center for Technology and Society. He is also a non-resident senior fellow at the Peterson Institute for International Economics and a research associate of the National Bureau of Economic Research. He served as a Senior Economist at the Council of Economic Advisers in 2011–2012. Branstetter has conducted research in the domains of innovation, the economics of intellectual property, international technology transfer and international trade and investment.

MIRA BURRI is a Senior Lecturer at the Faculty of Law of the University of Lucerne, Switzerland. She teaches international intellectual property, media, and Internet and trade law. Mira's current research interests are in the areas of digital trade, culture, copyright, data protection and Internet governance. Mira is the principal investigator of 'The Governance of Big Data in Trade Agreements' project, which is sponsored by the Swiss National Science Foundation. She consults for the European Parliament, UNESCO and others on issues of digital innovation and cultural diversity. Mira has co-edited the publications *Trade Governance in the Digital Age* (Cambridge University Press 2012) and *Big Data and Global Trade Law* (Cambridge University Press 2020). She is the author of *Public Service*

* Correct as of 2020.

Broadcasting 3.0: Legal Design for the Digital Present (Routledge 2015). Mira's publications are available at: http://ssrn.com/author=483457.

ANTONIA CARZANIGA is Counsellor in the Trade in Services and Investment Division at the World Trade Organization (WTO). She is an economist with a BSc degree from Bocconi University, Italy, and an MA degree from the College of Europe, Belgium, and the London School of Economics, UK. She has worked in the WTO since 1998. She is the Secretary of the WTO Council for Trade in Services and deals, inter alia, with issues relating to the movement of natural persons (mode 4), various transport services and e-commerce. She has conducted many technical assistance activities focused on services trade and the disciplines of the General Agreement on Trade in Services, including for economies seeking to accede to the WTO. Ms Carzaniga has published extensively on matters relating to trade in services and has contributed to many expert fora, conferences and academic seminars.

CRISTINA CHAMINADE is a full Professor in Innovation Studies at Lund University (Sweden) and Adjunct Professor at Aalborg University (Denmark). She holds a BA and PhD in Economics from the Autonomous University of Madrid (UAM). The focus of her research is on global networks and the processes of knowledge creation and adoption that underpin innovations and the transformations towards sustainable forms of living (economic, social and environmental). She has actively worked on innovation in developing countries such as China, India, South Africa, Thailand and Brazil for over 20 years. She has been an advisor to international organizations such as the European Commission, UNCTAD, OECD and UN-ECLAC. She has published in international journals, refereed books and handbooks in the fields of innovation, development studies and knowledge management such as research policy, industry and innovation, innovation and development and european planning studies. She is editor of the *Journal of Innovation and Development*, the *International Journal of Innovation* and the *Journal of Sustainability Research.*

LAURIE CIARAMELLA is Assistant Professor at Telecom ParisTech, and Affiliated Research Fellow at the Max Planck Institute for Innovation and Competition (MPI). Prior to that, she was Senior Research Fellow at the MPI, affiliated with the Innovation and

Entrepreneurship research group. Laurie obtained her PhD in Economics from Mines ParisTech-PSL in 2017. She also holds a Masters degree in Economics of Markets and Organizations from the Toulouse School of Economics. In her research, Laurie conducts empirical studies in economics of innovation, with a focus on the determinants and consequences of markets for technology. She is particularly interested in the interplay of these markets and taxation, digital transformation and firm strategy. Laurie's PhD dissertation received the Best Dissertation award, finalist of the TIM division of the Academy of Management 2018 in Chicago.

NIGEL CORY is an associate director at the Information Technology and Innovation Foundation covering trade policy at the Information Technology and Innovation Foundation. He focuses on cross-border data flows, data governance, intellectual property, and how they each relate to digital trade and the broader digital economy. He previously worked as a researcher in the Southeast Asia Program at the Center for Strategic and International Studies. Prior to that, he worked for eight years in Australia's Department of Foreign Affairs and Trade, which included positions working on G20 global economic and trade issues and the Doha Development Round. Cory also had diplomatic postings in Malaysia, where he worked on bilateral and regional trade, economic and security issues, and in Afghanistan, where he was the deputy director of a joint US–Australia provincial reconstruction team. Cory holds an MA degree in public policy from Georgetown University and a BA degree in international business and commerce from Griffith University in Brisbane, Australia.

MERCEDES DELGADO is Associate Professor of Strategy and Innovation at Copenhagen Business School and Research Scientist at the MIT Innovation Initiative. She serves as Senior Institute Associate at the Institute for Strategy and Competitiveness at Harvard Business School. Delgado's research focuses on the relationship between the regional business environment and the performance of inventors, firms, regions and countries. She examines the role of regional clusters – geographic concentrations of related industries, firms and supporting institutions – in job creation, innovation, entrepreneurship, inclusivity and resilience. Delgado has developed new methods for defining and mapping industry clusters and the supply chain economy, providing tools to help firms, practitioners and policymakers create regional and national strategies.

JEFF C. DODD is the Director of the BBG Information Policy Institute, Houston, Texas. He is the author of *Modern Licensing Law* (Thomson West 2019) and a new edition of *Drafting Effective Contracts* (Wolters Kluwer 2020), both of which he previously co-authored with the late Professor Raymond T. Nimmer of the University of Houston Law Center. He and Lorin Brennan are updating Professor Nimmer's *Information Law* and *The Law of Computer Technology* (both with Thomson West 1985) and are planning new editions for both. He has written and lectured extensively on licensing and information law topics, has been an adjunct at the University of Law Center and has been a lecturer at Beijing Normal University. He is currently a partner at Hunton Andrews Kurth, LLP.

JACOB DUBBERT was an extern with the Office of the Chief Economist at the United States Patent and Trademark Office (USPTO). He is currently a Research Economist in the Business Research Division at the University of Colorado, Boulder, where he focuses on researching and forecasting the Colorado and US economies. His research interests include international trade, economic policy and machine learning. Jacob holds an MA in Global Finance, Trade and Economic Integration from the University of Denver and a BA in Finance from Colorado State University.

HOLGER ERNST is full Professor of Business Administration, especially technology and innovation management at the WHU – Otto Beisheim School of Management, in Vallendar, Germany. He is a regular Visiting Professor and a member of the Center for Research in Technology and Innovation at the Kellogg School of Management at Northwestern University, USA. He is also Honorary Professor and Principal Fellow within the Faculty of Business and Economics at the Melbourne Business School, The University of Melbourne, Australia. Professor Ernst has published about 50 papers in the fields of innovation, technology, new product development and intellectual property management in leading journals such as *Journal of Marketing, Journal of Product Innovation Management, Research Policy* and others. He has won multiple research and best teacher awards. He is also a member of the editorial boards of

Journal of Product Innovation Management, *Creativity and Innovation Management* and *Journal of Knowledge Management*. Professor Ernst is co-founder of PatentSight GmbH, a LexisNexis Company, located in Bonn, Germany. He advises and speaks to corporations worldwide and he supports start-ups as a business angel.

LISA C. FRIEDMAN received her PhD in biochemistry from the University of Wisconsin–Madison. Her professional career spans work in the biotechnology and software industries, with special expertise in network science. She is a cofounder of PatentVector LLC.

ALEXANDER V. GICZY is a Data Scientist (Addx Corporation) with the Office of the Chief Economist at the United States Patent and Trademark Office (USPTO) and was previously a patent examiner in the field of aerospace systems. Prior to joining the USPTO, Alex served 25 years in the United States Air Force, holding numerous leadership positions in systems development and acquisition, systems engineering and space operations. His research interests include machine learning, innovation policy and technology development. Alex holds an MS in Business Analytics from the George Washington University, an MA in Public Policy from Harvard University, and a BS in Astronautical Engineering from the United States Air Force Academy.

KAYLA GRANT is Development Operations Consultant at the Inter-American Development Bank, Washington, DC.

CARSTEN C. GUDERIAN is Senior Project Leader at PatentSight GmbH, a LexisNexis company, in Bonn, Germany, and Lecturer at the Friedrich-Alexander-University Erlangen-Nuremberg in Fürth, Germany. Carsten's research focuses on patent analytics and patent valuation.

JOSÉ GUIMÓN is Associate Professor of Economics at the Autonomous University of Madrid (UAM) and Researcher at the UAM-Accenture Chair in Economics and Management of Innovation. He works regularly as a policy analyst/consultant for international organizations such as the OECD, the European Commission and the World Bank. He sits on the Executive Committee of the European Forum for Studies of Policies for Research and Innovation (Eu-SPRI Forum).

JORGE GUTIERREZ is a licensed attorney in Panama, specialized in intellectual property. In 2018, he worked as a Young Professional at the Intellectual Property, Government Procurement and Competition Division of the World Trade Organization (WTO). In this capacity he supported the work of the WTO Secretariat with matters relating to The Agreement on Trade-Related Aspects of Intellectual Property Rights (TRIPS), by planning, coordinating and delivering technical assistance and capacity-building activities, and assisting in preparations for TRIPS Council meetings, among other duties. Gutierrez holds an MA in Intellectual Property, Social Networks and New Technologies from ESADE, Spain, as well as a Law degree and an MA in Procedural Law from the Universidad Catolica Santa Maria La Antigua in Panama.

MARGARET KYLE (PhD, MIT Economics) studies innovation, productivity and competition, including R&D productivity in the pharmaceutical industry, specifically the role of geographic and academic spillovers; the firm-specific and policy determinants of the diffusion of new products; generic competition; and the use of markets for technology. Recent work examines the effect of trade and IP policies on the level, location and direction of R&D investment and competition. She currently holds the Chair in Markets for Technology and Intellectual Property at MINES ParisTech and is a member of the Conseil National de Productivité in France. She is an associate editor at the *International Journal of Industrial Organization* and a Research Fellow at the Centre for Economic Policy. She previously held positions at Carnegie Mellon University, Duke University, London Business School and the Toulouse School of Economics. She has also been a Visiting Scholar at the Federal Reserve Bank of San Francisco, the University of Hong Kong and Northwestern University.

MARY LAFRANCE is the IGT Professor of Intellectual Property Law at the William S. Boyd School of Law, University of Nevada, Las Vegas. She previously taught at Florida State University, in both the College of Law and the School of Motion Pictures, Television, and Recording Arts. She received her JD with High Honors from the Duke University School of Law, where she served as Executive Editor of the *Duke Law Journal*. She simultaneously earned her MA in Philosophy from the Duke University School of Graduate Studies. Prior to teaching, she clerked for Judge Harry T. Edwards of the United States Court of Appeals for the DC

Circuit, and practised law for three years with the Washington, DC office of Fried, Frank, Harris, Shriver & Jacobson. In addition to her law review articles and book chapters, Professor LaFrance has authored or co-authored six books, including *Intellectual Property Cases and Materials* (Thomson West 2018), *Understanding Trademark Law* (Carolina Academic Press 2019), *Understanding Intellectual Property Law* (Carolina Academic Press 2019), *Global Issues in Copyright Law* (West 2009), *Entertainment Law on a Global Stage* (West 2015), and *Copyright Law in a Nutshell* (West 2017).

TRAVIS J. LYBBERT, a Professor at the University of California, Davis in the Agricultural and Resource Economics Department, has published research on topics in applied microeconomics ranging from poverty dynamics, climate change and childhood nutrition to technology adoption, intellectual property and innovation policy. Collaborating with researchers, students, NGOs, governments, and private firms, he has lived and worked in India, Haiti, and throughout Sub-Saharan Africa, North Africa and Europe. He currently serves as Co-Editor of the *American Journal of Agricultural Economics.* He was a Fulbright Scholar in Morocco before earning his MS (2000) and PhD (2004) in Applied Economics from Cornell University.

JOSCELYN MAGDELEINE is an Economic Affairs Officer in the Trade in Services and Investment Division of the World Trade Organization. His sectoral responsibilities include health-related services and many business services. He is also responsible for the Services Integrated-Trade Intelligence Portal (I-TIP services) database. Before joining the Trade in Services and Investment Division in 2014, he was responsible for trade in services statistics-related issues in the WTO's Statistics Group. He notably contributed to the *UN Manual on Statistics of International Trade in Services.* He has participated in many technical assistance and capacity-building activities on GATS as well as on trade in services statistics in Africa, Asia, the Middle East, Latin America and South Eastern Europe. Before joining the WTO in 2003 he worked in the OECD for seven years, mainly on services-related issues.

KEITH E. MASKUS is Professor of Economics and former Associate Dean for Social Sciences at the University of Colorado, Boulder, USA. He has been a Lead Economist in the Development Research Group at the

World Bank. He is also a Research Fellow at the Peterson Institute for International Economics, a Fellow at the Kiel Institute for World Economics, and an Adjunct Professor at the University of Adelaide. He has been a Visiting Professor at the University of Bocconi and a visiting scholar at the CES-Ifo Institute at the University of Munich and the China Center for Economic Research at Peking University. He serves also as a consultant for the World Bank and the World Intellectual Property Organization and recently chaired a panel of the National Research Council on intellectual property management in standards-setting organizations.

ANDREAS MAURER is Chief of the International Trade Statistics Section at the WTO. He studied economics with a specialization in public finance and statistics/econometrics at the University of Hohenheim and holds a doctorate (Dr.oec.) in economics. In 1990, he joined the United Nations Economic Commission for Europe. He was editor-in-charge of the *Statistical Journal of the UN ECE*. Since 1994, he has worked with GATT/WTO. His current interests include measuring trade in services flows, trade in value added and digital trade.

WOLF R. MEIER-EWERT is Counsellor in the Intellectual Property, Government Procurement and Competition Division of the World Trade Organization (WTO), which is responsible for the administration of the Agreement on Trade-related Aspects of Intellectual Property Rights (TRIPS Agreement). In this capacity he gives legal advice in relation to intellectual property and the TRIPS Agreement to members and observers of the WTO and deals with TRIPS-related dispute settlement cases among WTO members. He serves as the Secretary to the TRIPS Council, the governing body of the TRIPS Agreement, and was Secretary to the Special Session of the TRIPS Council, the negotiating group dealing with TRIPS negotiations under the Doha Round.

Mr. Meier-Ewert is a graduate of the University of Oxford, UK, where he studied Politics, Philosophy and Economics (PPE) and holds a Law degree from the Ludwig-Maximilian University in Munich, Germany. He has widely lectured on TRIPS and WTO-related matters.

THOMAS NEUBIG was appointed Deputy Head of CTPA's Tax Policy and Statistics Division in May 2014. He has over 30 years' experience as an economist in both government and the private sector. He has spent the last 20 years at EY where he founded and lead a group of 34 tax policy economists, statisticians and survey specialists. Mr Neubig is EY's Director of Quantitative Economics and Statistics, where he serves as an advisor to numerous public and private clients on federal, state and global tax policy issues, including revenue and economic impact. He holds a BA degree in Economics from Kalamazoo College and a PhD in Economics from the University of Michigan.

KEITH NURSE is Principal of the Sir Arthur Lewis Community College in St. Lucia, Senior Advisor on Structural Policies and Innovation at the OECD Development Centre, member of the executive bureau of the UN Committee for Development Policy and former WTO Chair and Senior Fellow at the University of the West Indies.

ERICK S. OH was, from 2004 to 2019, an International Trade Analyst in the Services Division, Office of Industries, at the United States International Trade Commission, a US government agency tasked with providing information and analysis on issues of trade and competitiveness to the US Trade Representative and the US Congress. While at the USITC, Mr Oh wrote on a wide variety of services trade issues but his particular focus was audiovisual services, including online content. He was a major contributor to many USITC reports, including US–Mexico-Canada Trade Agreement: Likely Impact on the US Economy and on Specific Industry Sectors, Inv. TPA-105-003 (April 2019); Recent Trends in US Services Trade 2018 Annual Report (June 2018); Global Digital Trade 1: Market Opportunities and Key Foreign Trade Restrictions, Inv. 332-561 (July 2017); Trans-Pacific Partnership Agreement: Likely Impact on the US Economy and on Specific Industry Sectors, Inv. TPA-105-001 (May 2016); Recent Trends in US Services Trade: 2015 Annual Report, Inv. 332-345 (May 2015); Digital Trade in the US and Global Economies, Part 1, Inv. 332-531 (July 2013), and Digital Trade in the US and Global Economies, Part II, Inv. 332-540 (August 2014). While at the USITC, Mr Oh also published working papers and trade briefings on a range of topics, including Nigeria's film industry, and the growing services sectors in India and Vietnam.

NICHOLAS A. PAIROLERO is an Economist with the Office of the Chief Economist at the United States Patent and Trademark Office. His research interests include the economics of innovation, intellectual property and applied microeconomics. Nick holds a BBA in Economics and Mathematics from the University of Wisconsin Eau Claire, an MA in Economics from Indiana University, Bloomington, and a PhD in Economics from Indiana University, Bloomington.

ROBERTA PIERMARTINI is Chief of Trade Costs Analysis at the WTO. Her research focuses on trade and trade policy analysis. Her papers have been published in *The American Economic Journal* and the *Journal of International Economics* among others and she has authored various books. She is one of the lead authors and coordinators of the World Trade Report (WTR) and WTO-WBG publications on trade and poverty. She is author of 'A Practical Guide to Trade Policy Modelling' (WTO 2012) and 'An Advanced Guide to Trade Policy Modelling' (WTO 2016). She has served the WTO Dispute Settlement in several Panel and Arbitration cases. Prior to joining the WTO in 2000, she was Lecturer in Economics and Statistics at the University of Southampton and Research Fellow in the research division of Confindustria. She has also taught at the University of Geneva and LUISS. She holds a PhD in Economics from the University of Southampton.

ROBERTA RABELLOTTI is Professor of Economics at the University of Pavia and also holds a position as Adjunct Professor at the University of Aalborg. Her research is focused on innovation in developing countries, clusters, global value chains (GVC), and foreign direct investment (FDI) and multinationals. She has published widely in international journals and her last book was *Upgrading to Compete: Global Value Chains, Clusters, and SMEs in Latin America* (Harvard University Press 2007).

GAÉTAN DE RASSENFOSSE is Assistant Professor Tenure Track in Science & Technology Policy at EPFL (Lausanne, Switzerland). He joined the Institute of Technology and Public Policy at the College of Management of Technology at EPFL in late 2014. Prior to that, he was a research fellow then a senior research fellow at the University of Melbourne (Australia) from 2010 to 2014. He was affiliated with the Melbourne Institute of Applied Economic and Social Research at the Faculty of Business and Economics. Gaétan obtained a PhD in Economics from the Université libre de Bruxelles (Belgium), Solvay

Brussels School of Economics and Management in 2010. The overarching objective of Gaétan's research is to provide the policy environment that best addresses the needs of the knowledge economy. This objective is met by providing sound empirical evidence on research questions related, for example, to intellectual property issues, to the measurement of intangible capital, and to higher education systems to name but a few topics of interest. His work has appeared in international peer-reviewed scientific journals, such as *Strategic Entrepreneurship Journal, Journal of Economics & Management Strategy*, *Research Policy* and *European Economic Review.*

MARCO RICHTER is Managing Director at PatentSight GmbH, a LexisNexis company, in Bonn, Germany. He has been involved in patent analytics for more than 10 years. Marco consults for and collaborates with various firms, for example members of the DAX 30 (Germany), Nikkei 225 (Japan) and S&P 500 (USA).

MARTIN ROY is Counsellor in the Trade in Services and Investment Division of World Trade Organization. With the WTO since 2002, he has been involved in various functions relating to negotiations, technical assistance, dispute settlement, and policy research. He is the Secretary to the Special Session of the Council for Trade in Services. Between 2014 and 2016, he was senior advisor at the Office of the Chief Trade Advisor for Pacific Island Countries, in Vanuatu. Dr Roy has published widely on such topics as trade in services, foreign investment, and regional economic integration. He co-edited the *Research Handbook on Trade in Services*, published by Edward Elgar (2016), and *Opening Markets for Trade in Services: Countries and Sectors in Bilateral and WTO Negotiations*, published by Cambridge University Press (2008).

STELA RUBÍNOVÁ is a Research Economist at the Economic Research and Statistics Division of the World Trade Organization (WTO). She joined the WTO in 2016 and contributed to several publications, including the annual World Trade Reports. She also co-authored an ILO–WTO publication on *Investing in Skills for Inclusive Trade* and co-coordinated the World Trade Report 2019 on the Future of Services Trade. Stela's research topics are at the junction of international economic integration, global value chains, and economic growth. She holds a PhD in International Economics from the Graduate Institute of International and Development Studies, Geneva.

FLORIAN SELIGER is Senior Researcher in the Innovation Group at the KOF Swiss Economic Institute at ETH Zurich. In his work on empirical innovation economics, he combines firm and regional-level data with patent data. He is an experienced user of patent databases and innovation survey data. His research interests include knowledge spillovers, technology clusters and the internationalization of R&D. He is a project leader of international projects on patent data, including external collaborations with academic institutions in Switzerland and Germany.

ALICIA SHEPHERD is a creative industries consultant and graduate of the Sir Arthur Lewis Institute of Social and Economic Studies, University of the West Indies.

ERICA SMITH is a PhD graduate of the University of Agder, Norway and CEO of the Copyright Society of Composers, Authors & Publishers Inc. in Barbados.

MICHAEL D. SMITH is a Professor of Information Technology and Marketing at Carnegie Mellon University. He received his BSc in Electrical Engineering (summa cum laude) and his MSc Telecommunications Science from the University of Maryland, and received his PhD in Management Science and Information Technology from the Sloan School of Management at MIT. Professor Smith's research uses economic and statistical techniques to analyse firm and consumer behaviour in online markets – specifically markets for digital information and digital media products. Prior to receiving his PhD, Professor Smith worked extensively in the telecommunications and information systems industries, first with GTE in their laboratories, telecommunications and satellite business units, and subsequently with Booz Allen and Hamilton as a member of their telecommunications client service team. While with GTE, Professor Smith was awarded a patent for research applying fuzzy logic and artificial intelligence techniques to the design and operation of telecommunications networks.

LUCAS SPADANO is a partner at the Brazilian law firm Fialho Salles Advogados, focusing on international trade regulations, intellectual property and competition law. He is a PhD candidate in International Law (USP), currently taking part in the WTO PhD Support Program. He has an LLM (with merit) in International Business Law (London School of Economics); he also has Executive MBA (Fundação Dom Cabral); Bachelor of Laws (UFMG); and Bachelor of International Relations (PUC Minas) degrees.

LUIZA TÂNGARI COELHO is a Senior Associate at the Brazilian law firm Fialho Salles Advogados, focusing on intellectual property law, data protection and commercial agreements. She has an LLM in Commercial Law (University of Cambridge); she also has Specialization in Intellectual Property Law (University of South Africa/WIPO) and Bachelor of Laws (UFMG) degrees.

ANTONY TAUBMAN is Director of the WTO's Intellectual Property, Government Procurement and Competition Division. He formerly directed the Global Intellectual Property Issues Division of WIPO (including the Traditional Knowledge Division and Life Sciences Programme), covering IP and genetic resources, traditional knowledge and folklore, the life sciences, and related global issues including public health and climate, the environment, climate change, human rights, food security, bioethics and indigenous issues. He earlier held appointments in the Australian diplomatic service and worked in private practice as a patent attorney, and he has held a number of academic and teaching positions. He has published widely on international IP law and policy, and cognate policy and legal questions. His education encompasses law, international relations, computer science, mathematics, philosophy, classical Greek and theology.

RAHUL TELANG is Professor of Information Systems and Management at the Heinz College at Carnegie Mellon University and at the Tepper School of Business, with an interest in how information and communication technologies, and associated digitization of information impact consumers, business and policies. His research has a particular focus on how digitization (and associated piracy) in copyrighted industries is affecting the incentives of content providers, distributors and users, and the economics of information security and privacy. Dr Telang has published extensively in many top management and policy journals like *Management Science*, *Marketing Science*, *ISR*, *MIS Quarterly*, *Journal of Industrial Economics*, *Journal of Policy and Management*, and NBER chapters. He held senior editor positions at *ISR* (Information Systems

Research) and *MIS Quarterly*. Dr Telang provides extensive consulting and speaking at various firms.

ANDREW A. TOOLE is the Chief Economist at the US Patent and Trademark Office (USPTO) and a Research Associate at the Centre for European Economic Research (ZEW). Dr Toole joined the USPTO with experience in the private sector, academia and government. While completing his PhD in Economics at Michigan State University, Andrew Toole was a Senior Economist for Laurits R. Christensen Associates, where he conducted studies on total factor productivity, cost and price analysis and competitive strategy. In 1998, Dr Toole went to Stanford University as a postdoctoral student before becoming a faculty member at Illinois State University and Rutgers University in New Jersey. As an academic researcher, Dr Toole was asked to advise on science and technology policy issues for institutions such as the US National Academies of Science, US National Institutes of Health, and the US Department of Agriculture (USDA). In 2010, he joined the Science Policy Branch of USDA's Economic Research Service. His research focuses on the economics of innovation, intellectual property, and related science and technology policies. Dr Toole has published in the *Journal of Law and Economics*, the *Review of Economics and Statistics*, *Research Policy*, *Management Science*, and many other peer-reviewed journals.

ANDREW W. TORRANCE is Earl B. Shurtz Research Professor at the University of Kansas School of Law, and the winner of a 2015 University Scholarly Achievement Award at the University of Kansas. He received his PhD in Biology from Harvard University in 1997, JD from Harvard Law School in 2000, and BSc from Queen's University (Canada) in 1991. He joined the University of Kansas School of Law in 2005. Torrance teaches and conducts research in patent law, intellectual property, innovation, food and drug regulation, biotechnology law, biodiversity law, biolaw, and empirical, experimental, and big data approaches to the law. Specific research foci include open, user and collaborative innovation, design, and legal issues surrounding genes, biotechnology, genetically-modified organisms, synthetic biology, conservation biology, and de-extinction.

LEE TUTHILL is a senior staff member of the WTO responsible for telecommunications, ICT services, and electronic commerce. In these areas, she follows policy, regulatory practices, and trends in technology and business models. She is responsible for keeping up to date on how ICT trade and e-commerce developments relate to the WTO and General Agreement on Trade in Services (GATS). She frequently conducts multi-stakeholder national and regional workshops on e-commerce work taking place within the WTO. For many years, she has also provided technical assistance to telecommunications/ICT regulators on the implementation of GATS provisions (including the disciplines of the GATS Annex on Telecommunications and the Reference Paper commitments on sector regulation). She also helps governments who are negotiating WTO accession or free trade agreements with the technical aspects of drafting their commitments in the sectors she covers. She has worked at the WTO since 1990 and graduated from Columbia University in 1980 with an MA in International Affairs.

JAYASHREE WATAL was Counsellor in the Intellectual Property, Government Procurement and Competition Division of the WTO from 2001 to 2019, contributing to work on TRIPS and public health, TRIPS-CBD, Patents, Undisclosed information, Economics of TRIPS, IP and Transfer of Technology, IP and Climate Change, and IP and Competition Policy.

She currently holds a part-time Adjunct Professor position at the Georgetown University Law Centre, the position of Honorary Professor at the National Law University, Delhi, and has been a member of the Governance Board of the Medicines Patent Pool, a non-profit organization based in Geneva since 2015.

Ms Watal holds post-graduate degrees in both law and economics and, prior to joining the WTO, she had more than 22 years of experience in government in India. She represented India at a crucial stage in the Uruguay Round TRIPS negotiations from 1989 to 1990.

She is the co-editor of two WTO books: *A Handbook on the TRIPS Agreement* (Cambridge University Press 2012) and *The Making of the TRIPS Agreement* (WTO 2015). She has also authored *Intellectual Property Rights in the WTO and Developing Countries* (Oxford University Press, India and Kluwer Law International, 2001) and several peer-reviewed journal articles on issues related to the law/economics of intellectual property rights.

JACQUES DE WERRA is Professor of Contract Law and of Intellectual Property at the Law School of the University of

Geneva, Switzerland. He authored a doctoral thesis in Swiss and comparative copyright law, which he completed as a Visiting Scholar at the Max-Planck Institute for Intellectual Property, Competition and Tax Law in Munich in 1996. He then practised law in Switzerland, before obtaining an LLM degree from Columbia Law School in New York City in 2001 and being admitted to the New York bar in 2002. Jacques researches, publishes and discusses on topics related to various aspects of intellectual property law, contract law, particularly on the commercialization of intellectual property assets with the use of transfer of technology, licensing and franchising, IT and Internet and digital law, as well as alternative dispute resolution mechanisms for IP and technology disputes.

SACHA WUNSCH VINCENT is Head of the Composite Indicator Research Section, Economics and Statistics Division, and Co-Editor of the Global Innovation Index (GII) at the World Intellectual Property Organization (WIPO). He joined WIPO as Senior Economist in 2010 to help set up WIPO's economics work under the Chief Economist, including the World Intellectual Property Report and the GII. Before joining WIPO, he was an Economist and Co-Leader of the Innovation Strategy Project at the OECD Directorate for Science, Technology and Industry. Prior to that, he was the Swiss National Science Fellow at the Berkeley Center for Law and Technology, University of California, Berkeley, and the Peterson Institute for International Economics, Washington, DC. He is currently preparing a book on 'Harnessing Public Research for Innovation in the 21st Century: An International Assessment of Knowledge Transfer Policies' with Anthony Arundel and Suma Athreye for Cambridge University Press. He holds an MA in International Economics from the Maastricht Economic Research Institute on Innovation and Technology, University of Maastricht, and a PhD in Economics from the University of St Gallen, Switzerland. He teaches international economics at Sciences Po Paris and the World Bank Institute.

PETER K. YU is Regents Professor of Law and Communication and Director of the Center for Law and Intellectual Property at Texas A&M University. Born and raised in Hong Kong, he previously held the Kern Family Chair in Intellectual Property Law at Drake University Law School and was Wenlan Scholar Chair Professor at Zhongnan

University of Economics and Law in Wuhan, China. He served as a Visiting Professor of law at Bocconi University, Hanken School of Economics, Hokkaido University, the University of Haifa, the University of Helsinki, the University of Hong Kong and the University of Strasbourg.

NIKOLAS J. ZOLAS is a Senior Economist with the Center for Economic Studies at the US Census Bureau. Nikolas's research interests are in innovation, intellectual property and technology transfer. His work has been published in *Research Policy*, *Science*, *Journal of Regional Science* and more. Nikolas received his PhD from the University of California, Davis. Prior to receiving his PhD, Nikolas started a non-profit agency and worked in finance.

PREFACE

It is now more than 25 years since the WTO TRIPS Agreement entered into force, setting intellectual property (IP) standards at the centre of multilateral trade rules. The quarter-century since then has seen a fundamental transformation in the scale, diversity and very nature of cross-border commercial transactions in knowledge and knowledge products. An array of technological, economic, social and policy factors has driven this transformation and diversification. The disruptive impact of technological change – the prospects that it brings for sustainable development and for a more equitable world, along with concerns about its potential to displace and disenfranchise, and to entrench inequities – has placed it at the centre of policy debates and practical initiatives about economic and social development, and indeed a host of wider public policy issues today. The framing of the United Nations Sustainable Development Goals (SDGs) in 2015 – a blueprint for international cooperation and national action towards an ambitious set of targets in 2030 – was striking for the high degree of recognition of the need for the development and implementation of new technologies to address fundamental development needs. Innovation, as such, was recognized as a development goal in itself.

As international officials charged with providing policy support to developing country members of the WTO, we have been increasingly struck by the demand from a wide range of policymakers and officials for a fresh, up to date and inclusive information platform to support a truly contemporary discussion and practically relevant planning of technical cooperation that reflects the current understanding of the economic, legal and policy aspects of trade in knowledge today. The TRIPS Agreement was concluded in the absence of any understanding of the dramatic impact of the development of the Internet and increasing global access to digital networks. Indeed, it is a piquant historical irony that Tim Berners-Lee was in the process of inventing the World Wide Web at CERN, in Geneva, a few minutes away from the negotiating rooms where the text of the TRIPS Agreement was being hammered out at exactly the same time. Yet TRIPS did not account for the revolutionary upheaval in the way knowledge would be created, disseminated and traded once the Web had reached the wider community; its negotiating roots could be found in attempts in the 1970s and 1980s to develop a code on counterfeit trade, with a concentration on IP as part of the added value in traded physical goods, rather than as a tradable good in itself. As an agreement on 'trade-related aspects' of intellectual property rights, TRIPS set the stage for the impending fundamental transformation of the relationship between IP and trade.

The volume is intended to serve as a conceptual and empirical foundation for a renewed set of policy discussions, capacity building and technical assistance for governments seeking to engage with the knowledge economy for development, through new trade, business and employment opportunities. It seeks to review the legal character and economic implications of international transactions that facilitate the transfer or diffusion of new knowledge and intangible content, through traditional trade channels and new forms of business and knowledge transfer. To provide a complete picture, we have aimed to include legal, policy and economic analysis in a coherent manner. Thus we sought accounts of how knowledge crosses international borders in different ways, and how to measure these flows, as well as the analysis of legal and policy scholars reviewing the evolving laws, regulations and policies that govern such trade, and analysing the legal character of knowledge transactions in today's international economy.

In a call for papers, we set out several broad research questions:

1. How can we measure different forms of global cross-border flows of knowledge and knowledge products, including digital content? What can we say from the relevant data about the scale, and geographical and time trends (for example, pre-TRIPS and post-TRIPS) of such flows?
2. What legal and policy questions are raised by current trends in cross-border knowledge flows?
3. What can we say about the effects of knowledge flows on economic development, growth and productivity; domestic innovation; technology transfer; trade, especially high-tech trade and trade in digital content; and the development opportunities afforded by new avenues for trade and employment?

4. What is the relationship of such knowledge flows to improved creation of and access to global public goods, especially technologies for agriculture, health and climate change, and (information and communication technology) ICT?
5. What can we say about the legal and economic character of trade in digital content covered by intellectual property rights (IPRs), including issues arising from global or regional regulatory frameworks, new business models for content distribution, and cross-border licensing and enforcement?
6. What is the current experience in specific sectors, and in markets for IPRs as such, and what insights does this experience offer policymakers?

We were delighted at the strong, positive response elicited by this call for essays, and the willingness of the leading international scholars whom we invited to contribute. While we cannot expect this broad and ambitious set of questions to have been definitively answered, we believe that the scholarly work collected in this volume should establish a stronger and more up-to-date empirical, theoretical and methodological basis for a vital continuing international conversation centred on these questions. We hope that policymakers and scholars will continue to return to these questions, armed with greater insights and greater curiosity sparked by an encounter with this book.

The book project was greatly enhanced by several peer-review sessions, in particular the Seminar on Intellectual Property and Knowledge Flows in a Digital Era, convened at the WTO in November 2018, as a follow up to the call for papers. This Seminar drew together over 40 policymakers from developing and least developed countries around the world, who were joined by 20 internationally renowned economist lawyers and policymakers. Their discussions on how to map and assess the impact of knowledge flows across borders and charting their legal, economic and policy dimensions helped inform and consolidate the scheme for this book and served to strengthen and make more practical and relevant the contributions that are now gathered together in this collection. The Seminar considered five broad themes that in turn helped to shape this book: mapping the interface between trade, intellectual property rules and knowledge flows; measuring trade in knowledge; the impact of knowledge flows on trade and development; policy, regulatory and legislative frameworks; and the way forward on trade rules and economic implications for cross-border knowledge flows.

Addressing the Seminar, the WTO Deputy Director General responsible for this field, Mr Xiaozhun Yi, remarked that

> The TRIPS Agreement was a landmark recognition of the importance of the knowledge component of trade. Yet in the years since conclusion, digital disruption has utterly transformed the interplay between trade and knowledge. This radical transformation creates a compelling need to update our understanding of the context for TRIPS rules and the intellectual property system within the framework of trade and development policy. We need to fundamentally update both our theoretical understanding, and the empirical, factual base we work from.
>
> This is important, too, because in this period, development policy has laid increasing emphasis on the knowledge component of trade, and has raised practical questions of how developing economies can make best use of the opportunities provided by the knowledge economy: SDG 9, notably, identifies innovation as such as a goal for sustainable development.
>
> The WTO's technical assistance activities have sought to respond to evolving demand from developing country Members for capacity building in these areas, but in a relatively ad hoc way, largely as an adjunct to existing programme structures, and these activities have demonstrated the unmet demand and practical need for more systematic capacity building on an updated base of information.[1]

This demand follows the disruptive effect of technological change which has impacted significantly on the area of trade involving IP rights, and the exercise of policy options under the TRIPS Agreement, opening up new avenues for development as IP in itself becomes a tradable good and IP plays a pivotal role in dispersed international production chains and in facilitating knowledge transfer. Policymakers therefore confront an entirely new set of challenges integrating TRIPS measures into trade policies that respond to a digitally transformed knowledge economy; these challenges extend to basic capacity to measure and to map the IP dimension of trade, and thus to develop an integrated understanding of how the IP system, and new forms of trading in knowledge, can function in the contemporary international economy to service diverse national development priorities.

Recognizing the need for this initiative to retool and rebase the WTO's technical assistance in the TRIPS area, responding to the fundamentally transformed technological and trade landscape, the themes of this book were also the subject of a focused session at the WTO's Aid for Trade Global Review 2019. Hence the initiative for this book was elaborated in

[1] See www.wto.org/english/news_e/news18_e/trip_08nov18_e.htm.

dialogue with policymakers and officials from across the developing world and is intended to provide a scholarly, but practical and forward-looking, resource as the foundation for a new generation of technical assistance and policy dialogue.

This collaborative and consultative background, but more importantly the remarkable quality, timeliness and cross-disciplinary character of the authors' contributions, inspires hope that this volume – and the associated resources at www.wto.org/trade-in-knowledge – will indeed help to catalyse a fresh, contemporary approach to policy development and technical assistance in the complex, but critical, area of today's trade in knowledge, where the IP system and knowledge flows interact in ever more diverse ways.

We are profoundly grateful to the authors who have so generously devoted their time and efforts to produce invaluable new scholarship and policy insights. Our opening chapter seeks to outline each of their contributions and to set them into the broader framework of this book and the aspirations we have for it, and we trust that this will encourage the reader to explore their work in full, beyond the chapters contained here, as among the roll of authors are many who have made a major contribution to scholarship and policy development. We count ourselves as most fortunate to have among these authors invaluable colleagues who are also new or long-established friends, and we thank them for their support and their patience as this project moved forwards.

For his encouragement and support, we thank Deputy Director-General Yi, and also record our warm thanks to our colleagues, Anthony Martin and Heather Sapey-Pertin of the WTO's Information and External Relations Division for their advice, support and patience, Karyn Russell who provided cheerful and efficient administrative support throughout the editorial process and Giovanni Bertinelli and Francesco Hernandez Fernandez for their scrupulous attention to final editorial corrections.

At Cambridge University Press, we are indebted to Kim Hughes for her encouragement and support at a critical early stage.

Co-editors
Antony Taubman
Jayashree Watal

1

Thematic Overview: Charting the Evolution of Knowledge Flows

ANTONY TAUBMAN AND JAYASHREE WATAL

Introduction: Trade in Knowledge Today

The Nexus: Knowledge Flows, Trade and Intellectual Property

Understanding cross-border flows of knowledge, often associated with transactions involving intellectual property (IP), is essential to analysing how modern economies grow and evolve, and how international trade can underpin technological development. How to stimulate knowledge flows and make more effective, systematic use of them is an immediate practical concern for contemporary policymakers and analysts seeking to frame and implement policies for economic and technological development, that strengthen innovation systems and tap into indigenous creative and innovative capacity. Trade is understood to serve as a major conduit for the knowledge dissemination and technology spillovers that are essential for sustainable development today. And the IP system has been crafted and implemented ostensibly to facilitate both innovation and the dissemination of the fruits of innovation. Trade in knowledge as such – transactions specifically over the licensing or transfer of IP rights, for instance – has become a practical reality and a major source of dynamism and disruption. The complex and dynamic interaction between the IP system and international trade is therefore critical to our understanding of knowledge flows and their contribution to development.

Yet technological change – digital disruption – is today itself increasingly a factor reshaping and diversifying the ways in which knowledge is developed, managed, transacted and disseminated. Accordingly, in the quarter-century since the WTO was established, and since its Agreement on Trade-Related Aspects of Intellectual Property Rights ('TRIPS') came into force, both the knowledge dimension of trade and the functioning of the IP system have been radically transformed. Many salient aspects of these developments have been closely studied by scholars. Yet, when surveying available material to respond to WTO members' increasing interest in understanding these complex phenomena, we found few resources that look at knowledge flows, trade patterns and the evolution of the IP system in an holistic way, while responding also to the development implications of technological change.

Hence the WTO Secretariat initiated a dialogue between policymakers and analysts, including a call for papers, several workshops and a peer review process, to fill this gap in available materials, an effort culminating in the present edited collection of readings and cutting-edge analysis. This volume forms a central part of the Secretariat's efforts to build an up-to-date, inclusive and empirically well-founded information platform to support policy development by its members in this critical but challenging area.

Structure

The book is organized in four substantive parts, corresponding to four dimensions of the need for systematic understanding of cross-border knowledge flows or 'trade in knowledge':

(i) an overview of the conceptual framework for trade, IP and international knowledge flows
(ii) possibilities and challenges for measuring trade in knowledge
(iii) the impact of knowledge flows on trade and development
(iv) considerations for the governance frameworks that apply to these knowledge flows.

The present chapter provides a general introduction to the book, along with a thematic overview of the individual chapters contained in each of these parts. A concluding chapter then aims to draw together observations and insights from the substantive chapters and to offer ideas for future directions in research and policy dialogue.

Background

Knowledge flows, and their trade and development impacts, have come to the forefront of contemporary trade policy and trade relations. Governments seek to clarify and redefine their economic and development interests in the light of the disruptive effects of technological change, the changing patterns of production and trade, and fundamental shifts in innovative and technological capacity.

The qualitatively more diverse and quantitatively higher cross-border knowledge flows since the 1990s have in part been associated with a process of diversification of production capacity, associated with the rapid development of emerging economies, notably in Asia. This evolution was, in turn, partly driven by the ICT revolution which so dramatically improved rapid and secure communications that it enabled the rise of global production chains or value chains – a transformation that Baldwin has termed 'the second unbundling', as physical steps in the production process (following the 'first unbundling', which had separated consumers from producers). As he has phrased it:

> Globalization accelerated again from around 1990, when the information and communication technology (ICT) revolution radically lowered the cost of moving ideas. This launched globalization's next phase—call it the 'second unbundling' since it involves the international separation of factories. Specifically, radically better communications made it possible to coordinate complex activities at distance. Once this sort of offshoring was feasible, the North–South wage gap that had arisen during the first unbundling made it profitable.
>
> The offshoring of production stages to low-wage nations changed globalization, but not just because it shifted jobs overseas. To ensure that the offshored stages meshed seamlessly with those left onshore, rich-nation firms sent their marketing, managerial, and technical know-how along with the production stages that had been moved offshore. As a consequence, the second unbundling—sometimes called the 'global value chain revolution'—redrew the international boundaries of knowledge. The contours of industrial competitiveness are now increasingly defined by the outlines of international production networks rather than the boundaries of nations.[1]

Perhaps not entirely coincidentally, economists – notably Paul Romer – were at the same time recognizing that knowledge was a key and endogenous parameter in a country's economic development, and could no longer be considered an external factor when modelling economic growth. As he observed at a 1992 World Bank conference on development:

> All too often, economists concerned with the economy as a whole have been willing to treat the economics of ideas as a footnote to the rest of

[1] Richard Baldwin, *The Great Convergence*, Cambridge, MA: Harvard University Press, 2016, 5–6.

> economic analysis – important for understanding some of the details but not something that changes how we think about big policy questions. A neoclassical model with perfect competition and exogenous technological change continues to frame many, if not most, policy discussions of growth and development. Ideas are routinely ignored … ideas are extremely important economic goods, far more important than the objects emphasized in most economic models. In a world with physical limits, it is discoveries of big ideas (for example, how to make high-temperature superconductors), together with the discovery of millions of little ideas (better ways to sew a shirt), that make persistent economic growth possible. Ideas are the instructions that let us combine limited physical resources in arrangements that are ever more valuable.[2]

He argued at that time that it is necessary to 'take seriously the economic opportunities presented by the potential for producing new ideas and for diffusing existing ideas to the widest possible extent. In so doing, we must recognize that ideas are economic goods which are unlike conventional private goods and that markets are inherently less successful at producing and transmitting ideas than they are with private goods'.[3]

Just at the time that such economic analysis was emphasising the necessity – and the significance for policymakers – of incorporating knowledge into models of growth and development, trade negotiators, led by the then industrialized countries, negotiated the TRIPS Agreement in order to increase legal certainty and predictability in the transfer of knowledge. Formally concluded in 1994 and entering into force the following year, its text had been essentially settled by 1992.[4] The Agreement laid out minimum standards for the protection, use and enforcement of intellectual property rights that all WTO members would have to follow, while also incorporating provisions on technology transfer for least-developed countries and express scope for policymakers to craft laws to facilitate the flow of knowledge. The incorporation of the TRIPS Agreement into the package of international trade law that came into effect upon the formation of the WTO in 1995 meant that it

[2] Romer, Paul M., 'Two Strategies for Economic Development: Using Ideas and Producing Ideas', Proceedings of the Annual World Bank Conference on Development 1992, Supplement, Washington, DC, World Bank Economic Review, 1993, at 63.

[3] Ibid., 89.

[4] For individual negotiators' accounts of the TRIPS negotiations, and a thematic overview of the negotiations, see Jayashree Watal and Antony Taubman, *The Making of the TRIPS Agreement: Personal Insights from the Uruguay Round Negotiations*, Geneva: WTO, 2015, available at: www.wto.org/english/res_e/booksp_e/trips_agree_e/history_of_trips_nego_e.pdf.

comprised a core element of the emerging legal and economic framework for what were to be the largest global transfers of knowledge in the period from the 1990s to the present day.

The period since 1995 has seen a fundamental transformation not only in the character and impact of digital technologies, but also in the geographical distribution of innovators and associated IP right owners, especially patents. Over this period, due specifically to the digital revolution, creative cultural content that used to be traded as physical goods are now sold on digital platforms online directly to markets across the globe – a burgeoning 'trade in knowledge' that frees valuable content from the physical carrier media once relied upon to transport it. Such 'digital disruption' offers new opportunities for development, as small traders and creative industries in the developing world can potentially overcome traditional obstacles to trade, although significant challenges remain, with concerns about the potential effects on beneficial competition of dominant online platforms and the difficulty of establishing alternative avenues for knowledge trade. Equally, the management of IP and IP licensing transactions constitute significant elements of dispersed global production chains and play a key role also in the knowledge spillovers resulting from IP-based transactions.

Conceptual Framework

Part I of this book sets out the conceptual framework about what we consider to be trade in knowledge in relation to trade in goods, services and intellectual property. We note the growing importance of trade in intangibles, distinguishing the delivery of knowledge-intensive services from the charges for the use of IP such as licence fees and royalties. We also note the rise in trade of digital products and services, and the IP dimension of such trade, in view of the fact that much of this trade is constituted as transactions in IP rights, whether through the purchase of licences or the transfer of ownership. Finally, this part looks at the existing IP framework for trade in knowledge, analysing both the TRIPS Agreement itself in its contemporary context, as well as provisions in subsequent trade agreements that have bearing both on IP in the digital environment and on trade in digital products; it then broadly points to the emerging policy issues and possible gaps in the regulatory framework thus far.

Antony Taubman's introductory chapter sets the framework for the book. He charts the evolution and diversification of trade in knowledge that has taken place in the quarter-century since the TRIPS Agreement came into force. Entirely new markets have come into being and, arguably, the very character of 'trade' is in need of reconsideration. For instance, the disruptive effect of digital technology has meant that much of the content formerly conceived of as 'added value' embedded in physical carrier media, traded and measured as 'goods', is now traded in the form of specific licences that use IP rights covering the content that is now increasingly accessed online in digital form. Taubman outlines how these new forms of exchange in valuable intangible content confront fundamental assumptions about the nature of trade and its interaction with the IP system, forcing a rethink of what constitutes the 'trade-related aspects' of intellectual property. The issues examined include the principle of territoriality of IP rights and the segmentation of markets according to national jurisdictions; the structuring of cross-border commercial exchanges into the two discrete categories of 'goods' and 'services'; the emerging disparity in regional trade agreements between provisions on digital IP standards and on digital products and e-commerce; and the significance of IP rights being treated as assets in investment treaties. The chapter concludes that – whatever formal or legal overlay is applied to these new trading arrangements – it is essential to understand that this is now trade in IP licences as such, rather than trade in goods that have an IP component as an adjunct or ancillary element. Just as Romer and others demonstrated the need for economic growth theory to incorporate intangible knowledge as an endogenous factor, rather than maintaining it as exogenous to models of growth, trade policy must similarly work to incorporate an understanding of the trade in IP licences itself within cross-border commercial exchanges as an integral element of international trading relations. This means treating the exchange and licensing of IP rights systematically and effectively as 'endogenous' to trade. This is essential for an accurate empirical picture of trade relations today, given the economic significance both of dispersed global value chains and of trade in 'pure' IP content as such, particularly in the creative sectors.

Lee Tuthill, Antonia Carzaniga and Martin Roy look at the ways digital technologies have stimulated the information component of services trade and consequently enhanced trade in both goods and services that embody knowledge. They illustrate the role that ICTs have taken on as conduits for digital and digitally-enabled trade. Their chapter briefly describes six important digital developments, namely the cloud, data analytics, (so-called 'big data'), Internet of Things (IoT), artificial intelligence, robotics and three-dimensional (3D) printing. These technologies are transforming the tradability of services, increasing the growth of cross-border services supplied electronically, across a wide range of sectors, from medical, to educational, financial, audiovisual or professional services. This chapter covers, in broad strokes, the landscape of policy challenges that governments confront as they seek to adapt, including policies that could potentially disrupt the growth of cross-border digital trade such as localization of data. Finally, the chapter provides illustrations of ways negotiators of trade rules have begun to shape new legal frameworks via regional trade agreements (RTAs) that elaborate upon and, in some respects, extend beyond existing multilateral trade rules. For example, in some cases, WTO members with no GATS commitments in basic telecommunication services made RTA commitments on the sector, with no limitations. However, trade disciplines allow countries to take measures to pursue legitimate policy objectives, provided that they are not applied in a manner that would constitute a means of arbitrary or unjustifiable discrimination or a disguised restriction on trade.

Wolf R. Meier-Ewert and Jorge Gutierrez explore how regulatory responses to emerging IP issues in digital trade may develop at the international level. In particular, the authors examine how existing mechanisms might influence the chances of developing internationally agreed rules in this regard. The authors note that the primacy of state sovereignty in intellectual property up to the late nineteenth century gave way to the important World Intellectual Property Organization (WIPO) treaties, which still retained some independence of member states and based international regulatory responses directly on national experience. While more regulatory sovereignty was ceded in TRIPS, the WIPO Copyright Treaty and the WIPO Performances and Phonograms Treaty, the adoption of non-binding instruments (such as the WIPO Joint Recommendations in the area of trademarks) show the limits of decision-making by consensus. International non-state solutions such as the Uniform Domain-Name Dispute-Resolution Policy (UDRP) established by the Internet Corporation for Assigned Names and Numbers (ICANN) have introduced separate, technically determined solutions to specific IP issues. Proliferating free trade agreements (FTAs) have emerged as a new platform to agree to IP-related regulatory responses that can be used to project the national solutions of a few dominant FTA partners. However, these FTAs have also served to give legally binding status to internationally agreed non-binding recommendations.

The authors go on to highlight how these diverse approaches are apparent in recent IP-regulatory responses to emerging digital issues that are particularly relevant for digital business models, including inter alia Internet service provider (ISP) liability, 'safe harbour' provisions and the issue of orphan works, where there appears to be less agreement. Still further away from reaching any kind of agreement are the emerging issues of online exhaustion, data mining and IP-related questions of artificial intelligence.

Measuring Trade in Knowledge

Part II of this book discusses the possibilities and challenges for measuring trade in knowledge and what these measurements tell us about recent trends in cross-border knowledge flows. It benefits from chapters contributed by some of the leading researchers in the field. Their work measures both absolute and relative cross-border flows, and trends both in terms of dominant technologies as well as geographical distribution using different metrics. The two key sources of data explored are the balance-of-payments (BoP) statistics collected by the International Monetary Fund (IMF), and patent statistics.

Andreas Maurer and Joscelyn Magdeleine focus on an analysis of the statistics on IP-related transactions recorded as goods and services in international balance-of-payments data – in effect, an incomplete measure of trade in IP as such, although a measure with its shortcomings. Their chapter opens this part of the book because this has been the standard means of measuring cross-border knowledge flows through trade:[5] accordingly, it provides the baseline for improved – more accurate and comprehensive – measurements of cross-border payments for charges for the use of IP, and the authors helpfully identify how statistics could be made more complete and accurate. They chart how licence fees for the use of IP have increased more than four-fold since 1995, twice as fast as exports of high-tech goods and 1.5 times faster than the overall increase of trade in commercial services. This trade, which is driven in part by global production arrangements, remains highly concentrated geographically, with the US and the EU (28) accounting for more than 76 per cent of the receipts in 2016. However, they note how the data suffer from serious lacunae in that only a very small number of mainly

[5] See https://data.worldbank.org/indicator/BM.GSR.ROYL.CD.

OECD countries report complete information, and there are several definitional problems that prevent a full understanding of the dimension, direction and other details of trade in IP-related products. The authors conclude by making several recommendations to consider in order to improve the statistical basis, including the creation of a new international dataset covering international IP-related flows.

Throwing some doubts over the conclusions that can be drawn from an uncritical view of the BoP statistics described in the previous chapter, Thomas Neubig and Sacha Wunsch-Vincent show how tax planning by multinational enterprises has seriously distorted the measurement of cross-border IP flows and affected national measurements of imports, exports, GDP and productivity. The main data sources assessing these flows are described and the main distortions to these flows are assessed. Focusing on the implications of differing taxation regimes, the chapter describes the tax effects on cross-border IP measures in more detail and measures the magnitude of and trends in the tax distortions. The authors estimate that overall tax-induced mis-measurement could be more than 35 per cent of the Charges for Use of Intellectual Property (CUIP), being more for individual countries, particularly those with high tax rates. The authors suggest some initial possible approaches to reducing mis-measurement distortions.

Elucidating general patterns of the more valuable technical knowledge flow across borders from patent citations and patents network data, Andrew W. Torrance, Jevin D. West and Lisa C. Friedman test three specific hypotheses designed to shed light on such flows. The first is general, and is inspired by a growing interest in technology transfer between the developed and developing world: the net flow of more valuable technical knowledge tends to be from more developed to less developed countries. It transpires that the importance of citing developed world patents is much greater on average than citing developing world patents throughout the entire time period from 1985 to 2018. From 2010 onwards, the disparity narrows somewhat, in large part due to China. The second hypothesis concerns the trajectory of pharmaceutical knowledge flow between developed and developing countries. Developing world pharmaceutical patents cited by developed world patents also exhibited a general rising trend. However, the average importance of cited developing world patents remained consistently far above that of the developed world level, again in no small measure due to China. This may mean that while smaller numbers of pharmaceutical patents are filed by developing countries, these tend to be more important inventions.

Overall, pharmaceutical patent trends in citations, aggregate importance and mean importance do not appear to diverge meaningfully from those for patents across all technological fields. The third hypothesis concerns the trajectory of climate change mitigation knowledge flow (especially from developed to developing countries) after the 1997 Kyoto Protocol and the 2015 Paris Agreement on climate change. Looking only at wind-power patents, the authors reject conclusions from earlier more general studies and tell us that there is no clear evidence that the Kyoto Protocol influenced any of the metrics used to characterize wind technology patent knowledge flows but there are some positive trends after the Paris Agreement, which, given how recent these data are, should be treated with great caution. One striking observation apparent from the analyses in this chapter is that US patents make up a huge proportion of patent citations, patent importance and technical knowledge flow within the developed world. Similarly, China has recently come to dominate patent citations, patent importance and technical knowledge flow within the developing world.

Laurie Ciaramella, Gaétan de Rassenfosse and Florian Seliger provide a long-term view on the sources of knowledge flow between developed and developing nations. The authors rely on patent data to explore three potential sources of cross-border knowledge flows: R&D collaboration, technology sourcing and technology transfer. R&D collaboration is measured by looking at patents that are co-invented or co-applied for by parties in two different countries. Technology sourcing is measured by patents that are applied for by a party in one country but invented in another country. Technology or knowledge transfer is measured using information on the transfers of ownership (i.e. sales) of patents. All three sources provide very consistent conclusions. First, knowledge flows with East Asia, particularly China, are occurring more frequently. Second, knowledge flows are increasingly concentrated in information and communication technologies. Third, while the United States and Canada traditionally have greater patenting activity with Asia than with Europe, the share of activity between Europe and Asia has been increasing in recent years. Fourth, greater patenting activity between the United States and Canada and Asia implies that the US/Canada region is more likely to benefit from reverse knowledge flows as China progresses towards becoming a technological leader.

Jacob Dubbert, Alexander V. Giczy, Nicholas A. Pairolero and Andrew A. Toole provide a valuable survey of empirical studies on cross-border trade in knowledge that use IPRs data. This review finds that most studies use IPRs data, primarily patent documents, as direct indicators of innovation, technology transfer and knowledge flows. Most of the direct indicators are constructed using patent counts, patent citations, licensing and royalty payments, and patent families. The authors also find IPRs data are also used in indirect ways to characterize the relationship between two or more entities (e.g. countries, industries, firms) and serve to measure the degree of technology transfer or knowledge flow. Studies also use IPRs data to construct indexes of country-level IPRs strength, various metrics of IPRs intensity, technological proximity and technology transfer or knowledge flow through inventor mobility across countries. The authors conclude that IPRs data are a valuable source of information for learning about technology transfer and knowledge flows across borders. These data can help to inform the evidence base for policymaking so long as decision-makers are aware of the limitations of such data, such as territoriality, missing contexts and variability, so that not too much is read into the findings.

Erick S. Oh focuses in his chapter on recent developments in the digital content industry. He opens his review with a brief discussion of the data limitations that challenge the analysis of this market, and continues with overviews of the key characteristics, important trends and competitive landscapes in each of the major digital content sectors – video games, video on demand (VoD), digital music, and e-publishing (primarily e-books). He describes how more than half of the global digital content market is for video games, China surpassing the US in 2017 as the largest contributor to this sector. The next most important sector is VoD, where the US has about 60 per cent of the global market, thanks to the domination of a few US companies. While this market is getting increasingly competitive, the new entrants are again American entities. China is the second largest consumer of VoD, with that market mainly serviced by Chinese companies. The last two sectors are smaller and their growth is hampered to some extent by copyright infringement issues. Oh also explains how artificial intelligence has been used to good effect to increase market penetration in these different areas. The chapter ends with a short summary of intellectual property rights issues and barriers that are currently affecting the global digital content industry, providing a valuable conceptual framework overview for the issues that are dealt with in Part III of this volume, such as the chapter by Smith and Telang.

Vito Amendolagine, Cristina Chaminade, José Guimón and Roberta Rabellotti measure cross-border knowledge flows through yet another variable, namely foreign direct investment in R&D. The authors provide an overview of R&D FDI during the period 2003–2017, analysing key trends of greenfield investments and acquisitions by region and industry. Their main finding is that R&D FDI is highly concentrated in a few large emerging countries such as China and India, and in just a few regions and cities within these countries. Such FDI is also confined to a handful of industries, notably ICT and chemicals. The authors build their analysis on the assumption that learning opportunities for low- and middle-income countries (LMICs) are larger when multinational enterprises (MNEs) collaborate in innovation with local firms, universities and public research institutes, and focus on inward R&D FDI as a driver of economic development and catching-up for LMICs. Their chapter delves into the motivations and implications of this type of FDI, building on a critical review of the existing literature. Finally, the authors provide suggestions for a future research and policy agenda, focusing on the opportunities and challenges for LMICs.

Holger Ernst, Carsten C. Guderian and Marco Richter examine the metric of mergers and acquisitions to provide insights into cross-border knowledge flows. They demonstrate how novel patent analytics based on standardized international patent data available to policymakers and managers can help trace specific knowledge flows via mergers and acquisitions. Mergers shape both current and future knowledge flow, inter alia, by affecting the incentives and capabilities of the merged firm to innovate. The European Commission's decision to approve the Dow/DuPont merger shows how to measure relevant knowledge flows by means of novel patent analytics, moving beyond conventional patent indicators. Such patent analytics are used in this chapter to trace and assess cross-border knowledge flows. Their analysis – consistent with other chapters in this part – finds that high-quality patents are still largely developed in the US and Europe. However, Asian countries such as China, Japan and the Republic of Korea are catching up rapidly in terms of patent strength and patent quality. The destinations of global patent flows have also changed significantly over time. The authors also show that China has become an important destination for patents, reflecting its increasing role as an important knowledge destination market for many countries, especially Germany. They demonstrate how policymakers and managers can use future-oriented, quantitative patent analytics to improve policy decisions related to cross-border knowledge flows and innovation.

Impact of Knowledge Flows on Trade and Development

Part III of this book deals with the impact of knowledge flows on trade and development. Some chapters are focused on trade and more particularly on what we can learn from the effect of knowledge inflows on trade and also the effect of trade on creating more knowledge, particularly highlighting the case of global production chains. Others provide specific policy guidance to LMICs on what they should do to further enhance inflows of knowledge. We begin this Part with a comprehensive survey of the literature from two of the leading scholars on technology flows who tell us what economists have found so far with respect to the theory and empirical evidence on the impact of international knowledge flows on international trade, growth, productivity and innovation of the recipient country.

Keith E. Maskus and Lee Branstetter consider the key lessons presented by more than two decades of past and ongoing empirical research on international knowledge flows, including their own earlier work (which itself is a leading contribution to scholarly understanding of the field). They recognize the disparities in the emerging and developing world between those countries with sufficient size, economic dynamism and the necessary complementary skills to learn deeply from the global stock of knowledge, and those countries without such advantages. The insights gained help them explain why the income and productivity gains from information globalization do not diffuse as widely as basic models would suggest. The important question of how R&D investments have been globalized, primarily by MNEs, and the implications for knowledge flows are discussed. They demonstrate the crucial role played by investments in human capital and the acquisition of technological capabilities in technology receiving countries. Empirical economic research amply demonstrates that knowledge acquisition and use increasingly requires complementary technical skills within an economy. Achieving broad skill endowments may not be feasible in poor countries for some time, suggesting that investing in deeper skills that may be deployed in global information networks could be a better development strategy. The authors also draw lessons from interesting experimental work aimed at improving education delivery in India through the use of artificial intelligence (AI). Together, these insights point to the need for a broader understanding of how knowledge is transmitted and could be better absorbed in the current era. Maskus and Branstetter conclude with some policy inferences, including that the measured effect of local IPR (and other policies) on the actual incidence of technology transfer tends to be highest in the richer developing countries because these are precisely the places where local skill levels support a significant degree of technology transfer.

Margaret Kyle and Mercedes Delgado focus on cross-border knowledge flows through international trade in the post-TRIPS era. They examine trade patterns following the introduction of intellectual property (IP) rights, with a specific focus on a country's compliance with TRIPS. The authors compare how imports and exports of IP-intensive products changed versus a control group of products for which IP is less critical. Using data from 1993 to 2016 for 151 countries, they show that both exports and imports of IP-intensive goods increased after TRIPS compliance relative to a control group of products. Reflecting the diversifying global landscape for innovation and technology diffusion, in contrast with broad assumptions of a north–south divide, this increase was not confined to high-income countries: developing countries also benefitted and increased their imports of high-IP products from the most innovative countries. They conclude that if trade is associated with knowledge diffusion and technology transfer, then TRIPS may have achieved some of its aims. However, the authors strike a note of caution: whether the increased trade represents increased access or merely higher prices remains an important issue for future work.

Roberta Piermartini and Stela Rubínová have done seminal work for their chapter, showing how global production chains can facilitate the access to foreign non-codified knowledge, by intensifying communication between foreign firms and domestic suppliers. Patents and scientific publications are a public source of codified knowledge. However, not all knowledge can be codified and part of it diffuses only via face-to-face communication and direct transfer. To benefit from knowledge generated elsewhere, firms often need to have access also to the non-codifiable part. This boosts innovation. Using industry-level R&D and patent data for a sample of 29 countries for the period 2000–2008, the authors show that production linkages can be an important driver of knowledge spillovers, especially when the intermediate input suppliers are sufficiently integrated in the supply chain. Quantitatively, they show that international knowledge spillovers from such production chains are larger than previously estimated. Furthermore, they show that while knowledge spillovers diminish with geographical distance, distance has become less important as production chains have become more globalized.

Nikolas J. Zolas and Travis J. Lybbert, use an original algorithmic concordance that links patent classification to industry and product classifications to look at global value chains (GVCs) from the opposite angle to the previous chapter: how do patents affect trade and, more specifically, the organization and structure of GVCs? We know that patents play an important role in the global economy through their impact on technology diffusion, knowledge transfer and competition. The authors suggest that as production has become fragmented into coordinated processes that span the globe, the role of patents has evolved. Patents can transmit technical knowledge and facilitate upstream and downstream licensing arrangements, thereby increasing the flow of intermediate and final goods and catalyzing knowledge spillovers across sectors and regions. Using the World Input-Output Database as the basis for various GVC measures, the authors find that increased international patenting inflows are associated with greater value-added production, but that this positive effect is driven entirely by industries in high-income countries. They also find some evidence of heterogeneity in these effects by region and sector-specific R&D intensity. They are cautious about important limitations of this exploratory analysis and implications for future research.

Michael D. Smith and Rahul Telang synthesize the academic literature to help policymakers better understand the empirical evidence of both the impact of piracy on worldwide trade in copyrighted goods and the effectiveness of various strategies for protecting intellectual property from the threat of piracy. While the digital revolution has made it easier for small creators and innovators to have a larger global audience, it has also led to increased piracy of creative content. The authors find convincing empirical evidence, including from their own work, that suggests that (1) piracy harms sales in legal markets in the vast majority of settings in which it occurs, (2) lost revenue from piracy impacts producers' incentives to innovate and create new content; more specifically, there is emerging evidence that reduced revenue from piracy is causing a reduction in both the quantity and quality of content produced by the copyright industries, (3) anti-piracy measures can be effective at changing consumer behaviour; in particular, each of the major stakeholders in content delivery – governments, right holders, platforms, and ISPs – can play a role in changing consumer behaviour. Moreover, the literature suggests that active enforcement is important to influencing consumer behaviour and that anti-piracy measures are likely to have a stronger impact on digital sales channels than on physical channels. However, the authors conclude that more empirical research, particularly field experiments, are needed to replicate and refine these results to better inform policymakers.

Keith Nurse and his co-authors assess the challenges and opportunities for creative industries in developing countries, especially as it relates to making the transition to a digital creative economy and to the adoption of blockchain technologies. The music industry is used as a case study because it is this sector that has experienced the greatest level of digital disruption and it is also among the first to embrace blockchain technology. The authors explore blockchain technologies as one element of the digital economy that has the capacity to present opportunities for these countries to increase market penetration and deepen global value-addition. They identify four potential interventions that would enhance participation in the digital marketplace: promoting distribution of music on key platforms; building institutional and human resources in the creative industries to tap into the opportunities in the digital and blockchain arenas; employing targeted marketing strategies suitable for the various genres and styles of creative content on digital platforms; and strengthening the legal, technological and institutional infrastructure for collective management of copyright, through collective management organizations that stimulate creativity and musical diversity through the creation of works of local genres, generate royalties, and also undertake support activities such as education, awards and social-welfare actions.

Policy, Regulatory and Legislative Frameworks

Part IV sets out an analysis of the policy, legal and regulatory frameworks that govern cross-border knowledge flows. Partly due to the intangible quality of knowledge flows, and in view of the general character of knowledge as a public good, knowledge flows are particularly sensitive to policy and legal settings, both within national jurisdictions and in the international sphere. It is, after all, the IP system itself that defines exclusive rights over knowledge products, such as inventions and technical knowhow, that would otherwise be non-excludable and non-rivalrous public goods: in other words, it is the very existence of IP laws that create and define the packages of knowledge that can be traded internationally. The efficiency and effectiveness of international knowledge flows therefore depend in part on how national regulatory and legal systems define and administer IP rights, and in part on how international rules provide for reasonable and workable interoperability between IP systems that are still essentially domestic and national in character. This part of the book explores the regulatory responses to the challenges posed by new technologies, as domestic regulators and international negotiators seek to adapt and supplement existing rules to the contemporary context for knowledge flows and transactions in IP rights and digital products.

Mary LaFrance examines the legal regimes that govern the streaming of music and audiovisual works in the United States and the European Union. The author concludes that although these legal systems have already undergone considerable change during the Internet era, they must continue to evolve in order to address the challenges presented by licensed and unlicensed streaming. For example, with respect to licensed streaming, the number of licenses needed is greater, and using them effectively requires tracking the utilization of each work as well as linking each work to all of the rights holders entitled to compensation. Due to their greater bargaining power, larger rights holders can typically negotiate favourable licenses, leaving independent artists on their own to protect their rights. Within the EU, consumer demand for borderless streaming has highlighted the need for multi-territorial licensing. In the case of unlicensed streaming, neither the US nor the EU have imposed filtering or monitoring obligations on ISPs that host user-provided infringing content; and the law in these jurisdictions seems to be trending in opposite directions. Paradoxically, if ISPs are required to monitor and filter their content, this is likely to favour the larger ISPs that can afford to create and invest in this technology, while creating a barrier to entry for newer services.

Mira Burri discusses the depth of disruptive changes needed in trade law and policies, given the trajectory of the digital transformation of international trade. In order to do this, she examines existing regulatory frameworks – both at the international and at the regional and bilateral levels. She is, in particular, interested in an understanding of the new templates for electronic commerce and for this the chapter focuses on the most advanced model so far – that of the Comprehensive and Progressive Agreement for Transpacific Partnership (CPTPP) and the United States–Mexico–Canada Agreement (USMCA). She goes on to contextualize and assess the impact of the existing legal framework, as shaped in recent times almost predominantly by preferential trade agreements. She asks whether there are better ways to address the challenges of the data-driven economy and what the essential elements of a working regulatory model should be. In conclusion, she suggests a return to the multilateral forum of the WTO and briefly sketches viable paths to do so.

Nigel Cory explores three interrelated topics: first, the role of data flows generally and the impact of policies that act as barriers to their movement across borders; second, how the intersection of intellectual property rights, data flows and digitalization raises new challenges for copyright enforcement and protection of trade secrets; and finally how data flows and digital trade can be indirectly affected by policies that restrict the Internet-based platforms and services that are key agents in facilitating and managing data flows, services and digital intellectual property. The author concludes that while data and digital technologies have transformed how organizations trade, especially in knowledge-intensive goods and services, many policymakers are struggling to adapt domestic and international rules and norms. This is evident in the ever-growing gap between technological innovation and domestic/international policy frameworks, which allows countries to enact policies that detract from the potential economic and social benefits of these technologies. He views intellectual property as crucial to supporting innovation and asserts that policymakers will soon face a key choice in deciding whether they want to embrace a truly global market for digitally enabled trade in goods and services and be willing to push back on the emerging threat of digital protectionism.

Lucas Spadano and Luiza Coelho provide a basic understanding of how multilateral, plurilateral and bilateral trade agreements could affect cross-border knowledge flows. In particular, the authors examine whether the current multilateral disciplines are sufficient to regulate and encourage cross-border knowledge flows, or whether new trade rules to further promote such flows are needed. The question is discussed, particularly, in the light of new trends identified in recent plurilateral and bilateral agreements. The authors describe how the current international trade legal system regulates cross-border knowledge flows. The relevant WTO disciplines are explained briefly, alongside current trends in bilateral and plurilateral trade agreements. They discuss possible reasons for reforming or updating current multilateral trade rules and conclude that there is a need for such reform.

Jacques de Werra and Jeff C. Dodd view knowledge-based IP transactions as vitally important to the modern global economy. The focus of their chapter is on cross-border trade in IP and information products that manifests itself through licensing. There is no internationally recognized general statement of the commercial legal principles dealing with this unique but common transactional form of licence nor on the unique but common qualities of knowledge-based intangibles. Various private ordering regimes have emerged to address discrete types of transactions, whether by industry or other groups. One form of private ordering, cross-border licensing practices – which they term 'information law merchant', modelled on the cross-jurisdictional *lex mercatoria* developed by European traders in the medieval period – covers only a limited number of participants who routinely trade in certain types of information assets. Effective participation in many forms of international commercial IP transactions often requires access to specialized legal knowledge, extensive commercial experience, and elaborate contract forms, creating barriers to entry for new actors, disadvantaging smaller firms, increasing transaction and performance costs, and fostering disputes. Another form of private ordering relates to FRAND licensing across different jurisdictions. Recent developments show a piecemeal and fragmented development of FRAND licensing terms and conditions (beyond the issue of the financial remuneration or royalties), which provide no firm foundation for addressing the trade in IP assets. The authors conclude that international organizations that deal with IP issues should undertake a project to address the general principles relating to international IP commercial contracts.

Peter K. Yu focuses on the legal frameworks governing the cross-border flows of machine-generated data in an era when the Internet of Things has slowly transformed into the 'Internet of Everything'. Data generated or collected by networked sensors, interconnected devices, and intelligent machines is highly valuable. The author's view is that if countries began to create new rights in these data – whether based on the EU proposal or other proposals – the cross-border flow of such data would raise questions about the need for new trade standards. He highlights two sets of challenges concerning the development of new trade standards for regulating the cross-border flow of machine-generated data: (1) national policy developments and (2) international norm setting. He identifies policy questions that have to be addressed before the creation of a new national regime for the protection of machine-generated data. He then turns to the potential complications that would arise in the international norm-setting arena. Taken together, these two sets of challenges show how the protection, regulation and overall governance of machine-generated data may not fit well with the existing international trade regime.

Looking Forward

Part V comprises a forward-looking chapter that reviews the current status of our understanding of knowledge flows in trade, considers what we have learned about the gaps in our conceptual understanding and empirical data, and considers what can be done to address these gaps. The chapter discusses the possible directions for building a stronger empirical and theoretical platform to support further policy dialogue and research. This includes improving the reach and quality of statistics, and improving the analysis of available data, including through greater integration of different forms of data (such as measurement of the value and trends of trade as a proxy for knowledge transactions, and more nuanced and granular analysis of IP statistics). Policy and legal analysis need to 'unbundle' the knowledge component from various proxies for it (such as trade in IP-rich goods, trade in knowledge-intensive services, and trade in IP rights for such goods as software and creative content). This would help address such shortcomings as the distorting effect of taxation arrangements and the mismatch between trade statistics and the true character of cross-border commercial transactions and the related flow of valuable knowledge. More importantly, it would provide a surer foundation for policymakers to identify and implement positive opportunities to leverage indigenous knowledge resources and incoming knowledge flows for sustainable development and welfare-enhancing trade and economic policy. These developments pose challenges for policy coherence and international governance, given the diversification of approaches at the domestic level and in the emerging patchwork of bilateral and regional agreements, in contrast with the policy coherence and interoperability between jurisdictions that was brought about by the WTO TRIPS Agreement. The chapter discusses the prospects for identifying, at least in principle, a potential role for multilateral institutions to update and consolidate the governance framework for knowledge flows, or whether it is more feasible and realistic to work towards policy coherence through dialogue and cooperation, supported by a forward-looking research agenda.

Conclusions

The dialogue between scholars, analysts and policymakers that led to the elaboration of this volume, and the process of editing their excellent and broad-based contributions, have reaffirmed our firm conviction of the significant value of contemporary cross-disciplinary research in this critical area, as well as its importance for policymakers seeking to grasp and identify the need and potential directions for this vital research agenda. We close with an overview of some of the more compelling areas for future work in this area.

Metrics. At a time when trade policy interests and settings are ever more influenced by close attention to trade balances and the impact of dispersed production and value chains, it is striking that some of the most valuable elements of international trade – those that entail transactions purely in knowledge as such – are among the most poorly measured, both in terms of specific bilateral flows and general international patterns. There are 'known unknowns' – such as full data on international trade for consumer licences for IP content, and on the intangible components of dispersed development and production chains – that, if addressed, could significantly alter perceptions of trade balances and trade policy priorities.

The making of rules. The conventional legal paradigm for IP law and related regulations governing the knowledge economy – epitomised by the TRIPS Agreement and its implementation – is the articulation of an international, multilateral set of rules which national legislation subsequently implements. However, the emerging international framework has become ever more complex, with overlapping and potentially conflicting rules flowing from bilateral and regional agreements, the de facto reach of domestic laws of the major players and the kind of private ordering that may result in an information law merchant as suggested in this book.

Regulatory impacts. In 1992, Romer observed that 'we must recognize that ideas are economic goods which are unlike conventional private goods and that markets are inherently less successful at producing and transmitting ideas than they are with private goods'.[6] This observation underscores the strong sensitivity to regulatory structures of the dissemination of usable knowledge; to some extent, it is the regulatory system – and specifically IP laws – that enable markets in ideas to develop and that structure and define those markets. Regulatory intervention in a range of areas doubtless is a key factor determining how successfully markets function to ensure that ideas are generated and are disseminated and used effectively for the overall public benefit, and regulation can distort or inhibit knowledge flows, sometimes in unexpected ways.

Shifting production and innovative capacities. The mobility of knowledge and of knowledge workers, the possibility of dynamic knowledge networks not defined by national boundaries or geographical distance and the unbundling of production capacity, together with the

[6] At 89.

evolution of a number of developing and transition economies as centres of knowledge production and technological innovation, all contribute to fast-evolving and ever-diversifying ecosystems for innovation and the production and dissemination of knowledge. These factors are reshaping how, where and by whom innovation takes place, how and where the resultant new knowledge is developed, transacted and disseminated, and how countries can benefit directly and indirectly through technology spillovers.

New ways of trading. The World Wide Web was invented by Tim Berners-Lee at CERN, in Geneva, exactly at the time that TRIPS negotiators were concluding the text of an agreement which essentially assumed that the IP component of trade largely comprised value added in traded physical goods. Since then, through the massive expansion and diversification of the Internet as a common platform for the exchange of intangible content, intellectual property rights – whether through transfer of ownership or diverse forms of licensing – have emerged as widely traded goods in themselves, both between firms and in consumer markets. The practical convergence of the 'two IPs' – the Internet protocol and intellectual property – since that time has opened up entirely new markets (and important non-market avenues) for the dissemination of knowledge and creative content, greatly facilitating knowledge flows and creating new possibilities for economic development and more equitable access to international markets.

A COVID-19 Epilogue

This project had already been completed when the first reports emerged of a novel coronavirus that rapidly escalated into the pandemic that has since convulsed societies across the globe, caused widespread death and suffering and brought chaos to national economies and to international trade.

No attempt is made here to assess or respond to the gravity and severity of this fundamental upheaval and its impact on and implications for the issues explored in this volume. Nonetheless, it is clear that the value of innovation systems and the equitable dissemination of the benefits of new knowledge production is more acutely understood than ever, and that the disruption of trade and potentially of established production chains is likely to accentuate the need and demand for more effective sharing and absorption of knowledge through digital platforms and through the licensing and other transmission of knowledge products as policymakers seek first to understand and then to adapt to the 'new normal'.

The editors therefore express the hope that the ideas and possibilities explored in this volume will help to illuminate the difficult path ahead through a more complex policy landscape.

Bibliography

Baldwin, Richard, *The Great Convergence: Information Technology and the New Globalization*, Cambridge, MA: Harvard University Press, 2016.

Romer, Paul M., 'Two Strategies for Economic Development: Using Ideas and Producing Ideas', *Proceedings of the World Bank Annual Conference on Development Economics 1992*, Supplement, Washington, DC: World Bank Economic Review, 1993.

Watal, Jayashree and Taubman, Antony, *The Making of the TRIPS Agreement: Personal Insights from the Uruguay Round Negotiations*, Geneva: WTO, 2015.

PART I

Conceptual Framework

2

The Shifting Contours of Trade in Knowledge: The New 'Trade-Related Aspects' of Intellectual Property

ANTONY TAUBMAN

Abstract

This chapter charts the evolution and diversification of trade in knowledge that has taken place in the quarter-century since the WTO TRIPS Agreement came into force. Entirely new markets have come into being, potentially redefining the very character of 'trade'. The disruptive effect of digital technology has led to much of the content – formerly conceived of as 'added value' embedded in physical carrier media, traded and measured as 'goods' – can be traded in the form of specific licences that use IP rights covering the content that is increasingly accessed online in digital form. These new forms of exchange in valuable intangible content confront fundamental assumptions about the nature of trade and its interaction with the IP system, forcing a rethink of what constitutes the 'trade-related aspects' of intellectual property. The issues examined include the principle of territoriality of IP rights and the segmentation of markets according to national jurisdictions; the structuring of cross-border commercial exchanges into the two discrete categories of 'goods' and 'services'; the emerging disparity in regional trade agreements between provisions on digital IP standards and on digital products and e-commerce; and the significance of IP rights being treated as assets in investment treaties. Whatever formal or legal overlay is applied to these new trading arrangements – it is essential to understand that this is now trade in IP licences as such, rather than trade in goods that have an IP component as an adjunct or ancillary element. TRIPS came about at a time when economic growth theory incorporated intangible knowledge as an endogenous factor, rather than maintaining it as exogenous to models of growth. Trade policy must similarly work to incorporate an understanding of the trade in IP licences itself within cross-border commercial exchanges as an integral element of international trading relations: sale and licensing of IP rights can then be considered 'endogenous' to trade. This is essential for an accurate empirical picture of trade relations today, given the economic significance both of dispersed global value chains and of trade in 'pure' IP content as such particularly in the creative sectors.

Overview: The New 'Trade-Related Aspects' of IP

Growing recognition of the economic significance of the IP system and of the knowledge component of trade led negotiators, a generation ago, to formulate the WTO TRIPS Agreement. TRIPS ostensibly addressed the 'trade-related aspects' of IP rights and integrated the IP system into the framework of multilateral trade law, but it was concluded before the effects were felt of the impact of digital technologies on how knowledge-rich products – tangible and intangible – are traded and disseminated. In the quarter-century since TRIPS came into force, trade in knowledge – the tangible and intangible ways valuable content is disseminated through commercial channels – has dramatically evolved and diversified. Entirely new markets have come into being for valuable content defined and protected by IP, and IP licences governing knowledge constitute one form of linkage in dispersed value chains. Consequently, the 'trade-related aspects' of IP have evolved and diversified, to the point that trade in IP rights as such is commonplace and defines major consumer markets for creative content.

The emerging trade in IP rights as such, and the digital products defined and traded through IP rights, suggests that the very character of what is conceived of as 'trade' needs reconsideration. For instance, from a trade perspective, valuable content (such as musical works, software or literary works) was earlier conceived as 'added value' embedded in physical carrier media, the physical objects that were traded and counted as 'goods'. Trade in music, software or literature would be measured through the physical transfer of such goods, and transactions defined by the transfer of ownership over such physical objects. The disruptive effect of digital technology means that much of this content is now traded digitally. The individual transactions that make up the trade increasingly take the form not of transfer of ownership of carrier media, but of specific licences that combine contractual undertakings with limited licences to use IP rights covering the traded content. Established notions of ownership and property are under strain. Trade in content as such, valued for its own sake, therefore increasingly supersedes trade in the physical carrier media that had earlier served as a proxy for trade in valuable intangible goods such as musical and literary works, software and games. These new markets and new forms of exchange in valuable intangible content confront fundamental assumptions about the nature of trade and its interaction with the IP system, forcing a rethink of what constitutes the 'trade-related aspects' of IP.

This dynamic context, and the disruptive effect of technological change, have implications for the principle of territoriality of IP rights and the segmentation of IP markets according to national jurisdiction; the structuring of cross-border commercial exchanges into the two discrete categories of 'goods' and 'services'; the emerging disparity in regional trade agreements between digital IP standards and provisions on digital products and e-commerce; and the significance of IP rights also being treated as assets in investment treaties.

Whatever formal or legal overlay is applied to these new trading arrangements, it is essential to build an understanding of their character, in part, as trade in IP licences as such, rather than viewing the IP component as an adjunct, ancillary or extraneous element. Just at the time TRIPS was being negotiated, Romer and others demonstrated the need for economic growth theory to incorporate intangible knowledge as an endogenous factor. Today, trade policy must similarly work to incorporate an understanding of the IP dimension of cross-border commercial exchanges as an integral element of trading relations – and ideally count them more comprehensively and effectively in the trade balance statistics that can influence trade policy choices. This means treating the exchange and licensing of IP rights systematically and effectively as 'endogenous' to trade. This shift in framing the 'trade-related aspects' of IP – indeed, considering the IP-related aspects of trade – is essential for an accurate empirical picture of trade relations today, given the economic significance both of dispersed global value chains and of trade in 'pure' IP content as such, particularly in the creative sectors. Such a move need not challenge formal positions as to the categorization of trade in digital products. Instead, it may be more productive to accept the diverse range of interactions between the IP system and trade, and build an understanding on empirical observation of diverse phenomena, rather than a priori formal categorization.

'Old Town Road' and New Trade Routes

The song 'Old Town Road', by the rapper Lil Nas X (Montero Hill), set new sales records in 2019, even as it resisted definition within the music business's established categories. For an unprecedented 19 weeks, the song topped the Billboard Hot 100 , the principal music industry listing of currently popular recordings in the United States – the original *Billboard* magazine 'hit parade' dating back to the 1930s. The Recording Industry

Association of America (RIAA) later certified the song as 'diamond', representing confirmed sales of 10 million units; it reached this milestone in record time.[1] And the song defied conventional musical genres: blending elements of hip hop, trap and country music. 'Old Town Road' was initially listed on Billboard's Hot 100 and on its R&B/hip hop chart, as well as on its country music chart, but was reportedly removed from the latter on the grounds that it 'does not embrace enough elements of today's country music to chart in its current version', a decision that sparked controversy, it remained on the rap charts.[2] At the time, the songwriter argued that the 'song is country trap. It's not one, it's not the other. It's both. It should be on both [charts]'.[3]

The song was built on the foundation of a beat created by Kiowa Roukema (under the handle YoungKio), a Dutch musician. He had encountered – when browsing YouTube algorithmic recommendations – the instrumental track '34 Ghosts IV' produced by Nine Inch Nails (composed by Trent Reznor and Atticus Ross). He combined a trap rhythm with a banjo riff sampled from the Nine Inch Nails track. In turn, Mr Hill obtained this beat from BeatStars, an online market for instrumental audio clips to be used by recording artists and songwriters. While he was reported to have 'purchased' or 'bought' the beat, in fact he took out a standard, non-exclusive licence – a 'basic lease' for USD 30, which gave limited rights to use the clip for recording music that was capped by a permitted number of copies, and limited rights to audio streams and broadcasting rights of the resulting musical work. BeatStars is an international marketplace for intellectual property licences, the territory of application of which is defined as 'the world'. It reportedly hosts over 1.5 million beats, audio clips available for licensing, that are posted by music producers from around 160 countries, and has paid over USD 50 million to producers such as Mr Roukema – although it is very unlikely that these payments will be counted as exports of goods or services from the countries in which they work. The Nine Inch Nails track had been released under a Creative Commons licence, with a positive encouragement for the material to be used for non-commercial

[1] Rania Aniftos, 'Lil Nas X's "Old Town Road" Is the Fastest Song in History to Be Certified Diamond by the RIAA', *Billboard*, 22 October 2019.

[2] Hubert Adjei-Kontoh, 'Lil Nas' song was removed from Billboard for not being "country" enough. But who gets to decide categories?', *The Guardian*, 2 April 2019.

[3] Andrew Chow, 'Lil Nas X Talks "Old Town Road" and the Billboard Controversy', available at https://time.com/5561466/lil-nas-x-old-town-road-billboard/.

purposes. However, the right to use the sample in 'Old Town Road' was only cleared retrospectively through a telephone call. The original musical composition was credited to Hill and Roukema as well as to Trent Reznor and Atticus Ross: of the four credited songwriters, only the last two had actually met, and the first two were separated by an ocean.

Mr Hill initially released the song independently (signing to an established record label, Columbia, only after its breakout success) and promoted it through extensive use of social media, including the newly popular avenue of TikTok. He encouraged its use in video clips by other users, and gained attention to the track through a variety of Internet memes. The groundswell of interest thus generated led to its popularity in more conventional settings, in particular those used by Billboard and other industry sources to measure success. The Billboard Hot 100 measure includes traditional retail sales of physical media (such as CDs), as well as digital downloads, streaming and on-demand access.[4]

'Old Town Road' exemplifies how digital technology has transformed the music industry in particular in the period since the WTO TRIPS Agreement was concluded in 1994, some five years before the song's creator and performer was born. This transformation is evident in terms of how the song was composed and disseminated, the interplay between creators' rights and user rights as its components came together, the geographically dispersed cluster of rights over the song's ingredients (the very process of its composition and production resembling a global value chain), the significance of digital platforms including a global marketplace for IP licences unsupported by physical carrier media, the song's non-conformity with established genres, and even the manner of measuring its success, all taken together, offer illuminating insights into the impact of digital disruption on this sector. It demonstrates how entirely new forms of trading in creative content are supplanting traditional business models and challenging traditional genres.

'Old Town Road' exemplifies trends that can be said to be transforming the very nature of trade, and the linkages between the intellectual property (IP) system and international trade:

- the development of online commercial markets for licences in IP content as such, enabling seamless trading in a global space, and transforming the notion of 'trade-related aspects' of IP rights;

[4] See www.billboard.com/p/billboard-charts-legend.

- the diversification and informality of the means of creation, dissemination, reuse and consumption of digital content;
- the multiple uses of the Internet as a packet-switched network, and the transmission of packets of data structured by the Internet protocol (TCP/IP), for diverse creative, cultural, social and commercial purposes, and the correspondingly diverse legal statuses of those packets of data, which may variously be construed as in the public domain, subject to fair use or user rights, or bound by contractual obligations and IP rights;
- the blurring of boundaries: between producer and user of creative content, between established genres, between distinct distribution channels, and between the distinct national jurisdictions under which IP rights are recognized and enforced; and
- the challenge of tracking and measuring international commercial transactions that entail the licensing of IP content no longer embedded in the physical carrier media – discs, tapes, printed publications such as sheet music – that once could comprise the totality of creative content traded internationally.

From Trade in Atoms …

GATT and the 'Trade in Goods' Paradigm

The multilateral trade agreements that came into force on the establishment of the WTO in 1995 were negotiated and concluded in an effectively pre-Internet age, with scant consideration of how digital technologies were likely to reshape not only the directions and composition of trade, but even transform the very legal and economic character of commercial transactions that constitute trade.

The interaction between trade and the IP system, and the general acceptance of the significance of the intangible component of trade, had only slowly taken root in a multilateral system of trade rules that originally focused on trade in physical goods – informally, 'things you could drop on your foot'. In 1947, the General Agreement on Tariffs and Trade (the GATT) established a rule, essentially, of non-interference and of non-discrimination between trade law and IP law: the IP system was held at arm's length. Thus, GATT Article XX, on general exceptions, accepted that contracting parties may choose to protect IP within their domestic systems, without requiring this. At the same time, it provided that IP protection should not be a disguised restriction on trade, and should not discriminate against imported goods (the GATT being a trade-in-goods agreement, discrimination was construed in terms of goods and not of persons): in effect, protect IP if you wish, but do no harm to trade in physical goods. GATT jurisprudence confirmed that measures to enforce IP at the border could fall foul of the principle of non-discrimination, effectively setting limits on the impact of IP measures on trade in goods.[5]

One strand of IP – loosely, the unfair competition/geographical indication (GI) nexus – found some, tentative, recognition in the original GATT text. The obligation under Article IX.6 to cooperate to prevent the use of trade names that would 'misrepresent the true origin of a product, to the detriment of such distinctive regional or geographical names of products of the territory of a contracting party as are protected by its legislation' recalls the trade-relatedness of geographical indications and the mechanism for communicating names protected under domestic law points towards a later mandate to negotiate a multilateral GI register, but there are no obligations positively to protect such terms.

Over time, trade policy began to register the relevance of IP issues more widely. Thus a GATT inventory of non-tariff barriers to trade compiled in 1968 included a notification by the United Kingdom of Italy's local working requirements for patents (invoking the Paris Convention for the Protection of Industrial Property), and of the manufacturing clause in US copyright law.[6] A more sustained and structural shift to recognizing the intangible value that IP embeds in traded goods can be traced more concretely to past GATT work on counterfeit trade beginning in the 1970s. The United States sought to introduce a requirement to act against trade in counterfeit goods within the GATT Tokyo Round negotiations: an early proposal was headed 'Agreement on the Sanctions to be Imposed Upon the Importation of Counterfeit Merchandise',[7] and dealt with international trade in *articles* that bore a spurious trademark or were made in violation of copyright. A subsequent version, submitted jointly with Canada, the European Community and Japan, proposed an 'Agreement

[5] See United States – Section 337 of the Tariff Act of 1930, Report by the Panel adopted on 7 November 1989, L/6439 – 36S/345.

[6] GATT documents COM.IND/4 (30 August 1968) and COM.IND/4/Corr.1 (26 September 1968).

[7] GATT document MTN/NTM/W/204, Multilateral Trade Negotiations – Group 'Non-Tariff Measures' – Sub-Group 'Customs Matters' – Commercial Counterfeiting – 11 December 1978.

on Measures to Discourage the Importation of Counterfeit Goods',[8] which only addressed international trade in imported goods bearing a false representation of a trademark. These proposals were unsuccessful in that they failed to produce an immediate negotiating outcome, but they helped shape the negotiating mandate for the subsequent Uruguay Round negotiations – the Punta del Este Declaration of 20 September 1986. This negotiating mandate – within the broader category of 'trade in goods' – referred to '[t]rade-related aspects of intellectual property rights, including trade in counterfeit goods' and established the negotiating objective of developing 'a multilateral framework of principles, rules and disciplines dealing with international trade in counterfeit goods'. Hence, for historical and practical reasons, the essential notion of IP and international trade that the TRIPS mandate addressed was still centred on the idea that IP was embedded in physical goods, and that the infringing trade to be suppressed was trade in infringing goods.

This practical assumption that international trade relating to IP was embedded in physical goods finds a strong echo in the earlier multilateral conventions on IP administered by the World Intellectual Property Organization (WIPO). Thus, the Paris Convention deals with 'articles', 'products', and 'goods' as either embodiments or infringements of IP. Until its revision in 1958, Paris had not recognized service marks at all, in line with the past understanding in many countries that trademarks were reserved for goods only. What was arguably the first truly 'trade-related' agreement on intellectual property – the Madrid Agreement for the Repression of False or Deceptive Indications of Source on Goods of 1891 – squarely addressed trade in goods in a manner that has consonance with the one positive obligation related to IP in the original GATT, the requirement under Article IX.6 to cooperate 'with a view to preventing the use of trade names in such manner as to misrepresent the true origin of a product'.

In this 'analogue' age, it was, indeed, the case that goods served as proxies especially for consumer access to the content protected and defined by IP rights. Hence, for most consumers, music, books, journals, cinematic works, and even consumer software and games, were traded internationally almost exclusively on physical carrier media – optical and vinyl discs, recorded tape, film stock, newsprint, bound volumes, sheet music and so on. And guidelines for measuring international trade in

[8] GATT document L/5382, Agreement on Measures to Discourage the Importation of Counterfeit Goods, 18 October 1982.

goods recognize such material as traded goods: '[a]s a general guideline, media, whether or not recorded, is included in international merchandise trade statistics at its full transaction value, except for media used for carrying customized software or software written for a specific client or originals of any nature, which should in principle be excluded.'[9] One exception concerns international 'newspapers and periodicals sent under direct subscription'[10] – though they entailed the passage of valuable physical goods across borders, these were counted as trade in services, the physical shipment of the publications being conceptually subordinate to the provision of a subscription service.

Commercial transactions defined by the exchange of ownership of these physical things – these bundles of atoms – therefore served as proxies for the acquisition of access to valued intangible content (such as music, literature, films and software). The reliance on physical carrier media as the means of dissemination meant that international trade in musical and literary works could readily be tracked and relatively accurate trade statistics maintained, by monitoring the quantity and value of physical media that passed through customs procedures on a country's boundary. Hence recorded media (recorded discs, tapes and film stock, published books, newspapers) have been counted and valued separately from blank media (blank discs, tape and film stock, paper, newsprint); their 'full transactional value' incorporates the licence acquired to use the recorded content, normally limited to certain private uses. Broadcasting and other forms of wired and wireless transmission – on domestic and cross-border networks – also provided the public with access to some categories of material, but not in a form susceptible to individual transactions concerning ownership of a right to continued access to a specific work.[11]

In categorizing trade in goods for customs valuation and statistics, the Harmonized Commodity Description and Coding Systems (HS) classification of traded goods distinguishes between recorded and unrecorded optical media, magnetic media and photographic media. Clear differences in value are apparent depending on whether blank or recorded media are traded. Thus, in 2018, a global total of 13.8 billion imports of

[9] United Nations, *International Merchandise Trade Statistics: Concepts and Definitions 2010*, New York: IMTS, 2010, p. 15.

[10] Ibid., p. 21.

[11] The lack of such a right was a factor behind the negotiation of what were termed the 'WIPO Internet treaties' in 1996, notably producing a new right of distribution – see 'IP in the Digital Marketplace: The Effect of Exhaustion', *infra*.

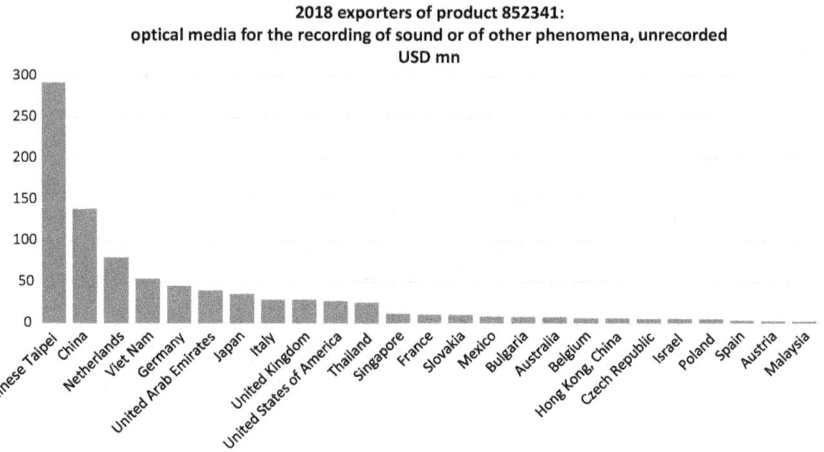

Figure 2.1 List of exporters in recorded optical discs in 2018
Source: ITC Trade Map.

recorded optical discs (HS code 852349) was reported, as against 2.1 billion imports of unrecorded (blank) optical discs (HS code 852341). The contrasting two patterns of exports (see Figures 2.1 and 2.2) illustrate a kind of 'value chain' in international trade, as intangible content is added to the blank discs, greatly enhancing their value, with the export profile of the more valuable recorded media being dominated by developed countries.

Historical Legal Questions: What Are You Purchasing?

Prefiguring the manner in which we need today to consider the implications of digital disruption for trade in knowledge products such as musical works, earlier technological changes – such as the development of soundrecording and broadcasting technologies – led to similar issues concerning the very character of trade in copyright works. Hence, this question arose at a time when radio technology made it possible for a sound recording – then normally distributed on gramophone records – to be widely broadcast to the public beyond the original, private, context in which such records had been played. Until the advent of broadcasting, the only ways of gaining access to a musical performance were either being physically present at the performance or by means of access to a physical object, the recorded disc. Hence the question arose, with resonance still today: if you do buy a recorded physical carrier medium, such

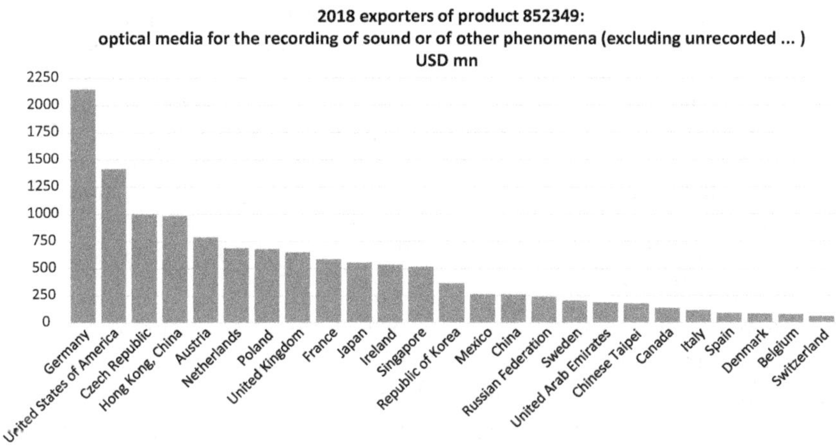

Figure 2.2 List of exporters in unrecorded optical discs in 2018
Source: ITC Trade Map.

as a gramophone record or an optical disc, what are you actually purchasing? What is the very nature of that transaction? Is it essentially the purchase of a physical thing, a 'chattel' in the legal jargon, something that you have property rights over and can sell and pass on to others? Is it the purchase of a rather limited private right to use the content, to use the intangible content? Is it a combination of the two? And how is the nature of this transaction affected by the introduction of new technologies for disseminating content?

In an earlier age, when radio broadcasting was a disruptive new technology, a US court developed an intriguing way of answering these questions. In the 1930s, the musician Fred Waring, bandleader of the Pennsylvanians, ran into difficulty enforcing an agreement with his record company, the Victor Talking Machine Company. His band's recorded music was licensed for gramophone production provided the ensuing records were labelled 'not licensed for radio broadcast'. The broadcast market was a separate, valuable source of income. The radio station WDAS purchased the disc and broadcast these recordings contrary to the asserted licence conditions. This led the court to construe the significance of technological disruption for rights and entitlements linked to intangible content:

> The problems involved in this case have never before been presented to an American or an English court. They challenge the vaunted genius of the law to adapt itself to new social and industrial conditions and to the

> progress of science and invention. For the first time in history human action can be photographed and visually re-portrayed by the motion picture. Sound can now be mechanically captured and reproduced not only by means of the phonograph for an audience physically present, but, through broadcasting, for practically all the world as simultaneous auditors. Just as the birth of the printing press made it necessary for equity to inaugurate a protection for literary and intellectual property, so these latter-day inventions make demands upon the creative and ever-evolving energy of equity to extend that protection so as adequately to do justice under current conditions of life.[12]

In this particular case, the challenge of technological disruption led the court to conclude that the licence restricting the use of the gramophone record was an 'equitable servitude'[13] on a chattel. The physical disc was sold by the gramophone company to a radio station. Waring himself was not a party to this transaction, and could not interfere with the sale of the disc as such. Even so, he was entitled as a matter of equity to enforce his interest in the recorded content contained on the disc and could restrain certain uses of the disc, despite the separate transfer of ownership of the disc as personal property (the 'chattel').

> [No] valid reason exists why the restriction attached to the manufacture and sale of the records in this case should not be enforced in equity . . . in a sense the plaintiff was not imposing a restriction in connection with a sale by him of a chattel. The chattel here consisted of the phonograph record. This the plaintiff never owned. What he granted was merely the incorporeal privilege of reproducing the rendition of the song indented upon the chattel sold by the Talking Machine Co. The reservation or restriction imposed by him was to limit the extent of this privilege. The title to the physical substance and the right to the use of literary or artistic property which may be printed upon or embodied in it are entirely distinct and independent of each other.[14]

The court then upheld the complaint on the basis that the radio station's use of the recording was an act of unfair competition. This somewhat experimental construction of the law did not find more general or lasting acceptance, and the law evolved to recognize a growing bundle of distinct IP rights applicable to recordings and performances as such.[15] The case is

[12] Fred Waring *v.* WDAS Station Inc. 194 A. 631 (Pa. 1937) 433.

[13] Zechariah Chafee, 'Equitable Servitudes on Chattels' (1928), *Harvard Law Review* 41: 945.

[14] Waring *v.* WDAS, p. 447.

[15] The need for ideas of equity and balance to adjust to such technological impact is discussed in Antony Taubman, 'Nobility of Interpretation: Equity, Retrospectivity, and

cited here, nonetheless, as an instructive historical insight into the continuing challenges, in a changing technological environment, of applying legal principles that seem better adapted to deal with property interests in tangible goods, as against claims or interests relating to intangible content. Defining and articulating the limits of such claims over embedded content when distributed by means of the sale of a physical thing, a chattel, remains a task for the policymaker or the courts confronted with today's new technological possibilities.

Exhaustion of IP Rights and the Scope of Markets

Indeed, considering the trade dimension in particular, in the contemporary commercial and legal environment, the relationship between the physical carrier medium and the rights governing the content it carries has increasing significance for determining the extent to which goods carrying IP-protected content can be traded, domestically and across borders. Key to the creation and structure of such borderless markets for IP content is the question of exhaustion of IP rights, particularly copyright. The term 'exhaustion' refers to the generally accepted principle in IP law that a right owner's exclusive right to control the distribution of a protected item lapses after the first act of distribution, when the right holder is assumed to have received a fair commercial return. On an international level, given the generally jurisdictionally defined and bound character of IPRs, it refers to the extent to which distinct authorization is required for IP-protected items to cross borders and to pass to distinct IP jurisdictions. The scope of exhaustion of rights forms the central pivot of the interaction between domestic jurisdictions and global markets for products defined or governed by IP rights.

The TRIPS negotiators were unable to bridge between contrasting views that exhaustion should apply nationally (meaning that an IP-protected product can be further sold within the same jurisdiction, but can not be imported even if legitimately acquired with the IP owner's consent in a foreign market), or internationally (meaning that the IP-protected item, once sold, can be imported into other jurisdictions even if

Collectivity in Implementing New Norms for Performers' Rights' (2005), *Journal of Intellectual Property* Law 12: 351, available at https://digitalcommons.law.uga.edu/jipl/vol12/iss2/2.

the IP right is separately in force there).[16] Thus this question was left open under TRIPS for national authorities to regulate (provided non-discrimination is respected), a matter confirmed in the 2001 Doha Declaration on the TRIPS Agreement and Public Health.[17] The central question, considering the policy dimension of exhaustion, is the extent to which the existence of jurisdictional boundaries constrains the free flow of IP-protected material, and to what extent the holder of an IP right should be able to bar its flow across borders.

The approach taken to exhaustion of IP rights embedded in tangible goods will determine whether there can be, effectively, a single global market for physical goods carrying IP-protected material, superseding distinct domestic markets defined by IP rights granted under national legal systems. In turn, the contours of such markets can depend on the character of the underlying transaction when a physical good is purchased that carries content protected by IP rights. Two recent US Supreme Court decisions have considered this question when determining the effective reach of IPRs across jurisdictions when goods are traded internationally, and thus the degree to which IPRs can shape international trade flows for knowledge content defined and protected as IP.

The international dimension of the *Kirtsaeng*[18] case concerned whether textbooks lawfully sold abroad with the consent of the copyright owner (at a lower price than the domestic versions) could be imported and sold in the US. The domestic copyright law of the US provides that 'the owner of a particular copy or phonorecord lawfully made under this title, or any person authorized by such owner, is entitled, without the authority of the copyright owner, to sell or otherwise dispose of the possession of that copy or phonorecord'.[19] This provision codifies the 'first sale' doctrine under US law, under which a

[16] TRIPS Agreement, Article 6. For an account on the negotiation of this issue, see David Fitzpatrick, 'Negotiating for Hong Kong', in Jayashree Watal and Antony Taubman, *The Making of TRIPS*, Geneva: WTO, 2015, pp. 285–291.

[17] Para. 5 of the Doha Declaration on the TRIPS Agreement and Public Health confirmed that the 'effect of the [TRIPS] provisions … relevant to the exhaustion of intellectual property rights is to leave each member free to establish its own regime for such exhaustion without challenge, subject to the MFN and national treatment provisions of Articles 3 and 4'.

[18] Kirtsaeng *v.* John Wiley & Sons, Inc., 568 US 519 (2013).

[19] 17 US Code §109 (a).

copyright holder is not entitled to restrain further sales once a first sale has been made. The international aspect of the case therefore hinged on whether the phrase 'lawfully made under this title' was limited in reference to copies made within the US, or was not geographically restricted; the majority held that it was 'nongeographical', and that the domestic statute defined a standard of lawfulness, while not requiring a copy to be made in the United States to benefit from this exhaustion of the distribution right. A majority found that physical books containing copyright works, imported into the United States in the so-called 'grey market', were not infringements of US copyright law and could thus legitimately enter the domestic market.

A host of policy questions lay behind this seemingly narrow question. Notably, from the point of view of the interplay between IPRs and trade law and policy, the majority held that the copyright statute aimed at a principle of 'equal treatment' between foreign and domestically produced works: 'the "equal treatment" principle is difficult to square with a geographical interpretation that would grant an American copyright holder permanent control over the American distribution chain in respect to copies printed abroad but not those printed in America.'[20] The majority decision draws an analogy between the purchaser's rights over the imported copyright-protected textbook, and ownership of a 'chattel' (a tangible item of property), rather than viewing the physical book as being essentially a carrier medium for protected content and licensed IP and thus giving primacy to the IP dimension of the original transaction. In the *Waring* case noted above, a copyright restriction on radio broadcast of a sound recording was construed as an 'equitable servitude on a chattel'.[21] Such a construction sees the essential nature of the transaction as transfer of ownership of the physical object, while enjoyment of the possession of a physical copy of the recording was subject to continuing liability to the originator of the sound recording.[22]

Dissenting, Justice Ginsberg argued that 'lawfully made under this title' refers to 'instances in which a copy's creation is governed by, and conducted in compliance with, Title 17 of the US Code'. She argues

[20] *Kirtsaeng*, n. 18 *supra*, 3.

[21] Waring *v.* WDAS Broad. Station Inc., 194 A. 631, 638 (1937).

[22] See Antony Taubman, 'TRIPS Encounters the Internet: An Analogue Treaty in a Digital Age, or the First Trade 2.0 Agreement?', in Mira Burri and Thomas Cottier (eds), *Trade Governance in the Digital Age*, Cambridge: Cambridge University Press, 2015, p. 314.

that, since US copyright law is not extraterritorial, it is anomalous 'to speak of particular conduct as "lawful" under an inapplicable law'. Her dissent sets out the essential policy question as follows:

> Because economic conditions and demand for particular goods vary across the globe, copyright owners have a financial incentive to charge different prices for copies of their works in different geographic regions. Their ability to engage in such price discrimination, however, is undermined if arbitrageurs are permitted to import copies from low-price regions and sell them in high-price regions.[23]

At the international level, she outlined the divergent positions as follows:

> In the absence of agreement at the international level, each country has been left to choose for itself the exhaustion framework it will follow. One option is a national-exhaustion regime, under which a copyright owner's right to control distribution of a particular copy is exhausted only within the country in which the copy is sold ... Another option is a rule of international exhaustion, under which the authorized distribution of a particular copy anywhere in the world exhausts the copyright owner's distribution right everywhere with respect to that copy ... The European Union has adopted the intermediate approach of regional exhaustion, under which the sale of a copy anywhere within the European Economic Area exhausts the copyright owner's distribution right throughout that region ... Section 602(a)(1), in my view, ties the United States to a national-exhaustion framework. The Court's decision, in contrast, places the United States solidly in the international-exhaustion camp.
>
> Strong arguments have been made both in favor of, and in opposition to, international exhaustion ... International exhaustion subjects copyright-protected goods to competition from lower priced imports and, to that extent, benefits consumers. Correspondingly, copyright owners profit from a national-exhaustion regime, which also enlarges the monetary incentive to create new copyrightable works.[24]

A subsequent Supreme Court decision, *Impression Products*,[25] concerning the aftermarket for used printer cartridges, addressed the question of international exhaustion of patent rights in a case that had some similarities with (and referred to) *Kirtsaeng*. The international dimension of the case pivoted on whether patent-protected cartridges sold abroad could be

[23] *Kirtsaeng*, p. 43.

[24] Ibid.

[25] Impression Products, Inc. *v.* Lexmark International Inc., 581 US 1523 (2017).

refilled and then sold in the United States, and the domestic dimension concerning whether conditions imposed on the subsequent use by the purchaser of cartridges could be enforced under patent rights. In both circumstances, the majority of the Court held that a sale of a patented product (even in a foreign jurisdiction) by the patent holder exhausted the patent rights. Thus the patent could not be used to prevent downstream resale or importation of a refilled cartridge. The majority decision revisited the policy considerations it had discussed in *Kirtsaeng*, in particular the common law 'refusal to permit restraints on the alienation of chattels'. In the domestic market, it found that,

> In sum, patent exhaustion is uniform and automatic. Once a patentee decides to sell—whether on its own or through a licensee—that sale exhausts its patent rights, regardless of any post-sale restrictions the patentee purports to impose, either directly or through a license.[26]

And when the patented article is sold internationally and then imported to the United States, the outcome was the same:

> An authorized sale outside the United States, just as one within the United States, exhausts all rights under the Patent Act ... exhaustion occurs because, in a sale, the patentee elects to give up title to an item in exchange for payment. Allowing patent rights to stick remora-like to that item as it flows through the market would violate the principle against restraints on alienation. Exhaustion does not depend on whether the patentee receives a premium for selling in the United States, or the type of rights that buyers expect to receive. As a result, restrictions and location are irrelevant; what matters is the patentee's decision to make a sale.[27]

Again, Justice Ginsberg dissented from the majority finding on the international dimension , arguing that the overseas sale operated independently of the US patent system: 'US patent protection accompanies none of a US patentee's sale abroad—a competitor could sell the same patented product abroad with no US-patent-law consequence. Accordingly, the foreign sale should not diminish the protections of US law in the United States.'[28]

In the Court's analysis, it is the act of selling an article that exhausts the patent right, and the fundamental aversion to restraints on the use of

[26] Ibid., p. 1535.
[27] Ibid., p. 1538.
[28] Ibid., p. 1539.

physical chattels once sold forms the legal foundation for exhaustion – the exhaustion rule 'marks the point where patent rights yield to the common law principle against restraints on alienation'. Hence it is the transfer of rights over physical property – and the consequent common law right to use and resell it without constraint from the 'remora-like' patent rights – that characterizes the essential transaction, not the fact that it is a sale undertaken within the panoply of applicable patent rights – in fact, the sale means that the product 'is no longer within the limits of the [patent] monopoly' and instead becomes the 'private, individual property' of the purchaser. But, again, the analysis may differ in cases where there is no tangible product, the transfer of ownership of which triggers the exhaustion of rights. Instead, the transaction may potentially be construed as the purchase of a limited licence, essentially defined in terms of a limited entitlement to use the patented invention within the scope of the exclusivity granted to the patent holder (the contrasting case of exhaustion of rights over intangible products is considered in 'IP in the Digital Marketplace: The Effect of Exhaustion').

In this context, it is noteworthy that the majority decision in *Impression Products* takes care to distinguish the nature of the licence from the sale of a physical product.

> A patentee can impose restrictions on licensees because a license does not implicate the same concerns about restraints on alienation as a sale. Patent exhaustion reflects the principle that, when an item passes into commerce, it should not be shaded by a legal cloud on title as it moves through the marketplace. But a license is not about passing title to a product, it is about changing the contours of the patentee's monopoly: The patentee agrees not to exclude a licensee from making or selling the patented invention, expanding the club of authorized producers and sellers. See General Elec. Co., 272 U. S., at 489–490. Because the patentee is exchanging rights, not goods, it is free to relinquish only a portion of its bundle of patent protections. A patentee's authority to limit licensees does not, as the Federal Circuit thought, mean that patentees can use licenses to impose post-sale restrictions on purchasers that are enforceable through the patent laws. So long as a licensee complies with the license when selling an item, the patentee has, in effect, authorized the sale. That licensee's sale is treated, for purposes of patent exhaustion, as if the patentee made the sale itself. The result: The sale exhausts the patentee's rights in that item ... A license may require the licensee to impose a restriction on purchasers, like the license limiting the computer manufacturer to selling for non-commercial use by individuals. But if the licensee does so—by, perhaps, having each customer sign a contract promising not to use the computers in business—the sale nonetheless exhausts all patent

> rights in the item sold … The purchasers might not comply with the restriction, but the only recourse for the licensee is through contract law, just as if the patentee itself sold the item with a restriction.[29]

Already, therefore, for trade in goods, it is impossible to understand the full range of their legitimate tradability internationally – the extent to which there is a downstream market – without careful analysis of the applicability and the effective scope of IP rights covering certain goods and the circumstances in which they are considered no longer to bind a purchaser (the exhaustion question). These cases draw on a legal tradition against restraints on the alienation of chattels (or constraints on dealing with a physical good once legitimately purchased); in both the cases just discussed, the majority drew on the roots of the common law, citing the seventeenth-century jurist Lord Coke on this question:

> [If] a man be possessed of … a horse, or of any other chattell … and give or sell his whole interest … therein upon condition that the Donee or Vendee shall not alien[ate] the same, the [condition] is voi[d], because his whole interest … is out of him, so as he hath no possibilit[y] of a Reverter, and it is against Trade and Traffi[c], and bargaining and contracting betwee[n] man and man: and [*539] it is within the reason of our Author that it should ouster him of all power given to him.[30]

Pivotal, for these recent decisions, was a longstanding principle that favoured freedom to trade in legitimately purchased and owned physical goods, as against an approach that would favour the claims of the holder of intangible IP rights, rights seen perhaps as more contingent, less concrete.

These cases illustrate how technological change and the growing value given to intangible content when carried on physical carrier media continues to raise a tangle of legal and policy questions. As new technologies fundamentally alter how creative works are distributed and made available to the public, established legal frameworks are put into tension. In a forward-looking mood in the 1930s, the *Waring* court had proclaimed that 'there is no reason … why an ancient generalization of law should be held invariably to apply to cases in which modern conditions of commerce and industry and the nature of new scientific inventions make restrictions highly desirable. Mere aphorisms should not be permitted to fetter the law in furthering proper social and economic purposes.'[31]

29 Ibid., p. 1535.

30 Edward Coke, *Institutes of the Laws of England: Containing the Exposition of Many Ancient and Other Statutes*, 1628, p. 223.

31 *Waring*, n. 12 *supra*.

Similar challenges for the adaptability of the law arise today as digital technology radically transforms the way valuable intangible content is traded and disseminated, to the extent that the physical carrier medium – the 'chattel' – can be dispensed with altogether. The advent of trading of IP-protected materials as intangible content on digital platforms has raised the issue of whether the answer to this question can and should be different depending on whether IP is embedded in a physical carrier medium (such as a book or optical disc) or simply traded as a licensed copy of a digital file. Digital disruption has raised the parallel question over the extent of downstream control over commercial reuse that an IPR can and should confer: in particular, whether and when rights over digital content are exhausted, limiting the right holder's entitlement to restrain further distribution of the protected digital work – in short, can legitimately purchased digital copies be resold (bearing in mind that the nature of the 'purchase' is essentially a limited IP licence)? One of the central trade policy questions in considering the implications of digital disruption is whether an intangible product, with similar properties for the consumer as its tangible counterpart, should be treated in the same way, or be treated differently, on the basis that it is essentially a bundle of intangible rights, with no physical substrate that can be 'owned' as a chattel. Would the Supreme Court have ruled differently if the textbooks concerned were e-books, and no tangible product was imported? Would both national exhaustion and digital exhaustion apply in such a case? The digital dimension of exhaustion is discussed in 'IP in the Digital Marketplace: The Effect of Exhaustion', below.

… To Trade in Bits

The Internet Protocol as a Trade Pact?

In 1990, as TRIPS negotiators progressed towards a final text, 0.05 per cent of the world's population used the Internet; in 2018, the ITU reported that the Internet was accessible by over 51 per cent of a population that had since grown by over 2 billion. Thus, following the rapid recent uptake of the Internet in the developing world – and despite enormous disparities and troubling inequities in access – for the first time most people on the planet have access to the Internet. The emergence of Internet connectivity – from its roots in ARPANet, a US Government defence project, through a narrow band of academics and research scientists, to reach a global public – has already, in myriad ways, transformed social relations, political dynamics and cultural life; it has opened up new opportunities for economic and social development, to the extent that Internet access is now recognized as a measure of progress towards attainment of the UN Sustainable Development Goals.

One TRIPS negotiator has since observed that 'the Internet was not then upon us [and the] negotiators did not indulge in futurology'.[32] The Chair of the Uruguay Round Negotiating Group on TRIPS recalls that the negotiations proceeded unaware of the contemporaneous invention of the World Wide Web at CERN, nearby in Geneva.[33] It was around the time of formal adoption of the TRIPS text, in 1994, that the implications of global connectivity through the Internet began to enter mainstream consciousness, as its use rapidly broadened beyond the research and academic communities. It was in this period that consumers (initially in a handful of developed countries, later more equitably distributed) were first gaining access to the Internet and the World Wide Web in particular, and the Internet was gaining wider practical use in many countries as a means of cultural, social and commercial exchange. When the TRIPS negotiations commenced, there were 2,308 Internet hosts in existence, primarily research and academic institutions,[34] and the user base was narrow and almost entirely comprised of academics and scientific researchers. By the time TRIPS entered into force, the number of Internet hosts had grown to 5,846,000, and the growth has proceeded exponentially since then, exceeding 1 billion by 2014. The user base grew still more sharply, from roughly 40 million in 1995 to over half the world's population by 2018.

Reflecting on the transformative impact of digital connectivity, in a commentary serendipitously published on 1 January 1995, the very day the TRIPS Agreement entered into force, Nicholas Negroponte predicted a fundamental transformation in the way we communicate, transact business and share content, summarized simply as 'bits, not atoms'. As he described this phenomenon, it had fundamental implications for the

[32] David Fitzpatrick, 'Negotiating for Hong Kong', in Watal and Taubman, *The Making of TRIPS*, pp. 285–291.

[33] Lars Anell, 'Keynote speech at the TRIPS Symposium, 26 February 2015', in Watal and Taubman, *The Making of TRIPS*, pp. 285–291.

[34] See www.isc.org/solutions/survey/history.

way in which we assess the value of goods, and the way that we conduct transactions in goods through trade:

> When returning from abroad, you must complete a customs declaration form. But have you ever declared the value of the bits you acquired while traveling? Have customs officers inquired whether you have a diskette that is worth hundreds of thousands of dollars? No. To them, the value of any diskette is the same – full or empty – only a few dollars, or the value of the atoms . . . Our mind-set about value is driven by atoms. The General Agreement on Tariffs and Trade is about atoms. Even new movies and music are shipped as atoms. Companies declare their atoms on a balance sheet and depreciate them according to rigorous schedules. But their bits, often far more valuable, do not appear. Strange.[35]

This paradigm of trade and value – rooted in physical goods, or 'atoms'– was at that very time on the point of a major pivot, the implications of which are still becoming apparent today. Technological change and the dramatic shift towards the free flow of information were putting pressure on the established copyright system, but were also removing information-based constraints on trade and creating entirely new ways of trading in knowledge products. Buyers and sellers could find each other much more readily, across the globe. New forms of widespread trading in intangible content were created, once it was possible when reaching substantial consumer markets to detach such content from the physical substrate or 'atom-based' proxy that had served as a vehicle for transactions in this content.

The rapid dissemination of establishment of the Internet created the pathways for IP-protected content to be disseminated in the form of packets defined according to the TCP/IP protocol. It enabled the development of a unique, apparently seamless, multifunctional international trading environment, a digital counterpart to the borderless trading domain in the 'analogue' world that multilateral trade rules are crafted to support.

A combination of this necessarily rigid, uniform protocol and a set of single, unambiguous addresses (the domain name system and the Internet Protocol (IP) logical addresses to which domain names point), creates a reliable system of exchanging and forwarding data to predictable addressees with confidence that the data will be intelligible to the recipient. The universality, the flexibility, the adaptability and openness

[35] Nicholas Negroponte, 'Bits and Atoms', *Wired*, 3, 1 January 1995.

of the Internet – what Zittrain calls a generative grid[36] – flows paradoxically from this rigid orthodoxy. The essence of the Internet is therefore a protocol, not any particular collection of hardware or network of data conduits – it is a rule rather than an assemblage of pluming. This provides an instructive metaphor for the more general function of international rules as underpinning greater flows of information, cultural exchanges and trade:

> Electronic commerce presents major policy contradictions for many governments. On one hand, the creation of the [TCP/IP] as a harmonised protocol for data exchange sets the stage for explosive growth of Internet-based commerce in a virtual global community and marketplace. On the other hand, the trade policies and strategies of governments are embedded in notions of territoriality . . . Governments must avoid fragmentation of the emerging global online market because of incompatible approaches to rule making among nations. The best way to do this is through negotiating effective multilateral rules. In key respects, the TCP/IP is a metaphor for good rule making. Just as the TCP/IP is a set of rules which makes globalised data exchange possible, so good trade rules facilitate global commerce, including electronic commerce.[37]

For the evolving trade in knowledge, the TCP/IP protocol was the equivalent, for intangible content defined in terms of its informational content, of the creation of the standard container for trade in physical goods. Thus the *Economist* has observed that, as a harmonised network for international exchanges, the Internet operates in a manner similar to an open international trade regime: 'the internet is as much a trade pact as an invention . . . Just as a free-trade agreement between countries increases the size of the market and boosts gains from trade, so the Internet led to greater gains from the exchange of data and allowed innovation to flourish.'[38] The rise of Internet commerce has illustrated how rules operate to promote international exchanges and, paradoxically, how a backbone of rules-based harmonization may provide a basis for diversity in cultural expression and diffusion of information. The trade policy significance was evident as early as 1998, when the WTO's Geneva Ministerial Declaration on Global Electronic Commerce[39] recognized the 'new opportunities for trade' that were then already unfolding.

[36] Jonathan Zittrain, 'The Generative Internet' (1974), *Harvard Law Review* [2006]: 119.

[37] Department of Foreign Affairs and Trade, *Driving Forces on the New Silk Road*, Canberra: Department of Foreign Affairs and Trade, 1999, p. 85.

[38] 'The Web's New Walls', *The Economist*, 2 September 2010.

[39] WT/MIN(98)/DEC/2, 25 May 1998.

The 'atoms to bits' shift predicted by Negroponte in 1995 has since eventuated to a considerable extent, transforming both domestic markets and international trade – not merely opening up new avenues for trading and thus competing in the supply of established goods and services, but also creating altogether new forms of commercial transaction, novel possibilities for exchanging value through new trading platforms. This transformation was most immediately apparent in the development of new practical means of supplying intangible content, notably the now widely-used platforms for consumer access to e-books and other publications, software applications, music and audiovisual works. But at a conceptual level, it redefined or at least diversified the very character of the commercial transactions that constitute trade in valuable intangible content, or the 'purchase' of such content (which is, in fact, generally the acquisition of a restricted use licence, defined by IP, by technological measures, by contract, or more typically by a combination of these). As debate continued about whether 'digital products' should be considered goods or services,[40] or something else[41], other business models emerged, blurring the boundaries of established forms of transaction in such IP-defined and IP-protected content, such as streaming subscriptions, 'freemium' shareware and in-app purchases. While many have the essential character of services, uncertainty remains over digital products that are analogous to traditional physical products containing essentially the same content. Equally, IP rights as such are increasingly traded as discrete items,[42] whether through dedicated IP exchanges established as well-defined marketplaces,[43] or in a broader sense of a 'market' for IP rights, such as the emerging 'market for brands', comprising purchase, franchising or licensing of trademarks and brands as the subject of

[40] '[T]here was still a lack of clarity with regard to the classification under GATT or GATS of certain products which can be delivered both in electronic form and on a physical carrier'. Summary by the Secretariat of the Issues Raised, Dedicated Discussion on Electronic Commerce under the Auspices of the General Council on 15 June 2001, WTO document WT/GC/W/436 (6 July 2001); despite continuing debate and a voluminous scholarly literature, the question remains unresolved at a formal level.

[41] See, e.g., WTO, Communication from Indonesia and Singapore, Preparations for the 1999 Ministerial Conference: Work Programme on Electronic Commerce, WT/GC/W/247, 9 July 1999.

[42] OECD, 'Intellectual Property Market', in OECD, *Science, Technology and Industry Outlook*, 2012, OECD Publishing, at dx.doi.org/10.1787/sti_outlook-2012-24-en.

[43] See, e.g., www.ip-marketplace.org/, maintained by the Danish Patent and Trademark Office; and Asia IP Exchange (AsiaIPEX) developed by the Hong Kong Trade Development Council, available at www.asiaipex.com.

commercial transactions in their own right,[44] and the growth of markets for technology as such, 'disembodied from physical goods'.[45]

Creating New Markets for IP

The transformative effect of digital technologies on trade in knowledge products has been profound throughout the period of implementation of the TRIPS Agreement. The scale of this trade in IP is remarkable, as is its impact in many sectors. For many consumers, the most evident manifestation is in the form of online platforms for access to digital content, such as music downloads, apps, and e-books. In 2001, the global recorded music industry[46] reported revenues of USD 23.2 billion for sales of physical media; this total has fallen steadily since then, reaching USD 4.7 billion in 2018. Digital downloads only registered a significant proportion from 2004, peaked in 2012 at USD 4.3 billion, and fell to USD 2.3 billion in 2018. Streaming revenues rose sharply more recently, at USD 8.9 billion in 2018 well exceeding the revenues from both physical media and downloads. In the book sector, the Association of American Publishers reports that in the US market in 2018, for the second successive year, 'publisher sales to online retail channels exceeded sales to physical retail channels with sales to online retail at \$8.03 billion and sales to physical retail at \$6.90 billion'.[47] In a Chinese market of over USD 1 billion in 2016, digital editions reportedly accounted for around 28[48] per cent. A survey of the publishing market in 2018 indicated the highest revenue share from digital editions in Japan (24.5 per cent), Sweden (23.2 per cent), the Republic of Korea (22.5 per cent) and the US (19.4 per cent).[49]

Despite only coming into existence with the introduction of the iPhone in 2008, app stores have become major commercial platforms

[44] Carl Benedikt Frey, Atif Ansar and Sacha Wunsch-Vincent, 'Defining and Measuring the "Market for Brands": Are Emerging Economies Catching Up?', Economic Research Working Paper No. 21, 2014.

[45] Ashish Arora and Alfonso Gambardella, 'Ideas for Rent: An Overview of Markets for Technology' (2010), *Industrial and Corporate Change* 19, 3: 775–803, available at https://ssrn.com/abstract=1617051.

[46] International Federation of the Phonographic Industry (IFPI), Global Music Report 2019 // State of the Industry, available at www.ifpi.org/recording-industry-in-numbers.php.

[47] AAP StatShot Annual Report for Calendar Year 2018, 21 June 2019.

[48] WIPO, 'The Global Publishing Industry in 2016: A Pilot Survey', available at www.wipo_ipa_pilotsurvey_2016.

[49] WIPO, *The Global Publishing Industry in 2018*, Geneva: World Intellectual Property Organization, 2020.

creating new international marketplaces for intangible content. One industry report reported that some 115 billion transactions took place in 2019 on the two major app stores, such as Google Play and the Apple iOS App Store.[50] By one estimate, app store revenues were USD 120 billion in 2019, rising 110 per cent since 2016.[51] This major area of international commercial activity is striking in its scale, given that this category of commerce did not exist before 2008; and yet much of this trade is not reported in existing trade statistics,[52] the chief source of data currently the private sector itself, many details (such as the distribution of revenue to authors and app developers worldwide) being treated as confidential business information. A WTO report comments:

> It is not clear to what extent these transactions are recorded in current trade statistics, but their value is now a major component of revenues in the content industries, and a share of these earnings is redistributed to app developers, musicians, authors and other creators internationally. A clearer picture of these sizeable revenue flows would improve our understanding of the pattern of international trade in these sectors, and could lead to a more accurate understanding of how economies benefit from this form of international trade, as internet platforms serve to connect content developers across the globe with consumers in multiple jurisdictions.[53]

The WTO report examines the transformational effect of trade in digitizable goods (defined as physical goods that can be digitalized) including 'cinematograph film; traditionally printed matter such as books, pamphlets, maps, newspapers, journals, periodicals, postcards and personal greeting message or announcement cards; video games; computer software; and recorded media such as musical records, tapes and other sound or similar recordings'[54] and concludes that imports of such goods in physical form has fallen to 0.8 per cent of WTO members' total imports, by contrast with the proportion of 2.9 per cent in 2000 (see Figure 2.3).

[50] Sensor Tower, Q4 2019 Store Intelligence Data Digest, available at https://go.sensortower.com/Q4-2019-Data-Digest.html.

[51] App Annie, State of Mobile 2020, available at https://www.appannie.com/en/go/state-of-mobile-2020/.

[52] On the difficulties of measuring this trade, see Joscelyn Magdeleine and Andreas Maurer, 'Measuring International Intellectual Property Transactions in a Globalized World: Current Challenges and Possible Improvements', Chapter 5 in this volume, and Erick S. Oh, 'The Global Digital Content Landscape', Chapter 10 in this volume.

[53] WTO, *World Trade Report 2018: The Future of World Trade: How Digital Technologies are Transforming Global Commerce*, Geneva: WTO, 2018, p. 98.

[54] Ibid., p. 92.

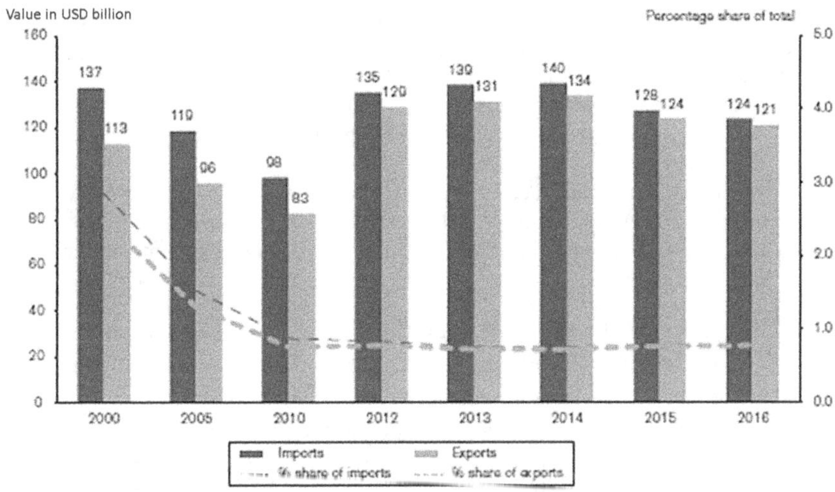

Figure 2.3 Value and share of trade in physical form of digitizable goods
Source: WTO, 2018.

The advent of widespread access to digital platforms has, indeed, created entirely new markets for content. One example is the market for caller tunes, the music played to those calling a mobile telephone. This is a major source of revenue for the predominantly domestic music sector in developing countries such as India, where, reportedly, over a billion transactions a day are undertaken domestically,[55] and with revenue from foreign markets reportedly comprising 10 per cent of this income stream. Plainly, TRIPS negotiators could not have anticipated not merely the scale and importance, but even the very existence of this particular marketplace for highly specific licences for musical works.

In contrast, with trade in such content when included on physical media, 'purchase' of digital content generally does not lead to a transfer of ownership, but rather simply entails a conditional and limited licence for access. Thus, the 2018 terms and conditions for Google Play refer to 'purchase of content' and a 'sale contract', but then stipulate:

> License to Use Content. After completing a transaction or paying the applicable fees for Content, you will have the non-exclusive right, solely as expressly permitted in these Terms and associated policies, to store, access, view, use, and display copies of the applicable Content on your

[55] See www.comviva.com/news-events/comvivas-crbt-platform-delivers-1-billion-caller-tunes-every-day-india.htm.

> Devices or as otherwise authorized as part of the Service for your personal, non-commercial use only. All rights, title and interest in Google Play and Content not expressly granted to you in the Terms are reserved. Your use of apps and games may be governed by the additional terms and conditions of the end user license agreement between you and the Provider.
>
> Violation of License Terms. If you violate any of the Terms, your rights under this license will immediately terminate, and Google may terminate your access to Google Play, the Content or your Google Account without refund to you.[56]

Similarly, Apple's Licensed Application End User License Agreement opens with the clear statement that '[apps] made available through the App Store are licensed, not sold, to you ... Licensor grants to you a nontransferable license to use the Licensed Application on any Apple-branded products that you own or control and as permitted by the Usage Rules...'[57] And Amazon's Kindle Store stipulates that 'Kindle Content is licensed, not sold, to you by the Content Provider', and grants 'a non-exclusive right to view, use, and display ... Kindle Content' solely as permitted.

A much broader policy debate surrounds this instance of the shift 'from asset to access', or the development of 'an economy built around access relations' shifting from 'a property regime based on the idea of broadly distributed ownership to an access regime based on securing short-term limited use of assets controlled by networks of suppliers'.[58] A recent critical analysis of the implications of trading 'property rights for conditional privileges' argues that the 'baseline for property rights should be a function of the law, not contingent on the kindness of copyright holders and retailers'[59] and calls for the law to recognize purchasers' property rights over digital property, akin to property rights over chattels. For immediate analysis of the trade policy and economic implications, however, it remains the case that the very legal character of trade in digital content is, on the whole, significantly different from trade in corresponding physical carrier media, in terms of the formal transfer of ownership, in terms of the contingent character of access to content,

[56] Google Play Terms of Service, 5 February 2018, available at https://play.google.com/about/play-terms/index.html.

[57] See www.apple.com/legal/internet-services/itunes/dev/stdeula/.

[58] Jeremy Rifkin, *The Age of Access*, New York: Penguin Putnam, 2000, p. 4.

[59] Aaron Perzanowski and Jason Schultz, *The End of Ownership: Personal Property in the Digital Economy*, Cambridge, MA: MIT Press, 2016, p. 187.

and in terms of the further reach of applicable IP rights over the downstream use of and trade in the content to which access is procured.

. . . *And New Trade Opportunities?*

At least at the level of principle, the resultant technological transformation of commercial practice has the potential both to improve prospects for equality of commercial conditions for enterprises around the globe regardless of their geographical location (the kind of market access that would be favoured, in principle, by trade policy), and to ensure more efficient, and more transparent, competition in domestic markets.[60] The resultant new forms of trading, in principle, open up new prospects for socially beneficial competition and for international market access as a de facto form of trade liberalization. In particular, the interconnectivity afforded by the Internet protocol suite, has opened up new opportunities for participation in international commercial activity, notably by enterprises in developing countries and by micro, small and medium-sized enterprises (MSMEs). A recent position paper submitted by several WTO member governments observes that:

> Digital technology is transforming the global economy. This transformation presents new opportunities to promote inclusive economic growth, including by connecting rural to urban economies; opening new channels of trade for landlocked countries; facilitating the participation of women and micro enterprises in the formal economy; providing micro, small and medium-sized enterprises (MSMEs) access to a global consumer base; and facilitating cross-border trade in services previously considered not technically feasible.[61]

The statistics, such as they are, provide some evidence that developers across the world may be taking advantage of these opportunities. Apple claimed in January 2020 that its App Store 'provides developers of all sizes access to customers in 155 countries. Since the App Store launched in 2008, developers have earned over $155 billion, with a quarter of those

[60] D. Van Welsum, W. Overmeer and B. Van Ark, 'Unlocking the ICT Growth Potential in Europe: Enabling People and Businesses', The Conference Board for the European Commission, 2013.

[61] WTO, *Trade Policy, The WTO and the Digital Economy*, Communication from Canada, Chile, Colombia, Côte d'Ivoire, the European Union, the Republic of Korea, Mexico, Montenegro, Paraguay, Singapore and Turkey JOB/GC/116, JOB/CTG/4, JOB/SERV/248, JOB/IP/21, JOB/DEV/42 (13 January 2017).

earnings coming from the past year alone'.[62] Alphabet reports that 'over $80 billion has been earned by developers around the world from Google Play, [which has] over 2 billion active monthly users'.[63]

The practical implications for the creative industries – and development prospects – in a developing country context were set out in a recent ITC study considering the prospects for this sector in Rwanda,[64] which concluded:

> digitization has contributed to the robust growth of creative industries in recent years, generating $2.25 trillion in revenue and 29.5 million jobs globally. It has also made digital export in the creative industries more accessible to small and medium-sized enterprises, including those from developing countries. Digital export in creative industries could underpin overall developing countries exports, providing a channel to leverage their rich culture and heritage for economic growth and diversification. Developing countries have already gained a foothold in the global creative export market. They account for 53% of worldwide exports of creative goods, amounting to $265 billion in export revenue. Although developed economies still dominate global trade in creative services, momentum is building in developing countries, with least developed countries' share in exports of personal, cultural and recreational services growing 22.7% a year since 2012.

New platforms, tailored to specific needs, can open up these prospects further, for instance sites promoting local music such as Famemix in Rwanda, or Jokotext and MusikBi in Senegal. Despite these promising trends, considerable hurdles of course impede opportunities to benefit from these new avenues for trade in knowledge, particularly in the developing world, including shortcomings in digital infrastructure, lack of equitable access to established trading platforms, and the inevitable lag in the legal and regulatory framework in responding effectively to the distinctive characteristics of these new forms of trade. The following section reviews these evolving characteristics of intangible trade in knowledge products.

[62] 'Apple rings in new era of Services following landmark year', 8 January 2020, available at www.apple.com/newsroom/2020/01/apple-rings-in-new-era-of-services-following-landmark-year/.

[63] 'Alphabet Q4 2019 Earnings Call, February 3, 2020', available at https://abc.xyz/investor/static/pdf/2019_Q4_Earnings_Transcript.pdf.

[64] International Trade Centre, *Creative Industries in Rwanda: Digital Paths to Global Markets*, Geneva: ITC, 2019.

But What Constitutes 'Trade in BITS'?

Regulating Trade-Related Aspects of IP in the Digital Environment

The conclusion of a multilateral trade agreement on the 'trade-related aspects' of IP rights, in the form of the TRIPS Agreement, was, in effect, a recognition of the need to address what was already a complex interplay between international trade and the IP system; even at a time when that very interplay was in the process of radical transformation. Earlier, the IP system had been seen, conventionally, to be at odds with the objectives of market liberalization for trade in goods, so that IP protection had been conceived as an allowable exception under the GATT (Article XX), and not a positive obligation. When the TRIPS Agreement inverted this logic, and made application of high standards of IP protection a requirement within the WTO trade law system, critics of TRIPS viewed it as the intrusion of non-trade issues into the trading system in tension with the goal of market liberalization,[65] by imposing 'behind the border' standards rather than opening up trade. Yet the preamble to TRIPS set the IP system in the context of international trade, recording WTO Members' desire 'to reduce distortions and impediments to international trade, and taking into account the need to promote effective and adequate protection of intellectual property rights, and to ensure that measures and procedures to enforce intellectual property rights do not themselves become barriers to legitimate trade'.

Hence, the advent and implementation of the TRIPS Agreement spurred a reconsideration of the complex and diversifying interaction between IP and trade. Yet, emerging as it did from within the trade-in-goods paradigm, the Agreement as originally conceived was not negotiated in anticipation of the massive, widespread tradability of IP rights as such, and did not envisage the sale of an IP licence as constituting the essential value at the heart of commercial transactions constituting international trade. The evolving diversification of commercial transactions dealing with intangible content, fuelled by the disruptive impact of digital technology – and the transformation both of content industries and of the opportunities for creative and innovative firms across the globe – suggests that it is timely to reconsider the 'trade-related aspects' of the IP system in the light of the dramatic transformations which have proceeded in parallel

[65] E.g. A. Panagariya, 'TRIPS and the WTO: An Uneasy Marriage', in K. Maskus (ed.), *The WTO, Intellectual Property Rights and the Knowledge Economy*, Cheltenham: Edward Elgar Publishing, 2004, pp. 42–53.

with the implementation of the TRIPS Agreement across the WTO membership over the past quarter-century. These developments suggest that the evolution of the IP system and the digital environment together compel a reconsideration of what constitutes 'trade'.

Even as the ink had barely dried on the TRIPS Agreement, digital disruption of trade in IP content posed a range of challenges for the international IP system and above all for an agreement that sought to deal with the interplay between IP and international commerce – the pace of technological innovation effectively forcing a redefinition, in practice, of the 'trade-related aspects' of IP rights. The challenges posed confronted some fundamental concepts – on the face of it, at least, a kind of technological dilution or even abolition of national borders, with conceptual and practical difficulties in correlating the exercise and enforcement of IP rights with distinct and well-defined national jurisdictions, testing the longstanding principle of territoriality of IP rights and licences granted under them. Furthermore, the detachment of IP content from the physical carrier media that had conventionally served as a proxy for trade in IP rights made it possible for the general consumer to enter the market for pure licences in IP.

Trade in Digital Products

Governments have long debated how WTO rules should apply to digital products: how they are taxed, valued and classified, and whether differential treatment of digital trade amounts to discrimination. For instance, what happens when the 'same' content is conveyed across the same border, but through electronic transmissions as a digital product, rather than as content embedded on a physically traded good? What is functionally the very same software package, for instance, may be downloaded or purchased on a disc; and a package purchased on a disc may be partially or fully upgraded over the Internet as part of the same commercial transaction. The packet-switching technology and dispersed architecture of the Internet could mean that different elements of this content could pass undetected through many different jurisdictions. No distinct package or assemblage of atoms is presented to customs officials for clearance at a defined border. This uncertainty over the 'real world' characteristics of such products leads to the specific question of how digital products should fall within the conventional categories of goods and services. Early in the WTO debate, one delegation pointed out that 'it was difficult to see how a distinction between "goods" and "services" could be handled in practice, even if agreed on in theory. As the transmitted bytes of data streams consisted only of ones and zeroes, the delegation raised the questions how it was possible to decide for each individual case whether a particular transmission was covered by goods or services disciplines?'[66]

And, indeed, an early paper by Indonesia and Singapore, discussing the need for legal certainty in classification, speculated about the possibility of a third category of trade, that of trade in IP as such, which would be consonant with the increasing attention given to the contents, rather than the platform on which the contents are delivered:

> In attempting to classify digitized products one possible criterion that has been raised is to consider whether the product has a tangible counterpart in the physical world. This criterion could then be applied to over-the-counter purchases of books, music and software even if such purchases were delivered as digitized products and not in terms of their physical counterparts. An alternative is to just consider the contents themselves. Books, music and software are not in themselves new commercial products. It is just that prior to the advent of e-commerce, they were treated as goods because they had to be delivered in the form of a carrier media, be it paper, cassettes or diskettes etc. and those carrier media were classified as goods. Now that those forms of tangible carrier mediums are no longer necessary maybe what we need to consider is whether the software and music would continue to be classified as goods, or it might be more appropriate for them to be classified as services.
>
> It may also not be a coincidence that all these three examples, without a carrier medium are intangible goods considered under the ambit of intellectual property rights. Could such products then be simply considered as trade in intellectual property rights and not be classified as a good or a service? What is paramount though is that the criteria for classification should provide legal certainty on how the good, the service or the intellectual property right is to be treated.[67]

Meanwhile, the trade in digital products has grown apace and a massive body of practical experience has accumulated. This may indicate either that no definitive position is needed, is feasible or desirable under international trade law; or it may imply that the question may ultimately be resolved in a more ad hoc way, through pragmatic negotiation, through dispute settlement or through the accumulation of bilateral

[66] General Council, 'Interim Review of Progress in the Implementation of the Work Programme on Electronic Commerce, Communication from the Chairman of the Council for Trade in Goods', WT/GC/24, 12 April 1999, p. 3.

[67] WTO document WT/GC/W/247, note 41 above, paras 10–14.

and regional trade agreements dealing with digital products, with potentially diverse forms of classifications applicable to a widening array of such products. To be sure, WTO dispute settlement has effectively confirmed that services delivered over the Internet are indeed covered by GATS obligations, despite the positions taken by some governments in WTO policy discussions that either an express common understanding would be desirable, or specific, additional commitments concerning Internet-supplied services would be required before any obligations came into effect.[68]

Recent bilateral and regional trade agreements have, in any case, addressed the issue in different ways.[69] A number of recent agreements have established rules expressly addressing trade in digital products, defining such products and regulating their trade in terms that are similar, but not identical. In general, such agreements indicate, in various formulations, that any definition of a digital product is without prejudice to Parties' views on whether trade in digital products through electronic transmission should be categorized as trade in services or goods. But the scope of definition of 'digital products' differs, including on apparent coverage of content included on carrier media. The Comprehensive and Progressive Agreement for Trans-Pacific Partnership (CPTPP)[70] and the recent agreement between Canada, Mexico and the United States (variously styled by its parties T-MEC, CUSMA and USMCA)[71] both define a digital product as 'a computer programme, text, video, image, sound recording or other product that is digitally encoded, produced for commercial sale or distribution, and that can be transmitted electronically'. The Australia–Japan Economic Partnership Agreement defines the term similarly but expressly excludes products 'that are fixed on a carrier medium'[72] (in effect, the 'chattels' discussed above). By contrast, the Republic of Korea–US Free Trade Agreement defines digital products in otherwise identical terms, but 'regardless of whether they are fixed on a carrier medium or transmitted electronically'.[73] Given that the principal

[68] See the summary of the debate in Sasha Wunsch-Vincent, 'The Internet, Cross-Border Trade in Services, and The GATS – Lessons from US-Gambling', *World Trade Review* 5, 3: 319–356, p. 323.

[69] For a general discussion of trade agreements in this area, see Mira Burri, 'Adapting Trade Rules for the Age of Big Data', Chapter 20 in this volume.

[70] Article 14.1.

[71] Article 19.1.

[72] Article 13.2.

[73] Article 15.9.

undertaking applied to trade in digital products is one of non-discrimination, such divergences in definitional scope may have limited practical impact – beyond reinforcing a general liberalization of such trade – but they clearly betoken some divergence as to the trade law significance of digital content embedded on a traded physical carrier medium. Since, also, some provisions require treatment of digital products that is no less favourable to 'like' digital products, to the extent that the definition includes content on carrier medium, this non-discriminatory principle may have implications for traded 'chattels' that have traditionally been treated as traded goods – particularly if physical carrier media are subject to tariffs or other constraints at the border which are not applied to their intangible counterparts.

The Comprehensive and Economic Trade Agreement (CETA) between the EU and Canada takes a different approach to dealing with trade in parcels of digital content. It does not refer to digital products, but, in its e-commerce chapter, defines a 'delivery' as 'a computer program, text, video, image, sound recording or other delivery that is digitally encoded', a phrasing closely analogous to that of other agreements' definition of 'digital product'. Despite the substantive overlap in these definitions, this choice of terminology seemingly emphasizes the means of transmission, and not the treatment or categorization of digital content as such. Indeed, the term 'delivery' may perhaps allude to a trade in services framework.[74] In any event, as in other trade agreements, a key element concerns the exclusion of 'a customs duty, fee, or charge on a delivery transmitted by electronic means'.

Chapters on electronic commerce or digital trade in recent trade agreements are generally framed with the proviso that their terms are without prejudice to the parallel rules on IP. If the protection of IP – and the approach taken to the question of exhaustion – is to prevail in this way over parallel, newly crafted obligations to treat digital products (including, potentially, 'like' digital products traded on physical carriers), this may provide a basis for differential treatment between intangible and tangible versions of the same content in some circumstances. More generally, and at the very least, this kind of provision may betoken the need for a more coherent view, from a trade policy point of view, of the IP dimension of transactions for digital products.

[74] For instance, Article XXVIII of the WTO General Agreement on Trade in Services defines supply of a service to include its 'delivery': (c) 'measures by Members affecting trade in service include measures in respect of . . .'.

Beyond Trade in Goods?

Taken together, these developments – in technology, in business patterns (particularly new ways of linking content providers with content consumers) and in international agreements – raise probing questions about the very character of trade, its essential legal and economic characteristics, and how it is to be measured and classified. In particular, the development of international digital platforms that permit the trading of pure content means that the commercial nature of the transaction is decreasingly less likely to be defined by the transfer of ownership in a physical thing; the true character of the transaction emerges more clearly as the acquisition of a licence or contract over content defined by IP rights.

The WTO's multilateral trade agreements – and the overarching Agreement Establishing the WTO itself – do not venture an express formal definition of what constitutes 'trade' as such. A dispute settlement panel has observed that 'although the preamble to the WTO Agreement refers in particular to expanding trade in goods, it does not give sufficiently precise information on the terms which we must interpret'.[75] And this may be inevitable, as trade policy has long wrestled with the boundaries of the kind of commercial transactions that are validated as 'trade', which in turn raises deep questions of economic value.

By one recent, standard definition, 'trade' is the 'exchange of goods between two individuals or nations . . . the basic component of economic activity . . . undertaken for mutual advantage'.[76] Naturally, such a definition begs the question of what is counted as a 'good' – and how material and enduring it must be. The intuitive tendency to associate economic value with the outcomes of productivity only when captured in lasting tangible form – the proverbial 'things you can drop on your foot' – is already apparent in Adam Smith's reference, in the *Wealth of Nations*, to the intangible or ephemeral product of 'players, opera-singers, opera-dancers, etc'. as producing 'nothing which could afterwards purchase or procure an equal quantity of labour. Like the declamation of the actor, the harangue of the orator, or the tune of the musician, the work of all of them perishes in the very instant of its production'.[77]

[75] Panel Report, EC – Asbestos, para. 8.48.

[76] *Oxford Dictionary of Economics*, 4th ed., Oxford: Oxford University Press, 2013.

[77] Adam Smith, *An Inquiry into the Nature and Causes of the Wealth of Nations*, Henry Frowde (ed.), Oxford: Oxford University Press, 1909 (1776).

In more recent times, the increasing recognition of the value of the intangible component of commercial transactions – and its consequential significance for economic growth and trade policy – inevitably led to a reframing of what constitutes 'trade', resulting most consequentially in the incorporation of trade in services within the framework of multilateral trade law through the vector of the General Agreement on Trade in Services,[78] and parallel developments in numerous bilateral and regional trade agreements. Thus, in Goode's dictionary, trade 'usually refers to the sale and distribution of goods and services across international borders. There are many different ways of doing this, but there must be a commercial element for a transaction to qualify as trade'. By one definition, a good is 'any physical object, natural or manmade, or service rendered, that could command a price in a market'.[79] A more precise technical definition of tradeable goods in the context of statistics is found in the recommendation that 'international merchandise trade statistics record all goods which add to or subtract from the stock of material resources of a country by entering (imports) or leaving (exports) its economic territory'.[80]

The definitions of these concepts begin to count – literally count – when used to define statistics. In balance-of-payments statistics, goods are defined as 'physical, produced items over which ownership rights can be established and whose economic ownership can be passed from one institutional unit to another by engaging in transactions . . . The production of a good can be separated from its subsequent sale or resale'.[81] And services are defined as 'the result of a production activity that changes the conditions of the consuming units, or facilitates the exchange of products or financial assets. Services are not generally separate items over which ownership rights can be established and cannot generally be separated from their production'.[82]

Notably, there are certain cases in which the passage of physical goods across borders is counted as a service, not because of their inherent nature or value, but because of the nature of the commercial transaction that leads to their shipment, specifically 'newspapers and periodicals sent

[78] See Lee Tuthill, Antonia Carzaniga and Martin Roy, 'How Digitization is Transforming Trade', Chapter 3 in this volume, for a general overview of the trade in services dimension.

[79] G. Bannock, R. E. Baxter and E. Davis, *Dictionary of Economics*, London: Penguin, 2004.

[80] United Nations, International Merchandise Trade Statistics: Concepts and Definitions 2010, ST/ESA/STAT/SER.M/52/Rev.3 Statistical Papers Series M No. 52, 12.

[81] IMF, *Balance of Payments and International Investment Position Manual*, Washington, DC: International Monetary Fund, 2009, p. 119.

[82] Ibid.

under direct subscription' and 'media used for carrying software customized or written for a specific client or originals of any nature, where identified'.[83] In other words, whether a transaction is classed as a good or service in these cases will in turn depend not on the characteristics of the physical good itself, but rather the commercial context within which the good is shipped. This is a telling reminder that, again, it is the character and legal context of the way in which value is defined and exchanged that determines the nature of 'trade', rather than the objective characteristics of any object, tangible or otherwise, that is transmitted in the course of, or as a consequence of, the transaction.

The extent to which IP rights define and govern transactions in both physical and digital products can significantly shape both domestic and international trade in these materials, specifically when physical goods embody IP-protected content and when digital products are defined and transacted in the form of IP licences. Hence the applicable IP rights can form an inherent part of the context of commercial transactions and in turn define the very nature of the market for such products. Their significance is particularly evident when considering the effect of exhaustion of IP rights, and more generally as to whether conceptual and legal preference is to be given to the tangible character of traded goods, or whether the IP dimension is to prevail.

On the domestic plane, the interplay between IP and trade in goods was considered by the US Court of Appeals for the Federal Circuit in the *ClearCorrect* case[84], concerning the authority of the International Trade Commission under the Tariff Act to 'remedy only those unfair acts that involve the importation of "articles" as described in 19 USC § 1337(a)'. The case concerned whether this authority extended to the electronic transmission of digital data, when a digital data model for the alignment of teeth, transmitted from Pakistan to the United States, was argued to be an importation of an article infringing a US patent and thus subject to border measures as a form of unfair competition. The ITC had held that 'the digital data sets at issue . . . are true articles of international commerce that are imported into the United States, and their inclusion within the purview of section 337 [of the Tariff Act] would effectuate the central purpose of the statute'.[85] However, on appeal to the Federal

[83] International Merchandise Trade Statistics: Concepts and Definitions 2010, note 80, 21.
[84] ClearCorrect Operating, LLC *v.* International Trade Commission, 810 F.3d 1283 (Fed. Cir. 2015).
[85] Ibid., p. 1304.

Circuit, the majority opinion found that 'articles' means 'material things', acknowledging that 'electronic transmissions have some physical properties—for example an electron's invariant mass is a known quantity'[86] – but arguing that 'commonsense dictates that there is a fundamental difference between electronic transmissions and 'material things'. The majority saw this as a policy matter for Congress, which 'is in a far better position to draw the lines that must be drawn if the product of intellectual processes rather than manufacturing processes are to be included within the statute'.[87]

In her dissent, Judge Newman argued that the Tariff Act was 'enacted to provide additional support to domestic industries that dealt in new and creative commerce, by providing an efficient safeguard against unfair competition by imports that infringe United States patents or copyrights'.[88] She argued that the digital datasets were patentable inventions: '[i]t is now beyond debate that digital goods are subject to the patent law, and it is beyond debate that digital goods can be imported' and 'the intention to omit unforeseen, later-discovered technologies cannot be imputed to this statute'.[89]

This case highlights one of the central trade policy questions in considering the implications of digital disruption: whether an intangible product, with similar properties for the consumer as its tangible counterpart, should be treated in the same way, or should be treated differently, on the basis that it is essentially a bundle of intangible rights, with no physical substrate that can be 'owned' as a chattel; or, more succinctly, how far we can indeed apply the majority, avowedly 'commonsense', view in *ClearCorrect* that there is indeed 'a *fundamental* difference between electronic transmissions and material things' (emphasis added).

IP in the Digital Marketplace: The Effect of Exhaustion

One consequential question for trade and IP policy is whether, to what extent and how, digital disruption can and should create single markets for content that transcend national borders. Can digital markets for content defined by IP rights be forged internationally, for the mutual

86 Ibid., p. 1287.
87 Ibid., p. 1302, citing its decision in Bayer AG *v.* Housey Pharm., Inc., 340 F.3d 1367, 1374 (Fed. Cir. 2003).
88 Ibid., p. 1304.
89 Ibid., p. 1307.

benefit of the creators and consumers of creative content, while still compatible with IP systems defined and structured on a territorial basis? Digital disruption has created practical possibilities for global markets for IP-protected digital content, and to some extent technological development has enabled the de facto eradication of the national borders that used to enable IP right holders to segment markets for IP content according to geographical boundaries. Indeed, this leads to competing expectations – right holders seeking to maintain downstream control over the distribution of content to other jurisdictions, consumers of content expecting immediate access to a global single market of content, with a corresponding single global licence.

In the past analogue context, we have seen how the US Supreme Court drew an analogy between the purchaser's rights over the imported copyright-protected textbook and ownership of a 'chattel' (a tangible item of property), rather than viewing the physical book as being essentially a mere carrier medium for protected content and licensed IP. And in earlier US jurisprudence, a copyright restriction on radio broadcast of a sound recording was construed as an 'equitable servitude on a chattel',[90] seeing the essential nature of the transaction as ownership of the physical object, while 'enjoyment of the possession of a physical copy of the recording was subject to continuing liability to the originator of the sound recording'.[91]

The advent of digital technologies, and the trading in digital copies of copyright works in particular, inevitably leads to a recalibration of the market and a redefinition of the relationship between content producer, downstream trader and consumer. How should the treaty negotiator, the domestic legislator, the court respond? Is this a technical matter of applying established principles in a novel context, or are new or adjusted principles needed? The approach taken to the exhaustion of rights over purely digital content provides an instructive test case: does the right holder have a different entitlement to reach through the original transaction and to control downstream distribution, depending on whether the content is carried on physical media or is despatched as bundles of data on a packet-switching network?

[90] Waring *v.* WDAS Broad. Station Inc., 194 A. 631, 638 (1937).

[91] Antony Taubman, 'TRIPS Encounters the Internet: An Analogue Treaty in a Digital Age, or The First Trade 2.0 Agreement?', in Mira Burri and Thomas Cottier (eds), *Trade Governance in the Digital Age*, Cambridge: Cambridge University Press, 2015, p. 314.

On-demand delivery of digital copies of copyright material was not directly addressed in the TRIPS negotiations, which had concluded effectively in 1991, given the acknowledged lack of awareness among negotiators as to the impending impact of the Internet on the content industries. Thus, how to regulate on-demand delivery of protected works, performances and sound recordings became a central issue in the work at WIPO, which resulted in the adoption of the two new copyright treaties in December 1996, the WCT and WPPT. The principal purpose of these so-called 'Internet Treaties' was to adapt international rules for the protection of copyright and the rights of performers and producers of sound recordings to the digital revolution, in particular, the distribution of copyright material over the Internet.

WCT Article 8 on 'Right of Communication to the Public' is the most important element in the WCT building on the platform established by TRIPS. It is intended to cover on-demand delivery of protected works over the Internet, a scenario captured in the carefully negotiated wording 'the making available to the public or their works in such a way that members of the public may access these works from a place and at a time individually chosen by them'. The Basic Proposal, commenting on what became Article 8, explains the different scope and effect of the distinct rights of communication and of distribution:

> It should be pointed out that no rights are exhausted in connection with communication to the public. Should communication of a work result in the reproduction of a copy at the recipient end, the work may not be communicated further to the public or distributed to the public without authorization. Exhaustion of rights is only associated with the distribution of tangible copies.[92]

The text of the provision as contained in the Basic Proposal was adopted without any changes, and a similar approach was followed in WPPT Articles 10 and 14 (which deal respectively with the analogous right of making available fixed performances and phonograms). The 2012 Beijing Treaty on Audiovisual Performances in its Article 10 (Right of Making Available of Fixed Performances) extended this right also to performers of performances fixed in audiovisual fixations. The overall effect is to create different conditions for the further sale of IP-protected content, depending on whether it is provided as a distribution or a communication.

[92] Basic Proposal, CRNR/DC/4, para. 10.20.

At the level of domestic jurisprudence, the European Court of Justice (ECJ) has concluded that 'exhaustion of right applies to the tangible object into which a protected work or its copy is incorporated if it has been placed onto the market with the copyright holder's consent'.[93] However, further commercial use – in this case, transfer to a new medium – is still caught by the copyright owner's rights, as it amounts to a new form of commercial use not covered by the original copyright licence.

A more recent ECJ decision considered the implications of the distinction between physical and digital transmission of copyright works. The *Tom Kabinet* case[94] concerned a system of trading in e-books, which entailed selling second-hand e-books which had been legitimately purchased from the publishers. In addressing whether the purchaser of an e-book was entitled to resell it in this way, the case turned on whether, in the terms of Directive 2001/29/EC (the Infosoc Directive, which directly applied the WCT terminology) the supply of an e-book was a 'distribution to the public', akin to the second-hand sale of a physical book (implying exhaustion of rights associated with the further sale, since it was assumed that the right holder received sufficient remuneration from the first sale), or a 'communication to the public' (for which the WCT had expressly precluded exhaustion of rights) – in the latter case, the first sale of the e-book would not bring with it the entitlement of the purchaser then to sell the e-book to a third party.

The ECJ concluded that 'the supply to the public by downloading, for permanent use, of an e-book is covered by the concept of "communication to the public" and, more specifically, by that of 'making available to the public of [authors'] works in such a way that members of the public may access them from a place and at a time individually chosen by them'. This ruled out the exhaustion of rights following the initial supply of the e-book. The Court's decision was based on its interpretation of the Infosoc Directive, but was supported by policy considerations that emphasized the distinct economics of trade in hard copies and in e-books. Thus the court analysed both the WCT and the *travaux préparatoires* of the Infosoc Directive itself to conclude that the legislators had intended the rule of exhaustion to apply only to distribution of tangible objects incorporating the copyright work, such as printed books on a material medium, and not to the online communication of works:

[93] *All Posters*, C-419/13, 22 January 2015, curia.europa.eu/juris/liste.jsf?num=C-419/13.

[94] European Court of Justice, Decision of 19 December 2019, C-263/18 – Nederlands Uitgeversverbond et al. *v.* Tom Kabinet Internet BV et al. ('Tom Kabinet').

> interactive on-demand transmission was a new form of exploitation of intellectual property, in relation to which the Member States were of the view that it should be covered by the right to control communication to the public, while stating that it was generally accepted that the distribution right, which applies exclusively to the distribution of physical copies, does not cover such transmission.[95]

The court set out the policy distinction between digital and material supply of books in these terms:

> The supply of a book on a material medium and the supply of an e-book cannot, however, be considered equivalent from an economic and functional point of view ... dematerialised digital copies, unlike books on a material medium, do not deteriorate with use, and used copies are therefore perfect substitutes for new copies. In addition, exchanging such copies requires neither additional effort nor additional cost, so that a parallel secondhand market would be likely to affect the interests of the copyright holders in obtaining appropriate reward for their works much more than the market for second-hand tangible objects, contrary to the objective [of establishing a high level of protection of authors, allowing them to obtain an appropriate reward for the use of their works, including when a communication to the public takes place].[96]

The result had been different in an earlier ECJ case addressing digital exhaustion, the *UsedSoft* case, which turned on whether digital copies of software, legitimately purchased as downloads (not on physical media such as discs), could be resold to third parties. In that case, the Court had concluded that the right of distribution could be exhausted when the software is sold either on a physical carrier medium (such as a CDROM) or as a software download with an unlimited period of use:

> the right of distribution of a copy of a computer program is exhausted if the copyright holder who has authorised, even free of charge, the downloading of that copy from the internet onto a data carrier has also conferred, in return for payment of a fee intended to enable him to obtain a remuneration corresponding to the economic value of the copy of the work of which he is the proprietor, a right to use that copy for an unlimited period.[97]

It therefore concluded that

> An author of software cannot oppose the resale of his 'used' licences allowing the use of his programs downloaded from the internet. The

[95] Ibid., para. 43.
[96] Ibid., para. 58.
[97] *UsedSoft*, C-128/11, 3 July 2012, available at www.curia.europa.eu/juris/liste.jsf?num=C-128/11.

> exclusive right of distribution of a copy of a computer program covered by such a licence is exhausted on its first sale.

This would only apply, however, if the nature of the transaction was effectively a true sale of the program, with transfer of ownership, even if it was formally structured as the acquisition of an IP licence. The transfer, thus, must be definitive, in that the transferor (or first proprietor) must delete the original copy, and the transfer must correspond with the same bundle of rights as initially transferred. The Court cites a definition of a 'sale' as 'an agreement by which a person, in return for payment, transfers to another person his rights of ownership in an item of tangible or intangible property belonging to him'.[98]

The *TomKabinet* decision explains why the outcome is different for computer programs as against e-books. Computer programs are dealt with by a *lex specialis*, the Computer Programs Directive 2009/24, which expressly provided for the exhaustion of rights regardless of whether computer programs are supplied as downloads or in tangible form. It found that it was 'abundantly clear the intention of the European Union legislature to assimilate, for the purposes of the protection laid down by [the Software Directive], tangible and intangible copies of computer programs.' And, expounding the policy rationale for this distinction, it clarified that 'from an economic point of view, the sale of a computer program on a material medium and the sale of a computer program by downloading from the Internet are similar, since the online transmission method is the functional equivalent of the supply of a material medium. Accordingly, interpreting Article 4(2) of Directive 2009/24 in the light of the principle of equal treatment justifies the two methods of transmission being treated in a similar manner'. From a policy perspective, therefore, the Court justifies the distinction in terms of the inherently different economic character of markets for books and for computer programs: books naturally deteriorate with further use and distribution, while computer programs do not. These considerations are assumed to be factored into the remuneration originally received by the right holder upon the first sale. Thus these contrasting decisions – applying different treatment to the extent to which two digital products can be further traded after purchase – hinge on interpretation of both treaty and statute, and on policy and economic rationale.

Within the domestic market in the United States, it is well established that physical copies of recorded music or of software, for instance on

[98] Ibid., p. 42.

optical discs, can be sold on to third parties: the Supreme Court confirmed this in the two decisions discussed above, with reference to the restraints on the alienation of chattels. Digital files can be resold if they are carried on a physical platform such as an MP3 player.[99] But what if the IP content is not carried on a physical chattel?

The *ReDigi* case[100] dealt with the application of the US 'first sale' doctrine to a marketplace developed for the reselling of lawfully purchased and downloaded digital music files. ReDigi had developed a market for such files which operated by transferring files to the purchaser while deleting them from the seller's computer, so that after 'data migration' the seller would no longer retain a copy of the digital file that they had sold. US copyright law (USC Section 109(a)) sets out the 'first sale doctrine' as follows: 'the owner of a particular copy or phonorecord lawfully made under this title, or any person authorized by such owner, is entitled, without the authority of the copyright owner, to sell or otherwise dispose of the possession of that copy or phonorecord'.

The case therefore turned in part on whether reselling digital music files fell within this exception to copyright – in effect, whether the right to object to such reselling had been exhausted (as it undoubtedly has for copyright works sold on physical media). The trial court and appeals court considered a range of legal and policy questions in reaching the conclusion that such reselling, against the authority of the original right holder, was not permitted under US copyright law. In essence, the finding was that the data migration process necessarily entails making copies of the digital files, copies that are not authorized by the right holder. When the purchaser downloads a file to their data storage, that storage becomes a new, unauthorized phonorecord. A range of policy issues were raised by the defendants, and in amici briefs, notably on the economic benefits that would flow from an effective secondary market for digital files. The appeal court declined to venture into issues which it saw as policy questions to be settled by Congress, but nonetheless pointed out that 'the establishment of ReDigi's resale marketplace would benefit some, especially purchasers of digital music, at the expense of others, especially rightsholders, who, in the sale of their merchandise,

[99] US Copyright Office, 'A Report of the Register of Copyrights Pursuant § *104* of the *Digital Millennium Copyright Act*', 2001, available at www.copyright.gov/reports/studies/dmca/sec-104-report-vol-1.pdf.

[100] Capitol Records, LLC *v.* ReDigi Inc., No. 16-2321 (2nd Cir. 2018), available at https://law.justia.com/cases/federal/appellate-courts/ca2/16-2321/16-2321-2018-12-12.html.

would have to compete with resellers of the same merchandise in digital form, which, although second hand, would, unlike second hand books and records, be as good as new'.[101] Further, the court argued that a secondary market could be sustained by selling digital files on storage media such as thumb drives. But concerning a market purely in digital content as such, the court concluded that '[i]f ReDigi and its champions have persuasive arguments in support of the change of law they advocate, it is Congress they should persuade. We reject the invitation to substitute our judgment for that of Congress'.

The extent of 'digital exhaustion' – and the rationales for it to converge with or diverge from exhaustion of rights over content embedded in physical carrier media ('chattels') – are emblematic of the unresolved policy tensions for the IP system and international trade, in the light of the technology-driven trend towards a global marketplace for knowledge products, on the one hand, and the maintenance of territorially-based systems for defining and giving effect to IPRs, on the other. Even as the US courts have favoured international exhaustion of IPRs when embedded in physical carrier media, potentially opening up international trade for such knowledge products in the form of a secondary market, the question of whether purely digital content can be traded the same way also appears to be unsettled, with divergent views in two major jurisdictions, the EU and the US. And the *ClearCorrect* case has shown the difficulty of defining the perceived boundaries, even within the law of one jurisdiction, of what can be construed as a traded article, when it is no longer necessary to rely on a physical carrier medium as a platform for valuable content to be traded internationally.

Unbundling the Packets: Analysing the IP Dimension of Trade in Digital Products

'Big Data' or Small Packages?

This chapter has explored how rights over valuable intangible content can shape the nature and extent of markets both for physical media and for digital products. This interlacing of IP law and the law governing trade in goods means that decisions on the formulation and application

[101] Plaintiffs-Appellees, 15 16 *v.* 17 18 ReDigi Inc., John Ossenmacher, Larry Rudolph, AKA Lawrence S. Rogel, No. 16-2321, Document 188-1, p. 34, available at www.supremecourt.gov/DocketPDF/18/18-1430/90519/20190304145955525_00000003.pdf.

of IP law and policy taken by trade negotiators, by legislators and by the courts can significantly shape the structure of domestic and international trade. We cannot therefore understand the nature of trade and the contemporary international marketplace without analysing the IP component, and the extent to which a licence or contract under an IP right defines the scope of legitimate trade in physical and digital products.

The most immediate observation that can be derived from the growth of trade composed essentially by IP licences is that it is erroneous to consider 'trade in bits' as simply a cross-border flow of packets of data analogous to the flow of containers of traded goods. Discussions about the trade policy implications of e-commerce have underscored the need to differentiate different forms of data flow. An examination of the characteristics of digital-enabled 'trade in IP', the trade in 'digital products' and digital 'deliveries' demonstrates the difficulties of defining, regulating, tracing and measuring such trade. Given the designedly dispersed character of the Internet as a widely distributed packet-switching network, most digital products are not sent as clear, bounded bodies of data in a single, discrete transmission over a dedicated, permanent connection between source and destination. The flow of data is complex, heterogenous in content and subject to distinct legal constraints.

Consider the data packets involved in a single Internet transaction over the purchase of a single downloaded song, app or e-book, by a consumer in one jurisdiction from a commercial site in another, non-contiguous, jurisdiction. These packets of data, all defined by the TCP/IP protocol, would typically include:

- data on available content for purchase from the site, and the applicable terms and conditions (information that is normally freely accessible to the public over the Internet, although not all of it necessarily in the public domain)
- information concerning the purchaser, including personal details and credit card details (subject to privacy and confidentiality considerations)
- transmission from the purchaser to the supplier, for instance legally confirming adherence to licensing terms and conditions and ostensibly entering into a contract
- metadata concerning the digital product or downloaded file
- rights management information relating to copyright content (information which itself may be protected in accordance with the requirements of the WCT and similar standards in bilateral agreements) and

- the data packets constituting the actual digital file for which access and a licence to use have been purchased (normally the subject of IP rights or contractual obligations constraining its field of use and subsequent dissemination, copying and possibly onward sale, depending on the applicable exhaustion regime).

In a normal transaction – one of the uncountable billions of such transactions taking place each year – none of these data would pass from vendor to purchaser as a discrete bundle or package, or a single 'file'. Indeed, the very design and logic of the Internet not only makes this unlikely, but makes it difficult to predict just what pathway across the Internet individual packets of data would take. The digital product itself – such as the mp3 file, e-book file, – is dispatched through numerous data packets over the Internet. These packets of digitized information may follow different routes to reach their destination, potentially passing through different territories, before being reconstructed within the digital device of the purchaser once the packets are all received. Thus the 'digital product' or 'delivery' referred to in recent trade agreements normally only exists in a coherent package in the memory of devices at either end of the transaction – plainly, none of the individual packets of data variously transmitted between the two end nodes will constitute transmission of the digital product or full delivery as such. Moreover, the transaction may entail a continuing right to download a purchased digital product perpetually, or for a distinct period or number of times.

What is ultimately significant, therefore, in understanding this transaction is not the complex and diverse flow of data packets, but rather the relationship between the purchaser and the vendor, and the nature of the rights to use data that are transferred or licensed in this process and the limitations on those rights, and the transfer of ownership (if any), however ownership is construed.

It is natural to speak of having 'purchased' an e-book, a song or an app, and some authors have argued that terms such as 'buy' or 'purchase', when applied to digital transactions, may be positively misleading.[102] And it is counterintuitive to suggest that the essence of the commercial transaction – the 'trade' – involving a digital product does not constitute the electronic transmission of data as such, but rather the legal relationship between the purchase of a limited IP licence or contract. Yet even

[102] See, for instance, Aaron Perzanowski and Jason Schultz, n. 59 *supra*, 84–101.

when ‘analogue’ transactions were based on the purchase of physical carrier media, it was generally fallacious to assume that transfer of ownership of the physical platform – the book, the disc, the tape – brought with it unhindered rights to use the embedded content: for instance, purchase, and ownership, of a CD or DVD did not confer a right of public performance of the musical or cinematic work it carried. And the purchase of content in foreign jurisdictions also did not bring with it an entitlement to trade it in jurisdictions that applied national exhaustion to the exercise of IP rights, even when the content was embedded in a physical carrier medium, a chattel.

Thus it is suggested that it is impossible to reach a clear understanding of the inherent characteristics of many digital transactions without information on the legal relationship, including IP licences and contractual undertakings, that is established between the supplier and the purchaser. While statistics may be relatively accurate, if never fully complete, for business to business transactions, it becomes extremely difficult to measure or even gauge the full extent of business to consumer licences for IP that number in the billions internationally within a host of different and evolving business models.

Shedding Light: A Quantum Theoretical Approach to IP?

The question of whether digital products should be classed as goods or services has not been definitively resolved at the multilateral level, whether by agreement or in the course of dispute settlement. The complex character of digital products, as outlined above, and the different categories of data despatched over networks, may give some illustration of the inherent difficulty in reaching a definitive position on this matter without considering the specific practical circumstances and legal context of digital products – just as the international despatch of some physical goods can yet be measured as part of services trade in some circumstances (as cited in GATT and the ‘trade in goods’ paradigm above), when the legal character of the underlying transaction makes this the more appropriate choice. And, indeed, as noted, a number of recent trade agreements have defined and regulated ‘digital products’ expressly without taking a position on whether they should be classed as goods or services (Trade in digital products, above). Add to this complex analytical framework the differing potential effects of applicable IP rights and the shortcomings of an overly deterministic approach become evident. An improbable metaphor – that of the conception of light in quantum theory – may unexpectedly assist in creating a more enabling framework for understanding these diverse forms that IP may take in practice.

A central insight of the quantum theory view of light is wave-particle duality – light can exhibit the behaviour of both waves and of particles or packets ('quanta'), and may be observed and measured in either form. Concerning wave-particle duality, Einstein and Infeld observed:

> It seems as though we must use sometimes the one theory and sometimes the other, while at times we may use either. We are faced with a new kind of difficulty. We have two contradictory pictures of reality; separately neither of them fully explains the phenomena of light, but together they do.[103]

Without placing *any* significant emphasis on this admittedly tenuous metaphor, it suggests an analogous way of viewing IP rights, and indeed the diverse packets of data that are despatched in association with the delivery of digital products. Rather than assuming one single, exhaustive position as to how to categorize the essential character of IP rights and digital products in today's technological and economic context and in a diversifying international trading system, it would be better to accept that they have a range of different properties in practice, which can be observed variously from different vantage points and will be more or less pertinent to the legal and commercial context of trade. Thus the grant, regulation and enforcement of the very same IP right may, in principle, be conceived in the international legal space as

- a conditional exception to trade law disciplines, as a kind of behind-the-border domestic regulatory measure that may need to be justified under trade law as non-discriminatory and not trade-restrictive
- a component of market access,[104] and a means of avoiding distortions to trade[105]

[103] Albert Einstein and Leopold Infeld, *The Evolution of Physics*, Cambridge: Cambridge University Press, 1938, p. 278, available at https://archive.org/details/evolutionofphysi033254mbp/.

[104] Economic and Trade Agreement between the Government of the United States of America and the Government of the People's Republic of China, January 2020, Article 2.1: 'Each Party shall ensure fair and equitable market access to persons of the other Party that rely upon intellectual property protection.'

[105] Preamble, TRIPS Agreement.

- a determinant of the legitimacy of traded goods[106]
- a tradable service in itself when service delivery entails the licensing of access to the IP
- a tradeable good, to the extent that purchase of access to and delivery of the material covered by the IP right is deemed a 'good' as such
- an avenue for cooperation in research and development, and a bespoke vehicle for transfer of technology[107]
- an asset, the express subject of investment disciplines[108]
- a component of and an obstacle to the exercise of human rights,[109] and
- as a subsidy.[110]

Physicists cannot directly observe fundamental particles, and can only understand their character by observing their behaviour. In a roughly analogous way, rather than first seeking to define the essence of an IP right in the international trade law and policy space, and then to work out towards its practical manifestations, it may be more illuminating instead to observe how IP rights behave in international commerce, and on that basis accept that – depending on the context and purpose of this observation. Thus IP rights may manifest behaviour as:

- transacted property
- traded goods
- services
- the subject of market regulation
- an element of expectations of market access
- the content of technology transfer or equitable sharing of benefits
- investment assets

[106] Preamble, and Article 41, TRIPS Agreement.

[107] Jayashree Watal and Letitia L. Caminero, 'Least-Developed Countries, Transfer of Technology and the TRIPS Agreement', in C. Correa and X. Seuba (eds), *Intellectual Property and Development: Understanding the Interfaces*, Singapore: Springer, 2019.

[108] Lahra Liberti, 'Intellectual Property Rights in International Investment Agreements: An Overview', OECD Working Papers on International Investment, 2010/01, OECD Publishing, available at http://dx.doi.org/10.1787/5kmfq1njzl35-en.

[109] United Nations, Committee on Economic, Social and Cultural Rights, General Comment No. 17 (2005), The right of everyone to benefit from the protection of the moral and material interests resulting from any scientific, literary or artistic production of which he or she is the author (Article 15, para. 1 (c), of the Covenant), E/C.12/GC/1712 January 2006.

[110] DS353: United States – Measures Affecting Trade in Large Civil Aircraft – Second Complaint.

- subsidies, or
- a constraint on trade, technology transfer or fair competition.

More succinctly, 'Old Town Road', the song discussed in the introduction above, exemplifies how music can manifest the characteristics of distinct categories, depending on the vantage point of the listener, without being solely confined to either category, as the songwriter observed: 'It's not one, it's not the other. It's both.'[111] In other words, rather than insisting on one exclusive categorization, it may be both more practically useful and more empirically sound to observe its behaviour, and to use that understanding as the basis for drawing up new rules or updating old ones.

Whatever formal or legal overlay is applied to the new trading arrangements for IP, facilitated by new technologies, it is essential to build an understanding of their character, in part, as trade in IP licences as such, rather than viewing the IP component as an adjunct or ancillary element.

The implications for trade policy, and for economic and social development, are profound. In parallel with the TRIPS negotiations, and the contemporaneous invention of the World Wide Web, Paul Romer and other economists were addressing the need for economic growth theory to incorporate knowledge, technological knowhow and human capital as endogenous factors, rather than maintaining it as exogenous to models of growth. The resultant 'endogenous growth theory' recalled the importance for human development and economic growth of the institutions and policy settings that promote the development and dissemination of new knowledge. As Romer expressed the analytical task in these terms when accepting the 2018 Nobel Prize for Economics:

> The human condition emerges from a never-ending contest between the dismal Malthusian economics of objects and the unrealized possibilities of the economics of ideas. For centuries, economists took sides and followed Thomas Malthus. A paper I published finally turned it into a fair fight. Economists no longer have to assume that Malthus wins before exploring the question posed by title I chose for my Nobel lecture: 'On the possibility of progress' ... In my paper[112] ... all I did was make the trivial observation that ideas belong to neither of the standard analytical categories: private goods and public goods ... I showed that this observation has consequences; big consequences; the biggest possible consequences.

[111] 'Lil Nas X Talks "Old Town Road" and the Billboard Controversy', n. 3 *supra*.

[112] Paul Romer, 'Endogenous Technological Change' (1990), *Journal of Political Economy* 98, 5, Part 2: S71–S102.

> The unique characteristics of ideas make material progress possible, but that's not all. Ideas matter not just for what humans have, but also for how they are. During the Pleistocene, human nature evolved in a Malthusian world of objects. We developed an ugly tendency to split humanity into 'us' and 'them'. A world that also includes ideas justifies a new mindset that treats all humans with the dignity and respect that we offer to 'us'. It is a world in which we may derive net material benefits from the presence of others.[113]

Romer has argued that endogenous growth theory enables a shift from the zero-sum mindset that is focused on the inherently rivalrous domain of atoms, and an acceptance of mutual interest in a positive-sum conception of human progress and economic growth – recalling the 'mutual interest' that the TRIPS Agreement itself sets as an objective for the IP system in its Article 7.

Trade law and trade policy have conventionally viewed the operation of IP rights as, in effect, exogenous. The shifting contours of trade in knowledge – the emergence of widespread trade in IP rights as such, as traded content is detached from chattels, and the integral and essential role of IP licensing in defining and enabling knowledge flows though dispersed global value chains – suggest that trade policy analysis must similarly work to incorporate an understanding of the IP dimension of cross-border commercial exchanges as an integral element of trading relations. This means treating the exchange and licensing of IP rights systematically and effectively as 'endogenous' to trade. Such a shift in framing the 'trade-related aspects' of IP – turning instead to consider the IP-related aspects of trade – is essential for an accurate empirical picture of trade relations today, especially given the economic significance both of dispersed global value chains and of trade in 'pure' IP content as such, particularly in the creative sectors.

To work towards such understanding is not an abstract or academic exercise. It is, for instance, essential if developing countries are to benefit from knowledge spillovers from their engagement in global value chains. And it is essential to the creation, evolution and regulations of global digital markets that would enable fair and feasible access to creators across the globe, most critically from developing countries and from least developed countries (LDCs). For instance, the recent ITC report *Creative Industries in Rwanda: Digital Paths to Global Markets* identifies the

[113] Paul Romer, *Nobel Lecture: On the Possibility of Progress*, 5 February 2019, available at https://paulromer.net/prize/.

remarkable opportunities offered to the Rwandan cultural industries that have been opened up by the evolution of digital trading platforms, while identifying 'common challenges for small businesses exporting creative products and services in developing countries . . . [including] the need for fair revenue sharing with artists; [and] access to, and costs of, operating on global platforms'. For instance, concerning sustainable development of the creative industries:

> Creative industries involve a complex network of artists, creators, producers, distributors, platforms and intermediaries. Fair sharing of revenue has been a critical issue, as artists and creators are often individuals or small businesses and have less bargaining power against the networks and platforms that often dominate the distribution channels. Digitization is exacerbating this problem, as 'winner-take-all' is a common strategy for digital companies.[114]

This report calls for 'policymakers and industry players to take action to ensure inclusive and sustainable development of the creative sector'.

Romer, in one of his breakthrough papers, underscored the importance of integrating the knowledge component of economic growth into wider policy development in these terms:

> We will be able to rejoin the ongoing policy debates about . . . the feedback between trade policy and innovation, the scope of protection for intellectual property rights, the links between private firms and universities, the mechanisms for selecting the research areas that receive public support, and the costs and benefits of an explicit government-led technology policy. . . In a developing country like the Philippines, what are the best institutional arrangements for gaining access to the knowledge that already exists in the rest of the world? In a country like the United States, what are the best institutional arrangements for encouraging the production and use of new knowledge?[115]

Those concluding observations, published the very year the TRIPS Agreement was concluded, seemed to make the assumption – perhaps better empirically grounded at the time – that a stark distinction existed between the interests of a country like the Philippines which is seen in this case entirely as a recipient, as a beneficiary of other people's technology or knowledge, and a country like the US which is seen as

[114] International Trade Centre, *Creative Industries in Rwanda: Digital Paths to Global Markets*, Geneva: ITC, 2019, p. viii, available at www.intracen.org/uploadedFiles/intracenorg/Content/Publications/Rwanda%20Digital%20exports_final_Low-res.pdf.

[115] Paul Romer, 'The Origins of Endogenous Growth' (1994), *Journal of Economic Perspectives* 8, 1: 3–22, p. 22.

the source of innovation for others. Today's international knowledge economy is more heterogeneous and less polarised, as many developing countries work their way up the ranks of innovative capacity, strengthen their indigenous innovation capacity and recognize and value traditional knowledge systems. The consequential value is all the more evident, then, of building the IP dimension integrally into trade policy, in a coherent, inclusive and empirically up-to-date manner.

Bibliography

AAP StatShot Annual Report for Calendar Year 2018, 21 June 2019.

Adjei-Kontoh, Hubert, 'Lil Nas' Song was Removed from Billboard for Not Being "Country" Enough. But Who Gets to Decide Categories?', *The Guardian*, 2 April 2019.

Anell, Lars, 'Keynote Speech at the TRIPS Symposium, 26 February 2015', in Jayashree Watal and Antony Taubman, *The Making of TRIPS*, Geneva: WTO, 2015, pp. 285–291.

Aniftos, Rania, 'Lil Nas X's "Old Town Road" is the Fastest Song in History to be Certified Diamond by the RIAA', *Billboard*, 22 October 2019.

Arora, Ashish and Gambardella, Alfonso, 'Ideas for Rent: An Overview of Markets for Technology' (June 2010), *Industrial and Corporate Change* 19, 3: 775–803, available at https://ssrn.com/abstract=1617051 or http://dx.doi.org/dtq022.

Bannock, Graham, Davis, E. and Baxter, R. E., *The Penguin Dictionary of Economics*, London: Penguin, 2004.

Chafee, Zechariah, 'Equitable Servitudes on Chattels' (June 1928), *Harvard Law Review*, 41, 8: 945.

Chow, Andrew, 'Lil Nas X Talks "Old Town Road" and the Billboard Controversy', available at https://time.com/5561466/lil-nas-x-old-town-road-billboard/.

Coke, Edward, *Institutes of the Laws of England: Containing the Exposition of Many Ancient and Other Statutes*, 1628.

Department of Foreign Affairs and Trade, *Driving Forces on the New Silk Road*, Canberra: Department of Foreign Affairs and Trade, 1999.

The Economist, 'The Web's New Walls', *The Economist*, 2 September 2010.

Einstein, Albert and Infeld, Leopold, *The Evolution of Physics*, Cambridge: Cambridge University Press, 1938, available at https://archive.org/details/evolutionofphysi033254mbp/.

Fitzpatrick, David, 'Negotiating for Hong Kong', in Jayashree Watal and Antony Taubman, *The Making of TRIPS*, Geneva: WTO, 2015, pp. 285–291.

Frey, Carl Benedikt, Ansar, Atif and Wunsch-Vincent, Sacha, 'Defining and Measuring the "Market for Brands": Are Emerging Economies Catching Up?', Economic Research Working Paper No. 21, 2014.

IMF, *Balance of Payments and International Investment Position Manual*, Washington, DC: International Monetary Fund, 2009, p. 119.

International Federation of the Phonographic Industry (IFPI), 'Global Music Report 2019 // State of the Industry', available at www.ifpi.org/recording-industry-in-numbers.php.

International Trade Centre, *Creative Industries in Rwanda: Digital Paths to Global Markets*, Geneva: ITC, 2019.

Liberti, Lahra, 'Intellectual Property Rights in International Investment Agreements: An Overview', *OECD Working Papers on International Investment*, January 2010, OECD Publishing, available at http://dx.doi.org/10.1787/5kmfq1njzl35-en.

Negroponte, Nicholas, 'Bits and Atoms' (January 1995), *Wired* 3, 1.

OECD, 'Intellectual Property Market, in OECD Science, Technology and Industry Outlook', 2012, OECD Publishing, available at dx.doi.org/10.1787/sti_outlook-2012-24-en.

Panagariya, A., 'TRIPS and the WTO: An Uneasy Marriage', in K. Maskus (ed.), *The WTO, Intellectual Property Rights and the Knowledge Economy*, Cheltenham: Edward Elgar Publishing, 2004, pp. 42–53.

Perzanowski, Aaron and Schultz, Jason, *The End of Ownership: Personal Property in the Digital Economy*, Cambridge, MA: MIT Press, 2016.

Rifkin, Jeremy, *The Age of Access*, New York: Penguin Putnam, 2000, p. 4.

Romer, Paul, 'Endogenous Technological Change' (October 1990), *Journal of Political Economy* 98, 5, Part 2: S71–S102.

Romer, Paul, 'The Origins of Endogenous Growth' (1994), *Journal of Economic Perspectives* 8, 1: 3–22.

Romer, Paul, *Nobel Lecture: On the Possibility of Progress*, 5 February 2018, available at https://paulromer.net/prize/.

Smith, Adam, *An Inquiry into the Nature and Causes of the Wealth of Nations*, Henry Frowde (ed.), Oxford: Oxford University Press, 1909 (1776).

Taubman, Antony, 'Nobility of Interpretation: Equity, Retrospectivity, and Collectivity in Implementing New Norms for Performers' Rights' (2005), *Journal of Intellectual Property Law* 12, 351, available at https://digitalcommons.law.uga.edu/jipl/vol12/iss2/2.

Taubman, Antony, 'TRIPS Encounters the Internet: An Analogue Treaty in a Digital Age, or the First Trade 2.0 Agreement?', in Mira Burri and Thomas Cottier (eds), *Trade Governance in the Digital Age*, New York: Cambridge University Press, 2015, p. 314.

United Nations, Committee on Economic, Social and Cultural Rights, General Comment No. 17 (2005), 'The right of everyone to benefit from the protection of the moral and material interests resulting from any scientific, literary or artistic production of which he or she is the author' (Article 15, para. 1 (c), of the Covenant), E/C.12/GC/1712 January 2006.

United Nations, *International Merchandise Trade Statistics: Concepts and Definitions 2010* (IMTS 2010), New York: United Nations, 2010, p. 15.

United Nations, 'International Merchandise Trade Statistics: Concepts and Definitions' 2010, ST/ESA/STAT/SER.M/52/Rev.3 Statistical Papers Series M No. 52, 12.

US Copyright Office, 'A Report of the Register of Copzrights Pursuant § 104 of the *Digital Millennium Copyright Act*, 2001', available at www.copyright.gov/reports/studies/dmca/sec-104-report-vol-1.pdf.

Van Welsum, D., Overmeer, W. and van Ark, B., 'Unlocking the ICT Growth Potential in Europe: Enabling People and Businesses', The Conference Board for the European Commission, Brussels: European Commission, 2013.

Watal, Jayashree and Caminero, Letiti, 'Transfer of Technology and the TRIPS Agreement', in C. Correa and X. Seuba (eds), *Intellectual Property and Development: Understanding the Interfaces*, Singapore: Springer, 2019.

WIPO, 'The Global Publishing Industry in 2016: A Pilot Survey', 2016, available at www.wipo_ipa_pilotsurvey.

WIPO, *The Global Publishing Industry in 2018*, Geneva: World Intellectual Property Organization, 2020.

WTO, *Trade Policy, The WTO and the Digital Economy*, Communication from Canada, Chile, Colombia, Côte d'Ivoire, the European Union, the Republic of Korea, Mexico, Montenegro, Paraguay, Singapore and Turkey JOB/GC/116, JOB/CTG/4, JOB/SERV/248, JOB/IP/21, JOB/DEV/42 (13 January 2017).

WTO, *World Trade Report 2018: The Future of World Trade: How Digital Technologies are Transforming Global Commerce*, Geneva: WTO, 2018.

Wunsch-Vincent, Sasha, 'The Internet, Cross-Border Trade in Services, and the Gats – Lessons from US-Gambling' (2006), *World Trade Review* 5, 3: 319–356, p. 323.

Zittrain, Jonathan, 'The Generative Internet' (1974), *Harvard Law Review* 119, 7.

3

How Digitization is Transforming Trade

LEE TUTHILL, ANTONIA CARZANIGA AND MARTIN ROY*

Abstract

This chapter looks at the ways new digital trends and technologies have stimulated the information component of services trade and consequently enhanced trade in goods and services that embody knowledge. It illustrates the role that ICTs have taken on as conduits for digital and digitally-enabled trade and describes recent digital developments such as cloud services, large scale data analytics, Internet of things, artificial intelligence, robotics, and three-dimensional printing. It presents the relevant trade data and then covers, in broad strokes, the landscape of policy challenges that governments confront as they seek to adapt, and examples of ways trade negotiators have begun to shape new legal frameworks. The rise of such technologies and corresponding growth in services that trade internationally by means of the global movements of information has led policymakers to believe a new or enhanced legal regime could be needed. Not always well understood, digital trends can lead to exaggerated fears and cataclysmic predictions. Over-reaction to these transformations can hold the risk of disproportionate policy responses, which may harm not only trade, but also the sharing of knowledge across borders. One significant challenge, the article nevertheless raises, is that international trade rules are founded on the premise that national governments can implement them at or within their borders. Yet, many of the policy and legal responses that arise from an unanticipated shift in services trade from commercial presence to cross-border supply, have a variety of interjurisdictional consequences. Therefore, whatever trade rules may be employed, existing or new, the article concludes that enhanced efforts at collaboration among governments will be needed to complement and coordinate national initiatives.

* The views expressed are the authors' own and should not be attributed to any WTO member or the WTO Secretariat. The authors would like to extend thanks to Joscelyn Magdeleine, Justine Lan and Kian Cassehgari Posada for valuable input and assistance.

Introduction – Information in Trade and Trade in Information

The expression 'knowledge is power', attributed to Sir Francis Bacon, is a point worth applying to trade. Knowledge embedded in goods and services arises from innovation, expertise and creativity. It creates value and motivates society to trade. In short, knowledge is a power that drives markets.

Digitization is transforming trade. At the core of such a transformation are the various information and communication technology (ICT) products that provide the basic infrastructure for digital supply. Technological knowledge is intrinsic to those ICT goods and services. Digitization has, in particular, vastly increased opportunities for trade in information or knowledge-intensive services. Services trade, for its part, has long been characterized as knowledge and information intensive, and, as a result, has proven easily amenable to trade by electronic means. So-called knowledge services range from the professions and research and development to education and consultancy. Once information at the core of such services is digitized, it can be supplied via digital media in both domestic and international settings. Information services such as databases, news agency services, or media platforms can now offer the desired content online directly to consumers, wherever they may be located. In addition, ICT services arising from technological knowhow, such as telecommunication and computer services are not only key to facilitating further trade in knowledge and information-intensive services, but are also traded themselves, not only across borders but also by means of establishment by foreign suppliers.

Moreover, goods embody knowledge services in the form of, for example, design services or software programming that form an important part of the value chain of their production. More recently, as the services component of goods production has grown, the incidence of knowledge services associated with merchandise goods has also increased. Manufacturing is increasingly reliant on service inputs and progressively supplying services alongside goods, in a process referred to as 'servicification'. Together with the deployment of ICT tools, this allows producers to become better informed of and more responsive to their customers' needs, which in turn facilitates innovation and sustainability, and to maintain mutually beneficial long-term relations. Consequently, greater digitization and the further evolution of ICTs have increased the contribution of intellectual property and other forms of knowledge to trade. WIPO estimates that, on average, 30.4 per cent of the production value of global value chains is generated by intangible capital in the form of technology, design and brand value, as well as workers' skills and managerial knowhow.[1]

This chapter looks at the ways new digital trends and technologies have stimulated the information component of services trade and consequently enhanced trade in goods and services that embody knowledge. It first illustrates the role that ICTs have taken on as conduits for digital and digitally-enabled trade.[2] It briefly describes recent digital developments, namely the cloud, data analytics, (so-called 'big data'), Internet of Things (IoT), aka machine-to-machine (M2M) communications, artificial intelligence, robotics, and three-dimensional (3D) printing (aka additive manufacturing). It covers, in broad strokes, the landscape of policy challenges that governments confront as they seek to adapt. Finally, the chapter provides illustrations of ways negotiators of trade rules have begun to shape new legal frameworks via regional trade agreements (RTAs) that elaborate upon, and in some respects extend beyond, existing multilateral trade rules. While the focus of this chapter is primarily on trade in services, some of the implications for trade in merchandise are also noted.

ICT – the Conduits for Digital Trade

From Physical Proximity to Phone and Fax

Early research on trade in services, including studies by trade officials laying the groundwork for services trade negotiations in the late 1980s, revealed that services were commonly traded via physical proximity of the supplier to the consumer. Among the reasons for this feature was frequent customization, or personalization, for example, of legal advice or accountancy services to clients. This meant that location of a firm or of an individual service provider in the country where the services were to be offered was necessary to facilitate direct interaction and negotiation with clients on the desired features. Another reason for physical proximity was the degree to which a number of services were not considered storable, given their generally intangible nature, and, as such, not easily

[1] WIPO, *World Intellectual Property Report 2017: Intangible Capital in Global Value Chains*, Geneva: WIPO, 2017, p. 11.

[2] This chapter uses interchangeably terms such as 'digitally-enabled trade', 'digitally-impacted trade', 'online trade' and similar. As the equivalent term in the WTO context is 'e-commerce', as defined by the Work Programme on Electronic Commerce, the latter is also used, in particular with reference to discussions in the WTO.

transmittable across borders. Services, such as a consultant's advice, if not provided in person, could be conveyed by a phone call or by mail. In essence, services trade traditionally relied on personal interaction or was embedded in physical carrier mediums. Both of these options incurred costs in terms of setting up a commercial establishment, travelling to the consumers' market or transporting items by physical means.

Indeed, the customization and non-storability of services led to the creation of a new paradigm for trade. The General Agreement on Trade in Services (GATS) re-engineered trade disciplines to cover services traded not only across borders but rather by four different modes of supply. The first concerned trade across borders (also known as cross-border supply, or mode 1, in GATS parlance), but the other three modes of supply extended the definition of trade to the consumer moving into physical proximity with the supplier (consumption abroad, mode 2), the establishment of a business abroad (commercial presence, mode 3) and an individual supplier or the foreign employee of an enterprise engaged in services physically visiting the client's country (movement of natural persons, mode 4).

Services supplied by phone and fax were acknowledged as means to cross-border trade.[3] However, in a gesture towards the evolving digital technologies, the GATS Annex on Telecommunications recognized the sector's 'dual role as a distinct sector of economic activity and as the underlying transport means for other economic activities', and subjected telecommunications to specific trade disciplines. Such disciplines referred to trade that was facilitated, even then, by communications networks used by companies to supply services. Market reforms inspired further innovation in telecommunications, such as a surge in mobile services and broadband Internet technology.

From Telephony to Data Networks and Internet

Early networks for corporate communications managed corporate affairs across global subsidiaries and affiliates as well as with global customers and suppliers. These drove the emerging trade in so-called 'value-added

[3] As cited in the first and subsequently revised guidelines for scheduling of market access commitments in services (documents MTN.GNS/W/164, Scheduling of Initial Commitments in Trade in Services: Explanatory Note, dated 3 September 1993, and MTN.GNS/W/164/Add.1, dated 30 November 1993 and revised as S/L/92, adopted by the Council for Trade in Services on 23 March 2001).

networks services', allowing firms to outsource, instead of self-service, their communication needs. They offered their clients services such as email, database and data processing services.

Commercialization of the Internet began at the turn of the 1990s, primarily as vehicle for email and some relatively limited information services. It was accessed on lines dialled-in over the public telephony networks. Despite slow speeds and the relatively high cost to consumers, Internet uptake nevertheless grew at rates faster than any previously encountered technological innovations. Growth was so phenomenal that the expression was coined that an Internet year was equivalent to three months.[4] Even then, Internet growth was already accompanied by concerns about policy and legal frameworks keeping pace with its development and the transformation in human activity. Internet access as we know it today, however, was not possible until the introduction of the World Wide Web in 1991 and easily accessible web browsers (Mosaic in 1992 and Netscape in 1994) permitting more accessible use and more sophisticated websites with greater volumes of information. Speeds and capacity (bandwidth) to more easily permit business applications, such as online ordering, and encryption to permit customer accounts, purchase transactions and payment mechanisms, first arose in the early 2000s. Broadband Internet, both fixed and mobile, is growing in the developed world, and is still emerging in the developing world where penetration rates remain low.

With the advent of newer technologies, not only the Internet, but, subsequently, platforms and other services overlaid on a better and faster Internet had a multiplier effect on economic activity, leading to what some observers see as digital disruption and to a redefinition of commercial models and trade patterns. The feasibility of offering some of the most popular services over the Internet today, e.g. music and film distribution, had to await not only higher capacity bandwidth, but also the emergence of new business models in the entertainment industry. These industries had long considered the Internet mainly to be a vehicle for piracy or revenue loss. The rise of mobile services as the telephony of popular choice, and now of mobile Internet, was one of the single most unanticipated phenomena in communications – not only because the reduced cost and mobile Internet technology was not foreseen by many observers, but also because it contributed to

[4] Attributed to Tim Berners-Lee, chief inventor of the Web technologies, in a 1996 interview in the *WWW Journal*.

vastly expanding the penetration of communications technologies in developing countries.

Evolving High-Capacity Internet

The advance that truly makes digital business and trade a reality is higher speed, higher-capacity Internet, characterized by more powerful bandwidth. This was accomplished by, for example, fibreoptic cable rollout by telephone operators, as well as the introduction of Internet by way of the upgrade of networks previously dedicated to cable television. In mobile telephony, the highest bandwidth offerings currently possible, known as fifth generation, or 5G, are just beginning to be introduced in most countries. Other advances discussed below and heralded today as leading to a transformation and redefinition of trade ultimately rely on high-capacity Internet for their existence and commercial viability.

The expansion of knowledge in the form of technological knowhow has led ICT infrastructure services to become vehicles of ICT-enabled trade for other knowledge and information-intensive services. These trends have impacted trade more generally, in a number of ways:

- First, they have enhanced the tradability of services, thereby expanding export opportunities for both developed and developing countries. It is increasingly easier and less costly to export services across borders, either as final products or as intermediate products for the production of another service or a good. For suppliers across a range of services, cross-border supply becomes either a new – or more interesting – alternative, or a complement to the supply of services through a commercial presence abroad (mode 3) or the temporary movement of persons (mode 4).
- Second, the increased performance of ICT network services, in combination with innovations in logistics, have enabled an enormous expansion of global value chains. Information-intensive services, such as computer, research and development, advertising, telecommunications, and financial and professional services serve as enablers of global value chains.
- Third, ICT services underpin flows of communications in the form of data flows across borders, which have skyrocketed in recent years. Cross-border data flows, boosted by basic and value-added telecom services, such as data processing and storage via large capacity cloud technology, allow companies not only to sell their goods and services,

but also to coordinate their logistics and the activities of their subsidiaries and partner offices across the globe.[5]

- Fourth, ICT services, and more specifically the Internet, constitute the backbone for key pillars of e-commerce such as online retail and wholesale trade, whether cross-border or domestic. Indeed, without increased capacity and speed, and the lower communication costs brought about by improvements in telecom and computer services, the sale of goods online as it stands today, including inventory management, would not be possible.[6]

The future holds much more potential than we can imagine today. This is evident in the still low uptake of broadband Internet, particularly in the developing world, and in the even lower uptake of mobile Internet. Although twice as many mobile-broadband subscriptions exist per 100 inhabitants in developed countries than in developing countries, and four times as many in developed countries than in least-developed countries (LDCs), the growth rate of mobile-broadband subscriptions was the highest in LDCs and developing countries, at over 50 per cent and 30 per cent, respectively, from 2016 to 2017. Over the same period, the growth of fixed-broadband subscriptions climbed by over 40 per cent and 10 per cent in LDCs and developing countries, respectively, as compared to less than 5 per cent in developed countries. Mobile broadband is also increasingly more affordable worldwide. Mobile-broadband prices fell from 32.4 per cent to 14.1 per cent of gross national income (GNI) per capita in LDCs, from 11.6 per cent to 6 per cent in developing countries, and from 1 per cent to 0.7 per cent in developed countries, from 2013 to 2016.[7]

Digital Trends to Watch

The six digital trends taking shape today that appear as most transformative are cloud technologies, the Internet of Things (IoT), large-scale data analytics (also known as big data), artificial intelligence, robotics and three-dimensional (3D) printing.

[5] L. Tuthill, 'Cross-border Data Flows: What Role for Trade Rules?', in P. Sauvé and M. Roy (eds), *Research Handbook on Trade in Services*, Cheltenham: Edward Elgar Publishing, 2016.

[6] M. Roy, 'The Contribution of Services Trade Policies to Connectivity in The Context of Aid for Trade', WTO Staff Working Paper, ERSD-2017-12, 2017.

[7] International Telecommunications Union (ITU), 2017 'ICT Facts and Figures 2017', available at www.itu.int/en/ITU-D/Statistics/Pages/facts/default.aspx.

These developments, although diverse, are characterized, first and foremost, by significant overlap and synergies. Second, some represent new commercial models for super-charged versions of relatively long-existent types of computer services. And last, but not least, the terms used for these developments do not represent services, in themselves, but rather are generic expressions that encompass families of evolving technologies that can be deployed to supply a wide array of services, most with which we have long been familiar.

To illustrate these points, 'cloud services', for example, are essentially a commercially generated term that denotes configurations of networks and equipment by which service suppliers can offer high-capacity storage, data processing and delivery options to their customers. Large-scale data analytics was born out of the coming of age of the cloud's massive storage and computing capacity. Robotics and IoT can only be realized in conjunction with data network and transmission services and are subsequently used to supply a vast array of services offerings. Artificial intelligence and robotics result in large part from sophisticated algorithms and software. IoT, for its part, creates data that becomes fodder for more powerful data processing capacities. As it becomes increasingly commercialized, they will be deployed via chips or intelligent, software-embedded devices performing many different functions and services. Most often, these technologies will rely on wire-based technologies, such as satellite or mobile links, connected to data networks, typically the Internet, permitting information to be transmitted.

However, the data only become commercially viable once interpreted by means of data processing methodologies. Finally, 3D printing results from an extension of advanced software and design services into the realm of equipment capable of producing replicas of physical objects. While such software may be inserted into printing equipment via a physical cartridge, again it can also be linked to ICTs when it is transmitted virtually to network-enabled printers.

Impacts – Redefining Trade?

The most direct impact of this family of technological developments is to expand the universe, and, more specifically, the amplitude of services that can be traded. At the same time, they are also not without implications for goods production and trade. The ease by which these digital trends can augment global services trade is directly attributable to their being, by their very nature, networked technologies. They are conveyed by networks, like the Internet, which, in turn, are global in nature. The economic activities arising from these developments will be made available to other businesses by 'next-generation' digital service suppliers. By extension, given the information intensity of most services, a great many customers of these digital services will, themselves, be suppliers of services. Moreover, the variety of services that can ultimately be supplied in this chain is boundless.

Another transformative implication of the networked nature of these trends is that the potential for trade via remote supply will be even further enhanced, and at a reduced cost, permitting even greater segmentation of value chains across borders than is the case today. Such segmentation of production, for example, in the research and development sector, IT services and business support services has already shown signs of increasing the participation of developing countries in global trade.

Yet, many of the digital trends and associated challenges can lend themselves to exaggeration, outsized fear for the future and cataclysmic predictions. A case in point is the early notion that e-commerce would lead to the death of intermediaries, with consumers ordering directly from factories. Instead, a new breed of online intermediaries evolved.

Economic Significance of Digitally-Enabled Trade

Among the most significant impacts of digital technologies is the reduction of trade costs and greater ease of market entry. The trade data appear to support these implications. Advances in information and communications technology are transforming the tradability of services, increasing the growth of services supplied electronically cross-border, across a wide range of sectors, from medical, to educational, financial, audiovisual or professional services. This is reflected, in the first instance, in the growing relative importance of services in total trade. Measured on a balance-of-payments (BoP) basis, trade in services now accounts for 23 per cent of total trade in goods and services, compared to 19 per cent in 1995. The strong growth of trade in services is largely a result of the Internet revolution.[8]

[8] BoP statistics do not cover all four modes of services supply defined by the GATS, as it excludes mode 3. Among other modes of supply, cross-border trade (mode 1) is estimated to account for 27 per cent of world trade in services, compared with 15 per cent for mode 2, 5 per cent for mode 4, and 53 per cent for mode 3 (WTO World Statistical Review 2018, WTO, Geneva, available at https://doi.org/10.30875/0ab3aa40-en).

Moreover, technological advances and increased tradability have led to significant change in the composition of trade in services. 'Other commercial services', which lend themselves more easily to digitisation, have increased significantly and now account for 54 per cent (in 2017) of global trade in commercial services and include some of the most dynamic components of world trade today, compared with less than 40 per cent in 1995, and 47 per cent in 2005. By contrast, the relative share of travel and transport in BoP statistics has diminished considerably.

Not surprisingly, services that have experienced strong growth consist of services that can be supplied electronically and that have benefitted significantly from the increased efficiency of digital networks. These are also services intensive in digitized information and technological knowledge. Between 2005 and 2017, exports of the fastest-growing subcategory, 'telecommunications, computer, and information services' increased at an annual average rate of 13.3 per cent; exports of these services now account for 10 per cent of world exports, compared with 7.8 per cent in 2005. Most of the trade in this category pertained to computer services, which had an annual growth rate of 17.6 per cent over the same period.

Exports of what may be referred to as 'IP services' (i.e. charges for the use of intellectual property not included elsewhere) exhibited an average annual growth rate of 11 per cent over the same period. With 10 per cent growth in 2017, this was the fastest-growing service category. This knowledge-intensive category includes charges for the use of proprietary rights (e.g. patents, trademarks, copyrights, franchises, and rights arising from research and development) as well as charges for the authorized reproduction and/or distribution (through licensing agreements) of produced software originals, as well as fees and charges for the authorized reproduction/distribution, through licensing agreements, of produced audiovisual originals or prototypes (for example, cinematographic works and sound recordings) and related rights pertaining to recordings of live performances and radio, television, cable and satellite broadcasts.[9]

A vast array of information-intensive services is captured in the category of 'other business services', which accounted for 23 per cent of total services exports in 2017. These services, which grew at an average

[9] United Nations Statistical Commission (2010), *Manual on Statistics of International Trade in Services* (MSITS 2010) 2010, United Nations publication, 2010, available at https://unstats.un.org/unsd/publication/Seriesm/seriesM_86Rev1e.pdf.

annual pace of 11 per cent between 2005 and 2017, include, for example, research and development services as well as professional, advertising and management consulting services.

Many developing countries are taking greater advantage of direct export opportunities offered by new technologies enabling the digital supply of services. Their share of global trade in services has risen from 28 per cent in 2005 to 34 per cent in 2017. Exports of developing countries are concentrated in 'other commercial services' (44 per cent in 2017), in contrast to transport (20 per cent), travel (33 per cent), and goods-related services (3 per cent). With 13.7 per cent of world exports, India ranked as a top global exporter of computer services in 2017, second only to the European Union.

Potential for Digital Disruption?

While, on the one hand, changing trade patterns are seen as a boost to developing economies, this transition may, on the other hand, be perceived as disruptive of the status quo in industrial economies. Advanced economies could, in the not too distant past, count on having a comparative advantage in technology, information and skills needed for a knowledge economy. Certainly, economic disruption can occur through the demise of certain economic actors, but also through the creation of new ones. However, it is possible that the shift of capital, skills and technologies required for growth and comparative advantage in trade could well be smoother for less advanced countries without legacy technologies and industries, permitting them to transition directly to new economic models. Many developing countries, have, for example, moved directly into mobile communications, without having built fixed telecommunication networks, and they have secured mobile banking and payments methods for citizens that never had a bank account. Meanwhile, such services have been much slower to take hold in developed countries where legacy telecommunications and banking services were widely available.

The implications of technological development for manufacturing are most apparent in robotics and 3D printing, which lead to concomitant implications for goods trade. While robotics can make possible the remote provision of services, such as surgical operations, its most transformative applications have, to date, taken hold on factory floors in the manufacturing industry. By lowering the costs of production, competitive advantage can be enhanced, yet the transition from labour-intensive to capital-intensive manufacturing can be disruptive, particularly in the job market and in developing countries. For 3D printing, compared with robotics, commercial applications are still in their infancy. Nevertheless, the potential for 3D applications to transform manufacturing industries is vast, if not sometimes overstated, at least in the near-term outlook.

Twenty-First-Century Trade Rules?

Challenges

The Internet blurs geographic boundaries, raising issues about the proper application of private international law, including jurisdiction, applicable law, and the recognition and enforcement of foreign judicial rulings, that some domestic and international trade rules may not be well equipped to address. Even international trade rules, for example, are founded on the premise that national governments will implement them at their borders or within their own territories. Some of the policy and legal questions that arise also stem from an unanticipated shift in services trade away from commercial presence to cross-border supply.

It is, moreover, incumbent on trade negotiators to discuss not only aspects of digital technologies that directly impact trade, but also to address issues less directly related to trade that touch on other public policy concerns. For example, a rise in cross-border data flows is an intrinsic and essential result of trade conducted via new technologies. Yet, controversies underpin policy concerns linked to a great many digital trade flows and transactions, most notably those with a bearing on so-called non-trade matters, such as privacy, cybersecurity and protection against fraud, hacking and other cybercrimes.

The rise of cloud computing, IoT, data analytics and other services that internationally transfer and store data has led some policymakers to believe a new or enhanced legal regime could be needed to handle data moved across borders. With more companies building or outsourcing data centres around the world, questions may arise about the relevance of server location in determining jurisdiction in certain matters, such as judicial proceedings, or even WTO proceedings. The jurisdictional issues can best be explained by an ongoing case involving Microsoft. It came about after a 2013 drug trafficking investigation during which the FBI issued a Stored Communications Act (SCA) warrant for emails that belonged to a US citizen that Microsoft had stored on a server in Ireland. Microsoft argued that it could not turn over the data stored outside the US and that the SCA did not cover such cases. The core of the issue is whether a government can compel a service provider to hand over data, even if this is stored in another country.

Competition issues may also arise due to network effects. It is easiest to illustrate this effect by looking at social media, where the more users sign up on, for instance, Facebook, the more attractive it is for others to sign up, and the more attractive it is for advertisers to position ads on that platform. In effect, the value of a product or a service increases as more users subscribe to it.

The Existing Framework – WTO Rules

The General Agreement on Trade in Services

The GATS makes no distinction regarding different technological means through which a service may be supplied. The supply of services through electronic means is covered by the Agreement in the same way as all other means of supply. This has been confirmed by WTO jurisprudence. For example, in *US – Gambling*,[10] the Panel concluded that:

> mode 1 includes all means of delivery. We are of the view that when a Member inscribes the word 'None' in the market access column of its schedule for mode 1, it commits itself not to maintain measures which prohibit the use of one, several or all means of delivery under mode 1 in a committed sector or sub-sector. This is especially so in sectors and sub-sectors where cross-border supply is affected essentially if not exclusively through the Internet.[11]

In that context, online trade falls within the scope of GATS, and therefore trade restrictions, as well as domestic regulations affecting electronic supply of services, are subject to GATS obligations, disciplines and commitments.

[10] Appellate Body Report, *United States – Measures Affecting the Cross-Border Supply of Gambling and Betting Services*, WT/DS285/AB/R, adopted 20 April 2005, DSR 2005:XII, p. 5663 (and Corr.1, DSR 2006:XII, p. 5475); Panel Report, *United States – Measures Affecting the Cross-Border Supply of Gambling and Betting Services*, WT/DS285/R, adopted 20 April 2005, as modified by Appellate Body Report WT/DS285/AB/R, DSR 2005:XII, p. 5797.

[11] Panel Report, *United States – Measures Affecting the Cross-Border Supply of Gambling and Betting Services*, at para. 6.287. A 'none' inscription in a schedule signifies that no restrictions are applicable.

As most GATS disciplines apply only to committed services, the most advantageous conditions for the digital supply of information-intensive services are achieved when relevant commitments exist and when those are as open as possible. The fact that most commitments date from negotiations concluded over 20 years ago represents the single most important gap in the WTO coverage of electronic commerce[12] in services. Updating these commitments would be possible, should WTO members decide to do so, given the considerable levels of liberalization in place that has not been bound in GATS schedules. However, in order to most effectively undertake commitments that reflect the current realities of global online trade, some services classification issues may also need to be addressed. But many online services available today are not explicitly mentioned by their common or commercial names, in the 1991 classification list currently used for GATS commitments. Examples include not only various 'cloud' services, search engines, web hosting or mobile applications, but also many information services such as social networks and blogs or media services such as magazines, news or other virtual information platforms. Are some of these entirely new services, or do they relate to existing services classification if interpreted in generic terms? Are some of these hybrids combining various services sub-categories together in a manner that can ultimately be linked to an existing classification?

To some extent, WTO dispute settlement panels have already faced such issues. In *China – Publications and Audiovisual Products*,[13] for example, the Panel and the Appellate Body noted that the service entry of 'Sound Recording Distribution Services', in the context of China's GATS Schedule, did not expressly exclude any particular form of distribution, i.e. it did not indicate that the commitment was limited to the physical distribution of sound recordings embedded in physical media, and thus concluded that the entry also covered electronic

[12] As will be discussed below, e-commerce is broadly defined in the WTO, so as to include all forms of digital trade online as well as digital inputs to goods or services that are ultimately delivered physically.

[13] Appellate Body report, *China – Measures Affecting Trading Rights and Distribution Services for Certain Publications and Audiovisual Entertainment Products*, WT/DS363/AB/R, adopted 19 January 2010, DSR 2010:I, p. 3; Panel Report, *China – Measures Affecting Trading Rights and Distribution Services for Certain Publications and Audiovisual Entertainment Products*, WT/DS363/R and Corr.1, adopted 19 January 2010, as modified by Appellate Body Report WT/DS363/AB/R, DSR 2010:II, p. 261.

distribution.[14,15] Also, in the case on *China – Electronic Payment Services*,[16] the Panel dealt with an integrated set of services that together made up an electronic payments system. It ultimately found that the legal requirements China maintained on electronic payment networks for payment card transactions and the suppliers of those services (modes 1 and 3) were inconsistent with its commitments under the GATS.

Electronic networks have also made possible digitally-enabled trade that cuts across a great many sectors of activity. Not all of these sectors would be considered 'knowledge services', but a great many are. Some of these are already subject to GATS commitments by WTO members. For example, as Annex 1 indicates, the main subsectors of the computer services sector, which entails very high IP content, have been committed in 80 to 89 schedules. Between 72 per cent and 79 per cent of these commitments are unrestricted (i.e. without limitations) for cross-border supply.

In terms of enabling services, subsectors of telecommunication services, also a quintessentially electronic service, have also attracted a relatively high number of GATS commitments, though those tend to be subject, in comparison with computer services, not only to more limitations in mode 1, but also mode 3. For example, 65 per cent of commitments on data transmission are subject to limitations or are 'unbound' (i.e. uncommitted) with respect to mode 1, and this figure reaches 78 per cent for mode 3.

A total of 103 WTO members have committed in whole or in part, in their schedule of specific commitments, to the telecom Reference Paper's regulatory principles, which are aimed at fostering competition, transparency and predictability in telecom markets and which have led to the extensive innovation in digital infrastructure and services witnessed

[14] Panel report, *China – Measures Affecting Trading Rights and Distribution Services for Certain Publications and Audiovisual Entertainment Products*, at para. 7.1265, as upheld by the Appellate Body report, *China – Measures Affecting Trading Rights and Distribution Services for Certain Publications and Audiovisual Entertainment Products*, at paras 375–413.

[15] The Panel also noted that 'digital or electronic distribution' of sound recordings includes distribution both through the Internet and by other electronic means. Panel report, *China – Measures Affecting Trading Rights and Distribution Services for Certain Publications and Audiovisual Entertainment Products*, at paras 7.1148–7.1153.

[16] Panel Report, *China – Certain Measures Affecting Electronic Payment Services*, WT/DS413/R and Add.1, adopted 31 August 2012, DSR 2012:X, p. 5305.

today.[17] Moreover, the access and use disciplines of the Annex on Telecommunications form an integral part of the GATS. The applicability of the Annex and Reference Paper were clarified in the findings of the GATS case on *Mexico – Telecoms*.[18]

The GATT and Associated Agreements

Regarding trade in goods, even if not specifically mentioned in any provision, goods sold or marketed by electronic means but delivered physically across borders are without question subject to the existing WTO rules. These rules apply also to knowledge-embodying digital products that are internationally traded by means of a physical support, such as data or software recorded in a DVD. The GATT and other goods texts, such as the agreements on technical barriers to trade, trade-related investment measures, rules of origin, customs valuation, all apply to goods that are physically delivered even if traded electronically. Like the GATS, these agreements are drafted in a technology neutral manner.

The more recently concluded Trade Facilitation Agreement (TFA) provides for electronic ways of expediting and facilitating government procedures by, inter alia, encouraging members to accept paper or electronic copies of supporting documents required for import, export or transit formalities. The Information Technology Agreement (ITA) also has important and positive implications for electronic trade. By eliminating tariffs on IT products that are important components of the digital infrastructure, it makes them more affordable and readily available.

Possible Multilateral Rules through the Prism of Regional Trade Agreements?

Conduits for Digital Trade – Telecommunications Rule-Making

Compared to the GATS, in the RTAs, WTO members have expanded their commitments for the telecom sector, as well as extended the regulatory disciplines beyond those in the Reference Paper and

[17] The Reference Paper on Basic Telecommunications (WTO Job document 2104, dated 24 April 1996).

[18] Panel report, *Mexico – Measures Affecting Telecommunications Services*, WT/DS204/R, adopted 1 June 2004, DSR 2004: IV, p. 1537.

Telecom Annex.[19] The majority of RTAs cover more services and provide a greater degree of market openness and foreign ownership than that provided for in GATS commitments. In some cases, WTO members with no GATS commitments in basic telecommunication services made RTA commitments on the sector, with no limitations. The most important reason for this is that governments have continued sector reforms and were able to commit to these in RTAs at a time when WTO negotiations are blocked.

Out of the 307 notified and non-notified RTAs (as of March 2018), 83 contain a stand-alone chapter on telecommunications with telecoms regulatory principles. RTAs between developing and developed countries make up 51 per cent of RTAs with a stand-alone chapter on telecoms, while RTAs between developing countries as well as RTAs between developed countries represent 44 per cent and 5 per cent respectively. The four participants most frequently involved in RTAs with a telecom component are Chile, the United States, Singapore and the European Union.

A number of RTAs broaden the scope of the Reference Paper obligations beyond basic telecommunications, to cover all telecom services, thereby promoting fair and transparent competition for all forms of telecommunications. The provisions also add clarity to the scope of application of the WTO regulatory disciplines, by covering explicitly many services and situations not spelled out in the GATS disciplines, and by extending benefits to value-added telecom services that do not fall within the scope of the GATS Reference Paper. Another RTA expansion on GATS provisions includes requirements for major suppliers to provide leased circuit services at 'capacity-based, cost-oriented prices'. Leased circuits are used by many digital service providers to create virtual networks to deliver their services. In the GATS Telecom Annex, the standard is vaguer, requiring 'reasonable and non-discriminatory' terms and conditions. Further, some RTAs contain new provisions dealing with regulatory issues not addressed – at least, not explicitly – in GATS disciplines. In addition, considering that broadband technology is increasingly both mobile and global, a number of RTAs contain provisions encouraging cooperation to foster fair and transparent pricing with respect to international mobile roaming rates and technological alternatives to roaming services. Such provisions were intended to enable

[19] This subsection draws in part on material prepared on 'telecommunications regulatory issues' for the *World Trade Report 2018*, Geneva: WTO, 2018, pp. 182–184.

end-users, including business users, to use their mobile handset or other device for voice, data or messaging services while outside their territory at reasonable cost.

Experiments in E-Commerce Rule-Making

E-commerce provisions have become an increasingly common feature of RTAs over the past 10 years. Out of 275 RTAs notified to the WTO (as of May 2017), 75 contain e-commerce chapters or provisions. Although this is a relatively small share, accounting for just over 20 per cent of all notified RTAs, the number is growing. Membership of these RTAs is increasingly more diverse, more recently involving agreements exclusively between developing countries.

The e-commerce chapters in RTAs normally deal with similar themes. Some address issues, such as cooperation, transparency and non-discrimination, which already exist in these agreements, but whose scope is extended to explicitly cover e-commerce. Some RTAs include provisions addressing topics more specific to e-commerce, such as information flows, electronic authentication, paperless trade, and consumer and data protection.

In terms of information flows, the ability to transfer data across borders is essential not only to electronic commerce, but also to trade in knowledge that is digitized. The GATS Annex on Telecommunications provides that 'each Member shall ensure that service suppliers of any other Member may use public telecommunications transport networks and services for the movement of information within and across borders'. While this provision is relevant, it ensures suppliers' rights to access the underlying telecommunications used as a means to transfer information, but only applies to the extent that the suppliers involved are service suppliers taking advantage of GATS commitments.

Of the RTAs with an e-commerce chapter, only a third deal with cross-border information flows. Generally, RTAs contain soft provisions on cooperation or best endeavour provisions to avoid unnecessary barriers to electronic information flows. Very few RTAs, to date, have binding commitments. The CPTPP and the revised Singapore–Australia Agreement, for instance, provide that the parties shall allow the cross-border transfer of information by electronic means, including personal information, when this activity is for the conduct of the business of a covered person. However, they also allow the parties to adopt measures that are inconsistent with this obligation to achieve a legitimate public policy objective, provided that the measures are not applied in an arbitrary or unjustifiable manner and do not impose restrictions greater than what is required to achieve the objective concerned.

Requirements to locate data centres, servers or other computing facilities within one's territory are a form of data flow restriction that may, at most, make data transfer impossible, or, at the least, require duplicate facilities to be established that might not otherwise be needed from a commercial standpoint. Such requirements, depending on how they are designed and implemented, might, under some circumstances, already be disciplined by specific commitments under the GATS. Nonetheless, explicit disciplines on localization are found only in very recently negotiated RTAs, such as the CPTPP, the Japan–Mongolia Agreement and the third revision of the Singapore–Australia Agreement. All three of these prohibit the adoption of such measures. However, not unlike data flows provisions, they recognize the rights of the parties to adopt or maintain infringing measures necessary to achieve legitimate public policy objectives, provided that they are not applied in a manner that would constitute a means of arbitrary or unjustifiable discrimination or a disguised restriction on trade.

Conclusions

Digital technologies discussed in this chapter have resulted in a shift in services trade from physical to virtual forms of supply that are enabling knowledge- and information-intensive services to be traded cross-border. They also have important implications for the manufacturing sector, particularly, but not only, IoT and 3D printing technologies. Sophisticated data analytics has already demonstrated the capability to enhance knowledge of customers, their preferences and purchasing habits in ways that are only beginning to bear potential for transforming both goods and services trade.

Albert Einstein is often quoted as saying, 'information is not knowledge', but, rather, it becomes knowledge with imagination, analysis, innovation and experience. A corollary is that raw data is not information until it has been processed and transformed in an intelligible and useful form; that is, data itself is not knowledge, but rather is transformed into knowledge. Digitization makes this process easier and more rapid.

Over-reactions to these transformations hold the risk of disproportionate policy responses which may harm not only trade, but also the associated transmission of knowledge across borders. In many respects, the most salient features of the technologies behind today's digitization, and its continued potential, are less a uniqueness of technologies themselves, but rather the effect of greatly enhanced potential for trade.

In what ways does this transformation require new or enhanced rules of trade and engagement?

Whatever trade rules may be employed, existing or new, one salient point is that strengthened and enhanced efforts at cross-border collaboration among governments may be needed to complement national initiatives.

Bibliography

International Telecommunications Union (ITU), 2017 "ICT Facts and Figures 2017", available online at https://www.itu.int/en/ITU-D/Statistics/Pages/facts/default.aspx.

Roy, Martin. (2017), "The Contribution of Services Trade Policies to Connectivity in The Context of Aid for Trade", WTO Staff Working Paper, ERSD-2017-12.

Tuthill, Lee (2016), "Cross-border Data Flows: What Role for Trade Rules?", in Sauvé and Roy (eds), *Research Handbook on Trade in Services*, Edward Elgar, Cheltenham, UK.

United Nations et al. (2010), Manual on Statistics of International Trade in Services 2010.

WIPO, World Intellectual Property Report 2017: Intangible Capital in Global Value Chains, Geneva, 2017.

WTO, Appellate Body Report, China – Measures Affecting Trading Rights and Distribution Services for Certain Publications and Audiovisual Entertainment Products, WT/DS363/AB/R, adopted 19 January 2010, DSR 2010:I.

WTO, Appellate Body Report, United States – Measures Affecting the Cross-Border Supply of Gambling and Betting Services, WT/DS285/AB/R, adopted 20 April 2005, DSR 2005:XII, p. 5663 (and Corr.1, DSR 2006:XII, p. 5475).

WTO, Panel Report, China – Certain Measures Affecting Electronic Payment Services, WT/DS413/R and Add.1, adopted 31 August 2012, DSR 2012:X, p. 5305.

WTO, Panel Report, China – Measures Affecting Trading Rights and Distribution Services for Certain Publications and Audiovisual Entertainment Products, WT/DS363/R and Corr.1, adopted 19 January 2010, as modified by Appellate Body Report WT/DS363/AB/R, DSR 2010:II, p. 261.

WTO, Panel report, Mexico – Measures Affecting Telecommunications Services, WT/DS204/R, adopted 1 June 2004, DSR 2004:IV, p. 1537.

WTO, Panel Report, United States – Measures Affecting the Cross-Border Supply of Gambling and Betting Services, WT/DS285/R, adopted 20 April 2005, as modified by Appellate Body Report WT/DS285/AB/R, DSR 2005:XII, p. 5797.

WTO, Reference Paper on Basic Telecommunications (WTO Job document 2104, dated 24 April 1996).

A3.1

Specific commitments across selected sectors, by modes of supply number of schedules with specific commitments (out of 152)

		Mode 1			Mode 2			Mode 3			Mode 4	
		Full	Partial	Unbound	Full	Partial	Unbound	Full	Partial	Unbound	Full/ Partial	Unbound
Business services												
Professional services												
Legal services	77	25%	66%	9%	35%	60%	5%	13%	82%	5%	97%	4%
Accounting/auditing/ bookkeeping services	88	42%	40%	18%	55%	36%	9%	27%	72%	1%	92%	8%
Engineering services	89	55%	30%	15%	71%	17%	12%	48%	49%	2%	97%	3%
Computer services												
Consultancy services related to the installation of computer hardware	84	79%	7%	14%	85%	6%	10%	79%	20%	1%	98%	2%
Software implementation services	89	74%	13%	12%	81%	12%	7%	71%	28%	1%	97%	3%
Data processing services	87	72%	15%	13%	80%	13%	7%	70%	29%	1%	97%	3%
Database services	80	78%	9%	14%	86%	8%	6%	75%	24%	1%	97%	3%
Other	62	71%	26%	3%	74%	23%	3%	63%	37%	0%	98%	2%
R&D services												
R&D services on natural sciences	42	71%	17%	12%	69%	19%	12%	64%	36%	0%	95%	5%

Other business services												
Advertising services	70	61%	29%	10%	64%	29%	7%	50%	49%	1%	100%	0%
Management consulting	83	80%	11%	10%	84%	10%	6%	80%	19%	1%	100%	0%
Communication services												
Postal services	14	36%	57%	7%	57%	36%	7%	21%	71%	7%	79%	21%
Courier services	65	54%	34%	12%	60%	34%	6%	43%	57%	0%	95%	5%
Telecommunication services												
Voice telephone services	100	24%	70%	6%	51%	44%	5%	18%	81%	1%	95%	5%
Packet-switched data transmission services	93	34%	62%	4%	55%	41%	3%	21%	78%	1%	96%	4%
Circuit-switched data transmission services	94	35%	60%	5%	56%	40%	4%	22%	76%	2%	96%	4%
Private leased circuit services	89	36%	61%	3%	58%	39%	2%	24%	75%	1%	97%	3%
Online information and database retrieval	85	50%	45%	5%	63%	29%	8%	37%	60%	2%	98%	2%
Online information and/or data processing	70	55%	38%	7%	69%	23%	8%	42%	56%	1%	97%	3%

Source: WTO analysis based on GATS Schedules – available at i-tip.wto.org/services.

4

Intellectual Property and Digital Trade – Mapping International Regulatory Responses to Emerging Issues

WOLF R. MEIER-EWERT AND JORGE GUTIERREZ

Abstract

This chapter explores how regulatory responses to emerging IP issues in digital trade may develop at the international level and in particular how existing mechanisms might influence the chances of developing internationally agreed rules in this regard. The primacy of state sovereignty in intellectual property up to the late 19th century gave way to the important WIPO treaties, which still retained some independence of member states and based international regulatory responses directly on national experience. While more regulatory sovereignty was ceded in TRIPS, the WIPO Copyright Treaty and the WIPO Performances and Phonograms Treaty, the adoption of non-binding instruments (such as the WIPO Joint Recommendations in the area of trademarks) show the limits of decision making by consensus. International non-state solutions such as the Uniform Domain-Name Dispute-Resolution Policy (UDRP) established by the Internet Corporation for Assigned Names and Numbers (ICANN) have introduced separate, technically determined solutions to specific IP issues. Proliferating free-trade agreements (FTAs) have emerged as a new platform to agree to IP-related regulatory responses that can be used to project the national solutions of a few dominant FTA-partners. However, these FTAs have also served to give legally binding status to internationally agreed non-binding recommendations. These diverse approaches are apparent in recent IP-regulatory responses to emerging digital issues that are particularly relevant for digital business models, including inter alia Internet service provider (ISP) liability, "safe harbour" provisions and the issue of orphan works, where there appears to be less agreement. Still further behind to reaching any kind of agreement are the emerging issues of online exhaustion, data mining and IP-related questions of artificial intelligence.

Introduction

The genesis of international regulation in any subject area is complex and multifaceted. Whether a particular rule or practice succeeds in garnering international agreement is influenced by varying constellations of interests, stakeholders and institutions, and the fragile interaction between national jurisdictions and regional or international agreements. Internationally agreed regulation is particularly advanced in the area of intellectual property (IP), where detailed treaties set binding international standards on subject matter, scope of protection and enforcement of most types of IP rights. International registration systems exercise a harmonizing influence on procedures and formalities. The intangible nature of IP meant that it was one of the first regulatory areas to react to the challenges posed by digital networks and their consequences for territoriality and the reproduction of digital works. While many of the principles underlying existing IP regulation proved sufficiently adaptable to the digital world, many IP-related issues that have emerged since the advent of the Internet and digitization are triggering new or adapted regulatory responses at various levels. Some matters have already resulted in international agreements or uniform multilateral practices. Other – more recent – issues are still receiving different treatment in different jurisdictions and international consensus on how to regulate them is not (yet) in sight.

To understand how international regulatory responses to IP-related challenges in the area of digital trade might develop at the international level, and what factors influence the locus and nature of such responses, this chapter first describes the rule-making processes that have shaped the international IP regime since its origins in the late nineteenth century, including recent examples of tools and legal instruments that address digital challenges. The chapter then reviews the status of selected current digital issues, including ISP liability and online exhaustion, from the perspective of mechanisms that might lead to internationally agreed responses.

The Changing Pattern of International Rule-Making in Intellectual Property

The proverbial lag of regulatory and policy responses to technological developments is a frequently evoked stereotype that has become particularly popular – and true – in the area of digital technologies, where the rate and profundity of change has reached breakneck speed. This 'tech lag' phenomenon merely describes the time delay that national institutions face in identifying, formulating, issuing and implementing relevant policy or regulatory reactions to technological developments.

However, even further complexity is usually associated with *international* regulatory responses, which – while having the advantage of disproportionate regulatory synergy across different markets – encounter myriad additional challenges as to legitimate fora, compatibility of legal systems, enforcement and adjudication of disputes.

The Early Ideal of Universal Codification and the Primacy of Sovereign Treatymaking

The WIPO Paris and Berne Conventions, together with the TRIPS Agreement, form the foundations of today's international IP system. Their substantive and institutional development largely shaped the advancement of internationally agreed IP rules during the twentieth century.

The Berne and Paris Conventions as the Foundation of International IP Regime

The Berne and Paris Conventions resulted from the intangible nature – and hence easy international mobility – of inventions and literary works. The popularity of 'Universal Exhibitions' in the second half of the nineteenth century, and the corresponding surge of international exchange of industrial inventions and literature, soon united the relevant actors – industrialists and authors/publishers[1] – to call for 'universal' unified regulation of authors' and inventors' rights. The resulting intergovernmental organizations (the Berne and Paris Unions) and conventions remained the prime locus for formulating international IP rules for the next century.

While the early ideal of truly universal codification[2] soon gave way to more realistic – and moderate – objectives, the early spirit of finding

[1] For the role of the *Association Artistique et Littéraire* (ALAI) in the initiation of the Berne Union, see Ricketson and Ginsburg, (2006), pp. 49–58.

[2] See the programme of the Vienna Patent Congress 1873, Appendix A, *Webster's Report*, page 400 (cited in Ricketson (2015), p. 34): 'All the views, however, even those of the partisans of patent protection, unite invariably and unexceptionably in this, that the protection of the rights of inventors needs new forms corresponding to the altered international commercial relations; and the solution of this question of reform should not be aimed separately as hitherto, by each state of the great commercial area, but rather, that a complete solution common to all states should be accomplished by international agreement.'; regarding the Berne Convention, see the debate of the German motion in favour of a universal codification at *Actes 1884*, pp. 28–29, cited in Ricketson and Ginsburg (2006), p. 138.

common rules through the exchange of technical experts directly at the international level remained reflected in the institutions' structure and operations.[3] Exemplifying a form of international regulatory activity, these conventions – and the institutions administering them – provided a unique intergovernmental forum for technical experts in the relatively well-defined areas of IP to discuss and strive to formulate common regulatory solutions directly at the international level, which – if successful – became international treaty law.

Participants in these deliberations were mostly like-minded national IP experts that subscribed to the common goal of international harmonization around appropriate subject matter principles and solutions. The iterative process of successive treaty revisions of the Paris and the Berne Conventions, which remained the focus of efforts up until the second half of the twentieth century, further reflects the lingering spirit that a 'universal regulation' of the entire area of industrial property or copyright could be contained in a single body of rules agreed among sovereign states.

Political and policy considerations did influence divergent national positions. Yet in expert deliberations, and certainly in the dynamics of revision conferences, it is clear that the limitation of the treaty scope to the relatively confined area of IP and the traditional influence of practical technical questions (rooted in the early influence of authors, publishers and inventors) meant that the influence of strategizing and external political considerations could remain limited.

The historical context of these treaties is complex and cannot be viewed in a simple linear pattern. Yet these arguably dominant traits of the early stages of international IP treatymaking help explain the surprisingly early and dynamic genesis of these conventions, which represent – then, as today – a degree and depth of international codification unparalleled in any other area of private law. The early and successful establishment of the Berne and Paris Unions with their expert-driven and unified regulatory approach made this model of sovereign treatymaking the natural focus for international IP regulation for most of the twentieth century, next to which alternative institutions – or even alternative approaches to treatymaking in this area – remained limited in scope.[4]

[3] The unions were organized in 'groups of experts' that formed the precursors to today's WIPO Standing Committees.

[4] This is not to diminish alternative efforts such as the Universal Copyright Convention (UCC), that pursued equally 'universal' ambitions.

By the time digitization and the Internet emerged in the 1990s, however, this traditional model of consensus-based treaty revisions based on expert opinion had reached certain limits. Concerns of developing countries had dominated the revision conferences in the 1960s and 1970s, and the iterative revisions of entire conventions had become difficult – and, while still hoped for in the 1990s, effectively came to a halt after the 1971 revision of the Berne Convention.[5] The emerging and accelerating technological changes, and the corresponding new means of exploitation, now led to more divergent national solutions and approaches that could no longer be easily bridged by national expert discussions at the international level, as had been the case in the early years.

Hence the provisions of the 1971 Berne Convention remained far from the original ideal of 'uniformity of protection' with implications for coverage of emerging digital issues. Gaps persisted, in particular with regard to a right of distribution of copyright protected works. The formulation of a number of protected rights still permitted considerable variations in national interpretation.[6] Given the wide discretion left to countries with regard to copyright exceptions, and the lack of clarity as to whether software fell within the scope of the Convention, much of the effective protection of authors was effectively left to the application of national treatment.

While member countries maintained the characteristically expert-driven approach in the context of WIPO by establishing committees of government experts on a number of salient issues – such as computer software as early as the 1970s and 1980s – these efforts did not bear fruit until after the conclusion of the TRIPS negotiations, when some of the work from the 'guided development'[7] period served as a basis of the 1996 WIPO Internet Treaties.

TRIPS: A Continuation of Unified Expert-Driven Treatymaking

Although the inclusion of IP subject matter in the multilateral negotiations of the GATT Uruguay Round represented a significant shift from the historical pattern of treatymaking, the methodology and the outcome of the negotiations of the TRIPS Agreement still resemble the model of

[5] See the account of 'uneasy truce' that no one wanted to reopen by beginning new debates, in Ricketson and Ginsberg (2006), p. 140.

[6] This was the case in the areas of reproduction, broadcasting and cable distribution. See Ricketson and Ginsberg (2006), p. 138.

[7] Ricketson and Ginsberg (2006), p. 143.

unified expert-driven treatymaking. The factors that facilitated the shift of focus from WIPO to the GATT/WTO have been amply commented upon.[8] From the perspective of international IP regulatory activity, these factors fall into two categories: those related to the limits of the traditional locus and methodology of international IP regulation in WIPO; and those relating to the systemic dynamics of multilateral trade negotiations. For WIPO, the lack of progress since the last revisions of the Paris and Berne Conventions in 1967 and 1971 respectively meant that there was little prospect that remaining gaps in protection, notably on enforcement and dispute settlement, could be closed in the traditional fashion in the foreseeable future. The protracted experience of the last revision conferences, and the failure of attempts to conclude 'special agreements' in the 1980s – notably on software[9] – opened some Member countries' minds to alternative approaches of treatymaking, although much convincing remained to be done before agreement on negotiating a comprehensive IP instrument in GATT was reached in the course of the Uruguay Round.[10]

In the trade negotiations area, the characteristic trade-off dynamic of the Uruguay Round negotiations meant that, in contrast to the WIPO context, non-IP considerations were able to exercise more considerable – and more direct – leverage on countries' willingness to discuss IP. At the time, this concerned first and foremost the question of whether a fully-fledged TRIPS outcome should be part of the Uruguay Round *at all*. The mandate to negotiate comprehensive 'standards and principles concerning the availability, scope and use of trade-related IPRs' was agreed in April 1989[11] – after considerable hesitation on the part of a number of both developed and developing countries – only when the prospective benefits of the Uruguay Round in areas such as textiles, agriculture and tariffs became clearer, and a refusal to negotiate on IP would have endangered the benefits of the overall outcome.[12] It is less evident that this trade-off leverage had any effect on individual substantive IP questions in the same way as is argued in the context of recent bilateral treaties.[13] Rather, it seems that negotiating countries on the whole saw IP negotiations *as a whole* as a trade-off for lucrative agricultural market

[8] Ibid., p. 155, note 44.
[9] Ibid., p. 144.
[10] See Otten (2015).
[11] GATT Document MTN/TNC/11, Uruguay Round – Trade Negotiations Committee – Mid-Term Meeting, 21 April 1989.
[12] Otten (2015), pp. 62 and 74.
[13] See 'Regional Trade Agreements: Regulatory Responses to Digital Challenges' below.

access offers, hence requiring progress on the latter before continuing the former during the successive negotiation sessions.[14] Negotiations on individual IP issues remained largely guided by the – offensive or defensive – substantive interests, patiently explained by IP experts, of the negotiating countries who lined up in groups – often defying the traditional north–south narrative – of common positions around copyright, enforcement or geographical indications, to name just a few.[15]

From the perspective of international IP regulation, therefore, and despite this new context of international IP regulation in the Uruguay Round, the substantive outcome on IP within the TRIPS Agreement followed in many ways the characteristics of the treatymaking process under the WIPO Conventions. Although the negotiations moved much faster and in a less formal manner, and took place outside the WIPO ecosystem of government expert committees and working groups, national IP experts played a central role in the framing and the conduct of TRIPS negotiations. Furthermore the historic ideal underlying the conventions, namely of 'universal codification' seems to have been even more successful in the unifying edifice of the TRIPS Agreement. Incorporating *tel quel* not only most of the provisions of the Berne and Paris Conventions, but also parts of the Rome Convention and the Washington Treaty, and supplying significant substantive additions and clarifications, the TRIPS Agreement remains the single most comprehensive international treaty on IP today – covering substantive protection and enforcement of most conventional categories of IP in a single treaty.

Although negotiated just as early digitization issues were arising,[16] the TRIPS Agreement contains few specific regulatory responses in this area. Notable is the first international confirmation that software is covered by copyright, resolving an issue discussed in WIPO in the 1980s. The specific formulation 'whether in source or object code' clarified that protection extended also to the machine-readable binary code in which software was usually distributed – which some national jurisprudence had excluded,[17] hence rendering protection ineffective. By stipulating protection 'as literary works', Article 10.1 TRIPS ensured that computer

[14] See the account of the Brussels breakdown of negotiations in Otten (2015), p. 67.

[15] See the country experiences reported in Watal and Taubman (2015) *The Making of the TRIPS Agreement* (WTO 2015).

[16] Although signed only in 1994, the bulk of the TRIPS text was negotiated already in the 1980s. See Gervais (2012).

[17] See Blomqvist (2014), p. 88.

programs – with their arguably functional character – would not be categorized as works of applied art, which would have permitted a reduced minimum term of protection,[18] or even exclusion from protection altogether – albeit while risking material reciprocity – under the Berne Convention (1971).[19] TRIPS Article 10.2 on 'compilations of data and other material' – while deciding against requiring *sui generis* database protection at the international level[20] – specifically acknowledges that compilations of data or other material 'whether in machine-readable or other form' are to be protected if they constitute intellectual creations by reason of selection or arrangement, even if the data or the material itself is not copyright protected.

Against this – admittedly simplistic and selective – account charted above it would seem that, despite the institutional shift from a body exclusively dedicated to IP into the multilateral trade regime, the TRIPS negotiations represent nevertheless the culmination of the traditional model of international IP regulation in which (i) largely expert-driven negotiations directly at the international level develop rules in pursuit of – ideally – (ii) a unified and universal body of rules in the shape of conventions or comprehensive texts, that are then agreed to as (iii) international treaties by sovereign states. The limits of this model arguably showed already in the earlier slowdown after the conventions' last revisions and it could be argued that it was only the context of the trade-offs available in the Uruguay Round that achieved the renewed momentum. The TRIPS outcome nevertheless shows the continued salience and attractiveness of the 'universal sovereign treaty model' in the early 1990s, although other – more limited – selective subject matter agreements would also have been possible, and were in fact contemplated.[21]

The Emergence of New Modes of Regulatory Responses

The culmination of the model described above coincided with the early development of the World Wide Web, and therefore did not address the new issues raised by widespread use of the Internet, particularly the

18 Article 7(4) Berne Convention (1971).

19 Article 2(7) of the Berne Convention (1971); see also Blomqvist (2014). For an overview of the negotiating dynamics on copyright protection of software at the time of the Uruguay Round, see Wager (2015).

20 See the background in Gervais (2012).

21 See the GATT 1982 and 1986 Ministerial Declarations with a mandate for a code on counterfeit goods only.

online distribution of protected works. In responding to these challenges, the traditional model began to give way to more varied regulatory responses.

The WIPO Internet Treaties: An Issue-Driven International Solution

Although work on the challenges presented by new technological developments had begun in WIPO already in the 1970s, progress had been slow, and momentum was lacking particularly once the Uruguay Round mandate to negotiate a comprehensive IP agreement had taken shape in late 1989. As TRIPS did not address many of the new technology issues in detail, momentum returned to WIPO where an astonishing spurt of concerted effort produced the WIPO 'Internet Treaties', namely the WIPO Copyright Treaty (WCT) and the WIPO Performances and Phonograms Treaty (WPPT), less than two years after the Uruguay Round concluded.[22] The Internet Treaties took significant steps towards adapting international rules for the protection of copyright and the rights of performers and producers of sound recordings to the digital revolution, and in particular to the distribution of copyright material over the Internet.[23]

These treaties establish an international agreement[24] that storage of works in a digital form in an electronic medium constitutes a reproduction. Despite alternative approaches discussed in the run-up to the Diplomatic Conference, signatories ultimately agreed that the respective reproduction rights, of authors, performers and of phonogram producers – as well as the permitted exceptions – fully apply to the digital environment.[25] While this ensured that digital exploitation and storage was covered by the traditional reproduction concept, the specific mention of the applicability of permitted exceptions, and a certain leeway in interpreting the term 'storage', was understood to permit justified exceptions regarding transient or incidental reproductions,[26] as may occur in

[22] The WCT and the WPPT were adopted on 20 December 1996 and entered into force on 6 March 2002 and 20 May 2002, respectively.

[23] Wager (2015).

[24] By March 2020, the Internet Treaties had been signed by 104 countries.

[25] For copyright, see Article 1(4) WCT and agreed statement. For performers' and phonogram producers' rights, see Articles 7 and 11 of the WPPT that confirm and expand the reproduction rights provided for in Article 7.1 (for performers) and Article 10 (for phonogram producers) of the Rome Convention, and the accompanying agreed statement.

[26] See WIPO Handbook (2004), 5.220 and 5.563.

the operation of digital networks.[27] An agreed statement to the TRIPS-style three-step test that was now introduced to cover exceptions of the Internet Treaties and the Berne Convention[28] explicitly highlighted the objective to permit the development of new exceptions and limitations appropriate for the digital network environment.[29]

The treaties further enshrine the central principle that the transmission of works in digital networks is the object of an exclusive right of the author or other rights owner. In formulating this 'right of making available' in a manner that captured the technological specificity of Internet distribution, yet remained neutral as to which traditional rights were the basis of this new obligation, the treaties bridged considerable diversity that existed in national jurisdictions as regards the recognition and application of a distribution right or a right of communication to the public.[30] As the Berne Convention (1971) coverage of both these rights was limited,[31] the Internet Treaties further endeavoured to fill these gaps by explicitly extending the right of communication to the public to cover the making available of works in digital networks (Article 8 WCT, Articles 10 and 14 WPPT), and by explicitly stipulating a distribution right (Article 6 WCT, Articles 8 and 12 WPPT), thus clarifying the hitherto heterogenous interpretation of the international standard.

This so-called 'umbrella solution'[32] – to formulate a new making available right in a 'neutral, legal characterization-free description'[33] – ensured

[27] This permitted, in principle, the same treatment as for 'ephemeral fixations' by broadcasting organizations under Article 15.1 (c) of the Rome Convention (1961).

[28] It is Article 10(2) WCT that extends the test to govern exceptions and limitations to all Berne Convention rights.

[29] The agreed statement to Article 10 WCT – also covering Article 16(2) WPPT – reads: 'It is understood that the provisions of Article 10 permit Contracting Parties to carry forward and appropriately extend into the digital environment limitations and exceptions in their national laws which have been considered acceptable under the Berne Convention. Similarly, these provisions should be understood to permit Contracting Parties to devise new exceptions and limitations that are appropriate in the digital network environment. It is also understood that Article 10(2) neither reduces nor extends the scope of applicability of the limitations and exceptions permitted by the Berne Convention.'

[30] See WIPO Handbook (2004).

[31] In the Berne Convention (1971) a distribution right is only explicitly granted with respect to cinematographic works (Article 14(1)(i)), although some jurisdictions considered such a right a necessary – and thus implicit – corollary of the right of reproduction. The right of communication to the public only extends to certain forms of communication of works (Article 11*bis*(1)).

[32] The term was reportedly coined by Mihály Ficsor, Secretary of the Diplomatic Conference. See Schlesinger (2010), p. 180.

[33] Mihály Ficsor (2002), § C.8.06.

that both possible bases for such an obligation – the right of communication to the public and the distribution right – were now equally enshrined in the international standard of copyright protection. This artful solution gave national legislatures considerable flexibility in characterizing the exclusive rights involved.[34] While Article 10 WCT associates the new right of making available with the right of communication to the public – and many countries have chosen to implement that way[35] – the negotiation history[36] and subsequent commentary[37] clarifies that the 'umbrella solution' equally permits signatories to implement the making available right through applying the exclusive distribution right to electronic transmissions of works.[38]

Indeed, in that regard, the United States observed that:

> a 'distribution' approach more closely approximates the real market impact of on-demand and other online transactions, in which the recipient of the transmission often ends up with a copy of a work that he or she did not have before.[39]

The United States therefore saw no need for legislative action to implement the new right, since 'its broad reading of the distribution right, in conjunction with the reproduction right [. . .] would cover the act of "making available" as that is defined in the WCT (and the WPPT)'.[40]

Some of the challenges that would be raised by the implementation of these new rights, and which do indeed occupy courts and law-makers today – such as ISP liability and the question of online exhaustion – were anticipated in some of the agreed statements adopted with the Internet Treaties. The newly confirmed right of distribution was accompanied by a statement seeking to clarify that the 'copies' subject to the distribution (and

[34] See Schlesinger (2010).

[35] Ibid. See also an early Survey on Implementation Provisions of the WCT and the WPPT, document SCCR/9/6, 25 April 2003, which mentions that the right of making available had been implemented as a right of communication in 19 out of 39 laws reviewed, and 'under or in conjunction with' the right of distribution in only five out of 39 laws reviewed.

[36] WIPO Handbook (2004), 5.226.

[37] Schlesinger (2010) and von Lewinski (2015), § 8.10.10.

[38] Schlesinger (2010), p. 181. For the WPPT, see von Lewinski (2015), § 8.10.10.

[39] Schlesinger (2010).

[40] Ibid. See also US Copyright Office (2016), pp. 74–75 confirming the sufficiency of current statute: 'In general, where a party offers members of the public access to a work in the form of a download, the offer implicates the right of distribution.' '. . . Congress understood such conduct to be an infringement of the distribution right.'

rental) right were *tangible* objects.[41] Together with the traditional understanding, expressed in the notes of the Basic Proposal, that 'no rights are exhausted in connection with communication' and that 'exhaustion of rights is only associated with the distribution of tangible copies',[42] this provides the dogmatic background for asserting that in countries that consider 'making available' a communication to the public, electronic copies made available in digital networks would not be subject to exhaustion. However, the basic tenet of the 'umbrella solution' – namely that, despite the wording of Article 8 WCT, countries are free to implement the new exclusive making available right by extending the distribution right to cover electronic transmissions – leaves the dogmatic context more ambiguous for those who, like the United States, consider online downloads an act of distribution.

This tension is recognized in some characterizations of the agreed statement, which seems to imply that countries' freedom of choice regarding the implementation of the new right includes the freedom to have exhaustion apply to electronic copies 'distributed' through the making available right.

> The question may emerge whether this Agreed Statement [concerning Articles 6 and 7] conflicts with the 'umbrella solution' for transmissions in interactive digital networks, and, particularly, whether or not it excludes application of the right of distribution to such transmissions. The answer to this question is obviously negative. The Agreed Statement determines only the minimum scope of application of the right of distribution; it does not create any obstacle for Contracting States to exceed that minimum.[43]

As regards the issue of ISP liability, the new making available right in Article 8 WCT was accompanied by an agreed statement clarifying that the provision of physical infrastructure did not in itself amount to an act

[41] 'Concerning Articles 6 and 7: As used in these Articles, the expressions "copies" and "original and copies", being subject to the right of distribution and the right of rental under the said Articles, refer exclusively to fixed copies that can be put into circulation as tangible objects.'

[42] See the Basic Proposal [. . .] to be Considered by the Diplomatic Conference (CRNR/DC/4 of 30 August 1996), para. 10.20: 'It should be pointed out that no rights are exhausted in connection with communication to the public. Should communication of a work result in the reproduction of a copy at the recipient end, the work may not be communicated further to the public or distributed to the public without authorization. Exhaustion of rights is only associated with the distribution of tangible copies.'

[43] Mihály Ficsor (2005), p. 11.

of communication within the meaning of the treaty,[44] which is intended to clarify the issue of the liability of service and access providers in digital networks.[45] However, other than stating the rather obvious fact that providing infrastructure is not communicating to the public, this agreed statement is not determinative of who is liable for infringements of the exclusive right of making available stipulated in Article 8 WCT.

This brief – and selective[46] – overview of some of the Internet Treaties' achievements in crafting creative regulatory responses to the challenges the digital environment posed for copyright and related rights highlights a certain departure from the traditional treatymaking pattern identified earlier. The negotiators did not pursue international regulation of copyright or related rights in a 'unified and universal body of rules', i.e. by pursuing another revision of the traditional conventions, but deliberately chose separate instruments (making use of the Berne Article 20 provision for special agreements), with their own treaty administration,[47] that could be acceded to individually.[48] Although this is certainly not to suggest an abandonment of consistency with the existing body of rules,[49] this formal separation of instruments permitted a more focused – and arguably more ambitious – regulatory response to the specific challenges posed by new communication technology, and thus avoided the concerns associated with reopening the Berne Convention.

The Internet Treaties, like the Uruguay Round conclusion a few years earlier, also coincided with a geopolitical situation more favourable to market opening, multilateral cooperation and to embracing technological

[44] See agreed statement concerning Article 8, 'It is understood that the mere provision of physical facilities for enabling or making a communication does not in itself amount to communication within the meaning of this Treaty or the Berne Convention. It is further understood that nothing in Article 8 precludes a Contracting Party from applying Article 11*bis*(2)'.

[45] WIPO Handbook (2004), 5.567.

[46] For a full overview of the regulatory breadth of the Internet Treaties, see the respective sections of the WIPO Handbook (2004).

[47] See Article 15 WCT and Article 24 WPPT for arrangements of the respective assemblies.

[48] Note that membership of the Berne or Rome Conventions was not a condition for eligibility to join the Internet Treaties (see Article 17 WCT and Article 26 WPPT). In March 2020, the WCT and WPPT were in force in 97 out of a total of 104 contracting parties, while the 1971 Paris Act of the Berne Convention was in force in 188 contracting parties.

[49] Indeed, the elaborate provisions on relationships with other treaties emphasize the link with the Berne and Rome Conventions, respectively, and ensure that the Internet Treaties may not be interpreted in a manner that is inconsistent with their individual preceding conventions. See Article 1 WCT and Article 1 WPPT.

change, which influenced countries' willingness to agree on complex legal issues in an international forum. Many former communist or socialist economies were actively studying and seeking to establish societies based on market economy principles, which sometimes served as an inspiration for traditional developing countries to pursue similar ambitions.[50] The conclusion of the TRIPS Agreement, which reconfirmed, unified and further built on the Berne and Paris Conventions, may thus have helped overcome regulatory stagnation in the field of IP, and represented a new platform from which new solutions for the challenges posed by the accelerating technological developments could be developed in the Internet Treaties. In some areas, countries were prepared to agree solutions that had not yet been legislated or contemplated in the national jurisdictions, and thus again represent expert-driven, substantive international law-making, rather than agreement on a lowest common denominator of existing national solutions.[51]

From a regulatory point of view, the issue-driven Internet Treaties thus represent a particularly successful instance of treatymaking that was able to benefit from thorough expert preparation in substance and favourable geopolitical circumstances to achieve consensus on a rapid and relatively comprehensive response to the copyright challenges of new communication technologies. While countries were able to build on this success to some extent with the conclusion of 'the 3rd WIPO Internet Treaty'[52] – the Beijing Treaty on Audiovisual Performances in 2012 – achieving treaty-level consensus on regulatory responses to digital challenges soon became more difficult and gave rise to the use of non-binding regulatory instruments.

The Emergence Of Non-Binding Instruments – the Joint Recommendations

While work on the Internet Treaties was successfully concluded, alignment of interests in other areas was more elusive. Increased commercial Internet

[50] Otten (2015), Wager (2015).

[51] The obligations on technical protection measures and digital rights management information (Articles 11–12 WCT and Articles 18–19 WPPT) have not been treated here. For an example of discussions in the context of subsequent implementation of these obligations see Geist (2010), and Ficsor (2009).

[52] See Mihály Ficsor, 'The WIPO Internet Treaties and Copyright in the "Cloud"', paper presented at the ALAI Congress in Kyoto, 2012.

use and the emergence of new trademark laws and registration authorities, among other factors caused by technological and commercial developments, had brought into sharp focus the need for clarity on the practical definition of 'well-known' marks whose scope of protection in Article 6*bis* Paris Convention had just been extended by Article 16 of the TRIPS Agreement.[53] Based on a mandate to study 'all questions of relevance to the correct application of Article 6*bis*' from the 1996–1997 WIPO Programme[54] a Committee of Experts on Well-Known Marks – later the Standing Committee on Trademarks, Industrial Designs and Geographical Indications (SCT) – developed draft provisions. Up until its third session in 1997 the Committee of Experts foresaw the adoption of these draft provisions either through an international instrument or a recommendation by the WIPO General Assembly, 'once sufficient agreement had been reached on such conclusions'.[55]

However, at around the same time WIPO members officially embraced the need to adapt to the pace of change in the field of industrial property by considering new options – i.e. other than treaties – for agreeing international common principles:

> Given the practical imperative for accelerated development and implementation of certain international harmonized common principles and rules in industrial property law, the future strategy for this main program includes consideration of ways to complement the treaty-based approach [. . .] If Member States judge it to be in their interests so to proceed, a more flexible approach may be taken towards the harmonization of industrial property principles and rules, and coordination of

[53] See Kur (2013) remarking that 'It was not uncommon during that phase that fortune-seekers succeeded in registering famous marks like "Dior" or "Cartier" and others, in order to extract money from the true proprietors when they tried to get a foothold on the same market. This of course created concern among the trademark community in the Western world, leading to warnings directed at the political instances in those countries that they were in violation of their obligations under Article 6bis Paris Convention and of Article 16 TRIPS, threatening to compromise their access to WTO membership. Trying to achieve what was expected of them most governments were keenly interested in obtaining specific and secure guidelines for checking which marks were to be considered as "well-known" in the meaning of the international agreements and hence must be excluded from trademark protection.'

[54] WIPO Document AB/XXVI/2, Item 03(5).

[55] Memorandum on Protection of Well-Known Marks at the Third Session of the Committee of Experts on Well-Known Marks, 20–23 October 1997, WIPO Document WKM/CE/III/2: 'Therefore, [. . .] it is left open whether those draft provisions would be adopted in the form of a recommendation of the said bodies or in the form of an international instrument such as a Protocol to the Trademark Law Treaty.'

administration, so that results can be achieved and applied more rapidly, ensuring earlier practical benefits for administrators and users of the industrial property system.[56]

Under this approach, WIPO member states agreed three non-binding recommendations[57] between 1999 and 2001. In 1999, the Paris Union Assembly and the WIPO General Assembly adopted the Joint Recommendation Concerning Provisions on the Protection of Well-Known Marks (JR 1999), which provided criteria for the determination of whether a mark qualifies as 'well-known'[58] and established remedies for conflicts between well-known marks and other marks, business identifiers and domain names.[59] Its relevance for digital trade arises from its recommended prohibition on requirements for use or registration of the mark in the member state as a condition for it to be considered well known[60] there, while recommending the recognition of use and promotion or advertising – including on the Internet – as factors counting in favour of the well-known status of a mark.[61] Thus the JR 1999 significantly shores up the right owners' position in the digital marketplace, since advertising and use of the mark on the Internet is privileged vis-à-vis actual local use in the relevant member state.[62]

The newly created SCT had also started more general work on 'Trademarks and the Internet' at its second session in 1999 which developed into the Joint Recommendation Concerning Provisions on the Protection of Marks, and Other Industrial Property Rights in Signs, on the Internet (JR 2001) adopted in 2001. These recommendations attempted to harmonize the interpretation and meaning of 'trademark use' that had remained undefined in the Paris Convention and the TRIPS Agreement,

[56] WIPO Program and Budget for the biennium 1998–1999, document A/32/2-WO/BC/18/2, p. 86.

[57] Joint Recommendation Concerning Provisions on the Protection of Well-Known Marks (1999), a Joint Recommendation on Trademark Licenses (2000) and a Joint Recommendation Concerning the Protection of Marks, and Other Industrial Property Rights in Signs, on the Internet (2001).

[58] JR 1999, Article 2.

[59] JR 1999, Articles 4–6.

[60] JR 1999, Article 2(3)(i).

[61] JR 1999, Article 2(1)(b)(2) and (3). Note that 'promotion' was separately mentioned as a factor counting towards well-known status, also to overcome any ambiguity of whether promotion and advertising were regarded as 'use' of the mark. See the (explanatory – not 'agreed') Notes on Article 2, available at www.wipo.int/edocs/pubdocs/en/wipo_pub_833-accessible1.pdf.

[62] See Kur (2013).

and had come into sharper focus with the contradiction between the principle of territoriality of rights and the global nature of the Internet.

> The present provisions are intended to be applied in the context of determining whether, under the applicable law of a Member State, use of a sign on the Internet has contributed to the acquisition, maintenance or infringement of a mark or other industrial property right in the sign, or whether such use constitutes an act of unfair competition, and in the context of determining remedies.[63]

In substance, the JR 2001 recommends resolving the question of whether Internet use of a sign can be considered as use in a certain territory on the basis of whether it constitutes a 'commercial effect' according to a list of factors.[64] It also recommends a 'notice and avoidance of conflict' procedure for avoiding conflicts of right holders of identical or similar rights granted in different countries and their use over the Internet, under which right owners and other legitimate users are exempt from liability until they are notified of a conflicting right.[65] It recommends that remedies for infringement be limited, as far as possible, to the territory in which the right is recognized, and only be available if the allegedly infringing use of the sign can be deemed to have taken place in that territory. In other words, the JR 2001 proposes that the 'commercial effect' of Internet use should serve as a yardstick for determining a 'proportionate' remedy.[66]

As international regulatory responses, the Joint Recommendations depart further from the traditional treatymaking model. They pursue distinct solutions to specific details within a single IP discipline, not a unified body of rules. And they are non-binding 'soft law', not binding international treaty instruments agreed to by sovereign states. The need for acceleration of rule-making to ensure 'earlier practical benefits for administrators and users'[67] that is cited in support of this new approach also seems to suggest that the traditional expert-driven process that would have been necessary to ensure consensus for binding treaty provisions may have given way to more interest-driven results[68] that representatives could accept in the absence of binding commitments.

[63] JR 2001, Preamble.
[64] Article 3 JR 2001.
[65] Article 9 JR 2001.
[66] WIPO Handbook (2004) 5.751.
[67] WIPO Program 1998–1999 (n. 56).
[68] Kur (2013) observes: 'Driven not least by international stakeholders' associations, the text is pointedly right-holder friendly, without offering much legal certainty in return.'

Their non-binding nature may have facilitated their adoption but has not impeded their influence on national IP policymaking. Indeed, the standing of these instruments as recommendations from two authoritative WIPO bodies has led to their direct incorporation into legislative projects in some countries,[69] or to them being taken into account in national[70] jurisprudence. More recently, their inclusion in IP chapters of Free Trade Agreements have turned these non-binding recommendations into binding and enforceable commitments of an increasing number of countries.[71]

A Technically-Determined Solution to Specific IP Issues: The UDRP

The contemporaneous privatization of the hitherto government-run structure of the Domain Name System (DNS) and the creation of the Internet Corporation for Assigned Names and Numbers (ICANN) led to the creation of an entirely different IP-related regulatory response in the area of the Internet's infrastructure.

The use of domain names as 'user friendly' labels to connect to numerical Internet Protocol addresses on the global Internet inevitably led to conflicts with the existing territorial protection of trademarks under the national laws.[72] The National Science Foundation (NSF) was authorized to permit commercial activity on the NSFNET – the non-military part of the Internet it was administering – in 1992,[73] and the ensuing interest of commercial actors led to a rapid expansion of the Internet.[74] Network Solutions Inc. (NSI), a private company in charge of registering and administering the most valuable generic Top Level Domains (gTLDs)[75] – including .com – on behalf of the NSF on a first come, first served basis, originally saw no substantive role for the

[69] See for example the Trade Marks Act of the Republic of India, Chapter II, 11(6) to (10) referring to JR 1999.

[70] See section 9.3.3 *The Long Arm of Non-Binding Decisions at WIPO*, in Kwakwa and Talbott (2013).

[71] See below Regional Trade Agreements: Regulatory Responses to Digital Challenges.

[72] See generally Dinwoodie (2000).

[73] See Scientific and Advanced-Technology Act of 1992; Pub. L. 102-476 § 4(9), 106 Stat. 2297, 2300 (codified at 42 USC § 1862 (a)).

[74] For an overview of the Domain Name System and the evolution of its governance structure, see Petillion and Janssen (2017), chapter 2.

[75] NSI, a private American company, had received a directive from the InterNIC in 1993 to administrate the generic Top Level Domain Names (gTLDs): COM, EDU, GOV, INT, NET, ORG and MIL. See Haas (2009).

registration authority in the resolution of such disputes.[76] However, as disputes over the Internet's naming system soared[77] and criticism over the absence of competition in the registration process grew – and as NSI began charging user fees for domain name registration[78] – NSI introduced a first Domain Name Dispute Policy in 1995. Based on the contractual relationship between the domain name applicant and the registrar, to which it was annexed, this policy sought to avoid liability and prevent potential lawsuits of third parties against NSI.[79]

NSI's role as sole DNS registrar, and its Domain Name Dispute Policy, attracted sustained criticism over its monopoly position and, from the trademark community, its archaic dispute policy. The policy's approach to resolving conflicts between trademarks and domain names on the basis of registration priority[80] stood in stark tension with the long-standing US first-to-use tradition, by which rights in a mark are based on first use, not registration.[81] While the Clinton administration's ensuing decision to 'privatize' the Internet, and NSI's subsequent loss of registrar monopoly with the creation of ICANN and a new governance structure, was taken in the much larger policy context of Internet governance,[82] the tension between the 'commercial' trademark owner community and the 'academic' engineering community that had created the network was a visible part of this defining period for the Internet's naming system.

76 Response to RFC (Request for Comments) 1561 from March 1994: 'In case of a dispute between domain names registrants as to the rights to a particular name, the registration authority shall have no role or responsibility other than to provide the contact information to both parties. The registration of a domain name does not have any trademark status. It is up to the requester to be sure he is not violating anyone else's trademark', cited in Haas (2009).

77 In a 1998 Wired.com article, Dave Graves, Network Solutions' director of business affairs, is quoted: 'Our dispute policy has been invoked about 1,700 times in the two years that it has been in existence', he said, 'Compared to a database of over 1.6 million domain names, that represents about one-tenth of 1 percent.' See Stutz (1998).

78 Petillion and Janssen (2017) Chapter 2, n 57. NSI was permitted to charge USD 50 per year per second-level domain.

79 Haas (2009). See also INTA White Paper (1997) Section E. NSI Dispute Policy: What Happens When Domain Names and Trademarks Conflict.

80 Haas (2009): 'NSI determined the "creation date" of the domain name registration. If it was prior to the trademark, no action was taken.'

81 For a thorough conceptual discussion of this tension see Dinwoodie (2000), p. 515.

82 For the larger context see the introductions to the US Green Paper (1998), and the US White Paper (1998).

The International Trademark Association's (INTA) 1997 White Paper,[83] in criticizing the state of affairs under the NSI policy, opined that

> At the threshold is the issue that the Internet was not created solely for commercial enterprise and that domain names should not be the exclusive province of trademark owners. Thus, those with legitimate non-trademark interests in second level domain names have to be accommodated along with the rights of trademark owners. Similarly, the interests of owners of trademarks which exist in commerce concurrently for non-related products or services must be considered as do those of famous marks. Finally, it is not necessary to have a second level domain name to do business effectively or successfully on the Internet, and thus while it may be preferable to acquire the second level domain name of your choice, it is not an absolute right and may have to bend to accommodate competing interests.[84]

INTA's preferred solution was thus *not* to create a separate substantive domain name dispute resolution policy at all. Rather, a *sui generis* approach would permit a workable procedural approach to domain registration and disputes, while all substantive issues 'will be left to the courts and trademark tribunals' and their already growing body of domain name dispute jurisprudence,[85] thus ensuring that traditional trademark law would apply to these conflicts.

The NSI's director of business affairs disagreed with trademark lawyers' criticism of their revised Dispute Policy.

> '[T]here's nothing at all in law that says having a trademark and the rights to that trademark also provide an automatic right to a domain name,' said Graves. 'There's nothing that says that.'[86]

The alternative governance model known as gTLD-MoU – competing with the much-criticized[87] US Department of Commerce's Green Paper proposal of 30 January 1998[88] – built on previous criticism of NSI's dispute policy. It focused on a self-regulatory and market-driven mechanism enforced by administrative challenge panels (ACP) that would reside within WIPO's Arbitration and Mediation Center.[89]

[83] INTA White Paper (1997).
[84] INTA White Paper (1997).
[85] INTA White Paper (1997).
[86] David Graves, NSI cited in Stutz (1998).
[87] Petllion and Janssen (2017), chapter 2, A.2.b.(3)(a).
[88] US Green Paper (1998).
[89] Petillion and Janssen (2017), chapter 2, A.2.b.(3)(a). See also Komaitis (2010), p. 75.

While this MoU, as well as the envisaged governance association with the International Telecommunications Union (ITU), did not garner the required governmental support of the United States,[90] many of the characteristics of its dispute resolution approach[91] would be replicated in the Uniform Domain Name Dispute Resolution Policy (UDRP) that was developed under WIPO auspices and eventually adopted by ICANN under the arrangements of the US Department of Commerce's White Paper of 5 June 1998,[92] in which the Clinton administration's privatization policy for the DNS was settled.

The US White Paper's solution to the 'Trademark Dilemma'[93] was to ask WIPO to initiate a 'balanced and transparent' process to develop a uniform approach to resolving trademark/domain name disputes involving cyberpiracy (not conflicts between competing trademarks), albeit with precise recommendations that sought to address problems and criticism identified under previous experiences. These included the maintenance of an up-to-date database of domain name owners' contact information that should be accessible to trademark owners in order to identify and contact potential infringers, and development of process to exclude famous trademarks from being used as domain names except by the trademark holder. It further recommended that, at the time of registration or renewal, domain name registrants submit 'infringing domain names' to a court of law in a certain jurisdiction,[94] while for cases 'involving cyberpiracy and cybersquatting' they would submit to and be bound by the alternative dispute resolution systems that the new corporation (i.e. ICANN) would adopt following the WIPO process.[95]

[90] Ibid. See also US White Paper (1998).

[91] See Komaitis (2010): 'The proposal conceived of a mechanism that would be hybrid in nature, would not replace traditional means of adjudication and would see administrative panels adjudicating disputes under certain objective standards and criteria.'

[92] US White Paper (1998).

[93] US White Paper (1998), section 8.

[94] '1) Domain registrants pay registration fees at the time of registration or renewal and agree to submit infringing domain names to the authority of a court of law in the jurisdiction in which the registry, registry database, registrar, or the "A" root servers are located.' US White Paper (1998) Recommendations.

[95] '2) Domain name registrants would agree, at the time of registration or renewal, that in cases involving cyberpiracy or cybersquatting (as opposed to conflicts between legitimate competing rights holders), they would submit to and be bound by alternative dispute resolution systems identified by the new corporation for the purpose of resolving those conflicts. Registries and Registrars should be required to abide by decisions of the ADR system.' US White Paper (1998) Recommendations.

Finally, the rights of both domain name registrants and trademark owners under national laws should remain unaffected.[96]

After a brisk process of nine months, and taking into account reactions to an interim report,[97] WIPO delivered its final report[98] to ICANN on 30 April 1999, which – after an equally brief commenting period and a number of amendments[99] – on 26 August 1999 adopted the UDRP.[100] On 1 January 2000, a one-member panel decided the first domain name dispute under the UDRP, which has since governed well over 40,000 cases.[101]

The UDRP is a mandatory policy between a registrar and its customer and is included in registration agreements for all ICANN-accredited registrars. It thus applies for second-level domain name registrations in all generic Top Level Domains (gTLDs) (e.g., .com, .net and .org) and those country code top level domains (ccTLDs) that have elected to adopt the Policy.[102] Under its mandatory administrative proceedings, 'complainants' (trademark owners) request cancellation, transfer or other changes to infringing domain name registrations in cases where (i) the domain name is identical or confusingly similar to a trademark or service mark in which the complainant has rights; (ii) if the domain name owner does not have rights or legitimate interests in respect of the domain name; and (iii) if the domain name has been registered and is being used in bad faith.[103] Complaints are heard and decided by independent administrative panels (not the registrar)[104] upon whose recommendation the registrars will cancel or transfer the domain name – thus providing a single system for *adjudication* and *enforcement*.

This brief sketch of the UDRP's genesis provides a glimpse of the complex interaction of interests that led to the creation of this unique regulatory

96 '4) Nothing in the domain name registration agreement or in the operation of the new corporation should limit the rights that can be asserted by a domain name registrant or trademark owner under national laws.' US White Paper (1998) Recommendations.

97 *The World Intellectual Property Organization (WIPO) publishes its Interim Report on the Internet Domain Name Process*, 22 December 1998, Press Releases PR/1998/149.

98 WIPO, *Final Report of the WIPO Internet Domain Name Process*, 30 April 1999, available at www.wipo.int/amc/en/processes/process1/report/finalreport.html.

99 Komaitis (2010), p. 82.

100 ICANN, Uniform Domain Name Dispute Resolution Policy (UDRP), adopted 26 August 1999, available at www.icann.org/resources/pages/schedule-2012-02-25-en.

101 See www.wipo.int/wipo_magazine/en/2017/05/article_0008.html.

102 Isenberg (2017).

103 See www.icann.org/resources/pages/policy-2012-02-25-en.

104 See paras 4(e) and (h), UDRP (n. 100).

instrument.[105] As the United States' decision to privatize the DNS opened the registration process up to competition and multiple registrars, it became important to ensure the uniform 'global' application of dispute resolution procedures across different gTLDs.[106] Early proposals to ensure this by requiring applicants to submit to personal jurisdiction at the place of the root 'A' server met with scepticism, as this was seen 'as an inappropriate attempt to establish US trademark law as the law of the Internet'.[107] Hence the realization in the US White Paper that accepting jurisdiction of 'an alternative dispute resolution body is likely to be at least somewhat less controversial'.[108] Finally, it was the common view among the engineering community that registrars' involvement in resolving these disputes should be minimal.

The UDRP clearly represents an international regulatory response to a digital IP challenge that differs entirely from the traditional treatymaking model. The unique constellation of a single global infrastructure – the DNS, that identifies servers and websites throughout the Internet – which is administered by a private corporation – ICANN, that is itself governed by a consensus-based multi-stakeholder model – created its own set of necessities and opportunities. The drive for a 'supra-national' uniform solution to domain name disputes was not motivated by aspirations of creating a 'unified and universal body of rules' for IP, but by the need – and the technical possibility – for uniform pragmatic solutions to a narrowly focused practical problem that occurred in the same fashion throughout the world, wherever a gTLD was registered. The UDRP is not an international treaty agreed by sovereign nations, nor even a national legislative act, but rather a set of standard terms that are included in the contractual relationship between applicant and registrar at the time of a gTLD registration. The single global infrastructure, and the individual contract with each domain name applicant during the registration process, permitted this unique contractual solution that enables conflict resolution and implementation in a single instance. This constellation

[105] See the critical accounts of the processes involved in the privatization of the Internet and the creation of ICANN and the UDRP in Komaitis (2010). Chapter 5; Petillion and Janssen (2017), chapter 2; and Helfer and Dinwoodie (2001).

[106] The US Green Paper (1998) had still envisaged allowing different registrars to develop their own dispute resolution mechanisms.

[107] US White Paper (1998). The original root 'A' server, and the subsequent additional root servers were located in the United States. See 'History of the Root Server System Report from the ICANN Root Server System Advisory Committee (RSSAC)', 4 November 2016, available at www.icann.org/en/system/files/files/rssac-023-04nov16-en.pdf.

[108] US White Paper (1998).

is, however, also responsible for the narrow scope of application of the UDRP that focuses on providing a 'quick and cheap' solution to the most obvious cases.[109]

WIPO's involvement provided a deliberative process with extensive involvement of WIPO member state governments, intergovernmental organizations, professional associations, corporations and individuals, as well as a panel of experts.[110] This process – not least due to the time pressure under which it was conducted – cannot be compared to the iterative process of committee meetings that led to earlier international treaties,[111] and was only the precursor to the subsequent internal ICANN stakeholder consultations and amendments of the Policy before its adoption in August 1999.[112] While the UDRP has drawn repeated criticism – in terms of scope of application,[113] procedural justice[114] and judicial oversight[115] – it is undisputed that this unique supra-national instrument has been a successful tool to resolve thousands of domain name disputes over the course of the last two decades.[116] Although recourse to national courts remains a theoretical possibility under the Policy, the efficiency of the dispute resolution providers and the undeniable pecuniary advantages of arbitration means that few UDRP awards are challenged in courts.[117]

Regional Trade Agreements: Regulatory Responses to Digital Challenges

Bilateral and regional treaties (collectively regional trade agreements or RTAs) that regulate aspects of IP law are not a new phenomenon.[118] However, the recent dramatic increase in the number of those that address IP, and the degree of depth and detail of the IP provisions they

109 Dinwoodie (2000), p. 511.
110 See WIPO Final Report (n. 98), paras 26–31 for the 'Mechanics of the WIPO Process'.
111 For doubts on WIPO's 'capacity to engage in a balanced consultative process' under these circumstances, see Helfer and Dinwoodie (n. 105), p. 177.
112 For a critical account of the ICANN process see above at n. 105.
113 See Helfer and Dinwoodie (2001).
114 See Helfer and Dinwoodie (2001), Geist (2001), Geist (2002).
115 Petillion and Janssen (2017).
116 de Werra (2016).
117 See Petillion and Janssen (2017) and Helfer and Dinwoodie (2001). For a recent reversal of a UDRP award by the Paris Court of Appeal, see Pôle 5, chapter 1, Monsieur X./Team Reager AB et Stone Age Limited of 8 November 2016.
118 For an account of bilateral IP treaties in force at the time of the conclusion of the Paris Convention, see Ricketson (2015), p. 2.02.

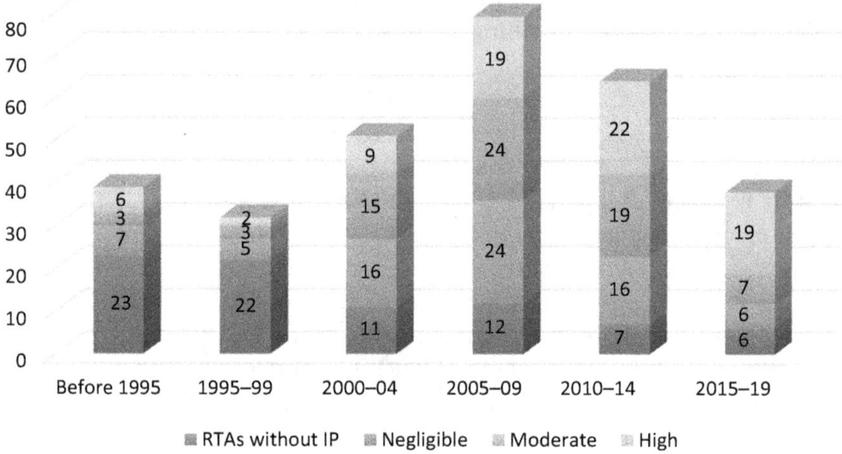

Figure 4.1 RTAs with increased IP content over time
Source: Valdés and McCann (2014) and WTO RTA Database.

contain, has made them a primary source of international regulatory responses to IP issues in recent decades (see Figure 4.1).[119]

Since 2000, IP-intensive RTAs have grown in a distinct hub-and-spoke architecture – originally around the North American Free Trade Agreement (NAFTA), the European Free Trade Association (EFTA) and the European Union – and have encouraged the convergence of domestic IP regimes among the respective RTA signatories linked to a common hub.[120] Higher standards agreed in such RTAs have fed back into the international arena, as countries tend to 're-export' such commitments in subsequent RTAs in order to achieve deeper integration and to lock in domestic reforms.[121]

Implementing these commitments into domestic law usually leads to a non-discriminatory application of these new IP standards to all WTO member nationals, as the most-favoured nation (MFN) principle enshrined in the TRIPS Agreement does not permit general exceptions[122]

[119] For a systematic quantitative analysis of IP provisions in RTAs, see Valdés and Tavengwa, (2012) and Valdés and McCann (2012).

[120] Valdés and McCann (2014) p. 36, and charts 6 and 7.

[121] Valdés and McCann (2014), p. 39.

[122] Article 4 of the TRIPS Agreement provides that '[w]ith regard to the protection of IP, any advantage, favour, privilege or immunity granted by a Member to the nationals of any other country shall be accorded immediately and unconditionally to the nationals of all other Members'. Exemptions exist only for general judicial assistance arrangements

for RTAs as are foreseen in GATT or GATS,[123] where deeper integration in goods and services trade can be targeted exclusively to RTA partners. But even for provisions that fall outside the scope of the TRIPS MFN obligation,[124] crafting national IP provisions that exclude third country nationals may be exceedingly costly and complex, considering that national treatment obligations are also contained in the Berne and Paris Conventions.[125] Therefore, while RTAs themselves only bind their respective parties, the multilateral context and the practicalities of implementation favour the creation of a unilateral 'international standard' that RTA signatories apply to most, if not all, trading partners.

The proliferation of RTAs with elaborate IP chapters leads to noteworthy results. Unlike the 'spaghetti bowl'[126] of preferential trading relationships created by the more permissive GATT and GATS rules, the 'lasagne effect'[127] of strict TRIPS MFN means that third countries outside the RTA can benefit from the higher IP standards that RTA signatories have negotiated among themselves, without having to provide the same level of protection. Third country nationals can benefit from higher IP standards agreed in an RTA – such as the availability of software patents or patent term extensions – by virtue of the TRIPS MFN and national treatment obligations without having to provide such standards

(Article 4(a)), protection dependent on reciprocity under the Berne or Rome Conventions (Article 4(b)), in respect of the rights of performers, producers of phonograms and broadcasting organizations not provided under this Agreement (Article 4(c), and deriving from notified international IP agreements that entered into force prior to the WTO Agreement (Article 4(d)). Contrary to GATT and GATS, the TRIPS Agreement does not contain a general MFN exemption for free trade agreements.

123 See GATT Article XXIV and GATS Article V for exemptions from the respective MFN obligation for customs unions or free trade areas (or a corresponding interim agreement), or agreements liberalizing trade in services between or among parties, under certain conditions.

124 See the limited exemptions from TRIPS MFN in Article 4(a)–(d), n. 122.

125 See Article 5(1) Berne Convention (1971) and Article 2(1) Paris Convention (1967).

126 The term was initially used by Bhagwati (1995) to denote the plethora of individual RTA trading relationships between WTO members that are permitted by the MFN exceptions under GATT and GATS, and thus create a complicated web of relationships much like a spaghetti bowl.

127 See Taubman (2008) and Taubman (2019). The absence of general exceptions from the TRIPS MFN obligation means that additional substantive obligations agreed in an RTA lead to a general 'ratcheting up' of that country's IP obligations vis-à-vis nationals of all other WTO members. Thus, in contrast to the situation of the GATT/GATS spaghetti bowl described at n. 126, IP commitments in RTAs add general layers to the TRIPS obligations of that member, much like – to extend Bhagwati's food metaphor – in a lasagne dish.

to nationals of the RTA signatories. This means, inversely, that the value of accepting an IP commitment in RTA negotiations – for instance in exchange for market access in a certain agriculture sector – should take into account its non-discriminatory scope of application. While – in the sphere of trade in goods – the benefits of a lower tariff for beef or rice can be limited to an RTA trading partner in accordance with the exceptions to the MFN principles under the GATT, the situation is different under TRIPS. The more limited scope of exceptions to MFN in TRIPS means that bilateral IP commitments such as specific digital enforcement standards will have to be made available to nationals of all members; and their scope and impact is thus more difficult to ascertain.

Against that background, the regulatory impact of provisions in RTAs goes well beyond the jurisdictions of signatories and has contributed significantly to an internationalization of certain approaches to emerging IP issues – including in the digital sphere. As the frequency and complexity of IP chapters in RTAs grow at dramatic speed, detailed qualitative analysis of IP commitments remains a challenge. Quantitative analysis shows a broad distribution of IP topics addressed in RTAs (see Figure 4.2).

RTAs frequently address digital IP issues concerning copyright law, trademark law, IP enforcement, and technology-specific, trade-related matters such as the ISP liability. RTA commitments on copyright include clarifying the application of existing remedies to online enforcement or undertaking to target specific copyright violations in the online environment.[128] Many IP chapters refer to the WIPO Internet

[128] **Example:** China–Korea, Republic of: Section J, Article 15.28 Each Party *shall take effective measures to curtail repetitive infringement of copyright and related rights on the Internet or other digital network.* . . . Section K, Article 15.30: Under the established structure of this Agreement, each Party shall, upon request of the other Party, and in addition to the already existing forms of cooperation: . . . (ii) exchanges and cooperation on online copyright enforcement

Side letter – Example: Korea, Republic of–US: Confirmation letter (Online Piracy Prevention): The Parties agree on the objective of shutting down Internet sites that permit the unauthorized reproduction, distribution, or transmission of copyright works, of regularly assessing and actively seeking to reduce the impact of new technological means for committing online copyright piracy, and of providing generally for more effective enforcement of IPRs on the Internet. The Republic of Korea agrees that internet piracy of works and other subject matter protected by copyright . . . The Republic of Korea agrees to issue as soon as possible, but no later than six months after the date the Agreement enters into force, a policy directive establishing clear jurisdiction for a division or joint investigation team to engage in effective enforcement against online piracy. . .

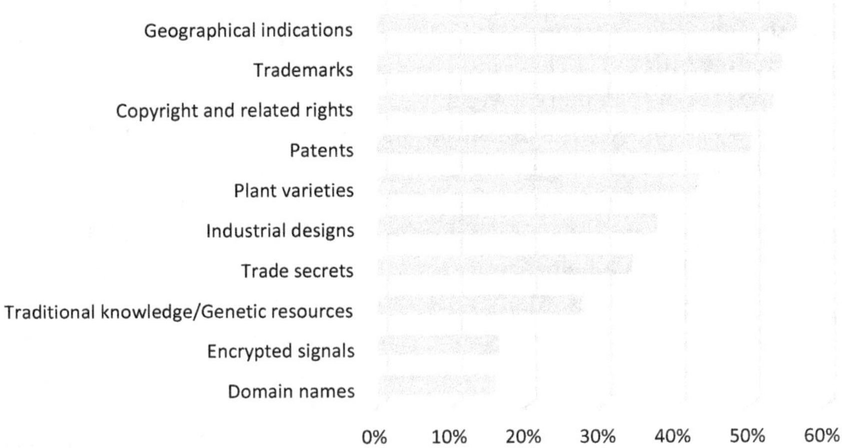

Figure 4.2 Specific IP provisions in RTAs[129] with IP
Source: Valdés and McCann (2014) and WTO RTA Database.

Treaties,[130] variously *requiring compliance* with, *affirming existing obligations* pursuant to and *requiring accession* to these treaties.[131] Some of the most detailed copyright provisions concern technical protection measures (TPMs), reflecting the considerable variety in national implementation of the general obligation to provide for TPMs under the WIPO Internet Treaties. Notably RTAs negotiated with the participation of the United States contain detailed provisions in this regard that may define the subject matter of TPM protection,[132] require protection

[129] RTAs that have been notified to the WTO and are in force 2019.

[130] See Valdés and McCann (2014), p. 15.

[131] **Example:** EFTA–Peru: Chapter 6, Article 6.4.3 The Parties to this Agreement which are not a party to one or more of the agreements listed below shall ratify or accede to the following multilateral agreements within one year from the date of entry into force of this Agreement: (a) WIPO Performances and Phonograms Treaty of 20 December 1996 (WPPT); and (b) WIPO Copyright Treaty of 20 December 1996 (WCT).

Example: CETA: Article 20.7.1 The Parties shall comply with the following international agreements: (a) Articles 2 through 20 of the Berne Convention for the Protection of Literary and Artistic Works, done at Paris on 24 July 1971; (b) Articles 1 through 14 of the WIPO Copyright Treaty, done at Geneva on 20 December 1996; (c) Articles 1 through 23 of the WIPO Performances and Phonograms Treaty, done at Geneva on 20 December 1996; and [. . .].

[132] **Example:** Korea, Republic of–US: Article 18.4.7 (f). Effective technological measure means any technology, device, or component that, in the normal course of its operation, controls access to a protected work, performance, phonogram, or other protected subject matter, or protects any copyright or any rights related to copyright.

of TPMs independently of any underlying copyright infringement[133] and sometimes specify the legal remedy that must be available against the circumvention (i.e. 'hacking') of such TPMs.[134]

In the area of trademark law, RTA commitments frequently refer to the 2001 WIPO Joint Recommendation on marks and signs on the Internet (JR 2001), either *affirming* its importance, or providing *hortatory* language on applying it.[135] As mentioned above, this mechanism has helped spread and multiply pledges to apply the non-binding JR 2001 among RTA signatories and thus helped – to some extent – turn soft into hard law among RTA signatories. Many RTAs also contain provisions on domain names and trademark use on the Internet that address the bad-faith registration or use of a domain name that is confusingly similar to a trademark or, in the case of EU – CARIFORUM States the Economic Partnership Agreement (EPA), a trademark or a geographical indications (GI).[136] Some of these provisions make explicit reference to ICANN's UDRP as a model for how such conflicts should be resolved.

Finally, on enforcement, RTA provisions range from general commitments on cooperation and best efforts to address Internet piracy, to

[133] **Example:** US–Singapore: Article 16.4.7(d). Each Party shall provide that a violation of the law implementing this paragraph is independent of any infringement that might occur under the Party's law on copyright and related rights.

[134] **Example:** CPTPP: Chapter 20, Article 20.66: Technological Protection Measures

1. In order to provide adequate legal protection and effective legal remedies against the circumvention of effective technological measures that authors, performers, and producers of phonograms use in connection with the exercise of their rights and that restrict unauthorized acts in respect of their works, performances, and phonograms, each Party shall provide that a person who: (a) knowingly, or having reasonable grounds to know, circumvents [. . .]; or (b) manufactures, imports, distributes, offers for sale or rental to the public, or otherwise provides devices, products, or components, or offers to the public or provides services, that: [. . .] is liable and subject to the remedies provided for in Article 20.81.18 (Civil and Administrative Procedures and Remedies).

[135] See US–Singapore: Article 16.2(b) (shall give effect to JR 1999) and EU –CARIFORUM, Article 145 (shall endeavour to apply JR 2001).

[136] **Example:** CPTPP: Chapter 18, Article 18.28.1 In connection with each Party's system for the management of its country-code top-level domain (ccTLD) domain names, the following shall be available: (a) an appropriate procedure for the settlement of disputes, based on, or modelled along the same lines as, the principles established in the Uniform Domain-Name Dispute-Resolution Policy, as approved by the Internet Corporation for Assigned Names and Numbers (ICANN).

2. In connection with each Party's system for the management of ccTLD domain names, appropriate remedies shall be available at least in cases in which a person registers or holds, with a bad faith intent to profit, a domain name that is identical or confusingly similar to a trademark. See also EU–CARIFORUM Article 145.

providing specific remedies or adopting specific interpretations of elements for criminal liability.[137] Among the most elaborate provisions in this area are commitments relating to the liability of ISPs for IP infringements committed by their users, or via their platforms, which are discussed in detail below.[138]

The impact of bilateral treaties on the international normative landscape of IP regulation has produced a considerable body of literature by academia and international organizations over recent decades[139] which provide a rich and detailed discussion of the strategic and institutional particularities involved in their conclusion. The present chapter concentrates on several distinctive characteristics of RTAs as international regulatory responses to emerging digital challenges.

The inclusion of IP chapters in RTAs does not directly advance the goal of a unified body of IP rules for universal application, as did the early international IP conventions. Nevertheless, most of these IP chapters are expressly situated in the context of the multilateral IP treaties by reaffirming their importance, exhorting compliance with them, or specifically recognizing their precedence over the RTA rules.[140] The focus of RTA IP chapters – when they venture beyond general affirmations – is on regulating IP areas or issues outside the scope of the multilateral rules, or where those rules provide discretion for national implementation. In some cases, this will mean inciting partners to adopt international standards they had hitherto not joined on their own account, thus reinforcing linkages to the international IP treaties and increasing their membership. In areas where no examples of international codification exist, the dynamic of RTA IP negotiations will typically be to assess whether to resist or accept demands for adoption of particular regulatory IP approaches that already exist in one of the RTA partners – leading to what is often referred to as 'transplantation'.[141]

[137] See digital enforcement measures contained in Australia–Chile; Dominican Republic–Central America–United States Free Trade Agreement (CAFTA-DR); EC; EU–Colombia; EU–Republic of Korea; EU–Peru; Japan–Peru; Japan–Switzerland; Republic of Korea–United States; Mexico–Nicaragua; North American Free Trade Agreement (NAFTA); United States–Australia; United States–Bahrain; United States–Chile; United States–Colombia; United States–Morocco; United States–Panama; United States–Oman; United States–Peru; United States–Singapore.

[138] Section 3.1.2.

[139] See Seuba (2015) and note 8.

[140] See examples for TRIPS and WIPO treaties' affirmation in RTAs in Valdés and McCann (2014), paras 45–54.

[141] Valdés and McCann (2014), para. 150. Seuba (2015), p. 63.

The distribution of interests in these negotiations is distinct from international rule-making not only because of the limited number of participants – where differences in negotiating capacity take on greater significance – but also because RTAs are typically negotiated across a number of trade-related areas, inviting linkages and trade-offs across different subject areas that have been ostensibly absent, or at least more difficult to bring to bear, in traditional international negotiations that have been focused on IP.

These elements also impact on the degree of expert participation in these negotiations, a factor which had arguably enabled the traditional international treatymaking process to develop or adapt original solutions to specific IP issues, such as in the WCT and the WPPT. The time pressure associated with RTA negotiations and the constellation of interests described above indicates that the predominant perspective in RTA IP negotiations is the assimilation of systems by adoption, not necessarily the development of new substantive solutions to IP challenges. It seems that it is only in negotiations between partners with strongly divergent interests in a particular area that RTA negotiators attempt to craft creative solutions espousing common principles.[142]

Conclusion

The mechanisms of international regulatory responses to emerging IP issues have evolved significantly in the digital era. For most of the twentieth century the institutionalized deliberative process of the traditional treatymaking model provided an ecosystem in which systemic considerations and comparative assessment enabled a broader and potentially more comprehensive assessment of regulatory solutions that often led to a common, and sometimes original, multilateral outcome.

The arrival of digitization and online distribution represents a significant acceleration and proliferation of technological change. The corresponding speed and urgency of regulatory reaction could be argued to have tilted the balance – also in the international process described above – towards demands for individual short-term responses which are difficult to resist, thus reflecting the realisation that 'it is easier to reach a shared understanding on specific issues, where there is a demonstrable and manageable need for international action, than to achieve a

[142] See the provisions on geographical indications in CETA, US–Republic of Korea and the United States–Mexico–Canada Agreement (USMCA).

shared understanding across the whole range of IP, which now underlies most economic and cultural activities'.[143]

Thus, coinciding with the advent of the digital era, this traditional treatymaking scenario has given way to more varied landscape where a variety of tools and legal instruments embody regulatory responses to digital challenges. The preceding section sought to identify the factors that shape different regulatory responses to new issues.

Ready for a Common Regulatory Response? – Selected Emerging Digital Issues

In the global, potentially seamless markets for digital products that have been created by digital communication technologies, common – or at least interoperable – regulatory solutions to IP issues are essential to ensure the viability of digital business models through which much of the continuously increasing share of online trade is conducted. This part briefly surveys several salient digital IP issues with regard to an available international regulatory response.

ISP Liability

The degree of liability of ISPs for IP infringements by their users directly impacts the viability of digital platforms in a global market. A common international approach to this question would therefore be particularly valuable. Indeed, the pervasive view that the important role in facilitating access justifies a certain privilege for ISPs, requiring their action and collaboration only when they are notified of infringing content by rights holders, was developed through years of jurisprudence and – once the 'right of making available' had been established by the WCT and WPPT[144] – led to national legislative responses centred on similar, yet not identical, principles.

Regulatory Approaches in National Legislation

Two early legislative implementations of the WCT and the WPPT, the US Digital Millennium Copyright Act (DMCA) (1998) and the European

[143] See 'Acceptance Speech by Francis Gurry on his Reappointment', WIPO Assemblies 2014, 8 May 2014, available at www.wipo.int/about-wipo/en/dgo/speeches/a_53_dg_speech.html.

[144] See 'The WIPO Internet Treaties: An Issue-Driven International Solution' above.

E-Commerce Directive (2000), enshrined systems of ISP liability limitations into national law. Their evolution and case law – from the perspective of music streaming – are the subject of Chapter 19 of this volume.[145] This chapter identifies aspects that illustrate similarities and differences with regulatory responses taken in other jurisdictions.

United States and European Union The US DMCA[146] establishes limitations on the copyright liability of online service providers[147] that maintain a policy providing for termination of network services for repeat infringers in appropriate circumstances[148] and do not interfere with standard technical measures used by copyright owners to identify and protect copyrighted works.[149] For such service providers, 'safe harbours' are available for transitory communications,[150] system caching,[151] storage of information on systems or networks at the direction of users (i.e. hosting),[152] and information location tools (i.e. search engines).[153] A notice and take-down procedure[154] prescribes the conditions under which the ISP can be considered to have actual knowledge of infringing material on its services, and monetary liability is waived, if after receiving the notification, the ISP quickly removes or blocks access to the material identified in the notification,[155] while the subscriber has the possibility of

145 LaFrance (2020), Chapter 19 in this volume.
146 Public Law 105–304, 28 October 1998.
147 Service providers are defined in section 512(k)(1)(A) as 'an entity offering the transmission, routing, or providing of connections for digital online communications, between or among points specified by a user, of material of the user's choosing, without modification to the content of the material as sent or received'.
148 17 USC § 512(i)(1)(A).
149 17 USC § 512(i)(1)(B).
150 17 USC § 512 (a). Transitory Communications are activities where the service provider acts as a 'mere conduit' of digital information from one point to another including transmissions, routing and connection services.
151 17 USC § 512 (b). System caching is the activity carried out by a service provider, when it retains, for limited time, copies of material that has been uploaded by a third party to be transmitted to an Internet user, in order to simplify interactions online and reduce the service provider bandwidth requirements.
152 17 USC § 512 (c).
153 17 USC § 512 (d).
154 17 USC § 512(c)(3) for hosting services and 512(d) for information location tools.
155 As an additional safeguard for the ISP for this diligent action, section 512(g)(1) establishes that there will be no liability to any third party if the ISP took down allegedly infringing material in 'good faith'.

counter-notification[156] to respond to any erroneous or fraudulent notifications. The act permits injunctions against ISPs that may include ordering the ISP to restrain from providing access to the infringing material or activity, thus restraining the service provider from providing access to a subscriber who is engaging in infringing activity and is identified in the order or any other injunctive relief necessary to prevent infringement.[157]

This DMCA approach to ISP liability, as developed and confirmed in subsequent case law, set a relatively high threshold for knowledge of the ISP necessary to trigger its obligation to act,[158] and has expressly excluded an obligation to monitor or filter content on its own accord,[159] that has recently come under criticism.[160]

In the European Union, broad exemptions from ISP liability – covering also IPRs beyond copyright, as well as unfair competition and criminal acts – were established in the E-commerce Directive.[161] Under the Directive an information society service provider can enjoy exemption from liability for mere conduit,[162] caching[163] and hosting[164] of third-party

[156] 512(g)(1). If a counter notification is filed in compliance with the requirements, and the copyright owner does not file an action seeking court order against the subscriber, the service provider has to re-grant access to the material within 10–14 business days after receiving the notification. Knowing misrepresentation that material is an infringement incurs liability for subsequent injury (section 512(f)).

[157] Section 512(j).

[158] See the discussion of 'actual' and 'red flag' knowledge in Viacom Int'l, Inc. *v.* YouTube, Inc., 676 F.3d 19 (2nd Cir. 2012); Capitol Records, LLC *v.* Vimeo, LLC, 972 F. Supp. 2d 500, 523 (SDNY 2013); Capitol Records, Inc. *v.* MP3tunes, LLC, 821 F. Supp. 2d 627, 633–634 (SDNY 2011) ('MP3tunes I'). See also the references in LaFrance (n. 145).

[159] Section 512(m)(1). See also Viacom Int'l, Inc. *v.* YouTube, Inc., 676 F.3d 19 (2nd Cir. 2012) and Capitol Records, LLC *v.* Vimeo, LLC, 972 F. Supp. 2d 500, 523 (SDNY 2013).

[160] See *Artists Urging Reforms of the DMCA Safe Harbor: 'Our Culture Is At Stake'* (14 March 2017), available at https://blog.jipel.law.nyu.edu/2017/03/artists-urging-reforms-of-the-dmca-safe-harbor-our-culture-is-at-stake/.

[161] Directive 2000/31/EC of the European Parliament and of the Council of 8 June 2000 on certain legal aspects of information society services, in particular electronic commerce, in the Internal Market ('Directive on electronic commerce').

[162] Article 12 E-commerce Directive provides that 'where an information society service is provided that consists of the transmission in a communication network of information provided by a recipient of the service, or the provision of access to a communication network', ISPs will not be liable if the ISP does not initiate the transmission; the ISP does not select the receiver of the transmission; and the ISP does not select or modify the information contained in the transmission.

[163] Article 13.

[164] Article 14.

information. Exemption from liability for caching and hosting is conditional on the service provider acting expeditiously to remove or to disable access to the information, upon obtaining 'actual knowledge or awareness' of illegal activity or information.[165] Under the E-commerce Directive, member states were expressly prohibited from imposing a general monitoring obligation on ISPs,[166] although monitoring obligations under national law 'in a specific case' – arguably including content already identified as infringing (the so-called 'stay down' obligation) – were expressly contemplated.[167] The 2001 Directive on Copyright in the Information Society (InfoSoc Directive)[168] that implemented the WCT and WPPT did require that injunctions can be addressed to ISPs 'whose services are used by a third party to infringe a copyright or related right',[169] but otherwise left the remaining question of what liability ISPs retained in the area of copyright infringements largely to member states.[170]

Characteristically, these early systems focused on establishing the conditions for *liability exemptions* for ISPs, rather than clarifying the boundaries of (primary or secondary) copyright *liability* of ISP for their activities. The specific ISP liability for injunctions to take down or disable access to infringing material – available under both the DMCA and the E-commerce directive[171] – was a recognition of *accountability* for terminating, not *liability* for committing,[172] third-party infringements and was not systemically embedded to the overall conceptual regime of

165 For caching, see Article 13(e). For hosting, see Article 14.

166 Article 15.1 'Member States shall not impose a general obligation on providers, when providing the services covered by Articles 12, 13 and 14, to monitor the information which they transmit or store, nor a general obligation actively to seek facts or circumstances indicating illegal activity.'

167 Recital 47: (47) 'Member States are prevented from imposing a monitoring obligation on service providers only with respect to obligations of a general nature; this does not concern monitoring obligations in a specific case and, in particular, does not affect orders by national authorities in accordance with national legislation.'

168 Directive 2001/29/EC of the European Parliament and of the Council of 22 May 2001 on the harmonization of certain aspects of copyright and related rights in the information society.

169 Article 8.3 InfoSoc Copyright Directive.

170 EU Parliament (2018).

171 For the EU, see Article 8(3) Copyright Directive (for copyright) and Article 11, 3rd sentence Enforcement Directive (for other IPRs). For the US, see DMCA section 512(j).

172 EU Parliament (2018), 20, 'Precisely put, Article 8(3) Copyright Directive is not about a provider liability, but helping duties. Husovec called this "accountable, not liable".' See Husovec (2016).

liability for copyright infringement. It reflected the then current perception of intermediaries as passive participants in the transmission of information, without any technical capacity to monitor third-party content,[173] who are nonetheless well placed to help in terminating the infringements of other – third-party – infringers.[174]

There has thus developed a rich body of subsequent jurisprudence and debate to calibrate the exact balance of obligations between right owners and ISPs, to ensure systemic consistency with the concepts of primary and secondary liability for copyright infringements and to take account of the dramatically increased economic impact and technological ability of ISPs today.[175] In the US context, where monitoring duties of ISPs had been categorically excluded by legislation, the main area of engagement was the precise contours of the knowledge – 'red flag' or actual – required to trigger the ISPs' obligations to take action and how primary liability could be established for ISPs falling outside the safe harbour.[176] In the European Union, this also included the contemplation of certain ISP monitoring duties – which remained available under national systems – a thorough debate of weighing different fundamental rights and more recently, the 'value gap' discussion.[177]

Although these two early systems of ISP 'safe harbours' were conceptually very similar, their subsequent reception in jurisprudence and debate has clearly pulled in different directions. Despite growing criticism, US jurisprudence interpreting the DMCA has maintained a broad scope of the 'safe harbour' and a high threshold for triggering ISP liability for removal of infringing material. In stark contrast, in the European Union, the contemplation of certain monitoring duties[178] and

[173] Rotaru (2017).

[174] See InfoSoc Directive, Recital 59 *in fine*: 'In the digital environment, in particular, the services of intermediaries may increasingly be used by third parties for infringing activities. In many cases such intermediaries are best placed to bring such infringing activities to an end.'

[175] LaFrance (2020), Chapter 19 in this volume.

[176] See the discussion of 'actual' and 'red flag' knowledge in Viacom Int'l, Inc. *v.* YouTube, Inc., 676 F.3d 19 (2nd Cir. 2012); Capitol Records, LLC *v.* Vimeo, LLC, 972 F. Supp. 2d 500, 523 (SDNY 2013); Capitol Records, Inc. *v.* MP3tunes, LLC, 821 F. Supp. 2d 627, 633–634 (SDNY 2011) ('MP3tunes I'). See also LaFrance (2020), Chapter 19 in this volume.

[177] See the succinct overview of the value gap argument in Senftleben (2020).

[178] See EU Parliament (2018) p. 17 on the lack of decisive CJEU jurisprudence on the scope of Article 15 E-Commerce Directive.

the Court of Justice of the European Union's (CJEU's) development of sector-specific liability rules for the right of making available[179] prepared the ground for a significant reversal of direction in the 2019 Directive on Copyright in the Digital Single Market (DSMD)[180] which European member states will have to implement by 2021.

Significantly, the DSMD establishes primary copyright liability for large commercial platforms carrying user-generated content[181] for unauthorized acts of making available or communication to the public unless best efforts were made to obtain authorization, to ensure unavailability (i.e. monitors and filters) of specific identified works in accordance with high industry standards of professional diligence, and operates a 'notice and stay down' system – all this while maintaining availability of content which is – including by virtue of exceptions such as criticism or parody – non-infringing.[182] This paradigm-shifting rebalancing of the burden of monitoring the Internet for copyright violations – from the right owners to the hitherto more privileged ISPs – is setting ISP liability on a new course in the European Union, and is already shifting the debate towards the merits of the expected large-scale application of automated algorithmic enforcement.[183]

Non-Signatories of the WIPO Internet Treaties The early systems of safe harbours for ISP liability set up by the US and the EU, including the subsequent jurisprudence and debate, have also influenced national regulatory approaches in other jurisdictions – including in non-signatories of the WIPO Internet Treaties, which did thus not necessarily have the 'making available' right defined in their legislation. They also sought to balance the obligations of right owners and ISPs concerning online copyright infringement.

[179] CJEU of 8 September 2016, C-160/15 – GS Media/Sanoma; CJEU of 26 April 2017, C-527/15 – Brein/Wullems (Filmspeler); CJEU of 14 June 2017, C-610/15 – Ziggo/Brein.

[180] Directive (EU) 2019/790 of the European Parliament and of the Council of 17 April 2019 on copyright and related rights in the Digital Single Market and Amending Directives 96/9/EC and 2001/29/EC, *O.J.* (L 130) 92.

[181] See Article 17(1) and Article 17(6) for the definition of 'online content-sharing service provider' and the scope of application.

[182] Articles 17(4) and 17(7).

[183] See Senftleben (2020) and Schwemer and Schovsbo (2020).

India India, a non-signatory of the Internet Treaties until 2018,[184] introduced successive ISP safe harbours in a 2008 amendment to its Information Technology Act 2000 (IT Act), and in a 2012 amendment of its Copyright Act 1957.

The 2008 amendment of the IT Act introduced a broad liability exemption for intermediaries whose functions were limited to providing access to a communication system as long as they observed 'due diligence' in discharging their functions, and expeditiously removed or disabled access to the offending material upon receiving actual knowledge or on being notified by a government agency.[185] Uncertainty on the extent of 'due diligence', and on the broader question of whether this safe harbour would be available also regarding copyright violations led to jurisprudence contemplating broad monitoring duties for ISPs. In *Super Cassettes Industries Limited* v. *MySpace Inc.*,[186] the Single Judge Bench of the Delhi High Court (HC) granted an interim injunction on the grounds that there was no safe harbour for intermediaries under the Copyright Act[187] and implied that intermediaries should screen all user-generated content to check for infringement prior to making the content available online.[188] Although the Division Bench upheld the eligibility of the ISP for safe harbour under the IT Act,[189] uncertainty remains around how to ensure harmonious interpretation of the different statutes in different scenarios, and what degree of knowledge is necessary to trigger ISP action.

A copyright-specific safe harbour was added in the 2012 amendment of the Copyright Act, which expressly pursued the aim of implementing the Internet Treaties.[190] It introduced an exemption from secondary liability for copyright infringement for 'transient or incidental storage' of material unless the ISP is 'aware or has reasonable grounds' for believing that such storage is of an infringing copy.[191] A notice and take-down procedure requires that access must be withheld upon

[184] India acceded to the Internet Treaties on 25 September 2018. The treaties entered into force for India on 25 December 2018.

[185] See Articles 2(w) and 79(1)–(3) Information Technology Act (2000) as amended.

[186] In Super Cassettes Industries Limited *v.* MySpace Inc. & Another, IA Nos. 15781/2008 &3085/2009 in CS (OS) No. 2682/2008.

[187] Agarwal and Agarwal (2017).

[188] Kumar (2014).

[189] Agarwal and Agarwal (2017), 187.

[190] See statement by the Indian Copyright office, available at http://copyright.gov.in/.

[191] 52.1(c) Copyright Act 1957, as amended.

receiving a written complaint from the right owner for 21 days, awaiting a court order.[192]

The coexistence of these two Indian safe harbour regimes, in s. 79 of the IT Act and in s. 52.1(c) the Copyright Act, for which jurisprudence has developed different knowledge standards[193] and whose respective scope of application have not been clearly delineated[194] means that concrete litigation outcomes continue to rely on courts applying and interpreting principles of copyright liability and statute concordance, rather than on a predictable tool to preserve ISP business models.

Brazil Not being a signatory to the Internet Treaties, judges and prosecutors in Brazil had to identify and interpret national law in order to encompass the concept of 'making available' by platforms and ISPs. In the absence of specific rules before 2014, the application of general principles of civil law akin to strict liability had led to a number of private agreements between copyright holders and ISPs that established voluntary notice and take-down procedures that reflected industry demands.[195]

Against this background, the vigorous discussion around a controversial far-reaching 2008 proposal regarding internet activities more generally,[196] followed by an elaborate public consultation during 2008–2009 and a protracted legislative process, led to the adoption of the 2014 Law No. 12.965, also known as the 'Marco Civil da Internet'[197] which sets out the regulatory framework for internet activities, and presents a complex compromise with regard to ISP liability. ISP activities of 'mere conduit' are exempted from liability[198] without the conditions required in other jurisdictions. Internet application providers (i.e. content hosts) are exempt if they remove content upon receipt of a specific judicial order.[199]

[192] 52.1(c) Copyright Act 1957, as amended.
[193] Sethia (2017), Saha and Saha (2018).
[194] Agarwal and Agarwal (2017). See also Vodafone India Ltd *v.* RK Productions, 2013 (54) PTC 149 (Mad), in which the Madras High Court upheld the application of s. 79 IT Act to copyright infringement.
[195] Zingales (2015).
[196] The so-called 'Azeredo Bill' proposed three-year mandatory data retention and other duties for ISPs, as well as the criminalization of access to data 'without authorization of the legitimate owner'. See Zingales (n. 195).
[197] Law No. 12.965 of April 23, 2014, available in English at www.publicknowledge.org/assets/uploads/documents/APPROVED-MARCO-CIVIL-MAY-2014.pdf.
[198] Article 18.
[199] Article 19.

Only material that constitutes a breach of privacy[200] must be removed at the simple – extra-judicial – requests of an interested party.[201] While the retention of a judicial notice as a requirement for ISP action was seen as a success of the civil rights movement,[202] this was achieved at the cost of a carve-out of liability for copyright and related rights violations, which is excluded from the safe harbour provisions described above pending specific legislation.[203] The National Congress's discussions of an amendment of the Copyright Bill currently contemplate the instruments of 'notice and notice' – an obligation on the ISP to notify the alleged infringer upon receiving a notification by the right holder, and a proposal to provide right holders with a remuneration right for each improper use.[204]

In the absence of a specific law as required by the statute, courts continue to rely on general principles of secondary copyright liability, under which the current practice remains of the removal of infringing material upon extra-judicial notification by the right holder.[205]

The above examples illustrate areas of commonality, but also of considerable variety that continues to exist in national ISP safe harbour regimes. Common ground seems to exist for establishing the susceptibility of ISPs to injunctions for removing access to infringing material, although there is considerable diversity as to whether such liability is rooted in secondary liability for copyright infringement or whether it is a general 'helping duty' due to an ISP's practical ability to terminate infringement by a third party. A certain commonality also exists with respect to the types of ISP activities that may benefit from a safe harbour, with caching and hosting being identified in most regimes, while location services are already more infrequently covered. Beyond these – rather basic – concepts, considerable variety exists with respect to the degree of ISP knowledge required to trigger cooperation, the nature of the ISP's cooperation that might be triggered, and, in particular, the question of how ISP activity outside the safe harbour would incur liability for copyright infringement.

[200] Essentially private acts of nudity or sexual activity (also known as 'revenge-porn').
[201] Article 21.
[202] Mulholland (2018).
[203] See Article 19.2 'Application of the provision in this article to infractions of copyright or related rights depends on a specific legal provision, which must respect freedom of expression and other guarantees set forth in article 5 of the Federal Constitution.'
[204] Mulholland (2018) at 1.9.
[205] Ibid.

The latter question is further complicated by the rapid economic and technological development of Internet enterprises that provide access and host content, representing business models that have long surpassed the original perception of passive access providers with little technological means to control or monitor the content to which they provide access.

Provisions in Regional Trade Agreements

Considering the interest of Internet companies in minimizing the cost of compliance with diverse liability regimes in different markets – and reflecting the role of RTAs described earlier in this paper – it is no surprise that provisions on ISP liability occur with increasing frequency and depth in recent RTAs (Table 4.1). In line with the purpose of this chapter, the following examples are by no means exhaustive but attempt to briefly illustrate the assimilation of regulatory responses in the field of ISP liability under current RTAs.

As is to be expected from the hub-and-spoke architecture described above, the RTAs with the US and the EU largely reflect their domestic systems and approaches to the issue. While early agreements with these partners may contain individual provisions regarding ISPs,[206] more elaborate RTAs such as CETA, EU–Republic of Korea, US–Singapore, US–Republic of Korea, TPP and USMCA contain elaborate specific obligations that essentially mirror the entire domestic EU and US systems described in the previous section.

Beyond the EU and US agreements, general provisions regarding ISP cooperation in RTAs take the form of permissive contemplation of limiting ISP liability[207] or individual provisions requiring that user identity can be obtained from the ISP in the context of Internet copyright enforcement,[208] or that ISP liability shall be limited to encourage cooperation with right holders.[209]

[206] See, for example, EU–CARIFORUM States EPA: Section 2, Article 158 (permit injunctions against ISPs).

[207] 'China–Australia Article 11.20: Service Provider Liability Each Party may take appropriate measures to limit the liability of, or remedies available against, internet service providers for copyright infringement by the users of their online services or facilities, where the internet service providers take action to prevent access to the materials infringing copyright in accordance with the laws and regulations of the Party.'

[208] China–Republic of Korea, Article 15.29 and Japan–Switzerland, Article 126.2.

[209] Japan–Switzerland, Article 126.1.

Table 4.1 *Selected ISP provisions in selected EU and US RTAs*

	EU–Republic of Korea	CETA	US–Republic of Korea	USMCA
Liability of ISPs	Article 10.62 The Parties recognise that the services of intermediaries may be used by third parties for infringing activities. To ensure the free movement of information services and at the same time enforce intellectual property rights in the digital environment, each Party **shall provide** for the measures set out in Articles 10.63 through 10.66 for intermediary service providers where they are in no way involved with the information transmitted.	Article 20.11(1) Subject to the other paras of this Article, each Party **shall provide limitations** or exceptions in its law regarding the liability of service providers, when acting as intermediaries, for infringements of copyright or related rights that take place on or through communication networks, in relation to the provision or use of their services.	Article 18.10(30) 1. For the purpose of providing enforcement procedures . . . each Party **shall provide** . . . : (a) legal incentives for service providers to cooperate with copyright [fn 35: and related rights] owners in deterring the unauthorized storage and transmission . . .; and (b) limitations in its law regarding the scope of remedies available against service providers for copyright infringements that they do not control, initiate, or direct, ...[fn 36: without prejudice to general defences for copyright infringement].	Article 20.88: Legal Remedies and Safe Harbors 1. The Parties recognize the importance of facilitating the continued development of legitimate online services operating as intermediaries and, in a manner consistent with Article 41 of the TRIPS Agreement, providing enforcement procedures that permit effective and expeditious action . . . This framework of legal remedies and safe harbors **shall include**: (a) legal incentives for Internet Service Providers to cooperate with copyright owners

Table 4.1 (*cont.*)

	EU–Republic of Korea	CETA	US–Republic of Korea	USMCA
				to deter the unauthorized storage and transmission of copyrighted materials . . .; and (b) limitations in its law that have the effect of precluding monetary relief against ISPs for copyright infringements that they do not control, initiate or direct . . .
ISP functions covered	Article 10.63 '**mere conduit**' 1. Where . . . service . . . consists of the transmission in a communication network . . . Article 10.64 '**caching**' 1. Where an information society service . . .	Article 20.11(2) The limitations . . . (a) shall cover at least the following functions: (i) **hosting** of the information at the request of a user of the hosting services; (ii) **caching** carried out through an automated	Article 18.10(30) 1.(b) . . . (i) These limitations shall preclude monetary relief and provide reasonable restrictions on court-ordered relief . . . for the following functions, and shall be confined to those functions:	Article 20.88 2. The limitations described in para. 1(b) shall include limitations in respect of the following functions: (a) **transmitting, routing, or providing connections** for

consists of the transmission in a communication network of information provided by a recipient of the service, . . . Article 10.65 **'hosting'** 1. Where an information society service . . . consists of the storage of information provided by a recipient of the service, the Parties shall ensure that the service provider is not liable for the information stored . . .	process, when the service provider: . . . (iii) **mere conduit**, which consists of the provision of the means to transmit information provided by a user, or the means of access to a communication network; and (b) may also cover other functions, including providing an information location tool, . . .	(A) **transmitting, routing**, or providing connections for material without modification of its content, or the intermediate and transient storage of such material in the course thereof; (B) **caching** carried out through an automatic process; (C) **storage** at the direction of a user of material residing on a system or network controlled or operated by or for the service provider; and (D) referring or linking users to an online location by **using information location tools**, including hyperlinks and directories.	material without modification of its content or the intermediate and transient storage of that material done automatically in the course of such a technical process; (b) **caching** carried out through an automated process; (c) **storage**, at the direction of a user, of material residing on a system or network controlled or operated by or for the Internet Service Provider; and (d) referring or linking users to an online location by **using information location tools**, including hyperlinks and directories.

Table 4.1 (*cont.*)

	EU–Republic of Korea	CETA	US–Republic of Korea	USMCA
Conditions to qualify for limitation of liabilty	Article 10.66 (2) The Parties **may establish obligations** for information society service providers to promptly inform the competent authorities of alleged illegal activities undertaken or information provided by recipients of their service, or to communicate to the competent authorities, at their request, information enabling the identification of recipients of their service with whom they have storage agreements.	Article 20.11(4) Each Party **may prescribe** in its domestic law, conditions for service providers to qualify for the limitations or exceptions in this Article. Without prejudice to the above, each Party may establish appropriate procedures for effective notifications of claimed infringement, and effective counter-notifications by those whose material is removed or disabled through mistake or misidentification.	Article 18.10(30) 1.(b)(v) With respect to functions referred to in clauses (i)(C) and (D), the limitations **shall be conditioned** on the service provider: (A) **not receiving a financial benefit** directly **attributable to the infringing activity**, in circumstances where it has the right and ability to control such activity; (B) **expeditiously removing or disabling access** to the material residing on its system or network on obtaining actual knowledge of the infringement or becoming aware of facts or circumstances from which the infringement	Article 20.88 3. To facilitate effective action to address infringement, each Party **shall prescribe in its law** conditions for Internet Service Providers to qualify for the limitations described in para. 1(b), (a) With respect to the functions referred to in para.s 2(c) and 2(d), these conditions shall include a requirement for Internet Service Providers to **expeditiously remove or disable access** to material residing on their networks or systems upon obtaining actual knowledge of the

was apparent, such as through effective notifications of claimed infringement in accordance with clause (ix); and (C) publicly designating a representative **to receive such notifications**.	copyright infringement or becoming aware of facts or circumstances from which the infringement is apparent, such as through receiving a notice of alleged infringement from the right holder or a person authorized to act on its behalf. (b) An Internet Service Provider that removes or disables access to material in good faith under subpara. (a) shall be exempt from any liability for having done so, provided that it takes reasonable steps in advance or promptly after to notify the person whose material is removed or disabled.

Table 4.1 (*cont.*)

	EU–Republic of Korea	CETA	US–Republic of Korea	USMCA
Prohibition of requiring monitoring	Article 10.66 No general obligation to monitor 1. The Parties **shall not impose** a general obligation on providers, when providing the services covered by Articles 10.63 through 10.65, to monitor the information which they transmit or store, nor a general obligation to actively seek facts or circumstances indicating illegal activity	Article 20.11(3) The eligibility for the limitations or exceptions referred to in this Article **may not be conditioned** on the service provider monitoring its service, or affirmatively seeking facts indicating infringing activity.	Article 18.10(30) 1.(b)(vii) Eligibility for the limitations in this subpara. **may not be conditioned** on the service provider monitoring its service, or affirmatively seeking facts indicating infringing activity, except to the extent consistent with such technical measures.	Article 20.88 7. Eligibility for the limitations in para. 1 **shall not be conditioned** on the Internet Service Provider monitoring its service or affirmatively seeking facts indicating infringing activity, except to the extent consistent with the technical measures identified in para. 6(b).

The geographical reach and overlap of the elaborate EU and US agreements illustrates the successful exportation and thus a high degree of assimilation among the relevant RTA partners that will arguably contribute to seamless digital markets in which the basic determinants of ISP liability will be the same, providing some of the desired legal certainty sought by businesses. Although the purpose of each RTA may have been to export the domestic system, countries subject to both obligations will likely comply by adopting the 'higher' standard, illustrating the *de facto* cumulative effect of RTA IP obligations that are formulated as minimum standards. Past experience indicates that signatories of these RTAs are likely to include substantively similar provisions in future agreements further extending the hub-and-spoke architecture, and thus reinforcing this trend of a common regulatory response by virtue of RTAs.

Online Exhaustion

The question whether exhaustion – the principle that once an IP-protected good has legitimately entered distribution channels, its further distribution (e.g. of a second-hand book) no longer requires the agreement from the original right owner – could also apply to downloaded digital products (e.g. e-books or software) is determinative for whether a potentially significant global market for 'second-hand' digital products could exist.

Exhaustion in International Treaties

While the concept of exhaustion – or, for that matter, territoriality – is not explicitly mentioned in the Paris or Berne Conventions,[210] a number of interpretations have taken the territoriality of IP protection arguably implied in these conventions to indicate a preference for national exhaustion.[211] In the TRIPS context, the intense yet inconclusive discussion of pharmaceutical parallel imports led to the exclusion of exhaustion from dispute settlement considerations[212] which leaves WTO members free to

[210] See Article 4*bis* Paris Convention and Article 5 Berne Convention.

[211] See Gervais (2012), para. 2.99. See also Gosh and Calboli (2019). Regarding the Paris Convention, see German Federal Supreme Court, Centrafarm and Dirk de Fluiter *v.* Eli Lilly & Co., 8 IIC 64 (1977) – *Tylosin* (supporting national exhaustion); and Tokyo High Court, 27 IIC 550 (1996) (rejecting implications for exhaustion).

[212] Article 6 TRIPS Agreement.

establish its own regime for exhaustion without challenge.[213] Where TRIPS text does – indirectly – articulate the concept, exhaustion is formulated exclusively with respect to goods, put on the market by, or with the consent of, the right holder.[214] As has been described above,[215] the discussion on exhaustion during the negotiations of the Internet Treaties led to the agreed statement concerning Articles 6 and 7 of the WCT, affirming that only physical copies were subject to the new distribution right. While this has generally been understood to mean that exhaustion does not apply to digital products downloaded from the Internet (i.e. 'made available' rather than 'distributed'), the purported flexibility of the 'umbrella solution' as a background to the making available right would also seem to permit a more nuanced interpretation.[216]

National Jurisprudence on Online Exhaustion – Filling the Gaps?

In the absence of international agreement on these issues, the role of the courts in applying domestic law can be significant in determining the scope of exhaustion in practice. The increasing use of electronic channels for the purchase of digital products raises the question whether legal distinctions associated with the different modes of online and offline transfer should continue to apply where they create counter-intuitive distinctions between otherwise – from the consumer perspective – identical products.[217] In the words of the EU Advocate General Spuznar:

> The digitisation of content and the development of the new means of supplying that content to users made possible by the internet have upset the balance that existed in the analogue environment between, on the one hand, the interests of copyright holders and, on the other hand, the interests of users of the works. The rule of the exhaustion of the right of

[213] See Doha Declaration on TRIPS and Public Health WT/MIN(01)/DEC/W/2 of 14 November 2001, para. 5(d): 'The effect of the provisions in the TRIPS Agreement that are relevant to the exhaustion of IPRs is to leave each Member free to establish its own regime for such exhaustion without challenge, subject to the MFN and national treatment provisions of Articles 3 and 4.'

[214] See footnote 13 to Article 51 TRIPS, excluding from the obligation of border measures 'imports of goods put on the market in another country by or with the consent of the right holder. This formulation tracks Article 6.5 of the Treaty on Intellectual Property in Respect of Integrated Circuits (1989) which has been incorporated into the TRIPS Agreement by virtue of Article 35 TRIPS Agreement'.

[215] See 'The WIPO Internet Treaties: An Issue-Driven International Solution' above.

[216] Ibid.

[217] For a more elaborate discussion and background, see Taubman (2020).

> distribution is one of the instruments that help to maintain that balance. The question is whether the balancing of the interests involved also requires the application of that rule in the case of the supply of works by downloading.[218]

In the landmark case *UsedSoft*,[219] the Court of Justice of the European Union decided in the affirmative that copies of software that had been legitimately acquired and downloaded could be resold if the transfer had been definitive and no residual copy remained with the seller. While the decision was taken in the specific context of the EU Software Directive,[220] and hence much of its appreciation centred around its characterization of software licensing as tantamount to a 'first sale' under Article 4(2) of the Software Directive,[221] the Court expressly rejected the Commission's argument drawn from the WCT background above and confirmed:

> In those circumstances, it must be considered that the exhaustion of the distribution right under Article 4(2) of Directive 2009/24 concerns both tangible and intangible copies of a computer program, and hence also copies of programs which, on the occasion of their first sale, have been downloaded from the internet onto the first acquirer's computer.[222]

Subsequent European jurisprudence has been reluctant to apply this approach outside the scope of the Software Directive and, in the recent *Tom Kabinet*[223] case relating to second-hand e-books, expressly rejected the assimilation of tangible and intangible copies under the Copyright Directive,[224] citing – inter alia – its purpose as implementing Articles 6(1) and 8 WCT and referring the agreed statement in that regard.

Although this appears as a reversal to the traditional view that exhaustion is limited to the distribution of tangible copies only, the tension of this approach with the economic reality is apparent in the Advocate General's opinion in this case:

> The foregoing considerations lead me to conclude that arguments, of both a legal and a teleological nature, are in favour of recognition of the rule of

[218] *Tom Kabinet*, C-263/18, Opinion of Advocate General Szpunar, para. 79.

[219] *UsedSoft*, C-128/11, 3 July 2012, available at curia.europa.eu/juris/liste.jsf?num=C-128/11.

[220] Directive 2009/24/EC of the European Parliament and of the Council of 23 April 2009 on the legal protection of computer programs.

[221] See Hilty et al. (2013).

[222] *UsedSoft*, C-128/11, 3 July 2012, para. 59.

[223] *Tom Kabinet*, C-263/18, 19 December 2019.

[224] *Tom Kabinet*, C-263/18, para. 56.

> exhaustion of the distribution right with respect to works supplied by downloading for permanent use. In particular, the permanent possession by the user of a copy of such a work shows the similarity of that mode of supply with the distribution of tangible copies. However, I am of the view that, as EU law now stands, the arguments to the contrary should prevail. These are, in particular, the arguments [. . .] concerning the EU legislature's clear intention that downloading should be covered by the right of communication to the public, the limitation of the distribution right to acts of transfer of ownership of a copy, and the right of reproduction.[225]

A similar tension between the limits of existing legislation and the realities of digital trade is apparent in the US jurisprudence related to this question in the cases *ReDigi* and *ClearCorrect*. In *ReDigi*[226] the 2nd Circuit Court of Appeals in New York rejected applying exhaustion to lawfully purchased iTunes tracks that were transferred to the purchasing customer while ensuring deletion from the seller's network. It argued that uploading the music files on ReDigi's server 'inevitably involved' the creation of new *unauthorized* phonorecords by reproduction, which are excluded from the scope of exhaustion, and rejected a *fair use* defence in light of the negative impact the use would have on the music market.

The *ClearCorrect*[227] case did not concern exhaustion as such, but rather whether the International Trade Court (ITC) had jurisdiction to bar the import of digital datasets related to teeth aligning models.[228] The Federal Circuit found that 19 US Code § 1337(a) – relating to importation of 'articles' – limited the ITCs jurisdiction to 'material things' and did not include the ability to bar digital imports. In a dissenting opinion, Judge Newman argued for a broad interpretation of 'articles' to include intangible products, citing several US statutes and administrative statements that had already assimilated tangible and intangible articles and goods.[229]

Prospects for a Common Regulatory Response

This national jurisprudence highlighted above illustrates the increasing tension between the traditional approach to exhaustion as applying only

[225] *Tom Kabinet*, C-263/18, Opinion of Advocate General Szpunar, para. 79.

[226] Capitol Records, LLC et al. *v.* ReDigi Inc., No. 16-2321 (2nd Cir. 2018).

[227] ClearCorrect Operating, LLC *v.* ITC, No. 2014-1527, Slip Op. at 3 (Fed. Cir. November 10, 2015).

[228] Discussed in Taubman, Antony, 'The Shifting Contours of Trade in Knowledge: The New "Trade-Related Aspects" of Intellectual Property', Chapter 2 in this volume ('Beyond Trade in Goods?', p. 62).

[229] Ibid., at 1304 *et seq.*

to tangible products and the reality of pervasive digitization. While sympathetic to considering the new business models that challenge traditional exhaustion, the courts consider themselves constrained by existing statutes that enshrine the traditional distinction between tangible and intangible products under copyright. In their efforts to fill existing gaps by creative solutions, no common approach has yet emerged around which initiatives for an international regulatory response could coagulate.

Characteristically, in the European context, many of the arguments resisting a relaxation of exhaustion centre around the interpretation of the WCT's 'right of making available' as a communication to the public, and hence the exclusion of downloaded products from exhaustion under the guidance of the agreed statement to Article 6 WCT. As highlighted above in the section the Internet Treaties, WCT signatories that have chosen the alternative means of implementing the 'right of making available' as a form of the distribution right[230] should feel less constrained by such considerations to apply exhaustion in the digital context. Considerations of compelling WCT interpretation in this regard are thus notably absent from the US jurisprudence cited above.

Any recalibration of the balance of interests between right holders and users with regard to digital products will need to be addressed in light of economic realities, taking into account the purpose and objective of the tool of exhaustion. In digital situations that emulate offline exhaustion – such as a permanent transfer of a digital product with no residual copy, as elaborated in *UsedSoft* – court opinions and policy considerations have shown sympathy for an application of the same principle. It is recognized that in the absence of accessible evidentiary tools to verify such conditions on a large scale as would be required for, say, the monitoring of a particular e-book copy, the application of online exhaustion will need further consideration. However, the new technologies that have upset the traditional balance in the analogue world may yet be instrumental in establishing a new balance. If technologies like blockchain could create a reliable technical standard for evidence for how many copies continue to exist of a particular digital product, this may help address the evidentiary side of a concept of online exhaustion and help spur a common regulatory response in this area.

[230] See the references to the US implementation above at nn. 40 and 41.

New Issues – Rapidly Approaching: Data Mining and Artificial Intelligence

Rapid progress in technology and its widespread use means that the next issues requiring a – preferably common – regulatory response are already approaching. Among them are the questions of how to address the increasing commercial and ethical relevance of 'big data', and how to address the occurrence of artificial intelligence (AI) in the traditionally human-centric system of intellectual property protection.

Big Data and Emerging Data Mining Exceptions

Cutting across a number of different disciplines, the policy approaches to harnessing the welfare potential of using 'big data' collection and use have often been characterized as being similar to that of IP – namely striking the right balance between incentivizing the creation (i.e. collection) of data while ensuring sufficient access and benefit for users from the general public. Seeking to contribute to the latter, the practice of text and data mining – i.e. provisions intended to permit the analysis of large volumes of digital text and data to identify patterns, trends and correlations – has been recognized in legislative initiatives in Europe,[231] and under the *fair use* principle in the United States.[232] The, as yet divergent and incomplete, regulatory approaches in this area reflect that the application of IP protection or exceptions to large collections of data have not yet been fully settled. Challenges lie not only in different approaches to traditional database approaches – such as a *sui generis* database right in the European Union[233] – but also stem from the evolving nature of data collections that resist categorization in traditional IP right categories.[234]

Artificial Intelligence in a Human-Centric IP System

AI tools and their outputs pose a number of conceptual challenges to the IP system which has traditionally rewarded inventive and creative

[231] See Articles 3 and 4 of the DSM Directive and the background to criticism of its limited scope in EU Parliament (20018a) and EU Parliament (20018b), and Benhamou (2020).

[232] See Authors Guild *v.* HathiTrust, 755 F.3d 87 (2nd Cir. 2014), White *v.* West (SDNY 2014), Fox *v.* TVEyes (SDNY 2014), Authors Guild *v.* Google, 770 F.Supp.2d 666 (SDNY 2011).

[233] See Benhamou (2020) and Gervais (2019).

[234] See Gervais (2019) 'Beyond the protection of software used to collect and process Big Data corpora, copyright's traditional role is challenged by the relatively unstructured nature of the non-relational (noSQL) databases typical of Big Data corpora.'

activity associated with humans. AI tools, such as machine learning, big data analysis and evolutionary algorithms pose questions as to IP ownership, standards for IP protection criteria such as 'obviousness'[235] and 'originality', as well as the protectability of AI outputs. Responses to these challenges have so far triggered clarifications in patent examination guidelines[236] and isolated national jurisprudence applying existing concepts,[237] but broader conceptual engagement with AI at the policy level remains at an early stage.

At the international level, at the time of writing, WIPO launched a public consultation process on AI and IP policy to identify the most pressing questions likely to face IP policymakers in this area.[238] While responses to the first issues paper[239] suggest that considerable clarification is still necessary to properly frame the relevant questions, international coordination in this area could benefit from considerable WIPO groundwork on AI that reaches back as far as the early 1990s.[240]

Conclusion

The mechanisms that influence the creation of international regulatory responses to emerging IP issues have undergone significant change since the advent of the digital era. The primacy of state sovereignty in international affairs in the nineteenth and twentieth centuries, coupled with the unique demands of rapid internationalization of arts and technology at the turn of the century, led to a dominance of international organizations as the forum for developing and agreeing international regulatory responses in the area of IP. The favouring of consensus decisions and

[235] Abbott (2018).

[236] See, for example, Singapore's April 2019 AI-related revision of Examination Guidelines for Patent Applications.

[237] See patent applications in the name of an IT tool 'DABUS' filed in multiple jurisdictions by The Artificial Inventor Project (artificialinventor.com). In November 2019 the EPO rejected two such applications (EP 18275 163 and EP 18275174) on the basis of the requirement that an inventor designated in the application has to be a human being, not a machine (see www.epo.org/news-issues/news/2020/20200128.html).

[238] See WIPO press release PR/2019/843 of 13 December 2019.

[239] See MPI (2020) for an elaboration of the conceptual challenges.

[240] See WIPO Worldwide Symposium on the Intellectual Property Aspects of Artificial Intelligence held at Stanford University 25–27 March 1991, available at www.wipo.int/edocs/pubdocs/en/wipo_pub_698.pdf.

the iterative process of revising the treaties created a situation in which technical regulatory responses developed and experienced at the national level could be directly translated into binding international rule-making.

Coinciding with the advent of the digital era, this scenario has given way to a more varied landscape where a variety of tools and legal instruments embody regulatory responses to digital challenges. While TRIPS, the WCT and the WPPT are examples of the traditional model of multilaterally negotiated treaties in existing institutions, the adoption of non-binding instruments – such as the Joint Recommendations – shows the limits of consensus and momentum in this model. International non-state solutions such as ICANN and the UDRP emerge as separate, technically determined solutions to specific IP issues. Proliferating FTAs emerge as a new platform to formulate and agree IP-related regulatory responses that can be used to project the national solutions of one FTA-partner but can also serve to give legally binding status to internationally agreed non-binding recommendations.

Today, these different modes of international regulation co-exist and interact, reflecting 'the reality of a multi-speed and multi-tiered world in which multilateralism, while being the highest expression of inclusiveness and legitimacy, is nevertheless the slowest solution'.[241]

This chapter shows how these diverse approaches interact in recent IP regulatory responses to emerging digital issues that are particularly relevant for digital business models. In the relatively mature area of ISP liability, global regulatory responses show broad agreement in principle that limitation of liability is essential for the viability of Internet platforms and the important functions they perform in the global digital marketplace. While the methodology on conditions and sanctions of the various 'safe harbour' models still varies, broad agreement in principle has meant that the concept has been included in bilateral and regional trade agreements. Whether this means that this issue is closer to becoming an international rule will have to be assessed in light of the recent policy changes at the domestic level – notably under the European Digital Single Market Directive (DSM Directive or DSMD). Still further behind are the emerging issues of online exhaustion, data mining and IP-related questions of artificial intelligence. As regards the former, domestic jurisprudence in different countries is still struggling to find a consistent

[241] See Gurry acceptance speech 2014 (n. 143).

understanding of under what evidentiary circumstances the offline concept can be applied to digital works. With regard to the latter two, a conceptually consistent policy approach is yet to unite the hitherto diverse regulatory reactions ranging from IP office guidelines on IP ownership to data mining exceptions in national law.

Bibliography

Abbott, R., 'Everything is Obvious' (2018), *UCLA Law Review* 66, 2, available at https://ssrn.com/abstract=3056915 or http://dx.doi.org/10.2139/ssrn.3056915.

Agarwal, Devika and Agarwal, Radhika, 'Delhi High Court Upholds Safe Harbour for Intermediaries in Copyright Disputes' (2017), *Journal of Intellectual Property Law & Practice* 12, 5: 366–368, available at https://doi.org/10.1093/jiplp/jpx040.

Benhamou, Yaniv, 'Licensing Big Data: A Holistic Analysis Based on a Three-Step Approach' (2020), available at www.researchgate.net/publication/339140374_Licensing_Big_Data_a_holistic_analysis_based_on_a_three-step_approach.

Bhagwati, Jagdish, 'US Trade Policy: The Infatuation with Free Trade Agreements', in J Bhagwati and A Krueger, The Dangerous Drift to Preferential Trade Agreements, Washington, DC: AEI Press, 1995.

Blomqvist, Jorgen, *A Primer on International Copyright and Related Rights*, Cheltenham: Edward Elgar Publishing, 2014.

Dinwoodie, Graeme B., '(National) Trademark Laws and the (Non-National) Domain Name System' (2000), *University of Pennsylvania. Journal of International Law* 495, 21, available at https://scholarship.law.upenn.edu/jil/vol21/iss3/2.

EU Parliament (2018), DG for Internal Policies, (Nordemann) *Liability of Online Service Providers for Copyrighted Content – Regulatory Action Needed?* 2018 (PE 614.207).

EU Parliament (2018a), DG for Internal Policies, (Geiger et al.) *The Exception for Text and Data Mining (TDM) in the Proposed Directive on Copyright in the Digital Single Market – Legal Aspects* 2018 (PE 604.941).

EU Parliament (2018b), DG for Internal Policies, (Rosati) *The Exception for Text and Data Mining (TDM) in the Proposed Directive on Copyright in the Digital Single Market – Technical Aspects* 2018 (PE 604.942).

Ficsor, Mihály, *The Law of Copyright and the Internet: the 1996 WIPO Treaties, Their Interpretation and Implementation*, Oxford: Oxford University Press, 2002.

Ficsor, Mihály, 'Copyright In The Digital Environment: The WIPO Copyright Treaty (WCT) And The WIPO Performances And Phonograms Treaty (WPPT) in WIPO/CR/KRT/05/7', February 2005, available at www.wipo.int › mdocs › arab › wipo_cr_krt_05 › wipo_cr_krt_05_7.

Ficsor, Mihály, 'Only once more — and then Merry Christmas and Happy New Year to everybody, including Professor Geist and his devoted followers: the 1996 WIPO Diplomatic Conference, the WIPO Treaties and the balance of interests', Barry Sookman, 23 December 2009, available at www.barrysookman.com/2009/12/23/only-once-more-and-then-marry-christmas-and-happy-new-year-to-everybody-including-professor-geist-and-his-devoted-followers-the-1996-wipo-diplomatic-conference-the-wipo-treaties-and-the-balanc/.

Ficsor, Mihály, 'The WIPO Internet Treaties and Copyright in the "Cloud"', paper presented at the 2012 ALAI Congress in Kyoto.

Geist, Michael A., 'Fair.Com?: An Examination of the Allegations of Systemic Unfairness in the ICANN UDRP', August 2001, available at https://ssrn.com/abstract=280630.

Geist, Michael A., 'Fundamentally Fair.com? An Update on Bias Allegations and the ICANN UDRP', 2002, available at http://aix1.uottawa.ca/~geist/fairupdate.pdf.

Geist, Michael A., 'The Case for Flexibility in Implementing the WIPO Internet Treaties: An Examination of the Anti-Circumvention Requirements', 2010, available at www.irwinlaw.com/sites/default/files/attached/CCDA%2008%20Geist.pdf.

Gervais, Daniel, *The TRIPS Agreement - Drafting History and Analysis*, 4th ed., London: Sweet & Maxwell, 2012.

Gervais, Daniel, 'Exploring the Interfaces Between Big Data and Intellectual Property Law' (2019), *Journal of Intellectual Property, Information Technology and Electronic Commerce Law*, 10, 22: para. 1.

Gosha, Shuba and Calboli, Irene, *Exhausting Intellectual Property Rights – A comparative Law and Policy Analysis*, Cambridge: Cambridge University Press, 2019.

Haas, Marie-Emmanuelle, *The origin of the UDRP: NSI's 1995 domain name dispute policy*, (domainesinfo.fr 2009) available at www.me-haas.eu/wp-content/uploads/2014/03/The-origin-of-the-UDRP.pdf

Helfer, Laurence R. and Dinwoodie, Graeme B., 'Designing Non-National Systems: The Case of the Uniform Domain Name Dispute Resolution Policy' (2001), *William and Mary Law Review* 43: 141, available at https://scholarship.law.wm.edu/wmlr/vol43/iss1/7.

Hilty, Reto, Köklü, Kaya and Hafenbrädl, Fabian, 'Software Agreements: Stocktaking and Outlook Lessons from the UsedSoft *v.* Oracle Case from a Comparative Law Perspective' (2013), *International Review of Intellectual Property and Competition Law* 44: 263–292.

Husovec, Martin, 'Accountable, Not Liable: Injunctions Against Intermediaries', 2 May 2016, TILEC Discussion Paper No. 2016-012, available at https://ssrn.com/abstract=2773768 or http://dx.doi.org/10.2139/ssrn.2773768.

Inta White Paper, *The Intersection of Trademarks and Domain Names*, International Trademark Association, 18 August 1997, available at www.ntia.doc.gov/legacy/ntiahome/domainname/not-emailed/INTA-whitepaper.htm.

Isenberg, Doug, *These Countries Have Adopted the UDRP*, 1 June 2017, CircleID, available at www.circleid.com/posts/20170601_these_countries_have_adopted_the_udrp/.

Komaitis, Konstantinos, *The Current State of Domain Regulation: Domain Names as Second-Class Citizens in a Mark-Dominated World*, New York: Routledge, 2010.

Kumar, Aakanksha, 'Internet Intermediary (ISP) Liability for Contributory Copyright Infringement in USA and India: Lack of Uniformity as a Trade Barrier' (2014), *Journal of Intellectual Property Rights* 19: 272–281.

Kur, Annette, 'Not Prior in Time, But Superior in Right: How Trademark Registrations Can be Affected by Third Party Interests in a Sign' (2013), *International Review of Intellectual Property and Competition Law* 44, 7: 790–814, available at https://ssrn.com/abstract=2253888.

Kwakwa, Edward and Talbott, Autumn, 'The Influence of the World Intellectual Property Organization on the European Union', in Ramses Wessel and Steven Blockmans (eds), *Between Autonomy and Dependence: The EU Legal Order under the Influence of International Organizations*, The Hague: Asser Press/Springer, 2013.

LaFrance, Mary, *Streaming of Music and Audiovisual Works*, Chapter 19 in this volume, 2020.

von Lewinski, Silke, 'Article 14 WPPT – Right of Making Available of Phonograms', in Jorge Reinbothe and Silke von Lewinski, *The WIPO Treaties on Copyright: A Commentary on the WCT, the WPPT and the BTAP*, Oxford: Oxford University Press, 2015.

MPI, *Comments of the Max Planck Institute for Innovation and Competition of 11 February 2020 on the Draft Issues Paper of the World Intellectual Property Organization on Intellectual Property Policy and Artificial Intelligence* 2020, available at www.ip.mpg.de/fileadmin/ipmpg/content/stellungnahmen/2020-02-11_WIPO_AI_Draft_Issue_Paper__Comments_Max_Planck.pdf.

Mulholland, Caitlin, *Secondary liability of service providers in Brazil: The effect of the Civil Rights Framework*, (responsabildadecivil.org) 29 March 2018, available at www.responsabilidadecivil.org/single-post/2018/03/29/Secondary-liability-of-service-providers-in-Brazil-the-effect-of-the-Civil-Rights-Framework.

Otten, Adrian, 'The TRIPS Negotiations: An Overview', in Jayashree Watal and Antony Taubman (eds), *The making of the TRIPS Agreement*, Geneva: WTO, 2015, pp. 55–79.

Petillion, Flip and Janssen, Jan, *Competing for the Internet: ICANN Gate – An Analysis and Plea for Judicial Review through Arbitration*, Alphen aan den Rijn, Netherlands: Kluwer, 2017.

Ricketson, S., *The Paris Convention for the Protection of Industrial Property – A Commentary*, Oxford: Oxford University Press, 2015.

Ricketson, S. and Ginsburg, J., *International Copyright and Neighbouring Rights – The Berne Convention and Beyond*, 2nd ed., Oxford: Oxford University Press, 2006.

Rotaru, Vasile, *Accountable Algorithmic Copyright Enforcement*, PIR 2017/2018, available at www.academia.edu/37432171/ACCOUNTABLE_ALGORITHMIC_COPYRIGHT_ENFORCEMENT.

Saha, Ishaan and Saha, Oieshi, 'Safe Harbour Law In India: Raising the Red Flag in the Wake of Myspace v. Super Cassettes' (2018), *Journal of Intellectual Property Law & Practice* 13, 5: 393–399, available at https://doi.org/10.1093/jiplp/jpx192.

Schlesinger, Michael, 'The Right of Making Available and its Implementation in National Law and Case Law', in Hugh Hansen (ed.), *Intellectual Property Law and Policy*, Vol. 11, Oxford: Hart, 2010.

Schwemer, Sebastian and Schovsbo, Jens, 'What is Left of User Rights? – Algorithmic Copyright Enforcement and Free Speech in the Light of the Article 17 Regime', forthcoming in Paul Torremans (ed.), *Intellectual Property Law and Human Rights*, 4th ed., Alphen aan den Rijn, The Netherlands: Wolter Kluwers, 2020.

Senftleben, Martin, 'Institutionalized Algorithmic Enforcement – The Pros and Cons of the EU Approach to UGC Platform Liability' (2020), *Florida International University Law Review* 14, available at http://ssrn.com/abstract=3565175.

Sethia, Aradhya, 'The Troubled Waters of Copyright Safe Harbours in India' (2017), *Journal of Intellectual Property Law & Practice* 12, 5: 398–407, available at https://doi.org/10.1093/jiplp/jpx017.

Seuba, Xavier, 'Substantive and Jurisdictional Challenges Arising from Bilateralism in Intellectual Property' in CEIPI – ICTSD, *What Institutional Environment for the Development and Enforcement of IP Law?*, November 2015, CEIPI – ICTSD Series: Global Perspectives and Challenges for the Intellectual Property System; Issue No. 1, pp. 57–68.

Stutz, Michael, 'NSI Tweaks Domain Name Dispute Rules', wired.com 2 December 1998, available at www.wired.com/1998/02/nsi-tweaks-domain-dispute-rules/.

Taubman, Antony, *The Lasagne Effect: Bilateral, Regional and Multilateral Standards, and the Settlement of Disputes Over Trade and Intellectual Property*, Society of International Economic Law Inaugural Conference, Geneva, July 2008.

Taubman, Antony, 'Discontent Industries? Creative Works and International Trade Law: Making Sense of "Analogue" IP Rules in a Digital Age', 9 November 2019, available at https://ssrn.com/abstract=3566680.

Taubman, Antony, 'Digital Disruption: Reshaping Markets for IP', forthcoming in Robert D. Anderson, Nuno Pires de Carvalho and Antony Taubman, *Competition Policy and Intellectual Property in Today's Global Economy*, Cambridge: Cambridge University Press, 2020.

US Copyright Office, *The Making Available Right in the United States – A Report of the Register of Copyrights*, 22 February 2016.

US Green Paper, National Telecommunications and Information Administration (NTIA), *A Proposal to Improve Technical Management of Internet Names and Addresses – Discussion Draft 1/30/1998*, available at www.ntia.doc.gov/legacy/ntiahome/domainname/dnsdrft.htm.

US White Paper, US Department of Commerce, *Statement of Policy on the Management of Internet Names and Addresses*, 5 June 1998, available at www.ntia.doc.gov/federal-register-notice/1998/statement-policy-management-internet-names-and-addresses.

Valdés, R. and McCann, M., 'Intellectual Property Provisions in Regional Trade Agreements: Revision and Update', WTO Staff Working Paper ERSD-2014-14, Geneva: World Trade Organization, 2014.

Valdés, R. and Runyowa, T., 'Intellectual Property Provisions in Regional Trade Agreements', WTO Staff Working Paper ERSD-2012-21, Geneva: World Trade Organization, 2012.

Wager, Hannu, 'Copyright: A Nordic Perspective', in Jayashree Watal and Antony Taubman (eds), *The making of the TRIPS Agreement*, Geneva: WTO, 2015, pp. 321–340.

Watal, J. and Taubman, A. (eds) (2015), 'The Making of the TRIPS Agreement: Personal Insights from the Uruguay Round Negotiations', Geneva: WTO, 2015, available at https://doi.org/10.30875/00344762-en.

De Werra, Jacques, 'Alternative Dispute Resolution Mechanisms for Solving Trademark Disputes (Mediation, UDRP, Arbitration)', in Irene Calboli and Jacques de Werra (eds), *The Law and Practice of Trademark Transactions: A Global and Local Outlook*, Cheltenham: Edward Elgar Publishing Ltd, 2016, pp. 293–322, available at https://archive-ouverte.unige.ch/unige:82027.

WIPO, *Final Report of the WIPO Internet Domain Name Process*, 30 April 1999, available at www.wipo.int/amc/en/processes/process1/report/finalreport.html.

WIPO, *Intellectual Property Handbook*, 2nd ed., Geneva: World Intellectual Property Organization, 2004.

Zingales, N., 'The Brazilian Approach to Internet Intermediary Liability: Blueprint for a Global Regime?' (2015), *Internet Policy Review* 4, 4: DOI: 10.14763/2015.4.395.

PART II

Measuring Trade in Knowledge

5

Measuring International Intellectual Property Transactions in a Globalized World: Current Challenges and Possible Improvements

JOSCELYN MAGDELEINE AND ANDREAS MAURER*

Abstract

Trade in IP products (IPP) has grown rapidly over the past decades and at an accelerating pace in recent years. Advances in information and communications technologies (ICTs), and the possibilities offered by digitization and new business models, have widened opportunities for such trade, shaping production networks in goods and services and global value chains. This paper describes the importance of such trade. It depicts current concepts and methods used to compile official statistics in a global value chain environment and to describe characteristics of traders in IP products. In considering what we ca learn from cross-border knowledge flows from IMF Balance of payments data and other statistical frameworks, it concludes with an outline for a way forward to improve the information base.

Introduction

Intellectual property (IP) is defined as 'the rights relating to: literary, artistic and scientific works, performances of performing artists, phonograms, and broadcasts, inventions in all fields of human endeavour, scientific discoveries, industrial designs, trademarks, service marks, and commercial names and designations, protection against unfair competition, and all other rights resulting from intellectual activity in the industrial, scientific, literary or artistic fields'.[1] It is described as 'one of the most readily tradable properties in the digital marketplace'.[2] Thus, IP is an essential component of the production of goods and

* Thanks go to Florian Eberth and Barbara d'Andrea for providing statistics and text on high-tech goods and IP trade.

1 See www.wipo.int/treaties/en/text.jsp?file_id=283854#P50_1504.

2 See www.businessdictionary.com/definition/intellectual-property.html.

services, particularly for those that are innovative or creative. It is traded internationally:

i. embedded in the value of traded goods and services
ii. through international licensing transactions, or
iii. through the sales/transfer of ownership in IP rights (including the results of Research and Development – R&D, assignment of IP portfolios through acquisition, or rights on computer programs, cinematographic works or sound recordings).

Trade in IP products (IPP)[3] has grown rapidly over the past decades and at an accelerating pace in recent years. Advances in information and communications technologies (ICTs), and the possibilities offered by digitization and new business models, have widened opportunities for such trade, shaping production networks in goods and services and global value chains.

Statistically, the *Manual on Statistics of International Trade in Services* 2010 (MSITS2010) as well as the revised *Balance of Payments Manual*, 6th edition (BPM6) and accompanying compilation guidance have clarified the concepts of intellectual property in statistical frameworks. They present a classification system of related receipts and payments, depending on how IP is transacted internationally (embedded in products, licensing, sales or transfer of ownership of IP rights), and at what level of detail (see Box 5.1). However, globalization, digitalization and tax optimization have contributed to blur the way transactions are recorded and compiled into relevant statistics for policymakers, research and for businesses themselves.

MSITS2010 catalogues research and development services as well as transactions in computer software, audiovisual and cultural products. Compilation guides of the BPM6 and MSITS2010, as well as the Guide to Measuring Global Production of the Conference of European Statisticians, which deals with national accounting aspects, provide further guidance as to how compilers could approach some of the challenging measurement issues arising from the globalization of the economy. But activities of multinational enterprises (MNEs) make it more complex to value international transactions and assess related transfers of ownership.

[3] These products include research and development, computer software and information services, audiovisual and other cultural products, franchises and trademarks.

The shortage of data makes it difficult to answer important policy questions. For instance, to what extent are less developed economies benefiting from the expansion of trade and investment in technology? What are the characteristics of firms which are engaging in IP international transactions? What is the role of small and medium-sized enterprises in IP trade?

This chapter will review what developments are needed for compiling relevant statistics to respond to these important questions. The first part of the chapter will present some general trends in international transactions pertaining to IP. The second part will review the concepts and definitions related to IP which are currently available in trade in goods and services statistics, and report on the current data availability. The third part will illustrate some of the measurement challenges that compilers face to develop such data. Linkages between balance-of-payments IP-related transactions, foreign direct investment (FDI) and foreign affiliates statistics (FATS) will be shown. The fourth part will explore possibilities offered by statistics on trade by enterprise characteristics in relation to trade in IP. The final part will sketch a possible way forward for the collection and compilation of data (e.g. improve or create new surveys, finding synergies) to provide a better understanding of the economics of trade, global value chains and IP.

Importance of Intellectual Property in International Trade

Different types of statistics can be used to assess the importance of IP in international trade. These cover customs statistics (trade in high-tech and branded goods, and specific goods such as recorded optical media and printed publications) and the balance-of-payments (BPM6) for services (including charges for the use of intellectual property and research and development services). For intra-firm transactions, FDI statistics and FATS are useful frames. Quantitative indicators such as patent applications, grouped by family, filed abroad by country of origin, valued by citations, patent applications with at least one applicant from abroad, patent assignments across borders, etc. are a complementary data source. In this chapter we focus on transactions recorded as goods and services in the balance of payments.

Since 1995, the value of exports in high-tech goods, which includes a very large share of IP, has increased significantly. For developed countries, it increased by nearly 80 per cent, while their share of this global trade decreased from 72 to 51 per cent. In contrast, the developing

Table 5.1 *Exports of high-tech goods 1995, 2000, 2010, 2015–2017*[4]

(Billion US dollars and percentage)

	Value ($bn) High-tech goods					
Reporter group	1995	2000	2010	2015	2016	2017
World	**586**	**966**	**1286**	**1480**	**1437**	**1480**
Developed economies	424	634	689	741	744	762
Developing economies & CIS	162	331	597	739	693	718
	Share (%) High-tech goods					
Reporter group	1995	2000	2010	2015	2016	2017
World	**100**	**100**	**100**	**100**	**100**	**100**
Developed economies	72	66	54	50	52	51
Developing economies & CIS	28	34	46	50	48	49

Source: WTO, UN Comtrade data.

economies' share increased by 75 per cent, its value growing more than four times to reach USD 718 billion in 2017 (see Table 5.1).

Trade in charges for the use of IP, which includes licence fees for the use of IP, has increased more than twice as fast as exports of high-tech goods. The increase in such trade is more than four-fold since 1995, which is 1.5 times faster than the overall increase of trade in commercial services. It accounted for USD 398 billion in 2017 (Figure 5.1). Also, Figure 5.2 shows the increase of transactions relating to R&D services, computer and information and audio-visual services, which was even stronger, in particular since 2005 (no comparable statistics are available for previous years for these services categories).

Transactions referring to the use of IP are highly concentrated. As seen from Figure 5.3, in 2016, the biggest traders alone, the US and the EU (28), held a share of more than 76 per cent. Almost half of the European Union's receipts of charges and licensing fees originated from within the EU, and receipts from the United States accounted for an additional 20 per cent. Similarly, in the case of the United States, around 40 per cent of receipts were arising from exports to EU member countries, in particular Ireland and the United Kingdom (at this time a member of the EU), as well as from exports to Switzerland and Canada. Data on payments also reflect

[4] For high-tech goods, the OECD-Definition in document OCDE/GD(97)216) is applied.

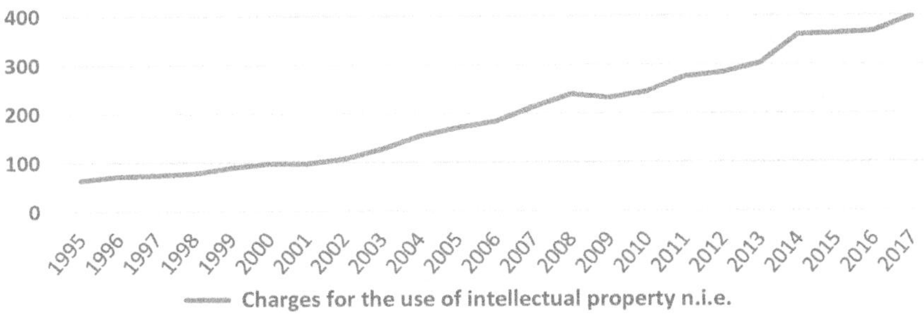

Figure 5.1 World international transactions relating to charges for the use of intellectual property, n.i.e., 1995–2017 (billion US dollars)
Source: ITC, UNCTAD, WTO, 2018.

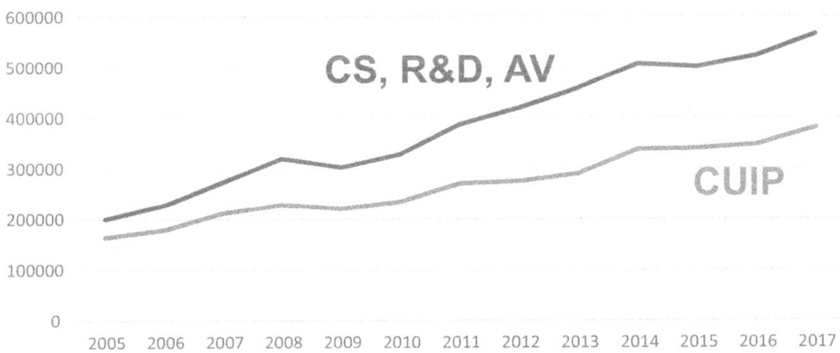

Figure 5.2 World international transactions relating to charges for the use of intellectual property n.i.e. (CUIP), computer services (CS), research & development (R&D) and audio-visual services (AV), 2005–2017 (Source: IMF)
Source: ITC, UNCTAD, WTO, 2018.

these trends. US data reflect that a large share of IP international transactions takes place within multinational enterprises.

Concepts Pertaining to IP-Related International Transactions and Current Data Availability

Relevant international statistical guidelines strove to cover innovation and related IP flows in one way or the other, whether in economic statistics (*System of National Accounts 2008*, BPM6, Manuals on Statistics of International Trade in Services, *OECD Handbook on Deriving Capital Measures of IPPs*, *OECD Handbook on Economic Globalization Indicators*), specialized statistics on innovation and

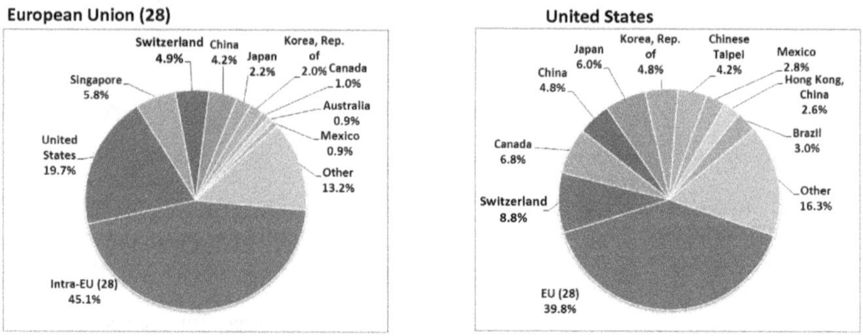

Figure 5.3 European Union (28) and the United States – charges for the use of intellectual property, n.i.e., receipts by main partner, 2016[5]

Source: WTO World Trade Statistical Review (WTSR 2018), data are sourced from Eurostat and OECD.

research and development (*Frascati Manual, Oslo Manual*), as well as quantitative data on patents, trademarks, etc.

IP products can be accessed or produced in various ways: within the firm, or through a diffusion process such as accessing open source IP or knowledge, IP acquired from other economic entities (outsourcing of R&D, licensing for the use of IP), or through the purchase of new innovative products (materials, software etc.). We will focus in this chapter on the market international transactions involving IP. In economic statistics, IP is generally described as taking the following forms:

- Intellectual property-related products (IPPs), which can take the form of
  - produced assets:
    - computer software and databases, audio-visual products (music, movies, television and radio programmes)
    - outcomes of research & development (R&D)
    - exploration rights (in general no international related transactions as the client will normally have an entity resident in same economy as owner of rights (in principle government entity) and
  - non-produced assets (use of trademark).
- Exchanges of tangible products:
  - intellectual property embedded in goods transactions, e.g. cultural or creative goods (mass-produced),
  - R&D results embedded in goods (e.g. industrial processes),
  - originals/blueprints exchanged on physical media.

[5] See *World Trade Statistical Review*, WTO, 2018, p. 54.

- Exchanges of intangible products (transactions in intangibles):
  - downloaded products which have a goods equivalent, the difference being the media through which it is delivered/transmitted to clients (i.e. electronic transmission rather than CDs, DVDs or other physical media).
- Licences for the use of intellectual property, generally transactions between the owner of originals and producers, distributors which replicate the original, and trademark payments (including franchising type transactions when not possible to separate IP component from other types of transactions, e.g. services).
- Transfers of blueprints etc. to producers (most probably also in the form of a licence) or directly to households such as for 3D printing.

How has this translated in international guidelines for the recording of international transactions, and what is the underlying data availability? Up to 2008, the concepts and definitions of the *Balance of Payments, 5th edition* (BPM5) were used for compiling statistics on international transactions. Under the BPM5, sales/transfer of IP products (whether results of R&D, or computer programs, cinematographic works or sound recordings) were recorded indistinguishably as capital account transactions under the item acquisition/disposal of non-produced, non-financial assets.

But for other IP-related transactions, as shown in Table 5.2, data availability greatly improved during the late 1990s–early 2000s. For example, by 2010 there were 138 economies reporting receipts for the item royalties and licence fees and 155 for payments. Reporting for royalties and licence fees even surpassed related items, such as computer and information services, in particular on the payments side (142 economies, of which around two-thirds reported computer services separately) or audiovisual and related services (approximately 80). Only 69 economies reported data for research and development services and for advertising and market research services. In terms of breakdowns, many agencies developed estimates for franchises and similar rights (approximately 35–40 reporters, mainly EU and/or OECD economies), separately from other royalties and licence fees. Only a handful of economies went a step further in breaking down royalties and licence fees into more detailed subcategories. These included Australia (industrial processes, computer software, music), Canada (trademarks, franchises, patents and industrial design, copyrights and related rights, software and other royalties), New Zealand (software royalties and licence fees) and the United States (trademarks, franchise fees, industrial processes, books, records and tapes,

Table 5.2 *Reporting of BPM5 intellectual property-related items, 2010*

	Receipts	Payments
S262 Computer and information services	133	142
S263 Computer services	94	106
S264 Information services	75	94
S266 Royalties and licence fees	138	155
S891 Franchises and similar rights	34	38
S268 Other business services	167	174
S273 Miscellaneous business, professional and technical services	107	112
S277 Business and management consultancy, public relations services	50	66
S278 Advertising, market research, etc.	68	73
S279 Research and development services	69	68
S280 Architectural, engineering, other technical consults	68	64
S287 Personal, cultural and recreational services	123	133
S288 Audiovisual and related services	76	82
S289 Other personal, cultural and recreational services	73	80
S895 Personal services, education	28	28
S896 Personal services, health	27	28

Source: IMF.

broadcasting and recording of live events, general use computer services, industrial engineering services). However, as can be seen, this was far from closing the gap in terms of information needs relating to international IP-related transactions. In addition, there were many issues pertaining to the delineation between different items.

BPM6, which was released in 2008, introduced major conceptual improvements. A consistent complement to BPM6 is MSITS2010. The MSITS2010 provides for more details than BPM6 and introduces more detail for some items. Both these manuals represent a major step forward to respond to information needs. First, originals (i.e. the IP product over which ownership rights can be established, e.g. the master copy of a film, music, software, patented result of R&D) are now considered as produced assets (i.e. the result of a (creative) production process). The results of research and development (R&D) such as patents, copyrights, and industrial processes are now treated as produced assets and included in research and development services (under other business services). Likewise, sales/transfer of IP rights are identified separately under the services that produce them (e.g. computer software originals are identified as a separate category under computer services). The only IP-related product that remains under the capital account relates to marketing assets such as brand names, trademarks, logos, etc.

Second, the breakdown of the item 'other business services' is reorganized, enabling the separate identification of research and development services (R&D). This provides more visibility to an important item in terms of international trade, which was previously neglected in international statistical guidelines. Third, the delineation is clarified between goods, services and different types of licences for use for some of the most important IP-related products in international transactions (i.e. R&D, computer and audio-visual services). Box 5.1 summarizes the treatment of intellectual property in BPM6 and MSITS2010 guidelines.

The classification of transactions relating to the use of those originals (copies, reproduction or distribution rights) will depend on several factors. Charges for the use of intellectual property in MSITS2010 and BPM6 cover the charges for use of proprietary rights (patents, trademarks, copyrights, industrial processes and designs, franchises, etc.) whether the rights result from research and development, marketing, advertising or other creative or cultural activities (computer software, music, films, books, etc.). This item corresponds to the item royalties and licence fees in BPM5. Charges for the use of intellectual property includes licensing receipts or payment for reproduction and/or distribution of computer software, audiovisual products or other products (i.e. the transactions between the owners of the original/rights and producers who either reproduce the products or embed them in other products). However, it is important to note that the item as defined in BPM6 and MSITS2010 (i.e. charges for the use of intellectual property not included elsewhere) does not cover the value of end-user licences or copies themselves (i.e. the licence component of music, video or software sold at the level of the consumer).

Transactions with an end-user licence/copies which are sold on a physical media (such as a music CD, or a movie on a DVD) will either be classified under goods if they are mass-produced products with a licence for perpetual use (in Box 5.1 identified as non-customized products provided on physical media with right to perpetual use) or as services (i.e. depending on the type of product, under computer software, audiovisual services etc.) if the sale entails the subsequent payment(s) of periodic licence fees, for example, for updates. If they are customized products, they will be classified as services. All copies delivered or distributed electronically (downloading, online consumption, streaming) will be classified under the relevant services. These are products of great interest in

BOX 5.1 TREATMENT OF INTELLECTUAL PROPERTY IN BALANCE-OF-PAYMENTS STATISTICS

	Use of intellectual property		Sale or purchase of intellectual property ownership rights[a]
Franchises and trademarks	*Charges for the use of intellectual property n.i.e.*		Balance-of-payments capital account
Outcomes of research and development	*Charges for the use of intellectual property n.i.e.*		Research and development services
Computer software products; audiovisual and related products	**Licence to use excluding reproduction and distribution**[b]	**Licence to reproduce and/or distribute**[c]	
(a) Customized products of all types	Relevant service item[d]	*Charges for the use of intellectual property n.i.e.*	
(b) Non-customized products, downloaded or otherwise electronically delivered	Relevant service item[d]		Relevant service item[d]
(c) Non-customized products provided on physical media with periodic licence fee	Relevant service item[d]		
(d) Non-customized products provided on physical media with right to perpetual use	Goods		

[a] Covers the case where there is a change of economic ownership of the whole of the intellectual property right in question and the seller no longer has any

BOX 5.1 *(cont.)*

rights or obligations associated with the intellectual property. This case also includes second or subsequent outright sales of intellectual property rights.

[b] Covers the case where a specific product is supplied with the right to use the intellectual property embodied in it, but not to copy it for further distribution. The transactions should be classified under the appropriate goods and services items.

[c] Covers the case where authority to reproduce and/or distribute the intellectual property is delegated by its owner.

[d] The relevant item is classified under either computer services or audiovisual and related products, depending on the nature of the content provided. For example, the sale or purchase of a copy of a software package that is mass-produced, and is obtained by an individual to load onto a single computer is covered by a licence to use that excludes reproduction and distribution. If a manufacturer pays for the right to include the software on the computers that it produces, then the payment would be a licence to reproduce and/or distribute (charges for the use of intellectual property provided by the owner of the original).

Source: Table III.1 in *Manual on Statistics of International Trade in Services*, 2010 edition.

the context of trade in digitized products.[6] Corresponding international transactions, when they occur, will be reported indistinguishably in the relevant item together with the other transactions likely to fall under these services (e.g. computer services, services provided by firms/individuals for the shooting of a movie, transactions in originals, etc.).

The relevant items in the most detailed breakdown provided by MSITS2010 are shown in Table 5.3, together with the number of those reporting each individual item for receipts and payments. Although the number of those reporting in BPM5 and BPM6/MSITS2010 has not drastically changed for the main item of interest here, that is charges for the use of intellectual property not included elsewhere (hereafter n.i.e.) (still in the range of 140 for receipts and 160 for payments), those reporting other main items have increased substantially. Research and development show the highest increase, with 50 per cent more reporters (up to approximately 100). The second-best performer is computer

[6] See Erick S. Oh, 'The Global Digital Content Landscape', Chapter 10 in this volume.

Table 5.3 *Reporting of BPM6/MSITS2010 intellectual property-related items, 2015*

	Receipts	**Payments**
8 Charges for the use of intellectual property, n.i.e.	142	161
8.1 Franchises and trademarks licensing fees	19	21
8.2 Licences for the use of outcomes of research and development	18	17
8.3 Licences to reproduce and/or distribute computer software	16	17
8.4 Licences to reproduce and/or distribute audiovisual and related products	15	15
8.4.1 Licences to reproduce and or distribute audiovisual products	7	8
8.4.2 Licences to reproduce and/or distribute other products	6	7
9 Telecommunications, computer, and information services	180	181
9.2 Computer services	116	134
9.2.1 Computer software	10	10
of which: 9.2.1.a Software originals	7	7
9.3 Information services	102	110
9.3.2 Other information services	19	23
10 Other business services	177	181
10.1 Research and development services	100	106
10.1.1 Work undertaken on a systematic basis to increase the stock of knowledge	26	25
10.1.1.1 Provision of customized and non-customized R&D services	25	24
10.1.1.2 Sale of proprietary rights arising from R&D	25	25
10.1.1.2.1 Patents	8	8
10.1.1.2.2 Copyrights arising from R&D	7	7
10.1.1.2.3 Industrial processes and designs	7	8
10.1.1.2.4 Other	6	7
10.1.2 Other	23	22
10.2 Professional and management consulting services	129	138
10.2.2 Advertising, market research, and public opinion polling	35	34
10.3 Technical, trade-related and other business services	161	162

Table 5.3 (*cont.*)

	Receipts	Payments
10.3.1 Architectural, engineering, scientific and other technical services	35	35
10.3.1.1 Architectural services	25	24
10.3.1.2 Engineering services	26	25
10.3.1.3 Scientific and other technical services	24	24
11 Personal, cultural, and recreational services	142	154
11.1 Audiovisual and related services	89	96
11.1.1 Audiovisual services	7	7
of which: 11.1.1. Audiovisual originals	6	6
11.1.2 Artistic related services	7	7
11.2 Other personal, cultural, and recreational services	116	121
11.2.1 Health services	26	26
11.2.2 Education services	25	26
11.2.3 Heritage and recreational services	23	24

Source: IMF.

services, now representing over 110 reporters for receipts and 130 for payments, followed by audiovisual (around 90). Surprisingly the number of reporters of advertising, market research and public opinion polling has markedly decreased, from 70 down to 35 reporters. However, it is important to note that for many of these items, developing countries, particularly those in Africa, do not report any data.

While we have described above substantial improvements in the reporting of some main IP-related items, it is also important that we analyse further the level of development of statistics at the more detailed level introduced by MSITS2010. There, even though MSITS2010 and a number of other guidelines were released, and policymakers have referred to the need to obtain further details, the picture is rather disappointing. Only a very small number of reporters (mainly OECD or EU countries) have compiled information for those. As shown in Table 5.3, only 15–20 economies report details for charges for the use of intellectual property, 25 report details for research and development services (of which many are shown as having a zero value!), and fewer than 10 economies report data on sales or the transfer of proprietary rights. Finally, data broken down by counterparts in the transactions is available in 40–50 economies (mainly OECD and EU countries). Consequently, it is important that users of the data and compilers further discuss the data gaps and identify ways to better respond to information needs.

It is also important to state that IP-related trade can also take place through the temporary presence of natural persons (referred to as 'mode 4' delivery of services in the parlance of the General Agreement on Trade in Services). Very little information is available separately for mode 4, but the WTO Secretariat recently released an experimental dataset on Trade in Services by Modes of Supply (TISMOS).[7] The economic transactions involving this mode of trade are indistinguishably covered in the balance-of-payments items indicated above. They are most likely important in the following items: computer services, professional and technical services (consultancy, advertising, architectural, artistic, education and health services (see Table 5.3)). When it comes to obtaining counts on mode 4 persons, the main area of interest will be on persons travelling abroad in the context of service contracts that they deliver either on their own behalf or on behalf of their employer. Again, very little data are available, but guidance is prepared on developing international labour mobility statistics.[8] It is hoped that these guidelines will improve data availability enabling an analysis of mode 4, where in many cases an individual's knowledge of the person is important in delivering the service.

The distinction between the Extended Balance of Payments Services (EBOPS) 2010 categories from a reporter's perspective may not always be clear (for example software versus research and development, or sales of IP rights versus licensing for use of IP). The suggested granularity of the breakdown of the R&D item is also often seen as challenging by compilers. When it comes to collecting the information, there are basically two main ways of gathering information: reporting by commercial banks of international transactions made by their clients (international transaction reporting system) and the use of surveys. The latter offers more options to collect detailed data as covered in this chapter. Given the level of detail sought and the complexity of the subject, one needs to clearly draft appropriate guidance for respondents, which may be particularly difficult when an international transaction reporting system is used (and probably also for general trade in services surveys). But the refined classification as presented in MSITS2010 should provide a solid point

[7] An experimental data set was released on 31 July 2019; see 'WTO launches trade in services dataset by sector and mode of supply', available at www.wto.org/english/news_e/news19_e/serv_31jul19_e.htm.

[8] See *UNECE Guide on International Labour Mobility Statistics.*

of departure for compilers. Interestingly, the US is spearheading developments on implementing these concepts. It has issued an enterprise survey collecting detailed information on international transactions relating to intellectual property.[9]

Also, recent developments in business strategies, and the blurring of activities is rendering the collection and compilation of information difficult. There are new major players involved (e.g. telecommunications companies, Internet service providers) in distributing IP products, which may contribute to the blurring of fields of activities. This may complicate the identification of the sample of enterprises to survey. There are also a few borderline issues concerning the rights acquired by transmitters such as TV companies and radio stations, when the contractual arrangements allow for multiple transmissions. Where the fees are paid on a 'pay as you go' basis, for example a royalty payment is made every time a song is played on a radio station, these should be recorded under audiovisual services while a one-off fee paid for unlimited air-time should be recorded as being equivalent to a licence to reproduce (charges for the use of intellectual property n.i.e.). Finally, although flows between enterprises (whether affiliated or unaffiliated) should be accounted for in financial statements, they may not always be identifiable as specific IP-related transactions.

As for the technological means of delivery, it is important to note that trade involving IP increasingly takes place online through e-commerce. The flow of IP-protected information is an item of increasing concern to service suppliers around the world, and, in particular, in relation to flows taking place through the Internet or other types of data networks. These data flows may reflect the actual service being provided (i.e. music being downloaded, film being streamed, blueprint), the transfer of a copy of the original on which the recipient will be entitled to make copies for distribution or sale, or refer to the information essential to service suppliers to be able to manage customer relations and data or to enable the international payments associated with sales, etc. Statistics on IT-enabled transactions and e-commerce should also become an important complementary source of information when considering IP-related transactions.[10] It is therefore important to take these developments into

[9] For transaction types covered, see USBEA BE-120, 'General Instructions', p. 24.

[10] A related project on measuring trade in ideas attempts to categorize transactions related to IP to analyse further which of these transactions are available in data collection systems of national statistical offices to build statistical indicators.

account when developing strategies to improve the quality and relevance of statistics relating to IP international transactions.

Additional Measurement Challenges in GVCs

The establishment of global value chains is a driving force for the increase of transactions in IP. International competition forces firms to increase their efficiency and develop new products. This phenomenon poses additional significant measurement challenges for the items identified in the previous section.

Outside MNEs, IPP-related transfers or payments are tracked using market transactions and the identification of IPP ownership is usually less problematic. Yet, the analysis of IPP use in production still typically requires a complete picture of the global production chain (e.g. 'factoryless goods producers', 'virtual manufacturing').

However, within MNEs it is more complicated. First, intra-firm transactions (i.e. within multinationals) may be affected by (i) the use of transfer pricing and/or more general tax planning issues which distorts the valuation of trade transactions, and (ii) decisions where to establish multinational affiliates or headquarters[11]. Transfer prices, being the cost at which assets are transacted between the divisions of one firm, may significantly differ from the actual 'real' market transaction values, negotiated by separate firms at arm's-length from one another. Also, the distinction between flows recorded as trade in services and flows recorded as property income may not always be clear-cut. For example, R&D-related transactions or transactions relating to the use of an asset between affiliated enterprises are not always observable. They may also be channelled through convoluted chains of affiliates. Often, payments that are not explicitly recorded, but that are implicitly related to R&D or the use of an underlying asset are instead recorded as property income. In principle, an imputed payment should be recorded (either as a payment for R&D services or charges for the use of intellectual property n.i.e.). Hence, more often than not, it is unlikely that such imputations will be made in practice. Nevertheless, if compilers do make such imputations, they should ensure that counterpart transactions (in particular international transactions) should be coherent, requiring coordination with other statistics agencies.

[11] See Thomas Neubig and Sacha Wunsch-Vincent, 'A Missing Link in the Analysis of Global Value Chains: Cross-Border Flows of Intangible Assets, Taxation and Related Measurement Implications', Chapter 6 in this volume.

Second, defining the location of the economic ownership of IP assets may be an additional barrier to the appropriate measurement of (international) transactions, with the fragmentation of activities, rendering transactions hardly identifiable.[12] Indeed, multinationals may choose to register their patents, industrial processes or originals in one country rather than another based on 'benefit maximizing' considerations. Patents could be registered:

- with the parent company; as the ultimate beneficiary, the parent company often financing directly or indirectly (via an affiliate) the acquisition or production of the IPP (i.e. the original)
- with an affiliate using the IP in its production
- with an affiliated intermediary which could be the original producer or could be a Special Purpose Entity (SPE) whose sole purpose is to register assets and act as the legal owner of IPPs, therefore obtaining the revenues of IPP copies or licences to use or reproduce. SPEs are usually established in view of optimizing the overall post-tax MNE profits.

The country of registration will be where the legal ownership is established. But this does not mean that the country of registration is necessarily the same as that of the economic owner of the IP (i.e. the entity that draws benefits and may encounter losses from the ownership of the asset, whether the producer of the original or the entity providing or using the services or copies of the original). Not all countries may be able to clearly identify these aspects.

As shown above, although recent international statistical standards clarified the classification of transactions, they failed to provide clear recommendations as to how to compile the information. When transactions are not observed directly, ownership and the recording of intra-group IPP transfers become uncertain and can only be based on certain

[12] In national accounts and the balance-of-payments statistics, the recording of product transactions is done based on economic ownership change, which is a fundamental principle. Economic ownership is defined in para. 3.26 of the SNA as follows: 'The economic owner of entities such as goods and services, natural resources, financial assets and liabilities is the institutional unit entitled to claim the benefits associated with the use of the entity in question in the course of an economic activity by virtue of accepting the associated risks'. As indicated in the *Guide to Measuring Global Production*, accepting associated risks involves the owner's responsibility for maintenance of the asset, which can entail paying for fees to maintain patents, copyrights or other registrations of the IPP in question. The benefits can usually be derived from embedding IPP in its own production and therefore the subsequent sales of goods or services, or alternatively by licensing other parties for the right to use the IPP in their production processes.

conventions. The *Guide on Measuring Global Production* provides some guidelines in relation to global production arrangements, from the perspective of national accounts, as well from the perspective of the trade in services and balance-of-payments statistics. This complements the compilation guidance drafted by the UN expert group on the compilation of trade in services statistics.

The *Guide on Measuring Global Production* provides a decision tree to determine the economic ownership of IPP and related IPP transactions. 'The starting point is the observation of IPP output or IPP ownership at the level of a certain unit. The obtained information is examined in four different steps:

1. Control ownership of the unit: is the unit member of an MNE (yes/no)?
2. Is the unit the producer of the IPP (yes/no)?
3. What is the main kind of activity (in terms of ISIC) of the unit, or, is the unit expected to use the IPP in its production process (yes/no)?
4. Does the unit receive income related to IPPs, or, does the unit pay for the use of IPPs (royalties and licences) (yes/no)?'

Of course, to be able to use such a decision tree, appropriate source data are needed. Nevertheless, compilers are strongly advised to implement this decision tree, as this should enable the compilation of relevant and internationally consistent data.[13] Following the establishment of these more detailed guidelines, some specially targeted enterprise surveys should help improve the data situation when it comes to the more detailed information sought on IP, intra-firm transactions and location of ownership of IP (e.g. trade in service, FATS surveys, surveys used for the collection of R&D data).

More research is needed on how to compile IPP-related transactions when SPEs are involved. A clear and separate identification of the IPP income flows received by IPP-holding SPEs should be classified under a separate heading such as 'IPP related services provided by SPEs' as the provision of these services does not really reflect economic transactions. Such a practice will help to support the correct interpretation of economic statistics where these entities are located, as well as help improve the data in other countries, whether the related MNEs are established there (parent companies or affiliates) or not, as well for countries where companies have unrelated/arm's-length transactions.

[13] Given the difficulties in compiling the information, it is not recommended to reroute the ownership of IP by SPEs.

However, many countries/compilers will not be able to collect such (detailed) information accurately. Also, the increase in the response burden should be acknowledged. A solution for these could be to complement their more general data collection systems with the information collected and disseminated by countries that will be engaging in a more detailed and sophisticated data collection system (most probably the countries which have interest in this information, that is the ones where research and development, and more broadly IP, is significant and where multinationals are involved). However, this can only function if there is efficient cooperation between compilers of different countries. In addition, it will be necessary to have detailed bilateral information published by countries that will be engaging in a detailed data collection system.

Finally, an alternative global production arrangement is receiving increased attention in the statistical community. Although it is not a new channel, global producers and distributors are making rapid and increasing use of the opportunities offered by e-commerce. Consequently, the development of new business models for transactions in intangibles has been observed in recent years. This is described in international statistical guidelines as 'merchanting of services' (see MSITS2010 and UNECE *Guide to Measuring Global Production*). It can be described as follows: an intermediary located in one country arranges the supply of services/IP between suppliers and consumers located in other countries, without itself being engaged in operational activities. For example, a firm or establishment (i.e. the entity engaged in the merchanting of services) is created in a jurisdiction with the sole purpose of distributing copies of IP-protected material to other countries on behalf of a client in a third country. This is expected to be applied by MNES, but is not limited to those. At the time of writing, only an attempt has been made to conceptualize this practice for statistical purposes, but it seems that this way of doing business is of importance for several major service trading economies. Gathering further information on these types of transactions may also shed more light on how IP is traded.

Characteristics of IP Traders

The first sections of this chapter deal with issues relating to the classification, collection and recording of information on international transactions related to IP. But how can we understand better the characteristics of those engaged in such transactions? How can we analyse the transactions with respect to the size of enterprises, their activities and the relationships between supplying firms and recipients/clients? These are important questions for trade and other policymakers. They would need this type of information to improve their decision-making when it comes to determining export strategies as well as for trade negotiations.

Trade by enterprise characteristics (TEC), compiled to complement the traditional merchandise and services trade statistics, can eventually respond to the questions raised in the previous paragraph. Data on international merchandise trade and trade in services are presented according to enterprise size class (measured in number of employees) and type of ownership (domestic whether with only local activities or multinationals and foreign-controlled affiliates). Data on merchandise trade by enterprise characteristics have been available for a number of years (collected in certain economies since 2006), and one would need to focus on high-technology product groups (e.g. aerospace, computers, electronics and telecommunications, pharmaceuticals, scientific instruments, chemicals), or relevant specific technology-intensive industries, to analyse merchandise trade related to IP. Statistics on Services Trade by Enterprise Characteristics (STEC) have received greater attention in recent years. Eurostat and the OECD recently released a compiler's guide to produce such data.[14] One important feature of such a dataset is that it does not require the addition of a response burden on reporters. However, one needs to have the necessary legal framework and data collection system in place enabling data linking between trade in services, micro data and enterprise characteristics. Keeping in mind confidentiality constraints, it would be useful to break down the information to a level of interest to analysts and policymakers.

The level of detail recommended for the type of economic activity is aggregated and it will probably be difficult to suggest more detailed activities given the infancy of this new way of presenting trade statistics. Nevertheless, the current recommendations do suggest a level of disaggregation of services products that would be extremely useful in our context, as this would separately identify charges for the use of intellectual property n.i.e. and research and development services. Although these two items are of high relevance, other recommended items may also be useful (computer, audiovisual services, etc.).

Finally, presenting the information by type of ownership would also be extremely useful to understand the role of multinationals in

[14] See *Compilers Guide for Statistics on Services Trade by Enterprise Characteristics* (STEC), OECD and Eurostat, 2017 edition.

knowledge diffusion. This can either be analysed in the context of TEC and STEC (Services Trade by Enterprise Characteristics), as well as looking more closely at foreign direct investment statistics and FATS.

For FDI statistics, it would be interesting to analyse foreign investment in knowledge-intensive activities, as well as to obtain a better understanding of the role of SPEs in that context. In the absence of statistics applying the economic ownership principle, it would be useful to gather more detailed information with respect to SPEs that are used to register assets and act as the legal owner of IPPs, therefore obtaining the revenues of IPP copies or licences to use or reproduce.

Other sources that should be examined to obtain a better understanding of MNE operations with respect to IPPs are operational data portraying the activities of affiliates (sales, exports and imports, employment, assets) as captured by FATS. The information is presented according to the main sector of affiliates' activities and enables the analysis of the performance of domestic- and foreign-controlled enterprises. It can be particularly interesting to obtain information pertaining to the eventual ownership of IP assets and transactions in IPPs, such as sales of products with embedded IP and licensing agreements, whether domestic or international (in the latter case, linking to balance-of-payments data).

Conclusion – A Way Forward

This chapter has shown that trade in IP products has grown rapidly over the past decades and at an accelerating pace in recent years, driven by the development of global production arrangements, as well as the digitization of the economy. While concepts in statistical frameworks have been clarified, data collection and compilation do not keep pace. At the time of writing we are far from having a full picture of international transactions pertaining to IP. Main BPM6/MSITS2010 items are compiled (computer services, audiovisual services, charges for the use of intellectual property, n.i.e.) but, in most cases, we do not have the necessary details (let alone breakdowns by trading partner) to conduct a thorough analysis of international IP transactions. The only item that presents a notable recent increase in reporting is research and development services. Also, as the section entitled 'Additional Measurement Challenges in GVCS' has shown, several challenges remain when it comes to compiling these items. As has been outlined, one of the main issues is the valuation of intra-firm transactions, which is particularly striking for IP-related transactions. The other important issue pertains to the identification of the ownership of IP rights, and more particularly to the economic relevance of SPEs being identified as owners of IP rights in economic statistics. Finally, the section entitled 'Characteristics of IP Traders' has highlighted the need to obtain more information for better trade and IP policy analysis, and decision-making (size of firms, relationship between firms, type of global production arrangements etc.).

Based on the points raised in this chapter, we suggest some steps that could be explored to improve the data situation:

- It is advised to implement BPM6 recommendations, including for the services items of interest by all reporting jurisdictions. Only this would allow implementation of the level of detail recommended in MSITS2010 (including data broken down by partner).
- Find synergies between relevant data collection and compilation methods based on existing compilation guidelines (*BPM6 Compilation Guide, MSITS2010 Compilers Guide, UNECE Guide on Measuring Global Production*, etc.) with mechanisms established for other related statistical needs (audiovisual, culture, creativity, e-commerce). Specific questions should be added in (trade in services) surveys, and if deemed necessary, specific surveys could be developed. Innovative sources of information could also be explored (e.g. big data).
- It is crucial to better understand the (emerging) business models to address compilation issues (ownership of IP rights, who trades with whom, intermediary platforms in e-commerce, etc.). Existing international guidance, such as the *Frascati Manual* and the UNECE *Guide to Measuring Global Production*, should be followed. More information on SPEs and their role in global production arrangements needs to be gathered (including through FDI statistics and FATS).
- Given the importance of knowing more about the characteristics of the firms that trade in IP products, it is suggested that ways of developing statistics on trade broken down according to enterprise characteristics, focusing on items of interest in the context of IP (computer, audiovisual services etc.) should be found.
- This cannot be done efficiently without the promotion of cooperation at the national level for defining priorities and needs, and finding synergies for data collection and compilation (i.e. need for coherence and reducing the burden of data collection). This needs to be accompanied by a policy push if it is to succeed (engaging those authorities

and policymakers that deal with trade, IP, innovation and related industry and technology policies). There should also be cooperation at the international level to ensure the comparability of the data, to promote and assist in the development of relevant statistics, and to help compilers exchange information and experiences, such as data-sharing arrangements and further guidelines based on practical experience.

To respond to information needs, there is also the need to create a new international dataset covering international IP-related flows (including relevant services items as well as merchandise statistics to cover embedded IP). For example, work could be done in the context of the OECD–WTO Trade in Value Added (TiVA) initiative to better measure IP embedded in traded products.

Bibliography

OECD and Eurostat, *Compiler's Guide for Statistics on Services Trade by Enterprise Characteristics (STEC)*, 2017 edition.

UNECE, *Guide on International Labour Mobility Statistics*, Geneva and New York, 2018.

WTO, *World Trade Statistical Review*, Geneva: WTO, 2018.

6

A Missing Link in the Analysis of Global Value Chains: Cross-Border Flows of Intangible Assets, Taxation and Related Measurement Implications

THOMAS NEUBIG AND SACHA WUNSCH-VINCENT*

Abstract

Global fragmented production and associated trade in intermediate products has changed how economists study globalization and how new public policies are shaped. This creates a need for understanding cross-border flows of disembodied knowledge, often associated with intellectual property (IP). However, data on these international IP-related knowledge flows, specifically, cross-border payments for use of IP, are distorted. The chapter shows how tax planning by multinational enterprises has seriously distorted the measurement of cross-border IP flows, with tax-induced mismeasurement potentially exceeding 35% of global Charges for Use of Intellectual Property (CUIP), and more for individual countries, particularly high-tax-rate countries. This chapter describes the trend of increased cross-border trade in ideas, assessing the main data sources and distortions to these flows. The chapter analyses the tax effects on cross border IP measures and the magnitudes and trends in the tax distortions. It concludes with some possible avenues for reducing mismeasurement distortions, directed at national statisticians, national tax administrations, policymakers and analysts, and academics.

Introduction

The phenomenon of global fragmented production and associated trade in intermediate products, including intangible assets, has changed how economists study globalization and how new public policies are shaped.

In this light, understanding cross-border flows of disembodied knowledge, often associated with intellectual property (IP), is essential to analysing how modern economies operate. Unfortunately, available data

* The views expressed in this article are those of the authors and do not necessarily reflect the views of the World Intellectual Property Organization or its member states.

to document these international IP-related knowledge flows – namely cross-border payments for IP[1] – are distorted. Indeed, IP-related tax avoidance strategies have biased measures of trade, GDP and productivity.

As this chapter shows, tax planning by multinational enterprises has seriously distorted the measurement of cross-border IP flows and affected the national measurement of imports, exports, GDP and productivity. The tax-induced mismeasurement could be more than 35 per cent of global Charges for Use of Intellectual Property (CUIP) and more for individual countries, particularly high-tax-rate countries.

The chapter is structured as follows. In the first section, the trend of increased cross-border trade in ideas is described. The main data sources assessing these flows are portrayed in the second section. In the third section, the main distortions to these flows are assessed. Then, in more detail, in the fourth section, the tax effects on cross-border IP measures are described and the magnitudes and trends in the tax distortions are presented. Finally, in the last section, the chapter discusses some initial possible approaches to reducing mismeasurement distortions.[2]

The Rise of Cross-Border Trade in IP

Technology, business innovations, and falling trade costs have transformed the organization of global production. The unbundling of the production process and the geographical dispersion of different stages of production are the key elements of this transformation.

Increasingly, multinational enterprises (MNEs) source input and technology from suppliers worldwide. This reflects a fragmentation of the production process in the manufacturing and services industries, with increases in task-based manufacturing, intermediate trade and the outsourcing of services. As a result, a greater number of countries participate in global production and innovation networks.[3] Manufacturers exposed to these networks experience technological and organizational learning, possibly leading to industrial upgrading.

[1] See Joscelyn Magdeleine and Andreas Maurer, 'Measuring International Intellectual Property Transactions in a Globalized World: Current Challenges and Possible Improvements', Chapter 5 in this volume.

[2] The underlying findings of this chapter were produced to inform the WIPO World Intellectual Property Report 2017, on 'Intangible Capital in Global Value Chains', WIPO (2017).

[3] WIPO (2011).

It is now a common assumption that intangible assets in the form of technological knowledge, software and other types of know-how are key in the analysis of increasingly fragmented production. The causes and consequences of this cross-border trade in ideas are manifold:

- As firms focus on their core competitive advantage, they purchase essential technologies from third parties rather than developing themselves, also propelling the vertical disintegration of knowledge-based industries.[4]
- The increasing existence of 'technology markets', backed by (i) new business models such as IP licensing, (ii) information technologies, (iii) more legal and practical experience with technology transactions, and (iv) increased IP protection worldwide allow for such technology transactions to increasingly take place.
- The operations of MNEs have led to more intra-company transfers of technology, also because of increased foreign direct investment.
- Factoryless production is on the rise in which firms outsource their manufacturing activities but control the underlying IP (including the brand name) and hence control the production and value chain outcome.
- The mix of productive assets in business has shifted decisively since 1990 to the point where a majority of capital investment in developed economies is in technology, software, design, creative works, brands, human capital and business organization. About half of these intangible investments are 'owned' via formal IP rights.[5]

These factors have spurred an increase in both inter-company and intra-company trade in disembodied know-how. Such knowledge is frequently subject to registered IP, such as patents and industrial designs, and unregistered IP, such as copyright and trade secrets. As a result, ensuring the accurate measurement of exports and imports of the trade in IP is essential.[6]

Importantly, the types of market-based transactions of IP include the outright sale of originals, the temporary licensing of copies/technology,

[4] See Arora et al. (2001) and WIPO (2011), chapter 2.

[5] Estimates of business intangible investment for the United Kingdom and the role of IP rights are estimates in work commissioned by the UK IPO, see https://assets.publishing.service.gov.uk/government/uploads/system/uploads/attachment_data/file/554480/Investment-in-Intangibles.pdf.

[6] OECD (2014).

but also more complex arrangements such as cross-licensing deals, patent pools and joint R&D ventures or cost-sharing arrangements.

For measurement purposes these exchanges can take various formalized, market-based transactions of which some entail explicit pecuniary transactions – including notional payments for intra-corporate IP transfers among headquarters and company affiliates – and others involve the sharing of technology without explicit payment from buyer to the seller (see Table 6.1 for a taxonomy). In all likelihood, some of the below transaction types involve self-declared estimates or are unrecorded in

Table 6.1 *Taxonomy of formalized and informal technology transactions*

	Financial transaction status and degree of documentation	Type of transfer	Legal status of transfer
Formalized IP-based transactions or sharing agreements	**Pecuniary and recorded**	Market-based transactions with one buyer paying seller. Transactions among headquarters and affiliates involving notional estimates of the transaction.	Commercial licensing of a specific technology with contract and payment/sale or purchase of a patented industrial process. Intra-company transfers.
	Nonpecuniary but recorded	Mutual sharing of technology.	Cross-licensing, patent pools.
Informal technology sharing	**Nonpecuniary and unrecorded**	Non-market-based use of third-party technology with no associated payment. IP infringement.	Implicit, unwritten cross-licensing arrangements or covenants not to sue. Consent decrees. Unrecorded intra-company transfers. Patent infringement or piracy.

existing statistics, hence biasing estimates of trade in IP, mostly downward.

It is important to recognize that only (i) pecuniary, market-based, authorized transactions or (ii) self-declared, notionally valued IP transactions are captured by official statistics. Even in these two cases, the proper valuation of licensing transactions is complex, leaving room for arbitrariness or misreporting reflecting tax or other considerations.

Available Data on Cross-Border IP-Related Flows

Two official sources exist to trace cross-border IP flows, namely (i) international trade data that set out cross-border receipts and payments for the purchase or use of IP, and (ii) tax data.

As regards the former, these international trades in services data are now commonly available through the balance-of-payment (BoP) statistics at the level of countries collected by the International Monetary Fund (IMF) and available in the World Development Indicators (WDI) database, and at the level of the OECD – and a few non-OECD economies – as technology balance-of-payment data.

In addition, a limited number of specific countries publish these data in a more fine-grained fashion – also capturing intra-company transfers – based on specific quarterly, annual or other surveys. The United States (US), in particular, has been publishing detailed intra- and inter-firm data on IP flows for some time. Only a few national data sources allow for such a breakdown, namely Canada, Finland, Israel, Italy, Japan, the Netherlands, Poland, Sweden and the US. Yet, even for these few high-income economies, not all of these data are detailed enough for the analysis of intra-corporate IP flows.

The most widely reported metric on disembodied technology trade relates to the international receipts and payments for the 'authorized use of intangible assets and proprietary rights'.[7] One advantage of these data is that most countries publish them in a timely and regular (yearly or quarterly) manner. In recent years, significant progress has been achieved

[7] The IMF defines royalties licences and fees (RLF) as including 'international payments and receipts for the authorized use of intangible, non-produced, non-financial assets and proprietary rights ... and with the use, through licensing agreements, of produced originals or prototypes ...'. See International Monetary Fund, Balance of Payments Statistics Yearbook and data files, available at https://databank.worldbank.org/metadata glossary/africa-development-indicators/series/BX.GSR.ROYL.CD.

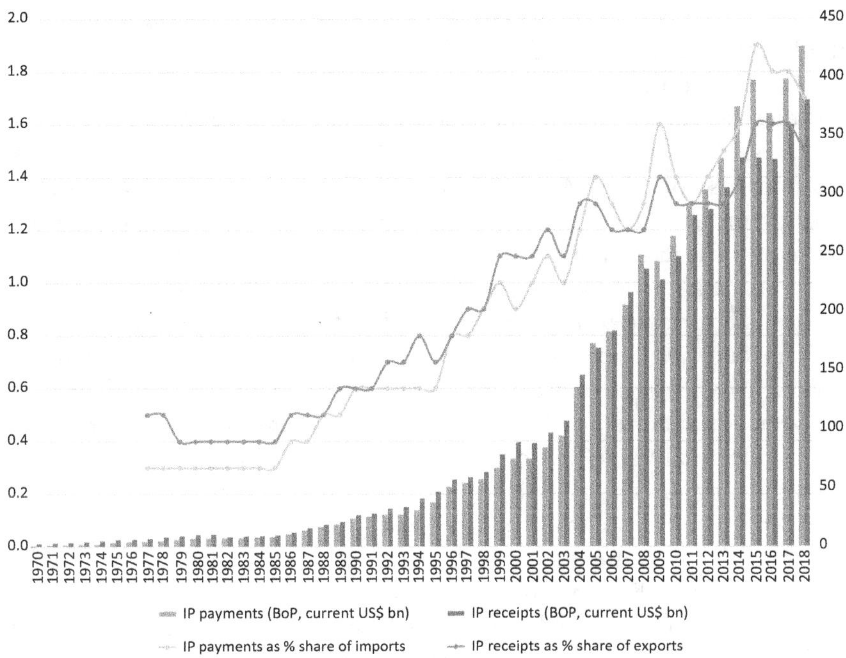

Figure 6.1 Royalties Licences and Fees (RLF) receipts and payments, in USD billion and as share of trade
Source: Authors based on World Development Indicators.

to deliver more reliable data on cross-border technology payments (IMF, 2009, UN et al., 2011). Steps have been taken to improve international accounting standards of national accounts and BoP to better record transactions of firms participating in global production (de Haan et al., 2014, and UN ECE, 2015).

The associated data show that the rise of global value chains (GVC) has coincided with increasing cross-border trade in ideas and IP across countries since the 1990s in high-income countries and then as of the 2000s in upper-middle-income countries mostly through Asian economies, particularly China.[8] In 1990, 62 countries reported making licensing payments but by 2015, this number had increased to more than 120 countries (see Figure 6.1).

The US has the largest amount of receipts (exports) followed by the Netherlands and Japan. Ireland has the largest amount of payments

[8] See Athreye et al. (2012), WIPO (2011a) and IMF (2011).

(imports) followed by the Netherlands and the US. The US and Japan are the largest net exporters of IP services while Ireland and China are the largest net importers. A number of tax havens do not report RLF receipts, but there are other reasons for this discrepancy discussed below.

The OECD's Technology Balance of Payments (TBP) follows the same methods as for the IMF BoP manuals.[9] The magnitude of Ireland's surplus in technology receipts stands out. It is known that the strong presence of foreign affiliates (particularly US and UK firms) and related intra-firm transactions play a role in Ireland, potentially also affected by tax transfer pricing of MNE internal-related party transactions.

For countries where detailed data are available, it is known that IP-related payments mostly consist of intra-firm payments, i.e. payments between subsidiaries and company headquarters. The US Bureau of Economic Analysis (BEA) data show that the majority of IP payments and thus imports – slightly more than 70 per cent of all recorded payments in 2015 – consist of intra-firm payments.

Another government source of royalty data are derived from corporate tax returns. For instance, the US Internal Revenue Service (IRS) Statistics of Income publishes annual corporate tax statistics, which include royalties received by industry. The Australian Taxation Office requires certain taxpayers to complete an annual international dealings schedule, which contains information on international related party transactions, which can include dealings in intangible assets.

That said, corporate tax data are not as comprehensive as data from administrative surveys, since some royalties will be received or paid by non-corporations.

Key Distortions

The statistical measures of cross-border IP flows are distorted by a number of factors.[10] This section identifies some of the key distortions.

Incomplete Reporting

Global flows of IP, measured in the Balance of Payments as Charges for the use of intellectual property (CUIP), not included elsewhere, totalled

[9] OECD (1990).

[10] Some of the most important distortions were initially reported in Madeuf (1984) and OECD (1995).

USD 319 billion receipts and USD 359 billion payments in 2015. The USD 40 billion discrepancy between total receipts and payments indicates a statistical problem. Many countries do not report CUIP receipts and/or payments, thus contributing to an undercount. Countries such as the Bahamas, Bermuda and the Cayman Islands, which are home to many MNE affiliates with IP-holding structures, have not reported royalty receipts.

Some of the other under-reporting distortions include:

- Incomplete surveying: frequently, only firms with R&D activities are surveyed for their royalty receipts and payments, whereas other companies might also license in technology, hence leading to an underestimation (OECD, 2005).[11]
- Difficulty of separating disembodied from embodied technology flows: as described in OECD (2005), intangible IP flows often take place in conjunction with, or in addition to, high-technology exports or imports or direct investments. While they ought to be reported as technology payments or receipts, in principal, in reality they are often difficult to identify separately from a firm's other transactions.
- Payment for intangibles via channels other than technology payments: if payment is made through channels other than technology payments, e.g. payments in the form of profits, dividends or overcharging for capital goods, then the payments for intangibles are not recorded appropriately (OECD, 2005).
- Disaggregation: international transfers of IP 'bundles' which generate economic value can often be assessed as individual rights which on their own have lesser total value. The individual rights can be reassembled at their destination. Complementarities between individual IP rights can significantly increase the value of the individual holdings.
- Tacit and non-pecuniary IP flows, and, of course, straight-out infringements of IP rights of third parties, which are unauthorized, result in undercounting of cross-border IP flows.

[11] In some countries, surveys concerning the TBP are combined with R&D surveys (same sample). So the collected data could be underestimated, especially as far as payments are concerned, since firms without any R&D of their own which import technology from abroad are not taken into account.

Non-Valuation Measurement Issues

Individual countries' national statistics could reflect IP activity that could exaggerate the amount of real economic activity occurring in some countries, while understating it in other countries. Four types of issues are described below.

- First, Special Purpose Entities (SPE) are often used for IP or financial holding companies which can increase measured inflows and outflows, as a result of serving as an intermediary or flow-through.[12]
- Second, characterization of cross-border IP flows can affect measured CUIP. While imports and exports of CUIP should net, if there is transformation in the character of the payments, such as from royalties to dividends, on one side of the transaction, then the relative IP position of countries would be distorted.
- Third, profits from IP associated with contract manufacturing undertaken in other countries can increase the exports from the country of the contractor.
- Fourth, combining the provision of services (annual flows) with the acquisition of capital investments (stocks) can provide a misleading picture of a country's IP capabilities.

Valuation and Tax Issues

One of the important IP measurement issues results from multinational enterprises' tax planning and organizational structures. IP often plays a critical role in this planning. Favourable government policies, including lower tax rates for certain tax IP income, so-called 'patent boxes', increase the likelihood of tax-induced investment and potential profit-shifting.

The amount and valuation of cross-border IP flows is affected by countries' tax rules. Illegally evading taxes often results in undercounting of the related economic activity. Differential tax treatment of royalties and dividend payments may result in changing the character of payments to reduce taxes. More important are the distortions from the mispricing of transactions between related parties in different taxing jurisdictions to reduce a MNE's global tax liability.

Lower effective tax rates on IP investments can attract additional real investment in research and development. Low tax rates can encourage

[12] Rassier (2015).

more registrations of patents in countries. Low marginal tax rates can encourage multinational enterprises to shift taxable income and reported financial profit from higher-tax-rate countries to lower-tax-rate countries. These tax effects, particularly base erosion and profit-shifting effects, can distort the measurement of cross-border intellectual property receipts, payments and assets.

Several specific tax factors can distort national statistics from IP. The most well-known, and possibly the most important, factor is transfer mispricing. Transfer mispricing is where non-arm's-length valuations are used for related party transactions. Arm's-length prices between unrelated entities are often not available as comparables for valuation of related party transactions due to the unique nature of many intangibles. This can distort national statistics towards higher valuations in low-tax-rate countries and lower valuations in high-tax-rate countries.[13] The presence of tax-motivated transfer mispricing is found in numerous empirical studies, and is particularly strong among R&D-intensive firms.[14] Beer et al. (2018) report the rate of the percentage change in the transfer price in response to a one-percentage point change in a country's tax rate ranges from 0.5 to 6.0, with intangible transactions at the higher end.

Another tax planning approach is the strategic location of valuable IP in low-tax-rate affiliates. MNEs can conduct their research and development activities in one country, but transfer the ownership of the patent or other IP to a country where the future income streams will be taxed at a low tax rate. Since valuation of transfers of unique IP is difficult due to lack of comparable transactions, especially when the IP is not fully developed, significant future profits can be shifted to low-tax-rate jurisdictions. Several studies report high responsiveness of patent and trademark applications to tax rate differences.[15] Karkinsy and Reidel (2012) find a one-percentage point increase in the corporate tax rate reduces the probability of patent applications in a country by 3.5 per cent.

The responsiveness of the location of intangible income to tax rates is greater when the location of the future income can be separated from the location of the actual value creation or R&D activity. A number of

[13] Guvenen et al. (2017).

[14] Clausing (2003), Christea and Nguyen (2016), Hebous and Johannesen (2015), Liu et al. (2017).

[15] Grubert (2003), Dischinger and Riedel (2011), Karkinsky and Riedel (2012), Griffith et al. (2014), Dudar and Voget (2016).

countries have introduced so-called 'patent box' tax rules providing lower tax rates for certain types of intangible income, compared to their ordinary corporate tax rates. Studies found that patent box tax rates have a greater location effect on reporting of intangible income, but much less effect on actual local R&D activity, when the tax rules don't require an 'economic nexus' linking actual R&D activity with intangible income.[16] The OECD/G20 Base Erosion and Profit-shifting (BEPS) project, and the subsequent BEPS Inclusive Framework, requires the 115 member countries to have an economic nexus requirement on patent box tax regimes to prevent harmful tax competition.[17]

Several other potential distortions can result from the quantity of activity being mismeasured, even if the prices used are market prices. Structuring of business operations, entities and transactions may result in less measured economic activities in certain countries. In some cases, the structuring may facilitate transfer mispricing, but may result from tax minimizing strategies to avoid income tax in a jurisdiction, minimize withholding taxes or simply take advantage of lower tax rates.

The Location of Cross-Border IP Receipts and Tax Rates

The OECD/G20 BEPS project addressed the disconnect between the location of taxable income and the location of value creation. The project instituted standards to prevent harmful tax competition, updated standards for tax treaties and transfer pricing, and instituted new country-by-country reporting of MNEs for improved transfer pricing administration, among other changes.

Information from the World Development Indicators on cross-border Charges for the Use of Intellectual Property (CUIP) has not previously been used to assess profit-shifting from transfer mispricing and the strategic location of IP, which have been estimated to be the main channels of base erosion and profit-shifting. Cross-border IP receipts should be strongly related to prior R&D expenditures.

A simple analysis examines whether corporate tax rates, including tax rates for certain intangible income, affect the relationship of cross-border IP receipts and prior year R&D expenditures across countries. Figure 6.2 shows a high ratio for several countries with low tax rates or tax regimes

[16] Evers et al. (2013) and European Commission (2015).

[17] See www.oecd.org/tax/beps/beps-about.htm.

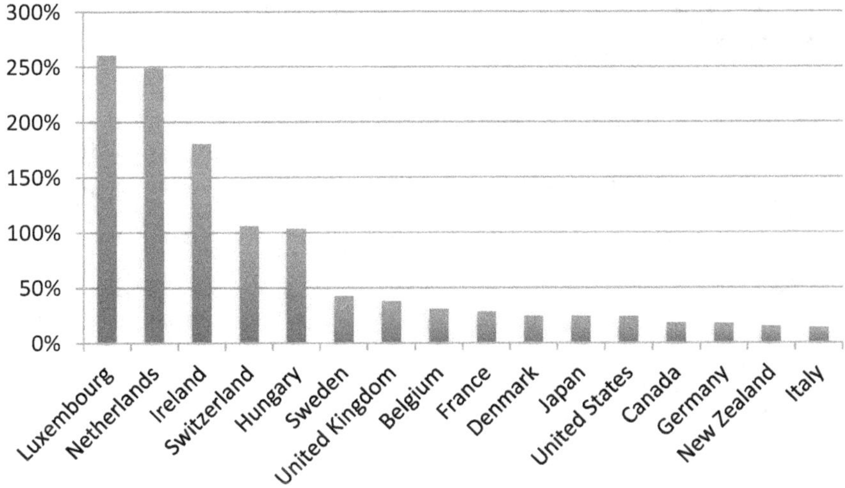

Figure 6.2 Charges for the use of IP as a percentage of lagged R&D, 2016
Source: World Bank World Development Indicators (datacatalog.worldbank.org/dataset/world-development-indicators) and authors' calculations.

providing low effective taxation of IP. Luxembourg, Netherlands and Ireland have ratios exceeding 175 per cent while Japan, Germany and the US have ratios below 25 per cent.

Regression analysis of CUIP, R&D, outbound FDI and tax rate data for 29 OECD countries from 2005 to 2016 finds that a one-percentage point lower tax rate on IP income increases the ratio of IP income to lagged R&D expenditures by 5–7 per cent (Table 6.2). This is consistent with other empirical findings showing greater transfer mispricing in R&D-intensive sectors and the strategic location of IP in countries with low tax rates. It is unlikely that non-tax explanations can fully account for the consistent pattern of higher IP receipts relative to prior year R&D expenditures recorded in countries with lower tax rates. Future research could use this type of data to determine if the OECD/G20 BEPS project and implementation of anti-avoidance rules by countries since 2014 are reducing tax-motivated distortions in the IP flows and national statistics.

The regression finds the general corporate tax rate to be statistically significant, but there is a larger effect when the intangible tax rate is used. The differential between the general and intangible tax rate has a larger effect than the intangible rate by itself. The ratio of countries' outbound foreign direct investment (FDI) to GDP is positive and statistically significant. High relative outbound FDI is expected to be associated with

Table 6.2 *Regression results of excess cross-border receipts to tax rates*

	Dependent variables					
Explanatory variables	**CUIP/ R&D**	**CUIP/ R&D**	**CUIP/ R&D**	**In (CUIP/ R&D)**	**In (CUIP/ R&D)**	**In (CUIP/ GDP)**
Intercept	0.517	0.652	0.588	−1.142	−1.669	−5.963
	0.092	0.063	0.087	0.249	0.344	0.299
General corporate tax rate	−0.012		−0.016		−0.031	−0.066
	0.003		0.003		0.013	0.011
Intangible tax rate		−0.019		−0.049		
		0.002		0.009		
Differential between			0.021		0.065	0.067
general & intangible tax			0.003		0.012	0.01
Outbound FDI % of GDP	0.018	0.014	0.013	0.028	0.025	0.024
	0.001	0.001	0.001	0.006	0.006	0.005
In (R&Dt-1/ GDPt-1)						2.275
						0.118
R2 adj.	0.353	0.429	0.429	0.199	0.208	0.585
N	348	348	348	348	348	348

Source: World Bank World Development Indicators (datacatalog.worldbank.org/dataset/world-development-indicators) and authors' calculations.

greater cross-border activity, but also reflects countries with significant SPEs, which often facilitate tax planning.

A number of alternative specifications were tested. The last column shows when CUIP as a percentage of GDP is an absolute rather than a ratio to lagged R&D expenditures, with a slightly larger tax differential effect. Time fixed effects don't affect the size of the coefficients. The coefficient on the tax rate differential variable declines with country fixed effects, suggesting most of the effect occurs across countries rather than within individual countries.

Magnitudes and Trends in Tax Distortions of Cross-Border Flows in National Statistics

Ideally there would be a comprehensive database of unconsolidated firm-level data over multiple years with which to econometrically estimate the effects of corporate tax rate differentials on profit-shifting. Such a database doesn't exist, so researchers have turned to aggregate national statistics as well as available firm-level databases. The BEPS project requires large MNEs to file country-by-country reports (CbCR) of their economic activity and taxes by individual firms with tax administrations. The OECD will provide aggregated tables of the CbCRs starting in 2019.

The most-used global firm-level database, ORBIS, has millions of financial account records for consolidated and unconsolidated entities globally, both domestic only and multinational enterprises. However, the database is missing companies from many parts of the world, since MNEs headquartered in Europe accounted for 69 per cent of the affiliated firms in the database, and of the affiliates with key financial information 78 per cent were located in Europe. Thus, the coverage of the US, BRIC countries and low-income countries is far from complete. Further, some of the affiliates that had been flagged in parliamentary inquiries for large amounts of profit-shifting were not included in the database or did not include financial information.[18] Further, to estimate the revenue consequences of profit-shifting, only financial data, not tax return, information was available.

Researchers have turned to several types of country-level aggregate data sources to assess the general magnitude of profit-shifting, or have used elasticity estimates from individual firm data matched with country-level aggregate data. Table 6.3 shows seven estimates of the annual global

[18] OECD BEPS Action 11 report (2015).

Table 6.3 *Estimates of global and low-income country fiscal effects from profit-shifting*

Fiscal estimate approach	**Scope**	**Magnitude (billions)**
OECD Aggregate tax rate differential 2015	Global	100–240 (4–10% of CIT)
IMF CIT efficiency 2014	Global	5% of CIT
UNCTAD Offshore investment matrix 2015	Global	200 (8% of CIT)
Clausing excess income in low tax countries 2016	Global	279 (20% of CIT)
Cobham and Jansky tax haven spillover 2018	Global	494 (24% of CIT)
Crivelli, Keen and DeMooij tax haven spillover 2016	Global	647 (32% of CIT)
Torslov, Weir and Zucman high profit-to-wage ratios of foreign-owned firms 2018	Global	10% of CIT
IMF CIT efficiency 2014	Developing countries	13% of CIT
UNCTAD offshore investment matrix 2015	Developing countries	66–120 (7.5–14% of CIT)

revenue loss, and two estimates of annual losses in low-income countries, from base erosion and profit-shifting.

These estimates were done at an aggregated basis so do not separate profit-shifting from transfer mispricing and the strategic location of intangible assets from the strategic location of debt and other profit-shifting tax minimization strategies,[19] although transfer pricing and the strategic location of intangibles have been estimated to be the primary drivers of BEPS.

What is clear is that profit-shifting is occurring as a result of multiple tax minimization strategies of MNEs and does affect the measurement of cross-border IP flows and trade in services, both in quantity and valuation.

[19] The BEPS Action 11 report (2015) provides detailed information about these different analyses and the limitations of such estimates.

Estimates at the global or regional basis have to rely on aggregate country statistics, since individual firm information across countries is incomplete. More detailed analysis using administrative records, including tax return information, could potentially provide estimates with a smaller range and greater reliability, but would still be estimates, since profit-shifting has to be separated from shifts in real economic activity.

To provide a general magnitude of the potential mismeasurement of cross-border IP flows for this chapter, we suggest starting from a global net revenue loss of overall profit-shifting. Table 6.3 shows a wide range from 4 to 32 per cent of global corporate tax revenues lost due to BEPS. Starting from a 10 per cent estimate of roughly USD 250 billion in 2015, the total loss can be shared down to the proportion attributable to intellectual property (see Table 6.4). The revenue loss from IP is then grossed back up to the magnitude of CUIP affected. Based on a number of critical assumptions, the amount of profit-shifting from cross-border CUIP flows in 2015 could conservatively be in the order of USD 120 billion annually. This results in an understatement by at least 35 per cent of the total trade in CUIP. This profit-shifting represents a disconnect between the location of measured IP profits and the location of where the economic activity generating the IP resides.

The starting point of total global net revenue lost from base erosion and profit-shifting of USD 250 billion (line 1 in Table 6.4) assumes that

Table 6.4 *Estimate of global profit-shifting of cross-border CUIP flows*

	USD billions
1. Net global revenue loss from total profit-shifting, 2015	250
2. Exclude losses from tax shifting of interest income/expense (33%)	-83
3. Net global revenue loss from non-interest profit-shifting	168
4. Share of net global revenue loss from CUIP before adjustments (3%)	5
5. Adjustment for higher profit-shifting elasticities for IP (2x)	+5
6. Net global revenue loss from CUIP profit-shifting	10
7. Average tax rate differential, weighted by trade flows	÷8.3%
8. Global net profit-shifting of cross-border CUIP flows	121
9. Average of exports and imports in CUIP, 2015	÷349
10. Net profit-shifting as per cent of trade in CUIP	35%

Source: Calculations by authors, described in text.

profit-shifting has continued to increase since the levels earlier in the decade on which the empirical estimates were based. The estimate assumes (line 2) that roughly one-third of the total global revenue loss is from the strategic location of both internal and external debt, consistent with some firm-specific analyses. This reduces the potential revenue loss from non-interest profit-shifting to USD 168 billion (line 3).

CUIP is only a small share of total international trade. Although the distinction between goods and services is increasingly blurred, roughly 70 per cent of international trade is in goods, not services. Data on the underlying detail of trade in services in the EU28 countries and the United States shows that CUIP, not included elsewhere in national statistics, was only eight per cent of total trade in services. This leaves CUIP as only 3 per cent of total measured trade subject to potential transfer mispricing and other non-interest profit-shifting strategies. Assuming that CUIP has the same potential for profit-shifting as non-CUIP trade, then there would a global annual net revenue loss of USD 5 billion associated with CUIP (line 4), but that is an unreasonable assumption.

Empirical research has found profit-shifting to be significantly higher in intangibles-related activity, as described above. The responsiveness of cross-border IP flows to profit-shifting from corporate tax rate differentials is assumed to be two times the responsiveness of other profit-shifting, an elasticity of at least -2.0. This adjustment increases the annual global revenue loss from cross-border CUIP flows to USD 10 billion (lines 5 and 6).

Any estimate of the potential government revenue lost from profit-shifting depends on the tax rate differential between the countries from which and to which the profit was shifted. The amount of shifted profit will thus be the annual revenue loss from profit-shifting related to IP divided by the appropriate weighted average tax rate differential. Assuming the tax rate differential on IP flows is 8.3 percentage points[20] (line 7) results in an estimate at around USD 120 billion CUIP flows annually (line 8) or about 35 per cent of total trade in CUIP, at 2015 levels (lines 9 and 10). Modifications to any of these assumptions would change the estimate, either higher or lower, but we believe that this is a conservative estimate of the understatement of global CUIP.

It should be noted that while profit-shifting is zero-sum globally, the mismeasurement of global CUIP is unlikely to be zero-sum, and highly

[20] BEPS Action 11 report (2015), p. 206.

likely to be understated. Fetzer et al. (2017) note that CUIP is a major area of asymmetry in trade in services statistics from national statistical agencies,[21] which is apparent in the large discrepancy between total global receipts and payments of CUIP in Table 6.3. Tax minimization by MNEs in related party transactions results in overcharges for imported services to high-tax-rate countries (payments) and undercharges for exported services (receipts), and the reverse for low-tax-rate countries.

Mismeasurement for Individual Countries

Given the current data limitations of measuring tax-induced profit-shifting,[22] attempting to estimate the CUIP mismeasurement for individual countries would not be reliable. However, the direction of the biases is clear, with understatement of net exports by high-tax-rate countries and overstatement of net imports by low-tax-rate countries. Several of the recent estimates of global revenue loss from profit-shifting have also made estimates of overall profit-shifting for individual countries, but the mix of IP and non-IP tax distortions is likely to vary by country.

Using US BEA annual surveys of US-based multinational firms and their affiliated firms abroad, Clausing (2016) estimated – econometrically – profit-shifting from the US to other countries. She found that 82 per cent of the 'excess' income is booked in seven low-tax-rate ('tax haven') countries: Bermuda, Cayman Islands, Ireland, Luxembourg, the Netherlands, Singapore and Switzerland. Extending her analysis to the global profits of Global 2000 firms, she estimated that higher-tax-rate headquarter countries booked USD1.1 trillion of profits in low-tax-rate countries in 2012.

Dowd et al. (2017) report significant profit-shifting into tax haven countries by US multinationals based on tax return data. They estimate that profit-shifting between foreign affiliates is highly non-linear with respect to corporate tax rates with very high elasticities in shifting to tax havens. Guvenen et al. (2017) estimate, based on US MNE data and an assumption that profit is related to sales, that profit-shifting reduces earnings on direct investment abroad of US multinationals by 65 per cent or USD 280 billion, with most coming from tax havens and from R&D-intensive industries.

[21] Fetzer et al. (2017), p. 13.

[22] OECD BEPS Action 11 report (2015).

Main Trends in Cross-Border IP Profit-Shifting

Estimates of the tax losses from profit-shifting have not been made across time; although there are some indications that profit-shifting has been increasing over time. Grubert (2003) examined tax return and other data for US MNEs and found higher levels of profit-shifting over time. Guvenen et al. (2017) also find a significant increase in profit-shifting by US MNEs since 2000.

Clausing (2016) estimated the trend in revenue loss due to income shifting from the United States, showing a rapid rise after 2001 from under USD 20 billion to over USD 110 billion in 2012. Her estimated trend assumes a constant elasticity of profit-shifting to corporate tax differentials, so the trend reflects the doubling of income of foreign affiliates between 2004 and 2012 plus a continuing decline in average foreign effective tax rates, which are the incentive to shift profits out of the US. The variation in corporate tax rates among OECD countries has increased significantly between 2000 and 2017.

An important question is whether significant changes in the international tax environment and national governments' tax policies and administration will reverse what appears to be the prior trend toward more profit-shifting, particularly affecting cross-border IP flows. Tax authorities are focusing on these issues much more closely, as are more academic researchers, which will assist national account statisticians in improving their measurements.

Possible Approaches to Improve Measures of Cross-Border IP Flows

Recent global and national initiatives in the areas of tax policy and tax administration are expected to reduce the amount of tax-induced profit-shifting, and thus will reduce future distortions in the measures of cross-border IP flows. Additional steps by various stakeholders could further improve national statistics of cross-border IP flows.

Potential Actions of National Statisticians

1. ensure implementation of improvements in data on better classification and new IP flow disaggregation
2. further extension of the work on SPEs as part of the OECD's Benchmark Definition of Foreign Direct Investment and IMF's BPM6, plus improvements in the measurement of intangible investments, including capitalization of investments

3. closer cooperation with tax authorities, and qualified academic researchers, on economic activities of MNEs, including potential agreements to secure better information from tax return data, as is currently done in some countries
4. where possible, linking tax return data at the firm level with business financial account data would provide important insights. For example, linked data could be used to better evaluate the effects of tax patent box claims on the effectiveness on R&D and revenue impacts
5. more focus on MNE activity, both inbound and outbound, including consideration of cost-beneficial imputations in satellite accounts. Additional work on identifying appropriate imputation methodologies is needed
6. linking national satellite accounts on the stock of intangible assets with trade data would provide better understanding of the location of creation and uses of IP.

Potential Actions of National Tax Administrations

1. closer cooperation with national statisticians and qualified academic researchers, including potential agreements to share tax return information on MNEs, as appropriate
2. analysis and aggregated publication of future country-by-country reporting data of MNEs
3. analysis and publication of aggregate tax return information from MNEs and domestic only firms, and details on income and expenses from intellectual property.

Potential Actions of National and International Policymakers and Analysts

1. recognize the importance of empirical data on cross-border IP flows and support adequate resources for the collection and analysis of such data
2. increase transparency of tax incentives, particularly for the use of IP transactions by firms, such as declaration of the number of patents for which incentives are claimed
3. increase transparency of IP ownership, which could improve markets for trading of IP and more consistent valuations
4. reduce incentives (both tax and non-tax) for profit-shifting through changes to national rules and as part of international agreements

5. adhere to the BEPS Inclusive Framework minimum standards on harmful tax practices, increased transfer pricing documentation, and revised transfer pricing guidelines
6. support increased revenue mobilization in low-income countries through training and collaborative tax administration initiatives
7. support improved dispute resolution mechanisms to resolve potential double tax situations arising out of multiple countries claiming taxing rights to the same cross-border income with subsequent adjustments to national statistics.

Academics

1. increase focus on profit-shifting in low-income countries, including IP cross-border flows
2. increase analysis of governmental incentives for IP and their potential for distortions of reported cross-border IP flows, including improved measures of embedded IP
3. increase analysis of factors contributing to affiliate profitability. If imputations are needed, what are appropriate estimation methodologies of affiliate profitability?

Conclusions

As described in this chapter, intangible assets play a critical role in how the modern economy operates with global fragmented production and associated trade in intermediate products. Understanding cross-border flows of IP knowledge flows is essential to analysing how modern economies operate. This in turn calls for better metrics of charges for the use of IP, since they are distorted by several factors, particularly MNE tax planning to reduce their global tax liabilities.

Cross-border IP-related transfer mispricing and other tax minimization strategies distort current trade data, including cross-border IP payments, total imports and exports, GDP and productivity of individual countries. The empirical literature on profit-shifting, plus new analysis of CUIP flows, show their sensitivity to tax rates. The general magnitude of the measurement distortions between countries due to tax-induced profit-shifting is conservatively estimated at 35 per cent of total Charges for the Use of Intellectual Property. These distortions have been increasing over time.

Recent global initiatives, such as the OECD/G20 BEPS project and the recommendations suggested in this chapter will hopefully reduce tax-induced profit-shifting and improve global and national measurement of IP. Better national statistics on cross-border IP flows will help empirical-based policymaking.

Bibliography

Arora, Ashish, Fusfuri, A. and Gambardella, A., 'Markets for Technology and their Implications for Corporate Strategy' (2001), *Industrial and Corporate Change* 10, 2: 419–451.

Athreye, S. and Yang, Y., 'Disembodied Knowledge Flows in the World Economy', Background Report to the WIPO 2011 World Intellectual Property Report. Published as WIPO Economic Research Working Papers, No. 3, Geneva: WIPO, 2012.

Beer, Sebastian, de Mooij, Ruud A. and Liu, Li, 'International Corporate Tax Avoidance: A Review of Channels, Magnitudes and Blind Spots', IMF Working Paper No. 18/168, 2018.

Clausing, K. A., 'Tax-Motivated Transfer Pricing and US Intrafirm Trade Prices' (2003), *Journal of Public Economics* 87, 9–10: 2207–2223.

Clausing, K. A., 'The Effect of Profit-Shifting on the Corporate Tax Based in the United States and Beyond' (2016), *National Tax Journal* 69, 4: 905–934.

Cobham, Alex and Jansky, Petr, 'Global distribution of revenue loss from corporate tax avoidance: reestimation and country results' (2018), *Journal of International Development* 30, 2: 206–232.

Cristea, Anca and Nguyen, Daniel, 'Transfer Pricing by Multinational Firms: New Evidence from Foreign Firm Ownerships' (2016), *American Economic Journal: Economic Policy* 8, 3: 170–202.

Crivelli, Ernesto, Keen, Michael and de Mooij, Ruud A., 'Base Erosion, Profit-Shifting, and Developing Countries', Oxford University Centre for Business Taxation Working Paper WP 15/09, 2015.

De Haan, M., Connolly, M., Peltola, R. and Dimova, T., 'Measuring Global Production in the National Accounts and the Balance of Payments', 24–30 August 2014, Paper Prepared for the IARIW 33rd General Conference, Rotterdam, the Netherlands.

Dischinger, M. and Riedel, N., 'Corporate Taxes and the Location of Intangible Assets within Multinational Firms' (2011), *Journal of Public Economics* 95: 691–707.

Dowd, Tim, Landefeld, Paul and Moore, Anne, 'Profit-Shifting of U.S. Multinationals' (2017), *Journal of Public Economics* 148: 1–13.

Dudar, Olena and Voget, Johannes, 'Corporate Taxation and Location of Intangible Assets: Patents vs Trademarks', No. 16-015, ZEW Discussion Papers, ZEW – Center for European Economic Research, 2016.

European Commission, 'Patent Boxes Design, Patents Location and local R&D', IPTS Working Papers on Corporate R&D and Innovation, No. 6/2015, 2015.

Evers, L., Miller, H. and Spengel, C., 'Intellectual Property Box Regimes: Effective Tax Rates and Tax Policy Considerations' (2013), *ZEW Discussion Papers* No. 13-070.

Fetzer, James J., Mataloni, Jr., Raymond J. and Thompson, Sarahelen, 'BEA's Initiative to Expand and Reconcile Trade in Services Statistics: New Detail for Improved Analysis', mimeo, 11 April 2017, available at www.gtap.agecon.purdue.edu/resources/download/8436.pdf.

Griffith, Rachel, Miller, Helen and O'Connell, Martin, 'Ownership of Intellectual Property and Corporate Taxation' (2014), *Journal of Public Economics* 112: 12–23.

Grubert, Harry, 'Intangible Income, Intercompany Transactions, Income Shifting, and the Choice of Location' (2003), *National Tax Journal* 56, 1: 221–242.

Guvenen, Fatih, Mataloni, Jr., Raymond J., Rassier, Dylan G. and Ruhl, Kim J., 'Offshore Profit-shifting and Domestic Productivity Measurement', National Bureau of Economic Research Working Paper No. 23324, 2017.

Hebous, Shafik and Johannesen, Niels, 'At Your Service! The Role of Tax Havens in International Trade with Services', CESifo Working Paper Series No. 5414, CESifo Group Munich, 2015.

IMF, *Balance of Payments and International Investment Position Manual, Sixth Edition (BPM6)*, Washington, DC: International Monetary Fund, 2009.

IMF, Balance of Payments Statistics Yearbook and data files, available at https://databank.worldbank.org/metadataglossary/africa-development-indicators/series/BX.GSR.ROYL.CD, n.d.

IMF, 'Changing Patterns of Global Trade', (Strategy, Policy, and Review Department Paper), 2012, available at www.imf.org/external/pubs/ft/dp/2012/dp1201.pdf.

IMF, 'Spillovers in International Corporate Taxation', IMF Policy paper, Washington, DC: IMF, 2014.

Karkinsky, T. and Riedel, N., 'Corporate Taxation and the Location of Patents within Multinational Firms' (2012), *Journal of International Economics* 88, 1: 176–185.

Liu, Li, Schmidt-Eisenlhor, Tim and Guo, Dongxian, 'International Tax Avoidance and Transfer Mispricing: Evidence from Linked Tax-Trade Statistics in the UK', Oxford Centre for Business Taxation Working Paper No. 17/02, 2017.

Madeuf, B. 'International Technology Transfers and International Technology Payments: Definitions, Measurement and Firms' Behaviour' (1984), *Research Policy* 13, 3: 125–140.

OECD, *Proposed Standard Method of Compiling and Interpreting the Technology Balance of Payments Data (TBP Manual)*, Paris: OECD Publishing, 1990.

OECD, *Transfer Pricing Guidelines for Multinational Enterprises and Tax Administrations, Organisation For Economic Co-operation And Development*, Paris: OECD Publishing, 1995.

OECD, *Measuring Globalisation: OECD Handbook on Economic Globalisation Indicators 2005*, Paris: OECD Publishing, 2005.

OECD, *Handbook on Deriving Capital Measures of Intellectual Property Products*, Paris: OECD Publishing, 2014.

OECD, *Measuring and Monitoring BEPS, Action 11 – 2015 Final Report*, OECD/G20 Base Erosion and Profit-shifting Project, Paris: OECD Publishing, 2015, available at http://dx.doi.org/10.1787/9789264241343-en.

Rassier, Dylan G., 'Characteristics of Special Purpose Entities in Measures of U.S. Direct Investment Abroad', 2015, available at www.bea.gov/papers/pdf/characteristics-of-special-purpose-entities-in-measures-of-us-direct-investment-abroad.pdf.

Torslov, Thomas, Wier, Ludvig and Zucman, Gabriel, 'The Missing Profits of Nations', NBER Working Paper No. W24701, 2018.

United Nations Economic Commission for Europe (UNECE), *Guide to Measuring Global Production*, Geneva: United Nations Economic Commission for Europe (in particular, Chapter 7 on International transactions in intellectual property products), 2015, available at www.unece.org/fileadmin/DAM/stats/publications/2015/Guide_to_Measuring_Global_Production__2015_.pdf.

UN, IMF, OECD, Eurostat, UNCTAD, UNWTO and WTO, *Manual on Statistics of International Trade in Services 2010 (MSITS2010)*, Geneva, Luxembourg, Madrid, New York, Paris and Washington, DC: United Nations, IMF, OECD, Statistical Office of the European Union, United Nations Conference on Trade and Development, World Tourism Organization and WTO, 2011.

UNCTAD, *World Investment Report 2015: Reforming international investment governance*, UN Reference: UNCTAD/WIR/2015, 2015b.

WIPO, 'The Changing Nature of Innovation and Intellectual Property, Chapter 1', in *World IP Report 2011*, Geneva: WIPO Economics and Statistics Division, 2011, pp. 23–72.

WIPO, *World Intellectual Property Report 2017: Intangible Capital in Global Value Chains*. Geneva: World Intellectual Property Organization, 2017.

7

Global Ebbs and Flows of Patent Knowledge

ANDREW W. TORRANCE, JEVIN D. WEST
AND LISA C. FRIEDMAN

Abstract

We use patent citation data to map the flows of technical knowledge, and in particular to test three hypotheses. First, that the net flow of technical knowledge tends to be from more developed to less developed countries. Second, that the trajectory of climate change-mitigation knowledge flow increased (especially from developed to developing countries) after the 1997 Kyoto Protocol and the 2015 Paris Agreement on climate change. Third, that the trajectory of pharmaceutical knowledge flow increased after the conclusion of the TRIPS Agreement. We find that massive amounts of technical information are exchanged, among countries around the world, in sometimes surprising patterns. Developed country patents supply a disproportionate amount of patent citations compared to patents from developing countries, and the importance of technical knowledge thereby transferred is disproportionately high. However, we observe some evidence that this imbalance in knowledge flow may be beginning to reverse itself, as developing country patents have become increasingly cited by those in developed countries, and the importance of developing world patents has grown. We did not discern evidence that the Kyoto Protocol has spurred knowledge flow in climate-mitigation technology, but found some preliminary evidence consistent with an effect by the Paris Agreement. We did find evidence consistent with the possibility that the TRIPS Agreement may have spurred pharmaceutical (and more general) knowledge flow.

Introduction

Patents and patent applications contain rich sources of scientific and technical information. By their very name, patents – derived from a Latin word meaning 'open' – make their information freely available to the public. They describe new devices, machines, systems, molecules and even living organisms, as well as methods for making and using them. Transfer of technical knowledge among people, firms, institutions and governments has long relied upon the information patent documents (hereafter simply 'patents') disclose. One may take advantage of a feature of patent law to track the flow of technical ideas among patents by constructing a network from the citations that patents make to and from each other. The result is a patent citation network. The worldwide patent citation network is immense, with almost half a billion citations among more than 100 million patents. In this chapter, we use the worldwide patent citation network to infer the flow of technical information among countries.

Technical knowledge flows among inventors, organizations (e.g. firms, research institutes, universities) and countries. Patent citation data can be used to estimate these flows. Here we focus on knowledge flow among countries or other jurisdictions, calculating pairwise citations – both raw and importance-weighted – to and from them. This method offers new insights into global patterns of technical knowledge flow.

Our study suggests that the use of big patent data and hierarchical mapping network approaches may offer new, and potentially useful, insights into the flow of technical knowledge among countries and other patent jurisdictions, within specific technologies, and over defined periods of time.

Scientific and technical publications, and the citations among them, may be envisioned as forming a vast network. In this network, publications are 'nodes', while citations among nodes are 'links'. One source of such publications is patents and patent applications. The architecture of such a patent network represents millions of individual choices inventors, and patent agents or attorneys who represent them, have made about how to situate inventors' new ideas within the wider context of existing knowledge. If the computationally-challenging task of constructing a patent citation network is done successfully, the resulting lattice of interlinked inventions may hold within its structure immense amounts of valuable information concerning the evolution of, and relationships between, technologies.

There are myriad approaches to building a patent citation network. We use eigenvector centrality and hierarchical graphical approaches to construct comprehensive citation networks. This results in several salutary features useful for analysing not only network structure at defined moments in time but also changes in network structure over time. The network contains millions of 'natural technology clusters' grouped together by their citations, with these natural technology clusters running the gamut of granularity from the most specific technology areas to the most inclusive areas. In part by virtue of the nested organization of its natural technology clusters, the structure of the patent citation network holds a wealth of information about where knowledge is generated, where it flows and how patterns have already, and likely shall in the future, change.

In addition to elucidating general patterns of technical knowledge flow, we also test three specific hypotheses designed to shed light on flow of technological information among countries. The first is general, and is inspired by a growing interest in technology transfer between the developed and developing world:

1. The net flow of technical knowledge tends to be from more developed to less developed countries.

The other two hypotheses investigate two particular fields of technology – climate-change mitigation technology (with wind power technology as a proxy) and pharmaceutical technology – which several prominent international agreements (e.g. the 1995 World Trade Organization ('WTO')[1] Agreement on Trade-Related Aspects of Intellectual Property Rights ('TRIPS'))[2] (which, *inter alia*, mandated protection for pharmaceutical technology), and the Framework Convention on Climate Change's Kyoto Protocol and Paris Agreement (dealing, *inter alia*, with climate-change mitigation technology) were expected by many to encourage and increase technical knowledge transfer, especially from developed countries to developing countries. These more specific hypotheses are:

2. The trajectory of climate-change mitigation knowledge flow increased (especially from developed to developing countries) after the 1997 Kyoto Protocol[3] and the 2015 Paris Agreement[4] on climate change; and
3. The trajectory of pharmaceutical knowledge flow increased after the conclusion of the TRIPS Agreement.

We find that massive amounts of technical information are exchanged, among countries around the world, in sometimes surprising patterns.

[1] The WTO is an international organization dedicated to the promotion and administration of trade among countries around the world. (See www.wto.org/index.htm.)

[2] Administered by the WTO, the TRIPS is a multilateral trade agreement that attempts to standardize intellectual property rights among WTO members. (See www.wto.org/english/tratop_e/trips_e/trips_e.htm.)

[3] The Kyoto Protocol is a 1997 treaty intended to implement the 1992 United National Framework Convention on Climate Change. (See https://unfccc.int/process-and-meetings/the-kyoto-protocol/what-is-the-kyoto-protocol/what-is-the-kyoto-protocol.)

[4] The Paris Convention is a 2015 treaty intended to implement the 1992 United National Framework Convention on Climate Change. (See https://unfccc.int/process-and-meetings/the-paris-agreement/the-paris-agreement.)

Background

Overview

In this study, we focus on an important subset of the worldwide network of scientific and technical knowledge composed of granted patents and patent applications (collectively referred to as 'patents' unless otherwise noted). The eigenvector centrality approach we use to construct and analyse the worldwide patent citation network results in estimates for each patent of its 'importance' within the context of the network. The dataset on which we primarily rely here is the 'PATSTAT' database compiled, annotated and maintained by the European Patent Office ('EPO').[5] The importance approach can be used to study not only the worldwide patent system, but also national and regional patent systems. It also allows comparisons between jurisdictions of choice (e.g. the United Kingdom and Japan, the United States and the European Patent system[6]).

Previous Research

We published the first patent citation network study to use the importance approach in 2017.[7] Entitled *All Patents Great and Small: A Big Data Network Approach to Valuation* (2017) this project focused on the United States ('US') patent system. Facilitated by availability of high-quality, weekly-updated patent data for bulk downloading, this research project offered confirmation that the eigenvector centrality approach works well for patent citation networks. However, the US patent system is only a subset of the worldwide patent system. For this chapter, we constructed a global patent citation network that incorporates not only US patents, but all patents from other countries and jurisdictions located within the PATSTAT database.

5 In the past, we have also used bulk patent data provided by the United States Patent and Trademark Office ('USPTO'). See Andrew W. Torrance and Jevin D. West, 'All Patents Great and Small: A Big Data Network Approach to Valuation', 20 *Virginia Journal of Law & Technology* 466 (2017).

6 Here 'European Patent system' refers to the regional patenting authority governed by the European Patent Convention (EPC).

7 See Andrew W. Torrance and Jevin D. West, 'All Patents Great and Small: A Big Data Network Approach to Valuation', 20 *Virginia Journal of Law & Technology* 466 (2017).

International Climate Agreements

The UN Framework Convention on Climate Change ('UNFCCC') has given rise to two major implementing agreements: the Kyoto Protocol (1997) and the Paris Agreement (2015). The time period covered by our data allows some consideration of effects these treaties may have had in knowledge transfer in climate-mitigation technology, represented here by wind power technology.

The main technology transfer provision in the Kyoto Protocol is found in Article 10(c), which requires countries to 'promote, facilitate and finance, as appropriate, the transfer of, or access to, environmentally sound technologies, know-how, practices and processes pertinent to climate change, in particular to developing countries, including the formulation of policies and programmes for the effective transfer of environmentally sound technologies that are publicly owned or in the public domain'.[8] Notably, Article 10(c) also encourages countries to develop programmes that 'create an enabling environment' for the private sector to transfer environmentally sound technologies to developing countries.[9] This provision, however, does not require participation by the private sector. The Kyoto Protocol also imposes a duty on the developed countries to the Agreement to establish policies for technology transfer that minimize adverse economic, social and environmental impacts on developing countries.[10]

The Kyoto Protocol as a whole has received criticism for not effectively reducing greenhouse gas emissions, even by the former executive secretary of the UN Climate Secretariat, Yvo de Boer.[11] Despite this criticism, de Boer has suggested that the Kyoto Protocol has achieved success by laying the foundation for technology transfer of environmentally sound technologies.[12] About a third of all projects related to the Clean Development Mechanism[13] involve some sort of technology

[8] Kyoto Protocol to the United Nations Framework Convention on Climate Change Article 10(c), 11 December 1997, UN Doc FCCC/CP/1997/7/Add.1, 37 ILM 22 (1998) (hereinafter Kyoto Protocol).

[9] *Id.*

[10] Kyoto Protocol, *supra* n. 8, Article 4, ¶ 14.

[11] David Adam, 'Analysis: Has the Kyoto Protocol Worked?', *The Guardian* (7 December 2008, 7:01 PM EST), available at www.theguardian.com/environment/2008/dec/08/kyoto-poznan-environment-emissions-carbon ('Has Kyoto worked? "In terms of emission reductions achieved, the answer would be no", De Boer said.').

[12] *Id.*

[13] Kyoto Protocol, *supra* n. 8, Article 12.

transfer from developed to developing countries.[14] Moreover, projects that involved some form of technology transfer under the Kyoto Protocol have accounted for 59 per cent of estimated annual emissions reductions, suggesting that projects involving technology transfer may indeed have larger effects than those projects lacking technology transfer.[15] The rate of technology transfer does differ among types of projects; projects related to energy distribution, hydro, cement, fugitive emissions, transport and energy efficiency have low rates of technology transfer, ranging from 0 to 27 per cent, while projects involving tidal power, CO_2 capture, agriculture, HFCs and energy-efficient households have much higher technology transfer rates, ranging from 56 to 100 per cent.[16] The types of technology transfer (transfer of equipment, knowledge, or both) also differ between project types.[17]

In 2015, most of the world's countries agreed to the Paris Agreement, an implementation treaty intended to update the Kyoto Protocol. Article 10 of the Paris Agreement sets out goals related to technology transfer by using the 'Technology Mechanism' created by the UNFCCC.[18] The Paris Agreement reinforces the importance of technology transfer in the effort to reduce greenhouse gas emissions and combat climate change,[19] requires parties to the agreement to 'strengthen cooperative action on technology development and transfer',[20] and requires parties to provide financial support for the facilitation of access to technology to developing countries.[21] In Article 11, the Agreement emphasizes the use of technology transfer to assist developing countries in capacity building.[22] The Agreement also contains accountability mechanisms wherein developing countries must report information related to the technology received through technology transfer

[14] Zhong Fa Ma, 'The Effectiveness of Kyoto Protocol and the Legal Institution for International Technology Transfer', 37 *Journal of Technology Transfer* 75, 83 (2010).

[15] Stephen Seres, *Analysis of Technology Transfer in CDM Projects* 7 (2008), available at http://cdm.unfccc.int/Reference/Reports/TTreport/TTrep08.pdf.

[16] *Id.* at 24.

[17] *Id.* at 13.

[18] UN Framework Convention on Climate Change, Adoption of the Paris Agreement, Article 10, 12 December 2016, UN Doc. FCCC/CP/2015/10/Add.1, available at http://unfccc.int/files/home/application/pdf/paris_agreement.pdf. (hereinafter Paris Agreement).

[19] *Id.* at Article 10 ¶ 1.

[20] *Id.* at Article 10 ¶ 2.

[21] *Id.* at Article 10 ¶ 5.

[22] *Id.* at Article 11 ¶ 1.

and developed countries must report information related to technology they have transferred to developing countries.[23]

Methods

In this chapter, we provide only a brief summary of the methods by which we construct and analyse the worldwide patent citation network we use to estimate technical knowledge flow. A detailed explanation of these methods is available in our 2017 article, *All Patents Great and Small: A Big Data Network Approach to Valuation.*[24]

Network Analysis

Patents often cite other patent documents. Over time these citations accumulate.[25] A patent citation network spanning all patent systems in the world is a valuable tool for studying worldwide patterns of scientific information flow dynamics, including those elucidating technological innovation, patenting effort, and national and international patent law regimes. Major technical barriers have hampered efforts to calculate a worldwide patent citation network. We present a powerful new approach to patent citation network calculation based on big data and network analytics. In our 2017 article, *All Patents Great and Small: A Big Data Network Approach to Valuation*, we provided several lines of evidence demonstrating the accuracy and explanatory power of our approach as applied to the US patent corpus.[26] For this chapter, we applied these methods to the construction of a worldwide patent citation network, encompassing the patent systems of all major countries and jurisdictions, based on the fall 2018 PATSTAT bibliographic data that include more than 112,331,073 million patent documents connected by 265,303,432 patent citations. We provide a brief description of the structure of this network, and then highlight novel insights it provides about the worldwide evolution of technological fields and comparative differences in

[23] *Id.* at Article 13 ¶¶ 9, 10.

[24] See Andrew W. Torrance and Jevin D. West, 'All Patents Great and Small: A Big Data Network Approach to Valuation', 20 *Victoria Journal of Law & Technology* 466 (2017).

[25] Because citations accumulate over time, all other factors being equal, older patents tend to have attracted more citations than more recent ones. A consequence of this pattern of accumulation over time is that metrics based on citations tend to be biased downwards as time approaches the present.

[26] See Andrew W. Torrance and Jevin D. West, 'All Patents Great and Small: A Big Data Network Approach to Valuation', 20 *Victoria Journal of Law & Technology* 466 (2017).

patenting behaviour among countries and regions. In addition, we present an overview of original network analytics approaches to analysing large datasets. These offer promising new, powerful and efficient approaches for constructing and analysing complex networks like the worldwide patent citation network.

Patent Citations

Citations to and from patents tend to be indicators of both private value to their owners and social value to society more generally.[27] Patent citations have been widely used in patent valuation analysis.[28] They can be informative about firm value,[29] useful in assisting universities to predict which of the patents they own will most likely be licensed[30] and indicative of whether a patent application will be granted.[31] Patent citations have been found to correlate well with likelihood of litigation[32] and patent value.[33] Beyond economic value alone, forward citations can provide good estimates of the technological importance of inventions disclosed in patents.[34]

27 Manuel Trajtenberg, 'A Penny for Your Quotes: Patent Citation and the Value of Innovations', 21 *Rand Journal of Economics* 172 (1990).

28 Bronwyn H. Hall, Adam B. Jaffe and Manuel Trajtenberg, *Market Value and Patent Citations: A First Look* (National Bureau of Economic Research, Working Paper No. 7741, 2000); Dietmar Harhoff, Katrin Cremers, Francis Nairn, Frederic M. Scherer and Katrin Vopel, 'Citation Frequency and the Value of Patented Inventions', 81 *Review of Economics and Statistics* 511, 511 (1999); Jean O. Lanjouw and Mark Schankerman, 'Characteristics of Patent Litigation: A Window on Competition', 32 *Rand Journal of Economics* 129 (2001).

29 Bronwyn H. Hall, Adam Jaffe & Manuel Trajtenberg, 'Market Value and Patent Citations', 36 *Rand Journal of Economics* 16 (2005).

30 Bhaven N. Sampat and Arvids A. Ziedonis, 'Patent Citations and the Economic Value of Patents', in H. F. Moed, W. Glänzel and U. Schmoch (eds), *Handbook of Quantitative Science and Technology Research*, p. 277.

31 Alfons Palangkaraya, Elizabeth Webster & Paul H. Jensen, 'Misclassification Between Patent Offices: Evidence From a Matched Sample of Patent Applications', 93 *Rev. Econ. & Stat.* 1063 (2011).

32 Jean O. Lanjouw and Mark Schankerman (2003) 'Enforcing Patent Rights: An Empirical Study', in *Empirical Economics of Innovation and Patenting*, 2003-03-14–2003-03-15, p. 14, available at http://eprints.lse.ac.uk/58574/ ('The probability of litigation increases with ... forward citations per claim ... the likelihood of a suit falls with the number of backward citations per claim.')

33 John R. Allison, Mark A. Lemley, Kimberly A. Morre and R. Derek Trunkey, 'Valuable Patents', 92 *The Georgetown Law Journal* 435, 451 (2004).

34 Mark P. Carpenter, Francis Narin and Patricia Woolf, 'Citation Rates to Technologically Important Patents', 3 *World Patent Information* 160 (1991); Francis Narin, Elliot Noma and Ross Perry, 'Patents as Indicators of Corporate Technological Strength', 16 *Res. Pol'y*

One limitation of our approach is that it is very difficult to parse inventions originating in a country from those originating elsewhere. To illustrate, imagine all of the patent applications were filed in Nigeria. Some of these patent applications claim technologies invented by locals; however, other Nigerian patent applications claim inventions that arose in other countries, but were allowed to be filed as Nigerian patent applications under the Paris Convention or the Patent Cooperation Treaty. Both of these categories of patents count as Nigerian for the purposes of our analyses. In the future, more granular data may allow these two types of patents to be distinguished easily, at which time more detailed analysis will be possible.

There may also be bias in the number of developing world patent citations due to institutional limitations in the developing world. It requires considerable capacity, both technological and human capital, to collect and search *prior art* from other countries, leading, perhaps, to more patent citations in patents filed in the developed world than in the developing world. Our methods minimize this bias by focusing more on patent importance than on raw patent citations; this reduces the influence of large numbers of patent citations and of citations computed on a per patent basis because quality of citation tends to trump quantity of citation.

An approach that could be used in the future would be to increase the size of the analytical unit used to construct patent citations networks to patent families rather than relying on individual patents and patent applications. Such an approach might help to dispel the illusion that, when large US, European and Japanese companies, such as those in the pharmaceutical industry, increasingly choose to file foreign versions of their patents in developing world countries (e.g. China, India, Brazil), this necessarily indicates increases in technological advancement there.

An 'Importance' Approach

The most powerful way currently known to weight citations accurately is to construct a patent citation network in which the position of each patent helps determine its value. To analyse our patent network, we use

143 (1987); Michael B. Albert, D. Avery, Francis Narin and Paul R. McAllister, 'Direct Validation of Citation Counts as Indicators of Industrially Important Patents', 20 *Res. Pol'y* 251 (1991).

the Eigenfactor metrics[35], which have become the gold standard in ranking scholarly journals.[36] The algorithm captures a random walker following hyperlinks (links) from webpage (nodes) to webpage. The Eigenfactor algorithm captures a random process on scholarly citation networks.[37] For patent citation networks, we use a modified version of the Eigenfactor algorithm called the article-level Eigenfactor (ALEF).[38] To calculate the ALEF scores, we use methods described by West and Vilhena (2014)[39] and West et al. (2016)[40] By sewing together the citations from the countries represented in PATSTAT, we offer a better understanding of how patents organize by country and technology areas at very fine, subcommunity scales. This complements the human-curated, patent classification systems and provides a different lens for how to evaluate patent influence and technology trends.

Patent Networks and Knowledge Flow

This particular focus of this study involves a comprehensive analysis of the flow of technical knowledge within the worldwide patent system.[41] It does so using two metrics. The first of these is based upon raw citations,

[35] Jevin D. West, Theodore C. Bergstrom and Carl T. Bergstrom, 'The Eigenfactor Metrics: A Network Approach to Assessing Scholarly Journals', 71 *College & Research Libraries* 236 (2010).

[36] They are now included in Thomson-Reuters' Journal Citation Reports (JCR). The underlying algorithm is similar to the PageRank algorithm developed by the founders of Google, Larry Page and Sergey Brin. Lawrence Page, Sergey Brin, Rajeev Motwani and Terry Winograd, 'The PageRank Citation Ranking: Bringing Order to the Web, Stanford InfoLab', 1999, available at http://ilpubs.stanford.edu:8090/422/1/1999-66.pdf.

[37] The algorithm was placed first in North America and second worldwide in Microsoft Research's WSDM Cup Challenge, a 2015 contest whose goal was to statically rank tens of millions of articles from the scholarly literature. The contest provided additional evidence of the advantages of using the network rather than just counting raw citations. Microsoft Research, WSDM Cup Challenge, 2015, available at www.microsoft.com/en-us/research/publication/wsdm-cup-2016-entity-ranking-challenge/.

[38] Jevin D. West, Ian Wesley Smith and Carl T. Bergstrom, 'A Recommendation System Based on Hierarchical Clustering of an Article-Level Citation Network', 2 *IEEE Transactions on Big Data* 113 (2016).

[39] Jevin D. West and Daril A. Vilhena, 'A Network Approach to Scholarly Evaluation', in Blaise Cronin and Cassidy R. Sugimoto (eds), *Bibliometrics & Beyond: Metrics-Based Evaluation*, 2014, pp. 151–166.

[40] See US Patent No. 9,589,051, at [0032] (filed 1 February 2013).

[41] We do not purport to demonstrate herein that the technical information disclosed in patent documents is meaningful. Instead, we simply show the flows of such information via citations, both raw and weighted.

which is the number of times one patent cites a different patent. The second is importance, which reflects not simply the number of citations, but the relative influence of each citation. For every available national (e.g. New Zealand, Italy, Brazil), regional (e.g. the European Patent Convention), and international (e.g. Patent Cooperation Treaty) patent jurisdiction, we enumerated the citations to and citations from all national and jurisdictional pairs as well as the importance of these citations.

Data

Based on the United Nations classification[42], we divided countries and jurisdictions into two categories: developed and developing. In addition, we grouped patents originating under the jurisdiction of the European Patent Convention ('EPC') as developed. Turkey and Serbia are both usually classified as developing countries despite being members of the EPC; however, because their contributions to the EPC are still quite minor, their inclusion is unlikely to affect the results.

It is difficult to categorize climate-change mitigation technology because it encompasses a diverse array of more internally-consistent technological fields, such as solar power, carbon sequestration, energy efficiency, hydro-electric power, tidal power, power system design, high-efficiency engines, power management software and wind power. Wind power technology is the largest and most coherent of these fields. Consequently, we used wind power technology, a cluster of about 33,186 patents, as a proxy to represent all climate-change mitigation technologies.[43]

It is comparatively easier to classify pharmaceutical technology because of its relatively high internal coherence as a technological field. We identified a large natural cluster having 4,526,982 patents that includes a large majority of patents covering pharmaceutical technologies.[44]

Caveat Regarding Recent Patent Data

For all figures showing filing, citation and importance trends for pharmaceuticals or climate-mitigation technologies, the decay in values that occurs towards the right-hand side of the graphs is a data artefact. Because most

[42] See Table A, available at www.un.org/en/development/desa/policy/wesp/wesp_current/2014wesp_country_classification.pdf.

[43] These patents are identified in our network as Cluster 1: 168.

[44] These patents are identified in our network as Cluster 3.

patents experience a lag in publication, recent data tends to underestimate total numbers. Both citations and importance accumulate over time, meaning that, as measurements of these approach the present day, they will tend to decrease in magnitude. Thus, we tend to avoid making conclusions about these data for periods of time close to the present day.

Results

We derive estimates of technical knowledge flow from the structure and dynamics of the worldwide citation network. The information disclosed in patents certainly does not represent the sum total of technical knowledge. Important alternative information sources include the scientific literature, webpages and data available on the Internet, and knowledge residing within the heads of scientists and engineers. Nevertheless, patents are indeed one of the major sources of technical knowledge. We examine worldwide technical knowledge flow, but also flow between developed and developing countries, in general, and for the specific technological fields of wind power and pharmaceuticals. For the latter, we estimate flow of technical knowledge of all kinds, as well as flows in the specific technological fields of wind power (as a proxy for climate-change mitigation technologies) and pharmaceuticals and biotechnology. To illustrate our methods and data, we begin with the pairwise technical knowledge flow between the US and China.

An Illustrative Example: China

The pattern of citations between China and the US provides an illustration of our results based on both raw citations and citations weighted for importance. Consider the citation patterns between Chinese and US patent documents. Chinese patent documents have cited US patents or patent applications on 2,209,396 occasions, while US patent documents have cited Chinese documents only 592,154 times. Thus, Chinese patent documents cite US patent documents 3.73 times more often than US patent documents cite Chinese patent documents.

The second metric is importance. Chinese patents have cited US patents that have a mean importance of 6.91. By comparison, US patents have cited Chinese patents that have a mean importance of 1.46. This yields an importance ratio of about 4.73:1 in favour of US patents. More broadly, the mean importance of all US-cited patents is 21.63 compared to a mean importance of 0.84 for all cited Chinese patents. This yields an importance of ratio of about 25.75:1, again in favor of US patents.

One interpretation of these results is that US technical knowledge embodied within patents has flowed much more robustly towards, rather than from, China. Furthermore, measurements of knowledge flow derived from raw patent citations substantially underestimate the magnitude of this knowledge flow.

Trends in Patent Numbers

The rise in patents and patent applications over the past half century has been prodigious (Figure 7.1). Since 1970, they have increased from just under 500,000 to a high point of more than 5,500,000 in 2017. During the same time period, the overall increase in US patent numbers has been from about 65,000 to over 725,000. Both US and worldwide patent numbers have swelled 11-fold in this interval.

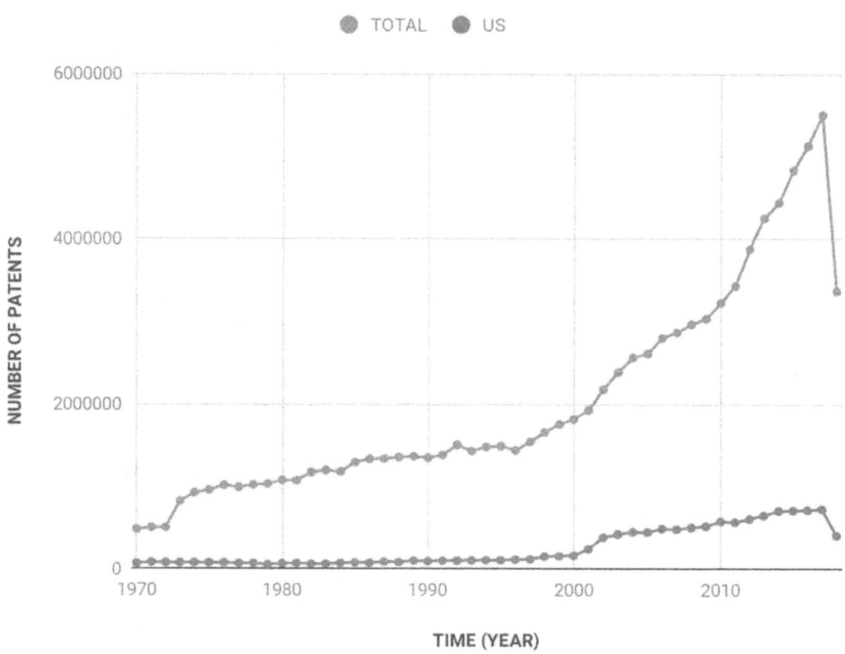

Figure 7.1 Trends in patent numbers
Source: Authors' analysis.

Numbers of both worldwide and US patents declined substantially after 2017. This fall is almost certainly an artefact caused by incomplete data. The fall 2018 PATSTAT dataset analysed for this chapter was released in October 2018, so it lacks patent data for at least the final quarter of 2018. In addition, there are delays by many national and international patent authorities in providing the most recent patent data to the European Patent Office for incorporation into PATSTAT. Accurate patent numbers for 2018 will become clearer with the passage of time. In the meantime, we suggest that these most recent numbers be regarded with scepticism.

Trends in Interjurisdictional Patent Citations

Over the 50-year period starting in 1970, there are noticeable patterns in the proportion of patent citations made to patents within the same jurisdiction ('intrajurisdictional' citation) and those made to patents in other jurisdictions ('interjurisdictional' citation) (Figure 7.2). This pattern provides a window on the flows of technical knowledge among countries. It also sets a baseline for comparing trends in more specific technological fields, like wind power and pharmaceuticals. Figure 7.2 depicts an initial interjurisdictional citation rate of about 13 per cent in 1970. This modest level remained within a narrow range until it

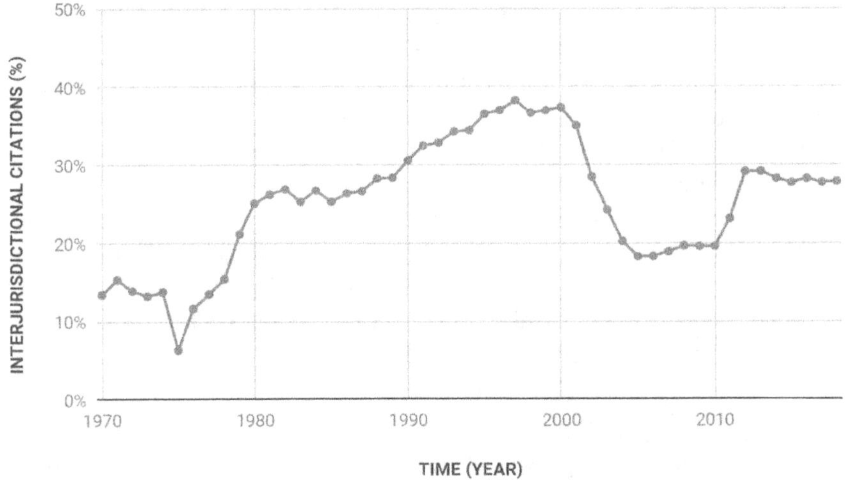

Figure 7.2 Rates of interjurisdictional citation
Source: Authors' analysis.

plummeted to about 6 per cent in 1975, after which it grew rapidly, more than quadrupling to about 27 per cent in 1982. After several years of relative stability, the rate began rising again in 2008, growing to about 38 per cent in 1997, fluctuating little until 2001, when it began to plummet, reaching about 18 per cent in 2005. It changed little until 2010, after which it rose sharply to about 29 per cent in 2012, moving little through 2018.

Three broad, but contrasting, changes in rates of knowledge flow emerge from Figure 7.2. The first is the remarkable decades-long increase in rates of interjurisdictional citation from 1975 to 1997, during which technical knowledge flow increased more than six-fold. This was reversed by a precipitous fall of more than 50 per cent between 2000 and 2005. Finally, interjurisdictional citations rose suddenly by about 45 per cent between 2010 to 2012. To generalize, technical knowledge flow was relatively stable, grew prodigiously, stabilized, fell rapidly, stabilized, grew rapidly again and then stabilized again.

Knowledge Flow between the Developing and Developed World

A major focus of this chapter is technical knowledge flow between developed and developing countries. As noted in the above section on methodology,[45] we have employed a United Nations taxonomy that divides countries around the world into the categories of developed and developing[46]. In our analysis, there are 38 developed countries and jurisdictions (including the EPC area) and 198 developing countries.

A vital principle for interpreting the patent citation data presented below is that, as one approaches the current day (2019 at the time of writing), deficiencies in data collected from patent offices around the world become more serious. Some patent offices report their data with alacrity, but others report theirs at a more sluggish pace.[47] Consequently, citation data decrease in completeness as one approaches the present. Another interpretive principle concerns patent citation and importance data. As described in the above subsection on network analysis,[48] citations naturally accumulate with the passage of time. Thus, a relative

[45] P. 224 *supra*.

[46] See Table A, available at www.un.org/en/development/desa/policy/wesp/wesp_current/2014wesp_country_classification.pdf.

[47] Personal communications with EPO staff responsible for PATSTAT.

[48] P. 224 *supra*.

dearth of citations by more recent patents is to be expected. Because citations among patents in the worldwide patent citation network are the basis for calculating importance, both citation numbers and importance are impacted by recency; confidence in the accuracy of both increases as time before the present day increases.

Raw Citations

The number of raw patent citations provides a straightforward metric of knowledge flow. From 1985 to 2005, there were very few patent citations between developed world patents and developing world patents (Figure 7.3). Nevertheless, until 2006, the number of citations from developed to developing countries was almost twice as large as in the other direction. After 2005, rates of citations in both directions rose markedly, but much more rapidly for citations from developing to developed country patents. In addition, the polarity of citations reversed in 2006, with many more citations thereafter from developing to developed country patents. Also depicted in Figure 7.3 are numbers of citations from US to developing world patents and from China to

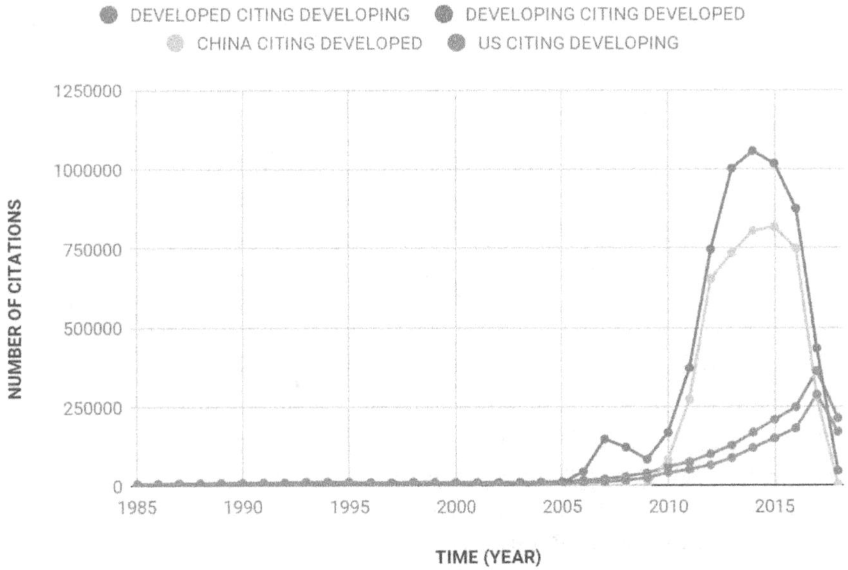

Figure 7.3 Patent citations between developed and developing countries
Source: Authors' analysis.

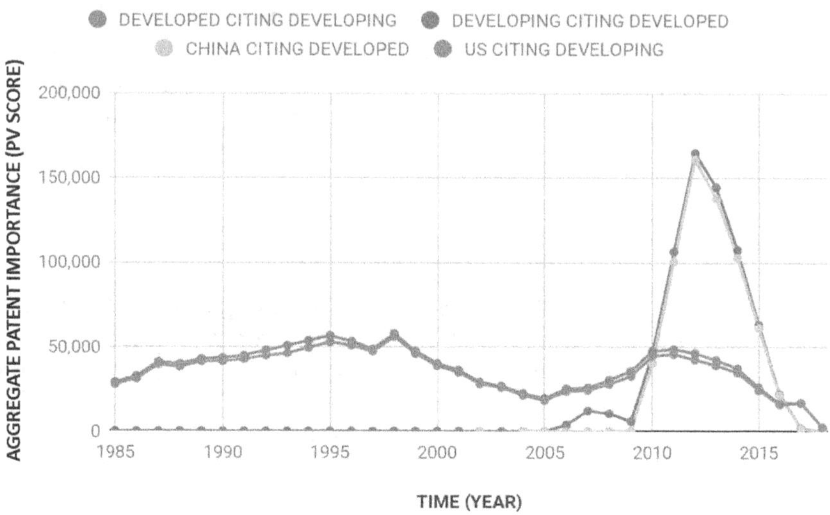

Figure 7.4 Importance of citing patents between developed and developing countries
Source: Authors' analysis.

developed world patents. Since 2011, China has accounted for the majority of citations from developing to developed world patents, while the US accounted for the majority of citations from developed to developing world patents since at least 1985.

Citations Weighted by Importance

As discussed in the above section on methodology,[49] patent citations weighted by their importance in the worldwide patent citation network may provide a more accurate metric for technical knowledge flow than do raw patent citations. Figure 7.4 shows the aggregate importance of developed country patents citing developing country patents, and vice versa. In addition, it depicts US patents citing patents in the developing world and Chinese patents citing patents in the developed world. From 1985 to 2005, the total importance of developed world patents remained far greater than those in the developing world, with the former ranging from 19,545 to 57,701, and the latter from 0 to 21. Beginning in 2006, the importance of developing country patents became substantially greater,

[49] P. 224 *supra*.

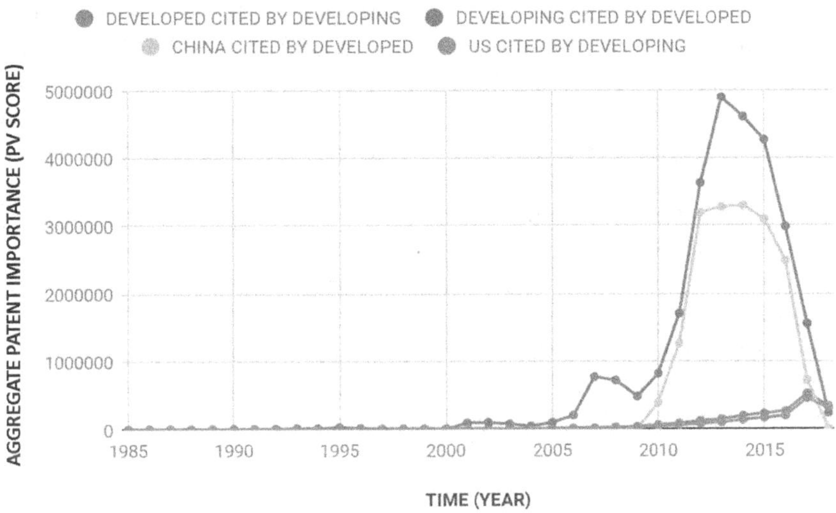

Figure 7.5 Importance of cited patents between developed and developing countries
Source: Authors' analysis.

almost equalling the importance of developed country patents by 2010, and subsequently dwarfing them until 2016. Figure 7.4 also illustrates that the patterns in cited patent importance in developed and developing countries are overwhelmingly accounted for by the contributions of US and Chinese patents.

Figure 7.5 illustrates the aggregate importance of developed country patents cited by developing country patents, and vice versa. The pattern for cited patents is noticeably different from that for citing patents. The aggregate importance of developed world patents cited by developing world patents increased from 5,213 in 1985 to 15,332 in 1998, before subsiding gradually to 11,224 in 2005. Beginning in 2006, though, their total importance rose rapidly, almost 50-fold, to 524,657 in 2017. The trend was strikingly similar for US patents being cited by developing world patents, with US patents again accounting for most of the importance. The aggregate importance of developing world patents cited by developed world patents increased rapidly, from a negligible 1.14 in 1985 to 1672,98 only two years later, in 1987. After remaining relatively stable until 1991, their importance began to rise rapidly once again, reaching 32,020,25 in 1995. This reflected a rise in importance of more than 28,000 times in a decade. By 1998, their importance had fallen sharply by almost 10 times, to 3714,60. With several temporary interruptions, importance rose rapidly, reaching a high of 4893464,10 in 2013, before shallowly subsiding. Until 1992, the importance of these cited developing world patents lagged well behind that of cited developed world patents, but, from 1993 to 1996, the former surmounted the latter. After falling below cited developed world patents in importance again until 2000, cited developing world patents established and maintained a huge lead in importance over those from the developed world. The pattern for Chinese patents shows substantial differences. After some initial fluctuations at very low levels from 2002 to 2006, the importance of these Chinese patents began a remarkable rise, reaching above 3,000,000 by 2012, and accounting for a majority of developing world patent importance by 2011. To put this prodigious rise in perspective, from 2002 – the first year for which we have Chinese data – to 2014, the aggregate importance of Chinese patents cited by patents in the developed world increased by more than 180,000 times.

An alternative method of measuring knowledge flows is to consider mean, rather than aggregate, importance. Figure 7.6 shows the mean importance of developed country patents citing developing country patents, and vice versa. The mean importance of citing developed world patents remains above 4.0 until 2000, after which it declines gradually. The mean importance of citing developed world patents is

Figure 7.6 Mean importance of citing patents between developed and developing countries

Source: Authors' analysis.

much greater than citing developing world patents throughout the entire time period from 1985 to 2018. In fact, until 2010 this difference is one or two orders of magnitude. From 2010 onwards, the disparity narrows somewhat. The trend for citing US patents parallels that for developed world patents, though the former is consistently substantially greater than the latter.

The trend for citing developing world patents is distinctly dissimilar to that of citing developed world patents. From 1988 until 2004, the importance of citing developing world patents fluctuated near a value of zero, after which it increased rapidly, pausing for several years after 2006 before reaching a high of 0.29 in 2011, and, then, decreasing steadily thereafter. From 2010 until 2017, citing developing world patents maintained importances only several times smaller than those for citing developed world patents. For all years in which Chinese patent data are available, the mean importance of citing Chinese patents was greater than the importance of citing developing world patents.

Figure 7.7 illustrates the mean importance of developed country patents cited by developing country patents, and vice versa. Except for the first two years of data, 1985 and 1986, developing world patents cited by developed world patents have been substantially more important than developed world patents cited by those in the developing world. From 1987 to 2018, this difference has remained at about half an order of

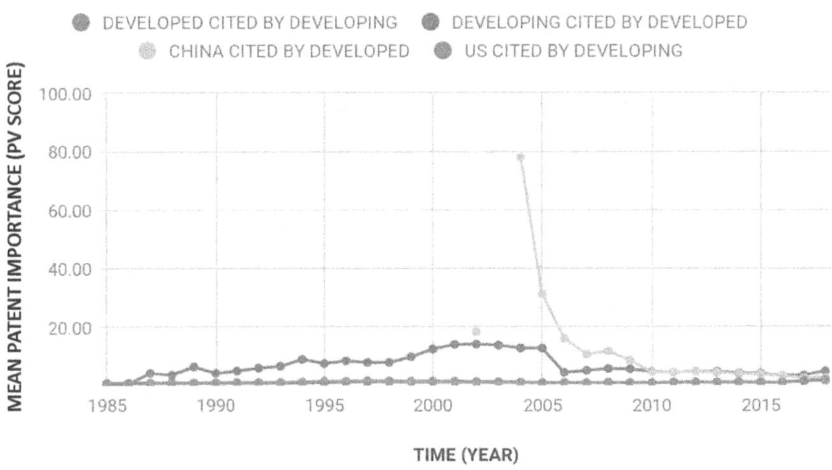

Figure 7.7 Mean importance of cited patents between developed and developing countries

Source: Authors' analysis.

magnitude, and the mean importance of these patents has consistently been very high, ranging from a low of 3.41 in 2016 to a high of 14.20 in 2002. The mean importance of these patents demonstrated a robust growth trend from 1987 to 2002, remained steady until 2005, fell by more than 50 per cent in 2006 and thereafter stayed relatively flat through 2018.

The mean importance of cited Chinese patents was substantially higher than cited developing world patents during the period in which Chinese data first became available, moved almost in lockstep with cited developing world patents from 2010 until 2016 and then fell substantially below the latter in 2017 and 2018.

The trends in mean patent importance for both cited developing world and US patents showed much less fluctuation. Starting at around 1.0 in 1985, they rose gradually to new highs in 1997, then declined gently back down to about 1.0 in 2005, remained relatively close to that level until 2016 and, finally, increased rapidly in 2017 and 2018. Throughout almost the entire period from 1985 until 2018, the mean importance of cited developed patents was higher than cited US patents.

Knowledge Flow in Specific Technologies

In addition to exploring general trends in technical knowledge flow, we also examine two particular technologies: wind power and pharmaceuticals. Figure 7.8 illustrates the trends in patents in these two technological fields over time, and compares them with trends for all patents.

Figure 7.8 Trends in total, wind power and pharmaceutical patents over time
Source: Authors' analysis.

Pharmaceutical patent numbers comprise approximately 2.5 per cent and 5 per cent of all patents. Wind power patents lag far behind this amount, consistently making up less than 0.1 per cent of all patents. From 1970 until 2018, both total patents and pharmaceutical patents increased in numbers by about an order of magnitude. By contrast, wind power patents increased by about two orders of magnitude over the same period of time.

Wind Power Technology

Figure 7.9 depicts the growth over time of wind power patents. Numbers of patents in this technology cluster remained quite modest for almost three decades from 1970, not rising above 100 until 1980, nor above 200 until 1999. From 1998 until 2006, numbers of patents grew more than 3.5-fold, from 183 to 656. Then, from 2006 to 2012, these numbers accelerated substantially to 33,134, an almost five-fold increase. As explained above, the decay in numbers since 2012 is difficult to interpret, likely reflecting not a decline in wind power patents, but, rather, incomplete reporting of recent data from national patent offices.

Figure 7.10 shows the interjurisdictional patent citation rate between developed and developing countries for wind power technology. The number of patents in this technology field is a small subset of all patents across all technologies. Though characterized by more fluctuations, the pattern in Figure 7.10 is generally similar to that for all technological

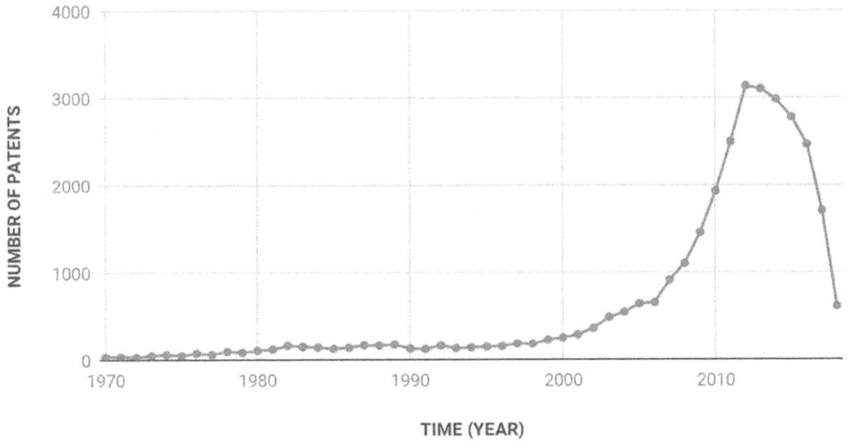

Figure 7.9 Trend in wind power patents over time
Source: Authors' analysis.

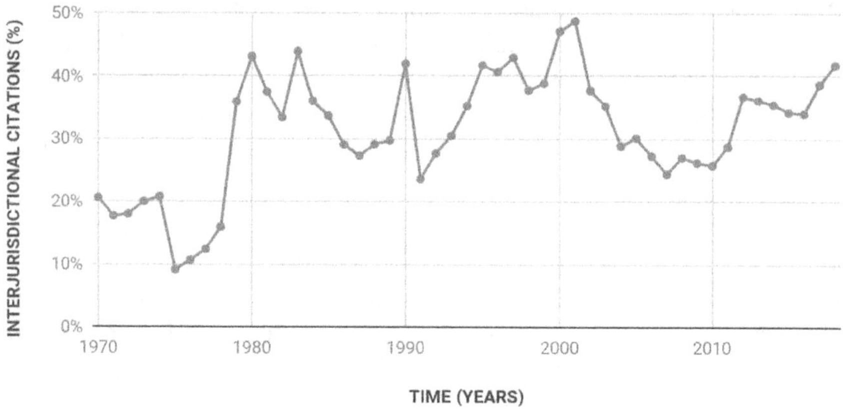

Figure 7.10 Rates of interjurisictional citations for wind technology
Source: Authors' analysis.

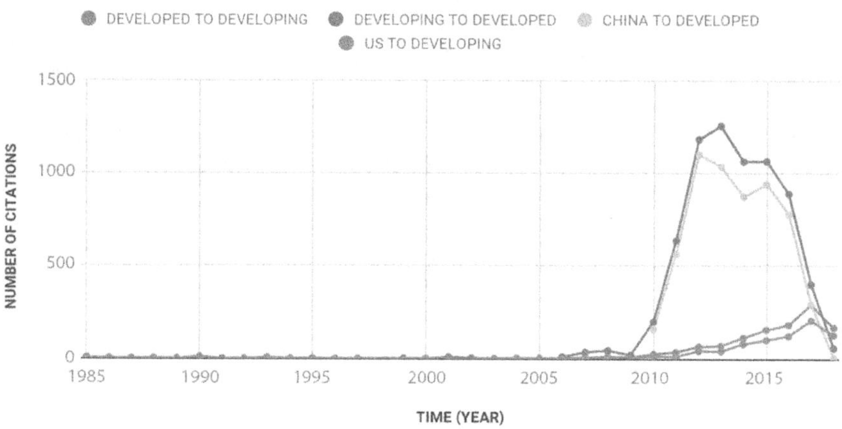

Figure 7.11 Wind power patent citations between developed and developing countries
Source: Authors' analysis.

fields (Figure 7.2), and replicates the overall rise-fall-rise pattern, though its rate of interjurisdictional citation tends to shift higher throughout.

Figure 7.11 illustrates trends in the aggregate citations between wind power patents originating in the developed and developing world. It also includes citations from US patents to those in the developing world as well as citations from Chinese patents to those in the developed world. There were very few patent citations between 1985 and 2006; in fact, there were no more than 10 per year until 2006, when there were 11 citations from developing world patents to developed world patents. Patent citations from developing to developed world patents reached 201 in 2010 before reaching a peak of 1,256 in 2013, after which they subsided. From 2010 onwards, China accounted for the vast majority of these patent citations. Patent citations from developed to developing world patents finally exceeded 10 in 2008, then rose substantially, jumping more than an order of magnitude to 294 in 2017. Patent citations from US patents to developing world patents accounted for a large majority of this number during every year from 2007 to 2018, except in 2011.

Figure 7.12 shows the aggregate importance of developed country wind power patents citing developing country patents, and vice versa. There are several gaps in this data. Importances of developed world patents cited by developing world patents are only continuous from 1990 onwards, and US patents cited by developing world patents from 2004. Importances of developing world patents cited by developed world patents are only continuous beginning in 2006, and Chinese patents cited by developed world patents later, from 2010. Nevertheless, several trends are noticeable. For developed world wind power patents cited by those in the developing world, importances vary over a range spanning almost two orders of magnitude, from a low of 0.59 in 1996 to a high of 53.81 in 2012. Over

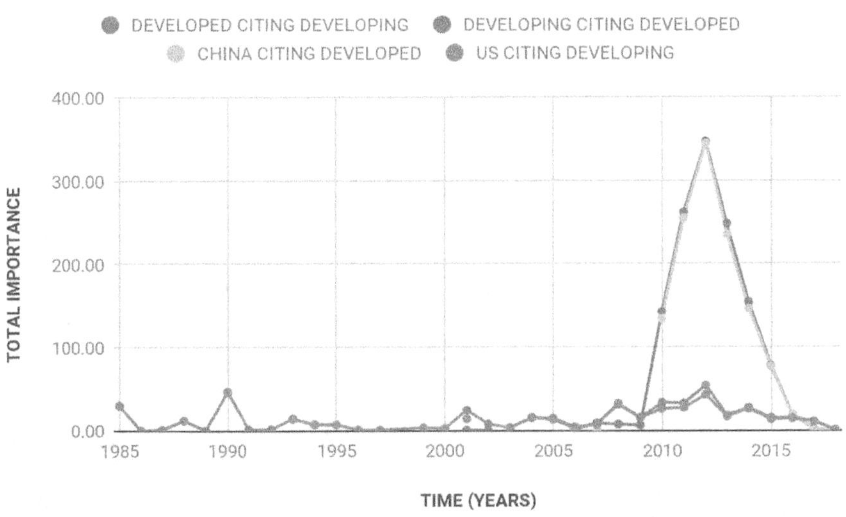

Figure 7.12 Importance of citing wind power patents between developed and developing countries.
Source: Authors' analysis.

this same time period, from 1996 to 2012, the dominant trend is upwards, though this rise is interrupted by several large reversals in direction. After 2012, the trend is downwards. For all spans of time during which developed world and US data are both available, cited US wind power patents account for almost all importance in the developed world.

The pattern for cited developing world wind power patents is quite different. After 2006, when continuous cited developing world data begins, there is a rapid rise in importance to 2007, a substantial reversal in trend until 2009, and then a rapid rise to a maximum of 346.61 in 2012. Continuous data for cited Chinese wind power patents begins in 2010, accounting for almost all developing world patent importance until 2018.

Figure 7.13 illustrates the aggregate importance of developed country wind power patents cited by developing country patents, and vice versa. The aggregate importance values of cited wind power patents are approximately an order of magnitude greater than those for citing wind power patents. There is continuous importance data for developed country wind power patents cited by those in developed countries. Aggregate importances range from a low of 0.25 to a peak value of 273.44, representing a difference of three orders of magnitude. From 1985 until 2009, these importances fluctuated frequently within a range from 0.25 to 8.87. Then, after 2009, they exhibited a rapid rise to the peak value of 273.44 in

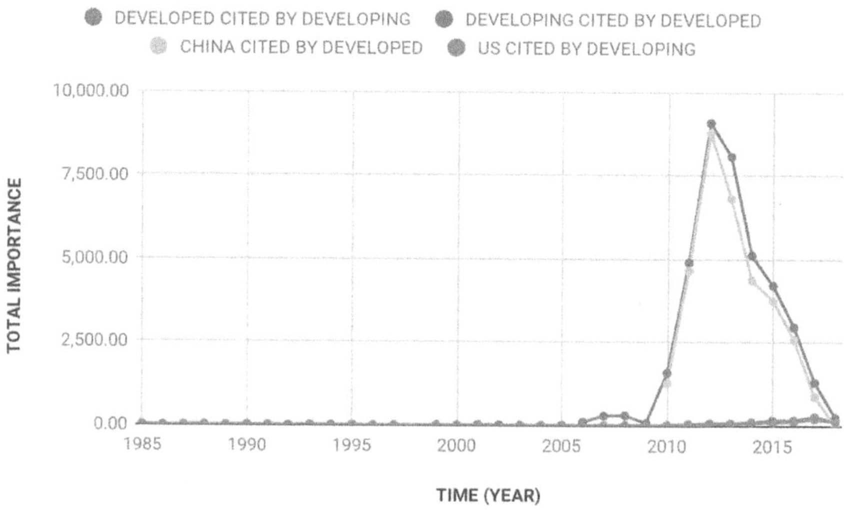

Figure 7.13 Importance of cited wind power patents between developed and developing countries
Source: Authors' analysis.

2017 before falling in 2018. Data for the importances of cited US patents – incomplete until 2004 – showed a similar trajectory to that for the developed world, though US importances tended to be substantially lower.

Aggregate importance data for developing world patents cited by those in the developed world are scarce prior to 2006, after which patent importances rose and fell substantially until 2009. From an aggregate importance of 74.06 in 2009, they then rose sharply, reaching a maximum of 9,092.57 in 2012, an almost 123-fold increase in only three years. After 2012, aggregate importance fell rapidly. The trend for importance of cited Chinese patents closely tracked that for cited developing world patents, though importances for these Chinese patents were consistently a bit lower.

Figure 7.14 shows the mean importance of developed country patents citing developing country patents, and vice versa. Here, there is continuous importance data for developed country wind power patents citing developing country patents. Mean importance fluctuates from lows of zero in 1986 and 1989 to a high of 7.08 in 1994, but there is no clear directional trend.

Figure 7.15 reveals the mean importance of developed country wind power patents cited by developing country patents, and vice versa. The

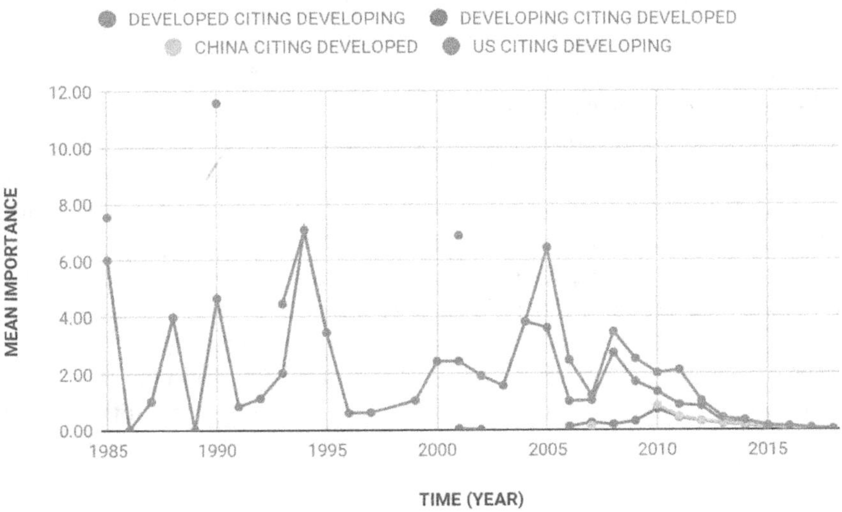

Figure 7.14 Mean importance of citing wind technology patents between developed and developing countries

Source: Authors' analysis.

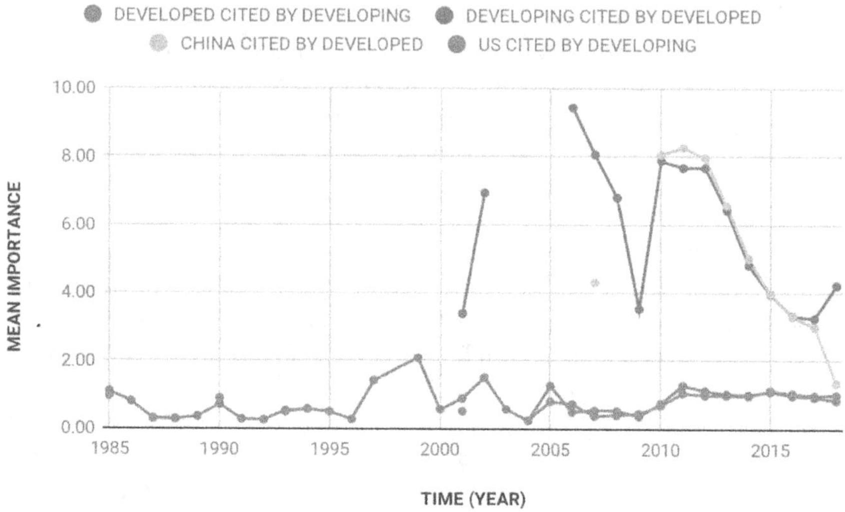

Figure 7.15 Mean importance of cited wind technology patents between developed and developing countries
Source: Authors' analysis.

only continuous mean patent importance data from 1985 to 2018 pertains to developed world patents cited by developing world patents. These mean values fluctuated between a low of 0.23 in 2004 and a high of 2.08 in 2009, but without any overall rising or falling trend. Values for US mean patent importances – for which data is discontinuous until 2004 – tracked developed world values relatively closely throughout the time period. Continuous mean importance data for cited developing world patents begins in 2006. These mean importances were consistently far higher than those for cited developed world patents, with maximum and minimum values of 9.45 and 3.00 respectively. From 2006 to 2009, these values dropped precipitously, recovering suddenly in 2010, then declining substantially until 2017, and finally recovering modestly in 2018. From 2010 onwards – when continuous Chinese data are available – mean importances for cited Chinese wind power patents closely tracked those for developing world patents, diverging substantially only in 2018.

Pharmaceutical Technology

Figure 7.16 depicts the growth over time of pharmaceutical patents. Numbers of patents in the pharmaceutical technology cluster have grown

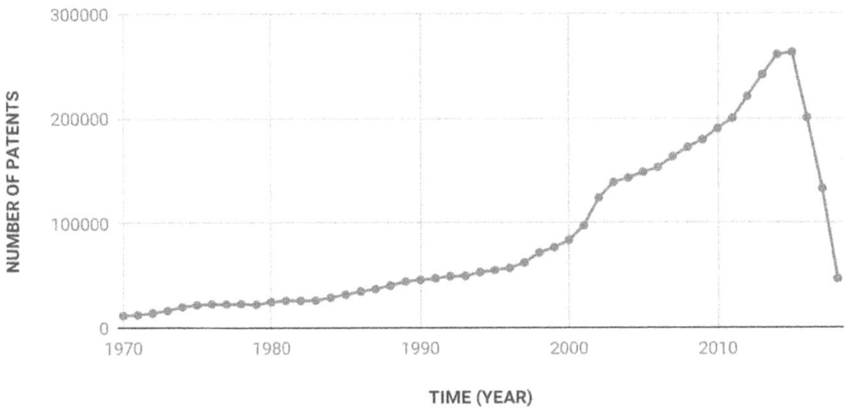

Figure 7.16 Trend in pharmaceutical patents over time
Source: Authors' analysis.

every year since 1970 with the exception of a brief pause from 1976 to 1979. Rates of growth accelerated noticeably after 1996, a year with 57,017 patents, to 138,934 by 2003, for a seven-year increase of almost 2.5 times. Then, from 2003 to 2015, they almost doubled again, reaching 263,059. In contrast to wind power patents, the decay in numbers of pharmaceutical patents did not begin until after 2015. These too are difficult to interpret, likely reflecting not a decline in pharmaceutical patents, but incomplete data reporting by national patent offices.

Figure 7.17 shows the interjurisdictional patent citation rate between developed and developing countries for pharmaceutical technology. Although the number of patents in this technology field is a small subset of all patents across all technologies, as can be seen in Figure 7.16, it includes far more patents than does wind power (Figure 7.10). The pattern in Figure 7.17 is strikingly similar to that for all technological fields (Figure 7.2), replicating the overall rise-fall-rise pattern. However, as for wind power patents, the rate of interjurisdictional citation of pharmaceutical patents has shifted higher during every time period except from 1975 to 1978.

Figure 7.18 illustrates trends in the aggregate citations between pharmaceutical patents originating in the developed and developing world. The number of raw patent citations in pharmaceutical technology made by patents in the developed world to those in the developing world rose steadily, roughly quadrupling during the two decades from 1985 to

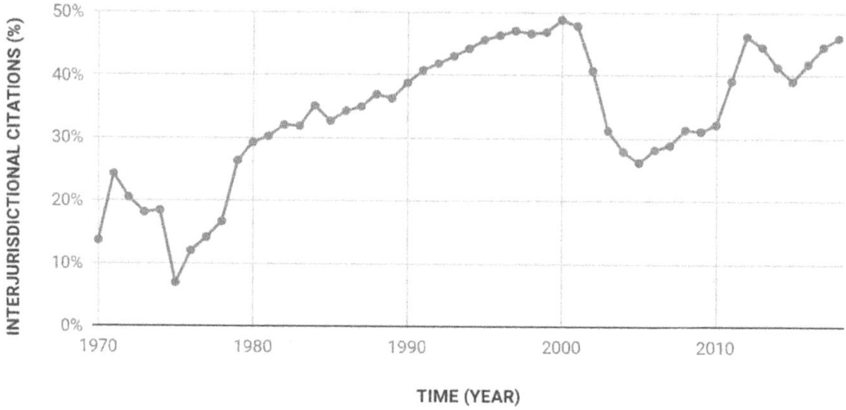

Figure 7.17 Rates of interjurisdictional citation for pharmaceutical technology
Source: Authors' analysis.

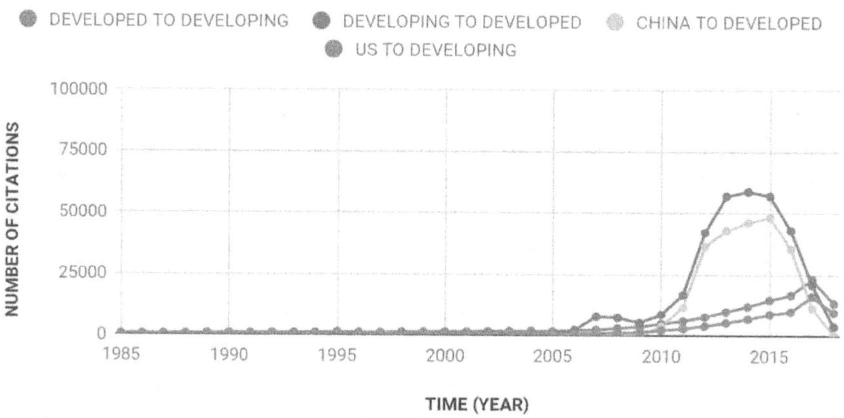

Figure 7.18 Pharmaceutical patent citations between developed and developing countries
Source: Authors' analysis.

2005. Then, the growth trajectory accelerated, rising by more than an order of magnitude, from 1656 in 2005 to 22,935 in 2017. Citations of US pharmaceutical patents by developing world patents rose in a similar pattern, consistently accounting for about half of all developed world citations.

With the exception of 1986, complete citation data for developing world pharmaceutical patents cited by developed world patents exists for

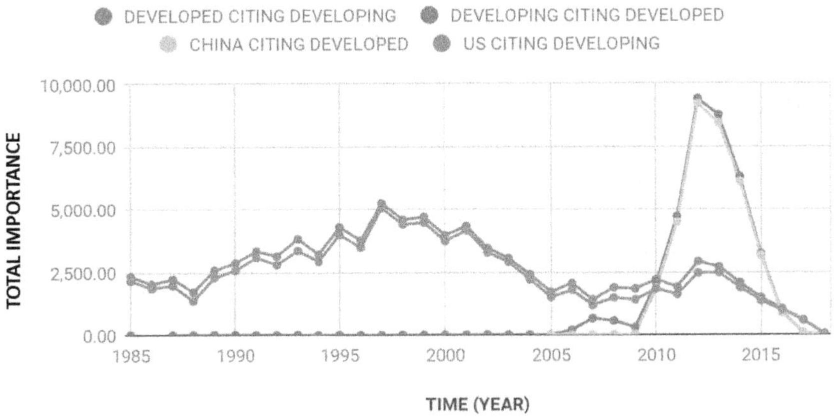

Figure 7.19 Importance of citing pharmaceutical patents between developed and developing countries
Source: Authors' analysis.

the entire time period from 1985 to 2018. This trend shows far more volatility than that for cited developed world patents. Until 1995, it lags behind cited developed world patents, pulling even in 1995, but then falling behind again – sometimes far behind – until pulling even for a second time in 2006. From 2004 until 2007, these citations grew more than 35-fold, from only 215 to 7,660, they fell back down to 5,206 in 2009, before reaching a peak of 58,849 in 2014, and then decreased substantially thereafter. Data for cited Chinese pharmaceutical patents is available from 2005 onwards. Starting with a paltry two citations in 2005, these Chinese citations rose very rapidly, accounting for a large majority of developing world citations from 2011 to 2017.

Figure 7.19 shows the aggregate importance of developed country pharmaceutical patents citing developing country patents, and vice versa. Despite frequent fluctuations, the aggregate importance of developed world pharmaceutical patents that cite developing world patents generally rose from 1985 to 1997, reaching a peak of 5,249.41, subsided thereafter down to 1,398.12 in 2007, reversed direction again after 2007 to climb back to 2,910.64 in 2012, and then declined steadily until 2018. The aggregate importance of US patents closely matched this pattern, and always accounted for a large majority of developing world aggregate importance.

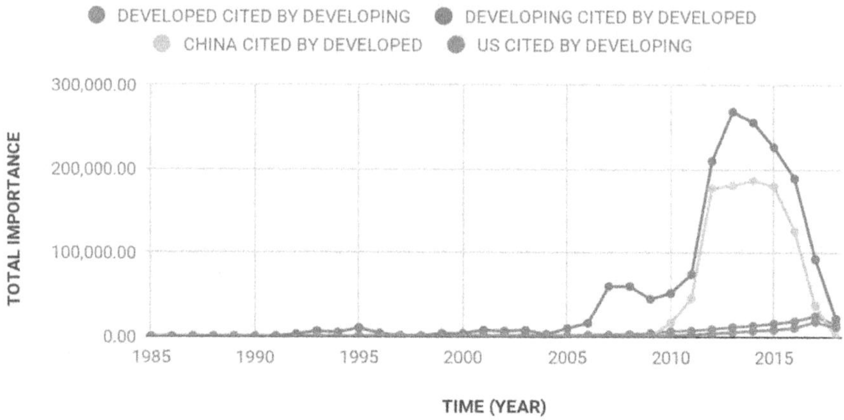

Figure 7.20 Importance of cited pharmaceutical patents between developed and developing countries
Source: Authors' analysis.

Including small fluctuations in value, the aggregate importance of developing world pharmaceutical patents that cite developed world patents remained very low in the two decades from 1985 to 2005. Starting in 2006, these importance values rose substantially. From 0 in 2005, importance rose to 644.22 in 2007, declined to 293.79 by 2009, and then rocketed upwards, exceeding the value for developed country patents citing developing country patents by 2011, and reaching a maximum of 9,396.83 in 2012, before declining sharply again. Aggregate Chinese importance remained very low until 2009, and then closely tracked the value for all developing country patents, accounting for almost all their importance.

Figure 7.20 illustrates the aggregate importance of developed country pharmaceutical patents cited by developing country patents, and vice versa. The aggregate importance values of cited pharmaceutical patents are approximately an order of magnitude greater than those for citing pharmaceutical patents. The trend in aggregate importance of developed country pharmaceutical patents cited by developing country patents was steadily upwards from 382.38 in 1985 to 25,645.84 in 2017, a prodigious rise of almost two orders of magnitude. The aggregate importance of US patents rose in a similar trajectory. For most of the period from 1985 to 2018, the US value accounted for a majority of developing world aggregate patent importance, but its fraction of importance did slip below 50 per cent from 2005 to 2014.

The trend for developing world pharmaceutical patents cited by developed world patents also exhibited a general rising trend, but experienced more fluctuations. Although slightly above the aggregate importance for developed world pharmaceutical patents in 1987, the importance of developing world patents slipped below the developed world level from 1988 until 1991. Beginning in 1992, it rose well above the aggregate importance of developed country patents, declining again after 1995 and drawing close to even with developed country importance in 1997 and 1998. After this, aggregate importance of cited developing world patents remained consistently above the developed world level, and usually at about an order of magnitude above. From a very low aggregate importance of 11.71 in 2005, it reached a high of 186,952.43 in 2014, for an increase of more than four orders of magnitude in less than a decade. From 2011 to 2016, aggregate Chinese importance made up a majority of developing world importance.

Figure 7.21 shows the fvmean importance of developed country patents citing developing country patents, and vice versa. After an initial decline, the mean importance of developed world pharmaceutical patents that cite those from the developing world fluctuated above and below 4.00 from 1989 to 1997, after which it declined steadily from 5.14 in 1997 towards zero in 2018. The mean importance of citing US pharmaceutical patents was consistently higher than that for developed country patents. It also declined after 1985, losing almost half its importance by 1998, then rebounded to reach a new high in 1995, declined sharply in 1996, and then reached another new high in 1997. With several fluctuations, the trend in mean importance from 1997 onwards declined steadily towards zero in 2018.

Mean developing world patent importances stayed near zero from 1985 until 2005. Next, they spiked upwards to 0.10 in 2006, declined modestly until 2009, and then rose sharply again, reaching 0.28 in 2011, before declining towards zero in 2018. The pattern for Chinese patents citing developed world patents started higher than that for developing world patents, at 0.43 in 2006, converging on the developing world patent importance trend by 2012.

Figure 7.22 reveals the mean importance of developed country pharmaceutical patents cited by developing country patents, and vice versa. The trend in mean importance for developed world pharmaceutical patents cited by developing world patents remained quite flat,

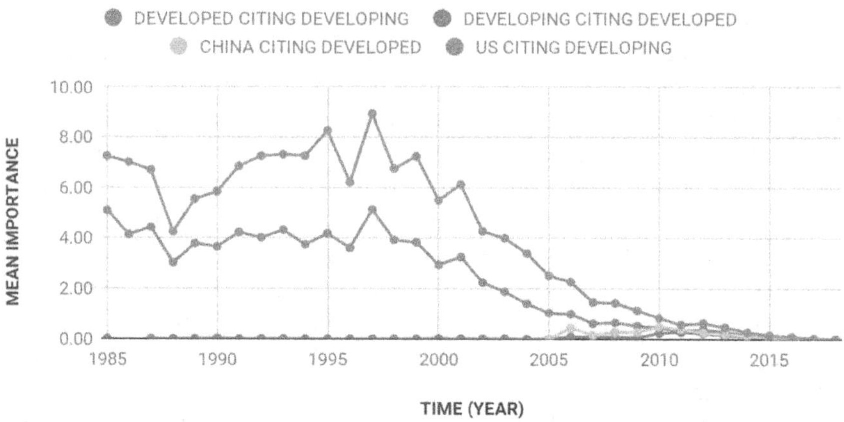

Figure 7.21 Mean importance of citing pharmaceutical patents between developed and developing countries
Source: Authors' analysis.

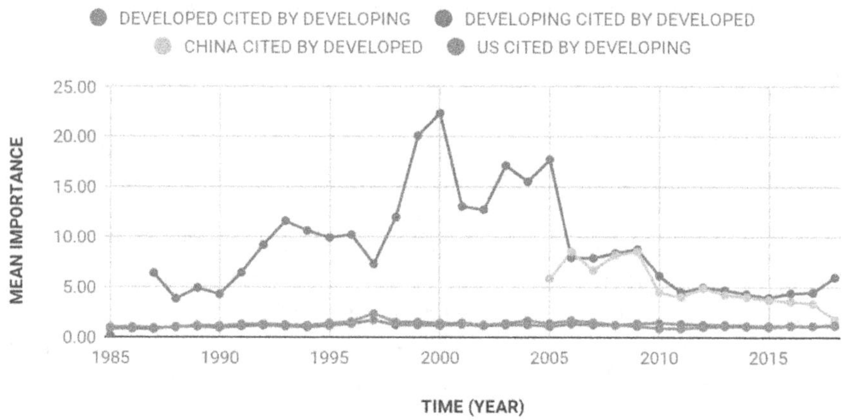

Figure 7.22 Mean importance of cited pharmaceutical patents between developed and developing countries
Source: Authors' analysis.

almost always just above 1.0, from 1985 to 2018, with the exception of a modest peak in 1997. The trend for US patents was quite similar, except for a modest decline from 2006 to 2011. With the exception of 1985, the mean importances for developing country patents cited by developed world patents were consistently about five times to an order of magnitude larger than those for developed world patents. Punctuated by substantial fluctuations, developing country patent importances, though fluctuating substantially, generally rose rapidly after 1985, reaching a maximum of 22.35 in 2000, and then generally declined thereafter. The mean importance of Chinese pharmaceutical patents started well below that for developing world patents, then converged on the developing world values, before falling well below them from 2016 onwards.

Worldwide Knowledge Flow among All Countries

One way to analyse international patent knowledge flow is to use a radial diagram in which almost all countries and jurisdictions in the world are arrayed around the circumference of a circle.[50]

The radial diagram in Figure 7.23 shows the flow of citations to and from developed and developing countries measured by importance. All citations from patents of one country to those of another country are summed together. The thicker the lines between countries, the more citations between them, relative to other links. In the radial diagrams shown in this chapter, we show 75 per cent of all the links measured by importance. We removed a portion of the links to highlight the key patterns. We adopt this practice because including all patent citation links in a radial diagram can make major patterns of knowledge flow difficult to see due their high density.

The dark grey two-letter codes represent developed countries. The light grey colours represent developing countries. The two-letter code 'WO' represents the PCT, which accepts patent applications from applicants in almost all countries; because it belongs neither to the developed nor the developing world, the WO is situated in Figure 7.23 between the two categories of countries or regional filing authorities. Because the PCT is an international filing system, not a final destination of patent applications, it is difficult to construe as a node of knowledge flow as such; with that caveat, it is included for completeness' sake.

Figure 7.24 illustrates patent knowledge flow from two perspectives: from developed countries' patents to developing countries' patents (the left-hand radial diagram); and, from developing countries' patents to developed countries' patents (the right-hand radial diagram). The figure's lines do not represent the sum of links as they do in Figure 7.23.

[50] See http://well-formed.eigenfactor.org/radial.html.

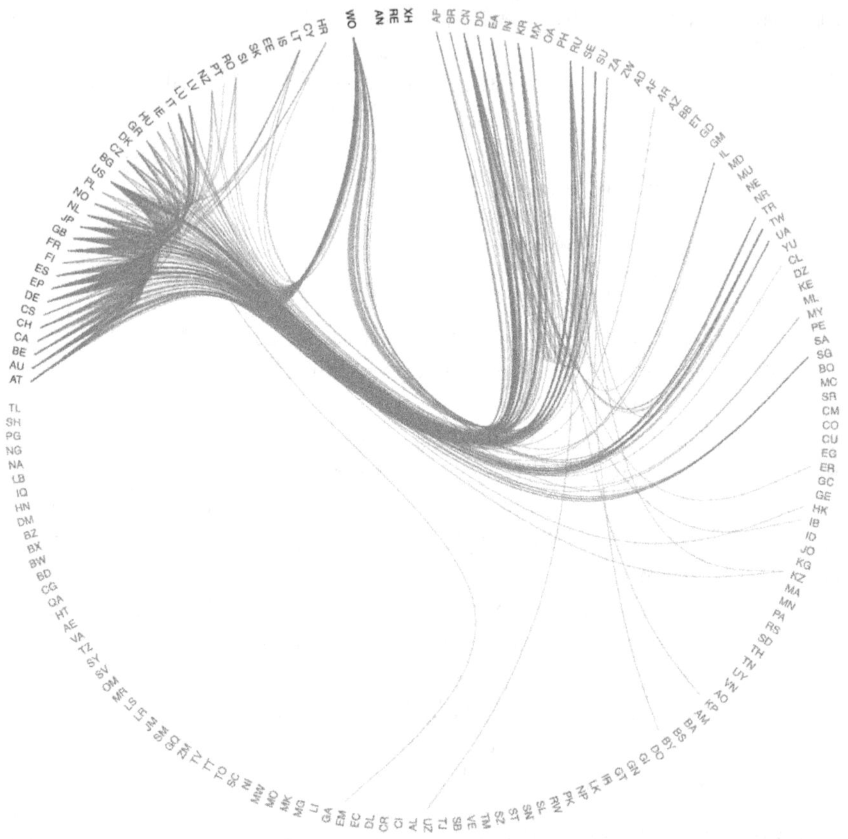

Figure 7.23 Radial diagram of international knowledge flow
Source: Authors' analysis.

Nor do they include citations from developed world patents to other developed world patents or developing world patents to other developing world patents. The presence or absence of lines linking countries does represent whether or not there is substantial important patent knowledge flow.

The radial diagram in Figure 7.24 reveals several interesting patterns. Not all developed countries possess a substantial number of patents that are cited regularly by those in developing countries, as discussed earlier in the chapter. Less surprisingly, the converse is also true; not all developing countries possess significant holdings of patents. Patent knowledge flows from the patents of 20 developed countries to the

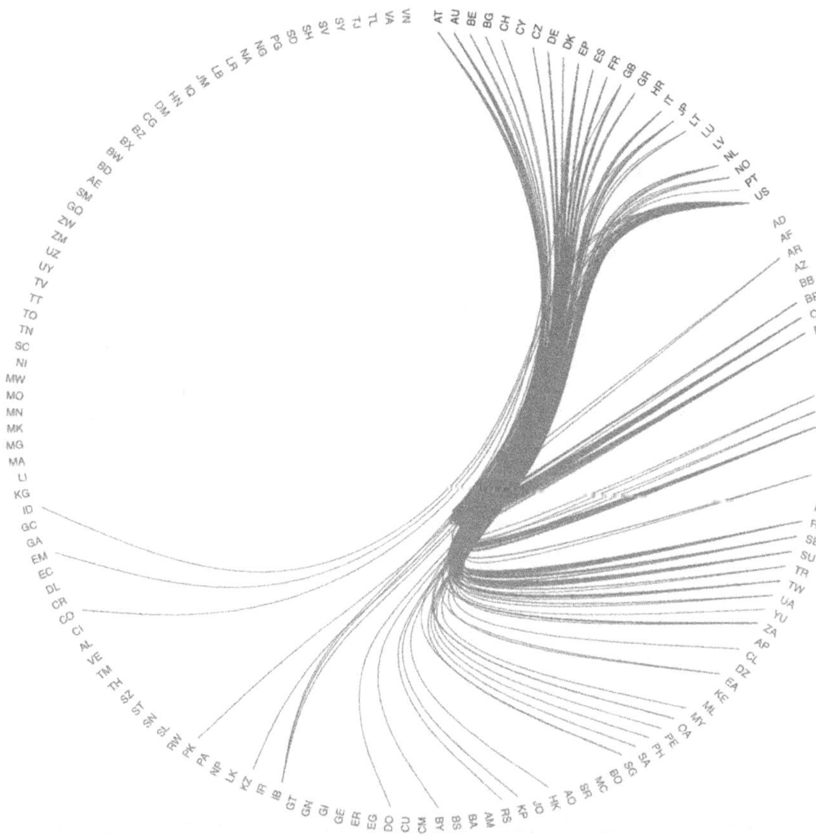

Figure 7.24 Directional knowledge flow between developed and developing world countries
Source: Authors' analysis.

patents of 35 developing countries. By contrast, patent knowledge from the patents of only 21 developing countries flows to the patents of only 16 developed countries. In other words, not only is there less patent knowledge flow from developing countries' patents to developed countries' patents, there is substantially less participation by patent systems in both developed and developing countries in knowledge flow from developing to developed countries. One stark contrast is that a much higher fraction of developed world countries' patent systems participate in patent knowledge flow in both directions (that is, developed to developing world and developing to developed world) than do those in the developing world. This reveals in a new light considerable opportunties for growth in

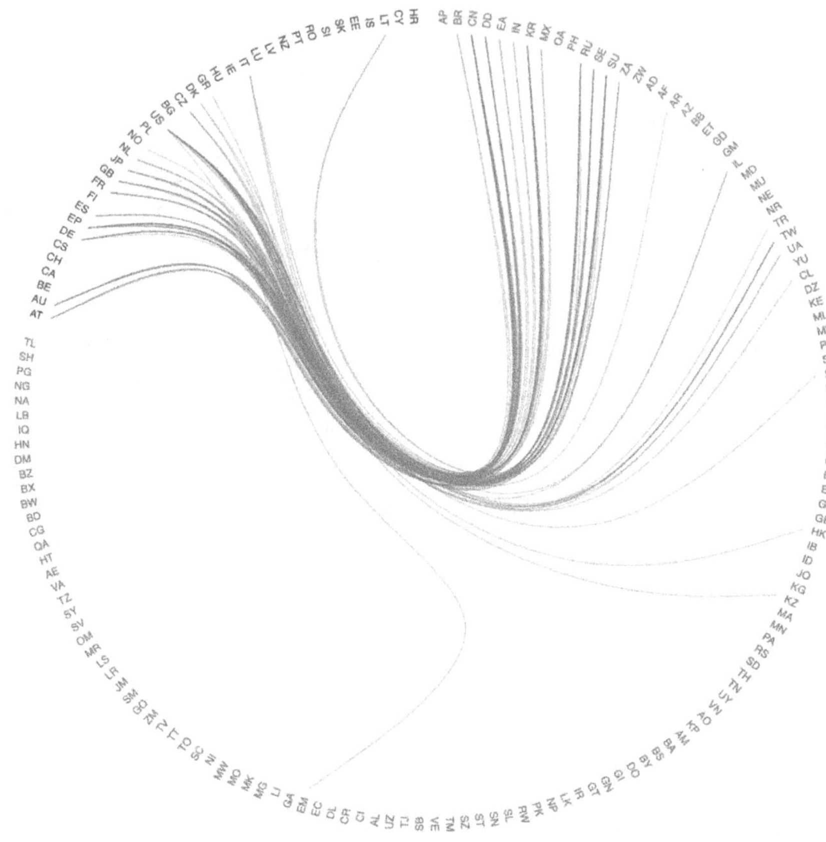

Figure 7.24 (*cont.*)

contributions developing world countries may make to worldwide patent knowledge flow – contributions capable of increasing for all technological innovation and the benefits therefrom.

Discussion

Knowledge Flow between More and Less Developed Countries

Fluctuating Interjurisdictional Citation Rates

Interjurisdictional patent citation generally grew robustly between 1970 and 2000, roughly quadrupling from about 10 per cent in 1970 to almost 40 per cent in 2000 (Figure 7.2). This parallels the growth in patents during the same period (Figure 7.1), which also approximately quadrupled. It is also consistent with the increasing availability of scientific, technical and patent documents, data, and other information with improvements in information technology, such as personal computers, the Internet, and the World Wide Web. However, the similarity between interjurisdictional citations and patent numbers ends around 2000, after which patent numbers not only continued to increase, but accelerated, reaching almost 6,000,000 in 2017, while citations decreased sharply, halving by 2005. Interjurisdictional citations did subsequently increase again, including a particularly rapid rise from 2010 to 2012, before remaining stable at about 30 per cent.

The sharp decline and recovery in interjurisdictional citations defies easy explanation. The 2000–2003 global recession might seem a likely candidate to have influenced the drop in citations after 2000. However, if so, it is odd that rates of patent citations declined while numbers of patents continued to climb. The drop in citations did not correspond with the WTO–TRIPS amendments, which were finalized in 1995, nor with any other major changes in international, US, or European patent law. Similarly, it is difficult to explain the subsequent recovery in the rate of patent citations, which also did not coincide with any obvious explanatory external legal or economic event. Another possible explanation is missing patent data, but there is no evidence of this.

It is possible that the post-2000 decline in interjurisdictional patent citation rates is a consequence of the natural accumulation of citations over time. This is certainly true for *numbers* of patent citations. As a patent ages, it tends to attract more citations. Thus, younger patents tend to have attracted fewer citations than older ones. However, it is not obvious why the *rate* of interjurisdictional patent citation rates would be similarly affected. Perhaps it is more likely that a patent will be cited by other patents in the same jurisdiction due to their proximity to one another. But, if this were so, then the rapid recovery in the rate of interjurisdictional patent citations after 2010 is confounding.

Towards More Balanced Knowledge Flow

Until 2005, there were considerably more developed world patent citations to developing world patents than vice versa, though overall numbers of worldwide patent citations were fairly stable at a much lower level than in recent years (Figure 7.3). After 2005, two striking changes occurred. First, the total number of patent citations worldwide rocketed upwards by about two orders of magnitude. Second, the pattern of patent citation between developed and developing countries reversed, with developing country patents citing developed country patents much more frequently than vice versa. In fact, this pattern reversal occurred despite the rapid growth in patent citations of developing countries by developed countries. After 2009, China accounted for most of the increasing citations from developing world patents.

One implication of these patterns is that, in recent years, patent systems in the developing world have become much more aware of the relevance to their own patents of developed world patents. Another is that the same phenomenon applies in the developed to developing world direction, but to a lesser extent. Nevertheless, the citation data from 2015 onwards suggest that developing world patents may be reducing their citations of those from the developed world while the latter continues to increase its citations of developing world patents. If these trends were to continue, the magnitude of citations between developed and developing world patents would appear likely to equalize, at least briefly.

Developing countries appear to be increasing rapidly as sources of technical information for the developed world, and to be relying less themselves on technical information from the developed world. This suggests that, while technical knowledge has been flowing robustly from developed countries to developing countries in recent years, this dependency has begun to lessen, leading towards more balanced knowledge flow.

A Patent Importance Perspective

A Cautionary Illustration

It may be preferable to rely on importance measures than on raw citations, as the latter can yield misleading estimates of technical knowledge flow. Consider the citation patterns between Chinese and US patent documents. Chinese patent documents have cited US patents or patent applications on 2,209,396 occasions, while US patent documents have cited Chinese documents only 592,154 times. This represents a major imbalance because Chinese patent documents cite US patent documents 3.73 times more often than US patent documents cite Chinese patent documents.

However, when the importance of these citations is taken into account, this skewed citation pattern becomes more uneven, reaching a difference of almost an order of magnitude because the importance of

Chinese-to-US citations is 15,261,498 while the importance of US-to-Chinese citations amounts to only 861,941. By this measurement, the importance of the US patents cited by Chinese patents is 17.7 times as great as the importance of the Chinese patents cited by US patents.

One interpretation of these results is that US technical knowledge embodied within patents has flowed much more robustly to, rather than from, China. Furthermore, in selecting accurate measurements of this knowledge flow, those relying on raw citations may vastly underestimate the magnitude of this skewed knowledge flow. It may be advisable to rely more on importance-weighted citations than raw citations for measuring knowledge flow.

Estimating Knowledge Flow from Importance

Aggregate importance of citations adds a different perspective. We examined aggregate importance from two perspectives: developed world patents that cite developing world patents (Figure 7.4) and vice versa (Figure 7.5). In the first case, developed world patents maintained far higher importance from 1985 to 2010, after which the importance of developing world patents raced ahead. The sustained rise in importance of developing world patents citing developed world patents occurred after 2005. Throughout the time period measured, US patents accounted for the vast majority of developed world patent importance. Similarly, after 2009, Chinese patents contributed the vast majority of developing world patent importance.

One implication of this pattern is that citation of developed world patents has recently become a very strong indicator of importance for developing world patents. In fact, since 2010, citation of developed world patents has tended to be strongly associated with the importance of developing world patents. By contrast, the relatively modest fluctuations in the importance of developed world patents that cite developing world patents suggests little effect on the importance of the former. These results also reveal the disproportionate importance of US and Chinese patents within the wider categories of developed and developing world patents, respectively.

Whether developed world patents were cited by developing world patents seems not to have had a substantial effect on the importance of the former. There may have been an increase in the most recent years, but even this rise has been modest. Again, it is the importance of developing world patents that appears to have been affected; beginning after 2000, and especially after 2009, developing country patents cited by those in developed countries have increased prodigiously in importance. Again, US patents have consistently accounted for much of developed world patent importance, and, after 2009, Chinese patents have played a similar role among developing world patents.

As with citations flowing in the other direction, being cited by developed world patents appears to have been a strong indicator of developing world patent importance, whereas the importance of developed world patents seems to have been affected little by citations from developing world patents.

An examination of mean patent importances tells a different story. Mean importances of developed world patents citing those in the developing world dwarfed those of developing world patents citing developed world patents from 1985 until 2010, though this disparity began to decrease steadily after 1997, and mean importances approached convergence from 2010 onwards (Figure 7.6). Mean importances for US patents were substantially higher than those for all developed world patents, but showed a very similar trend to the latter. Similarly, mean Chinese patent importances were above those for developing countries, but held to a similar trajectory.

There was a reversal of roles for developing country patents cited by developed world patents. After 1986, the mean importance of developing world patents remained well above the mean importance of developed world patents cited by developing world patents (Figure 7.7). The mean importance of US and developed world patents was very similar throughout the time period measured, whereas mean importances of Chinese patents were initially much higher than those for the developing world, but rapidly converged with them.

The results for mean patent importance provide little evidence that developing world patents that cite developed world patents tend to be more important, though the modest bump in importance after 2009 might suggest an incipient change. On the other hand, mean importances of developing world patents cited by developed world patents have been noticeably higher than vice versa.

Climate Mitigation Technology Knowledge Flow

In addition to general trends of citation and importance spanning all areas of technology, we also examine two particular technological fields: wind power and pharmaceuticals. First, we explore wind power technology. We test the hypothesis that the trajectory of climate-change mitigation knowledge flow increased (especially flow from developed to developing countries) after the 1997 Kyoto Protocol[51] and the 2015 Paris Agreement[52] on climate change.

Evidence of Knowledge Flow in Wind Power Technology

The relatively small number of patents in the field of wind power technology makes it challenging to make fine-grained comparisons to overall trends in patent citations and importance. More generalized comparisons must suffice, and, at this level, the trends and patterns for wind technology patents generally resemble those for all technologies combined. The growth trajectory is similar and strongly upwards in both wind power patents (Figure 7.9) and all patents (Figure 7.1), although the rapid acceleration of wind patents lags several years behind that observed for both all patents and pharmaceutical patents (Figure 7.16). The pattern in rates of interjurisdictional citation (Figure 7.10) is similar for both, though the upward shift in rates for wind power patents suggests more knowledge flow between the developed and developing world in this technological field, and a generally upward trend after 2010. Patterns of citations (Figure 7.11), aggregate importance (Figures 7.12 and 7.13), and mean importance (Figures 7.14 and 7.15) are not meaningfully different from those for all patents. And, while there is no clear evidence that the Kyoto Protocol influenced any of the metrics used to characterize wind technology patent knowledge flow, Figure 7.10 does illustrate a sharp reversal in the trajectory of interjurisdictional citation rate for wind power patents one year after the successful 2015 negotiation of the Paris Agreement. This latter observation must be treated with caution, however, because it is the product of very recent patent data that is likely incomplete, and, thus, may constitute a biased sample. Furthermore, correlation is not causation, so one must be circumspect about attributing this increase to the Paris Agreement. The paucity of recent data will be solved by the passage of time, which will allow more complete data, accumulation of citations and more accurate estimates of importance.

[51] The Kyoto Protocol is a 1997 treaty intended to implement the 1992 United National Framework Convention on Climate Change. (See https://unfccc.int/process-and-meetings/the-kyoto-protocol/what-is-the-kyoto-protocol/what-is-the-kyoto-protocol.)

[52] The Paris Convention is a 2015 treaty intended to implement the 1992 United National Framework Convention on Climate Change. (See https://unfccc.int/process-and-meetings/the-paris-agreement/the-paris-agreement.)

Pharmaceutical Technology Knowledge Flow

Defining 'Pharmaceutical'

The WTO–TRIPS Agreement entered into force on 1 January 1995.[53] In addition to establishing a minimum level of patent protection in member countries, it represented a step towards the standardization of patent law worldwide. One technology field particularly affected by this standardization was pharmaceutical drugs. Many in the pharmaceutical industry hoped that the TRIPS Agreement would increase the potency of patent protection around the globe, while many, including those in developing countries, wished for enhanced access to powerful medicines and information about how to make and use them. It is challenging to quantify the latter knowledge flow of technical information.

As described in the above section on methodology,[54] we use eigenvector centrality to attempt to measure knowledge flow among countries, including in the field of pharmaceutical drugs. A challenge in doing so successfully relates to the complexity of 'pharmaceutical drugs' as a category of technology. Our method of classifying technologies relies on the hierarchical structure of patent citation network our method produces. In this network, there are approximately 100 million relatively discrete technology clusters. These clusters tend to be nested within larger, more inclusive, technology clusters, with all clusters ultimately nested, either directly or indirectly, within the largest, most inclusive, cluster, which is the entire network itself. These clusters may be thought of as 'natural' technology groups because they form as a result of the structure of the network. This contrasts with technology groups resulting from classification systems such as the IPC and CPC schemes, which are human constructs into which each patent application is placed, often as the consequence of a human decision.

The clustering method of technology classification we employ is not congruent with schemes such as the IPC or CPC. Rather, traditional categories of technology are often dispersed among IPC or CPC categories. In other words, our classification of 'pharmaceutical drug' is unique. Consequently, we focused our analysis on a particular natural technology cluster, not any derived from the IPC or CPC schemes. In our network

[53] The WTO TRIPS Agreement allowed staged implementation by different groups of WTO members. Thus, many developing countries did not adopt all TRIPS provisions until years after its initial entry into force.

[54] P. 224 *supra*.

we have defined a large natural cluster that comprises the vast majority of patents traditionally classified as falling within pharmaceutical technology.[55] We use this cluster to represent 'pharmaceutical technology' in the following analyses.

Evidence of Knowledge Flow in Pharmaceutical Technology

The World Health Organization ('WHO') has stated that, of all the WTO agreements, TRIPS 'is expected to have the greatest impact on the pharmaceutical sector and access to medicines'.[56] Although more than 40 countries lacked patent protection for pharmaceuticals prior to the TRIPS negotiations,[57] a result of the Agreement was to make availability of such protection mandatory, though the necessity to comply was phased in for certain countries and TRIPS does afford WTO members some degree of discretion in implementation,[58] (and least developed country members have no such obligations until at least 2033). The TRIPS Agreement did come into force in 1995, but there was no single date upon which all pharmaceutical inventions became patent eligible subject matter. This complicates the interpretation of citation and PV-weighted citation because some developing country members brought in patent protection for pharmaceuticals in 1995, or even beforehand, while others waited until as late as 2005 to do so.

Our analyses do offer some evidence consistent with the suggestion that knowledge flow in pharmaceutical technology increased after relevant TRIPS obligations began to apply from 1995. The increase in pharmaceutical patents accelerated soon after 1995, maintaining a much higher growth rate until 2015 (Figure 7.16). However, the trend for all patents across all technological fields showed an even more impressive growth rate after 1996 (Figure 7.2), suggesting that pharmaceutical technology, despite its acceleration, has actually been a laggard compared with the more general trend after 1995. Although the rate of interjurisdictional citation for pharmaceutical technology (Figure 7.17) has closely mirrored the shape for all patents (Figure 7.3), from 1979 onwards the rate of cross-border citation in pharmaceutical patents has been substantially higher. This suggests that knowledge flow is especially strong in pharmaceutical technology, and, if the post-2005 trend is

[55] This cluster roughly corresponds to CPC A61K.

[56] See www.who.int/medicines/areas/policy/wto_trips/en/.

[57] See www.who.int/medicines/areas/policy/wto_trips/en/.

[58] See www.who.int/medicines/areas/policy/wto_trips/en/.

indicative, likely to grow stronger. On the other hand, pharmaceutical patent trends in citations (Figure 7.18), aggregate importance (Figures 7.19 and 7.20) and mean importance (Figures 7.21 and 7.22) do not appear to diverge meaningfully from those for patents across all technological fields. It should be noted that any causal effects the TRIPS Agreement might have had could have been masked by the staggered entry into legal force in various countries of its full legal obligations germane to pharmaceutical drugs.[59]

Conclusions

Employing eigenvector centrality and hierarchical network methods to examine technical knowledge flow offers advantages over traditional methods based only on raw patent citations. A primary advantage is that neither patent numbers nor raw citations are capable of reflecting the importance of the technical knowledge that does flow from patent to patent, party to party, and country to country.

Developed country patents supply a disproportionate amount of patent citations compared to patents from developing countries, and the importance of technical knowledge thereby transferred is disproportionately high. However, we observe some evidence that this imbalance in knowledge flow may be beginning to reverse itself, as developing country patents have become increasingly cited by those in developed countries, and the importance of developing world patents has grown. If this observation does foreshadow a sustained shift in patent citations and patent importance, technical knowledge via patents from the developing to the developed world may soon become an important factor in global knowledge flow.

Our results failed to discern evidence that the Kyoto Protocol has spurred knowledge flow in climate-mitigation technology, but they did generate some preliminary evidence consistent with an effect by the Paris Agreement. We did find evidence consistent with the possibility that the TRIPS Agreement may have spurred pharmaceutical (and more general) knowledge flow.

One striking observation apparent from the analyses in this chapter is that US patents make up a huge proportion of the patent citations, patent importance and technical knowledge flow within the developed world.

[59] See www.wto.org/english/tratop_e/trips_e/factsheet_pharm04_e.htm.

Similarly, China has recently come to dominate patent citations, patent importance and technical knowledge flow within the developing world. These two phenomena may change over time, leading to less influence by one or both countries. In the meantime, it may be possible to use the US and China as relatively accurate proxies for patent analyses involving the developed and developing worlds, respectively, without sacrificing inordinate resolving power. The use of worldwide patent data and hierarchical mapping network approaches offer new, and potentially useful, insights into the flow of technical knowledge among countries and other patent jurisdictions, within specific technologies, and over defined periods of time.

Bibliography

Albert, Michael B., Avery, D., Narin, Francis and McAllister, Paul R., 'Direct Validation of Citation Counts as Indicators of Industrially Important Patents' (1991), *Res. Pol'y* 20: 251.

Allison, John R., 'Valuable Patents' (2004), *Georgetown Law Journal* 92, 435: 451.

Carpenter, Mark P., Francis Narin and Woolf, Patricia, 'Citation Rates to Technologically Important Patents' (1991), 3 *World Patent Information* 3: 160.

Hall, Bronwyn H., Jaffe, Adam B. and Trajtenberg, Manuel, 'Market Value and Patent Citations: A First Look', 2000, *National Bureau of Economic Research*, Working Paper No. 7741.

Hall, Bronwyn H., Jaffe, Adam and Trajtenberg, Manuel, 'Market Value and Patent Citations' (2005), *Rand Journal of Economics*, 16: 36.

Harhoff, Dietmar, Narin, Francis, Scherer, F. M. and Vopel, Karin, 'Citation Frequency and the Value of Patented Inventions' (1999), *Econ. & Stat* 81, 511.

Lanjouw, Jean O. and Schankerman, Mark, 'Characteristics of Patent Litigation: A Window on Competition' (2001), *Rand Journal of Economics* 32, 1: 129–151.

Lanjouw, Jean O. and Schankerman, Mark, 'Enforcing Patent Rights: An Empirical Study', in *Empirical Economics of Innovation and Patenting*, 2003, p. 14, available at LES Research Online, http://eprints.lse.ac.uk/58574/.

Narin, Francis, Noma, Elliot and Perry, Ross, 'Patents as Indicators of Corporate Technological Strength' (1987), *Res. Pol'y* 16: 143.

Page, Lawrence, Brin, Sergey, Motwani, Rajeev and Winograd, Terry, 'The PageRank Citation Ranking: Bringing Order to the Web, Stanford InfoLab', 1999, available at http://ilpubs.stanford.edu:8090/422/1/1999-66.pdf.

Palangkaraya, Alfons, Webster, Elizabeth and Jensen, Paul H., 'Misclassification Between Patent Offices: Evidence From a Matched Sample of Patent Applications' (2011), *Review of Economics & Statistics* 93: 1063.

Sampat, Bhaven N. and Ziedonis, Arvids A., 'Patent Citations and the Economic Value of Patents', in *Handbook of Quantitative Science and Technology Research 277*, H. F. Moed, W. Glänzel, and U. Schmoch (eds), Berlin: Kluwer Academic Publishers, 2004.

Seres, Stephen, 'Analysis of Technology Transfer in CDM Projects, 7', 2008, available at http://cdm.unfccc.int/Reference/Reports/TTreport/TTrep08.pdf.

Torrance, Andrew W. and West, Jevin D., 'All Patents Great and Small: A Big Data Network Approach to Valuation' (2017), *Virginia Journal of Law & Technology* 20, 3: 466–504.

Trajtenberg, Manuel, 'A Penny for Your Quotes: Patent Citation and the Value of Innovations' (1990), *Rand Journal of Economics* 21: 172–187.

West, Jevin D. and Vilhena, Daril A., 'A Network Approach to Scholarly Evaluation', in *Bibliometrics & Beyond: Metrics-Based Evaluation*, Blaise Cronin and Cassidy R. Sugimoto (eds), Cambridge, MA: MIT Press, 2014, pp. 151–166.

West, Jevin D., Bergstrom, Theodore C. and Bergstrom, Carl T., 'The Eigenfactor Metrics: A Network Approach to Assessing Scholarly Journals' (2010), *College & Research Libraries* 71: 236.

West, Jevin D., Wesley Smith, Ian and Bergstrom, Carl T., 'A Recommendation System Based on Hierarchical Clustering of an Article-Level Citation Network' (2016), *IEEE Transactions on Big Data* 2, 2: 113–123.

Zhong, Fa Ma, 'The Effectiveness of the Kyoto Protocol and the Legal Institution for International Technology Transfer' (2010), *Journal of Technology Transfer* 37: 75, 83.

8

Sources of Knowledge Flow between Developed and Developing Countries

LAURIE CIARAMELLA, GAÉTAN DE RASSENFOSSE AND FLORIAN SELIGER

Abstract

This chapter provides a long-term view on the sources of knowledge flow between developed and developing nations. It relies on patent data to explore three potential sources: R&D collaboration, technology sourcing, and technology transfer. All three sources provide a very consistent message. First, knowledge flows with East Asia, particularly China, are occurring more frequently. Second, knowledge flows are increasingly concentred in information and communication technologies. Third, the United States & Canada had traditionally larger patenting activity with Asia than Europe, but the share of activity between Europe and Asia has been increasing in recent years. Fourth, larger patenting activity between the United States & Canada and Asia implies that the US–Canada region is more likely to benefit from reverse knowledge flows as China progresses towards becoming a technological leader.

Introduction*

R&D globalization is a defining feature of modern innovation systems and a major driver of productivity growth (Eaton and Kortum, 1996; Thomson and de Rassenfosse, 2016). Innovating firms set up R&D labs abroad or cooperate with foreign partners in order to tap into an ever more globally dispersed knowledge frontier and to reduce R&D costs (Harhoff et al., 2014).

From the viewpoint of host countries, policymakers are keen to attract foreign R&D. The knowledge that flows from foreign R&D may be

* Part of the work outlined in this chapter was funded thanks to a grant by the Swiss National Science Foundation (application number 100018_169584, entitled 'Globalization of R&D: Technology Cluster, Performance and Risk'). The authors are grateful to Andy Toole and Jayashree Watal for helpful comments.

appropriated by local firms and raise their productivity level. If appropriation takes place without local firms contributing to the cost of the research, one talks of 'knowledge spillovers'. Appropriation can also occur in the context of a transaction on the market for technology (Arora et al., 2004).

The existence of cross-border knowledge flows has been well documented in the academic literature. Most of the literature tracks knowledge flows by means of patent citations, where citations are measured between a citing and a cited country, industry or firm (see, e.g., Jaffe and Trajtenberg, 1999; Maruseth and Verspagen, 2002; Peri, 2005). The vast majority of studies focus on developed economies – literature on developing economies is scarcer (see, e.g. Svensson, 2007). For developing countries, attracting foreign knowledge from more developed regions is both crucial and challenging. It is crucial because knowledge flows from the technology frontier are a key source of learning (Griffith et al., 2004; Seliger, 2016). It is challenging because developing countries lack the knowledge base and infrastructure to fully benefit from them.

This chapter contributes to the literature on cross-border knowledge flows in two ways. First, it puts the spotlight on flows between developed and developing economies. Second, it focuses on some potential sources of knowledge flows rather than on documenting their existence. We explore three potential sources: R&D collaboration, technology sourcing and technology transfer.[1] We quantify these sources by means of patent data. In contrast to prior studies that focus on patents filed at selected patent offices in the United States or Europe, our analysis considers 52 patent offices around the world.

R&D collaboration is measured by looking at patents that are co-invented or co-applied by parties in two different countries. Technology sourcing is measured by patents that are applied by a party in one country but invented in another country. Finally, knowledge transfer is measured using information on the transfers of ownership (i.e. sales) of patents.

We find that there has been a large shift towards R&D collaboration and technology sourcing with Asian countries (especially China) in the last two decades. Asia is today the only significant area for R&D collaboration and technology sourcing for Western economies. We also find that R&D collaboration and technology sourcing mainly take place in the

[1] Other sources of knowledge transfer exist, such as the mobility of R&D personnel (e.g. Lenzi, 2010). Our analysis is silent on this and other sources.

information and communication technology (ICT) sector and especially in computer technology. Regarding patent transfers, we document an important increase in the last decade, although overall levels remain low. East Asia is the largest recipient region among developing countries. Patent transfers from developing to developed economies also exist, although the volumes are more modest, reaching about a third of the volumes of the opposite direction.

Method and Data

In contrast to studies that seek to assess the *effect* of knowledge flows on the sending or receiving country, this chapter focuses on the *sources* of knowledge flows. It is well-documented that interpersonal and interfirm collaboration raise knowledge flows between the parties involved (Agrawal et al., 2006; Gomes-Casseres et al., 2006; Singh, 2005). We discuss the three potential sources in turn.

Measuring R&D Collaboration with Patent Data

Cross-border R&D collaboration occurs when firms from different countries work together on an invention or when inventors from different countries work together. These aspects can be measured by looking at applicant–applicant and inventor–inventor pairs of the patent documents, respectively (see Guellec and de la Potterie, 2001; Picci, 2010; Picci and Savorelli, 2018). In the context of the present study, one applicant (inventor) must come from a developed country and the other applicant (inventor) from a developing country.

Consider for example the case of patent application number FR2965057A1 filed on 22 September 2010. This patent is co-applied by two organizations, namely the Soils and Fertilizers Research Institute (Vietnam) and the Institut de Recherche pour le Développement (France). This patent is most likely the result of R&D collaboration between these two institutes.

Note that the term 'collaboration' is more appropriate for inventor–inventor pairs than for applicant–applicant pairs. The fact that a patent is co-applied does not necessarily imply that applicants are on equal footing. The patent could be fully developed by a subsidiary and co-applied by the subsidiary and the headquarter. Our data do not include ownership information and we are thus unable to assess whether patents arise from collaboration between two related entities. As we will see, however, insights obtained from applicant–applicant pairs are very similar to insights obtained from inventor–inventor pairs.

Most research in the field relies on the count of patents filed at major patent offices, such as the European Patent Office (EPO) or the United States Patent and Trademark Office (USPTO). However, the patenting activity at these offices may not necessarily be representative of the overall situation across the globe.

By contrast, the present analysis exploits the worldwide count of priority filings put forward by de Rassenfosse et al. (2013). This patent count identifies all priority patent applications filed worldwide and assigns them to the country of residence of the applicant and/or inventor. A priority patent application is the first patent application that is filed to protect an invention, anywhere in the world. The implementation of this count is quite challenging because of missing data on the inventors' and applicants' countries of residence. The authors have proposed a technical solution for recovering missing information on countries of residence that involves exploiting patent family information. Briefly, the technical solution involves looking for information on the countries of residence of applicants and inventors in the subsequent patent applications that belong to the same family.[2] Subsequent filings are typically made in other jurisdictions (i.e. at other patent offices) than the priority filing but this need not be the case. The 'worldwide count of priority filings' considers 52 patent offices and seeks to impute potential missing country information (for more details, see A8.2).

Measuring Technology Sourcing with Patent Data

We measure technology sourcing by considering patents for which applicants and inventors are located in different countries. In our context, one country needs to be a developed country and the other needs to be a developing country. Such patents can indicate R&D offshoring or external R&D contracting. In the case of R&D offshoring, the inventor works for a foreign subsidiary, whereas the patent is filed by the mother company. In the case of R&D contracting, a firm contracts out research to an R&D supplier.

[2] A family of patents is a set of patents that are related to each other through common priority patent applications. The original data in de Rassenfosse et al. (2013) have recently been updated and improved thanks to an EPFL-ETH Zurich project funded by the Swiss National Science Foundation.

Consider for example patent application number DE102011014441A1, filed on 18 March 2011. The sole applicant is the Germany-based automotive company Daimler AG and the inventors are all located in Pune, India. The Daimler group has an R&D centre in Pune, and the patent application is therefore the result of R&D offshoring.

The literature usually identifies three main motives for technology sourcing. First, the technology-seeking motive relates to firms tapping into frontier knowledge that is not available in their home country. Second, the market-seeking motive relates to firms seeking to enter new markets and involves adapting home technology to local specificities. Third, the cost-reduction motive relates to performing R&D tasks in a country with cheaper labour (Chung and Alcácer, 2002; Dunning and Lundan, 2008). The data at hand do not allow us to distinguish between the various motives but we note that one or more of these motives may be at play.

The count again relies on priority filings with imputed applicant and inventor country information. We exclude patents that were also co-applied (i.e. patent applications that have been filed by applicants from both the developing and developed countries). This restriction ensures that we exclude patents arising from technology collaboration and, therefore, that we identify more accurately cases of technology sourcing.

Measuring Technology Transfer with Patent Data

We measure technology transfer using detailed information on the transfers of ownership, i.e. the sale of rights. We rely on the register of the European Patent Office (EPO) for patent *applications*, and on the register of the German Patent Office (DPMA) for *granted* European (EP) patents. Indeed, once a European patent application has been granted by the EPO, it is transformed into a bundle of national patents. This implies that, before grant, a transfer of patent ownership should be registered at the EPO, while after grant, the transfer has to be registered in national offices of countries in which the patent has been validated.[3] Germany is the country with the largest proportion of validated EP patents (95 per cent in 2003). It is therefore the most complete source for post-grant changes of ownership of European patents (Harhoff et al., 2009).

It should be mentioned that registering a transfer of patent ownership is mandatory neither at the EPO, nor at the DPMA. There are

[3] It should be noted that it is still possible to register the transaction at the EPO during the nine-month period following the grant of the patent.

nevertheless strong incentives for patent purchasers to register patent acquisitions, as the lack of registration may have severe consequences. Indeed, in many European countries, the non-registration of patent transfers considerably hinders the enforcement of patent rights in case of litigation (see Ciaramella et al., 2017 for a more detailed discussion). In comparison with the amounts at stake before courts, the costs of registering a transfer of ownership are negligible.[4]

Note that the countries of patent protection (in our setting, European countries), and of patent ownership are distinct. For example, it is possible for a European patent to be owned by a US firm and transferred to a Chinese firm. Thus, we will be able to provide a global view of patent transfers even using EP patents alone.

Consider for example patent application number EP1905886A1, filed on 2 April 2008. This patent was developed by the Germany-based company AMTEC Wäschereimaschinen GmbH. It was then transferred on 7 July 2010 to Supreme Machinery Manufacturing Co. LTD, based in Thailand.

Empirical large-scale research investigating the transfers of patent ownership is recent. It started with Serrano (2010), which provides insights on the sale of US patents. Several studies have contributed to this emerging stream of literature, most of them focusing on the market for US patents (e.g. Galasso et al., 2013; De Marco et al., 2017). Literature on European patents is scarcer (see Boesenberg and Egger, 2017 and Ciaramella et al., 2017 for notable exceptions).

Descriptive Statistics

R&D Collaboration

Figure 8.1 provides an overview of the proportion of patents co-applied between core European applicants and applicants from developing countries, by region (Panel A) and by technology field (Panel B).[5] The number of co-applied patents grew from 16 in 1980 to 1,501 in 2010, leading to a compound annual growth rate (CAGR) of 16.3 per cent. To put that figure in perspective, collaboration between core European applicants and

[4] The cost of registering a transfer of ownership at the EPO is EUR 100. There is no cost for registering a transfer of patent ownership at the DPMA since 2002.

[5] A8.1 explains how we allocate countries to groups of developed and developing countries. A8.3 discusses the allocation of patents to technological fields.

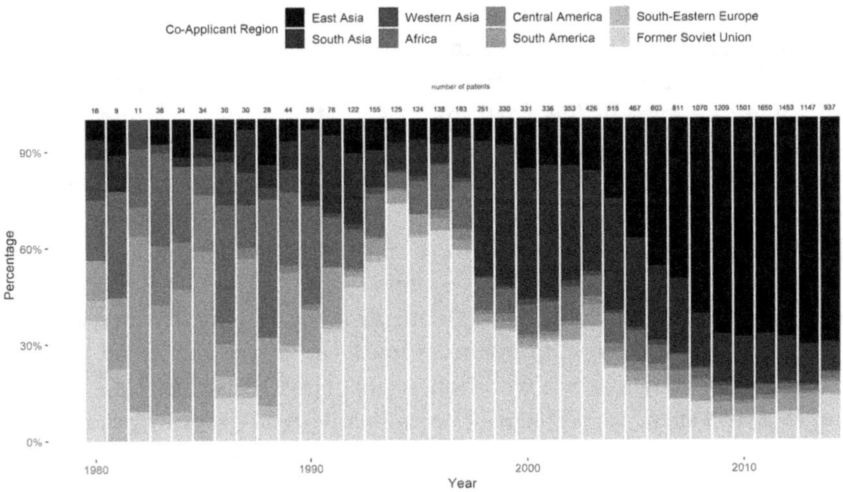

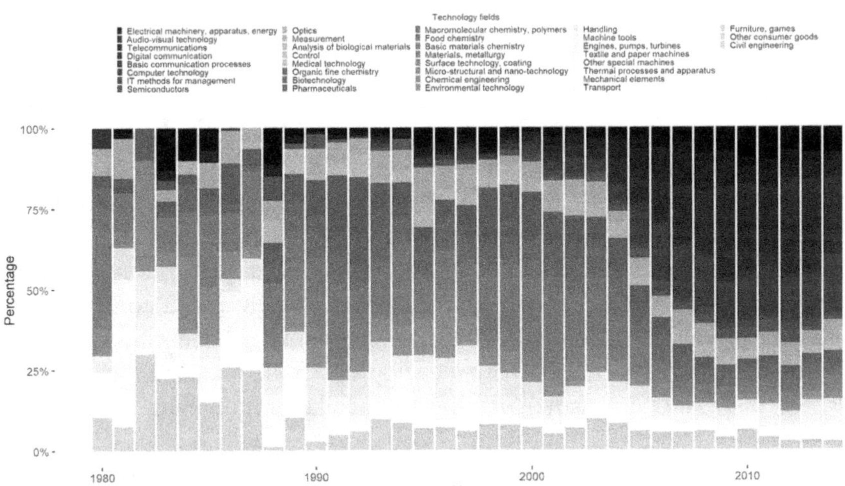

Figure 8.1 R&D collaboration (applicant criterion), by region and technology

Panel A. Patents co-applied between Core Europe and developing countries, by region in percentage.

Panel B. Patents co-applied between Core Europe and developing countries, by technology field in percentage.

Source: EPO PATSTATA database.

Note: The figures above each bar indicate the total number of patents that were co-applied with developing countries.

US applicants increased from about 500 patents in 1980 to more than 5,000 patents in 2010 and experienced a CAGR of 8 per cent. Thus, from a European perspective, collaboration with developing countries amounts to about one-third of the extent of collaboration with the United States. However, the growth rate has been more than twice as high.

Regarding the regional breakdown, most of the growth in collaboration is driven by firms located in East Asia, notably China. Collaboration with Russia and other former Soviet Union countries is low and oscillates at around 100 patents since the 2000s. Finally, collaboration with Africa, Central and South America has slightly increased in total numbers, although it remains at low levels. As a proportion, patents arising from collaboration with non-Asian countries is shrinking fast – it represents a mere 17 per cent in recent years. Asia has now become the dominant collaborating partner among all developing regions.

A strikingly similar pattern is obtained when looking at patents co-applied between US and Canadian applicants and applicants from developing countries (not shown), at least for recent years. The CAGR is higher than for Europe, reaching 24 per cent, and the breakdown in the 2010–2014 period is the following: East Asia (57 per cent); South Asia (33 per cent); Western Asia (<1 per cent); Africa (1 per cent); Central America (1.3 per cent); South America (2.2 per cent); South-Eastern Europe (<1 per cent); former Soviet Union (5.3 per cent). However, contrary to Europe, the United States and Canada had their main focus on Asian partners since the 1990s. In addition, although the number of priority filings is smaller for the United States and Canada compared to Europe (67,412 vs 113,952 in 2010), these countries have a much larger number of co-applications with developing countries (3,829 vs 1,501). Thus, from a US/Canadian perspective, collaboration with developing countries is almost as important as collaboration with Europe.

Panel B of Figure 8.1 breaks down the collaboration between core European applicants and applicants from developing countries by technology field. We allocate single technological fields into five technology sectors (see Schmoch, 2008): information and communication technologies (ICT) and electrical engineering; instruments; chemistry and pharmaceuticals; mechanical engineering; and other fields. Collaboration in ICT accounts for the majority of collaboration with developing countries in recent years (65.6 per cent in 2010). Historically, collaboration occurred mainly in pharmaceuticals and chemistry (58.1 per cent in 1990) but this sector has been marginalized, in relative terms, with the rise of communication and computer technologies. Similar findings emerge for the United States and Canada (not reported). However, the rise in the proportion of ICT started earlier (United States and Canada: 29 per cent in 2000, Europe: 10.7 per cent in 2000).

Figure 8.2 provides an overview of the proportion of patents co-invented between inventors from developed countries and inventors from developing countries, by region. Panel A focuses on core European inventors and Panel B focuses on US and Canadian inventors. Cross-border inventor collaboration looks very similar to cross-border firm collaboration over time. The similar pattern between cross-border firm collaboration and cross-border inventor collaboration should not come as a surprise. Indeed, a patent co-applied by firms in two countries very often involves inventors from these two countries.

Comparing Panel A with Panel B, it seems that European inventors as a whole have a collaboration network that is more geographically dispersed than North American inventors – the latter focus on Asia to a greater extent. However, similar to co-applications, the share of patents co-invented with Asia among total co-invented patents has increased strongly also in Europe. Looking at technology fields (not reported) suggests a pattern that is very similar to Panel B of Figure 8.1. The greater reliance on Asia for North America translates into a greater share of patents co-invented in information and communication technologies.

Technology Sourcing

The present section looks at patents sourced internationally. Figure 8.3 shows patent filings from applicants in Core Europe (Panel A) and the United States and Canada (Panel B) that are developed by inventors located in developing countries. The overall pattern is again very similar to the findings in Figure 8.1 and Figure 8.2. However, South Asia seems to be a bit more important for technology sourcing activities of North American applicants compared to East Asia, at least in recent years (the share of 'sourced' patents is 57 per cent for South Asia, compared to 30 per cent for East Asia in 2014). In A8.4, Figure A8.1 Panel A provides a complementary view. It shows a Sankey diagram of technology sourcing between developed regions and developing regions for the year 2014.[6] We can see that the United States and Canada account for the majority of technology sourcing from developing countries.

[6] Sankey diagrams are a specific type of flow diagram, in which the width of the arrows is shown proportionally to the flow quantity.

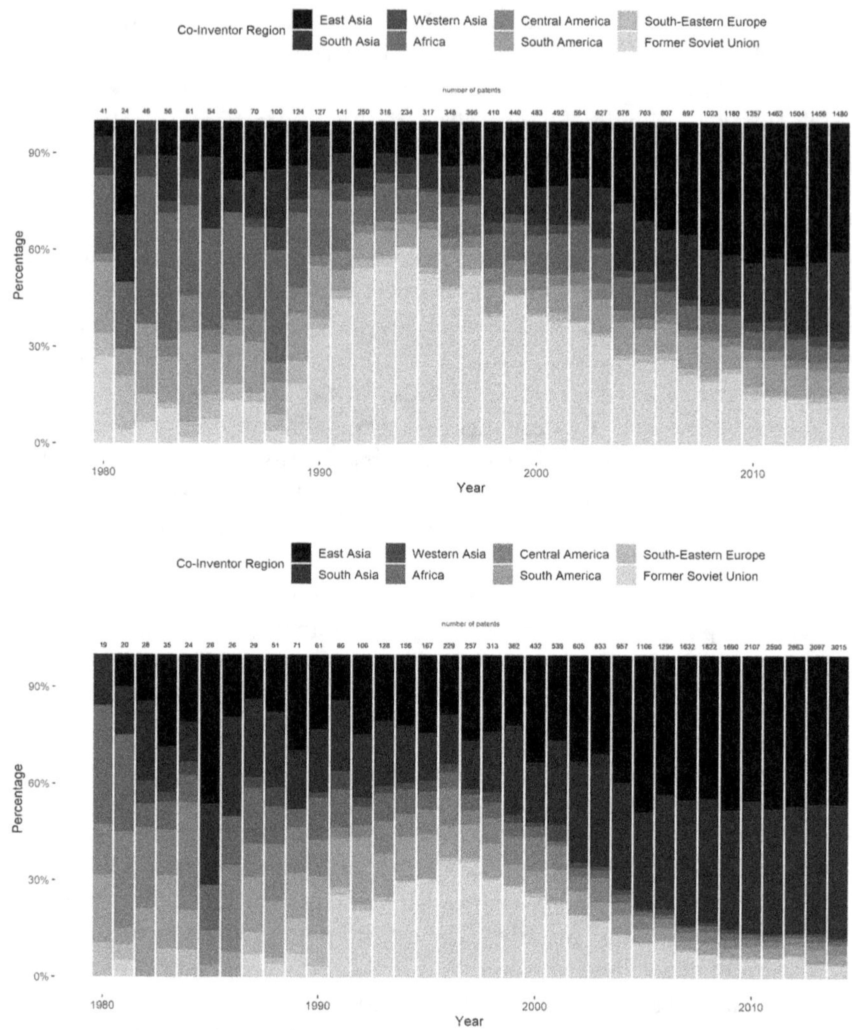

Figure 8.2 R&D collaboration (inventor criterion), by region

Panel A. Patents co-invented between Core Europe and developing countries, by region in percentage.

Panel B. Patents co-invented between the United States and Canada and developing countries, by region in percentage.

Source: EPO PATSTATA database.

Note: The figures above each bar indicate the total number of patents that were co-invented with developing countries.

The numbers of patents sourced by the United States and Canada dropped significantly during the 2008 global financial crisis.[7] Comparing the numbers of patents in Panel B of Figure 8.3 with those in Panel B of Figure 8.2 reveals that technology sourcing was more sensitive to the crisis than R&D collaboration. Firms in the United States and Canada had dramatically reduced their technology sourcing activities during the crisis. One possible explanation is that collaboration projects establish medium to long-term relationships that are more resilient to changing financial conditions. The number of patents filed by US and Canadian applicants with inventors in developing countries again increased strongly after the crisis period had ended.

As already discussed in the section on method and data,[8] we exclude co-applied patent filings in order to measure technology sourcing more accurately. Nevertheless, it is instructive to compare 'pure' technology sourcing (excluding co-applications) with technology sourcing including co-applications (which is suggestive of R&D collaboration). The former has become less common for East Asia relative to the latter. This suggests that firms from developed economies increasingly rely on R&D collaboration in East Asia in order to tap into local knowledge. In China, for example, finding local collaboration partners helps mitigate political and bureaucratic risks (Gassmann and Han, 2004). It is also sometimes a prerequisite imposed by the government to gain access to the Chinese market. In contrast, R&D offshoring to South Asia might still offer a large potential for saving costs.

Figure 8.4 shows technology sourcing by developing countries from developed countries. It presents the number of patents applied by developing countries and invented in developed countries (again excluding co-applied patents). The figures show a dominance of East Asian countries. Regarding the United States and Canada as host countries, the dominance is particularly visible. East Asia is the most active region in terms of sourcing technologies from developed countries, and it mainly does so in the United States. Interestingly, South Asian applicants are not very active when it comes to technology sourcing. Regarding technology sourcing from Europe, former Soviet Union countries still play a role. South America, which had a couple of patents with US and Canadian inventors in the past, has been marginalized, in relative terms. In A8.4,

[7] Not only the number of patents with US applicants and inventors abroad decreased in 2008–2009, but also the number of total patent filings.

[8] P. 267 *supra*.

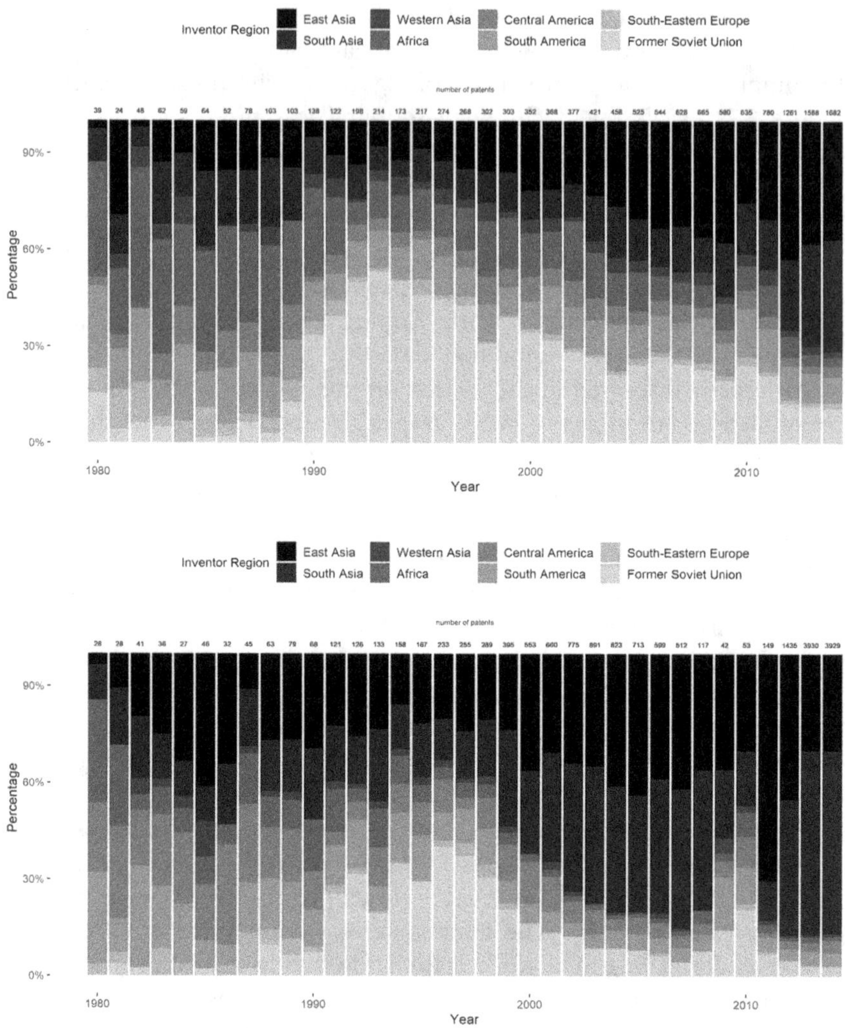

Figure 8.3 Technology sourcing from developing countries

Panel A. Patents applied by Core Europe and invented in developing countries, by region in percentage.

Panel B. Patents applied by the United States and Canada and invented in developing countries, by region in percentage.

Source: EPO PATSTATA database.
Note: The figures above each bar indicate the total number of patents that were 'sourced' from developing countries.

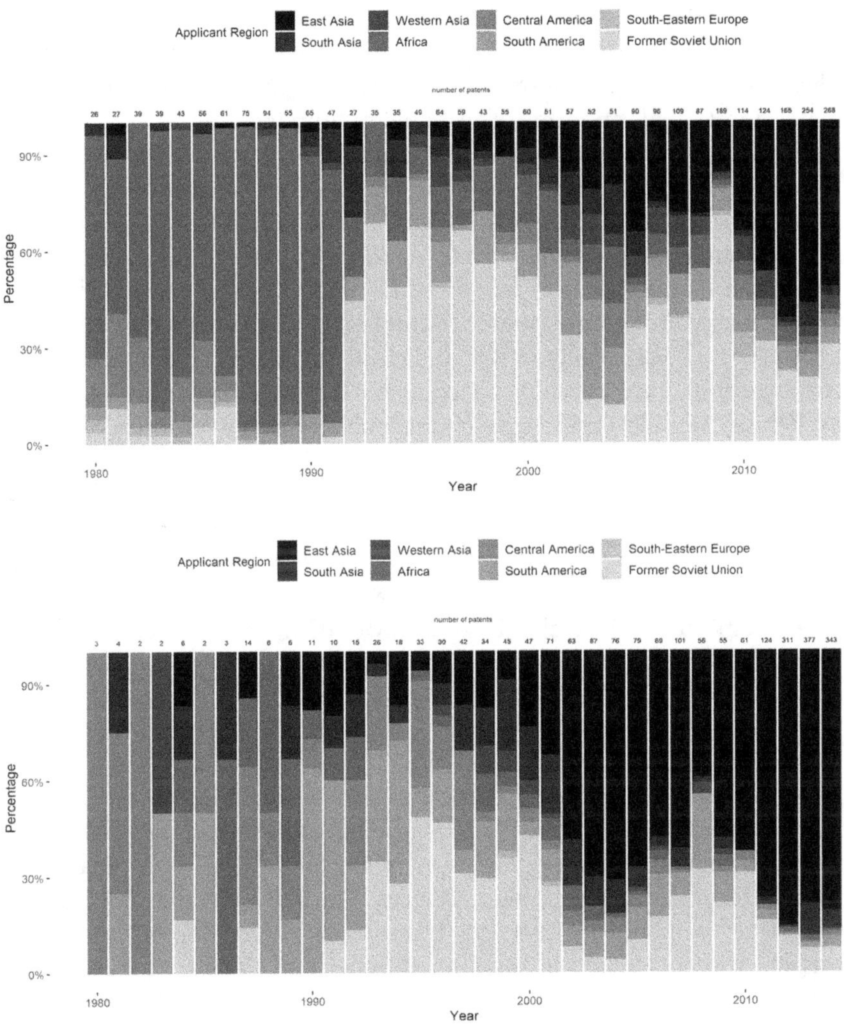

Figure 8.4 Technology sourcing from developed countries

Panel A. Patents invented in Core Europe and applied by developing countries, by region in percentage.

Panel B. Patents invented in the United States and Canada and applied by developing countries, by region in percentage.

Source: EPO PATSTATA database.
Note: The figures above each bar indicate the total number of patents that were 'sourced' from developed countries.

Figure A8.1 Panel B shows a Sankey diagram of technology sourcing of developing regions from developed regions for the year 2014. It further illustrates the dominance of the link between East Asia and the United States and Canada in terms of technology sourcing.

Figure 8.4 illustrates that East Asian companies increasingly source technologies in countries that are at the forefront of science and R&D. The reverse might not be true, at least in the past: Western companies might source technologies from developing countries for different reasons, for example in order to reduce R&D costs. However, the fact that developed economies source technologies mainly from East Asia and South Asia, and especially in ICT and electrical engineering, suggests that Asian regions have developed a comparative advantage in terms of the availability of skills and technological sophistication over other developing regions. Asian regions have certainly learned some of the knowledge brought in by Western firms (Li, Li and Shapiro, 2012). The fact that only East Asia, especially China, sources technologies at a larger scale reflects the sheer size of the country. It may also be a consequence of the Chinese strategy of building up its own R&D capabilities by drawing on knowledge from abroad (see also Hou and Mohnen, 2013; Nepelski and De Prato, 2015).

Technology Transfer

In this section, we focus on the transfers of ownership, i.e. the sales of rights of European patents. Panel A of Figure 8.5 shows the transfers of European patents from original owners located in Core Europe, to new owners located in developing countries. Panel B of Figure 8.5 follows the same logic. It displays the transfers of European patents from original owners located in the United States and Canada to developing countries.

In terms of overall volumes, patents transferred from Europe to developing countries have increased over the last decade. However, the overall activity is rather marginal. The year during which the largest number of patents were transferred from Core European to developing countries is 2013, during which 68 patents changed ownership to developing countries. Transfers arising from the United States and Canada represent a similar volume to transfers arising from Core Europe.

In terms of recipient regions, Panel A of Figure 8.5 shows that African countries were the most important destination region for patent transfers originating from Core Europe in the late 1990s, attracting

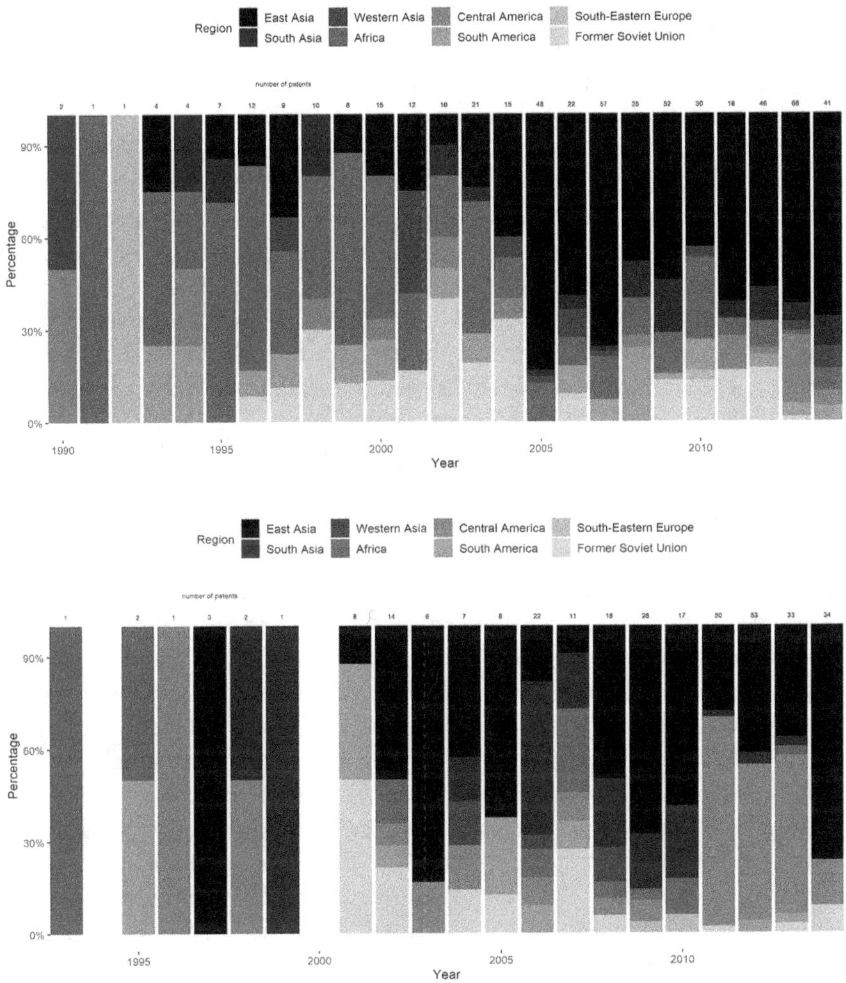

Figure 8.5 Technology transfers to developing countries

Panel A. Patents transferred from Core Europe to developing countries, by region in percentage.

Panel B. Patents transferred from United States and Canada to developing countries, by region in percentage.

Source: EPO PATSTATA and DPMA.
Note: The figures above each bar indicate the total number of patents that were transferred to developing countries. Empty bars indicate that the number is zero in the respective year.

around 40 per cent of transfers.[9] The pattern changed in the early 2000s, with the drastic increase of the proportion of East Asian countries as recipients of patents transferred to developing countries. In 2014, 83 per cent of these transfers were made to a new owner located in an East Asian country.

Panel B of Figure 8.5 shows the shares of developing countries regions as recipients of patent transfers originating from the United States and Canada, by year. Similar to transfers originating from Core Europe countries, the share of East Asian countries as recipients of transfers originating from the United States and Canada has increased over the last two decades. Central American countries are also an important destination in recent years for patent transfers originating from the United States and Canada.

Figure 8.6 focuses on developing countries as sources of patent transfers. Panel A presents the shares of developing regions as origin countries for patent transfers to Core Europe countries. Africa was the dominant origin region in the pre-2000 period, although this result should be interpreted with caution as the absolute numbers are very low. In more recent years, the shares are balanced, and there is no absolute dominance of a particular region. East Asia, Central America, Africa and the Former Soviet Union are the most important origin regions. Taking the average absolute volumes in the entire period, the number of patents transferred from developing countries to Core Europe is twice as small as the number of patents transferred from Core Europe to developing countries.

Panel B of Figure 8.6 displays the shares of developing regions as origin countries for patent transfers to the United States and Canada. Asian countries account for the bulk of the activity, although former Soviet Union countries are also well represented. In terms of absolute volumes, transfers from developing countries to the United States and Canada are more than three times less important than transfers to developing countries from US and Canadian owners in most of the recent years.

Concluding Remarks

This chapter studied the sources of cross-border knowledge flows through the lens of patent data. The various patent counts presented can be interpreted as proxies for R&D collaboration (co-applications

[9] The absolute volumes are nevertheless very low.

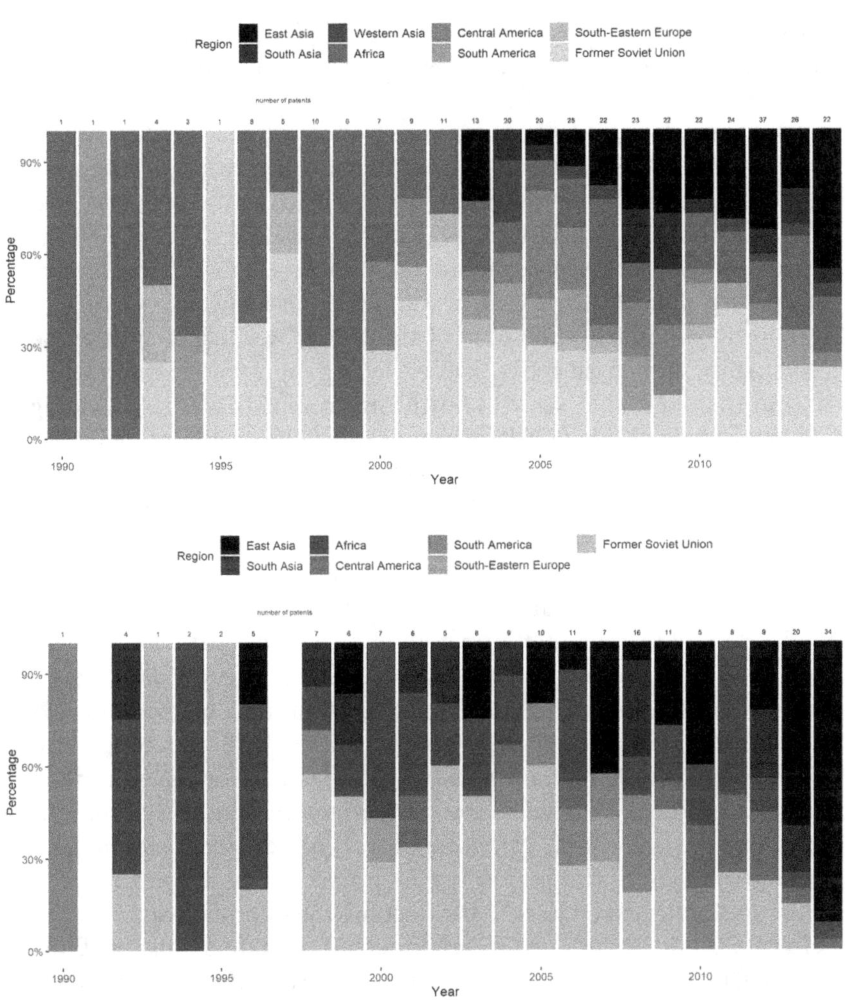

Figure 8.6 Technology transfers from developing countries

Panel A. Patents transferred from developing countries to Core Europe, by region in percentage.

Panel B. Patents transferred from developing countries to United States and Canada, by region in percentage.

Source: EPO PATSTATA and DPMA
Note: The figures above each bar indicate the total number of patents that were transferred to developed countries. Empty bars indicate that the number is zero in the respective year.

and co-inventions), technology sourcing (applicant and inventor from different countries) and technology transfer (patent transferred across countries).

A few caveats must be borne in mind when interpreting these results. First, the analysis is subject to the well-known limitation of patent data (Griliches, 1998). Not all inventions are patented, not all patented inventions are useful and patents vary widely in quality. Second, effective knowledge transfer involves more than co-developing or transferring patents (e.g. Liu, 2017). Third, the majority of transfers occur within developed economies, and some of the trends we document may be a consequence of the rising GDP of developing economies. Finally, lack of data on the ownership structure of firms prevents us from providing a more fine-grained analysis (for instance, by differentiating technology sourcing into R&D offshoring or R&D contracting).

Notwithstanding these limitations, a consistent message emerges across the three indicators. The main finding is that R&D activities and patent transfers have been concentrating in recent years. First, on the regional level, East Asia, and to a lesser extent South Asia, have risen as the developing regions that attract almost all of the patenting activities from developed regions. Regarding patent transfers, East Asia has become over the last decade the largest recipient region among developing countries, for transfers coming both from the United States and from Europe. In terms of volumes, transfers going to developing countries are almost three times as large as transfers originating in developing economies. East Asia, Central America and the Former Soviet Union are the major origin regions for this last type of transfers in recent years. Second, on the technological level, ICT has become the dominant sector.

In addition, although the developments are quite similar in Europe and the United States and Canada, we see some striking differences. First, the United States and Canada traditionally have greater patent activities with Asia, whereas this is a relatively new phenomenon for Europe. Second, the United States and Canada started to focus on ICT earlier than Europe. Finally, Central American countries remain an important destination for patent transfers originating from US and Canadian owners (although numbers are admittedly small).

Two additional findings are worth discussing. First, technology sourcing seems to be more sensitive to economic conditions than R&D collaboration. Firms in the United States and Canada dramatically reduced their technology sourcing activities during the global financial crisis.

Second, we observe more and more 'reverse' knowledge flows, whereby firms in developed regions source technologies from developing economies. Here again China is leading the charge. We can expect that Asian countries that attract foreign patent activities are benefiting from knowledge flows from the more developed countries, thereby raising their own technological base. China is already at the stage at which it sources technologies from developed countries to a large extent. Given that East Asia will continue to progress towards becoming a technological leader, US and Canadian firms seem to be in a better position than European firms to benefit from the rising sophistication of East Asia. They have a larger and better-established network of patent applicants and inventors in this region and are thus better placed to benefit from potential 'reverse' knowledge flows.

Bibliography

Agrawal, A., Cockburn, I. and McHale, J., 'Gone But Not Forgotten: Knowledge Flows, Labor Mobility, and Enduring Social Relationships' (2006), *Journal of Economic Geography* 6, 5: 571–591.

Arora, A., Fosfuri, A. and Gambardella, A., *Markets for Technology: The Economics Of Innovation and Corporate Strategy*, Cambridge, MA: MIT Press, 2004.

Bösenberg, S. and Egger, P. H., 'R&D Tax Incentives and the Emergence and Trade of Ideas' (2017), *Economic Policy* 32, 89: 39–80.

Chung, W. and Alcácer, J., 'Knowledge Seeking and Location Choice of Foreign Direct Investment in the United States' (2002), *Management Science* 48, 12: 1534–1554.

Ciaramella, L., Martínez, C. and Ménière, Y., 'Tracking Patent Transfers in Different European Countries: Methods and a First Application to Medical Technologies' (2017), *Scientometrics* 112, 2: 817–850.

De Marco, A., Scellato, G., Ughetto, E. and Caviggioli, F., 'Global Markets for Technology: Evidence from Patent Transactions' (2017), *Research Policy* 46: 9: 1644–1654.

de Rassenfosse, G., Dernis, H., Guellec, D., Picci, L. and de la Potterie, B. van P., 'The Worldwide Count of Priority Patents: A New Indicator of Inventive Activity' (2013), *Research Policy* 42, 3: 720–737.

Dunning, J. H. and Lundan, S. M., *Multinational Enterprises and the Global Economy*, Cheltenham: Edward Elgar Publishing, 2008.

Eaton, J. and Kortum, S., 'Measuring Technology Diffusion and the International Sources Of Growth' (1996), *Eastern Economic Journal* 22, 4: 401–410.

European Patent Office, *Patstat - Worldwide Patent Statistical Database - Autumn 2016*, Vienna: European Patent Office, 2016.

Galasso, A., Schankerman, M. and Serrano, C. J., 'Trading and Enforcing Patent Rights' (2013), *The RAND Journal of Economics* 44, 2: 275–312.

Gassmann, O. and Han, Z., 'Motivations and Barriers of Foreign R&D Activities in China' (2004), *R&D Management* 34, 4: 423–437.

Gomes-Casseres, B., Hagedoorn, J. and Jaffe, A. B., 'Do Alliances Promote Knowledge Flows?' (2006), *Journal of Financial Economics* 80, 1: 5–33.

Griffith, R., Redding, S. and Reenen, J. Van, 'Mapping the Two Faces of R&D: Productivity Growth in a Panel Of OECD Industries' (2004), *Review of Economics and Statistics* 86, 4: 883–895.

Griliches, Z., 'Patent Statistics as Economic Indicators: A Survey', in: *R&D and Productivity: The Econometric Evidence*, Chicago: University of Chicago Press, 1998, pp. 287–343.

Guellec, D. and de la Potterie, B. van P., 'The Internationalisation of Technology Analysed with Patent Data' (2001), *Research Policy* 30, 8: 1253–1266.

Harhoff, D., Hoisl, K., Reichl, B. and de la Potterie, B. van P., 'Patent Validation at the Country Level—The Role of Fees and Translation Costs' (2009), *Research Policy* 38, 9: 1423–1437.

Harhoff, D., Mueller, E. and Van Reenen, J., 'What Are the Channels For Technology Sourcing? Panel Data Evidence from German Companies' (2014), *Journal of Economics & Management Strategy* 23, 1: 204–224.

Hou, J., and Mohnen, P., 'Complementarity between In-House R&D and Technology Purchasing: Evidence from Chinese Manufacturing Firms' (2013), *Oxford Development Studies* 41, 3: 343–371.

International Monetary Fund, *World Economic Outlook: Challenges to Steady Growth*, Washington, DC: IMF, 2018.

Jaffe, A. B. and Trajtenberg, M., 'International Knowledge Flows: Evidence from Patent Citations' (1999), *Economics of Innovation and New Technology* 8, 1–2: 105–136.

Lenzi, C., 'Workers' Mobility and Patterns of Knowledge Diffusion: Evidence from Italian Data' (2010), *The Journal of Technology Transfer* 35, 6: 651–670.

Li, J., Li, Y. and Shapiro, D., 'Knowledge Seeking and Outward FDI of Emerging Market Firms: The Moderating Effect of Inward FDI' (2012), *Global Strategy Journal* 2, 4: 277–295.

Liu, Y., 'Promoting Cross-Border Knowledge Transfer For New Product Development in MNCS: A Process View' (2017), *The Journal of Technology Transfer* Early Access View.

Maruseth, P. B. and Verspagen, B. 'Knowledge-Spillovers in Europe: A Patent Citation Analysis' (2002), *Scandinavian Journal of Economics* 1044: 531–545.

Nepelski, D. and De Prato, G., 'International Technology Sourcing Between a Developing Country and the Rest of the World' (2015), *A Case Study of China. Technovation* 35: 12–21.

Peri, G., 'Determinants of Knowledge Flows and Their Effect on Innovation' (2005), *Review of Economics and Statistics* 87, 2: 308–322.

Picci, L., 'The Internationalization of Inventive Activity: A Gravity Model Using Patent Data' (2010), *Research Policy* 39, 8: 1070–1081.

Picci, L. and Savorelli, L., 'The "Inventor Balance" and the Functional Specialization In Global Inventive Activities' (2018), *Economics of Innovation and New Technology* 27, 1: 39–61.

Schmoch, U., Fraunhofer Institute for Systems and Innovation Research, Karlsruhe, Germany, June 2008, available at www.wipo.int/export/sites/www/ipstats/en/statistics/patents/pdf/wipo_ipc_technology.pdf.

Seliger, F., 'What Determines International and Inter-Sectoral Knowledge Flows? The Impact Of Absorptive Capacity, Technological Distance and Spillovers' (2016), KOF Working Paper, available at https://doi.org/10.3929/ethz-a-010737145.

Serrano, C. J., 'The Dynamics of the Transfer and Renewal Of Patents' (2010), *The RAND Journal of Economics* 41, 4: 686–708.

Singh, J., 'Collaborative Networks as Determinants of Knowledge Diffusion Patterns' (2005), *Management Science* 51, 5: 756–770.

Svensson, R., 'Knowledge Transfer to Emerging Markets Via Consulting Projects' (2007), *The Journal of Technology Transfer* 32, 5: 545–559.

Thomson, R. and de Rassenfosse, G., 'R&D Offshoring and Home Industry Productivity' (2016), available at https://papers.ssrn.com/sol3/papers.cfm?abstract_id=2812184.

United Nations, *World Economic Situation and Prospects*, New York City: United Nations, 2018.

A8.1

Allocation of Developed and Developing Countries to Regions

The allocation of developed and developing countries to regions is based on the country classification in the World Economic Situation and Prospects report (United Nations, 2018) and per capita nominal GDP figures from the World Economic Outlook Database (International Monetary Fund, 2018). The former classifies all countries of the world into developed economies, economies of transition and developing economies, mainly reflecting the basic economic conditions of the whole region. Geographical regions for developing economies are North Africa, Central Africa, East Africa, Southern Africa, West Africa, East Asia, South Asia, Western Asia, the Caribbean, Mexico and Central America, and South America. Economies of transition comprise countries in South-Eastern Europe and from the former Soviet Union (including Russia). For simplicity, we treated transition countries as developing economies.

The country classification is in some respects problematic as some regions of developing countries also comprise high-income countries (for example, Israel in Western Asia and the Republic of Korea and Singapore in East Asia). Therefore, we adapted the country classification and excluded countries from developing regions if they have a per capita nominal GDP that lies above the world average in 2017. In our analysis, we grouped all African regions into 'Africa' as the co-patenting shares are tiny for smaller regions. We also built one group for 'Central America' including the Caribbean and Mexico and other countries in Central America.

For the developed economies, we used two groups of countries: 'Core Europe' and 'United States and Canada'. Core Europe comprises all European Union member states (28) as well as Iceland, Norway and Switzerland. Other developed countries (Australia, New Zealand, Japan) are not considered in the chapter.

The patent filings are assigned to countries (and to regions) based on the applicants' and inventors' country codes in PATSTAT (European Patent Office, 2016). As the country codes are missing for many priority filings, we impute them using the method described in A8.2.

The following table shows the groups of countries we used to allocate patent filings to different world regions.

Table A8.1 *Groups of countries used in the chapter**

Developed countries	**Developing countries**			
Core Europe	***South-Eastern Europe***	**Egypt**	**Zimbabwe**	**Cuba**
Austria	Albania	Eritrea	***East Asia***	Dominican Rep.
Belgium	Bosnia and Herzegovina	Ethiopia	China	El Salvador
		Eswatini		
Bulgaria	Montenegro	Gabon	Fiji	Guatemala
Croatia	Serbia	Gambia	Indonesia	Guyana
Cyprus	North Macedonia	Ghana	Kiribati	Haiti
Czech Republic	***Former Soviet Union***	Guinea	Lao People's Dem. Rep.	Honduras
Denmark	Armenia	Guinea-Bissau	Malaysia	Jamaica
Estonia	Azerbaijan	Kenya	Mongolia	Mexico
Finland	Belarus	Lesotho	Myanmar	Nicaragua
France	Georgia	Liberia	Papua New Guinea	Suriname
Germany	Kazakhstan	Libya	Philippines	***South America***
Greece	Kyrgyzstan	Madagascar	Samoa	Bolivia
Hungary	Republic of Moldova	Malawi	Solomon Islands	Brazil
Iceland	Russian Federation	Mali	Thailand	Colombia
Ireland	Tajikistan	Mauritania	Timor-Leste	Ecuador
Italy	Turkmenistan	Mauritius	Vanuatu	Paraguay
Latvia	Ukraine	Morocco	Vietnam	Peru
Lithuania	Uzbekistan	Mozambique	**South Asia**	Venezuela
Luxembourg	***Africa***	Namibia	Afghanistan	
Malta	Algeria	Niger	Bangladesh	
Netherlands	Angola	Nigeria	Bhutan	
Norway	Benin	Rwanda	India	

* Editors' note: the authors' classification as set out in this table is for the purpose of the authors' scholarly analysis in the context of this chapter only and does not necessarily reflect formal legal or political status, nor the views of the WTO, its members or its Secretariat.

Table A8.1 (*cont.*)

Developed countries	**Developing countries**			
Core Europe	***South-Eastern Europe***	**Egypt**	**Zimbabwe**	**Cuba**
Poland	Botswana	Sao Tome and Principe	Iran	
Portugal	Burkina Faso	Senegal	Nepal	
Romania	Burundi	Sierra Leone	Pakistan	
Slovakia	Cabo Verde	Somalia	Sri Lanka	
Slovenia	Cameroon	South Africa	***Western Asia***	
Spain	Central African Rep.	Sudan	Iraq	
Sweden	Chad		Jordan	
Switzerland	Comoros	Togo	Syrian Arab Rep	
United Kingdom	Congo	Tunisia	Turkey	
United States and Canada	Côte d'Ivoire	Uganda	Yemen	
USA	Dem. Rep. of the Congo	United Rep. of Tanzania	***Central America***	
Canada	Djibouti	Zambia	Belize	

A8.2

Information on Inventors' and Applicants' Countries of Residence in Priority Filings

Patent statistics are based on so-called priority filings. Priority filings are the first filings within a patent family that might comprise multiple filings in different jurisdictions. We impute missing inventor (applicant) country codes using the method described in de Rassenfosse et al. (2013). Basically, their algorithm looks for equivalents and subsequent filings in the same family (preferring filings that are closer in time to the first filing) and uses the country codes from these filings if the priority filings' inventor (applicant) country code is missing. Subsequent filings are typically made at other patent offices. The algorithm browses 52 patent offices in order to impute missing information. To be more precise, it first selects all priority filings of a given patent office in a given year, so the first information source is the priority filing itself. For each filing that has missing information on the inventor's (applicant's) country of residence, it looks into six additional sources of information. The sources are browsed subsequently in order to retrieve missing information. The algorithm stops looking into those sources once it has found the country information in one of them. Source 1 is the priority document itself, whereas sources 2 and 3 exploit family linkages. Sources 4 to 6 look into country information of applicants, thereby assuming that the applicant's country is most likely to be identical with the inventor's country. Source 7 uses the country of the priority office for the country of residence of the inventor (applicant) if all other sources do not provide information. The following list provides more detailed information on the sources. If the interest lies in the applicant's country of residence rather than the inventor's country of residence, the sources are browsed in the same way starting with the applicant's country of residence in the priority document (as indicated in parentheses for each source).

- Source 1: Uses the inventor's (applicant's) country of residence from the priority document itself.
- Source 2: If no information on the inventor's (applicant's) country of residence is available from the priority document, the earliest direct equivalent is browsed. A direct equivalent is a second filing claiming the priority application in source 1 as sole priority.

- Source 3: If no information on the inventor's (applicant's) country of residence is available in the direct equivalents, the other second filings of the same family are browsed. The second filings considered in this source claim more than the priority document.
- Source 4: If no information on the inventor's (applicant's) country of residence is available in the other subsequent filings, the applicant's (inventor's) country of residence from the priority document is used.
- Source 5: If no information on the applicant's (inventor's) country of residence is available from the priority document, the earliest direct equivalent is browsed for this information.
- Source 6: If no information on the applicant's (inventor's) country of residence is available in the direct equivalents, the other second filings of the same family are browsed.
- Source 7: If the information is still missing, the country of the priority office is used for the inventor's (applicant's) country of residence.

In our context, we are interested in priority filings including more than one applicant (inventor) country or one applicant and one inventor being located in different countries. Of course, priority filings can have mixed applicant (inventor) teams with applicants (inventors) coming from more than one region of developing countries. These filings are then counted separately for each region. These cases are rare, but we checked the results using fractional counting (by assigning a weight to each developing country taking into account the relative size of the inventor team for each country). The results are very similar to the results reported in the main part of the paper.

A8.3

Allocation of Technology Fields to Patent Filings

The International Patent Classification (IPC) that is used to categorize patents according to their technological content provides a good starting point for an analysis by technologies. However, the IPC is highly technical, with hundreds of subclasses and groups. Therefore, we use more aggregated technology fields that have been assigned to IPC codes of patent filings based on the 'Concept of a Technology Classification for Country Comparisons' (Schmoch, 2008).

As patent filings usually have several IPC codes that correspond to several technologies, we use the weights from PATSTAT. It considers the degree to which a patent belongs to a certain technology field based on its IPC codes. To give an example, patent filing WO2018126352A1 is assigned to IPC Codes C09K9/00, G01K11/16 and H01B13/00. The technology classification uses only the first four digits. Here, C09K corresponds to 'Basic materials chemistry', G01K to 'Measurement' and H01B to 'Electrical machinery, apparatus, energy'. This means that the respective filing counts one-third for 'Basic materials chemistry', one-third for 'Measurement', and one-third for 'Electrical machinery, apparatus, energy'. The filing's weights that are calculated in this way can be found in PATSTAT. In our analysis, we sum them up by technology field (and year, region).

A8.4

Sankey Diagrams

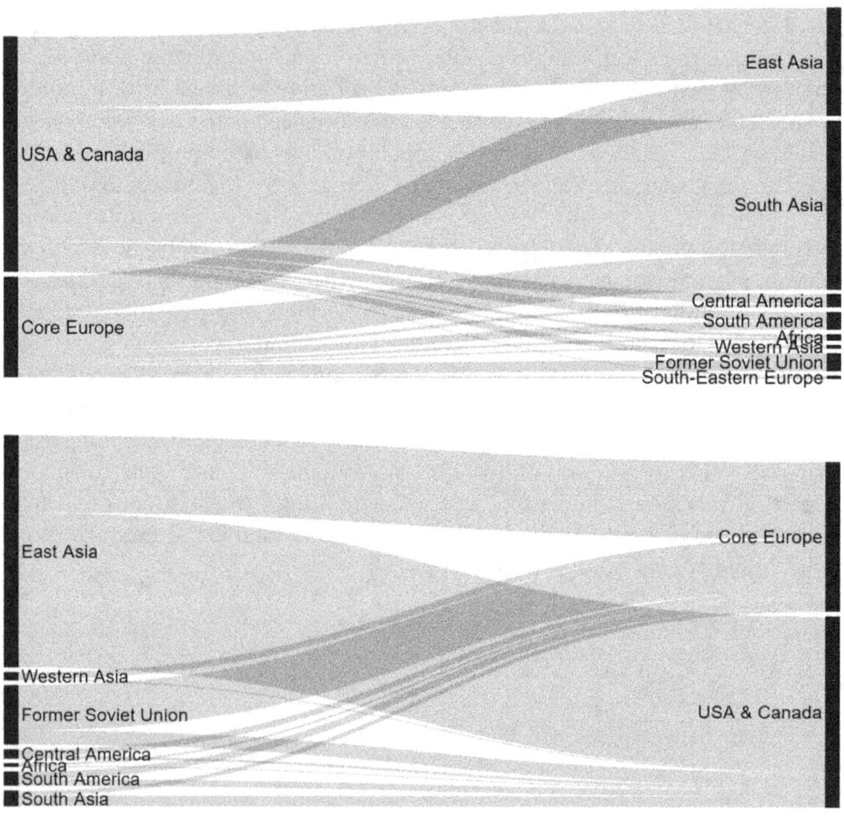

Figure A8.1 Links between the United States and Canada/Core Europe and developing countries

Panel A. Patents applied by the United States and Canada/Core Europe and invented in developing countries, by region, priority year 2014.

Panel B. Patents applied by developing countries and invented in the United States and Canada/ Core Europe, by region, priority year 2014.

9

Using Intellectual Property Data to Measure Cross-Border Knowledge Flows

JACOB DUBBERT, ALEXANDER V. GICZY, NICHOLAS A. PAIROLERO AND ANDREW A. TOOLE*

Abstract

This chapter surveys the landscape of empirical studies on cross-border trade in knowledge that use data on intellectual property rights (IPRs). Our discussion critically evaluates whether these data support the empirical findings in the studies by identifying where IPRs data are particularly useful and where these data have limitations. Additionally, we discuss the potential value of making greater use of IPRs assignment data. The goal of the chapter is to provide a reference to help policymakers evaluate the trade in knowledge literature, particularly the interpretation of IPRs-based evidence for policy decisions.

Introduction

Globalization and digitization have fundamentally changed the volume, form and content of international trade and cross-border information flows. Traditional determinants of trade such as natural resource endowments and transportation costs are becoming less important. Intangible assets increasingly define product characteristics and add value to tradable outputs. At the same time, customers are demanding more diverse and sophisticated products in international markets.

While scholars have incorporated many of these features into their empirical studies, our work at the US Patent and Trademark Office (USPTO) identified a need to synthesize this literature for those working

* We are grateful to Jayashree Watal, Nigel Cory and Andrew Torrance for helpful comments on an earlier version of this chapter. We also thank the participants in the 'Globalization and Intellectual Property' session at the January 2019 Allied Social Sciences Association (ASSA) meetings in Atlanta, GA. The views expressed in this chapter are the authors' and do not necessarily represent the views of the United States Patent and Trademark Office.

in policy environments. Policymakers generally welcome new insights from academic work, particularly when those insights help to formulate evidence-based policymaking. However, establishing evidence-based policy requires a significant amount of time and energy to review the various academic arguments and assess the credibility of the underlying data. Our experience also revealed that most of the new studies on trade in knowledge use intellectual property rights (IPRs) data, particularly information from patent documents, to proxy for theoretical concepts and to support the validity of their underlying arguments.[1] As intangible assets, IPRs data are potentially quite valuable as metrics for technology transfer and knowledge flows, but they are also specific legal rights that can complicate and limit their interpretation as evidence for economic policy.

This chapter surveys the landscape of empirical studies on cross-border trade in knowledge that use IPRs data. Based on a thorough search of the literature, we identify and categorize the types and uses of IPRs data. Our discussion critically evaluates whether these data support the empirical findings in the studies by identifying where IPRs data are particularly useful and where these data have limitations. The final section of the chapter discusses the potential value of making greater use of IPRs assignment data. The goal is to provide a reference to help policymakers evaluate the trade in knowledge literature, particularly the interpretation of IPRs-based evidence for policy decisions.

Scope, Literature and Economic Concepts

To keep the breadth of literature reviewed manageable, we imposed a set of restrictions. First, we defined 'cross-border trade' to mean international trade flows between sovereign nations as opposed to trade between states, provinces or territories within a single country. Second, all studies must include an empirical component that used IPRs data.[2]

[1] Measurement is critical for documenting the relationship between the flow of knowledge, technology transfer, innovation and economic activity. IPRs data are commonly used to proxy for knowledge flows and innovation because these data are widely accessible in machine-readable form, contain a rich set of information such as who owns the intellectual property and, when used carefully, allow for comparisons across countries.

[2] Our discussion of the uses of IPRs data in the literature is agnostic about the source; however, our discussion of underutilized IPRs data is United States centric since the authors are most familiar with USPTO data sources. Several resources are available for learning more about USPTO IPRs data. The USPTO Office of the Chief Economist releases several datasets and corresponding working papers describing the data, available

Third, we interpret trade to mean exchange through market and non-market transactions, although our coverage of each of these forms of trade is incomplete due to our focus on empirical studies using IPRs data.[3] Finally, and most significantly, there is the challenge of defining knowledge flows, whether in physical goods or information. For our purposes, knowledge is information that improves understanding *and* creates value as reflected in better economic outcomes for the recipients, their markets and their countries.

To construct our literature set, we identified studies using Google Scholar and followed up on the references found within these studies. Applying our restrictions, we identified and reviewed over 40 studies, both published and unpublished; however, we do not claim to be fully comprehensive in our coverage.

The literature attempts to characterize trade in knowledge using a wide variety of economic concepts and a diversity of empirical constructs. Trade in knowledge is seen as taking place through the movement of individuals, through market transactions between firms, through cross-border transfers within multinational firms, through indirect exchange across borders (e.g. intermediaries and online sellers), through foreign aid and through disembodied knowledge spillovers.[4] Some studies consider how country-level institutions and policies affect the flow of knowledge.

As might be expected, the segment of the literature that uses IPRs data focuses predominantly on the information contained in patent documents. Patent documents, whether from submitted applications or granted patents, provide a rich source of information on inventions. Among other things, patent documents reveal the technology owner on record,[5] the owner's location, dates such as the filing date, citations made

at https://www.uspto.gov/economics. Additionally, data on several other characteristics of IPRs are available in bulk form, available at https://bulkdata.uspto.gov/ and https://www.patentsview.org.

3 This limitation means we do not cover illicit trade in counterfeit goods, digital piracy or trade secrets. It also means we do not consider knowledge spillovers through certain disembodied forms such as journal publications, Internet downloads, television signals and so forth.

4 We interpret the category of 'foreign aid' quite broadly to include the work of foundations such as the Bill and Melinda Gates Foundation, non-governmental organizations and government aid programmes. Our search of the literature did not find any studies in this category that use IPRs data to characterize trade in knowledge.

5 There are many reasons why the owner on record from the patent document may not be the current owner of the patent. See Graham et al. (2018a) for further information.

to prior patents and non-patent literature, the names of inventors, location information for inventors, technological classification codes and more. IPRs metrics constructed from patent documents start with simple counts of patents, citations, classifications and inventors. This information is sometimes combined with other data to construct relationships between patents and patenting entities such as patent 'families' or 'equivalents', patent portfolios, measures of technological 'proximity' and country-level indexes of IPRs strength.

Beyond patent documents, a handful of studies in the literature use cross-border financial transactions reflecting licensing and royalty payments for patents, copyrighted works and trademarks. Table 9.1 lists the major studies we identified along with a brief summary of each paper's focus including the authors' names, publication date, time period covered, country coverage, topic, IPRs data used and the economic concepts proxied by the IPRs data.

The literature, however, does not take advantage of all available IPRs data to construct empirical metrics for characterizing trade in knowledge. Using patent documents extensively, the literature does not exploit the information in patent or trademark assignment databases. Assignment databases contain information on the sale, transfer and other forms of conveyance between parties of patent and trademark rights (see 'Underutilized Sources of Data for Trade in Knowledge' below[6]). Our survey also highlights the need for an authoritative, transparent and reproducible source for patent inventor disambiguation.[7]

The Uses of Intellectual Property Rights Data

In the literature, IPRs data are used as direct indicators of innovation as well as cross-border technology transfer and knowledge flows. They are also used indirectly to construct other indicators and to serve as variables that moderate the flow of technology or knowledge across borders. This section is organized by direct and indirect uses of IPRs data in the literature.

[6] P. 312 *infra.*

[7] Disambiguation is the process of creating unique identifiers that connect IPRs owner and inventor records. It addresses the extensive problems of text field matching. A simple example is fixing a misspelled name that would otherwise lead someone to conclude that the misspelling represents two owners or inventors instead of one.

Table 9.1 *Trade in knowledge: summary of selected literature*

Author	Time period	Coverage	Topic	IP data dependent variable	Dependent variable concept	IP data independent variable	Independent variable concept
Agrawal et al. (2011)	1981–2000	India	Inventor mobility	Patent citations (USPTO)	Measure knowledge flows	Patent inventor location (USPTO)	Measure the flow of skilled labour
Athreye and Yang (2011)	1998–2007	19 OECD countries	IP reform	OECD technology balance of payments; licensing revenue fees; WDI licensing revenue fees	Measure international flows of technology (intellectual property licences and sales)	Ginarte Park index	Identify the strength of intellectual property rights
Belitz and Molders (2016)	1990–2008	77 advanced and developing countries	R&D spillovers			Patent counts (WIPO)	Stock of knowledge that, when combined with import data, proxies for knowledge transfer
Branstetter (2001)	1983–1989	US and Japan	R&D spillovers	Patent counts (USPTO)	Proxy for the production of new knowledge		
Branstetter et al. (2006)	1982–1999	16 countries	IP reform	BEA RLF data; foreign patent counts (WIPO)	Measure technology transfer from parent firm to foreign affiliate [intrafirm	US patent counts (USPTO); Ginarte Park index	Identify patent intensive multinational affiliate companies;

Table 9.1 (*cont.*)

Author	Time period	Coverage	Topic	IP data dependent variable	Dependent variable concept	IP data independent variable	Independent variable concept
					licensing] in intellectual property reforming country; measure technology transfer from domestic to foreign countries and vice versa		identify intellectual property reforming countries and the date of reform
Branstetter et al. (2011)	1982–1999	24 countries	IP reform	BEA RLF data	Technology transfer	BEA RLF data	Identify technology intensive firms
Cai et al. (2017)	2005	28 countries	R&D spillovers			Patent counts (USPTO); patent citations (USPTO)	Measure innovation; measure knowledge flows
Eaton and Kortum (1996)	1988	19 OECD countries	Int. trade	Patent applications by reporting country and country of residence (WIPO)	Measure technology transfer from domestic to foreign countries and vice versa	Maskus and Penubarti measure of IP strength	Identify the strength of intellectual property rights
Fons-Rosen et al. (2017)	1998–2008	Belgium, Finland, France, Italy, Norway and Spain	R&D spillovers	Patent counts (USPTO)	Measure innovation	Firm-level patent portfolio technology shares	Develop a technology closeness measure

Ho et al. (2017)	1998–2009	China	IP reform	Patent counts (USPTO)	Measure of domestic pharmaceutical innovation	Number of patent stocks per 1,000 employees in pharmaceuticals	Existing knowledge stock
Hu and Jaffe (2003)	1977–1999	US, Japan, Republic of Korea and Chinese Taipei	R&D spillovers	Patent citations (USPTO)	Measure knowledge flows	Firm-level patent portfolio technology shares	Develop a technology closeness measure
Ivus (2010)	1962–2000	24 OECD and 55 developing countries	IP reform/trade			Ginarte Park index	Identify the strength of intellectual property rights
Javorcik (2002)	1989–1994	Eastern Europe and Former Soviet Union countries	IP reform			Ginarte Park index	Identify the strength of intellectual property rights
Johnstone et al. (2011)	1988–2005	50 countries	Variables, proxies and measurement	PATSTAT patent families	Measure technology transfer from priority country to additional countries		
Kim et al. (2009)	1975–1998	US	Inventor mobility	Patent citations (USPTO)	Measure knowledge flows	Patent inventor location (USPTO)	Measure the flow of skilled labor
Kuznar (2012)	1995–2011	15 EU countries and US	Variables, proxies and measurement	OECD technology balance of payments; licensing revenue fees	Measure international flows of technology (intellectual property licenses and sales)		

Table 9.1 (*cont.*)

Author	Time period	Coverage	Topic	IP data dependent variable	Dependent variable concept	IP data independent variable	Independent variable concept
MacGarvie (2006)	1986–1992	8 countries	Int. trade	Patent citations (EPO)	Measure knowledge flows	Patent classifications (EPO)	Measure technological proximity between firms
Miguelez et al. (2010)	1990–2006	Europe	Inventor mobility	Patent inventor location (EPO)	Measure the flow of skilled labour		
Miguelez (2018)	1990–2010	88 countries	Inventor mobility	Patent inventor location (WIPO)	Measure the flow of skilled labour and co-inventorship	Patent counts (WIPO); firm and country patent portfolio technology shares	Measure innovation; measure technological proximity between firm or countries
Moser et al. (2011)	1865–1914	14 original member countries of the Paris Convention and 14 that joined after US accession in 1887	IP reform	US patents by foreign nationals (USPTO)	Technology transfer		
Nakamura (2001)	1982–1988	Japan	Int. trade	Patent counts (USPTO)	Measure innovation	Licensed technology imports	
Oettl and Agrawal (2008)	1980–2000	Germany and Canada	Inventor mobility	Citations (USPTO)	Measure knowledge flows	Patent counts (USPTO); patent inventor	Measure existing stock of innovation;

						location (USPTO); firm and country patent portfolio technology shares	measure the flow of skilled labour; measure technological proximity between firm or countries
Peri (2005)	1975–1996	147 European and North American subnational regions	R&D spillovers	Patent citations (USPTO)	Measure knowledge flows		
Piermartini and Rubinova (2014)	2000–2008	29 countries	R&D spillovers	Patent counts (WIPO)	Measure innovation	Ginarte Park index	The extent of patent protection
Popovici (2006)	1963–1999	US and 12 countries with US subsidiaries	IP reform	Patent citations made and received (USPTO); patent classifications (USPTO)	Measure knowledge flows; originality and generality of patents		
Riker (2014)	2006 and 2012	33 countries	IPR reform	US cross-border RLFS (BEA)	Measure the strength of intellectual property rights in foreign countries		
Sjoholm (1996)	1973–1986	Sweden	Int. trade	Patent citations	Measure knowledge flows	Patent counts	Existing stock of patents or knowledge

IPRs Data as Direct Indicators

IPRs data are often used as direct indicators of innovation, technology transfer and knowledge flows. The indicators are constructed using patent counts, patent citations, licensing and royalty payments and patent families.

Patent Counts

Several studies use patent counts to measure innovation outputs.[8] For example, Fons-Rosen et al. (2017) analyse the impact of foreign competition on domestic firm innovation, which is proxied by firm patent counts. Additionally, Peri (2005) measures the impact of research and development spillovers on domestic innovation, again with innovation captured by patent counts. This is a standard approach in the literature and builds on two basic facts: first, the flow of new patents is positively correlated with innovation; and second, patent data are widely available in research ready datasets (see Pakes and Griliches, 1980; Griliches, 1998).

A well-developed literature describes a number of limitations regarding the use of patent counts or weighted counts to represent innovation. First, the distribution of valuable patents is highly skewed (Pakes, 1986; Griliches, 1998; Harhoff et al., 2003). Therefore, depending on the underlying motives, an increase in patent counts or patent counts weighted by citations may not reflect an increase in valuable innovation. Second, there are significant differences in legally patentable subject matter across jurisdictions and legal interpretations change over time (Pavitt, 1988; Cohen et al., 2002). This makes temporal and international comparisons of innovation through patent counts challenging. Additionally, the value of a patent right is different across technologies for a variety of reasons, such as variations in the cost of imitation (Pavitt, 1988; Cohen et al., 2002). Therefore, the degree to which patents represent innovation is not the same across industries, and this limits the usefulness of comparing patent counts across industries, and possibly technologies within an industry. As noted by many researchers, these concerns highlight the need for further research on non-patent-based measures of innovation (Sampat, 2018).

Counts of foreign patent filings relative to domestic filings are used in the literature to proxy for technology transfer (i.e. the movement of technology across borders). Branstetter et al. (2006) use World

[8] Ho et al. (2017); Fons-Rosen et al. (2017); Peri (2005); Cai et al. (2017); Nakamura (2001).

Intellectual Property Organization (WIPO) patent data to estimate whether country-level IPRs legal reform has any impact on foreign patent filings relative to domestic filings. They contend that a post-reform increase in foreign filings relative to domestic filings is consistent with an inflow of technology from multinational parents to affiliates due to the reform. They further contend that these filings may indicate the transfer of *new* technical knowledge rather than existing knowledge. (They use technology licensing flows to proxy for existing knowledge transfer within multinationals.) Similarly, Moser et al. (2011) use USPTO patent counts by foreign nationals, and Eaton and Kortum (1996) use WIPO patent counts to measure technology transfer and diffusion.

Despite the claims made by these authors, it is unclear whether a relative increase in foreign filings (or foreign patent counts in the case of Moser et al. (2011) and Eaton and Kortum (1996)) actually captures technology transfer. It is well known that companies file patents abroad for strategic purposes,[9] or companies may produce the good domestically for export to the foreign jurisdiction. Both of these alternatives undermine the interpretation of patent counts as technology transfer. Of course, when companies use their patented technologies in foreign jurisdictions, they may provide this technology to a foreign affiliate for local production, and that may constitute a form of technology transfer. To know which interpretation of patent counts is appropriate one needs to understand the motivations that led to the foreign patenting filing and have richer information on company choices and behaviours after filing abroad.

Patent Citations

Several papers use patent citations to proxy for knowledge flows.[10] These authors interpret each citation given by a focal patent to other patents or non-patent sources as an indicator of knowledge flowing from those cited sources to the creative process yielding the current invention. For example, MacGarvie (2006) uses citations from domestic firm patents to foreign firm patents to capture the transfer of knowledge from foreign

9 Blind et al. (2009) suggest that firms pursue strategic filing for a variety of reasons including protecting technological knowledge, blocking competitors and generating revenue through negotiation and exchange of patents with other firms. The strategic use of patents is supported in the literature based on survey and other empirical evidence. For example, survey evidence from Cohen et al. (2000) finds that blocking competitors and preventing lawsuits are two important motives for seeking patent protection.

10 MacGarvie (2006); Peri (2005); Popovici (2006); Sjoholm (1996); Cai et al. (2017); Hu and Jaffe (2003); Oettle and Agrawal (2008); Agrawal et al. (2011); Kim et al. (2009).

countries. The paper focuses on how imports influence knowledge flows to the importing firm from the exporting foreign country. In another example, Peri (2005) studies how innovation depends on research and development knowledge 'spillovers' by using patent citations as a direct indicator of spillovers.[11]

There are several critiques in the literature regarding the use of patent citations to capture knowledge flows (Peri, 2005; MacGarvie, 2006; Jaffe and de Rassenfosse, 2017). Perhaps the most obvious critique is that patent citations only capture a narrow form of potential knowledge flows – knowledge that gets codified into patent documents, particularly granted patent documents. Conceptually and empirically, knowledge flows through many channels that patents do not capture such as interpersonal relationships, professional networks, scientific and industry publications and more (Cohen et al., 2002). The narrowness of citations as a metric for knowledge flows is particularly concerning for the strand of the literature that studies spillovers from research and development. This strand uses patent citations as a proxy for all channels of knowledge flows, which is likely to underestimate the general contribution of spillovers and overestimate the importance of patent citations as a single channel for these flows.

Two other issues affecting how to interpret citations are the entity who cites the patent document and the specific procedures used by the relevant patent office to report citations. Peri (2005) points out that citation metrics become less informative when patent office employees (i.e. the patent examiners) add citations. At the USPTO, an examiner often finds *prior art* that the applicant did not cite, and this adds citations unrelated to the knowledge used in the inventive process.[12] Also, applicant submitted citations may get reported as examiner added citations. This happens because patent documents do not list duplicate citations between the applicant and the examiner. When a citation is entered by the examiner and the applicant, it shows up as an examiner citation on the USPTO published patent document.[13] Moreover, in the US, patent attorneys and agents often add a large proportion of the citations to the patent

[11] Knowledge spillovers take place when valuable information benefits a third party who did not invest in the production of that information or pay for access to that information.

[12] In general, *prior art* is defined by WIPO as 'all the knowledge that existed prior to the relevant filing or priority date of a patent application, whether it existed by way of written and oral disclosure'. For a detailed list of *prior art* definitions by country, see https://www.wipo.int/export/sites/www/scp/en/national_laws/prior_art.pdf.

[13] https://www.uspto.gov/web/offices/pac/mpep/s1302.html.

application. While the extent of this issue is unknown, it would be incorrect to attribute attorney/agent added citations as knowledge flows used by inventors as part of the inventive process. Also, if a foreign patent office records a citation, the citation may show up as an applicant citation at the USPTO. In this case, the citation would not represent a knowledge flow. Finally, applicants may list references for strategic reasons (Atal and Bar, 2010). These considerations suggest that differentiation between applicant and examiner citations, which some authors do, is still not enough to ensure good measurement of knowledge flows using patent citations.

Additional issues arise when interpreting patent citations as international knowledge flows (Jaffe and de Rassenfosse, 2018). One important issue is the differences in laws and policies across jurisdictions. US law requires patent applicants to report all relevant *prior art* if it is known at the time of application (i.e. the 'duty of candor'). US patent owners may lose their patent right if a court finds that they purposely withheld relevant citations. In contrast, for applications to the European Patent Office, examiners add all citations. This leads to international differences in citation practices that will affect interpretation. Further, Bacchiocchi and Montobbio (2010) find evidence of 'home bias' in patent citations. That is, a patent's citations tend to reflect sources available in the specific home jurisdiction. For these reasons, citations may only weakly transmit information about cross-border knowledge flows.

Recall that citations are used to capture knowledge flows that influenced the inventor and led to a patent. However, the relevance and importance of the information contained in patent citations to the original inventive process is unclear. Based on a survey of patent inventors, Jaffe et al. (2000) find that about one-fourth of the citations on patents signalled meaningful knowledge flows, half had no meaningful relationship to the inventive process and the remaining quarter fell somewhere in between these extremes. Roach and Cohen (2013) find evidence of 'errors of omission' (reported knowledge flows with no corresponding citations) and 'errors of commission' (observed citations with no corresponding reported knowledge flows). Moreover, applicants may purposely add excessive citations to confuse the examiner or to protect themselves against future patent litigation (Cotropia et al., 2013).[14] In a recent article, de Grazia et al. (2018) introduce a metric to

[14] The presumption of validity describes the reluctance of the courts to overrule a patent examiner's consideration of *prior art* in patent litigation. *Prior art* considered by the patent examiner during examination is only used to invalidate a patent in litigation if

assess the technical relevance of patent citations using the language contained in the claims of the focal patent and the claims of the cited patents.[15] The paper shows that examiner citations are more similar to the focal patent than citations provided by applicants. While this work moves in the direction of linking patents based on technical information content, it cannot tell us if the technical information was available or used by the inventors in the inventive process; nor can it address problems related to who adds citations to the patent document.

Finally, there is evidence that less novel inventions are more likely to have many citations to previous patents (Trajtenberg et al., 1997). This empirical observation casts doubt on the interpretation of citations in some studies. For instance, while a domestic firm that cites many foreign patents could be the recipient of knowledge flows from abroad, as in MacGarvie (2006), these cites may be related to less novel inventions rather than capturing valuable knowledge flows. If less novel inventions have more citations to previous patents, the results related to IPRs reform in developing counties, such as those in Branstetter et al. (2011), also come into question. Suppose intellectual property reform in developing countries reduces imitative activity and increases domestic incentives to innovate. If this innovation is novel, it may have fewer citations to prior patents, not more. This would lead to the somewhat counterintuitive conclusion that fewer citations to foreign countries (i.e. less knowledge flow) is associated with greater welfare.

Licensing and Royalty Payments

Kuznar (2012) and Athreye and Yang (2011) use the Organisation for Economic Cooperation and Development (OECD) technology balance-of-payments data to capture technology transfer. These data contain 'commercial transactions related to international technology and know-how transfers'.[16] Kuznar (2012) notes that licensing and royalty payment

there is 'clear and convincing evidence'. For this reason, applicants may strategically submit *prior art* by submitting a large number of citations. Given a limited amount of time provided to the examiner to examine the patent application, this may increase the likelihood that relevant *prior art* is not used in an examiner's rejection. This art would then enjoy the presumption of validity in later patent litigation (Cotropia et al., 2013).

[15] Recall the claims portion of a patent document is where the invention is precisely described. See Younge and Kuhn (2016) and Arts et al. (2017) for other recent papers that apply natural language processing methods to patent documents.

[16] OECD is an intergovernmental economic organization with about 36 member countries. Their data comprise 'money paid or received for the acquisition or use of patents,

statistics are also available for non-OECD countries from the International Monetary Fund's (IMF) Balance of Payments Statistics. However, both sources use very broad definitions that are overly inclusive from the perspective of capturing knowledge flows. Large portions of the IMF's licensing and royalty payments are intrafirm flows between parent companies and their subsidiaries due to differences in taxes and transfer pricing practices. Further, the OECD technology balance of payments data include 'technology related services and industrial R&D carried out abroad'.

Branstetter et al. (2006) use the Bureau of Economic Analysis (BEA) survey of US Direct Investment Abroad and Balance of Payments Survey to capture technology transfer within multinational firms; in particular, intrafirm royalty payments for intangible assets.[17] The licensing flows are used to examine whether intellectual property reform increases international technology transfer within multinational companies. To account for the influence of tax regimes on the licensing and royalty payments data, Branstetter et al. (2006) control for country income tax and withholding tax rates.

Athreye and Yang (2011) use the MERIT-CATI[18] and Thompson Financials SDC Platinum[19] databases to capture technology agreements and licensing royalties. The MERIT-CATI database records technology agreements that are reported in the media; including financial and technical press. Therefore, the MERIT-CATI technology agreements likely over-represent valuable and more impactful technology agreements. The Thompson Financials database contains a variety of metadata on technology agreements (for example, exclusivity and fee descriptions); however, since the technology agreements are voluntarily disclosed, the data may be subject to biases related to firm strategy.

Overall, royalty and licensing data are useful for capturing payments associated with IPRs protecting intangible assets. The details and pitfalls of this type of data are discussed in greater depth elsewhere in this

licenses, trademarks, designs, inventions, know-how and closely related technology services and for industrial R&D carried out abroad'. See OECD publication number 2087228.

17 A detailed description of this data is contained in Mataloni (1995).

18 To the best of our knowledge, this data source is discontinued.

19 The data is available here https://www.refinitiv.com/en/products/sdc-platinum-financial-securities.

volume.[20] One of the unresolved issues with licensing and royalty data is whether these transactions actually represent valuable knowledge flows and/or technology transfers. For instance, much of the knowledge or underlying technology embodied in licensed patents is already known through public disclosure of the patent documents. Further, the technology needed to produce licensed copyrighted materials such as music, movies and software may not be available to the licensee. Nevertheless, the licensing and royalty data would show significant financial flows. These financial flows would surely overestimate knowledge flows or technology transfer.

Patent Families

International patent families are groups of patent documents that typically share three key features: (1) the patents come from the same applicant (e.g. IBM); (2) the patents share a similar (or the same) invention concept;[21] and (3) the patents are filed in multiple jurisdictions. Johnstone et al. (2011) use international patent families to measure technology transfer.[22] They note three ways technology flows could be measured using family relationships. First, technology may flow from the inventor location/country to the priority office location/country.[23] Second, technology could flow from the inventor location/country to additional offices located throughout the world. Third, technology may flow from the priority jurisdiction to additional offices abroad. Whether these linkages reflect international technology transfer is unclear for many of the same reasons discussed previously. Rather than technology transfer, companies often have strategic motives for filing similar patents abroad and thereby creating patent families (Dechezlepretre et al., 2017). Further, this type of metric is necessarily restricted to technology transfers within the same firm. Again, richer information is needed to understand the connections between international patent filing strategies and

[20] See in particular Chapter 5 (Maurer and Magdeleine) in this volume.

[21] The invention concept for a patent is described in the patent specification part of the patent document. While patent claims legally define the invention, patents in the same family rarely share the exact same claims due to legal differences within and across jurisdictions.

[22] WIPO provides a definition of patent families (see https://www.wipo.int/ipstats/en/statistics/glossary.html); however, there are many different definitions used in the literature. Martinez (2011) provides an overview of the different definitions and the importance of each.

[23] The priority office jurisdiction is the location where the first patent application is filed.

firm operational decisions. Technology transfer could be taking place if the companies involved built foreign production facilities, educated foreign workers and otherwise shared new technical information that created value in the receiving country.

IPRs Data and Indirect Indicators

Intellectual property data are used in indirect ways to characterize the relationship between two or more entities (e.g. countries, industries and firms) and to serve as moderating variables that influence the degree of technology transfer or knowledge flow. In particular, IPRs data are used to construct indexes of country-level IPRs strength, various metrics of IPR intensity, technological proximity and technology transfer or knowledge flow through inventor mobility across countries.

Indexes of Intellectual Property Strength

Various country-level indexes of IPRs strength appear in the literature. By far the most popular is the Ginarte Park index.[24] Branstetter et al. (2006) and Branstetter et al. (2011) use changes in the Ginarte Park index to investigate the effect of IPRs reform on a variety of economic outcomes. The advantage of indexes is the ability to summarize a large number of complex laws and policies into a single indicator. The disadvantage is that one cannot usually tell which component of the index is driving the suggested results and the weighting schemes are quite arbitrary. In this regard, indexes are blunt empirical constructs and rarely produce the detailed and specific conclusions needed for setting evidence-based policy.

Intellectual Property Intensity

Several papers construct metrics of IPRs 'intensity' that separate industries or companies into groups based on the extent to which they use

[24] Ginarte and Park (1997) use the unweighted sum of five separate scores to create their index. These are: coverage (inventions that are patentable); membership in international treaties; duration of protection; enforcement mechanisms; and restrictions. Other indexes include Maskus and Penubarti (1995), Mansfield (1995) and Riker (2014). Maskus and Penubarti (1995) use an index developed by Rapp and Rozek (1990) which measures the relative strength of patent laws across countries based on business surveys and patent laws, ranking them on a scale from 1 to 5; however, they correct the index for measurement error and endogeneity by adopting an instrumental variables approach.

IPRs (Ivus, 2010; Javorcik, 2002; and Branstetter et al., 2006). Ivus (2010) draws on the work of Cohen et al. (2000) to characterize the IPRs intensity by industry.[25] This is used to account for policy effects on trade that are common across patent-intensive and non-patent-intensive industries. Javorcik (2002) uses the Mansfield (1995) classification to measure the impact of intellectual property strength on the decision to undertake foreign direct investment and the composition of foreign direct investment. Branstetter et al. (2006) use a measure of firm-level patent intensity to estimate the differential impact of intellectual property reform on technology transfer between affiliates of patent-intensive and non-patent-intensive parents. A multinational parent is patent intensive if it has 'at least as many US patent applications as the parent of the median affiliate in the reforming country over the same period' (Branstetter et al., 2006). The key assumption in this work is that the IPRs data used to construct the intensity metric is exogenous (i.e. not correlated with un-modelled influences affecting the outcome being studied).

Technological Proximity

The trade and knowledge literature uses IPRs data to construct metrics of technological proximity, which is the idea of 'closeness' in technological knowledge or use between two entities such as firms, industries or countries. MacGarvie (2006) uses patent technology classifications to identify the proximity of a firm's patent portfolio to a foreign country's technological profile.[26] Because technological proximity is one reason for observing greater patent citations between domestic companies and other jurisdictions, MacGarvie (2006) includes this metric as a control variable when examining the relationship between imports and firm knowledge flows (as captured by citations to the foreign country).[27]

[25] Cohen et al. (2000) develop a measure of intellectual property reliance at the industry level, based on the responses of R&D managers to questions on the effectiveness of different appropriability mechanisms for protecting innovation.

[26] A country's technology profile is constructed using the set of patents held by that country (MacGarvie, 2006). Technological proximity is calculated using the cosine distance metric introduced by Jaffe (1986).

[27] Similar approaches are used in other work. See, for instance, Miguelez (2016), Fons-Rosen et al. (2017) and Oettl and Agrawal (2008).

Patent Inventor Location

Several papers use inventor locations on patent documents to proxy for the mobility of skilled labour. In this context, cross-border knowledge flows take place through the movement of people who, presumably, bring specialized technical knowledge from one country to another. Oettl and Agrawal (2008) use the location of inventors on USPTO patents to identify instances of inventors moving from a firm to a foreign country. They do not perform disambiguation of the inventor names (see fn. 7) and this leads to either overestimation or underestimation of knowledge flows. Overestimation will occur when two inventors with the same name patent in different countries. In this case, they incorrectly treat two different people as if they were the same inventor. Underestimation will occur when an inventor moved abroad but, due to the lack of disambiguated names, their method misses this person because of name variations on the patent documents. Oettl and Agrawal (2008) take a few steps to minimize the first type of error; however, their approach is relatively simplistic.[28] The authors believe the second type of error should not bias their results since errors in name records are unlikely to be correlated with the tendency to cite a patent. While plausible, this assertion remains untested.

Miguelez (2018) uses inventor residence and nationality data from WIPO patent documents for an analysis of how skilled migration impacts international patent collaboration. In their work, an incidence of the migration of skilled labour is captured when an inventor on a WIPO application has a different residence and nationality. Miguelez (2018) follows Kerr (2008) and treats each inventor observation as an instance of skilled migration, rather than disambiguating the inventors. Another limitation of their approach is that migration is not counted if the inventor changes citizenship to the residence country.[29] Finally, as noted by Miguelez (2018), tracking skilled migration with patented inventions is quite limited as it is restricted to individuals who are observed multiple times as inventors in patent data.

Agrawal et al. (2011) use inventor location data to estimate the impact of inventor diaspora on knowledge flows. Their inventor identification strategy does not depend on disambiguation, but

[28] A name with multiple patents is only identified as the same inventor if the patents cover inventions in similar fields. See Oettl and Agrawal (2008, p. 1247) for a precise definition of 'similar fields'.

[29] Since in this case the nationality would be the same as the residence.

creatively (yet noisily[30]) identifies non-Indian residents who are Indian inventors by their last names.[31] In other work, Miguelez et al. (2010) use WIPO inventor locations to track skilled migration across regions of Europe over time. They employ the Soundex algorithm for inventor disambiguation, noting that Trajtenberg et al. (2006) and Kim et al. (2009) use the same algorithm. Finally, Kim et al. (2009) use USPTO inventor location data to estimate the impact of foreign research experience on knowledge flows (as captured through citations).

This research highlights the need for an authoritative, transparent and reproducible method for disambiguating inventor names (and other similar information like owner names) on patent documents. One source for disambiguated patent inventor and patent owner information for US granted patents is PatentsView.[32] PatentsView is free Web-based data visualization and analysis platform sponsored by the USPTO Office of the Chief Economist (www.patentsview.org). It uses a sophisticated open source algorithm for disambiguation with downloadable files available in bulk or through an application programming interface (API).[33]

Underutilized Sources of Data For Trade in Knowledge

Our literature search revealed that IPRs assignment datasets are underutilized as sources for learning about international technology transfer and knowledge flows. Patent and trademark assignment datasets contain various types of transactions between an existing owner (the assignor) and a recipient (the assignee). Some of these transactions, particularly those involving the buying and selling of patents and trademarks across borders, may reflect international technology transfer or knowledge flows. Other transaction types, such as those involving assignments of patents and trademarks as collateral to financial institutions, may be

[30] For example, as noted by the authors, Indian women who emigrate from India and change their last name (for example with marriage) are not identified as emigrating from India. Despite this, the authors note that measurement errors in their name data will bias the result downward.

[31] See Agrawal et al. (2011), p. 48.

[32] Another option is the PATSTAT product offered by the European Patent Office also includes some disambiguated data.

[33] A full description of the algorithm and results is on PatentsView, available at https://www.patentsview.org.

useful for understanding how banking relationships influence cross-border technology transfer.[34]

To illustrate potential uses of the US assignment datasets, we analysed patent and trademark transactions flowing in four location-based directions: US assignor to US assignee; US incoming (foreign assignor to US assignee); US outgoing (US assignor to foreign assignee); and foreign assignor to foreign assignee. To construct these comparisons, we required the location information for each transacting party. Because patent assignors are not required to report their addresses, we used the inventor and assignee information from PatentsView, which contains the city and country of patent inventor(s) and owner(s) at the date of grant.[35] For the trademark assignment dataset, the assignor addresses are not available after 1992 due to a change in USPTO requirements. However, the trademark assignment dataset contains a 'nationality' field for assignors and assignees that is consistent over time. We used this field to identify locations.

Figures 9.1 and 9.2 show the comparisons for patents and trademarks, respectively. With the PatentsView data, Figure 9.1 provides a comparison of inventor country-of-residence to assignee-at-grant (i.e. owner) location rather than directly representing transactions. The figure shows that cross-border assignments, US incoming or US outgoing, occur for utility and design patents, but they are much fewer in number than US to US or foreign to foreign. From 1976 through 2017, approximately 1.2 million cross border assignments took place for utility patents and about 200,000 for design patents. For trademarks, Figure 9.2 covers a much longer time interval, from 1899 to 2018. Across all conveyance types, there were about 1 million cross-border transactions. Most of these were cross-border ownership assignments

[34] See Graham et al. (2018a, 2018b) for detailed descriptions of the USPTO datasets on assignments. The Patent Assignment Dataset is available at https://www.uspto.gov/learning-and-resources/electronic-data-products/patent-assignment-dataset and the Trademark Assignment Dataset is available at https://www.uspto.gov/learning-and-resources/electronic-data-products/trademark-assignment-dataset.

[35] PatentsView's bulk data download, available at https://patentsview.org/download/data-download-tables. We used 'rawassignee', 'rawinventor' and 'rawlocation' datasets for the analysis. Also, PatentsView data may be used to establish a chain of assignors by assuming (1) the assignee-at-grant is the assignor of the first non-employee-to-employer assignment and (2) subsequent assignors are the previous transaction's assignees. However, because assignment recordation is voluntary, these assumptions will introduce noise into the chain of ownership.

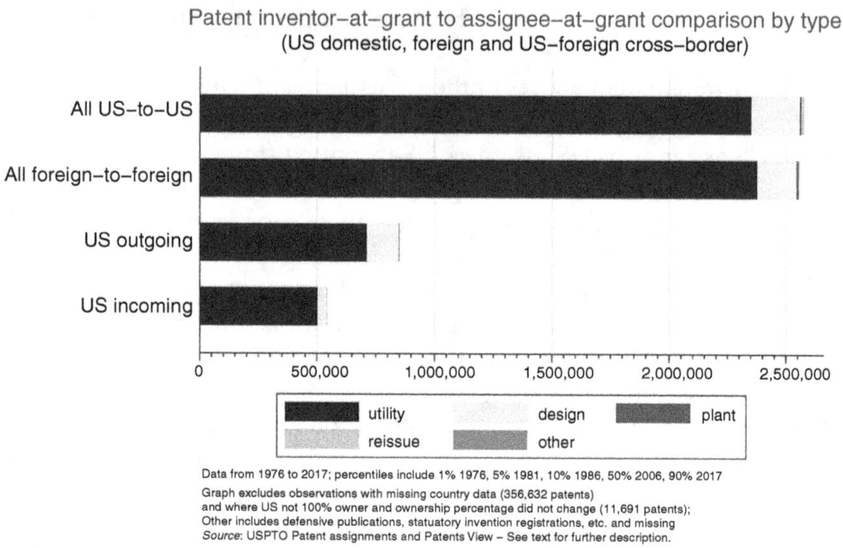

Figure 9.1 USPTO patent assignments at grant, 1976–2017

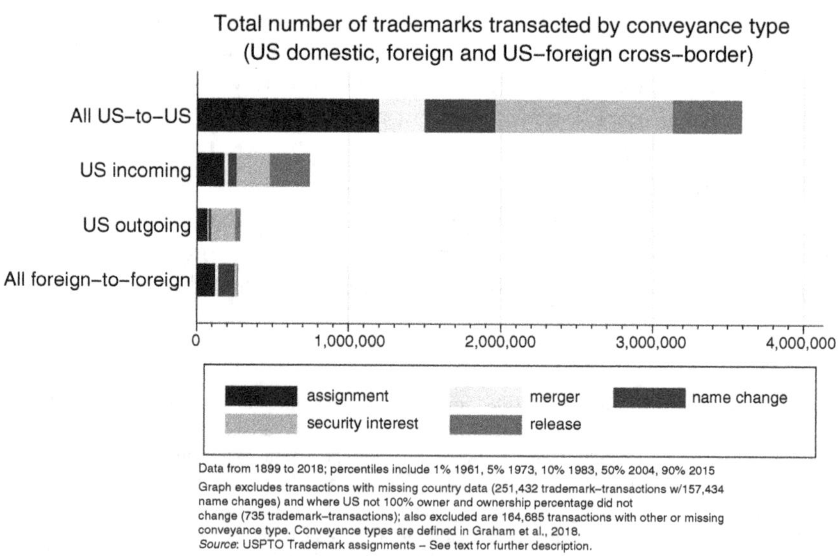

Figure 9.2 USPTO trademark assignments, 1899–2018

and security interest assignments related to financial institution collateral.

There are some limitations of the US assignment databases. Perhaps the most significant is that IPRs owners are not legally required to report patent or trademark transactions to the USPTO. Nevertheless, there are a couple of reasons to think the data are informative. First, failure to record a patent assignment renders it void against subsequent purchasers or mortgagees, although US case law allows for retroactive recording through *nunc pro tunc* ('now for then') (Graham et al., 2018a). Recording trademark assignments provides *prima facie* evidence of the transaction and limits the ability of an unrecorded assignee to take certain legal actions (Graham et al., 2018b).

Assignment datasets suffer from many of the same limitations discussed previously in this chapter for IPRs data. First, the transaction records are missing context. That is, the information on patent and trademark assignments does not include any of the terms of the legally binding contracts associated with these transactions. Those contract terms will reflect the sellers' and buyers' intentions and thereby govern the degree to which the transactions can be interpreted as technology transfer or knowledge flows. Second, IP rights are binding only within specific jurisdictions and patent documents publicly disclose the inventions eighteen months after initial filing.[36] This suggests that patent transactions need to involve some kind of non-public exchange of valuable information to constitute cross-border technology transfer or knowledge flows. Third, it is conceptually unclear how selling and buying trademarks, which represent product and service brands, constitutes cross-border technology transfer or knowledge flows. It is possible that trademark transactions are associated with the introduction of new products or services into a foreign market. This case may represent some kind of technology transfer or knowledge flows, but it is hard to be sure.

Conclusion

Our chapter surveyed the landscape of empirical studies on cross-border trade in knowledge that use IPRs data. We found authors using IPRs data, primarily patent documents, as direct indicators of innovation,

[36] Trademark applications are made public immediately after filing.

technology transfer and knowledge flows. Most of the direct indicators are constructed using patent counts, patent citations, licensing and royalty payments and patent families. We also found IPRs data used in indirect ways to characterize the relationship between two or more entities (e.g. countries, industries and firms) and to serve as moderating variables that influence the degree of technology transfer or knowledge flow. Here, authors used IPRs data to construct indexes of country-level IPRs strength, various metrics of IPR intensity, technological proximity and technology transfer or knowledge flow through inventor mobility across countries.

Our assessment is that IPRs data are a valuable source of information for learning about technology transfer and knowledge flows across borders. These data can help to inform the evidence base for policy-making as long as decision-makers keep in mind a number of important caveats. These caveats include the following considerations:

- IPRs data reflect territorial legal rights that make international comparisons difficult. Rather than accepting empirical results at face value, these results need to be supplemented with legal and operational realities. Variation in the laws and policies across jurisdictions are further complicated by variations in the treatment of intellectual property by the regional intellectual property offices and the statistical authorities.
- IPRs data rarely reveal the underlying motivations of the entities (e.g. governments, non-for-profits and for-profit companies) for seeking protection or undertaking transactions. These motivations shape the meaning of the IPRs data. Further, one often needs to know more than the IPRs data reveal by themselves. It is particularly important to know about the decisions intellectual property owners, sellers and buyers make after filing, receiving or selling intellectual property assets.
- Each of the varieties of IPRs data considered in this chapter, including the patent and trademark assignments datasets that we highlight as underutilized, have many specific limitations related to quality and coverage. Much of the literature on international trade in knowledge uses IRPs data, but IPRs data are very difficult to use correctly, even when the research intent is clear and reasonable.
- Finally, for all IPRs data, it will be important to develop a transparent, reliable and reproducible method for disambiguating data elements such as inventor and owner names.

Policymakers need experts who know the origin, nature and nuances of the specific IPRs data. These experts can review any empirical findings before gleaning policy insights to help minimize the risk of unknown errors or incorrect interpretations.

Bibliography

Agrawal, A., Kapur, D., McHale, J. and Oettl, A., 'Brain drain or brain bank? The impact of skilled emigration on poor-country innovation' (2011), *Journal of Urban Economics* 69, 1: 43–55.

Arts, S., Cassiman, B. and Gomez, J., 'Text Matching to Measure Patent Similarity' (2017), *Strategic Management Journal* 39, 1: 62–84.

Atal, V. and Bar, T., 'Prior Art: To Search or Not to Search' (2010), *International Journal of Industrial Organization* 28, 5: 507–512.

Athreye, S. and Yang, Y., 'Disembodied Knowledge Flows in the World Economy', Working Paper No. 3, WIPO Economic Research Working Papers, World Intellectual Property Organization, 2011.

Bacchiocchi, E. and Montobbio, F., 'International Knowledge Diffusion and Home-Bias Effect: Do USPTO and EPO Patent Citations Tell the Same Story?' (2010), *The Scandinavian Journal of Economics* 112, 3: 441–470.

Belitz, H. and Molders, F., 'International Knowledge Spillovers through High-Tech Imports and R&D of Foreign-Owned Firms' (2016), *The Journal of International Trade & Economic Development* 25, 4: 590–613.

Blind, K., Cremers, K. and Mueller, E., 'The Influence of Strategic Patenting on Companies' Patent Portfolios' (2009), *Research Policy* 38, 2: 428–436.

Branstetter, L.G., 'Are Knowledge Spillovers International or Intranational in Scope? Microeconometric Evidence from the U.S. and Japan' (2001), *Journal of International Economics* 53, 1: 53–79.

Branstetter, L. G., Fisman, R. and Foley, C. F., 'Do Stronger Intellectual Property Rights Increase International Technology Transfer? Empirical Evidence from U.S. Firm-Level Panel Data' (2006), *Quarterly Journal of Economics* 121, 1: 321–349.

Branstetter, L., Fisman, R., Foley, C. F. and Saggi, K., 'Does Intellectual Property Rights Reform Spur Industrial Development?' (2011), *Journal of International Economics* 83, 1: 27–36.

Cai, J., Santacreu, A. M. and Li, N., 'Knowledge Diffusion, Trade and Innovation Across Countries and Sectors', FRB St. Louis Working Paper No. 2017–29, 2017, available at https://ssrn.com/abstract=3078549.

Cohen, W., Nelson, R. and Walsh, J., 'Protecting their Intellectual Assets: Appropriability Conditions and Why U.S. Manufacturing Firms Patent (or

Not)', NBER Working Paper No. 7552, National Bureau of Economic Research, 2000.

Cohen, W., Nelson, R. and Walsh, J., 'Links and Impacts: The Influence of Public Research on Industrial R&D' (2002), *Management Science* 48, 1: 1–23.

Cotropia, C. A., Lemley, M. A. and Sampat, B., 'Do Applicant Patent Citations Matter?' (2013), *Research Policy* 42, 4: 844–854.

Dechezlepretre A., Meniere, Y. and Mohnen, M., 'International Patent Families: from Application Strategies to Statistical Indicators' (2017), *Scientometrics* 111, 2: 793–828.

DeGrazia, C., Frunkin, J. and Pairolero, N. A., 'Embracing Invention Similarity for the Measurement of Vertically Overlapping Claims', USPTO Working Paper No. 2018-01, 2018, available at https://ssrn.com/abstract=3166042.

Eaton, J. and Kortum, S., 'Trade in Ideas. Patenting and Productivity in the OECD' (1996), *Journal of International Economics* 40, 3–4: 251–278.

Fons-Rosen, C., Kalemli-Ozcan, S., Sorensen, B. E., Villegas-Sanchez, C. and Volosovych, V., 'Foreign Investment and Domestic Productivity: Identifying Knowledge Spillovers and Competition Effects', NBER Working Paper No. 23643, National Bureau of Economic Research, 2017.

Ginarte, J. and Park, W. (1997) 'Determinants of Patent Rights: A Cross-national Study' (1997), *Research Policy* 26, 3: 287–301.

Graham, S. J. H., Marco, A. C. and Myers, A.F., 'Patent Transactions in the Marketplace: Lessons from the USPTO Patent Assignments Dataset' (2018a), *Journal of Economics and Management Strategy* 27, 3: 343–373.

Graham, S. J. H., Marco, A. C. and Myers, A. F., 'Monetizing Marks: Insights from the USPTO Trademark Assignments Dataset' (2018b), *Journal of Economics and Management Strategy* 27, 3: 403–432.

Griliches, Z., 'Patent Statistics as Economic Indicators: A Survey', in Zvi Griliches (ed.), *R&D and Productivity: The Econometric Evidence*, Chicago: University of Chicago Press, 1998, pp. 287–343.

Harhoff, D., Scherer, F. and Vopel, K., 'Exploring the Tail of Patented Invention Value Distributions', in Ove Granstrand (ed.), *Economics, Law and Intellectual Property*, Berlin: Kluwer Academic Publishers, 2003, pp. 279–309.

Ho, C.-U., Li, X. and Zhou W., 'Foreign Direct Investment Spillovers and Pharmaceutical Innovation: The Role of Intellectual Property Rights', Asian Development Bank Institute, Working Paper 775, 2017.

Hu, A. G. Z. and Jaffe, A. B., 'Patent Citations and International Knowledge Flow' (2003), *International Journal of Industrial Organization* 21, 6: 849–880.

Ivus, O., 'Do Stronger Patent Rights Raise High-tech Exports to the Developing World?' (2010), *Journal of International Economics* 81, 1: 38–47.

Jaffe, A. B., 'Technological Opportunity and Spillovers from R&D: Evidence from Firms' Patents, Profits, and Market Value' (1986), *American Economic Review* 76, 5: 984–999.

Jaffe, A. B. and de Rassenfosse, G., 'Patent citation data in social science research: Overview and best practices', NBER Working Paper No. 21868, National Bureau of Economic Research, 2017.

Jaffe, A. B., Trajtenberg, M. and Fogarty, M. S., 'Knowledge Spillovers and Patent Citations: Evidence from a Survey of Inventors' (2000), *American Economic Review* 90, 2: 215–218.

Javorcik, B. S., 'The Composition of Foreign Direct Investment and Protection of Intellectual Property Rights: Evidence from Transition Economies' (2002), *European Economic Review* 48, 1: 39–62.

Johnstone, N., Hascic, I. and Watson, F., 'Annex A: Methodological Issues in the Development of Indicators of Innovation and Transfer in Environmental Technologies', in *Invention and Transfer of Environmental Technologies*, OECD, 2011.

Kerr, W., 'Ethnic Scientific Communities and International Technology Diffusion' (2008), *Review of Economics and Statistics* 90, 3: 518–537.

Kim, J., John, Lee S. and Marschke, G. (2009) 'International Knowledge Flows: Evidence from an Inventor-Firm Matched Data Set', in Richard Freeman and Daniel Goroff (eds), *Science and Engineering Careers in the United States: An Analysis of Markets and Employment*, Chicago and London: NBER and The University of Chicago Press, 2009.

Kuznar, A., 'Intangibles in Economies and International Trade', 2012, available at https://ssrn.com/abstract=2953588.

MacGarvie, M., 'Do Firms Learn from International Trade?' (2006), *Research in Economics and Statistics* 88, 1: 48–60.

Mansfield, E., 'Intellectual property protection, foreign direct investment and technology transfer', International Finance Corporation Discussion Paper No. 27, 1995.

Martinez, C., 'Patent families: When do different definitions really matter?' (2011), *Scientometrics* 26, 1: 39–63.

Maskus, K. E. and Penubarti, M., 'How Trade Related are Intellectual Property Rights?' (1995), *Journal of International Economics* 39, 3–4: 227–248.

Mataloni, R. J., 'A Guide to BEA Statistics on U.S. Multinational Companies' (1995), *Survey of Current Business* 75, 3: 38–55.

Miguelez, E., 'Inventor Diasporas and the Internationalization of Technology' (2016), *The World Bank Economic Review* 32, 1: 41–63.

Miguelez, E., Moreno, R. and Surinach, J., 'Inventors on The Move: Tracing Inventors' Mobility and Its Spatial Distribution' (2010), *Regional Science* 89, 2: 251–274.

Moser, P., Bilir, K. and Talis, I., 'Do Treaties Encourage Technology Transfer? Evidence from the Paris Convention', 2011, available at https://ssrn.com/abstract=1893052.

Nakamura, T., 'International Knowledge Spillovers and Technology Imports: Evidence from Japanese Chemical and Electric Equipment Industries' (2001), *Journal of the Japanese and International Economies* 15, 3: 271–297.

OECD (1990), *Proposed Standard Method of Compiling and Interpreting Technology Balance of Payments Data: TBP Manual*, Paris: OECD Publishing, available at https://doi.org/10.1787/9789264065567-en.

Oettl, A. and Agrawal, A., 'International Labor Mobility and Knowledge Flow Externalities' (2008), *Journal of International Business Studies* 39, 8: 1242–1260.

Pakes, A., 'Patents as Options: Some Estimates of the Value of Holding European Patent Stocks' (1986), *Econometrica* 54, 4: 755–784.

Pakes, A. and Griliches, Z., 'Patents and R and D at the Firm Level: a First look', NBER Working Paper No. 561, National Bureau of Economics Research, 1980.

Pavitt, K., 'Uses and Abuses of Patent Statistics', in A. F. J. Van Raan (ed.), *Handbook of Quantitative Studies of Science and Technology*, Amsterdam, The Netherlands: Elsevier Science Publishers, 1988, pp. 509–536.

Peri, G., 'Determinants of Knowledge Flows and their Effect on Innovation' (2005), *The Review of Economics and Statistics* 87, 2: 308–322.

Piermartini, R. and Rubinova, S., 'Knowledge Spillovers through International Supply Chains', WTO Staff Working Paper No. ERSD-2014-11, World Trade Organization, 2014.

Popovici, I., 'Impact of Intellectual Property Rights Reforms on the Diffusion of Knowledge through FDI', Economic Research Working Paper Series 6-2-2006, Florida International University, 2006.

Rapp, R. T. and Rozek, R. P., 'Benefits and Costs of Intellectual Property Protection in Developing Countries' (1990), *Journal of World Trade* 24, 5: 75–102.

Riker, D., 'Intellectual Property Rights and International Receipts of Royalties and Licensing Fees', Office of Economics Working Paper No. 2014-08C, U.S. International Trade Commission, 2014.

Roach, M. and Cohen, W. M., 'Lens or Prism? Patent Citations as a Measure of Knowledge Flows from Public Research' (2013), *Management Science* 59, 2: 504–525.

Sampat, B. N., 'A Survey of Empirical Evidence on Patents and Innovation', NBER Working Paper No. 25383, National Bureau of Economic Research, 2018.

Sjoholm, F., 'International Transfer of Knowledge: The Role of International Trade and Geographic Proximity' (1996), *Weltwirtschaftliches Archiv* 132, 1: 97–115.

Trajtenberg, M., Henderson, R. and Jaffe, A., 'University Versus Corporate Patents: A Window on the Basicness of Invention' (1997), *Economics of Innovation and New Technology* 5: 19–50.

Trajtenberg M., Shiff G. and Melamed R., 'The "names game": harnessing inventors' patent data for economic research', NBER Working Paper No. 12479, National Bureau of Economic Research, 2006.

Younge, K. A. and Kuhn J. M., (2016) 'Patent-to-Patent Similarity: A Vector Space Model', 2016, available at https://ssrn.com/abstract=2709238.

A9.1

Detailed Description of Analysis of Assignment Data for Exemplary Analysis

The analysis involved several steps, beginning with aggregating trademark assignor and assignees to the country level. For patents, inventors-at-grant and assignors-at-grant were grouped at the country level. This resulted in country counts for each trademark transaction and for each granted patent. For the trademark assignment dataset, the country was determined by using the nationality field, then the country address field and then the state address field.[37] These fields resulted in a mix of countries and geographic areas (e.g. US states were present in the 'nationality' field) which were normalized and disambiguated.[38] For the PatentsView data, the countries were listed by two-digit country codes. Next, we merged the country counts with the number of trademark properties involved in the transaction and the conveyance type. The effective date[39] of the transaction is in the assignor data file for trademarks. Since each transaction may involve assignors, we used the last chronological date as the transaction's effective date, or, if missing, the last chronological acknowledgement date.

[37] Although for this study we did not parse the text of address fields, these fields along with the postal code field may contain information that could be used to impute the country when missing.

[38] Normalization was done to the level where an ISO 3166-1 two-digit country code existed, with the exception that US territories having a country code were labeled as US; WIPO country names and two-letter codes were also used. Disambiguation between country of Georgia and the US state of the same name was done by assuming the US state unless there was information to indicate otherwise. The data do contain errors, e.g. the address may be in Germany or the Republic of Korea but the country is listed as Georgia; future researchers should be aware of such data quality issues if they are examining specific countries.

[39] As noted by Graham et al. (2018a, 2018b), there is a lag between the transaction's recordation date and the effective date. The papers suggest use of the recordation date. Although we did not, one may impute the effective date from the recordation date, using the lag; the imputation should be by conveyance type, since the lag varies by this variable.

10

The Global Digital Content Landscape

ERICK S. OH*

Abstract

This chapter focuses on recent developments in the digital content industry. It begins with a brief discussion of the data limitations that challenge the analysis of this market, and continues with overviews of the key characteristics, important trends, and competitive landscapes in each of the major digital content sectors – video games, video on demand (VoD), digital music, and e-publishing (primarily e-books). The chapter ends with a short summary of intellectual property rights issues or barriers that are currently affecting the global digital content industry.

Introduction

In recent years, advances in mobile device technologies as well as in mobile and fixed-broadband Internet have enabled consumers to access almost limitless amounts of online content. Central to this move to digital delivery are cloud infrastructure and services that provide content creators with the scale of computing power needed to meet increasingly customized consumer demands for digital content. As a result of these technology and infrastructure innovations, the boundaries between creative content industries, social media and e-commerce have blurred. Besides being able to share personal news and photos with friends and family on sites such as Facebook and Twitter, users can now post their own live video streams for public viewing, read and react to news stories tailored to their interests and receive product recommendations via

* This chapter is the result of the ongoing professional research of USITC staff and is solely meant to represent the opinions and professional research of its authors. It is not meant to represent in any way the view of the US International Trade Commission, any of its individual Commissioners, or the United States government.

targeted ads based on previous online search queries. Nonetheless, although cloud innovations have allowed more people to access increasingly personalized content, often at low or no cost, content creators continue to face significant challenges. These include the protection of copyrighted materials against online pirates and concerns regarding online intermediaries' handling of user-generated content.

This chapter focuses on recent developments in the digital content industry. It begins with a brief discussion of the data limitations that challenge the analysis of this market, and continues with overviews of the key characteristics, important trends, and competitive landscapes in each of the major digital content sectors – video games, video on demand (VoD), digital music and e-publishing (primarily e-books). The chapter ends with a short summary of intellectual property rights issues/barriers that are currently affecting the global digital content industry.

The Availability of Data on the Digital Content Market

Consistent and robust international trade statistics on cross-border trade in digital content are limited. Outside of a handful of reports,[1] comprehensive quantitative analysis of digital trade and e-commerce in general have been largely confined to studies done within OECD countries and have relied on privately gathered data that vary substantially depending on the method of measurement, thus making systematic global trade analyses impossible. With only a few countries gathering data on e-commerce, and with such data being almost non-existent for most developing countries, key questions regarding policy design and regulation remain unanswered.[2] Moreover, there is no consensus definition of

[1] For examples, see World Economic Forum, *Digital Transformation of Industries: Digital Enterprise*, January 2016 and A. Grimm, 'Trends in US Trade in Information and Communications Technology (ICT) Services and in IT-Enabled Services', (Washington, DC: US Bureau of Economic Analysis (BEA)), May 2016. Grimm (2016) does present the term 'Potentially Internet and Communications Technology (ICT)-Enabled Services', which includes service types predominantly delivered remotely over ICT networks. 'Potentially ICT-enabled services' include ICT services as well as a variety of other ICT-enabled services, including insurance and financial services, charges for the use of intellectual property, and professional and management consulting services, among others. However, the BEA cannot definitely identify the value of US digital trade because official trade statistics do not contain information on the mode of delivery of services.

[2] UNESCAP, *Asia-Pacific Trade and Investment Report 2016: Recent Trends and Developments*, (Bangkok, Thailand: United Nations Economic and Social Commission for Asia and the Pacific), November 2016.

Table 10.1 *Global digital content revenues, by sector and subsector, 2017*

Sector	Revenue (million USD)
Video games	
Downloads	11,126
Mobile	38,718
Online	13,148
Total video games	62,992
Video on demand	
Downloads	3,465
Pay-per-view	3,824
Streaming	16,428
Total VoD	23,717
Music	
Downloads	2,692
Streaming	9,394
Total music	12,085
E-publishing	
E-books	11,354
E-magazines	1,784
E-newspapers	3,500
Total e-publishing	16,638
Grand total	115,432

Source: Statista, 'Digital Media' database.
Note: Totals may not be exact due to rounding.

digital content trade or e-commerce, generally, complicating efforts to separate domestic and cross-border digital content trade numbers.[3]

To limit inconsistent approaches to digital content trade data, this chapter will largely rely on global and national revenue numbers from one source, Statista, an online statistics company. According to Statista data, the global digital content market – video games, VoD, digital music and e-publishing – reached USD 115.4 billion in total revenue in 2017, an increase of about 11.2 per cent from 2016. This market was dominated by video games, with about USD 63.0 billion in revenue that year (Table 10.1). The United States led in most digital content sectors by

[3] J. Nicholson, 'Digital Trade in North America', Washington, DC: US Department of Commerce, 5 January 2018.

relatively large margins. However, in the video games sector, China's revenue surpassed the United States for the first time in 2017 – making it the world's largest market – primarily buoyed by its strong mobile games subsector.[4]

Video Games

Video games delivered over the Internet include downloads of full-format games and add-on content, as well as game subscriptions, mobile application (app) games, social network games, other online and cloud-based games[5] and e-sports.[6] Most video games today are delivered online and are available in multiplayer formats (Box 10.1).

Competitive Landscape

Supported by increasingly robust cloud infrastructure and faster broadband speeds, games played on mobile devices via social media platforms (e.g. Facebook) have opened the industry to a wider demographic of consumers. The industry's primary drivers of demand are diverse – they include individuals (particularly women) who use social media games[7] to engage with friends and family; casual gamers who download freemium games to their mobile devices and make in-app microtransaction purchases[8] to enhance their gaming experiences; and avid viewers and players of e-sports or online video game competitions who use video streaming platforms such as Twitch and Machinima and attend live arena events to connect with gamers all over the world.[9]

[4] Statista, 'Digital Media' database, at www.statista.com/study/44526/digital-media-report/ accessed 17 July 2018.

[5] W. Cai et al., 'A Survey of Cloud Gaming: Future of Computer Games', University of British Columbia, 2016, p. 7606. Thanks to cloud gaming, players can rent games on demand and share replays from their games with friends without frequent hardware upgrades.

[6] P. Lee and D. Stewart, 'eSports: Bigger and Smaller Than You Think', Deloitte, 2016. E-sports are video game competitions that are often played before live audiences and broadcast over the Internet. The most popular e-sports tournaments can offer large cash prizes and professional sponsorships for the best players/teams.

[7] Some of the most popular social media games include *FarmVille*, *Mafia Wars* and *The Sims Social*.

[8] F. Blau, 'Social Status: New Markets and Rising Incomes', IBISWorld, July 2016, 7–8. Players typically pay a few dollars or less to reach a higher level of the game or to purchase a service, such as being able to unlock new maps, gain additional 'lives', or access virtual currency.

[9] Accenture, 'The Pulse of Gaming', 2014, 16–18.

BOX 10.1 DIGITAL VIDEO GAMES SECTOR SNAPSHOT[a]

Global digital video games revenue: USD 63.0 billion in 2017.

- What the Statista revenue data measures:
  - Downloads (online sales of video games for gaming consoles or PCs/laptops via direct download).
  - Mobile games (gaming apps for mobile devices such as smartphones and tablets; paid app-downloads (single purchases); and freemium games that are free to download, but allow in-app purchases).
  - Online Games (freemium internet browser games (that don't require installation) with in-game purchases for additional premium content or functionalities; and massive multiplayer online games (MMOG games)).
- What the Statista revenue data does not measure:
  - Games on physical data carriers (e.g. CD-ROM), access fees to gaming networks, free offers, and in-game advertising.

Top 5 digital video game markets, by revenue, 2017

China	USD 18.0 billion
United States	USD 15.7 billion
Japan	USD 10.7 billion
United Kingdom	USD 2.6 billion
Republic of Korea	USD 2.2 billion

Industry leaders by overall game revenue (including physical), 2017, (Total = USD 94.1 billion):

- Tencent (China) – USD 18.1 billion
- Sony (Japan) – USD 10.5 billion
- Apple (USA) – USD 8.0 billion
- Microsoft (USA) – USD 7.1 billion
- Activision Blizzard (US) – USD 6.5 billion

Sources: Statista, 'Digital Media: Video Games', June 2018; Newzoo, 'Top 25 Public Game Companies Earn USD 94.1 Billion in 2017', 9 May 2018; Statista, 'Digital Media' database, accessed 17 July 2018.

[a] Footnotes will currently remain outside of the boxes for space reasons.

The global popularity of mobile games that employ newer technologies such as augmented reality[10] was evidenced by the widely popular freemium app game *Pokémon GO*, which drew as many as 290 million monthly active users during mid-2016.[11] Overall, it is expected that more

[10] M. Gurman, 'Apple's Next Big Thing: Augmented Reality', *Bloomberg.com*, 20 March 2017.

[11] Statista, 'Digital Media Report', June 2018; B. Barrett, 'Pokémon Go Is Doing Just Fine', *Wired.com*, 18 September 2016.

powerful mobile devices will continue to drive gaming revenues, particularly for firms that can incorporate more advanced technologies (e.g. virtual reality) into their products and services.[12]

Cloud technology has allowed the video game industry to better customize gaming experiences through increased consumer engagement (similar to personalizing one's digital video selections on Netflix or one's streaming music playlist on Spotify). Further, 'games as a service', or cloud gaming, has contributed to fierce market competition by enabling gaming companies to provide regular updates – including new content, events or options for downloadable content – that can be tailored to an individual gamer's preferences[13] in an effort to keep users engaged.[14]

Lastly, the popularity of video games as a spectator sport has grown dramatically in the past two years. E-sports fuse the multiplayer game experience with real-world physical sports, attracting viewers (primarily younger fans) as well as investors looking to back gaming teams and tournaments. Major game publishers and online retailers – including Activision Blizzard (US), Tencent (China) and Alibaba (China) – have made significant investments in e-sports in recent years. E-sports are most popular in Asia: China accounted for 57 per cent of all e-sports viewing in 2016. However, the main enabler for the initial growth and popularity of e-sports was the US-based Twitch, a live-streaming video platform which

[12] Statista, 'Digital Media: Video Games', 2016; SuperData Research and Unity Technologies, 'Can't Stop, Won't Stop: 2016 Mobile and VR Games', 2017, 16–17. Although technologies such as virtual reality (VR) remain a relatively nascent subsector, total revenue from VR gaming reached about USD 1.8 billion in 2016. Gamers were initially slow to adopt the technology, but by the end of 2016, nearly 6.3 million VR devices were shipped to consumers worldwide. Growing acceptance of VR gaming has largely been driven by the presence of high-quality manufacturers such as Facebook (Oculus Rift), Google (Daydream VR), HTC (Vive), PlayStation (VR) and Samsung (Gear VR).

[13] Accenture, 'The Pulse of Gaming', 2014, 4–6. Downloadable content is extra content available for video game users to download from the Internet (either free or for a fee), and can be distributed by the game's official publisher, console online markets (e.g. content purchased through Microsoft Xbox Live's or Sony PlayStation's online networks) or a third-party platform. This content generally enhances or completes the video game's features (e.g. introducing new levels, characters, or items). For example, Steam, which is owned by Valve (US), is a primary distribution platform for PC gamers. Steam offers games and updates for purchase, as well as a platform for multiplayer gaming, video streaming and other social networking services.

[14] F. Blau, 'Social Status: New Markets and Rising Incomes', *IBISWorld*, July 2016, 16. Customers may abandon a game if they are concerned about inadequate technical support, lack of updates, questionable data security or rising transaction costs and fees.

was acquired by Amazon for USD 970 million in 2014.[15] The rise of professional gamers as social media stars (rivaling professional athletes in terms of followers) is one factor that suggests that industry revenues will continue to mushroom: Newzoo, a video game market research company, forecasts that revenues from e-sports will reach USD 905.6 million in 2018, up from an estimated USD 13.1 million in 2012.[16]

Global Markets

The digital video games sector remains heavily concentrated in Asian, US and European markets. China, the United States and Europe together accounted for about USD 43.7 billion (69.4 per cent) of the global digital video game market in 2017, with China alone generating about USD 18.0 billion of the total,[17] largely due to its rapidly growing mobile gaming subsector. The United States recorded about USD 15.7 billion in digital video game revenue in 2017, followed by Europe with USD 10.0 billion.[18]

The largest subsegment of the digital video game sector for China, the United States and Europe was mobile games. Mobile gaming revenue reached a new high in 2017, generating USD 38.7 billion globally, an increase of about 10.6 per cent over the previous year. Mobile gaming revenue accounted for roughly 53.2 per cent and 41.8 per cent of overall digital video game revenue in the United States and Europe, respectively. The digital video game market in China, however, was almost entirely driven by mobile games, which comprised about 80.2 per cent (USD 14.4 billion) of China's digital video game market in 2017. Further, Chinese mobile gaming revenue accounted for more than half of the entire Chinese digital content market (including VoD, digital music and e-publications) in that year. Companies derived this revenue from China's huge mobile gamer population, which reached 402.7 million users in 2016 (more than the entire population of the United States).[19] Many industry analysts credit the worldwide growth in mobile games to the high performance of contemporary smartphones and tablets, which

[15] T. Bradshaw, 'Esports Viewing Shoots Up', *FT.com*, 8 May 2017; Accenture, 'The Pulse of Gaming', 2014, 16; P. Lee and D. Stewart, 'eSports: Bigger and Smaller Than You Think', *Deloitte*, 2016.

[16] Newzoo, 'Global Esports Economy Will Reach $905.6 Million in 2018 as Brand Investment Grows by 48%', 21 February 2018; T. Bradshaw, 'Esports Viewing Shoots Up', *FT.com*, 8 May 2017; Newzoo, 'Global ESports Market Report 2017', 2017.

[17] Statista, 'Digital Media: Video Games', June 2018.

[18] Statista, 'Digital Media: Video Games', June 2018.

[19] Statista, 'Digital Media: Video Games', June 2018.

allow very computation-intensive applications and games.[20] For further information on the Brazilian, Chinese, European, Indian, Indonesian and Russian digital video game markets, including market data, industry players and policies and regulatory measures (where reported), see Appendix H of the USITC's *Global Digital Trade I: Market Opportunities and Key Foreign Trade Restrictions* report (August 2017).[21]

Video

Digital video or video on demand (VoD) includes content from broadcast TV, cable TV, movies, sporting events, music videos and user-generated short-form videos (e.g. live streaming, vlogs) (Box 10.2).

Competitive Landscape

The evolving competitive landscape in the VoD market has required content providers to quickly adapt to the tastes of their consumers. This is particularly the case for younger, more tech-savvy millennials who often expect instant access to more personalized, higher-quality content at lower cost, and are generally more willing to forego conventional service providers.[22] Streaming – accessing content such as movies, TV programming and videos directly over the Internet without downloading it – generated the majority of VoD revenue in 2017. The growing global popularity and market strength of US-based streaming VoD providers have put increasing pressure on traditional/local broadcast and pay-TV companies both in the United States and abroad. Consequently, many traditional cable providers have started offering 'skinny' bundle options that provide customers with more flexible digital channel packages at lower prices.[23] These packages typically provide live streaming of some of the most popular cable and broadcast channels, in addition to on-demand content for additional fees.[24] In an effort to match the services available from subscription streaming providers, many broadcasters have established or are revamping their own VoD channels in conjunction with their traditional service offerings in order

[20] Statista, 'Digital Media: Video Games', 2016; S. Perez, 'App Annie: Android to Top iOS', *TechCrunch.com*, 29 March 2017.

[21] US International Trade Commission, *Global Digital Trade I: Market Opportunities and Key Foreign Trade Restrictions*, August 2017, 419–423.

[22] Strategy+Business, *Global Entertainment and Media Outlook 2016–2020*, 2016, 11–15; T. Amobi, 'Industry Surveys: Media', *S&P*, September 2016, 75.

[23] T. Amobi, 'Industry Surveys: Media', September 2016, 52–54.

[24] T. Amobi, 'Industry Surveys: Media', September 2016, 52–54.

BOX 10.2 VOD SECTOR SNAPSHOT

Global VoD revenue: USD 23.7 billion in 2017.

- What the Statista revenue data measures:
  - Downloads (video content that is purchased in a one-time transaction and permanently accessible after purchase).
  - Pay-per-view (time-limited access to premium video content that requires a usage-based one-time payment – videos can be downloaded or streamed).
  - Streaming (subscription-based video on demand (SVoD) services, e.g. Netflix and Amazon Prime Video).
- What the Statista revenue data does not measure:
  - Revenue from cable and satellite pay TV subscriptions.
  - Video advertising, ad-based content and services and user-generated content.

Top 5 video on demand markets, by revenue, 2017	
United States	USD 13,484 million
China	USD 1,659 million
United Kingdom	USD 1,450 million
Germany	USD 1,397million
France	USD 634 million

Industry leaders by overall VoD revenue (est.), 2016, (Total = USD 25 billion):

- YouTube/Google (USA) – USD 4 billion
- Netflix (USA) – USD 3.8 billion
- Facebook (USA) – USD 1.8 billion
- Amazon Prime (USA) – USD 0.9 billion
- Hulu (USA) – USD 0.7 billion

Sources: Statista, 'Digital Media: Video on Demand', June 2018; Arthofer et al., 'The Future of Television', Boston Consulting Group, 20 September 2016, 14–15; F. Richter, 'Netflix Reaches 130 Million Subscribers', Statista, 17 July 2018.

Note: Company-level revenue totals will not match Statista's global/country-level estimates due to sources' differing accounting methodologies. Also, some companies' streaming revenue comes primarily from advertisers (YouTube), while others rely on subscriptions (Netflix).

to offer their content whenever and wherever viewers may wish to watch (no matter the device).[25] Lastly, traditional providers with vast content libraries are entering into mergers with telecoms (and vice versa,

[25] A. Brown, 'iPlayer Will Be Revamped to Compete with Netflix and Amazon Prime, BBC confirms', *Express.co.uk*, 7 April 2018.

e.g. AT&T's USD 109 billion proposed merger with Time Warner)[26] or acquiring other cable/broadcasting companies in order to consolidate their video catalogues and/or distribution capabilities (e.g. Disney acquiring 21st Century Fox for USD 71 billion)[27] (Figure 10.1).[28]

Nonetheless, the popularity of streaming video content, a cloud-enabled service that requires fast connection speeds, continues to grow. Leading online video providers such as Netflix and Amazon Prime are constantly making greater investments to expand the range of exclusive content and services offered to their growing multinational user base. Netflix, in an effort to build on widely popular and critical hit series such as *Stranger Things*, *The Crown* and *Orange is the New Black* spent more than USD 10 billion in cash on streaming content in the twelve months ending in July 2018, with a good portion of those investments earmarked for productions in specific regions or countries.[29] Although Netflix is the current market leader among subscription VoD service providers, it continues to face increasing competitive pressure from Amazon Prime Video, which notably beats Netflix in terms of subscribership in major markets such as Germany, India and Japan.[30] Reportedly, this is because Amazon, unlike Netflix (whose scope largely caters to 'global' audiences), has reached out to international markets primarily through partnership programmes with niche local video services, giving customers access to both global and local content from the start.[31] To illustrate, Amazon has vied for rights to the Indian Premier League cricket events, which consistently capture that country's highest viewership ratings (but later lost to Star India Sports, a subsidiary of Fox).[32] Other burgeoning rivals for global subscription streaming revenue include Disney, Facebook and

[26] *Economist.com*, 'AT&T's Merger With Time Warner Goes On Trial', 17 March 2018. This estimated merger total also includes debt.

[27] *Economist.com*, 'Traditional TV's Surprising Staying Power', 9 February 2017; J. Disis and H. Gold, 'Disney Wins Antitrust Approval to Purchase Most of Fox', *Money.cnn.com*, 27 June 2018.

[28] A. Brown, 'iPlayer Will Be Revamped to Compete with Netflix and Amazon Prime, BBC confirms', *Express.co.uk*, 7 April 2018.

[29] F. Richter, 'Netflix Splurges Cash on Content', Statista, 17 July 2018.

[30] A. Levy, 'Amazon Prime is Beating Netflix in 3 Countries', *BusinessInsider.com*/The Motley Fool, 17 February 2018.

[31] N. Granados, 'The Battle For Video Entertainment Goes Global: Who Will Win?', *Forbes.com*, 20 February 2018.

[32] S. Herrera, 'Netflix and Amazon Go Global: The Impact of Content Localization of Video Streaming', Media and Entertainment Journal (Spring 2017), 2–4; E. Smith, 'How Cricket is Going Global with Netflix and Amazon', *NewStatesman.com*, 24 September 2017.

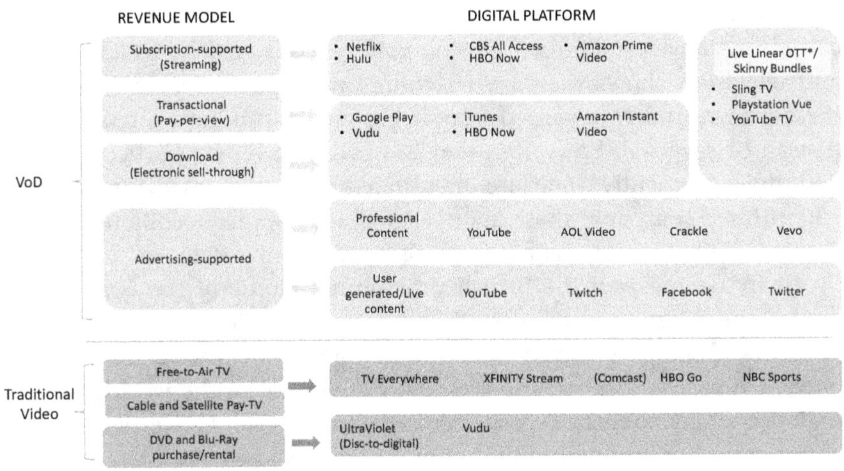

Figure 10.1 Breakout of the video on demand (VoD) ecosystem, by types of providers (non-exhaustive)

Sources: Compiled by the US International Trade Commission; Arthofer et al., 'The Future of Television', Boston Consulting Group, 2016, 8.

Note: [a] Live linear over-the-top (OTT) service or 'skinny bundles' combine VoD services with traditional broadcast and pay-TV content.

YouTube. Reportedly, Disney[33] – whose content library includes brands from Pixar, Marvel and Lucasfilm – will discontinue offering most of its content on Netflix in 2019 and soon after begin their own streaming channels, and Facebook and YouTube are increasing spending on original video content.[34]

As more and more content is stored on the cloud, digital video providers increasingly conduct data analytics, allowing them to better customize their extensive online catalogue of titles to each customer's perceived preferences or interests. For example, Netflix provides personalized content recommendations to its customers based on their past viewing sessions. In the past, Netflix could record that a customer rented

[33] S. Meredith, 'After Exiting Battle for Fox, Comcast Fires "Warning Shot" to Disney over Sky Takeover, analyst says', *CNBC.com*, 20 July 2018. In late July 2018, Disney reportedly had won its bid to acquire British broadcaster Sky (a subsidiary of Fox). This proposed acquisition will allow Disney to access overseas consumers more directly.

[34] P. La Monica, 'Netflix Still Wears the Streaming Crown', *Money.cnn.com*, 3 January 2018; *Economist.com*, 'Mass Entertainment in the Digital Age is Still About Blockbusters, Not Endless Choice', 11 February 2017; T. Sepalla, 'YouTube Reportedly Plans to Spend "Hundreds of Millions" on Red Originals', *Engadget.com*, 23 February 2018.

a DVD but it did not know if they even watched it. Now its algorithms can estimate viewers' future viewing preferences based on which movies and television shows they are watching on its platform, how many of these programmes are viewed from beginning to end, how often they are paused or reversed, how often they are searched for by particular users and how frequently they are mentioned on social media platforms. Algorithms analysing these data also guide Netflix's content investments.[35] For example, analysis of user preference data led Netflix to invest in a remake of the British programme *House of Cards* and even guided the selection of the cast.[36]

Lastly, although Western video streaming providers are denied market entry, China has fostered the growth of a handful of the world's largest digital content companies (e.g. Alibaba, Tencent).[37] However, as these companies start to incorporate more AI technologies like their Western counterparts, their ability to offer the content their viewers most want has started to conflict with official government censors. This has resulted in penalties for some of the country's largest digital media providers, including providers of live streaming,[38] which has grown to be extremely popular in a country where more than 95 per cent of Internet users are on mobile.[39] To illustrate, news aggregation and video content platform

[35] World Economic Forum, *Digital Transformation of Industries: Digital Enterprise*, January 2016, 10.

[36] Z. Bulygo, 'How Netflix Uses Analytics to Select Movies', (2014), accessed 28 June 2017; L. Shaw, 'Netflix's Pursuit of TV Domination Has a New Step', Bloomberg News, 21 April 2015; A. Swanson, 'The Power of Big Data in China', Cheung Kong Graduate School of Business, 28 July 2015.

[37] Economist Intelligence Unit, 'Digital Upheaval: How Asia-Pacific is Leading the Way in Emerging Media Consumption Trends', 22 January 2018, 4, 7–8.

[38] Economist Intelligence Unit, 'Digital Upheaval: How Asia-Pacific is Leading the Way in Emerging Media Consumption Trends', 22 January 2018, 4, 7–8. Content generated from social media apps that allow individuals to make live broadcasts to a network of streaming viewers. Often, these Internet broadcasters can solicit electronic payments (microtransactions) from their viewers in the form of fungible tokens (or 'virtual gifts'). In many cases, these live streaming broadcasts can offer an informal network/community of support for people with similar backgrounds and interests. In China, live streaming has been particularly popular among migrant workers looking to connect with others that originate from the same region. One of the most popular live streaming apps is QQ, a chat platform owned by Tencent.

[39] Economist Intelligence Unit, 'Digital Upheaval: How Asia-Pacific is Leading the Way in Emerging Media Consumption Trends', 22 January 2018, 4, 7–8; *Economist.com*, 'China's New Craze for Live-Streaming', 9 February 2017; A. Lee, 'China's Booming Live Streaming Industry May Have Reached Its Peak', *Scmp.com*, 20 December 2017; P. C. Ho, 'China Removes 370 Live-streaming Apps', *Technode.com*, 18 April 2018. However,

Toutiao, with 120 million daily users, had its mobile app suspended for three weeks in April 2018 over alleged conduct violations – it previously received a 24-hour government ban for similar violations in December 2017.[40] Toutiao is unique in that unlike other rigidly monitored media outlets, it uses AI algorithms to create personalized news and video feeds for its users. However, industry observers see a conflict between this business model and China's government directives. Interestingly, as a way to retain and attract new investors (and deflect losses caused by the government shutdowns), Toutiao has expanded abroad, including paying USD 1 billion to acquire US lip-syncing app Musical.ly in November 2017, among other acquisitions.[41]

Global Markets

The global VoD industry has grown rapidly over the past few years, reaching USD 23.7 billion in 2017, an increase of 16.9 per cent from 2016.[42] The United States generated about USD 13.5 billion in VoD revenue in 2017, accounting for about 57.0 per cent of the global VoD market that year.[43] Video streaming accounted for USD 9.3 billion of US VoD revenue in 2017, about 4.5 times the revenue generated by either pay-per-view or video downloads (each earning about USD 2.1 billion that year). Similarly, the VoD market in Europe, which accounted for USD 5.8 billion in revenue in 2017, was also dominated by video streaming, which accounted for about 69.7 per cent (USD 4.0 billion) of European digital VoD revenue. By comparison, European pay-per-view and video downloads accounted for only USD 1.1 billion and USD 650 million, respectively, in 2017.[44] China generated about USD 1.7 billion in total VoD revenue

in April 2018, China's Ministry of Culture and Tourism inspected over 4,900 live streaming apps and removed 370 from app stores for failing to comply with regulations. Other larger live streaming platforms such as Huajiao, Douyu, Huya, 6.cn and Panda.tv are also undergoing investigations for content 'harmful to public morality'. Notably, some mobile game apps faced similar 'conduct/values'-related government penalties after random selection searches done by the Ministry of Culture.

[40] E. Feng and Y. Yang, 'Chinese Unicorns Tripped up by Content Crackdown', *FT.com*, 29 April 2018.

[41] E. Feng and Y. Yang, 'Chinese Unicorns Tripped up by Content Crackdown', *FT.com*, 29 April 2018. Other major content platforms to have faced government censorship penalties include Baidu, Sina Weibo and Tencent, among others.

[42] Statista, 'Digital Media' database, accessed 17 July 2018.

[43] Statista, 'Digital Media' database, accessed 17 July 2018.

[44] Statista, 'Digital Media: Video-on-Demand', June 2018.

in 2017, an increase of 22.3 per cent from 2016, making it the second largest country market for VoD that year (behind the United States).[45] Video streaming accounted for USD 1.2 billion of total VoD in China in 2017, an increase of about 20.9 per cent from 2016.[46] The digitally-focused market research firm eMarketer estimated that close to 229 million people in China will view video content through a subscription streaming service in 2018 and more than two-fifths of China's digital video viewers will use a subscription service by 2019. Continued growth in the streaming subsector is expected due in large part to increasing investments in homegrown content by major Chinese video streaming providers such as Baidu's iQiyi, Alibaba's Youku and Tencent's Tencent Video.[47] For further information on the Brazilian, Chinese, European, Indian, Indonesian and Russian VoD markets, including market data, industry players, and policies and regulatory measures (where reported), see Appendix H of the USITC's *Global Digital Trade I: Market Opportunities and Key Foreign Trade Restrictions* report (August 2017).[48]

Music

Digital music encompasses streamed or downloaded content such as recorded songs, concerts (live and recorded), online radio and podcasts (Box 10.3).

Competitive Landscape

The global music industry has been primarily driven by digital streaming in recent years as companies such as Spotify (Sweden), Apple Music (US) and Amazon Music (US) continue to expand their share of the global market. As of October 2017, these three companies accounted for 63 per cent of the over 162 million digital music subscribers worldwide.[49] In 2011, only 13 per cent of global digital music revenue came from

[45] The Chinese government blocks access to most Western digital and social media providers, including Facebook, Google and Netflix.

[46] Statista, 'Digital Media: Video-on-Demand', June 2018.

[47] *eMarketer.com*, 'China's Subscription OTT Video Market Is Booming', 18 January 2018.

[48] US International Trade Commission, *Global Digital Trade I: Market Opportunities and Key Foreign Trade Restrictions*, August 2017, 423–428.

[49] A. Nicolaou and H. Kuchler, 'Facebook Looks to Change the Tune with Move into Music', *FT.com*, 6 March 2018; M. Mulligan, 'Amazon Is Now the 3rd Biggest Music Subscription Service', *Musicindustryblog.wordpress.com*, 14 July 2017.

BOX 10.3 DIGITAL MUSIC SECTOR SNAPSHOT

Global digital music revenue: USD 12.1 billion in 2017.

- What the Statista revenue data measure:
  - Downloads (paid downloads of professionally produced single tracks or albums/compilations that are permanently accessible after purchase).
  - Streaming (subscription-based (without any advertising) or ad-supported unlimited access to music streaming services).
- What the Statista revenue data do not measure:
  - Video downloads, video streaming, audio books and Internet radios.

Top 5 digital music markets, by revenue, 2017

United States	USD 6,314 million
United Kingdom	USD 791 million
Germany	USD 784 million
Japan	USD 590 million
China	USD 571 million

Industry leaders by market share of global music streaming subscribers, October 2017, %, (Total = 162.6 million subscribers):

- Spotify (Sweden) – 36 per cent
- Apple Music (USA) – 17 per cent
- Amazon Music (USA) – 10 per cent
- QQ Music (China) – 6 per cent
- Deezer (France) – 4 per cent

Sources: Statista, 'Digital Media: Digital Music', June 2018; Nicolaou and H. Kuchler, 'Facebook Looks to Change the Tune with Move into Music', *FT.com*, 6 March 2018.

Note: Company-level revenue totals will not match country-level estimates due to sources' differing accounting methodologies.

streaming services, versus 72 per cent from downloads. By 2017, this ratio had shifted to 71 per cent from streaming versus 20 per cent from downloads (Figure 10.2).[50]

Among the top three providers, Amazon was the second most widely used streaming music app (behind Spotify and ahead of Apple) in 2017. Amazon Music, which has grown at a particularly rapid rate since 2016, also has the largest installed base of weekly active users when it comes to pure subscription services (Spotify benefits from a large installed base of free users). As with Amazon Prime Video, Amazon Music's streaming

[50] IFPI, *Global Music Report*, 2018, 10–11, 52; T. Bundgaard et al., 'The Beat of Progress: The Rise of Music Streaming', *McKinsey Quarterly*, November 2016, 2. The remaining 9 per cent came from downloads of ringtones.

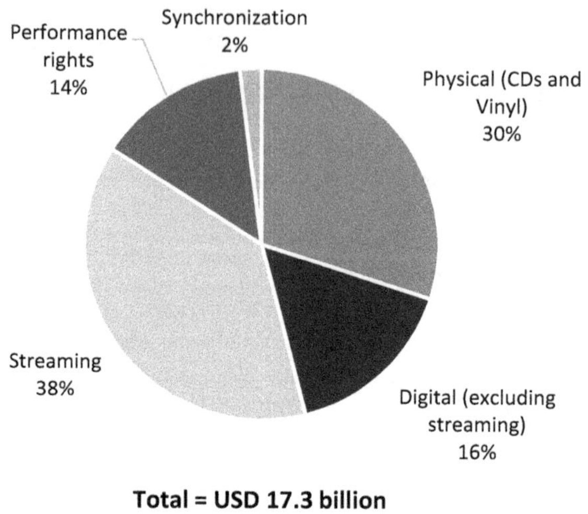

Figure 10.2 Global music revenue, by segment, 2017

Source: International Federation of the Phonographic Industry (IFPI), *Global Music Report*, 2018, 11.
Note: Due to differing accounting methods, global revenue data from the International Federation of the Phonographic Industry (IFPI) and Statista will not match. For the sake of consistency across sectors, we will rely on Statista data for this section unless otherwise noted. Synchronization is the licensing of artistic material to other media outlets for royalty payments (e.g. using copyrighted music for a TV commercial or a video game).

subscribers are concentrated in a handful of key markets – the United States, Japan, Germany and the United Kingdom.[51] Unlike Spotify or Apple, Amazon benefits from having a large preexisting base of Prime (shopping) subscribers that simply need to add a music app to start using one of its services (Amazon Prime Music, which offers a relatively small song library to all Prime members at no additional charge, or Amazon Music Unlimited, which is available for an additional fee and is more similar to Spotify or Apple Music in terms of service and offerings).[52] Moreover, many analysts point to Amazon's Echo – the market leader among smart speakers – as an additional reason for Amazon's strong music streaming growth. However, precise up-to-date subscriber

[51] M. Mulligan, 'Amazon Is Now the 3rd Biggest Music Subscription Service', *Musicindustryblog.wordpress.com*, 14 July 2017.

[52] M. Mulligan, 'Amazon Is Now the 3rd Biggest Music Subscription Service', *Musicindustryblog.wordpress.com*, 14 July 2017.

numbers are difficult to estimate, as Amazon generally doesn't disclose such information.[53]

Similar to VoD, music streaming services have benefited greatly from the development of AI and more advanced data analytics, particularly recommendation algorithms. Music is particularly well suited to the use of such algorithms, since it provides a very large catalogue to choose from – about 30 million songs – compared to the thousands of existing film and television titles. Further, listening to a poor song recommendation, which lasts 3–4 minutes, may not matter as much as watching a poor film recommendation, which can last one or more hours.[54] Spotify has been an innovator in developing such algorithms. The company analyses billions of users' playlists to create a Discover Weekly playlist – a feature used by 100 million customers – which includes 30 songs that are most liked by users with similar interests. As the playlist is only a couple of hours in length and changes every Monday, it provides a fresh and concise set of music that keeps listeners engaged.[55]

The perceived 'value gap' between earnings from platforms that provide digital music to users for free (such as YouTube) and earnings from subscription streaming services (such as Spotify and Apple Music) has been a source of contention within the music industry for several years. According to IFPI, the estimated annual revenue that Spotify generates per user is more than 20 times that offered by YouTube. IFPI argues that due to inconsistent application of liability laws, some platforms are not providing artists/music labels with the remuneration they deserve.[56] Nonetheless, YouTube remains the leading streaming music app among teens, with Spotify a close second.[57] Google has emerged in the subscription streaming subsector as its paid Play Music service has an estimated 5 million subscribers.[58] Another social media player, Facebook, has also entered the digital music arena, having set up music licensing agreements with Universal Music Group (the world's largest music label)

[53] E. Niu, 'Amazon Has More Music Subscribers Than You Think', *Fool.com*, 4 April 2018. The company recently stated that they had 'tens of millions' of music subscribers.

[54] *Economist.com*, 'How to Devise the Perfect Recommendation Algorithm', 9 February 2017.

[55] *Economist.com*, 'How to Devise the Perfect Recommendation Algorithm', 9 February 2017.

[56] IFPI, *Global Music Report*, 2018, 26–27.

[57] D. Pierce, 'Spotify, Amazon, Apple or YouTube? The Streaming-Music Showdown', *Wsj.com*, 24 June 2018. However, Spotify is the most used among all users.

[58] M. Mulligan, 'Is YouTube Serious About Music Subscriptions This Time Round?', *Musicindustryblog.wordpress.com*, 17 May 2018.

and Sony/ATV (the sector's biggest publisher) in the first half of 2018. These licences would allow Facebook (and Instagram) users to attach music files to their personal video clips, a service that may be particularly popular with younger consumers among whom Facebook use is declining. However, it is too early to determine if Facebook will become a traditional music video destination that rivals YouTube.[59]

The infringement of intellectual property rights, particularly copyrights, remains a constant barrier to digital music industry growth. As technology and consumption patterns have evolved, so have the ways in which pirates acquire illegal content. Stream ripping, or the downloading of streamed music for illegal use and distribution, is the fastest growing form of music copyright infringement globally. The recording industry has coordinated a global strategy to address this practice, including directing legal action against the largest ripping sites in several countries (with some of the most recent legal victories occurring in coordination with US, UK and German industry partners).[60]

Global Markets

The global digital music industry has grown steadily over the past few years, reaching USD 12.1 billion in 2017, an increase of 22.3 per cent from 2016.[61] Together, the United States, Europe and China accounted for about 83 per cent of the global digital market (USD 10.0 billion) in 2017. The United States generated about USD 6.3 billion in digital music revenue in 2017, accounting for about 52.2 per cent of the global digital music market that year.[62] Music streaming accounted for about 80 per cent or USD 5.0 billion of US digital music revenue in 2017, compared to about USD 1.3 billion in revenue from downloads. The European digital music market (which accounted for USD 3.1 billion in revenue in 2017) was also dominated by music streaming. Nearly 80 per cent (USD 2.5 billion) of European digital music revenue was generated by the streaming subsector in 2017, while downloads accounted for only USD 642 million.[63] China generated about USD 571 million in total digital

59 A. Nicolaou and H. Kuchler, 'Facebook Looks to Change the Tune with Move into Music', *FT.com*, 6 March 2018. Notably, most music industry executives view Facebook as a 'clean slate' and are cautiously optimistic that such a partnership can help close the digital value gap.

60 IFPI, *Global Music Report*, 2018, 42.

61 Statista, 'Digital Media' database, accessed 17 July 2018.

62 Statista, 'Digital Media' database, accessed 17 July 2018.

63 Statista, 'Digital Media' database, accessed 17 July 2018.

music revenue in 2017 (an increase of 25.8 per cent from 2016), making it the fifth largest country market for digital music that year.[64] Streaming accounted for 91.4 per cent or USD 522 million of the Chinese digital music market in 2017, an increase of about 25.2 per cent from 2016.[65] Although streaming revenue was proportionally higher in China than in other top markets, the majority of Chinese users reportedly prefer ad-based music streaming, which generally shows a low willingness to pay for such digital content. For this reason, the average revenue per user in China in 2017 was only USD 0.92, compared to average revenue per user in the United States of USD 39.57.[66] For further information on the Brazilian, Chinese, European, Indian, Indonesian and Russian digital music markets, including market data, industry players, and policies and regulatory measures (where reported), see Appendix H of the USITC's *Global Digital Trade I: Market Opportunities and Key Foreign Trade Restrictions* report (August 2017).[67]

E-Publishing

E-books, a subsector of e-publishing, include digital or electronic versions of consumer trade titles (encompassing adult fiction and nonfiction, young adult, and children's genres), as well as educational textbooks and professional or scientific publications (including journals) (Box 10.4).

Competitive Landscape

Unlike the digital content sectors discussed above, the global e-book industry has largely experienced moderate to slow growth in recent years. Although Amazon leads the global e-book market, a rapidly burgeoning market for self-published or independently published e-books is expected to drive future growth. This is particularly true in developing markets (e.g. India) where Amazon's Kindle does not yet have a dominant presence.

The recent rise in e-book prices likely has contributed to traditional e-book publishers' sales declines. Amazon's Kindle Store was initially

[64] The Chinese government blocks access to most Western digital and social media content providers, including Facebook, Google and Netflix.

[65] Statista, 'Digital Media: Video-on-Demand', June 2018.

[66] Statista, 'Digital Media: Digital Music', June 2018.

[67] US International Trade Commission, *Global Digital Trade I: Market Opportunities and Key Foreign Trade Restrictions*, August 2017, 428–432.

BOX 10.4 E-BOOKS SUBSECTOR SNAPSHOT

Global e-books revenue: USD 11.4 billion in 2017.

- What the Statista revenue data measure:
  - Paid downloads of digital or electronic versions of printed books, which can be accessed and read with the help of various devices such as e-Readers (e.g. Kindle), tablets, smartphones or computers).
- What the Statista revenue data do not measure:
  - Paid downloads of digital or electronic versions of magazines and newspapers.
  - Open-access literature, ad-based content and services, bundle subscriptions and digital paid content on websites.

Top 5 e-book markets, by revenue, 2017

United States	USD 5,297 million
Japan	USD 1,177 million
China	USD 1,109 million
United Kingdom	USD 784 million
Germany	USD 453 million

Industry leaders by US e-book revenue (est.), 2018, (Total = USD 3,600 million):

- Amazon (USA) – USD 2,340 million
- Apple (USA) – USD 464 million
- Barnes & Noble (USA) – USD 338 million
- Kobo (Japan/Canada) – USD 126 million
- Google (USA) – USD 86 million

Sources: Statista, 'Digital Media' database, accessed 17 July 2018; McGinley, 'E-Book Publishing in the US', *IBISWorld*, June 2018, 16.

Note: Due to differing accounting methods, USA-company level and national/global revenue data estimates from IBISWorld and Statista will not match. For the sake of consistency across sectors, we will rely on Statista data for this section unless otherwise noted.

successful with e-books priced at USD 9.99 or lower. Such low prices likely helped e-books (particularly Kindle e-books) to gain mainstream popularity.[68] However, Amazon now allows e-book publishers to set

[68] D. McGinley, 'Bookworms: The Growing Popularity of E-readers', *IBISWorld*, December 2016, 7. Concurrent declines in electronic component prices, which made the Kindle and similar e-book reading devices more affordable for consumers to buy, added to their fast rise in popularity.

their own Kindle e-book prices (after conflicts with traditional publishers, including multiple lawsuits), resulting in significant e-book price increases in established markets like the United States and the United Kingdom.[69]

While price increases may have contributed to a decline in traditional publishers' e-book sales, prices vary widely depending on the market and publisher. In the United States and other similarly mature e-book markets, the ratio of hardcover book prices to e-book prices is about 1:0.78, which is much higher than in developing markets. In China, for instance, this ratio is about 1:0.25.[70] Further, although most traditional publishers release the majority of new e-books on large platforms such as Amazon or Kobo at relatively high price points, almost half of all e-books are sold at price points of less than USD 5.40, with the least expensive e-books coming from independent publishers. Hence, the impact of price on the global competitive landscape is difficult to assess.[71]

A second, and more debated, reason for the industry's relative decline is that consumers may be tiring of using dedicated digital media to read books, with some readers preferring print books as a relief from an increasingly digital world. There are several arguments for and against this reasoning. Those that support it note that, by contrast with video and music content, no electronic device is inherently needed to read a book. Moreover, despite certain price and convenience factors (including the growing catalogue of free e-books), it is argued that e-book reading devices, including smartphones and tablets, simply have not delivered the long-form reading experience needed to completely replace physical books.[72] Other industry observers, however, assign more weight to the e-book industry's closed technological platforms and strict digital rights management policies.[73] Publishers, in these observers' views, have tied the user's reading experience to the vendor's closed environment in a way

[69] D. McGinley, 'Bookworms: The Growing Popularity of E-readers', *IBISWorld*, December 2016, 8. Incidents included an antitrust suit with charges of price collusion brought against major book publishers and Apple in 2012 by the US government, and a series of negotiating conflicts between Amazon and Hachette Book Group in 2014.

[70] Statista, 'Digital Media: ePublishing', 2016.

[71] P. Anderson, '2017 Global Ebook Report: As Many Stories as Markets', *PublishingPerspectives.com*, 15 May 2017.

[72] J. Milliot, 'As E-book Sales Decline, Digital Fatigue Grows', *PublishersWeekly.com*, 17 June 2016; E. Spinak, 'eBooks – Global Market and Trends – Part II', *Blog.scielo.org*, 22 June 2016; J. Anand, 'Amazon Kindle Sales Up 200% in India', *Gadgetsnow.com*, 19 February 2016.

[73] M. Masnick, 'The Stagnation of eBooks', *Techdirt.com*, 5 October 2015.

that inconveniences customers. Once customers have purchased their e-readers, they are locked into their chosen brand's format – for example, Amazon's e-books are unusable on Nook devices and vice versa.[74] E-books are also bound by digital rights management policies set by vendors which limit transfers, while a traditional book can be passed repeatedly from reader to reader.[75]

Amazon continues to dominate the global e-book industry. As of February 2017, Amazon accounted for 82 per cent of all English-language e-book sales (406 million units) in the United States and in four other predominantly English-speaking countries: Australia, Canada, New Zealand and the UK.[76] Within those English-speaking markets (where firm-level e-book data are most comparable), Amazon's e-book sales were followed by those of Apple iBooks (US) (10 per cent); Barnes & Noble Nook (US) (3 per cent); Google Play (US) (less than 3 per cent); and Ratuken Kobo (Japan/Canada) (2 per cent).[77] In terms of US revenue, Amazon was also the clear market leader with revenue estimated to reach about $2.34 billion in 2018 – five times larger than revenues earned by its next largest competitor, Apple.[78]

Finally, the market prominence of independent e-book authors has grown. Between 2014 and 2015, almost 460,000 new e-book titles were published worldwide, with 75 per cent of these being published on three platforms for independent authors: Smashwords (US), Amazon's CreateSpace (which offers publishing via the Kindle Store and paperback) and Lulu (US).[79] The top self-publishing platform, Smashwords, generated about 437,000 titles by 127,500 individual authors in 2016.[80] Moreover, self-published authors made up 20–35 per cent of all international sales by major e-book retailers (Amazon, Apple, Kobo and Barnes & Noble) in that year, with independent authors accounting for about 42 per cent of Amazon's e-book sales as

[74] M. Masnick, 'The Stagnation of eBooks', *Techdirt.com*, 5 October 2015.

[75] C. Meadows, 'Consumers Believe They Have More Rights', *Teleread.com*, 26 May 2016.

[76] *AuthorEarnings.com*, 'February 2017 Big, Bad, Wide and International Report', 2017; R. Wischenbart et al., *Global eBook*, *Global-ebook.com*, 2016, 14; E. Spinak, 'eBooks – Global Market and Trends – Part I', *Blog.scielo.org*, 22 June 2016; E. Spinak, 'eBooks – Global Market and Trends – Part III', *Blog.scielo.org*, 27 July 2016.

[77] *AuthorEarnings.com*, 'February 2017 Big, Bad, Wide and International Report', 2017.

[78] D. McGinley, 'E-Book Publishing in the US', IBISWorld, June 2018, 16.

[79] E. Spinak, 'eBooks – Global Market and Trends – Part I', *Blog.scielo.org*, 22 June 2016.

[80] M. Coker, 'Smashwords Year in Review 2016 and 2017 Preview', *Blog.smashwords.com*, 31 December 2016.

of mid-January 2016.[81] However, the future economic sustainability of independent e-book publishers remains uncertain, as their products are usually priced well below market averages (often publishing for free) and lack the advertising and commercial exposure traditional e-publishers can provide.[82]

Global Markets

The global e-book industry has grown moderately over the past few years, reaching about USD 11.4 billion in 2017, an increase of about 4.7 per cent over the previous year. US e-book sales were about $5.3 billion in 2017, accounting for about 46.5 per cent of the global market.[83] Notably, US e-book revenues for traditional publishers[84] fell by about 16 per cent in 2016 compared to the previous year.[85] The e-book market in Europe, which posted USD 2.5 billion in sales in 2017, is also stagnating. This is particularly true in mature markets such as the United Kingdom and Germany due to market saturation.[86] China, the third-largest consumer of e-books behind the United States and Japan, generated about USD 1.0 billion in e-book revenue in 2017.[87] For further information on the Brazilian, Chinese, European, Indian, Indonesian and Russian e-book markets, including market data, industry players, and policies and regulatory measures (where reported), see Appendix H of the USITC's *Global Digital Trade I: Market Opportunities and Key Foreign Trade Restrictions* report (August 2017).[88]

[81] *AuthorEarnings.com*, 'February 2017 Big, Bad, Wide and International Report', 2017; *AuthorEarnings.com*, 'February 2016 Author Earnings Report', 2016.

[82] M. Coker, '2018 Book Publishing Predictions – Are Indie Authors Losing their Independence?', *Huffingtonpost.com*, 5 January 2018.

[83] Statista, 'Digital Media' database, accessed 17 July 2018.

[84] 'Traditional publishers' refers to established publication houses with major print operations, such as the global book industry's five largest English-language publishers – Penguin Random House (US), Hachette Livre (France), HarperCollins (US), Macmillan (Germany) and Simon & Schuster (US).

[85] J. Milliot, 'The Bad News about E-books', *Publishersweekly.com*, 20 January 2017; E. Spinak, 'eBooks – Global Market and Trends – Part I', *Blog.scielo.org*, 22 June 2016; *AuthorEarnings.com*, 'February 2016 Author Earnings Report', 2016.

[86] Statista, 'Digital Media: ePublishing', June 2018.

[87] Statista, 'Digital Media' database, accessed 17 July 2018.

[88] US International Trade Commission, *Global Digital Trade I: Market Opportunities and Key Foreign Trade Restrictions*, August 2017, 432–436.

Intellectual Property Rights Issues

To address digital piracy and intermediary liability concerns (Box 10.5), a country needs a strong legal framework and effective enforcement.[89] As Internet penetration increases in both developed and developing countries, digital piracy has reportedly also been rising rapidly among Internet users. For example, according to the Motion Picture Association of America (MPAA), 'Online piracy is the most significant threat to the [US film] industry generally and [its] exports more significantly.'[90] The music industry reportedly also suffers from a major revenue-erosion problem as a result of stream ripping sites, which illegally download music streams for distribution, and other methods that provide unauthorized access to content.[91]

Some key markets are implementing strong intellectual property laws and/or increasing enforcement of IPRs through local law enforcement agencies or domestic courts while the situation remains problematic in other markets. Most EU countries have specific laws and enforcement agencies targeting digital piracy. For example, in coordination with the FBI, law enforcement in the United Kingdom and the Netherlands raided and shut down Sharebeast, a large music sharing site, for violating copyright laws.[92] Moreover, Europe is in the process of pursuing new means to combat piracy through the EU

[89] Depending on the content, digital piracy can occur through a variety of means and devices. For example, digital piracy of films includes unauthorized recordings made in movie theatres of first-run motion pictures that are distributed worldwide via the Internet. Digital piracy of software includes pirate servers that allow users to play unauthorized versions of cloud-based entertainment software, as well as online distribution of software and devices that allow for 'game copiers' and mod chips, enabling users to play pirated games on physical consoles. Digital piracy of music includes a user joining a file-sharing network and downloading unauthorized copies of copyrighted music for free, or paying a fee to join a file-sharing network not authorized to distribute copyrighted music and then downloading that music. Office of the US Trade Representative, *2018 Special 301 Report*, April 2018; Recording Industry Association of America, 'About Piracy', *Riaa.com*, accessed 8 February 2017.

[90] US International Trade Commission, hearing transcript, Washington, DC, 4 April 2017, 35 (testimony of Joanna McIntosh, MPAA).

[91] Office of the US Trade Representative, *2017 Out-of-Cycle Review of Notorious Markets*, January 2018.

[92] Office of the US Trade Representative, *2017 Out-of-Cycle Review of Notorious Markets*, January 2018.

BOX 10.5 DEBATE SURROUNDING INTERNET INTERMEDIARY LIABILITY FOR ADDRESSING COPYRIGHT INFRINGEMENT[a]

Most countries have 'notice and takedown' provisions in their domestic copyright protection laws or implementing regulations that hold Internet intermediaries[b] liable if they continue to display content after notification from the copyright holder under certain circumstances. While these laws place some responsibility for IPR protection on intermediaries, they also generally include 'safe-harbour' provisions that limit liability upon compliance with 'notice and takedown' procedures. Some intermediaries act automatically upon notification from a copyright holder of infringing material and emphasize their rapid processing of notice and takedown requests. For example, Google reports that it processes takedown notices in less than six hours on average.[c]

Content industries generally advocate placing increased responsibility on Internet intermediaries, particularly ISPs, to implement 'notice and staydown'. They note that infringing material on a website can easily be reinstated as current copyright protection laws keep intermediaries' responsibilities narrowly defined, with negative effects on content industries.[d]

On the other hand, Internet intermediaries generally resist calls for increased legal responsibility, such as requirements to search for and delete copies of infringing material on their platforms before it is posted or to block the posting of new copies in the future. Internet industry representatives contend that regulatory measures and policies aimed at increasing intermediaries' responsibilities would impede digital trade for intermediary firms in markets where such measures are enforced.[e]

[a] This information is also presented in the US International Trade Commission's *Global Digital Trade I: Market Opportunities and Key Foreign Trade Restrictions*, August 2017 report.

[b] Some examples of Internet intermediaries are Internet services providers (ISPs), search engines, hosting services, social networks, online forums and online platforms.

[c] C. Hall, 'How Many Copyright Takedown Notices Does Google Handle?' *Bizjournals.com*, 7 March 2016.

[d] US International Trade Commission, hearing transcript, Washington, DC, 4 April 2017, 137 (testimony of George York, RIAA) and US International Trade Commission, *Global Digital Trade I: Market Opportunities and Key Foreign Trade Restrictions*, August 2017, 297–298.

[e] US International Trade Commission, hearing transcript, Washington, DC, 4 April 2017, 141–244 (testimony of Ari Giovenco, Internet Association).

Digital Single Market platform and other reforms.[93] By contrast, enforcement of digital piracy laws in China and Russia reportedly remains problematic.[94]

New measures and voluntary initiatives to prevent and deter digital content piracy are being implemented in key markets. These include accelerating official responses to infringement complaints; the increased use of commercial licensing arrangements between platform companies and right holders; developing new technologies to identify or prevent infringing uses; and increased reliance on cooperative procedures involving private and public actors focused on reducing digital piracy.[95]

Bibliography

Accenture, 'The Pulse of Gaming', 2014.

Amobi, T., 'Industry Surveys: Media', *S&P*, September 2016.

Anand, J., 'Amazon Kindle Sales Up 200% in India', *Gadgetsnow.com*, 19 February 2016.

Anderson, P., '2017 Global Ebook Report: As Many Stories as Markets', *PublishingPerspectives.com*, 15 May 2017.

Arthofer, F. et al., 'The Future of Television', Boston Consulting Group, 2016.

AuthorEarnings.com, 'February 2016 Author Earnings Report', 2016.

AuthorEarnings.com, 'February 2017 Big, Bad, Wide and International Report', 2017.

Barrett, B., 'Pokémon Go Is Doing Just Fine', *Wired.com*, 18 September 2016.

Blau, F., 'Social Status: New Markets and Rising Incomes', *IBISWorld*, July 2016.

Bradshaw, T., 'Esports Viewing Shoots Up', *FT.com*, 8 May 2017.

Brown, A., 'iPlayer Will Be Revamped to Compete with Netflix and Amazon Prime, BBC confirms', *Express.co.uk*, 7 April 2018.

Bulygo, Z., 'How Netflix Uses Analytics to Select Movies', (2014), available at www.researchgate.net/publication/324046341_The_Rise_of_Embedded_Analytics_Empowering_Manufacturing_and_Service_Industry_With_Big_D.

93 European Commission, 'Questions and Answers', updated 24 January 2017.

94 USTR's *2018 Special 301 Report* states that India, China, and Russia have egregious commercial-scale digital piracy because certain websites in these countries host, operate or direct parties to violate IPRs. Office of the US Trade Representative, *2018 Special 301 Report*, April 2018.

95 Office of the US Trade Representative, *2017 Out-of-Cycle Review of Notorious Markets*, January 2018 and US International Trade Commission, *Global Digital Trade I: Market Opportunities and Key Foreign Trade Restrictions*, August 2017, 291–301.

Bundgaard, T., Karlsson, A., Lau, A. and Pereira, A., 'The Beat of Progress: The Rise of Music Streaming', *McKinsey Quarterly*, November 2016.

Cai, W. et al., 'A Survey of Cloud Gaming: Future of Computer Games', (University of British Columbia, 2016), 7606.

Coker, M., '2018 Book Publishing Predictions – Are Indie Authors Losing their Independence?', *Huffingtonpost.com*, 5 January 2018.

Coker, M., 'Smashwords Year in Review 2016 and 2017 Preview', *Blog.smashwords.com*, 31 December 2016.

Disis, J. and Gold, H., 'Disney Wins Antitrust Approval to Purchase Most of Fox', *Money.cnn.com*, 27 June 2018.

Economist Intelligence Unit, 'Digital Upheaval: How Asia-Pacific is Leading the Way in Emerging Media Consumption Trends', 22 January 2018, p. 4.

Economist.com, 'China's New Craze for Live-Streaming', 9 February 2017.

Economist.com, 'How to Devise the Perfect Recommendation Algorithm', 9 February 2017.

Economist.com, 'Mass Entertainment in the Digital Age is Still About Blockbusters, Not Endless Choice', 11 February 2017.

Economist.com, 'Traditional TV's Surprising Staying Power', 9 February 2017.

Economist.com, 'AT&T's Merger With Time Warner Goes On Trial', 17 March 2018.

eMarketer.com, 'China's Subscription OTT Video Market Is Booming', 18 January 2018.

European Commission, 'Questions and Answers: Digital Single Market Strategy', Fact sheet, updated 24 January 2017.

Feng, E. and Yang, Y., 'Chinese Unicorns Tripped up by Content Crackdown', *FT.com*, 29 April 2018.

Granados, N., 'The Battle For Video Entertainment Goes Global: Who Will Win?', *Forbes.com*, 20 February 2018.

Grimm, A., 'Trends in U.S. Trade in Information and Communications Technology (ICT) Services and in IT-Enabled Services', (Washington, DC: US Bureau of Economic Analysis), May 2016.

Gurman, M., 'Apple's Next Big Thing: Augmented Reality', *Bloomberg.com*, 20 March 2017.

Hall, C., 'How Many Copyright Takedown Notices Does Google Handle?', *Bizjournals.com*, 7 March 2016.

Herrera, S., 'Netflix and Amazon Go Global: The Impact of Content Localization of Video Streaming', Media and Entertainment Journal (Spring 2017).

Ho, P. C., 'China Removes 370 Live-streaming Apps', *Technode.com*, 18 April 2018.

International Federation of the Phonographic Industry (IFPI), *Global Music Report*, 2018, available at www.ifpi.org/ifpi-global-music-report-2018/.

La Monica, P., 'Netflix Still Wears the Streaming Crown', *Money.cnn.com*, 3 January 2018.

Lee, A., 'China's Booming Live Streaming Industry May Have Reached Its Peak', *Scmp.com*, 20 December 2017.

Lee, P. and Stewart, D., 'eSports: Bigger and Smaller Than You Think', *Deloitte*, 2016.

Levy, A., 'Amazon Prime is Beating Netflix in 3 Countries', *BusinessInsider.com/* The Motley Fool, 17 February 2018.

Masnick, M., 'The Stagnation of eBooks', *Techdirt.com*, 5 October 2015.

McGinley, D., 'Bookworms: The Growing Popularity of E-readers', *IBISWorld*, December 2016.

McGinley, D., 'E-Book Publishing in the US', *IBISWorld*, June 2018.

Meadows, C., 'Consumers Believe They Have More Rights', *Teleread.com*, 26 May 2016.

Meredith, S., 'After Exiting Battle for Fox, Comcast Fires "Warning Shot" to Disney over Sky Takeover, analyst says', *CNBC.com*, 20 July 2018.

Milliot, J., 'As E-book Sales Decline, Digital Fatigue Grows', *PublishersWeekly.com*, 17 June 2016.

Milliot, J., 'The Bad News about E-books', *PublishersWeekly.com*, 20 January 2017.

Mulligan, M., 'Amazon Is Now the 3rd Biggest Music Subscription Service', *Musicindustryblog.wordpress.com*, 14 July 2017.

Mulligan, M., 'Is YouTube Serious About Music Subscriptions This Time Round?', *Musicindustryblog.wordpress.com*, 17 May 2018.

Newzoo, 'Global ESports Market Report 2017', 2017.

Newzoo, 'Top 25 Public Game Companies Earn $94.1 Billion in 2017', 9 May 2018.

Newzoo, 'Global Esports Economy Will Reach $905.6 Million in 2018 as Brand Investment Grows by 48%', 21 February 2018.

Nicholson, J., 'Digital Trade in North America' (Washington, DC: US Department of Commerce), 5 January 2018.

Nicolaou, A. and Kuchler, H., 'Facebook Looks to Change the Tune with Move into Music', *FT.com*, 6 March 2018.

Niu, E., 'Amazon Has More Music Subscribers Than You Think', *Fool.com*, 4 April 2018.

Office of the US Trade Representative, *2017 Out-of-Cycle Review of Notorious Markets*, January 2018.

Office of the US Trade Representative, *2018 Special 301 Report*, April 2018.

Perez, S., 'App Annie: Android to Top iOS', *TechCrunch.com*, 29 March 2017.

Pierce, D., 'Spotify, Amazon, Apple or YouTube? The Streaming-Music Showdown', *Wsj.com*, 24 June 2018.

Recording Industry Association of America (RIAA), 'About Piracy', *Riaa.com*, 8 February 2017.

Richter, F., 'Netflix Reaches 130 Million Subscribers', Statista, 17 July 2018.

Richter, F., 'Netflix Splurges Cash on Content', Statista, 17 July 2018.

Sepalla, T., 'YouTube Reportedly Plans to Spend "Hundreds of Millions" on Red Originals', *Engadget.com*, 23 February 2018.

Shaw, L., 'Netflix's Pursuit of TV Domination Has a New Step', Bloomberg News, 21 April 2015.

Smith, E., 'How Cricket is Going Global with Netflix and Amazon', *NewStatesman.com*, 24 September 2017.

Spinak, E., 'eBooks—Global Market and Trends—Part I', *Blog.scielo.org*, 22 June 2016.

Spinak, E., 'eBooks—Global Market and Trends—Part II', *Blog.scielo.org*, 22 June 2016.

Spinak, E., 'eBooks—Global Market and Trends—Part III', *Blog.scielo.org*, 27 July 2016.

Statista, 'Digital Media: ePublishing', 2016.

Statista, 'Digital Media: Video Games', 2016.

Statista, 'Digital Media', database, 17 July 2018.

Statista, 'Digital Media: Digital Music', June 2018.

Statista, 'Digital Media: ePublishing', June 2018.

Statista, 'Digital Media Report', June 2018.

Statista, 'Digital Media: Video Games', June 2018.

Statista, 'Digital Media: Video-on-Demand', June 2018.

Strategy+Business, *Global Entertainment and Media Outlook 2016–2020*, 2016.

SuperData Research and Unity Technologies, 'Can't Stop, Won't Stop: 2016 Mobile and VR Games', 2017.

Swanson, A., 'The Power of Big Data in China', Cheung Kong Graduate School of Business, 28 July 2015.

UNESCAP, *Asia-Pacific Trade and Investment Report 2016: Recent Trends and Developments*, Bangkok, Thailand: United Nations Economic and Social Commission for Asia and the Pacific, November 2016.

US International Trade Commission (USITC), *Global Digital Trade I: Market Opportunities and Key Foreign Trade Restrictions*, Washington, DC: USITC, August 2017.

US International Trade Commission (USITC), Hearing transcript in connection with Inv. No. 332–561, *Global Digital Trade I: Market Opportunities and Key Foreign Trade Restrictions*, Washington, DC: USITC, 4 April 2017, p. 35 (testimony of Joanna McIntosh, MPAA); 137 (testimony of George York, RIAA); 141–144 (testimony of Ari Giovenco, Internet Association).

Wischenbart, R. et al., *Global eBook, Global-ebook.com*, 2016.

World Economic Forum, *Digital Transformation of Industries: Digital Enterprise*, January 2016.

11

Cross-Border Knowledge Flows through R&D FDI: Implications for Low- and Middle-Income Countries

VITO AMENDOLAGINE, CRISTINA CHAMINADE, JOSÉ GUIMÓN AND ROBERTA RABELLOTTI*

Abstract

R&D related foreign direct investments represent a powerful mechanism for cross-border knowledge sharing that can stimulate the process of technological catch-up. However, low-income countries and smaller middle-income countries remain largely excluded from this kind of global flows of knowledge. In this chapter, we discuss the motivations and implications of this type of FDI for low- and middle-income countries, building on a critical review of the existing literature, and analyze the trajectory of R&D FDI during the period 2003-2017 by region and industry. The data is used as a point of departure to discuss potential policies specially tailored for low- and middle-income countries and their capacity to attract and anchor R&D related FDI for technological catch up. The chapter concludes with an outline of a future research agenda.

Introduction

Foreign direct investment (FDI) has long been considered an important channel through which international technology transfer unfolds (Abramovitz, 1986). Through FDI, multinational enterprises (MNEs) increasingly act as global orchestrators of knowledge by tapping into diverse knowledge clusters and allowing connections between knowledge sources across distant locations. However, FDI is a very heterogeneous phenomenon, and the potential for cross-border knowledge exchange depends crucially on the type of activities that MNEs decide to offshore to each particular location (Narula and Dunning, 2010).

* Acknowledgements: The authors would like to thank Antonio Vezzani at the EU JRC in Seville for providing data about companies included in the R&D Investment Scoreboard.

It seems self-evident that FDI related to research and development (R&D) represents the type of investment with the highest potential for cross-border knowledge flows, since its purpose is precisely to access, generate and potentially diffuse knowledge within global innovation networks. Therefore, it is not surprising that attracting R&D FDI has become a high priority for policymakers throughout the world.[1]

The current global innovation landscape, characterized by increased technological capabilities in emerging economies coupled with open models of innovation, modularization and high technological complexity, is influencing the way that MNEs organize their R&D activity – from a centralized and hierarchical organization towards one that is more loosely structured around global innovation networks. Such networks include the R&D centres established by MNEs, collaborating both among each other and with other firms, universities and public research institutes in the different countries, regions and clusters where they are located.[2]

With the spread of global innovation networks, national, regional and local innovation systems influence and are increasingly influenced by R&D-related investments undertaken by MNEs. On the one hand, MNEs are considered as key actors characterized by superior technological resources in the location where they establish their subsidiaries, potentially generating knowledge spillovers (Javorcik, 2004). On the other hand, MNEs take advantage of their international investments to tap into local knowledge pools, embedding in technological hubs and creating networks with local actors (Marin and Arza, 2009). Therefore, their R&D-related location decisions are highly influenced by the innovation performance of the different national or regional innovation systems, particularly when investments respond to knowledge-seeking strategies.

In this chapter, we focus on inward R&D FDI as a driver of economic development and catching-up for low- and middle-income countries (LMICs). The following section on cross-border knowledge flows through R&D FTI delves into the motivations and implications of this type of FDI, building on a critical review of the existing literature. The next section[3]

[1] The high relevance of R&D FDI for policymakers was already confirmed in 2005 when the United Nations Conference on Trade and Development (UNCTAD) chose 'Transnational Corporations and the Internationalization of R&D' as the thematic focus of the World Investment Report (UNCTAD, 2005). This report, in turn, spurred a growing interest on the topic in subsequent years, both in policy as well as in academic circles.

[2] The concept of 'global innovation network' is analysed further in Chaminade et al. (2016).

[3] P. 357 *infra*.

provides an overview of R&D FDI during the period 2003–2017, analysing key trends of greenfield investments and acquisitions by region and industry. The final section[4] provides suggestions for a future research and policy agenda, focusing on the opportunities and challenges for LMICs.

Cross-Border Knowledge Flows through R&D FDI: Motivations and Impact on Low- and Middle-Income Countries

MNEs have traditionally located their offshore R&D centres in developed countries. However, since the late 1990s a significant amount of R&D FDI is directed towards LMICs. Scholars from economic geography, international business and innovation studies have tried to shed light on the motivations of MNEs to locate R&D investments in low- and middle-income countries, as well as on the impact of such investments on the innovation performance of host countries.[5] The rest of this section summarizes key findings of this strand of research.

Motivations Driving R&D FDI to Low- and Middle-Income Countries

The factors that influence the location of MNEs' R&D centres are many, including traditional drivers such as market size and factor costs, as well as knowledge-seeking motivations such as the availability of qualified engineers and scientists and, more generally, the possibility to tap into disperse 'global knowledge reservoirs' (Kafouros et al., 2012).

There are several reasons that help explain the growing attractiveness of low- and middle-income countries as locations of R&D FDI. First, the substantial increase in public investments in R&D in emerging countries and the availability of new, high-quality scientific infrastructure, particularly in certain metropolitan areas in China and India (Crescenzi and Rodríguez-Pose, 2017). Second, the large pools of highly skilled personnel available at relatively low cost combined with the shortage of highly skilled scientists and engineers in developed countries, as illustrated with the case of investments in IT and software services in India (Arora and Bagde, 2006) or biotechnology investments in China (Haakonsson, 2013). Third, the return migration of engineers, scientists and managers, who can play a bridging role between developing and developed

[4] P. 367 *infra*.

[5] For recent reviews, see Cantwell (2017), Lema et al. (2015) and Mudambi et al. (2018).

countries (Saxenian, 2006). Fourth, the large and dynamic markets of new emerging powers like China and India, which offer great opportunities for large-scale commercialization of different products and services and for incremental innovation aimed at adapting products to the domestic markets (Chen, 2008). Finally, and related to this last point, the obligation to conduct R&D in the country as a precondition to access the local market through FDI (Lema et al., 2015).

This mixture of market-seeking, efficiency-seeking and knowledge-seeking motivations leads to different types of offshore R&D centres located in LMICs. While some of them focus on creating new products (or adapting existing ones) to respond to local demand (Wang et al., 2012), others have the main purpose of reducing costs by conducting routine research activities that were previously performed in a high-income country at a higher cost (Reddy, 1997). Generally, earlier studies have shown that such R&D centres tend to focus (at least initially) on lower-end and routine R&D activities, given the weak technological capabilities of LMICs relative to high-income countries. In the words of Thursby and Thursby (2006), R&D activities by MNEs in low- and middle-income countries normally involve 'familiar science' (i.e. applications of science currently used by the firm and/or its competitors) rather than 'new science' (i.e. novel applications of science), which hitherto remained concentrated in the core high-income countries.

However, more recent studies show that some middle-income countries are increasingly engaging in more advanced R&D activities (e.g. D'Agostino and Santangelo, 2012). This often results from an evolutionary, learning-based upgrading whereby MNE subsidiaries gradually move from adaptation to the market of products already developed in the headquarters to conducting applied research and even basic research, developing new knowledge and technological competences along the way. In the international business literature, this phenomenon has been described as a progressive shift from the traditional *market-seeking* or *efficiency-seeking* investments going to middle-income countries towards more strategic *knowledge-seeking* FDI. In some instances, this knowledge-seeking behaviour has led to *reverse innovation*, whereby innovations generated by MNE subsidiaries in middle-income countries are subsequently re-used to cater for global markets (Govindarajan and Ramamurti, 2011; Von Zedtwitz et al., 2015). A well-known example of the latter is the pocketsize ultrasound scan developed by General Electric in China with rural doctors in mind, which has rapidly reached a global market.

Impact of R&D FDI in Low- and Middle-Income Countries

R&D FDI is especially relevant for LMICs as part of a process of catching-up by absorbing foreign knowledge. Indeed, the attraction of R&D FDI can enhance economic and social progress by facilitating the transfer of foreign knowledge and fostering the kind of structural changes that lead to an increasing participation in higher value-added activities within global value chains. Eventually, it may have a positive spillover effect on the R&D efforts of local firms,[6] create new opportunities for local talent and lead to the emergence of technology start-ups.

However, attracting R&D FDI remains a difficult task for low- and middle-income countries. Besides the obvious difficulties involved in competing with the most advanced innovation systems and technological hubs of developed countries, the existing literature points to various factors that may deter MNEs from locating R&D activities in low- and middle-income countries. These include the complexity of coordinating increasingly disperse structures as well as the high political risks and uncertainty in legal reforms common to many low- and middle-income countries. In particular, several studies have underlined that weak intellectual property (IP) regimes LMICs might be a significant hindrance, especially for more advanced types of R&D, to the extent that it harms MNEs' ability to appropriate the returns of such investments. For example, an empirical study for 2002–2006 by Chuang and Lin (2011) finds that the degree of IP protection in host countries has a significant negative influence on the overseas R&D activities of MNEs in emerging economies. However, the other side of the coin is that stronger IP regimes may diminish the scope for imitation and learning, creating an additional barrier for catching-up.[7]

Moreover, the benefits from R&D FDI are far from automatic. The upgradation process depends crucially on parallel efforts by host countries to improve their domestic technological capabilities and absorptive capacities[8]. In some instances, the impact might even be negative. Along these lines, Bruche (2009) stresses how R&D centres established by MNEs in developing countries may attract the best local scientists and engineers, leading to an *in-situ brain drain* that deprives local companies

[6] For example, Qu et al. (2013) finds that inward R&D FDI has a positive effect on the R&D efforts of Chinese firms, based on an empirical study of 12,309 manufacturing firms in the ICT sector.

[7] See Branstetter and Maskus (Chapter 13 in this volume).

[8] For further discussion on the crucial role of absorptive capacity for international knowledge transfer see Branstetter and Maskus (Chapter 13 in this volume).

of human capital. Other authors have also cautioned that MNEs might lead to a *crowding-out* of local firms, engage in a research agenda of little relevance to the local economy and divert scarce resources from more useful purposes (Pearce and Papanastassiou, 2009).

All in all, the existing literature suggests that R&D FDI provides opportunities for knowledge transfer to LMICs. Nevertheless, the extent of the impact in terms of learning and upgrading depends both on the motivation of the MNE, as well as on the quality of the host country's innovation system.

R&D FDI In Low- and Middle-Income Countries: An Overview

In this section, we first offer an overview of R&D FDI globally, and then focus on investments going towards LMICs. We consider both greenfield FDIs and cross-border acquisitions, over the period 2003–2017.

Data on greenfield investments are provided by FDI Markets, a database maintained by the Financial Times Group, which collects worldwide cross-border deals since 2003. For each investment, it gives information about the date and the location (country, region and city) of the deal, the name, the geographical origin, the industrial sector of specializations of the investor and the business activity undertaken with the investment project. In this chapter, we make use of this last piece of information to identify the investments in activities related with R&D. In particular, following Crescenzi et al. (2013), we consider deals in research and development (R&D) as well as in design, development and testing (DDT), defining them as R&D&DDT greenfield investments.

Data on cross-border acquisitions comes from Zephyr, a database maintained by Bureau van Dijk, providing name, sector and geographical origin of both the acquirers and the target companies, date and status of the deal and ownership share transferred from the target to the acquirer. We include in our analysis acquisitions of at least 10 per cent of the target's ownership, following the UNCTAD definition of FDI.[9] Identifying R&D-related acquisitions is not an easy task (Piscitello et al., 2015). Following Ahuja and Katila (2001), we focus on acquisitions involving a target company with some patenting activity[10] in the five years preceding

[9] Available at http://unctad.org/en/Pages/DIAE/Foreign-Direct-Investment-(FDI).aspx.

[10] We consider INPADOC (International Patent Documentation) families containing all the patent applications filed by the target company at any patent office that share the same priority date and protect a single invention (Martinez, 2010). The advantage of

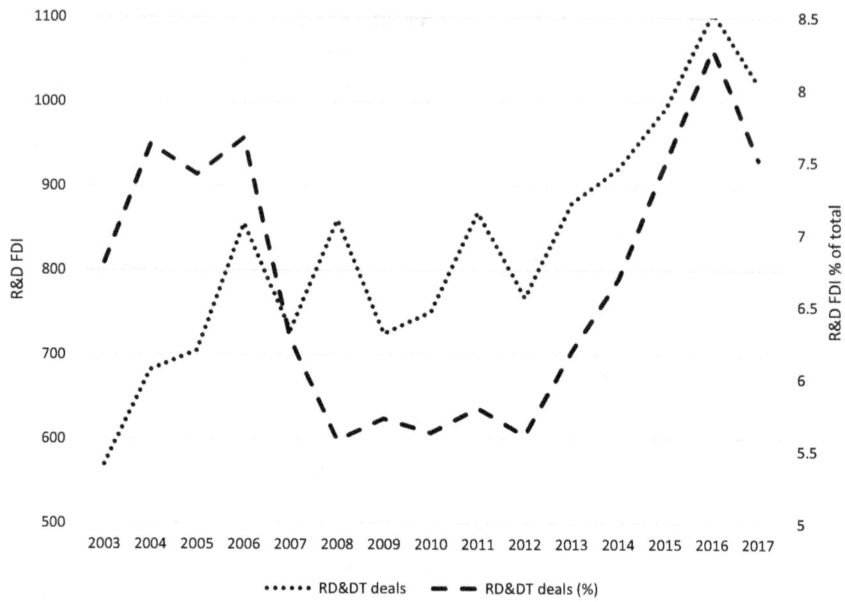

Figure 11.1 Dynamics of R&D&DDT greenfield investments (total and %)
Source: fDi Markets.

the acquisition, as an indication of previous R&D activity. To facilitate the search, we restrict our analysis on R&D-related acquisitions undertaken by the top 1,000 global companies by R&D expenditure.[11] These companies account for 65 per cent of global business expenditures in R&D (UNESCO, 2018) and have undertaken more than 40 per cent of all R&D greenfield investments according to fDi Markets.

Greenfield Investments

In the period 2003–2017, global R&D&DDT greenfield investments have increased 1.8 times, from 570 deals in 2003 to 1020 deals in 2017 (Figure 11.1). The growing relevance of investments in R&D-related activities becomes even more evident if we consider their share out of the total number of greenfield investments (indicated on the right vertical

employing INPADOC families rather than patent applications to individual patent offices is to count all the patents filed by a firm and, at the same time, avoid the double counting for the same invention (see for example Amendolagine et al., 2018).

11 Based on the R&D Investment Scoreboard, available at https://iri.jrc.ec.europa.eu/scoreboard/2017-eu-industrial-rd-investment-scoreboard.

Table 11.1 *Geographical distribution of R&D&DDT FDI (total and %)*

Region	DDT	R&D	Total R&D&DDT
Low- and middle-income	3,951 (42.0)	1,151 (38.0)	5,102 (41.0)
High-income	5,453 (58.0)	1,879 (62.0)	7,332 (59.0)
Africa	179 (1.9)	38 (1.2)	217 (1.7)
Latin America	534 (5.7)	127 (4.2)	661 (5.3)
North America	1,149 (12.2)	405 (13.4)	1,554 (12.5)
Europe	3,286 (35.0)	1,063 (35.1)	4,349 (35.0)
Asia	4,085 (43.4)	1,349 (44.5)	5,491 (43.7)
Oceania	171 (1.8)	48 (1.6)	219 (1.8)
Total	9,404 (100.0)	3,030 (100.0)	12,434 (100.0)

Source: fDi Markets.

axis). From 2008 to 2017, the share has risen from 5.6 to 7.5 per cent, reaching a peak in 2016 (8.3 per cent).

In terms of geographical distribution, Table 11.1 indicates that the largest share of greenfield R&D&DDT FDI is hosted by Asian countries (44 per cent), followed by Europe (35 per cent) and North America (12 per cent). Considering the disaggregation between LMICs and high-income countries, 59 per cent of the R&D investments (7,332 deals) go to the advanced economies and the remaining 41 per cent (5,102 deals) to LMICs. Considering the disaggregation between R&D and DDT, in low- and middle-income countries, 23 per cent of deals correspond to R&D (77 per cent in DDT) while the share goes up to 26 per cent in high-income countries (74 per cent in DDT). Thus around three-fourths of R&D&DDT FDI projects are really related to DDT.

Table 11.2 provides industry-specific details.[12] LMICs receive large shares of global R&D&DDT investments in just two sectors: software & IT services (47 per cent) and communications (41 per cent). In these two sectors the share of R&D relative to DDT investments is lower than the average: 10 and 21 per cent respectively. In contrast, in the chemical sector more than 50 per cent of investments are in R&D. By region, Asia hosts 53 per cent of R&D&DDT investments in electronics and 44 per cent in

[12] The industrial classification is based on fDi Markets and corresponds to the Standard Industrial Classification. Automotive aggregates Automotive OEM and Automotive Components; Electronics: Consumer Electronics, Electronic Components and Semiconductors; Chemicals: Biotechnology and Pharmaceuticals.

Table 11.2 *Geographical and sectoral distribution of R&D&DDT FDI (total and %)*

Region	Software & IT services	Chemicals	Electronics	Communi-cations	Automotive	Machinery	Others
Low- and middle-income	1,843 (47.0)	679 (36.8)	508 (40.0)	474 (40.7)	358 (40.0)	248 (37.3)	992 (37.1)
High-income	2,079 (53.0)	1164 (63.2)	764 (60.0)	691 (59.3)	535 (60.0)	416 (62.7)	1,683 (62.9)
Africa	79 (2.0)	32 (1.7)	12 (0.9)	23 (2.0)	12 (1.3)	5 (0.7)	54 (2.0)
Latin America	232 (5.9)	101 (5.5)	44 (3.4)	77 (6.6)	45 (5.0)	22 (3.3)	140 (5.2)
North America	378 (9.6)	286 (15.5)	127 (10.0)	137 (11.8)	146 (16.3)	89 (13.4)	391 (14.6)
Europe	1,413 (36.0)	645 (35.0)	403 (31.7)	405 (34.8)	314 (35.2)	246 (37.0)	923 (34.6)
Asia	1,741 (44.4)	762 (41.4)	675 (53.1)	488 (41.8)	372 (41.7)	293 (44.2)	1,103 (41.2)
Oceania	79 (2.0)	17 (0.9)	11 (0.9)	35 (3.0)	4 (0.5)	9 (1.4)	64 (2.4)
Total	3,922 (100.0)	1,843 (100.0)	1,272 (100.0)	1,165 (100.0)	893 (100.0)	664 (100.0)	2,675 (100.0)

Source: fDi Markets.

software and IT services. Europe is particularly attractive to the machinery industry (37 per cent) and software & IT services (36 per cent) while North America attracts a large share of R&D investments in the automotive industry (16 per cent) and in chemicals (15 per cent).

Focusing now on LMICs, the main destinations of R&D&DDT greenfield investments are India and China, which receive respectively 36 per cent (1,843) and 30 per cent (1,502) of the total number of investments going to this group of economies. It is worth noticing that India is particularly attractive for DDT investments, which represent more than 80 per cent of R&D&DDT FDI going to the country. In China, the share of DDT is substantially lower, at 69.5 per cent. Other significant host countries, albeit with a much lower share, are Brazil (5 per cent), Mexico (3 per cent) and Russia (almost 3 per cent) (Table 11.3). Altogether these five large middle-income countries represent as much as 77 per cent of all R&D&DDT investments going to LMICs.

In terms of countries of origin, 95 per cent of R&D&DDT investments going towards LMICs comes from high-income countries, mainly from the US (46.5 per cent), Germany (9.3 per cent), Japan (7.1 per cent), the UK (5.8 per cent) and France (4.6 per cent), which altogether represent around three out of four deals. In particular, the US undertakes 60 per cent of the deals in India, 44 per cent in Mexico and 43 per cent in China. Its main investment sectors are software & IT services, electronics and, particularly in China, chemicals. Germany undertakes 13 per cent of greenfield investments in Vietnam and 12 per cent in Mexico, mostly focusing on chemicals and software & IT services. Japan is relatively more present in Thailand and Vietnam, where it represents, respectively, 42 and 22 per cent of the deals and, in this case, the main sectors are automotive and rubber (Thailand) and software & IT services (Vietnam).

Global cities identified following Goerzen et al. (2013),[13] attract about 38 per cent of global R&D greenfield investments, with the share increasing to 41 per cent in LMICs and reaching 49 per cent in Asia. Table 11.4 lists the major global cities attracting R&D FDI in LMICs. In Africa, Johannesburg is the most important global city, hosting 10 per cent of all R&D FDI directed to the continent. In Asia, Bangalore is the global city

[13] Goerzen et al. (2013) identify 122 global cities around the world defined by the following characteristics: (i) a high degree of interconnectedness to local and global markets (through, for instance, major financial centres, headquarters of international institutions, or international transportation nodes); (ii) a socio-cultural cosmopolitan environment; (iii) a large endowment of advanced producer services (such as finance, law or advertising).

Table 11.3 *R&D&DDT greenfield investments towards low- and middle-income countries: main host and home countries (total and %)*

	USA	Germany	Japan	UK	France	Others	Total
India	1109 (60.2)	138 (7.5)	77 (4.2)	104 (5.6)	58 (3.1)	357 (19.4)	1843 (100)
China	659 (43.3)	175 (11.5)	152 (10.0)	66 (4.3)	67 (4.4)	404 (26.5)	1523 (100)
Brazil	106 (38.8)	25 (9.1)	13 (4.8)	16 (5.9)	20 (7.3)	93 (34.1)	273 (100)
Mexico	76 (43.9)	21 (12.1)	5 (2.9)	6 (3.5)	8 (4.6)	57 (32.9)	173 (100)
Russia	62 (42.2)	16 (10.9)	6 (4.1)	5 (3.4)	12 (8.2)	46 (31.3)	147 (100)
Malaysia	48 (35.0)	11 (8.0)	11 (8.0)	11 (8.0)	2 (1.5)	54 (39.4)	137 (100)
Thailand	20 (18.3)	10 (9.2)	46 (42.2)	5 (4.6)	4 (3.7)	24 (22.0)	109 (100)
Vietnam	26 (25.0)	14 (13.5)	23 (22.1)	9 (8.6)	5 (4.8)	27 (26.0)	104 (100)
Total	2372 (46.5)	476 (9.3)	365 (7.1)	298 (5.8)	237 (4.6)	1354 (26.5)	5102 (100)

Source: fDi Markets.

Table 11.4 *Global cities attracting R&D&DDT greenfield investments in low- and middle-income countries (total and %)*

Global cities	Total FDI (%)	Main sectors (total FDI)
Africa		
Johannesburg (ZA)	22 (10.1)	Software & IT services (8); chemicals (5)
Cairo (EG)	16 (7.4)	Software & IT services (7); communications (4)
Cape Town (ZA)	14 (6.4)	Software & IT services (9)
Total	217 (100)	Software & IT services (79); chemicals (32)
Asia		
Bangalore (IN)	597 (15.0)	Software & IT services (319); electronics (79)
Shanghai (CN)	543 (13.6)	Chemicals (150); software & IT services (77)
Beijing (CN)	241 (6.0)	Software & IT services (86); communications (37)
Mumbai (IN)	92 (2.3)	Software & IT services (33); chemicals (32)
Ho Chi Minh (VN)	50 (1.2)	Software & IT services (23); electronics (7)
Total	3979 (100)	Software & IT services (1410); chemicals (523)
Europe		
Moscow (RU)	47 (15.9)	Chemicals (13); software & IT services (10)
St Petersburg (RU)	24 (8.1)	Software & IT services (15); machinery & electronics (2)
Total	295 (100)	Software & IT services (143); chemicals (34)
Latin America & Caribbean		
Sao Paulo (BR)	68 (11.1)	Software & IT services (30); chemicals (18)
Rio de Janeiro (BR)	33 (5.4)	Software & IT services (9); communications (8)
Mexico City (MX)	30 (4.9)	Software & IT services (10); chemicals (8)
Bogota (CO)	21 (3.4)	Software & IT services (6); communications (6)
Buenos Aires (AR)	19 (3.1)	Software & IT services (10); communications (5)
Total	610 (100)	Software & IT services (211); chemicals (90)

Source: fDi Markets.

with the largest share of R&D greenfield FDI (15 per cent of the investments), followed by Shanghai (14 per cent) and Beijing (6 per cent). Russian global cities, i.e. Moscow and Saint Petersburg, are attracting greenfield investments in software & IT services and chemicals. In Latin America, R&D FDI are concentrated in Sao Paulo and Rio de Janeiro, which receive investments in software & IT services, chemicals and communications.

To conclude, Table 11.5 lists the companies with more than 20 R&D greenfield FDIs in LMICs. The largest investor is IBM with 108 investments (31 in China and 28 in India), followed by Microsoft with 78 investments and Intel with 63 – all mainly operating in IT and software services. An interesting difference between IBM and the other two investors is that IBM focuses on DDT (only 9 R&D investments) while both Microsoft and Intel invest a larger share in R&D (27 and 38 per cent respectively). There are three German multinationals in the list: Siemens, Bosch and BASF. Huawei Technologies, from China, is the only company in the list not coming from a high-income country, and it has made 29 deals, mainly concentrated in Bangalore (India) and Johannesburg (South Africa). Among the companies with a largest share of their activities in R&D are DuPont (51 per cent) and Samsung (47 per cent).

Acquisitions

Applying the selection criteria defined in the above overview section on R&D FDI in LMICS,[14] we have identified 45 R&D-related cross-border acquisitions, corresponding to 11 per cent of all acquisitions made by top R&D spenders in LMICs over the period 2003–2017. Table 11.6 provides a summary of those deals. The main destinations are China (11 deals), Brazil (8), Russia (6), India (5) and Turkey (5). In China, acquisitions took place mainly in the electronics industry (5 deals), followed by food and metals (two deals each), and originated from countries such as Germany, the Republic of Korea, Switzerland and the US (2 deals each).

Two notable acquisitions in India were undertaken in Bangalore by two leading US technology companies: IBM and Twitter. In both cases, the target companies were endowed also with patents filed with non-Indian patent offices (USPTO and PCT). The company acquired by Twitter in 2015 is Zipdial, a small start-up offering companies a special phone number, which their brands can use in print ads or TV commercials.

[14] P. 357 *supra*.

Table 11.5 *Top R&D&DDT investors in low- and middle-income countries (total FDI)*

	Total FDI	Main sectors	Main host countries	Main global cities
IBM (US)	108	Software & IT services (102)	China (31); India (28)	Beijing (15); Bangalore (10)
Microsoft (US)	78	Software & IT services (75)	China (33); India (15)	Shanghai (9); Bangalore & Beijing (7)
Intel (US)	63	Electronics (41)	China (23); India (11)	Bangalore (8); Beijing (5)
Siemens (DE)	41	Software & IT services (14)	China (17); India (11)	Bangalore (4); Beijing & Mumbai (2)
General Electrics (US)	38	Machinery (8)	China (13); India (12)	Bangalore (6); Shanghai (6)
DuPont (US)	37	Chemicals (16)	China (11); India (10)	Shanghai (9)
Robert Bosch (DE)	37	Automotive (20)	India (14); China (9)	Bangalore (8); Ho Chi Minh (4)
SGS (CH)	33	Business services (25)	China (7); India (6)	Mumbai (6); Shanghai (6)
BASF (DE)	30	Chemicals (26)	China (11); India (8)	Shanghai (8); Mumbai (3)
Intertek Group (UK)	30	Business services (28)	India (6); China (5)	Ho Chi Minh (2); Shanghai (2)
Samsung (KR)	30	Electronics (23)	India (7); China (6)	Hanoi (2)
Hewlett-Packard (US)	29	Software & IT services (18)	China (9); India (5)	Bangalore (3); Beijing (2)
Huawei Technologies (CN)	29	Communications (29)	India (8); South Africa (3)	Bangalore (7); Johannesburg (3)
Motorola (US)	25	Communications (16)	China (12); India (5)	Beijing (5); Bangalore (2); St Petersburg (2)
Honeywell (US)	24	Machinery (5)	China (10); India (5)	Shanghai (4); Bangalore (2)
General Motors (US)	22	Automotive (22)	China (9); India (5)	Shanghai (5); Bangalore (3)
Nokia (FI)	22	Communications (15)	India (7); China (6)	Mumbai (4); Bangalore (3)

Source: fDi Markets.

Table 11.6 *R&D-related acquisitions in low- and middle-income economies*

Target economy	Number	Main sectors	Main economies
China	11	Electronics (5); food, metals (2)	Germany, Republic of Korea, Switzerland, US (2)
Brazil	8	Chemicals (5)	USA (3)
Russia	6	Various sectors	India (2)
India	5	Business services (2); chemicals (2)	France (2); US (2)
Turkey	5	Furniture (2)	US (2)
Malaysia	2	Electronics (2)	Japan, Chinese Taipei (1)
Mexico	2	Chemicals (2)	Germany, US (1)
Argentina	1	Coke & petroleum	France
Bulgaria	1	Metals	Sweden
Indonesia	1	Machinery	Japan
Serbia	1	Chemicals	Germany
South Africa	1	Business services	Germany
Thailand	1	Electronics	Japan
Total	45		

Source: Bureau van Dijk, Zephyr, at www.bvdinfo.com/en-gb/our-products/data/economic-and-ma/zephyr.

Customers can call the number and hang up before they are charged for the call, while brands can phone or send text messages about their business to the 'missed callers'. This type of service is particularly valuable in LMICs, where prospective customers may not have the money for the call. In other words, the start-up is targeting the potentially vast market segment of low-income consumers, leading to a diversification of the traditional business of a tech company such as Twitter.

In China, the most innovative target (by number of patents) is *Tianning flavour & fragrance Jurong*, within the Eastern-side of Jangsu province, acquired in 2017 by the Irish Kerry Group. This company is the largest Chinese producer of food ingredients, with a strong R&D capacity, holding a large number of patents registered at the Chinese patent office. The main reason for this acquisition was the interest of the Kerry Group to enter into the very large Chinese market for food, given that the acquired company is the main supplier of flavours and fragrances of some of the Chinese leading beverage and food groups. The focus on the Chinese market explains why the patent activity of the company has a clear domestic orientation. Another interesting acquisition in China was undertaken by Trumpf, a German family-owned business in machine tools for metal processing, buying its rival Jangsu JingFang Yuan. This is a rare case of an acquisition backed by the Chinese government in an industry classified as key by Beijing authorities.

There are also some cases of south–south technology-driven acquisitions, such as that undertaken by Mahindra and Mahindra, an Indian multinational car-manufacturing corporation headquartered in Mumbai, which acquired Erkunt Traktor Sanayii AS, a Turkish tractor maker. Through this acquisition, Mahindra aims at increasing its globalization reach, entering the large Turkish market, but also diversifying its portfolio, taking advantage of the strong technological capability of the target in its field of specialization.

In sum, what the previous data show is that R&D-related investments (whether greenfield or acquisitions) towards LMICs are not ubiquitous. Rather, they are highly concentrated in a handful of countries, industries and cities which have managed to reach a certain level of technological capability in particular industrial fields. This has important implications in terms of policies, as will be discussed next.

Towards a New Research and Policy Agenda

This section aims to link the main contributions of the existing literature discussed in the above section on 'Cross-Border Knowledge Flows through R&D FDI'[15] and the empirical evidence presented in the above section on 'R&D FDI in LMICs',[16] pointing to promising avenues for a future research and policy agenda.

Engaging in More Comprehensive Analyses of Impact Channels

Learning opportunities for LMICs are larger when MNEs collaborate in innovation with local firms, universities and public research institutes. Indeed, the formation of linkages that enable an intense participation of local actors in innovation networks is a critical condition for spillovers to unfold (Amendolagine et al., 2019). As discussed in the above section on 'Motivations Driving R&D FDI to LMICs',[17] the modes and directions of cross-border knowledge flows are shifting from unilateral North–South

[15] P. 354 *supra*.
[16] P. 357 *supra*.
[17] P. 354 *supra*.

knowledge transfer to mutual learning relations, but we still lack conclusive evidence of the magnitude and implications of such shifts.

Future research should continue to analyse the interplay between absorptive capacity, linkages and spillovers, a line of research that has produced substantial insights but still needs further empirical grounding. For instance, while the existing literature points to significant spillover effects associated with R&D FDI, it does not clarify the type of technology being transferred and whether it is appropriate for LMICs. In order to maximize spillovers, developing countries should aim at strategically aligning inward R&D FDI with the capabilities of their local industries and human capital. To address these issues, there is a clear need for micro studies investigating the mechanisms for knowledge transfer and spillovers in different geographical contexts.

Moreover, although the impact of R&D FDI can be expected to be different depending on the entry mode,[18] most of the literature tends to focus on greenfield FDI, without sufficiently considering the case of cross-border acquisitions. This can be explained by the relatively small number of R&D-related acquisitions in LMICs and the difficulties of measuring R&D-related cross-border M&As, as discussed in the above section on 'Cross-Border Knowledge Flows through R&D FDI'.[19] Future efforts to develop new measurement frameworks and databases of such investments would be most welcome[20] as they will enable further research comparing the motivations and impact of both modes of entry.

Acknowledging the Heterogeneity of Low- and Middle-Income Countries

As shown in the above section on 'Cross-Border Knowledge Flows through R&D FDI',[21] R&D-related FDI reaching developing countries is strongly concentrated in large middle-income economies like China, India and Brazil. The governments of these large upper-middle-income

[18] While greenfield R&D FDI is generally attributed to be a net positive impact on the host country, the impact of cross-border R&D-related acquisitions is more controversial in view of concerns that the acquiring firm might discontinue or delay the acquired firm's pre-merger R&D activity to align it with its own research agenda and avoid duplications (Buehler et al., 2017).

[19] P. 354 *supra*.

[20] A promising line of research would be to use indicators of patent quality for this purpose, along the lines of Ernst et al. (2019), Chapter 12 in this volume.

[21] P. 354 *supra*.

countries, especially China, have successfully used their market size as a bargaining tool, by introducing local content requirements related to R&D and coordinating procurement and technology policies with approvals for foreign investments in order to build local capabilities.[22] They have actively encouraged foreign investors in manufacturing to open up R&D centres as well, in a process that Lema et al. (2015) refer to as 'trading market access for technology'. In parallel, as discussed by Manning (2008), these countries have also 'customized' their institutions and business networks in specific clusters or 'islands of excellence' to meet the needs of foreign investors in R&D.

However, it is not always easy for other smaller or lower-income countries to either attract R&D FDI or to enforce linkages and knowledge spillovers. In particular, future research should explore further the case of lower-income countries that remain largely excluded from global innovation networks. A deeper understanding of the interplay between building absorptive capacity and opening the economy to international investments in low-income countries is dearly needed (Chaminade et al., 2018). For example, from a policy perspective, it is questionable whether low-income countries that lack absorptive capacity should invest public money to attempt to attract R&D-related FDI in the face of other more pressing societal challenges.

Adopting Systemic, Time-Sensitive and Multi-Level Approaches to Guide Public Policies

The priority for any country aiming to attract R&D FDI is to improve the quality of its national innovation system, as this will obviously make it more attractive to foreign investors. In particular, a salient finding in the existing literature is the paramount importance of enhancing the quality of universities, so that they train highly skilled researchers and become relevant partners for research collaborations with the R&D centres of MNEs (Belderbos et al., 2016; Guimón and Salazar-Elena, 2015; Pietrobelli and Rabellotti, 2011). As emphasized in the above section on 'Impact of R&D FDI in LMICs',[23] the quality of the IP rights regime is

[22] According to Dachs (2017, p. 6), 'with the expansion of European and US MNEs into Asia, local content requirements in R&D (mandatory technology transfer, mandatory joint ventures, requirements to perform R&D in the host country) gained some prominence as a policy tool'.

[23] P. 356 *supra*.

another important element influencing the location choice of R&D centres by MNEs.

Only when a certain level of technological capability has been built can other direct policy interventions to attract R&D-related FDI be considered. This sequential, step-wise approach is paramount. Without a certain quality of the national innovation system, it is very difficult, if not impossible, for LMICs to attract and benefit from R&D FDI (Chaminade et al., 2018; Lema et al., 2018).

More 'direct' policy interventions aimed at providing targeted incentives to foreign investors in R&D might include tax credits, direct subsidies and public-private partnerships. In this regard, it is important to highlight that despite the growing use by governments of financial and tax incentives to attract R&D FDI, the debate around their effectiveness remains unresolved.[24] Based on the case of Chile, Guimón et al. (2018) illustrate the advantages of targeting incentives to specific projects that demonstrate potential for building knowledge-intensive linkages with local actors in selected technology fields or industries where there is already a threshold level of absorptive capacity that can facilitate the transfer of knowledge.

Governments can also make use of 'soft' policy instruments aimed at FDI promotion, including marketing campaigns, international missions, and 'after care' services. The latter is particularly important to foster an evolutionary technological upgrading of existing MNE subsidiaries, as Medcof (2007) and Chen (2008) discuss in relation to the case of China. Another policy option for LMICs is to negotiate provisions in international agreements that promote a more intense knowledge sharing by MNEs. Indeed, the scope of international investment agreements can be expanded beyond their traditional focus on protecting the interests of MNEs, by including also more references to their obligation to contribute to national science and innovation objectives, as suggested in Bellak and Leibrecht (2016) and Chaminade (2015).

In sum, governments of LMICs aiming to attract R&D FDI should adopt a systemic policy approach that takes into consideration the diversity of policy instruments. A combination of financial, regulatory and soft instruments needs to be grouped together within a coherent policy mix that responds to each country's structural and institutional conditions.

[24] For recent reviews of the evidence on the impact of incentives on R&D FDI location decisions see Belderbos et al. (2016) and Bellak and Leibrecht (2016).

Moreover, a multilevel governance approach that considers the regional and local dimensions is critical to better guide policymaking. Indeed, as discussed above,[25] R&D FDI LMICs is very concentrated in just a few regions and cities. This regional concentration of R&D FDI accentuates the already acute polarization of innovation systems in LMICs.[26] In view of the self-reinforcing process whereby agglomeration economies drive the regional clustering of innovation activity by both local and foreign-owned firms, it would be relevant for future research to monitor the regional concentration of R&D FDI and to reflect on possible policies to promote a more balanced technological development across regions. Thus, while debates about the impact and policy implications of R&D FDI in the innovation systems and international business literatures tend to focus on national economies and national policy responses, more emphasis on cities and regions would be necessary to properly address those challenges, drawing more extensively on insights from economic geography.

Conclusions

During the last two decades, some middle-income countries have attracted an increasing share of R&D FDI, becoming important nodes within global innovation networks. These investments represent a powerful mechanism for cross-border knowledge sharing that can stimulate the process of technological catch-up. However, R&D FDI LMICs is still very concentrated in just a few large emerging countries, and in just a few regions and cities within these countries. Meanwhile, low-income countries and smaller middle-income countries remain largely excluded from this kind of global flow of knowledge. In view of these trends, future research and policy analysis should place the focus on the possibilities for fostering a more balanced distribution of R&D FDI across countries and regions. In this chapter, we have pointed out several promising avenues for a future research agenda that provides a more nuanced analysis of impact channels and policy options, building on contributions from international business, economic geography and innovation studies.

[25] P. 368 *supra*.

[26] Recent research has found that the levels of agglomeration of innovation in China, India and Russia significantly exceed those found in the US and the EU (Crescenzi and Jaax, 2017; Crescenzi and Rodríguez-Pose, 2017).

Bibliography

Abramovitz, M., 'Catching Up, Forging Ahead, and Falling Behind' (1986), *Journal of Economic History* 46: 385–406.

Ahuja, G. and Katila, R., 'Technological Acquisitions and the Innovation Performance of Acquiring Firms: A Longitudinal Study' (2001), *Strategic Management Journal* 23: 197–220.

Amendolagine, V., Giuliani, E., Martinelli, A. and Rabellotti, R., 'Chinese and Indian MNEs' Shopping Sprees In Advanced Countries. How Good is it For Their Innovation Output?' (2018), *Journal of Economic Geography* 18: 1149–1176.

Amendolagine, V., Presbitero, A., Rabellotti, R. and Sanfilippo, M., 'Local Sourcing in Developing Countries: The Role Of Foreign Direct Investments and Global Value Chains' (2019), *World Development* 113: 73–88.

Arora, A. and Bagde, S., 'The Indian Software Industry: The Human Capital Story', in DRUID Conference 2006, Copenhagen.

Belderbos, R., Sleuwaegen, L., Somers, D. and De Backeri, K., 'Where To Locate Innovative Activities in Global Value Chains: Does Co-Location Matter?' (2016), *OECD Science, Technology and Industry Policy Papers* 30.

Bellak, C. and Leibrecht, M., 'The Use of Investment Incentives: The Cases of R&D-Related Incentives and International Investment Agreements', in A. T. Tavares-Lehmann, Perrine Toledano, Lise Johnson and Lisa Sachs (eds), *Rethinking Investment Incentives: Trends and Policy Options*, New York, Chichester: Columbia University Press, 2016.

Bruche, G., 'The Emergence Of China and India as New Competitors in MNCS' Innovation Networks' (2009), *Competition & Change* 13: 267–288.

Buehler, B., Coublucq, D., Hariton, C., Langus, G. and Valletti, T., 'Recent Developments at DG Competition: 2016/2017' (2017), *Review of Industrial Organization* 51: 397–422.

Cantwell, J., 'Innovation and International Business' (2017), *Industry and Innovation* 24: 41–60.

Chaminade, C. (ed.), *Technology driven FDI by emerging MNEs in Europe*, Lund: Lund University, 2015.

Chaminade, C., De Fuentes, C., Harirchi, G. and Plechero, M., 'The Geography and Structure of Global Innovation Networks: Global Scope and Regional Embeddedness', in R. Shearmur, C. Carrincazeaux, and D. Doloreux (eds), *Handbook on the Geographies of Innovation*, Cheltenham: Edward Elgar Publishing, 2016.

Chaminade, C., Lundvall, B.A. and Haneef, S., *Advanced Introduction to National Innovation Systems*, Cheltenham: Edward Elgar Publishing, 2018, chapter 10.

Chen, Y.-C., 'Why Do Multinational Corporations Locate Their Advanced R&D Centres in Beijing?' (2008), *Journal of Development Studies* 44: 622–644.

Chuang, W. B. and Lin, H. L., 'Overseas R&D Activities and Intellectual Property Rights – a Longitudinal Study of Multinational Enterprises in Emerging Economies' (2011), *Technology Analysis & Strategic Management* 23: 159–173.

Crescenzi, R. and Jaax, A., 'Innovation in Russia: The Territorial Dimension' (2017), *Economic Geography* 93: 66–88.

Crescenzi, R., Pietrobelli, C. and Rabellotti, R., 'Innovation Drivers, Value Chains and the Geography of Multinational Corporations in Europe' (2013), *Journal of Economic Geography* 14: 1053–1086.

Crescenzi, R. and Rodríguez-Pose, A., 'The geography of innovation in China and India' (2017), *International Journal of Urban and Regional Research* 41: 1010–1027.

D'Agostino, L. M. and Santangelo, G. D., 'Do Overseas R&D Laboratories in Emerging Markets Contribute to Home Knowledge Creation?' (2012), *Management International Review* 52: 251–273.

Dachs, B., 'Internationalisation of R&D: A review of drivers, impacts, and new lines of research', MPRA Paper No. 83367, 2017.

fDi Markets, a service from the Financial Times, (n.d.), available at www.fdiintelligence.com/fdi-markets.

Goerzen, A., Asmussen, C. G., Nielsen, B. B., 'Global Cities and Multinational Enterprise Location Strategy' (2013), *Journal of International Business Studies* 44: 427–450.

Govindarajan, V. and Ramamurti, R., 'Reverse Innovation, Emerging Markets, and Global Strategy' (2011), *Global Strategy Journal* 1: 191–205.

Guimón, J. and Salazar-Elena, J. C., 'Collaboration in Innovation between Foreign Subsidiaries and Local Universities: Evidence From Spain' (2015), *Industry and Innovation* 22: 445–466.

Guimón, J., Chaminade, C., Maggi, C. and Salazar-Elena, J. C., 'Policies to Attract R&D-Related FDI in Small Emerging Countries: Aligning Incentives with Local Linkages and Absorptive Capacities in Chile' (2018), *Journal of International Management* 24: 165–178.

Haakonsson, S., 'Offshoring of Innovation: Global Innovation Networks in the Danish Biotech Industry', in T. Pedersen, L. Bals, and P. D. Ørberg Jensen (eds), *The Offshoring Challenge: Strategic Design and Innovation for Tomorrow's Organization*, London: Springer, 2013.

Javorcik, B., 'Does Foreign Direct Investment Increase the Productivity of Domestic Firms?' (2004), *In search of spillovers through backward linkages, American Economic Review* 94: 605–627.

Kafouros, M. I., Buckley, P. J. and Clegg, J., 'The Effects of Global Knowledge Reservoirs on the Productivity of Multinational Enterprises: The Role of International Depth and Breadth' (2012), *Research Policy* 41: 848–861.

Lema, R., Quadros, R. and Schmitz, H., 'Reorganising Global Value Chains and Building Innovation Capabilities in Brazil and India' (2015), *Research Policy* 44: 1376–1386.

Lema, R., Rabellotti, R. and Sampath, P. G., 'Innovation Trajectories in Developing Countries: Co-evolution of Global Value Chains and Innovation Systems' (2018), *The European Journal of Development Research* 30: 345–363.

Manning, S., 'Customizing Clusters: On the Role of Western Multinational Corporations in the Formation of Science and Engineering Clusters in Emerging Economies' (2008), *Economic Development Quarterly* 22: 316–323.

Marin, A. and Arza, V., 'The Role of Multinational Corporations in National Innovation Systems In Developing Countries: From Technology Diffusion to International Involvement', in Bengt-Åke Lundvall, K. J. Joseph, Cristina Chaminade and Jan Vang (eds), *Handbook of Innovation Systems and Developing Countries*, Cheltenham: Edward Elgar, 2009.

Martinez, C., 'Insight into Different Types of Patent Families', *OECD Science, Technology and Industry Working Papers 2010/2*, Paris: OECD Publishing, 2010.

Medcof, J. W., 'Subsidiary Technology Upgrading and International Technology Transfer, with Reference to China' (2007), *Asia Pacific Business Review* 13: 451–470.

Mudambi, R., Narula, R. and Santangelo, G. D., 'Location, Collocation and Innovation by Multinational Enterprises: A Research Agenda' (2018), *Industry and Innovation* 25: 229–241.

Narula, R. and Dunning, J. H., 'Multinational Enterprises, Development and Globalisation: Some Clarifications and a Research Agenda' (2010), *Oxford Development Studies* 38: 263–287.

Pearce, R. and Papanastassiou, M., 'Multinationals and National Systems of Innovation: Strategy and Policy Issues', in R. Pearce and M. Papanastassiou (eds), *The Strategic Development of Multinationals Subsidiaries and Innovation*, Basingstoke: Macmillan Publishers, 2009.

Pietrobelli, C. and Rabellotti, R., 'Global Value Chains Meet Innovation Systems: Are There Learning Opportunities For Developing Countries?' (2011), *World Development* 39: 1261–1269.

Piscitello, L., Rabellotti, R. and Scalera, V., 'Chinese and Indian acquisitions in Europe: the relationship between motivation and entry mode choice', in A. Risberg, D. King and O. Meglio (eds), *The Routledge Companion to Merger and Acquisition*, London: Routledge, 2015.

Qu, Z., Huang, C., Zhang, M. and Zhao, Y., 'R&D Offshoring, Technology Learning and R&D Efforts of Host Country Firms in Emerging Economies' (2013), *Research Policy* 42: 502–516.

Reddy, P., 'New Trends in Globalization Of Corporate R&D and Implications For Innovation Capability in Host Countries: A Survey from India' (1997), *World Development* 25: 1821–1837.

Saxenian, A., 'The New Argonauts', in *Regional Advantage in a Global Economy*, Cambridge, MA: Harvard University Press, 2006.

Thursby, J. and Thursby, M., 'Where Is the New Science in Corporate R&D?' (2006), *Science* 314: 1547–1548.

UNCTAD, *World Investment Report 2005: Transnational Corporations and the Internationalization of R&D*. Geneva: United Nations Commission for Trade and Development 2005.

UNESCO Institute for Statistics (2018) Global Investments in R&D Fact Sheet No. 50, June 2018, UIS/FS/2018/SCI/50 https://unesdoc.unesco.org/ark:/48223/pf0000265401.

Von Zedtwitz, M., Corsi, S., Søberg, P.V. and Frega, R., 'A Typology of Reverse Innovation' (2015), *Journal of Product Innovation Management* 32: 12–28.

Wang, J., Xue, L. and Liang, Z., 'Multinational R&D in China: From Home-Country-Based to Host-Country-Based' (2012), *Innovation* 14: 192–202.

12

The Innovation Environment and Knowledge Diffusion: Improving Policy Decisions through Patent Analytics

HOLGER ERNST, CARSTEN C. GUDERIAN AND MARCO RICHTER*

Abstract

The introduction of intellectual property standards under the 1995 WTO TRIPS Agreement aimed to facilitate secure cross-border knowledge transfer. Standardized international patent data available to policymakers and managers can trace specific knowledge flows, for example those that occur frequently via mergers and acquisitions. Mergers shape current as well as future knowledge flows, for example by inter alia *affecting the incentives and capabilities to innovate. Regulatory authorities in Europe have begun to examine these merger-related impacts on future knowledge flows to prevent potentially negative effects on consumers. One of the key challenges is how to measure these knowledge flows more accurately to make better decisions on important mergers. This chapter reviews an actual application of such a merger-related analysis of future knowledge flows: the European Commission's approval decision of the Dow/DuPont merger. It shows how to measure relevant knowledge flows by means of novel patent analytics, moving beyond conventional patent indicators. In addition, it presents patent analytics using these novel patent measures to depict other potential analyses tracing and assessing knowledge flows in different contexts. It also*

* The authors thank the WTO, in particular Jayashree Watal, former Counsellor in the Intellectual Property, Government Procurement and Competition Division, for valuable feedback and support in drafting this chapter. The authors thank Julia Röchner, Christopher S. Baldwin, Professor James G. Conley, Center for Research in Technology and Innovation, Kellogg School of Management at Northwestern University, as well as Rahul Kapoor and Dennis Zimmermann for valuable research support. Furthermore, the authors would like to thank Cyril Hariton, Economist at the Chief Competition Economist Team of the Directorate-General Competition at the European Commission for various insights on the European Commission Decision M.7932. We also thank the reviewers of this chapter and participants of the WTO Seminar on 'IP and Knowledge Flows in a Digital Era' in November 2018 in Geneva, Switzerland, for their valuable review suggestions.

shows where new knowledge has originated and how it has spread to other geographical regions. Countries are clearly interdependent when it comes to knowledge flows. It demonstrates how policymakers and managers can use future-oriented, quantitative patent analytics to improve policy decisions related to cross-border knowledge flows and innovation.

Introduction

The introduction of the international intellectual property standards under the 1995 Agreement on Trade-Related Aspects of Intellectual Property Rights (TRIPS) of the World Trade Organization (WTO) set the minimum standards for national regulation of intellectual property. It extended and made more precise the nature of the protection of intangible assets in national jurisdictions, covering the most commonly applied intellectual property regimes like patents, copyrights, and trademarks that codify and protect intellectual assets, including knowledge. In theory, TRIPS set the foundation to enable safe cross-border transfer of intellectual property-protected knowledge. It has resulted in more international trade to countries were knowledge is protectable, for example by patents (Maskus and Penubarti, 1995). To put it differently, trade follows the cross-border protection and flow of knowledge via patents (Rafiquzzaman, 2003).

To ensure the efficiency of these knowledge and trade flows, regulatory authorities dealing with competition and innovation monitor firms' innovative positions to prevent monopolistic imbalances of power resulting in negative effects for consumers (Buehler et al., 2017; Teece, 1992). Mergers and acquisitions are strong drivers for firms to achieve monopolistic competitive positions with significant impact on innovation, knowledge flows and trade (Cassiman and Colombo, 2006; Katz and Shelanski, 2005). Mergers and acquisitions shape current as well as future knowledge flows, for example by changing research and development (R&D) incentives and innovation capabilities (Buehler et al., 2017; European Commission, 2017a). Examining these merger-related knowledge flows is also part of the regulatory, institutional monitoring under competition law. The key challenge is how to measure knowledge flows to improve the quality of these important policy decisions.

Shorter product life cycles, industrial convergences, increased technological dynamism and intensified competitive pressure have led to a surge of intellectual property rights as evidenced by worldwide increasing patent applications and grants (Arora and Gambardella, 2010; Ernst,

2017; Ernst et al., 2016; see also Figure 12.3 in this chapter). Consequently, patents have become an objective information source for analytical approaches, spanning diverse purposes such as regulatory decisions or technology/innovation valuations (Ernst, 2003; Ernst, 2017; Hall et al., 2005). Reasons for patents to be seen as valuable information sources include their timely availability in a systematic, standardized and hence internationally comparable manner (for example, Basberg, 1987; Brockhoff, 1992; Pavitt, 1985).

Policymakers dealing with competition and innovation have used patent data to trace cross-border knowledge flows and international trade (Branstetter et al., 2015; Branstetter and Maskus, 2018; Jaffe and Trajtenberg, 1999). However, conventional patent analytics is subject to decisive limitations. For example, data not harmonized for patents' legal status cannot discern active (granted and pending) from inactive (unmaintained or lapsed) patents in longitudinal datasets, leading to bias and imprecise measurement of patent indicators related to knowledge flows. Moreover, conventional patent quality measures, for example whether patents have foreign counterparts (Branstetter et al., 2015), are limited in their meaningfulness. They cannot distinguish the relevance of the respective geographical areas where protection is sought (Ernst, 2003; Ernst and Omland, 2011).

In this chapter, we present novel patent indicators that allow the measurement of the level and impact of knowledge flows more precisely. The new indicators move beyond conventional measures of patent quality, which allows policymakers to gain better and more robust insights. We outline and explain these new patent indicators in the section on methodological foundations: the Patent Asset Index.[1] We continue with the review of an actual application of these new patent indicators in a section[2] on merger-related knowledge flow analysis conducted by the European Commission in the Dow/Dupont Merger Approval Decision (European Commission, 2017c). The European Commission analysed how the potential merger of Dow/DuPont would change the innovation environment, particularly if it would stifle future new knowledge creation and commercialization (European Commission, 2017a). For the first time, novel patent quality indicators introduced by Ernst and Omland (2011) were used to draw inferences and justify their decision, affecting future international knowledge flows in the crop protection industry.

[1] See https://www.patentsight.com/.

[2] P. 381 *infra*.

We conduct additional patent analyses using the same novel patent quality measures the European Commission applied in their Dow/DuPont merger approval decision to illustrate other applications for tracing cross-border knowledge flows in the following section on the innovation environment, which addresses measuring current and future cross-border knowledge flows via novel patent analytics.[3] We shift our analyses from the firm- to the country-level to reveal new insights. We identify the top countries where new technological knowledge originated and how it spread to other countries. This allows us to trace cross-border flows of new technological knowledge over time. We further examine how knowledge developed in one country is subsequently adapted and used in other geographical regions. We compare the results for 2000 and 2015, tracing changes in knowledge flows over a 16-year time period. With these analyses, we demonstrate how policymakers and managers can trace and shape the future innovation environment and cross-border knowledge flows by using advanced patent analytics. We conclude our chapter by presenting additional options for policymakers in institutions dealing with competition, innovation or intellectual property to use advanced patent analytics in the concluding discussion section.[4]

Methodological Foundations: The Patent Asset Index

The Patent Asset Index is a new and objective method to evaluate the quality of patents and measure their innovation strength (Ernst and Omland, 2011). The Patent Asset Index considers not only the quantity of patents, but also their quality. This is crucial as only few key patents really matter; most other patents have little or no economic value at all (Gambardella et al., 2008). Thus, comparing the size of firms' patent portfolios alone does not reveal anything about their patenting or innovative strength. The Patent Asset Index enables us to identify the strength of patents in an objective, reliable and consistent manner. The Patent Asset Index of a patent portfolio is defined as the aggregate strength of all the patents the portfolio contains. The strength of each individual patent is measured by its Competitive Impact.

The Competitive Impact consists of two dimensions: Technology Relevance and Market Coverage. Technology Relevance is based on forward citations. Patent offices investigate all patent applications to

[3] P. 387 *infra*.
[4] P. 396 *infra*.

check on which prior patents new inventions are based. If a patent is of significance for the technical development in a field, subsequent patents will build on it and patent offices will frequently cite it as *prior art*. Technology Relevance measures whether a patent has been cited more often than other patents from the same technology field and year. The method also considers that international patent offices follow different citation rules (Ernst and Omland, 2011).

Market Coverage measures the total size of the worldwide markets for which patent protection exists. The more patents firms own in important markets, as indicated by high Market Coverage values, the more valuable the patents are, because innovators spend more on multi-market protection via patents if they believe an invention is more valuable. Thus, the scope of international patent protection is an important indicator of patent value. Market Coverage is calculated based on granted and pending, hence valid patents per country adjusted for each market's size. The size of each market is estimated using the countries' gross national incomes relative to the US gross national income as the largest global economy (Ernst and Omland, 2011). Alternatively, Market Coverage may also be calculated based on industry-specific market size data.

The following example illustrates the calculation of the Patent Asset Index and its sub-components Technology Relevance, Market Coverage and Competitive Impact. Dyson Ltd., a British manufacturer of a wide range of white goods such as bagless vacuum cleaners, owned 599 patent families[5] with at least one active member (i.e. at least one patent in the patent family was granted or pending and had not yet lapsed) on 31 December 2015. Its portfolio size is therefore 599. These 599 patent families had an average Technology Relevance of three, i.e. Dyson's patent families were cited three times more than an average patent family worldwide. The Market Coverage was two, i.e. Dyson's worldwide protection across many markets was thrice as high as for an average patent family worldwide. Multiplying Market Coverage and Technology Relevance yields Dyson's average Competitive Impact with a value of six. Hence, the quality of the overall Dyson patent portfolio was on average six times higher than the average for all patent families worldwide. Its patent portfolio is therefore of very high quality. Multiplying the

[5] Patent families are 'a set of either patent applications or publications taken in multiple countries to protect a single invention by a common inventor(s) and then patented in more than one country' (European Patent Office, 2017).

Competitive Impact of six (Quality) with the Portfolio Size of 599 (Quantity) results into an overall Patent Asset Index of 3594 for Dyson.[6]

The Patent Asset Index methodology was validated in a scientific study (Ernst and Omland, 2011). Patents with high Competitive Impacts have higher values when compared to a randomly chosen control group of patents (Ernst and Omland, 2011). As stated above, the indicators may be calculated for any selected group of patents, for example single patents, firms' patents belonging to single business units, entire firms' portfolios, multiple firms' patents, patents from entire technological fields, entire countries' patents or any other patent selection.

Merger-Related Knowledge Flows: The European Commission's Dow/Dupont Merger Approval Decision

Innovation as the New Key Concern in Merger Approval Decisions

In accordance with the European Union merger regulations, mergers subject to certain preconditions (for example mergers of large conglomerates) require approval by authorities prior to their implementation (European Commission, 2016). In the European Union, these authorities include the Directorate-General for Competition at the European Commission and its Chief Competition Economist's team. It 'enforces competition law in the areas of antitrust, merger control, and state aids' (Buehler et al., 2017, p. 397) by 'evaluating the economic impact of [the Directorate-General's] actions' (Buehler et al., 2017, p. 398) since 2003 (referred to in the remainder of this text as the European Commission). Similar regulatory authorities responsible for clearing mergers exist in other jurisdictions also.

The European Commission applied alternative assessment criteria in their approval decision (Buehler et al., 2017; Ersbøll et al., 2018). In the past, the predominant factor was price effects. It assumed that mergers would reduce rivalry and hence incentives to compete on prices, which negatively affects consumers (Buehler et al., 2017). Since the European Commission's objective is to prevent such negative effects for consumers, it aimed to avoid price increases after mergers. Research has found ambiguous effects of mergers on consumers: while they can reduce competition and lead to higher prices, they can also spur innovation

[6] The figures reported for Dyson Ltd's Competitive Impact and Patent Asset Index were rounded to match each other for illustrative purposes. This results in deviations to the exact values.

resulting in additional new products and benefits for consumers (Aghion et al., 2005; Arrow, 1962; Buehler et al., 2017).

Recently, the predominant focus of these merger assessments has shifted to competition and innovation.[7] According to Margrethe Vestager, European Commissioner for Competition, 'Innovation has become "so important" for future competition "because the viability of the product line depends on your ability to keep on innovating"' (Sebag, 2017). It became the European Commission's objective to ensure consumers' access to continued flows of improved and new products, i.e. preventing the stifling of innovation induced by reduced rivalry and lower incentives to invest in R&D after mergers (Buehler et al., 2017; Coublucq and Hariton, 2018). This line of argument is often referred to as the theory of harm in the innovation context (Farrell and Shapiro, 2010). In approving the Dow Chemical Company versus DuPont Company USD 130 billion merger, the European Commission created what law firms termed a novel theory of harm by applying forward-looking patent analytics to assess the impact of the merger on the level of future innovation (Ersbøll et al., 2018). Dow and DuPont were US-based firms in the chemical industry and announced their merger of equals on 11 December 2015 (Bertuzzi et al., 2017; Buehler et al., 2017; The Dow Chemical Company, 2015).[8]

The first assessment used qualitative evidence, including internal documents and a general market investigation (Bertuzzi et al., 2017; Buehler et al., 2017; European Commission, 2017a). It showed that only five chemical firms – Bayer, BASF, Dow, DuPont and Syngenta – were active in crop protection and capable to innovate in various regions globally, covering 'the entire R&D process, from discovery of new active ingredients [. . .], their development, testing[,] regulatory registration, to their manufactur[ing] and sale' (European Commission, 2017c). The number of firms with these comprehensive internal capabilities reduced from over 40 to these five firms in the past 50 years, showing a substantial concentration in the crop protection industry (Buehler et al., 2017; Coublucq and Hariton, 2018; Ersbøll et al., 2018).[9] Moreover, high entry

[7] Innovation concerns have been part of the European Commission's concerns in merger regulation for a long time. The Dow/DuPont decision built on this past practice by using new data and data analytics to investigate this issue. The authors thank Cyril Hariton from the European Commission for pointing this out. See also Deisenhofer (2017).

[8] As effects, including potential impediments, on European Economic Area member states and customers were expected, clearance by the European Commission was required.

[9] The essential components in crop protection are the active ingredients; hence, their discovery and development are the focal objectives in crop protection-related R&D and innovation management (for example, Buehler et al., 2017).

barriers existed, including long innovation cycles, substantial R&D investments, high risks, and the need for well-endowed R&D organizations capable of developing new active ingredients. On average, the development of a new active ingredient requires an investment of USD 240 million over 8 to 10 years (Coublucq and Hariton, 2018). In addition, the target market for crop protection products was large in 2017, with USD 51 billion globally or USD 10 billion in the European Economic Area (Coublucq and Hariton, 2018). With substantial overlaps in R&D capabilities and potential post-merger R&D reductions evident from internal documents like the integration plan, the European Commission decided to conduct a detailed investigation into the effects of the merger on future innovation (Coublucq and Hariton, 2018).

Approach of the European Commission in the Dow/DuPont Merger

In the European Commission's detailed investigation, patent data were used (Bertuzzi et al., 2017; Buehler et al., 2017). As simple patent counts are insufficient for meaningful analyses (Ernst, 1996; Ernst et al., 2016; Lerner and Seru, 2017; Paul et al., 2017), the European Commission decided to use the Patent Asset Index and its constituent indicators, especially the Technology Relevance, as objective, reliable and accessible measures for innovations (Buehler et al., 2017; European Commission, 2017a). To tailor the analyses to the specific preconditions of the Dow/DuPont merger, the European Commission chose the PatentSight Business Intelligence analytics software as the data source. The database interface allows users to query for patents and conduct analyses based on filter and measure selected options, including firms' entire or subsets portfolios (Guderian, 2019). In contrast to alternative patent databases, the Business Intelligence analytics software enables the tracing of annual patent data information for each year since 2000 and incorporates patents' legal and ownership status. Moreover, it provides patent information at the patent family level. The PatentSight database and the novel patent indicators described above (see the above section on 'Methodological Foundations'[10]) allow the evaluation of current as well as future knowledge flows by measuring firms' knowledge bases and potential areas of overlap. If strong overlaps and incentives for merging parties to reduce future innovation exist, the regulating authorities may

[10] P. 379 *supra*.

disapprove mergers or request amendments, including divestments of certain business areas of the merged parties.

The European Commission focused their analyses on all patents filed and active in Europe between 2000 and 2015. Patent quality was considered by analysing patent citation-based measures instead of simple patent counts, as the quality of patents in crop protection is heterogeneous, making simple patent counts insufficient (Buehler et al., 2017; European Commission, 2017a). As argued by the European Commission, firms with highly cited patents were likely to have higher levels of commercial success (Coublucq and Hariton, 2018).

The European Commission therefore focused their analyses on the top 10 per cent of quality patents as measured by the Patent Asset Index (Ernst and Omland, 2011). This generated subsamples of the merger parties' entire patent portfolios, as suggested by prior research (Buehler et al., 2017; Ernst, 1996; Ernst, 2003; Hall et al., 2005). The reasons for the European Commission to follow this approach were that the top 10 per cent of quality patents represent the highest probability of blockbuster patents[11] and more than 50 per cent of overall patent value as measured via the External Patent Asset Index[12] in the technology field. '[P]atents with . . . [below-]median quality do not bring significant value to firms' (Buehler et al., 2017, p. 409).

Results and Implications

The European Commission's evaluations ascertained that Dow and DuPont were strong and important innovators in terms of total external citation-based measures (Buehler et al., 2017). As can be seen in Figure 12.1, with a combined share of 50 to 60 per cent in the top 10 per cent of the most valuable patents globally as measured by the Patent Asset Index, the two merging parties would have a dominant position, which would reduce competition and hence innovation in the future, particularly in the crop protection industry (Buehler et al., 2017; Ersbøll et al., 2018). 'In particular, the [European Commission] assessed competition taking place (a) at so-called "innovation spaces" within the

[11] Blockbuster patents are patents protecting knowledge that is highly valuable and relevant for their owners, including those that result directly in revenues.

[12] The External Patent Asset Index is a derivative measure of the Patent Asset Index (Ernst and Omland, 2011), where the constituent indicator Technology Relevance is calculated based on patents' citations stemming from patents that are not part of the patent owners' portfolios.

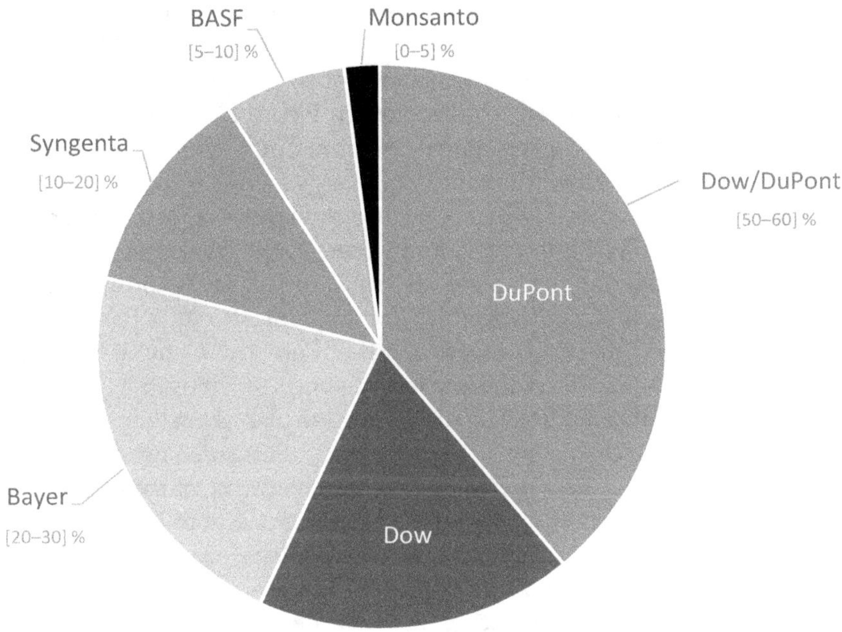

Figure 12.1 Percentage shares in top 10 per cent most valuable crop protection patents as measured by the Patent Asset Index
Source: Own illustration, following European Commission (2017a), data provided by PatentSight GmbH, a LexisNexis company (2018).

crop protection industry, i.e., lines of research that transcend the downstream crop protection product markets, and (b) at the industry level overall' (Ersbøll et al., 2018, p. 9). Moreover, the merger parties had 'significant combined share of research' (Buehler et al., 2017, p. 407), i.e. significant combined patents on new crop protection active ingredients in selective herbicides and insecticides (for details on the herbicides and insecticides, see Ersbøll et al., 2018). They had 'similar research capabilities and a number of overlapping lines of research [(product pipelines)] for new active ingredients' (Buehler et al., 2017, p. 403). The analyses revealed that the merger would have significant effects on future knowledge flows and would likely reduce innovation-based competition with negative implications for consumers in the crop protection industry. Hence, European Commission's inference on 27 March 2017 required substantial amendments to the original merger plan, including the divestment of the global pesticide business and its corresponding R&D entity of the merging parties to maintain knowledge flows, innovation and competition in the crop protection industry (for example, European Commission, 2017c; FMC Corporation, 2017).

Following the approval decision, the process of concentration in the chemical industry continued, as illustrated in Figure 12.2. The acquisition of Syngenta AG by the China National Chemical Corporation (ChemChina) in 2017 and Bayer AG and Monsanto Company's merger was cleared by the European Commission and other regulation authorities in 2018 (European Commission, 2017b; European Commission, 2018). Herein, the merger approval decisions continued to incorporate knowledge flow considerations measured via novel patent indicators. The law firm Arnold & Porter Kaye Scholer LLP stated that they 'expect that the [European Commission] will continue to scrutinize closely the impact of mergers on innovation competition in industries that are R&D intensive, in particular where there are just a few large competitors' (Ersbøll et al., 2018, p. 3). Firms that are actually or potentially subject to these decisions have also made use of similar innovation and knowledge flow analyses based on patent data to better prepare mergers and acquisitions as well as approval decisions.

The European Commission's approach, however, was also criticised. Petit (2019) thought that the merger approval decision was based on R&D outputs like patents instead of R&D inputs like R&D expenditures, because '[p]redictions of firm conduct in relation to R&D outputs are more speculative than predictions in relation to R&D inputs' due to 'a number of intervening events/factors that have an effect' on R&D output

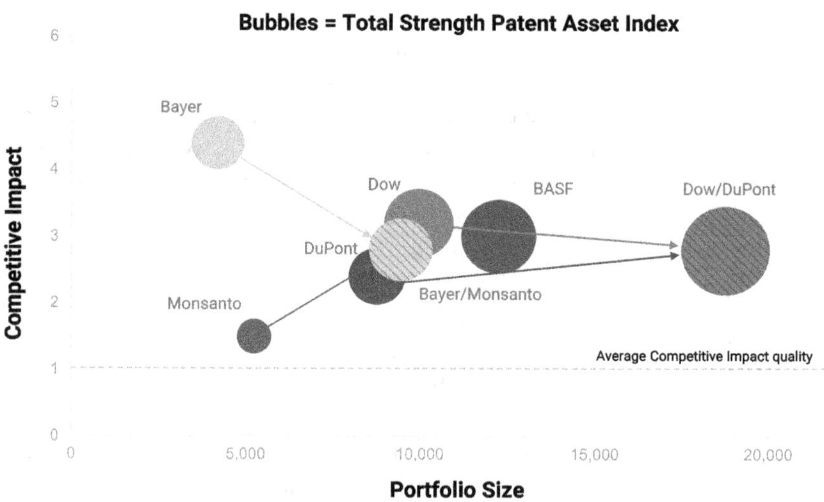

Figure 12.2 Process of concentration in the chemical industry
Source: Own illustration, data provided by PatentSight GmbH, a LexisNexis company (2018).

(Petit, 2019, p. 915). However, patents are a good indicator of R&D output if their quality is assessed objectively, for example through the Patent Asset Index (Ernst, 2001; Ernst, 2003; Ernst and Omland, 2011; Griliches, 1990). In addition, the Patent Asset Index has become the standard in the chemical industry, as 8 out of the top 10 players rely on this indicator to assess overall patent portfolio strength (European Commission, 2017a). The endorsement of the Patent Asset Index by Dow's former Chief Technology Officer who said that the Patent Asset Index 'provides an accurate view of the impact and efficiency of an enterprise's investment in innovation' (Petit, 2019, p. 915) served as another good argument for the European Commission to use it in its analyses (Buehler et al., 2017).

For the first time, the European Commission's competition authority relied on these novel patent quality indicators in their decision to approve the merger of two large conglomerates. As mergers and acquisitions occur, they affect future knowledge flows, transfer and dependencies. Regulatory authorities have therefore begun to assess innovation-related aspects of mergers and acquisitions to prevent the stifling of innovation. The Dow/DuPont case serves as a good example of how competition authorities can measure future knowledge flows through patent data. Applying these novel and objective indicators of patent quality, we analyse cross-border knowledge flows and knowledge dependencies in the following section.

The Innovation Environment: Measuring Current and Future Cross-Border Knowledge Flows via Novel Patent Analytics

Advancing from merely counting the number of patents or simple patent quality measures like the existence of foreign counterparts to US patents, novel indicators (see 'Methodological Foundations: The Patent Asset Index' and 'Merger-Related Knowledge Flows: The European Commission's Dow/DuPont Merger Approval Decision') provide ample opportunities for policymakers to base their cross-border trade-related decisions on objective patent data (Alich, 2018; Ernst, 2003; Ernst, 2017; Ernst and Omland, 2011). We present descriptive statistics on the same indicators the European Commission applied in the Dow/DuPont merger approval decision to depict how international knowledge flows can be tracked and assessed.

To begin, we present the development of the patent landscape during the 16-year period from 2000 to 2015 for the top 15 countries as measured via the Patent Asset Index and its Competitive Impact (see 'Methodological

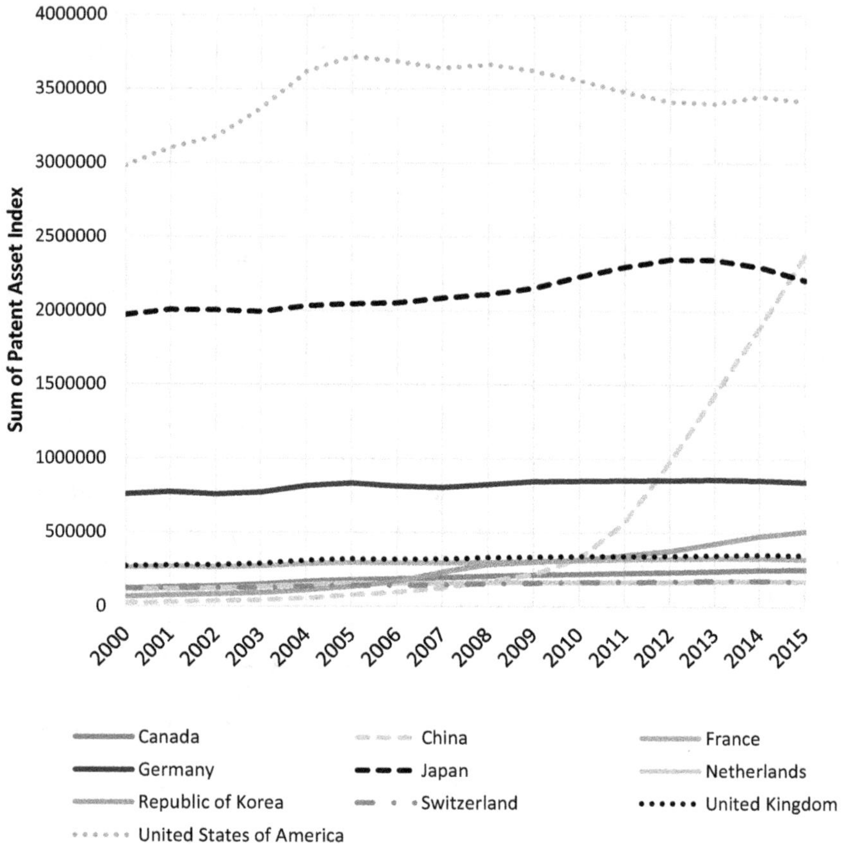

Figure 12.3 Sum of Patent Asset Index (top) and average Competitive Impact (bottom): development from 2000 to 2015 for top 10 countries by Patent Asset Index in 2015

Source: Own illustration, data provided by PatentSight GmbH, a LexisNexis company (2018).

Foundations: The Patent Asset Index'). For each year, we analysed all valid (granted and active) patents from the 15 countries in that particular year. As can be seen in Figure 12.3, there was an overall increase in terms of patent strength as measured by the Patent Asset Index for all countries. While Germany, Japan and the United States, the countries with the highest Patent Asset Index values in 2000, grew by 12, 12 and 15 per cent, respectively, Canada and the Republic of Korea grew much more rapidly by 111 and 687 per cent, respectively. The highest increase in the Patent Asset Index, however, occurred in China, which grew by 11.173 per cent from a Patent Asset Index of 21.097 in 2000 to a Patent Asset Index of 2.378.200 in 2015.

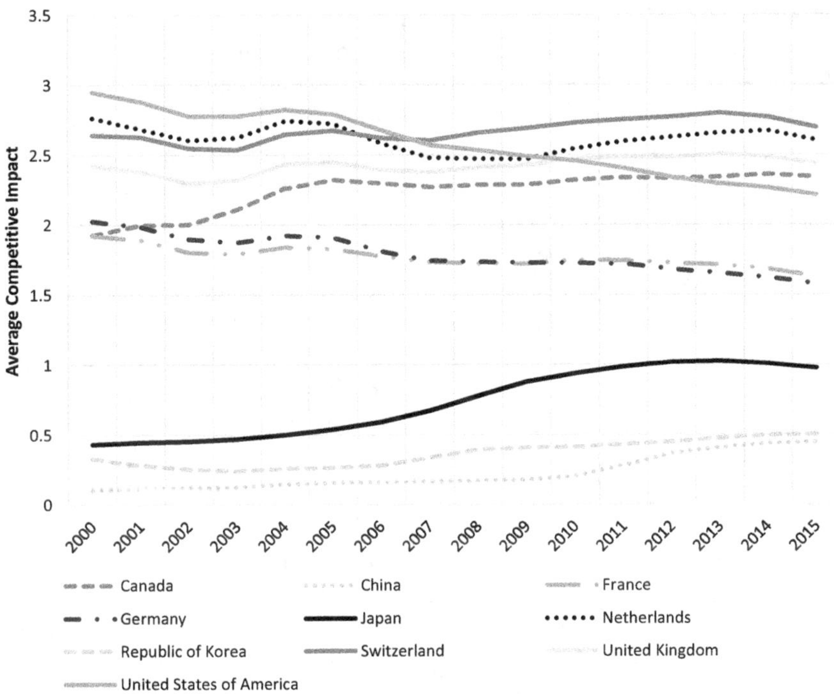

Figure 12.3 (*cont.*)

This moved China from tenth place out of 15 countries in 2000 to second place in 2015.

The above illustrates the growing patent quality and patenting strength for the top 15 countries, which includes some of the largest global economies. As patents protect knowledge, these figures underline that the importance of knowledge is growing in all business environments. In terms of patent quality, as measured by the average Competitive Impact (see 'Methodological Foundations: The Patent Asset Index') for all patents originating from their respective countries, divergent growth rates may also be detected. Major growth occurred in Asia, with China growing by 341 per cent from 2000 to 2015, followed by Japan growing by 125 per cent and the Republic of Korea by 53 per cent. By contrast, Canada grew by 21 per cent, while most of the European countries, apart from Switzerland and the United Kingdom which had moderate growth rates, endured losses: of 6 per cent for Netherlands, 15 per cent for France and 22 per cent for Germany. The US, too, had to cope with a loss of 25 per cent. It must be noted that the tremendous growth rates of patent quality in Asian countries, especially in China, are due to an overall absolute lower level of patent quality in these countries compared to Europe and the US in 2000. By 2015, China, Japan and the Republic of Korea still had average Competitive Impact values below the global average. Despite lower or even negative growth rates, the US and Europe still created, on average, better-quality patents than the three Asian countries in 2015.

Nevertheless, the tremendous growth of patent strength in Asia, especially China, indicates that the locus of knowledge creation and innovation has shifted, becoming more dispersed globally. It also shows that the commercialization of knowledge has increasingly focused on new and emerging economies. The growing globalization of knowledge flows, as evidenced in these patent figures, has and will have a profound effect on competitive positions of regions and hence global trade flows.

In addition, we conducted two analyses directly measuring cross-border knowledge flows based on the novel patent indicators the European Commission used in their Dow/DuPont merger approval decision. First, we investigated where the patents protecting new knowledge originated and how they spread to other countries, i.e. where the patents were also registered besides their country of origin. These statistics present cross-border knowledge flows, i.e. where knowledge originated and how it was transferred to other countries. As focal countries of origin, we chose Germany, Japan and the US, representing countries from America, Asia and Europe, and known to be active in knowledge creation and patenting. We measured the cross-border knowledge flows via patent families by looking at the top 10 countries in 2015 where patents originating from the three focal countries were also registered, granted and maintained. We traced the share of active patents in these other countries where patents were also registered over 16 years from 2000 to 2015. We measured the original country using the inventor addresses as documented in the priority patent.[13] The top 10 countries' positions were measured by the Patent Asset Index (see 'Methodological Foundations: The Patent Asset Index') based on active patents in other countries that originated from the three focal countries, respectively.

As can be seen in Figures 12.4, 12.5 and 12.6 for Germany, Japan and the US respectively, the highest shares of patents were not only protected in the respective country of origin, but also in the US and China. Growth

[13] Since multiple inventors with different addresses can jointly file patents, patent families can account for more than one country of origin. Compared to all patents used in the analyses, the figure is relatively low. Hence, this issue can be neglected.

of patenting predominantly moved to Asian economies like China, Chinese Taipei and the Republic of Korea. By contrast, technology transfer towards Europe and Japan declined. For example, patents that originate in Germany and represent 9 per cent of the German Patent Asset Index were also registered in China in 2000. This figure grew by 40 percentage points to 49 per cent in 2015. Similarly, this figure grew by 17 percentage points, from 6 per cent to 23 per cent for the Republic of Korea and by seven percentage points, from 69 per cent to 76 per cent for the US. By contrast, declines were detected for Italy (-23 percentage points), Japan (-17 percentage points), France (-8 percentage points) and the United Kingdom (-5 percentage points). In terms of cross-border knowledge flows, we see

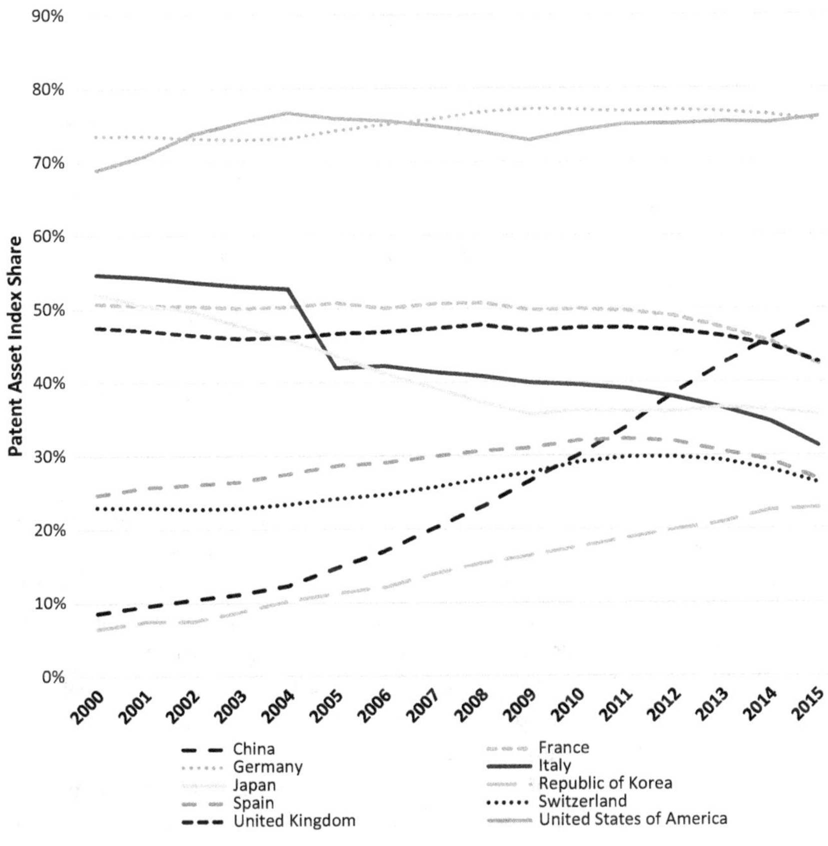

Figure 12.4 Top 10 countries where German patents spread in terms of the Patent Asset Index from 2000 to 2015
Source: Own illustration, data provided by PatentSight GmbH, a LexisNexis company (2018).

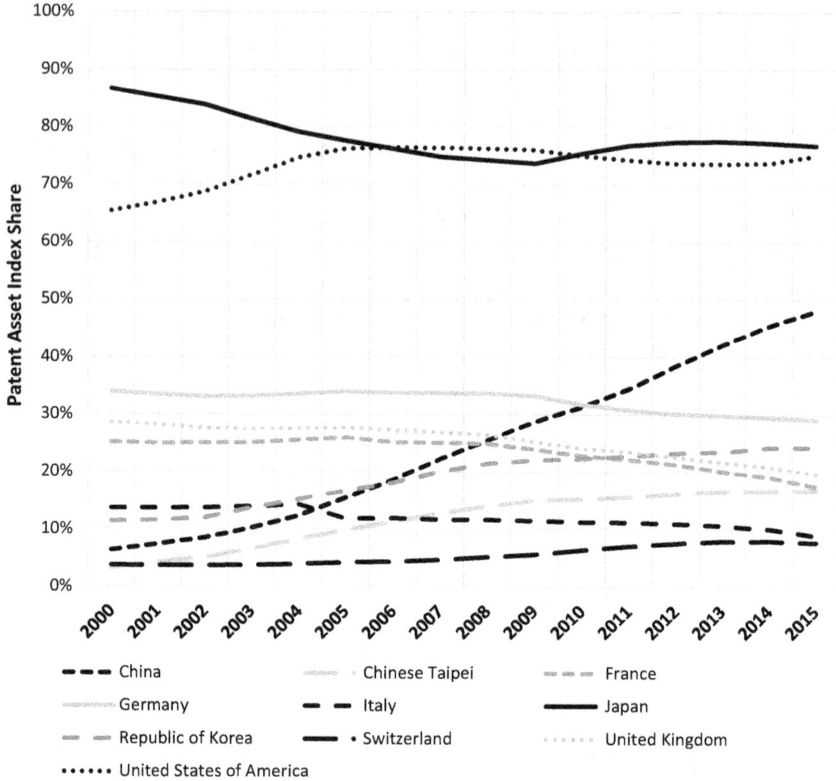

Figure 12.5 Top 10 economies where Japanese patents spread in terms of the Patent Asset Index from 2000 to 2015

Source: Own illustration, data provided by PatentSight GmbH, a LexisNexis company (2018).

that knowledge originating in Germany was increasingly transferred to Asian countries and the US, but less to European countries.

For patents that originated in Japan, while only 6 per cent of the Japanese Patent Asset Index were also registered and became active in China in 2000, this figure grew by 42 percentage points to 48 per cent in 2015. Similarly, this figure grew by 14 percentage points from 3 per cent to 17 per cent for Chinese Taipei, by 13 percentage points from 11 per cent to 24 per cent for the Republic of Korea, and by 10 percentage points from 65 per cent to 75 per cent for the US. By contrast, declines were detected for Japan itself (-10 percentage points), the United Kingdom (-9 percentage points), France (-8 percentage points), Germany (-5 percentage points) and Italy (-5 percentage points). For patents that originated in the US, only 7 per cent of those in the US Patent Asset Index were also registered and became active in China in 2000. This figure grew by 26 percentage points to 33 per

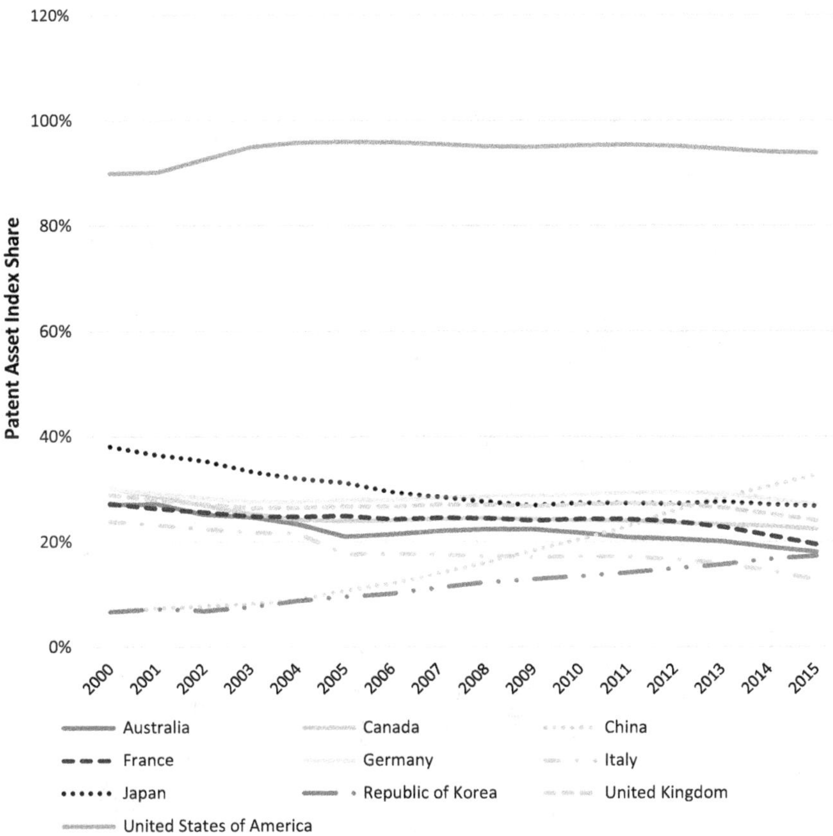

Figure 12.6 Top 10 countries where US patents spread in terms of the Patent Asset Index from 2000 to 2015

Source: Own illustration, data provided by PatentSight GmbH, a LexisNexis company (2018).

cent in 2015. Similarly, this figure grew by 10 percentage points from 7 per cent to 17 per cent in the Republic of Korea from 2000 to 2015. By contrast, declines were detected for Japan (-11 percentage points), Italy (-11 percentage points), Australia (-9 percentage points), Canada (-8 percentage points) and France (-8 percentage points). In terms of cross-border knowledge flows, we see that knowledge originating in Japan had been increasingly transferred to Asian countries and the US, but to a lesser extent to European countries. Similarly, US knowledge flows to Asia increased, while they decreased for Europe.

As can be seen in Table 12.1 for 2015, patents that represent 62 per cent of the Patent Asset Index of patents that originated in France had patents as *prior art* that came from Germany. In contrast, patents that

Table 12.1 *Technological dependence measured via Patent Asset Index percentage changes between 2000 and 2015 in prior art from selected countries' origination*

		Cited country origin									
	2015	**Australia**	**Canada**	**China**	**France**	**Germany**	**Italy**	**Japan**	**Republic of Korea**	**United Kingdom**	**United States of America**
Country of origin	Australia	56.31%	45.87%	31.68%	42.91%	61.08%	21.39%	70.42%	27.81%	57.98%	95.65%
	Canada	20.80%	70.51%	37.10%	43.72%	58.30%	21.11%	72.83%	35.46%	55.72%	97.58%
	China	2.70%	7.63%	51.80%	7.16%	12.44%	3.51%	27.68%	12.97%	8.64%	27.70%
	France	11.82%	27.70%	23.21%	71.48%	61.60%	19.57%	68.49%	20.41%	43.85%	90.24%
	Germany	10.19%	23.08%	20.41%	37.80%	88.82%	18.07%	72.24%	18.15%	39.02%	87.46%
	Italy	12.13%	26.46%	24.20%	40.99%	63.53%	56.75%	65.52%	20.21%	40.37%	87.37%
	Japan	3.63%	11.95%	14.30%	14.66%	31.10%	5.66%	94.18%	20.72%	17.99%	67.57%
	Republic of Korea	6.23%	22.83%	31.50%	19.89%	33.87%	8.96%	81.50%	78.61%	25.34%	77.13%
	United Kingdom	20.00%	41.52%	32.27%	46.68%	63.70%	21.99%	73.89%	28.52%	76.03%	96.20%
	United States of America	17.88%	43.76%	28.06%	38.80%	54.31%	18.02%	71.40%	28.79%	50.61%	98.70%

		Cited country origin									
	2000	**Australia**	**Canada**	**China**	**France**	**Germany**	**Italy**	**Japan**	**Republic of Korea**	**United Kingdom**	**United States of America**
Country of origin	Australia	42.38%	19.13%	1.74%	32.89%	49.49%	10.88%	50.64%	2.83%	43.91%	87.64%
	Canada	7.92%	46.97%	2.09%	27.49%	42.09%	9.11%	52.85%	3.13%	33.86%	93.75%
	China	7.19%	18.27%	17.81%	26.06%	39.99%	9.36%	61.88%	10.48%	31.54%	80.86%
	France	4.13%	9.50%	1.13%	64.38%	52.75%	10.85%	52.65%	2.35%	33.69%	84.44%

	Germany	3.32%	8.07%	0.76%	28.76%	84.90%	10.97%	57.11%	2.14%	30.80%	79.86%
	Italy	3.82%	8.82%	0.86%	31.86%	55.32%	46.03%	51.37%	2.23%	30.89%	80.32%
	Japan	1.46%	4.21%	0.51%	12.26%	26.50%	4.06%	70.93%	2.18%	15.12%	57.43%
	Republic of Korea	2.57%	9.64%	2.30%	16.62%	29.45%	6.41%	74.10%	27.39%	20.15%	77.54%
	United Kingdom	7.11%	13.66%	1.55%	32.87%	50.83%	10.61%	56.42%	3.25%	67.73%	90.02%
	United States of America	5.21%	16.14%	1.77%	24.69%	39.89%	8.32%	58.70%	3.71%	32.16%	96.64%

		Cited country origin									
	Percentage Point Changes	Australia	Canada	China	France	Germany	Italy	Japan	Republic of Korea	United Kingdom	United States of America
Country of origin	Australia	13.94	26.73	29.94	10.02	11.58	10.52	19.78	24.98	14.07	8.01
	Canada	12.87	23.55	35.01	16.22	16.22	12.00	19.98	32.33	21.86	3.83
	China	-4.48	-10.64	33.98	-18.90	-27.55	-5.85	-34.21	2.49	-22.91	-53.16
	France	7.70	18.21	22.08	7.09	8.86	8.72	15.84	18.06	10.16	5.79
	Germany	6.87	15.01	19.65	9.04	3.92	7.10	15.13	16.00	8.22	7.61
	Italy	8.32	17.64	23.34	9.13	8.21	10.72	14.15	17.98	9.48	7.05
	Japan	2.17	7.74	13.79	2.39	4.60	1.60	23.26	18.54	2.87	10.13
	Republic of Korea	3.66	13.19	29.20	3.27	4.42	2.55	7.40	51.22	5.19	-0.41
	United Kingdom	12.89	27.86	30.72	13.80	12.88	11.38	17.47	25.27	8.30	6.18
	United States of America	12.67	27.61	26.29	14.11	14.42	9.69	12.70	25.08	18.45	2.06

Source: Own illustration, data provided by PatentSight GmbH, a LexisNexis company (2018).

represent only 38 per cent of the Patent Asset Index of patents that originated in Germany had patents as *prior art* that stem from France. Hence, the French economy was building more heavily on German technological knowledge than vice versa in 2015. Most countries rely most intensely on knowledge that is created in their home market. The US plays a key role in knowledge creation because it is a major source of globally-used breakthrough technologies. It becomes apparent that the interdependencies have become more intense over time. China, for example, reduced its knowledge dependency on other countries between 2000 and 2015, while creating more dependency of others on its technological knowledge. China has therefore increasingly developed into another important global source for new technological knowledge.

Discussion

Given the increasing importance of innovation for future knowledge flows and competitiveness, novel patent-based metrics allow policymakers to better assess the impact of strategic decisions, such as mergers and acquisitions, and policies on innovation, future knowledge flows and trade. Moving beyond simple patent counts and patent citations to new and more sophisticated patent indicators on patent strength and patent quality improves, for example, the tracing and assessment of technology-based innovations, their cross-border dispersion from their home countries, as well as cross-border knowledge interdependencies. This chapter presents these novel patent analytics as applied in commercial transactions such as mergers and acquisitions to draw inferences and evaluate important cross-border knowledge flows. WTO members could use patent analytics to make better decisions on encouraging cross-border knowledge flows.

We presented the Dow/DuPont merger approval by the European Commission as a case to illustrate the application of patent analytics. Using smart patent indicators such as the Patent Asset Index and its constituent indicators (see 'Methodological Foundations: The Patent Asset Index'; Ernst and Omland, 2011) and focusing the analyses on carefully selected subsets of the merging parties' patent portfolios, the European Commission was able to detect a threat to future innovation, knowledge flows and competition, and hence demanded adjustments of the corporate merger plan prior to approval.

Moreover, using the same patent indicators applied by the European Commission, we assessed and traced the direction and dependencies of cross-border knowledge flows. We found that high-quality patents are still largely developed in the US and Europe. However, Asian countries such as China, Japan and the Republic of Korea are catching up rapidly in terms of patent strength and patent quality. The destinations of global patent flows have also changed significantly over time. This shows the changing significance of certain markets and impacts on knowledge transfer and patent protection. Our analyses have shown that China has become an important destination for patents, reflecting its increasing role as an important knowledge destination market for many countries, especially Germany.

In addition, we examined how countries build on other countries' technological knowledge protected by patents. These mutual interdependencies and their intensities have increased from 2000 to 2015. The majority of countries continued to rely most intensely on their own and knowledge originating in the US. China has reduced its own dependence on foreign knowledge and has increasingly begun to develop technologies that other countries build on.

The merger approval case yields various implications for policymakers. Policymakers need to prepare themselves up-front to address potential implications of mergers pro-actively. Policymakers can address concerns regarding innovation and future competition, develop, and assess best strategic options to mitigate risks and concerns that usually come with these large transactions. The novel patent analytics indicators presented in this chapter offer a valid, proven and usable tool for this kind of analysis.

Our analysis on cross-border knowledge flows offers interesting further insights for policymakers.[14] We have shown a major shift from established markets such as the US, Japan and Germany towards rising economies in Asia, especially China, regarding the quality, origin and destination of technological knowledge. In light of these developments, policymakers should implement strategies to increase countries' own technological capabilities and make them more attractive as destinations for new, technology-based products and applications. This is important to secure the future competitiveness of nations. Since the origin of technology creation has increasingly become globally dispersed, policymakers should encourage and support the establishment of overseas R&D activities to overcome the dominant home-country orientation.

[14] We have only presented a restricted number of analyses within the scope of this chapter. Many more detailed analyses based on patent data are possible, especially more fine-grained analyses at the industry-, technology- and inventor-level (for example, Ernst, 2003; Ernst, 2014; Ernst, 2017; Guderian, 2019).

This is critically important because technology-based innovations are often context-specific and may therefore only occur in specific international or emerging markets and not in established (home) markets (Dubiel and Ernst, 2012). Furthermore, changes of global patenting patterns over time indicate the rise of new competitors that may disrupt established business practices that have been historically developed in restricted geographical areas (Subramaniam et al., 2015). Based on early and robust insights from patent analyses, these allow policymakers to timely initiate strategic responses to these potential threats.

In times when international trade flows face potential risks even by important WTO members, the WTO must continue to protect intellectual property among its members. The TRIPS Agreement has been an immense success story since its introduction, enabling cross-border knowledge flows and providing cross-border trade opportunities and innovation incentives by allowing countries, firms and individuals to profit from their knowledge. As presented in this chapter, patent analytics supports relevant decision-making in international trade and cross-border knowledge flows, which would not have been possible without the WTO and its TRIPS Agreement that ensures international intellectual property standards, ultimately enabling their analytics.

Bibliography

Aghion, P., Bloom, N., Blundell, R., Griffith, R. and Howitt, P., 'Competition and Innovation: An Inverted-U Relationship' (2005), *The Quarterly Journal of Economics* 120, 2: 701–728.

Alich, H., 'Innovationskraft der Schweiz wird überschätzt [Switzerland's Innovativeness is Overestimated]', Tages-Anzeiger, 18 January 2018, available at www.tagesanzeiger.ch/wirtschaft/standardinnovationskraft-der-schweiz-wird-ueberschaetzt/story/27557633.

Arora, A. and Gambardella, A., 'Ideas For Rent: An Overview of Markets For Technology' (2010), *Industrial and Corporate Change* 19, 3: 775–803.

Arrow, K., 'Economic Welfare and the Allocation of Resources for Invention', in R.R. Nelson (ed.) (National Bureau of Economic Research), *The Rate and Direction of Economic Activities: Economic and Social Factors*, Princeton, NJ: Princeton University Press, 1962, pp. 609–626.

Basberg, B. L., 'Patents and the Measurement of Technological Change: A Survey of the Literature' (1987), *Research Policy* 16, 2–4: 131–141.

Bertuzzi, A., Blanco Thomas, S., Coublucq, D., Jonckheere, J., Tew, J. and Deisenhofer, T., 'Dow/DuPont: Protecting Product and Innovation

Competition' (2017), Competition Merger Brief 2/2017, European Commission, 1–8.

Branstetter, L. and Maskus, K. E., *Global Knowledge Flows, Absorptive Capacity, and Capability Acquisition: Old Ideas, Recent Data, and New Approaches*, Geneva: WTO Book on Trade in Knowledge, 2018.

Branstetter, L., Li, G. and Veloso, F., 'The Rise of International Coinvention', in A. B. Jaffe and B. F. Jones (eds), *The Changing Frontier. Rethinking Science and Innovation Policy*, Chicago: University of Chicago Press, 2015, pp. 135–168.

Brockhoff, K. K., 'Instruments For Patent Data Analyses in Business Firms' (1992), *Technovation* 12, 1: 41–59.

Buehler, B., Coublucq, D., Hariton, C., Langus, G. and Valletti, T., 'Recent Developments at DG Competition: 2016/2017' (2017), *Review of Industrial Organization* 51, 4: 397–422.

Cassiman, B. and Colombo, M. G., *Mergers and Acquisitions. The Innovation Impact*, Cheltenham: Edward Elgar Publishing, 2006.

Coublucq, D. and Hariton, C., 'Patent Analysis in Merger Control: Why and How?', Presentation at PatentSight Summit 2018, Bonn, Germany, 17 May 2018.

Deisenhofer, T., 'Assessing Innovation Effects in Dow/Dupont – Breaking New Ground or Déjà-Vu?', Presentation at the Global Seminar Series of the American Bar Association, 5 May 2017.

Dubiel, A. and Ernst, H., 'Industrial R&D Centers in Emerging Markets: Motivations, Barriers and Success Factors', in T. Pedersen, L. Bals, P. D. Ørberg Jensen and M. M. Larsen (eds), *The Offshoring Challenge: Strategic Design and Innovation for Tomorrow's Organization*, London: Springer, 2012, pp. 191–209.

Ernst, H., *Patentinformationen für die strategische Planung von Forschung und Entwicklung* [Patent Information for the Strategic Planning of Research and Development], Wiesbaden: DUV-Verlag, Wiesbaden, 1996.

Ernst, H., 'Patent Applications and Subsequent Changes of Performance: Evidence From Time-Series Cross-Section Analyses on the Firm Level' (2001), *Research Policy* 30, 1: 143–157.

Ernst, H., 'Patent Information For Strategic Technology Management' (2003), *World Patent Information* 25, 3: 233–242.

Ernst, H., 'Die Patentabteilung als Motor des Technologiemanagements: Bestandsaufnahme und Ausblick [The Patent Department as Motor of Technology Management: Status Quo and Outlook]', in C. Schultz and K. Hölzle (eds), *Motoren der Innovation. Zukunftsperspektiven der Innovationsforschung. Festschrift zum* 65. Geburtstag von Prof. Dr. Hans Georg Gemünden [Motors of Innovation. Future Perspectives in Innovation Management. Commemorative for Prof. Dr. Hans Georg Gemünden's 65th Birthday], Wiesbaden: Springer Fachmedien, 2014, pp. 39–55.

Ernst, H., 'Intellectual Property as a Management Discipline' (2017), *Technology & Innovation* 19, 2: 481–492.

Ernst, H. and Omland, N., 'The Patent Asset Index – a New Approach to Benchmark Patent Portfolios' (2011), *World Patent Information* 33, 1: 34–41.

Ernst, H., Conley, J. G. and Omland, N., 'How to Create Commercial Value from Patents: The Role of Patent Management' (2016), *R&D Management* 46, S2: 677–690.

Ersbøll, N., Gavala, A., Iverson, T. and Naydenova, L., *2017 EU Merger Enforcement Year in Review*, Arnold & Porter Kaye Scholer LLP, 2018, pp. 1–35.

European Commission, 'Competition Policy Brief. EU Merger Control and Innovation' (2016), available at http://ec.europa.eu/competition/publications/cpb/2016/2016_001_en.pdf.

European Commission, Case M.7932 – Dow/DuPont. Merger Procedure Regulation (EC) 139/2004, (2017a), European Commission, Brussels, Belgium, 27 March 2017.

European Commission, 'Mergers: Commission Clears ChemChina Acquisition of Syngenta, Subject to Conditions', Press Release (2017b), IP/17/882, European Commission, Brussels, Belgium, 5 April 2017.

European Commission, 'Mergers: Commission Clears Merger between Dow and Dupont, Subject to Conditions', Press Release (2017c), IP/17/772, European Commission, Brussels, Belgium, 27 March 2017.

European Commission, 'Mergers: Commission Clears Bayer's Acquisition of Monsanto, Subject to Conditions', Press Release (2017d), IP/18/2282, European Commission, Brussels, Belgium, 21 March 2018.

European Patent Office, 'Patent Families', 2017, available at www.epo.org/searching-for-patents/helpful-resources/first-time-here/patent-families.html.

Farrell, J. and Shapiro, C., 'Antitrust Evaluation of Horizontal Mergers: An Economic Alternative to Market Definition' (2010), *The B.E. Journal of Theoretical Economics* 10, 1: Article 9.

FMC Corporation, 'FMC Corporation Completes Transformative Transactions with DuPont', Press Release, FMC Corporation, Philadelphia, 1 November 2017.

Gambardella, A., Harhoff, D. and Verspagen B., 'The Value of European Patents' (2008), *European Management Review* 5, 2: 69–84.

Griliches, Z., 'Patent Statistics as Economic Indicators: A Survey' (1990), *Journal of Economic Literature* 28, 4: 1661–1707.

Guderian, C. C., 'Identifying Emerging Technologies with Smart Patent Indicators: The Example of Smart Houses' (2019), *International Journal of Innovation and Technology Management* 16, 2: 1950040.

Hall, B. H., Jaffe, A. and Trajtenberg, M., 'Market Value and Patent Citations' (2005), *The RAND Journal of Economics* 36, 1: 16–38.

Jaffe, A. B. and Trajtenberg, M., 'International Knowledge Flows: Evidence From Patent Citations' (1999), *Economics of Innovation and New Technology* 8, 1–2: 105–136.

Katz, M.L. and Shelanski, H. A., 'Merger Policy and Innovation: Must Enforcement Change to Account for Technological Change?' (2005), *Innovation Policy and the Economy* 5: 109–165.

Lerner, J. and Seru, A., 'The Use and Misuse of Patent Data: Issues For Corporate Finance and Beyond' (2017), *National Bureau of Economic Research Working Paper* 24053: 1–127.

Maskus, K. E. and Penubarti, M., 'How Trade-Related Are Intellectual Property Rights?' (1995), *Journal of International Economics* 39, 3–4: 227–248.

Paul, J. C., Kacedon, D. B. and Lindop, R. L., 'Court Permits Evidence from Damages Expert that Relies on Forward Citation Analysis, Comparable Settlement Agreements, and Preference for Lump Sum Agreements. LES Insights', 3 January 2017, available at www.finnegan.com/en/insights/court-permits-evidence-from-damages-expert-that-relies-on.html?news=98a4d4ad-22bd-438b-b6da-4a53f57fa594.

Pavitt, K., 'Patent Statistics As Indicators of Innovative Activities: Possibilities and Problems' (1985), *Scientometrics* 7, 1 2: 77–99.

Petit, N., 'Innovation Competition, Unilateral Effects and Merger Policy' (2019), *Antitrust Law Journal* 82, 3: 873–919.

Rafiquzzaman, M., 'The Impact of Patent Rights on International Trade: Evidence from Canada' (2003), *Canadian Journal of Economics* 35, 2: 307–330.

Sebag, G., 'Dow-DuPont Shows How Innovation Is EU's New M&A Battleground', Bloomberg Markets, 28 March 2017, available at www.bloomberg.com/news/articles/2017-03-28/dow-dupont-shows-how-innovation-is-eu-s-new-m-a-battleground.

Subramaniam, M., Ernst, H. and Dubiel, A., 'From the Special Issue Editors: Innovation for and from Emerging Markets' (2015), *Journal of Product Innovation Management* 32, 1: 5–11.

Teece, D. J., 'Competition, Cooperation, And Innovation: Organizational Arrangements For Regimes Of Rapid Technological Progress' (1992), *Journal of Economic Behavior & Organization* 18, 1: 1–25.

The Dow Chemical Company, 'DuPont and Dow to Combine in Merger of Equals' 11 December 2015, available at www.dow.com/en-us/news/press-releases/dupont-and-dow-to-combine-in-merger-of-equals.

PART III

Impact of Knowledge Flows on Trade and Development

13

Global Knowledge Flows, Absorptive Capacity and Capability Acquisition: Old Ideas, Recent Evidence and New Approaches

LEE BRANSTETTER AND KEITH E. MASKUS*

Abstract

In this chapter, we reconsider the key lessons presented by more than two decades of empirical research on international knowledge flows. We begin by reviewing some of the key empirical findings and policy lessons from that literature. We then build on this review by pointing out the importance and uneven distribution across developing countries of absorptive capacity, which may help explain the uneven diffusion of knowledge across these countries. We also consider the implications of growing R&D globalization, the potentially declining importance of international manufacturing value chains, the rise of global trade in services, and the new opportunities opened up by AI-enhanced learning technologies.

Introduction

We begin with a pair of fundamental observations. First, in an era of global economic integration unprecedented since the Second World War, extraordinary progress has been made. Despite contemporary undercurrents of discontent, the founders of the postwar economic order would surely be delighted to see the degree to which their vision of a world knit together by commerce was realized by the early twenty-first century. This era has made great contributions to human well-being, in large part a result of increasing diffusion of knowledge to the developing world.

Second, despite this progress the gap in incomes between the richest and poorest nations remains immense (Jones, 2014b). While people in some major emerging countries have experienced considerable income

* This chapter draws upon a number of papers, including ones previously published by the authors. Branstetter wishes to acknowledge funding from the CMU Portugal Programme, and joint research with Ray Fisman, Fritz Foley, Britta Glennon, Brad Jensen, Guangwei Li and Kamal Saggi, from which many of the ideas discussed herein are drawn.

growth, in much of the developing world that progress has been slow and uneven, leaving many millions in poverty (Collier, 2007). Growth economists point to persistent technological gaps between nations as the primary source of these large income gaps (Acemoglu, 2009). This situation begs the question of why technology has not diffused sufficiently to eliminate these gaps, or seems only to be doing so in particular regions. What unseen barriers could be standing in the way of universal technological convergence?[1]

The language we traditionally use to describe these phenomena may itself be a source of misunderstanding. We speak of international 'knowledge *flows*', suggesting knowledge resembles a liquid that will easily and beneficently flow downhill in the absence of impediments. Indeed, the greater the gap in income (and technology) between nations, the more rapidly the liquid embodying knowhow should flow. Our terminology implies that all we need is a channel, like the ancient Roman aqueducts, and open receptacles in poor developing countries, and gravity will do the rest. This appealing metaphor makes it easy to understand how critics of market-led globalization might conclude that some infernal barrier, set up by the currently rich nations, is somehow impeding the natural flow of knowledge. The Northern insistence on stronger intellectual property rights (IPRs) is often viewed in this light.

Unfortunately, this physical metaphor is highly inaccurate in describing how knowledge really flows across countries – or more often fails to do so. The truth is that economically valuable knowledge is 'sticky', often at least partly tacit (Polanyi, 1958) and resides principally in human beings. In one of the earliest studies of international technology transfer within multinational firms, Teece (1977) pointed to the surprising difficulty of moving knowledge across national boundaries, even within the same enterprise. Successful transfer of technology requires the acquisition of capabilities both by the transferor and transferee (Sutton, 2000). It requires an expensive investment by the receiving party in absorptive capacity (Cohen and Levinthal, 1989, 1990; Arora and Gambardella, 1990, 1994). It also often requires the willing, active cooperation of the parties possessing the knowledge.

Crucially, the successful acquisition of frontier technological knowledge often requires the prior mastery of more basic knowledge and skills, a cumulative process. Finally, successful technology transfer

[1] Recognizing the challenges that the modern world presents to economic theory, Elhanan Helpman titled his thoughtful 2004 book, *The Mystery of Economic Growth*.

requires coordinated capabilities among many individuals. When we consider the scale and complexity of the human capital investment required to support international 'knowledge flows', the mystery of its difficulty begins to fade.

In this chapter we reconsider the key lessons presented by more than two decades of empirical research on international knowledge flows – a scientific enterprise in which we have both actively participated. Our point of departure is to place context around the disparities in the emerging and developing world between those countries with sufficient size, economic dynamism and the necessary complementary skills to learn deeply from the global stock of knowledge, and those countries without such advantages. The insights gained help explain why the income and productivity gains from information globalization do not diffuse as widely as basic models would suggest.

We begin in the following second part by reviewing briefly the primary empirical results and policy lessons from recent literature. We also highlight ongoing research questions that are expanding our understanding of key questions. In the third part,[2] we turn to the important question of how R&D investments have been globalized, primarily by multinational enterprises (MNEs), and the implications for knowledge flows. With this background, in the fourth part,[3] we discuss the crucial role played by investments in human capital and the acquisition of technological capabilities in technology-receiving countries. In this context, we emphasize the important work of Jones (2014b) regarding the nature of human capital in absorbing and improving knowledge. In particular, his work emphasizes that knowledge acquisition and use increasingly require complementary technical skills within an economy. Achieving broad-skill endowments may not be feasible in poor countries for some time, suggesting that investing in deeper skills that may be deployed in global information networks could be a better development strategy. We also draw lessons from interesting experimental work aimed at improving education delivery in India through the use of artificial intelligence (AI). Together, these insights point to the need for a broader understanding of how knowledge is transmitted and could be better absorbed in the current era. We draw policy inferences in the concluding fifth part.[4]

[2] P. 412 *infra*.

[3] P. 418 *infra*.

[4] P. 424 *infra*.

How Does Technology Move Across Borders?

Technology Diffusion: Channels and the Role of IPRs

For most developing economies, accessing and deploying international technologies is the primary source of new information, productivity gains and economic growth (Keller, 2004). International technology diffusion is therefore a major determinant of global technical change and increasing such flows is a critical part of development policy. It is equally vital to adapt technologies to local conditions and learn how to use and improve them. Countries seeking access to foreign technologies therefore build into their innovation systems the entire policy complex involving skill accumulation, investment, competition, R&D support and intellectual property rights.

It has long been recognized that an important channel of acquiring technological information is trade in high-technology goods and services (Coe et al., 1997). Imported capital goods and technical intermediate inputs can directly improve productivity by being placed into production processes. A second is foreign direct investment (FDI), by which multinational enterprises (MNEs) transfer to their subsidiaries newer and more productive technological information (Markusen, 2002). MNEs often indirectly increase local productivity through sharing with upstream suppliers best standards in producing intermediate inputs (Javorcik, 2004). Yet a third is technology licensing, which typically involves the transfer of production or distribution rights and the associated technical information and know-how. A fourth is the cross-border movement of engineers and technicians (Hovhanissyan and Keller, 2015).

One important factor determining how readily technologies may be diffused through these various channels is the scope of IPRs in recipient countries. On the one hand, patents, trademarks and enforceable contracts for licensed trade secrets can reduce the information costs and uncertainty of technology transfer (Hoekman et al., 2005). They can also limit the tendency of recipient firms to expropriate technology opportunistically (Antras, 2005). On the other hand, if patents have extensive scope, say through broad claims and a ban on experimental use, they can make it more costly for domestic firms to imitate foreign technologies.

Recent empirical evidence suggests that technology movements to emerging and middle-income economies are generally enhanced by IPR protection. For example, in the first study of the trade impacts of TRIPS reforms, Ivus (2010) analysed the growth of high-technology exports from 24 OECD countries to 55 developing countries. Taking the 18 countries with larger policy reforms as the reference group, she found that high-technology exports to those nations grew significantly faster than low-technology exports. The stronger patent rights increased the value of OECD exports of patent-sensitive goods to those countries by 8.6 per cent. More recent studies find strong evidence that such reforms also raise the exports of high-technology goods from middle-income economies (Delgado and Kyle, 2013, Chapter 14 in this volume). This result suggests that such countries are able to incorporate foreign technical information into the greater production of exportable goods. Maskus and Yang (2018) also found a pro-export impact and showed that potential sources of this learning include inward patent applications, incoming FDI and intra-firm trade in high-technology intermediates.

Regarding FDI, recent evidence suggests that IPR reforms could affect multiple activities of MNEs. One prominent study analysed the impacts on licensing of US parents with affiliates after patent law changes in 16 emerging economies (Branstetter et al., 2006). The authors found that royalty payments to parents rose by 34 per cent on average, mostly reflecting an increased volume of technology sold rather than higher royalty charges. There was also a significant increase in R&D investments at local subsidiaries. Both of these effects were much stronger in high-technology industries.

A related analysis found significantly positive increases after patent reforms in affiliate sales, net plant and equipment and employee compensation among affiliates of US MNEs (Branstetter et al., 2011). Further, they found that value added in local firms rose significantly, especially in technology-intensive sectors. There was also strong evidence that firms in these countries expanded the range (or 'extensive margin') of products exported to the United States after patent rights were broadened.

To summarize, the best available evidence supports the claim that patent reforms have positive effects on inward technology transfer through market-based channels. They raise imports of high-technology goods and may also stimulate export growth. Stronger IPRs expand the local activities of multinational firms, while increasing licensing to both affiliated and unaffiliated parties. They particularly stimulate such responses among high-technology firms.

While these are important benefits, they must be qualified. First, to date, these impacts have been found only in larger and middle-income countries. There is little evidence of such effects in the poorest and smallest developing economies, where the limited amounts of technology transfer render patents of little relevance. Second, to date, there are no serious studies of any potential restrictive impacts of IPR reforms in poor countries. Local firms may have to change product lines or close down if they cannot adapt to the new competitive environment post-reforms, a possibility about which systematic evidence is absent. Finally, the available measures of technology diffusion are indirect and may miss considerable amounts of formal and informal knowledge transfers.[5]

Despite the flaws in data, it does seem that there has been little supply response in much of the developing world, even as developing countries have adopted stronger IPR protection. Put differently, formal technology markets are unresponsive to such reforms in poor countries, while updated legal regimes have had little detectable impact on domestic technology use or adaptation. This observation may puzzle advocates of strong global IPR protection but, as we argue later in the chapter, it largely reflects the lack of absorptive capacity and complementary human skills in such societies.

The Rise (and Possible Fall) of Extensive Production Networks

We consider briefly a special case of FDI and trade that embodies considerable technology sharing and diffusion, the development over the last few decades of extensive global and regional supply chains. Baldwin (2016) discussed the ability of multinationals to separate even narrow stages in the vertical production chain of many products and to place those stages in various locations. This second great 'unbundling', in this case of production stages from one another and from headquarters services performed in the home country of an MNE, was facilitated by the emergence of sophisticated information and communication technologies (ICT), trade and investment liberalization in emerging economies, and reductions in shipping costs. A canonical example of this fragmentation is the North American automobile industry, which developed sharp specialization by stages of production across the member countries of NAFTA. Other industries that developed extensive international production chains include microelectronics, household appliances, textiles and apparel. The remarkable growth in trade involving such networks may be seen in the rapid increase in international value added embodied in the exports of increasingly interlinked economies.[6]

[5] Many of the chapters in this volume analyse such data and their shortcomings.

[6] This growth is documented in the OECD's online Trade in Value Added (TiVA) database, available at www.oecd.org/sti/ind/measuring-trade-in-value-added.htm.

The dramatic outsourcing of production stages created significant amounts of manufacturing jobs in those developing countries that established linkages to global value chains. This is the essence of the early stages of China's industrial transformation, while manufacturing employment grew rapidly in Vietnam, Indonesia, Mexico, Poland and many other emerging economies. A similar statement would apply to the development of tradeable services in India. For such countries the rapid growth of such sectors and networks constitutes the major economic development story of our time.

Some of the more labour-intensive stages in supply chains may be described as shallow and footloose, with relatively little effective technology transfer (Baldwin and Lopez-Gonzalez, 2013). However, production chains often involve trade in sophisticated intermediate inputs, investment in new capital goods and processes, and procurement of locally produced inputs. In this context, because final goods must be produced with reliability and quality, MNEs at the centre of networks cannot risk being exposed to shoddy inputs, varying production standards and indifferent assembly. Such firms, therefore, find it important to transfer their best technological information, insist on high-quality process standards and demand timely deliveries. In turn, a distinctive feature of global and regional value chains is the purposeful sharing of technological knowledge among network partners.

Evidence suggests that the emergence of these complex supply relationships undergirds both the transfer of manufacturing employment and the diffusion of technology to emerging nations (Baldwin, 2016; OECD, 2017). Indeed, it seems that industries in countries that are closely linked to international value chains become more innovative, as measured by foreign patent applications (Piermartini and Rubínová, 2018, and Chapter 15 in this volume). However, this same literature points out the clear importance of partner countries investing in human capital and appropriate skills on the part of the domestic workforce in order to achieve such gains. We emphasize this again in the following section on the internationalization of R&D spending and teams.

Thus, the employment, productivity and knowledge gains from integration with supply chains have been significant in the emerging world. Whether this process may spread to more developing countries is increasingly debatable, however. A primary caution, as we discuss below, is that the impending explosion of AI technologies in manufacturing portends even greater replacement of lower-skilled manufacturing and service jobs, including in poor countries.

The Globalization of R&D

The Fundamental Need for International Research Collaboration

One focus of the literature on global knowledge flows has been on what might narrow the technological gap between developed and developing economies. This gap would necessarily close faster if the developed world experienced a profound and persistent slowdown in the rate of innovation. Could this ever happen?

For most of the postwar period, productivity growth in the Western countries, Japan and the rest of industrial East Asia seemed robust enough that economists believed in a sustainable innovation process that would support income growth forever. The idea arose from the 'endogenous growth' concepts of Romer (1986, 1987), Aghion and Howitt (1992) and Grossman and Helpman (1990, 1991). The basic idea was that R&D efforts would combine with a growing pool of knowledge, sustaining high returns to R&D investment forever. This faith was reinforced in the mid-1990s as, at least in the United States, there was a pronounced acceleration of productivity growth driven by the diffusion of ICT.

At the same time, however, younger growth economists questioned the view that the technological frontier was really endless. Jones (1995a, 1995b) pointed out that, despite rising research intensity in Western economies, there were flat or declining productivity growth rates outside the ICT sector. He developed several 'semi-endogenous' growth models, in which various factors might prevent increases in R&D from permanently raising the innovation rate. Kortum (1997) came to similar conclusions, suggesting that within particular knowledge domains there were a limited number of good ideas and that, once these had been harvested, diminishing returns to R&D would set in.

Jones (2009) again made a significant contribution, modelling a plausible mechanism that would reduce the productivity of research effort over time. The knowledge base upon which human inventors build is constantly expanding. However, human inventors must first master the knowledge built up by previous generations before they can extend it, a daunting task in today's economy. Human technological knowledge is so vast that even the brightest individuals can only reach the frontier, after years of advanced education, by specializing in a narrow piece of that knowledge. Unlike the past, successful invention today increasingly requires the bringing together of complementary pieces of frontier knowledge. In turn, successful innovation requires ever larger teams, with associated costs of coordination. In essence, the mountain of knowledge is rising, but each new generation has to start at the base. The patterns of collaboration suggested by the model in Jones (2009) have been confirmed by evidence in patent documents (Branstetter et al., 2008, 2015).

In the wake of the global financial crisis, it became increasingly evident that the rate of productivity growth in the US and other developed economies has slowed sharply (Byrne et al., 2016). Jones's work suggests that even if the current wave of digital innovation brings a boost in productivity growth, it will be a temporary reprieve from a looming fundamental slowdown in innovation arising from this 'burden of knowledge'. A more lasting escape would require a transformation of human capital formation or the structuring of knowledge, so that new innovators can rise from the base of the mountain to its peak much more quickly. This would entail better understanding of interrelationships between bodies of knowledge, a task that makes the formation and management of ever larger teams more effective. Alternatively, it would require a large increase in the number of intelligent individuals willing to engage in innovative work that can be purchased or shared without raising the costs of innovation.

From the Product Cycle to International Co-Invention: Innovation in the Global South

International economists have long studied the 'product cycle', in which a manufactured good would be invented and initially manufactured in the most advanced industrial economies (Vernon, 1966). Over time, production would shift to less advanced economies as the technology embodied in the product became more standard and routine. Theoretical work on the impact of IPR reform in developing countries put this notion of a product cycle at the centre of a stylized model of the global economy with an industrialized 'North' and a developing 'South'. Important early research by Helpman (1993) developed several variants of a North–South general equilibrium product-cycle model in which Northern innovation expands the range of differentiated goods produced in the world while Southern imitation leads to North–South production shifting.

Lai (1998) extended Helpman's model to allow both the level of FDI and Northern innovation to respond to changes in the strength of Southern IPR protection. This model is further extended in work by Branstetter and Saggi (2011) to the case where innovation, FDI and imitation are all endogenously determined – in other words are all determined within an economy. In these extensions, in any equilibrium with a positive rate of imitation, North–South FDI does not lead to equal wages in the two regions. A lower wage in the South creates an incentive to move production of existing varieties there, but MNEs doing so through FDI incur a higher risk of imitation when they move production to the South.

Imitation is a costly activity that requires deliberate investment on the part of Southern firms seeking to copy Northern products. Stronger IPR protection in the South increases these costs, reducing imitation and lowering the risks faced by MNEs. Production shifting allows for a reallocation of Northern resources towards innovative activity. Under certain assumptions, a strengthening of Southern IPR protection enhances Southern industrial development because the increase in North–South FDI more than offsets the decrease in Southern imitation.[7] To the extent that empirical work on global knowledge flows has been guided by general equilibrium trade models, the international product-cycle model has been the most influential.

Obviously, these models assumed that innovation was concentrated in the 'North'. This remained a reasonable assumption through the 1990s, given the enduring concentration of R&D expenditure and patenting in the developed countries.[8] However, that long-standing truth is now changing, driven in part by the significant rise in human capital outside of the Western world.

This rise is perhaps most pronounced in China and India, though growth in R&D expenditures and patenting is visible elsewhere in the developing world. Indian and Chinese students combined earned 18 per cent of doctorates in science and engineering from US universities in 2016.[9] At home, China graduates more than four times as many

[7] In this literature the innovation response of Southern firms to stronger IPRs is usually absent. A notable exception is He and Maskus (2012), who present a model in which FDI may result in 'reverse' spillovers from South to North. The general absence from these models of induced Southern innovation reflects, in part, the lack of unambiguous evidence to date that stronger IPRs stimulate a significant rise in domestic innovation (Lerner, 2002).

[8] The emergence of the Republic of Korea and Chinese Taipei as innovating economies in the 1990s coincided with the arrival of these economies to income levels equalling those of the poorer European OECD member states and a degree of human capital accumulation that exceeded nearly all of them. In other words, by the time they had emerged as important innovators, the Republic of Korea and Chinese Taipei were no longer developing countries.

[9] National Science Foundation, National Center for Science and Engineering Statistics, *Survey of Earned Doctorates.*

bachelor's-level engineers as the United States. China's participation in international comparisons of student achievement suggests that its educational system meets reasonably high standards for a developing country at China's income level.[10] Applications from Indians made up 62 per cent of new H-1B visa applications in 2016,[11] and the rapid expansion of Indian engineering schools has been documented by Arora and Gambardella (2005). If we view the large number of Indian and Chinese students pursuing graduate education at American research universities as the extreme right tail of a distribution of science and engineering talent, most of which remains at home, then this suggests a massive amount of human capital is available in China and India. This factor has surely accelerated the development of advanced capabilities in manufacturing and modern services work, allowing China and India to become such successful exporters of manufactured goods and services, respectively.

The impact of this human capital accumulation on the global distribution of innovative activity is harder to judge. Within China, there has been sharp growth in R&D spending and an explosion of patenting. China now grants more invention patents to domestic inventors than any other patent office in the world. These raw numbers suggest a rapid shift in the locus of global innovative activity toward the South, and to China in particular. It must be noted, however, that specific government edicts and subsidies designed to reward patenting explain some of this trend. There is also evidence that the novelty standards required for a patent grant in China have fallen (Branstetter et al., 2015; Branstetter et al., 2018).

Researchers traditionally have used the propensity of inventors to take out patents in multiple countries as a measure of patent quality. US firms tend to apply for foreign patents for about 50 per cent of their domestic inventions, and around one-third of US patents eventually obtain a grant in at least one other country (Branstetter et al., 2015). Impressive though China's 'Great Wall' of patents appears to be, the fraction of these inventions for which domestic Chinese inventors seek foreign patent protection is small. For only about 5 per cent of domestic patent applications do Chinese inventors even go through the trouble of applying for protection abroad, and the fraction of Chinese patents that have been granted in foreign jurisdictions is only about 1–2 per cent of the total

[10] See Freeman and Huang (2015) for an overview of China's massive mobilization of science and engineering talent.

[11] According to USCIS Fiscal Year 2016 Annual Report to Congress: 'Characteristics of H-1B Specialty Occupation Workers.'

(Branstetter et al., 2015), although these numbers may have changed since this study.

Analysis of the international patents granted to China-based inventors and India-based inventors reveals the disproportionate role played by multinational corporations in channelling the efforts of inventors based in these countries into new patented inventions. Branstetter et al. (2015) show that, through the mid-2010s, a majority of patents with at least one inventor located in India or China at the time of patent application are assigned to a MNE based outside those countries. Interestingly, a large fraction of these patents is generated by teams of inventors with addresses in multiple countries. Branstetter et al. (2015) refer to this as international co-invention, and suggest that international teams provide a unique way of combining high levels of 'raw talent' in emerging economies with the complementary skills necessary to generate frontier innovation.

The Role of Multinationals in an Era of R&D Globalization

Jones's (2014a) model of the 'knowledge trap' points to the challenges facing MNEs that seek to generate new innovations solely through the efforts of indigenous inventors in developing countries. Frontier innovation requires a suite of specialized skills, not all of which are embodied in the local staff. Branstetter et al. (2018a) provide an alternative, simpler model of the same idea. Prior to the advent of the Internet, and the diffusion of software-enabled engineering design tools that can facilitate collaboration among geographically distant co-inventors, the limited skills and experience of local inventor teams in developing countries strictly limited the degree to which they could participate in the advanced innovative activities of global firms. To be sure, complementary skills exist elsewhere within the MNE, but before the advent of the global Internet, the 'high-bandwidth' information sharing required among members of an inventor team effectively required that seasoned researchers resident in advanced industrial countries be dispatched, often for long periods, to emergent R&D centres in developing countries or vice versa. Either movement was expensive for the employees and the enterprise. It is therefore not surprising that, in the pre-Internet era, relatively few patents had international inventor teams, and very few of those contained significant numbers of inventors based in developing countries. It is especially interesting to note that, even as the number of US patents granted to inventors from Chinese Taipei and the Republic of

Korea shot up in the late 1980s and 1990s, very few of these patents contained inventors who were not from those economies.

Modern ICT has therefore played a critical role in facilitating international R&D collaboration. Now, talented young engineers in a developing country no longer need to possess the full suite of capabilities necessary to engage in frontier research. Instead, they can specialize in a subset of these capabilities, and 'import' the rest by collaborating with team members based in developed countries. Using the comprehensive database on US MNEs maintained by the US Bureau of Economic Analysis, Branstetter et al. (2018b) document a sharp rise in the share of emerging markets in US MNE R&D expenditure and patenting that is coincident with the diffusion of these technologies. Interestingly, this shift is not uniform across industries. ICT itself plays an important role in this growing globalization of R&D. Branstetter et al. (2018b) present evidence consistent with the view that ICT innovation is more 'modular', meaning that innovation in components of a system can take place more or less independently. This is because standard interfaces and system architectures allow independently developed ICT hardware components (or bits of software) to interact effectively with one another. It is also true that software-based engineering tools are especially well developed in these domains. Finally, the growing importance of software and ICT as drivers of innovation across multiple industries has created a shortage of engineers in advanced countries, which has prompted US multinationals to take special advantage of the growing numbers of engineers available for hire in developing countries.

Branstetter et al. (2015) document the disproportionately important role played by MNEs in generating the international patents assigned to Chinese and Indian inventors. They also show a significant quality difference between MNE-guided invention and the patents of domestic companies based on forward citations. Interestingly, this quality gap does not seem to fade over time. On the other hand, the authors document the striking degree to which the quality of invention generated by all-Chinese inventor teams employed by a multinational firm has converged to the quality of invention generated by inventor teams based in the MNEs' home countries.

Branstetter et al. (2018b) point to a potential mechanism by which this convergence in quality can be achieved. They observe that when MNE affiliates begin conducting R&D in a new technical domain, the number of inventor-team members based in advanced countries tends to be high. As this research programme proceeds, the fraction of advanced-country inventors declines. The authors take this as evidence suggesting that repeated international collaboration is a mechanism of transferring specific knowledge from the MNE's central R&D facility (or more advanced nodes in its network) to the relatively new hubs based in developing countries.

In light of the concern that insufficient human resources in the industrialized nations could bring about a long and substantial decline in the global rate of innovation, the 'bridging function' played by MNEs is a potentially critical one. It could take decades for today's emerging markets – let alone the poorest countries – to develop the full complement of skills required for frontier innovation. MNE-mediated international inventor teams relax that constraint, allowing the increasingly large numbers of engineers with high levels of basic skill and talent emerging from the universities of developing countries to join a truly globalized R&D system that connects them to the complementary skills they need to be productive. Indeed, MNE-based global R&D networks could accelerate the global rate of innovation or, at least, limit its decline. In the long run, the MNE-employed engineers in developing countries will acquire a fuller complement of skills, enabling some of them to form their own innovative teams.

The policy environment required to encourage the development of MNE-centred R&D networks seems clear enough. First, developing countries must educate their citizens up to the level that they can usefully contribute to such networks. This is a challenge with which many developing countries struggle, and where new learning technology may play a constructive role. We address that in the next section. Second, developing countries need to offer a stable and attractive policy environment for MNEs that includes a commitment to global openness and transparent protection of intellectual property rights. Third, and importantly, the governments of developed countries need to view the emergence of these networks as a source of benefit, not a 'hollowing out' of internal innovative capacity.

International Knowledge Flows in the Age of AI

A New (Post-) Industrial Revolution?

Until recently, artificial intelligence was viewed as an esoteric branch of engineering with immense theoretical promise but enormous practical challenges, and with little in the way of tangible results. The decisive turning point came in the 1990s, with the rise of 'machine learning' as the increasingly dominant approach within AI.

This approach largely bypassed efforts to fully codify the rules of human decision-making. Instead, statistical algorithms were developed that allowed computers to construct their own decision-making 'rules', provided they reproduced human judgements with high fidelity. With massive datasets, algorithms were soon capable of approaching human levels of accuracy in image recognition and speech-to-text translation. These advances opened the way for autonomous vehicles and conversational digital assistants. Related algorithms were able to detect anomalies and find heretofore unrecognized patterns in large, complex datasets, opening up the field of big data analytics.

The ability of algorithms to learn from and find patterns within enormous datasets grew as ever larger amounts of data were captured by the Internet. This process went into overdrive with the rise of 'cloud computing', the rapid diffusion of powerful handheld devices that allow billions of people to be connected to the Internet, and the so-called 'Internet of Things' that increasingly links devices to the Internet (Gubbi et al., 2013; Regalado, 2014). With the rise of machine learning, the petabytes of data collected on the Internet could now be sliced and diced with increasing ease and sophistication.

The expanding universe of smart devices, monitoring their own performance in real time under all the unpredictable conditions that obtain in the real world, effectively turns the entire planet into an information laboratory, generating reams of data that can be used in the next generation of (software-enabled) product development. Picking through these data to find salient patterns requires ever more powerful machine learning, AI and large-scale data analytics. It also brings in a completely new engine to drive technological progress in the design of new industrial and consumer products.

This engine is also driving innovative progress in a growing range of personal and business services. An ever-greater fraction of human life in advanced countries is conducted online. Business services are increasingly internet-enabled, digitally-driven activities, offered via mobile devices to a global client base. For the first time in history, a large part of the service economy is now subject to the same kind of meticulous measurement as activity on the factory floor became in an earlier age. The exponentially growing domains of data, and the expanding opportunity to run 'experiments' in real time, provide a new resource for the efficient creation of new and better products and services. This opportunity extends far beyond the conventional boundaries of manufacturing. Industrial firms have now entered a new era that fundamentally transforms business across the economy (Brynjolfsson and McAfee, 2014).

The Decline of Manufacturing Employment in the Digital Age

Improving machine learning, along with the agility of robotic hands, implies that a new wave of manufacturing automation is likely to come, and may already be here. Increasingly automated assembly lines are less likely to travel across borders in search of inexpensive labour and, even when they do, they will bring fewer jobs for human workers. This has significant implications for traditional channels of international technology transfer. The preceding sections have highlighted the important role played by FDI, the unbundling of manufacturing value chains and the creation of supplier linkages connecting indigenous manufacturing firms in developing countries (and their workers) to foreign purchasers with a well-developed understanding of advanced manufacturing. As manufacturing's share of employment declines throughout the world, this traditional channel of knowledge transfer will become necessarily less important. Development strategies based on the attraction and expansion of local manufacturing will need to be rethought.

A growing literature has pointed to emerging signs of 'premature deindustrialization' (Rodrik, 2016). In many cases, these changes are not the result of a policy failure, but rather reflect global shifts in the technology of production. While manufacturing firms will adapt their technology of production to reflect local factor prices, the rapidly growing capabilities of machines are likely to accelerate the pace at which advanced technology is incorporated into production, even in relatively poor countries. In this case, 'technology transfer' may increasingly limit the ability of traditional channels to foster the local development of human capabilities. As this trend unfolds, its force will be complemented by the likely slowdown of the shift of manufacturing from advanced to developing countries. Baldwin (2016) provides a comprehensive description of the unbundling, but makes clear that this process has natural limits. Once all the manufacturing that was 'movable' from the leading nations of the West had been moved, the spectacular growth in intermediate goods trade that has characterized recent decades would logically slow.

A Rise of Digital Services Trade?

While AI and its assorted technologies are likely to accelerate the decades-long shrinkage of employment in manufacturing, the advance of ICT could power substantial growth in international services trade. Recent studies have pointed to the rising importance of business services exports for the United States and other advanced industrial nations (Jensen, 2011; Council of Economic Advisors, 2012). Thanks to advances in digitization, modern telecommunications and the convenience of international air travel, an increasing array of business services can be exported to foreign clients. Available data strongly suggest that international trade in business services has grown rapidly and that they play a major role in the expanding services trade surplus of the United States.[12]

Services exports, as measured in the official data, have expanded dramatically, doubling between 1997 and 2007, and resuming rapid growth after the global financial crisis. Services exports now account for nearly 30 per cent of US exports. This growth was disproportionately driven by business services, broadly defined. Despite this rapid growth, the measured export intensity of even the most theoretically tradable parts of the service sector remains far lower than in manufacturing. According to recent disaggregated data from the Census Bureau analysed by Jensen (2011), the ratio of exports to sales in tradable business services is between 90 per cent and 78 per cent lower than in manufacturing. This lower ratio reflects a number of factors, including pervasive market access barriers in important trading partners that are considerably more restrictive than most remaining tariffs on trade in goods. It also reflects the reality that the ICT revolution making services increasingly tradable is still relatively recent and exporters around the world are still catching up to the possibilities it has opened up. Nevertheless, it is probable that business services and other ICT-supported services will eventually become as intensively traded as manufactured goods.

While this analysis is based on US export trends, the benefits of a substantial increase in business services trade will be global. Further, the impact on welfare may be greatest in developing countries where the quality and availability of business services is most constrained. Interesting evidence on this point comes from a randomized experiment in India (Bloom et al., 2013). Researchers randomly selected a set of Indian textile factories to receive a complimentary five-month programme of consulting services from a leading international firm. Upon arriving in these factories, the researchers and consultants found that productivity was hampered by poor management practices. Over the

[12] While trade in services has traditionally been poorly measured, in recent years the Bureau of Economic Analysis has made considerable strides in categorizing and measuring US international transactions in disaggregated services, including in the areas of producer, business and IT services.

next five months, the consultants worked with the firms to implement successful management practices used in the West. When the project ended, the 'treated' factories had cut product defects in half, substantially reduced inventories and increased output, while the control factories saw little change. The authors calculated that profit increases of the treated factories resulting from these performance improvements exceeded USD 200,000 per year.

Given the magnitude of the improvement, why had the firms not adopted these practices earlier? The authors' results suggest that informational barriers were the primary factor explaining the lack of adoption. What is true for India is likely to be true throughout the developing world. By reducing barriers to trade in services, developing countries can help their own firms move towards the productivity frontier achieved in the West. By increasing the range of and quality of services inputs that can be imported, developing country firms can increase their productivity. In fact, these gains would be analogous to the positive impact of enhanced market access to imported capital goods and industrial intermediate inputs on emerging market firm growth and productivity documented by many studies (e.g. Goldberg et al., 2010).

A related possible source of developing country gains from services trade is highlighted in Jones (2014a). This paper shows how the incentives of firms in developing countries to invest in specialized human capital can be reduced when the local stock of complementary specialists is limited. Jones notes that MNEs could, in principle, link specialists located in different countries together in production or development teams that could coordinate their effort in real time. This raises the incentives for investment in specialized human capital wherever these international networks exist. Expanding international services trade should facilitate the development of international value chains in services industries, and that creates a broader range of sectors in which the 'knowledge trap' can be ameliorated by globalization. Thus, while the rise of AI may reduce learning opportunities through the reduced importance of manufacturing value chains, it may help increase learning opportunities by supporting the emergence of globalized services value chains.

Those opportunities will only be realized if contemporary concerns over data privacy and the global reach of the largest digital services companies can be addressed without unnecessary impediments being placed on the global flow of data and the scope of operations of the best digital services providers (Branstetter, 2016). China is perhaps the world's most open large developing country when it comes to trade in conventional goods, but arguably is the most 'digitally protectionist' major economy in the world. Continued erosion of pro-digital-trade norms and practices could be as injurious to global welfare as the trade wars of the 1930s.[13]

AI and Human Capital Formation

Among the most exciting potential applications of AI are the prospects for machine learning to amplify and accelerate human learning. This essay began with a strong emphasis on the role of human capital constraints as a barrier to international knowledge flows. These barriers have remained significant, despite the impressive progress many emerging and developing countries have made recently in improving school enrollment and completion rates. This paradox arises partly because enrollments and graduations are not the same as learning. A growing body of evidence suggests that the productivity of developing countries in converting investments of time and money in education into real human capital remains low (Hanushek and Woessman, 2015). For instance, in India, over 50 per cent of students in Grade 5 cannot read at the second-grade level, despite primary school enrollment rates of over 95 per cent (Pratham, 2017). Further, there have been limited improvements in learning outcomes in the past decade, despite substantial increases in education spending (Muralidharan, 2013). The low return on conventional investments in education raises the distressing possibility of human capital barriers that can never be lowered at a politically feasible price, permanently stunting growth and development.

In this context, it is useful to mention the recent work of Muralidharan et al. (2018).[14] These authors present experimental evidence on the impact of AI-driven, computer-aided learning software on the learning of a sample of Indian school children randomly selected into a supplemental instructional programme using an AI-based instructional software. The authors find that students in the treatment group scored significantly higher in maths and Hindi language relative to other

[13] The potential welfare costs of data protection are not yet well understood and are just now becoming the subject of extensive analysis. An early entrant (Bauer et al., 2014) finds, in a CGE framework, that recently implemented and newly proposed restrictions, including economy-wide requirements for data localization, in several countries (including China and the EU) could generate substantial losses in domestic investment and real GDP. Losses of that type would surely mount if such restrictions became globally common as AI and related services take on premier roles in sharing knowledge.

[14] This section borrows heavily from Muralidharan et al. (2018).

students. The learning gains were achieved at a lower cost per student than in the public schooling system. Moreover, in earlier work, Muralidharan (2012) found that providing performance bonuses to teachers also led to significant test-score gains.

A key feature of the experimental software is its ability to use the ever-growing volumes of data generated by the students interacting with it to benchmark the learning level of every student and dynamically customize the material being delivered. A second noteworthy feature is its ability to analyse data to identify patterns of student errors and precisely target content to alleviate learning problems that may be difficult to address in the classroom. The ability of the software to personalize learning is critical because of the extreme heterogeneity the authors find among their students in terms of content mastery.

The software studied by Muralidharan et al. (2018) is just one example of a wave of AI-driven, computer-aided learning systems that have been shown to generate significant learning gains. In the United States, Kenneth Koedinger has led an effort to develop similar systems, focused on mathematics. Large-scale randomized control trials conducted in the US have shown that these computer tutors can substantially accelerate student learning (Pane et al., 2014). For decades, education researchers have thought that small-group tutoring generates the best learning conditions possible but have struggled to solve the key challenge that small-group tutoring by regular teachers is 'too costly for most societies to bear on a large scale' (Bloom, 1984). AI-driven computer learning systems may offer the best chance yet of achieving this 'first-best' approach to learning on a global scale and at a politically feasible cost. If so, the set of potential innovators available for emergent knowledge and innovation networks could be vastly expanded.[15]

Conclusion

In this chapter we have set out a number of points to help guide thinking about the present and future of international knowledge flows. We noted the importance of international trade, FDI, licensing and global value chains as formal mechanisms of technology transfer and their sensitivity to local economic and social conditions. To a significant degree, however,

[15] One could also imagine AI algorithms streamlining the innovation process itself, amplifying human cognitive effort in the same way that three hundred years of industrial progress have amplified human physical effort.

these channels are being complemented by the growth of MNE-centred R&D networks that actively build international research teams. Indeed, there are reasons to anticipate the shift in manufacturing employment to developing countries to moderate, with activity shifting towards services and other knowledge-based activities over time in those countries that are prepared to participate.

In this context, the language we typically use to describe international knowledge 'flows' downplays the significant investments in specific human capital required to transfer advanced capabilities from a set of firms and individuals located in a developed country to a different set of firms and individuals located in a developing country. Firms and individuals can only make these investments profitably when they are already equipped with an appropriate level of prior knowledge, and we suggest that the uneven geography of convergence can be explained, in part, by large gaps in knowledge capital across countries. These gaps are far larger than commonly measured school enrollment statistics would suggest. Jones (2014b) makes a compelling case that the real variation in human capital may be sufficiently large to explain global differences in incomes and growth performances.

This view helps explain the limited degree to which the conventional mechanisms of international knowledge transfers have supported technology diffusion in recent decades, at least to areas beyond China, India and other major emerging economies. Foreign firms will only transfer advanced technology to their subsidiaries where the skills of the local workforce and the level of sophistication in supplying and purchasing industries make that transfer profitable. Likewise, they will only invest in the capabilities of their local suppliers when the technology gaps are not too large. The measured effect of local IPRs (and other policies) on the actual incidence of technology transfer tends to be highest in the richer developing countries because these are the sites where the local skill level supports a significant degree of technology transfer. In the poorer developing countries, the low level of absorptive capacity among local firms and workers makes the *de jure* level of IPR protection less relevant.

If that argument is valid, then the pathway to a more equitable income distribution is clear – accelerate human capital formation in developing countries. Heretofore, that worthy goal has seemed all but impossible, given the limited resources available to developing countries to invest in their young and the remarkably low productivity with which those resources have been converted into economically valuable skills in those countries. However, new developments in technology – especially

AI-driven, computer-aided learning systems – may have brought us a powerful new tool with which to address the fundamental impediments limiting global knowledge flows and convergence. The new tools may well prove to be more limited in their capabilities and more subject to challenges than our early hopes suggest. Nevertheless, the promise suggested by recent research should compel the attention of policymakers and encourage efforts to exploit an important opportunity.

However, technology alone is likely to prove insufficient. While AI-driven learning systems may accelerate the formation of basic human capital in developing countries, these technologies will not eliminate the challenge developing countries – especially smaller ones – face in acquiring the full range of specialized skills an ever more sophisticated global economy will demand. But rising levels of international services trade could lessen this challenge by allowing developing countries to specialize in subsets of these capabilities, effectively importing the rest. This chapter has stressed the degree to which advances in information technology may enable a growing degree of international trade in knowledge-intensive services. This will create new export opportunities for advanced countries. In addition, developing countries caught in the 'knowledge trap' will have the opportunity to specialize, and gain from trade, reducing the range of capabilities required to escape that trap.

The globalized R&D networks being created by leading multinationals offer an example of how this international division of labour could work in practice. The latest technological revolutions may be limiting the ability of traditional channels of technology diffusion to continue to operate as they have in the past. But the same revolutions are opening up new opportunities for technology diffusion. Ensuring that these opportunities are fully realized will require a revitalized WTO, capable of coordinating policy in a digital age of expanding data flows. To be effective in this role, the WTO itself will need to become more knowledgeable of these emerging technologies and international trade opportunities. We see this volume as a step in this direction. For all of us, much remains to be done.

Bibliography

Acemoglu, Daron, *Introduction to Modern Economic Growth*, Princeton, NJ: Princeton University Press, 2009.

Aghion, Philippe and Howitt, Peter, 'A Model of Growth through Creative Destruction' (1992), *Econometrica* 60, 2: 323–351.

Antras, Pol, 'Incomplete Contracts and the Product Cycle' (2005), *American Economic Review* 95, 4: 1054–1073.

Arora, Ashish and Gambardella, Alfonso, 'Complementarities and External Linkages: The Strategies of Large Corporations in Biotechnology' (1990), *Journal of Industrial Economics* 38, 4: 361–379.

Arora, Ashish and Gambardella, Alfonso, 'The Changing Technology of Technological Change' (1994), *Research Policy* 23, 5: 523–532.

Arora, Ashish and Gambardella, Alfonso, *From Underdogs to Tigers? The Rise and Growth of the Software Industry in Brazil, China, India, Ireland, and Israel*, Oxford: Oxford University Press, 2005.

Baldwin, Richard, *The Great Convergence: Information Technology and the New Globalization*, Cambridge, MA: Harvard University Press, 2016.

Baldwin, Richard and Lopez-Gonzales, Javier, *Supply-Chain Trade: A Portrait of Global Patterns and Several Testable Hypotheses*, Cambridge: NBER working paper, 2013.

Bauer, Matthias, Lee Makiyama, Hosuk, van der Marel, Erik and Verschelde, Bert, *The Costs of Data Localisation: Friendly Fire on Economic Recovery*, Brussels: European Center for International Political Economy, 2014, ECIPE Occasional Paper 2014/3.

Bloom, Benjamin, 'The Two-Sigma Problem: The Search for Methods of Group Instruction as Effective as One-on-One Tutoring' (1984), *Educational Researcher* 13, 6: 4–16.

Bloom, Nick, Eifert, Benn, Mahajan, Aprajit, McKenzie, David and Roberts, John, 'Does Management Matter? Evidence from India' (2013), *Quarterly Journal of Economics* 128, 1: 1–51.

Branstetter, Lee, 'TPP and Digital Trade', in Kathryn Cimino-Isaacs, Jeffrey Schott and Steven Weisman (eds), *Assessing the TPP Volume 2: Innovations in Trading Rules*, Washington, DC: Peterson Institute for International Economics, 2016, chapter 6.

Branstetter, Lee, Conti, Rafaele and Zhang, Huiyan, 'Welcome to the Jungle: An Initial Expedition into China's Patent Thicket', 2018, CMU Working Paper.

Branstetter, Lee, Fisman, Ray and Fritz Foley, C., 'Do Stronger Intellectual Property Rights Increase International Technology Transfer? Empirical Evidence from US Firm-Level Panel Data' (2006), *Quarterly Journal of Economics* 121, 1: 321–349.

Branstetter, Lee, Fisman Ray, Fritz Foley, C. and Saggi, Kamal, 'Does Intellectual Property Rights Reform Spur Industrial Development?' (2011), *Journal of International Economics* 83, 1: 27–36.

Branstetter, Lee, Jensen, J. Bradford and Glennon, Britta, 'Knowledge Transfer Abroad: The Role of U.S. Inventors within Global R&D Networks' (2018a), NBER Working Paper No. 24453.

Branstetter, Lee, Jensen, J. Bradford and Glennon, Britta, 'The IT Revolution and the Globalization of R&D' (2018b), NBER Working Paper No. 24707.

Branstetter, Lee, Kuriakose, Smita, Goddard, John and Goldberg, Itzhak, 'Knowledge Absorption and Innovation in ECA: Links to Trade, FDI, and Knowledge Flows', in *The Second Report on the Knowledge Economy in Eastern Europe and Central Asia*, The World Bank, 2008.

Branstetter, Lee and Saggi, Kamal, 'Intellectual Property Rights, Foreign Direct Investment and Industrial Development' (2010), *Economic Journal* 121, 555: 1161–1191.

Branstetter, Lee, Li, Guangwei and Francisco, Veloso, 'The Rise of International Co-Invention', in Adam Jaffe and Benjamin Jones (eds), *The Changing Frontier: Rethinking Science and Innovation Policy*, Chicago: NBER and University of Chicago Press, 2015.

Brynjolfsson, Erik and McAfee, Andrew, *The Second Machine Age: Work, Progress and Prosperity in a Time of Brilliant Technologies*, New York: W.W. Norton, 2014.

Byrne, David, Fernald, John and Reinsdorf, Marshall, 'Does the United States Have a Productivity Slowdown or a Measurement Problem?' (2016), *Brookings Papers on Economic Activity* 47: 109–182.

Coe, Richard, Helpman, Elhanan and Hoffmaister, Alexander W., 'North–South R&D Spillovers' (1997), *The Economic Journal* 107, 440: 134–149.

Cohen, Wesley and Levinthal, Daniel, 'Innovation and Learning: The Two Faces of R&D' (1989), *Economic Journal* 99, 397: 569–596.

Cohen, Wesley and Levinthal, Daniel, 'Absorptive Capacity: A New Perspective on Learning and Innovation' (1990), *Administrative Science Quarterly* 35, 1: 128–152.

Collier, Paul, *The Bottom Billion: Why the Poorest Countries are Failing and What Can Be Done About It*, Oxford: Oxford University Press, 2007.

Cook, Philip, Dodge, Kenneth, Farkas, George, Fryer, Roland, Guryan, Jonathan, Ludwig, Jens, Mayer, Susan, Pollack, Harold and Steinberg, Laurence, 'Not Too Late: Improving Academic Outcomes for Disadvantaged Youth', Institute for Policy Research Working Paper 15-01, Northwestern University, 2015.

Council of Economic Advisors, *Economic Report of the President 2012*, Washington DC: Government Printing Office, 2012.

Delgado, Mercedes, Kyle, Margaret and McGahan, Anita M., 'Intellectual Property Protection and the Geography of Trade' (2013), *Journal of Industrial Economics* 61, 3: 733–762.

Freeman, Richard and Huang, Wei, *China's Great Leap Forward in Science and Engineering*, NBER Working Paper No. 21081, Cambridge, MA: NBER, 2015.

Goldberg, Pinelopi, Khandelwal, Amit, Pavcnik, Nina and Topalova, Petia Topalova, 'Imported Intermediate Inputs and Domestic Product Growth: Evidence from India' (2010), *Quarterly Journal of Economics* 125, 4: 1767–2010.

Grossman, Gene R. and Helpman, Elhanan, 'Comparative Advantage and Long-Run Growth' (1990), *American Economic Review* 80, 4: 796–815.

Grossman, Gene R. and Helpman, Elhanan, 'Quality Ladders in the Theory of Growth' (1991), *Review of Economic Studies* 58, 1: 43–61.

Gubbi, Jayavardhana, Buyya, Rajkumar, Marusic, Slaven and Palaniswami, Marimuthu, 'Internet of Things (IoT): A Vision, Architectural Elements, and Future Directions' (2013), *Future Generation Computer Systems* 29, 7: 1645–1660.

Hanushek, Eric and Woessman, Ludger, *The Knowledge Capital of Nations: Education and the Economics of Growth*, Cambridge, MA: MIT Press, 2015.

He, Yin and Maskus, Keith E., 'Southern Innovation and Reverse Knowledge Spillovers: A Dynamic FDI Model' (2012), *International Economic Review* 53, 1: 281–304.

Helpman, Elhanan, 'Innovation, Imitation and Intellectual Property Rights' (1993), *Econometrica* 61, 6: 1247–1280.

Hoekman, Bernard M., Maskus, Keith E. and Saggi, Kamal, 'Transfer of Technology to Developing Countries: Unilateral and Multilateral Policy Options' (2005), *World Development* 33, 10: 1587–1602.

Hovhanissyan, Nune and Keller, Wolfgang, 'International Business Travel: An Engine of Growth?' (2015), *Journal of Economic Growth* 20, 1: 75–104.

Ivus, Olena, 'Do Stronger Patent Rights Raise High-Tech Exports to the Developing World?' (2010), *Journal of International Economics* 81, 1: 38–47.

Javorcik, Beata Smarzynska, 'Does Foreign Direct Investment Increase the Productivity of Domestic Firms? In Search of Spillovers through Backward Linkages' (2004), *American Economic Review* 94, 3: 605–627.

Jensen, Bradford, *Global Trade in Services: Fear, Facts, and Offshoring. Peterson Institute for International Economics*, Washington, DC: Peterson Institute for International Economics, 2011.

Jones, Benjamin, 'The Knowledge Trap: Human Capital and Development Reconsidered' (2014a), Northwestern University Working Paper.

Jones, Benjamin, 'The Human Capital Stock: A Generalized Approach' (2014b), *American Economic Review* 104, 11: 3752–3777.

Jones, Benjamin F., 'The Burden of Knowledge and the Death of the Renaissance Man: Is Innovation Getting Harder?' (2009), *Review of Economic Studies* 76, 1: 283–317.

Jones, Charles I., 'R&D-Based Models of Economic Growth' (1995a), *Journal of Political Economy* 103: 759–784.

Jones, Charles I., 'Time Series Tests of Endogenous Growth Models' (1995b), *Quarterly Journal of Economics* 110: 495–525.

Keller, Wolfgang, 'International Technology Diffusion' (2004), *Journal of Economic Literature* 42, 3: 752–782.

Kortum, Samuel, 'Research, Patenting, and Technological Change' (1997), *Econometrica* 65, 6: 1389–1419.

Lai, Edwin L. C., 'International Intellectual Property Rights Protection and the Rate of Product Innovation' (1998), *Journal of Development Economics* 55, 1: 133–153.

Lerner, Joshua, '150 Years of Patent Protection' (2002), *American Economic Review Papers and Proceedings* 92, 2: 221–225.

Markusen, James R., *Multinational Firms and the Theory of International Trade*, Cambridge MA: MIT Press, 2002.

Maskus, Keith E. and Yang, Lei, 'Domestic Patent Rights, Access to Technologies and the Structure of Exports' (2018), *Canadian Journal of Economics* 51, 2: 483–509.

Muralidharan, Karthik, 'Long-Term Effects of Teacher Performance Pay: Experimental Evidence from India' (2012), Working Paper, UC-San Diego.

Muralidharan, Karthik, 'Priorities for Primary Education Policy in India's 12th 5-Year Plan' (2013), *India Policy Forum 2012–2013* 9: 1–46.

Muralidharan, Karthik, Singh, Abhijeet and Ganimian, Alejandro, 'Disrupting Education? Experimental Evidence on Technology-Aided Instruction in India' (2018), Working Paper.

Organisation for Economic Cooperation and Development, *OECD Skills Outlook 2017: Skills and Global Value Chains*. Paris: OECD, 2017.

Pane, John, Griffin, Beth, McCaffrey, Daniel and Karam, Rita, 'Effectiveness of Cognitive Tutor Algebra I at Scale' (2014), *Educational Evaluation and Policy Analysis* 36, 2: 127–144.

Piermartini, Roberta and Rubínová, Stela, *How Much Do Global Value Chains Boost Innovation?* World Trade Organization, manuscript, 2018.

Polanyi, M., *Personal Knowledge: Towards a Post-Critical Philosophy*, Chicago: University of Chicago Press, 1958.

Pratham. 2017. *Annual Status of Education Report 2016*, Pratham, New Delhi.

Regalado, Antonio, 'The Internet of Things' (2014), *MIT Technology Review*, July/August.

Rodrik, Dani, 'Premature Deindustrialization' (2016), *Journal of Economic Growth* 21: 1–33.

Romer, Paul, 'Increasing Returns and Long Run Growth' (1986), *Journal of Political Economy* 94: 1002–1037.

Romer, Paul, 'Growth Based on Increasing Returns Due to Specialization' (1987), *American Economic Review* 77: 56–62.

Sutton, John, 'Rich Trades, Scarce Capabilities: Industrial Development Revisited', Keynes Lecture, 2000. *Proceedings of the British Academy*, 2001.

Teece, David J., 'Technology Transfer by Multinational Firms: The Resource Cost of Transferring Technological Know-how' (1977), *Economic Journal* 87, 346: 242–261.

Vernon, Raymond J., 'International Trade and International Investment in the Product Cycle' (1966), *Quarterly Journal of Economics* 80, 2: 190–207.

14

Trade in Intellectual Property-Intensive Goods

MERCEDES DELGADO AND MARGARET KYLE*

Abstract

Intellectual property rights are common, if controversial, components of trade agreements, and existing evidence on the effects of the introduction of IP rights is mixed. We assess the extent to which the TRIPS Agreement is associated with an increase in trade of knowledge-intensive products. Our approach compares how trade in IP-intensive goods changed relative to trade in a control group of products following a country's compliance with the TRIPS Agreement. This allows us to isolate the effect of IP protection from changes in trade that result from other aspects of WTO membership, such as reductions in tariffs and improved terms of trade. We also explore differences across IP-intensive sectors, and differences across countries. We find that adoption of the TRIPS Agreement is associated with increased trade in IP-intensive products in both developing countries and high-income countries. Overall, developing countries have seen greater access to innovation exported from the most innovative countries, and these countries have also participated in the global market for innovative products through their own exports.

Introduction

Intellectual property (IP) rights are common, if controversial, components of trade agreements. Members of the World Trade Organization (WTO) agree to comply with the terms specified in the 1994 Trade-Related Aspects of Intellectual Property Rights (TRIPS) Agreement. This Agreement requires legal protections for many knowledge-intensive products, including biopharmaceuticals, information and communication

* The authors thank Michael Porter for providing access to the International Cluster Competitiveness Project (ICCP) data, and to Rich Bryden for valuable research assistance. All errors and omissions are the responsibility of the authors.

technologies, and creative outputs, with the explicit objective of improving the 'transfer and dissemination of technology, to the mutual advantage of producers and users of technological knowledge'.[1] In this chapter, we assess the extent to which the introduction of IP rights is associated with an increase in trade of knowledge-intensive products.

Existing evidence on the effects of the TRIPS Agreement is somewhat mixed. Several papers point to increased trade, including Maskus and Penubarti (1995), Rafiquzzaman (2002) and Ivus (2010). Others, such as Fink and Primo Braga (1999), Smith (1999) and Co (2004), are more sceptical: they find that IP has a negative or insignificant relationship with trade. In previous work (Delgado et al., 2013), we found that trade in high-IP products groups increased following TRIPS implementation, and we observed important differences between imports and exports, countries, and sectors. This chapter updates that earlier analysis.

Our approach compares how trade in IP-intensive goods changed relative to trade in a control group of products following a country's compliance with the TRIPS Agreement. This allows us to isolate the effect of IP protection from changes in trade that result from other aspects of WTO membership, such as reductions in tariffs and improved terms of trade. We also explore differences across IP-intensive sectors, and differences across countries.

The Link between IP and Trade

A natural question to consider, which we discuss only briefly here, is why IP is included in trade agreements at all. Indeed, some countries are deeply suspicious of the motives of countries and industries that lobby most intensively for IP provisions. McCalman (2001, 2005) estimates that the TRIPS Agreement resulted in substantial transfers of income from other countries to the US, for example. Weissman (1996) discusses the efforts of the pharmaceutical industry to add IP to the agenda of multilateral trade negotiations. While there is little doubt that countries and industries generally act in their own interests, rather than global interests, there are nevertheless some reasons to believe that including IP in trade agreements can raise total welfare.

First, IP has long been a tool of industrial policy employed by countries to gain advantages in certain areas. The US is notorious for having

[1] Part 1, Article 7 of Annex 1C of the Marrakesh Agreement to establish the World Trade Organization, available at www.wto.org/english/docs_e/legal_e/27-trips_03_e.htm.

denied copyright protection to foreign authors until the late 1800s, allowing the country cheap access to the works of Charles Dickens and other prominent British writers. Between 1969 and 1993, Canada permitted the compulsory licensing of pharmaceuticals, which likely contributed to the development of its generic drug sector. Trade agreements restrict the use of government subsidies to support domestic firms, and harmonization of IP laws similarly limits the ability of governments to use these laws as protectionist instruments. Of course, this argument is more palatable for countries that have already had the opportunity to use such instruments during their industrialization and development; developing countries today would not be able to do so (Correa, 2015). Relatedly, IP laws can function as non-tariff barriers to trade even if they are not part of an explicit industrial policy. Translation fees, institutional differences, etc. can all raise costs for foreign firms. Even if IP provisions of trade agreements do not eliminate these entirely, harmonization can contribute to a reduction in trade frictions.

Historically, multilateral agreements have explicitly addressed these concerns. For example, the Paris Convention for the Protection of Industrial Property of 1883 was one of the first treaties to require contracting parties to treat domestic and foreign entities in the same way, thus removing IP as a tool of protectionism; the Berne Convention for the Protection of Literary and Artistic Works in 1886 served a similar role for copyright. The Patent Cooperation Treaty, first signed in 1970, established a unified procedure for patent applications in participating countries. While not explicitly trade agreements, these treaties nonetheless have the effect of reducing trade frictions in IP-intensive goods. More recently, intellectual property has been included as a chapter in many bilateral and multilateral trade deals. The North American Free Trade Agreement (NAFTA) of 1994, for example, was among the first to specify minimum IP provisions required for Canada, Mexico and the US.[2] Similarly, membership in the European Union (EU) is conditional on complying with EU-wide standards for IP.

The argument outlined above essentially applies the same logic to IP-protected products as to any others: the global trade system is improved by removing protectionism and non-tariff barriers. However, IP's primary role (at least as stated by most countries) is to promote innovation. Knowledge, ideas and innovation are non-rivalrous: while any cake I eat

[2] See chapter 17 of NAFTA, available at https://can-mex-usa-sec.org/secretariat/assets/pdfs/usmca-aceum-tmec/agreement-eng.pdf.

denies someone else the consumption of that cake, my use of a cake recipe does not prevent any other baker from producing a similar cake. The non-rivalrous nature of knowledge means it is a public good, and also that, in general, too little will be produced. Innovation is often costly because it involves many failures, and everyone would prefer to let others fail and eventually benefit from another's success, or to free ride. IP allows the owners of patents, copyrights and trademarks to prevent free-riding. It attempts to balance the dynamic benefits (incentives to innovate or create) with the static costs of reduced supply, higher prices, or restricted use. Other policies to promote innovation include research subsidies, tax credits for research and development (R&D) and innovation prizes.

At a global level, free-riding is also a potential problem. Domestic innovation policies are costly, either because they require direct government outlays, reduced tax revenue or losses to consumers of IP-protected goods. Each country would prefer that other governments incur these costs, while benefiting from the positive results of those foreign policies (Kyle et al., 2017). A similar issue arises in defence spending and environmental policies. Just as NATO and the Paris Agreement on climate change require member countries to make some contribution to the common good, multilateral IP agreements also force each country to share the burden of providing innovation incentives.

Finally, dynamic benefits may result from an increase in the transfer and dissemination of knowledge through trade, and IP agreements may increase trade in knowledge-intensive products. Countries may learn from importing as well as exporting or foreign direct investment (Grossman and Helpman (1991, 1995), Eaton and Kortum (1996, 2002), Bretschger (1997), Keller (1998, 2002a, 2002b), Branstetter (2001, 2006), Saggi (2002), Furman et al. (2002), MacGarvie (2006) and Branstetter et al. (2006)). A large literature associates trade and knowledge flows in cross-sections of countries and industries (see, e.g. Bernard and Jensen (1999) and Hallward-Driemeier et al. (2002)) as well as within specific sectors and countries (Bloom et al. (2016), Park et al. (2010), Padoan (1998), Keller (2002a, 2002b) and Eaton et al. (2004), among others).

Based on this body of evidence that trade is associated with knowledge flows, we focus in this chapter on whether IP agreements increase trade, and thus the dissemination of knowledge. Innovators may be more willing to export to markets where they enjoy IP protection, and this can be a net increase in access to innovative products if domestic imitation is costly or time-consuming. They may also increase foreign direct investment where IP protects them against spillovers to local firms. If IP facilitates contracting over knowledge and innovation (Gans and Stern, 2010), we expect markets for technology to develop and increase measured imports and/or exports.

The TRIPS Agreement

IP emerged as a prominent issue during the Uruguay Round of multilateral trade negotiations under the General Agreement on Tariffs and Trade (GATT), starting in 1986. At the conclusion eight years later, in 1994, the WTO agreements replaced GATT and required their adoption, including of the TRIPS Agreement, by the membership. The lengthy negotiations reflect the difficulty in reconciling the divergent interests of so many countries, and IP was certainly one such area.

This agreement specifies minimum levels of protection in many domains, as well as enforcement procedures and dispute resolution. TRIPS requires compliance with the main provisions of WIPO's Paris and Berne Conventions, and specifies or clarifies protection for copyright, patents, trademarks, geographical indications, trade secrets and industrial designs. For patents, these requirements include a minimum term of 20 years of protection from the filing date, and the availability of patents for all fields of technology with three exceptions: inventions contrary to public order and morality; some diagnostic, therapeutic, and surgical methods for human or animal treatment; and plant and animal inventions. Importantly, TRIPS requires protection for pharmaceutical products. For copyright, TRIPS specifies a minimum term of 50 years, and requires that computer programs and collections of data be protected by copyright. Further details, including those pertaining to enforcement and dispute resolution, are available on the WTO's overview of the TRIPS Agreement.[3]

Many countries, both developed and developing, required new legislation in order to comply with TRIPS obligations. For example, in late 1994, the US changed its term of patent protection from 17 years post-grant to 20 years from the date of application in order to comply with TRIPS. While many developing countries (DCs) and least developed countries (LDCs) had some existing IP protection,[4] TRIPS required more substantial increases in the scope and length of such protection. In acknowledgement of their differing needs, and specific difficulties they might face, DCs and

[3] See www.wto.org/english/tratop_e/trips_e/intel2_e.htm.

[4] For example, Brazil was among the initial 11 signatories of the Paris Convention. Haiti, Liberia and Tunisia signed the Berne Convention in 1886.

LDCs were permitted transition periods and other accommodations in complying with the TRIPS Agreement when they became members. Countries that declared themselves as developing in 1995 received an extension to 1 January 2000. Developed countries that joined in 1995 had to be compliant by 1 January 1996. Countries that did not previously provide product patent protection in specific technologies, and for which significant legislative changes were therefore necessary, received an additional five years to comply. For countries that joined the WTO after 1995, TRIPS compliance was a requirement at the time of accession.

LDCs, as defined by the United Nations, initially had a TRIPS compliance date of 1 January 2006. In 2005, the transition period was lengthened to 2013 for most TRIPS provisions, and to 2016 for pharmaceutical patents. In 2013 and 2015, further extensions – to 1 July 2021 for most TRIPS provisions and 1 January 2033 for pharmaceuticals – were negotiated.[5] Countries that graduate from LDC status prior to these dates should be compliant when they are no longer in the LDC category. In addition to time extensions, WTO members have some flexibilities available under TRIPS concerning compulsory licensing, parallel imports and exceptions to patent rights. One particular use of these flexibilities has been to enable access to affordable pharmaceuticals – see t'Hoen (2018) for a detailed description of their use in practice.

In this chapter, we focus on TRIPS compliance dates as critical for trade in IP-intensive products. We estimate TRIPS compliance dates based on a country's membership date, status as LDC, and information provided by the WTO regarding transition periods (see Table A14.1). While LDC status is straightforward, as the UN definition applies, the WTO allowed other countries to declare whether they would use the transition periods made available to developing countries. For countries that joined that WTO in 1995, we identify the subset that requested a transition period based on information from the WTO's website.[6] This list has some surprises: it includes Israel and the Republic of Korea, but not Romania or South Africa. Unfortunately, information on transition periods for countries that subsequently joined is less readily available. As in our earlier work, we rely on efforts by Hamdan-Livramento (2009) and Park (2008) to assess each country's compliance with its TRIPS obligations, but these indices are not available for more recent years. For countries that joined the WTO in the last 10 years, we therefore used Trade Policy Reviews

[5] See www.wto.org/english/tratop_e/trips_e/ldc_e.htm.
[6] A list is provided at www.wto.org/english/tratop_e/trips_e/tripfq_e.htm.

from the WTO to evaluate whether DCs that were not compliant in 2009, based on these prior indices, have subsequently changed their IP laws. For new WTO members, we assumed that accession was possible only if these countries had proven TRIPS compliance when they joined.[7] Due to the additional transition periods negotiated in 2013 and 2015, no LDC was required to be TRIPS compliant by the end of our data (2016), so we are unable to estimate a post-TRIPS relationship for LDCs.

TRIPS compliance is an oversimplification of the 'true' IP situation in many countries. IP takes many forms (copyright, patents, trademarks, etc.), and determining whether a country actually met its compliance deadline requires careful legal analysis. Some countries provided IP protection prior to their compliance deadlines, for example. Others may have TRIPS-compliant laws, but fail to enforce them aggressively. Transparent and objective information on these points can be difficult to obtain, and researchers occasionally reach different conclusions.

Empirical Approach and Data

Our first approach considers a country's total exports or imports in high-IP sectors relative to a control sector. We describe the construction of the high-IP and control categories below. We test whether exports or imports increased more post-TRIPS compliance in high-IP products, compared to the control group of products. To do so, we estimate regressions that control for country income group-sector-year effects. That is, we allow for fixed differences between high-income countries and developing countries within each sector that vary by year. For details on the econometric specifications, see our earlier paper (Delgado et al., 2013). This analysis concerns whether access to technology (through imports) and production of technology (through exports) is related to IP.

Our second approach focuses on exports from high-income economies to developing economies. We aggregate each developing economy's imports from a group of high-income economies that had the 20 highest numbers of US patents in 1993 (see Table 14.1). As before, we are interested in whether imports of high-IP products increased more

[7] Economists will be rightfully worried about the endogeneity of policy choices here, including the decision to join the WTO and to change IP laws. The differences-in-differences approach we take should address some of the bias. We also examined pre-TRIPS trade trends to confirm the validity of our control sector. However, the usual caveats remain.

Table 14.1 *List of economies by economy-type**

High-income		**Developing (D)**		**Least developed**
Top 20 Innovative**	**Other High-Inc.**	**Upper-middle Inc. (D-High)**	**Lower-middle & low-Inc. (D-Low)**	**(LD)**
Australia	*Antigua and Barbuda*	*Argentina*	Albania	Afghanistan
Austria	*Bahrain*	*Botswana*	Armenia	Angola***
Belgium	*Barbados*	*Brazil*	*Belize*	Bangladesh
Canada	*Brunei Darussalam*	Bulgaria	*Bolivia*	Benin
Hong Kong, China	Croatia	*Chile*	*Cameroon*	Burkina Faso
Denmark	*Cyprus*	*Colombia*	Cape Verde*	Burundi
Finland	Czech Rep.	*Costa Rica*	*China*	Cambodia
France	*Estonia*	*Cuba****	*Congo*	Central African Rep.
Germany	Greece	*Dominica*	*Côte d'Ivoire*	Chad***
Israel	Hungary	*Dominican Rep.*	Ecuador	Gambia
Italy	Iceland	*Fiji*	*Egypt*	Guinea
Japan	Ireland	*Gabon*	*El Salvador*	Guinea-Bissau***
Netherlands	*Kuwait*	*Grenada*	*Eswatini* *Ghana*	Haiti***
Rep. of Korea	Liechtenstein***	*Jamaica*	Georgia	Lao P.D.R.
Norway	Luxembourg	Kazakhstan	*Guatemala*	Lesotho
Spain	*Macao, China****	Latvia	*Guyana*	Liberia
Sweden	*Malta*	Lithuania	*Honduras*	Madagascar
Switzerland	New Zealand	*Malaysia*	*India*	Malawi
United Kingdom	Oman	*Mauritius*	*Indonesia*	Mali
USA	Portugal	*Mexico*	Jordan	Mauritania
	Qatar	Montenegro	*Kenya*	Mozambique
	Saudi Arabia	*Namibia*	Kyrgyzstan	Myanmar***

* Editors' note: the authors' classification as set out in this table is for the purpose of the authors' scholarly analysis in the context only of this chapter and does not necessarily reflect formal legal or political status, nor the views of the WTO, its members or its Secretariat.

Table 14.1 (*cont.*)

High-income		**Developing (D)**		**Least developed**
Top 20 Innovative**	**Other High-Inc.**	**Upper-middle Inc. (D-High)**	**Lower-middle & low-Inc. (D-Low)**	**(LD)**
	Singapore	North Macedonia	Maldives*	Nepal
		Panama		
	Slovakia	*Peru*	Mongolia	Niger
	Slovenia	*Poland*	*Morocco*	Rwanda
		Romania	*Nicaragua*	Senegal
	Trinidad and Tobago	Russian Federation	*Nigeria*	Sierra Leone
	United Arab Emirates	*Saint Kitts and Nevis*	*Pakistan*	Solomon Islands***
		Saint Lucia	*Papua New Guinea*	Togo
		Saint Vincent & the Grenadines	*Paraguay*	Uganda
		Seychelles	*Philippines*	United Rep of Tanzania
		South Africa	Rep. of Moldova	Vanuatu
		Suriname	Samoa*	Yemen
			Sri Lanka	
		Turkey		
		Uruguay	Tajikistan	
		Venezuela	*Thailand*	
			Tonga	
			Tunisia	
			Ukraine	
			Viet Nam	
			Zimbabwe	

Notes: List of WTO members as of 2016. High-income economies based on the World Bank classifications as of 2009. All economies but Croatia remain in the high-income group as of 2016 (www.worldbank.org/en/publication/wdr2016). Economies in *italics* are economies self-designated as 'developing' when they joined WTO. The list of least developed economies can be accessed at www.un.org.

* Cape Verde, Maldives and Samoa moved from Least Developed to Developing in 2007, 2011 and 2014 respectively.

** Top-20 high-income innovative economies in terms of USPTO patents as of 1993.

*** WTO members excluded from the empirics because of missing or poor data.

than imports of control products following TRIPS compliance. Again, our regressions control for sector-year effects. The purpose of this analysis is to assess whether IP increases the dissemination of technology from rich economies to poorer ones.

The United Nations Commodity Trade Statistics database (UN Comtrade) provides the nominal value of country trade in US currency for reasonably detailed product categories. As in Feenstra et al. (2005), we estimate imports using reported exports. After converting the figures into 2016 dollars using the US Price Deflator for Gross Domestic Product, we construct one dataset of exports and one of imports, for each country-product category-year, based on SITC Rev. 3 definitions. The dataset includes those economies that were members of the WTO by 2016, resulting in an economy-level panel that describes the imports and exports between 151 economies from 1993 to 2016 (see Table 14.1).[8] We further classify economies using the World Bank definition of 'high income', the UN definition of 'least developed', and all others as developing. We exclude a small number of WTO members from our analysis due to the poor quality of their Comtrade data.[9]

High-IP Products

We use the group of high-IP-intensity products identified in Delgado et al. (2013). We started with a list of (four-digit NAICS (North American Industry Classification System)) industries with above-average IP intensity in the US (based on patents, trademarks or copyrights) described in a report by the Economics and Statistics Administration (ESA) and the USPTO.[10] To define the high-IP group of traded products, we match the NAICS industries to the Comtrade product categories (SITC Rev. 3). To define subsets of our high-IP product group, we use the Delgado et al. (2016) clustering approach that creates groups (called 'clusters') in a way that industries in the same cluster are more similar to each other than to those in other groups. They identify a set of 51 clusters of industries related by knowledge, skills, inputs, demand and other linkages.[11] We focus on

[8] For an economy-year that is not available in the data, we estimate their exports and imports using other economies' reported imports from and exports into the economy.

[9] The excluded economies are Angola; Chad; Cuba; Guinea-Bissau; Haiti; Liechtenstein; Macao, China; Myanmar; The Solomon Islands; and Chinese Taipei.

[10] ESA-USPTO Report, US Department of Commerce, 2012.

[11] We use two cluster databases: the *industry cluster* data from the US Cluster Mapping Project (USCMP, n.d.; Delgado et al., 2016); and the *traded-products cluster* data from the

clusters with the highest patent intensity: *Information Technology and Analytical Instruments*, *Communications Equipment and Services*, *Medical Devices*, *Chemical Products* and *Biopharmaceuticals*.[12] The products in these clusters are a subset of the broad high-IP group.[13] This cluster approach allows a more refined mapping of related traded products into meaningful groups of high-IP intensity.

Control Group: Non-IP-Intensive Products

Our empirical approach relies on a control group of products for which IP (and TRIPS implementation) is less important. This provides a benchmark that captures how trade between countries changed independently of TRIPS. The control group of low-IP products is the same as that in Delgado et al. (2013). It is based on the set of clusters with the lowest IP intensity and excludes a few products in these clusters that have high-IP. The control group includes mainly consumable and unprocessed (semi-processed) products.

Tables 14.2a, 14.2b and 14.2c summarize the product grouping. Delgado et al. (2013) provides additional details on the construction of both the high-IP and the control group. Table 14.3 presents summary statistics for the variables used in the analysis.

Empirical Results

Our goal is to highlight the important findings, so we provide a non-technical summary of the results in Table 14.4.[14] Each cell in Table 14.4 represents the estimated 'difference-in-difference' of the natural log of trade in high-IP products before and after TRIPS implementation, relative to the control group of products before and after TRIPS implementation. In columns, we present the results for an analysis of exports to the world, imports from the world and finally imports from the most innovative

International Cluster Competitiveness Project (ICCP). The ICCP uses the set of 51 benchmark cluster definitions developed by Delgado et al. (2016) and maps them into clusters of related traded products (SITC Rev. 3) in countries.

[12] The ESA-USPTO Report identifies as high-patent intensive industries with five or more patents per 1,000 workers per year. We look for industry clusters that have a patent intensity well above this value (more than 15 patents per 1,000 workers).

[13] Within high-IP clusters there may be some products with low IP-intensity. We correct this by dropping a few products that have low-IP based on the ESA-USPTO Report. The SITCs included in the final clusters are listed in the Appendix.

[14] Detailed tables with regression results are available from the authors.

Table 14.2a *Definition of high-IP group (SITC Rev. 3 Labels and Codes)*

High-patent products (most of which are also high-trademark)	
Crude fertilizers: 277, 278	Metalworking machinery: 73
Organic & inorganic chemicals: 51, 52	General machinery: 7413-9, 7421-3, 7427, 743-9
Dyeing materials: 53	Office machines: 75
Medicinal & pharmaceutical products: 54	Telecommunications: 76
Essential oils & perfume materials: 55	Electrical machinery: 77
Chemical materials & products: 59	Professional apparatus: 87
Rubber manufactures: 6214, 625, 6291-2	Photographic apparatus: 881-2, 884, 8853-4
Power-generating machinery: 71	Miscellaneous mfg.: 8931, 89332, 8939, 8941-3, 8947, 8952, 89591, 897-8, 8991-6
Machinery for industries: 721-3, 7243, 7248, 725-8	
High-trademark products (with low-patent/copyright)	
Dairy products & beverages: 022–024, 111, 1123	Manufactures of metals: 66494, 69561-2, 69564, 6963, 6966, 6973
Crude rubber: 231-2	
Pulp & waste paper: 251	Road vehicles: 784, 78531, 78536
Plastics: 57, 5813-7, 582, 583	Furniture: 82
Paper & related articles: 64	Footwear: 85
High-copyright products (most of which are also high-trademark)	
Cinematographic film: 883	Printed matter & recorded media: 892, 8986-7

Notes: Authors' categorization based on ESA-USPTO Report (US Department of Commerce, 2012).

high-income countries into developing (upper-middle, lower-middle and low-income) countries. In rows, we show the results for all high-IP products and then for each high-IP cluster of particular interest.

We begin with the relationship between TRIPS implementation and trade in all high-IP products. All countries see an increase in exports: holding all other variables constant, the estimated difference-in-difference is 0.915 compared to the control group. We also see an increase in the value of imports, though this change is smaller than for exports. Importantly, this increased trade in innovative products is not confined to rich countries. Since we expect imports from the most innovative

Table 14.2b *Definition of high-IP clusters (SITC Rev. 3 Codes)*

Biopharmaceuticals Medicinal & pharmaceutical products: 5147, 5157-8, 5411, 5413-6, 54199, 542 Diagnostic substances: 54192-3, 59867, 59869	**Medical devices** Surgical and dental instruments and supplies: 54191, 74183, 78531, 78536, 8721-4 Optical Instruments & ophthalmic goods: 8711, 8714, 8719, 8841-3
Upstream chemicals Agricultural chemicals: 5911-3 Industrial Gas: 5112, 5222 Inorganic & organic chemicals: 5221, 5223-6, 5231-8, 5243, 5249, 525, 5988, 2321, 5111, 5113-4, 5121-4, 5137-9, 5145-6, 5148, 5154-6, 5161-3, 5169, 5981, 5984	**Downstream chemicals** Dyes, pigments and coating: 531, 5322, 5331, 5334-5, 5514, 5977, 59865, 59891, 89591 Explosives: 5931-2 Personal care and cleaning products: 5323, 5531-5, 5541, 55421-3, 5543, 5914, 5983 Processed chemical products: 5513, 5933, 5972, 59733, 59861 59863-4, 59893-4, 59896-7, 59899, 882-3
ICT: Information technology & communications equipment	
Communications equipment: 7641, 76424-5, 7643, 76481-2, 77882-4, 7649, 77811, 77817	Electronic components: 7722-3, 7761-2, 7768 Medical apparatus: 7741-2, 8996
Information Technology & Analytical Instruments Audio & video equipment: 7611-2, 7621-2, 7628, 7633, 76381-4, 76421-3, 76426, 77885 Computers & peripherals: 7521-3, 7526-7, 7529, 7591, 75997, 881	Process & lab instruments: 8713, 87311, 87313, 87315, 87319, 87321, 87329, 8742-4, 8746-7, 8749, 8853-4 Semiconductors: 5985, 7763-4 Software reproducing: 8984-7

Notes: These high-IP clusters are mutually exclusive and are a subset of the High-IP group defined in Table 14.2a.
Sources: US Cluster Mapping Project (USCMP, n.d.), the International Cluster Competitiveness Project (ICCP, n.d.) and ESA-USPTO Report (2012).

countries to be associated with the most important technologies and innovations, we are especially interested to see that imports of high-IP products from these countries increase significantly more than imports of the control group in developing countries, and especially in the subset of lower-middle and low-income ('DC-low') countries. Developing

Table 14.2c *Definition of control group of low-IP products (SITC Rev. 3 Labels and Codes)*

Food & live animals: 01, 03, 041-5, 05, 061, 071-2, 074-5, 08	Manufactured goods by material: Leather (61); cork & wood (63); textiles (6511-4, 652, 654-9); non-metallic minerals (661-2, 6633, 6639, 6641-5, 6648 66491-3, 66495-6); iron & steel (67); non-ferrous metals (6821-6826, 68271, 683, 6841, 68421-6, 685-689); and metals (6911-2, 69243-4, 6932-5, 694, 6975, 699)
Crude materials, inedible, except fuels: 21, 22, 244, 261-5, 268-9, 273, 28, 292-7, 29292– 3, 29297-9	
Mineral fuels, lubricants & related materials: 32-4	
Animal & vegetable oils, fats and waxes: 41-3	Miscellaneous: Prefabricated buildings (811-2); travel goods (83); and apparel & accessories (84)

Sources: USCMP (n.d.), ICCP (n.d.) and the ESA-USPTO Report (2012).
Notes: Low-IP products contained in low-IP clusters.

countries see very similar increases in both exports and imports.[15] This confirms the results in our earlier paper: broadly speaking, IP is associated with increased trade in products that are IP-intensive.

Next, we focus on four clusters of high-IP products. Trade in biopharmaceuticals is especially sensitive to TRIPS compliance, which is perhaps not surprising given the importance of patent protection for this sector. As before, we see substantial increases for exports and imports, including imports from the most innovative countries. This suggests greater access as well as greater production for the export market in developing countries. Chemicals show a similar pattern. In contrast, although exports of medical devices have increased, the difference with the control group is

[15] The magnitude of the effect of TRIPS implementation on trade of high-IP products is meaningful. Based on the estimated coefficients reported in Table 14.4, we expect the change in the dollar value of country exports of high-IP products to be 2.5 times higher following TRIPS compliance than the change in exports of the control group. The dollar value of imports of high-IP products from the high innovative countries increases about 1.4 times more than imports of the control group in developing countries. We find similar magnitude of the post-TRIPS effects when we compute simple means of annual exports/imports across countries before and after TRIPS for high-IP products versus the control group. On average, countries increase trade in both groups of products after TRIPS, but the increase in the mean of exports of the high-IP products is about three times higher than that of the control group. And the increase in the mean of imports from the most innovative countries into developing countries is about 1.1 times higher for high-IP products than the control group.

Table 14.3 *Descriptive statistics*

	All countries N=3,577		High-inc. countries N=1,074		Developing countries N=1,838	
	Mean	**Std. dev.**	**Mean**	**Std. dev.**	**Mean**	**Std. dev.**
Multilateral trade: Exports$_{it}$ to or Imports$_{it}$ from world by country *i* in year *t* (USD 2016), 1993–2016						
Ln High-IP exports$_{it}$	20.803	3.233	23.522	2.437	20.376	2.777
Ln Bio exports$_{it}$	16.702	4.336	20.224	3.282	16.093	3.714
Ln Medical Devices exports$_{it}$	15.510	4.332	18.863	3.280	14.981	3.876
Ln Chemicals exports$_{it}$	18.505	3.504	21.246	2.516	18.069	3.174
Ln ICT exports$_{it}$	18.260	3.687	21.465	2.892	17.641	3.174
Ln Control exports$_{it}$	22.010	2.389	23.531	1.833	21.822	2.359
Ln High-IP imports$_{it}$	22.061	2.358	23.935	1.946	21.740	2.074
Ln Bio imports$_{it}$	19.158	2.725	21.040	2.247	18.751	2.459
Ln Medical Devices imports$_{it}$	17.763	2.685	19.878	2.203	17.341	2.368
Ln Chemicals imports$_{it}$	19.877	2.346	21.593	1.905	19.674	2.106
Ln ICT imports$_{it}$	20.218	2.649	22.372	2.184	19.832	2.324
Ln Control imports$_{it}$	21.889	2.169	23.485	1.876	21.597	1.930
Imports from high-income innovative countries into developing country *i* in year *t* (USD 2016), 1993–2016						
Ln High-IP imports$_{it}$					21.105	2.177
Ln Bio imports$_{it}$					18.115	2.688
Ln Medical Devices imports$_{it}$					16.885	2.495
Ln Chemicals imports$_{it}$					18.853	2.330
Ln ICT imports$_{it}$					19.223	2.306
Ln Control imports$_{it}$					20.321	2.071
Strength of IPR protection variables						
Post-TRIPS$_{it}$	0.564	0.496	0.826	0.379	0.615	0.487
Post-TRIPS Years$_{it}$	4.808	5.935	7.938	6.540	4.718	5.431
Ln GDP$_{it}$ (bill USD 2016)	3.440	2.327	5.121	2.032	3.096	2.182

Notes: Trade data are sourced from the UN Comtrade database. Real GDP data are sourced from IMF. IPR protection variables are computed by the authors based on multiple sources.

Table 14.4 *Post-TRIPS estimated effect on trade of high-IP sectors, 1993–2016*

Post-TRIPS effect: High-IP sector vs control (difference in estimated coefficients)						
	Exports to world		**Imports from world**		**Imports from high-income innovative countries**	
High-IP sector	All countries	DC	All countries	DC	DC	DC-low (lower-middle/low)
	1	2	3	4	5	6
High-IP	0.915**	0.896*	0.130*	0.191**	0.340*	0.415*
Biopharma	1.632**	1.490**	0.628**	0.645*	0.971**	1.420**
Medical Devices	0.871	0.656	0.286**	0.331**	0.604*	0.791*
Chemicals	1.041**	1.206**	0.174**	0.245**	0.370**	0.421**
ICT	0.878*	0.786	0.233**	0.333**	0.482**	0.565*

Notes: Y= Ln(country-year real dollar value of world export/import in sectors) in Columns 1 to 4; and Y=Ln(country-year real dollar value of sector imports from High-inc. innovative countries) in Columns 5 and 6. The table reports the difference in the estimated coefficients of *High-IP Sector*Post-TRIPS vs Control*Post-TRIPS* on Y. Columns 1 and 3 report the estimated Post-TRIPS effect on world exports/imports across all countries ever compliant. In Columns 2, 4 and 5 the reported *Post-TRIPS* effect is for developing countries (i.e. the difference between *DC*High-IP Sector*Post-TRIPS* and *DC*Control*Post-TRIPS*); and in Column 6 for the subset of developing countries with lower-middle and low-income. (i.e. the difference between *DC-Low*High-IP Sector*Post-TRIPS* and *DC-Low*Control*Post-TRIPS*).

To estimate the *Post-TRIPS* effects all the specifications include intercept, Ln GDP (interacted by sector), and income group-sector-year fixed effects. Specifically, Columns 1–4 estimate Equation (1), Column 5 estimates Equation (2) and Column (6) estimates Equation (3) in section IV of Delgado, Kyle and McGahan (2013).

** Significant at the 1 per cent level, *significant at the 5 per cent level.

not statistically significant. However, imports of medical devices did go up. Finally, trade in information and communication technologies (ICT) also generally increased following TRIPS compliance. While the increase in exports by developing countries is not statistically different from the increase in exports of the control group, imports did grow by more, and in particular from the most innovative countries to developing markets.

While our high-IP sector definitions differ slightly from those used in our earlier work, we find stronger evidence of increased IP-associated trade in these sectors compared to our results using data through 2009. This suggests that the impact of TRIPS implementation may have been gradual, and is more apparent over time.

Discussion and Conclusion

We find that adoption of the TRIPS Agreement is associated with increased trade in IP-intensive products. Both developing countries and high-income countries realized these increases, so the gains do not appear to be highly unequal. While we see some differences between patterns of exports and imports, it appears that overall, developing countries have seen greater access to innovation exported from the most innovative countries, and these countries have also participated in the global market for innovative products through their own exports.

Although the strength and breadth of IP protection is more nuanced in practice than our relatively crude test based on TRIPS compliance, we nevertheless find that such compliance is empirically meaningful. The relationship we show is not the effect of WTO membership on trade, which is reflected in our control group. Rather, we demonstrate an additional boost to trade in the most innovative products associated with the TRIPS commitment – even though many countries were previously signatories to the WIPO Paris and Berne Conventions or had some IP protection prior to full TRIPS compliance. It is also possible that the enforcement and dispute resolution requirements of TRIPS enhanced the impact of IP legislation. It is also worth noting that the TRIPS exceptions granted to developing countries do not seem to have substantially undermined the gains they realized from implementing stronger IP protection. This suggests some scope for policy flexibility.

An important caveat to our findings is that we focus on the value of trade, which reflects both price and quantity of products traded. This is especially problematic when discussing IP, which by design permits IP owners to exploit market power. Consider two (admittedly extreme) examples. Prior to TRIPS, a country did not grant product patents on pharmaceuticals and generic firms produced drugs for the domestic market. Following TRIPS compliance, a foreign firm applies for a patent, which blocks domestic production of a new pharmaceutical, and the country now imports this drug instead. Similarly, a country may import the same number of smartphones following TRIPS compliance as in the preceding period, but the newer versions of those same smartphones may now have higher prices due to patent protection. In both cases, our data record an increase in trade of high-IP products post-TRIPS, but access to innovation has not changed. We leave better measures of access to innovative products as an essential area of future research.

Bibliography

Bernard, A. B. and Bradford Jensen, J., 'Exceptional Exporter Performance: Cause, Effect, or Both?' (1999), *Journal of International Economics* 4, 1: 1–25.

Bloom, N., Draca, M. and Van Reenen, J., 'Trade Induced Technical Change? The Impact of Chinese Imports on innovation, IT and Productivity' (2016), *Review of Economic Studies* 83, 1: 87–117.

Branstetter, L., 'Are Knowledge Spillovers International or Intranational in Scope?: Microeconometric Evidence from the U.S. and Japan' (2001), *Journal of International Economics* 53, 1: 53–79.

Branstetter, L., 'Is Foreign Direct Investment a Channel of Knowledge Spillovers? Evidence from Japan's FDI in the United States' (2006), *Journal of International Economics* 68, 2: 325–344.

Branstetter, L., Fisman, R. and Foley, F., 'Do Stronger Intellectual Property Rights Increase International Technology Transfer? Empirical Evidence from U.S. Firm-Level Data' (2006), *Quarterly Journal of Economics* 121, 1: 321–349.

Bretschger, L., 'International Trade, Knowledge Diffusion and Growth' (1997), *The International Trade Journal* 11, 3: 27–348.

Co, C. Y., 'Do Patent Rights Regimes Matter?' (2004), *Review of International Economics* 12: 359–373.

Correa, C., 'Intellectual Property: How Much Room is Left for Industrial Policy?,' UNCTAD Discussion Paper No. 223, 2015.

Deardorff, A., 'Welfare Effects of Global Patent Protection' (1992), *Economica* 59: 35–51.

Delgado, M., Kyle, M. and McGahan A., 'Intellectual Property Protection and the Geography of Trade' (2013), *Journal of Industrial Economics* 61, 3: 733–762.

Delgado, M., Porter, M. E. and Stern, S., 'Defining Clusters of Related Industries' (2016), *Journal of Economic Geography* 16, 1: 1–38.

Eaton, J. and Kortum, S., 'Trade in Ideas: Patenting and Productivity in the OECD' (1996), *Journal of International Economics* 40, 3–4: 251–278.

Eaton, J. and Kortum S., 'Technology, Geography and Trade' (2002), *Econometrica* 70, 5: 1741–1770.

Eaton, J., Kortum, S. and Kramarz, F., 'Dissecting Trade: Firms, Industries, and Export Destinations' (2004), *American Economic Review* 94, 2: 150–154.

Feenstra, R. C., Lipsey, R. E., Deng, Haiyen, Ma, Alyson C. and Mo, Hengyong, 'World Trade Flows: 1962–2000' (January), NBER Working Paper No. 11040 (2005), available at www.nber.org/papers/w11040.

Fink, C. and Primo Braga, C. A., 'How Stronger Protection of Intellectual Property Rights Affects International Trade Flows', The World Bank Working Paper No. 2051, Washington, DC: World Bank (1999).

Furman, J. L., Stern, S. and Porter, M. E., 'The Determinants of National Innovative Capacity' (2002), *Research Policy* 31, 6: 899–933.

Gans, J. and Stern, S., 'Is There a Market for Ideas?' (2010), *Industrial and Corporate Change* 19, 3: 805–837.

Ginarte, J. and Park, W., 'Determinants of Patent Rights: A Cross-National Study' (1997), *Research Policy* 26, 3: 283–301.

Grossman, G. M. and Helpman, E., 'Trade, Knowledge Spillovers and Growth' (1991), *European Economic Review* (Papers and Proceedings), 35, 3: 517–526.

Grossman, G. M. and Helpman, E., 'Technology and Trade', in G. Grossman and K. Rogoff (eds), *Handbook of International Economics*, Vol. III, Amsterdam: North Holland, 1995.

Hallward-Driemeier, M., Iarossi, G. and Sokoloff, K. L., 'Exports and Manufacturing Productivity in East Asia: A Comparative Analysis', NBER Working Papers 8894, National Bureau of Economic Research, Inc., 2002.

Hamdan-Livramento, I. M., 'How Compliant are Developing Countries with Their TRIPS Obligations?', CEMI Working Paper 2009-001, 2009.

International Cluster Competitiveness Project (ICCP) of the Institute for Strategy and Competitiveness (n.d.), Harvard Business School.

Ivus, O., 'Do Stronger Patent Rights Raise High-Tech Exports to the Developing World?' (2010), *Journal of International Economics* 81, 1: 38–47.

Keller, W., 'Are International R&D Spillovers Trade-related? Analyzing Spillovers among Randomly Matched Trade Partners' (1998), *European Economic Review* 42, 8: 1469–1481.

Keller, W., 'Trade and the Transmission of Technology' (2002a), *Journal of Economic Growth* 7: 5–24.

Keller, W., 'Geographic Localization of International Technology Diffusion' (2002b), *American Economic Review* 92: 120–142.

Kyle, Margaret, Ridley, David and Zhang, Su, 'Strategic Interaction among Governments in the Provision of a Global Public Good' (2017), *Journal of Public Economics*, 156. 10.1016/j.jpubeco.2017.10.009.

Maskus, K. E. and Penubarti, M., 'How Trade-Related Are Intellectual Property Rights?' (1995), *Journal of International Economics* 39: 227–248.

McCalman, P., 'Reaping What you Sow: An Empirical Analysis of International Patent Harmonization' (2001), *Journal of International Economics* 55: 161–186.

McCalman, P., 'Who Enjoys TRIPs Abroad: An Empirical Analysis of Intellectual Property Rights in the Uruguay Round' (2005), *Canadian Journal of Economics* 38: 574–603.

MacGarvie, M., 'Do Firms Learn from International Trade?' (2006), *Review of Economics and Statistics* 88, 1: 46–60.

Padoan, P. C., 'Trade, Knowledge Accumulation and Diffusion: A Sectoral Perspective' (1998), *Structural Change and Economic Dynamics* 9, 3: 349–372.

Park, W. G., 'International Patent Protection: 1960–2005' (2008), *Research Policy* 37: 761–766.

Park, A., Yang, D., Shi, X. and Jiang, Y., 'Exporting and Firm Performance: Chinese Exporters and the Asian Financial Crisis' (2010), *Review of Economics and Statistics* 92, 4: 822–842.

Rafiquzzaman, M., 'Impact of Patent Rights on International Trade: Evidence from Canada' (2002), *Canadian Journal of Economics* 35: 307–330.

Rose, A., 'Do We Really Know that the WTO Increases Trade?' (2004), *American Economic Review* 94, 1: 98–114.

Rose, A., 'The Effect of Membership in the GATT/WTO on Trade: Where Do We Stand?', in Z. Drabek (ed.), *Is the World Trade Organization Attractive Enough for Emerging Economies?*, London: Palgrave Macmillan, 2010.

Saggi, K., 'Trade, Foreign Direct Investment, and International Technology Transfer: A Survey' (2002), *World Bank Research Observer* 17, 2: 191–235.

Smith, P. J., 'Are Weak Patent Rights a Barrier to US Exports?' (1999), *Journal of International Economics* 48: 151–177.

t'Hoen, E., 'Practical Applications of the Flexibilities of the Agreement on Trade-Related Aspects of Intellectual Property Rights', Doctoral Dissertation, University of Groningen, The Netherlands, 2018.

Taylor, M. S., 'TRIPS, Trade and Technology Transfer' (1993), *International Economic Review* 26, 3: 625–637.

Taylor, M. S., 'TRIPS, Trade and Growth' (1994), *International Economic Review* 35, 2: 361–381.

US Cluster Mapping (n.d.), Institute for Strategy and Competitiveness, Harvard Business School, available at http://clustermapping.us.

US Department of Commerce, *Intellectual Property and the U.S. Economy: Industries in Focus* (2012), available at www.uspto.gov/sites/default/files/news/publications/IP_Report_March_2012.pdf.

Weissman, R., 'A Long, Strange TRIPS: The Pharmaceutical Industry Drive to Harmonize Global Intellectual Property Rules, and the Remaining WTO Legal Alternatives Available to Third World Countries' (1996), *University of Pennsylvania Law Review* 17, 4: 1069–1125.

A14.1

Table A14.1 *Classification criteria for a country's TRIPS compliance*

1. WTO member countries in 1995 not self-designated as developing:
The estimated compliance year is 1995 for most countries; and 1996 for Portugal, Iceland, Slovakia and the Czech Republic (based on Ginarte and Park (1997) and Park (2008)).

2. WTO member countries *after* 1995:
Their estimated compliance year is their membership date, in accordance with WTO rules.

3. WTO member countries in 1995 that self-designated as developing:
The estimated year of compliance is 2000. There are some exceptions since TRIPS granted extensions for countries that did not provide product patent protection in a particular area of technology as of 2000 (see above discussion in 'The Link between IP and Trade'). We draw on Park (2008) and Hamdan-Livramento (2009) to identify countries that may be using these exceptions or are not compliant by their deadlines. Based on Hamdan-Livramento (2009), 11 countries achieved TRIPS compliance after 2000 (Brazil, Kenya and Uruguay are compliant in 2001; Mauritius in 2002; Ghana and Sri Lanka in 2003; Chile, India, Pakistan and Paraguay in 2005; and Egypt in 2006). Using Park (2008), we identify three additional countries that did not have TRIPS compliance by 2005 (Nigeria, Papua New Guinea and Tunisia). Based on Trade Policy Reviews conducted by the WTO, we concluded that Nigeria has yet to comply, while Papua New Guinea and Tunisia had complied by 2010.

4. LDC countries:
They are classified as non-compliant for the entire period of analysis. Initially, LDC countries were required to comply by 2006. This deadline was extended to 2016 for biopharmaceutical products and 2013 for all others after the Doha Declarations. In 2013 and 2015, further extensions – to 1 July 2021 and 1 January 2033 for pharmaceuticals – were negotiated. Park (2008) and

Table A14.1 (*cont.*)

Hamdan-Livramento (2009) confirm that most of these countries either do not have patent laws or that their systems for patent enforcement are not in compliance with TRIPS.

Notes: The main criteria are the WTO transition periods for compliance. Countries self-designated as 'developing' are listed in Table 14.1. Ginarte and Park's (1997) Index of Patent Rights measures the strength of IP protection and enforcement in 121 countries at five-year intervals updated through 2005 (Park, 2008). We use two components of the index: the strength of enforcement of patent protection and the patent-coverage. Hamdan-Livramento (2009) investigates the TRIPS implementation of 53 countries based on various types of IP protection, and reports estimates of the date of compliance.

15

Knowledge Spillovers through International Supply Chains

ROBERTA PIERMARTINI AND STELA RUBÍNOVÁ

Abstract

Patents and scientific publications are a public source of codified knowledge. To benefit from this knowledge in their research and development, firms often need to have access also to its non-codifiable part that diffuses only via face-to-face communication and direct transfer. This chapter shows that international supply chains can facilitate access to foreign non-codified knowledge and thus provide a boost to innovation through international knowledge spillovers. Using industry-level R&D and patent data for a sample of 29 countries for the period 2000–2008, we estimate the importance of knowledge that is diffused and absorbed thanks to international production linkages. We show that production linkages are especially conducive to knowledge spillovers when firms in the knowledge-receiving country are both sourcing from and selling to the international supply chain. In addition, we find that not only countries at the technology frontier, but also middle-income countries can benefit from research spending abroad. Finally, our results suggest that knowledge diffusion has become less localized as international supply chains have become more global.

Introduction

International supply chains can be a powerful channel for technology transfer. One reason is that they intensify contacts between foreign firms and domestic suppliers. When a foreign firm and a local supplier are part of the same production chain they need to interact and coordinate to guarantee a smooth functioning of the chain. This face-to-face communication will facilitate the transfer of non-codified knowledge.[1] A recent

[1] The literature on knowledge transfer has explained that while the codified part of innovation (contained for example in a patent or in a publication) is likely to be available to any scientist, there is a part of knowledge that is tacit and diffuses only via personal contact.

study by Hovhannisyan and Keller (2015) finds that a 10 per cent increase in business travel increases patenting in the destination country by about 0.2 per cent. Another argument is that foreign outsourcing firms are more willing to transfer the know-how and technology required for an efficient production of the outsourced input, because they will eventually consume that input and they need to assure compatibility with their own production process. As Baldwin and Lopez-Gonzalez (2013) state 'When Toyota makes car parts in Thailand, they do not rely on local know-how; they bring Toyota technology, Toyota management, Toyota logistics and any other bits of know-how needed since the Thai-made parts have to fit seamlessly into the company's production network.' Both these arguments suggest that trade resulting from international supply chains has a higher potential for facilitating technology transfer than other types of trade.

Understanding the determinants of knowledge spillovers[2] is important because the diffusion of knowledge across countries may be a powerful engine of growth and is a crucial factor in explaining global income distribution. Countries have different levels of productivity not only because they differ in terms of their own investment in research and development (R&D), but also because of their differences in the extent to which they benefit from research done abroad. If supply chains facilitate the diffusion and absorption of knowledge and know-how, then adopting policies that foster participation in supply chains, such as attracting vertical foreign direct investment (FDI) or establishing supplier development programmes, may be justifiable.

Previous studies have pointed out that trade in intermediate inputs may generate knowledge spillovers, by showing that a country's total factor productivity (TFP) increasingly benefits from research done abroad, the more that country imports intermediate goods.[3] However, if a country imports high-tech inputs, TFP may increase because these

[2] Not all knowledge transfer, including a transfer through supply chains, represents knowledge spillovers in the traditional economic sense. A supplying firm may need to invest into upgrading its production technology to meet the request of its customer. The existence of a demand for a higher-quality product provides an incentive for this investment, but it is linked to the supplier's ability to invest in technology upgrading. Spillovers are the part of technology upgrading for which the firm does not pay (or pays a lower cost than the initial cost of the technology).

[3] The pioneering work of Keller (2002a) finds that foreign R&D accounts for around 20 per cent of the total effect of R&D investment on productivity in eight OECD countries. Using international input-output data for 32 countries at the industry-level, Nishioka and Ripoll (2012) find significant spillovers from R&D-intensive industries from G5 countries.

inputs have higher price-adjusted quality and/or because they enhance the productivity of other factors of production.[4] In these cases, TFP increases do not necessarily imply that the importing country has acquired the knowledge embodied in the imported intermediates.[5]

In this chapter, we try to capture the actual knowledge flows between countries through international supply chains, by focusing on innovation instead of total factor productivity. We show that a country's capacity to innovate increasingly benefits from research done abroad as supply chain linkages strengthen. In doing so, we provide a lower-bound estimate of the potential benefits from participation in international supply chains, but we measure the actual transfer of knowledge that stays in the country even when the supply chain link is cut.

The rest of the chapter is organized as follows: the second section discusses the analytical framework. The third section describes the data and our empirical approach. The fourth section shows some stylized facts. The fifth section discusses our results. The final section concludes.

How does Knowledge Created Abroad Cross International Borders?

To analyse how R&D activity in one country influences innovative output of another country, we rely on a standard assumption. That is, innovation depends not only on private and excludable inputs such as R&D investment, but also on the public stock of knowledge generated in the past and by the R&D investment undertaken anywhere around the world (Romer, 1990; Grossman and Helpman, 1991a, 1991b; Eaton and Kortum, 1999). Once an idea is discovered it may become a public good and, as such, it inspires and drives new inventions. In this framework, research performed abroad that generates new profitable inventions also enhances productivity of research performed at home, thus generating international positive externality – knowledge spillovers. It is often assumed that although a country can draw upon both a domestic and

[4] Firm-level studies for Chile and Hungary (Kasahara and Rodrigue, 2008; and Halpern et al., 2015) document that using foreign intermediate inputs increases plant productivity.

[5] When a firm outsources a specific task, for example sewing a car seat, it may just lend the technology of that particular task. Therefore, the host country loses the technology when the car manufacture leaves. This type of technology flow – that Baldwin (2012) describes as 'technology lending' rather than technology spillovers – also provides countries with an opportunity for rapid industrial development, but this growth may stop if the offshoring company moves to another country.

foreign stock of knowledge, the latter is less accessible. Eaton and Kortum (1999) find that research performed abroad is about two-thirds as powerful in generating innovation as domestic research. This means that each dollar spent abroad in research has approximately the same effect on domestic innovation as USD 0.75 spent at home.

There are several reasons why foreign knowledge may be more difficult to draw upon than its domestic counterpart. As Keller (2004) summarizes in his review of the literature on technology diffusion, even if knowledge is non-rival and codified for public use, some knowledge is only partially codifiable. The non-codified part of knowledge can be nevertheless essential for follow-up innovations. This type of knowledge is often transferred through face-to-face communication and therefore the degree of such interactions between researchers will be a crucial determinant of knowledge spillovers. It is, in general, assumed that interactions between researchers located in different countries are more difficult, and so is the transmission of non-codified knowledge.

Our hypothesis is that the accessibility of foreign knowledge depends on supply chain linkages between countries. International production-sharing involves a high degree of interdependency between producers from different countries, as the production of a good in one country depends on a timely delivery of inputs from a factory abroad and these inputs need to be perfectly compatible with the domestic production line. Consequently, high-skilled personnel often flow within multinational firms across borders to assure technological as well as managerial cohesion across production units in different countries. For instance, as pointed out in Pisano and Shih (2012), a new design can only be properly manufactured if the designer and the manufacturer interact, while new ideas for innovative design can only be generated if the designer understands the manufacturing process. Therefore, we expect that countries whose production processes are more interdependent interact more, and that this in turn facilitates the transfer of knowledge.

Estimating International Knowledge Spillovers: Empirical Methodology

Translating the theoretical framework into an empirical model, we test whether domestic innovations (that we measure as *the number of patent applications* of a certain country) depend not only on the stock of *domestic R&D* expenditure but also on the *foreign R&D pool* accessible to domestic researchers. To test our assumption that the accessibility of foreign R&D expenditure depends on supply chain linkages between a foreign knowledge source country and the home country, we measure foreign R&D pool as a weighted average of R&D investments of foreign countries, where the weights are indexes of supply chain linkages between the foreign and the domestic country. If our assumption is correct, we expect to find that the variable *foreign R&D pool* has a positive and significant effect on innovation.

We construct four measures of international supply chain linkages that capture different degrees of supply chain integration. All of them measure the use of foreign intermediates' inputs into production in the home country, but for progressively narrower purposes – the use in overall domestic production, the production for exports, the production for exports to the source country and the production of intermediate inputs for exports to the source country. While the first two measures capture a one-way flow from a foreign country to the home country, the other two measures focus on reciprocal relationships where goods cross the same frontier at least twice – first as an input, then embodied in exported goods.

We estimate the empirical model accounting for country-specific determinants of innovation (such as the size of the home market which influences the profitability of patenting an innovation, the level of economic development, human capital and the institutional environment) and industry-specific determinants (such as the differences between the propensities to patent innovation across industries or the differences in the importance of incremental innovation).

Our baseline analysis is run on a cross-section of averages over the period 2000–2008 for 29 countries and 8 broad manufacturing industries. This is the largest possible sample for which data for all our variables are available and has the advantage of covering a sufficiently recent time period. This allows us to capture the latest structural changes that took place in the world, with the emergence of new global players such as China. The sample covers the three main production networks in the world, namely Factory Asia, Factory North-America and Factory Central-Eastern Europe.[6] The sample covers 13 industries which account for more than 90 per cent of business R&D spending in manufacturing.[7]

[6] In our sample, Factory Asia is represented by China, Chinese Taipei, Japan and the Republic of Korea; Factory North-America by Canada, Mexico and the United States; and Factory Central-Eastern Europe by Austria, Germany, Czech Republic, Hungary, Poland, Romania, Slovak Republic, and Slovenia.

[7] OECD average in 2008.

Global R&D Expenditures and Innovation

Table 15.1 reports the share of total R&D expenditures (domestic and foreign) and patent applications by industry based on our data sample. Electronics account for the largest share of R&D expenditures as well as the largest share of patent applications. Transport equipment and chemicals also account for a large share of R&D expenditures.[8]

Table 15.2 reports the share of total R&D expenditures and patent applications by country. R&D expenditures are very concentrated. The United States, Japan and Germany account for 67 per cent of total R&D expenditures in our sample, and, together with China, France, the Republic of Korea and the United Kingdom, they add up to almost 90 per cent. Patent applications are similarly concentrated in those countries. The last column shows the relative importance of the foreign R&D pool to home R&D spending. The foreign R&D pool matters relatively more in countries that are highly integrated in international supply chains, both in large rich countries such as Germany, France or Belgium and in smaller or poorer economies such as Czech Republic or Chinese Taipei.

Table 15.1 *Summary of main variables by industry, average over the period 2000–2008*

Industry	R&D expenditures % of total	Patent applications % of total	Foreign R&D pool % of own R&D
Petroleum products	0.92	10.61	9.57
Chemicals	21.35	25.12	137.93
Rubber and plastics	2.11	2.66	18.39
Metal products	4.08	6.77	140.85
Other mineral products	1.14	4.31	8.34
Electrical machinery	38.31	32.70	207.86
Transport equipment	23.26	5.53	203.82
Other machinery	8.82	12.31	69.32

Source: Authors' calculations.

[8] Full industry definitions are in A15.1, Table A15.3.

Table 15.2 *Summary of main variables by economy, average over the period 2000–2008*

Economy	R&D expenditures % of total	Patent applications % of total	Foreign R&D pool % of own R&D
Australia	0.53	1.24	29.27
Austria	0.77	0.93	105.44
Belgium	0.73	1.00	170.66
Canada	1.59	2.01	119.39
Czech Republic	0.28	0.12	107.79
Estonia	0.01	0.02	12.08
Finland	0.18	1.02	85.63
France	5.04	5.05	169.94
Germany	10.15	14.53	251.40
Greece	0.05	0.07	15.40
Hungary	0.13	0.16	109.51
China	7.65	2.28	100.24
Chinese Taipei	2.04	0.13	121.39
Ireland	0.18	0.33	102.87
Italy	1.58	2.16	123.92
Japan	20.22	19.88	88.98
Republic of Korea	4.81	3.46	100.13
Mexico	0.26	0.14	99.04
Netherlands	1.00	3.48	144.19
Poland	0.14	0.10	89.88
Portugal	0.07	0.06	99.66
Romania	0.06	0.03	39.97
Russia	0.69	0.58	15.71
Slovak Republic	0.03	0.03	99.15
Slovenia	0.09	0.09	57.85
Spain	0.97	0.88	111.12
Turkey	0.26	0.19	57.77
UK	4.00	4.68	168.97
USA	36.51	35.34	145.12

Source: Authors' calculations.

Quantifying Knowledge Spillovers through International Supply Chains: Our Results

Our results confirm our predictions. We find a positive and statistically significant effect of foreign R&D on domestic innovation through international supply chain linkages.[9] The economic significance can be gauged by comparing this effect to that of domestic R&D spending. The R&D expenditure of a supply chain partner can be up to 3.3 per cent as powerful in boosting innovation as domestic R&D spending. This is the case for the strongest production linkages which are, for example, links between the United States and Canada in transport equipment, the United States and Mexico in transport equipment and electrical machinery, or China and Chinese Taipei in electrical machinery[10]. Put differently, our estimate suggests that if the United States doubles its R&D in transport equipment, the number of patents in that industry in Canada increases by 0.4 per cent. Overall, our estimates suggest that if all supply chain partners double their R&D expenditures, the number of patent applications in the average country would increase by 18 per cent. Note that this is an estimate of a pure positive externality effect. It is the extent to which a country can benefit from R&D investment done abroad through the non-rival output (knowledge) this investment generates. Our estimated impact is therefore economically sizeable.

Moreover, we find much larger estimates when we focus only on knowledge spillovers from the United States, Japan and Germany. We showed that these countries account by far for the largest share of innovation and R&D expenditures in our sample. They are also the main headquarter economies in the three supply chain clusters covered by our data. Hence, we expect that having strong supply chain linkages with these innovation hubs is especially important for knowledge spillovers. The estimates show indeed a stronger relationship – for countries with the strongest supply chain linkages with the innovation hubs, R&D expenditures by the innovation hubs can be up to 13 per cent as powerful as domestic R&D spending in boosting innovation[11]. In addition, we find that not only countries at the technology frontier, but also middle-income countries, can benefit from research spending by the innovation hubs. In fact, the effect is stronger for countries in the lower half of the income distribution. In other words, supply chain integration with Germany is more important for Hungary than for Austria and supply chain integration with the United States is more important for Mexico than for Canada.

[9] See A15.1, Table A15.3 for the regressions results.

[10] See A15.1, Table A15.2 for the list of 10 most connected country-industries by the type of supply chain linkages.

[11] See A15.1, Table A15.4 for the regression results.

Finally, we find that linkages that involve inputs crossing the same border back and forth are the most important channels of pure knowledge spillovers. This is the case in which firms in the home country import an intermediate input from the foreign country, process it and re-export the processed good back to the foreign country. This finding has a simple theoretical explanation. That is, when an intermediate input is specifically designed to match the needs of a single final good producer (as is likely to be the case if a component is imported from and re-exported to the same country), the final good producer may 'hold-up' the supplier.[12] One way to reduce the risk of the hold-up problem is for the final good producer to reduce the cost of investment required for the customization of the input to its own need and monitor production. This includes providing the technology required for the customization (which will reduce the cost of investment) and increasing face-to-face interaction to ensure the adequate investment in technology learning by the local supplier.[13] Both options imply larger knowledge spillovers.

Knowledge Spillovers Decay with Distance, but Less So when Supply Chains Linkages are Strong

One established finding of the empirical literature is that knowledge spillovers are not global but local. In other words, global knowledge is not a public good from which anyone can source; rather, the extent to which a country benefits, in terms of productivity growth, from the knowledge created abroad falls with its distance from the knowledge-originating country.[14]

[12] This is because after the investment, the good has little market value outside the contractual relationship. Therefore, the input supplier has little bargaining power and the producer of the final good can breach the contract. Anticipating this possibility, the input supplier will under-invest, and thus outsourcing would be inefficient.

[13] Tirole (1998).

[14] Keller (2002b), estimates that, at a distance of 162km between the sender and the receiver, 50 per cent of foreign knowledge gets to the receiver, while at 2,000km only 5 per cent of knowledge is absorbed. Using the number of patents as a measure of innovation, Bottazzi and Peri (2003) find that spillovers are localized and exist only within a distance of 500km. In their exponential specification, they find that doubling R&D spending in a region would increase the output of new ideas in other regions at 200km by 0.8 per cent. An earlier study by Jaffe et al. (1993), that uses patent citations as a measure of technological spillovers, also emphasizes that knowledge spillovers are local. They find that US patents are more often cited in other US patents than in patents of other countries.

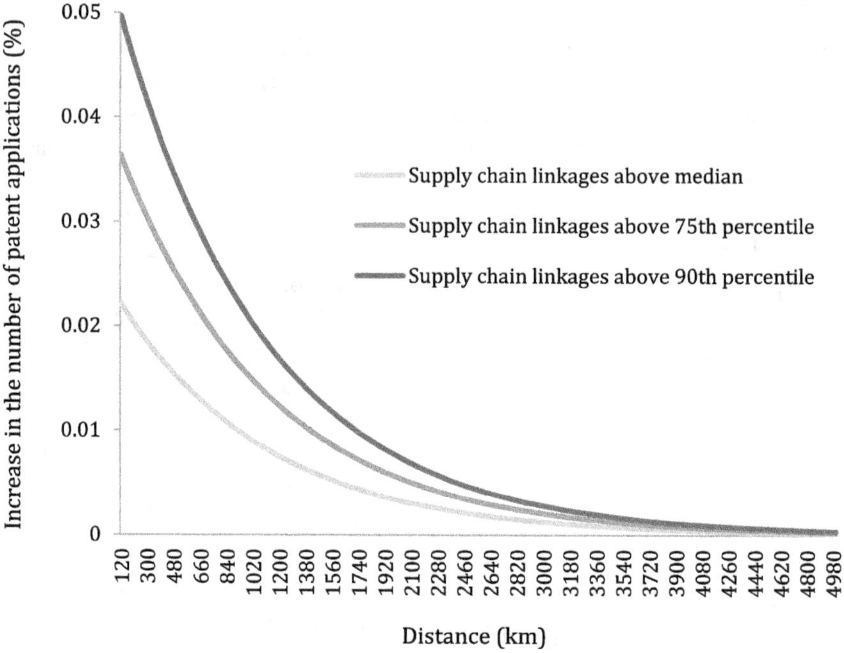

Figure 15.1 R&D spillovers by distance and the intensity of supply chain linkages, the effect of a 10 per cent increase in foreign R&D spending
Source: Authors' calculations.

To test whether our results are confounded by other factors driven by geographical distance, we calculate a distance-weighted foreign R&D pool[15] and add it in our regression beyond our supply chain-weighted foreign R&D pool. We find that our variable, the supply chain-weighted foreign R&D pool, is the most robust determinant knowledge spillover.[16]

Finally, in Figure 15.1, we show our estimates of the relationship between knowledge spillovers and distance. As is well known, knowledge spillovers decay with distance. However, in addition we show that

[15] Following the existing literature (Keller, 2004 and Bottazzi and Peri, 2003), we calculate this alternative measure using the distance between largest cities in thousands of kilometres based on data from CEPII.

[16] In line with previous literature we find a positive and significant coefficient for the distance-weighted pool within the EU. Using only this subsample, both R&D pools become statistically insignificant when we include them together in one regression. The imprecision might be driven by multicollinearity because the two pools are highly correlated within the EU sample. See A15.1, Table A15.5 in the Appendix for the regression results.

knowledge spillovers are less localized when supply chain linkages are strong. For example, the average effect of doubling R&D spending in countries at 200km distance and with supply chain linkages above the median is an increase in the number of patents by 0.24 per cent. When the R&D spending is done in a country with supply chain linkages above the 90th percentile, the increase doubles to 0.5 per cent. These effects are sizable and higher than those estimated by previous literature. Since supply chains have become more extensive in recent decades, this result shows that they may also be an explanation for the evidence that knowledge spillovers have become less localized over time.

Conclusion

Our paper investigates how international production networks affect the diffusion of knowledge in a sample of 29 economies. We focus on a very narrow definition of knowledge diffusion: we assume that there is international knowledge diffusion when knowledge created abroad affects domestic innovation. Despite this narrow definition, we find evidence that production networks are an important driver of knowledge transfers. In particular, we find evidence that knowledge spillovers occur especially between countries with strong supply chain linkages. We do not find evidence of pure knowledge spillovers through the mere imports of inputs. We estimate that the spillovers from doubling R&D expenditures by all supply chain partners increase the number of patent applications in a country by 18 per cent (given our narrow definition of knowledge spillovers, this number is impressively large). We find that supply chain connections with the main innovators – the United States, Japan and Germany – are especially important for knowledge spillovers.

Our findings have important implications. First, the rapid development of complex international supply chains among high-income countries can explain why knowledge spillovers have become less localized between the periods 1973–1983 and 1986–1995.[17]

Second, our finding can also help to explain the emergence of economies such as China, Singapore and the Republic of Korea as major

[17] Keller (2002b) estimates that knowledge flows at a distance of 2,000 km between senders and receivers increased from 5 per cent to 50 per cent between the periods 1973–1983 and 1986–1995. It may not be a coincidence that precisely the period between 1985 and 1995 witnessed the fastest growth of supply chains – a period that Baldwin (2012) identifies as the 'second unbundling'.

contributors to the pool of technological innovations since 1985. While previously some of these economies had served as a production platform for developed economies (without a deeper involvement in the production chain), the emergence of the 'factory Asia' and the strong development of production networks in the region have increased their capacity to innovate. Our findings show that production networks have not just provided a stronger incentive to innovate, thus increasing the amount of resources spent in R&D (which we control for), but that they have also increased the flow of foreign R&D absorbed by these economies.

In general, the scope of knowledge spillovers is crucial to determine income distribution among countries. Economic literature has so far stressed that while global spillovers foster convergence at the level of cities, regions or even countries, local spillovers can lead to convergence clusters and thus permanently different levels of income between groups of countries. Our finding suggests that convergence across countries is likely to occur along the production chain lines. This is clearly an interesting avenue for further research. There are also important policy implications. If spillovers of knowledge occur through certain types of supply chain participation, there is an economic rationale for governments to intervene to foster these connections.

Bibliography

Baldwin, R., 'Trade and Industrialisation after Globalisation's 2nd Unbundling: How Building and Joining a Supply Chain are Different and Why It Matters', CEPR Discussion Paper No. 8768, 2012.

Baldwin, R. and Lopez-Gonzalez, J., 'Supply-Chain Trade: A Portrait of Global Patterns and Several Testable Hypotheses', CEPR Discussion Paper No. 9421, 2013.

Bloom, N., Schankerman, M. and van Reenen, J., 'Identifying Technology Spillovers and Product Market Rivalry' (2013), *Econometrica* 81, 4: 1347–1393.

Bottazzi, L. and Peri, G., 'Innovation and Spillovers in Regions: Evidence From European Patent Data', IGIER Bocconi University Working Paper No. 215, 2002.

Bottazzi, L. and Peri, G., 'Innovation and Spillovers in Regions: Evidence From European Patent Data' (2003), *European Economic Review* 47: 687–710.

Bottazzi, L. and Peri, G., 'The International Dynamics of R&D and Innovation in the Short and in the Long Run', NBER Working Paper No. 11524, 2005.

Braun, M., 'Financial Contractibility and Asset Hardness', Unpublished manuscript. Harvard University, 2003.

Cameron, A. C. and Trivedi, P. K., *Regression Analysis of Count Data*, Cambridge: Cambridge University Press, 1998.

Coe, D. T. and Helpman, E., 'International R&D Spillovers' (1995), *European Economic Review* 39, 5: 859–887.

Eaton, J. and Kortum, S., 'International Technology Diffusion: Theory and Measurement' (1999), *International Economic Review* 40, 3: 537–570.

Griliches, Z., 'Patent Statistics as Economic Indicators: A Survey' (1990), *Journal of Economic Literature* 28, 4: 1661–1707.

Grossman, G. M. and Helpman, E., 'Trade, Knowledge Spillovers, and Growth' (1991), *European Economic Review* 35, 2–3: 517–526.

Grossman, G. M. and Helpman, E., 'Trade, Knowledge Spillovers, and Growth' (1991a), *European Economic Review*, 35, 2–3: 517–526.

Grossman, G. M. and Helpman, E., *Innovation and Growth in the Global Economy*, Cambridge, MA. The MIT Press, 1991b.

Halpern, L., Koren, M. and Szeidl, A., 'Imported Inputs and Productivity' (2015), *American Economic Review* 105, 12: 3660–3703.

Hovhannisyan, N. and Keller, W., 'International Business Travel: An Engine of Innovation?' (2015), *Journal of Economic Growth* 20, 1: 75–104.

Jaffe, A. B., Trajtenberg, M. and Henderson, R., 'Geographic Localization of Knowledge Spillovers as Evidenced by Patent Citations' (1993), *The Quarterly Journal of Economics* 108, 3: 577–598.

Javorcik, B., 'Does Foreign Direct Investment Increase the Productivity of Domestic Firms? In Search of Spillovers through Backward Linkages' (2004), *American Economic Review* 94, 3: 605–627.

Kasahara, H. and Rodrigue, J., 'Does the Use of Imported Intermediates Increase Productivity? Plant-Level Evidence' (2008), *Journal of Development Economics* 87, 1: 106–118.

Keller, W., 'Are International R&D Spillovers Trade-Related?: Analyzing Spillovers among Randomly Matched Trade Partners' (1998), *European Economic Review* 42 8: 1469–1481.

Keller, W., 'Trade and the Transmission of Technology' (2002a), *Journal of Economic Growth* 7: 5–24.

Keller, W., 'Geographic Localization of International Technology Diffusion' (2002b), *American Economic Review* 92: 120–142.

Keller, W., 'International Technology Diffusion' (2004), *Journal of Economic Literature* 42, 3: 752–782.

Keller, W., 'International Trade, Foreign Direct Investment and Technology Spillovers', in B. Hall and N. Rosenmerg (eds), *Handbook of the Economics of Innovation*, Amsterdam: Elsevier North Holland Publishers, 2010.

Lichtenberg, F. R. and Pottelsberghe de la Potterie, B., 'International R&D Spillovers: A Comment' (1998), *European Economic Review* 42, 8: 1483–1491.

Lybbert, T. and Zolas, N., 'Getting Patents and Economic Data To Speak To Each Other: An "Algorithmic Links with Probabilities" Approach for Joint Analyses of Patenting and Economic Activity', WIPO Economics & Statistics Series Working Paper No. 5, October 2012.

Manski, C. F., 'Identification of Endogenous Social Effects: The Reflection Problem' (1993), *Review of Economic Studies* 60: 531–542.

Maskus, K. E., Neumann, R. and Seidel, T., 'How National and International Financial Development Affect Industrial R&D' (2012), *European Economic Review* 56: 72–83.

Newman, C., Rand, J., Talbot, T. and Tarp, F., 'Technology Transfers, Foreign Investment and Productivity Spillovers' (2015), *European Economic Review* 76: 168–187.

Nishioka, S. and Ripoll, M., 'Productivity, Trade And The R&D Content of Intermediate Inputs' (2012), *European Economic Review* 56, 2012: 1573–1592.

OECD, *OECD Patent Statistics Manual*, Paris: OECD, 2009.

Park, W. B., 'International Patent Protection: 1960–2005' (2008), *Research Policy* 37: 761–766.

Piermartini, R. and Rubínová, S., 'Knowledge Spillovers through International Supply Chains', WTO Working Paper ERSD-2014-11. Geneva: WTO, 2014.

Pisano, G. P. and Shih, W. C., *Producing Prosperity: Why America Needs a Manufacturing Renaissance*, Boston, MA: Harvard Business School Publishing, 2012.

Romer, P. M., 'Endogenous Technological Change' (1990), *Journal of Political Economy* 98, 5: 71–102.

Timmer, M., Dietzenbacher, E., Los, B., Stehrer, R. and de Vries, G. J., 'An Illustrated User Guide to the World Input–Output Database: The Case of Global Automotive Production' (2015), *Review of International Economics* 23, 3: 575–605.

Tirole, J., *The Theory of Industrial Organization*, Cambridge, MA: The MIT Press, 1988.

A15.1

Table A15.1 *Industry descriptions*

Industry	ISIC	Description
Petroleum products	23	Manufacture of coke, refined petroleum products and nuclear fuel
Chemicals	24	Manufacture of chemicals and chemical products
Rubber & plastics	25	Manufacture of rubber and plastics products
Metal products	27 to 28	Manufacture of basic metals and of fabricated metal products, except machinery and equipment
Other mineral products	26	Manufacture of other non-metallic mineral products
Electrical machinery	30 to 33	Manufacture of office, accounting and computing machinery, of electrical machinery and apparatus n.e.c., of radio, television and communication equipment and apparatus and of medical, precision and optical instruments, watches and clocks
Transport equipment	34 to 35	Manufacture of motor vehicles, trailers and semi-trailers and of other transport equipment
Other machinery	29	Manufacture of machinery and equipment n.e.c.

(*source:* authors' analysis)

Table A15.2 *10 most connected economy-pair-industries by the type of supply chain linkages*

	I2P – Imports to produce			**I2E – Imports to export**		
Rank	**Economy**	**Partner**	**Industry**	**Economy**	**Partner**	**Industry**
1	CHN	TPKM	Electronics	CAN	USA	Transport
2	CAN	USA	Transport	CHN	TPKM	Electronics
3	CHN	JPN	Electronics	MEX	USA	Electronics
4	CHN	KOR	Electronics	CHN	JPN	Electronics
5	USA	CAN	Transport	CHN	KOR	Electronics
6	MEX	USA	Electronics	FRA	GER	Transport
7	USA	CHN	Electronics	TPKM	JPN	Electronics
8	FRA	GER	Transport	TPKM	USA	Electronics
9	USA	CAN	Chemicals	MEX	USA	Transport
10	CHN	USA	Electronics	TPKM	CHN	Electronics

	I2RE – Imports to re-export			**I2REP – Imports to re-export into production**		
Rank	**Economy**	**Partner**	**Industry**	**Economy**	**Partner**	**Industry**
1	CAN	USA	Transport	CAN	USA	Transport
2	MEX	USA	Electronics	MEX	USA	Transport
3	MEX	USA	Transport	MEX	USA	Electronics
4	TPKM	CHN	Electronics	TPKM	CHN	Electronics
5	CAN	USA	Chemicals	AUT	GER	Transport
6	CAN	USA	Metal	HUN	GER	Transport
7	AUT	GER	Transport	USA	CAN	Transport
8	CAN	USA	Electronics	KOR	CHN	Electronics
9	FRA	GER	Transport	FRA	GER	Transport
10	KOR	CHN	Electronics	CAN	USA	Chemicals

Notes: Chemicals – ISIC 24, Metal – ISIC 27 to 28, Electronic – ISIC 30 to 33, Transport – ISIC 34 to 35
Source: Authors' analysis

Table A15.3 *Knowledge spillovers through supply chains – regressions results*

Weight:	**I2P**	**I2E**	**I2RE**	**I2REP**
	(1)	**(2)**	**(3)**	**(4)**
Foreign R&D pool	0.0007	0.0007	0.0029*	0.0042**
	(0.0010)	(0.0009)	(0.0017)	(0.0018)
Domestic R&D	0.141**	0.139**	0.132**	0.129**
	(0.0551)	(0.0561)	(0.0546)	(0.0524)
Observations	225	225	225	225

Country-clustered standard errors in parentheses.

Statistical significance level: *** p-value<0.01, ** p-value <0.05, * p-value <0.1

The dependent variable is the number of patent applications. All regressions include country and industry dummies.

See Piermartini and Rubínová (2014) for more details on the methodology.

Table A15.4 *Knowledge spillovers from main innovators – regression results*

Knowledge-receiving country group:	**All other (non-G3)**	**GDP per capita below median**
	(1)	**(2)**
R&D pool from G3	0.015***	0.018**
	(0.0054)	(0.0093)
Domestic R&D	0.111***	0.105**
	(0.0380)	(0.0447)
Observations	193	117

Country-clustered standard errors in parentheses.

Statistical significance level: *** p-value <0.01, ** p-value <0.05, * p-value <0.1

The dependent variable is the number of patent applications. All regressions include country and industry dummies.

Main innovators, the G3, are the United States, Japan and Germany.

See Piermartini and Rubínová (2014) for more details on the methodology.

Table A15.5 *The distance decay of knowledge spillovers*

	Full Sample			EU Sample		
	(1)	**(2)**	**(3)**	**(4)**	**(5)**	**(6)**
Foreign R&D pool_GVC	0.0042**		0.0044**	0.0084*		0.0078
	(0.0018)		(0.0018)	(0.0045)		(0.0053
Foreign R&D pool_distance		-0.0056	-0.0061*		0.0200*	0.0081
		(0.0035)	(0.0036)		(0.0110)	(0.0152)
Domestic R&D	0.124**	0.154***	0.133**	0.125	0.165*	0.132
	(0.055)	(0.055)	(0.057)	(0.098)	(0.089)	(0.099)
Observations	225	225	225	91	91	91

Country-clustered standard errors in parentheses.

Statistical significance level: *** p-value <0.01, ** p-value <0.05, * p-value <0.1

The dependent variable is the number of patent applications. All regressions include country and industry dummies.

EU Sample includes Austria, Belgium, Finland, France, Germany, Greece, Ireland, Italy, The Netherlands, Portugal, Spain and the United Kingdom.

See Piermartini and Rubínová (2014) for more details on the methodology.

16

How do Patents Shape Global Value Chains? International and Domestic Patenting and Value-Added Trade

NIKOLAS J. ZOLAS AND TRAVIS J. LYBBERT*

Abstract

Intellectual property plays an important role in the global economy through its impact on technology diffusion, knowledge transfer and competition. As production has become fragmented into coordinated processes that span the globe, the role of patents has evolved. Patents can transmit technical knowledge and facilitate upstream and downstream licensing arrangements, thereby increasing the flow of intermediate and final goods and catalyzing knowledge spillovers across sectors and regions. We exploit an algorithmic concordance that links patents to industry and product classifications to estimate how patents affect the organization and structure of Global Value Chains (GVCs). Using the World-Input Output Database as the basis for various GVC measures, we find that increased international patenting inflows are associated with greater value-added production, but that this positive effect is driven entirely by industries in high-income countries. We also find some evidence of heterogeneity in these effects by region and sector-specific R&D intensity. We conclude with discussion of important limitations of this exploratory analysis and implications for future research.

Introduction

Potential linkages between patents and international trade motivated the negotiation of the Agreement on Trade-Related Aspects of Intellectual

* Any opinions and conclusions expressed herein are those of the authors and do not necessarily represent the views of the US Census Bureau. We thank participants at the World Bank and Peterson Institute Conference on Global Value Chains, the 2015 Patent Statistics for Decision Makers Conference, the WTO Seminar on IP and Knowledge Flows in a Digital Era, and seminar participants at UC Berkeley, UC Davis, the Max Planck Institute and Inter-American Development Bank (IADB). We also thank Russell Hillberry, Dietmar Harhoff, Andy Toole and Mingzhi Xu for valuable feedback and suggestions. All remaining errors are our own.

Property Rights (TRIPS Agreement) as part of the Uruguay Round of the GATT that concluded in 1994. Since the conclusion of the TRIPS Agreement, numerous studies have analysed the role of patenting institutions on the composition and quantity of trade flows. These findings suggest that the increased use of patents and other forms of intellectual property (IP) have stimulated imports in knowledge-intensive and high-tech goods for several countries (Braga and Fink, 1999; Vichyanond, 2009; Awokuse and Yin, 2010; Ivus, 2010). The close relationship between patenting, investment and trade partly reflects similarities in the costs and benefits of each activity and how they shape technology transfer.

Coe and Helpman (1995) demonstrate the important effects of foreign R&D on domestic productivity, highlighting the contributions of international knowledge spillovers, in which both patents and trade figure prominently. However, the precise nature of the relationship between patents and trade is not fully understood. In modelling international patent flows, economists have traditionally relied on 'gravity'-type models, where flows are determined by the relative size (GDP) of countries, as well as distance and other country-specific variables (see Slama, 1981; Bosworth, 1984; Harhoff et al., 2007; Eaton et al., 2004; Zolas, 2014). Relatively little is known about the dynamics, spatial and industry patterns, and economic implications of this important relationship between patenting and the structure of global trade. This gap in our understanding stems principally from our inability – until recently – to connect patenting and trade at a high enough resolution to account for substantial industry-level heterogeneity.

While our understanding of how the knowledge embedded within patents gets transferred abroad is still somewhat rudimentary, the production processes generated, in part, from this knowledge have undergone a radical shift. Advances in communication and transportation technology, along with a reduction in trade barriers, have enabled what Richard Baldwin calls the 'great unbundling', with different stages of the production chain sliced into tinier fragments and spread more broadly around the world (Baldwin, 2006). At the most basic level, these production processes begin with raw materials being converted into basic inputs, which are then combined with more and more intermediate inputs until the final good is assembled. However, at a deeper level, the process is much more complicated and entails product, input and knowledge flows moving back and forth, horizontally and vertically. Numerous models have been proposed that help explain the production and ownership decisions of these processes such as Costinot et al. (2013) and Antras and Chor (2013), along with the impact of these value chains on trade flows (Baldwin and Venables, 2010; Yi, 2003; Harms, Lorz and Urban, 2012). The findings point to various determinants of value chain composition including the complexity of the process as captured by the number of distinct production stages and the position of the product within the supply chain relative to the final retail stage (‘*Upstreamness*’), which importantly shape both the volume of trade flows and global income distribution.

In this chapter, we explore the relationship between new quantitative measures of global value chains (GVCs) and patents across industries and countries.[1] We use the algorithmic matching techniques proposed by Goldschlag et al. (2019) to link the technology classes of patent flows from the PATSTAT database with the industry codes found in the input-output tables from the World Input-Output Database (WIOD). In doing so, we can test the impact of patent flows on different features of GVCs. Because the GVC measures we use are especially relevant to contemporary global supply chains, they provide a much better basis for testing the relationship between trade and patents than traditional trade measures such as gross exports and imports.

Given the scope and complexity of this topic, our approach is intentionally modest and intends to provide initial exploratory evidence related to broader efforts to understand international innovation systems (e.g. Fromhold-Eisebith, 2007). In undertaking an exploratory exercise, we face a number of data limitations. We cannot observe in our data the complex structure and ownership of multinational firms and can only differentiate patents by industry and not by use or by product versus process. Although the patterns we unveil are broadly relevant to current and future value chains, we necessarily rely on data from the past few decades and therefore cannot empirically test for how more recent innovations in the current digital era alter these patent–GVC relationships. Finally, we do not have pure exogenous variation in patent flows with which to identify the pure causal impact of patents on GVCs and instead lean on a weaker, predictive causality strategy. Despite these limitations, this exploratory analysis provides some intriguing initial insights that have both policy and research relevance.

1 For a more extensive and more technical version of the analysis in this chapter, we refer readers to Lybbert et al. (2019).

Using country-industries (a given industry in a specific country) as our unit of analysis, we show that increased patent inflows and outflows from abroad are associated with increased value-added production in the form of exports. Through disaggregated analysis, we find that this effect is driven by impacts in high-income countries. Industries in middle-income countries, by contrast, experience greater production fragmentation as a result of international patent flows. We find some evidence of additional heterogeneity in these effects by region and sector. We detect relationships between patents and changes in the structure of GVCs as captured by other measures as well. While these analyses do not test whether patent flows benefit country-industries through their effect on GVCs because our focus is on changes in GVC measures rather than total production value, they do suggest a direct link between patent policies and the structure and functioning of value chains.

Conceptual Framework: The Structure of GVCs and Patent Flows

The 'great unbundling' (Baldwin, 2006) has dramatically changed the structure and management of production across most sectors and countries and altered the flow of both tangible and intangible assets across borders. The complex GVCs that have emerged in recent decades present both a challenge and an opportunity for firms seeking to upgrade their engagement, position and profitability in these chains. Competitive pressures and ever-evolving technological frontiers in this digital era will continue to shape GVCs. As they navigate these challenges and opportunities, firms face an array of strategic and tactical considerations, including incentives shaped by regulatory and legal systems.[2] Since firms in a given industry face many common forces and incentives, these firm-level decisions map into industry-level GVC patterns that are quite distinct.

A vast academic, policy and practitioner literature has emerged alongside these rapidly evolving GVCs. This work, now spanning decades, provides a rich conceptual basis for understanding GVCs, empirical GVC measures and analysis of their functioning, performance and effects, and detailed policy recommendations for countries and industries seeking to upgrade their position in GVCs. While this work demonstrates the long reach of GVCs (i.e. firms with no link – direct or indirect – to GVCs are increasingly rare), it also suggests the particularly prominent role of

[2] See Neubig and Wunsch-Vincent, Chapter 6 in this volume for a discussion of incentives arising from tax law.

GVCs in developing countries because fragmented production stages can create more manageable opportunities and facilitate initial entry. Consequently, value-added trade contributes significantly more to GDP in developing countries (30 per cent on average) than in developed countries (18 per cent on average) (UNCTAD, 2013 report).

Efforts aimed at upgrading and enhancing value-added trade are particularly relevant to the analysis in this chapter. A standard progression of upgrading begins with processes (e.g. improving manufacturing efficiency) then shifts to products (e.g. product innovation, quality improvements), and culminates with functional upgrading (e.g. innovation from upstream design stages to downstream distribution stages). While firm-level decisions are central to any progression of upgrading, measures of GVC performance tend to focus more on aggregate input-output tables because of data available. These tables, though coarse, have the advantage of being accessible and have consequently become the basis for a family of GVC measures. We use three such measures to capture for each country-industry (i.e. a given industry in given country) its value-added exports as a share of total exports (VAX Ratio, *VAX* hereafter), the complexity of production based on the number of distinct stages in the GVC (*NStages*), and its position relative to the final retail stage (*Upstreamness*). Increases in the *VAX* signal effective upgrading as the value-added composition of trade is higher, whereas decreases in the *VAX* signals increased production fragmentation (i.e. lower value-added contributions by a given country-industry). While upgrading and enhancing the share of value-added contributed by a country-industry is a popular industrial strategy, this does not imply that a declining *VAX* signals unfavourable economic conditions. To the contrary, integration into the global economy can simultaneously lower the *VAX* and increase total value creation by dramatically expanding total exports. Upgrading is more difficult to discern in the *NStages* and *Upstreamness* measures given the familiar non-linearities of the 'smile curve' that suggests that value-added is highest in upstream and downstream production stages and lowest in the middle stages. It is important to note that an increase in any of these GVC measures would indicate whether the GVC is undergoing increased complexity (from adding additional production stages) or moving further downstream from the final good. Either way, an increase is not necessarily good or bad for the underlying country-industry as the overall effect is a function of many other factors. In the global economy, a country-industry can prosper with either a rising or declining *VAX* as long as total productivity – the translation of inputs into value – is increasing.

In this chapter, we explore the empirical relationship between patents and GVCs at the country-industry level as captured by these measures. We estimate elasticities for each measure with respect to patents flowing – both domestically and internationally – to and from a given country-industry. These elasticities assess how sensitive the GVC measures are to changes in patent flows. While this is novel as an empirical exploration, others have probed this relationship from different angles. For example, WIPO (2017b) documents the importance of intellectual property more broadly defined ('intangible capital') in contemporary GVCs. By attributing value-added production in GVCs to tangible and intangible capital and labour, the report shows that about a third of production value is due to intangible capital, which is more than the value attributable to tangible capital. Building on the work of Gereffi et al. (2005), the report describes how the nature of knowledge and information flows required by GVCs – especially their complexity and codification in transferrable packets, along with the capabilities of the firms involved – shape the organizational and governance structure that emerges in the GVC.

While our empirical analysis cannot capture either the richness of GVC governance or the full breadth of intangible capital (we restrict our focus to patents), the conceptual underpinnings of ownership along GVCs are nonetheless relevant. Consider what models of property rights in production processes along value chains imply about how firm-level incentives and management may shape the GVC measures we use. Antras and Chor (2013) model production ownership by a parent firm in production chains and offer conditions for patenting abroad. Patenting denotes ownership of the product or process within the production chain, ensuring that the technical knowledge embedded within the product or process flows to the subsidiary through licensing or ownership. In this framework, a firm patents to ensure that the production process is completed according to the exact specification embedded within the patent. More generally, patenting in the intended production location provides the parent firm with an ownership stake in production inputs, processes or outputs. Even when this patent-based ownership stake falls short of a subsidiary relationship, it can serve to reduce contractual frictions associated with fragmented and outsourced production. Thus, patents in the Antras and Chor (2013) framework facilitate knowledge transfer and reduce contractual frictions. When a firm patents in a jurisdiction with the intent of producing in that location, patenting thereby leads to potentially higher value-added production in this target destination. Beyond the Antras and Chor model, however, if we allow for non-productive patenting motives (e.g. defensive patenting to block competitors' access to inputs, processes or markets), the relationship between patenting and value-added production is more complex and may push in the opposite direction.

Our analysis aggregates firm-level patenting and GVC decisions to the country-industry level. While this complicates the direct application of firm-level models to our analysis, many of the forces and incentives faced by firms in a given country and industry share common features. This translates, albeit imperfectly, firm-level decisions into distinct country-industry GVC patterns. The relationship between patent flows and GVC measures at the country-industry level reflects the average firm-level relationship, which – according to the firm's patenting intent – can be either positive as suggested by the Antras and Chor model or negative as suggested by non-productive motives such as defensive patenting. Thus, how (or even whether) patents shape GVCs at the country-industry level is unclear a priori. Our empirical exploration aims to shed light on this relationship.

Data and Construction of Global Value Chain Measures

In this section, we describe the measures we use to understand the relationship between patenting and GVCs at country-industry level. GVCs are often complex, intricate and vary by firm and product. Country-industry measures of GVCs cannot capture all this richness and resolution, but are nonetheless useful as coarse measures of certain components of value chains. For our analysis, we rely on three different GVC measures that have been documented in the literature, namely: the *VAX* – the ratio of value-added production to the total value of exports; *NStages* – the number of stages in the production process; and *Upstreamness* – the mean-distance (in production stages) from the final good. We construct each of these measures from the same source data: the World Input-Output Database (WIOD) as described in Timmer et al. (2015), which covers 42 countries and 35 industries and yields a 1435 × 1435 input-output matrix for each year from 1995 to 2011. The WIOD sample contains 27 EU countries and 15 other major countries. Of the 35 industries, 14 are in manufacturing.

Our methodology for constructing the value-added trade data follows the multi-country, multi-product methodology first established in Johnson and Noguera (2012) and used in their subsequent working paper (Johnson and Noguera, 2017). Our methodology for the number of production stages, *NStages* and *Upstreamness* measures come from Fally (2012) and Antras et al. (2012). We merge these GVC measures

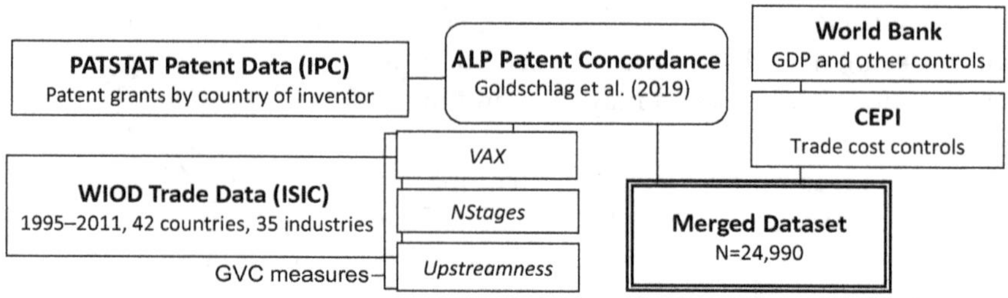

Figure 16.1 Construction of final merged dataset from PATSTAT and WIOD data
Source: Authors' analysis.

at the country-industry-year level with patent grant data from PATSTAT and control variables from other data sources as described below. For a detailed description of our application of these methods to construct these measures, see the more technical analysis in Lybbert et al. (2019). The following subsections provide a brief summary of the construction and intuition of each of the measures. Figure 16.1 heuristically depicts the construction of the final dataset we use in this analysis.

Value-Added Trade: VAX

The process proposed by Johnson and Noguera (2012) for constructing the *VAX* measure uses input-output tables and assumes a circular process of production where inputs and outputs are continuously transferred from one country-industry to another, implying an infinite number of production stages. To simplify the process, they assume a sequential two-stage production process where intermediate goods are only used to produce final goods (as opposed to other intermediate goods). The *VAX* ratio consists of separate components that further break down the value chain, such as the share of intermediate goods shipped elsewhere and then shipped back, and the share of intermediate goods that are consumed in a third country as a final good. While we do not break down the *VAX* ratio into each of the components, we want to point out that movements in the *VAX* ratio are going to be driven primarily by differences in the share of intermediate goods produced elsewhere.[3]

[3] Using the terminology in Johnson and Noguera (2012), movements in the *VAX* will mostly be driven by 'reflected' exports and the gap between 'absorbed' exports and 'net absorbed'.

Between 1995 and 2011, the aggregate *VAX* across our sample of countries declined by 5.6 per cent, indicating increased fragmentation as the share of value-added exports over gross exports has fallen. This decrease is mostly being driven by the fact that gross export flows for these countries have outpaced value-added export flows. Value-added exports have grown by 177 per cent over this period, while gross exports have increased by 194 per cent. Meanwhile, patent flows over this time period for the same set of countries has increased by 93[4] per cent.

As a preliminary perspective on the unconditional relationship between *VAX* and international patent flows see Figure 16.2 (left). In this figure, we plot annual *VAX* measures and patent flows by sector over the period 1995–2011.[5] We provide a trend line for each sector group to indicate the (unconditional) time trend in this relationship. Although purely descriptive, the patterns in this plot indicate a negative association between patents and *VAX* for nearly all sectors (the exception is 'Electrical & Machinery') – with total international patent grants increasing and *VAX* decreasing (i.e. production fragmentation increasing) over this period. In the empirical analysis below, we move beyond these unconditional, descriptive patterns and towards estimated effects with a degree of causal inference.

Production Stages: NStages

Our empirical analysis captures both inter- and intra-industry flows, and one measure of interest for global value chains is the number of production stages required to generate the final product. Holding aggregate value constant, more production stages for the same product would indicate less value-added per stage. To determine the number of production stages, we

4 Another takeaway is that the movements in the *VAX* ratio differ from the results found in Johnson and Noguera. This is due to a variety of reasons having to do with different data sources being used, different countries and different industries, as well as a longer time horizon of the data. In Johnson and Noguera (2017), the authors have a brief discussion in the footnotes discussing how the WIOD database fails to capture some important changes to the *VAX* ratios over the time period and how their study relies on the variability accrued over a four-decade long period. Besides the difference in time horizon, between the Johnson and Noguera data (30 years versus 16 years in the WIOD), Johnson and Noguera also pay particular attention to Asian countries which underwent rapid industrialization during their time frame, while the WIOD focuses mainly on European countries.

5 The R&D intensity of sectors is based on the OECD R&D intensity taxonomy (Galindo-Rueda and Verger, 2016). For the same plot disaggregated by sector rather than sector R&D intensity groups, see A16.1.

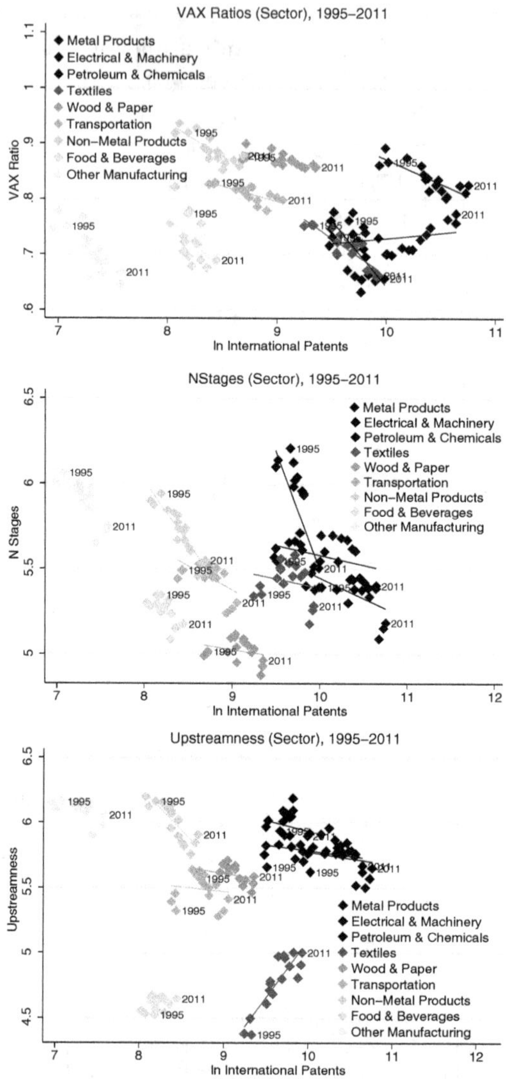

Figure 16.2 Yearly *VAX*, *NStages* and *Upstreamness* and international patent flows by sector

Source: VAX figures calculated using WIOD data (2013 Release) and the methodology described in Johnson and Noguera (2012). *NStages* figures calculated from same source data using methodology described in Fally (2012). *Upstreamness* figures calculated from same source data using methodology in Fally (2012) and Antras et al. (2013).

Note: The sectors are colour coded and ordered according to their patent intensity: darker colours correspond to patent intensity.

implement the methodology introduced by Fally (2012), who develops a measure for the weighted-average number of locations involved sequentially in the production of a good. The measure is constructed on the assumption of sequential production.

We plot the unconditional relationship between international patents and *NStages* broken out by sector in Figure 16.2 (middle). Between 1995 and 2011, we find that the number of production stages for each country-industry in our sample has declined on average by roughly 7.5 per cent indicating increased consolidation in the production process over this time period. We see similar declines and movements across all sectors with 'Petroleum & Chemicals' seeing the largest decline.

Distance from Final Good: Upstreamness

As a final GVC measure, we use the average distance from the final product for each country-industry. As the 2017 WIPO report (WIPO 2017b) demonstrates, value added follows a U-shaped 'smile curve' with respect to distance from the final good: processes further from and closer to the final good tend to have higher value-added content. Our measure of *Upstreamness*, which is based on Antràs et al. (2012),[6] increases as a given country-industry moves to more upstream positions in its value chain. The steps to develop this measure are somewhat similar to the steps undertaken in the metric of *NStages*, as it is a recursive process that captures the mean distance of each within-country intermediate input from the final good by tabulating the intermediate input shares of each country-industry.

Between 1995 and 2011, the average *Upstreamness* for all of the country-industries in the WIOD declined by 2.2, indicating that more production was happening further downstream. Figure 16.2 (right) plots the relationship between patents and measures of *Upstreamness* by sector and finds some variability in this unconditional relationship. Most sectors have similar responses to international patents (a steady decline), but 'Textiles' sees an increase in *Upstreamness* and 'Food & Beverages' has almost zero change.

The figures indicate that the average number of production stages and the average distance of each country-industry from the final good has been declining over this period. Since the *VAX* also declined over these years, these overall changes suggest that the increased production

[6] This measure is very similar to the measure of *downstreamness*, which is separately identified in Antras and Chor (2013) and Fally (2012).

fragmentation (declining *VAX*) has – on average – taken a specific form. Specifically, this pattern could be explained either by increased fragmentation in upstream stages that is partly offset by the emergence of fewer and higher-value stages further downstream (hence, declining *NStages* and *Upstreamness*). Or this result could be an indication that the upstream production process in the destination country is consolidating and producing less value-added than before. Our econometric analysis below seeks to control for the various confounding factors that complicate meaningful interpretation of these unconditional correlations.

Patent and Other Data

As our measure of patent flows, we use the number of granted patents in a given year and associated with a given industry. To distinguish between domestic and international patents, we define the origin of the patent as the inventor's country as listed on the patent application.[7] Thus, international patent inflows represent the number of patents granted by one country to foreign inventors.[8] International patent outflows represent the number of patents granted in a foreign country to home country inventors. We construct aggregate unilateral versions of these patent flow measures along with domestic patent grants using the PATSTAT database available from the European Patent Office (EPO) with supplementary data provided by the World Intellectual Property Organization (WIPO). In order to associate a given patent with a given industry, we must concord the classification system used for patents into the industry classifications used in the WIOD database. The industries for the WIOD databases are organized by ISIC Rev. 3, with most groupings occurring at the two-digit level. The database combines the 60+ two-digit level ISIC classes into more aggregate classes to fit the 35 industry groups of the

[7] In cases where multiple inventor countries are listed on the patent, we take the modal inventor country as the origin. We randomly assign inventor country in cases where two or more countries appear in this field with equal frequency. Although PATSTAT does not list the country of origin for all inventors, fewer than 5 per cent of the patents in our sample (i.e. to and from countries represented in WIOD) are missing this information. We see no statistical differences in technological field (IPC) between patents with and without inventor country of origin.

[8] Given our focus in this analysis on patent grants in a given country-industry, it is not necessary to account for patent families that relate to a common invention. There are surely other empirical angles one might take to addressing questions about patents and GVCs that would leverage patent family information and structure, but that is beyond the scope of this work.

WIOD. To concord the patent data organized by International Patent Classification (IPC) to the industry data organized by ISIC, we use the probabilistic concordance developed in Lybbert and Zolas (2014).

For control variables, we use GDP and GDP per capita measures from the World Bank, trade proxies, such as distance, border dummies, language dummies and colonial history from CEPII. To explore more directly heterogeneity by income level, we disaggregate our analysis by high- and middle-income countries as defined by the World Bank.[9]

Value-Added Trade and Patents: Analysis and Results

Our exploration begins with an aggregate look at the impact of patent flows on a country-industry's value-added trade. This analysis is at the country-industry level and considers both domestic and international patents. As we describe our empirical approach, recall from above that our GVC measures relate specifically to a given industry in a given country and, as a data-weighted average of firm behaviour in a given country-industry, captures aggregate value chain patterns.

Estimation Approach

We first evaluate how international patent inflows, international patent outflows and domestic patents are associated with changes in the *VAX*. We then estimate the similar specifications to test the relationship between these patent flows and *NStages* and *Upstreamness*. Our specification in each case produces elasticities of these measures with respect to changes in patent flows of different kinds (e.g. percentage change in the *VAX* for every 1 percent change in international patent inflows). Specifically, we estimate these elasticities using the following specification:

$$ln\, GVC_{ikt} = \alpha + \beta_{in}\, ln\, PAT_{ikt}^{in} + \beta_{out} \ln PAT_{ikt}^{out} + \beta_{dom} \ln PAT_{ikt}^{dom} + X_{it} + \delta_{ik} + \delta_t + \epsilon_{ikt}$$

where GVC_{ikt} is one of our three GVC measures for industry i and country k in year t; PAT_{ikt}^{in} and PAT_{ikt}^{out} are international patent inflows

[9] These classifications are available at https://datahelpdesk.worldbank.org/knowledgebase/articles/906519-world-bank-country-and-lending-groups. Note that the WIOD data does not include low-income countries, for which patent statistics are also sparse. Hence, our income comparison is between high- and middle-income categories.

and outflows, respectively; X_{it} is a vector of country-specific control variables (GDP, GDP per capita and WTO membership); δ_{ik} denotes industry-country fixed effects, and δ_t denotes year fixed effects. With these fixed effects included, our estimated patent flow elasticities (β_{in}, β_{out}, β_{dom}) capture variation *within* country-industry (i.e. controlling for average differences in GVC measures by country-industry) accounting for the overall yearly average level of these measures.

In addition to estimating this equation for all countries in our sample, we also estimate it separately for high-income and middle-income countries in order to allow these elasticities to vary by level of economic development as an important dimension of heterogeneity. We explore two additional dimensions of heterogeneity in the relationship between patent flows and GVCs by estimating this specification separately by sector and region of the world.

In this empirical exploration, we seek to understand whether and how patent flows and GVC measures are associated with each other. Because we do not exploit pure exogenous variation in patent flows, we caution against strict causal interpretations of our estimated elasticities. We argue, however, that a weaker form of causality (in addition to simple statistical associations) may be justified. The choice of a given firm to apply for patent protection in a given jurisdiction is clearly endogenous as it is a function of the firm's perceptions of future market conditions, including factors that likely influence our GVC measures. Patent grants, on the other hand, lag behind initial applications by a few years on average. Moreover, the actual lag length (and whether the patent is ultimately granted at all) is subject to a degree of random variation, which introduces exogenous variation into patent grants that is not present in endogenous patent applications.[10] By using patent grants as our measure of patent flows, we avoid in part the endogeneity arising from strategic patent application decisions. On this basis, our patent flow elasticities capture a form of 'Granger causality' (i.e. predictive causality): if patent grants in a given country-industry are associated with changes in the GVC position of that country-industry even though the patent

[10] Patent examination lags and outcomes in the US, Japan and Europe have been analysed in some detail, but little systematic work has been done to characterize patent examination in other offices. The data that are available suggest significant heterogeneity across countries and sectors (e.g. WIPO, 2017a). While some of this variation can be explained by observable factors such as technological class and inventor origin (e.g. Harhoff and Wagner, 2009), much of the variation in examination delays is stochastic (i.e. unexplained).

application decision randomly pre-dated the grant by up to several years, we can conclude that patent grants are not only *associated* with GVC position, but that *predictive causality* likely runs from patent flows to GVC position. Because we match patents to our GVC measures based on their grant date, any such effect is essentially contemporaneous, which implies that our results capture the short-term relationship between patent flows and GVCs rather than a longer-run dynamic and interdependent relationship between the two.

Our interpretation of the coefficients is relatively straightforward. In the case of the *VAX*, a decrease indicates that relatively less value-added production is occurring in country *i* and industry *j*, which suggests that production is becoming more fragmented in value terms. Hence, a negative β coefficient in equation (1) – that is, a negative patent-GVC elasticity – implies that an increase in the corresponding patent flow is associated with greater dispersion of the production process across GVCs. For *NStages* and *Upstreamness*, respectively, a positive β coefficient suggests that patent flows lead to an expansion of production stages, which is consistent with increased complexity, and to the country-industry shifting its production position in the GVC downstream (i.e. further away from the final good).

Results

To facilitate the presentation of results, we show estimated elasticities graphically and report the associated numeric estimates in full tables of results in the Appendix. In Figure 16.3, we show the estimated elasticities for *VAX*, *NStages* and *Upstreamness* with respect to patents flowing from different sources. The estimated elasticity for 'All' country-industries in the data provide the main results, which we then disaggregate along the dimensions of income (high- vs middle-income countries), sector categories, and geographic regions of the world. These results suggest several interesting patterns in the relationship between patents and GVCs.

Consider first the *VAX* results. Overall, we see that the *VAX* for a given country-industry increases with both inflows and outflows of international patents to/from that country-industry. These movements are mostly small in magnitude on a year-to-year basis.[11] This is

[11] Given a mean growth of international patents of 93.5 per cent over the period 1995 to 2011, our baseline coefficient suggests that the cumulative impact of patent inflows added an additional 0.10 percentage points to the *VAX* ratio, while the cumulative impact of patent outflows contributed an additional 0.18 percentage points to the *VAX* ratio.

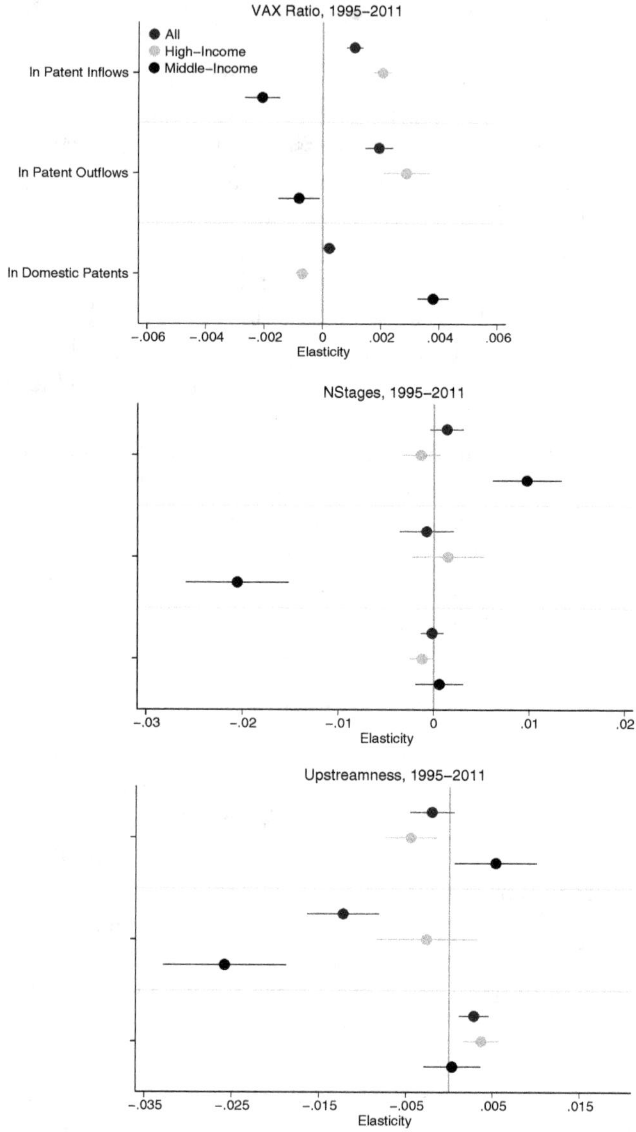

Figure 16.3 Estimated unilateral elasticities for *VAX*, *NStages* and *Upstreamness* with respect to patents with 95 per cent confidence intervals based on robust standard errors

Source: Authors' calculations.

Notes: All regressions include country-industry fixed effects, year fixed effects and country-level control variables GDP, GDP per capita and WTO membership. Results reported in A16.1, Tables A16.1 and A16.2.

unsurprising given the limited cumulative movements in the *VAX* over this period (-5.6 per cent overall or -0.35 per cent per year on average) relative to the changes in patent output. The overall effect of domestic patents is more modest, but still significantly positive at the 5 per cent level. Interestingly, high- and middle-income countries experience different effects between patents and GVCs. For middle-income countries, international patents flowing into and out of country-industries *reduce* the *VAX* and lead to more fragmentation for middle-income countries, while domestic patenting related to a given country-industry is associated with increase in the *VAX*. This suggests that while domestic patenting enables country-industries to enhance their value-added position in GVCs, international patenting (patent inflows) fragments their value-added production. It is important to note, however, that a declining *VAX* does not imply that the country-industry is not benefiting from GVCs – only that its value-added share of total exports is relatively declining. Income per capita and employment gains and other improvements can also accompany the structural transformations that are associated with production fragmentation captured by a declining *VAX*.

The other two panels in Figure 16.3 indicate similarly heterogeneous results for high- and middle-income countries with elasticities for *NStages* and *Upstreamness*. The *NStages* elasticities are statistically zero, except for middle-income countries. International patent inflows increase the number of production stages in country-industries in these middle-income countries, while the estimated elasticity with respect to outflows is strongly negative. Elasticities of *Upstreamness* also suggest some stark differences between high- and middle-income countries. Whereas this elasticity for patent inflows is negative for high-income countries, it is positive for middle-income countries. For patent outflows, all three elasticities are negative, with the middle-income estimate significantly larger in magnitude. Middle-income countries see no relationship between the *Upstreamness* of their country-industries and domestic patents, but high-income countries see a positive relationship.

To complement the breakdown by income level, we explore heterogeneity in the patent–GVC relationship by sector and by region of the world in Figures 16.4 and 16.5. While there is some variation across sectors in terms of magnitude and significance, most of the sectors share similar signs for patent inflows and domestic patents. While the confidence intervals on these coefficients often overlap, indicating that there is no statistically measureable difference by sector, there are some pronounced exceptions to this pattern – particularly with patent outflows. The

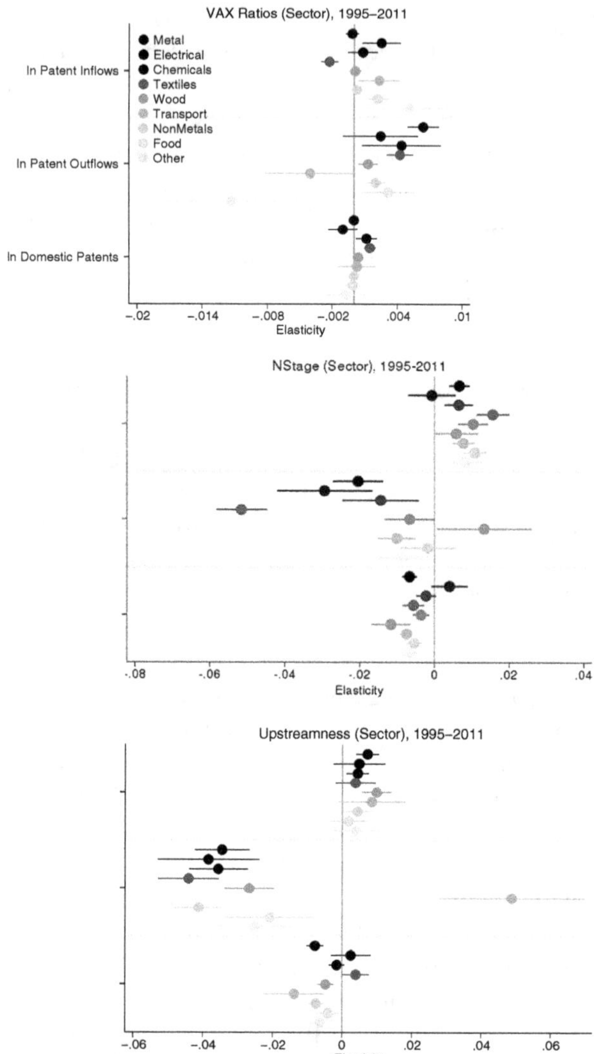

Figure 16.4 Regression coefficients for *VAX*, *NStages* and *Upstreamness* based on patent flows by sector

Source: Authors' calculations.

Notes: Confidence intervals based on robust standard errors clustered by industry in parentheses. All results based on within country-industry regressions and include country regressors of GDP, GDP per capita and WTO membership which are not reported here, along with country-industry fixed effects and yearly fixed effects. The sectors are colour coded and ordered according to their patent intensity, with the darker colour being the most patent intensive and the lighter colour being the least.

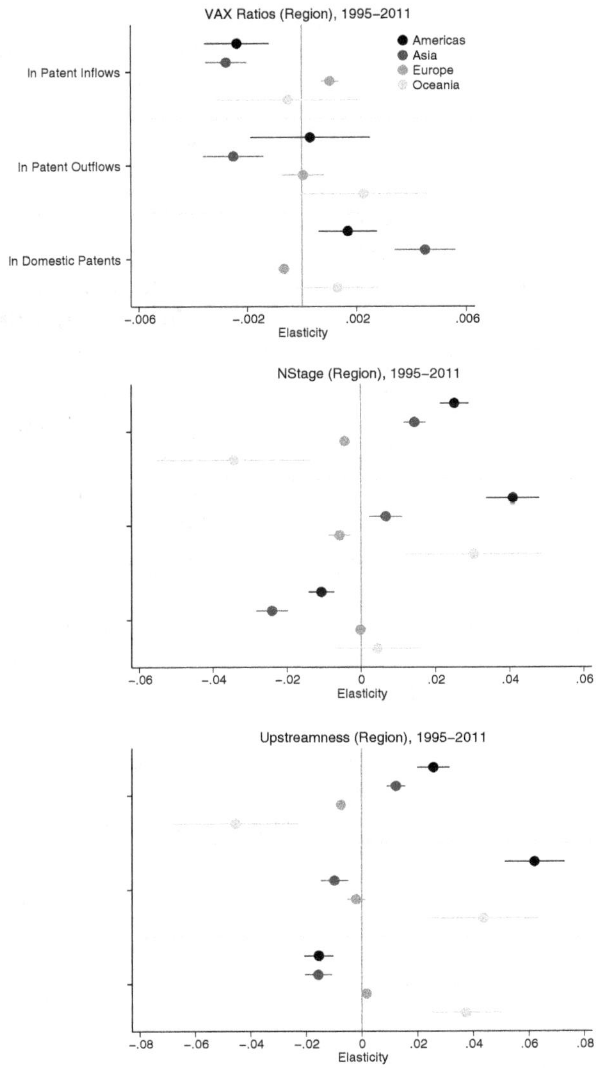

Figure 16.5 Unilateral regression coefficients for *VAX*, *NStages* and *Upstreamness* based on patent flows by region

Source: Authors' calculations.

Notes: Confidence intervals based on robust standard errors clustered by industry in parentheses. All results based on within country-industry regressions and include country regressors of GDP, GDP per capita and WTO membership which are not reported here, along with country fixed effects, industry fixed effects and yearly fixed effects. Colouring indicates level of patent intensity with dark grey being the most patent intensive (Americas) and light grey being the least patent intensive (Oceania).

coefficients on patent outflows for 'transportation' manufacturing differs significantly from the other sectors across all GVC outcomes with regard to patent outflows. We see a lower VAX ratio (greater fragmentation), more stages of production and further upstream production for 'transportation' manufactured goods when patents flow out of a given country-industry to the broader GVC. This seems to be consistent with the 'just in time' production system that was famously developed by Toyota, which spread throughout manufacturing sectors in the 1980s and 1990s.

We find even more pronounced variation in the effects of patent flows on GVC measures by region (Figure 16.5). Since the variation in estimated coefficients by region reflects all regional differences – including structural factors, income levels, policy environments, etc. – we cannot attribute different coefficients to a specific or simple determinant, but there are, nonetheless, some intriguing patterns in Figure 16.5. The patent flow elasticities for European countries tends to be relatively modest in magnitude, but also precisely estimated (i.e. smaller confidence intervals on the coefficients).[12] The estimated elasticities for the Americas and Asia are more likely to share the same sign than other regions, although they are often significantly different in magnitude. Patent inflows increase production fragmentation (decrease the *VAX*) in the Americas and Asia, but decrease fragmentation in Europe. The pattern of regional patent elasticities is qualitatively very similar for *NStages* and *Upstreamness*, with patent inflows increasing both measures in Asia and the Americas and decreasing both in Europe and Oceania. Domestic patents have the opposite effect across these regions. Although more a first step than the final word, this considerable regional variation in the effect of patents on GVCs is nonetheless intriguing – and merits future attention.

Discussion and Conclusion

The 'great unbundling' that has played out over the past several decades has created complex GVCs that span the planet and raise a host of interesting and important questions. In this chapter, we tackle one such question – and a relatively narrow one at that: what role do patents play in the organization and structure of GVCs? Our empirical analysis aimed at addressing this question is distinctly exploratory in nature. While the

[12] More generally, the more heterogeneous a region is the larger is its confidence interval.

results are much more a 'first step' than the 'last word', they nonetheless offer some intriguing patterns and nascent insights.

We find that international patent inflows and outflows both increase value-added trade on average, but that this effect is driven primarily by industries based in high-income countries. Indeed, these international patent flows have the opposite effect in middle-income countries where they lead to greater production fragmentation and declining value-added trade as share of exports, which can also be consistent with productivity enhancing integration into GVCs. Our results suggest that the relationship between patents and GVCs composition and structure is similarly distinct across high- and middle-income countries. While this analysis cannot pin down the mechanisms behind these heterogeneous results, candidate mechanisms include different compositions of patents, different patenting motives or strategies, and differential capacity to absorb new knowledge and technologies between high- and middle-income countries. Understanding how such differences systematically shape firm-level strategy and thereby alter the effect of patent flows on GVCs remains an important priority for future research. When we decompose estimated patent elasticities by sector and region, we see further dimensions of heterogeneity. Taken as a whole, the results suggest that both international and domestic patent flows can shape GVCs in ways that are statistically detectable and may therefore be relevant for the design, implementation and impact of innovation policy.

Several important limitations of this analysis merit some discussion and suggest potential next steps for future analysis along these lines. Because the opportunity to empirically test the relationship between patents and GVCs is new and as yet unexplored, we have opted for an essentially inductive approach in this chapter. As the evidence base deepens, it will be important to develop an analytical framework – perhaps formalized as a theoretical model – with which to generate testable hypotheses and through which to provide a richer interpretation of results. Such a framework would help to articulate the relationships and mechanisms that map patent flows into effects on GVCs. Since developing such a framework is beyond our scope here, we hope that our exploratory empirical work and the dominant country-industry patterns it detects prompts other work in this direction.

As is always the case in applied research, there is more we could do with more and better data. The source input-output data used to construct the GVC measures we use are complex and difficult to collect and construct. As these data become more widely available, empirical research into GVCs will continue to expand rapidly, which is likely to bring additional improvements in these data sources and modelling approaches. In our case, these input-output data are essentially non-existent for low-income countries, which is why we currently restrict our focus to high- and middle-income countries. During the years covered in this analysis, patent flows to, from and within low-income countries were very sparse, which would have limited the estimation of similar specifications for low-income countries even if their input-output data were available. Going forward, however, it will become increasingly important to understand the innovation and GVC dynamics in these low-income economies, many of which are changing rapidly. This is a critical research priority since the experience of middle-income countries over the past few decades may be a poor guide to the future prospects and possibilities faced by today's low-income countries.

In addition to improved input-output data, better measurement of cross-border trade in ideas (e.g. licensing and royalties) and more widely available firm-level data would help generate richer policy-relevant insights. Like our disaggregated analysis by income class, sector or region, which provides a clearer view of the heterogeneity hidden in average estimates, firm-level analysis would open the door to yet higher-level heterogeneity analyses to further unpack aggregate relationships and underlying mechanisms.

While better data – perhaps combined with case study-type analyses – might provide cleaner and more convincing estimates of the causal impact of patent flows on GVCs, it is important to note that there is an even more fundamental challenge to this and any other empirical exercise: data analysis is always backward-looking. This limitation makes it difficult for this analysis to fit the 'Digital Era' theme of this volume. The years covered in our analysis clearly pre-date the digital era as it is now understood and anticipated, which suggests that the patterns we detect may not be indicative of future relationships in which GVCs are more fully integrated into the digital economy. Given the candidate explanations we have in mind for the existence of (statistically-detectable) linkages between patents and GVCs, however, we believe the continued march into the digital era will only amplify the importance of this relationship.

Finally, for tractability, we have opted here for an essentially static, contemporaneous and uni-directional analysis. That is, we have sought to estimate the contemporaneous effect of patent flows on GVCs. Aside from the lags between patent applications and grants, which we leverage for predictive causality as described above, we do not introduce any dynamics between these moving and interdependent pieces. Consider, in conclusion, the opposite direction in this relationship – from changes in GVCs and value-added trade to patent-based (or more general) innovation. Given the intended effects of policy instruments aimed at upgrading a given country-industry's GVC position, understanding how enhanced GVCs shape subsequent innovation is potentially more interesting and more important. For example, how might greater production fragmentation impact domestic and international patenting? In a basic model of offshoring, increased production fragmentation allows the domestic firm to reallocate more workers towards higher-end production processes, which include R&D-intensive industries. We would expect countries that increase production fragmentation over time by becoming more integrated in GVCs to thereby benefit with higher levels of innovation. This would suggest that a declining *VAX* may lead to higher future levels of innovation and patent output. A richer understanding of these relationships, including through detailed case studies and firm-level microdata, is not only a laudable research pursuit, but one with clear and compelling policy implications. Results from such inquiries may ultimately help to guide innovation policies and strategies to stimulate investments in upgrading GVCs in ways that reflect important heterogeneity across countries, regions and sectors.

Bibliography

Antras, Pol and Chor, Davin, 'Organizing the Global Value Chain' (2013), *Econometrica* 81, 6: 2127–2204.

Antras, Pol, Chor, Davin, Fally, Thibault and Hillberry, Russell, 'Measuring the *Upstreamness* of Production and Trade Flows' (2012), *American Economic Review Paper and Proceedings* 102, 3: 412–416.

Awokuse, T. O. and Yin, H., 'Intellectual Property Rights Protection and the Surge In FDI In China' (2010), *Journal of Comparative Economics* 38, 2: 217–224.

Baldwin, R., 'Globalisation: The Great Unbundling(s)' (2006), *Economic Council of Finland* 20, 3: 5–47.

Baldwin, Richard and Venables, Anthony, 'Relocating the Value Chain: Offshoring and Agglomeration in the Global Economy', NBER Working Paper No. 16611, 2010.

Bosworth, Derek, 'Foreign Patent Flows To and From the United Kingdom' (1984), *Research Policy* 13, 2: 115–124.

Coe, David and Helpman, Elhanan, 'International R&D Spillovers' (1995), *European Economic Review* 35, 5.

Costinot, Arnaud, Vogel, Jonathan and Wang, Su, 'An Elementary Theory of Global Supply Chains' (2013), *Review of Economic Studies* 80: 109–144.

Eaton, Jonathan, Kortum, Samuel and Lerner, Josh, 'International Patenting and the European Patent Office: A Quantitative Assessment', Patents, Innovation and Economic Performance: OECD Conference Proceedings, 2004.

Fally, Thibault, 'Production Staging: Measurement and Facts', Boulder, Colorado: University of Colorado Boulder Mimeo, 2012.

Fink, Carsten and Braga, Carlos A., 'How Stronger Protection of Intellectual Property Rights AJects International Trade Flows. World Bank, Intellectual Property and Development: Lessons from Recent Economic Research' (1999) 10.1596/1813-9450-2051.

Fromhold-Eisebith, M., 'Bridging Scales in Innovation Policies: How to Link Regional, National and International Innovation Systems' (2007), *European Planning Studies* 15, 2: 217–233.

Galindo-Rueda, F. and Verger, F., 'OECD Taxonomy of Economic Activities Based on R&D Intensity', OECD Science, Technology and Industry Working Papers, 2016/04, Paris: OECD Publishing, 2016.

Gereffi, Gary, Humphrey, John and Sturgeon, Timothy, 'The Governance of Global Value Chains' (2005), *Review of International Political Economy*, 12, 1: 78–104, DOI: 10.1080/09692290500049805.

Goldschlag, Nathan, Lybbert, Travis J. and Zolas, Nikolas J., 'Tracking the Technological Composition of Industries with Algorithmic Patent Concordances' (2019), *Economics of Innovation and New Technology*, DOI: 10.1080/10438599.2019.1648014.

Harhoff, Dietmar, Hoisl, Karin, Reichl, Bettina and Pottelsberghe De La Potterie, Bruno Van, 'Patent Validation at the Country Level: The Role of Fees and Translation Costs' (2007), *Research Policy* 38, 9: 1423–1437.

Harhoff, Dietmar and Wagner, Stefan, 'The duration of patent examination at the European Patent Office' (2009), *Management Science* 55, 12: 1969–1984.

Harms, P., Lorz, O. and Urban, D., 'Offshoring Along the Production Chain' (2012), *Canadian Journal of Economics/Revue canadienne d'économique*, 45: 93–106. https://doi.org/10.1111/j.1540-5982.2011.01688.x.

Ivus, O., 'Do Stronger Patent Rights Raise High-Tech Exports to the Developing World?' (2010), *Journal of International Economics* 81, 1: 38–47.

Johnson, Robert C. and Noguera, Guillrmo, 'Accounting for Intermediates: Production Sharing and Trade in Value Added' (2012), *Journal of International Economics* 86, 2: 224–236.

Johnson, Robert C. and Noguera, Guillermo, 'Fragmentation and Trade in Value Added Over Four Decades' (2017), *The Review of Economics and Statistics* 99, 5: 896–911.

Kim, Kiheung, 'Technology Transfer: The Case of the Korean Electronics Industry', The Hawaii Intenational Conference, 1998.

Kim, Linsu, *Imitation to Innovation – The Dynamics of Korea's Technological Learning*, Boston: Harvard Business School Press, 1997.

Kim, Linsu, 'Technology Transfer & Intellectual Property Rights – The Korean Experience', Intellectual Property Rights and Sustainable Development, UNCTAD-ICTSD project on IPRs and Sustainable Development, June 2003.

Lybbert, T. J. and Zolas, Nikolas, 'Getting Patents and Economic Data to Speak to Each Other: An "Algorithmic Links With Probabilities" Approach for Joint Analyses of Patenting and Economic Activity' (2014), *Research Policy* 43, 3: 530–542.

Neubig, Thomas and Wunsch-Vincent, Sacha, 'A Missing Link in the Analysis of Global Value Chains: Cross-Broder Flows of Intangible Assets, Taxation and Related Measurement Implications', in *WTO Trade in Knowledge* (forthcoming). World Trade Organization, 2018.

Primo Braga, C. and Fink, C., 'How Stronger Protection of Intellectual Property Rights Affects International Trade Flows' World Bank Policy Research Working Paper No. 2051, 1999.

Slama, Jiri, 'Analysis by Means of a Gravitation Model of International Flows of Patent Applications in the Period 1967–1978' (1981), *World Patent Information* 3, 1: 2–8.

Timmer, Marcel, 'The World Input-Output Database (WIOD): Contents, Sources and Methods' WIOD Working Paper No. 10, 2012.

Timmer, M. P., Dietzenbacher, E., Los, B., Stehrer, R. and de Vries, G. J., 'An Illustrated User Guide to the World Input–Output Database: The Case of Global Automotive Production' (2015), *Review of International Economics*, 23: 575–605.

UNCTAD, 'Global Value Chains: Investment and Trade for Development' in *World Investment Report 2013*, Geneva: UNCTAD, 2013.

Vichyanond, J., *Intellectual property protection and patterns of trade: Center for Economic Policy Studies*, Princeton, NJ: Princeton University Press, 2009.

WIPO, 'Patents' in *World Intellectual Property Indicators*, Geneva: WIPO, 2017a.

WIPO, *World Intellectual Property Report*, Geneva: WIPO, 2017b.

World Bank, *Measuring and Analyzing the Impact of GVCs on Economic Development*, Washington, DC: World Bank Group, 2017.

Yi, Kei-Mu, 'Can Vertical Specialization Explain the Growth of World Trade?' (2003), *Journal of Political Economy* 111, 1: 52–102.

Yi, Kei-Mu, 'Can Multi-Stage Production Explain the Home Bias in Trade?' (2010), *American Economic Review* 100, 1: 364–393.

Zolas, Nikolas, 'International Patenting with Heterogeneous Firms', CES Working Paper No. 14–28, 2014.

A16.1

Appendix Tables and Figures

Table A16.1 *Country-Industry Regressions on* VAX *Ratio, 1995–2011*

	(1) **ln VAX_{ikt}** **(All)**	(2) **ln VAX_{ikt}** **(High-Income)**	(3) **ln VAX_{ikt}** **(Middle-Income)**
ln PAT_IN_{ikt}	0.00110***	0.00207***	-0.00206***
	(0.000146)	(0.000164)	(0.000303)
ln PAT_OUT_{ikt}	0.00195***	0.00288***	-0.000808*
	(0.000243)	(0.000405)	(0.000355)
ln PAT_DOM_{ikt}	0.000226*	-0.000701***	0.00380***
	(0.000106)	(0.000115)	(0.000268)
ln GDP_{it}	0.0640***	0.110***	-0.0145+
	(0.00298)	(0.00350)	(0.00755)
ln GDP_PC_{ikt}	-0.0615***	-0.116***	0.0188**
	(0.00304)	(0.00368)	(0.00709)
WTO_{it} (1/0)	-0.00191*	0.0318***	0.000376
	(0.000761)	(0.00738)	(0.000996)
Country-Industry FEs	Yes	Yes	Yes
Year FEs	Yes	Yes	Yes
Observations	24,990	16,660	8,330
R-squared	0.952	0.957	0.933

Source: authors' analysis as described in the chapter text
Robust standard errors clustered by industry in parentheses. *, **, and *** denotes significance at 5, 1 and 0.1% confidence level

Table A16.2 *Country-Industry Regressions on* NStages *and* Upstreamness, *1995–2011*

	NStages			***Upstreamness***		
	(1) **ln $NStages_{ikt}$** **(All)**	**(2)** **ln $NStages_{ikt}$** **(High-Income)**	**(3)** **ln $NStages_{ikt}$** **(Middle-Income)**	**(4)** **ln $Upstream_{ikt}$** **(All)**	**(5)** **ln $Upstream_{ikt}$** **(High-Income)**	**(6)** **ln $Upstream_{ikt}$** **(Middle-Income)**
$\ln PAT\_IN_{ikt}$	0.00135	-0.00134	0.00973***	-0.00202	-0.00446**	0.00530*
	(0.000889)	(0.00100)	(0.00183)	(0.00130)	(0.00157)	(0.00241)
$\ln PAT\_OUT_{ikt}$	-0.000767	0.00148	-0.0205***	-0.0122***	-0.00261	-0.0258***
	(0.00144)	(0.00188)	(0.00272)	(0.00210)	(0.00294)	(0.00358)
$\ln PAT\_DOM_{ikt}$	-0.000167	-0.00121+	0.000591	0.00284**	0.00369***	0.000344
	(0.000602)	(0.000666)	(0.00127)	(0.000879)	(0.00104)	(0.00167)
Country FEs	No	No	No	No	No	No
Industry FEs	No	No	No	No	No	No
Country-Industry FEs	Yes	Yes	Yes	Yes	Yes	Yes
Year FEs	Yes	Yes	Yes	Yes	Yes	Yes
Observations	24,990	16,660	8,330	24,990	16,660	8,330
R-squared	0.952	0.959	0.938	0.911	0.907	0.921

Source: authors' analysis as described in the chapter text

Robust standard errors clustered by industry in parentheses. *, **, and *** denotes significance at 5, 1 and 0.1% confidence level. All sets of regressions include country regressors of GDP, GDP per capita and WTO membership which are not reported here, but are available upon request.

17

The Enforcement of Intellectual Property Rights in a Digital Era

MICHAEL D. SMITH AND RAHUL TELANG*

Abstract

While the recent diffusion of broadband Internet access has significantly improved the productivity of users, it has also made it hard to enforce intellectual property for digital goods like movies and music. Internet access makes it easy for users to infringe digital content and has undermined the property rights of creators. We first provide evidence and review methods adopted by researchers to quantify the revenue losses in these industries and outline the challenges in quantifying these numbers. We then discuss how poor enforcement of intellectual property undermines creators' incentives to create the goods and innovation, hurting society's broader wellbeing. We review current research in this space and discuss the respective roles of government, rights holders, ISPs and platforms in enforcing the rights. The role can be demand side (where demand of infringing goods is reduced) or supply side (where supply of infringing content is reduced). We outline the short-term and long-term effectiveness of various policies and stakeholders in different counties.

Introduction

The diffusion of broadband Internet access has facilitated a dramatic growth in e-commerce trade, first through the diffusion of broadband landline connections and more recently through the diffusion of broadband mobile connections. Lin (2015), for example, finds a direct correlation between increased Internet use and global trade, estimating that a

* The authors thank the editors of this volume for helpful comments on this research. This research was conducted as part of Carnegie Mellon University's Initiative for Digital Entertainment Analytics (IDEA), which receives unrestricted (gift) funding from the Motion Picture Association of America. This research was conducted independently without any oversight or editorial control.

10 per cent increase in a country's Internet use causes a 0.2–0.4 per cent increase in international trade from that country.

As a result of these technological developments, e-commerce transactions have become an important part of worldwide trade and economic development. Today in developed countries close to 12 per cent of all retail transactions occur online.[1] Moreover, goods produced by the copyright industries represent a particularly vital and growing category of overall trade. For example, a 2015 report by the World Intellectual Property Organization (WIPO, 2015) showed that, across studies in 42 different countries, the copyright industries make up an average of 5.2 per cent of country-level GDP, with a high of 11 per cent in the United States and a low of 2 per cent in Brunei.

Goods produced by the copyright industries fall into the broad economic category of information goods. Information goods have two important economic characteristics that enhance their attractiveness for trade in online markets. First, they are non-rivalrous, which means that consumption by one person doesn't impede simultaneous consumption by someone else. Second, information goods can be replicated with perfect accuracy at near zero marginal cost. These two characteristics give them unique scale and scope advantages for trade over a worldwide digital communications network, and have made them an important and growing part of digital trade.

However, these same characteristics also introduce unique challenges for worldwide trade by making it easy for digital pirates to make unauthorized copies of information goods. Trade in pirated goods isn't a new phenomenon of course. Piracy and the counterfeiting of physical goods has always been part of worldwide trade, whether from the sale of pirated DVDs in Mumbai or fake Rolex watches in New York. The growth of broadband has made trade in counterfeit goods much easier. The goods can be advertised on a variety of popular Internet platforms greatly increasing the scale and scope of such trade. In fact, an OECD report estimates that in 2013 worldwide trade in counterfeit physical goods reached USD 461 billion, approximately 2.6 per cent of global trade (OECD/EUIPO, 2016).

However, digital piracy represents a unique and growing threat to producers of information goods. A recent survey of customers by the European Commission found that 68 per cent of respondents watched

[1] See www.statista.com/statistics/534123/e-commerce-share-of-retail-sales-worldwide/.

films via 'free downloads', and half did so weekly (EC, 2013). And there are good reasons to believe that the availability of free content online is cannibalizing sales in paid channels. For example, legal music sales fell by 50 per cent in the decade following the introduction of the pirate network Napster (Liebowitz, 2014), home entertainment sales of movies fell by over 25 per cent in the four years after the widespread diffusion of the BitTorrent protocol (Danaher et al., 2017), and according to a report by Digital TV Research, in 2017 alone streaming services lost an estimated USD 31.8 billion to piracy compared to USD 46.5 billion in total revenue (Digital TV Research, 2017).

There are many reasons why information goods face an increased threat from infringement. For one, information goods can be replicated with little cost and with almost no loss of quality. The reproduction does not require special skills or equipment, making it possible for even an individual user to supply them. Second, information goods can be readily downloaded with a click of a button reducing the transaction cost to almost zero. Finally, the global nature of the Internet ensures the scope of digital piracy is not limited to local markets anymore. A Hollywood movie can be copied and hosted on a server in Eastern Europe but can be readily downloaded by US consumers, hurting the sales even in the US market. Given the anonymity of the Internet, it is very hard for law enforcement to arrest and prosecute individuals providing digital pirated content online. Moreover, the global nature of the Internet means that the prosecution of offenders frequently involves cooperation across multiple jurisdictions, increasing the difficulty in bringing pirates to justice. These factors make digital piracy significantly more pernicious to the copyright industries than prior threats from physical piracy.

Given the importance of trade in goods produced by the copyright industries, and given the unique challenges in protecting that trade from piracy in digital markets, our goal in this chapter is to synthesize the academic literature to help policymakers better understand the empirical evidence of both the impact of piracy on worldwide trade in copyrighted goods and the effectiveness of various strategies for protecting intellectual property from the threat of piracy.

To conduct this analysis, we note that for there to be a need to protect trade in copyrighted goods, it first must be the case that (1) piracy harms sales in legal markets; (2) lost revenue from piracy impacts producers' incentives to innovate and create new content; and (3) anti-piracy measures can be effective at changing consumer behaviour. As such, we discuss the empirical evidence for these three questions below, starting with the impact of piracy on legal trade.

Our analysis of these three questions shows that, first, the presence of piracy harms legal trade in almost all of the settings that have been studied in the academic literature. In our review of the literature, 26 out of 29 studies published in peer-reviewed academic journals found statistically and economically significant harm from piracy. Second, there is growing empirical evidence in the literature that the lost sales from piracy reduce the incentives producers have to create new products, and that these reduced incentives could be disproportionately large on some types of culturally important entertainment goods. Finally, we note that many studies in the literature show that anti-piracy policies can be effective, such that even small changes in the relative cost of consuming pirated content versus legal content can cause substantial changes in consumer behaviour.

The Impact of Piracy on Legitimate Demand

As we noted above, for there to be a need to protect the copyright industries from pirated content, it first must be the case that pirated content has an impact on legal sales.

Unfortunately, answering this question is complicated both theoretically and empirically. From a purely theoretical perspective, the impact of piracy is indeterminate: piracy could have a negative, positive, or no impact on sales. A negative impact of piracy could occur if individuals who would have otherwise purchased the content choose to consume the content in (free) pirate channels instead.

Piracy could have a positive impact on sales if increased consumption of piracy led to increased awareness of the content among consumers (who presumably would choose legal channels to consume after becoming aware of the product). Alternatively, piracy could increase consumption in other channels and/or complements. For example, some have argued that even though music piracy might decrease music sales, it could also lead to increased concert ticket sales.

Lastly, piracy could have no impact on legal sales if the sorts of individual who pirate were unlikely to make legal purchases in the first place. In short, there are reasonable theoretical arguments that piracy could help, hurt, or have no impact on sales. Ultimately, the true impact of piracy on sales is an empirical question.

Unfortunately, answering this question is complicated by three main factors. First, it is difficult to directly observe the amount of piracy committed online. This is due to the not particularly surprising fact that most pirates take steps to hide their activity. Second, we can only directly observe the sales that actually occur in the market, not the sales that *would have* occurred if not for piracy – what economists refer to as the counterfactual. Third, and related, observational data are almost always contaminated by unobserved factors that impact both the independent and dependent variables. These omitted variables cause bias in our estimates on the impact of piracy on sales.

However, several papers in the literature have tried to overcome these challenges using a variety of methods. Several studies address the endogeneity between individual preferences to consume movies and the observed piracy and legal consumption at an individual level by creating a panel of behaviour over several years and then accounting for unobserved differences in consumer preferences using individual fixed effects (Rob and Waldfogel, 2007; Waldfogel, 2010; Bai and Waldfogel, 2012; Herz and Kiljanski, 2018). Other studies (e.g. Zentner, 2006; Liebowitz, 2008) have used (presumably exogenous) cross-country or cross-city variation in piracy levels to identify the impact of piracy on sales.

Another method for dealing with the endogeneity between observed piracy and observed sales is to use a natural experiment. In a natural experiment, an event occurs that impacts only one part of the market in a way that is unrelated to future sales. In this way the 'natural' experiment mimics a controlled experiment where a researcher would randomly choose which subjects to treat. An example of this approach is Danaher et al. (2010), who used NBC's decision to remove their television content from the Apple iTunes store as an exogenous shock to the supply of NBC content and compared the levels of piracy for NBC content (the group treated by the natural experiment) to levels of piracy for untreated networks that were similar to NBC: ABC, CBS and FOX.

A final related method of dealing with the endogeneity between piracy and sales is to use an instrumental variable that proxies for exogenous shifts in the dependent variable. For example, Oberholzer and Strumpf (2007) used such an approach to analyse the impact of music piracy on sales in the US. Their instrument was the incidence of school holidays in Germany under the argument that German school holidays are uncorrelated with sales in the United States, but that when German school children are away from school they have more time to engage in piracy, which in a globally interconnected marketplace makes it easier for US consumers to access pirated content.

However, while the literature uses different approaches to analyse the impact of piracy on legal sales, the results from this literature are notably similar. We are aware of 29 peer-reviewed academic studies analysing the impact of piracy on sales. Of these studies, three find no impact of piracy on sales (see Table A17.1 in the Appendix) and 26 find both a statistically and economically negative impact of piracy (see Table A17.2 in the Appendix).[2]

If one were to take all of these results at face value, the conclusion would be that piracy harms sales in the vast majority of settings where it occurs. This includes books, where Reimers (2016) finds that anti-piracy enforcement results in a 14 per cent increase in legal sales; movies, where Herz and Kiljanski (2018) find that one pirate viewing displaces approximately 0.37 units of paid viewings; and music, where Bender and Wang (2009) find that a 1 per cent increase in the rate of piracy caused music sales to decline by 0.6 per cent.

These results also seem to suggest that piracy is more harmful early in the content release cycle versus later in the release cycle. For example, Ma et al. (2014) find that pre-release movie piracy causes a 19.1 per cent drop in theatrical sales, but Smith and Telang (2009) find no impact of movie piracy when a movie is broadcast on television (which typically occurs several years after its theatrical premiere).

It is also important to recognize that these lost sales are only part of the problem for the copyright industries. This is because piracy impacts the willingness to pay of all customers, even the ones who choose to remain in legal channels. As noted by Smith and Telang (2016), 'piracy creates a new alternative for consumers that competes on not just price but also on timeliness, quality, and usability — the same factors the entertainment industries have relied on to execute their business models'.

However, the fact that piracy harms sales in legal channels is not the only necessary condition for piracy to be harmful to overall social welfare. In the next section, we discuss the second necessary condition: that piracy impacts creative output.

The Impact of Piracy on Innovation and Creative Output

Although piracy appears to harm sales in almost all settings analysed in the academic literature, this doesn't necessarily mean that piracy harms overall social welfare. The reason for this is that, although lost revenues represent a decline in welfare for producers, piracy *could* result in a far larger increase in welfare consumers by allowing them to access content

[2] These tables are adapted and updated from Danaher, Smith and Telang (2017).

that they otherwise would not have been able to access, leading to significantly larger consumption. In this way, lost sales from piracy could be modelled as a mere wealth transfer from producers to consumers.

However, producers could respond by shrinking their output and investments as their profitability is eroded. This will hurt innovation and creative output, and will lower consumer welfare as well.[3] Indeed, for piracy to be harmful to social welfare it must be the case that the reduced revenues from piracy cause producers to invest less in the market, resulting in fewer and lower quality content than otherwise would have occurred.

However, while it is well understood, theoretically, that strong intellectual property rights protection is necessary for invention and creative output, the empirical evidence on the role of the strength of IPRs (especially for copyright) and creativity is not well developed (see a National Research Council report highlighting the lack of empirical documentation on short- and long-run effects of copyright (NRC 2013)). Indeed, proving that piracy results in lower output and lower quality output is in many ways significantly more challenging.

Besides the fact that it is extremely difficult to observe the counterfactual of how much creative output would have occurred in the absence of piracy, it is difficult to disentangle the impact of piracy on the marketplace from the impact of other changes to content (especially the cost to produce and distribute) that are occurring at the same time. In fact, Handke (2012) and Waldfogel (2012) both find that following the introduction of Napster, there was no significant change in the quality and quantity of music.

However, the lack of a change in music output and music quality after Napster doesn't necessarily mean that increased piracy had no impact on industry quality and output. New distribution and production technologies that accompanied Napster meant that new music is more likely to be made and distributed. Both authors acknowledge these challenges.

In short, to analyse whether piracy *alone* has an impact on creative output, one needs a setting where you can tease out the impact of piracy on creative output from other simultaneous technological changes in the cost of creative output. Fortunately, there is a burgeoning literature that is attempting to do this.

[3] It is also the case that piracy could harm consumers by exposing them to increased risks from malware, as shown in Telang (2018).

One approach, adopted by Telang and Waldfogel (2018), is to use a time period in a market where production costs were not declining, but where piracy became rampant. They find such a setting in Bollywood movie production in the early- and mid-1980s. This setting is useful for two reasons. First, movies are useful to study because their investment is significantly larger than music, and therefore a decrease in revenue may have a larger impact on output. Second, the Indian market for movies in the early- and mid-1980s is useful to study because the introduction of the VCR in India during this time frame represents a discrete change in the ease of piracy without a collinear change in the cost of production or the ease of distribution (as was the case with the diffusion of Napster). Specifically, prior to the widespread deployment of the VCR in India, it was relatively difficult to pirate movies. However, after the VCR, movie-piracy became widespread in India.

Telang and Waldfogel (2018) use this setting and ask whether this increase in piracy made a difference to revenue in the Indian movie market and the quality and quantity of movies produced by Bollywood. Their results with respect to revenue, reproduced in Figure 17.1, show that revenue was relatively flat in Bollywood throughout the 1970s, but began a sharp drop starting around the time the VCR was introduced in the

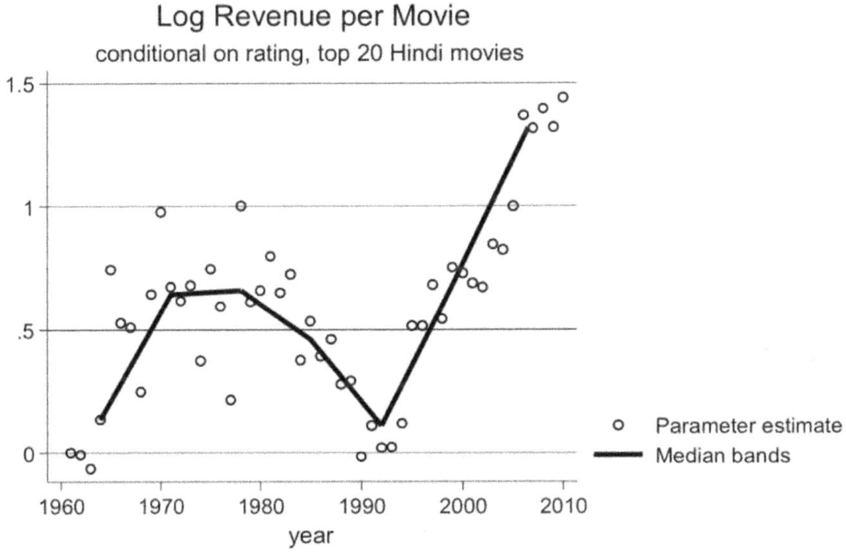

Figure 17.1 Bollywood revenue (log scale), 1960–2010
Source: Telang and Waldfogel, 2018.

early-1980s. This revenue drop continued until the late 1990s, when revenue recovered as Bollywood movies gained access to worldwide markets.

Telang and Waldfogel (2018) then ask whether this decrease in revenue had an impact on both the production and quality of Indian movies. They measure production as the number of movies produced per year by Bollywood based on different source indices (see Figure 17.2) and quality as the average IMDb rating of the movies produced in each year (see Figure 17.3). Figure 17.2 shows that, as with revenue, movie output was increasing in the two decades prior to the 1980s and then started to fall in the middle of the 1980s, recovering in the early- to mid-1990s. Figure 17.3 displays similar results with respect to the quality of movies as measured by IMDb ratings. IMDb ratings of movies released in the 1960s and 1970s were relatively stable, but experienced a sharp decline in the early 1980s, recovering somewhat in the late 1990s.

These results are consistent with the revenue results above, suggesting that the decreased revenue available from movie investment in Bollywood led to a decrease in investment in movies being made in Bollywood that exhibited itself in a drop in both quantity and quality.

Another way to measure the impact of piracy on creative output is to compare domestic output across countries with relatively high and low

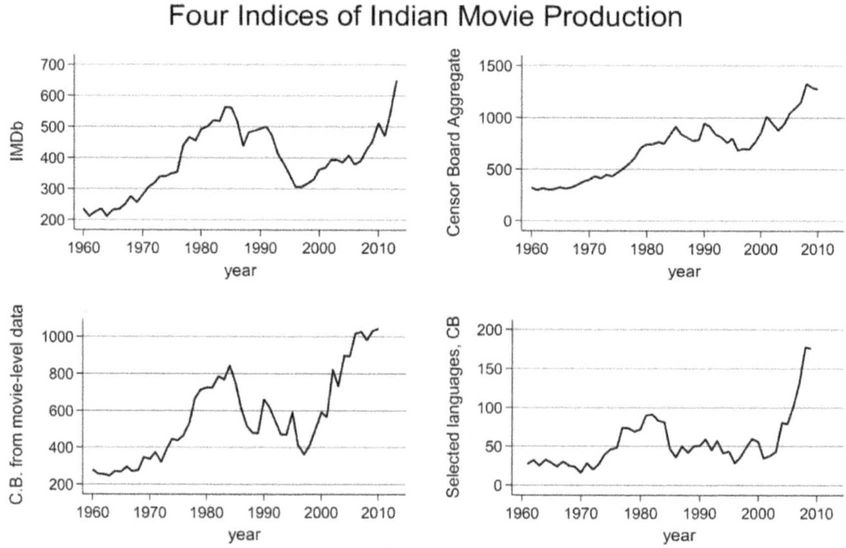

Figure 17.2 Indices of Indian movie production, 1960–2010
Source: Telang and Waldfogel, 2018.

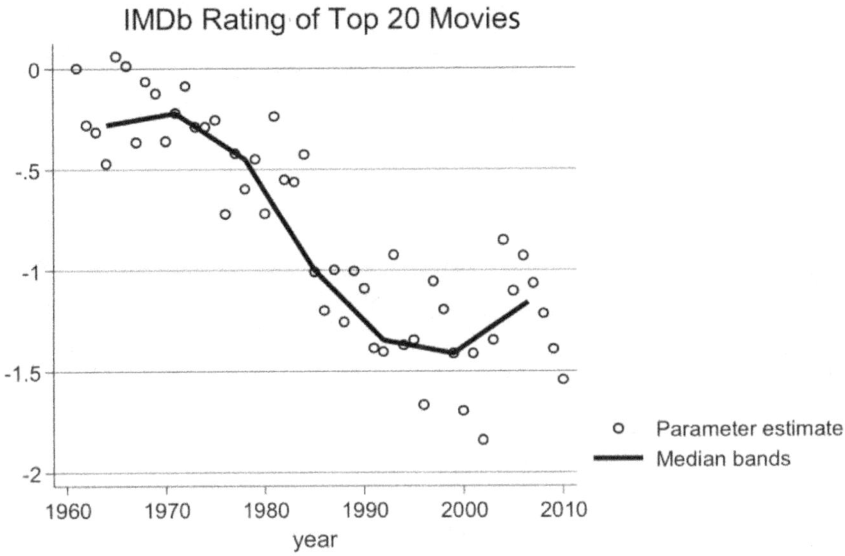

Figure 17.3 IMDb rating of top 20 Bollywood movies
Source: Telang and Waldfogel, 2018.

piracy before and after the widespread availability of piracy in a market. Danaher and Smith (2017) adopt this strategy by analysing the production of award-winning independent films in a local market. The motivation is that, if piracy is impacting the production of high-quality movies, one would expect it to have a larger impact on production in high piracy markets versus low piracy markets.

Danaher and Smith (2017) explore this hypothesis by comparing the number of Academy award-winning movies in Mexico, Italy and Spain (countries with a relatively high incidence of piracy) versus Germany, the UK and France (countries with a low incidence of piracy). Their results, reproduced in Table 17.1, show suggestive evidence that there was a larger drop in award-winning movies in high piracy countries after 2007 (16 award-winning movies before versus 8 after) versus the decline in high piracy countries after 2007 (61 award winning movies before versus 57 after). While not conclusive, this is suggestive that lost revenues from piracy had an impact on creativity and overall output.

In short, there is strong empirical evidence that piracy harms revenue available to the copyright industries and there is emerging evidence that this reduced revenue is causing a reduction in both the quantity and quality of content produced by the copyright industries. Given these two findings, there may be a need for policymakers to protect trade by

Table 17.1 *Academy awards by country, pre-/post-piracy*

Academy awards by country, pre-/post-piracy				
	1995–2006		2007–2014	
	Number of award winning movies	Total awards	Number of award winning movies	Total awards
Germany	22	40	10	15
UK	21	35	33	68
France	12	14	14	20
Mexico	4	7	1	1
Italy	8	10	2	2
Spain	4	6	3	3

Source: Danaher and Smith, 2017.

increasing the strength of intellectual property enforcement. In the next two sections, we first discuss the challenges to intellectual property enforcement and the options currently being pursued by governments to ensure adequate intellectual property enforcement, and then the available empirical evidence of the effectiveness of these efforts.

Policy Responses to Piracy

One way to categorize the available policy responses to piracy is to identify the parties who might be able to intervene in the transmission of pirated content – governments, right holders, online platforms and Internet service providers (ISPs) – and then consider the various strategies these parties could take to influence both the supply of and demand for pirated content.

Governments

At the top level, governments are able to create and enforce laws governing both the suppliers and the consumers of pirated content. As noted in the prior section, governments may wish to provide strong intellectual property rights protection as a way to maximize overall social welfare by ensuring a healthy market for content creation. Governments have served this role in a variety of ways. For example, most developed economies provide legal structures for IPRs protection, including enabling the prosecution of both individuals providing pirated content and those consuming pirated content.

In the United States, for example, Title 17 of the US Code provides criminal penalties for copyright violations. Specifically, Title 17 defines copyright infringement as a felony and provides up to five years imprisonment and up to a USD 500,000 fine for first-time offenders. Other governments have created laws that seek to limit access to infringing content online either by shutting down well-known pirate sites, requiring ISPs to block access to such sites, or by notifying individuals of potential penalties for consuming copyrighted content. For example, in the context of site shutdowns, on 19 January 2012, the US Federal Bureau of Investigation seized the domain name and assets of the file hosting site Megaupload.com, and charged its founder, Kim Dotcom, with a variety of crimes associated with the operation of this site. In the context of site blocking, various governments, including the UK, Australia, Brazil and Indonesia require ISPs to block access to well-known pirate sites. And in the context of notice sending programs, in 2009 the French government created an anti-piracy law called HADOPI that was designed to send a graduated set of notices to individuals found to be engaging in copyright infringement online.

However, a significant challenge associated with these government efforts is that they are expensive and there are no guarantees that they will be effective at changing consumer behaviour. For example, infringing content is likely to remain available on multiple other sites even after the shutdown of the initial site (e.g. Lauinger et al., 2013). Similarly, site blocking efforts at the ISP-level may not be effective because there are a variety of technical workarounds that users can employ (such as Virtual Privacy Network services) to get around these blocks. Finally, graduated response notice sending programs may not be effective at changing user behaviour because of limited enforcement and light penalties.

Right Holders

Right holders can play a role in protecting their own content against piracy in a variety of ways. First, they can implement educational campaigns to inform consumers about the risks of piracy, the harm piracy can cause to artists and the existence of legal alternatives to piracy. Second, they can adopt technical measures in digital files, also known as Digital Rights Management (DRM), to make it harder for users to make copies of those files. Third, they can change how their content is distributed and marketed to adapt to the presence of piracy in the marketplace. Many legal digital distribution channels were initially presented as direct responses to the presence of piracy in the market. For example, in a 2003 interview with CNN, Steve Jobs touted the advantages of the iTunes music store by observing that if you pirated, you were frequently 'spending an hour to download four songs that you could buy for under $4 from Apple, which means you're working for under minimum wage'.[4] Similarly, in a 2014 blog post, Spotify CEO Daniel Eck observed that Spotify 'was working day and night to recover money for artists and the music business that piracy was stealing away'. Rights holders have also changed their marketing practices in response to piracy, including reducing the time between various release windows and reducing prices for their content on legal distribution channels.

While these changes in distribution and marketing may be effective at increasing the attractiveness of legal content relative to pirated content, they also come at a cost. Reducing the delay between release windows may make it harder for firms to price discriminate across customers with different valuations – a key pricing strategy used by sellers of information goods. Likewise, adopting new digital channels can cannibalize sales in existing channels. Finally, given the high concentration of most Internet platform markets, adding content to online platforms can serve to increase their power in the market relative to the power of rights holders (see, for example, Smith and Telang, 2016, chapter 8).

In addition to educating customers about the risks of piracy and changing distribution and marketing strategies, right holders can bring direct legal actions against pirates. Most developed economies give right holders the ability to make civil claims associated with copyright violations. In the United States, for example, the law gives right holders the ability to take legal action against both infringing networks and individuals engaged in copyright infringements; and right holders have used both tactics in their fight against piracy.

In terms of lawsuits against individuals, in April 2003 the Recording Industry Association of America (RIAA) brought civil lawsuits against four individual college students for sharing music files through campus networks. These cases were settled out of court, with the defendants paying damages that were reported to be in the range of USD 12,500 to USD 17,000.[5] These cases were followed by numerous others, with the

[4] See www.cnn.com/2003/TECH/industry/04/29/jobs.interview/.

[5] See www.wired.com/2003/09/riaa-lawsuit-orgy-underway/.

Electronic Frontiers Foundation claiming that by July 2006 over 20,000 individuals had been sued by the music industry.

The challenge with fighting piracy by taking individuals to court is that such actions can backfire in the court of public opinion. Press coverage of the RIAA's lawsuits tended to focus on particularly sympathetic cases, including lawsuits against 'a 12 year old Manhattan schoolgirl', 'a working mom' and a '71-year-old grandpa'.[6] For this reason, in late 2008, the RIAA announced that it was dropping the strategy of mass lawsuits against individuals in favour of lawsuits against the networks themselves.[7]

These lawsuits, brought by the RIAA, the Motion Picture Association of America (MPAA), and their member companies, include suits against almost all of the best-known piracy platforms such as Napster, iMesh, Bearshare and Grokster. The latter case made it all the way to the US Supreme Court in the *MGM* v. *Grokster* case. In that case, the Court ruled in favour of copyright holders, stating that 'one who distributes a device with the object of promoting its use to infringe copyright, as shown by clear expression or other affirmative steps taken to foster infringement, is liable for the resulting acts of infringement by third parties'.

The challenge with lawsuits against networks supplying pirated content is two-fold. First, they are costly and time-consuming for rights holders. Second, it is not clear whether they are effective given that the networks that are shut down are typically replaced by new file-sharing networks: Napster begat Scour, which begat Aimster, which begat AudioGalaxy and so on. This process has been referred to as a game of 'Whac-a-Mole' by many industry observers.[8]

Platforms

The cases cited above concern platforms that were almost exclusively engaged in exchanging pirated content. But what about the role of online platforms that are only partially, and possibly even unwittingly, facilitating trade in infringing works? For example, sites like eBay, YouTube and Facebook provide public platforms where users can post products for

[6] See www.wired.com/2003/09/schoolgirl-settles-with-riaa/.

[7] See www.wired.com/2010/05/riaa-bump/.

[8] See, for example, www.nytimes.com/2012/08/05/sunday-review/internet-pirates-will-always-win.html; www.engadget.com/2015/05/15/european-commission-piracy/; and www.nytimes.com/2013/01/29/business/media/playing-whac-a-mole-with-piracy-sites.html.

sale, videos for public consumption or information for friends to view. Likewise, Google provides a platform where users can discover content online. These sites aren't promoted 'to infringe copyright' as in the Grokster example above. Nonetheless, they frequently facilitate access to infringing content. How should law-makers deal with these sites?

In the context of US law, the responsibility for policing content on such public platforms is typically shared between the right holders and the platform. The Digital Millennium Copyright Act explicitly exempts intermediaries from liability as long as they take down infringing content in a timely manner following a request from the right holder. Thus, the right holder has the responsibility of identifying infringing content and links, and the platform has the responsibility of taking this content down upon request. In some cases, the platform itself chose to put systems in place to pro-actively identify and take down files that match the audio or video fingerprint provided by right holders. For example, YouTube's Content ID allows right holders to provide YouTube with audio and video files of copyrighted works. YouTube then uses these files to create fingerprints of protected content and compares these fingerprints to content uploaded by users – flagging uploaded content that matches known copyrighted files.

The problem with these approaches is that they place an enormous burden on both right holders and platforms. From the perspective of right holders, they are required to take costly steps to police various online platforms searching for infringing content, and then send out 'takedown' notices to those sites, with the knowledge that much of the content that is taken down will quickly be replaced by new infringing links. On the other hand, the platforms themselves must develop systems and procedures to respond to the flood of notice and takedown requests. For example, Google processes close to 20 million takedown notices *per week* from right holders (see Figure 17.4).

Internet Service Providers

ISPs are important in anti-piracy efforts because they have a point of direct connection with individual customers: ISPs bill customers, provision IP addresses for their customers and provision bandwidth to their customers. Because of this, ISPs are frequently called on, either by courts or by right holders, to participate in anti-piracy efforts by identifying which subscriber is associated with an IP address that was observed

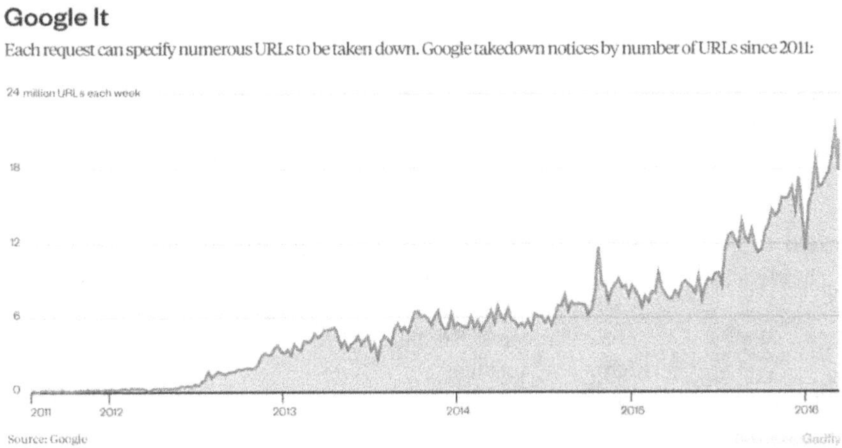

Figure 17.4 Google notice and takedown requests, 2011–2016
Source: Google Tranparency Report.[9]

infringing content, by delivering notices to infringers or by blocking known infringing sites as discussed above.

ISPs may have conflicting interests in cooperating with these requests, however. On the one hand, ISPs have incentives to ensure that their customers are satisfied with the service provided by the ISP, and many customers choose to have fast broadband connections to the Internet in part so they can engage in piracy. On the other hand, the bandwidth used by pirated content can be expensive to ISPs, occupying large proportions of their scarce bandwidth and potentially cannibalizing other legal (paid) services that the ISPs (particularly cable ISPs) provide.

A Taxonomy of Anti-Piracy Options

Synthesizing the different options described above, one can categorize potential anti-piracy policies along two axes. One axis involves the party or parties primarily involved in the action: governments, right holders, platforms, ISPs. The other axis concerns whether the anti-piracy action targets the individuals engaged in piracy (the demand-side) or the parties providing the infringing content (the supply-side). Table 17.2 graphically displays this categorization along with representative actions.

[9] See https://torrentfreak.com/google-asked-to-remove-100000-pirate-links-every-hour-160306/.

Table 17.2 *Taxonomy of anti-piracy options*

	Supply-side	Demand-side
Government	Site shutdowns (e.g. Megaupload); site blocking (e.g. UK, Australia); laws and legal structures	Graduated response programs (e.g. HADOPI)
Right holders	Lawsuits against pirate networks; takedown notices to search engines and other online platforms; Digital Rights Management	Educational campaigns; lawsuits against users; changes to marketing/ distribution
Platform	Removing or reducing the prominence of pirated content	Flagging potentially infringing content
ISP	Blocking access to known pirate sites (UK Blocking)	Notice sending programs (Copyright Alert System, CCUK)

Source: Authors' analysis.

From Table 17.4 and the discussion above, it is clear that there are many potential options for addressing digital piracy. What remains is evaluating which of these various options are actually effective at changing consumer behaviour. In the next section, we discuss several empirical studies that have attempted to do just that.

Empirical Evidence of the Impact of Anti-Piracy Programs

Supply-Side

As the name suggests, the supply-side interventions try to limit the availability of infringing content. This is done by either passing laws or by private efforts to make it hard for suppliers to supply infringing content online.

There are several studies in the literature on the effectiveness of government efforts to limit the supply of pirated content. The first such study is Danaher and Smith (2014b), who analyse the impact of the shutdown of Megaupload on sales of digital movies. As noted earlier, Megaupload was shut down on 19 January 2012 when the United States Department of Justice seized the domain name and servers of

Megaupload. The authors take advantage of the fact that there was significant heterogeneity in the popularity of Megaupload at a country-level. For example, nearly 17 per cent of Spanish Internet users and 11 per cent of French Internet users visited Megaupload in the month before it was shut down, versus only 2 per cent in Australia, Germany, and the UK. The authors then use this variation in the 'Megaupload Penetration Ratio' to evaluate whether the shutdown is causally related to a change in sales.

The authors find that countries with higher penetration ratios had the largest increase in legal sales after the site was shut down. As shown in Figure 17.5, there is a positive correlation between the Megaupload penetration ratio shown on the X-axis and the change in digital movie sales from the month before and after the shutdown as shown on the Y-axis. They estimate that Megaupload caused a 6.5–8.5 per cent increase in legal digital movie sales for the three major motion picture studios in their data.

However, government-ordered site shutdowns don't always have positive impacts on legal consumption either because of heterogeneity in product characteristics or because, in some cases, users find it easy to

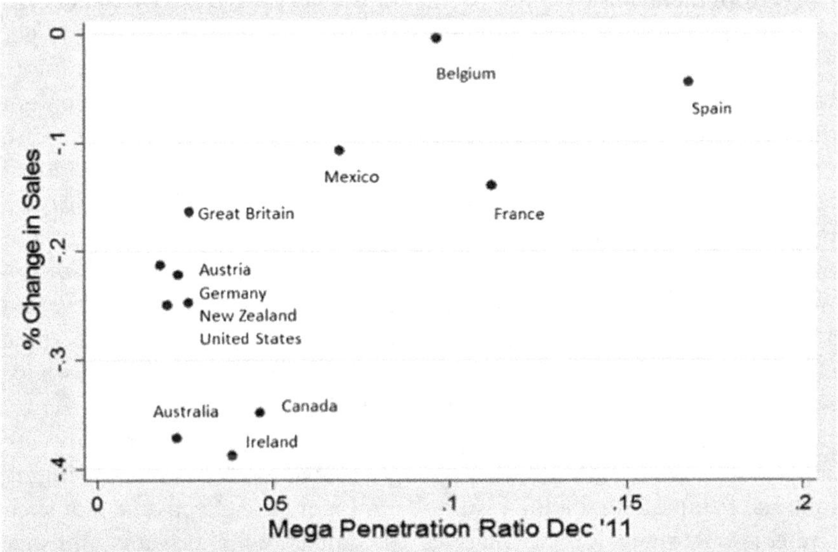

Figure 17.5 Post-shutdown change in weekly digital movie sales vs December 2011 Megaupload penetration

Source: Danaher and Smith, 2014b, p. 4, Figure 1.

discover other sites. For example, Peukert et al. (2017) analysed the impact of the Megaupload shutdown in the context of theatrical revenue. They found results very similar to Danaher and Smith's (2017) for movies in 'wide release'. However, they also found that niche movies and those released by independent studios did not benefit from (or were even hurt by) the shutdown. They argue that Megaupload may have served as an advertising vehicle for these lesser-known movies. Similarly, Aguilar et al. (2018) find that the shutdown of the kino.to website in Germany on 8 June 2011 had little impact on user behaviour as users simply switched to other well-known piracy sites.

Right holders, privately, have made a variety of efforts to limit the supply of pirated content. One notable strategy is using Digital Rights Management (DRM) technologies to make it more difficult for consumers to make copies of digital files. These technologies are designed to stop casual copying of digital files between users, and they have undoubtedly been successful in many contexts. However, DRM systems also carry notable risks for right holders. For example, DRM systems may decrease overall consumer utility by limiting their options for how legally purchased content can be consumed. Reduced utility of DRM-restricted content is consistent with Zhang (2018), who finds that when right holders removed DRM from their music content, digital music sales increased by 10 per cent overall and that sales of 'long tail' albums increased by far more (40 per cent) than more popular albums. In effect, consumers placed far more value on content they could play on a variety of devices than on content that was restricted. A second possible risk of DRM is that it could increase platform power by increasing consumer lock-in. Smith and Telang (2016) argue that once consumers have purchased DRM-protected content from a particular platform, they will be less likely to incur the complexity and overhead of using a different DRM technology from a competing platform. In this regard, some have argued that Apple's iTunes DRM systems created a strong lock-in to the iTunes platform, and increased the power of Apple at the expense of right holders. As of now, most of the music labels have moved away from the consumer-acing DRM.

In addition to using DRM protection, right holders can limit the supply of pirated content by using legal measures to remove infringing material from search engine results. To measure the effectiveness of such strategies, Reimers (2016) analyses the impact of a private publisher (RosettaBooks) who used services provided by Digimarc to take down infringing links on some of its content. Reimers finds that enforcement in this way increased sales of the protected electronic books by 14 per cent, but had no impact on sales of print books. Again, the difference between the response to electronic and print books likely reflects the fact that digital piracy is a closer substitute for legal digital channels than it is for legal physical channels.

Online platforms, such as search engines, can also play a role in the fight against IP theft by making pirated content harder to find in search results, as Google did when it changed its search algorithm to demote pirated content in August 2012 and again in October 2014.[10] Many have argued that efforts to change consumer behaviour by making it harder to find pirated content would fail because consumers would be relatively inelastic to increased search costs.[11] Sivan et al. (2018) use a laboratory experiment to analyse the impact of demoting pirated content in search results. The authors show that removing pirated content from the top page of search results can significantly increase the likelihood that users will consume through legal channels, and that these results apply even among users whose searches and prior behaviour reveal a desire to consume pirated content.

Finally, ISPs also play a particularly important role in protecting copyrighted content because they have a direct connection with the consumer. Because of this, it's not surprising that various governments have instituted programmes that have required ISPs to take actions to reduce consumers' ability to access piracy, and several papers in the literature have studied the effectiveness of these programmes. For example, Poort et al. (2014) find that when Dutch courts required ISPs to block access to the major torrent site The Pirate Bay and its mirror sites, there was very little change in overall downloading of pirated content. Similarly, Danaher, Smith and Telang (2018) find very little impact of the decision in the UK to block access to The Pirate Bay. In their results, when The Pirate Bay was blocked, users simply switched to other unblocked sites or started using VPNs to go around the blocks. However, when 19 sites were simultaneously blocked in the UK in November 2013 and when 52 sites were blocked in November 2014, the authors observe different results. Specifically, blocking many sites at once caused a 10 per cent increase in visits to legal subscription sites and an 11.5 per cent increase in visits to legal ad-supported sites. Aligning

[10] See https://publicpolicy.googleblog.com/2014/10/continued-progress-on-fighting-piracy.html.

[11] See, e.g., www.techdirt.com/articles/20130221/07560622055 and www.extremetech.com/extreme/192471-g.

these results with those reported by Poort et al. (2014) suggests that, to be effective, ISP-level blocking must impact a large number of sites. Light enforcement or the shutdown of a small number of sites may not sufficiently inconvenience users to have them change their behaviour. However, when a sufficient number of sites are blocked, consumers can be convinced to return to legal channels.

Together these results suggest that government efforts to reduce the supply of pirated content can be effective if it makes it sufficiently hard for users to find other pirated content relative to the cost (both direct and indirect) of accessing legal content.

Demand-Side

These interventions target users to induce behavioural changes so the demand for infringing content shrinks. Government regulations have played an important role. Adermon and Liang (2014) analyse the impact of the IPRED law in Sweden. The law significantly increased the likelihood that users engaged in piracy would be caught and prosecuted. The authors find that in the first six months after its enactment, the law caused overall Internet traffic in Sweden to decrease by 16 per cent and total music sales to increase by 36 per cent. However, the authors also find that the effect disappeared after six months, which they attribute to weak legal enforcement of the law.

The HADOPI law in France is another example of a demand-side government intervention. The HADOPI law created a government body that issues graduated notices to consumers found engaging in online piracy and imposes penalties if their behaviour does not change. Danaher, Smith et al. (2014a) analyse the impact of this law by comparing digital music sales before and after the law went into effect in France versus a control group of countries (the UK, Italy, Spain, Germany, Belgium). The results, summarized in Figure 17.6, show that awareness of this law caused a 20–25 per cent increase in French music sales relative to sales in the control group countries. The increase in sales was much larger in more heavily pirated genres of music (Rap, Hip-Hop, Rock, Pop) versus less heavily pirated genres (Christian, Classical, Folk, and Jazz), further suggesting a causal relationship between the law and the observed sales changes.

These results contrast those in Smith, where the author finds that graduated response laws implemented across six countries have no impact on theatrical revenue. However, the difference between the

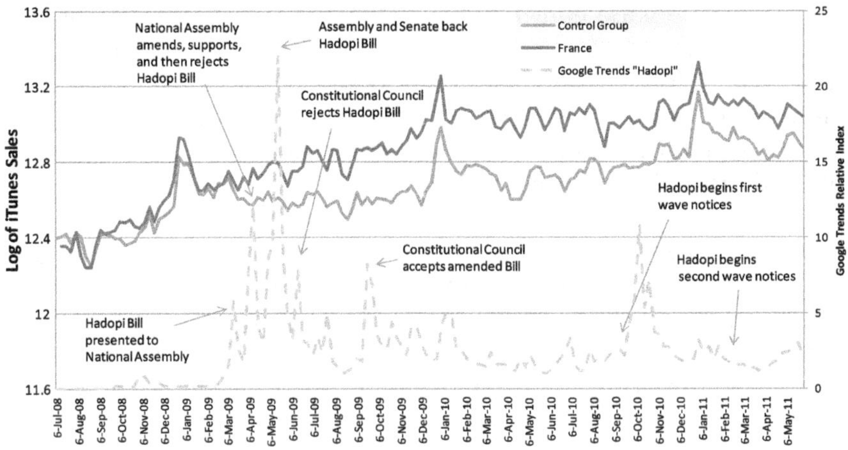

Figure 17.6 iTunes single track unit sales trends (2008–2011)
Source: Danaher et al., 2014a, p. 547, Figure 1.

findings in McKenzie and Danaher et al. (2014) could simply be due to the fact that digital piracy is a stronger substitute for digital sales channels than it is for physical sales channels (see also Danaher et al., 2010, 2015).

In short, the empirical evidence suggests that demand-side government policies can be effective at changing consumer behaviour, but that they need to be designed carefully such that enforcement is well-known among consumers and is effective.

Right holders can also play a role in influencing consumer behaviour with respect to piracy consumption. While in practice, this occurs both through lawsuits against individual users and through market-based measures to make legal content easier for consumers to purchase, studies in the literature have generally analysed the impact of market-based measures on consumer behaviour.

For example, Danaher et al. (2010) analyse the impact of NBC's decision to remove their television content from the iTunes store in December 2007. The authors compare piracy for NBC content before and after this date to piracy for a control group of content from ABC, CBS and FOX. They find that NBC's decision to remove its content from iTunes caused an 11.4 per cent increase in the demand for piracy of NBC content. In a similar way, Danaher et al. (2015) analyse ABC's decision to add its content to Hulu, showing that Hulu availability caused piracy on ABC content to decrease by 19 per cent.

Platforms can also influence the consumption of pirated content. For example, search engines can clearly differentiate between pirated and legal content in search results without changing search rankings. Sivan, Smith and Telang (2014) study this possibility by labelling infringing content with the flag 'this site may contain infringing content'. However, the authors find no significant change in user behaviour as a result of the flag.

ISPs have also played a role in notice sending activities. The Copyright Alert System (CAS) in the US was one such effort where right holders and ISPs worked together to identify infringing customers and send them notices (similar to the HADOPI effort). A similar programme (CCUK) is underway in the UK. The effectiveness of these programmes is not well understood yet.

ISPs can also influence user behaviour directly, potentially by targeting known pirates with special offers or other discounts on legal content. For example, de Matos, Ferreira and Smith (2017) use a randomized experiment to analyse whether targeting pirates with promotional offers – in their case free Subscription Video-On-Demand (SVOD) service – can have an impact on their piracy behaviour. They find that users who received the free SVOD offer decreased their BitTorrent usage by 18 per cent and their upload traffic by 45 per cent during the promotional period.

Discussion

Copyrighted goods are an increasingly important part of global trade and, because of their digital nature, are particularly vulnerable to infringement. However, for there to be a need to protect trade in copyrighted content, three important conditions must hold. First, the availability of infringement must harm sales in legal markets. Second, lost revenue from infringement must harm producers' incentives to innovate and create new content. Third, it must be the case that anti-piracy measures can be effective at changing consumer behaviour.

The empirical literature has analysed each of these questions. As shown in this chapter, the vast majority of the peer-reviewed papers in the literature find that piracy results in statistically significant harm to legal sales. While more nascent, the available literature also shows that lost revenue from piracy reduces the incentives that producers have to invest in copyrighted content, which may hurt overall social welfare. Finally, the literature shows that anti-piracy measures can be effective at changing consumer behaviour and that each of the major stakeholders in content delivery – governments, right holders, platforms and ISPs – can play a role in changing consumer behaviour. Moreover, the available empirical literature provides important guidance for policymakers in designing anti-piracy policy. Specifically, the literature suggests that active enforcement is important to influencing consumer behaviour and that anti-piracy measures are likely to have a stronger impact on digital sales channels than on physical channels. However, more empirical research, particularly field experiments, are needed to replicate and refine these results to better inform policymakers.

Bibliography

Adermon, Adrian and Liang, Che-Yuan, 'Piracy and Music Sales: The Effects of an Anti-Piracy Law' (2014), *Journal of Economic Behavior and Organization* 105: 90–106.

Aguiar, L., Claussen, J. and Peukert, C., 'Catch Me if You Can: Effectiveness and Consequences of Online Copyright Enforcement' *Information Systems Research*, Forthcoming.

Andersen, B. and Frenz, M., 'Don't Blame the P2P File-Sharers: The Impact of Free Music Downloads on The Purchase of Music CDs in Canada' (2010), *Journal of Evolutionary Economics* 20: 715–740.

Bai, J. and Waldfogel, J., 'Movie Piracy and Sales Displacement in Two Samples of Chinese Consumers' (2012), *Information Economics and Policy* 24, 3: 187–196.

Bender, M. T. and Wang, Y., 'The Impact of Digital Piracy on Music Sales: A Cross-Country Analysis' (2009), *International Social Science Review* 84, 3–4: 157–170.

Bhattacharjee, S., Gopal, R., Lertwachara, K., Marsden, J. and Telang, R., 'The Effect of Digital Sharing Technologies on Music Markets: A Survival Analysis of Albums on Ranking Charts' (2007), *Management Science* 53, 9: 1359–1374.

Bounie, D., Bourreau, M. and Waelbroeck, P., 'Piracy and the Demand for Films: Analysis of Piracy Behavior in French Universities' (2006), *Review of Economic Research on Copyright Issues* 3, 2: 15–27.

Danaher, B., Dhanasobhon, S., Smith, M. D. and Telang, R., 'Converting Pirates without Cannibalizing Purchasers: The Impact of Digital Distribution on Physical Sales and Internet Piracy' (2010), *Marketing Science* 29, 6: 1138–1151.

Danaher, Brett, Smith, Michael D., Telang, Rahul and Chen, Siwen, 'The Effect of Graduated Response Anti-Piracy Laws on Music Sales: Evidence from an Event Study in France' (2014), *Journal of Industrial Economics* 62, 3: 541–553.

Danaher, Brett and Smith, Michael D., 'Gone in 60 Seconds: The Impact of the Megaupload Shutdown on Movie Sales' (2014), *International Journal of Industrial Organization* 33: 1–8.

Danaher, Brett, Dhanasobhon, Samita, Smith, Michael D. and Telang, Rahul, 'Understanding Media Markets in the Digital Age: Economics and Methodology', in Avi Goldfarb, Shane M. Greenstein and Catherine E. Tucker (eds), *Economic Analysis of the Digital Economy*, Chicago: University of Chicago Press, 2015, pp. 385–406.

Danaher, Brett, Smith, Michael D. and Telang, Rahul, 'Copyright Enforcement in the Digital Age: Empirical Evidence and Conclusions' (2017), *Communications of the Association of Computing Machinery* 60, 2: 68–75.

Danaher, Brett and Smith, Michael D., 'Digital Piracy, Film Quality, and Social Welfare' (2017), *George Mason University Law Review* 24, 4: 923–938.

Danaher, Brett, Smith, Michael D. and Telang, Rahul, 'The Effect of Piracy Website Blocking on Consumer Behavior' Working Paper, Carnegie Mellon University, Pittsburgh, 2018, available at https://ssrn.com/abstract=2612063.

de Matos, Miguel Godinho, Ferreira, Pedro and Smith, Michael D., 'The Effect of Subscription Video-on-Demand on Piracy: Evidence from a Household-Level Randomized Experiment' (2017) *Management Science*.

De Vany, A. S. and Walls, W. D., 'Estimating the Effects of Movie Piracy on Box-office Revenue' (2007), *Review of Industrial Organization* 30: 291–301.

Digital TV Research, TV Piracy Forecasts, October 2017.

EC, *A Profile of Current and Future Audiovisual Audience*, European Union Publications, 2013, available at https://publications.europa.eu/en/publication-detail/-/publication/108c4160-1980-4bd5-8bf8-ce7f06da8449/language-en).

Handke, Christian, 'Digital Copying and the Supply of Sound Recordings' (2012), *Information Economics and Policy* 24: 15–29.

Hennig-Thurau, T., Henning, V. and Sattler, H., 'Consumer File Sharing of Motion Pictures' (2007), *Journal of Marketing* 71: 1–18.

Herz, Benedikt and Kiljański, Kamil, 'Movie Piracy and Displaced Sales in Europe: Evidence from Six Countries' (2018), *Information Economics and Policy* 43, C: 12–22, available at https://EconPapers.repec.org/RePEc:eee:iepoli:v:43:y:2018:i:c:p:12-22.

Hong, S.-H., 'Measuring the Effect of Napster on Recorded Music Sales: Difference-in-Difference Estimates Under Compositional Changes' (2013), *Journal of Applied Econometrics* 28: 297–324.

Hui, K. and Png, I., 'Piracy and the Legitimate Demand for Recorded Music' (2003), *Contributions to Economic Analysis & Policy* 2, 1: Article 11.

Lauinger, T., Szydlowski, M., Onarlioglu, K., Wondracek, G., Kirda, E. and Kruegel, C., 'Clickonomics: Determining the Effect of Anti-Piracy Measures for One-Click Hosting' Working Paper, Boston, MA: Northeastern University, 2013.

Lee, Jonathan F. 'Purchase, Pirate, Publicize: Private-Network Music Sharing and Market Album Sales' (2018), *Information Economics and Policy* 42: 35–55.

Liebowitz, S., 'Testing File-Sharing's Impact by Examining Record Sales in Cities' (2008), *Management Science* 54, 4: 852–859.

Liebowitz, S., 'The Impacts of Internet Piracy', in R. Watt (ed.), *The Economics of Copyright: A Handbook for Students and Teachers*, Cheltenham: Edward Elgar Publishing, 2014, 225–240.

Lin, Faqin, 'Estimating the Effect of the Internet on International Trade' (2015), *Journal of International Trade and Economic Development* 24, 3: 408–428.

Ma, Liye, Montgomery, Alan, Singh, Param and Smith, Michael D., 'The Effect of Pre-Release Movie Piracy on Box Office Revenue' (2014), *Information Systems Research* 25, 3: 590–603.

McKenzie, Jordi and David Walls, W., 'File Sharing and Film Revenues: Estimates of Sales Displacement at the Box Office' (2016), *B.E. Journal of Economic Analysis and Policy* 16, 1: 25–57.

McKenzie, Jordi, 'Graduated Response Policies To Digital Piracy: Do They Increase Box Office Revenues Of Movies?' (2017), *Information Economics and Policy* 38: 1–11.

Michel, N., 'The Impact Of Digital File Sharing On The Music Industry: An Empirical Analysis' (2006), *Berkeley Electronic Press: Topics in Economic Analysis & Policy* 6: Article 18.

National Research Council (NRC) 2013. *Copyright in the Digital Era: Building Evidence for Policy*, Washington, DC: The National Academies Press, 2013, https://doi.org/10.17226/14686.

Oberholzer, F. and Strumpf, K., 'The Effect of File Sharing on Record Sales. An Empirical Analysis' (2007), *Journal of Political Economy* 115, 1: 1–42.

OECD/EUIPO, *Trade in Counterfeit and Pirated Goods: Mapping the Economic Impact*, Paris: OECD Publishing, 2016.

OECD, *New Sources of Growth: Knowledge-Based Capital: Key Analyses and Policy Conclusions*, Paris: OECD Publishing, 2013.

Peitz, M. and Waelbroeck, P., 'The Effect of Internet Piracy on CD Sales: Cross-Section Evidence' (2004), *Review of Economic Research on Copyright Issues* 1, 2: 71–79.

Peukert, C., Claussen, J., and Kretschmer, T., 'Piracy and Box Office Movie Revenues: Evidence From Megaupload' (2017), *Information Economics and Policy* 52: 188–215.

Poort, J., Leenheer, J., van der Ham, J. and Dumitru, C., 'Baywatch: Two approaches to measure the effects of blocking access to The Pirate Bay' (2014), *Telecommunications Policy* 38: 383–392.

Reimers, I., 'Can Private Copyright Protection be Effective? Evidence from Book Publishing' (2016), *Journal of Law and Economics* 59: 411–440.

Rob, R. and Waldfogel, J., 'Piracy on the High C's: Music Downloading, Sales Displacement, and Social Welfare in a Sample of College Students' (2006), *Journal of Law and Economics* 49, 1: 29–62.

Rob, R. and Waldfogel, J., 'Piracy on the Silver Screen' (2007), *Journal of Industrial Economics* 55, 3: 379–393.

Sivan, Liron, Smith, M. D. and Telang, R., 'Do Search Engines Influence Media Piracy? Evidence from a Randomized Field Study', Working Paper, Pittsburgh: Carnegie Mellon University, 2018.

Smith, M. D. and Telang, R., 'Competing with Free: The Impact of Movie Broadcasts on DVD Sales and Internet Piracy' (2009), *Management Information Systems Quarterly* 33, 2: 312–338.

Smith, M. D. and Telang, R., *Streaming, Sharing, Stealing: Big Data and the Future of Entertainment*, Cambridge, MA: MIT Press, 2016.

Stevens, L. K. and Sessions, D. N., 'An Empirical Investigation Into the Effect of Music Downloading on the Consumer Expenditure of Recorded Music: A Time Series Approach' (2005), *Journal of Consumer Policy* 28, 3: 311–324.

Telang, Rahul, 'Does Online Piracy make Computers Insecure? Evidence from Panel Data', Workshop on Economics of Information Security, Innsbruck Austria, June 2018.

Telang, Rahul and Waldfogel, Joel, 'Piracy and New Product Creation: A Bollywood Story' (2018), *Information Economics and Policy* 43: 1–11.

Waldfogel, J., 'Music File Sharing and Sales Displacement in the iTunes Era' (2010), *Information Economics and Policy* 22, 4: 306–314.

Waldfogel, Joel, 'Copyright Protection, Technological Change, and the Quality of New Products: Evidence from Recorded Music since Napster' (2012), *Journal of Law and Economics* 55, 4: Article 1.

WIPO, WIPO Studies on the Economic Contribution of the Copyright Industries: Overview, 2014, available at www.wipo.int/export/sites/www/copyright/en/performance/pdf/economic_contribution_analysis_2014.pdf.

WIPO, *Guide on Surveying the Economic Contribution of the Copyright Industries*, revised edition, 2015, available at www.wipo.int/edocs/pubdocs/en/copyright/893/wipo_pub_893.pdf.

Zentner, A., 'File Sharing and International Sales of Copyrighted Music: An Empirical Analysis with a Panel of Countries' (2005), *Berkeley Electronic Press: Topics in Economic Analysis and Policy* 5, 1: Article 21.

Zentner, A., 'Measuring the Effect of File Sharing on Music Purchases' (2006), *The Journal of Law and Economics* 49: 63–90.

Zhang, Laurina, 'Intellectual Property Strategy and the Long Tail: Evidence from the Recorded Music Industry' (2018), *Management Science* 64, 1: 24–42.

A17.1

Peer-Reviewed Studies Analysing the Impact of Piracy on Sales

Table A17.1 *Peer-reviewed journal articles finding no statistical impact of piracy*

Citation	Primary Data	Result
Oberholzer and Strumpf (2007, *Journal of Political Economy*)	2002 OpenNap music downloads, 2002 US sales of popular albums	'[F]ile sharing has had no statistically significant effect on purchases of the average album in our sample.'
Smith and Telang (2009, *MIS Quarterly*)	2005–2006 Amazon DVD sales ranks and BitTorrent movie file downloads	'[T]he availability of pirated content at [television broadcast] has no effect on post-broadcast DVD sales gains.'
Andersen and Frenz (2010, *Journal of Evolutionary Economics*)	2006 survey of Canadian customers' file sharing and CD purchasing behaviour	There is 'no (statistical) association between the number of P2P files downloaded and CD album sales'.

Source: Authors' analysis.

Table A17.2 *Peer-reviewed journal articles finding that piracy harms sales*

Citation	Primary Data	Result
Hui and Png (2003, *Contrib. to Economic Analysis & Policy*)	1994–1998 IFPI worldwide CD sales data and physical piracy rates	'[D]emand for music CDs decreased with piracy, suggesting that "theft" outweighed the "positive" effects of piracy.'
Peitz and Waelbroeck (2004, *Rev. of Econ. Res. on Copyright*)	1998–2002 worldwide CD sales, IPSOS survey data for piracy downloads	Internet piracy may have been responsible for a 20% decrease in music sales between 1998–2002.
Stevens and Sessions (2005, *Journal of Consumer Policy*)	1990–2004 consumer spending on cassette tapes, LPs and CDs	'[T]he proliferation of peer-to-peer file sharing networks since 2000 has led to a *significant* decline in music format sales' (emphasis in original).
Zentner (2005, *Topics in Economic Analysis and Policy*)	1997–2002 country-level data on music sales and broadband usage	'countries with higher internet and broadband penetration have suffered higher drops in music sales'.
Bounie et al. (2006, *Rev. of Econ. Res. on Copyright*)	2005 survey of movie piracy and purchases from French universities	'[Piracy] has a strong [negative] impact on video [VHS and DVD] purchases and rentals' but statistically no impact on box office revenue.
Michel (2006, *Topics in Economic Analysis and Policy*)	1995–2003 US BLS micro Consumer Expenditure Survey data	'The relationship between computer ownership and music purchases weakened' due to piracy, potentially reducing CD sales by 13 per cent.

Table A17.2 (*cont.*)

Citation	Primary Data	Result
Rob and Waldfogel (2006, *Journal of Law and Economics*)	2003 survey of US college students piracy and purchase behaviour	'[E]ach album download reduces purchases by 0.2 in our sample, although possibly by much more.'
Zentner (2006, *Journal of Law and Economics*)	2001 survey of European music purchase and piracy behaviour	'[Piracy] may explain a 30 percent reduction in the probability of buying music.'
Bhattacharjee et al. (2007, *Management Science*)	1995–2002 Billboard 100 chart rankings, WinMX file sharing post-2000	P2P file sharing technologies have resulted in 'significantly reduced chart survival except for those albums that debut high on the charts'.
DeVany and Walls (2007, *Review of Industrial Organization*)	Box office revenue and the supply of pirated content for an unnamed movie	'[Piracy] of a major studio movie accelerated its box-office decline and caused the picture to lose about $40 million in revenue.'
Hennig-Thurau et al. (2007, *Journal of Marketing*)	2006 survey of German movie purchase and piracy intentions	Piracy causes 'substantial cannibalization of theater visits, DVD rentals [and] purchases responsible for annual revenue losses of $300 million in Germany.'
Rob and Waldfogel (2007, *Journal of Industrial Economics*)	2005 survey of U. Penn. students' movie purchase and piracy behaviour	'[U]npaid first [piracy] consumption reduces paid consumption by about 1 unit.'
Liebowitz (2008, *Management Science*)	1998–2003 Census data on broadband Internet use and music purchases	'[F]ile sharing appears to have caused the entire decline in record sales [observed from 1998 to 2003].'

Table A17.2 (*cont.*)

Citation	Primary Data	Result
Bender and Wang (2009, *International Social Science Review*)	1999–2007 Country-level annual recorded music sales	'For a one percent increase in piracy rate, music sales declined about 0.6 percent.'
Danaher et al. (2010, *Marketing Science*)	2007–2008 BitTorrent downloads of television torrents	'[T]he removal of NBC content from iTunes resulted in an 11.4% increase in piracy for its content'
Waldfogel (2010, *Information Economics and Policy*)	2009–2010 survey of Wharton students' music piracy and purchases	'[A]n additional song stolen reduces paid consumption by between a third and a sixth of a song.'
Bai and Waldfogel (2012, *Information Economics and Policy*)	2008–2009 survey of Chinese university students' movie behaviour	'[T]hree quarters of [Chinese students'] movie consumption is unpaid and . . . each instance of [piracy] displaces 0.14 paid consumption instances.'
Hong (2013, *Journal of Applied Econometrics*)	1996–2002 survey data from US BLS Consumer Expenditure Survey data	'[F]ile sharing is likely to explain about 20% of the total sales decline during the Napster period, mostly driven by . . . households with children aged 6–17.'
Danaher et al. (2014, *Journal of Industrial Economics*)	2008–2011 iTunes music sales in France and other European countries	The HADOPI anti-piracy law 'caused iTunes music sales to increase by 22–25% [in France] relative to changes in the control group [countries].'
Danaher and Smith (2014, *International Journal of Industrial Organization*)	2011–2013 Sales and rental data for movies in 12 European	'The shutdown of Megaupload and its associated sites caused digital revenues for

Table A17.2 (*cont.*)

Citation	Primary Data	Result
	countries from 3 major motion picture studios	three major motion picture studios to increase by 6.5–8.5%.'
Ma et al. (2014, *Information Systems Research*)	Box office revenue for All movies whose wide release occurred between February 2006 and December 2008	'Pre-release [movie] piracy causes a 19.1% decline in revenue compared to piracy that occurs post release.'
Adermon and Liang (2014, *Journal of Economic Behavior & Organization*)	Digital and physical music sales in Sweden, Norway and Finland from 2004 through 2009	The IPRED copyright reform in Sweden 'increased music sales by 36% during the first six months [after it was implemented]. Pirated music therefore seems to be a strong substitute to legal music [purchases]'.
McKenzie and Walls (2016, *B.E. Journal of Economic Analysis and Policy*)	State-level daily theatrical sales, torrent downloads for 166 films released in Australia from Jan. 2010 through Aug. 2011	BitTorrent 'downloads have a significant negative impact on [Australian] first-week box office' driven by 'downloading activity post-US release but pre-Australian release.'
Reimers (2016, *Journal of Law and Economics*	Electronic and physical book sales of RosettaBooks from Jan. 2010 to Dec. 2013	'I find a protection-related increase in sales of electronic books — the closest substitute for online piracy — of more than 14 percent.'
Lee (2018, *Information Economics and Policy*)	US sales and BitTorrent downloads of 2,109 music albums in 2008	'[T]he file sharing elasticity of sales is -0.02 for physical sales, [and] -0.04 for digital sales... [P]rivate-network piracy leads to a crowding out of

Table A17.2 (*cont.*)

Citation	Primary Data	Result
		legitimate sales . . . [but] the practical extent of these effects is quite small' (and mediated by artist popularity).
Herz and Kiljanski (2018, *Information Economics and Policy*)	September–October 2014 survey of movie consumption for 30,000 individuals in 6 European countries	'We document that one unpaid [pirated] (first) viewing of a movie displaces about 0.37 units of paid viewings . . . this implies that unpaid movies viewings reduced movies sales in Europe by about 4.4% during the sample period.'

Source: Authors' analysis.

18

The Digital Creative Economy and Blockchains: Options and Prospects for the Developing World

KEITH NURSE, ERICA SMITH, KAYLA GRANT AND ALICIA SHEPHERD

Abstract

The creative sector has emerged as a critical driver of digital trade and generates significant opportunities for economic diversification and competitiveness in developed and developing economies. The expansion of the digital creative economy creates not just new and alternative business models, it also generates new markets, which make creative industries a critical resource for economic development. This chapter assesses the challenges and opportunities for creative industries in developing countries, especially as it relates to making the transition to a digital creative economy and to the adoption of blockchain technologies which have the potential to address structural challenges such as big data management, financial inclusion and integration into global value chains.

Introduction

The creative sector has emerged as a critical driver of digital trade and generates significant opportunities for economic diversification and competitiveness in developed and developing economies. Digitalization has led to the convergence of information, communication technologies (ICTs), social media and creative industries and hence the growth of the digital creative economy, which is founded essentially on copyright law.[1] It can be argued that the economics behind digitally-delivered content products, in particular the negligible marginal costs for widespread duplication and distribution, make them ideal 'tradeables'.[2] It is also argued that the new

[1] For an introduction to the concept of the digital creative economy see Ruth Towse and Christian Handke, *Handbook on the Digital Creative Economy*, Edward Elgar Publishing, Cheltenham UK, 2013.

[2] Sacha Wunsch-Vincent (2006) The WTO, the Internet and Trade in Digital Products: EC–US Perspectives.

technologies and innovations have generated new business models, for example, advertisement-based and subscription-based revenue streams that utilize the Internet for online as well as offline trade and exploit the opportunities from the growing penetration rates of personal devices like smartphones, tablets and laptops. And all of this is facilitated and monetized through the expanding role of digital service providers (DSPs) that stream creative content like Spotify for music and Netflix for film.[3]

The key point is that the expansion of the digital creative economy creates not just new and alternative business models, it also generates new markets, which make creative industries a critical resource for economic development. For example, Keith Maskus argues that 'digital trade has the potential to be one of the most dynamic and innovative platforms for creative entrepreneurs and small enterprises to develop international marketing networks and increase sales'. He further asserts that 'countries and firms that are poised to build the electronic infrastructure for such activities and facilitate the development of e-commerce markets and digital trade routes will be the major beneficiaries'.[4]

One of the key and burgeoning features of the new digital economy, and one which has the potential to transform the creative sector, is the emergence of blockchain technologies that promises to expand digital transactions and improve cooperation among parties through building trust (i.e. decentralized validation, elimination of redundancy, immutable storage and encryption). Blockchain technologies are key innovations that have the potential to address some of the structural challenges evident in the creative industry, especially as they relate to big data management, financial inclusion and trade facilitation.

This chapter assesses the challenges and opportunities for creative industries in developing countries, especially as they relate to making the transition to a digital creative economy and to the adoption of blockchain technologies. The music industry is used as a case study because it is this sector that has experienced the greatest level of digital disruption and is also among the first to embrace blockchain technology. The chapter explores blockchain technologies as one element of the digital creative economy that has the capacity to present opportunities for these countries to increase market penetration and deepen global value-addition.

[3] See OECD (2015) Enquiries into Intellectual Property's Economic Impact. Paris: 225.

[4] Keith Maskus (2018) 'Fostering Innovation in Digital Trade', in Xavier Seuba, Christophe Geiger and Julien Penin (eds), *Intellectual Property and Digital Trade in the Age of Artificial Intelligence and Big Data*, Global Perspectives for the Intellectual Property System, CEIPI-ICTSD, Issue Number 5: 21.

The Rise of the Digital Creative Economy

In the wake of the global economic crisis, the creative sector has outperformed most other sectors. This is in part due to the growth of the digital economy, where intellectual property and trade in services have expanded as a share of global value added.[5] The creative industries generated USD 2,250 billion in revenue in 2013, accounted for 3 per cent of global GDP and employed 29.5 million persons, approximately 1 per cent of the world's active population. World exports of cultural and recreational services are such that Europe tops with USD 43 billion, followed by North America (USD 27 billion), Asia (USD 10 billion) and South, Central America and the Caribbean (USD 7 billion). Further behind are the Middle East (USD 2 billion), Africa and the Commonwealth of Independent States each at USD 1 billion (see Figure 18.1). Most developing countries operate with a large trade imbalance, the exception being countries like China, India, Brazil, Republic of Korea and Mexico that have strong industrial and export capabilities in creative goods, services and intellectual property, as well as large home and diasporic markets.[6]

Digital creative trade is also one of the fastest-rising components of global trade. In 2013, the digital creative economy contributed USD 200 billion to the digital economy, and drove sales of electronic devices worth USD 532 billion.[7] The key dimensions of this trade are captured in the following economic ways:

- physical goods sold on the internet (books, music, games and video)
- digital cultural content (e-books, music, video, games)
- online media advertising (for online media and free streaming services)
- digital advertising creation.[8]

Today, creative content accounts for a significant share of economic activity on ecommerce and ICT-enabled platforms. A key driver of this

[5] See UNDP/UNESCO (2013) *The Creative Economy Report 2013: Widening Local Development Pathways* UNDP/UNESCO, New York/Paris, pp. 161–163.

[6] Keith Nurse and Zhen Ye (2012) Youth Entrepreneurship and the Rise of the Creative Industries. UNIDO, Vienna, available at www.researchgate.net/publication/254956321_Creative_Industries_for_Youth_Unleashing_Potential_and_Growth.

[7] EY (2015) Cultural Times: The First Global Map of Cultural and Creative Industries, available at https://en.unesco.org/creativity/sites/creativity/files/cultural_times._the_first_global_map_of_cultural_and_creative_industries.pdf.

[8] See www.mckinsey.com/business-functions/mckinsey-digital/our-insights/digital-globalization-the-new-era-of-global-flows.

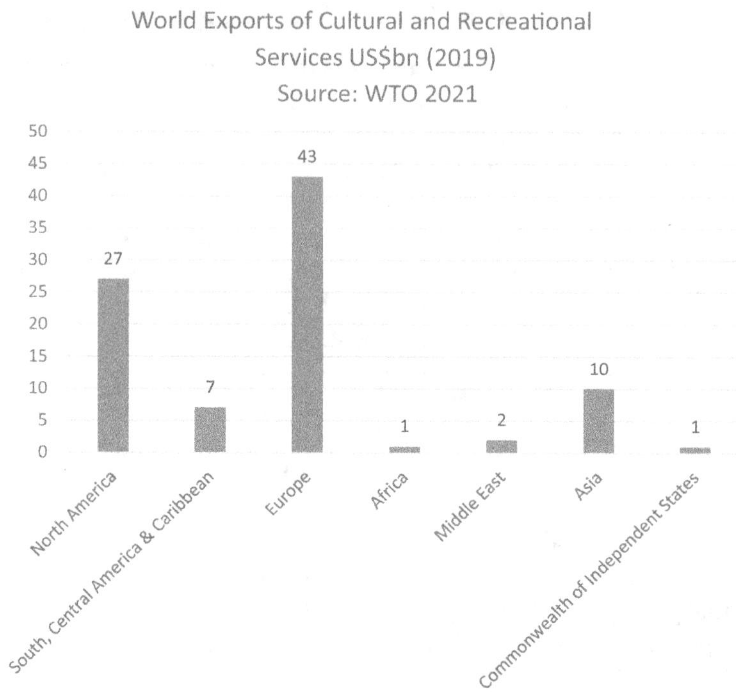

Figure 18.1 The economic contribution of cultural and creative industries by region, USD billion
Source: EY, 2015.

process has been the rapid growth of social media and networking which has facilitated a shift away from the passive consumer model to a prosumer and user-generated framework (e.g. YouTube, Facebook, Instagram, Snapchat, Flickr, etc). As such, the rise of the digital creative economy has generated significant earnings for top media companies as the fast-rising valuation of FAANGS stocks[9] illustrates. The new on-demand and online consumption models for the music industry have created increased possibilities for the distribution of content. For example, it was reported in June 2018 that there were 229.56 million paying music subscribers globally up 16 per cent over the figure for the year 2017. Of the total number of subscribers, Spotify had a market share

[9] The term FAANGS refers to the top tech stocks: Facebook, Apple, Amazon, Netflix Google (parent company Alphabet) and Spotify.

of 36 per cent, with Apple Music growing to 19 per cent.[10] In terms of valuation, Apple reached the USD 1 trillion mark[11] and Apple Music was valued at USD 10 billion.[12]

The FAANGS growth has largely come from the monetization of data. Data are increasingly viewed as the 'new oil' in reference to the rapid expansion of the digital knowledge economy. It is argued, 'that data have economic value at the macroeconomic level is mirrored by the fact that they are intensely valuable for firms that generate or collect them online. This value stems largely from the ability of firms to monetize data through selling their characteristics to advertisers'. Additionally, 'access to data also permits firms to tailor new products and services to meet the preferences of individual users, raising the value of data even more'.[13] This is becoming even more evident with the emergence of the new business models of firms like Netflix and Spotify that have challenged and supplanted traditional 'bricks and mortar' competitors. Indeed, the competitiveness of these firms comes in part from their capacity to leverage the data from their subscribers and users and in turn utilize that data to commission and produce new original programming targeted at these audiences.

The above analysis provides an overview of the rise of the digital creative economy. From this standpoint it can be argued that digital trade and entrepreneurship are key areas for the creative industries because of their potential to promote economic diversification and industrial upgrading. As such the key question is, given the inexorable rise of the creative digital creative economy, how can developing countries participate in this growth process and what role can trade-related copyright and blockchains play in global value chain integration and industry upgrading?

[10] Music Business Worldwide (2018, September 13). Apple Music gains global streaming subscription market share – as Spotify holds firm, available at www.musicbusinessworldwide.com/apple-music-gains-global-streaming-subscription-market-share-as-spotify-holds-firm/.

[11] Apple just became the first American public company to cross $1 trillion in value. (n.d.). Apple reaches $1 trillion value, available at https://money.cnn.com/2018/08/02/investing/apple-one-trillion-market-value/index.html.

[12] Apple Music Is Now Worth $10 Billion (n.d.), available at https://money.usnews.com/investing/stock-market-news/articles/2018-02-28/apple-inc-aapl-stock.

[13] Keith Maskus (2018) 'Fostering Innovation in Digital Trade', in Xavier Seuba, Christophe Geiger and Julien Penin (eds), *Intellectual Property and Digital Trade in the Age of Artificial Intelligence and Big Data*, Global Perspectives for the Intellectual Property System, CEIPI-ICTSD, Issue Number 5: 23.

Trade-Related Copyright and Digitalization

The significant increase in demand for creative content has been the key driver of the digital economy. It is estimated that as much as 70 per cent of the content on the Internet is creative content, much of which is amateur or user-generated content. Nonetheless, a key observation is that the burgeoning digital economy relies heavily on creative copyrighted content, which means that the commercialization of this has to necessarily take into account the balance between the interests of creators and that of users, as well as distributors, platforms or DSPs. The challenge of balancing all the interests involved is exemplified in the debates and controversies surrounding the EU Directive on Copyright in the Digital Single Market that is still under consideration and which aims to strengthen and update existing regulations to ensure an improved marketplace for the exploitation of digital and cross-border content. The Directive states in its explanatory memorandum that:

> Evolution of digital technologies has led to the emergence of new business models and reinforced the role of the Internet as the main marketplace for the distribution and access to copyright-protected content. In this new framework, rightholders face difficulties when seeking to license their rights and be remunerated for the online distribution of their works. This could put at risk the development of European creativity and production of creative content. It is therefore necessary to guarantee that authors and rightholders receive a fair share of the value that is generated by the use of their works and other subject-matter. Against this background, this proposal provides for measures aiming at improving the position of rightholders to negotiate and be remunerated for the exploitation of their content by online services giving access to user-uploaded content.[14]

Copyright is thus not only critical for legal purposes but also essential for creating the environment for investment and global trade particularly through licensing.

Copyright is thus a critical feature of the underlying conditions for the digital creative economy and its importance is manifest in how copyright industries have expanded in recent decades as exemplified by the contribution of copyright industries to GDP and employment in both developed and developing economies.[15] It is estimated that copyright

[14] Proposal for a Directive of the European Parliament and of the Council on Copyright in the Digital Single Market. COM/2016/0593 final – 2016/0280 (COD).

[15] Copyright industries include press and literature; music, theatrical productions, operas; motion picture and video, radio and television; photography; software and databases;

industries outpace traditional sectors like manufacturing, agriculture and pharmaceuticals in the US. They contribute 11 per cent of GDP and 8 per cent of employment, making the US the top performing copyright economy among developed economies. Data from 40 national studies commissioned by WIPO show that the average economic contribution of copyright industries hovers at around 5 per cent for GDP and employment with above-average performance in large developing economies like the Republic of Korea, Mexico and the Philippines along with high GDP shares for small states like those in the Caribbean.[16]

However, the impact of trade of copyright-related goods and services is far more difficult to assess, especially for developing countries. The key problem is with data capture, as digital trade involves mostly intangible trade in services and intellectual property which are notoriously difficult to collate without dedicated industry cooperation. In addition, the creative industries have been at the forefront of the digital transition and the growth of digital trade. For example, it is estimated that digitalization has led to a decline in trade of physical forms of creative goods like CDs, books and newspapers which together accounted for 2.7 per cent of total goods trade in 2000 but by 2016 had dropped to 0.8 per cent.[17]

Digitizable creative content such as music, for instance, has been subject to high levels of copyright infringement, by way of piracy, bootlegging, counterfeiting, unlicensed broadcasting, illegal downloading and unauthorized file sharing (e.g. Napster, Grokster, BitTorrent). The impact of the digital economy on the copyright and creative sector is well illustrated in the experience of the global recorded music sector. As Figure 18.2 shows, the sector experienced a steady decline from USD 20.5 billion in 2004 to a low of USD 14.3 billion in 2014 with a recovery thereafter climbing to USD 20.2 in 2019. The rise of digital revenue is the key growth trend, with streaming dominating such that by 2019 it accounted for more than half of total revenues.[18] Physical sound-carriers'

visual and graphic arts; advertising services; and copyright collective management societies. For further details see: WIPO, 'Guide on Surveying the Economic Contribution of Copyright Industries. 2015' (revised edition), available at www.wipo.int/edocs/pubdocs/en/copyright/893/wipo_pub_893.pdf.

[16] Countries such as Jamaica, St Lucia, St Kitts and Nevis, St Vincent and the Grenadines and Trinidad and Tobago benefit from copyright industries having a significant impact on GDP and employment.

[17] See www.wto.org/english/res_e/publications_e/world_trade_report18_e.pdf.

[18] IFPI (2020) Global Music Report – The Industry in 2019, available at www.ifpi.org/news/IFPI-issues-annual-Global-Music-Report.

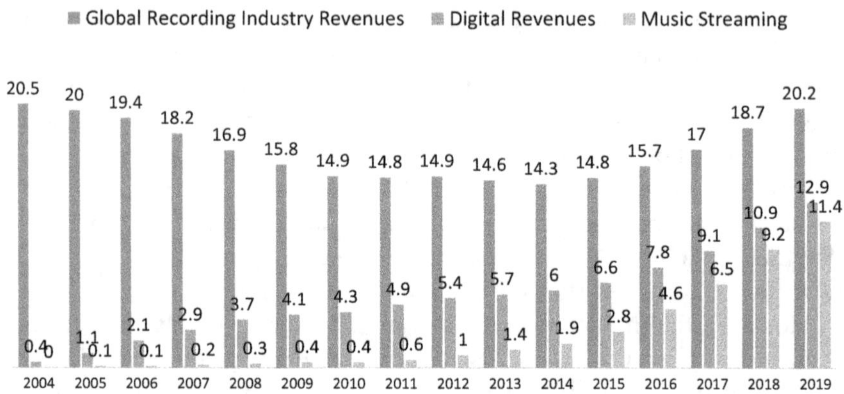

Figure 18.2 Global recorded music revenues, 2004–2019, USD billion
Source: IFPI, 2020.

share of the market plummeted from USD 20 billion in 2004 to a low of USD 14 billion in 2014.[19]

In the same period, revenue from digital sources climbed dramatically. Indeed, the year 2016 is considered an inflection year as digital revenue accounted for 50 per cent of total revenue, surpassing the combined earnings from physical format, performing rights and synchronization income (see Figure 18.3). At the end of 2019, streaming revenues accounted for 56.1 per cent of the global recorded music market with subscription audio streaming at 42 per cent of total revenues and ad-supported streams contributing 14.1 per cent. Downloads and other digital revenues were 7.2 per cent, thus making overall digital revenue 63.3 per cent of total revenues in the sector. Physical format sales continue to decline and contribute 21.6 per cent, followed by performing rights income (12.6 per cent) and synchronization revenue at 2.4 per cent.[20]

Digital Music and Royalties Collections

The shift towards the digital economy is also evident in global copyright collections. Global collections rose by 18.5 per cent between 2012

[19] IFPI (2017) Global Music Report 2017: Annual State of the Industry, available at www.ifpi.org/downloads/GMR2017.pdf.

[20] IFPI (2020) Global Music Report – The Industry in 2019, available at www.ifpi.org/news/IFPI-issues-annual-Global-Music-Report.

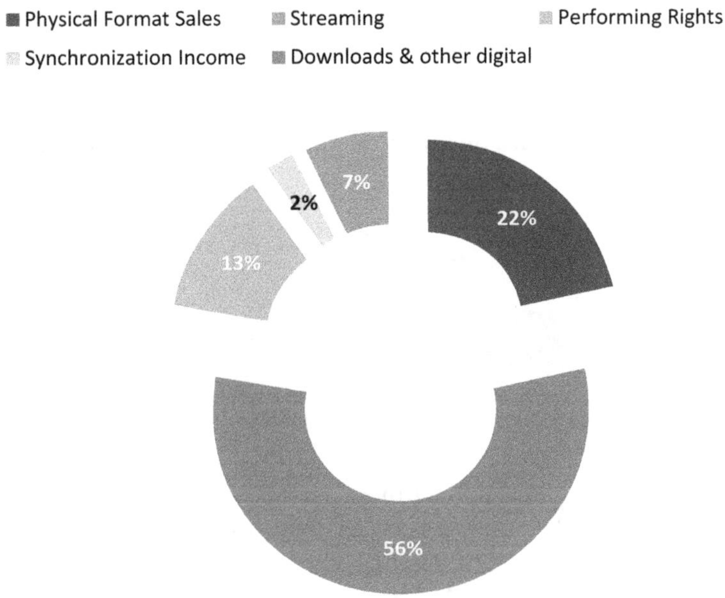

Figure 18.3 Global music revenues, 2019
Source: IFPI, 2020.

(USD 7.7 billion) and 2016 (USD 9.2 billion) of which 87.4 per cent of that growth was in the music industry. The increasing pivot around the digital economy is also evident, as collections in this sector rose above 50 per cent in 2016.[21]

The data on global music collections for 2017 from the International Confederation of Societies of Authors and Composers (CISAC) provide an interesting view on the impact of digital music as a share of total collections in the various regions (see Table 18.1). The global average for digital music is 15 per cent. The share of digital music collections as a share of total collections is highest in the Asia/Pacific region, with 24 per cent. North America is next at 17 per cent along with Africa, which is operating at a significantly lower level of collections. The two regions with the lowest shares for digital music collections are Europe (12 per cent) and Latin America and the Caribbean (9.5 per cent). What the data illustrate is that digital music is a significant factor in all regions.[22]

[21] Ibid.

[22] CISAC, Global Collections Reports (2018), available at www.cisac.org/Media/Studies-and-Reports/Publications/Royalty-Reports/2018-CISAC-Global-Collections-Report-EN.

Table 18.1 *Music collections by region, 2017 (Euro millions)*

	Global	Europe	USA/ Canada	Asia Pacific	Latin America & the Caribbean	Africa
Total music collections	8,336	4,349	2,123	1,258	538	69
Total digital music collections	1,248	535	363	307	51	12
Digital music share (%)	15	12	17	24	9.5	17

Source: CISAC.

The dominance of North America and Europe in music royalty collection is such that they collect six times that of the Latin America and Caribbean (LAC) region, 15 times that of the Asia/Pacific region and over 60 times that of Africa. When measured as a share of GDP, the gap narrows considerably to the point where the LAC region is just below half of the European average and on par with that of North America. The Asia-Pacific and Africa regions are close to a fifth of the European GDP share. The data therefore provide evidence to support a claim for a correlation between region and share of royalties' collection, with most developing countries having a largely under-developed market for copyright exploitation, featuring at the lower end of the scale. Table 18.2 aptly depicts this divide.[23]

A trade perspective is captured when global royalty collections are taken into account. Figure 18.4 shows that 78 per cent of the total global royalty collections in the creative industries is generated in Europe and North America.[24] The Asia-Pacific region has a share of 15 per cent, the bulk of which can be attributed to large economies like the Republic of Korea and China. As such, it can be argued that the impact on developing countries' exports and trade has been limited at best in spite of the significant impact of copyright-based industries on GDP and employment and the rapid expansion of global income from digital creative content.

[23] CISAC, Global Collections Report (2017), available at www.cisac.org/Media/Studies-and-Reports/Publications/Royalty-Reports/2017-Global-Collections-Report-EN.

[24] Ibid.

Table 18.2 *Average collection for copyright, by number of inhabitants across the globe*

Territory	Collections per head of population by region (USD)	Collections as a share of GDP by region	Percentage of total collections (%)
Europe	USD 5.79	0.028	56.8%
North America	USD 5.51	0.011	21.6%
Asia-Pacific	USD 0.38	0.006	14.8%
Latin America & Caribbean	USD 0.91	0.012	6.1%
Africa	USD 0.09	0.005	0.7%
World average	USD 1.48	0.014	100%

Source: CISAC.

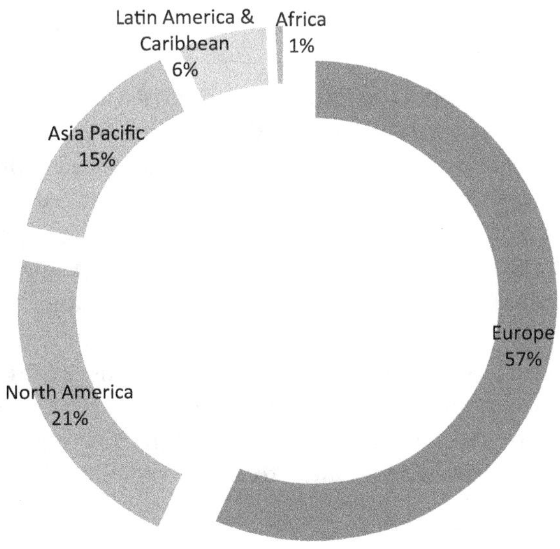

Figure 18.4 Global collections of royalties, share by regions, 2017
Source: CISAC, 2018.

In practice, what these changes have meant in terms of the operations of collective management organizations (CMOs) is that while the traditional CMO model continues to work effectively for conventional music use, such as performances at public premises and broadcasts, the massive number of performances on digital platforms tests the processing and administrative capacity of CMOs. To illustrate the current situation, in 2017, 6.6 trillion music performances were reported to the English CMO PRS for Music,[25] while Buzzangle[26] reported that there were 377 billion audio streams in the US alone in 2017. CMOs have had to continuously invest in more advanced technologies and increasingly work in collaborative arrangements to attain the resources necessary to address increased processing requirements. Examples of these collaborations are the International Copyright Enterprise (ICE), which is a joint venture owned by the English CMO; the PRS for Music; the German CMO, GEMA; and the Swedish CMO, STIM and MINT, another collaboration between the Canadian CMO, SOCAN and the Swiss CMO, SUISA.

In addition to the hurdles relative to CMOs, the level of remuneration earned by right holders now features as a prominent issue. Considering the massive quantity of music being consumed, remuneration appears to be on a divergent trajectory. To earn USD 1,260 on Apple Music, a signed artist needs 971,323 plays earning USD 0.0012 per play. To earn the equivalent on Spotify, 1,117,021 plays are required.[27] Yet another issue remains pertinent, one less discussed but of equal importance to both right holders and artists operating outside of mainstream music industries. There is an unquestionable lack of diversity in the music consumed globally, despite the overwhelming number of songs being produced.

The sheer increase in the number of recordings has contributed to the tectonic shifts in the ecosystem of the industry. It was reported that in 2017, of the music streamed globally, according to the Buzzangle report, 99 per cent came from 10 per cent of the music available. This issue can be defined as the genre gap, one which is of particular concern for developing countries as their content may well be increasingly marginalized in the digital arena. On the flipside, the genre gap can be viewed as an occasion for digital service providers based in the developing world to take advantage of the opportunity to build regional digital platforms and marketplaces.

[25] PRS for Music announces signing of new two-year multi-territory deal with Spotify for Europe (n.d.), available at www.prsformusic.com/press/2015/prs-for-music-announces-signing-of-a-new-two-year-multi-territory-deal-with-spotify-for-europe.

[26] BuzzAngle Music Admin (n.d.). News, available at https://radioconnects.ca/wp-content/uploads/2018/01/BuzzAngle-Music-2017-US-Report-Draft.pdf.

[27] McCandless, D. (2018, August 19). 'How Much Do Music Artists Earn Online – 2015 Remix', available at https://informationisbeautiful.net/visualizations/how-much-do-music-artists-earn-online-2015-remix.

Is Blockchain a Solution?

Given the issues outlined in the previous section, can blockchain technologies then offer viable solutions to the creative and music industries, especially in the case of developing economies? Blockchain has been touted as having a vast capacity to solve many global issues. Its value is advocated most vehemently in the area of inclusion: in finance it encourages inclusion through alternative modes of payments (bitcoins); for the democratic process, it facilitates identity verification, alleviating voter burden, and curtailing corruption vis à vis public projects; and in the area of trade, inclusion is enhanced through cost cuts.

Relative to the issue of the lack of financial inclusion in the sector, blockchain technologies can also be seen as having an emancipatory role for creative persons in all countries, where stringent banking regulations as a result of money-laundering and counter-terrorism (ML/CT) measures implemented after the 2008 crisis have left many unbanked.

With specific reference to developing countries, where CMOs and other music businesses are categorized as micro, small or medium-sized businesses (MSMEs), blockchain technologies may offer CMOs and right holders a more transparent and efficient solution for identifying and monitoring the use of works. Furthermore, it could enable the processing and handling of micropayments for music, a crucial element in the online music streaming industry. Other advantages include the capacity of blockchain technologies to formalize and secure new kinds of relationships in the digital world, and reduce associated transaction costs, such as those incurred in establishing trust between negotiating parties. Coupled with smart contracts, the process of access to end-users, prosumers and intermediaries is mostly automatic, thus faster and unfettered.

The move to the use of blockchain technologies could unleash new innovations in music industry business models with great potential for new revenue streams for artists and new trade media. Beyond creating payment efficiencies, blockchain technologies enlarge the entire ecosystem, allowing for the expansion of copyright trade. In effect, the benefits of blockchain allow 'licensing access to a catalogue so it can be offered by companies whose commercial activity is based on the exploitation of creative repertoires'.[28] This is consistent with the view that the music business is moving from a model based only on sales to one of access and

[28] Frederic Patissier (2009) *Financing Creative Industries: In Search for a New Approach.* Paris: CISAC, p. 4.

'monetizing' rights. It shifts control from intermediaries back to entrepreneurs, irrespective of the size of their operation. Blockchain's potential for upscaling also offers the added value of efficiency, security, immutability and transparency. Blockchain technologies further facilitate the inclusion of other emerging technologies, such as artificial intelligence and virtual reality, which can be built on top of blockchains to offer content creators a host of new avenues for content creation, distribution and monetization.

On account of the significance of the growing shift made possible by blockchains and other technologies, the future role of the CMO is certainly questionable. It is generally recognized that 'their value as collective bargaining agencies is undeniable – and their skill at TV, radio and local venue revenue collection is indispensable – but their future role in data and digital distributions may be less certain'.[29] However, CMOs have also been actively embracing the potential of blockchain.[30] Major CMOs are actively exploring the use of blockchain to improve their services; for example, the American giant, ASCAP; the French CMO, SACEM; and the English CMO, PRS for Music, are working on a joint project with IBM to use blockchain to improve data accuracy. The goal is to 'prototype how the music industry could create and adopt a shared, decentralized database of music works metadata with real-time update and tracking capabilities'.[31] In another case, a group comprising the tech start-up, JAAK, record companies, music publishers and a CMO collaborated to pilot the blockchain network, KORD, whose objective is to develop 'a single database providing royalty and intellectual property information'. Collaborations ensure 'greater opportunities for content commercialization and licensing opportunities'.[32] Major players such as Ernst and Young and Microsoft have also launched solutions for content

[29] Ibid.

[30] Pieter van Rijn, 'Collecting societies are struggling to keep up with the influx of millions of lines of data.' Music Business Worldwide May 13, 2018, available at www.musicbusinessworldwide.com/the-future-of-digital-performance-rights-management/.

[31] ASCAP (2017, April 7). *ASCAP, SACEM, and PRS for Music Initiate Joint Blockchain Project to Improve Data Accuracy for Rightsholders* [Press release]. Retrieved 16 October 2018, available at www.ascap.com/press/2017/04-07-ascap-sacem-prs-blockchain.

[32] Aswad, J. (2018, 2 May). JAAK Moves Ahead with Blockchain Pilot, Joined by BMG, Global Music Rights, Warner Music, available at https://variety.com/2018/biz/news/jaak-moves-ahead-with-blockchain-pilot-joined-by-bmg-global-music-rights-warner-music-others-1202794923/.

rights and royalties' management for the entertainment industry based on blockchain and smart contracts.[33]

It is anticipated that the future holds at least three likely scenarios for CMOs:

- In scenario one, collecting societies will decide that delivering, processing, reporting and analysing data is at the core of their business model and will thus invest and restructure accordingly, becoming data- and technology-driven companies in their own right. They will need to investigate and invest in the potential for new technologies, including blockchain, for example, to improve reporting timeliness and accuracy.
- Scenario two would result in collecting societies focusing on their current stronghold – negotiating collective blanket licence agreements, and administering and disbursing copyright royalties from media houses. This will necessitate the outsourcing of the management and the processing of digital music rights data and royalty distributions.
- In scenario three, there will be new entrants in the market with not only ample tech capabilities to handle collection from DSPs, but also with the capacity to extend vertically and handle negotiations. These new entrants, which are already emerging, will directly challenge traditional versions as they are entering with fresh eyes, new ideas and a willingness to invest in change.[34]

As was shown, scenario 1 is a reality, with the emergence of new business models with substantial investments in technology. One of the best-known examples is the American Music Rights Association (AMRA), which describes itself as a 'global digital music collection society, built on technology and trust'. AMRA is owned by a music publishing company that provides its technology, which was developed through funding from large investors including Google Ventures. Scenario 2 is also an actuality – for example, in Europe and Latin America where through the use of licensing hubs and administration back offices, CMOs have outsourced digital licensing and the associated processing and have internally focused on traditional core activities. However, scenario 3 is also gaining

[33] EY (2018, 20 June). *EY and Microsoft launch blockchain solution for content rights and royalties management for media and entertainment industry* [Press release], available at www.ey.com/en_gl/news/2018/06/ey-and-microsoft-launch-blockchain-solution-for-content-rights.

[34] Pieter van Rijn, 'Collecting societies are struggling to keep up with the influx of millions of lines of data.' Music Business Worldwide 13 May 2018, available at www.musicbusinessworldwide.com/the-future-of-digital-performance-rights-management/.

a lot of momentum. KORD, the previously mentioned collaboration, is one such case. It provides a shared data network of public record of rights and a fixed audit trail. It also connects identifying information from across the recording business, including labels, publishers, performing rights organizations, songwriters and their representatives, and builds a global database of IP rights for the music industry. In this framework, participating members have the sole authority to insert, update and remove personal information, and resolve conflicts, thereby facilitating control and real-time data production and analytics about the use and monetization of creator IP.[35]

Of these new business models, scenario 3 quickly supplants traditional intermediaries and forecasts the imminent rollout of blockchain.

The blockchain revolution might be led by either streaming players or digital retailers themselves. If companies such as Netflix, YouTube, Spotify, Amazon or Alibaba choose to transition their content distribution platforms to private blockchain platforms, this would blow open the use of the blockchain to a broad set of content generators and users, and in the process cut a wide swathe through the complex intermediation process.[36]

Beyond the operations of CMOs, the digital world will continue to spawn new models that will impact the existing content provider model, where artists and right holders will utilize blockchain to displace intermediaries and interface directly with end-users. For another example, of late Spotify, the global giant in the music distribution business, has launched a new service that will enable independent artists to upload music tracks to their digital platform directly – without any requirement for a third-party aggregator or record label. What Spotify is offering is a free service that does not require any upfront fees for uploads – no matter how many tracks are submitted, and no additional commission on the royalties generated by their music.[37] This is undoubtedly a game changer, which threatens to disrupt the marketplace for the top three transnational music companies/labels (Sony BMG, Universal Music Group

[35] Rhian Jones, 'Global music rights database pilot launched with top music companies' Music Business Worldwide 2 May 2018, available at www.musicbusinessworldwide.com/global-music-rights-database-pilot-launched-with-top-music-companies/.

[36] Kaj Burchardi and Nicolas Harle, 'The blockchain will disrupt the music business and beyond' *WIRED magazine*, 20 January 2018, available at www.wired.co.uk/article/blockchain-disrupting-music-mycelia.

[37] See www.musicbusinessworldwide.com/spotify-opens-the-floodgates-users-can-now-upload-tracks-to-the-streaming-platform-for-free/.

and Warner Music Group) and third-party digital aggregators/distributors such as CD Baby, TuneCore, Distrokid and Ditto – all of which require either a one-off upload fee or a yearly subscription payment from artists. It also pushes the envelope for competitors like Apple Music, SoundCloud, Google, Tencent, Deezer, Tidal and Pandora.

Options and Prospects for Developing Economies

The rapid growth of digitalization, and blockchain technologies in particular, is having a profound impact on the creative economy, music business and copyright administration. What is evident from the analysis is that one of the main beneficiaries are the digital service providers, which have been able to tap into new technologies such as blockchain to offer music businesses and musicians more attractive models. The music industry in developing countries therefore stands to benefit but only if these services are made available within their spaces, and if creative entrepreneurs have the capacity for quality access to these technologies, including Internet access.

In the developing world, digitalization is in fact growing rapidly. As Table A18.1 illustrates, there are a number of digital aggregators and music distribution services offering downloading and streaming services in Africa (e.g. Simfy Africa, Spinlet, BoomPlay), Latin America and the Caribbean (e.g. Claromúsica, Kuack Media Group), Asia (e.g. KKBOX, Saavn) and the Middle East and North Africa (e.g. Anghami). While data on earnings and trade flows are not readily available, what is evident is that there are market opportunities for these firms if the case of Anghami is generalizable. Anghami, the Lebanon-based DSP operating in 13 MENA countries with one million paying subscribers has been able to compete with Spotify and Deezer by drawing on local knowledge, low-tech consumer options and tie-ups with 'a vast network of independent label deals and partnerships with 29 mobile operators'.[38]

The case of Anghami illustrates that business models and strategy matter. It also suggests that some of the assumptions made about blockchain and its potential value to the music industry are subject to market conditions and future technological developments. For example, one of the key considerations in terms of bypassing intermediaries is that

[38] Murray (2019, 5 March). Why Anghami, With Over 1m Paying Users, Doesn't Feel Threatened By Spotify In The Middle East. Music Business Worldwide, available at www.musicbusinessworldwide.com/anghami-with-over-1m-paying-users-doesnt-feel-threatened-by-spotify-in-the-middle-east/.

consumers must be willing to transact online with cryptocurrency (or its equivalent), which presupposes awareness and confidence in virtual currencies, which have been notoriously unstable thus far. Similarly, there have also been some smart contract failures.[39] Of tremendous importance, given the volume of music available, there still remains the issue of diversity. Will it encourage consumers to move further away from the top 10 per cent of mainstream releases or simply reify the existing situation?

It remains to be seen if blockchain is truly disruptive in the sense that the current incumbents are actively engaging with the technologies and are thus able to offer significant competition to new entrants. Emerging CMOs in developing economies have different realities. This is because they are not actively participating in blockchain initiatives; neither are they owners or developers of technologies, and they lack financial and technical resources. Of course, this lag behind global technological trends is nothing new. This has been the case in the past and it appears that this will be the case in the future. The evidence suggests that developing economies will remain technologically dependent and so face a real chance at being at least partially displaced by blockchain technologies and new market entrants. Nonetheless, at present, there is substantial optimism about the transformative potential of blockchain and in particular its application to improve copyright royalty payments by regional right holders.

However, the analysis suggests that digitalization and the introduction of blockchains are no panaceas. Based on the current trajectories, developing countries are likely to experience a widening digital divide and a decline in the diversity of music to the disadvantage of non-mainstream, developing countries' music industries unless they develop and implement a roadmap for global value chain integration. This would require an innovative governance framework and a strategic industrial upgrading programme.[40]

In this regard, there are four key recommendations that developing countries can pursue to enhance participation in the burgeoning digital marketplace. The first area for implementation would be the promotion

[39] Lee, S. (2018, 11 July) Blockchain Smart Contracts: More Trouble Than They Are Worth? Available at www.forbes.com/sites/shermanlee/2018/07/10/blockchain-smart-contracts-more-trouble-than-they-are-worth/#45dc4e9a23a6.

[40] An example can be read at IADB (6 June 2018). 'The Open Music Initiative's New Toys', available at https://blogs.iadb.org/caribbean-dev-trends/en/the-open-music-initiatives-new-toys/.

and facilitation of the distribution of music on key platforms. This might be achieved through the facilitation of, and partnership with, digital aggregators. It might also mean making use of blockchain technologies and investing in business models which allow for direct-to-consumer relationships. The productive use of technologies could assist with closing some of the gaps in the music industries of developing countries, which are characterized by very few investors, record companies, music publishers and other key players.

Closely tied to the above would be to expand the institutional and human resources in the creative industries to tap into the opportunities in the digital and blockchain arenas. Improving access to finance should accompany incubator and accelerator mechanisms, which facilitate enterprise development and market integration. Strategic initiatives should also exploit the synergies between live and digital music, particularly in the social media realm.

Employing targeted marketing strategies suitable for the various genres and styles of creative content on digital platforms would be crucial. This can assist artists and right holders in establishing greater visibility on playlists and potentially in accessing higher incomes from royalties. It can also help the tailoring of strategies to service regional, diaspora and global markets.

Last but not least, it is imperative that developing countries recognize the role of CMOs in their music industries. Once this is understood to be positive, whether in the analogue or digital markets or both, then strengthening the legal, technological and institutional infrastructure for collective management would be important. An effective CMO stimulates creativity and musical diversity through the creation of works of local genres and generates royalties, but also undertakes to support activities such as education, awards and social welfare actions.

A18.1

Table A18.1 *Digital music providers in the developing world*[41]

Provider and services	Key target markets	Reach and strength
Simfy Africa: Streaming	Simfy Africa gives music fans access to over 16 million songs in the cloud. Users can listen to music, create playlists and share them via social networks. Launched in 2010, Simfy has rapidly grown to become one of the leading music streaming providers in Africa.	Depth of catalogue with a focus on African music, MNO partnerships, service fully optimized for local conditions.
KKBOX: Downloads Streaming	Reach the growing Asian music market with the largest digital music subscription service in the Asia region. Listeners can stream over 10 million music tracks from over 500 major and local music labels and publishers, both online and offline.	Local and regional focus. Zero-in on the music market in Japan; Chinese Taipei; Hong Kong, China; Macao, China; Singapore; Malaysia; and Thailand.
Anghami: Downloads Streaming	The number 1 streaming and download music service in the Middle East and North Africa.	Local and regional focus in the growing Middle Eastern and North African music market.
Spinlet: Downloads Streaming	Showcase your music to the growing African music market with Spinlet, the leading music download and streaming service in Africa.	

[41] Source: TUNECORE, Digital Music Distribution Stores, available at www.tunecore.com/digital-music-stores. Accessed 21 September 2018.

Table A18.1 (*cont.*)

Provider and services	Key target markets	Reach and strength
Claromúsica: Downloads Streaming	Powered by the leading wireless services provider in Latin America, Claromúsica gets your music heard in Mexico, Argentina, Colombia, and 12 other Latin American countries. Your fans can access your music when and however they want via Claromúsica's multi-platform experience.	Local focus. Music heard in major Latin American countries.
Saavn: Streaming	The number 1 digital music service in India with award-winning mobile features.	Local focus and reach. Known as 'India's Spotify', your music can reach over 11 million monthly users in a booming music streaming market.
Kuack Music Group: Streaming	Kuack allows mobile carrier services and major brands to offer music streaming services to their subscribers in Latin America and the Caribbean. The catalogue is available for streaming on Digicel, Virgin Mobile and other mobile services.	Kuack provides an opportunity to reach more fans in Latin America and the Caribbean.
BoomPlay Music: Downloads Streaming	Boomplay Music is currently the number 1 and fastest-growing music community, lifestyle and entertainment app with a focus on music that aims to build the largest and most sustainable digital music platform in pan-Africa and African diaspora markets.	With over 7 million users and a monthly growth rate of over 700k new users, Boomplay Music continues to be preloaded on the number one smartphone in Africa.

Bibliography

Aswad, J., 'JAAK Moves Ahead with Blockchain Pilot, Joined by BMG, Global Music Rights, Warner Music, Others', *Variety* , 2 May 2018.

Burchardi, Kaj and Harle, Nicolas, 'The Blockchain Will Disrupt the Music Business And Beyond' *WIRED magazine*, 20 January 2018.

CISAC Global Collections Report 2018 For 2017 Data, available at www.cisac.org/Newsroom/news-releases/digital-royalties-creators-top-eu1-billion-global-collections-rise-62-eu96.

EY, 'Cultural Times: The First Global Map of Cultural and Creative Industries', 2015, available at https://en.unesco.org/creativity/sites/creativity/files/cultural_times._the_first_global_map_of_cultural_and_creative_industries.pdf.

IADB, 'The Open Music Initiative's New Toys', 6 June 2018, available at https://blogs.iadb.org.

Jones, Rhian, 'Global Music Rights Database Pilot Launched With Top Music Companies' *Music Business Worldwide*, 2 May 2018.

Lee, S., 'Blockchain Smart Contracts: More Trouble Than They Are Worth?', Forbes, 11 July 2018.

Maskus, Keith, 'Fostering Innovation in Digital Trade', in Xavier Seuba, Christophe Geiger and Julien Penin (eds), *Intellectual Property and Digital Trade in the Age of Artificial Intelligence and Big Data, Global Perspectives for the Intellectual Property System*, CEIPI-ICTSD, Issue Number 5, 2018.

Murray, S., 'Why Anghami, With Over 1m Paying Users, Doesn't Feel Threatened By Spotify In The Middle East', *Music Business Worldwide*, 5 March 2019.

Nurse, Keith and Ye, Zhen, 'Youth Entrepreneurship and the Rise of the Creative Industries', Vienna: UNIDO, 2012.

OECD, *Enquiries into Intellectual Property's Economic Impact*, Paris: OECD Publishing, 2015.

Patissier, Frederic, *Financing Creative Industries: In Search for a New Approach*, Paris: CISAC, 2009.

Towse, Ruth and Handke, Christian, *Handbook on the Digital Creative Economy*, Cheltenham: Edward Elgar Publishing, 2013.

TUNECORE, Digital Music Distribution Stores, available at www.tunecore.com/digital-music-stores.

UNDP/UNESCO, *The Creative Economy Report 2013: Widening Local Development Pathways*, New York/Paris: UNESCO, 2013.

van Rijn, Pieter, 'Collecting Societies Are Struggling To Keep Up with the Influx of Millions of Lines of Data', *Music Business Worldwide*, 13 May 2018.

WIPO, 'Guide on Surveying the Economic Contribution of Copyright Industries. 2015', revised edition.

WTO, *World Trade Statistical Review* 2021. https://www.wto.org/english/res_e/statis_e/wts2021_e/wts2021_e.pdf.

Wunsch-Vincent, Sacha, *The WTO, the Internet and Trade in Digital Products: EC-US Perspectives*, Oxford: Hart Publishing, 2006.

PART IV

Policy, Regulatory and Legislative Frameworks

19

Streaming of Music and Audiovisual Works

MARY LAFRANCE*

Abstract

As digital dissemination has become an increasingly important means of exploiting music and audiovisual works, this has necessitated reform in copyright and related rights regimes in order to enable rightholders to receive the compensation to which they are entitled without unduly burdening users' ability to benefit from these innovative services. The legal regimes that govern streaming of music and audiovisual works in the United States and the European Union have already undergone considerable change to address these concerns, and further changes are likely in the future. In the United States, recent reforms have focused on protecting the rights of music and sound recording creators to receive compensation for the use of their works by licensed streaming services. However, the unlicensed digital dissemination of music and audiovisual works remains a serious problem, leading some observers to criticize the broad scope of the safe harbours that protect Internet intermediaries. In the European Union, recent reforms have focused on two areas: (1) facilitating cross-border licensing of digital dissemination in order to further the goal of a digital single market, and (2) protecting rightholders against unauthorized digital exploitation of their works. On the latter point, the recently adopted DSM Directive subjects Internet intermediaries to a greatly increased risk of infringement liability, in stark contrast to the strong safe harbours they continue to enjoy in the United States.

* The author has published some of this chapter's material in two law review articles. *See* Mary LaFrance, 'Music Modernization and the Labyrinth of Streaming', 2 *Bus. Entrepreneurship & Tax L. Rev.* 310 (2018); Mary LaFrance, 'An Ocean Apart: Transatlantic Approaches to Copyright Infringement by Internet Intermediaries', 47-2 *AIPLA* 267 (2019). The author would like to thank the participants in Brigham Young University's Copyright and Trademark Symposium (18–19 October 2018), and the World Trade Organization's Seminar on IP and Knowledge Flows in a Digital Era (5–6 November 2018), for their helpful comments on earlier versions of this work.

Introduction

The rapid rise of digital streaming has revolutionized the music and film industries.[1] Yet most national copyright regimes remain rooted in a system of exclusive rights and economic rewards based predominantly on transactions involving tangible goods, theatrical exhibitions and terrestrial broadcasts. This impairs the ability of copyright law to distinguish between infringing and non-infringing activities, and to channel appropriate compensation to right holders. In the new world of digital entertainment services, international cooperation is essential to developing systems for licensing musical works, sound recordings and audiovisual works, collecting and accurately distributing royalties, distinguishing between infringing and non-infringing transmissions, providing appropriate mechanisms for preventing infringement and enforcing the rights of content owners when infringement occurs.

This chapter examines the legal regimes that govern the streaming of music and audiovisual works in the United States and the European Union. Although these legal systems have already undergone considerable change during the Internet era, they must continue to evolve in order to address the challenges presented by licensed and unlicensed streaming.

United States

Legislative Background

As technological changes have transformed the entertainment industry, Congress has periodically updated the copyright laws in an effort to maintain the economic reward system that sustains the industry without discouraging technological innovation. Key legislation affecting sound recordings and audiovisual works has included the Sound Recording Act (SRA) of 1971,[2] the Digital Performance Right in Sound Recordings Act (DPRA) of 1995,[3] the Digital Millennium Copyright Act (DMCA) of 1998,[4] and, most recently, the Orrin G. Hatch-Bob Goodlatte Music Modernization Act of 2018 (MMA).[5]

[1] According to the RIAA, as of mid-2018, streaming accounted for 75 per cent of music industry revenues. RIAA, 'Mid-Year 2018 RIAA Music Revenues Report', 2018, p. 2.

[2] Pub. L. 92-140 (15 October 1971).

[3] Pub. L. 104-39, 109 Stat. 336 (1 November 1995).

[4] Pub. L. 105-304 (28 October 1998).

[5] Pub. L. 115-264, 132 Stat. 3676 (11 October 2018).

Sound Recording Act of 1971

Until the SRA was enacted in 1971, federal copyright law did not extend to sound recordings at all. A cause of action arose, if at all, under state law.[6] Because the SRA was aimed specifically at piracy of physical recordings, it recognized only the rights of reproduction and public distribution (although Congress later added a narrow adaptation right).[7] The SRA did not recognize any public performance right in sound recordings.[8]

Digital Performance Right in Sound Recordings Act of 1995

Public Performance of Sound Recordings As streaming revealed its potential to displace record sales, Congress enacted the 1995 DPRA to create a narrowly limited public performance right for sound recordings, applicable only to digital streaming of copyrighted sound recordings.[9] Section 114 creates two separate royalty schemes for sound recording performance royalties – one for noninteractive services, and one for interactive services.

Noninteractive services do not allow users to choose or predict which recording they will hear at any given time. These include satellite radio (SiriusXM) and radio-style streaming services (such as Pandora Free). Noninteractive services are eligible for a statutory licence that permits them to stream any copyrighted sound recording in exchange for paying a statutory royalty that is set through an administrative proceeding conducted by the Copyright Royalty Board (CRB). The royalties are collected and disbursed by SoundExchange, a non-profit collective. By law, the royalty proceeds are allocated 50 per cent to the record label, 45 per cent to the featured vocalists and musicians and 5 per cent to the non-featured performers (split equally between two groups – vocalists and musicians).[10] SoundExchange disburses royalties to the featured performers directly; royalties for non-featured performers are paid to their unions, which in turn distribute them to the performers.

[6] See, e.g., Cal. Penal Code § 653h (California's criminal record piracy statute).

[7] 17 USC §§ 106(1)-(3), 114(b).

[8] 17 USC § 114(a). In addition, the law only protected sound recordings created on or after 15 February 1972. Older recordings remained subject to state law.

[9] 17 USC §§ 106(6), 114(f)-(g). The DPRA was amended by the Digital Millennium Copyright Act of 1998. This discussion reflects the current statutes.

[10] 17 USC § 114(g)(2).

In contrast, *interactive services* allow listeners to choose the recordings they will hear – Spotify and Pandora Premium, for example – and are not eligible for the statutory licence. Instead, they must negotiate a licence from the copyright owner of each sound recording. The law gives record labels more control over licensing to interactive services because these services are more likely to displace record sales.[11] In contrast to the statutory royalty, recording artists are not guaranteed a share of the streaming royalty for their recordings. Instead, the terms of their recording contracts determine whether and to what extent they receive a portion of the record label's streaming royalty.

Compulsory Licence for Digital Phonorecord Deliveries The DPRA also extended the section 115 compulsory mechanical licence[12] to encompass the distribution of sound recordings by digital downloads, referring to these as 'digital phonorecord deliveries'. A service providing digital downloads of recordings can use the compulsory licence rather than negotiate a voluntary licence for the musical composition. (Of course, the service also needs a licence from the record label to copy and distribute the sound recording.) In addition, when a record label uses the compulsory licence to make a recording, that licence includes the right to distribute (or authorize distribution of) that recording by digital phonorecord delivery (in which case it is referred to as a 'pass-through' licence).

Although the DPRA's definition of 'digital phonorecord delivery' clearly encompassed downloads, it was less clear whether it also encompassed streaming, since it was unclear whether streaming involved making and distributing copies of sound recordings.

Digital Millennium Copyright Act of 1998

In 1998, Congress enacted the DMCA in order to limit the copyright liability of Internet service providers (ISPs) for transmitting, storing or providing access to infringing material. With respect to ISPs that host user-posted content, exemplified by YouTube, the section 512 'safe harbour' largely insulates eligible ISPs from liability for storing and transmitting their users' infringing content.[13] To qualify for the safe harbour, the

[11] The ability of interactive streaming to displace record sales has only increased in recent years, with the development of stream-ripping technologies.

[12] 17 USC § 115. Royalty rates for the compulsory licence are established by the CRB. In practice, even voluntary mechanical licences apply the compulsory rate.

[13] 17 USC § 512.

ISP must, among other things, implement a policy of terminating repeat infringers, and expeditiously remove any content that it knows is infringing, or where facts and circumstances make the infringement apparent.[14]

Because of this safe harbour, YouTube has become the most popular music streaming service in the world – larger than fully licensed services such as Spotify – as well as a popular platform for users seeking free access to films and television programmes.[15]

The Complexities of Licensed Music Streaming

Under the existing legislative scheme, music streaming services must obtain several kinds of licences, from different sources, and under different royalty regimes. First, they need public performance licences covering all copyrighted musical compositions embodied in the sound recordings they intend to stream. In this respect, they stand in the same legal position as radio and television broadcasters. However, streaming services incur additional royalty obligations that terrestrial broadcasters do not – specifically, the DPRA digital streaming royalty and, in the case of interactive services, a mechanical royalty for reproducing the musical composition embodied in the recording, as well as a master recording licence for reproducing the sound recording itself.

As discussed below, the most significant complaints regarding this regime have come from songwriters and publishers who believe that both their public performance royalties and their mechanical royalties are inadequate. Some of these complaints have now been addressed in the 2018 MMA.

[14] 17 USC §§ 512(c), (i)(1).

[15] According to a 2018 report by the International Federation of the Phonographic Industry (IFPI), nearly 50 per cent of the time spent listening to on-demand music streaming is on YouTube, more than all other music streaming services combined. IFPI, 'Music Consumer Insight Report', at 13 (2018). YouTube's free user-uploaded streaming service had 1.9 billion users in 2018, compared to Spotify's 170 million users. Lennon Cihak 'YouTube's Head of Music: "We're Not Discussing the Value Gap"', *Digital Music News*, 28 June 2018, available at www.digitalmusicnews.com/2018/06/28/youtube-lyor-cohen-value-gap/. A 2018 study of royalty payouts to a mid-size indie label shows that YouTube's free service (where some right holders receive a small share of ad revenues through Content ID) has nearly a 50 per cent market share, compared to Spotify's 30 per cent: '2018 Streaming Price Bible! Per Stream Rates Drop as Streaming Volume Grows. YouTube's Value Gap is Very Real', *The Trichordist* , 29 January 2019, available at https://thetrichordist.com/2019/01/29/2018-streaming-price-bible-per-stream-rates-drop-as-streaming-volume-grows-youtubes-value-gap-is-very-real/.

Public Performance Royalties for Musical Compositions

For the right to perform the underlying musical compositions, streaming services must obtain blanket public performance licences from each of the four domestic performance rights organizations (PROs) that represent songwriters and publishers in the United States (and their counterparts abroad, through affiliation agreements with foreign PROs). While a service could in theory get blanket licences from only the two largest PROs, ASCAP and BMI, this would leave significant gaps in their repertoires (e.g. Bruce Springsteen, Bob Seger and George and Ira Gershwin, all licensed through Global Music Rights (GMR)).

In negotiating with streaming services, ASCAP and BMI operate under the constraints of antitrust consent decrees dating from the 1940s.[16] A potential licensee that objects to the rates or terms of the proposed blanket licence can have the dispute adjudicated by the District Court for the Southern District of New York (the 'Rate Court'). While a dispute is pending, the PRO must allow the licensee to use its entire catalogue of music, but the royalty will not be payable until after the rate court proceeding (including any appeal) concludes. Most American songwriters and publishers cannot avoid the constraints of the consent decrees. Although the two other domestic PROs – SESAC and GMR – are not subject to consent decrees, they cherry-pick their members on an invitation-only basis.

Whereas the record labels have generally succeeded in obtaining favourable performance royalty rates from streaming services (either through direct negotiation with interactive services, or through CRB proceedings for the noninteractive services), the performance royalties received by songwriters and publishers through the efforts of their PROs have been considerably lower. Until recently, songwriters and publishers were unable to use this disparity to argue for higher royalties in the Rate Court, because section 114(i) prohibited sound recording royalties from being considered in those proceedings.[17] When several publishers attempted to withdraw their digital performance rights from ASCAP

[16] Second Amended Final Judgment, United States *v.* American Society of Composers, Authors and Publishers, Civ. Action No. 41-1395 (SDNY); [Amended] Final Judgment, United States *v.* Broadcast Music, Inc., Civil No. 64-Civ-3787 (SDNY); see United States Department of Justice, Antitrust Consent Decree Review – ASCAP and BMI 2014, available at www.justice.gov/atr/ascap-bmi-decree-review.

[17] 17 USC 114(i). Congress originally enacted this provision based on the songwriters' and publishers' concern that, in Rate Court proceedings, streaming services would cite their new obligation to pay royalties to record companies as an argument for reducing the

and BMI, so that they could negotiate directly with the streaming services, the Second Circuit ruled that this was not permitted by the consent decrees.[18] As discussed in '2018 Legislation: The Hatch–Goodlatte Music Modernization Act' below, the MMA has responded to this problem by repealing section 114(i).

Mechanical Royalties

Initially, it was not clear whether streaming services were required to pay mechanical royalties to the copyright owners of musical compositions. Eventually, a general consensus emerged that interactive streaming services must pay mechanical royalties.

Whereas record labels needed only a dozen or so mechanical licences for a traditional record album, interactive streaming services needed thousands, and needed them quickly, leading them to file massive numbers of compulsory licence notices (NOIs) with the Copyright Office. Because of the royalty expense, the challenges of identifying and locating the copyright owners in the absence of a reliable database, the uncertain state of the law and their haste to enter the market, interactive services often did not pay their mechanical royalties.[19] As a result, Spotify faced – and settled – massive lawsuits for its failure to pay.[20]

The challenge of locating all of the right holders for each sound recording prompted numerous proposals for the creation of a single database that (1) collects all of the metadata for every sound recording and musical composition, (2) is accessible to all rights holders and licensees and (3) can be updated as necessary. There were several

royalties payable for the musical works; they did not foresee that the record labels' royalties would be so much higher.

[18] Pandora Media, Inc. *v.* Am. Soc. of Composers, Authors and Publishers, 785 F.3d 73, 77 (2nd Cir. 2015); see also Statement of the Department of Justice on the Closing of the Antitrust Division's Review of ASCAP and BMI Consent Decrees (4 August 2016) (refusing to modify the decrees); see also Steven J. Gagliano, 'Consent Decrees in the Streaming Era: Digital Withdrawal, Fractional Licensing, and § 114(i)', 10 *Business, Entrepreneurship & The Law* 317, 321–322 (2017).

[19] See Jody Dunitz, 'The Easiest Way to Fix the Mechanical Royalty is to Get Rid of It', *Digital Music News* (25 September 2017), available at www.digitalmusicnews.com/2017/09/25/fix-streaming-mechanical/.

[20] Robert Levine, 'Spotify Settles Class Action Lawsuits Filed by David Lowery and Melissa Ferrick with $43.4 Million Fund' (26 May 2017), available at www.billboard.com/articles/business/7809561/spotify-settles-class-action-lawsuits-filed-by-david-lowery-and-melissa.

unsuccessful attempts to create such databases.[21] Key issues were how to require industry participants to contribute and update the relevant information, and who would be responsible for maintaining and funding the database.

Even when songwriters and publishers were paid their compulsory mechanicals, the royalty rates tended to be low, because the law required the CRB to set the rate based on four objectives: (1) maximizing availability of creative works, (2) giving the copyright owner a fair return and the licensee a fair income, (3) reflecting the copyright owner and licensee's relative contributions to the product and to the opening of new markets and new media and (4) minimizing disruption of the industries and prevailing industry practices.[22] The CRB used a complicated formula that was based largely on the revenues of the interactive service. While this approach may have been appropriate when streaming was a new industry, once it became the dominant mode of music exploitation songwriters and publishers argued that they should no longer be expected to subsidize these operations.[23]

In contrast, record labels have generally obtained better remuneration for the streaming of their recordings.[24] The labels can negotiate freely with interactive services, obtaining relatively favourable terms, including significant advances and, in the case of Spotify, equity interests, in addition to the negotiated performance royalties. In the case of noninteractive services, the record labels were limited to the statutory royalty, but the CRB was required to set that royalty according to a 'willing buyer/ willing seller' standard[25] that generally yielded a higher rate than the

[21] Several PROs in the US and Europe formed the International Music Joint Venture in 2000, but never succeeded in producing the database. In 2009, the European Commission established the Global Repertoire Database Working Group, but the effort collapsed in 2014. The World Intellectual Property Organization (WIPO) undertook to create the International Music Registry in 2011, but this effort failed as well. See Klementina Milosic, 'The Failure of the Global Repertoire Database', available at www.hypebot.com/hypebot/2015/08/the-failure-of-the-global-repertoire-database-effort-draft.html. The failures typically arose because of disputes over control of the database or choice of technological standards, leading one or more participants to withdraw their funding.

[22] 17 USC § 801(b)(1)(A)-(D).

[23] See, e.g., Daniel Sanchez, 'Exclusive Report: Spotify Artist Payments are Declining in 2017, Data Shows', *Digital Music News* (16 May 2017), available at www.digitalmusicnews.com/2017/05/16/spotify-audiam-low-rates/.

[24] See US Music Streaming Royalties Explained, available at www.manatt.com/Manatt/media/Media/PDF/US-Streaming-Royalties-Explained.pdf.

[25] 17 USC § 114(f)(2)(B). The exceptions are the older digital services – SiriusXM, Muzak and Music Choice – which are governed by the same rate-setting standard as section 115.

multi-factor test that the CRB applied to compulsory mechanical licences.

In late 2017, the CRB tweaked its formula for calculating the compulsory mechanical royalty for interactive services.[26] Although the new formula was an improvement, it still fell below the willing buyer/willing seller standard. Fortunately for songwriters and publishers, further relief was on the horizon, in the 2018 MMA.

2018 Legislation: The Hatch–Goodlatte Music Modernization Act

Some of the challenges presented by digital music streaming have now been addressed in the Orrin G. Hatch–Bob Goodlatte Music Modernization Act (MMA),[27] enacted in October of 2018. Title I, the Musical Works Modernization Act (MWMA), addresses mechanical and public performance royalties for digital streaming of musical compositions.[28]

The MWMA addresses both mechanical and public performance royalties. It requires interactive streaming services to obtain mechanical licences for the musical works embodied in the recordings that they stream,[29] thus ending any residual uncertainty over whether such licences are required. To facilitate the mechanical licensing process, the law requires creation of a non-profit mechanical licensing collective (similar to a PRO) to issue blanket mechanical licences to digital music services. While prior law allowed the party seeking a section 115 licence to file its notice of intent with the Copyright Office, once the collective becomes operational the interactive streaming services will be required to serve notice either on the copyright owner of the musical work or on the collective. In this way, even if the streaming service cannot identify the copyright owner(s) or determine their respective royalty shares, it must

17 USC § 114(f)(1). United States Copyright Office, *Copyright and the Music Marketplace* 81 (February 2015).

26 Copyright Royalty Board, Docket No. 16-CRB-0003-PR (2018-2022), (Phonorecords III) (22 December 2017), available at https://crb.gov/rate/.

27 Pub. L. No. 115–264, 132 Stat. 3676 (11 October 2018).

28 Title II, the CLASSICS Protection and Access Act (the CLASSICS Act), grants, for the first time, federal protection to pre-1972 sound recordings made in the US. Codified at 17 USC § 1401, the new protection strongly resembles copyright, but is not identical.

29 The compulsory licence requirement applies to 'digital phonorecord deliveries', which the MWMA redefines to expressly include interactive streaming as well as downloads, but not non-interactive streaming.

still pay the mechanical royalty to the collecting society, which will itself undertake the task of identifying the copyright owner(s) and, in the case of jointly owned works, determine the owners' respective royalty shares. To verify the accuracy of the royalty payments, copyright owners will have the right to audit the collective's records, and the collective will have the right to audit the records of the streaming services.

For the collective to allocate licence fees to the correct copyright owners, it will need an accurate database that identifies the copyright owners of the musical work(s) on each sound recording. To accomplish this, the MWMA requires the collective to create and maintain a database that identifies (1) the musical works embodied in individual sound recordings, (2) the copyright owners of those musical works, (3) the respective ownership shares of each of those copyright owners and (4) contact information for each of the owners. With respect to both the musical works and the sound recordings that embody them, the database will include, to the extent possible, the international standard codes that uniquely identify those works. In addition, the database will be available to the public, at no charge, in a searchable online format.

The MWMA also requires the CRB to use the 'willing buyer/willing seller' standard to determine the compulsory mechanical royalty rate under section 115, thus eliminating the four-factor test and applying the same standard that applies to the section 114 statutory royalty for record labels.

Finally, the MWMA revises section 115 to clarify that 'pass-through' compulsory licences are not available for interactive streaming, although they can still be used for digital downloads.

With respect to public performance rights in musical compositions, the MWMA changes the manner in which the Rate Court oversees the rates and terms of blanket licences issued to streaming services by ASCAP and BMI. As noted earlier, section 114(i) has prohibited the Rate Court from considering the (higher) performance royalties paid to record labels. The MWMA repeals section 114(i), and expressly permits the Rate Court to consider the sound recording performance royalties when setting the performance royalties for streaming the musical works.

Summary: US Law on Music Streaming

Until recently, outdated laws governing music streaming have impeded the efforts of songwriters and music publishers to negotiate market-rate public performance and mechanical royalties, while generally favouring the record labels. However, the 2018 MMA significantly improves this legal regime. The improved process for administering mechanical licences and setting compulsory royalty rates should help songwriters and music publishers to receive fair compensation. The mandate to create a publicly accessible music database should lead to the creation of an essential resource which can expand to include a worldwide repertoire linking recordings to their underlying musical works and to all of the creative participants who may be entitled to share in the proceeds of those works.

The new legislation does not, however, address concerns regarding ISPs such as YouTube and Facebook that host large quantities of user-posted sound recordings and music videos, yet avoid paying market-rate royalties because they enjoy the protection of the DMCA safe harbours. The music industry will continue to pressure law-makers to reconsider the scope of the safe harbours that enable these hosting services to generate significant advertising revenues from music and sound recordings while paying little or nothing to the right holders. These safe harbours are discussed in 'Intermediary Liability and the DMCA Safe Harbours' below.

US Law on Streaming of Audiovisual Works

In contrast to sound recordings, audiovisual works enjoy full federal copyright protection. Therefore, any digital transmission of a copyrighted work to the public – via download or streaming – is a copyright infringement unless it is licensed by the copyright owner or falls within a statutory exemption such as fair use or the DMCA safe harbours.

In defining the exclusive rights of copyright owners, federal copyright law does not use the terms 'making available' or 'communication to the public'. However, federal courts agree that the act of making a work available on the Internet for downloading constitutes public distribution, although they disagree on whether infringement liability requires proof of an actual download.[30]

Streaming a musical work, sound recording or audiovisual work on the Internet is a considered a public performance regardless of whether

[30] United States Copyright Office, 'The Making Available Right in the United States' 19–26, 29–36 (February 2016) ('Making Available Report') (discussing authorities). In contrast to the civil copyright statutes, 'making available' is specifically mentioned in the criminal provisions of federal copyright law, which criminalizes the knowing distribution of a work being prepared for commercial distribution 'by making it available on a computer network accessible to members of the public'; 17 USC § 506(a)(1)(C).

'the members of the public capable of receiving the performance or display receive it in the same place or in separate places and at the same time or at different times'.[31] The statutes do not directly answer the question of whether merely making a work available for streaming constitutes a public performance, or whether proof of actual streaming is required. In the context of traditional broadcasts, a public performance takes place anytime the transmission is *capable* of being received, even if none of the potential recipients is operating a receiving device at the time.[32] While neither Congress nor the courts have analysed the analogous question in the context of on-demand streaming, where no actual transmission occurs until requested by a user, the Copyright Office believes, as a policy matter, that making a work available for public streaming should be sufficient to constitute a public performance.[33]

Unlike musical compositions and sound recordings, there are no compulsory licences for audiovisual works, and no statutory schemes for directing royalty payments to anyone other than the copyright owner.[34] The main digital exploitation concerns for audiovisual works, therefore, are unlicensed transmissions, in the form of either downloads or on-demand streaming.

Most enforcement actions against unauthorized streaming involve only civil litigation. Federal law criminalizes wilful copyright infringement by *streaming* only if it is for purposes of commercial advantage or private financial gain; in contrast, criminal penalties may be imposed, in appropriate circumstances, for wilful infringements by copying or public distribution even in the absence of commercial or financial motives.[35] Proposed legislation to broaden the criminal provisions for infringing streaming was defeated in 2011.[36]

[31] 17 USC § 101.

[32] HR Rep. No. 94-1476, 94th Cong., 2nd Sess. 65 (1976).

[33] 'Making Available Report', *supra* n. 30, at 38–40.

[34] Commercially viable audiovisual works in the US are almost always created as works made for hire, with the performers, writers, directors or other creative participants retaining no share of the copyright. To the extent these parties are entitled to any share of the copyright owner's revenues from digital transmissions, it is only as a result of their contracts with the production company (which, in the case of unionized workers, incorporate the terms of collective bargaining agreements).

[35] 17 USC § 506(a)(1).

[36] S. 978, 112th Cong., 1st Sess. (2011).

Intermediary Liability and the DMCA Safe Harbours

In the DMCA safe harbours, Congress sought to limit the liability of Internet service providers (ISPs) for copyright infringement in order to avoid chilling the development of new technologies.[37] As a result, the largest user-generated content (UGC) providers, such as YouTube and Facebook, are largely insulated from liability under the DMCA.

To be eligible for *any* of the safe harbours, an ISP must adopt, 'reasonably implement' and inform its users of a policy that it will, 'in appropriate circumstances', terminate service to 'repeat infringers'.[38] These undefined terms leave much room for interpretation. If the ISP fails to qualify, it may be liable for direct, vicarious or contributory copyright infringement.

The safe harbour most relevant to hosting services is section 512(c), which protects an ISP from liability arising from storage of infringing material, at a user's direction, if it satisfies four conditions: (1) the ISP must not have actual knowledge of the infringing activity, and must not be aware of facts or circumstances that make the infringing activity apparent or, upon obtaining such knowledge or awareness, it must promptly remove or disable access to the infringing material; (2) an ISP that has the right and ability to control the infringing activity must not derive a direct financial benefit from it; (3) upon receiving an infringement notice that meets the statutory requirements, the ISP must promptly remove or disable access to the infringing material; and (4) the ISP must properly designate an agent to receive infringement notices.[39]

The first requirement has been frequently litigated – in particular, the 'red flag' provision that eliminates the safe harbour if a provider is 'aware of facts or circumstances from which infringing activity is apparent', but fails to take corrective action. In general, courts have been reluctant to impute such knowledge, on the theory that Congress did not intend to place a heavy burden on ISPs. Both the Second and Ninth Circuits, therefore, hold that red flag knowledge requires more than generalized awareness of infringing activity. Instead, the ISP must be subjectively aware of facts or circumstances that indicate *specific and identifiable* acts of infringement. As the Second Circuit explained in *Viacom Int'l, Inc.*

[37] UMG Recordings, Inc. *v.* Shelter Capital Partners LLC, 718 F.3d 1006, 1014 (9th Cir. 2013).

[38] 17 USC § 512(i).

[39] *Id.* § 512(c).

v. *YouTube, Inc.*: '[T]he actual knowledge provision turns on whether the provider actually or "subjectively" knew of specific infringement, while the red flag provision turns on whether the provider was subjectively aware of facts that would have made the specific infringement "objectively" obvious to a reasonable person.'[40] Without actual knowledge or awareness of specific infringing material, the courts have reasoned, it would not be feasible for the ISP to carry out its statutory obligation to remove or disable access to that material.

In both the Second and Ninth Circuits, a showing of 'wilful blindness' can satisfy either the actual or red flag knowledge requirement.[41] In this context, courts use a concept of 'wilful blindness' derived from a 2011 Supreme Court patent infringement opinion, which stated that a wilfully blind defendant is 'one who takes deliberate actions to avoid confirming a high probability of wrongdoing and who can almost be said to have known the critical facts'.[42]

It is difficult to reconcile some of the decisions applying the red flag test.

In *Capitol Records, LLC* v. *Vimeo, LLC*,[43] where the defendant ISP stored and streamed user-posted videos, the Second Circuit found neither actual nor red flag knowledge even though the defendant's own employees had viewed user-posted videos that contained 'all or virtually all of a recognizable, copyrighted song'.[44] Although it applied the *Viacom* standard, *Vimeo* held that the 'hypothetical "reasonable person" to whom the infringement must be obvious is an ordinary person – not endowed with specialized knowledge or expertise concerning music or the laws of copyright'. In this case, the employee might have viewed the video too briefly to know that the song was present in its entirety, or might have been viewing the video for a business purpose other than checking for infringement. The fact that some people would recognize the song does not mean that a hypothetical ordinary person with no musical expertise would recognize it. And the employee could not be expected to have copyright expertise, to distinguish between infringement and fair use, or to know whether the use was authorized or not. Finally, the ISP had no legal obligation to have its employees investigate these questions.[45]

40 Viacom Int'l, Inc. *v.* YouTube, Inc., 676 F.3d 19, 31 (2nd Cir. 2012).
41 UMG Recordings, Inc *v.* Shelter Capital Partners LLC, 718 F.3d 1006 (9th Cir. 2013); Perfect 10, Inc. *v.* CCBill LLC, 488 F.3d 1102, 1114 (9th Cir. 2007).
42 Global-Tech Appliances, Inc. *v.* SEB S.A., 563 US 754, 769 (2011).
43 826 F.3d 78 (2nd Cir. 2016).
44 *Id.* at 96.
45 *Id.* at 96–97.

In contrast, the same court imputed greater music expertise to the defendant in *EMI Christian Music Group, Inc.* v. *MP3tunes, LLC*,[46] holding that a jury could find that an ISP had red flag knowledge or wilful blindness as to four categories of music files: (1) those stored on domains identified in takedown notices as having 10 or more infringing files; (2) sideloads[47] of MP3s before January 2007, because the defendant knew that major record labels did not issue MP3 files before 2007; (3) certain sideloads by MP3tunes executives; and (4) works by the Beatles, because the defendant knew that there had been no legal online distribution of Beatles tracks before 2010.[48]

In a similar vein, in *Columbia Pictures Indus.* v. *Fung*[49] the Ninth Circuit imputed sufficient awareness to a defendant that operated a peer-to-peer file-sharing service utilizing BitTorrent. The court found that the red flag standard was satisfied because the defendant (1) had used his own service to download infringing material, (2) actively encouraged infringement by urging his users to upload and download particular copyrighted works, (3) assisted users seeking to watch copyrighted films, and (4) helped users burn copyrighted material onto DVDs. In the Court's view, the content at issue was 'sufficiently current and well-known that it would have been objectively obvious to a reasonable person' that it was copyrighted and not licensed to the general public.[50]

The second requirement for the safe harbour – that the defendant not derive a financial benefit from the infringing activity – applies only if the defendant had the 'right and ability to control the infringing activity'. Courts in both the Second and Ninth Circuits have held that this requires 'something more' than the ability to locate and remove infringing material and to terminate users' access. Were it otherwise, the mere fact that an ISP has the ability to comply with the safe harbour requirements (by monitoring its website, locating and removing infringing materials and blocking infringers' access) would expose the ISP to liability, which cannot be what Congress intended.[51] Instead, the ISP must exert

46 844 F.3d 79 (2nd Cir. 2016).

47 A sideload is a file transfer between two local devices, typically from a computer to a mobile device.

48 844 F.3d at 92–93.

49 710 F.3d 1020 (9th Cir. 2013).

50 710 F.3d at 1043.

51 See UMG Recordings, Inc. *v.* Veoh Networks, Inc., 665 F.Supp.2d 1099, 1112–11116 (CD Cal. 2009) (collecting cases), *aff'd*, 718 F.3d 1006 (9th Cir. 2013). The legislative history of § 512 evinces Congress's concern that ISPs would be discouraged from making voluntary

'substantial influence' over the activities of its users, which may involve either a high degree of control over their activities or purposeful conduct such as inducing the infringing activity.[52] In the *Fung* case, the defendant's inducing activity established the requisite degree of control.[53]

If an ISP does not qualify for the DMCA safe harbour, in most cases its liability for hosting or facilitating infringing activity will be determined under the common law standards for vicarious or contributory liability. In *BMG Rights Mgmt (US) LLC* v. *Cox Comm'n, Inc.*,[54] an Internet access provider was not eligible for the section 512(a) safe harbour, which protects ISPs that merely act as conduits for users that are transmitting infringing content, because it failed to terminate repeat infringers.[55] However, the Fourth Circuit held that the district court erred by instructing the jury that Cox could be contributorily liable if it 'knew or should have known' of its users' infringing activities. The court held that neither negligence nor recklessness was sufficient for contributory liability; instead, BMG must prove that the ISP was at least 'wilfully blind' to the infringing activity,[56] and the ISP's actual knowledge or wilful blindness must pertain to specific instances of infringing activity, rather than general knowledge that its users were engaging in such activity. Thus, even though Cox was not protected by the safe harbour, BMG still had to meet a high standard of proof to hold Cox contributorily liable, and the standard of proof that the court imposed was similar, if not identical, to the standard that applies to the safe harbour.

In contrast, for an ISP to be considered a *direct* infringer, courts require a 'volitional' act of infringement by the ISP itself, rather than simply by its users. In the ISP context, the meaning of volition is unsettled. One commentator infers from the case law that volition will *not* be found if the only way for the ISP to prevent the infringement is to police its users' activities.[57] In contrast, website operators engage in

efforts to monitor infringing activity if these efforts would place their safe harbor at risk. *Id.* at 1113 note 19 (citing H. Conf. Report 105–796, at 73 (8 October 1998)).

[52] *UMG Recordings*, 718 F.3d at 1030; *Viacom*, 676 F.3d at 38. The courts found no such influence in these cases.

[53] 710 F.3d at 1046.

[54] 881 F.3d 293 (4th Cir. 2018).

[55] Its stated policy was to terminate subscribers after 13 notices of infringement, but it did not enforce that policy.

[56] *Id.* at 308–10. The court did not define 'willful blindness' in this context, so it is unclear whether it meant to adopt the Supreme Court's *Global-Tech* definition.

[57] See Robert C. Denicola, 'Volition and Copyright Infringement', 37 *Cardozo L. Rev.* 1259, 1276 (2016).

volitional conduct – and thus can be liable for direct infringement – when they select the content for their users to stream or download.[58] In most cases, however, ISPs avoid liability as direct infringers, because courts ascribe the volitional conduct to the users, treating the ISPs as mere conduits or facilitators.[59]

YouTube offers some, but not all, copyright owners the opportunity to block or monetize their work through its automated monitoring system, Content ID. An eligible right holder delivers reference files containing the copyrighted materials and metadata to YouTube, which matches this data against user uploads, and gives the right holder the option to block, track or monetize the upload. Right holders must apply for participation, and YouTube acceptance is based on 'an evaluation of each applicant's actual need for the tools'. YouTube does not disclose how 'actual need' is assessed, other than to state that the applicant must own exclusive rights to 'a substantial body of original material that is frequently uploaded by the YouTube user community'.[60]

When Content ID is used, YouTube reportedly keeps 45 per cent of the advertising revenue, and the remaining 55 per cent is split among right holders, including the creator of the video, the record label, the songwriter and the publisher. If the songwriter or publisher uses a digital collection agency (such as CMRRA or Audiam), the agency takes a share as well.[61] Right holders cannot be sure of the amount of advertising revenue that forms the royalty base for YouTube's payments. According to one vendor, the pay-out for ad revenues with respect to a particular

[58] See *id.* at 1280 & n. 155. Examples include Warner Bros. Entm't *v.* WTV Sys., Inc., 824 F.Supp.2d 1003 (CD Cal. 2011); Arista Records LLC *v.* Usenet.com, Inc., 633 F.Supp.2d 124 (SDNY 2009); UMG Recordings, Inc., *v.* MP3.com, Inc., 92 F.Supp.2d 349 (SDNY 2000); Playboy Enters., Inc. *v.* Webbworld, Inc., 968 F.Supp. 1171, 1175 (ND Tex. 1997).

[59] See, e.g., BWP Media USA, Inc. *v.* T&S Software Assocs, Inc., 852 F.3d 436 (5th Cir. 2017); Perfect10, Inc. *v.* Giganews, Inc., 847 F.3d 657, 666–667 (9th Cir. 2017); Leonard *v.* Stemtech Int'l, Inc., 834 F.3d 376, 387 (3d Cir. 2016); Cartoon Network LP *v.* CSC Holdings, Inc., 536 F.3d 121, 131 (2nd Cir. 2008); CoStar Group, Inc. *v.* Loopnet, Inc., 373 F.3d 544, 551 (4th Cir. 2004); Religious Technology Center *v.* Netcom On-Line Comm'n Servs., Inc., 907 F.Supp. 1361 (CD Cal. 1995) (pre-DMCA case). But See Perfect 10, Inc. *v.* Amazon.com, 508 F.3d 1146 (9th Cir. 2007) (finding that framing and hyperlinking as part of an image search engine constitute a fair use of images because the use was highly transformative).

[60] See https://support.google.com/youtube/answer/3244015?hl=en; https://support.google.com/youtube/answer/1311402.

[61] Michael Raine, 'YouTube: Friend or Foe of the Music Industry?', *Canadian Musician* (9 May 2017), available at https://indepth.canadianmusician.com/youtube-friend-or-foe-of-the-music-industry/.

monetized video depends on how the viewer responds to the ad. In order for any ad revenues to be shared, the viewer must click on a banner or text ad, or watch a video commercial for a minimum period of time.[62] Thus, payment to right holders depends on the effectiveness of the advertisement in capturing the user's attention.

Right holders complain that '[g]etting your work into Content ID without the aid of a major backer is famously difficult'.[63] Independent musicians and songwriters, in particular, complain that Content ID only accepts applications from major record labels and a few independent artists. YouTube responds that all right holders can access Content ID through 'third party vendors', including Audiam, AdRev, Vydia, ONErpm, and aggregators such as CD Baby,[64] but these vendors charge the right holders 15–50 per cent of the ad revenues, and do not provide blocking services for those who choose not to monetize their content.[65] As of 20 February 2018, channels with fewer than 1,000 subscribers and 4,000 watch hours no longer qualify for this programme, and will be unable to monetize on their own.[66]

Monetization through Content ID is not true voluntary licensing, because, in many if not most cases, the DMCA safe harbours virtually ensure that the right holder's content will be available on YouTube even without the licence. In 2008, when Warner Music Group chose to remove rather than monetize its content, it reportedly spent USD 2 million over nine months trying to keep its content off YouTube.[67] In 2016, IFPI estimated that Content ID failed to identify 40 per cent of infringing works,[68] a figure contested by YouTube.[69]

62 Michael Raine, *supra* n. 61.

63 See www.plagiarismtoday.com/2018/05/02/youtube-beta-testing-content-id-for-everyone/.

64 See https://futureofmusic.org/blog/2016/05/17/how-get-your-music-content-id; Nicholas Salamone, 'YouTube for Musicians: How is All the $$ Made?', *DIY Musician* (12 June 2017), available at https://diymusician.cdbaby.com/youtube/youtube-musicians-made/.

65 Maria Schneider, 'Content ID is Still Piracy in Disguise', available at https://musictechpolicy.com/2016/07/31/guest-post-by-schneidermaria-content-id-is-still-just-piracy-in-disguise-an-open-letter-to-rightsholders-and-a-music-industry-ready-to-renegotiate-with-a-monster/; http://futureofmusic.org/blog/2016/05/17/how-get-your-music-content-id.

66 See https://support.cdbaby.com/hc/en-us/articles/211095163-Why-should-I-have-CD-Baby-help-me-monetize-my-music-on-YouTube-; http://diymusician.cdbaby.com/youtube/youtubes-channel-monetization-changes-wont-affect-much/.

67 See www.theverge.com/2016/6/3/11852146/music-industry-fighting-youtube-dmca.

68 'Music Industry Welcomes EC Copyright Proposal as a Good First Step', Music Ally (14 September 2016), available at http://musically.com/2016/09/14/music-industry-welcomes-ec-copyright-proposal-as-a-good-first-step/.

69 C. Muller, 'YouTube: No Other Platform Gives as Much Money Back to Creators', *The Guardian*, 28 April 2016, available at www.theguardian.com/music/musicblog/2016/apr/28/youtube-no-other-platform-gives-as-much-money-back-to-creators.

Users, on the other hand, complain that Content ID often blocks legitimate content. Problems include applicants that falsely claim copyright ownership.[70] In one notorious example, the creator of a 10-hour 'white noise' recording was the subject of five Content ID claims, all seeking to monetize his work.[71] Content ID is also not capable of distinguishing infringement from fair use.[72] Because a right holder's use of Content ID to block or monetize a user's posting does not constitute a DMCA takedown notice, the user cannot simply respond with a DMCA counter-notice.

YouTube is beta testing a new monitoring service called Copyright Match, which allows content owners to deliver reference files that YouTube will use to scan user uploads and identify matching content. Unlike Content ID, it does not offer the option to monetize or track analytics, and it can only recognize content that is identical to the reference files, rather than identifying uploaded content that contains portions of the reference files.[73] Furthermore, Copyright Match will not automatically block infringing content; the right holder must request it by sending a takedown notice. If a user asks YouTube to remove the content, but the channel files a counter-notice, YouTube will restore the content.[74]

European Union

Under the Directive on the Harmonization of Certain Aspects of Copyright and Related Rights in the Information Society (the 'Copyright Harmonization Directive'),[75] the streaming of music and audiovisual content in the EU implicates the non-exhaustible rights of 'communication' and 'making available' to the public. These rights belong to writers, performers, phonogram producers, film producers and broadcasters with respect to fixations of their works.

[70] Cory Doctorow, 'Like YouTube's Content ID System – for the Entire Internet', Motherboard (14 June 2018), available at https://motherboard.vice.com/en_us/article/mbk47b/europe-copyright-rules-content-id.

[71] See https://torrentfreak.com/musicians-white-noise-youtube-video-hit-with-copyright-complaints-180105/.

[72] Toni Lester and Dessislava Pachamanova, 'The Dilemma of False Positives: Making Content ID Algorithms More Conducive to Fostering Innovative Fair Use in Music Creation', 24 *UCLA Entertainment L. Rev.* 51, 64 (2017).

[73] See www.tubefilter.com/2018/05/01/youtube-content-match-copyright-tool-test/.

[74] See www.plagiarismtoday.com/2018/05/02/youtube-beta-testing-content-id-for-everyone/.

[75] Directive 2001/29/EC.

Cross-Border Licensing Issues

Despite the high degree of copyright and neighbouring rights harmonization within the EU, the streaming of music, sound recordings, and audiovisual works remains subject to territorial licensing, creating a serious obstacle to the full realization of the Digital Single Market.

Cross-border licensing for the streaming of audiovisual works remains an aspiration, while geo-blocking remains a reality. It is still common for audiovisual copyright owners to license their content on a country-by-country basis, and these contracts remain enforceable. Copyright owners – particularly in the case of audiovisual works – use these territorial restrictions to establish pricing for different markets and often to secure financing.[76] As long as these territorial restrictions continue, the concept of completely EU-wide video-on-demand cannot be realized. The European Commission has recommended addressing this through a stakeholders' dialogue and negotiation.[77] Even if this is successful with respect to EU right holders, it will not address contractual restrictions imposed by right holders in other countries; because copyright owners of US films and television programmes are unlikely to agree to EU-wide licensing,[78] cross-border streaming of these works would have to be addressed by EU-wide legislation.

According to Recital 29 of the Copyright Directive, the principle of exhaustion does not apply to services. Thus, territorial limitations on broadcast rights are enforceable. This has been confirmed in a series of cases upholding territorial restrictions on transmission of copyrighted content.[79] In particular, the CJEU upheld territorial restrictions on sports broadcast rights in *Football Ass'n Premier League Ltd and Others* v. *QC Leisure and Others*.[80] No cases have yet arisen with regard to streaming.[81]

[76] See Tambiama Madiega, European Parliamentary Research Service, *EU Copyright Reform: Revising the Principle of Territoriality* 4, 6–7 (September 2015).

[77] Impact Assessment, Proposal for a Regulation of the European Parliament and of the Council Laying Down Rules on the Exercise of Copyright and Related Rights Applicable to Certain Online Transmissions of Broadcasting Organisations and Retransmissions of Television and Radio Programmes; COM(2016)594, 2016/0284 (COD) (14 September 2016).

[78] See John Hopewell, 'E.U. Agrees to Cross-Border Access to Streaming Services', *Variety* (7 February 2017).

[79] Tambiama Madiega, *supra* n. 76, at 6 (collecting cases).

[80] (C-403/08 and C-429/08) (4 October 2011).

[81] The CJEU decision in UsedSoft GmbH *v.* Oracle Int'l Co. C-128/11 (3 July 2012), applied the exhaustion principle to allow, under certain conditions, the resale of software licences.

Nonetheless, there have been several small steps in the direction of a Digital Single Market for streaming services.

New rules permit the cross-border portability of digital subscriptions to services such as video on demand (e.g. Netflix and Spotify).[82] The rules enable users to access their subscription services throughout the EU rather than only in the member state where they live. However, a person living in one member state cannot subscribe to a service located in a different state. Thus, the availability of content on a particular platform will still be limited by territorial restrictions enforceable by geo-blocking.

In April 2019, the European Parliament and the Council of Europe adopted EU Directive 2019/789, to facilitate cross-border streaming of television and radio broadcasts. Modelled on the Cable and Satellite Directive, the new Directive extends the compulsory collective management rules for cable retransmission to equivalent digital retransmissions. Although the European Commission in 2016 had originally proposed adopting the 'country of origin' principle for rights clearance for all such transmissions,[83] the European Parliament voted to limit the country of origin rule to radio broadcasts, news, current affairs programming and programmes fully financed by the broadcaster. In addition, sports broadcasts are expressly excluded. Member states must implement the new Directive by 7 June 2021.

Music streaming in the EU remained subject to country-by-country licensing until the adoption of the 2014 Directive on Collective Management of Copyright and Related Rights and Multi-Territorial Licensing of Rights in Musical Works for Online Use in the Internal Market ('CMO Directive'),[84] which member states were required to implement by April 2016. The Directive facilitates the downloading and streaming of music and audiovisual works by making it easier for ISPs to obtain multi-territorial licences from collective management organizations (CMOs).

However, the Court relied on the original licence's resemblance to a sale, which would distinguish it from a territorially-restricted licence to stream content.

82 Regulation on the Cross-Border Portability of Online Content Services in the Internal Market, Regulation (EU) 2017/1128 (14 June 2017).

83 Proposal for a Regulation of the European Parliament and of the Council Laying Down Rules on the Exercise of Copyright and Related Rights Applicable to Certain Online Transmissions of Broadcasting Organisations and Retransmissions of Television and Radio Programmes, COM(2016)594, 2016/0284 (COD) (14 September 2016).

84 Directive 2014/26/EU.

In contrast to the US, with its handful of collecting societies, the EU has hundreds of CMOs engaged in licensing on behalf of authors and neighbouring right holders with respect to music, sound recordings and audiovisual works. Each country has its own CMOs, although a single CMO can represent several kinds of right holders.[85] The importance of CMOs has increased because streaming services need large numbers of licences from multiple right holders. In addition, in order to serve consumers throughout the EU, ISPs need multi-territorial rather than single-country licences.

Under the Directive, a qualified CMO is no longer restricted to single-country licensing; instead, it may engage in multi-territorial licensing, in some cases throughout the entire EU. The Directive also establishes rules to improve the transparency, governance and fiscal responsibility of CMOs. To qualify for multi-territorial licensing, a CMO must be able to handle large amounts of data, maintain an accurate database of works and right holders, and collect and disburse royalty payments accurately and efficiently. A qualifying CMO will be permitted to represent right holders from any member state, and to license their works throughout the EU. Because right holders will be able to choose their CMOs without regard to nationality, this should increase the competitiveness of CMOs. CMOs that do not qualify for multi-territorial licensing can continue to operate on a territorial basis, and its members can choose to remain with that CMO for domestic activities while transferring their multi-territorial rights to a different CMO. Alternatively, non-qualifying CMOs may make arrangements with multi-territorial CMOs to represent their members outside of the domestic territory.

As is true in the US, European songwriters and neighbouring right holders often fail to receive their streaming royalties because, despite multiple efforts, there is no comprehensive publicly available database linking authors and right holders to their recordings.[86] The new

[85] For example, PPL in the UK represents sound recording performers and producers, and PRS for Music represents songwriters and music publishers.

[86] Larry LeBlanc, 'SOCAN Co-Founds International Music Venture', *Billboard*, Vol. 113, Iss. 11 (17 March 2001); Tim Ingham, 'Global Repertoire Database on Course for 2014', *Music Week* (3 August 2012), available at https://search-proquest-com.ezproxy.library.unlv.edu/docview/1838679937/A718D91999684023PQ/6?accountid=3611; Lars Brandle, 'Collections Societies Pull the Plug on IMJV Project', *Billboard*, Vol. 114, Iss. 2 (26 January 2002).

Anonymous, 'Why Have Societies Pulled Funding?', *Music Week* (4 July 2014), available at https://search-proquest-com.ezproxy.library.unlv.edu/docview/1840890009/

federally-mandated database in the United States should spur collaboration with European entities.

Liability of Hosting Intermediaries

The EU is at a crossroads with respect to ISPs that host user-provided content. Numerous commentators have pointed to the 'value gap' – a reference to the failure of advertising-supported hosting services to provide fair compensation to right holders.

As discussed below, the copyright liability of hosting services is addressed in several existing Directives, and is one of the most controversial subjects addressed in the proposed Directive on Copyright in the Digital Single Market ('DSM Directive'). It has also drawn increasing judicial scrutiny.

Directives

The rules governing user-posted content are currently based on the Copyright Harmonization Directive[87] and the 2000 Directive on Certain Legal Aspects of Information Society Services (the 'E-Commerce Directive').[88] The proposed DSM Directive has encountered significant headwinds, with much of the controversy focused on the provisions addressing ISP liability.

Existing Directives Article 3 of the Copyright Harmonization Directive recognizes the exclusive and non-exhaustible 'communication' and 'making available' rights of authors, performers, phonogram producers, film producers and broadcasters. However, Recital 27 states '[t]he mere provision of physical facilities for enabling or making a communication does not in itself amount to communication within the meaning of this Directive'.

Articles 12–15 of the E-Commerce Directive address the liability of ISPs for information stored or transmitted through their platforms. Under Article 12, a 'mere conduit' that transmits user-provided information in a communications network (including any transient storage)

8DCA7F0115D84F64PQ/5?accountid=3611; Targeted News Service, *ASCAP, SACEM, and PRS for Music Initiate Joint Blockchain Project to Improve Data Accuracy for Rightsholders* (7 April 2017).

[87] Directive 2001/29/EC.

[88] Directive 2000/31/EC.

or provides access to such a network is not liable for the information transmitted if the ISP does not initiate the transmission, select the receiver, or select or modify the information transmitted. Article 13 provides a similar exemption for an ISP that temporarily caches information to facilitate transmission, if the ISP meets specified conditions. Under Article 14, the 'hosting' exemption, an ISP is not liable for storing information at the request of a user if (1) the ISP does not have actual knowledge of illegal activity or information and, if damages are requested, is not aware of facts or circumstances from which the illegal activity is apparent, or (2) upon obtaining such knowledge or awareness, the ISP acts expeditiously to remove or disable access to the information. Under all three of these Articles, however, a court or administrative agency may require an ISP to terminate or prevent an infringement.

With respect to any of the services described in Articles 12–14, Article 15 prohibits member states from imposing on ISPs a general obligation to monitor the information they transmit or store.

Recital 42 of the Directive limits the scope of these exemptions to cases where the ISP is engaged only in 'the technical process of operating and giving access to a communication network' for transmitting or caching user-provided information, stating that 'this activity is of a mere technical, automatic and passive nature, which implies that the information society service provider has neither knowledge of nor control over the information which is transmitted or stored'.

Unlike the DMCA, the E-Commerce Directive does not focus specifically on copyrighted works, encompassing other types of information as well.[89] A 2017 report commissioned by the European Parliament's Committee on the Internal Market and Consumer Protection (IMCO) raised the question whether there should be a separate set of rules for copyright infringements, arguing that these are often more easily assessed and detected than other violations, and that a number of member states had already implemented notice and action procedures for infringements.[90] The report also noted that search engines and 'participative platforms' do not fall clearly into any of the three exemptions, and were still in their infancy when the Directive was adopted in 2000.[91] It also questioned whether, in light of the 'practice and

[89] Thus, its coverage also overlaps with that of the Communications Decency Act in the US; 47 USC § 230.

[90] Directorate General for Internal Policies, *Providers Liability: From the eCommerce Directive to the Future*, IP/A/IMCO/2017-7 (October 2017), p. 18.

[91] *Id.*

social function of content intermediaries' today, passivity should continue to be a necessary condition for immunity.[92]

DSM Directive Since it was first proposed, the DSM Directive has generated tremendous controversy, leading to multiple revisions. One of the most hotly contested provisions has been Article 17, which addresses the copyright liability of online content sharing platforms.

As originally proposed by the European Commission (EC) in September 2016,[93] Article 13 (as it was then numbered) provided, in relevant part:

> Information society service providers that store and provide to the public access to large amounts of works or other subject-matter uploaded by their users shall, in cooperation with rightholders, take measures to ensure the functioning of agreements concluded with rightholders for the use of their works or other subject-matter or to prevent the availability on their services of works or other subject-matter identified by right-holders through the cooperation with the service providers. Those measures, such as the use of effective content recognition technologies, shall be appropriate and proportionate.[94]

Commentators raised strong objections to Article 13, arguing that it imposed a general monitoring obligation that was inconsistent with Articles 14 and 15 of the E-Commerce Directive, Articles 7, 8, 9, 10 and 14 of the Charter of Fundamental Rights of the European Union and CJEU case law.[95] The endorsement of 'effective content recognition technologies' raised concerns that the Directive would have an anti-competitive effect. Only the larger platforms would be capable of creating and implementing effective filtering technologies – YouTube's Content ID, for example.[96] Critics argued that the filtering obligation

[92] *Id.* at 19.

[93] Proposal for a Directive on Copyright in the Digital Single Market (14 September 2016), COM(2016)593, 2016/0280(COD), chapter 2, Article 13(1).

[94] *Id.*, Article 13(1).

[95] See, e.g., Sophie Stalla-Bourdillon et al., 'Open Letter to the European Commission – On the Importance of Preserving the Consistency and Integrity of the EU Acquis Relating to Content Monitoring within the Information Society', 30 September 2016, available at https://ssrn.com/abstract=2850483.

[96] Apple has created iTunes Match. Another technology is Audible Magic. Maria Schneider, 'Content ID is Still Piracy in Disguise', available at https://musictechpolicy.com/2016/07/31/guest-post-by-schneidermaria-content-id-is-still-just-piracy-in-disguise-an-open-letter-to-rightsholders-and-a-music-industry-ready-to-renegotiate-with-a-monster/.

would be unduly burdensome and costly for smaller providers, rendering them unable to compete.[97]

In May 2018, the Council of the European Union released its own version of the Directive, explicitly stating in Article 13 that content sharing services perform either an 'act of communication' or an act of 'making available' to the public when they give the public access to user-uploaded materials, and that, with respect to copyright infringement, they are not eligible for the Article 14 hosting exemption in the E-Commerce Directive.[98] In order to avoid infringement liability, the hosting service would be required *either* to 'prevent the availability' of unauthorized content, or satisfy *both* of the following conditions:

(1) make 'best efforts' to implement 'effective and proportionate measures' to prevent the availability of the specific materials sufficiently identified by right holders, *and*
(2) upon receiving notice from a right holder, expeditiously remove or disable access to the infringing materials and make best efforts to prevent their future availability through 'effective and proportionate measures'.[99]

After the European Parliament adopted a different variation, the draft Directive entered the trilogue process, leading to approval of a final text in February 2019. In a deeply divided vote, the European Parliament approved the Directive on 26 March 2019,[100] and the Council of Europe added its endorsement on 15 April.[101] The member states have two years to implement its provisions in their domestic laws.[102]

A threshold question is which ISPs are subject to the Directive. Article 2(6) defines an 'online content-sharing service provider' as 'a provider of an information society service of which the main or one of the main

[97] See Pamela Samuelson, 'The EU's Controversial Digital Single Market Directive – Part I: Why the Proposed Internet Content Filtering Mandate Was So Controversial', Kluwer Copyright Blog (10 July 2018).

[98] EU Council Proposed DSM Directive (25 May 2018), Title IV, chapter 2, Article 13 (1), (3).

[99] *Id.* Article 13(4).

[100] See Simon Casinader and Daniel R. Cartmell, 'Final Approval Given to EU Copyright Directive', *National Law Review* (27 March 2019), available at www.natlawreview.com/article/final-approval-given-to-eu-copyright-directive [http://perma.cc/4DAC-USEY] (noting that the vote was 348:274, with 36 abstentions).

[101] Press Release, European Council, *EU Adjusts Copyright Rules to the Digital Age* (15 April 2019).

[102] Casinader and Cartmell, *supra* n. 100.

purposes is to store and give the public access to a large amount of copyright-protected works or other protected subject matter uploaded by its users, which it organizes and promotes for profit-making purposes'.[103] According to the Recitals, whether a particular ISP deals with a 'large amount' of copyrighted works should be determined on a case-by-case basis, considering such factors as audience size and the number of files uploaded.[104] Recital 62 suggests how this should be interpreted:

> The definition of an online content-sharing service provider laid down in this Directive should target only online services that play an important role on the online market by competing with other online content services, such as online audio and video streaming services, for the same audiences.

Article 17 (formerly Article 13) now provides, in relevant part:

- An 'online content-sharing service provider performs an act of communication to the public or an act of making available to the public' when it gives the public access to copyrighted works uploaded by its users, and therefore must obtain authorization from the right holders.[105]
- An authorization obtained by the provider will also protect the user that uploaded the content, unless the user acted on a commercial basis or generated significant revenues.[106]
- With respect to copyrighted works, the provider's acts of communication or making available to the public are not eligible for the Article 14(1) hosting exemption.[107]
- The provider will be liable for unauthorized acts of communication or making available to the public unless it
  - made best efforts to obtain authorization, and
  - made best efforts to ensure unavailability of specific works for which the right holders provided the necessary information, and
  - acted expeditiously, upon receiving sufficient notice from the right holders, to remove the content or disable access to it, and made best efforts to prevent future uploads of that content.[108]

[103] The definition expressly excludes not-for-profit encyclopedias, not-for-profit educational and scientific repositories, online marketplaces, business-to-business cloud services and cloud services that allow users to upload content for their own use.
[104] Recital 63.
[105] Article 17(1).
[106] Article 17(2).
[107] Article 17(3).
[108] Article 17(4).

- These requirements must not prevent availability of content that is non-infringing, including content covered by exceptions or limitations such as quotation, criticism, review, caricature, parody or pastiche.[109]

The liability rules under Article 17 are significantly relaxed for a provider whose services have been available in the EU for less than three years with an annual turnover below EUR 10 million; such a provider is exempt from the requirements of ensuring unavailability and preventing future uploads.[110]

For other providers, the requirement to make 'best efforts' to obtain authorization apparently applies to *every* uploaded work, unless a copyright exception or limitation applies. This alone is a tremendous undertaking. Either the provider must request authorization for *all* uploaded content, or it must perform a preliminary copyright analysis on each work in an effort to identify which ones are non-infringing, and then request authorization for all of the others. In addition, it must make best efforts to block future uploads of any content identified by right holders.

On the other hand, the revised Directive allows room for interpretation on the question of whether a provider has satisfied its authorization/monitoring obligations. Compliance with the 'best efforts' and expeditious removal/disablement requirements of Article 17(4) is assessed under the principle of proportionality, considering, inter alia, the type, audience and size of the service, the types of subject matter uploaded, and the 'availability of suitable and effective means and their cost for service providers'.[111] In addition, Recital 66 states that providers should make their 'best efforts in accordance with the high industry standards of professional diligence'.

Article 17(8) states that the provisions of Article 17 'shall not lead to any general monitoring obligation'. This admonition is hard to reconcile with Article 17(4), which arguably imposes just such an obligation; it is hard to see how a provider can make 'best efforts' to obtain authorization for uploaded content, or to prevent future uploads, unless it monitors all its users' uploads. Even if Article 17(8) can be interpreted to impose only a 'best efforts' obligation to monitor user uploads, it is still a general monitoring obligation. However, Article 17(10) states that the

[109] Article 17(7).

[110] Article 17(6). Once it averages 5 million monthly visitors, however, such a provider must also 'make best efforts to prevent further uploads' of works identified by rights holders. *Id.*

[111] Article 17(5).

Commission will issue 'guidance on the application of' Article 17(4), after the Directive enters into force, and after holding further stakeholder dialogues to address 'best practices', noting that such practices must take 'special account' of 'the need to balance fundamental rights and . . . the use of exceptions and limitations'.

Some content sharing services will not even qualify for the limited protection of Article 17. According to Recital 62, it does not apply at all to 'service providers the main purpose of which is to engage in or to facilitate copyright piracy'.

Case Law

Until the new Directive is fully implemented, the contours of potential infringement liability of content sharing services will continue to be shaped by judicial interpretations of the existing laws governing the rights of copyright owners, users and Internet intermediaries. Both the Court of Justice of the European Union (CJEU) and courts in the individual member states have been active in attempting to reconcile the rights of copyright owners with the protections of the E-Commerce Directive. Even after implementation, the enforceability of the new Directive may be tested at the CJEU.

Decisions of the CJEU have strongly enforced the provisions of Articles 14 and 15 of the E-Commerce Directive, which protect content sharing services that qualify as hosting providers. However, the Court has also indicated that, in appropriate circumstances, it may find that their activities cross the line from hosting to direct infringement, in which case they are not eligible for these protections.

The CJEU has twice ruled that mandatory filtering violates EU law. In the *Scarlet/SABAM* ruling,[112] the Court held that an ISP could not be required to use filtering and blocking technology to prevent its users from downloading infringing content through peer-to-peer networks, because this would violate Article 15(1) of the E-Commerce Directive, infringe the freedom of the ISP to conduct its business and violate Article 3(1) of Directive 2004/48, which requires that measures for protecting intellectual property should not be unnecessarily complicated or costly. It would also violate the rights of users to protect their personal data and their freedom to receive or impart information, in violation of Articles 8 (right of privacy) and 11 (freedom of assembly and association) of the

[112] Judgment of the Court (Third Chamber) of 24 November 2011, Scarlet Extended SA *v.* Societe belge des auteurs, compositeurs et editeurs SCRL (SABAM), Case C-70/10.

Charter of Fundamental Rights of the European Union. Because the filtering technology might not adequately distinguish lawful from unlawful content, it could block lawful communications. Accordingly, requiring the ISP to install a filtering system would fail to strike a fair balance between intellectual property rights and the freedom to conduct business, the right to protect personal data, and the freedom to receive or impart information.[113]

A few months later, in the *SABAM/Netlog* ruling,[114] the CJEU applied this same rule to the social networking site Netlog, holding that a social network cannot be required to install a general filtering system, covering all its users, to prevent the unlawful use of copyrighted materials. It was undisputed that Netlog was a 'hosting service provider' entitled to the hosting exemption under Articles 14 and 15(1) of the E-Commerce Directive.[115] The filtering system proposed by SABAM would have required Netlog to (1) identify which of the files stored by its users are likely to contain materials claimed by the right holders, (2) determine which of those files are being stored or made available unlawfully, and (3) prevent the unlawful files from being made available.[116] This would impose a general monitoring obligation in violation of the hosting exemption.[117] It would also fail to strike a fair balance between the rights of intellectual property owners and Netlog's freedom to conduct business under Article 16 of the Charter,[118] and would infringe the users' rights under Articles 8 and 11 of the Charter.[119] It would also undermine the freedom of information by potentially blocking lawful communications.[120]

These rulings could make it difficult for member states to enforce a general monitoring obligation on content sharing platforms. The DSM Directive makes many of these services ineligible for the hosting exemption. However, because the *Sabam/Netlog* decision also relies heavily on the Charter, it will be more difficult to implement the DSM Directive so

[113] Scarlet/SABAM at [53].
[114] Judgment of the Court (Third Chamber), Belgische Vereniging van Auteurs, Componisten en Uitgevers CVBA (SABAM) *v.* Netlog NV, Case C-360/10 (16 February 2012).
[115] *Id.* at [27]–[34].
[116] *Id.* at [36].
[117] *Id.* at [38].
[118] *Id.* at [44]–[47].
[119] *Id.* at [48].
[120] *Id.* at [50].

as to narrow Articles 14 and 15(1) of the E-Commerce Directive in a way that conflicts with the Charter. Although the DSM Directive does not explicitly require filtering, it imposes obligations that may, as a practical matter, require service providers to adopt filtering mechanisms.

Nonetheless, the CJEU may be open to this remedy for certain hosting services that, like YouTube, engage in activities that take them beyond the role of passive service providers. In recent years, the court has widened the scope of liability for direct infringement by broadly interpreting the concept of a 'communication to the public' under Article 3 of the Copyright Harmonization Directive. In the *GS Media* case,[121] the Court held that hyperlinking to a website containing material placed there without the consent of the copyright owner could constitute a communication to the public if the party supplying the hyperlink knew, or should have known, that the content was unauthorized.[122] If the purpose of the hyperlink was commercial, this knowledge could be presumed, subject to rebuttal.[123] And in its *Filmspeler* decision,[124] the CJEU applied this concept to the distribution of a tangible good. The defendant in that case had, with a profit-making motive, sold a multimedia player on which he had knowingly installed add-ons that included hyperlinks to websites that provided infringing content.[125]

In 2017, the CJEU for the first time held an Internet intermediary liable for direct copyright infringement. In *Stichting Brein* v. *Ziggo BV and XS4All Internet BV*,[126] the intermediary was The Pirate Bay (TPB), a notorious peer-to-peer file sharing site. Even though the infringing content did not reside on TPB's website, TPB's activities with respect to that content were a 'communication to the public' within the meaning of Article 3(1) of the Copyright Harmonization Directive because an act of 'communication' occurs when a party plays an 'indispensable role' through 'deliberate intervention'. This requirement is satisfied where the party intervenes, 'in full knowledge of the consequences of his action', to provide other parties with access to a protected work. In this case, even though the infringing content was placed on the online sharing platform

[121] GS Media BV *v.* Sanoma Media Netherlands BV and Others, C-160/15 (8 Sept. 2016).
[122] *Id.* at [49].
[123] *Id.* at [51].
[124] Stichting Brein *v.* Jack Frederik Wullems, C-527/15 (26 April 2017).
[125] *Id.* at [51]–[53].
[126] C-610/15 (14 June 2017).

by TPB's users, by managing the platform TPB had intervened to provide access to that content in full knowledge of the consequences. Without this intervention, it would have been difficult or impossible for the users to access the materials; in addition, TPB indexed and classified the materials in different categories, periodically checked to make sure that materials were in the correct categories, deleted obsolete or faulty torrent files and actively filtered some content. This distinguished TPB's activities from a 'mere provision' of physical facilities for communication, within the meaning of Recital 27.

The communication was also 'to the public' – meaning a 'new' public beyond the initial public to whom the copyright owner had authorized communication.[127] In apparent support of this conclusion, the CJEU observed that TPB's operators (1) knew that their platform provided access to unauthorized copies of works, and (2) intended to make copyrighted works available to their users and to encourage their users to copy those works, for (3) a profit-making purpose.[128] To support this analysis, the CJEU relied on its holdings in *GS Media* and *Filmspeler*.[129] Applying this rule to TPB, the CJEU found that TPB knew that its platform was being used to infringe.[130] Because TPB was a direct infringer, it was appropriate to order Ziggo to block its users' access to this platform.

Thus, in *Ziggo* the CJEU introduced elements of knowledge, intent and profit motive into its analysis of whether a communication is 'to the public'. Because these have not previously been considered elements of direct copyright infringement, it is not clear why the CJEU imposed them here. The Court may have been trying to create a new liability standard specifically for Internet intermediaries. This seems to follow from its conclusion that the concept of a 'communication to the public' includes 'the making available and management, on the internet, of a sharing platform which, by means of indexation of metadata referring to protected works and the provision of a search engine, allows users of that platform to locate those works and to share them in the context of a peer-to-peer network'. By defining these services as an act of direct infringement, the Court removed service providers that meet this description from the 'hosting' category, and

[127] *Id.* at [44].
[128] *Id.* at [45]–[46].
[129] *Id.* at [32]–[33].
[130] *Id.* at [45].

thus eliminated their Article 14 hosting defence and their Article 15(1) protection from a general obligation to monitor.

A similar judicial development took place in June of 2018, although not at the CJEU level. Television station Puls 4 won a preliminary ruling from the Commercial Court in Vienna, Austria, holding YouTube liable for hosting infringing videos. The Court rejected YouTube's hosting defence under Article 14 of the E-Commerce Directive, concluding that YouTube was not a neutral hosting provider because it took an active role in 'sorting, filtering and linking' content and 'in particular by creating tables of contents according to predefined categories'.[131] The preliminary ruling could change before it becomes final, however, and if it does not, YouTube is likely to appeal. After *Ziggo*, the CJEU may be ready to treat YouTube as a direct infringer and as therefore ineligible for the hosting defence.

Conclusion

In both the US and the EU, licensed and unlicensed streaming present complex challenges for copyright and neighbouring rights regimes that were designed to address much older technologies. With respect to licensed streaming, the number of licences needed is greater, and using them effectively requires tracking the utilization of each work as well as connecting each work to all the right holders entitled to compensation. Due to their greater bargaining power, larger right holders can typically negotiate favourable licences, leaving independent artists on their own to protect their rights. Within the EU, consumer demand for borderless streaming has highlighted the need for multi-territorial licensing.

With respect to unlicensed streaming of user-provided content, however, the law in these jurisdictions is trending in opposite directions. In the US, courts interpreting the DMCA have set an increasingly high standard for the level of knowledge necessary to defeat the safe harbour, making it difficult to hold intermediaries liable. In the EU, the E-Commerce Directive's hosting exemption has functioned much like the DMCA safe harbours, but with the adoption of the new DSM Directive EU law has evolved toward imposing an affirmative obligation on ISPs to monitor and filter their content. A similar trend is seen in the European courts, which are scrutinizing the activities of hosting services more

[131] Scott Roxborough, 'YouTube Liable for Copyright Infringement, Austrian Court Finds in Preliminary Ruling', *Hollywood Reporter*, 6 June 2018, available at www.hollywoodreporter.com/news/youtube-liable-copyright-infringement-austrian-court-finds-1117828.

closely. It is not clear, however, whether or under what circumstances the imposition of a general monitoring obligation will be upheld by the CJEU. If ISPs are required to monitor and filter their content, this is likely to favour the larger ISPs that can afford to create and invest in this technology, while creating a barrier to entry for newer services.

Bibliography

Anonymous, 'Why Have Societies Pulled Funding?', *Music Week*, 4 July 2014, available at https://search-proquest-com.ezproxy.library.unlv.edu/docview/1840890009/8DCA7F0115D84F64PQ/5?accountid=3611.

Brandle, Lars, 'Collections Societies Pull the Plug on IMJV Project' (2002), *Billboard* 114: 2.

Casinader, Simon and Cartmell, Daniel R., 'Final Approval Given to EU Copyright Directive' (2019), *National Law Review*, available at www.natlawreview.com/article/final-approval-given-to-eu-copyright-directive [http://perma.cc/4DAC-USEY].

Cihak, Lennon, 'YouTube's Head of Music: 'We're Not Discussing the Value Gap', *Digital Music News*, 28 June 2018, available at www.digitalmusicnews.com/2018/06/28/youtube-lyor-cohen-value-gap/.

Denicola, Robert C., 'Volition and Copyright Infringement' (2016), 37 *Cardozo Law Review* 37: 1259.

Doctorow, Cory, 'Like YouTube's Content ID System – for the Entire Internet', *Motherboard*, 14 June 2018, available at https://motherboard.vice.com/en_us/article/mbk47b/europe-copyright-rules-content-id.

Dunitz, Jody, 'The Easiest Way to Fix the Mechanical Royalty is to Get Rid of It', *Digital Music News*, 25 September 2017, available at www.digitalmusicnews.com/2017/09/25/fix-streaming-mechanical/.

Future of Music Coalition, 'How to Get Your Music into Content ID', available at https://futureofmusic.org/blog/2016/05/17/how-get-your-music-content-id.

Gagliano, Steven J., 'Consent Decrees in the Streaming Era: Digital Withdrawal, Fractional Licensing, and § 114(i)' (2017), *Business, Entrepreneurship & The Law* 10: 317.

Hopewell, John, 'E.U. Agrees to Cross-Border Access to Streaming Services', *Variety*, 7 February 2017.

IFPI, Music Consumer Insight Report, 9 October 2018, 13.

Ingham, Tim, 'Global Repertoire Database on Course for 2014', *Music Week*, 3 August 2012, available at https://search-proquest-com.ezproxy.library.unlv.edu/docview/1838679937/A718D91999684023PQ/6?accountid=3611.

LaFrance, Mary, 'Music Modernization and the Labyrinth of Streaming' (2018), 2 *Business Entrepreneurship & Tax Law Review* 2: 310.

LaFrance, Mary, 'An Ocean Apart: Transatlantic Approaches to Copyright Infringement by Internet Intermediaries' (2019), 2 *AIPLA Quarterly Journal* 47: 2.

LeBlanc, Larry, 'SOCAN Co-Founds International Music Venture' (2001), *Billboard* 113: 11.

Lester, Toni and Pachamanova, Dessislava, 'The Dilemma of False Positives: Making Content ID Algorithms More Conducive to Fostering Innovative Fair Use in Music Creation' (2017), 24 *UCLA Entertainment Law Review* 24: 51.

Levine, Robert, 'Spotify Settles Class Action Lawsuits Filed by David Lowery and Melissa Ferrick with $43.4 Million Fund', 26 May 2017, available at www.billboard.com/articles/business/7809561/spotify-settles-class-action-lawsuits-filed-by-david-lowery-and-melissa.

Madiega, Tambiama, 'European Parliamentary Research Service, EU Copyright Reform: Revising the Principle of Territoriality' 4 (September 2015).

Milosic, Klementina, 'The Failure of the Global Repertoire Database', available at www.hypebot.com/hypebot/2015/08/the-failure-of-the-global-repertoire-database-effort-draft.html.

Muller, C., 'YouTube: No Other Platform Gives as Much Money Back to Creators', *The Guardian*, 28 April 2016, available at www.theguardian.com/music/musicblog/2016/apr/28/youtube-no-other-platform-gives-as-much-money-back-to-creators.

Music Ally, 'Music Industry Welcomes EC Copyright Proposal as a Good First Step', *Music Ally*, 14 September 2016, available at http://musically.com/2016/09/14/music-industry-welcomes-ec-copyright-proposal-as-a-good-first-step/.

Raine, Michael, 'YouTube: Friend or Foe of the Music Industry?', *Canadian Musician*, 9 May 2017, available at http://canadianmusician.com/features/archives/214#sthash.WTWPCRpA.dpbs.

RIAA, Mid-Year 2018 RIAA Music Revenues Report, 2018.

Roxborough, Scott, 'YouTube Liable for Copyright Infringement, Austrian Court Finds in Preliminary Ruling', *Hollywood Reporter*, 6 June 2018, available at www.hollywoodreporter.com/news/youtube-liable-copyright-infringement-austrian-court-finds-1117828.

Salamone, Nicholas, 'YouTube for Musicians: How is All the $$ Made?', *DIY Musician*, 12 June 2017, available at https://diymusician.cdbaby.com/youtube/youtube-musicians-made/.

Samuelson, Pamela, 'The EU's Controversial Digital Single Market Directive – Part I: Why the Proposed Internet Content Filtering Mandate Was So Controversial', Kluwer Copyright Blog, 10 July 2018.

Sanchez, Daniel, 'Exclusive Report: Spotify Artist Payments are Declining in 2017, Data Shows', *Digital Music News*, 16 May 2017, available at www.digitalmusicnews.com/2017/05/16/spotify-audiam-low-rates/.

Schneider, Maria, 'Content ID is Still Piracy in Disguise', 31 July 2016, available at www.musicanswers.org/content-id/.

Stalla-Bourdillon, Sophie et al., 'Open Letter to the European Commission – On the Importance of Preserving the Consistency and Integrity of the EU Acquis Relating to Content Monitoring within the Information Society', 30 September 2016, available at https://ssrn.com/abstract=2850483.

The Trichordist, '2018 Streaming Price Bible! Per Stream Rates Drop as Streaming Volume Grows. YouTube's Value Gap is Very Real', 29 January 2019, available at https://thetrichordist.com/2019/01/29/2018-streaming-price-bible-per-stream-rates-drop-as-streaming-volume-grows-youtubes-value-gap-is-very-real/.

United States Copyright Office, *Copyright and the Music Marketplace*, Washington, DC: United States Copyright Office, February 2015.

United States Copyright Office, *The Making Available Right in the United States*, Washington, DC: United States Copyright Office, February 2016.

'US Music Streaming Royalties Explained', n.d., available at www.manatt.com/Manatt/media/Media/PDF/US-Streaming-Royalties-Explained.pdf.

Targeted News Service, 'ASCAP, SACEM, and PRS for Music Initiate Joint Blockchain Project to Improve Data Accuracy for Rightsholders', 7 April 2017.

20

Adapting Trade Rules for the Age of Big Data

MIRA BURRI

Abstract

The chapter looks at some of the disruptive changes brought about digital technologies that matter for trade and trade policy. It then analyzes the responses that trade policy has formulated to address these changes. The chapter focuses in particular on the Comprehensive and Progressive Agreement for Transpacific Partnership (CPTPP), as the most advanced model so far and one that has now found continuation in the United States–Mexico–Canada Agreement (USMCA). The chapter goes on to contextualize and assess the impact of the existing legal framework, as shaped almost predominantly by free trade agreements. The chapter ultimately asks whether there are better ways to address the challenges of the data-driven economy and what the essential elements of a working regulatory model may be.

Introduction

Laws need to adapt to societal changes, including those triggered by technological advances.[1] It is often said that the transformations brought about by digital technologies are particularly far-reaching and demand changes in all fields of law, including in the area of international economic law.[2] The chapter seeks to explore the validity of these demands by

[1] See, e.g., John Gerard Ruggie, 'International Responses to Technology: Concepts and Trends', *International Organization* 29 (1975), 557–583; Thomas Cottier, 'The Impact of New Technologies on Multilateral Trade Regulation and Governance', *Chicago-Kent Law Review* 72 (1996), 415–436; Roger Brownsword and Karen Yeung (eds), *Regulating Technologies: Legal Futures, Regulatory Frames and Technological Fixes*, Oxford: Hart, 2008; Daniel Gervais, 'The Regulation of Inchoate Technologies', *Houston Law Review* 47 (2010), 665–705.

[2] See, e.g., Kauffman Taskforce on Law, *Innovation and Growth, Rules for Growth: Promoting Innovation and Growth through Legal Reform*, Kansas City, MO: Kauffman

looking first at some of the discrete technological developments in the broader context of digitization. While such an analysis cannot be comprehensive, as the scope of changes is vast and the fluidity of the environment high, we seek to give at least a sense of the trajectory of digital transformations and a sense of the depth of disruptive changes that matter for trade law and policies. In order to understand what needs to be changed in existing foreign trade policy, we also need to know what we have in terms of existing regulatory frameworks – both at the international and at the regional and bilateral levels. It is the objective of the chapter's second part to attend to this need. Here, in particular, an understanding of the new templates for electronic commerce is essential and this chapter will convey this knowledge by focusing on the most advanced model so far – that of the Comprehensive and Progressive Agreement for Transpacific Partnership (CPTPP). The chapter goes on to contextualize and assess the impact of the existing legal framework, as shaped in recent times almost predominantly by preferential trade agreements. In its last part, the chapter ultimately asks whether there are better ways to address the challenges of the data-driven economy and what the essential elements of a working regulatory model should be. It suggests a return to the multilateral forum of the WTO and briefly sketches viable paths to do so.

Understanding Digitally Fuelled Transformations

Digitization is the ability to express all information (be it audio, text, still or moving images) as binary digits; it frees information from the tangible medium and makes it networkable and easy to manipulate.[3] Digitization has allowed computers to talk a common language and has led to the emergence of the Internet as a network of networks that share bits of data through a common protocol.[4] As of the 1980s, on top of these technological foundations, a range of new information processing and

Foundation, 2011; Mira Burri and Thomas Cottier, 'Digital Technologies and International Economic Regulation: An Introduction', in Mira Burri and Thomas Cottier (eds), *Trade Governance in the Digital Age*, Cambridge: Cambridge University Press, 2012, pp. 1–14.

[3] See, e.g., Terry Flew, *New Media: An Introduction*, 2nd ed., Oxford: Oxford University Press, 2014.

[4] For an excellent, not too technical, explanation of all the underlying technologies, see James Grimmelmann, *Internet Law*, Oregon City, OR: Semaphore Press, 2016, chapter 1.

transmission technologies developed rapidly.[5] The Internet was created as an end-to-end, generative platform that allows 'permissionless innovation'.[6] As a consequence, we have witnessed in the past decades 'an explosion of goods and services in the IT industry', an amazing amount of new applications, new forms of content creation and communication.[7] There are multiple sources of data gathered over different periods of time that show the different beneficial effects of the global digital platform – for instance, through an increase in consumer welfare, as consumers are now able to search, compare and buy products and services on a global scale from a much greater variety of offerings. Other positive accounts relate to the inclusiveness of the platform, as the Internet has allowed not only big companies but also small and medium-sized enterprises (SMEs), as well as developing countries, to engage in global trade, because of the lower thresholds for participation and the real economic gains to be reaped.[8] This chapter cannot capture all these experiences but seeks to elaborate on those aspects of the digital economy that matter for trade and trade policy, and contemplates how this innovation environment can be sustained and fostered. For this purpose, we highlight here three aspects of the digital evolution that have triggered different regulatory challenges. We look in turn at (i) the process of convergence; (ii) the emergence and application of great amounts of data; and (iii) the Internet of Things.

5 Metcalfe's Law states that the value of a network to society is proportional to the square of the number of users of the network. For a great analysis of all these changes, see Constantijn van Oranje-Nassau et al., *Responding to Convergence, Prepared for the Dutch Independent Telecommunications and Post Regulator*, Oxford: RAND Corporation, 2008, pp. 6–7.

6 This is a phrase attributed to Vint Cerf, the father of the Internet. See Henry Chesbrough and Marshall Van Alstyne, 'Permissionless Innovation', *Communications of the ACM* 58 (2015), 24–26.

7 Jonathan L. Zittrain, *The Future of the Internet – and How to Stop It*, New Haven: Yale University Press, 2008.

8 For more examples see, e.g., Joshua P. Meltzer, 'Maximizing the Opportunities of the Internet for International Trade', *E15 Expert Group on the Digital Economy – Policy Options Paper* (2016). Facebook estimates that 50 million SMEs are on its platform, up from 25 million in 2013. To put this number in perspective, consider that the World Bank estimated there were 125 million SMEs worldwide in 2010. For small businesses in the developing world, digital platforms are a way to overcome constraints in their local markets. See James Manyika et al., *Digital Globalization: The New Era of Global Flows*, Washington, DC: McKinsey Global Institute, 2016, p. 7. See also Part II of this volume.

Convergence

We begin with one of the early regulatory dilemmas that digitization brought about that has to do with the process of *convergence*. The technological advances that drove digitization, such as increased transmission speed and storage capacity, allowed, already in the early years of digitization somewhere in the 1990s, for a single or similar set of services (such as TV, phone and Internet access) to be offered over different platforms – over cable, satellite or telecommunication networks, as well as enabling the bundling of distinct services onto a single platform.[9] This naturally triggered the erosion of the previously distinct boundaries between the media, the telecommunications and the IT sectors, ultimately leading to a convergence of their products, services and companies. Companies like Google, Facebook or Yahoo! are good examples in this context that not only transcend the conventional sectoral boundaries but also clearly illustrate the power of the few.[10]

Convergence is problematic from a regulatory perspective because it makes the existing legal frameworks for telecom and media outdated, especially if they are based upon technology-based classifications. Convergence also poses serious questions about appropriate regulatory design that is capable of reconciling the very different regulatory rationales, histories, rules and actors that these previously distinct sectors had. For example, we do not have media regulation for the same reasons for which we have telecom rules.[11] At the same time, many new services – such as the so-called 'over-the-top' services – like Skype, YouTube or Netflix – do not fall under any of the existing regulatory categories, yet effectively serve the same consumer needs and compete in the same markets. The regulator has thus to make important decisions as to the regulatory burden to be imposed on new (and old) companies, on the degree of competition and the safeguarding of essential societal objectives, such as freedom of speech and access to high-quality information.[12]

[9] van Oranje-Nassau et al. (2008).

[10] See, e.g., Anupam Chander, 'Facebookistan', *North Carolina Law Review* 90 (2012), 1807–1842.

[11] Broadcasting often had a strong public service rationale, driven by concerns about free speech, diversity of supply, decency, protection of minors, etc. Telecommunications markets were mostly ruled by economic and technical issues, including network access. See van Oranje-Nassau et al. (2008).

[12] See, e.g., van Oranje-Nassau et al. (2008); also Mira Burri, *Public Service Broadcasting 3.0: Legal Design for the Digital Present*, Abingdon: Routledge, 2015; and Orly Lobel, 'The Law of the Platform', *Minnesota Law Review* 101 (2016), 87–166.

We have seen regulatory reforms unfold due to convergence effects – the European Union, for instance, has twice adopted such reform packages and is now in the process of undergoing a third reform as part of its Digital Single Market Strategy.[13] At the international level however, there have not been any deliberate regulatory responses and, as a result, there is a mismatch between the rules framework and the market reality.

Data and Big Data

In contrast to convergence, data and big data appear as relatively new buzzwords in the contemporary debates of digitally driven economic growth and innovation.[14] Enabled by a new generation of digital technologies and because of their deep embeddedness in all facets of societal life, companies increasingly capture vast amounts of information about their customers, suppliers and operations. Millions of networked sensors are now implanted in the physical world in devices, such as mobile phones and cars, extracting, creating and communicating data. Multimedia and individuals with smartphones and on social networking sites only fuel this exponential growth of data and ultimately lead to accumulation of 'big datasets'.[15] Data have become so essential to economic processes that they are said to be the 'new oil'.[16] Like other factors of production, such as natural resources and human capital, it is increasingly the case that much of modern economic activity, innovation and

[13] See generally European Commission, 'A Digital Single Market Strategy for Europe', COM (2015) 192 final, 6 May 2015.

[14] Although there were some debates on data flows in the 1980s. See, e.g. Christopher Kuner, 'Regulation of Transborder Data Flows under Data Protection and Privacy Law: Past, Present and Future', *OECD Digital Economy Paper* 187 (2011); Susan Aaronson, 'Why Trade Agreements Are Not Setting Information Free: The Lost History and Reinvigorated Debate over Cross-Border Data Flows, Human Rights and National Security', *World Trade Review* 14 (2015), 671–700; also William J. Drake, Background Paper for the workshop on Data Localization and Barriers to Transborder Data Flows, 14–15 September 2016, World Economic Forum, Geneva.

[15] James Manyika et al., *Big Data: The Next Frontier for Innovation, Competition, and Productivity*, Washington, DC: McKinsey Global Institute, 2011. There are no clear definitions of small versus big data. Definitions vary and scholars seem to agree that the term of big data is generalized and slightly imprecise. One common identification of big data is through its characteristics of volume, velocity and variety, also referred to as the '3-Vs'. Increasingly, experts add a fourth 'V' that relates to the veracity or reliability of the underlying data. See Viktor Mayer-Schönberger and Kenneth Cukier, *Big Data: A Revolution That Will Transform How We Live, Work, and Think*, New York: Eamon Dolan/Houghton Mifflin Harcourt, 2013, p. 13.

[16] *The Economist*, 'The World's Most Valuable Resource Is No Longer Oil, but Data', print edition, 6 May 2017.

growth cannot occur without data.[17] A plethora of studies and expert reports point at the vast potential of data as a trigger for more efficient business operations, highly innovative societal solutions, and ultimately better policy choices.[18] The transformative potential is great and refers not only to new 'digital native' areas, such as search or social networking, but also to 'brick-and-mortar' businesses. The data gathered, for instance in manufacturing, can help improve processes, anticipate risks and prevent accidents; public sector administration can also be better structured, made more efficient and more citizen-oriented.[19]

The implications of big data and big data analytics are multiple and some of them far-reaching.[20] At a micro-level, for instance, the value of data changes the traditional relationship between consumers and producers. While in the past companies sold products to their customers in return for money and some negligible data, '[t]oday, transactions – and indeed every interaction with a consumer – produce valuable information. Sometimes the data itself is so valuable that companies such as *Facebook*, *LinkedIn*, *Pinterest*, *Twitter*, and many others are willing to offer free services in order to obtain it. [. . .] To maintain an edge in consumer data, user acquisition and user interaction are both critical'.[21] Data become, also, absolutely essential in terms of competition and market power. Some firms, like Apple, Google, Amazon, Facebook, Microsoft, General Electric or Baidu, have had a sizeable first-mover advantage in the field and have become 'analytics leaders', while at the same time establishing themselves as some of the most valuable companies in the world.[22] These companies have differentiated themselves through unique data sources, analytics talent and investment in data infrastructure. The same trend can be seen among younger companies, 'the next wave of disruptors' – that tend to be firms with business models predicated on data analytics, such as Uber, Flipkart, Airbnb, Snapchat,

[17] Manyika et al. (2011).

[18] See, e.g. Manyika et al. (2011); Mayer-Schönberger and Cukier (2013); Nicolaus Henke et al., *The Age of Analytics: Competing in a Data-Driven World*, Washington, DC: McKinsey Global Institute, 2016.

[19] See, e.g., Manyika (2011).

[20] Mayer-Schönberger and Cukier (2013). For a brief introduction on Big Data applications and review of the literature, see Mira Burri, 'Understanding the Implications of Big Data and Big Data Analytics for Competition Law: An Attempt for a Primer', in Klaus Mathis and Avishalom Tor (eds), *New Developments in Competition Behavioural Law and Economics*, Berlin: Springer, 2019.

[21] Henke et al. (2016), at 26.

[22] Henke et al. (2016), at 26.

Pinterest or Spotify.[23] It should be noted that the capacity to handle data increasingly also turns into a competitive advantage for countries and plays as a power move in the global political economy. For instance, China unveiled in 2016 that it is in possession of the world's fastest supercomputer, which is 40 times more powerful than the fastest computer of 2010.[24] Overall, companies as well as governments are encouraged to use the potential of data and to mobilize their resources aptly, so as to make the data-driven economy real.[25]

In the context of trade and trade policies, the growing importance of data for the digital economy has one crucial implication: Data *must* flow across borders. Many of the economic innovations based on digital technologies do rely on global data flows. Things like the app economy, the outsourcing of many services, the provision of digital products and streaming services, many cloud computing applications or the Internet of Things, would not function under restrictions on the cross-border flow of data.[26]

The Internet of Things

Our last example of the applications of digitization, and very much also in the sense of illustrating the far-reaching effects of big data, is the Internet of Things. We use it in particular to underline that although typically when we talk about the digital revolution, we mean intangibles, this should not always be the case. Indeed, increasingly, the connected world includes physical objects. Machinery, shipments, infrastructure and devices are equipped with networked sensors that enable them to monitor their environment, report their status, receive instructions and even take action based on the information received. This is what we understand as 'the Internet of Things' and it can be used in many ways to improve productivity, and enable new types of products and services – in health care, infrastructure and in the public sector.[27]

[23] Henke et al. (2016), at 26.

[24] See www.top500.org/list/2016/06/. The competition is ongoing and the Chinese supercomputer has been overtaken by two US and one Japanese computers.

[25] See, e.g., Manyika et al. (2011); Henke et al. (2016); Jacques Bughin et al., *Digital Europe: Pushing the Frontier, Capturing the Benefits*, Washington, DC: McKinsey Global Institute, 2016.

[26] See Anupam Chander, 'National Data Governance in a Global Economy', *UC Davis Legal Studies Research Paper* 495 (2016), at 2.

[27] Henke et al. (2016), 51–60.

The Internet of Things is one of the disruptive technologies that is also said to hold vast future potential. More than 9 billion devices around the world are currently connected to the Internet, including computers and smartphones, but this number is expected to increase dramatically within the next decade, with estimates ranging from 50 billion devices to one trillion. The potential for economic impact is equally astounding and ranges from USD 2.7 trillion to USD 6.2 trillion annually by 2025.[28] For this chapter's discussion, the importance of the Internet of Things for future digital innovation reminds us that we cannot simply concentrate on services regulation when we conceive of a regulatory framework for digital trade, but must include adequate rules for trade in goods as well.[29]

Interim Conclusion

Global digital trade is hard to stop at the border. It appears to be an essential element of many of the applications of the new digital economy that data must cross borders – often in a manner that is unrelated to a distinct service or business transaction, often crossing multiple times and residing in multiple jurisdictions. At the same time, digital content and applications have profound effects on individuals in a certain country as well as on its society as a whole. They may induce certain behavioural patterns, affect the conditions for diversity, social cohesion and democratic practice; they may influence consumer protection, financial stability and safety; they may impact on national security. Overall, digital trade can affect the capacity of domestic regulators to achieve their regulatory aims in many aspects and in many different areas. The increased centrality of data and the importance of cross-border data flows have brought about a new set of concerns. The sheer volume and the personal nature of

[28] Henke et al. (2016), 51–60.

[29] 3D printing is another pertinent example in this context. 3D printing belongs to a class of techniques known as additive manufacturing. Additive processes build objects layer-by-layer rather than through moulding or subtractive techniques. 3D printing can create objects from a variety of materials, including plastic, metal, ceramics, glass, paper and even living cells. With some techniques, a single object can be printed in multiple materials and colours, and a single print job can even produce interconnected moving parts (such as hinges or mesh). Current limitations of 3D printing include relatively slow build speed, limited object size, limited object detail or high materials cost. See Manyika et al. (2011), pp. 105–113; Kommerskollegium, *Trade Regulation in a 3D Printed World*, Stockholm: Swedish National Board of Trade, 2016; also Kommerskollegium, *No Transfer, No Production: Report on Cross-border Data Transfers, Global Value Chains, and the Production of Goods*, Stockholm: Swedish Board of Trade, 2015.

the information collected and used can be in itself worrying.[30] Big data methods provide a new and powerful means to sort, combine and analyse data. The inherent ability of such technologies to capture sensitive details from information that, to the average customer, might seem mundane or meaningless, is astounding.[31] Furthermore the practices behind big data are often not transparent and, as mentioned above, they are under the control of a few gatekeepers, such as Google, Facebook or Amazon.[32] Privacy policy reports in the US, as well as in the EU, point out that conventional methods of protecting users and their private sphere, such as anonymization and de-identification, are no longer effective.[33] The related concerns, such as discrimination or control over individuals' future activities, are multiple. The possible permanence of personal data also means that it can be potentially reused in the future for unanticipated purposes.[34] Privacy, which is a fundamental right under international human rights law and under the constitutions of many countries, as well as the EU Charter of Fundamental Rights, may be seriously endangered.[35]

Tensions between domestic and global rules in general, and between privacy and free data flows in particular, are bound to increase and policymakers will need to find appropriate frameworks to balance the trade-offs between these.[36] This may be particularly hard, as the

[30] Urs Gasser, 'Perspectives on the Future of Digital Privacy', *Zeitschrift für Schweizerisches Recht* 135 (2015), 335–448, at 349; also Urs Gasser, 'Recoding Privacy Law: Reflections on the Future Relationship Among Law, Technology, and Privacy', *Harvard Law Review* 130:2 (2016), 61–70.

[31] Gasser (2015); Daniel J. Solove, 'A Taxonomy of Privacy', *University of Pennsylvania Law Review* 154 (2006), 477–560, at 506.

[32] Gasser (2015), at 343–350; also see, e.g., Ariel Ezrachi and Maurice E. Stucke, *Virtual Competition: The Promise and Perils of the Algorithm-driven Economy*, Cambridge, MA: Harvard University Press, 2016.

[33] See US President's Advisory Council on Science and Technology, *Big Data and Privacy: A Technological Perspective*, Washington, DC, 2014; European Union Agency for Network and Information Security (ENISA), *Privacy and Data Protection by Design – from Policy to Engineering*, Brussels, 2014.

[34] Gasser (2015), at 353.

[35] See, e.g., Gasser (2015, 2016); Colin J. Bennett and Robin M. Bayley, 'Privacy Protection in the Era of "Big Data": Regulatory Challenges and Social Assessments', in Bart van der Sloot, Dennis Broeders, and Erik Schrijvers (eds), *Exploring the Boundaries of Big Data*, Amsterdam: University of Amsterdam Press, 2016, 205–227.

[36] See, e.g., Mira Burri and Rahel Schär, 'The Reform of the EU Data Protection Framework: Outlining Key Changes and Assessing Their Fitness for a Data-Driven Economy', *Journal of Information Policy* 6 (2016), 479–511; Mira Burri, 'Interfacing Privacy and Trade', *Case Western Journal of International Law* 53 (2021), 35–88.

approaches of the US and the EU[37] towards the protection of privacy are at this stage hardly reconcilable.[38]

Trade Policy Responses to the Digital Transformation

The Existing Regulatory Framework for Digital Trade

Digitization and digital trade do not happen in a regulatory vacuum. Despite the fact that they may call for adjustments of different kinds and depths, there are existing rules at the international level that they can be subsumed under. The law of the World Trade Organization (WTO) is at the core of this framework, which has been over time complemented by a number of bilateral and regional trade deals of preferential nature. We discuss these rules in turn and try to briefly explain what their relevance for the contemporary digital economy is, where legal adaptation has failed and where countries have managed to formulate some new rules as a response to the digital challenge.

The Law of the World Trade Organization

The WTO Agreements were negotiated and adopted during the Uruguay Round (1986–1994).[39] Despite a few updates – such as the Information Technology Agreement (ITA) – the WTO rules have so far not reacted in a forward-looking manner to the various changes triggered by

[37] The EU only strengthened the rules on personal data protection as of May 2018 by increasing the standards of protection, the scope of the covered addressees and the sanctions. See Regulation 2016/680 of the European Parliament and of the Council of 27 April 2016 on the protection of natural persons with regard to the processing of personal data by competent authorities for the purposes of the prevention, investigation, detection or prosecution of criminal offences or the execution of criminal penalties, and on the free movement of such data, and repealing Council Framework Decision 2008/977/JHA, OJ L [2016] 119/89 [GDPR].

[38] See C-362/14, Maximillian Schrems *v.* Data Protection Commissioner, judgment of 6 October 2015, ECLI:EU:C:2015:650; Irish High Court, Data Protection Commissioner *v.* Facebook Ireland Limited and Maximillian Schrems (Schrems II), 2016 No 4809 P., judgment of 3 October 2017 (the case has been referred to the CJEU). See also Paul M. Schwartz, 'The EU–US Privacy Collision: A Turn to Institutions and Procedures', *Harvard Law Review* 126 (2013), 1966–2009; Paul M. Schwartz and Daniel J. Solove, 'Reconciling Personal Information in the United States and European Union', *California Law Review* 102 (2014), 877–916.

[39] The WTO Agreements comprise the Marrakesh Agreement Establishing the World Trade Organization and the, annexed to it, General Agreement on Tariffs and Trade [GATT]; General Agreement on Trade in Services [GATS]; and the Agreement on Trade-Related Aspects of Intellectual Property Rights [TRIPS].

digitization. Nonetheless, WTO law does regulate digital trade in many ways – and this as a matter of 'hard' law, agreed upon by the now 164 members and enforceable through the mechanisms of the WTO's dispute settlement.

The WTO endorses far-reaching principles of non-discrimination: the *most-favoured nation* (MFN) and the *national treatment* (NT) obligations. They ban countries from discriminating between products and services coming from different WTO members (MFN) and from discriminating between foreign and domestic products and services (NT). The therewith created constraints on national regimes are substantial. Next to these general rules of the WTO architecture, specific WTO Agreements regulating trade in goods, trade in services, the protection of intellectual property rights, the provisions on subsidies, standards, government procurement or trade facilitation, include many rules that matter for the digital economy – either by endorsing and detailing the application of the non-discrimination principles or by specifically addressing certain issues.[40]

With regard to trade in IT products, the WTO secures one of the *most accommodating conditions for free trade*. In addition to the far-reaching framework of the GATT for trade in goods, the ITA provides for a special regime for trade in IT products and ensures that trade in communication equipment is duty free. The ITA was adopted after the completion of the Uruguay Round at the Singapore Ministerial Conference in 1996,[41] largely as a result of the pressure applied by the US IT industry. The proclaimed objective of the ITA is to 'achieve maximum freedom of world trade in information technology products'.[42] To this effect, the ITA signatories pledged to provide *zero tariffs* for selected IT products, such as computers, semi-conductors, semi-conductor manufacturing equipment, telecommunication apparatus, data-storage media and software.[43] Although only a plurilateral agreement, the ITA has been

[40] For a detailed analysis, see Mira Burri, 'The International Economic Law Framework for Digital Trade', *Zeitschrift für Schweizerisches Recht* 135 (2015a), 10–72; Mira Burri, 'The Regulation of Data Flows in Trade Agreements', *Georgetown Journal of International Law* 48 (2017), 408–448; Mira Burri and Thomas Cottier (eds), *Trade Governance in the Digital Age*, Cambridge: Cambridge University Press, 2012.

[41] WTO, Ministerial Declaration on Trade in Information Technology Products, WT/MIN (96)/16 (1996).

[42] *Id.*, at Preamble and para. 1.

[43] See WTO, *15 Years of the Information Technology Agreement: Trade, Innovation and Global Production Networks*, Geneva: World Trade Organization, 2012.

successful in creating a 'critical mass' and attracting the major stakeholders in both the developed and the developing world. Originally signed by 29 countries, the ITA currently lists 82 WTO members. Together, these members account for more than 97 per cent of global trade in IT products.[44] In 2015, 50 WTO members agreed on the expansion of the ITA to cover an additional 201 product lines that have been valued at over USD 1.3 trillion per year.[45] Overall and despite some flaws, the ITA can be deemed as truly successful and has made a real difference in trade practice. It ultimately provided for a very liberal regime for trade in IT-related hardware, which spurred competition and benefited consumers.[46] Together with the far-reaching commitments in the telecommunication services sector, the ITA boosted the emergence of global value chains for IT trade and substantially facilitated the worldwide spread and adoption of technological advances and the emergence of the data economy. It is one of the good examples that vividly shows how regulation matters for shaping innovation.[47] It is also a case that illustrates how some WTO members can move forward on issues that are important to them without having the support of the entire WTO membership.

The effects of the WTO are also palpable in the field of digital services. The GATS, similarly to the GATT, aims at protecting the equality of competitive opportunities for companies regardless of their origin and the origin of their services, and at facilitating the progressive liberalization of services markets. Its legal design is however different and allows for flexibility in committing through the so-called *specific* commitments accepted by individual WTO members and listed in their 'Schedules of Specific Commitments'. These schedules show the positive obligations of a member with regard to *national treatment* and *market access*.[48] The fairly flexible regime of the GATS allows for the opening of services markets but also for keeping them protected, partially or completely.

[44] WTO, *Id.*

[45] As reported by the WTO on the occasion of the expansion of the ITA (see WTO, available at www.wto.org/english/tratop_e/inftec_e/inftec_e.htm).

[46] Copenhagen Economics, *Expanding the Information Technology Agreement (ITA): Economic and Trade Impacts*, Final Report for the European Commission, 2010.

[47] Anupam Chander, 'How Law Made Silicon Valley', *Emory Law Journal* 63 (2014), 639–694.

[48] 'Market access' is articulated in Article XVI GATS and addresses quantitative restrictions to services trade. The 'national treatment' obligation, specified in Article XVII GATS, is of a broader, qualitative nature and bans discrimination between domestic and foreign services and service suppliers.

In terms of services sectors that are pertinent for the digital economy, one commonly reviews the telecommunications, the computer and related, and the audiovisual as well as the financial services sectors. The level of openness of these sectors varies substantially. One can maintain generally that while the regime for digital infrastructure and applications is liberal under the WTO, content-related services are almost uncommitted for.[49]

A deep intervention, which may substantially limit the regulatory space available domestically comes from the GATS rules on *computer and related services*. For computer and related services, which was a fairly new sector at the time of the Uruguay Round and thus largely devoid of either domestic regulation or trade barriers, a great number of WTO members have made far-reaching commitments for both market access and national treatment. The EU has, for instance, committed for all the listed subsectors: (a) consultancy services related to the installation of computer hardware; (b) software implementation services; (c) data processing services; (d) database services; maintenance and repair; and (e) other computer services.[50] The implications of these commitments are real and the wiggle-room available for domestic regulators is severely constrained. If we imagine a situation where the EU would like to install new measures with regard to search engines that somehow limit the market access or discriminate against foreign companies and their services, this may implicate a violation of WTO law – because search engines can be subsumed under 'data processing services'[51] and because the EU is fully committed to those. Localization requirements would be also GATS-inconsistent in the sectors where there are specific commitments made.[52] Yet, at least so far, such situations have not been tested before a WTO panel.

[49] Burri (2015a); Rolf H. Weber and Mira Burri, *Classification of Services in the Digital Economy*, Bern: Stämpfli, 2012.

[50] The EU has listed no limitations for the first three modes of supply (cross-border, consumption abroad and commercial presence) and remains unbound only for the presence of natural persons (mode 4). See WTO, European Communities and their member states, Schedule of Specific Commitments, Trade in Services, Supplement 3, GATS/SC/31/Suppl. 3 (1997).

[51] See Henry Gao, 'Googling for the Trade–Human Rights Nexus in China: Can the WTO Help?', in Mira Burri and Thomas Cottier (eds), *Trade Governance in the Digital Age*, Cambridge: Cambridge University Press, 2012, pp. 247–275; also Weber and Burri (2012), at 115.

[52] See, e.g., Cathleen Cimino et al., 'A Proposed Code to Discipline Local Content Requirements', *Peterson Institute of International Economics Policy Brief* 4 (2014); Holger P. Hestermeyer and Laura Nielsen, 'The Legality of Local Content Measures under WTO Law', *Journal of World Trade* 48 (2014), 553–592.

The EU and other WTO members have often looked for an 'escape' in this context by relying on one argument that has to do with the technical issue of services classification. Whenever they want to preserve policy space, WTO members would argue that such digital services should be classified as 'audiovisual services',[53] because of their inherent function as content platforms.[54] There is arguably room for interpretation and members make use of the lack of clear distinctions in the existing classification schemes, which is exacerbated by their pre-Internet origin. In the sector of audiovisual services, almost no WTO members have made commitments and thus remain relatively free to sustain discriminatory measures and adopt new ones.[55] This is the result of a pronounced and politically charged contention between trade and cultural interests that unfolded during the Uruguay Round of negotiations. It was associated with a rupture between the key negotiating parties – the EU and the US – on the question of how to regulate cultural matters and whether to make them subject to the rules of the WTO – the so-called 'exception culturelle' debate.[56] The current round of trade negotiations – the Doha Development Agenda – is unlikely to change things in the audiovisual services sector.[57] Despite the recognition, widely shared by key WTO members, that the audiovisual sector has changed dramatically,[58] in particular in the face of the sweeping transformations caused by the Internet, there is little agreement on the way forward.[59] This is a major

[53] 'Audiovisual services' include motion picture and videotape production and distribution services; motion picture projection service; radio and television services; radio and television transmission services and sound recording.

[54] See, e.g., WTO, Work Programme on Electronic Commerce, Submission by the European Communities WT/GC/W/497 (2003), at para. 7.

[55] WTO, Council for Trade in Services, Audiovisual Services, Background note by the Secretariat, S/C/W/310 (2010).

[56] See, e.g., Mira Burri, 'Trade versus Culture in the Digital Environment: An Old Conflict in Need of a New Definition', *Journal of International Economic Law* 12 (2009), 17–62; Mira Burri, 'The EU, the WTO and Cultural Diversity', in Evangelia Psychogiopoulou (ed.), *Cultural Governance and the European Union: Protecting and Promoting Cultural Diversity in Europe*, Basingstoke: Palgrave Macmillan, 2015b, pp. 195–204.

[57] See, e.g., Lee Tuthill and Martin Roy, 'GATS Classification Issues for Information and Communication Technology Services', in Mira Burri and Thomas Cottier (eds), *Trade Governance in the Digital Age*, Cambridge: Cambridge University Press, 2012, pp. 157–178.

[58] WTO, Communication from the European Union and the United States: Contribution to the Work Programme on Electronic Commerce, S/C/W/338 (2011).

[59] See, e.g., WTO, Communication from the European Communities and its Member States, Draft consolidated GATS Schedule, S/C/W/273 (2006).

setback for data as content and undermines the very liberal regime that the WTO has established with regard to infrastructure and some services sectors like telecom and computer and related services.

It may also be worth keeping in mind this specific case of juxtaposing trade and culture and how the distributional conflict between the US and the EU has played out. This situation may very well be replicated in the area of free data flows versus data protection, where the positions of the two key stakeholders also diverge profoundly.

Overall, while the WTO Agreements have fairly comprehensive rules and digital trade can be subsumed under the law of the GATT and the GATS, it is evident that legal adaptation under the auspices of the WTO has not progressed, at least so far. Despite the utility of the WTO's dispute settlement, illustrated in a number of Internet-related cases, such as *US–Gambling* and *China–Audiovisual Products*,[60] judicial transplants cannot replace political consensus on the substance, particularly in a complex and highly technical domain, such as digital trade. Legal certainty has been compromised. The classification dilemma, as often discussed in the field of services regulation and as particularly critical for the legal categorization of data flows, exposes vividly the disconnectedness of trade rules from trade practices and the state of paralysis in the WTO.[61] Many other issues discussed in the framework of the 1998 WTO Work Programme on Electronic Commerce have been left without a solution or even a clarification.[62] There is, for instance, still no agreement

[60] Panel Report, *United States – Measures Affecting the Cross-Border Supply of Gambling and Betting Services (US – Gambling)*, WT/DS285/R, adopted 10 November 2004; Appellate Body Report, *United States – Measures Affecting the Cross-Border Supply of Gambling and Betting Services (US – Gambling)*, WT/DS285/AB/R, adopted 7 April 2005; Panel Report, *China – Measures Affecting Trading Rights and Distribution Services for Certain Publications and Audiovisual Entertainment Products (China – Publications and Audiovisual Products)*, WT/DS363/R, adopted 12 August 2009; Appellate Body Report, *China – Measures Affecting Trading Rights and Distribution Services for Certain Publications and Audiovisual Entertainment Products (China – Publications and Audiovisual Products)*, WT/DS363/AB/R, adopted 21 December 2009.

[61] Online games, for instance, as a new type of content platform, could be potentially fitted into the discrete categories of computer and related services, value-added telecommunications services, entertainment or audiovisual services. The classification is not trivial, since it triggers different obligations. See Weber and Burri (2012). With specific regard to the classification of data flows, see Nivedita Sen, 'Understanding the Role of the WTO in International Data Flows: Taking the Liberalization or the Regulatory Path', *Journal of International Economic Law* 21 (2018), 323–348, in particular at 331–335.

[62] Sacha Wunsch-Vincent and Arno Hold, 'Towards Coherent Rules for Digital Trade: Building on Efforts in Multilateral versus Preferential Trade Negotiations', in Mira Burri

on a permanent moratorium on duties on electronic transmissions.[63] 2016 and 2017 were years of reinvigorated interest towards matters of electronic commerce but the statements by the WTO members did not yet point towards a clear negotiating mandate; instead, they again exposed some of the 'old' divides – between the willingness to create new rules or rather adhere to existing commitments; between the willingness to address trade barriers or rather preserve policy space.[64] The efforts to move towards a digital trade agreement under the WTO have been subsequently renewed under the Joint Statement Initiative of 2019 and despite great progress that was made, the outlines of a proper agreement remain still unclear and there are many points of disagreement between the parties.[65]

The overall lack of progress under the WTO has triggered forum-shopping – through bilateral, regional and plurilateral initiatives. Many of these efforts have also sought answers to the regulatory challenges posed by digital technologies.

Beyond the WTO: Free Trade Agreements

The regulatory environment for digital trade has been substantially influenced by free trade agreements (FTAs) and in particular by those led by the US. The United States has endorsed and attempted to ensure implementation of its so-called 'Digital Agenda'[66] through the FTA channel.

and Thomas Cottier (eds), *Trade Governance in the Digital Age*, Cambridge: Cambridge University Press, 2012, pp. 179–221, p. 181.

[63] The moratorium has only been temporarily extended several times; the last time for a period of two years following a decision taken during the Buenos Aires Ministerial Conference in 2017, subsequently extended to June 2019 by the WTO General Council in 2019.

[64] See, e.g., WTO Work Programme on E-Commerce, *Non-Paper from the United States*, WTO Doc JOB/GC/94 (2016); WTO Work Programme on E-Commerce, *Non-Paper from Brazil*, WTO Doc JOB/GC/98 (2016); WTO Work Programme on E-Commerce, *Communication from Canada, Chile, Colombia, Côte d'Ivoire, the European Union, the Republic of Korea, Mexico, Paraguay and Singapore, Trade Policy, the WTO and the Digital Economy*, WTO Doc JOB/GC/97/Rev.1 (2016); WTO, *Joint Statement on Electronic Commerce*, Buenos Aires Ministerial Conference 11th Session, WTO/MIN/(17)60 (2017).

[65] For a detailed analysis of the WTO members' positions, see Sen (2018), at 339–341; see also Henry Gao, 'Digital or Trade? The Contrasting Approaches of China and US to Digital Trade', *Journal of International Economic Law* 21 (2018), 297–321; Mira Burri, 'Towards a New Treaty on Digital Trade', *Journal of World Trade* 55 (2021), 77–100.

[66] See Sacha Wunsch-Vincent, 'The Digital Trade Agenda of the US: Parallel Tracks of Bilateral, Regional and Multilateral Liberalization', *Aussenwirtschaft* 1 (2003), 7–46.

The agreements reached since 2002 with Australia, Bahrain, Chile, Morocco, Oman, Peru, Singapore, the Central American countries[67] and more recently with Panama, Colombia and the Republic of Korea, all contain critical WTO-plus (going above the WTO commitments) and WTO-extra (addressing issues not covered by the WTO) provisions in the broader field of digital trade. The emergent regulatory template on digital issues is not, however, limited to US agreements, but has diffused and can be found in other FTAs as well, such as Singapore–Australia, Thailand–Australia, Thailand–New Zealand, New Zealand–Singapore, India–Singapore, Japan–Singapore and Republic of Korea–Singapore.[68] Australia, Japan, New Zealand and Colombia have been among the major drivers of this diffusion.[69]

Key aspects of digital trade are typically addressed in: (1) specifically dedicated e-commerce chapters; (2) the chapters on cross-border supply of services; and (3) the intellectual property chapters. In our discussion, we look only at the e-commerce chapters, as they contain deliberate responses to digital trade. The electronic commerce chapters have also evolved over time – from less to more binding and from a mere compensation for the lack of progress in the WTO towards new (and partially innovative) digital rule-making. In the former sense, they have included a clear definition of 'digital products', which treats digital products delivered offline as equal to those delivered online, so that technological neutrality is ensured. The chapters also recognize the applicability of WTO rules to e-commerce and establish a permanent moratorium on imposing duties on the import or export of digital products by electronic transmission. Critically, the e-commerce chapters ensure both MFN and NT for digital products trade; discrimination is banned on the basis that digital products are 'created, produced, published, stored, transmitted, contracted for, commissioned, or first made available on commercial

[67] The DR–CAFTA includes Costa Rica, El Salvador, Guatemala, Honduras, Nicaragua and the Dominican Republic.

[68] We have created a database (called TAPED) for all FTAs since 2000. The overall number of coded PTAs since 2000 until June 2019 is 345 (WTO notified 272); number that have e-commerce chapters: 77; number that have e-commerce provisions (including annexes): 182; number that have general data-related provisions: 24; data-related provisions for financial services: 69; for telecommunication services: 64; for data localization: 12. See Mira Burri and Rodrigo Polanco, 'Digital Trade Provisions in Preferential Trade Agreements: Introducing a New Dataset', *Journal of International Economic Law* 23:1 (2020).

[69] Based on own data, *Id.*

terms outside the country's territory' or 'whose author, performer, producer, developer, or distributor is a person of another party or a non-party'.[70]

The e-commerce chapters also include rules that go beyond the WTO. These cover different issues in the broader IT policy field, such as those for telecommunications policy, IT standards and interoperability, cybersecurity, electronic signatures and payments, paperless trading, self-regulation and e-government projects. More importantly for data flows, they seek to achieve some common ground rules for the digital marketplace, where increasingly inadequate and incompatible national regulations are seen as an important digital trade barrier.

The US–Republic of Korea FTA (KORUS) was first of a kind in this regard. It included 'Principles on Access to and Use of the Internet for Electronic Commerce', which detail rights for the consumers to: (a) access and use services and digital products of their choice; (b) run applications and services of their choice; (c) connect their choice of devices to the Internet; and (d) have the benefit of competition among network providers, application and service providers, and content providers.[71] Next to these fairly solid safeguards against censorship and other types of constrained access and use, the US–Republic of Korea FTA provides for free cross-border information flows and obliges the parties, although in a non-binding manner, 'to refrain from imposing or maintaining unnecessary barriers to electronic information flows across borders'.[72]

In the following, we look at the follow-up of the KORUS and the most comprehensive model that we have had so far – that of the CPTTP. Interestingly enough, the e-commerce chapter of the CPTPP has survived the TPP negotiations[73] in its entirety and without any change, and still reflects the efforts of the United States in this domain. So, in a sense, we

[70] See, e.g., US–Singapore FTA, Article 14.3; US–Australia FTA, Article 16.4. In many FTAs, digital products must not be fully produced and exported through one of the contracting parties of the bilateral FTAs to benefit from the non-discrimination obligations. This is an interesting way to avoid complex rules of origin.

[71] US–Republic of Korea, Article 15.7.

[72] US–Republic of Korea, Article 15.8: 'Recognizing the importance of the free flow of information in facilitating trade, and acknowledging the importance of protecting personal information, the Parties shall endeavor to refrain from imposing or maintaining unnecessary barriers to electronic information flows across borders.'

[73] The Trans-Pacific Partnership Agreement, available at https://ustr.gov/trade-agreements/free-trade-agreements/trans-pacific-partnership/tpp-full-text [hereinafter TPP].

have a far-reaching implementation of the US model, without the US participating in it.

The CPTPP

The Comprehensive and Progressive Agreement for Transpacific Partnership (CPTPP – also known as the TPP11 or TPP 2.0)[74] was agreed upon in 2017 among 11 countries in the Pacific Rim[75] and entered into force on 30 December 2018. The CPTPP represents 13.4 per cent of the global gross domestic product or USD13.5 trillion, making it the third largest trade agreement after the North American Free Trade Agreement and the single market of the European Union.[76] The CPTPP also, and importantly for us, represents a new level in the evolution of digital trade provisions in FTAs.

The CPTPP chapter on e-commerce has clearly created the most comprehensive model for digital trade regulation. It comprises 18 articles and includes new features, such as provisions on the domestic electronic transactions framework, personal information protection, Internet interconnection charge sharing, location of computing facilities, unsolicited commercial electronic messages, source code and dispute settlement.[77] In the following, we look more closely at the CPTPP provisions and how far they create binding rules for the signatories.

The CPTPP seeks for the first time to explicitly restrict the use of data localization measures. Article 14.13(2) prohibits the parties from requiring a 'covered person to use or locate computing facilities in that Party's territory as a condition for conducting business in that territory'. The soft language from KORUS on free data flows is now framed as a hard rule: '[e]ach Party shall allow the cross-border transfer of information by electronic means, including personal information, when this activity is for the conduct of the business of a covered person'.[78] The rule has a broad scope and most data that are transferred over the Internet are likely

[74] The Comprehensive and Progressive Agreement for Transpacific Partnership, full text available at http://international.gc.ca/trade-commerce/trade-agreements-accords-commerciaux/agr-acc/cptpp-ptpgp/text-texte/index.aspx?lang=eng.

[75] Australia, Brunei, Canada, Chile, Japan, Malaysia, Mexico, New Zealand, Peru, Singapore and Vietnam.

[76] Zachary Torrey, 'TPP 2.0: The Deal Without the US: What's New about the CPTPP and What Do the Changes Mean?', *The Diplomat*, 3 February 2018, available at https://thediplomat.com/2018/02/tpp-2-0-the-deal-without-the-us/.

[77] CPTPP Articles 14.5, 14.8, 14.12, 14.13, 14.14, 14.17 and 14.18, respectively.

[78] Article 14.11(2) CPTPP.

to be covered, although the word 'for' may suggest the need for some causality between the flow of data and the business of the covered person.

Measures restricting digital flows or localization requirements under Article 14.13 CPTPP are permitted only if they do not amount to 'arbitrary or unjustifiable discrimination or a disguised restriction on trade' and do not 'impose restrictions on transfers of information greater than are required to achieve the objective'.[79] These non-discriminatory conditions are similar to the strict test formulated by the GATS Article XIV and GATT Article XX, a test that is intended to balance trade and non-trade interests, but one that is also extremely hard to pass.[80] The CPTPP test differs from the WTO norms in one significant element: while there is a list of public policy objectives in the GATT and the GATS, the CPTPP provides no such enumeration and simply speaks of a 'legitimate public policy objective'.[81] This permits more regulatory autonomy for the CPTPP signatories. However, it also may lead to abuses and overall legal uncertainty. Further, it should be noted that the ban on localization measures is somewhat softened with regard to financial services and institutions.[82] An annex to the Financial Services chapter has a separate data transfer requirement, whereby certain restrictions on data flows may apply for the protection of privacy or confidentiality of individual records, or for prudential reasons.[83] Government procurement is also excluded.[84]

Pursuant to Article 14.17, a CPTPP member may not require the transfer of, or access to, source code of software owned by a person of another party as a condition for the import, distribution, sale or use of such software, or of products containing such software, in its territory. The prohibition applies, however, only to mass-market software or products containing such software.[85] This means that tailor-made products will be excluded, as well as software used for critical infrastructure

[79] Article 14.11(3) CPTPP.

[80] See, e.g., Henrik Andersen, 'Protection of Non-Trade Values in WTO Appellate Body Jurisprudence: Exceptions, Economic Arguments, and Eluding Questions', *Journal of International Economic Law* 18 (2015), 383–405.

[81] Article 14.11(3) CPTPP.

[82] See the definition of 'a covered person' in Article 14.1, which is said to exclude a 'financial institution' and a 'cross-border financial service supplier'.

[83] The provision reads: 'Each Party shall allow a financial institution of another Party to transfer information in electronic or other form, into and out of its territory, for data processing if such processing is required in the institution's ordinary course of business'.

[84] Article 14.8(3) CPTPP.

[85] Article 14.17(2) CPTPP.

and those in commercially negotiated contracts.[86] The aim of this provision is to protect software companies and address their concerns about loss of IP or cracks in the security of their proprietary code[87] – its real effect is, however, hard to predict.

These provisions illustrate an interesting development because it is evident that they do not simply entail a clarification of existing bans on discrimination, nor do they merely set higher standards, as is generally anticipated from trade agreements. Rather, they shape the regulatory space domestically and may actually lower certain standards. A commitment to lower standards of protection is particularly palpable in the field of privacy and data protection.

Article 14.8(2) requires every CPTPP party to 'adopt or maintain a legal framework that provides for the protection of the personal information of the users of electronic commerce'. No standards or benchmarks for the legal framework have been specified, except for a general requirement that CPTPP parties 'take into account principles or guidelines of relevant international bodies'.[88] A footnote provides some clarification in saying that: '[f]or greater certainty, a Party may comply with the obligation in this paragraph by adopting or maintaining measures such as a comprehensive privacy, personal information or personal data protection laws, sector-specific laws covering privacy, or laws that provide for the enforcement of voluntary undertakings by enterprises relating to privacy'.[89] Parties are also invited to promote compatibility between their data protection regimes, by essentially treating lower standards as equivalent.[90] Overall, the goal seems to be to prioritize trade over privacy rights. This commitment had been pushed by the US, which subscribes to a relatively weak and patchy protection of privacy. Timewise, this insertion was a consequence of the judgment of the Court of Justice of the European Union (CJEU) that struck down the EU–US Safe Harbor Agreement.[91]

[86] Article 14.17(2) CPTPP.

[87] It is interesting to note that China does demand access to source code from software producers selling in its market, so this provision may be interpreted as a reaction to this.

[88] Article 14.8(2) CPTPP.

[89] Article 14.8(2) CPTPP, footnote 6.

[90] Article 14.8(5) CPTPP.

[91] C-362/14, *Schrems*. Maximillian Schrems is an Austrian citizen, who filed a suit against the Irish supervisory authority (the Data Protection Commissioner), after it rejected his complaint over Facebook's practice of storing user data in the United States. The plaintiff claimed that his data was not adequately protected in light of the recent NSA revelations

While the attention is often exclusively focused on data protection, it should be noted that the CPTPP also has provisions on consumer protection[92] and spam control,[93] although they are fairly weak. The same is true for the newly introduced rules on cybersecurity. Article 14.16 is non-binding and identifies a relatively limited scope of activities for cooperation, in situations of 'malicious intrusions' or 'dissemination of malicious code', and capacity building of governmental bodies dealing with cybersecurity incidents.

Net neutrality is another important digital economy topic that has been given specific attention in the CPTPP, although the created rules are of non-binding nature. Article 14.10 states that

> [s]ubject to applicable policies, laws and regulations, the Parties recognize the benefits of consumers in their territories having the ability to: (a) access and use services and applications of a consumer's choice available on the Internet, subject to reasonable network management; (b) connect the end-user devices of a consumer's choice to the Internet, provided that such devices do not harm the network; and (c) access information on the network management practices of a consumer's Internet access service supplier.

While it is commendable that net neutrality is endorsed, this comes with many reservations, as evidenced from the above provision, from the domestic laws of CPTPP countries; from undefined situations that call for 'reasonable network management';[94] or from exclusive services. The obligations are ultimately not linked to legal remedies for situations, such as blocking or filtering content, and are unlikely to lead to a uniform approach across CPTPP countries.

The USMCA

After the withdrawal of the United States from the TPP, there was some uncertainty as to the direction the United States would follow in its trade deals in general and on matters of digital trade in particular. The renegotiated North American Free Trade Agreement (NAFTA), which is now

and this, despite the existing agreement between the EU and the US – the so-called 'safe harbour' scheme – that expressly sought to ensure that the United States provides for an adequate level of protection of the transferred personal data.

92 Article 14.17 CPTPP.

93 Article 14.14 CPTPP.

94 Article 14.10(a) CPTPP. Footnote 6 to this paragraph specifies that: 'The Parties recognise that an Internet access service supplier that offers its subscribers certain content on an exclusive basis would not be acting contrary to this principle.'

called the United States–Mexico–Canada Agreement, or USMCA, casts the doubts aside. The USMCA has a comprehensive electronic commerce chapter, which is now also properly titled 'Digital Trade' and follows all critical lines of the CPTPP in ensuring the free flow of data through a clear ban on data localization (Article 19.12), providing a non-discrimination regime for digital products (Article 19.4) and a hard rule on free information flows (Article 19.11). The USMCA appears particularly interesting in two aspects. The first is that it keeps the clause on exceptions that permits the pursuit of certain non-economic objectives. Article 19.11 specifies, very much in the sense of the CPTPP, that parties can adopt or maintain a measure inconsistent with the free flow of data provision if this is necessary to achieve a legitimate public policy objective, provided that the measure: (a) is not applied in a manner which would constitute a means of arbitrary or unjustifiable discrimination or a disguised restriction on trade; and (b) does not impose restrictions on transfers of information greater than are necessary to achieve the objective.[95] Furthermore, and departing from the standard US approach, the USMCA signals an acceptance of some data protection principles. While Article 19.8 remains soft on prescribing domestic regimes on personal data protection, it recognizes principles and guidelines of relevant international bodies, such as the APEC Privacy Framework and the OECD Recommendation of the Council concerning Guidelines governing the Protection of Privacy and Transborder Flows of Personal Data (2013).[96] The parties also recognize that these key principles include: limitation on collection; choice; data quality; purpose specification; use limitation; security safeguards; transparency; individual participation; and accountability,[97] and aim to provide remedies for any violations.[98] This is interesting because it goes beyond what the US may have in its national laws on data protection and also because it reflects some of the principles the European Union has advocated in the domain of the protection of privacy.

It should be finally noted that the models of the CPTPP and the USMCA have diffused in more recent years and their key norms on data flows can be found in the US–Japan Digital Trade Agreement, the updated

[95] Article 19.11(2). There is a footnote attached, which clarifies: 'A measure does not meet the conditions of this paragraph if it accords different treatment to data transfers solely on the basis that they are cross-border in a manner that modifies the conditions of competition to the detriment of service suppliers of another Party.'

[96] Article 19.8(2) USMCA.

[97] Article 19.8(3) USMCA.

[98] Article 19.8(4) and (5) USMCA.

Singapore–Australia FTA and the highly advanced Digital Economy Partnership Agreement between Chile, New Zealand and Singapore.

Deliberate Responses to the Digital Challenge: An Appraisal of the State of Affairs

Against the backdrop of failing legal adaptation under the auspices of the WTO, much has happened in preferential trade venues. Although not in a manner of a revolutionary change, there is a new emergent regime for digital trade. It includes a number of WTO-plus commitments and clarifies some issues that the WTO members could not agree on, such as a duty-free regime for electronic transactions. The FTAs also, and perhaps more importantly, tackle certain 'non-trade' or 'WTO-extra' issues, such as consumer protection, privacy and safeguards for the free flow of data. The CPTPP stands out with regard to digital trade, not only due to its high standards but also because of the breadth of issues covered that matter more or less immediately for the digital economy. The clear ban on localization measures and the subscription to a binding norm on free data flows with a potentially broad scope of application are unprecedented. It should also be noted that the CPTPP appears to take a first, although somewhat vague and insecure, step towards reconciling economic and non-economic interests as part of the e-commerce chapter, as it attempts some sort of a balance between free data flows and other public interests.

Overall, FTA partners do benefit from swifter solutions, from the deeper, as well as often clearer, provisions. It appears that FTAs work better, although not always, for reconciling diverging interests – on longstanding trade topics, such as classification, and in politically charged domains, such as audiovisual services. FTAs are also in a good position to address the new generation of trade barriers, such as localization measures, which are distorting digital innovation and which may lead to balkanization of the global digital space.[99]

[99] Digital trade has also been associated with a new palette of measures that inhibit digital trade. A number of studies in the last five years have tried to compile and analyse information on these new digital trade barriers. Some of them can be grouped under the so-called 'digital trade localization measures'. Others are not strictly trade measures and encompass issues relating to censorship, divergent approaches to data privacy and IP protection that different countries have adopted, that in different ways disrupt digital trade, increase the cost of doing business and hinder innovation. See United States International Trade Commission (USITC), *Digital Trade in the US and Global Economies, Part 1*, Investigation No 332–531 (Washington, DC: USITC, 2013); USITC,

FTAs' benefits may, however, be offset by the fact that a patchwork of multiple and overlapping agreements exacerbates the world's asymmetric wealth distribution and rule fragmentation, and does not contribute to the free cross-border flow of information on a global scale. It must be underscored in this context that although we concentrated here on the advanced template of the US and the follow-up CPTPP, many other countries, even developed ones like the members of the European Free Trade Association (EFTA), do not have a digital strategy and have not entered into any substantial WTO-extra commitments in their FTAs. In addition, it should be noted that FTAs may be undermining the value and impact of multilateral venues and the role of international law in general. Without engaging in the debate of preferentialism versus multilateralism, purely from the perspective of digital trade and its demands on seamlessness and interoperability,[100] the multilateral forum appears to be a more sensible solution.[101]

Concluding Remarks

Beyond the narrow question of the suitability of FTAs to address digital trade, there is a broader one on appropriate legal design. To be sure, the novel design that is needed is not of the type of rules that were discussed during the 1998 E-Commerce Work Programme of the WTO – it is less about ensuring market access but more about interfacing domestic regimes so as to provide interoperability and legal certainty. As noted

Digital Trade in the US and Global Economies, Part 2, Investigation No 332–540 (Washington, DC: USITC, 2014); For a detailed study of localization measures, see also OECD, *Emerging Policy Issues: Localisation Barriers to Trade*, TAD/TC/WP(2014)17/FINAL, 12 May 2015. For a country survey, see Anupam Chander and Uyên P. Lê, 'Data Nationalism', *Emory Law Journal* 64 (2015), 677–739. For a dynamic database, see the Digital Trade Estimates Project, available at http://ecipe.org/dte/.

100 Urs Gasser and John Palfrey, 'Fostering Innovation and Trade in the Global Information Society: The Different Facets and Roles of Interoperability', in Mira Burri and Thomas Cottier (eds), *Trade Governance in the Digital Age* (Cambridge: Cambridge University Press, 2012), 123–153.

101 One can, however, also point at the deficiencies of the WTO as a brick-and-mortar forum based on state-centric, top-down paradigm of rule-making. See in particular Sungjoon Cho and Claire R. Kelly, 'Are World Trading Rules Passé?', *Virginia Journal of International Law* 53 (2013), 623–666; also Mira Burri, 'The Governance of Data and Data Flows in Trade Agreements: The Pitfalls of Legal Adaptation', *UC Davies Law Review* 51 (2017a), 65–132, at 129–132.

earlier, digital trade has dramatically changed in the last 10 or so years. It is all about data and data flows now[102] and this radically changes the perspective on state sovereignty and international cooperation in the domain of trade governance.

While governments do have the right and the responsibility to protect interests and values important to their citizens, they also have a variety of tools available to achieve these goals and many of them can be congruent with the functional nature of the Internet and with the fostering of an open and innovative data economy.[103] Two issues appear paramount in this context and may be important for allowing a smart solution for digital trade rules that is also politically feasible. The first such avenue is to address cross-border data issues in trade agreements horizontally, and not in a manner directly related to a discrete service or a discrete transaction. There are various ways to do this – for instance, as part of the horizontal commitments of the services schedules; in the form of a Reference Paper attached to the schedules as an additional commitment under Article XVIII GATS; as part of a plurilateral trade in services agreement or more radically, as part of a dedicated digital trade agreement – which can either work on a MFN basis (like the ITA) or benefit only the signatories on a non-MFN basis (like the Government Procurement Agreement). Another important element of the solution will be to provide working mechanisms that may counterbalance the free flow of data and the non-economic concerns that the cross-border transfer of data raises. Personal data protection is likely to be critical here. It has been suggested in this context that it may be apt to differentiate between types of data, such as business, personal or sensitive data.[104] While such an exercise may allow for a special treatment and higher levels of protection of personal data and more liberal treatment of the rest, the exercise does come with many pitfalls. As noted earlier, big data can be incredibly miscellaneous and include a great amount of information of different types and from different sources. While not all this information is personal (i.e. data, such as name, gender, personal preferences, location, email or IP addresses) and identifies a person or permits

[102] The rhetoric of data flows is not necessarily new but now very present in trade discussions. For a historical account, see Drake (2016).
[103] Chander and Lê (2015), pp. 677–739; also Zittrain (2008).
[104] For a suggested taxonomy in this sense, see Sen (2018), pp. 343–347.

such identification,[105] it needs to be acknowledged that with the accumulation of data and with the affordances of big data analytics, much of this data can be 'turned' into personal information. Indeed, big data puts into question the very distinction between personal and non-personal data.[106]

Yet, we should not forget that trade law has over the years provided flexible and well-working mechanisms to reconcile different values. Article XX GATT and Article XIV GATS are great examples in this context. We may have also seen certain steps that pave the way in this direction. The CPTPP and now the USMCA are undoubtedly such stepping stones, as we showed above, and newer initiatives like the DEPA underscore this. It is also observable that states have increasingly realized the value of data and the critical importance of cross-border data flows. Even the most sceptical and cautious of parties, such as the EU, have been under pressure and have been rethinking their positions with regard to digital trade. For instance, the recent EU–Japan Free Trade Agreement says under the title 'Free Flow of Data' that: 'The Parties shall reassess the need for inclusion of an article on the free flow of data within three years of the entry into force of this Agreement.'[107] This has signalled a repositioning of the EU on data flows, which has been now fully endorsed in the ongoing negotiations of the EU with Australia, New Zealand and Tunisia, as well as in the 2021 post-Brexit treaty with the United Kingdom, where the parties

[105] The GDPR provides the following definition of personal data: 'personal data means any information relating to an identified or identifiable natural person ("data subject"); an identifiable natural person is one who can be identified, directly or indirectly, in particular by reference to an identifier such as a name, an identification number, location data, an online identifier or to one or more factors specific to the physical, physiological, genetic, mental, economic, cultural or social identity of that natural person'.

[106] 'As techniques like data fusion make big data analytics more powerful, the challenges to current expectations of privacy grow more serious. When data is initially linked to an individual or device, some privacy-protective technology seeks to remove this linkage, or "de-identify" personally identifiable information – but equally effective techniques exist to pull the pieces back together through "re-identification". Similarly, integrating diverse data can lead to what some analysts call the 'mosaic effect', whereby personally identifiable information can be derived or inferred from datasets that do not even include personal identifiers, bringing into focus a picture of who an individual is and what he or she likes. Many technologists are of the view that de-identification of data as a means of protecting individual privacy is, at best, a limited proposition.' See The White House, *Big Data: Seizing Opportunities, Preserving Values*, Executive Office of the President, May 2014, at 14.

[107] Article 8.81 EU–Japan FTA.

agree on free cross-border flows, coupled however with the EU's high standards of personal data protection.[108] Overall, there is a profound need to better understand the implications of the data economy for trade governance. Curbing 'digital protectionism' should be addressed as a priority in policy agendas, so as to enable a sustainable regulatory environment for the age of big data.

Bibliography

Aaronson, S., 'Why Trade Agreements Are Not Setting Information Free: The Lost History and Reinvigorated Debate over Cross-Border Data Flows, Human Rights and National Security' (2015), *World Trade Review* 14: 671–700.

Andersen, H., 'Protection of Non-Trade Values in WTO Appellate Body Jurisprudence: Exceptions, Economic Arguments, and Eluding Questions' (2015), *Journal of International Economic Law* 18: 383–405.

Bennett, C. J. and Bayley, R. M., 'Privacy Protection in the Era of "Big Data": Regulatory Challenges and Social Assessments', in B. van der Sloot, D. Broeders and E. Schrijvers (eds), *Exploring the Boundaries of Big Data*, Amsterdam: University of Amsterdam Press, 2016, pp. 205–220.

Brownsword, R. and Yeung, K. (eds), *Regulating Technologies: Legal Futures, Regulatory Frames and Technological Fixes*, Oxford: Hart, 2008.

Bughin, J., Hazan, E., Labaye, E., Manyika, J., Dahlström, P., Ramaswamy, S. and Cochin de Billy, C., *Digital Europe: Pushing the Frontier, Capturing the Benefits*, Washington, DC: McKinsey Global Institute, 2016.

Burri, M., 'Trade versus Culture in the Digital Environment: An Old Conflict in Need of a New Definition' (2009), *Journal of International Economic Law* 12: 17–62.

Burri, M., *Public Service Broadcasting 3.0: Legal Design for the Digital Present*, Abingdon: Routledge, 2015.

Burri, M., 'The International Economic Law Framework for Digital Trade' (2015a), *Zeitschrift für Schweizerisches Recht* 135: 10–72.

Burri, M., 'The EU, the WTO and Cultural Diversity', in E. Psychogiopoulou (ed.), *Cultural Governance and the European Union: Protecting and Promoting Cultural Diversity in Europe*, Basingstoke: Palgrave Macmillan, 2015b, pp. 195–204.

Burri, M., 'The Regulation of Data Flows in Trade Agreements' (2017), *Georgetown Journal of International Law* 48: 408–448.

Burri, M., 'The Governance of Data and Data Flows in Trade Agreements: The Pitfalls of Legal Adaptation' (2017a), *UC Davies Law Review* 51: 65–132.

[108] See Burri (2021).

Burri, M., 'Understanding the Implications of Big Data and Big Data Analytics for Competition Law: An Attempt for a Primer', in K. Mathis, and A. Tor (eds), *New Developments in Competition Behavioural Law and Economics*, Berlin: Springer, 2019, pp. 241–263.

Burri, M., 'Towards a New Treaty on Digital Trade' (2021), *Journal of World Trade* 55: 77–100.

Burri, M., 'Interfacing Privacy and Trade' (2021), *Case Western Journal of International Law* 53: 35–88.

Burri, M. and Cottier, T., 'Digital Technologies and International Economic Regulation: An Introduction', in M. Burri and T. Cottier (eds), *Trade Governance in the Digital Age*, Cambridge: Cambridge University Press, 2012, pp. 1–14.

Burri, M. and Polanco, R., 'Digital Trade Provisions in Preferential Trade Agreements: Introducing a New Dataset' (2020), *Journal of International Economic Law* 23: 1.

Burri, M. and Schär, R., 'The Reform of the EU Data Protection Framework: Outlining Key Changes and Assessing Their Fitness for a Data-Driven Economy' (2016), *Journal of Information Policy* 6: 479–511.

Chander, A., 'Facebookistan' (2012), *North Carolina Law Review* 90: 1807–1842.

Chander, A., 'How Law Made Silicon Valley' (2014), *Emory Law Journal* 63: 639–694.

Chander, A., 'National Data Governance in a Global Economy' (2016), *UC Davis Legal Studies Research Paper* 495.

Chander, A. and Lê, U. P., 'Data Nationalism' (2015), *Emory Law Journal* 64: 677–739.

Chesbrough, H. and Van Alstyne, M., 'Permissionless Innovation' (2015), *Communications of the ACM* 58: 24–26.

Cho, S. and Kelly, C. R., 'Are World Trading Rules Passé?' (2013), *Virginia Journal of International Law* 53: 623–666.

Cimino, C., Hufbauer, G. C. and Schott, J. J., 'A Proposed Code to Discipline Local Content Requirements' (2014), *Peterson Institute of International Economics Policy Brief* 4: 553–592.

Copenhagen Economics, *Expanding the Information Technology Agreement (ITA): Economic and Trade Impacts*, Final Report for the European Commission, 2010.

Cottier, T., 'The Impact of New Technologies on Multilateral Trade Regulation and Governance' (1996), *Chicago-Kent Law Review* 72: 415–436.

Drake, W. J., *Background Paper for the workshop on Data Localization and Barriers to Transborder Data Flows, 14–15 September 2016*, Geneva: World Economic Forum, 2016.

European Commission, 'A Digital Single Market Strategy for Europe', COM (2015) 192 final, 6 May 2015.

European Commission, 'Communication from the Commission to the European Parliament, the Council, the European Economic and Social Committee and the Committee of the Regions on the Mid-Term Review on the Implementation of the Digital Single Market Strategy A Connected Digital Single Market for All', COM(2017) 228 final, 10 May 2017.

European Union Agency for Network and Information Security (ENISA), *Privacy and Data Protection by Design – from Policy to Engineering*, Brussels, 2014.

Ezrachi, A. and Stucke, M. E., *Virtual Competition: The Promise and Perils of the Algorithm-driven Economy*, Cambridge, MA: Harvard University Press 2016.

Flew, Terry, *New Media: An Introduction*, 2nd ed., Oxford: Oxford University Press, 2014.

Gao, H., 'Googling for the Trade–Human Rights Nexus in China: Can the WTO Help?', in M. Burri and T. Cottier (eds), *Trade Governance in the Digital Age*, Cambridge: Cambridge University Press, 2012, pp. 247–275.

Gao, H., 'Digital or Trade? The Contrasting Approaches of China and US to Digital Trade' (2018), *Journal of International Economic Law* 21: 297–321.

Gasser, U., 'Perspectives on the Future of Digital Privacy' (2015), *Zeitschrift für Schweizerisches Recht* 135: 335–448.

Gasser, U., 'Recoding Privacy Law: Reflections on the Future Relationship Among Law, Technology, and Privacy' (2016), *Harvard Law Review* 130, 2: 61–70.

Gasser, U. and Palfrey, J., 'Fostering Innovation and Trade in the Global Information Society: The Different Facets and Roles of Interoperability', in M. Burri and T. Cottier (eds), *Trade Governance in the Digital Age*, Cambridge: Cambridge University Press, 2012, pp. 123–153.

Gervais, D., 'The Regulation of Inchoate Technologies' (2010), *Houston Law Review* 47: 665–705.

Grimmelmann, J., *Internet Law*, Oregon City, OR: Semaphore Press, 2016.

Flew, T., *New Media: An Introduction*, 2nd ed., Oxford: Oxford University Press, 2014.

Henke, Nicolaus et al., *The Age of Analytics: Competing in a Data-Driven World*, Washington, DC: McKinsey Global Institute, 2016.

Hestermeyer, H. P. and Nielsen, L., 'The Legality of Local Content Measures under WTO Law' (2014), *Journal of World Trade* 48: 553–592.

Kauffman Taskforce on Law, Innovation and Growth, *Rules for Growth: Promoting Innovation and Growth through Legal Reform*, Kansas City, MO: Kauffman Foundation, 2011.

Kommerskollegium, *No Transfer, No Production: Report on Cross-border Data Transfers, Global Value Chains, and the Production of Goods*, Stockholm: Swedish Board of Trade, 2015.

Kommerskollegium, *Trade Regulation in a 3D Printed World*, Stockholm: Swedish National Board of Trade, 2016.

Kuner, C., 'Regulation of Transborder Data Flows under Data Protection and Privacy Law: Past, Present and Future' (2011), *OECD Digital Economy Paper* 187.

Lobel, O., 'The Law of the Platform' (2016), *Minnesota Law Review* 101: 87–166.

Manyika, J., Chui, M., Brown, B., Bughin, J., Dobbs, R., Roxburgh, C. and Hung Byers, A., *Big Data: The Next Frontier for Innovation, Competition, and Productivity*, Washington, DC: McKinsey Global Institute, 2011.

Manyika, J., Henke, N., Bughin, J., Chui, M., Saleh, T., Wiseman, B. and Sethupathy, G., *The Age of Analytics: Competing in a Data-Driven World*, Washington, DC: McKinsey Global Institute, 2016.

Manyika, J., Lund, S., Bughin, J., Woetzel, J., Stamenov, K. and Dhingra, D., *Digital Globalization: The New Era of Global Flows*, Washington, DC: McKinsey Global Institute, 2016.

Mayer-Schönberger, V. and Cukier, K., *Big Data: A Revolution That Will Transform How We Live, Work, and Think*, New York: Eamon Dolan/ Houghton Mifflin Harcourt, 2013.

Meltzer, J. P., 'Maximizing the Opportunities of the Internet for International Trade', E15 Expert Group on the Digital Economy – Policy Options Paper, 2016.

Organization for Economic Co-Operation and Development (OECD), *Emerging Policy Issues: Localisation Barriers to Trade*, TAD/TC/WP(2014)17/FINAL, 2015.

Ruggie, J. G., 'International Responses to Technology: Concepts and Trends' (1975), *International Organization* 29: 557–583.

Schwartz, P. M., 'The EU–US Privacy Collision: A Turn to Institutions and Procedures' (2013), *Harvard Law Review* 126: 1966–2009.

Schwartz, P. M. and Solove, D. J., 'Reconciling Personal Information in the United States and European Union' (2014), *California Law Review* 102: 877–916.

Sen, N., 'Understanding the Role of the WTO in International Data Flows: Taking the Liberalization or the Regulatory Path' (2018), *Journal of International Economic Law* 21: 323–348.

Solove, D. J., 'A Taxonomy of Privacy' (2006), *University of Pennsylvania Law Review* 154: 477–560.

The Economist, 'The World's Most Valuable Resource Is No Longer Oil, but Data', print edition, 6 May 2017.

The White House, *Big Data: Seizing Opportunities, Preserving Values*, Washington, DC: Executive Office of the President, 2014.

Torrey, Z., 'TPP 2.0: The Deal Without the US: What's New about the CPTPP and What Do the Changes Mean?', The Diplomat, 3 February 2018, available at https://thediplomat.com/2018/02/tpp-2-0-the-deal-without-the-us/.

Tuthill, L. and Martin, R., 'GATS Classification Issues for Information and Communication Technology Services', in M. Burri and T. Cottier (eds), *Trade Governance in the Digital Age*, Cambridge: Cambridge University Press, 2012, pp. 157–178.

United States International Trade Commission (USITC), *Digital Trade in the US and Global Economies, Part 1*, Investigation No. 332–531, Washington, DC: USITC, 2013.

United States International Trade Commission (USITC), *Digital Trade in the US and Global Economies, Part 2*, Investigation No. 332–540, Washington, DC: USITC, 2014.

United States President's Advisory Council on Science and Technology, *Big Data and Privacy: A Technological Perspective*, Washington, DC, 2014.

van Oranje-Nassau, C., Cave, J., Van, M., Mandele, D., Schindler, R. and Hong, S. Y., *Responding to Convergence, Prepared for the Dutch Independent Telecommunications and Post Regulator*, Oxford: RAND Corporation, 2008.

Weber, R. H. and Burri, M., *Classification of Services in the Digital Economy*, Bern: Stämpfli, 2012.

World Trade Organization (WTO), *15 Years of the Information Technology Agreement: Trade, Innovation and Global Production Networks*, Geneva: World Trade Organization, 2012.

Wunsch-Vincent, S., 'The Digital Trade Agenda of the US: Parallel Tracks of Bilateral, Regional and Multilateral Liberalization' (2003), *Aussenwirtschaft* 1: 7–46.

Wunsch-Vincent, S. and Hold, A., 'Towards Coherent Rules for Digital Trade: Building on Efforts in Multilateral versus Preferential Trade Negotiations', in M. Burri and T. Cottier (eds), *Trade Governance in the Digital Age*, Cambridge: Cambridge University Press, 2012, pp. 179–221.

Zittrain, J. L., *The Future of the Internet – and How to Stop It*, New Haven: Yale University Press, 2008.

21

Trade in Knowledge and Cross-Border Data Flows: A Look at Emerging Digital Regulatory Issues

NIGEL CORY

Abstract

In contrast to the international trade issues around the movement of goods that defined 20th century globalization, trade in the 21st century is increasingly digital and knowledge-based, in large part, as digital technologies enable data-driven innovation, the ongoing disaggregation of production, and the increasing trade in services. Modern trade is more about the movement of bytes, ideas, information, and services, which are subject to a variety of non-tariff policies that affect digital and digitally enabled trade. However, the ever-growing gap between technological innovation and domestic and international policy frameworks shows that many policymakers are struggling to adapt rules and norms to today's digital economy, which detracts from the potential economic and social benefits of these technologies. In the years ahead, policymakers will face a key choice in deciding whether they want to be bold and adjust policies in order to embrace a truly global market for digitally enabled trade in goods and services.

Overview

Globalization in the twentieth century largely reflected the world that emerged from the Industrial Revolution. Trade was based on the movement of goods across borders, which was tangible, measurable, limited by physical infrastructure and heavily affected by trade policies such as tariffs.[1] But trade in the twenty-first century is increasingly digital and knowledge-based, in large part, as digital technologies enables data-driven innovation, the ongoing disaggregation of production and the

[1] Richard Baldwin, 'Globalization is close to its "holy cow" moment', *Chicago Booth Review*, April 30, 2018, available at http://review.chicagobooth.edu/economics/2018/article/globalization-close-its-holy-cow-moment.

increasing trade in services.[2] Modern trade is more about the movement of bytes, ideas and services, which are subject to a variety of non-tariff policies that affect digital and digitally-enabled trade. With roughly 3.6 billion people now connected to the Internet – over half the world's population – policies affecting data, digital platforms and services, and intellectual property are bound to play an integral role in shaping trade in the decades ahead.[3] This chapter analyses the digital nature of modern trade, a number of key policies that affect it, and the challenges facing policymakers as they deal with these issues in trying to support the ability of market participants to move data and digital content legally.

These digital trade policies are important as they help firms achieve economies of scale and network effects, which are critical to competing and succeeding in the global digital economy. In turn, these policies support broader economic competitiveness, innovation and productivity as they relate to the digital knowledge and information that is at the heart of value creation in the modern economy.[4] Knowledge – rather than labour, capital, or resource-intensive components – represents about one-half of current global trade flows; and this knowledge-intensive component is growing faster, at about 1.3 times the rate of labour-intensive flows.[5] It is a study in contrasts to put the rapidly growing size of global data flows alongside global merchandise trade, which has fallen from recent peaks in 2014.[6] Already, 22 per cent of global economic output can be attributed directly to digital commerce and it's expected

[2] Richard Baldwin, *The Great Convergence: Information Technology and the New Globalization*, Cambridge, MA: Harvard University Press, 2016.

[3] Mary Meeker, 'Internet Trends Report 2018' (Industry report, Kleiner Perkins, May 30, 2018), available at www.kleinerperkins.com/perspectives/internet-trends-report-2018.

[4] Daniel Castro and Alan McQuinn, 'Cross-Border Data Flows Enable Growth in All Industries' (Information Technology and Innovation Foundation, March 2015), available at www2.itif.org/2015-cross-border-data-flows.pdf.

[5] McKinsey Global Institute defines knowledge-intensive goods and services flows as those that have a high R&D component or utilize highly skilled labour. As such, they help transmit information, ideas or expertise among exchanging parties. James Manyika, Jacques Bughin, Susan Lund, Olivia Nottebohm, David Poulter, Sebastian Jauch, and Sree Ramaswamy, 'Global flows in a digital age: How trade, finance, people, and data connect the world economy' (McKinsey Global Institute, April, 2014), available at www.mckinsey.com/~/media/McKinsey/Featured%20Insights/Globalization/Global%20flows%20in%20a%20digital%20age/Global_flows_in_a_digital_age_Full_report%20March_2015.pdf.

[6] Victor Mulas, 'Value in Global Economy is Moving to Digital Business' (Washington, DC: World Bank. Slide 4 in the presentation on 'Startup Innovation Ecosystems as New Sources of Growth and Jobs'), www2.itif.org/2017-startup-ecosystems-mulas.pdf.

that the continued application of emerging digital technologies – such as cloud computing, data analytics, 3D printing and the Internet of Things (IoT) – will increase global GDP by another USD 2 trillion by 2020.[7]

Policymakers need to recognize that these trends are well under way and that domestic and international policy frameworks will need to adjust to maximize the social and economic benefits of digital technologies and global digital flows of knowledge. The challenge is to update intellectual property, trade, privacy and other public policy considerations for the digital era, but in such a way that still allows firms and individuals to maximize the benefits that come with data-driven innovation and commerce. The problem is that a growing number of countries are inadvertently – or intentionally, in the interests of protectionism – enacting policies that are unnecessary, burdensome and/or otherwise trade-distorting.

The chapter is broken into three sections that explore interrelated topics warranting careful analysis: first, the role of data flows generally and the impact of policies that act as barriers to its movement across borders; second, how the intersection of intellectual property rights, data flows and digitalization raises new challenges for copyright enforcement and protection of trade secrets; and finally how data flows and digital trade can be indirectly affected by policies that restrict the Internet-based platforms and services that are key agents in facilitating and managing data flows, services and digital intellectual property.

Cross-Border Data Flows

Up to the 1990s, globalization was mostly about goods crossing borders; now it also concerns know-how crossing borders, and this know-how is largely communicated through data flows.[8] That is because, while it may not always be visible, data have become integral to research and development processes and to the production and distribution of all manner of modern goods and services, whether they are purely digital, tied to a physical product or related to a professional service that requires in-person interaction. For example, e-commerce platforms such as Amazon

[7] Mark Knickrehm et al., 'Digital disruption: the growth multiplier' (Accenture Strategy report, January, 2016), available at www.accenture.com/_acnmedia/PDF-4/Accenture-Strategy-Digital-Disruption-Growth-Multiplier.pdf.

[8] Richard Baldwin, *The Great Convergence: Information Technology and the New Globalization*, Cambridge, MA: Harvard University Press, 2016.

and Alibaba were virtually non-existent 20 years ago, but now they facilitate approximately 12 per cent of the global trade in physical goods.[9] As more and more firms rely on digital platforms to engage with customers (wherever they are), data are increasingly shared and exchanged on an international basis.[10] Firms engaged in digital trade rely on data and data flows for a number of common business purposes, including monitoring production systems, managing global workforces, engaging and selling to customers, monitoring supply chains and providing real-time support for products in the field. For example, firms in virtually all industries use the highly sophisticated and automated tools involved in big data analytics to extract actionable insights from large datasets about customers, products and services in order to streamline business practices and increase efficiency.

Digital technologies have broadened the types of firms engaged in international trade by changing how firms engage in trade. Many tangible goods and services have been transformed into digital bytes, dramatically lowering the costs of accessing, producing and distributing them. For example, physical visits by people have been replaced by digital flows of email and messaging services, file-sharing services (such as DropBox), video-conferencing and collaborative work platforms (such as Slack). This 'second unbundling' of international trade (following the geographic separation of consumption and production of physical goods) has made services an increasingly important component of economic activity both as tradable 'products' in and of themselves, as well as in their role as intermediate goods in the network of production and trade in goods and services.[11] For small and medium-sized firms, these digital technologies have removed key barriers to international trade by dramatically lowering the cost and complexity of finding, accessing and

[9] Jacques Bughin and Susan Lund, 'The Ascendancy of International Data Flows', *VoxEU.org*, January 9, 2017, available at https://voxeu.org/article/ascendancy-international-data-flows.

[10] United Nations Conference on Trade and Development (UNCTAD), *Data Protection Regulations and International Data Flows: Implications for Trade and Development*, Geneva: UNCTAD, April, 2016, available at http://unctad.org/en/PublicationsLibrary/dtlstict2016d1_en.pdf.

[11] Richard Baldwin, 'Trade and Industrialisation after globalization's end unbundling: how building and joining a supply chain are different and why it matters' (National Bureau of Economic Research Working Paper 17716, December 2011), available at www.nber.org/papers/w17716.

delivering offerings to customers overseas.[12] These digital technologies also change how firms disaggregate and reallocate work tasks.[13] For example, multinational firms no longer have to pursue global trade through subsidiaries that largely replicated headquarter operations, as digital technologies allow companies to globalize in much leaner ways.

While the popular conception of data flows focuses on personal data, transaction information, search queries and social media posts, the reality is that data flows encompass a broader range of commercial exchanges and processes too.[14] A considerable amount of data flows are created as part of services between affiliates of the same firm, often relating to the supervision, control and organization of these affiliates. For example, the category of management services captures the data-intensive trade in services between related enterprises, whether from parent to subsidiary or vice versa.[15] The US Bureau of Economic Analysis provides insight into the underappreciated size of these intra-company data flows in its data tables on input-output use, which show sectors that produce and develop data as their main activity, who their key users are and how much they use these data-related services as a proportion of total

[12] For example, see: Asia Pacific MSME Trade Coalition (AMTC), 'Micro-Revolution: The New Stakeholders of trade in APAC' (AMTC, Singapore, February, 2018), available at https://static1.squarespace.com/static/5393d501e4b0643446abd228/t/5a83876b71c10b85cc1bd35d/1518569362142/MSME+Report-APAC.PDF.

[13] John Zysman and Martin Kenney, 'The Next Phase in the Digital Revolution: Intelligent Tools, Platforms, Growth, Employment', *Communications of the ACM* 61, no. 2 (2018): 54–63, available at https://cacm.acm.org/magazines/2018/2/224635-the-next-phase-in-the-digital-revolution/fulltext.

[14] Daniel Castro and Alan McQuinn, 'Cross-Border Data Flows Enable Growth in All Industries' (Information Technology and Innovation Foundation, March 2015), available at www2.itif.org/2015-cross-border-data-flows.pdf.

[15] This category includes services flowing from the parent to the affiliate enterprise company and vice versa and relates to the planning, organization and control of these enterprises. The World Bank's Trade in Services database classifies this as 'management services between related enterprises', which aligns with the US BEA's IO classification of 'management of companies and enterprises'. The *Manual on Statistics of International Trade in Services* 2010 states that trade in services transactions between related enterprises are recorded separately from unrelated enterprises. The category of trade in services between related enterprises therefore provides information on the value of services which are flowing between affiliated companies or enterprises in which a direct investment has taken place. It includes payments from the parent company to the affiliate establishment and vice versa. These payments hence relate to the general management costs of the related enterprises. Erik can der Marel, 'Disentangling the Flows of Data: Inside or Outside the Multinational Company?' (European Centre for International Political Economy, July, 2015), available at http://ecipe.org/app/uploads/2015/07/ECIPE-Data-Flows-final.pdf.

inputs.[16] These data show that many of the main data-producing sectors (e.g. software publishing, data processing, hosting and related services) are producing critical inputs for management purposes within companies – indeed, an estimated 13.1 per cent of total data inputs firms use supports enterprise management. This figure is surprising, as it is nearly equal to the data usage of data-service sectors themselves. Other business-support services that are essential to multinational firms are also identified as major data users: for example, data services account for an estimated 9.5 per cent of total inputs for administrative support, 6.9 per cent of the inputs for professional and business services and 5.4 per cent for financial and insurance services.[17] This shows that, whether directly or indirectly, data are one of the largest and most important inputs for modern business management. While firms in most other economies may not have the same level of access and use of technology as these firms in the United States, they are clearly heading in this same direction given the critical role of technology and data to modern competitiveness.

Barriers to Data Flows: Data Localization, Privacy and Cybersecurity

Data are central to the role the Internet and ICTs have played in boosting the gains from trade, including by increasing the marketplace for ideas and intellectual property. Just as a free trade agreement between countries increases the size of the market and boosts gains from trade, so the Internet leads to greater gains from the exchange of data, the ideas and goods/services embedded in them, and the innovations these support.[18] As policymakers consider the economic and societal value of data and

[16] These data provide detailed information on which sectors produce and develop data as their main activity, who are their key users and how much they use these data-related services (as a proportion of total inputs used). Of the former, a study shows that the main producers are software publishers, wired and wireless telecommunication carriers, data processing, hosting, and related services, Internet publishing and broadcasting and web search portals, custom computer programming services, computer systems design services, and other computer related services and that these sectors are also the most intensive users of data in production (as a percentage of total inputs). Erik can der Marel, 'Disentangling the Flows of Data: Inside or Outside the Multinational Company?' (European Centre for International Political Economy, July, 2015), available at http://ecipe.org/app/uploads/2015/07/ECIPE-Data-Flows-final.pdf.

[17] Erik can der Marel, 'Disentangling the Flows of Data: Inside or Outside the Multinational Company?' (European Centre for International Political Economy, July, 2015), available at http://ecipe.org/app/uploads/2015/07/ECIPE-Data-Flows-final.pdf.

[18] 'The web's new walls', *The Economist*, September 2, 2010, available at www.economist.com/node/16943579.

data flows, they should recognize that data will naturally flow across borders unless governments erect artificial barriers to stop it. While these cross-border data flows can raise legitimate public policy issues, such as data privacy and cybersecurity, policymakers need to carefully consider all of the available policy options to ensure they address data-related issues while still allowing data to flow freely.

Yet policymakers in a growing number of countries are instead enacting policies that create barriers to data flows. Despite the significant benefits to companies, consumers and national economies that arise from organizations being able to easily share data across borders, a growing number of countries are proposing or enacting barriers that make it more expensive and time-consuming, if not illegal, to transfer entire categories of data.[19] A recent Accenture report captured this trend and assessed the impact of what it calls 'digital fragmentation' (defined as the rise in restrictions on the free flow of data, information technology products, services and talent across country borders). It finds that 74 per cent of 402 chief information officers and chief technology officers surveyed expect to exit a geographic market, delay market-entry plans or abandon them altogether in the next three years as a result of increased barriers to globalization.[20]

The clearest example of a barrier to digital trade and knowledge transfers is data localization – whereby a country forces a firm to store its data within the country's borders. A growing number of countries are enacting data localization measures for accounting, tax and financial data; personal data; government and public data; data tied to emerging digital services; telecommunications data; and other data types.[21] At the heart of many of these data localization policies lies the reflexive, yet

[19] Nigel Cory, 'Cross-Border Data Flows: Where Are the Barriers, and What Do They Cost?' (Information Technology and Innovation Foundation, May, 2017), available at https://itif.org/publications/2017/05/01/cross-border-data-flows-where-are-barriers-and-what-do-they-cost.

[20] Accenture defines digital fragmentation as the rise in restrictions on the free flow of data, information technology products, services and talent across country borders. Accenture, '"Digital Fragmentation" Poses Threat to Businesses' Global Growth and Innovation According to Accenture Report', press release, 14 March 2018, available at https://newsroom.accenture.com/news/digital-fragmentation-poses-threat-to-businesses-global-growth-and-innovation-according-to-accenture-report.htm.

[21] Nigel Cory, 'Cross-Border Data Flows: Where Are the Barriers, and What Do They Cost?' (Information Technology and Innovation Foundation, May, 2017), available at https://itif.org/publications/2017/05/01/cross-border-data-flows-where-are-barriers-and-what-do-they-cost.

mistaken, belief among some policymakers that data are more private and secure when stored within a country's borders. In most instances, though, data localization mandates do not increase data security or commercial privacy.[22] The location of data can affect how organizations respond to lawful government requests for data. But controlling where organizations store data does not impact how organizations collect and use data (i.e. their privacy practices) or how they store and transmit data (i.e. their security practices). For example, as it relates to cybersecurity issues, such as data breaches, these can happen no matter where data are stored – data centres everywhere are exposed to similar risks. Such inadvertent disclosures are the result of security failures. A secure server in Colombia is no different from a secure server in Malaysia. Data security depends on the technical, physical and administrative controls implemented by service providers, which can be strong or weak, regardless of where data are stored.

This trend towards forced data localization has broad economic implications, because maximizing the value of data requires data to move freely. It undermines firm productivity and competitiveness, and ultimately an economy's productivity, by forcing firms to spend more than necessary on IT services. It also stops them from importing and analysing data from foreign countries (such as for trade in services provided remotely), which also impacts data-driven innovation. Data localization also threatens the role data play in modern research and development activities and potentially prevents companies from accessing the most-innovative services (as data-localization policies may keep innovative providers out of local markets).

Intellectual Property and the Digital Economy

In today's increasingly digital economy, intellectual property protection and enforcement are a critical part of the legal framework that needs to be in place in order to facilitate trade in knowledge-based goods and services. However, the territorial nature of intellectual property protections poses a major challenge, as intellectual property rights – patents, trademarks, trade secrets, industrial designs and copyrights – are only protected under domestic law in those countries where there are relevant laws, where

[22] Daniel Castro, 'The False Promise of Data Nationalism' (Information Technology and Innovation Foundation, December 2013), available at www2.itif.org/2013-false-promise-data-nationalism.pdf.

relevant material has been registered and where there is effective enforcement. While this has always been the case in intellectual property law, the global interconnected nature of the Internet brings this into stark relief for firms wanting to trade in intellectual property-protected material in multiple jurisdictions as protection and enforcement can vary significantly.

From a conceptual standpoint, intellectual property and digitally-enabled trade are closely interrelated in many respects, as for many modern goods and services, the latter won't take place without the former. An e-book, journal article, video, piece of source code or other digital product cannot be recognized and traded without intellectual property protections and enforcement. Likewise, e-commerce, more than other business systems, often involves selling goods and services (such as software, designs, training modules and other intangible but valuable content) that are based on intellectual property and its licensing which, if stolen or pirated, can destroy a business.[23] In reality, weak or non-existent intellectual property protection and enforcement represents a modern barrier to trade. For example, a US International Trade Commission survey shows that 75 per cent of large firms and 50 per cent of small to medium-sized enterprises (SMEs) in digital trade view intellectual property infringement as an obstacle to trade, with this being felt most keenly by content creators, large retail firms and SMEs in the digital communications sector.[24] Furthermore, a nation's benign or intentional lack of action on intellectual property potentially turns them into export platforms for piracy and cybertheft. For leading firms and economies that increasingly rely on intangible assets for a competitive advantage, this type of barrier matters because the knowledge and creativity required to create the goods and services exchanged in the twenty-first century – from smartphones, to biopharmaceutical drugs, to movies and music – are difficult to develop, but often very easy to steal or purchase for less than full-market value. But without fair payment, national and global innovation, and creativity output and trade, decreases.

Dealing with this modern trade issue is proving difficult as many policymakers are wedded to a traditional view that trade (only) involves

[23] 'Understanding How Intellectual Property (IP) Relates to E-Commerce', World Intellectual Property Organization website, accessed August 6, 2018, available at www.wipo.int/sme/en.

[24] United States International Trade Commission (USITC), *Digital Trade in the US and Global Economies, Part 1*, Washington, DC: USITC, 2013, available at www.usitc.gov/publications/332/pub4415.pdf.

manufactured goods facing tariffs when crossing borders. Given this traditional focus on the tangible, this outdated view is also often associated with the view that intellectual property is unrelated to trade, as it is supposedly a 'behind-the- border' issue where countries should have the freedom to affect policy however they want. As outlined, this narrow definition of trade refuses to acknowledge that what goes on 'behind the border' is central to shaping trade in the twenty-first century. In the modern digital economy, it does not make sense to suggest that reducing a tariff on a widget is legitimate in a trade agreement but that reducing the ability of a country (and its firms/citizens) to block, disrupt or steal another nation's goods and services – whether this involves policies which target data flows or online intellectual property enforcement – is not legitimate.

This has contributed to varying levels of intellectual property protection and enforcement around the world, as technological innovation has far outpaced the international framework of intellectual property and trade rules that govern digital issues, which remains largely predicated on rules and norms established in the 1990s when the Internet as we know it barely existed. The Agreement on Trade-Related Aspects of Intellectual Property Rights (TRIPS), which had been mostly negotiated by 1991[25] and came into force in 1995, set a minimum standard of protection and enforcement, but in its implementation at the domestic level varies in degree and effectiveness, especially as it relates to digital issues.[26] It is essentially an analogue-era treaty, in that a background consideration in the negotiation of TRIPS was that intellectual property was essentially treated as value added embedded in physical goods.[27] In 1996, the World Intellectual Property Organization (WIPO) Copyright Treaty and the WIPO Performances and Phonograms Treaty (known together as the Internet Treaties) were adopted, establishing international norms aimed

[25] See the accounts of the negotiations in Watal and Taubman (eds), *The Making of the TRIPS Agreement*, Geneva: WTO, 2015.

[26] It's essentially an analogue-era treaty, in that a central feature of TRIPS was that IP was embedded in physical goods. Antony Taubman, 'TRIPS Encounters the Internet: An Analogue Treaty in a Digital Age, or the First Trade 2.0 Agreement?' (July 1, 2012). Burri and Cottier (eds), *Trade Governance in the Digital Age*, Cambridge 2012, available at https://ssrn.com/abstract=2713086.

[27] Antony Taubman, 'TRIPS Encounters the Internet: An Analogue Treaty in a Digital Age, or the First Trade 2.0 Agreement?' (July 1, 2012). Burri and Cottier (eds), *Trade Governance in the Digital Age*, Cambridge 2012, available at https://ssrn.com/abstract=2713086.

at preventing unauthorized access to and use of creative works on the Internet or other digital networks.

Since then, there has not been a substantive debate at the multilateral level about how to update these agreements for the digital age, but there has been progress at the domestic level as countries pursue new intellectual property rules as part of domestic policymaking processes and at the bilateral and regional level as part of trade agreements. A few priority intellectual property issues have emerged in this gap between policy laggards and leaders, including non-existent or ineffective trade secret and source code protections and online piracy and counterfeiting due to non-existent or ineffective online intellectual property enforcement, both of which are discussed subsequently. In enacting stronger intellectual property protection, those countries that are policy leaders on this issue effectively remove impediments to the production, dissemination and sale of knowledge, including the sharing and sale of knowledge across borders via the Internet. From the perspective of a policymaker that has transitioned to a modern view of digital trade, these changes should be viewed as analogous to countries' reductions in tariffs that impede cross-border trade in goods.[28]

Enforcing Copyright Online through Website Blocking

While technology opens markets for international platforms and digital trade in legal, copyright-protected material, it likewise allows rapid and nearly cost-free duplication and global distribution of pirated content in countries with weak or non-existent intellectual property protections or enforcement. Measuring piracy – an illicit and therefore hard-to-track activity – is difficult. Yet, available evidence suggests that online copyright infringement remains prevalent, driven by the free and simple availability of illegal digital content. A NetNames report, 'Sizing the Piracy Universe', demonstrated that the number of users regularly accessing illegal copies of media content (such as songs and movies) and the amount of bandwidth consumed by infringing uses of content significantly increased between 2010 and 2013. This finding held true even in regions where there were

[28] Willian Zeile, *Research Spotlight Multinational Enterprises and International Technology Transfer*, Washington, DC: United States Department of Commerce, Bureau of Economic Analysis, September, 2014, available at https://apps.bea.gov/scb/pdf/2014/09%20September/0914_multinational_enterprises_and_technology_transfer.pdf.

growing numbers of legitimate distribution services for online content.[29] Piracy remains prevalent, in part, as it is a multibillion-dollar international business, relying on advertising, or to a lesser degree, paid subscriptions.

Piracy remains prevalent around the world despite the fact that many countries have signed international intellectual property treaties (as virtually every nation that acts as a haven for pirate sites is a member of the WTO and has thus agreed to TRIPS). Yet, for whatever reason, many countries have failed to implement and enforce these rules. The problem is that, given the Internet, countries that choose not to prioritize online copyright enforcement create a safe haven for those involved in piracy. This lack of effective online copyright laws and enforcement undermines legitimate trade in knowledge because commercial material must compete against free copies, which is untenable. This has led to a growing number of countries with stronger intellectual property protection working with Internet service providers (ISPs) in their countries to block websites (i.e. the ISP maintains a central list of websites that prevents its users from accessing blocked websites) that traffic in illegal content. This policy has proven to be an effective legal instrument to support legal digital economic activity in their domestic markets.

Improving copyright enforcement online through the blocking of websites engaged in disseminating large amounts of pirated material is emerging as one of the most useful tools to address digital piracy, yet it is also among the most contentious options. It touches upon a deep-seated ideological opposition in some parts of society about the role of government on the Internet (which is based on views commonly held by those involved in the Internet's early era). These people and advocacy organizations often oppose the application of rules that exist in the offline world to the online one, including for intellectual property (as explained below). Policymakers need to be aware of the potential for this ideological opposition to emerge, and, where necessary, respond by putting in place relevant checks and balances to account for other public interests. A growing number of countries recognize that legitimate concerns can be addressed alongside the central economic motivator that no copyright can be applied without efficient and effective enforcement.

Australia, Italy, the United Kingdom and 39 other countries currently utilize website blocking as a policy tool to reduce piracy and encourage

[29] David Price, 'Sizing the Piracy Universe' (industry report, Netnames, London, September 2013), available at https://illusionofmore.com/wp-content/uploads/2013/09/NetNames-Sizing_Piracy_Universe-Report-2.5.pdf.

consumption of legal content.[30] To be sure, website blocking is no silver bullet in the fight against digital piracy, but it should at least be one of the lead bullets, alongside other measures, such as policies that encourage the development of providers of legal media content online. This is evident in a 2016 study by Carnegie Mellon University that analysed consumer-level data over a few months (both pre-block and post-block) to look at how blocking 53 large-scale piracy websites in the United Kingdom affected consumer behaviour in terms of their consumption of illegal and legal content. The results found that the website blocking resulted in a 90 per cent decline in user visits to pirating sites, a 10 per cent increase in visits to legal ad-supported sites, and a 6 per cent increase in visits to subscription-based sites.[31] While there may be ways for users and piracy site operators to circumvent website blocking (e.g. through the use of a virtual private network), it is important to remember that the aim of website blocking is not to eliminate online piracy altogether, but to change consumers' behaviour by raising the cost – in terms of time and willingness to find alternatives sites or circumvention tools – to make the legal sources of content more appealing.[32] This study showed that website blocking can achieve this as most users are not willing or able to use tools to circumvent website blocks, and – if the website blocking covers a sufficient number of major piracy websites – search for alternative piracy websites.

Despite the growing use of and evidence about website blocking's effectiveness, and the fact that website blocking has been used by a growing number of countries without harming the free and open working of the Internet, misperceptions persist about website blocking. For example, some advocates contend that such policy tools should not apply to the Internet because they will be ineffective (addressed above),

[30] Motion Picture Association – Canada, 'Before the Canadian Radio-Television and Telecommunications Commission, in the matter of an application pursuant to Sections 24, 24.1, and 70(1)(a) of the Telecommunications Act, 1993 to disable on-line access to piracy sites' (industry submission, 29 March 2018), available at https://torrentfreak.com/images/mpa-can.pdf.

[31] Brett Danaher et al., 'Website Blocking Revisited: The Effect of the UK November 2014 Blocks on Consumer Behavior' (paper, Carnegie Mellon University, Pittsburg, 18 April 2016), available at http://ssrn.com/abstract=2766795.

[32] The study found that relatively few users circumvented the website blocks. While the study estimates that access to virtual private network sites increased by 30 per cent after the blocks, this was off a relatively small base. For example, users in the study made 86,735 visits to the piracy sites before they were blocked, but only 1,688 to VPN sites.

that website blocking is a form of censorship or that website blocking will be abused by content right holders.[33]

As mentioned earlier, many of these objections are based on a very skewed view of the Internet, one that does not recognize a role for government in extending laws that exist in the offline world to the online one. As it relates to this issue, the point needs to be made that website blocking is not antithetical to a free and open Internet. For example, even the most vocal proponents of Internet freedom recognize that it is legitimate to remove or to limit access to some materials online, such as child pornography. The International Criminal Police Organization's (INTERPOL) 190 members voted unanimously to promote the use of all technical tools, including website blocking, to fight child pornography, which many countries do, and this has not fundamentally altered the Internet. Similarly, countries use website blocking as part of efforts to address access to sites involved in malware, investment fraud, online gambling and terrorism.[34] Likewise, there is a clear public interest in curbing piracy as well.

Similarly, in the debate about protecting a free and open Internet, other opponents of website blocking fail to acknowledge that supporting the free flow of data does not have to mean support for the free flow of all data, regardless of its legal status. Some make the argument (in relation to a case involving the blocking of data flows related to patent-infringing material) that 'blocking data transmissions based on their content cuts against the general principles of the openness of the Internet, which has been a foundation of its success'.[35] Just as it is not a violation of free trade principles to block trade in banned products, such as elephant ivory or rhinoceros products, it is also not a violation of free trade principles to oppose digital trade in illegal digital goods, such as child pornography, email spam, Internet malware and pirated digital content.

[33] 'Content Blocking', Electronic Frontier Foundation website, accessed August 6, 2018, available at www.eff.org/issues/content-blocking; Adam Clark Estes, 'The Web Collectively Protests Congress's Censorship Law', *The Atlantic*, 16 November 2011, available at www.theatlantic.com/technology/archive/2011/11/web-collectively-protests-congresss-censorship-law/335366/.

[34] See a summary in: Nigel Cory, 'How Website Blocking Is Curbing Digital Piracy Without "Breaking the Internet"' (The Information Technology and Innovation Foundation, August, 2016), available at www2.itif.org/2016-website-blocking.pdf.

[35] Brent Kendall, 'Imports of Digital Goods Face Test', *Wall Street Journal*, 2 August 2015, available at www.wsj.com/articles/imports-of-digital-goods-face-test-1438554684.

As it relates to concerns over other interests and legal rights, some governments do cast too wide a net in the fight against illegal content on the Internet – for example, taking down or limiting access to content that is not misappropriated (from a copyright perspective), but simply upsetting to those in power. It is disingenuous of some opponents of digital intellectual property enforcement to equate the blocking of websites for piracy purposes with doing so for social or political purposes. The key issue about Internet freedom is not whether the Internet should be completely free or whether governments should have unlimited censorship authority, but rather when, where and how the appropriate lines should be drawn. What this shows is that policymakers need to put in place checks and balances, as is commonly the case with law-making, for website blocking. The fact that website blocking is used in so many countries where these checks and balances for other interests and legal rights exists (such as Australia and the United Kingdom) shows that countries can put in place an administrative or legal framework that includes appropriate language that ensures the website blocking regime is reasonable and proportionate (ensuring that alternative legal options have been considered), only targets those websites involved in large-scale copyright infringement (not accidental or minor instances or involving other interests, such as freedom of expression) and that there is a legal redress mechanism for respondents to challenge website blocking orders.

The Growing Cybertheft of Trade Secrets

A trade secret is confidential, commercially valuable information that provides a company with a competitive advantage, such as designs, codes, prototypes, methods of production, marketing strategies or chemical formulae. Trade secrets are fundamental building blocks that drive investment, innovation and economic growth. Recent empirical research points towards a positive relationship between the stringency of trade secret protection and economic indicators such as innovation, investment and trade.[36] Trade secrets are a particularly important form of

[36] Douglas Lippoldt and Mark Schultz, 'Uncovering Trade Secrets – An Empirical Assessment of Economic Implications of Protection for Undisclosed Data' (ParisL: Organisation for Economic Cooperation and Development (OECD) Trade Policy Papers, No. 167, 2014, OECD Publishing), available at http://dx.doi.org/10.1787/5jxzl5w3j3s6-en.

intellectual property for SMEs.[37] Whether a country has a legal framework that explicitly protects trade secrets clearly affects development, transfer and trade in knowledge.

The growing threat to trade secrets involves other businesses or nation states hiring hackers to remotely access a firm's computer systems to steal its most sensitive intellectual property and use it for their own advantage.[38] Modern technologies have created more ways to steal trade secrets that can be easily scanned, copied, downloaded or exfiltrated. Given that intellectual property can provide the majority of a company's value, cyber professionals call such breaches 'extinction-level events'.[39] Stealing intellectual property is a crime that is damaging to organizations and economies. Yet some countries and firms persist in stealing trade secrets because it's less expensive in time and resources than conducting their own research and development. For example, in the renewable energy sector, a Chinese firm bribed an official at their main American competitor to hand over the firm's source code for its wind turbine control software.[40] But intellectual property theft cuts into legitimate revenue for those who make or purchase licences for goods and services, which undermines the incentive for entrepreneurs to innovate, which slows the development of new inventions.[41]

[37] Marco Alexandre Saias, 'Unlawful Acquisition of Trade Secrets by Cyber Theft: Between the Proposed Directive on Trade Secrets and the Directive on Cyber Attacks', *Journal of Intellectual Property Law & Practice*, Volume 9, Issue 9, 1 September 2014, Pages 721–729, available at https://doi-org.ezproxylocal.library.nova.edu/10.1093/jiplp/jpu117; Katherine Linton, 'The Importance of Trade Secrets: New Directions in International Trade Policy Making and Empirical Research', *Journal of International Commerce and Economics*, 2 September 2016, available at https://ssrn.com/abstract=2893319.

[38] See Stephen Ezell, 'ITIF Filing to USTR on Section 301 Investigation of China's Policies and Practices Related to Tech Transfer, IP, and Innovation' (Information Technology and Innovation Foundation, 25 October 2017), available at https://itif.org/publications/2017/10/25/itif-filing-ustr-section-301-investigation-chinas-policies-and-practices; Jeff Ferry, 'Top Ten Cases of Chinese IP Theft', Coalition for a Prosperous America website, available at www.prosperousamerica.org/top_ten_cases_of_chinese_ip_theft.

[39] PWC, 'Adjusting the Lens on Economic Crime' (Industry report, PWC, Global Economic Crime Survey 2016), available at www.pwc.com/gx/en/economic-crime-survey/pdf/GlobalEconomicCrimeSurvey2016.pdf.

[40] Clare Sebastian, 'Chinese Trade Secret Theft Nearly Killed My Company', *CNNtech*, 23 March 2018, available at https://money.cnn.com/2018/03/23/technology/business/american-semiconductor-china-trade/index.html.

[41] IP Commission, 'The Report of the Commission on the Theft of American Intellectual Property', The National Bureau of Asian Research, May, 2013, available at www.ipcommission.org/report/ip_commission_report_052213.pdf.

Unfortunately, cyber-based trade secret theft is on the rise, with one in five companies in the European Union suffering at least one attempted theft of trade secrets in the past 10 years.[42] While the economic impact of trade secret theft is also hard to quantify, PricewaterhouseCoopers and the Center for Responsible Enterprise and Trade have estimated that it equals from 1 to 3 per cent of GDP in the United States and other advanced industrial economies.[43]

As the US National Counterintelligence and Security Center stated in its '2018 Foreign Economic Espionage in Cyberspace' report:

> China has expansive efforts in place to acquire U.S. technology to include sensitive trade secrets and proprietary information. It continues to use cyber espionage to support its strategic development goals—science and technology advancement, military modernization, and economic policy objectives. China's cyberspace operations are part of a complex, multi-pronged technology development strategy that uses licit and illicit methods to achieve its goals.[44]

The United States and Europe are the two most notable examples pointing towards best practices in trade secret protection and related activities. In 2016, the United States enacted the Defend Trade Secrets Act (DTSA), which created a new, private federal civil action for 'an owner of a trade secret that is misappropriated . . . if the trade secret is related to a product or service used in, or intended for use in, interstate or foreign commerce'.[45] DTSA provides a clear route for trade secret owners to pursue an action in federal court for trade secret misappropriation, whereas previously, firms had to largely rely on a patchwork of state laws. Similarly, the European Union released a directive in June 2016 to improve and harmonize trade secret protections across its member

[42] 'Study on Trade Secrets and Confidential Business Information in the Internal Market' (report prepared for the European Commission, April, 2013), available at https://ec.europa.eu/docsroom/documents/14838/attachments/1/translations/en/renditions/pdf.

[43] The Center for Responsible Enterprise And Trade (CREATe.org), 'Economic Impact of Trade Secret Theft: A framework for companies to safeguard trade secrets and mitigate potential threats' (Washington, DC: The Center for Responsible Enterprise And Trade (CREATe.org), February, 2014), available at www.innovation-asset.com/hubfs/blog-files/CREATe.org-PwC-Trade-Secret-Theft-FINAL-Feb-2014_01.pdf.

[44] Office of the Director of National Intelligence, *NCSC Releases 2018 Foreign Economic Espionage in Cyberspace Report*, Washington, DC: US National Counterintelligence and Security Center, 26 July 2018, available at www.dni.gov/files/NCSC/documents/news/20180724-ncsc-press-release-foreign-econ-esp-cyber.pdf.

[45] *Defend Trade Secrets Act of 2016*, 114th Congress, available at www.congress.gov/bill/114th-congress/senate-bill/1890/text.

countries.[46] Importantly, both the United States and European Union have enacted complementary legal changes that relate to the cyber-component of trade secret theft by enacting laws that make it a crime to access a computer without authorization or for a user to exceed their authorized access.[47]

But the problem is the growing policy gulf in terms of trade secret protection around the world.[48] A recent Organisation for Economic Cooperation and Development (OECD) report ranking trade secret protection in 37 countries shows the substantial gap between leaders in trade secret best practices (the United States, Canada, Lithuania, Japan and Spain) and the many laggards (including India, China, Indonesia, Russia and the Philippines).[49] In part, this is similar to other digital intellectual property issues, as TRIPS (the relevant multilateral agreement for trade secrets) does not set forth a detailed regime for protection and enforcement and it has not been updated since it came into force.[50] Again, similar to copyright online, bad actors (whether individuals, firms or nation states) can exploit weak protection and enforcement regimes in laggard countries to remotely launch operations to steal trade secrets, thus undermining international innovation and trade.[51] As knowledge

[46] 'Trade Secrets', European Commission website, accessed August 7, 2018, available at http://ec.europa.eu/growth/industry/intellectual-property/trade-secrets_en.

[47] 'Directive 2013/40/EU of the European Parliament and of the Council of 12 August 2013 on attacks against information systems and replacing Council Framework Decision 2005/222/JHA)', Office Journal of the European Union website, accessed August 7, 2018, available at http://eur-lex.europa.eu/LexUriServ/LexUriServ.do?uri=OJ:L:2013:218:0008:0014:EN:PDF.

[48] Douglas Lippoldt and Mark Schultz, *Approaches to the Protection of Trade Secrets*, Paris: Organisation for Economic Cooperation and Development, chapter in the report on 'Enquiring into Intellectual Property's Economic Impact', 2015, available at www.oecd.org/sti/ieconomy/Chapter3-KBC2-IP.pdf.

[49] Douglas Lippoldt and Mark Schultz, 'Uncovering Trade Secrets – An Empirical Assessment of Economic Implications of Protection for Undisclosed Data' (OECD Trade Policy Papers, No. 167, 2014, OECD Publishing), available at http://dx.doi.org/10.1787/5jxzl5w3j3s6-en.

[50] While Article 39(2) of TRIPS does not explicitly refer to trade secrets, it does refer to the 'protection of undisclosed information' in order to 'ensure effective protection against unfair competition'. Douglas Lippoldt and Mark Schultz, *Approaches to the Protection of Trade Secrets*, Paris: Organisation for Economic Cooperation and Development, chapter in the report on 'Enquiring into Intellectual Property's Economic Impact', available at www.oecd.org/sti/ieconomy/Chapter3-KBC2-IP.pdf.

[51] Kurt Calia et al., 'Economic Espionage and Trade Secret Theft: An Overview of the Legal Landscape and Policy Responses' (industry paper from Covington and Burling and the George Washington University Cybersecurity Initiative, September 2013), available at https://cchs.gwu.edu/sites/g/files/zaxdzs2371/f/downloads/Covington_SpecialIssueBrief.pdf.

becomes increasingly digital and more central to a firm's competitive advantage, and as supply chains and operations expand globally, this varied level of protection and enforcement only makes a firm's ability to use and protect its trade secrets that much harder.[52]

Regulatory Barriers to Trade on Internet Platforms and Internet-Based Services

Internet-based market platforms and intermediary services are key players and agents in global trade. Platforms aggregate supply and demand for buyers and sellers, whether this is for digitally copyrighted material, such as Apple's app store and Spotify, or e-commerce goods, such as Amazon, Flipkart and Mercado Libre. Firms and individuals can use these platforms and digital services as intermediary services and as final consumer goods, such as services for communications (e.g. Skype, Viber), finance (e.g. online point of sale credit), advertising (e.g. social networks and Google ads) and logistics (e.g. express delivery services). In essence, these platforms and services have changed how businesses use a range of services as a part of production and how consumers access and consume media and communicate. In broadcasting, so-called 'over-the-top' (OTT) service providers (such as Netflix, Hulu and HBO Go) deliver audio, video and other media over the Internet instead of being packaged with cable TV subscriptions. For messaging, OTT service providers (such as WhatsApp, WeChat, Skype and Facebook) provide instant-messaging services as an alternative to text-messaging services provided by traditional mobile telephone and data network operators.

The problem is that a growing number of countries are enacting discriminatory and restrictive regulations that affect the role that these platforms and services play in global digital trade. The cross-cutting nature of many of these digital services makes them susceptible to a range of behind-the-border barriers to trade, which can be enacted either in bad faith (for protectionist purposes) or inadvertently (due to poorly considered policymaking) as part of broader policy reviews, involving not only intellectual property, but also taxation, content moderation, general business licensing and registration, financial prudential oversight, law

[52] Kurt Calia et al., 'Economic Espionage and Trade Secret Theft: An Overview of the Legal Landscape and Policy Responses' (industry paper from Covington and Burling and the George Washington University Cybersecurity Initiative, September 2013), available at https://cchs.gwu.edu/sites/g/files/zaxdzs2371/f/downloads/Covington_SpecialIssueBrief.pdf.

enforcement and national security issues, and other issues. While these issues certainly can involve legitimate public policy concerns, such as how to address the dissemination of false information and how to ensure tax arrangements work in today's digital economy, many countries use these review processes as cover for trade protectionism, such as in Indonesia, Thailand and Vietnam.[53] The lack of internationally consistent terminology about how to define these platforms and digital services provides additional room for countries to apply laws and regulations in an unnecessarily restrictive and discriminatory fashion. While these trade-distorting policies vary by country and sector, the protectionist intent is usually evident when the resulting policy is vague, overly broad, involves little or no feedback from stakeholders and includes undue discretion for regulators.

Examples of these types of restrictions (many of which are used simultaneously) include:

- application of legacy regulatory frameworks for traditional broadcasting and telecommunication services to digital services
- excessive, opaque, and discriminatory licensing or registration requirements
- mandatory use of key local services (i.e. certain processes can only be performed by local firms, such as for payments)
- local (physical) office and staff (e.g. as a requirement for taxation purposes)
- local technology transfers
- forced local ownership of foreign firms
- local content requirement (for intangible products, such as videos and movies)
- local data storage, and
- forced contributions to funds for local content development (e.g. films).

Case Study: Local Content Requirements for Digital Goods and Services

While local content requirements have traditionally applied to films and TV shows, as more people consume content online, more countries

[53] Nigel Cory, 'Testimony Before the United States International Trade Commission on Global Digital Trade' (The Information Technology and Innovation Foundation, March 29, 2018), available at https://itif.org/publications/2018/03/29/testimony-united-states-international-trade-commission-global-digital-trade.

(Australia, Brazil and others) are considering extending these to digital video services.[54] For example, the European Union's (EU) 2007 Audiovisual Media Services Directive expanded the scope of previous directives requiring preferences for European content to also reach on-demand or streaming video services. Different EU members take different approaches – Austria, the Czech Republic, Spain and Italy require on-demand services to maintain a quota of European works in their on-demand libraries, while Wallonia (in Belgium), the Czech Republic, Italy and Spain require on-demand services to contribute to the financing of European audiovisual works.[55] Brazil has also proposed a range of restrictive measures on over-the-top services that distribute videos over the Internet, including that companies make an annual investment in local production (up to 4 per cent of revenue), and that companies include a minimum of local content. Such local content requirements disadvantage foreign platforms and advantage local platforms (which may have no intention of ever expanding internationally).

Case Study: Using Traditional Broadcasting and Telecommunications Rules to Disadvantage Digital Rivals

Many countries are applying traditional (and often poorly suited) broadcast and telecommunication regulations to target Internet-based services, often at the behest of incumbent telecommunication service and broadcast or cable television providers struggling to compete against digital competitors, who are often foreign firms. These local incumbents often call for governments to 'level the playing field' in terms of rules and regulations with Internet-based firms, even when the digital nature of these services means that they shouldn't be subject to traditional regulatory policy frameworks. For example, Vietnam's new draft cybersecurity law requires foreign enterprises providing telecommunication or Internet services to obtain business licences, establish local offices and locate Vietnamese personal data in Vietnam. Likewise, Indonesia is enacting

[54] See examples from Australia, Brazil, Canada, China, the EU (France, Italy, Poland, Spain), the Republic of Korea, Malaysia, Sri Lanka and Venezuela, among others. United States Trade Representative (USTR), *2013 National Trade Estimate Report*, Washington, DC: USTR, 2013.

[55] United States International Trade Commission (USITC), *Digital Trade in the US and Global Economies, Part 1*, Washington, DC: USITC, July, 2013, available at www.usitc.gov/publications/332/pub4415.pdf.

policies to force foreign firms to set up a permanent physical presence in Indonesia, including a local office and employees, as a condition of market entry and to comply with new tax requirements for digital firms. The regulation also effectively tries to install the Indonesian government as a gatekeeper of the Internet by including the requirement that foreign OTT firms apply for a licence to offer services in Indonesia. These sweeping, prescriptive and potentially discriminatory policy proposals contrast with the fact that OTT services have not typically required a licence or needed to pay any operating frees to operate in most markets.[56]

Conclusion

Data and digital technologies have transformed how organizations trade, especially in knowledge-intensive goods and services, yet many policy-makers are struggling to adopt domestic and international rules and norms. This is evident in the ever-growing gap between technological innovation and domestic/international policy frameworks, which allows countries to enact policies that detract from the potential economic and social benefits of these technologies. Within this, the growing importance of knowledge-based products and services for trade and economic growth means that intellectual property will remain crucial to supporting innovation. In the years ahead, policymakers will face a key choice in deciding whether they want to be bold and adjust policies in order to embrace a truly global market for digitally-enabled trade in goods and services, akin to the critical steps taken in the mid-twentieth century to create a global market for goods. This will require a new vision, bold leadership and a willingness to push back on the emerging threat of digital protectionism.

Bibliography

Accenture, '"Digital Fragmentation Poses Threat to Businesses" Global Growth and Innovation According to Accenture Report', press release 2018, available at https://newsroom.accenture.com/news/digital-fragmentation-poses-threat-to-businesses-global-growth-and-innovation-according-to-accenture-report.htm.

[56] Saku Rayuki et al., 'Indonesia and Thailand Target OTT Services', *Lexology*, 5 February 2018.

Asia Pacific MSME Trade Coalition (AMTC), 'Micro-Revolution: The New Stakeholders of trade in APAC', AMTC, Singapore, February 2018, available at www.asiantradecentre.org/talkingtrade//capturing-the-digital-opportunities-for-msmes.

Baldwin, Richard, 'Trade and Industrialisation after Globalization's End Unbundling: How Building and Joining a Supply Chain are Different and Why It Matters', National Bureau of Economic Research Working Paper No. 17716, December 2011, available at www.nber.org/papers/w17716.

Baldwin, Richard, *The Great Convergence: Information Technology and the New Globalization*, Cambridge, MA: Harvard University Press, 2016.

Baldwin, Richard, 'Globalization is Close to its "Holy Cow" Moment', *Chicago Booth Review*, 30 April 2018, available at http://review.chicagobooth.edu/economics/2018/article/globalization-close-its-holy-cow-moment.

Bughin, Jacques and Lund, Susan, 'The Ascendancy of International Data Flows', *VoxEU.org*, 9 January 2017, available at https://voxeu.org/article/ascendancy-international-data-flows.

Calia, Kurt, Fagan, David, Veroneau, John, Vetere, Gina, Eichensehr, Kristen, Cilluffo Frank and Beckner, Christian, 'Economic Espionage and Trade Secret Theft: An Overview of the Legal Landscape and Policy Responses', industry paper from Covington and Burling and the George Washington University Cybersecurity Initiative, September 2013, available at SpecialIssueBrief.pdf.

can der Marel, Erik, 'Disentangling the Flows of Data: Inside or Outside the Multinational Company?', European Center for International Political Economy, July 2015, available at http://ecipe.org/app/uploads/2015/07/ECIPE-Data-Flows-final.pdf.

Castro, Daniel, 'The False Promise of Data Nationalism', Information Technology and Innovation Foundation, December 2013, available at http://www2.itif.org/2013-false-promise-data-nationalism.pdf.

Castro, Daniel and McQuinn, Alan, 'Cross-Border Data Flows Enable Growth in All Industries' (Information Technology and Innovation Foundation), March 2015, available at www2.itif.org/2015-cross-border-data-flows.pdf.

'Content Blocking', Electronic Frontier Foundation website, 2018, available at https://www.eff.org/issues/content-blocking.

Cory, Nigel, 'How Website Blocking Is Curbing Digital Piracy Without "Breaking the Internet"', The Information Technology and Innovation Foundation, August 2016, available at www2.itif.org/2016-website-blocking.pdf.

Cory, Nigel, 'Cross-Border Data Flows: Where Are the Barriers, and What Do They Cost?', Information Technology and Innovation Foundation, May 2017, available at https://itif.org/publications/2017/05/01/cross-border-data-flows-where-are-barriers-and-what-do-they-cost.

Cory, Nigel, 'Testimony Before the United States International Trade Commission on Global Digital Trade', The Information Technology and Innovation Foundation,

29 March 2018, available at https://itif.org/publications/2018/03/29/testimony-united-states-international-trade-commission-global-digital-trade.

Danaher, Brett, Smith, Michael D. and Telang, Rahul, 'Website Blocking Revisited: The Effect of the UK November 2014 Blocks on Consumer Behavior', paper, Carnegie Mellon University, Pittsburg, 18 April 2016, available at http://ssrn.com/abstract=2766795.

Defend Trade Secrets Act of 2016, 114th Congress, available at www.congress.gov/bill/114th-congress/senate-bill/1890/text.

'Directive 2013/40/EU of the European Parliament and of the Council of 12 August 2013 on attacks against information systems and replacing Council Framework Decision 2005/222/JHA', Office Journal of the European Union website 2018, available at http://eur-lex.europa.eu/LexUriServ/LexUriServ.do?uri=OJ:L:2013:218:0008:0014:EN:PDF.

The Economist, 'The Web's New Walls', 2 September 2010, available at https://www.economist.com/node/16943579.

Estes, Adam Clark, 'The Web Collectively Protests Congress's Censorship Law', *The Atlantic*, 16 November 2011, available at https://www.theatlantic.com/technology/archive/2011/11/web-collectively-protests-congresss-censorship-law/335366/.

Ezell, Stephen, 'ITIF Filing to USTR on Section 301 Investigation of China's Policies and Practices Related to Tech Transfer, IP, and Innovation', Information Technology and Innovation Foundation, 25 October 2017, available at https://itif.org/publications/2017/10/25/itif-filing-ustr-section-301-investigation-chinas-policies-and-practices.

Ferry, Jeff, 'Top Ten Cases of Chinese IP Theft', Coalition for a Prosperous America website, 2018, available at https://www.prosperousamerica.org/top_ten_cases_of_chinese_ip_theft.

IP Commission, 'The Report of the Commission on the Theft of American Intellectual Property', *The National Bureau of Asian Research*, May 2013, available at www.ipcommission.org/report/ip_commission_report_052213.pdf.

Kendall, Brent, 'Imports of Digital Goods Face Test', *Wall Street Journal*, 2 August 2015, available at https://www.wsj.com/articles/imports-of-digital-goods-face-test-1438554684.

Knickrehm, Mark, Berthon, Bruno and Daugherty, Paul, 'Digital Disruption: The Growth Multiplier', Accenture Strategy report, January, 2016, available at https://www.accenture.com/_acnmedia/PDF-4/Accenture-Strategy-Digital-Disruption-Growth-Multiplier.pdf.

Linton, Katherine, 'The Importance of Trade Secrets: New Directions in International Trade Policy Making and Empirical Research', *Journal of International Commerce and Economics*, 2 September 2016, available at https://ssrn.com/abstract=2893319.

Lippoldt, Douglas and Schultz, Mark, 'Uncovering Trade Secrets – An Empirical Assessment of Economic Implications of Protection for Undisclosed Data',

Paris: Organisation for Economic Cooperation and Development (OECD) Trade Policy Papers, No. 167, OECD Publishing, 2014, available at http://dx.doi.org/10.1787/5jxzl5w3j3s6-en.

Lippoldt, Douglas and Schultz, Mark, *Approaches to the Protection of Trade Secrets*, Paris: Organisation for Economic Cooperation and Development, 2019, chapter in the report on 'Enquiring into Intellectual Property's Economic Impact', available at www.oecd.org/sti/ieconomy/Chapter3-KBC2-IP.pdf.

Manyika, James, Bughin, Jacques, Lund, Susan, Nottebohm, Olivia, Poulter, David, Jauch, Sebastian and Ramaswamy, Sree, 'Global flows in a Digital Age: How Trade, Finance, People, and Data Connect the World Economy', McKinsey Global Institute, April 2014, available at www.mckinsey.com/~/media/McKinsey/Global%20Themes/Globalization/Global%20flows%20in%20a%20digital%20age/Global_flows_in_a_digital_age_Full_report%20March_2015.ashx.

Meeker, Mary, 'Internet Trends Report 2018' (Industry report, Kleiner Perkins), 30 May 2018, available at www.kleinerperkins.com/perspectives/internet-trends-report-2018.

Mulas, Victor, 'Value in Global Economy is Moving to Digital Business', Washington, DC: World Bank. Slide 4 in the presentation on 'Startup Innovation Ecosystems as New Sources of Growth and Jobs', available at www2.itif.org/2017-startup-ecosystems-mulas.pdf.

Office of the Director of National Intelligence, *NCSC Releases 2018 Foreign Economic Espionage in Cyberspace Report*, Washington, DC: US National Counterintelligence and Security Center, July 26, 2018, available at www.dni.gov/files/NCSC/documents/news/20180724-ncsc-press-release-foreign-econ-esp-cyber.pdf.

Price, David, 'Sizing the Piracy Universe', industry report, Netnames, London, September 2013, available at https://www.netnames.com/assets/shared/whitepaper/pdf/netnames-sizing-piracy-universe-FULLreport-sept2013.pdf.

PWC, 'Adjusting the Lens on Economic Crime', Industry Report, PWC, Global Economic Crime Survey 2016, available at www.pwc.com/gx/en/economic-crime-survey/pdf/GlobalEconomicCrimeSurvey2016.pdf.

Rayuki, Saku, Chow, Peggy and Robinson, Mark, 'Indonesia and Thailand Target OTT Services' (2018), *Lexology*, 5 February.

Saias, Marco Alexandre, 'Unlawful Acquisition of Trade Secrets by Cyber Theft: between the Proposed Directive on Trade Secrets and the Directive on Cyber Attacks' (2014), *Journal of Intellectual Property Law & Practice* 9, 9: 721–729, available at https://doi-org.ezproxylocal.library.nova.edu/10.1093/jiplp/jpu117.

Sebastian, Clare, 'Chinese Trade Secret Theft Nearly Killed My Company', *CNNtech*, 23 March 2018, available at https://money.cnn.com/2018/03/23/technology/business/american-semiconductor-china-trade/index.html.

'Study on Trade Secrets and Confidential Business Information in the Internal Market', report prepared for the European Commission, April 2013, available at http://ec.europa.eu/internal_market/iprenforcement/docs/trade-secrets/130711_final-study_en.pdf.

Taubman, Antony, 'TRIPS Encounters the Internet: An Analogue Treaty in a Digital Age, or the First Trade 2.0 Agreement?', in M. Burri and R. Cottier (eds), *Trade Governance in the Digital Age*, Cambridge: Cambridge University Press, 2012, available at https://ssrn.com/abstract=2713086.

The Center for Responsible Enterprise And Trade (CREATe.org), 'Economic Impact of Trade Secret Theft: A framework for companies to safeguard trade secrets and mitigate potential threats', Washington, DC: The Center for Responsible Enterprise And Trade (CREATe.org), February 2014, available at https://create.org/wp-content/uploads/2014/07/CREATe.org-PwC-Trade-Secret-Theft-FINAL-Feb-2014_01.pdf.

'Trade Secrets', European Commission website, 2018, available at http://ec.europa.eu/growth/industry/intellectual-property/trade-secrets_en.

'Understanding How Intellectual Property (IP) Relates to E-Commerce', World Intellectual Property Organization website, 2018, available at www.wipo.int/sme/en/e_commerce/ip_ecommerce.htm.

United Nations Conference on Trade and Development (UNCTAD), *Data Protection Regulations and International Data Flows: Implications For Trade And Development*, Geneva: UNCTAD, April 2016, available at http://unctad.org/en/PublicationsLibrary/dtlstict2016d1_en.pdf.

United States International Trade Commission (USITC), *Digital Trade in the U.S. and Global Economies, Part 1*, Washington, DC: USITC, July 2013, available at www.usitc.gov/publications/332/pub4415.pdf.

United States Trade Representative (USTR), *National Trade Estimate Report*, Washington, DC: USTR, 2013.

Zeile, Willian, *Research Spotlight Multinational Enterprises and International Technology Transfer*, Washington, DC: United States Department of Commerce, Bureau of Economic Analysis, September, 2014, available at https://bea.gov/scb/pdf/2014/09%20September/0914_multinational_enterprises_and_technology_transfer.pdf.

Zysman, John and Kenney, Martin, 'The Next Phase in the Digital Revolution: Intelligent Tools, Platforms, Growth, Employment' (2018), *Communications of the ACM* 61, 2: 54–63, available at https://cacm.acm.org/magazines/2018/2/224635-the-next-phase-in-the-digital-revolution/fulltext.

22

Cross-Border Knowledge Flows under International Trade Agreements: A Need for New Multilateral Disciplines?

LUCAS SPADANO AND LUIZA TÂNGARI COELHO*

Abstract

Cross-border knowledge flows occur in many ways and are increasingly important for the world economy. In terms of international trade rules, knowledge flows are covered by different disciplines, both at the multilateral and at the plurilateral or bilateral levels. The purpose of this chapter is to provide a basic understanding of how such trade rules may affect cross-border knowledge flows. The chapter then discusses – particularly, in the light of new trends identified in recent plurilateral and bilateral agreements – whether the current multilateral disciplines are sufficient to regulate and encourage cross-border knowledge flows, or whether new trade rules to further promote such flows are needed.

Introduction: Trade and Flows of Knowledge

A significant body of scholarly literature has recently been developed with a focus on cross-border data flows. In this chapter, differently than those studies, we take a broader view that also considers other forms of knowledge flows.[1]

* The authors are grateful to Jayashree Watal, Antony Taubman, Lee Tuthill, Felipe Hees and Natalia Ruschel for valuable comments on an earlier draft.

[1] Knowledge, information and data are interrelated concepts. While their respective meanings are debatable and vary significantly across different fields of study, a well-known conception in information science, which we adopt for the purposes of this chapter, is that they are part of a sequential order: sets of data combine to make up pieces of information, which may be combined to assemble bodies of knowledge (Z. Papacharissi, 2015, p. 1096). The sequence is part of the so-called *Data-Information-Knowledge-Wisdom* (DIKW) pyramid, usually credited to organizational theorist Russell Ackoff – see I. Brodie and L. Brodie (2009), pp. 137–138.

There is an intricate relationship between knowledge flows and trade. First, knowledge is embodied in technological goods and 'human capital' that may be accessed through the provision of services.[2] Second, the purpose of knowledge creation, absorption and transfer – whether by academic, governmental, business or non-profit institutions – is generally to obtain developments and results that are ultimately traded as new products and processes that solve problems more efficiently.[3]

As is seen in Part II of this book, cross-border knowledge flows occur in many ways,[4] including by means of trade in knowledge-intensive goods,[5] technical assistance, research and development (R&D), licensing of intellectual property (IP) rights, knowledge embedded in products sold via e-commerce, technology spillovers from foreign direct investment, collaboration programmes where people exchange ideas and several others.

In terms of international trade rules, knowledge flows are covered by different disciplines, both at the multilateral and at the plurilateral or bilateral levels. The purpose of this chapter is to provide a basic understanding of how such trade rules may affect cross-border knowledge flows.

We then ask whether the current multilateral disciplines are sufficient to regulate and encourage cross-border knowledge flows, or whether new trade rules to further promote such flows are needed. The question is discussed, particularly, in the light of new trends identified in recent plurilateral and bilateral agreements.

The discussion is organized as follows. The next section seeks to describe how the current international trade legal system regulates cross-border knowledge flows. The relevant World Trade Organization (WTO) disciplines are explained briefly, alongside current trends in bilateral and plurilateral trade agreements. The following section, asking whether new trade rules are needed,[6] discusses possible reasons for a reform or update of current multilateral trade rules, and concludes with our views on the proposed question.

[2] OECD (1997); P. A. David (2005), p. 99.

[3] National Science Board (2018).

[4] See S. Athreye and Y. Yang (2011), explaining how measurements of 'technology trade', initially focused on the trade of technology-intensive goods, evolved to also encompass several forms of 'disembodied technology trade', including the transfer of know-how and of IP rights, services with technical content and R&D outsourcing.

[5] See, e.g., OECD (2010).

[6] P. 667 *infra*.

International Trade Rules Affecting Cross-Border Knowledge Flows

Several market access disciplines and behind-the-border regulations found in the WTO agreements and in free trade agreements (FTAs) may directly or indirectly impact the creation and exchange of knowledge (or data and information that may be combined to form knowledge).[7] Given that trade in goods and services is, to a greater or lesser degree, related to knowledge flows, all trade rules impact such flows, even if they do so indirectly.[8] Here we focus on selected provisions[9] that appear to have a closer connection to cross-border knowledge flows.[10]

We classify the relevant international trade rules into four categories: (a) access to technology-enabling goods and services; (b) incentives to the creation of knowledge; (c) transfer or dissemination of knowledge; and (d) exceptions that allow legitimate restrictions to knowledge flows.

We briefly analyse, under each category, provisions in the WTO agreements and in the following selection of seven FTAs: the Trans-Pacific Partnership (TPP, 2016);[11] the Free Trade Agreement between the United States of America and the Republic of Korea (KORUS, 2007); the Agreement between the United States of America, the United Mexican

[7] As explained above, we consider that the concept of knowledge encompasses information and data. Therefore, when we refer to knowledge flows throughout this chapter, we consider them to include information and data flows as well.

[8] See B. Hoekman et al. (2004, p. 3), stating that 'all exports bear some potential for transmitting technological information'.

[9] It is obviously not our purpose, within the limited scope of this chapter, to offer a comprehensive and detailed overview of all relevant legal provisions in different agreements. Rather, we simply pinpoint the essence of some provisions to the extent required for the purposes of the discussion at hand.

[10] There are many categories of legal provisions not covered herein that may substantially impact cross-border knowledge flows – for example, those relating to the protection of foreign direct investment under many FTAs, or those concerning technical standards or regulatory convergence. With respect to the latter, for an interesting take on the problematic implications of 'balkanized' standards in the area of information and communication technologies, see H. Liu (2014). Our choice to leave such categories out of the scope of the present discussion does not imply that they are any less relevant.

[11] After the Trump administration withdrew the United States from the TPP, the remaining participants signed the Comprehensive and Progressive Agreement for Trans-Pacific Partnership (CPTPP), also known as TPP-11, in March 2018. All substantial TPP provisions are incorporated by reference into the CPTPP, but some of them (which had been included essentially in the interests of the US) have been suspended. Here, we will refer to the text of the TPP and will note, where relevant, provisions suspended under the CPTPP.

States and Canada (USMCA, 2018); the Trade Agreement between the European Union and Colombia and Peru and Ecuador (2012); the Comprehensive Economic and Trade Agreement between Canada and the European Union (CETA, 2016); the Economic Partnership Agreement between the European Union and Japan (2018); and the China–Australia Free Trade Agreement (ChAFTA, 2015).

That illustrative sample includes representative agreements recently signed by the United States (US) and the European Union (EU) – given that these two jurisdictions tend to shape the future agenda of trade negotiations – that are typically regarded as the most advanced agreements to cope with the digital economy. The sample also includes agreements made between developed and developing countries, to highlight possible trends regarding provisions of interest to the latter. Finally, ChAFTA has been included to consider China's positions, as well as to assess at least one non-US or EU model.

Rather than discussing all market access commitments that go beyond the WTO, we focus mainly on selected legal disciplines or aspects that are not found in the WTO agreements.

Technology-Enabling Goods and Services

It is well known that certain goods have a special function of enabling access to information. Computers, telecommunication equipment and other information and communications technology (ICT) products are covered by the Information Technology Agreement (ITA), a WTO plurilateral agreement of 1996 that requires each member to eliminate customs duties for all products specified therein, on a most-favoured nation (MFN) basis. Today 82 WTO members are party to the ITA, which represents approximately 97 per cent of global trade in IT products.[12]

In 2015, in the light of new technological developments, 53 WTO members agreed to expanding the coverage of the ITA to an additional list of 201 products, including new-generation semi-conductors, GPS navigation systems, telecommunications satellites, touch screens and medical imaging products. The participant countries account for about 90 per cent of world trade in the new covered products, valued at over USD 1.3 trillion per year.[13]

[12] WTO (2017), p. 9.

[13] See www.wto.org/english/news_e/news15_e/ita_16dec15_e.htm.

Interestingly, the products covered by the ITA – both in the case of its original and expanded versions – are specified not only in an *Attachment A* covering specified tariff headings and subheadings under the Harmonized System (HS), but also in an *Attachment B* covering specific products 'wherever they are classified in the HS'.[14] In practice, the broader narrative description of products in Attachment B has proven valuable to ensure the applicability of the ITA commitments to a wide range of products (regardless of tariff classification issues), as shown in the *EC–IT Products* dispute.[15]

While there is room for further commitments – in terms of participation by other WTO members, non-tariff barriers and further coverage expansions in view of technological developments[16] – there is no question that the ITA contributes significantly to knowledge flows by expanding the trade of, and making more affordable, goods that not only embed high technology, but are also a crucial part of the infrastructure that enables access to the Internet and the opportunities that it entails.[17]

Certain services also have a key role in allowing the exchange of communications and payments, without which trade in goods and in other services would be difficult. An important set of multilateral rules in this respect is included in the GATS Annex on Telecommunications. The Annex contains general obligations (applicable regardless of specific commitments) to ensure that *users* of those services (i.e. firms that supply any services, such as banking, computer services or any others) will have access to telecommunications networks – which is of course a requisite to access the Internet – on a non-discriminatory basis.[18]

[14] See WT/MIN(96)/16, p. 6 and WT/MIN(15)/25, p. 4.

[15] See *EC – IT Products*, Reports of the Panel, WT/DS375/R, WT/DS376/R, WT/DS377/R, 16 August 2010 (finding that the EU should accord duty-free treatment to flat panel display devices, set-top boxes and multifunctional digital machines). That of course does not mean that the scope of the ITA is free from tariff classification debates. For example, contrast the results of *EC – IT Products* with *EC – Computer Equipment*, Report of the Appellate Body, WT/DS62/AB/R, WT/DS67/AB/R, WT/DS68/AB/R, 5 June 1998.

[16] The original and the expanded ITA provide for consultations on non-tariff barriers and periodic reviews of product coverage. See para. 3 of the Annex to WT/MIN(96)/16 and paras 10 and 11 of the Annex to WT/MIN(15)/25, p. 4.

[17] As observed by the WTO (2017, pp. 14 and 85), the ITA can be 'one of the drivers to the removal of barriers to Internet access', and 'can play an enabling role in technology diffusion and innovation. In the right circumstances, it can ultimately allow broader penetration of developing economies into global production networks and spur innovation in other sectors, thereby benefitting the economy as a whole'.

[18] See, in particular, para. 5 of the GATS Annex on Telecommunications.

With respect to specific provisions relating to technology-enabling goods and services, most of the analysed FTAs merely reinforce the GATS commitments on access to telecommunications infrastructure. The TPP is more detailed and includes, in its e-commerce chapter, specific principles recognizing the benefits of access and use of Internet services and applications by consumers (Article 14.10), as well as disciplines on the negotiations of Internet interconnection charge sharing by suppliers (Article 14.12). In addition, the TPP requires signatory parties to join the ITA (Article 2.17), which is an interesting and perhaps unusual direct contribution to WTO commitments.

Incentives for the Creation of Knowledge

Two important mechanisms that provide incentives for the creation of new knowledge and are regulated by WTO agreements concern R&D subsidies and IP rights. FTAs typically include additional IP-related obligations and, in some cases, scientific collaboration endeavours that may also encourage the creation of knowledge.

Incentives for R&D Activities

Although not easy to implement effectively, R&D-related subsidies may have a positive impact on knowledge creation (and also transfer), to the extent that they facilitate 'learning, technology acquisition, and dynamic comparative advantage where returns to such activities cannot be appropriated by private agents and hence will not be undertaken by any individual firm'.[19] Arguably, therefore, it is important for states to maintain some freedom to implement such policies. On the other hand, excessive or targeted subsidies may distort international technology markets and negatively impact knowledge flows. Trade rules, therefore, should seek to strike an optimal balance.

Initially, a balancing attempt was clearly reflected in Article 8.2(a) of the Agreement on Subsidies and Countervailing Measures (SCM), which allowed (by classifying as 'non-actionable') subsidies that, even though specific, involved 'assistance for research activities conducted by firms or by higher education or research establishments on a contract basis with firms', within certain limits depending on the type of research involved.[20]

[19] B. Hoekman et al. (2004), p. 13.

[20] For example, the Agreement allowed governments to cover up to 75 per cent of the costs of 'industrial research' – defined as 'planned search or critical investigation aimed at

However, lack of consensus among WTO members led to the expiry of such provisions at the end of 1999.[21] Currently, therefore, any R&D subsidy that falls within the definition of 'subsidy' under Article 1 and that meets the specificity criteria under Article 2 of the SCM Agreement is 'actionable', i.e. subject to countervailing measures or to challenge in the WTO dispute settlement when it provokes adverse effects to the interests of other WTO members. Nonetheless, only three WTO disputes so far appear to have directly addressed the issue of R&D subsidies – each of them involving export contingency or very specific subsidies to aircraft producers Bombardier, Boeing and Airbus.[22] This may indicate that, despite the expiry of Article 8.2(a), the SCM Agreement general rules (especially the concept of specificity) are, in practice, sufficient to allow governmental support to R&D activities.

Specifically with respect to agricultural goods, R&D subsidies are allowed without quantitative limitation under the so-called 'Green Box' category of the WTO Agreement on Agriculture (AoA), which includes support to 'research, including general research, research in connection with environmental products, and research programmes relating to particular products', provided that they do not involve direct payments to producers or processors, and also provided that, like other acceptable domestic support measures, they have no or minimal trade-distorting effects.[23]

At the multilateral level, therefore, WTO members keep reasonable freedom to adopt R&D subsidy policies, but at the same time there are constraints that help avoid distortions to trade in goods.

The analysed FTAs do not regulate such policies, with the exception of one atypical provision on R&D-related performance requirements found

discovery of new knowledge, with the objective that such knowledge may be useful in developing new products, processes or services, or in bringing about a significant improvement to existing products, processes or services'.

21 See Article 31 of the SCM Agreement.

22 See K. Maskus (2015), pp. 4–5. The referred disputes are DS222, DS316/317 and DS353. A more recent dispute between the European Union and Japan against Brazil involved a discussion of whether requirements to invest in R&D activities in Brazil, as a condition to receive subsidies directed to IT-related sectors, violated the national treatment obligation under the GATT. The Panel was unconvinced that R&D investment requirements *alone* created origin-based discrimination. See *Brazil – Taxation*, Panel Report, WT/DS472/R, WT/DS497/R, para. 7.227–7229, 30 August 2017.

23 See Annex 2, para. 2 and Articles 1(a), 6 and 7, of the Agreement on Agriculture.

in the investment liberalization provisions of the EU–Japan Agreement: Article 8.11(1)(j) prohibits any requirement, in connection with the operation or establishment of any enterprise, to achieve a given level or value of R&D in its territory.[24] On the other hand, Article 8.11(3) contains a clarification – which is standard in bilateral investment treaties and FTAs that contain investment chapters[25] – that advantages to investors may be conditioned on carrying out R&D in the territory of the recipient country, which, again, shows a concern in keeping policy space for incentives for local R&D activities.

Protection of IP Rights

The protection of IP rights over new technologies seeks to correct a market failure by granting temporary exclusive rights that should incentivize innovation and advancements in human knowledge, and provide a legal platform for innovators to license, assign and otherwise trade in new technologies. The ultimate expected result is that the protection of IP rights should lead to more technology development and transfer, so as to benefit not only inventors, but society as a whole.[26]

At the multilateral level, the TRIPS Agreement imposes on WTO members the adoption of minimum standards that imply a significant level of protection of IP rights. Such standards involve not only minimum terms of protection for patents, industrial designs, copyright and other IP rights, but also requirements that patents be available in all sectors (including for example pharmaceuticals, which were not protected in some countries prior to the TRIPS Agreement). There are also very comprehensive and detailed obligations on how IP rights should be enforced by administrative and judicial authorities in each country.[27]

At the plurilateral and bilateral levels, FTAs increasingly seek to further protect and regulate IP rights. All the selected agreements contain TRIPS-plus obligations. With the exception of ChAFTA, they require, for

[24] The origin of this text appears to be the provision on performance requirements included in the draft text of the failed Multilateral Agreement on Investment, negotiated within the OECD between 1995 and 1998. See www1.oecd.org/daf/mai/pdf/ng/ng987r1e.pdf.

[25] The same permission is found in the investment chapters of TPP (Article 9.10.3); USMCA (Article 14.10.3); KORUS (Article 18.11); CETA (Article 8.5.3); and the EU–Japan Agreement (Article 8.11.3).

[26] Such purposes are clearly reflected in Article 7 of the TRIPS Agreement.

[27] See, for example, Articles 10, 12 (on software), 25, 26 (on industrial designs), 27, 33, 34 (on patents) and 41 to 61 (on enforcement, including specific border measures and even criminal procedures) of the TRIPS Agreement.

example, minimum periods of market exclusivity for pharmaceutical and agricultural chemical products for which undisclosed test data concerning safety or efficacy has been submitted to national authorities – which presumably may incentivize innovation in such areas.

The TPP, KORUS and USMCA agreements further expand the scope of protection of IP rights. For example, they require signatories to prohibit (as a civil and criminal offence) the manufacture and marketing of devices used to decode encrypted program-carrying satellite and cable signals without authorization, as well as the wilful receipt and distribution of such signals.[28]

The optimal level of protection of IP rights – i.e. the one that strikes the right balance between incentives to innovation and benefits to society – is debatable.[29] There is no question, however, that safeguards against risks of overprotection are important to ensure that knowledge will be effectively disseminated. The trade agreements also provide for such safeguards, as will be discussed below.

Scientific Cooperation

While the WTO agreements do not refer explicitly to scientific cooperation,[30] it is interesting to note that several of the analysed FTAs contain best-endeavour undertakings to cooperate in specific areas of science, technology, research and innovation. They often refer as well to engaging the participation of the private sector and research institutions of each signatory country in such cooperation efforts.

Two of the selected agreements are worth highlighting in this respect. Aside from numerous cooperation provisions (e.g. on environment and sustainable development issues), CETA has a specific provision that reinforces a 1995 bilateral Agreement for Scientific and Technological

[28] The parties to the CPTPP have suspended the application of such requirements, provided for in Article 18.79 of the TPP.

[29] For a critical perspective on the level of protection established in the TRIPS Agreement, see A. Capling (2004, p. 179), arguing that the text reflects more the interest of technology-intensive sectors in developed countries than a 'measured consideration of costs and benefits within the global trade system'. See also J. M. Finger and J. Nogués (2002), pp. 321–339.

[30] The TRIPS Agreement, as discussed below, contains broad references to the promotion of innovation and technology transfer. Scientific cooperation may of course be one of the ways to do so. See, for example, WTO document IP/C/M/83/ADD.1, 30 January 2017, where, in a discussion concerning innovation models (item 12 of the agenda of the Council for TRIPS) members referred to collaborative scientific research projects, scientific cooperation scholarships and other topics.

Cooperation and seeks to enhance cooperative activities in such areas (Article 25.5).

The EU FTA with Colombia, Peru and Ecuador, in its turn, seems to include the most comprehensive set of scientific cooperation efforts. Its chapter on technology transfer refers, inter alia, to exchanging experiences and creating an adequate environment for the promotion of lasting relations between scientific communities, including through financing from public resources. The parties are also encouraged to facilitate the entry and exit of data and equipment used in R&D activities (Article 255), as well as the short-term entry and stay, specifically, of technical and scientific researchers (Article 128). Such provisions may be important not only to encourage the creation of knowledge and technological development in the common interest of the parties, but also knowledge flows facilitated by the movement of people involved in scientific projects.

Provisions Facilitating Cross-Border Flows of Knowledge

The above-mentioned mechanisms that contribute to the creation of knowledge may also contribute to its dissemination. The protection of IP rights in a foreign country, for example, may encourage technology licensing, and international scientific collaboration projects which by definition lead to the exchange of knowledge. There is some overlap, therefore, between the categories proposed here. In any event, the following types of provisions in trade agreements may directly contribute to the international transfer of knowledge.

Limits to the Protection of IP Rights

The minimum standards of protection of IP rights required at the multilateral level are counterbalanced with important safeguards to avoid overprotection. The latter include, for example, rules relating to the sufficiency of disclosure of patent applications, compulsory licensing of patents, fair use exceptions to copyright, access to knowledge in the public domain and avoiding anti-competitive abuse of the protection of IP rights.[31]

[31] For a full view of the available safeguards, see the following provisions of the TRIPS Agreement: first, fifth and sixth paras of the preamble, and Articles 7, 8, 9(2), 13, 14(6), 25(1), 26(2), 27(2), 27(3), 29(1), 30, 31, 37, 39(3), 40, 41(1), 41(5), 44(2), 48(1), 50(7), 59, 60, 66 and 67 (relating specifically to encouraging technology transfer to least-developed countries) and 73. See also Article 31*bis*, inserted as an amendment by a decision of the General Council (WT/L/641, 8 December 2005), which resulted from the Doha

While in most cases the exceptions and limitations are left to the discretion of each WTO member – i.e. there are few 'maximum' standards of protection[32] – one key mandatory safeguard in connection with knowledge flows is made explicit in Article 9.2 of the TRIPS Agreement, which provides that copyright protection *shall* extend only to expressions and 'not to ideas, procedures, methods of operation or mathematical concepts as such'. That provision avoids the risk of undue appropriation of disembodied knowledge at the pretext of protecting copyright. Part III of the TRIPS Agreement, on the enforcement of IP rights, also contains several mandatory safeguards to avoid abuse and protect due process rights of those accused of IP infringement.

The analysed FTAs, likewise, allow exceptions and limitations to IP protection. They all include, for example, permission for parties to freely determine their rules on the exhaustion of IP rights, and most of them expressly allow certain limitations to technological protection measures (TPMs). Some of the agreements also provide that the parties shall cooperate on policies concerning the fair use of IP for research, innovation and economic growth.

Generally, the FTAs expressly recognize the importance of a balance between IP rights and the public interest in areas such as public health, nutrition and technological development. The EU–Colombia/Peru/Ecuador Agreement (Article 196) refers furthermore to the promotion of education, culture, research, access to information and technology transfer. The TPP also refers to the 'importance of a rich and accessible public domain' (Article 18.15), and specifically requires parties to give due consideration to legitimate limitations or exceptions to copyright, including for 'teaching, scholarship, research, and other similar purposes' (Article 18.66).

It seems clear, therefore, that while on the one hand trade agreements guarantee a substantial level of protection of IP rights (and more significantly so in the case of FTAs), on the other hand they leave some room for parties to design their domestic rules in a way that may promote a reasonable balance of rights and obligations, and protect the legitimate interest of the public to access and benefit from new knowledge, the use

Declaration on the TRIPS Agreement and Public Health (WT/MIN(01)/DEC/2, 20 November 2001).

[32] See, for example, Article 8 of the TRIPS Agreement (providing that members *may* 'adopt measures necessary to protect public health and nutrition, and to promote the public interest in sectors of vital importance to their socio-economic and technological development, provided that such measures are consistent with the provisions of this Agreement').

of which, in the absence of the important above-mentioned safeguards, could be restricted by virtue of exclusive rights.

Technology Transfer and Performance Requirements

As noted earlier, the TRIPS Agreement acknowledges the importance of promoting international technology transfer. An interesting initiative in this respect has been the establishment of the Working Group on Transfer of Technology at the beginning of the Doha Round, with a mandate to examine ways to increase the flow of technology from developed to developing countries.[33] Similar endeavours – generally limited to recognizing the need to facilitate and encourage the transfer and dissemination of technology – are also usually included in the IP chapters of the selected FTAs.

Aside from such soft law provisions, Article 66.2 of the TRIPS Agreement obliges developed countries to 'provide incentives to enterprises and institutions in their territories for the purpose of promoting and encouraging technology transfer to least-developed country members in order to enable them to create a sound and viable technological base'.

A recent analysis of reports submitted by developed countries under Article 66.2 shows that LDCs have benefitted from projects involving capacity building, transfer of capital and technological know-how, and other incentives in diversified areas including environment/water, agriculture, IP and public health.[34]

From another angle, the investment chapters of most of the analysed FTAs prohibit performance requirements relating to the transfer of technologies, production processes, or other proprietary knowledge to the recipient country. The TPP (Article 14.17), USMCA (Article 19.16), and the FTA between EU and Japan (Article 8.73), furthermore, include in their respective e-commerce chapters a specific prohibition of requirements to disclose source codes owned by a person of another party.[35] The TPP (Article 14.13) and USMCA (Article 19.12) also prohibit requirements to 'localize' computing facilities in a national territory (in the case

[33] See www.wto.org/english/tratop_e/devel_e/dev_wkgp_trade_transfer_technology_e.htm.

[34] See J. Watal and L. Caminero (2018, pp. 14–25). The reports are submitted pursuant to a monitoring mechanism established by the Decision of the Council for TRIPS on the Implementation of Article 66.2, WTO Document IP/C/28, 20 February 2003.

[35] In the case of TPP, the applicability of the provision is limited to 'mass-market software', and excludes 'software used for critical infrastructure'. The USMCA provision applies not only to source code of software, but also to 'an algorithm expressed in that source code'.

of the TPP, subject to a specific exception for measures 'to achieve a legitimate public policy objective').

The traditional motivation behind such performance requirements is an attempt to induce the transfer of technology and, more recently, apparently, an idea to use 'smart industrial policy tools' to promote 'domestic digital firms and allow them to catch-up with the leading multinational firms'.[36] In practice, however, such policies run a risk of lowering the quality of technologies received, or perhaps even preventing investment (and relating knowledge flows) from occurring at all.[37]

Trade in Knowledge-Embedded Services

Many services are per se vehicles of knowledge flows, such as, inter alia, professional services, education, scientific and technical consulting (especially when technical personnel cross borders and transmit know-how), audio-visual and data processing services.

All such services are covered by the General Agreement on Trade in Services (GATS). However, market access and national treatment commitments under the GATS only apply to the extent that a member has entered them in its individual country schedule, with respect to specific service sectors and modes of supply.[38]

The service sectors are generally classified according to a comprehensive list compiled during the Uruguay Round to facilitate negotiations by ensuring cross-country comparability and uniformity of commitments undertaken. The list contains 12 sectors (including a residual category of 'other services not included elsewhere') and 160 subsectors defined as an aggregate of the more detailed categories contained in the 1991 provisional version of the United Nations Central Product Classification (CPC).[39]

As the WTO itself acknowledges, the liberalizing effects of the GATS have so far been relatively modest in most sectors, given that in most

[36] The African Group, which includes 43 WTO members, has recently highlighted such rationale, by reference to a Panel discussion in the WTO on 'Digital Industrial Policy and Development' – see WTO Document JOB/GC/133, 21 July 2017.

[37] See B. Hoekman et al. (2004, p. 11).

[38] There are four modes of supply, which correspond to the different ways of delivering services, as described in Article I.2 of the GATS: cross-border trade, consumption abroad, commercial presence and presence of natural persons.

[39] See https://unstats.un.org/unsd/tradekb/Knowledgebase/Sectoral-Classification-List-W120. The full Services Sectoral Classification List is available in WTO Document MTN.GNS/W/120, 10 July 1991. Also important is the Explanatory Note circulated by the GATT Secretariat on how to schedule initial commitments – see MTN.GNS/W/164, 3 September 1993.

cases commitments have remained limited to confirming conditions of market access that already existed.[40] Nonetheless, the legal structure required for desirable further commitments is already in place.[41]

Without delving into a detailed analysis of the GATS mechanics and commitments, one interesting aspect to highlight is its technological neutrality, i.e. the fact that the GATS does not contain any provisions that distinguish between the different technological means through which a service may be supplied.[42] WTO jurisprudence has confirmed that principle in *US – Gambling* and in *China – Audiovisual Services*.[43] While the applicability of technological neutrality under the GATS is not unanimously accepted,[44] it seems clear to us that the legal text of the GATS does not contain any indication that limits the means of delivery of services in any of the four modes of supply.

In view of the increasing economic relevance of services traded in digitized form,[45] the principle of technological neutrality may play a key role in ensuring that the agreed commitments remain applicable when services, together with the knowledge they embed, are delivered electronically.

With respect to the analysed FTAs, all of them contain further commitments on the liberalization of services,[46] and apparently maintain a

[40] The telecommunications sector is one important exception. Also, the binding effect of commitments in any service sectors (even if only to confirm existing market access conditions) is of course important to prevent protectionist backlashes.

[41] See www.wto.org/english/tratop_e/serv_e/gatsqa_e.htm.

[42] See the Progress Report adopted by the WTO Council for Trade in Services in 1999, stating the 'general view' that the GATS 'applies to all services regardless of the means by which they are delivered, and that electronic delivery can take place under any of the four modes of supply'. WTO Document S/L/74, 27 July 1999.

[43] *US – Gambling*, Panel Report, WT/DS285/R, 10 November 2004, para. 6.285 (finding that 'a market access commitment for mode 1 implies the right for other Members' suppliers to supply a service through all means of delivery, whether by mail, telephone, Internet etc., unless otherwise specified in a Member's Schedule'); *China – Audiovisual Services*, Appellate Body Report, WT/DS363/AB/R, 21 December 2009, para. 338 to 413 (finding that a 'sound recording distribution services' commitment encompasses distribution of sound recordings in both physical and non-physical forms, 'notably through electronic means').

[44] See, for example, J. Kelsey (2018, pp. 290–294), arguing that 'there is no credible source to support the concept' of technological neutrality.

[45] D. Castro and A. McQuinn (2015, p. 1) refer to an UNCTAD estimate that, as of 2009, about half of global trade in services were already enabled by digital technologies.

[46] They also include specific chapters on the temporary entry and stay of business persons, which may have a rather important role in promoting cross-border knowledge flows, but are not discussed here in further detail for space reasons.

technologically neutral stance. Notably, the FTAs signed by the US (the TPP, KORUS and USMCA), the EU–Japan Agreement, as well as the commitments made by Australia under the ChAFTA, adopt a 'negative list' approach, as opposed to the 'positive list' approach used in the negotiation of the GATS. This means that the commitments agreed in such FTAs apply to any services – in principle including new services that are developed over time, however they are delivered – unless exceptions are entered in the respective schedules. They may be, consequently, more suitable to encompass future technological development and tend to have a more positive impact on flows of knowledge embedded in services.[47]

E-Commerce and Data Flows

As early as 1998, WTO members realized that e-commerce was growing and creating new opportunities for trade. At the Second Ministerial Conference, in May 1998, Ministers adopted a Declaration on Global Electronic Commerce, which called for the establishment of a comprehensive Work Programme. They also agreed to 'continue their current practice of not imposing customs duties on electronic transmissions', a commitment that has been renewed by successive Ministerial Conferences since then.[48]

In the light of the outstanding development of the digital economy in recent years, and possibly also because of an interest in 'multilateralizing' developments in bilateral and plurilateral FTAs, the e-commerce discussions under the WTO are now more active than ever. Notably, at the latest Ministerial Conference in Buenos Aires, 71 members decided to 'initiate exploratory work together toward future WTO negotiations on trade-related aspects of electronic commerce'.[49]

All the analysed FTAs feature an e-commerce chapter, typically including provisions on issues such as the recognition of electronic

[47] However, that may not be the case if the parties enter reservations concerning 'new services', 'unrecognised or technically unfeasible services' or similar caveats. See, for example, Annex 8-B-II of the EU–Japan Agreement, pp. 165 and 174.

[48] See www.wto.org/english/tratop_e/ecom_e/ecom_e.htm. The Declaration on Global Electronic Commerce is available in WTO Document WT/MIN(98)/DEC/2, 25 May 1998. See also para. 5(c) of the GATS Annex on Telecommunications, with respect to the movement of information through telecommunications transport networks.

[49] See WTO Document WT/MIN(17)/60, 13 December 2017. For a helpful comprehensive list, prepared by a diversified group of WTO members, of all trade-related elements that could potentially be included in a new agreement on e-commerce, see WTO Document JOB/GC/116/Rev.2, 15 June 2017.

signatures, online consumer protection, unsolicited electronic messages and general legal frameworks governing electronic transactions. They all include a definitive obligation not to impose customs duties on electronic transmissions, except for ChAFTA (Article 12.3), where the commitment is attached to the WTO moratorium.

More interesting, for the purposes of our analysis, are the FTA provisions on data flows. Here, there is a notable difference between the approaches taken by the United States and the European Union.

Largely as a result of lobbying by influential Internet companies, the United States took the lead in promoting the free flow of digital information.[50] KORUS was the first FTA to include specific, albeit non-binding, language in that respect. Its Article 15.8 provides that parties 'shall endeavor to refrain from imposing or maintaining unnecessary barriers to electronic information flows across borders'. After that, the US succeeded in including binding language in the TPP, according to which parties 'shall allow the cross-border transfer of information by electronic means, including personal information, when this activity is for the conduct of the business of a covered person' (Article 14.11.2).[51] Although the US withdrew from the TPP, the CPTPP, signed by the 11 remaining participants, kept intact the previously agreed language on digital trade. A similar provision is also found in USMCA (Article 19.11).

In contrast, the European Union is focused on ensuring that the promotion of e-commerce will be compatible with appropriate standards of data protection, so as to ensure the confidence of users. The EU–Colombia/Peru/Ecuador Agreement is silent on data flows. CETA provides that the e-commerce chapter 'does not impose an obligation on a Party to allow a delivery transmitted by electronic means except in accordance with the Party's obligations' under the agreement (Article 16.2.2). The more recent EU–Japan Agreement, on the other hand, provides that the parties shall 'reassess, within three years' of its entry into force, 'the need for inclusion of provisions on the free flow of data' (Article 8.81).[52]

[50] For more details on how the United States constructed the 'digital trade agenda', including the influence of 'big tech' US companies, see J. Kelsey (2018), pp. 277–281.

[51] S. Aaronson and P. Leblond (2018), p. 255.

[52] This may be because, according to J. Kelsey (2018, pp. 280–281), Japan became the 'most active champion' of the digital trade agenda, proposing TPP-style provisions in its subsequent negotiations.

Finally, the ChAFTA, as expected in view of China's policies in the area of Internet regulation – such as the so-called 'Great Firewall' – does not expressly regulate data flows.

Another important digital trade-related aspect covered by FTAs concerns limitations of liability of Internet service providers ('ISPs'). Most analysed FTAs require signatories to provide for such limitations in domestic legislation, so that ISPs are not held liable for information transmitted by customers, as long as they act expeditiously to remove or to disable access to such information upon becoming aware that it violates a given right. The underlying rationale, as usually pointed out by players in the ISP industry, is that holding them liable for the acts of users could place an unreasonable burden on such companies, who in many cases lack control over individual content.[53] In other words, imposing excessive liability could 'kill the messenger' and incentives to the facilitation of networking between users, which is essential to promote increasingly important exchanges of data and information.

Exceptions that Allow Restrictions to Information and Data Flows

The other side of the coin of the liberalization of e-commerce and data flows is the concern about the protection of personal privacy and other non-trade values, which may lead to limitations to the principle of the free flow of data.

To the extent that said flows – as well as any other flows of knowledge embedded in services – are part of commitments to trade in services covered by the GATS, the general exceptions set forth in its Article XIV may be relevant. Such exceptions refer, inter alia, to measures necessary to secure compliance with laws or regulations relating to personal data, fraud and safety,[54] or to enforce any other laws otherwise consistent with

[53] See, e.g., the Computer & Communications Industry Association (CCIA) reply to the US Department of Commerce inquiry on Global Free Flow of Information on the Internet, Docket no. 100921457-0457-01, 2010, available at www.ntia.doc.gov/files/ntia/ccia_reply_to_doc-ntia_noi_on_global_free_flow_of_information.pdf. Along similar lines, the US has recently stated in the WTO that the lack of limitation of ISP liability for third-party content 'can suppress vibrant online forums and stifle innovation in services that depend on user engagement'. According to the US, 'trade rules can guarantee that merely storing, processing, or transmitting content does not make intermediaries legally liable for the content of that data, while still allowing for measures that ensure rigorous enforcement of intellectual property rights and criminal laws'. See WTO Document JOB/GC/178, 12 April 2018.

[54] See Article XIV(c)(ii) and (iii) of the GATS.

the GATS (e.g. laws on cybercrime). Pursuant to the GATS, in addition to being 'necessary', the measures must not be applied in a manner that constitutes 'a means of arbitrary or unjustifiable discrimination between countries where like conditions prevail, or a disguised restriction on trade in services'. Also important are the security exceptions provided for in Article XIV*bis* of the GATS, and the exception concerning security and confidentiality of messages provided for in para. 5(d) of the GATS Annex on Telecommunications.[55]

At the plurilateral or bilateral level, all the EU agreements, even when not requiring free data flows, include an explicit recognition of the importance of protecting the personal data of e-commerce users.[56] Furthermore, the FTA between the EU and Colombia/Peru/Ecuador includes a best-efforts undertaking for parties to develop domestic regulations for the protection of personal data (Article 164). CETA goes a step further and mandates parties to adopt measures for the protection of personal information, taking into account international standards of data protection (Article 16.4).

ChAFTA has a similar obligation, even though it is carefully softened by acknowledging 'differences in existing systems for personal information protection in the territories of the Parties', and by qualifying the measures of protection required as those that each one 'considers appropriate', taking into account international standards 'to the extent possible' (Article 12.8). KORUS merely acknowledges 'the importance of protecting personal information', in the same provision where parties endeavour to promote free information flows (Article 15.8).

The TPP and USMCA are more detailed in that respect. They require parties to adopt a legal framework for the protection of personal information that takes into account 'principles and guidelines of relevant international bodies' (TPP, Article 14.8; USMCA, Article 19.8). A footnote clarifies that there is significant flexibility to implement that

[55] Article XIV*bis* allows a member not to disclose information that it 'considers contrary to its essential security interests'. Para. 5(d) of the Annex on Telecommunications, as an exception to para. 5(c) obligation to allow service suppliers to move information through telecommunications networks within and across borders, permits measures 'necessary to ensure the security and confidentiality of messages, subject to the requirement that such measures are not applied in a manner which would constitute a means of arbitrary or unjustifiable discrimination or a disguised restriction on trade in services'.

[56] This is an expected reflection of the EU's own regulations on personal data protection, in particular the General Data Protection Regulation (GDPR), which recently entered into force.

obligation. 'Comprehensive privacy' laws, or even 'laws that provide for the enforcement of voluntary undertakings by enterprises relating to privacy' are sufficient. The provision further recognizes that parties may take different approaches to protecting personal information and, interestingly, urges them to develop 'mechanisms to promote compatibility between these different regimes'.[57] Both agreements also encourage cooperation on cybersecurity matters (TPP, Article 14.16; USMCA, Article 19.15).

The exceptions referred to above have a key role in the digital economy. While allowing legitimate controls to protect, for example, privacy rights and national security, they may strike an appropriate balance by ensuring that controls are not excessive (i.e. not beyond what is *necessary*) and not used as a disguised form of protectionism.

A Typology of Current Trade in Knowledge Rules

The discussion above shows that different types of trade rules are applicable to, and/or directly impact knowledge (including information and data) flows. In the synoptic table below (Table 22.1), we classify the main applicable provisions under four broad categories of trade disciplines relating to such flows. While there may admittedly be some overlap, the proposed categories are helpful to provide an overall comparative view of how cross-border knowledge flows are affected by the WTO agreements and FTAs.

Are New WTO Rules Needed?

On the basis of a broad understanding – as discussed in the previous section – of how WTO and FTA disciplines may affect knowledge flows, we address the question of whether the current WTO disciplines appear sufficient to promote such flows, or whether new trade rules, especially those identified in recent FTAs, should be multilateralized. We attempt to respond by reference to the categories of disciplines proposed in Table 22.1.

[57] This could be seen as a response to the EU largely unilateral 'adequacy decisions' under the GDPR, which determine whether other countries ensure an adequate level of data protection. See Article 45 of Regulation (EU) 2016/679.

Table 22.1 *Provisions relating to knowledge flows in WTO agreements and selected FTAs*

Provisions relating to knowledge flows in WTO agreements and selected FTAs			
Category	**WTO provisions**	**Common provisions in selected FTAs**	**Specificities of selected FTAs**
Technology-enabling goods and services	**Free trade of information technology products** (ITA; GATT, Article II) **Access to telecommunications infrastructure** (GATS, Annex on Telecommunications, para. 5)	**Reaffirmation of GATS commitments on access to telecommunications infrastructure**	**Obligation to take part in the ITA** (TPP, Article 2.17) **Obligations on access to internet services** (TPP, Article 14.10/USMCA, Article 19.10), and on **internet interconnection charge sharing** (TPP, Article 14.12)
Incentives to the creation of knowledge	**Permission for non-specific R&D subsidies** (SCM, Article 2 and expired Article 8.2(a); AoA, Annex 2, para. 2(a)) **Incentives to innovation through minimum standards of protection of IP rights** (TRIPS, Articles 10, 12, 25, 26, 27, 33, 34, 41 to 61, and others).	**Best efforts to strengthen cooperation in the areas of science, technology, research and innovation, including participation of private sector** **TRIPS-plus standards of protection of IP rights, in most cases including compliance with several international conventions,**	**Prohibition to condition investments on the achievement of a given level or value of R&D activities** (EU–Japan, Article 8.11.1) **Enhanced cooperation on science, technology, research and innovation** (CETA, Article 25.5)

and minimum periods of protection for undisclosed data concerning pharmaceutical and agrochemical products As an exception to the prohibition of certain investment-related requirements, **permission to condition advantages to investors on performing R&D locally** (except ChAFTA and EU–Colombia/Peru/Ecuador, which do not regulate performance requirements)	**Best efforts to promote lasting relations between scientific communities, including through financing from public resources, and capacity building** (EU–Colombia/Peru/Ecuador, Article 255) **Facilitation of temporary stay of short-term visitors, specifically for technical and scientific researchers** (EU–Colombia/Peru/Ecuador, Article 128) **Best efforts to facilitate the entry and exit of data and equipment used in R&D activities** (EU–Colombia/Peru/Ecuador, Article 255.6) **Prohibition (as civil and criminal offence) of manufacture and marketing of devices used to decode encrypted signals, and of distribution and wilful receipt of such**

Table 22.1 (*cont.*)

Provisions relating to knowledge flows in WTO agreements and selected FTAs			
Category	**WTO provisions**	**Common provisions in selected FTAs**	**Specificities of selected FTAs**
			signals (TPP, Article 18.79 [suspended under the CPTPP]/USMCA, Article 20.86/KORUS, Article 18.7)
Provisions relating to the transfer of knowledge, information and data flows	**Several provisions on technical cooperation** (GATS, Annex on Telecommunications, para. 6; TRIPS, Article 67) **Promotion of technology transfer** (TRIPS, Articles 7, 8(2), 40(1), 66.2) **Safeguards to avoid IP overprotection, and fair use exceptions** (TRIPS, Articles 8(1), 9(2), 13, 14(6), 25, 26(2), 27(2), 27(3), 30, 31, 31*bis*, 39(3), 40(2), 41 (1), 48(1), 50(7), 60	**Acknowledgement of importance of capacity building, technical assistance, exchange of information, experts and technology** **Cooperation on policies involving the use of IP for research, innovation and economic growth** **Safeguards to avoid IP overprotection, and exceptions – e.g. fair use policies, freedom to choose IP exhaustion rules, permission for limits on**	**Acknowledgment of need to maintain balance between IP protection and the public interest, especially regarding education, culture, research, public health, food security, environment, access to information and technology transfer** (EU–Colombia/Peru/Ecuador, Article 196), which contributes to the **aim to establish a sound and viable technological base** (idem, Article 197)

Commitments to trade in services that embed knowledge (GATS schedules of commitments) **Temporary agreement to keep e-commerce duty-free** (Ministerial decisions to maintain 'moratorium' on customs duties) **Information flows across telecommunications networks** (GATS, Annex on Telecommunications, para. 5(c))	**TPMs, permission for measures to prevent adverse effects to international transfer of technology** **Further commitments to trade in services that embed knowledge, and specific rules on the temporary presence of business persons** **In most cases, permanent agreement to keep e-commerce duty-free** **In most cases, mandatory ISP limitation of liability requirements** (optional provision in the case of ChAFTA; provision not included in EU–Japan; and applicability suspended in CPTPP) **Prohibition of investment-related requirements to transfer technology** (except ChAFTA and EU–Colombia/Peru/Ecuador)	**Recognition of the importance of a rich and accessible public domain, including databases of registered IP rights** (TPP, Article 18.15), and **endeavours to give due consideration to fair use of copyright, including for teaching, scholarship, and research purposes** (TPP, Article 18.66) **Exchange of experiences and information on practices and policies affecting transfer of technology** (EU–Colombia/Peru/Ecuador, Article 255.1) **Parties not obliged to allow free data flows, except where required under other provisions of the agreement** (CETA, Article 16.2.2). **Endeavour to refrain from imposing unnecessary barriers to cross-border**

Table 22.1 (*cont.*)

Provisions relating to knowledge flows in WTO agreements and selected FTAs			
Category	WTO provisions	Common provisions in selected FTAs	Specificities of selected FTAs
			data flows (KORUS, Article 15.8) **Obligation to allow cross-border data flows, including personal information** (TPP, Article 14.11.2/USMCA, Article 19.11) **Reassessment within 3 years of need for inclusion of provisions on the free data flows** (EU–Japan, Article 8.81). **Prohibition on requirement to disclose source code of software owned by a person of another party** (TPP, Article 14.17/EU–Japan, Article 8.73/USMCA, Article 19.16), **except**

			software used for 'critical infrastructure' (TPP, Article 14.17.2) **Prohibition of requirements to localize computing facilities** (TPP, Article 14.13/USMCA, Article 19.12)
Exceptions allowed to protect non-trade values/ legitimate restrictions to data flows	**Privacy/protection of personal data** (GATS, Article XIV(c)(ii)) **National security** (GATS, Article XIV*bis*) **Security and confidentiality of messages** (GATS, Annex on Telecommunications, para. 5(d))	**Acknowledgement of importance of, and in some cases obligation to adopt, a legal framework for the protection of personal information** **On telecommunications, obligation to ensure confidentiality of telecommunications and related traffic data** **Best efforts (or obligation, in the case of TPP and USMCA) to adopt measures to protect e-commerce consumers from fraudulent practices, and from unsolicited**	**Obligation to develop electronic commerce in a manner that is consistent with the international standards of data protection, to ensure the confidence of users of electronic commerce** (EU–Colombia/Peru/Ecuador, Article 164) **Best efforts to adopt non-discriminatory practices in protecting users of electronic commerce from personal information protection violations** (TPP, Article 14.8/USMCA, Article 19.8)

Table 22.1 (*cont.*)

Provisions relating to knowledge flows in WTO agreements and selected FTAs			
Category	**WTO provisions**	**Common provisions in selected FTAs**	**Specificities of selected FTAs**
		commercial electronic messages	**Measures to protect personal data may be limited to those that each party considers appropriate, taking into account differences in national systems** (ChAFTA, Article 12.8) **Cooperation on cybersecurity matters** (TPP, Article 14.16/ USMCA, Article 19.15/EU–Japan, Article 8.80)

Source: Author.

On Technology-Enabling Goods and Services

First, in relation to provisions promoting access to technology-enabling goods and services, such as information technology goods and telecommunications services that are required to access the Internet, there does not appear to be a need for new rules. There is of course room for deeper market access commitments under the existing rules, but the latter – in particular the plurilateral ITA and the GATS Annex on Telecommunications – already seem to provide a comprehensive and sufficient legal framework to facilitate the trade of such enablers of access to knowledge. It would also be very positive if future FTAs followed the example of the TPP, which offered a welcoming contribution to WTO commitments by requiring members to adhere to the ITA.

On Incentives for the Creation of Knowledge

Second, with respect to mechanisms to incentivize the creation (and further dissemination) of knowledge, one could argue that the SCM Agreement provisions defining R&D subsidies as non-actionable should be revived, in order to re-establish policy space for such measures that may be important to correct market failures and incentivize positive innovation externalities.[58] However, as discussed above, the rules that currently apply under the SCM Agreement, as well as under the Agreement on Agriculture, already seem to leave room for R&D subsidies that are not specific and, consequently, are not trade-distorting.

In our view, the current WTO rules provide a satisfactory normative framework to regulate R&D subsidies or, in the words of Keith Maskus, 'a sensible policy foundation' and an 'apparent equilibrium' that 'one should be cautious about disrupting'.[59]

Concerning the protection of IP rights, in view of the fact that FTAs typically require TRIPS-plus standards of protection, and include disciplines purportedly more suitable to the digital economy, one may wonder

[58] See B. Hoekman et al. (2004), p. 23.

[59] In a 2015 paper, K. Maskus (2015, pp. 1–10) discussed whether new WTO disciplines were needed for R&D subsidies. He proposed a number of 'basic principles' to sort out 'damaging subsidization' from 'properly designed programs' – including an assessment of whether they intend to protect the domestic industry or to resolve market failures by linking domestic firms with global innovation networks, and incentivizing the openness of public research grants to foreign competition – but concluded that they would work better as guidelines, as opposed to written in a revised SCM Agreement.

whether it would be desirable to multilateralize them.[60] In fact, by virtue of the most-favoured nation obligation in Article 4 of the TRIPS Agreement, which has no exception regarding FTAs, IP concessions made at the bilateral or plurilateral level will in most cases have to be multilateralized. But that is of course different than modifying the level of protection required by the TRIPS Agreement.

Here, a key question would be: does strengthening IP protection (to TRIPS-plus levels) really lead to more creation and dissemination of knowledge, and ultimately more welfare to society as a whole?

That is a difficult question to answer, especially in the absence of studies to inform whether TRIPS-plus obligations in FTAs lead to more innovation and cross-border knowledge flows, compared to standard FTAs.[61] It would not seem prudent, therefore, to propose a multilateralization of stronger levels of protection of IP rights at this stage.[62] Nor does there appear to be a need to adapt the TRIPS Agreement to the digital world.[63]

In bilateral or plurilateral negotiations, of course, it will remain up to each country to assess whether strengthening and/or regulating certain IP rights is desirable, which presumably will depend, among other aspects, on the overall bargain on the table and the level of development of the country in question.

[60] Stakeholders of the digital trade agenda, in particular online content industries, would probably argue so, given that they describe copyright infringement as a major barrier to such trade and consequently lobby for stronger protection of IP rights relating to the digital world, including, for example, punishment against users, and disciplines to protect 'self-help' mechanisms such as TPMs. See, e.g., W. J. Drake (2016), p. 11, and R. F. Fefer et al. (2018), pp. 15–17.

[61] See K. Maskus (2016, p. 5), noting precisely the lack of evidence to conclude whether TRIPS-plus standards 'increase innovation, technology flows and information spillovers'. See also D. Rodrik (2004, p. 35), arguing that the 'adverse effects on technological capacity' of the TRIPS Agreement and its more restrictive versions in FTAs still need to receive commensurate attention, compared to the issue of public health and access to essential medicines.

[62] Earlier, K. E. Maskus and J. H. Reichman (2005, pp. 36–39) had argued for a 'moratorium' on stronger protection of IP rights, by virtue of 'growing fears' of counterproductive effects of overprotection. They suggested that a long period of 'trial and error' would be needed for countries at different development stages to accommodate existing IP protection standards to their own systems of innovation. Hoekman et al. (2004, p. 16), furthermore, observe that economic literature commonly finds that the poorest countries are unlikely to benefit from strong IP rights.

[63] A. Taubman (2012) discusses whether the TRIPS has continuing value in the digital environment, and concludes that its 'analogue' framework, based on universal balancing principles and neutral with respect to any specific technical modes of exploiting IP rights, is probably 'an appropriate fit after all for a digital form of trade'.

One area where there would seem to be a stronger case for multilateralizing FTA provisions that may promote further access to knowledge is scientific cooperation. The agreements made by the EU, in particular, typically contain provisions to enhance cooperation on science, research and innovation. The FTA between the EU and Colombia/Peru/Ecuador, as seen above, features a number of provisions to incentivize scientific exchange, including through the temporary entry of scientific researchers, data and equipment. In spite of their best-efforts language, if effectively implemented, such incentives are bound to have a positive effect on knowledge flows.

A very recent and positive development relating to access to scientific knowledge, while not included in any FTAs so far, was the launch of cOAlition S. That is an initiative by 11 national research funding organizations in Europe, with the support of the European Commission and the European Research Council (ERC), to ensure that, as from January 2020, scientific publications on the results from research funded by public grants provided by the involved organizations will be published under open licences.[64] While a binding multilateral agreement of similar content would not appear realistic in the short term, this is perhaps an initiative well worth discussing and encouraging in the WTO.

On Provisions Facilitating Cross-Border Flows of Knowledge

Third, and finally, in the realm of provisions concerning the transfer of knowledge it is worth discussing the desirability of new multilateral trade rules in the following two areas:[65] (i) 'forced' technology transfer

[64] See www.scienceeurope.org/coalition-s. The initiative resembles an interesting academic proposal for a future WTO Agreement on Access to Basic Science and Technology (ABST), described by Hoekman et al. (2004, p. 27) as having 'considerable potential' to expand technology transfer to developing countries.

[65] Another area is the classification of services, which, as commented by many authors – see, e.g., N. Sen (2018, pp. 331–342), and M. Burri (2017, pp. 80–98) – is based on an outdated 1991 system that poses challenges with respect to the categorization of several Internet-based services. This problem may indeed affect the applicability of trade rules to certain knowledge flows, especially in the form of digital information flows (even though the outdating issue is not exclusive to the digital realm and does not concern only the GATS). The optimal solution, in our view, lies in the progressive negotiation of new commitments under the existing rules, as illustrated by the expanded ITA, which successfully accommodated new digital economy products. We also note that nothing in the legal text of the GATS requires parties to necessarily adopt a specific system of classification. Article XIX.3 only requires the establishment of negotiating guidelines and procedures. The Guidelines for Scheduling of Specific Commitments under the GATS (WTO

requirements; and (ii) commitments to free data flows in the light of mounting restrictions justified by non-trade values.

Technology Transfer Requirements

As discussed above, recent FTAs, including the TPP, USMCA, and the EU–Japan Agreement, prohibit so-called 'forced technology transfer' and 'disclosure of source code' requirements.

China seems to be a target of concerns relating to those measures. In 2017, the US initiated a Section 301 investigation into China's policies and practices relating to technology transfer, IP and innovation, which resulted in the unilateral imposition of tariffs and an ongoing 'trade war'. The US and the EU have also recently initiated WTO disputes against China (DS542 and DS549), challenging measures concerning the protection of IP rights and transfer of technology. The complaints are of violation of the national treatment principle under the TRIPS Agreement, as well as specific provisions on the protection of patents and trade secrets.

Prior to that, the United States was already relying on the WTO e-commerce Work Programme as part of a broader strategy to multilateralize the referred performance requirements and counter China's policies.[66] The question is, then, whether multilateralization would be desirable.

A first point to note in this respect is that, to the extent that the measures in question indeed involve the 'forced' transfer of technology, the current rules applicable under the TRIPS Agreement may be sufficient to curb them. The fact that WTO disputes have been initiated on the basis of TRIPS provisions to address China's policies appears to indicate, in itself, that new rules are not necessarily required.[67]

Second, regarding the prohibition of requirements to disclose source code, although profound discussions are still scarce, there is widespread criticism among activists (in particular against TPP) that the provision only served the interests of powerful US and Japanese companies, was not sufficiently debated and was 'thrown in at the last minute in an

document S/L/92, 28 March 2001), in their turn, provide that, where compatibility with the 1991 CPC is not possible, members may use their own classifications, if they give 'a sufficiently detailed definition to avoid any ambiguity as to the scope of the commitment'.

66 See, for example, WTO Document JOB/GC/94, 4 July 2016, paras 2.6 and 2.7.

67 It should be noted that Article 7.3 of China's Protocol of Accession to the WTO contains an explicit prohibition of technology transfer requirements. However, such provision is not mentioned in the requests for consultations that initiated either of the above-mentioned disputes.

obscure location' in the Agreement (i.e. in the e-commerce, rather than the IP, chapter).[68]

Third, even without discussing the merit of whether such measures are good or bad policy and whether they help or hurt knowledge flows, the fact is that they seem indeed to be misplaced in the ongoing WTO e-commerce discussions. Those types of measures are typically discussed as performance requirements relating to foreign investment,[69] and it should remain up to participants in FTAs or investment agreements to decide whether or not they are desirable obligations, as part of a greater bargain.

Developing countries, in particular, may have an interest in keeping policy space in this area. It is also worth remembering that technology transfer 'offsets' in government procurement in certain sectors (especially defence) are quite common even among developed countries, which seems to reinforce a conclusion that further discussion would be necessary before multilateralizing general prohibitions on technology transfer requirements.

Free Data Flows vs Data Protection Policies

Together with the celebration of the benefits and opportunities of data flows for the world economy, came increasing concerns, expressed by various governments and stakeholders, about the risks that they may pose for non-trade values, especially the protection of personal privacy and national security. Scandals such as the 2013 Snowden surveillance revelations and, more recently, Cambridge Analytica, did anything but lessen such concerns.

Policies like data protection regulations and localization requirements, while not new phenomena,[70] are clearly on the rise. Recent interesting papers have identified several types of data localization policies, enacted by dozens of countries.[71] As usually happens with public policies that

[68] See, e.g., Electronic Frontier Foundation, 'TPP Threatens Security and Safety by Locking Down US Policy on Source Code Audit', available at www.eff.org/pt-br/node/89193; and Software Freedom Law Center, 'TPP Article 14.17 & Free Software: No Harm, No Foul', available at www.softwarefreedom.org/blog/2015/nov/23/TPP-Article-14.

[69] They may also already be covered by obligations under the GATS and under trade in services chapters in FTAs, to the extent that they fall within the scope of the respectively agreed commitments.

[70] See W. J. Drake (2016), pp. 4–9.

[71] See A. Chander and U. P. Lê (2014), pp. 5–26, and N. Cory (2017), pp. 20–31. As Nigel Cory explains, data localization comes in many forms, from blanket bans on data

affect international trade, some of them probably aim at achieving legitimate goals, while others might be just an elegant disguise for protectionism or twenty-first century industrial policies.

To some extent, it seems, in reaction to such policies, many digital economy specialists and trade policy officials have recently commented that the WTO trade rules 'lack clarity', are 'woefully out of date' or 'have not kept pace with the complexities of the digital economy', which results in a 'pressing need' to adapt them to such contemporary reality.[72] Many note that the WTO agreements are silent on data flows,[73] and refer to more modern rules agreed in FTAs.

As a result, there are now proposals to create new trade rules to curb the perceived threats to free data flows, along the lines of those agreed in the e-commerce chapter of the TPP.[74] While such proposals could be submitted to different international fora, the trade arena appears to be preferred – as became the case with IP rights – by virtue of its 'teeth' that facilitate enforceability, in comparison to other regimes.

We are sceptical that any new, 'hard' trade rules can be a definitive panacea for that perceived threat, for a number of reasons. First, the barriers to cross-border data flows are very diversified and are enacted for radically different regulatory reasons, from taxation, payment card regulations, or traffic routing rules, to privacy, cybersecurity or censorship. Treating all such policies as birds of a feather that could be dealt with by a single set of rules will hardly be feasible.

Second, every country shares a concern to maintain certain policy space, at least with respect to security or other values, if not necessarily to privacy. Digital trade and privacy, or data protection, or cybersecurity, may be seen as a modern version of classic 'trade *and*...' debates, such as trade and environment, trade and public health or trade and labour. When such contrasting policy goals are at stake, the solution, at the end of the day, always lies at striking the right balance between them.

The practical consequence is that the 'free trade' rules will come with non-trade exceptions. The TPP itself provides a good example. While there is a prima facie obligation to allow free data flows, an exception

transfers to sector-specific restrictions covering personal data, accounting and tax information, telecommunications, mapping, online publishing data and others.

72 See, e.g., M. Burri (2017), pp. 126–131; N. Cory (2017), p. 14; S. Aaronson (2015), p. 678; R. F. Fefer et al. (2018), p. 29; N. Sen (2018), p. 338. For a different perspective, see A. Taubman (2012).

73 See, e.g., R. F. Fefer et al. (2018), p. 12.

74 The United states is one of the main proponents – see WTO Document JOB/GC/94, 4 July 2016.

permits any measures (inconsistent with the free data flow obligation) 'to achieve a legitimate public policy objective', provided that they are not applied in a discriminatory manner or as a disguised restriction on trade, and that the restrictions are not greater than required to achieve the objective.[75] Notably, the open-ended term 'legitimate public policy objective' means that it is easier to meet the requirements of the TPP exception than those of the GATS general exceptions under Article XIV, where the list of permitted non-trade policies is exhaustive.

Finally, we note that the current trade rules – to the extent that GATS commitments are applicable without national treatment limitations, concerning e.g. cross-border data processing services – are actually applicable to data localization measures. Whether a given measure will fall within a commitment and whether it will be justified under limitations or specific exceptions is something that may need to be settled on a case-by-case basis.[76]

Our scepticism regarding the high hopes for free data flow rules does not mean that a WTO agreement on e-commerce would not be important. Quite on the contrary. Legally, depending on how undertakings to maintain 'free' data flows are disciplined, they could become a very ingenious way to lock in a major and rare horizontal commitment to trade in cross-border services that are delivered electronically, in various sectors at the same time. Also, from a policy perspective, a new e-commerce agreement would perhaps send a positive message, important in these difficult times for global trade, that the WTO continues to lead the way to progressive trade liberalization.[77]

Conclusion

There is always room to improve laws and regulations. Law is always lagging behind social changes.[78] If domestic law faces that constant challenge, the more complex realm of international law (which requires understanding between representatives of two or many more different

[75] See Article 14.13.3 of the TPP. Article 19.11 of USMCA has similar language, but includes a necessity test.

[76] For an interesting brief discussion about this, see N. Sen (2018), pp. 335–338.

[77] That might explain why, when recently challenged, in a March 2018 episode of *BBC HARDtalk*, to show any sign of relevance of the WTO vis-à-vis current US policies, Director General Roberto Azevedo referred to the e-commerce negotiations, and rebutted that they are definitely not a mere 'detail', as Stephen Sackur had dismissively described.

[78] A. T. Vanderbilt (1951), p. 433.

jurisdictions) is certainly no different, particularly so in times of rapid changes constantly brought about by the revolution in information technology.

Improved commitments to existing multilateral rules, guidelines on issues such as R&D subsidies and policies on open access to science, as well as a possible new e-commerce agreement including undertakings to keep data flows free, as discussed in this chapter, could be very beneficial to cross-border knowledge flows. However, we believe that the perception of an urgent *need* for new multilateral legal disciplines is exaggerated, to the extent that it implies that the current rules are plainly insufficient. We have seen that WTO rules are already applicable to, and impact, knowledge flows in several ways. They have helped, and will continue to be important, to encourage such flows.

We also think it is advisable to avoid a capture of the free-data-flow discourse and momentum by sensitive and, in our understanding, unrelated issues – such as performance requirements and strengthening levels of protection of IP rights – which require much more discussion and, wherever they are negotiated, a broader exchange of concessions that ensures a balanced result. In our view, from a policy perspective, those issues are better left to bilateral or plurilateral negotiations at this stage.

A rush to impose changes in multilateral behind-the-border regulations that affect so-called digital industrial policies without properly understanding and measuring their impact is undesirable, as it could delay or even hamper potentially valuable multilateral results of the ongoing e-commerce negotiations. Further research is desirable to better understand the effect of both the rules (especially new rules adopted in FTAs, which still need to enter into force and be tested) and the policies they intend to regulate.

Bibliography

Aaronson, Susan, 'Why Trade Agreements are not Setting Information Free: The Lost History and Reinvigorated Debate over Cross-Border Data Flows, Human Rights, and National Security' (2015), *World Trade Review* 14, 4: 671–700.

Aaronson, Susan and Leblond, Patrick, 'Another Digital Divide: The Rise of Data Realms and its Implications for the WTO' (2018), *Journal of International Economic Law* 21: 245–272.

Athreye, Suma and Yang, Yong, 'Disembodied Knowledge Flows in the World Economy', WIPO Economic Research Working Paper No. 3, 2011.

Brodie, Ian and Brodie, Lyn, 'A knowledge-Information-Data Concept Model For Engineering Education' (2009), *Australasian Journal of Engineering Education* 15, 3: 137–144.

Burri, Mira, 'The Governance of Data and Data Flows in Trade Agreements: The Pitfalls of Legal Adaptation' (2017), *UC Davis Law Review* 51: 65–133.

Capling, Ann, 'Trading Ideas: The Politics of Intellectual Property', in B. Hocking and S. McGuire (eds), *Trade Politics*, 2nd ed., London: Routledge, 2004, pp. 179–193.

Castro, Daniel and McQuinn, Alan, 'Cross-border data flows enable growth in all industries' (2015), *Information Technology & Innovation Foundation*, February.

Chander, Anupam and Lê, Uyên P., 'Breaking the Web: Data Localization vs. the Global Internet', *Emory Law Journal, Forthcoming*, UC Davis Legal Studies Research Paper No. 378, March 2014.

Cory, Nigel, 'Cross-border Data Flows: Where Are the Barriers, and What Do They Cost?' (2017), *Information Technology & Innovation Foundation*, May.

David, Paul A., 'Koyaanisqatsi in Cyberspace: The Economics of an "Out Of Balance" Regime of Private Property Rights In Data And Information', in K. E. Maskus and J. H. Reichman (eds), *International Public Goods and Transfer of Technology under a Globalized Intellectual Property Regime*, Cambridge: Cambridge University Press, 2005, pp. 81–120.

Drake, William J., 'Data localization and Barriers to Transborder Data Flows', background paper, 14–15 September 2016, The World Economic Forum, Geneva.

Fefer, Rachel F., Akhtar, Shayerah Ilias and Morrison, Wayne M., 'Digital Trade and U.S. Trade Policy', *Congressional Research Service*, R44565, 11 May 2018.

Finger, Joseph Michael and Nogués, Julio J., 'The Unbalanced Uruguay Round Outcome: The New Areas in Future WTO Negotiations' (2002), *The World Economy* 25: 321–340.

Hoekman, Bernard, Maskus, Keith E. and Saggi, Kamal, 'Transfer of Technology to Developing Countries: Unilateral and Multilateral Policy Options', World Bank Policy Research Working Paper No. 3332, June 2004.

Kelsey, Jane, 'How a TPP-Style E-commerce Outcome in the WTO Would Endanger the Development Dimension of the GATS Acquis (and Potentially the WTO)' (2018), *Journal of International Economic Law* 21: 274–295.

Liu, Han-Wei, 'International Standards in Flux: A Balkanized ICT Standard-Setting Paradigm and its Implications For the WTO' (2014), *Journal of International Economic Law* 17: 551–600.

Maskus, Keith, 'Research and Development Subsidies: A Need for WTO Disciplines?', *E15Initiative. Geneva: International Centre for Trade and Sustainable Development (ICTSD) and World Economic Forum*, 2015.

Maskus, Keith, 'Patents and Technology Transfer through Trade and the Role of Regional Trade Agreements', Think-piece prepared for MCTI conference, East–West Center, January 2016.

Maskus, Keith E. and Reichman, Jerome H., 'The Globalization of Private Knowledge Goods and the Privatization of Global Public Goods', in K. E. Maskus and J. H. Reichman (eds), *International Public Goods and Transfer of Technology under a Globalized Intellectual Property Regime*, Cambridge: Cambridge University Press, 2005, pp. 3–45.

National Science Board, 'Invention, Knowledge Transfer, and Innovation', in *Science and Engineering Indicators 2018*, Alexandria, VA: National Science Foundation, 2018.

OECD, *National Innovation Systems*, Paris: OECD Publishing, 1997.

OECD, 'Trade in knowledge-intensive goods', in *Measuring Globalisation: OECD Economic Globalisation Indicators 2010*, Paris: OECD Publishing, 2010.

Papacharissi, Zizi, 'The Unbearable Lightness of Information and the Impossible Gravitas Of Knowledge: Big Data and the Makings of a Digital Orality' (2015), *Media, Culture & Society* 37, 7: 1095–1100.

Rodrik, Dani, 'Industrial Policy for the Twenty-First Century', Faculty Research Working Papers Series, RWP04-047, Harvard University, John F. Kennedy School of Government, November 2004.

Sen, Nivedita, 'Understanding the Role of the WTO in International Data Flows: Taking the Liberalization or the Regulatory Autonomy Path?' (2018), *Journal of International Economic Law*, 21, 2: 323–348.

Taubman, Antony Scott, 'TRIPS Encounters the Internet: An Analogue Treaty in a Digital Age, or the First Trade 2.0 Agreement?', in M. Burri and R. Cottier (eds), *Trade Governance in the Digital Age*, Cambridge University Press, 2012, pp. 299–322.

Vanderbilt, Arthur T., 'The Modernization of the Law' (1951), *Cornell Law Quarterly* 36, 3: 433–442.

Watal, Jayashree and Caminero, Leticia, 'Least-Developed Countries, Transfer of Technology and the TRIPS Agreement', Staff Working Paper ERSD-2018-01, World Trade Organization, 22 February 2018.

World Trade Organization (WTO), *15 Years of the Information Technology Agreement: Boosting Trade, Innovation and Digital Connectivity*, Geneva: WTO, 2017.

23

The Need for a Global Framework for Knowledge Transactions: Cross-Border Licensing and Enforcement

JACQUES DE WERRA AND JEFF C. DODD*

Abstract

Knowledge-based IP transactions are of vital importance to the modern global economy. The IP and information products that trade by license are no less important to this century than goods were to the last (and are now). Yet, there is still no recognized, general statement of the commercial legal principles dealing with the unique but common transactional form of license (like the unique transactional form of sale) and the unique but common qualities of knowledge-based intangibles. Various private ordering regimes have emerged to address discrete types of transactions, whether by industry or other groups. One form of private ordering – "information law merchant" – covers only a limited number of participants who routinely trade in certain types of information assets. Effective participation in many forms of international commercial IP transactions often requires access to specialized legal knowledge, extensive commercial experience, and elaborate contract forms, creating barriers to entry for new actors, disadvantaging smaller firms, increasing transaction and performance costs, and fostering disputes. Another form of private ordering relates to FRAND licensing. Recent developments show a piecemeal and equally fragmented development of FRAND licensing terms and conditions (beyond the issue of the financial remuneration or royalties) provides no firmer foundation for addressing the general commerce in IP assets.

In short, the authors believe that, just as international organizations created to foster global commercial trade and finance analyzed and fashioned frameworks of contractual principles for sales of goods and secured financing, those international organizations and the organizations created to foster intellectual property protection and access should undertake a project to address the general principles relating to international IP commercial contracts.

* Currently a partner at Hunton Andrews Kurth, LLP, but since that firm had no hand in the preparation of this chapter, nothing in this chapter should be attributed to it, its partners or clients (see full biography at p. xvii).

Introduction

The commercial global trade in knowledge-based intangible assets grows apace;[1] the transactions that constitute this trade[2] being defined, for the most part, by some form of licence.[3] While property-based laws and treaties have long been in place for the protection of knowledge-based intangible assets categorized as intellectual property (IP), the contractual principles governing the commercial arrangements by which cross-border trade in such knowledge-based intangible assets is conducted oddly has not been the subject of a similar systematic and comprehensive

[1] We describe some of the dimensions of the trade in knowledge-based intangible assets in 'The Importance of Global Trade in Information Assets' below. We use 'knowledge-based intangible assets' and 'information assets' interchangeably. We also have intentionally used these terms instead of referring to 'intellectual property' or specific types of intellectual property, for very often licences reference a technology without specifically identifying the underlying intellectual property directed to the technology (think of the commonplace software licence) or may cover a complex or hybrid of interrelated intellectual property rights in a bundle and/or other forms of knowledge or information that may or may not have specific protections under all relevant intellectual property regimes. So, while intellectual property rights would be comprehended by the terms 'knowledge-based intangible assets' and 'information assets', those rights do not mark precincts of licensing transactions in modern international commerce. The essential contractual elements of the licences relating to such transactions, as well as traditional intellectual property transactions, are identical. To be sure, there may well be discrete clauses in specific licences addressing particular matters associated with identified intellectual property (e.g. confidentiality as to trade secrets), but the contractual elements in modern commercial licences are common, unique, and identifiable. While policymakers may choose to winnow out some subsets of such transactions, the trade in all forms of information assets across boundaries is growing and is an important part of modern commerce. See 'Knowledge Networks and Markets', OECD Science, Technology and Industry Policy Papers, No. 7, pp. 7–11, 29–35 (OECD 2013), available at http://dx.doi.org/10.1787/5k44wzw9q5zv-en (discussing transactions in knowledge, technology and intellectual property markets with a focus on licensing). This chapter addresses this burgeoning trade and the unique form that the commercial contracts used to support that trade as a class. See R. Nimmer and J. Dodd, *Modern Licensing Law* §§1A:1-1A:26, Chapter 2A (Thomson Reuters 2019–2020 ed.).

[2] See discussion elsewhere in this volume of the legal character of this trade (Chapter 2) and of the challenges in measuring it (Chapter 4).

[3] We adopt the following definition of 'licence': 'A license is a contract (whether by express agreement or by implication in law) authorizing, transferring, or allowing a licensee's contractual right, power privilege or immunity with respect to uses of information or rights in information (including intellectual property and intellectual property rights) controlled or made available by or through a licensor without transferring all rights or interests with respect to such information or rights. This includes a focus on what rights, immunities, or uses are permitted (including by access) or withheld in reference to use of the information or rights, as well as what the licensee has agreed to do or not to do with respect to the information or rights.' Nimmer & Dodd, *Modern Licensing Law* (n. 1 above), §1.4.

approach.[4] Tensions between the globalism of IP transactions and the localism of the applicable regulatory frameworks governing them make contractual commercial arrangements for such transactions vulnerable to numerous legal challenges and uncertainties.[5] In spite of their global nature, these transactions remain susceptible to geographic fragmentation, for they are subject to many local rules that diverge significantly between jurisdictions. To take but one example, we note that the meaning and import of 'exclusivity' as to exclusive licences is not harmonized at the international level, whether as to standing to sue for infringement

[4] Our focus is on modern *commercial transactions* knowledge-based intangible assets – particularly intellectual property assets – as opposed to knowledge and technology transfers incident (and inherent) through movements of populations, particularly those skilled in crafts (or today 'knowledge workers') or through knowledge networks. For time out of mind migration of technology came with movement or migration of people. See, e.g., E. Kiriatzi and C. Knappett (ed.), *Human Mobility and Technological Transfer in the Prehistoric Mediterranean*, Cambridge University Press, 2016 (collection of articles describing how the prehistoric movement of technology across the Mediterranean, especially as to crafts, came with movement of peoples); N. Blackwell, 'Making the Lion Gate Relief at Mycenae: Tool Marks and Foreign Influence', *American Journal of Archaeology* Vol. 118, No. 3, pp. 451–488 (July 2014) (describing how stonecutting methods used on the Lion Gate Relief at Mycenae reflected possible Hittite-Mycenaean interaction). But knowledge also can inhere in and course through networks, formal and informal. See OECD, 'Knowledge Networks and Markets' (n. 1 *supra*) p. 7 ('knowledge networks and markets (KNMs) . . . [are] "arrangements which govern the transfer of various types of knowledge, such as intellectual property, know-how, software code or databases, between independent parties". This term has grown in popularity and can be applied to describe a very diverse set of knowledge sharing agreements, institutions, social relations, networks and infrastructures that aim to allow companies, organisations and individuals to safely engage in the meaningful exchange of knowledge and associated rights').

[5] See Sonia Baldia, 'The Transaction Cost Problem in International Intellectual Property Exchange and Innovation Markets', 34 *Northwestern Journal of International Law and Business* 1, 36–41 (2013) (discussing different hypotheses that show the tensions that can arise between uniform global contractual regimes and fragmented local IP regimes); see generally Michael Anthony C. Dizon, 'The Symbiotic Relationship Between Global Contracts and the International IP Regime', 4 *Journal of Intellectual Property Law and Practice* 559, 559–565 (2009); this is also evidenced by the recent WTO dispute initiated by the European Union against China with respect to certain Chinese measures pertaining to the transfer of foreign technology into China which are claimed to adversely affect the protection of the intellectual property rights of foreign companies transferring technology to China. G/L/1244 ; IP/D/39; WT/DS549/1 – China – Certain Measures on the Transfer of Technology – Request for consultations by the European Union, 6 June 2018. This dispute particularly raises the issue of whether a foreign importer of technology shall be held liable in case the licensed technology infringes on third-party IP rights: Article 24 of the Regulations of the People's Republic of China on the Administration of the Import and Export of Technologies requires that licensors of imported technology indemnify licensees for all liabilities for infringement resulting from the use of the transferred technology.

or even as to the rights and powers of the exclusive licensor and the exclusive licensee.[6] Similarly, the effect of the termination of a main licence on the sub-licence fragments along geographic and subject matter lines.[7] Other examples abound.

The absence of a uniform – or at least somewhat harmonized – international legal regime governing the commercial licensing of IP and other information assets has further led to various forms of private ordering. In this chapter we discuss two examples. The first, which we discuss in the following section below, is what can usefully be thought of as an 'information law merchant', a contemporary conception of the 'law merchant' or *lex mercatoria* developed through the customary practices of European traders in goods in the late Middle Ages. By one definition, law merchant or *lex mercatoria* comprises rules and principles 'which are developed primarily by the international business community itself based on custom, industry practice, and general principles of law that are applied in commercial arbitrations . . . in order to govern transactions between private parties, as well as between private parties and States, in transborder trade, commerce, and finance'.[8] We consider whether the emerging practice in licensing IP across national jurisdictions may be usefully considered a contemporary form of such a 'law merchant'.

This form of private ordering, observed among more sophisticated and active participants in the global trade in certain types of information assets, has meant that effective participation in many forms of international commercial IP transactions often requires access to specialized legal knowledge, extensive commercial experience and elaborate contract

[6] See Jacques de Werra, 'Can Exclusive Licensees Sue for Infringement of Licensed IP Rights? A Case Study Confirming the Need to Create Global IP Licensing Rules', *Harvard Journal of Law and Technology*, Vol. 30, 2017 (Symposium Issue), available at https://papers.ssrn.com/sol3/papers.cfm?abstract_id=2907655; under UK law, see John Liddicoat, 'Standing on the Edge: What Type of "Exclusive Licensees" Should Be Able to Initiate Patent Infringement Actions?', *International Review of Intellectual Property and Competition Law*, Vol. 48, No. 6, 2017, available at https://papers.ssrn.com/sol3/papers.cfm?abstract_id=2905761>. For a discussion of US law, see Nimmer & Dodd, *Modern Licensing Law* (n. 1 *supra*) p. 5.

[7] See Neil Wilkof, 'Will There Ever Be Clear Law About the Terminated Sublicense?', blogpost on Ipkat, 2 November 2012, available at http://ipkitten.blogspot.com/2012/11/will-there-ever-be-clear-law-about.html; see Nimmer & Dodd, *Modern Licensing Law* (n. 1 *supra*) §§9:26, 11:43, 15:38.

[8] Stephan Schill, 'Lex Mercatoria', in Rüdiger Wolfrum (ed.), *Max Planck Encyclopedia of Public International Law*, Vol VI, Oxford: Oxford University Press, 2012, p. 823.

forms. In turn, the need for specialist knowledge simply to trade effectively in IP creates barriers to entry for new actors, disadvantages smaller firms, increases transaction and performance costs, and fosters disputes. Even more fundamentally, technological advances have fostered commercialization of intangible knowledge-based assets that may be protected, in whole or in part, by one or more forms of IP where the commercial value lies in the collective intangible asset, not in the discrete types of IP protection accorded to the asset. Commercial transactions in such assets are increasingly conducted by commercial actors and lawyers, not IP specialists. Fragmented sets of practices cannot serve as a secure foundation for a commercial law relating to the unique, growing and diversifying international trade in knowledge-based intangible assets.

Our second example of private ordering in IP commercial arrangements concerns the various licensing frameworks for standard essential patents under fair, reasonable and non-discriminatory terms (FRAND). Patents protecting technologies that are integrated in technological standards (which are frequent in certain industries, and specifically in the telecom industry) become 'standard essential patents' (SEPs), in the sense that any company wishing to use and implement the relevant standards in its products would need a licence to use those patents. To overcome the problem of 'patent holdups' that SEP owners could otherwise interpose through infringement claims, standard-setting organizations (SSOs) develop not only technical standards, but also adopt IPR policies under which 'participants wishing to have their IPR included in the standard [are requested] to provide an irrevocable commitment in writing to offer to license their essential IPR to all third parties on fair, reasonable and non-discriminatory terms ('FRAND commitment')'.[9]

However, it remains uncertain today how to determine what licensing terms and conditions are 'fair, reasonable and non-discriminatory'.[10] As

[9] See the Guidelines on the applicability of Article 101 of the Treaty on the Functioning of the European Union to horizontal co-operation agreements (Text with EEA relevance), OJ C 11, 14.1.2011, p. 285, available at http://eur-lex.europa.eu/legal-content/EN/TXT/HTML/?uri=CELEX:52011XC0114%2804%29&from=EN. ('the Guidelines'), para. 269; for a (simplified) presentation of the key competition law issues of SEPs, see the Competition policy brief (Issue 8, June 2014) of the European Commission, Standard-essential patents, available at http://ec.europa.eu/competition/publications/cpb/2014/008_en.pdf (relating to the *Samsung* and *Motorola* cases, whereby this paper will focus on the *Samsung* case, see 'The Use of Arbitration to Solve FRAND Disputes' below).

[10] *See* OECD, 'Knowledge Networks and Markets' (n. 1 *supra*) p. 10 ('FRAND pledges have become the recent focus of contention in technology markets – particularly in ICT standards – because FRAND terms can be ambiguous, leaving considerable room for

we discuss below, deciding on the fairness and reasonableness of a licence must go beyond the issue of the financial remuneration due by the licensee to the licensor (even though this issue has logically attracted and continues to attract the attention of all stakeholders). FRAND must also apply to all other contractual terms and conditions of the licence agreement (including the term and termination of the licence, the choice of court provision, etc.). This is a difficult exercise which demonstrates the need to develop global guiding principles on these issues as well. In the absence of such guidance, local courts develop their own approach of what they consider to be FRAND terms and conditions which are not ideal models for a uniform set of principles for licensing transactions; moreover, courts tend to rely on the parties' proposed licensing terms, making court-validated FRAND terms no less the product of private ordering than other licences where the courts construe and enforce terms.

This leads us to conclude our chapter by arguing that the international organizations created to foster commercial trade and IP protection and access should undertake a project to address the general principles relating to international IP commercial contracts in cooperation with all stakeholders, including those who license to others and those who license from others (often overlapping constituencies), academia, governmental organizations, industry groups, and other relevant and interested participants. Commercial transactions involving IP and information assets are a substantial and increasing component of world trade, especially among developing countries; such a project could help foster and facilitate that trade.

We also discuss some of the possible issues that may result from the development of general contractual principles in commercial IP and information transactions. In 1980, the UN Convention on Contracts for the International Sale of Goods (1980, 'CISG')[11] was adopted in order to provide an optional[12] uniform international framework to govern international commercial[13] sales of *physical* goods. We submit that a corresponding international instrument relating to principles of international commercial transactions (especially licences) in knowledge-

disagreement between parties regarding the transferability of those pledges and the determination of an appropriate royalty rate in thicketed markets.')

[11] See www.uncitral.org/uncitral/en/uncitral_texts/sale_goods/1980CISG_status.html.

[12] Contracting parties can opt out of the CISG (Article 6).

[13] Consumer sales are excluded from the scope of the CISG (Article 2(a)).

based *intangible* assets (especially those protected by IP rights) would be no less important for this century's growing and crucial trade in such assets than was the similar recognition accorded to commercial transactions in tangible goods during the last century.

While Global Trade in Information Assets Grows the Commercial Law Relating to Such Transactions is Uncertain

The Importance of Global Trade in Information Assets

While both the global development and trade in information assets has grown substantially,[14] empirical data regarding the scope and dimensions of this trade is notoriously elusive, nebulous and difficult to measure comprehensively and accurately,[15] leaving us only glimpses based on various aspects of information transaction markets and indirect sets of

[14] See Chapter 9 this volume, as well as OECD, 'Knowledge Networks and Markets' (n. 1 *supra*) p. 17. See also T. Agthe et al., 'A Proposed UNICTRAL Project On Commercial Transactions In Intellectual Property', p. 2 (Submitted at UNCITRAL - Fourth International Colloquium on Secured Transactions Vienna, 15–17 March 2017). ('A recent study shows that: (i) from 1998 to 2013, the index of global exports in goods grew by about 20%, but royalty payments for IP more than quadrupled over the same period; and (ii) from 1990 to 2009 the share of developing countries in global technology payments doubled from approximately 13% to 26%. The US Chamber of Commerce identifies five benefits states obtain from increased IP commerce: (i) superior access to finance and venture capital; (ii) higher quality utilization of national human capital; (iii) increased local inventive activity; (iv) better access for local firms to technology: and (v) streamlined and enhanced access for the public to creative content. Realizing these benefits requires both enhanced IP protection and legal support for commercial transactions (e.g. "technology in-flows").'). See also USPTO, 'Intellectual Property and the US Economy: 2016 Update', US Economics and Statistics Administration and US Patent and Trademark Office, September 2016. Available at www.uspto.gov/sites/default/files/documents/IPandtheUSEconomySept2016.pdf ('The 2012 report Intellectual Property and the US Economy: Industries in Focus identified IP-intensive industries and quantified their contribution to the US economy. It found that in 2010 IP-intensive industries supported over 40 million jobs and accounted for about $5.06 trillion in value added; equivalent to 34.8 percent of US GDP. The current report provides updated results demonstrating that IP-intensive industries supported 45.5 million jobs and contributed $6.6 trillion in value added in 2014, equivalent to 38.2 percent of US GDP. In addition, the current report reinforces the earlier finding that IP use permeates all aspects of the economy with increasing intensity and extends to all parts of the US'), available at www.uspto.gov/sites/default/files/documents/IPandtheUSEconomySept2016.pdf.

[15] See Chapter 5 in this volume.

evidence.[16] In part this is due to the wide variety of information assets and types of information asset trades,[17] as well as the private nature of most transactions.[18] Also, as an historical matter, accounting and other standards have not adequately measured the value and importance of intangible assets to corporate enterprises. Investment in knowledge-based assets is not fully reflected on balance sheets, though investments in tangible assets certainly are. As Jonathan Haskel and Stian Westlake point out in *Capitalism without Capital*, the balance sheets of, say, Microsoft, record very small levels of investment in assets (plant,

[16] One indirect measure of the level of trade may be royalty receipts. Thus, for example, 'the [tax] returns of active [US] corporations reported gross royalty receipts increasing from USD 115.8 billion dollars in 2002 to USD 171 billion in 2008, reaching nearly 1% of total revenue. Over 5% of US receipts in the computer manufacturing industries now derives from royalties and license fees'. OECD, 'Knowledge Networks and Markets' (n. 1 *supra*) p. 11. Global charges for the use of intellectual property also march upward. See, e.g., https://data.worldbank.org/indicator/BM.GSR.ROYL.CD (charts and related data showing dramatic increase in charges for use of intellectual property from 1960–2017). Another view of information markets and their importance can be gathered by examining the patterns of what the OECD has termed 'knowledge sourcing strategies', not only by internal research and development but also by 'open innovation', that is the 'use of purposive inflows and outflows of knowledge' in the 'arms' length flow of innovation knowledge across the boundaries of individual organizations'. OECD, 'Knowledge Networks and Markets' (n. 1 *supra*) p. 21. Though the global financial crises in 2008 and the following years clearly had some impact on flows, the OECD has collected data showing the trends of businesses in various countries relying on transactions for outside (extramural) knowledge-based assets characterized as research and development, including through licences. OECD, 'Knowledge Networks and Markets' (n. 1 *supra*) p. 28.

[17] Acquisition of intangible assets takes, of course, various forms, including research and development, purchase and other similar arrangements, as well as assignment of IP rights through mergers and acquisitions. Although we do not frequently draw distinctions as to the form of commercial trade and acquisition of information assets in this chapter, we believe that licences are probably the most common – if not dominant – forms of commercial arrangement by which the trade and acquisition of information assets occurs. We can, of course, mention anecdotal evidence: just think of how most businesses acquire and access information assets such as software and information tools. Again data about the level of licensing compared to other transactional forms for trading in information assets only can be culled in bits from available research, but indirect evidence underscores the importance of licensing, over sales. See OECD, 'Knowledge Networks and Markets', n. 1 *supra*, pp. 48–49 (describing relative level of sales versus licences across certain countries).

[18] OECD, 'Knowledge Networks and Markets' (n. 1 *supra*) p. 11('Exact estimates of the size of the IP marketplace are difficult to produce because most transactions are based on confidential agreements and therefore go unreported in open sources of information and registers . . . Specific information on royalty and licensing income for the entire economy, including both international and domestic transactions, is notoriously more difficult to come by . . .').

equipment, etc.) that accounting standards measure relative to their market capitalizations, but clearly Microsoft, as with many modern companies, invests enormous amounts in intangible assets, in their information products through research and development, product design, and the human capital building the products and platforms generating its revenues and profits.[19] However, over time, 'intangible investment has, in most developed countries, been growing more and more important. Indeed, in some countries it now outweighs tangible investment'.[20]

Where is the Law?

With the growing importance of knowledge-based intangible assets to the modern global economies and of the commercial trade in such assets among developed and, increasingly, developing countries, we find it perplexing that there is no general legal framework relating to the contractual principles tailored to address the commercial arrangements – especially licences – by which cross-border trade in such unique assets is conducted. To be sure, many domestic and international treaties and laws are directed to IP; some may even feature a few provisions addressing contractual terms. Just as certainly, specific laws and comprehensive statements of contractual principles have been crafted to suit the particular characteristics of discrete types of commercial transactions in other assets. For example, as mentioned above in the introduction, the CISG (UN Convention on Contracts for the International Sale of Goods (1980)[21]) was designed for international commercial trade in sales of physical goods. Similar guidance applies to secured transactions[22] and equipment leasing.[23]

But a spotty, indirect treatment with principles governing very different types of commercial transactions in very different types of assets will

[19] Haskel and Westlake, *Capitalism without Capital* (Princeton: Princeton University Press, 2018), pp. 4–8.

[20] Haskel, *Capitalism without Capital* (n. 19 *supra*) p. 7. To be sure, there are variations by country, and the methods for measuring the amount of intangible investment are still being refined, *see* Haskel, *Capitalism without Capital* (n. 19 *supra*) pp. 24–35, chapter 3. but the technological leaps over the past couple of decades have led to a very different global economy, certainly in most developed and increasingly in developing countries.

[21] See www.uncitral.org/uncitral/en/uncitral_texts/sale_goods/1980CISG_status.html.

[22] See www.uncitral.org/uncitral/en/uncitral_texts/payments/Guide_securedtrans.html (Legislative Guide) and www.unis.unvienna.org/unis/en/pressrels/2016/unisl233.html (Model Law).

[23] See www.unidroit.org/english/documents/2008/study59a/s-59a-17-e.pdf.

not adequately facilitate or support the increasingly vital commercial trade of knowledge-based intangible assets. The form of the transactions involving tangible and intangible assets differs radically: a licence contemplates that the very subject of the transaction still remains tethered to the owner of the information asset and that its use will be conditioned in ways specified in the agreement. More fundamentally, essential attributes of the intangible assets that are the object of the licence are radically different from the attributes defining the tangible asset. Forcing commercial trade in information assets into the Procrustean bed of commercial legal principles tailored for the types and forms of transactions in very different assets in very different industries, heedless of the commercial practices of licensing or the unique and essential contours of information assets, would be unwise policy and would prove inimical to the growing and important trade in information assets.[24] We would not expect that a law governing transactions providing access to software would suit the trade in thoroughbred horses, pipes to be delivered to a drilling site, machinery, pencils or elaborately designed glass bottles that are to be filled with expensive premium whiskeys.[25] Why would we expect the opposite for information assets?[26]

So what does a practising lawyer do now when asked to compose a licence for, say, a software transaction, or, perhaps, a transfer of a patent on a bio-acetic acid process, or a musical composition or a trademark. Of course, she would turn to the forms and contractual precedents from other types of transactions as to assets that might be 'similar' though not identical to the

[24] *Cf.* G. Gilmore, 'On the Difficulties of Codifying Commercial Law', 57 *Yale Law Journal* 1341 (1948) ('The principal objects of draftsmen of general commercial legislation—by which I mean legislation which is designed to clarify the law about business transactions rather than to change the habits of the business community—are to be accurate and not to be original. Their intention is to assure that if a given transaction involving commercial paper is initiated, it shall have a specified result; they attempt to state as matter of law the conclusion which the business community apart from statute and as matter of fact gives to the transaction in any case.').

[25] *Cf.* K. N. Llewellyn, 'Across Sales on Horseback', 52 *Harv. L. Rev.* 725, 728–729 (1939) (Llewellyn explains what made the law of sales (and contracts for sales) of goods a discrete body of law: it focused on the transfer of property in goods and those transactions were recognized as being discrete from other transactions).

[26] See, e.g., L. Brennan and J. Dodd, *A Preliminary Review of the UNIDROIT Contracts Principles as Applied to Intellectual Property* presented at UNICTRAL Annual Meeting June 2009 (discussing the view that UNDROIT principles are inadequate for IP commerce). See also Nimmer and Dodd, *Modern Licensing Law* (n. 1 *supra*) §§8: 4–8: 30 (explaining why warranty law relating to sales of goods is inadequate for transactions in information assets).

subject of the current transaction. Those forms and precedents would have been crafted with regard to the IP laws governing such assets, the practices of those institutions trading in such assets, public policy considerations (such as competition law), and the demands of the clients and transaction. Certainly, she would have IP law to consider, for IP law can influence the shape and content of the contract. Certainly, she would need to be aware of public policy constraints, such as the applicability of competition law and policy. But as to the commercial heart of the licence – its fundamental nature as a contract – she does not have a commercial law framework fashioned to fit the unique aspects of transactions in IP (or knowledge-based intangibles). Yes, there might be generally applicable contractual principles, but those principles would not furnish rules fitted to the unique species of transactions in information assets. No default rules. No common terminology. No general remedies for contractual breaches tailored with a view to the types of harm flowing from a breach of a licence.

Contrast those circumstances with those of a commercial lawyer facing a commercial dispute involving sales of goods or being asked to draft a sales-of-goods contract. If a dispute erupted over the commercial terms of the sale of goods, the commercial lawyer, her clients and, as need be, the judge or arbitrator of the case would have a fairly comprehensive, recognized, identifiable set of laws, domestically and internationally, relating to the contractual principles applicable to such transactions to consult and apply, just as she would have had in framing the original commercial contract. The counterparties and their counsel would as well. They would know how and whether, for example, warranties had been created or disclaimed, what remedies would be available by default and what to modify, the common terminology to be employed to reduce, though never eliminate, the ambit of misunderstanding and the default set of rules that would apply barring agreement to the contrary.

That is, there is an identifiable background of sales-of-goods principles, fashioned with a view to the unique species of transactions and subject matter, on which commercial participants and their counsel can rely. This background law addresses a large class of assets – goods, from horses to machinery – and the particular commercial forms of transactions for transferring such assets – sales and contracts for sales. Laws governing sales-of-goods and ultimately an international sales-of-goods convention did not build multiple, narrowly crafted sales laws tailored to specific industries or goods. (Just imagine, a 'Sales of Horses Law', 'Sales of Industrial Machinery Law', 'Sales of Gas Law' and so forth!) Rather, comprehensive laws, domestic and international, relating to sales as a transactional form and goods as a subject matter were recognized because the basic principles applying to such transactions were not radically different as to the different types of assets that we call 'goods'. The principles recognized by such laws were largely malleable enough to yield to agreements struck by the parties and industry practices and customs, while allowing commercial lawyers and business counterparties in different locations and with different backgrounds to have a common basis and terminology for transacting business – across boundaries. That framework of principles informs those who participate in the commercial trade and those who draft, who interpret and who decide. Indeed, the legal recognition of comprehensive general commercial legal principles as to sales of goods facilitated the growth in goods-based trade.[27]

The IP and information products that trade by licence are now no less commercially vital than goods transferred in sales. Legal recognition of the unique legal principles concerning commercial transactions in information assets would undoubtedly have a positive effect on trade in information assets, similar to the effect that the legal recognition of the unique legal principles concerning sales-of-goods transactions had for trade in goods.[28]

Market Responses to the Absence of Adequate Commercial Law

The yawning absence of international legal regimes validating and supporting commercial licensing of IP and other information assets has led

[27] A fundamental shift in commercial law can have profound consequences to other changes. *Cf.* Harold J. Berman, *Law and Revolution,* p. 336 (Harvard University Press, 1983) ('There is also a danger of viewing the law always as a consequence of social and economic change and never as a constituent part of such change, and in that sense a cause of it. In fact, the new jurisprudence of the late eleventh and twelfth centuries provided a framework for institutionalizing and systematizing commercial relations in accordance with new concepts of order and justice. Without such new legal devices as negotiable bills of exchange and limited liability partnerships, without the reform of the antiquated commercial customs of the past, without mercantile courts and mercantile legislation, other social and economic pressures for change would have found no outlet. Thus, the commercial revolution helped to produce commercial law, but commercial law also helped to produce the commercial revolution. Indeed, what occurred was a revolutionary transformation not only of commerce but of the whole society in that total transformation commercial law, like feudal law and manorial law, had its origins and from it, like them, it took its character.') See also K. N. Llewellyn, 'Why We Need the Uniform Commercial Code', 10 *Florida. Law Review* 367 (1957) (describing the effect of recognition as to sales of goods and negotiable instruments transactions).

[28] Agthe et al., 'A Proposed UNICTRAL Project On Commercial Transactions In Intellectual Property', pp. 1–3 (n. 14 *supra*).

to various discrete forms of licences based on private ordering for particular types of information assets. Below we discuss the two examples of private ordering briefly introduced above. In the subsection immediately following, we address the 'information law merchant' that has cropped up among more sophisticated and active participants in the global trade in certain types of information assets. In the following subsection, we address a very different private ordering response: the development of FRAND licensing terms and conditions.

Information Law Merchant

Examples of Law Merchant The absence of comprehensive, recognized principles of commercial law dealing with the unique but common transactional form of licence (like the unique transactional form of sale) and the unique but common qualities of knowledge-based intangibles has led to the emergence of a mélange of custom,[29] practice, borrowed commercial law and bits of IP law, varying according to jurisdiction, industry sector, technology, speciality and practices of discrete sets of commercial participants routinely participating in the trade, somewhat in the fashion of an Information Law Merchant.[30]

[29] See Jennifer E. Rothman, 'The Questionable Use of Custom in Intellectual Property', *Virginia Law Review*, 93, available at www.virginialawreview.org/sites/virginialawreview.org/files/1899.pdf.

[30] For a description of the emergence of *lex mercatoria* among merchants in the late Middle Ages, see E. Hunt and J. Murray, *A History of Business in Medieval Europe 1200–1550*, pp. 96–97, Cambridge University Press, 1999. Law Merchant had ancient predecessors. Thus, records from Kanesh and Assur in Assyria indicate that credit arrangements among merchants and agreements between local rulers and merchants governed the conduct of business and the settlement of debts, especially when a merchant died, and heirs, business partners and counterparties had to sort through a web of debts, claims and commitments. See M. T. Larsen, *Ancient Kanesh: A Merchant Colony in the Bronze Age of Anatolia*, pp. 96, 116, 152–153, Cambridge University Press, 2015. Rulers wanted to harvest the tax revenues from the trade that caravans of merchant traders from other cities and regions would provide, so protection of caravans, maintenance of roads, and, importantly, recognition of the contracts and commercial law principles observed by merchants across boundaries was crucial to ensuring that the flow of trade continued. *Id.* at pp. 152–158. The Romans also recognized a form of law among merchants: 'Indeed, it was the jus gentium, the (customary) "law of nations," applicable to those who were not Roman citizens, that governed most types of commercial transactions within the Roman Empire, especially those involving the carriage of goods over long distances. Included in the customary law of commerce of the Roman Empire was the Sea Law of Rhodes, usually thought to date from about 300 BC, as well as the customs of maritime trade that had been developed subsequently by eastern Mediterranean traders. Some of the rules of the Roman customary law of commerce, as well as some of the rules of Roman civil law,

We could catalogue several examples, but let us focus on a few. For example, the transfers of IP assets in art transactions may take the form of a simple licence of copyrights as incidental part of the relationship between artist and dealer or patron that is otherwise focused on the work or image itself.[31] So too with many forms of 'entertainment'[32] or 'sports' arrangements, where character, services, venue, publicity, distribution may receive more attention than the transfer of rights – though the transfer is undoubtedly important.[33] Indeed, in some cases, the media of delivery of content and the content itself converge (so called 'technotainment'), so that the focus is less on specific IP rights, rather than the cluster of trademark, publicity and copyright interests that may be included in the media 'package' and on the rights and methods of distribution.[34] Freelance photographers are the authors and thus owners of the copyrights in their photographs, but when they grant rights with respect to the use of the photographs, they may just refer to the covered photographs in a licence, not specific copyrights, while including scope limitations keyed to the exclusive rights they have as copyright owners.[35] The distribution of software invariably is governed by an often-extensive licence, but here again the focus is not necessarily on specific IP, but rather on the programs comprising the software, with the licence regulating the use of the associated IP through terms that refer only to the software. In these transactions, the technology or content may be identified as the subject of the transfer and the licence and the rights conferred may not necessarily specify the IP rights covered. The licences indirectly,

had survived in the West from the fifth to the eleventh centuries, independently of the texts of Justinian; they are to be found, for example, in Lombard law as well as in customs of the merchants of Venice; which remained as a flourishing trading center throughout the period.' Berman, *Law and Revolution*, pp. 339–340 (n. 27 *supra*).

31 J. Bresler and R. Lerner, *Art Law: The Guide for Collectors, Investors, Dealers, & Artists*, New York: Practising Law Institute, 2013, pp 941–943 (PLI 4th ed.)

32 For the purposes of simplicity in this short treatment, we have tossed music, book, theatre, television and so forth into the 'entertainment' category. For a collection of articles and sample forms, see generally Counseling Clients in the Entertainment Industry 2018, 2 vols. (PLI Course Handbook).

33 27A *Am. Jur. 2nd Entertainment and Sports Law* §§1, *et seq.*

34 See, e.g., 'Technotainment' 2016: The Convergence of Sports Media (PLI Course Handbook).

35 See, e.g., Spinelli *v.* National Football League, 903 F.3d 18 193-94 (2nd Cir. 2018) ('Photographer hereby provides to AP a perpetual, irrevocable, transferable, worldwide, right and license to reproduce, edit, translate the caption of, prepare derivative works of, publicly perform, publicly display, load into computer memory, cache, store and otherwise use the Final Photos and to transfer or sublicense these rights to other entities.').

but effectively, govern the 'use' of any underlying IP by virtue of imposing control of the content or technology subject matter. Nonetheless, a licence or transfer is a vital part of the transaction; without such provisions no right to use the technology or content would be conferred.

Contrast this with university technology transfers, which often specifically identify the patents or patent applications that are the subject of the licence and define its scope. The classic example here features the transfer of promising biotechnology from a university to a start-up, with participation by the inventor-professor and, perhaps, some of her colleagues, through a licence covering not only the patents or inventions, but also materials and, potentially know-how, accompanied by a host of other obligations, rights and powers.[36]

However, the reach of a customary 'law' extends only to a limited number of participants.[37] Moreover, commercial transactions in knowledge-based assets – especially where IP is not specifically identified or where various IP rights may underlie the transaction – are increasingly conducted by commercial actors and lawyers, not IP specialists. Yet effective participation in many forms of international commercial IP transactions often requires access to specialized legal knowledge, extensive commercial experience and elaborate contract forms, creating barriers to entry for new actors, disadvantaging smaller firms, increasing transaction and performance costs, and fostering disputes.[38] Moreover,

[36] For but one of a host of examples, see, e.g. Harvard's Sample Licence, available at https://otd.harvard.edu/upload/files/Sample_License_Agreement_Exclusive_Patent_Rights.pdf.

[37] We note that the Law Merchant emerging in the eleventh and twelfth centuries might have had more universality than we are suggesting that Information Law Merchant may have. However, the late medieval law merchant subsisted among a small and identifiable group as to their commercial transactions at a limited number of locations. It related to a class of persons and the transactions that they undertook at certain locations. Berman, *Law and Revolution*, p. 341 (n. 27 *supra*) ('The law merchant, then, governed a special class of people (merchants) in special places (fairs, markets, and seaports); and it also governed mercantile relations in cities and towns.') Within that class and at those places, the 'law merchant shared with the other major legal systems of the time the qualities of objectivity, universality, reciprocity, participatory adjudication, integration, and growth'. *Id.*

[38] We are reminded of how Karl Llewellyn described the salutary effect of the adoption of a Negotiable Instruments Law at the end of the nineteenth century and the muddled state of the law before then:

Eighty years ago, bankers were swearing at the law of Bills and Notes (mostly Notes) and swearing by the two fat volumes of Daniel. Not that Daniel met the need. Paper ran across state lines, but law didn't. In addition, the law of the paper was tangled and often obscure: there were three or four different rules, for instance, on the 'anomalous indorser,' and what was the status of a 'referee in case of need'? Still, bankers and their lawyers simply had to make out with conflict and with obscurity. James Coolidge Carter had just

the trade is international; for among other things, the physics of granting rights in IP or transporting intangible digital information poses fewer challenges than the transport of physical items across distance. The fragmented sets of practices that we have described as 'Information Law Merchant' cannot serve as a secure foundation for a commercial law relating to the unique and growing – and broad-based – international trade in knowledge-based intangible assets.[39]

Scope: The Core of a Licence Although the shape, content and interpretation of licences in an industry are creatures of the practitioners and participants who regularly trade in the information assets common to the industry, we stress that commercial licences have a core, a spine if you will, that gives shape, support and structure to information transactions. That core is scope.

Certainly the form and content of the scope clause, as well as other terms, are framed by reference to practices in the trade as to a technology. Thus, for example, a software licence may tie scope to the number of 'concurrent users' at a particular location or on specific systems, where the scope provisions in a biotechnology licence may focus on fields of use versus others (e.g. treatment of pediatric oncology vs adult oncology), or territories. A licence with respect to a motion picture licence may have

led the Wall Street Bar and Wall Street Opinion into clear and conclusive understanding that to codify is to kill and that man's wit cannot in our system reach to produce by way of statutory language a workable clarity and reckonability together with a reasonable flexibility. It was all very sad, and there was nothing to do but go on suffering. It was the kind of thing on which everybody knew that Wall Street, like Papa, knows best. . . . Except that, then, in 1897, the National Conference of Commissioners on Uniform State Laws produced the uniform Negotiable Instruments Law. For twenty-five hundred pages of Daniel they proposed to substitute twenty-five pages of code language, much of which an ordinary man can understand. For forty or fifty divergent bodies of law they proposed to substitute a single body. Where possible, they proposed to simplify and clarify matters which the cases had left obscure. Wall Street knew indeed that these goals were impossible, but somehow the N. I. L. got passed, all over the country, and bankers started to live with it and to live by it. . . . Nevertheless, the legislatures kept adopting the N. I. L. and the governors kept signing it and the bankers not only lived under it but found they could rather easily train every last bank clerk to understand it reasonably well. If the surety was the ancient darling of the chancellor, surely the N. I. L. has become the commercial banker's darling. K.N. Llewellyn, 'Why We Need the Uniform Commercial Code', 10 *Florida Law Review*. 367, 37–68 (1957).

[39] Trust is an essential glue to the conduct of business. See generally, R. Botsman, *Who Can You Trust?*, New York: PublicAffairs, 2017, pp. 29–30, 59–68. But commercial transactions in goods remotely required legal frameworks supporting, validating and enforcing commercial agreements. Trust with teeth, in other words.

very specific scope limitations based on duration of use, theatres in which the motion picture may be featured, and the technological methods for public performance and promotion.

Yet, despite this variety, scope clauses have essential elements that provide a common, though unique, architectural core for licences. Let us take another look at the definition of licence that we adopted earlier:

> A license is a contract (whether by express agreement or by implication in law) authorizing, transferring, or allowing a licensee's contractual right, power privilege or immunity with respect to uses of information or rights in information (including intellectual property and intellectual property rights) *controlled or made available by or through a licensor without transferring all rights or interests with respect to such information or rights.* This includes a focus on what rights, immunities, or uses are permitted (including by access) *or withheld* in reference to use of the information or rights, *as well as what the licensee has agreed to do or not to do with respect to the information or rights.*[40]

As this definition makes clear, the essential nature of a licence is its conditionality. Information assets are provided by the licensor without transfer of all rights in those assets; the licensee's use lives within the confines of scope defined by uses permitted or denied and by what the licensee agreed to do or not do with respect to the information or rights. That a licence is subject to the limitations imposed by its scope means that uses outside of its ambit breach a contractual duty (express or implied) and, potentially, could give rise to infringement liability if the unsanctioned use would otherwise infringe the licensor's IP right. Otherwise put: a licence confers on the licensee a contractual immunity from suits, whether infringement, contractual or otherwise, by the licensor as to uses within the confines of scope. In essence, a licence 'invests the licensee with a contractual right or immunity as to actions that an infringement claim would otherwise lie, but the licensor maintains residual (often much more valuable) rights in the intellectual property'.[41]

This conditionality encased in scope is the core of the licence and explains the power of licences in information transactions and the reason why licences are so prevalent.[42] Take the example of a manufacturer of a tangible item as to which a patent covers some of the inventions

[40] See n. 3 *supra* (quoting Nimmer and Dodd, *Modern Licensing Law* (n. 1 *supra*) §1.4 (emphasis added)).

[41] Nimmer and Dodd, *Modern Licensing Law* (n. 1 *supra*) §1.11.

[42] See n. 17 *supra*.

embodied in that item. When it sells its product, its patent rights may be exhausted as to that item, but its patent rights – its power to exclude others from making or selling infringing products – remains intact. If it sold the patents, it would lose that power. Now if that company were in the business of providing information assets as a product – not a tangible item – one can readily see that its very business model depends on not transferring the intellectual property rights relating to those assets but rather controlling the rights even as it provides access over and over. Licences allow that control to be maintained. So while the vagaries of practice and custom by sophisticated participants in information transactions in an industry influence, if not determine, the contractual content of many terms of a licence, the structural form of a licence retains the core of conditionality – that is, it has a scope.

Inadequacy of Law Merchant and 'Current Law' So, while trade in information assets relies on the ubiquitous structure of a licence – a commercial form of transaction that has unique but identifiable and common essential elements – commercial parties strike the particular terms of a transaction based on their arrangement and the commercial practices of their industry or trading groups. Importantly, however, the Information Law Merchant does not address many recurring and important questions affecting the crucial and distinctive structure elements of licences generally, even scope provisions, regardless of the sophistication of the parties or their active participation in a trade of information assets. Nor should one expect that the Information Law Merchant, such as it is, would do so, for, by definition, it is based on the unique aspects of trade in information assets by participants in industries or in trading groups.

Even more importantly, the current state of the law relating to licensing does not provide comprehensive and international structural support to supplement Information Law Merchant by common interpretative principles for the essential and common licence transactional form used in information asset trade. Quite simply, there are no commercial laws or authoritative principles that create a recognized framework for the essential elements of licences – unlike, as we have noted, the sale of goods.

That does not mean laws are absent. There are numerous opinions and pronouncements – far too many to canvass here[43] – interpreting

[43] See generally R. Nimmer and J. Dodd, *Modern Licensing Law*, 2 volumes (covering US cases and statutes comprising licensing law).

licence terms – including the all-important scope provisions – in cases involving particular licences. However, judicial or administrative determinations vary in their interpretations of important licence terms by case and jurisdiction, and sometimes by subject matter.

Let us consider the example of the word 'exclusive' that often appears in scope clauses as but one example.[44] Many licences, even licences common in an industry, use the word 'exclusive' without great specification as to what, precisely, powers, privileges, immunities and duties that word is to comprehend.[45] These licences may contain many provisions designed to address industry-specific issues, but a word like 'exclusive', which appears in licences across industries, is assumed to have a known meaning. However, is the meaning of 'exclusive' so clear across jurisdictions – or even within one? Let us take the example of the United States. The difference between an exclusive and a non-exclusive licence generally is thought to lie in the extent to which the licensor is contractually permitted to grant licences to other parties covering the same scope and conditions. Thus, a pure non-exclusive licence does not restrict the licensor from subsequently licensing the same informational asset to other licensees.[46] In contrast, an exclusive licence is ordinarily considered

[44] We cite exclusivity as one example, but we could pick on others. 'Perpetual', 'irrevocable' and many other terms commonplace in licences do not necessarily have certain meanings. See, e.g., *Matter of Provider Meds, L.L.C.*, 907 F.3d 845 (5th Cir. 2018) (discussing meaning of 'perpetual' vs irrevocable and perpetual under Texas law). *See also* Nimmer and Dodd, *Modern Licensing Law, 2019–2020*, Eagan, MN: Thomson Reuters (n. 1 *supra*) §9:17. Other terms may be given very particular technical interpretations by, say, cases interpreting patent or other IP-specific licences, even though the interpretations are, in theory, based on contract terms and not patent (or other IP-specific) statutes and laws and may not be authortative in other contexts. See, e.g., Cascades AV LLC *v.* Evertz Microsystems Ltd., 335 F.Supp.3d 1088 (N.D. Ill. 2018) (reference to patents in licence does not include subsequent patents arising from divisional applications based on the original patent). See also Nimmer and Dodd, *Modern Licensing Law* (n. 1 *supra*) §6:13.

[45] See, e.g., Sample Publishing Agreement, submitted by Gail Ross, Ross Yoon Agency, Counseling Clients in the Entertainment Industry 2017 (PLI Course Handbook) ('Author grants to Publisher during the full term of copyright and any renewal or extensions thereof the exclusive right to publish the Work including the right to exercise or license the rights set forth in Paragraph 2 throughout the world in the English language and all other languages.').

[46] See, e.g., Spindelfabrik Suessen-Schurr, Stahlecker & Grill GmbH *v.* Schubert & Salzer Maschinenfabrik Aktiengesellschaft, 829 F.2d 1075, 1081, 4 USPQ 2d 1044 (Fed. Cir. 1987) (in a different context, affirming that even an affirmative grant of a right to use does not entail such an assurance).

to entail a commitment by the licensor that it will not engage in additional licensing covering the same informational subject matter within the same scope of application. However, does the use of the word 'exclusive' connote that the licensor will itself be precluded from using the underlying right or technology? Does it connote that other non-exclusive licences or other rights to use have not been previously granted and are subsisting?[47] What if the exclusive licensor grants a subsequent licence to a licensee who had no notice of the exclusive licence, or what if prior licences conferred powers to sub-licence and a sub-licence is granted? What are the consequences? Is the subsequent licence or sub-licence invalid, and the third party licensee or sub-licensee infringes the IP right? Is it merely a breach by the licensor? Does the exclusive licensee

[47] Some licences seem to contemplate that exclusivity implicitly provides assurances that the licensor has not granted rights to a third party within the scope of the exclusive licence or is not a party to an arrangement where a third party has retained rights. Thus, for example in the Harvard sample exclusive licence (Harvard's Sample Licence), available at https://otd.harvard.edu/upload/files/Sample_License_Agreement_Exclusive_Patent_Rights.pdf, Harvard reserves the right 'for itself and for other not-for-profit research organizations, to practice the Patent Rights and to use the Harvard Technology Transfer Materials within the scope of the license granted above, solely for research, educational and scholarly purposes' (Harvard Sample, Section 2.1.1) and 'the United States federal government retains rights in the Patent Rights pursuant to 35 USC §§ 200–212 and 37 CFR § 401 *et seq.*, and any right granted in this Agreement greater than that permitted under 35 USC §§ 200–212 or 37 CFR § 401 *et seq.* will be subject to modification as may be required to conform to the provisions of those statutes and regulations.' (Harvard Sample, Section 2.1.2). These exceptions would not be necessary if Harvard believed that 'exclusivity' allowed it to practice and third parties to retain rights without breaching the 'exclusivity' provision. Also, many universities are members of an initiative to foster transfers of rights as to licensed products that could result in significant public health benefits in developing countries. For a description of various global access initiatives, see C. Chen et al., 'The Silent Epidemic of Exclusive University Licensing Policies on Compounds for Neglected Diseases and Beyond' (2010), *PLoS Negl Trop Dis* 4, 3: e570, available at https://doi.org/10.1371/journal.pntd.0000570. Harvard has made such a commitment through its participation in the organization Universities Allied for Essential Medicines (https://uaem.org/). Thus, it may make an otherwise exclusive grant subject to a retained right to grant non-exclusive licences to non-profits and others for 'purposes of alleviating unmet health needs of local populations in' developing countries, see https://otd.harvard.edu/upload/files/Sample_Global_Access_Language.pdf. Again, if Harvard believed that exclusivity did not preclude future grants of non-exclusive licences it would not need to include such a provision. The point here is not to hold Harvard up as an example; many other licences, including many other university licences, include similar provisions. The point is that at least some licensing parties believe that such reservations are necessary or at least strongly advisable because of what 'exclusive' implies. That does not mean they are necessarily right.

have standing to bring action against the third parties? The law is not so clear as to these questions.[48]

In short, the term 'exclusive licence' has many colours. Characterizing a licence as 'exclusive' can potentially affect:

- the obligations the licensor owes to the exclusive licensee,
- the scope of privileges that the licensee can exercise,
- the obligations the licensee owes to the licensor,[49]
- the rights, powers and privileges the licensee has vis-à-vis third parties (including standing to pursue infringement claims),[50]
- the liabilities, rights and privileges third parties in the chain of 'title' from the licensor may have vis-à-vis the licensor and the licensee, and
- whether the transaction must be in writing or registered for purposes of enforceability or priority.[51]

[48] See generally, R. Nimmer and Dodd, *Modern Licensing Law* (n. 1 *supra*) §§5:4, *et seq.* See US Dept. of Justice and Fed. Trade Comm'n, *Antitrust Guidelines for the Licensing of Intellectual Property* §4.12. See also Kepner-Tregoe, Inc. *v.* Vroom, 186 F.3d 283, 51 U.S.P.Q.2d 1771 (2nd Cir. 1999); Finance Inv. Co. (Bermuda) Ltd. *v.* Geberit AG, 165 F.3d 526, 531-32, 49 USPQ 2d 1289, 42 Fed. R. Serv. 3d 515 (7th Cir. 1998) (a 'truly exclusive licensee' can enforce mark against third parties and exclusive licensor); CRC Press LLC *v.* Wolfram Research Inc., 149 F. Supp. 2d 500, 57 U.S.P.Q.2d 1220 (CD Ill 2000). See also *Milgrim on Licensing* §15.10 (1996) ('The word "exclusive" does not tell all. Exclusivity can be granted subject to material limitations.'); ICEE Distributors, Inc. *v.* J&J Snack Foods Corp., 325 F.3d 586, 66 USPQ 2d 1161 (5th Cir. 2003).

[49] See Nimmer and Dodd, *Modern Licensing Law* (n. 1 *supra*) §§5:28 to 5:62 (best efforts/ diligence). See, e.g., Mechanical Ice Tray Corp *v.* General Motors Corp, 144 F.2d 720, 62 USPQ 397 (CCA 2nd Cir. 1944) (existence of prior licence did not change character of licence as exclusive for purposes of implying a 'best efforts' obligation on the licensee); Vacuum Concrete Corp. of America *v.* American Mach. & Foundry Co., 321 F. Supp. 771, 772–73, 169 USPQ 287 (SDNY 1971) (duty on the part of exclusive licensee to exploit the subject matter of the licence with due diligence was implied in order to give meaning and effect to the contract as a whole).

[50] See Jacques de Werra, 'Can Exclusive Licensees Sue for Infringement of Licensed IP Rights? A Case Study Confirming the Need to Create Global IP Licensing Rules' (2017), *Harvard Journal of Law and Technology*, 30 (Symposium Issue), available at https://papers.ssrn.com/sol3/papers.cfm?abstract_id=2907655. See also Nimmer and Dodd, *Modern Licensing Law* (n. 1 *supra*) §§5:34–5:62.

[51] See Nimmer and Dodd, *Modern Licensing Law* (n. 1 *supra*) §§3:44 to 3:49, §§5:63 *et seq.* (statute of frauds). See also John G. Danielson, Inc. *v.* Winchester-Conant Properties, Inc., 186 F. Supp. 2d 1, 18, 62 USPQ 2d 1714 (D. Mass. 2002), *aff'd on other grounds*, 322 F.3d 26, 66 USPQ 2d 1065 (1st Cir. 2003) (non-exclusive copyright licence was not governed by the statute of frauds provision of 17 USCA §204). In addition to those listed, the characterization may also affect how a court or an agency examines the context in reference to antitrust issues. See, generally, US Dep't. of Justice and Fed. Trade Comm'n, Antitrust Enforcement and Intellectual Property Rights: Promoting Innovation and

Conclusion We end this section by observing that neither the available legal pronouncements nor what we have referred to as the Information Law Merchant have provided a sound, recognized framework for giving legal effect, across boundaries and industry, the licence contract that is generally used across boundaries and industries. We would not expect an Information Law Merchant among commercial participants in any given industry to address matters concerning 'exclusivity', much less the numerous other legal issues relating to the commercial aspects of licences generally. It is tailored, by industry and practice, to address questions common to those who trade in information assets in that industry, not to address questions relating to licensing law generally or to balance policies affecting the different interests of licensors and licensees as to many different information assets. Rather, those questions would remain properly dealt with within the framework of principles of a commercial licensing law dealing with the unique and common elements of licences that would support commercial trade in information assets across boundaries and industries. The 'law' now does not.

Fair, Reasonable and Non-Discriminatory (FRAND) Licensing Terms for Standard Essential Patents

Introduction Another form of specialized private ordering is progressively emerging as a result of the undertakings that certain industries (or subgroups) enter into when they participate in standards adopted by standard-setting organizations (SSOs). The process of standardization defines common technical standards[52] that must be used in order for a

Competition (04/2007); Department of Justice and Fed. Trade Comm'n, Antitrust Guidelines for the Licensing of Intellectual Property §4.1.2.

52 The interaction between IP law (and specifically patent law) and standardization is complex. See the definition of technical standards in the report of the International Telecommunication Union (ITU), Understanding patents, competition and standardization in an interconnected world (July 1, 2014), available at www.itu.int/en/ITU-T/ipr/Pages/Understanding-patents,-competition-and-standardization-in-an-interconnected-world.aspx ('the ITU Report'), p. 15: 'Technical standards generally refer to the establishment of norms and requirements for technical systems, specifying standard engineering criteria, methodologies or processes. The functionality of systems incorporating communicating parts is especially dependent on conformance with common standards. Here, we often speak of "compatibility standards", also known as "interoperability standards". These standards specify how technologies such as a mobile phone and a mobile network, or a compact disc and a compact disc player, interact with one another and work together successfully. Compatibility and interoperability standards are most common in the ICT and consumer electronics sectors, but their importance to other industry sectors is growing rapidly'; certain parts of the analysis presented here are derived from: Jacques

product to comply with the relevant technological standard (for instance Wi-Fi).[53] Technical standards integrate patented technologies owned by a wide range of companies, which thus become 'standard essential patents' (SEPs),[54] in the sense that any company wishing to use and implement the relevant standards in its products (which is then called an implementer) needs a licence to use those patents.[55] This creates the risk of 'patent holdup', i.e. the risk that the owners of such SEPs may unduly block the use of their patented technology by implementers through the use of (or threat of) infringement lawsuits unless they get potentially excessive royalty payments from implementers who want to comply with the relevant technical standard.[56]As a result, this type of behaviour has

de Werra, 'Patents and Trade Secrets in the Internet Age' (2015), 134 *Revue de Droit Suisse* II 146–164 (2015), available at https://papers.ssrn.com/sol3/papers.cfm?abstract_id=2684616.

53 Standards are of essential importance in the Information and Communication Technology (ICT) industry. See ITU Report (n. 52), p. 23, with a chart listing examples of international SSOs and consortia and their standards of relevance to ICTs.

54 For a general presentation, see (among multiple other publications) the comprehensive Report prepared for the European Commission (Directorate-General for Enterprise and Industry), Patents and Standards: A modern framework for IPR-based standardization, 2014, available at http://ec.europa.eu/growth/industry/intellectual-property/patents/standards/index_en.htm.

55 See the documents and presentations made at the recent Information Session on Patents and Standards (WIPO/IS/IP/GE/18) on 13 July 2018, available at www.wipo.int/meetings/en/details.jsp?meeting_id=47226 and the dedicated website, available at www.wipo.int/patent-law/en/developments/standards.html; see also the interesting guide published by the Japan Patent Office in June 2018: *Guide to Licensing Negotiations involving Standard Essential Patents*, available at www.jpo.go.jp/torikumi_e/kokusai_e/seps-tebiki_e.html; see also Commission Communication, *Defining the Union's approach to essential patents to standards*, 29 November 2017, COM (2017) 712 final, available at https://ec.europa.eu/docsroom/documents/26583?locale=en; for patents and standards, see the report Standards and Patents (doc. ref. SCP/13/2) prepared for the 13th session of WIPO's standing committee on patents (Geneva, March 23–27, 2009), available at www.wipo.int/edocs/mdocs/scp/en/scp_13/scp_13_2.pdf.

56 For a short description of the issue, see Judge Birss, in Unwired Planet International Ltd *v.* Huawei Technologies Co. Ltd & Anor [2017] EWHC 711 (Pat) (05 April 2017), available at www.bailii.org/ew/cases/EWHC/Patents/2017/711.html, at para. 83: 'The point of FRAND in standard setting is fairly easy to understand. Standards exist so that different manufacturers can produce equipment which is interoperable with the result that the manufacturers compete with one another. So the phone makers compete in the market for phones and the public can select a phone from any supplier and be sure (for example) that if it is a 4G phone, it will work with any 4G network. As a society we want the best, most up to date technology to be incorporated into the latest standards and that will involve incorporating patented inventions. While the inventor must be entitled to a fair return for the use of their invention, in order for the standard to permit interoperability the inventor must not be able to prevent others from using the patented invention

been scrutinized under competition law,[57] and measures have been taken to prevent such potentially abusive conduct.[58]

The SSOs that set or develop technical standards frequently develop IPR policies in order to address such potentially abusive behaviours.[59] Under such policies, 'participants wishing to have their IPR included in the standard [are requested] to provide an irrevocable commitment in writing to offer to licence their essential

incorporated in the standard as long as implementers take an appropriate license and pay a fair royalty. In this way a balance is struck, in the public interest, between the inventor and the implementers. The appropriate license is one which is fair, reasonable and non-discriminatory. That way a standard can safely incorporate the invention claimed in a patent without giving the inventor or his successors in title unwarranted power over those who implement the standard. Thus, the public interest is served because telecommunication standards can be set using the best and most up-to-date technical expedients available and the inventor's private interest is served because the FRAND undertaking ensures they or their successors will obtain a fair reward for their invention.'

57 Guidelines (n. 9), para. 269; for a (simplified) presentation of the key competition law issues of SEPs, see the Competition policy brief (Issue 8, June 2014) of the European Commission, Standard-essential patents, available at http://ec.europa.eu/competition/publications/cpb/2014/008.en.pdf (relating to the *Samsung* and *Motorola* cases, whereby this report will focus on the *Samsung* case); see also Jay P. Kesan and Carol Hayes, 'Standard Setting Organizations and FRAND Licensing', chapter 10, in R. Anderson, N. De Carvalho and A. Taubman (eds), *Competition Policy and Intellectual Property in Today's Global Economy* (WTO Internal Only), Cambridge: Cambridge University Press, 2021.

58 For an analysis, see Michela Angeli, 'Willing to Define Willingness: The (Almost) Final Word on SEP-Based Injunctions in Light of Samsung and Motorola' (2015), *Journal of European Competition Law & Practice*, 221–241.

59 This is what was done (by way of illustration) by the European Telecommunications Standards Institute (ETSI) in its IPR Policy. ETSI Intellectual Property Rights Policy (Annex 6 of the Rules of Procedure, 'ETSI IPR Policy'), available at www.etsi.org/images/files/IPR/etsi-ipr-policy.pdf; see also the webpage dedicated to IPR, available at www.etsi.org/index.php/about/iprs-in-etsi. The ETSI IPR Policy therefore provides for a mechanism of declaration by which the owners of standard essential patents commit to make their patents available to willing licensees under FRAND terms. See 6.1 of the ETSI IPR Policy ('[w]hen an ESSENTIAL IPR relating to a particular STANDARD or TECHNICAL SPECIFICATION is brought to the attention of ETSI, the Director-General of ETSI shall immediately request the owner to give within three months an irrevocable undertaking in writing that it is prepared to grant irrevocable licenses on fair, reasonable and non-discriminatory ("FRAND") terms and conditions under such IPR [. . .]'.); Article 15.6 of the ETSI IPR Policy (definition of 'ESSENTIAL'). Annex A to the ETSI IPR Policy (entitled 'IPR Licensing Declaration Forms') contains different forms to be completed and signed by the owner of the relevant IP rights under which such IP owner is invited to make a formal and binding statement according to which 'it and its AFFILIATES are prepared to grant irrevocable licenses under its/their IPR(s) on terms and conditions which are in accordance with Clause 6.1 of the ETSI IPR Policy, [. . .]'. See www.etsi.org/images/files/IPR/etsi-ipr-form.doc (the 'ETSI Declarations').

IPR to all third parties on fair, reasonable and non-discriminatory terms ("FRAND commitment")'.[60]

Plainly, the central element of the system is the very notion of FRAND licensing;[61] what shall be considered fair, reasonable and non-discriminatory licensing terms and conditions remains uncertain as of today[62] and will be discussed below. However, a preliminary legal issue relates to the legal nature and enforceability of the commitments ('undertaking'[63]) that are made by the owners of the relevant SEPs to the SSOs under the applicable governing law.[64]

By stating that the owners of SEPs are 'prepared to grant irrevocable licenses'[65] under their SEPS to third-party implementers (in the formal undertaking that they make to the SSOs), the issue is whether third-party beneficiaries could request the performance of such obligations, which in turn requires assessing whether these potential licensees (which have not directly entered into any contract with the owner of the relevant SEPs) can be considered as third-party beneficiaries. This issue, which obviously depends on the interpretation of the relevant declaration under the applicable law, remains disputed,[66] it being noted that granting – by

60 Guidelines (n. 9), para. 285, available at https://eur-lex.europa.eu/LexUriServ/LexUriServ.do?uri=OJ:C:2011:011:0001:0072:EN:PD.

61 For a Swiss perspective, see Rolf H. Weber, 'Competition Law versus FRAND Terms in IT Markets' (2011), *World Competition Law and Economics Review*, Vol. 34, No. 1, pp. 51–71; Rolf H. Weber/Salim Rizvi, 'FRAND – Versuch einer Strukturierung' (2011), *RJB/ZBJV*, pp. 433–462; Fabio Babey/Salim Rizvi, *Die Frand-Verpflichtung – Fair, Reasonable and Non-Discriminatory terms (FRAND) im Lichte des Kartellrechts*, WuW 2012, pp. 808–818.

62 See Doug Lichtman, 'Understanding the RAND Commitment' (2010), 47 *Houston Law Review*, pp. 1023–1050, p. 1031, available at http://papers.ssrn.com/sol3/papers.cfm?abstract_id=1783406 ('It is something of an outrage that the language of the RAND commitment offers so little guidance as to its proper interpretation.').

63 Further to the terminology referred to in the ETSI Declarations (n. 59).

64 The goal is not to analyse the relevant issues from the perspective of any specific national law, but rather to discuss these legal issues from a more fundamental and policy-oriented perspective (i.e. irrespective of the law that shall apply); the analysis will be made by reference to the ETSI Declarations even if they are to be interpreted under French law, as an example of the types of legal issues that can arise as a result of the commitments made by owners of SEPs.

65 ETSI Declarations (n. 59).

66 Admitting the validity of contractual commitments, see Microsoft Corp. *v.* Motorola, Inc., 854 F. Supp. 2d 993 (Dist. Court, WD Washington 2012), in which the Court agreed that Motorola (owner of SEP) through its letters to both the IEEE and ITU [as SSOs], has entered into binding contractual commitments to licence its essential patents on RAND terms (with references to prior case law: Research In Motion Ltd. *v.* Motorola, Inc., 644 F. Supp. 2d 788, 797 (N.D.Tex.2008) and Ericsson Inc. *v.* Samsung Electronics, Co., Civil

contract – rights to a third party is widely admitted at the global level. Under French law, which is of particular relevance for the discussion here (given that it is the law which governs the ETSI Declarations), the view is expressed that the commitments made by owners of SEPs under the ETSI Declarations can qualify as *stipulation pour autrui* within the meaning of Article 1205 of the New French Civil Code[67] (that is, identifying third-party beneficiaries of a contract, even when not expressly included as parties to the contract). The UK courts in the English case *Unwired Planet International Ltd* v. *Huawei Technologies Co. Ltd & Anor* ('*Unwired Planet*') have also accepted that the doctrine of *stipulation pour autrui* could be applied to ETSI even though Justice Birss admitted that the enforceability of the FRAND undertaking in French law is 'not a clear cut question'.[68]

Action No. 2:06-CV-63, 2007 WL 1202728, at *1 (ED Tex. 20 April, 2007)) and that Microsoft, as a member of both the IEEE and the ITU, is a third-party beneficiary of Motorola's commitments to the IEEE and ITU (with reference to ESS Tech., Inc. *v.* PC-Tel, Inc., No. C-99-20292 RMW, 1999 WL 33520483, at *4 (ND Cal. 4 November 4 1999)); these findings were reaffirmed in the subsequent decision Microsoft Corp. *v.* Motorola, Inc., 864 F. Supp. 2d 1023 (Dist. Court, WD Washington DC 2012); for an analysis of this case, see Kassandra Maldonado, 'Breaching RAND and Reaching for Reasonable: Microsoft *v.* Motorola and Standard-Essential Patent Litigation' (2014), 29 *Berkeley Tech. L.J.*, pp. 419–464, available at http://scholarship.law.berkeley.edu/btlj/vol29/iss4/4; for a contractual analysis of FRAND, see Roger G. Brooks/Damien Geradin, 'Interpreting and Enforcing the Voluntary FRAND Commitment' (July 20, 2010), available at http://ssrn.com/abstract=1645878; for the opposite view (considering that (common law) contract theory does not constitute the proper legal basis for analysing FRAND), see Jorge L. Contreras, 'A Market Reliance Theory for FRAND Commitments and Other Patent Pledges' (2015), to be published in *Utah Law Review* 2015, available at http://papers.ssrn.com/sol3/papers.cfm?abstract_id=2309023.

[67] On 1 October 2016, Order no. 2016-131 of 10 February 2016, modifying the French Civil Code provisions on contract law and the general regime and proof of obligations, entered into force, see www.trans-lex.org/601101/_/french-civil-code-2016/. See Christophe Caron, 'L'efficacité des licences FRAND: entre droit des brevets, droit civil et normalisation' (May 2013), *La Semaine Juridique, édition générale*, 21, 20 May, pp. 1006–1013, p. 1008 *et seq.*

[68] [2017] EWHC 711 (Pat) (5 April 2017), para. 146: 'Standing back I recognise that the enforceability of the FRAND undertaking in French law is not a clear-cut question. Prof Libchaber stated that there remains widespread uncertainty about the issue of whether the doctrine of "*stipulation pour autrui*" can be applied to ETSI. In my judgment it can be applied in that way and should be. The reason it should be applied is because the FRAND undertaking is an important aspect of technology standardisation. Holders of essential IPR are not compelled to give a FRAND undertaking but it serves the public interest that they make it clear whether or not they are doing so, and it serves the public interest that if they do, the undertaking is public, irrevocable and enforceable. To avoid hold up, implementers need to know that they can hold SEP owners to a FRAND obligation.'

The Development by Courts Of FRAND Licensing Terms: *Unwired Planet International Ltd* v. *Huawei* The analysis relating to the development by courts of FRAND licensing terms that will be made here will based on the case of *Unwired Planet International Ltd* v. *Huawei Technologies Co. Ltd & Anor* that was decided by the United Kingdom Court of Appeal in October 2018 (it being noted that appeals against the judgment were rejected by the UK Supreme Court in its decision of 26 August 2020).[69] This case has attracted a lot of attention[70] and is viewed as an important source in terms of development of global FRAND standards, even if the Court of Appeal has recognized the complexity of patent licensing contracts that can be structured in a variety of ways depending on the interests of the parties.[71] Contrary to the opinion of the

[69] Unwired Planet International Ltd. & Anor *v.* Huawei Technologies Co Ltd & Anor [2018] EWCA Civ 2344 (23 October 2018), available at www.bailii.org/ew/cases/EWCA/Civ/2018/2344.html; Cite as: [2018] EWCA Civ 2344 'the Unwired Planet Huawei Court of Appeal 2018 Judgment'; many decisions were rendered in this dispute, including: Unwired Planet International Ltd *v.* Huawei Technologies Co. Ltd & Anor [2017] EWHC 711 (Pat) (5 April 2017), available at www.bailii.org/ew/cases/EWHC/Patents/2017/711.html Cite as: [2017] EWHC 711 (Pat) 'the Unwired Planet Huawei April 2017 Judgment'; Unwired Planet International Ltd *v.* Huawei Technologies Co Ltd & Anor [2017] EWHC 1304 (Pat) (7 June 2017), available at www.bailii.org/ew/cases/EWHC/Patents/2017/1304.html (judgment dealing with the remedies to follow from the main judgment dated 5 April 2017 ([2017] EWHC 705 (Pat), 'the Unwired Planet Huawei June 2017 Judgment')).

[70] See Peter Picht, 'Unwired Planet v Huawei: A Seminal SEP/FRAND decision from the UK' (2017), *Journal of Intellectual Property Law & Practice*, 12, 10, pp. 867–880, available at https://doi.org/10.1093/jiplp/jpx152; see also Jorge Contreras, 'A New Perspective on FRAND Royalties: Unwired Planet v. Huawei', available at www.ssrn.com/abstract=2949449; 'Global Markets, Competition, and FRAND Royalties: The Many Implications of Unwired Planet v. Huawei', 16 *Antitrust Source* 17(1) (Aug. 2017), available at www.ssrn.com/abstract=3017850; Jacques de Werra, 'Les licences FRAND: chance ou risque pour l'harmonisation globale du droit des contrats de licence de brevets?' sic! 2019, pp. 77–83, available at https://archive-ouverte.unige.ch/unige:114455.

[71] Unwired Planet International Ltd. & Anor *v.* Huawei Technologies Co Ltd & Anor [2018] EWCA Civ 2344 (23 October 2018), para. 121: 'Patent licenses are complex and, with regard to the commercial priorities of the participating undertakings and the experience of the parties involved, may be structured in different ways, for example, be included in the license, the geographical scope of the license, the products to be licensed, and paid rates'; for an interesting analysis of the Unwired Planet Huawei April 2017 Judgment (note 62), see Mark Anderson, 'How To Draft A License Agreement That Is Fair, Reasonable, And Non-Discriminatory: A Ten-Point Plan' (2018), *Journal of Intellectual Property Law & Practice*, 13, 5: 377–392, available at https://doi.org/10.1093/jiplp/jpx212; also available at https://academic.oup.com/jiplp/article-pdf/13/5/377/24572778/jpx212.pdf.

Court of First Instance (Justice Birss), the Court of Appeal admitted the diversity of FRAND licence agreements so that there shall not be a single contract that could generally be considered as FRAND, while Mr Justice Birss stated to the contrary that 'for a given set of circumstances there will only be one set of FRAND terms and only one FRAND rate'.[72] One argument that Mr Justice Birss espoused for this view was that '[i]t will promote certainty and will enhance the normative aspect of FRAND'.[73] The Court of Appeal did not confirm this approach, which means that we cannot expect the decision of the Court of Appeal to offer a justification for the complete unification of FRAND licensing transactions.

The question is to identify which licensing contractual terms are covered by the FRAND obligations and how these obligations must be formulated. While the FRAND debate has essentially focused on the assessment and on the calculation of FRAND-compliant royalties,[74] patent licensing agreements must cover a range of other contractual terms and conditions for which the question of their compliance with FRAND also arises.[75]

These other components of a FRAND licence must indeed also be FRAND-compliant and may also raise quite complex legal issues that courts have to address (potentially by moving away from the clauses agreed upon by the parties). It must be noted from a contract law standpoint that it is generally not a standard practice that courts shall intervene in private dealings and shall thus define the content of contracts instead of the contracting parties unless exceptional circumstances justify such judicial interference.

72 Para. 164.

73 Para. 156.

74 See Gunther Friedl and Ann Christoph, 'Entgeltberechnung für FRAND-Lizenzen an standardessenziellen Patenten' (2014), *GRUR*, pp. 948–955.

75 See Jorge L. Contreras and David L. Newman, 'Developing a Framework for Arbitrating Standards-Essential Patent Disputes' (2014), *Journal of Dispute Resolution* 1, pp. 23–51, p. 39, referring to 'Non-Royalty FRAND Terms', available at http://papers.ssrn.com/sol3/papers.cfm?abstract_id=2335732; see also James H. Carter, 'FRAND Royalty Disputes: A New Challenge for International Arbitration?', in Arthur W. Rovine (ed.), *Contemporary Issues in International Arbitration and Mediation – the Fordham Papers 2013*, Leiden/Boston, 2013, pp. 67–78, p. 73 (holding that '[t]he paradigm license term in dispute naturally would be a royalty rate or rates, on the setting of which large amounts of money could turn; but there might be dozens of other disputed terms, many with complicated (but not readily apparent) financial implications. Patent license agreements can be complex documents').

The complexity of defining FRAND contractual terms (beyond the issue of royalties) can be illustrated by focusing on two contractual terms that have been discussed in the *Unwired Planet* v. *Huawei* case which respectively deals with (i) the irrevocable nature of the licence and (ii) the choice of court clause.

The Irrevocable Nature of the Licence The ETSI Declarations[76] provide that the owners of SEPs must be 'prepared to grant *irrevocable* licenses' (italics added). One can infer from the underlying objective of the FRAND commitment (and of the ETSI Declarations) that by stating that the licence shall be irrevocable, the ETSI Declarations pursued the goal to protect the licensee against an arbitrary unilateral termination of the licence by the licensor (and owner of SEPs).

In any event, leaving aside the interpretation of the concept of an irrevocable licence under French law,[77] this irrevocability raises the question of the conditions under which a FRAND-compliant licence can be terminated, which in turn refers to the law which shall govern the licence (it being noted that the ETSI Declarations do not prescribe that the licence agreements to be entered on FRAND terms and conditions shall be governed by French law).[78]

In the *Unwired Planet* v. *Huawei* case, the 'settled licence', i.e. the patent licence agreement which was validated as being FRAND by the High Court (fully disclosed in the *Unwired Planet Huawei* June 2017 Judgment as an Annex,[79] hereafter 'the Settled Licence') and was not challenged by the Court of Appeal is not declared to be irrevocable, contrary to what the ETSI Declarations require.[80] The Settled Licence was rather entered into for a defined period of time (i.e. until

[76] N. 50.

[77] Which has apparently not been discussed in the *Unwired Planet v. Huawei* case; for a discussion, see F. Ferro, 'The Nature Of FRAND Commitments Under French Contract and Property Law' (2018), *The Journal of Intellectual Property Law & Practice*, p. 988; M.-R. McGuire, 'Die FRAND-Erklärung' (2018), *Anwendbares Recht, Rechtsnatur und Bindungswirkung am Beispiel eines ETSI-Standards*, p. 128.

[78] McGuire (n. 77 *supra*) 133; it is, however, clear that in most cases the licence agreement will be entered between companies which will be located in different countries so this will be an international agreement for which the issue of the governing law will arise; the Settled Licence is governed by English law.

[79] Para. 70.

[80] Anderson (n. 71 *supra*) p. 382.

31 December 2020) and is thus not a perpetual licence.[81] The Settled Licence further provides for a termination clause (Section 6.2) by which

> [a] Party may terminate this Agreement by written notice if the other Party (or an Affiliate) at any time commits a material breach of any of its significant obligations under this Agreement (which shall expressly include any non-payment) and, in the event of a breach capable of remedy, fails to cure, or procure the cure of, such breach within thirty (30) days after receipt of a notice specifying the nature of such breach and requiring remedy of the same.

This contractual right of unilateral termination before the agreed date of expiry provided for in the Settled Licence could thus be incompatible with the requirement that the licence shall be irrevocable under the ETSI Declarations, because the term 'irrevocable' could be understood as meaning that the licence precisely cannot be terminated before its agreed date of expiry.[82] The Settled Licence further provides that '[t]he Parties agree that the failure to identify in this Agreement the breach of any particular obligation as a "material breach" does not preclude any Party from contending in the future that such breach is "material"'. This consequently means that the courts must decide what shall constitute a material breach of the Settled Licence that could lead to its termination under the conditions of Section 6.2.[83] In any event, the Settled Licence and its validation by the UK courts seems to indicate that, in spite of the requirement expressed in the ETSI Declaration that the licence shall be irrevocable, parties can agree that a FRAND patent licence agreement can still provide for a right of an early termination of the licence in case

[81] Ibid., p. 382.

[82] Ibid., p. 382.

[83] The concept of 'material breach' is not used in all legal systems, and particularly not under Swiss contract law. This however does not prevent that reference shall be made to international instruments that allude to the concept of 'material breach' which is related to the concept of fundamental breach under certain international instruments (i.e. the United Nations Convention on Contracts for the International Sale of Goods (Vienna, 1980) (CISG), Article 25, and the Unidroit Principles of International Commercial Contracts (2016), Article 7.3.1 (1) which provides that 'A party may terminate the contract where the failure of the other party to perform an obligation under the contract amounts to a fundamental non-performance', available at www.unidroit.org/instruments/commercial-contracts/unidroit-principles-2016) even if such instruments are not applicable to the international contract at issue. This is what was done by an arbitral tribunal in an award rendered in a dispute about a contract that was governed by Swiss law that was challenged before the Swiss Federal Court which upheld the award, see decision of the Swiss Federal Court in case 4A_240/2009 of 16 December 2009.

of material breach of the licence, leaving uncertainty as to what would constitute such a material breach and as to the consequences of such early termination of the licence. As a matter of principle, an early termination of a patent (or more generally any IP) licence agreement means that as of the effective time of the termination, the ex-licensee is no longer entitled to use the previously licensed patented inventions and is thus exposed to patent infringement consequences, including injunctive remedies. This would, however, seem delicate in a situation in which a licensor (owner of SEPs) would abusively terminate the licence on the grounds of a spurious claim of a material breach of the licence by the licensee. In such a case, the risk would be that the licensor could obtain injunctive relief after the early termination in order to re-negotiate and obtain better licensing terms from its ex-licensee in a new licence agreement that they would enter into (assuming the matter would be heard prior to, and separately from, consideration of the claimed licence infringement). The right of early termination thus raises difficulties for the licensee because this may create a risk of being exposed to injunctions in case of such early termination of the licence (which is essentially the same risk as the one that exists before a licence agreement is entered into). The view was expressed in the legal literature about the *Unwired Planet* v. *Huawei* case that the licensee could have insisted on an irrevocable licence on the SEP patents, 'in which the remedy for non-payment of the royalties would be simply to sue for damages, without the right to terminate the licence agreement'.[84] This shows in any event that FRAND licences, like other long-term contracts which remain in force over several years, will evolve over time. It is consequently necessary to anticipate as much as possible such potential evolutions and to adopt mechanisms that shall efficiently manage such potential evolution.[85]

Even if the licence was declared as irrevocable (in compliance with the ETSI Declarations), this might still be problematic depending on the law of contract that shall govern the licence agreement. Under certain national contract laws (including Swiss contract law, in the event that a

[84] Anderson (n. 71), p. 382.

[85] On the post-signing adjustment of SEP/FRAND licences (because of alteration in the set of licensed patents (an alteration may take the form of patent invalidation or, on the opposite, the confirmation of patent validity as a result of legal action, etc.), see Peter Picht, 'Post-signing adjustment of SEP/FRAND licenses' (2018), *les Nouvelles*, 99, available at https://ssrn.com/abstract=3164310.

licence agreement would be governed by Swiss law),[86] licence agreements can be validly terminated for just cause even if they are declared irrevocable by the parties, because a party to a long-term contract governed by Swiss law (a licence agreement is one of such contracts) has the unwaivable right to terminate the contract for just cause pursuant to a general principle anchored in Swiss contract law.[87] On this basis, a licence agreement on SEPs could or could not be irrevocable depending on the law governing the contract.

In any event, this discussion about the irrevocability of the licence to be granted by the SEP owner shows that courts can have different views on this issue. Even if the ETSI Declarations state that the licence shall be irrevocable, the UK courts validated the licence proposed by the parties even if it was not irrevocable but rather provided for a (quite standard) contractual provision permitting the early termination of the licence in case of an uncured material breach committed by one of the parties. This illustrates how national courts can define what they consider as FRAND terms in the absence of global standard principles that would guide them (even without binding them) in the definition of what shall constitute FRAND licensing terms. In this respect, one has to emphasize that courts 'cannot craft a set of FRAND terms out of thin air'[88] (as expressed by Mr Justice Birss). This consequently means that courts will (heavily) rely on the contractual terms that the parties will propose.[89]

This further means that FRAND terms are defined or at least co-defined by the parties to the FRAND dispute and that courts will not intervene intensively in the parties' dealings except with respect to the financial conditions of the licence (e.g. royalty rates and royalty calculation). Viewed from the broader perspective of the role of courts in contractual disputes, the reluctance of courts to intervene and to define independently the rights and obligations of contracting parties is fully understandable. This humble approach of courts is however problematic

[86] Which is relatively frequently chosen as governing law in international technology-related agreements, as resulting from a recent survey, see the Results of the WIPO Arbitration and Mediation Center International Survey on Dispute Resolution in Technology Transactions (March 2013), available at www.wipo.int/export/sites/www/amc/en/docs/surveyresults.pdf, p. 15.

[87] Marie-Noëlle Venturi Zen-Ruffinen, *La résiliation pour justes motifs des contrats de durée*, Fribourg 2007, p. 115 n. 330 *et seq*.

[88] Unwired Planet Huawei April 2017 Judgment, para. 169: 'Having now heard this trial I remain of the view that the court cannot craft a set of FRAND terms out of thin air.'

[89] Anderson (n. 71 *supra*) p. 387.

to the extent that it may have the consequence that individual clauses negotiated by specific parties in certain circumstances may ultimately become (after their adoption by courts) guiding references on a global basis for defining standard FRAND licensing terms.[90]

In sum, in spite of the requirement of irrevocability of the licence (reflected in the ETSI Declarations), one can admit that a licence shall be FRAND-compliant even if it provides (as this was done in the Settled Licence validated by the UK courts) that the licence can be terminated under certain justifiable circumstances most notably when a party breaches its contractual obligations (e.g. if the licensee does not pay the royalties due under the licence). This right of unilateral termination of the licence for just cause[91] appears reasonable under standard principles of commercial IP licensing law.

As reflected above, the recognition of such a right of early termination of the licence will ultimately depend on the law that shall govern the licence. For this reason, any court that would be invited to assess whether a given licence is FRAND-compliant should pay utmost attention to the conditions under which a licence can be terminated under the relevant law: even if a licence would provide that it would be irrevocable, such irrevocability might not be enforceable under the relevant governing contract law.

The Choice of Court Clause A second important aspect of *Unwired Planet* v. *Huawei* results from the geographic scope of the Settled Licence as set by Mr Justice Birss which is a worldwide licence and is thus not limited to the United Kingdom, noting that the Court of Appeal subsequently validated the global geographical scope of the FRAND licence.[92] Mr Justice Birss expressed the position relating to the exclusive choice of court clause that the parties had agreed upon that 'as a worldwide licence I think a jurisdiction clause purporting to oust the jurisdiction of foreign courts would not be appropriate'[93] and thus that the choice of court for the English courts (i.e. the High Court

90 Ibid., p. 389 ('the author strongly recommends that FRAND license negotiators do not treat the drafting in this case as a model for future FRAND license agreements').

91 I.e. termination only if there are objectively justifiable circumstances establishing that the party which terminates cannot reasonably be expected to continue to be bound by the contract.

92 According to Sections 1.21 and 2.1 of the Settled License.

93 Unwired Planet Huawei April 2017 Judgment, para. 594.

of England and Wales) should be non-exclusive, as was in any event reflected in the Settled Licence.[94]

While we may understand the deference to foreign courts shown by Mr Justice Birss, one can still wonder whether a non-exclusive choice of court agreement makes practical sense. A non-exclusive jurisdictional clause essentially means that the parties remain in a position to start judicial proceedings before other national courts outside of the United Kingdom for any 'disputes, differences or questions arising out of or relating to the interpretation or performance of this Agreement between the Parties', it being noted that the Settled Licence remains governed by 'the substantive law of England & Wales without regard to conflicts of law rules'.[95] This application of the law of England and Wales makes it natural and appropriate that the High Court of England and Wales shall have jurisdiction to decide on disputes by applying its own local law.

It is by contrast more complex and less obvious to submit a dispute governed by UK contract law to foreign (non-UK) courts also because this may lead to conflicting decisions: given the non-exclusivity nature of the choice of court clause, different courts in different countries may end up deciding differently even by applying the same (UK) law for which it is likely that they may call upon experts.[96] It consequently does not appear adequate to favour a system (resulting from the non-exclusive jurisdictional clause) by which parties could litigate the same issue (potentially the issue of the valid termination of the licence in the context of infringement proceedings initiated by the licensor) before different national courts (even though it could be expected that certain of these courts could suspend their proceedings in the expectation of the outcome to be decided by other courts).

On this basis, it is not a desirable outcome that non-exclusive choice of courts has been held FRAND-compliant in *Unwired Planet* v. *Huawei*.

[94] '9.3 The High Court of England and Wales shall have non-exclusive jurisdiction to finally settle all disputes, differences or questions arising out of or relating to the interpretation or performance of this Agreement between the Parties'.

[95] Settled License '9.1 This Agreement shall be governed by and construed in accordance with the substantive law of England & Wales without regard to conflicts of law rules'.

[96] For an illustration of the challenges resulting from the application of foreign law by a national judge, see the US case Bodum, USA, Inc. *v.* La Cafetiere, Inc., 621 F.3D 624 (7th Cir. 2010); for a discussion of this case, see Philip D. Stacey, *Rule 44.1, Bodum USA v. La Cafetiere, and the Challenge of Determining Foreign Law*, 6 Seventh Circuit Rev. 472 (2011), available at http://scholarship.kentlaw.iit.edu/seventhcircuitreview/vol6/iss2/5.

This might cause difficulties and might also be understood to mean that exclusive jurisdiction clauses would *not* be FRAND-compliant.

A further point that has not been discussed in *Unwired Planet* v. *Huawei* (at least not reflected in the court decisions so far) relates to the exclusive jurisdiction of courts to decide on disputes relating to the validity of patents (which results from the application of mandatory provisions of private international law). This exclusive jurisdictional power of the courts of the country of registration of the (licenced) patents may be problematic to apply.

From this perspective, by merely providing that the choice of court clause shall be non-exclusive, the Settled Licence does not solve the complexity of international IP patent licensing disputes in which both contractual and non-contractual issues are raised and in which the validity of the relevant patents is frequently disputed. Once the validity of the patents is in dispute, this may lead to the geographic fragmentation of the dispute: the courts in each country in which the patents have been registered have exclusive jurisdiction to decide on the validity of such rights.

This is the case under European law: pursuant to Article 24 para. 4 of the Brussels Regulation[97] (recast), in proceedings concerned with the registration or validity of patents, trade marks, designs, or other similar rights required to be deposited or registered, regardless of the domicile of the parties and irrespective of whether the issue is raised by way of an action or as a defence, exclusive jurisdiction is ascribed to the courts of the member state in which the deposit or registration has been applied for, has taken place or is deemed to have taken place under the terms of an EU instrument or an international convention. This means that as soon as the issue of the validity of the patents is raised (by way of an action or as a defence) no choice of court agreement would be valid and enforceable.

This does not prevent parties from validly agreeing on an exclusive choice of court clause in their IP licence agreement which would have the advantage of avoiding conflicting decisions of national courts on contractual issues relating to the licence agreement (such as the ones relating to the interpretation of the licence agreement), subject to the limit that such choice of court clause would not apply when the issue of the validity of the licensed patents would arise.

[97] Regulation (EU) No 1215/2012 of 12 December 2012 on jurisdiction and the recognition and enforcement of judgments in civil and commercial matters (recast).

From this perspective, the non-exclusive choice of court clause contained in the Settled Licence does not necessarily constitute a model for future FRAND licences, because such clause may contribute to a fragmentation of the future disputes that may result from the Settled Licence. Instead of validating a non-exclusive choice of court clause, a reasonable approach could be to privilege exclusive choice of court clauses under FRAND licensing terms and to bear in mind or even to carve out from the scope of the exclusive choice of court clause (to the extent required) disputes relating to the validity of the licensed patents (because such disputes would have to be submitted to courts in the countries of registration).

The Use of Arbitration to Solve FRAND Disputes Parties could avoid or at least significantly reduce the risk of an undesirable fragmentation of their FRAND dispute by submitting it to alternative dispute resolution mechanisms, and specifically to arbitration.[98] It is worth mentioning that the European Commission has devoted a specific chapter to alternative dispute resolution in its Communication to the Institutions on Setting out the EU approach to Standard Essential Patents of 29 November 2017.[99] The Commission has further expressed the view that alternative dispute resolution (ADR) mechanisms such as mediation and arbitration can offer swifter and less costly dispute resolution. While there can be no obligation for parties to use ADR, the Commission believes that the potential benefits of this tool are currently underexploited.[100] Market players do also confirm the importance of arbitration to settle global patent disputes, as reflected by Maria Varsellona, chief legal officer at Nokia, who stated that '[t]he use of independent arbitration to resolve differences in patent cases is a recognized best practice' (statement made

[98] See the short but telling statement made in the ppt presentation of Christian Loysau (ETSI) at WIPO (July 13, 2018 (WIPO/IS/IP/GE/18/D ETSI, available at www.wipo.int/edocs/mdocs/scp/en/wipo_is_ip_ge_18/wipo_is_ip_ge_18_etsi.pdf): 'Standardizations, patenting, licensing and disputes are global – court decisions are national'; see also Antje Baumann, 'Einschaltung von Schiedsgerichten zur Bestimmung der FRAND-Konditionen' (2018), *GRUR*, 145; Peter Picht, Schiedsverfahren in SEP/FRAND-Streitigkeiten – Überblick und Kernprobleme, Max Planck Institute for Innovation & Competition, Discussion Paper Nr. 13 of 14 October 2018, available at https://papers.ssrn.com/sol3/papers.cfm?abstract_id=3266546.

[99] See https://ec.europa.eu/docsroom/documents/26583.

[100] Communication, chapter 3.4, p. 11.

in connection with the rendering of an ICC arbitral award in a licensing dispute between Nokia and LG Electronics[101]).

The efficient use of arbitration in FRAND disputes can be illustrated by the high-profile *Samsung* v. *Apple* dispute which led to an EU antitrust procedure[102] that was resolved on 29 April 2014 by a decision of the EU Commission.[103]

By this decision, the Commission accepted the legally binding commitments made by Samsung (hereinafter 'the Commitments'),[104] which are of high importance because they illustrate the type of processes that have been validated in order to solve FRAND-related disputes.[105]

The relevant elements of the case are as follows: Samsung owns SEPs related to the 3G UMTS[106] standard (which is an industry standard for mobile and wireless communications). Samsung committed to license its SEPs on FRAND terms and conditions pursuant to the relevant ETSI rules. Samsung started to enforce certain of its UMTS SEPs against Apple in various EU countries (France, Germany, Italy, the Netherlands and the United Kingdom) in which it sought to obtain preliminary and permanent injunctions from the courts. The EU Commission initiated antitrust proceedings in order to investigate whether Samsung had failed to honour the commitment it gave to ETSI that it would license its SEPs on FRAND terms (i.e. whether Samsung has failed to honour its FRAND commitment in licensing negotiations, including by seeking injunctive relief before the courts of certain member states in relation to some of its SEPs). In the course of its investigation, the Commission preliminarily

101 See 'Nokia receives decision in patent license arbitration with LG Electronics', 18 September 2017, available at www.nokia.com/en_int/news/releases/2017/09/18/nokia-receives-decision-in-patent-license-arbitration-with-lg-electronics.

102 Case AT.39939 – *Samsung – Enforcement of UMTS standard essential patents*; see http://ec.europa.eu/competition/elojade/isef/case_details.cfm?proc_code=1_39939.

103 Commission Decision of 29 April 2014 relating to a proceeding under Article 102 of the Treaty on the Functioning of the European Union and Article 54 of the EEA Agreement (Case AT.39939 – Samsung – Enforcement of UMTS standard essential patents) (notified under document number C(2014) 2891 final), available at http://ec.europa.eu/competition/antritrust/case/dec_docs/39939/39939_1501_5.pdf (the summary of the decision was published in OJ 2014/C 350/08 of October 4, 2014).

104 The Commitments are available at http://ec.europa.eu/competition/antitrust/cases/dec_docs/39939/39939_1502_5.pdf.

105 This section of the article is derived from Jacques de Werra, 'The expanding significance of arbitration for patent licensing disputes: From post-termination disputes to pre-licensing FRAND disputes', *ASA Bulletin 2014*, vol. 32, no. 4, pp. 692–706, available at http://archive-ouverte.unige.ch/unige:46142.

106 Universal Mobile Telecommunications System.

concluded that Samsung's seeking of preliminary and permanent injunctions against Apple on the basis of its SEPs, in view of the exceptional circumstances of the case and in the absence of any objective justification, raised concerns as to the compatibility of the seeking of such injunctions with Article 102 of the Treaty on the Functioning of the European Union (TFEU). The exceptional circumstances were the UMTS standard-setting process and Samsung's commitment to license its SEPs on FRAND terms and conditions. The absence of objective justification related in particular to the fact that the potential licensee, i.e. Apple, was not unwilling to enter into a licence agreement for Samsung's SEPs on FRAND terms and conditions. By its decision of 29 April 2014, the Commission validated the Commitments made by Samsung[107] and decided that they shall be binding on Samsung (and Samsung's affiliates) for a period of five years and consequently concluded that there were no longer grounds for action by the Commission.

The Commitments are extremely interesting from a dispute resolution perspective, given that they provide for the submission to court proceedings or arbitration of FRAND disputes as part of a sophisticated and multi-step negotiation and dispute resolution mechanism. The Commitments first provide for the creation of a so-called 'Licensing Framework' the objective of which is to determine FRAND licensing terms between Samsung and potential licensees.[108] The Licensing Framework institutes a mandatory negotiation period (in principle 12 months) during which Samsung and the potential licensee are invited to negotiate on FRAND terms with a view to agreeing on a unilateral licence or a cross-licence. If the negotiations fail and if the parties do not agree on an alternative procedure for determining FRAND terms, the Commitments provide that 'the Parties shall submit the matter to arbitration or to court adjudication in order to determine the FRAND terms of a Unilateral License or, as applicable a Cross-License [. . .]'[109] in the course of a phase called 'Third Party Determination of FRAND Terms.'[110] The Parties are then invited to jointly decide whether they shall submit the FRAND dispute to arbitration or court adjudication

[107] See n. 103.

[108] The Commitments provide for the opportunities to negotiate cross-licences (in the case Samsung's licensees are also owners of SEPs).

[109] Ibid., clause 1.b.

[110] Ibid.

within a given time limit, whereby in the absence of agreement, the dispute will be submitted to courts.[111]

The Commitments provide for quite detailed rules on the arbitration proceedings. They first opt for institutional arbitration by indicating that 'the dispute shall be finally settled under the rules of arbitration of the ICC, unless the Parties mutually agree that the arbitration tribunal will be the patent mediation and arbitration center as established under Article 35(1) of the Agreement on a Unified Patent Court'.[112] Notably, the Commitments provide that '[a] non-confidential version of the arbitral decision shall be published within 90 days following the issuance of such decision' and that '[t]he non-confidential version of the arbitral decision may disclose the methodology relied upon by the arbitral panel to arrive at specific FRAND terms, but shall in no event disclose specific terms'.[113] This unusual element, which stands in obvious conflict with the basic tenet of confidentiality in commercial arbitration, is due to the requirement of transparency of FRAND decisions and awards reflected in the decision of the Commission of 29 April 2014.[114]

[111] Pursuant to the Commitments clause 10: '[t]he venue for the court adjudication procedure will be the Patent Court, High Court of England and Wales (or any successor court), or the UPC' [i.e. the Unified Patent Court as instituted by the Agreement on a Unified Patent Court of February 19, 2013, available at www.gov.uk/government/publications/agreement-on-a-unified-patent-court-19-february-2013].

[112] Ibid., clause 9.a. The reference to the Patent Mediation and Arbitration Centre to be established under the UPC (Article 35) is quite interesting because of the specificities of the Centre. It confirms the potential importance that this centre could gain as provider of arbitration and mediation services for IP (and specifically FRAND patent licensing) disputes in the future. The Centre has not been established yet and has not published its arbitration and mediation rules (that shall be adopted by the Centre pursuant to Article 35 para. 3 UPC); for an analysis, see Jacques de Werra, 'New Developments of IP Arbitration and Mediation in Europe: The Patent Mediation and Arbitration Center Instituted by the Agreement on a Unified Patent Court' (2014), *Revista Brasileira de Arbitragem*, pp. 17–35 (available at http://archive-ouverte.unige.ch/unige:39878); it also remains to be seen whether the Centre will adopt specific procedures and principles for FRAND disputes.

[113] Commitments clause 9.e.

[114] Decision of the Commission (note 103), para. 111 ('the publication of a non-confidential version of arbitration awards will contribute to the creation of a body of case-law upon which future FRAND determinations could draw. This should contribute to a principled and efficient solution of future FRAND disputes by arbitration tribunals'). The justification of the public disclosure of FRAND-related arbitral awards is debated in the legal literature. See Yoonhee Kim, 'Lifting Confidentiality of FRAND Royalties in SEP Arbitration' (2014), 16 *Columbia Science & Technology Law Review*, pp. 1–35, available at https://doi.org/10.7916/stlr.v16i1.3989. One issue to consider is the value and usefulness of the information contained in an arbitral award that shall potentially be disclosed

The Commitments further provide for a 'de novo appeal on issues of fact and law' against an arbitral award[115] before another arbitral tribunal,[116] whereby the 'appeal shall be treated as a separate arbitration'[117] in which the parties can 'agree to limit the issues to be considered on appeal'.[118] This constitutes another unusual feature of these proceedings which stands in sharp contrast to standard commercial arbitration practice. Interestingly, the Commitments state in this respect with regard to the seat of the arbitration that it 'will be in an EEA jurisdiction in which national laws permit Parties to agree to make an arbitration decision subject to appeal to a second arbitral tribunal'.[119]

Third, the Commitments indicate, as to the substantive scope of the jurisdictional power of the arbitral tribunal that '[t]he arbitral panel shall

to the public. In this respect, we may wonder if the publication of only the FRAND licensing rate would be relevant. See Kim, p. 32 ('[t]his Article does not argue that all patent licensing terms be known to the public: only a FRAND licensing rate calls for scrutiny in light of its public nature'). Knowing that the royalty rate will likely also reflect the validity of the licensed SEPs at issue, the relative value of the asserted patents both to the technical standard and to the infringing product. See Contreras and Newman (n. 75), p. 37. On this basis, it is uncertain whether the disclosure of the sole royalty rate could be of significant value. Another aspect relates to the non-discriminatory element of FRAND licensing. This requirement of non-discrimination presupposes that decision makers (and specifically arbitral tribunals) shall have access to other decisions and licences in order to ensure that this condition of non-discrimination is met. Carter (n. 75), p. 78. It however remains that non-discrimination does not necessarily imply that all the licensing terms and conditions and all the license agreements shall be identical. See Weber (n. 61), p. 56 (noting that the non-discrimination obligation 'does not exclude that licensing terms are dependent on the volume of the ordered goods or the creditworthiness of the licensee'). It would be worth considering the adoption of certain guidelines about the publication of FRAND-related arbitral awards (whereby certain confidential sections could be redacted in order to find an equitable balance between confidentiality and transparency) and to entrust a third party (potentially an arbitration institution) with the mission of communicating the relevant information to the arbitral tribunals, or even with the mission to review and scrutinize draft arbitral awards in order to ensure a certain consistency between the awards that shall be rendered under its supervision on FRAND licensing disputes. See Carter (n. 75), p. 78.

115 '[T]he first arbitral tribunal's decision' (according to the terminology of the Commitments, clause 9.f.).

116 '[T]he second arbitral tribunal' (according to the terminology of the Commitments, clause 9.f.i), whereby reference is also made to 'the second arbitral panel', clause 9.f.ii).

117 Commitments, clause 9.f.v.

118 Commitments, clause 9.f.iii.

119 Commitments, clause 9.d; the Commitments remain silent as to whether and under what conditions an appeal can be lodged against the award rendered on appeal by 'the second arbitral tribunal' which will ultimately depend on the law applicable in the jurisdiction of the seat of the arbitration.

take into account issues of validity, infringement, essentiality raised by the Parties in making the Third-Party Determination of FRAND Terms'.[120] This is interesting because it shows that arbitral tribunals[121] may have to take into account potential claims of invalidity of the disputed SEPs. This is of particular relevance to the extent that this confirms that it is legitimate that arbitral tribunals shall have the power to 'take into account' these issues.[122]

The *Samsung* case shows in any event that arbitration is viewed as a sustainable alternative to court litigation for solving FRAND disputes[123]

[120] Commitments, clause 9.g.

[121] It appears that this rule (in view of its systematic position in the Commitments) shall apply to both the 'first arbitral tribunal' and to the 'second arbitral tribunal'.

[122] The Commitments do not address the potential effects of an award rendered by the arbitral tribunal finding a SEP invalid. It should however be assumed that this will be limited to the parties, i.e. *inter partes* (and not *erga omnes*), also because of the wording of the Commitments which indicate that the arbitral tribunal shall 'take into account' these issues, and which does not indicate that the arbitral tribunals shall have the power to decide as such on the invalidity of a given SEP. For arbitration disputes submitted to the patent mediation and arbitration centre under the UPC, Article 35 para. 2 *in fine* UPC expressly provides that 'a patent may not be revoked or limited in mediation or arbitration proceedings' so that arbitral tribunals would not have the power to revoke a patent in that case. Another issue is to define under which (patent) law(s) the issues of (in)validity and (non-) infringements of SEPs will have to be decided in view of the clause of the Commitments providing that '[t]he arbitration will be governed by the laws of England and Wales'. (It is uncertain whether the goal of this provision was to address the law applicable to the relevant patent issues (particularly their infringement and their validity)). The question arises whether this provision was meant and was supposed to constitute a choice of law clause which could potentially mean that all issues that may arise in the arbitration (including issues of validity or infringement of the SEPs) should be decided under the laws of England and Wales. This would be possible in view of the freedom of the parties to select the governing law in international commercial arbitration. This flexibility and liberalism of arbitration stand in sharp contrast to the rigidity of choice of law rules which apply before (EU) national courts. Article 8 of the Regulation (EC) No 864/2007 of the European Parliament and of the Council of 11 July 2007 on the law applicable to non-contractual obligations (Rome II) indeed provides that '[t]he law applicable to a non-contractual obligation arising from an infringement of an intellectual property right shall be the law of the country for which protection is claimed' (Article 8 para. 1), whereby this choice of law rule is mandatory and thus cannot be derogated from by contract (Article 8 para. 3); on this issue (and on the comparative advantages of arbitration in terms of selection of the governing law), see Jacques de Werra, 'Arbitrating International Intellectual Property Disputes: Time to Think Beyond the Issue of (Non-) Arbitrability' (2012), *International Business Law Journal* 3, pp. 299–317, p. 307 *seq.*, available at http://papers.ssrn.com/sol3/papers.cfm?abstract_id=2149762.

[123] This is also confirmed by other antitrust proceedings relating to FRAND licensing, and particularly by the US case *In re Motorola Mobility LLC, and Google Inc.*, available at: www .ftc.gov/enforcement/cases-proceedings/1210120/motorola-mobility-llc-google-inc-matter;

and has been validated as such by competition authorities. It is therefore not surprising that efforts have been made by major institutions in order to address the needs of companies involved in FRAND licensing disputes and to conceptualize new dispute resolution mechanisms that shall be tailored to such disputes.[124] The WIPO Arbitration and Mediation Center has consequently established specific submission agreements that are adapted to FRAND Disputes[125] and the International Telecommunication Union (ITU) continues to be active on these issues.[126]

The implementation of FRAND commitments still raises major difficulties today and consequently continues to be discussed in the relevant fora. It is in any case important to ensure that fair and equitable dispute resolution mechanisms shall be adopted to solve FRAND patent licensing disputes, whereby arbitration could play a significant role in this context,

in its decision and order of 23 July 2013, available at www.ftc.gov/sites/default/files/documents/cases/2013/07/130724googlemotorolado.pdf, the Federal Trade Commission validated arbitration as a means 'to establish a License Agreement' (para. I.D) under SEPs owned by Motorola to willing licensees; arbitration is also selected by other technical bodies in order to solve FRAND-related SEPs licensing disputes; this is the case of the DVB (Digital Video Broadcasting) Project, available at www.dvb.org; Article 14.7 of its Statutes (also referred to as 'Memorandum of Understanding'), available at www.dvb.org/resources/public/documents_site/dvb_mou.pdf, provides for the submission to arbitration of disputes arising between Members about IPR licensing as follows: 'Each Member hereby agrees, on its behalf and on behalf of its affiliated companies, that, subject to clause 14.9 of this Article 14, all disputes with any other member of these statutes (MoU) regarding solely the terms and conditions of licenses arising in connection with the undertaking in this Article 14 shall be finally settled under the Rules of Conciliation and Arbitration of the International Chamber of Commerce by three arbitrators appointed in accordance with such Rules. Arbitration shall take place in Frankfurt, Germany.'

124 See Contreras and Newman (n. 75), p. 46 (group instituted under the aegis of the American Bar Association that is seeking to develop best practices for the arbitration of SEP disputes (called the 'ABA SEP Arbitration Project (ASAP)')).

125 See the specific submission agreements that are tailored to FRAND Disputes, available at www.wipo.int/amc/en/center/specific-sectors/ict/frand/; for a presentation, see Heike Wollgast and Ignacio de Castro, 'WIPO Arbitration and Mediation Center: New 2014 WIPO Rules' *ASA Bulletin* 2/2014, pp. 286–296, at p. 290 *seq.*

126 See the excellent report of the ITU, Understanding patents, competition and standardization in an interconnected world (1 July 2014), available at www.itu.int/en/ITU-T/ipr/Pages/Understanding-patents,-competition-and-standardization-in-an-interconnected-world.aspx; see also the site of the 'ITU Patent Roundtable', available at www.itu.int/en/ITU-T/Workshops-and-Seminars/patent/Pages/default.aspx. See also Xiaoping Wu, 'Interplay between Patents and Standards in the Information and Communication Technology (ICT) Sector and its Relevance to the Implementation of the WTO Agreements', WTO Working Paper ERSD-2017-08, 7 April 2017, available at www.wto.org/english/res_e/reser_e/ersd201708_e.pdf.

as evidenced by certain proposals which have suggested that arbitration shall be the exclusive dispute resolution mechanism for solving FRAND disputes in certain circumstances.[127]

Conclusion The debate about FRAND licensing shows that the transaction costs resulting from licensing negotiations can be very high,[128] which calls for a certain work of *legal* standardization. In order to be efficient, FRAND terms and conditions should be standardized at the international level in order to offer a global framework for this specific type of knowledge-based transaction. By way of example, and as discussed above, the supposedly irrevocable nature of the licence and the conditions under which a FRAND licence can be terminated unilaterally (particularly by the FRAND licensor) should ideally be harmonized at the global level in order to create standard fair, reasonable and non-discriminatory FRAND licensing terms. The process of global *technical standardization* which has led to the development of the concept of FRAND licensing terms and conditions should consequently lead to a global *legal standardization* of these terms and conditions (*substantive* legal standards) and to the standardization of the processes and mechanisms (*procedural* legal standards) which can lead to their use in a specific case, i.e. to the negotiation and conclusion of a FRAND-compliant licence agreement.

FRAND licensing thus shows the complexities of global harmonization of patent licensing transactions as to the substance (i.e. what shall be held as fair, reasonable and non-discriminatory licensing terms and conditions) and as to the processes (i.e. how shall FRAND licensing disputes be efficiently solved). Even if FRAND licensing terms and FRAND-related legal issues have specific features which cannot

[127] See Mark A. Lemley and Carl Shapiro, 'A Simple Approach to Setting Reasonable Royalties for Standard-Essential Patents' (2013), 28 *Berkeley Technology Law Journal*, pp. 1135–1166, available at http://btlj.org/data/articles2015/vol28/28_2/28-berkeley-tech-l-j-1135-1166.pdf, who have proposed that the standard-essential patent owner shall be obligated to enter into binding baseball-style (or 'final offer') arbitration with any willing licensee to determine the royalty rate; for a critical analysis of their proposal, see Pierre Larouch et al., 'Settling FRAND Disputes: Is Mandatory Arbitration a Reasonable and Non-Discriminatory Alternative?' (2014), *Journal of Competition Law & Economics*, pp. 581–610, available at http://jcle.oxfordjournals.org/content/10/3/581.abstract.

[128] See the interesting paper (under copyright law) of Peter S. Menell and Ben Depoorter, 'Using Fee Shifting: A Proposal to Promote Fair Use and Fair Licensing' (2014), 105 *California Law Review*, pp. 53–86, available at www.jstor.org/stable/23784367.

necessarily be found in other areas of intellectual property licensing, the discussion about FRAND licensing shows that the law of intellectual property licensing is still underdeveloped at the international and even regional level[129] and that this situation is inadequate.[130]

The discussion about FRAND licensing and the way national courts deal with this (as reflected in *Unwired Planet*) reveal the challenges of defining fair and reasonable licensing terms and conditions from a transnational perspective. It may appear surprising that the law governing IP licensing transactions remains largely unaffected by global trends of harmonization in spite of the unanimous understanding that intellectual property transactions as such, and licensing agreements in particular, are essential in today's interconnected world and economy, as demonstrated by this chapter. On this basis, FRAND licensing confirms the interest and even the need to develop common global standards of fair and reasonable licensing terms. This need is further confirmed by the development of compulsory licensing mechanisms which raise similar issues, i.e. what shall be the standard terms and conditions of a compulsory licence?[131] In the absence of source of global guidance,[132] local courts will most probably continue to establish their own standards, which may lead to conflicting solutions from a transnational

[129] This is (perhaps surprisingly) also the case within the European Union, see, e.g., Jacques de Werra, 'The Need to Harmonize Intellectual Property Licensing Law: A European Perspective', in Jacques de Werra (ed.), *Research Handbook on Intellectual Property Licensing*, Cheltenham: Edward Elgar, 2013, pp. 450–472, available at https://archive-ouverte.unige.ch/unige:29497.

[130] For a presentation of various perspectives of licensing practices in various countries and regions, and from various policy standpoints, see Jacques de Werra (ed.), *Research Handbook on Intellectual Property Licensing*, Cheltenham: Edward Elar Publishing, 2013, available at www.ip-licensing.info.

[131] It is worth mentioning that compulsory licensing mechanisms are also attracting increased scientific attention, see the collective book: Reto M. Hilty and Kung-Chung Liu (eds), 'Compulsory Licensing: Practical Experiences and Ways Forward', *MPI Studies in Intellectual Property and Competition Law No 22*, Munich 2015.

[132] Article 31 TRIPS does not define the detailed conditions under which compulsory licences shall be granted and many issues are still open; for instance, how can the patent owner and licensor control whether the compulsory licensee pays the adequate level of royalties (i.e. can there be an audit?)? Is there an implied warranty of validity or title of the patent owner? Can the compulsory licence be terminated beyond the scenario identified in Article 31 para. g TRIPS (which provides that 'authorization for such use shall be liable, subject to adequate protection of the legitimate interests of the persons so authorized, to be terminated if and when the circumstances which led to it cease to exist and are unlikely to recur [. . .]'), for instance because of a material breach committed by the licensee, etc.

perspective.[133] This is what results from the *Unwired Planet* case, which illustrates the risks resulting from the autonomous definition of FRAND terms by national courts.

Conclusion: Towards a Global Framework for Knowledge Transactions

We began our analysis with a description of the vital importance of knowledge-based IP transactions to the modern global economy. As we observed, the IP and information products that trade by licence are no less important to this century than goods were to the last (and are now). Yet, there is still no recognized, general statement of the commercial legal principles dealing with the unique but common transactional form of licence (like the unique transactional form of sale) and the unique but common qualities of knowledge-based intangibles.

Various private ordering regimes have emerged to address discrete types of transactions, whether by industry or other groups. We discussed

[133] See, by way of example, the dispute about the grant of a compulsory licence between Bayer and Natco in India as resulting from the Decision of the Intellectual Property Appellate Board ('IPAB') of Chennai of 4 March 2013 (OA/35/2012/PT/MUM); decision of the Controller of Patents Mumbai of March 9, 2012; appeals against the decision of the IPAB were dismissed by the Bombay High Court (see http://spicyip.com/2014/07/spicyip-tidbit-bombay-hc-dismisses-challenge-to-nexavar-compulsory-license.html) and by the Indian Supreme Court (which dismissed Bayer's Special Leave Petition, see www.globalhealthrights.org/wp-content/uploads/2015/11/Natco-v-Bayer.pdf. The FRAND licensing debate also raises the difficult question of the role of competition law in solving these issues at the crossroads of diverse legal fields, including contract law and intellectual property law (and also to the interactions between these two fields). For quite a vehement position criticizing the interference of competition law in the intellectual property system, see Robin Jacob, 'Competition Authorities Support Grasshoppers: Competition Law as a Threat to Innovation' (2013), *Competition Policy International* 9, 2, pp. 15–29 (concluding his paper (p. 26) by stating that '[t]he Competition Authorities should cease harassing inventive industries, remember that patents expire anyway and let the patent system do the job it was designed to do. Leave the ants alone'). While it is clear and undisputable that competition law is of key importance in this debate and that it must consequently not be underestimated, it still seems doubtful to admit that mechanisms which have been validated by competition authorities (such as the Commitments of Samsung commented above) shall be viewed as the ultimate standards of reference for all purposes, and specifically from a dispute resolution perspective. See Carter (n. 75), p. 72 *seq.* (scrutinizing the FTC's proposed and final consent orders in the US Motorola–Google dispute from an arbitration standpoint, whereby these comments can apply to other competition law proceedings in FRAND disputes). As discussed above, the Commitments raise complex issues which will need to be duly reflected upon in order to establish adequate and ideally global substantive and procedural standards for solving FRAND disputes.

two examples. One form of private ordering – 'information law merchant' – covers only a limited number of participants who routinely trade in certain types of information assets. As we observed, effective participation in many forms of international commercial IP transactions often requires access to specialized legal knowledge, extensive commercial experience, and elaborate contract forms, creating barriers to entry for new actors, disadvantaging smaller firms, increasing transaction and performance costs, and fostering disputes.[134] Our other example related to FRAND licensing. Our discussion of FRAND licensing revealed that the piecemeal and equally fragmented development of FRAND licensing terms and conditions (beyond the issue of the financial remuneration or royalties) provided no firmer foundation for addressing the general commerce in IP assets. While it is true that courts ultimately can validate the FRAND licensing terms in case of dispute between the parties, the limited experience so far shows that courts are unlikely to interfere significantly in the parties' proposed licensing terms;[135] thus, as with other licensing regimes, FRAND licensing constitutes a type of private ordering.

In short, we believe that, just as international organizations were created to foster global commercial trade and finance analysed and fashioned frameworks of contractual principles for sales of goods and secured financing, those international organizations and the organizations created to foster intellectual property protection and access should undertake a project to address the general principles relating to international IP commercial contracts.

That naturally leads to the questions of what form the product of such a project takes and what types of issues would such a product address. Let us address the second question first.

Space does not permit us to describe all of the issues that an instrument treating commercial transactions in IP (or information assets for that matter) might address.[136] Many are the recurring legal issues in international commercial transactions in information assets, especially

[134] See our discussion at n. 38, p. 699 *supra*.

[135] *Unwired Planet Huawei April 2017 Judgment*, [2017] EWHC 711 (Pat) (5 April 2017), para. 169: (opinion of Mr Justice Birss) ('Having now heard this trial I remain of the view that the court cannot craft a set of FRAND terms out of thin air').

[136] For a discussion of the issues to be addressed in, and a stalking horse start for, a model law, see L. Brennan and J. Dodd, 'A Concept Proposal for a Model Intellectual Property Law', in Jacques de Werra (ed.), *Research Handbook on Intellectual Property Licensing*, Cheltenham: Edward Elgar, 2013, pp. 257–280.

IP. Even a brief encounter with various treatises and treatments of licensing law[137] leaves one with at least two impressions: the volumes and volumes of discussion included in these (and other) treatises reflect the state of a far-too-complex Information Law Merchant[138] and many of the same types of legal issues relating to the commercial and contractual aspects of licences are covered. This suggests that a set of coherent principles relating to international IP commercial contracts could profitably be addressed and distilled for the guidance of courts, practitioners and participants. Here are just a few of those issues:

- Formation: Manner of forming an enforceable IP contract.
  - How can enforceable international IP contract be formed?
  - Should formation rules differ by different types IP (e.g. patent or copyright) or IP uses (e.g. assignment or licence)? If so, how are hybrid licences to be treated (i.e. licences relating to multiple or unidentified IP)?
  - How should territoriality of discrete IP rights be handled in a licence that potentially covers several – or many – jurisdictions?
  - Can licensees contract out of exhaustion of IP rights?
  - Are, or should there be, any formalities, e.g. a writing requirement or a registration requirement?
  - Can an IP contract be formed electronically?
  - Can an IP contract be formed by conduct, such as an implied licence, and if so how?
  - What formalities, if any, are needed to amend an IP contract?
  - Can an enforceable contract be formed if some terms are left open or to be later specified? If so which ones?
- Interpretation:
  - Should special interpretation rules exist for IP contracts?
  - Most importantly, what are the principles for interpreting scope? E.g.
    - Are incidental rights (e.g. know-how) implicitly covered? If so on what basis and to what extent?[139]

[137] See, e.g., J. Dratler, *Licensing of Intellectual Property*, New York: Law Journals Press, 1994; R. Milgrim and E. Bensen, *Milgrim on Licensing*, New York: Matthew Bender, 1991; Nimmer and Dodd, *Modern Licensing Law* (n. 1 *supra*).

[138] Again, we are reminded of Karl Llewellyn's description of the state of the law of negotiable instruments in the United States at the end of the nineteenth century. See n. 27 *supra*.

[139] Ancillary arrangements can be important in commercial transactions generally, so consideration might be given as to the composite of arrangements that might be included beyond the specific licence arrangement. *Cf.* Berman, *Law and Revolution*,

  - Are future improvements/new developments/new technologies covered?
  - Role of course of performance/industry practice/course of dealing.
- Implied Terms/Default Rules: One essential purpose of a commercial law is to provide default rules/terms that may be customarily included – unless the parties otherwise agree. Addressing the question of which default rules/terms are unique to IP contracts and should be recognized would be the most important task of the project. Potential Examples for IP contracts:
  - Exclusivity: What does the word 'exclusive' imply?[140]
  - Duration:
    - Duration vs commencement of other performance: future delivery or creation of IP/royalties?
    - What is the duration of an IP contract if not specified?
  - Geographic scope.
  - Transferability:
    - If the IP contract is silent, can a licensee transfer contractual rights or delegate contractual duties to another party?
    - Sub-licence? If the base licence is terminated or expires, what happens to sub-licences?

As to the form of the final product, we would expect that the organizations and entities undertaking this most important project for creating a framework for the commercial law of IP (or information assets) would ultimately determine the form. The important point here is that the project should develop a framework that would provide guidance as to general commercial law principles supporting IP transactions.[141]

However, we do think two major boundaries should be set on the scope of the project. First, the project should treat *commercial* law – not consumer transactions and should, as with other commercial laws, not prescribe specific contract terms. The commercial law should support contracts and not make them, setting forth, as default rules, the normal principles that generally would apply, while leaving virtually complete party autonomy to override the default rules by the parties. Commerce

p. 334 (n. 27). The Law Merchant governed not only the sale in the strict sense, but also other aspects of commercial transactions, including transportation, insurance, and financing.

[140] See text accompanying nn. 45–51 *supra.*

[141] Agthe et al., *A Proposed UNICTRAL Project On Commercial Transactions In Intellectual Property*, pp. 2–3 (n. 14).

on the terms that the parties agree should be respected in commercial transaction, just as it is under other bodies of commercial law. The idea would be to facilitate and support trade by reducing transaction costs, with a common framework, not frustrate trade on terms of the parties' own choosing.

Second, we firmly believe that the project would not seek to alter public policy requirements or IP regimes. Thus, laws and policies relating to competition, consumer protection or employment law would not be addressed. Nor would the project seek either to expand or restrict IP property rights or privileges. The idea, again, is to support commercial transactions in knowledge-based intangibles by addressing contractual principles, not the substance of IP property rights. Thus, it would not impose mandatory contract terms, but rather only provide a framework for contractual dealings.

In the final analysis, developing international recognition of such contractual principles undergirding global trade in knowledge-based intangible assets is such an important task, and is so vitally needed, that those who steer the project should avoid at all costs the temptations to build rigid rules that would straightjacket, not facilitate, party autonomy and commercial bargains or to tinker with public policy or property rights. The task of formulating a cross-border framework as we have described it is, as we have said above, no less important to commerce in this century than the task of recognizing and validating commercial transactions in tangible goods and in finance during the last century.

Bibliography

Agthe, Thilo C., Brennan, Lorin, Dodd, Jeff C. and Tosato, Andrea, 'A Proposed UNICTRAL Project On Commercial Transactions In Intellectual Property', Submitted at UNCITRAL – Fourth International Colloquium on Secured Transactions Vienna, 15–17 March 2017.

Anderson, Mark, 'How to Draft a License Agreement That Is Fair, Reasonable, and Non-Discriminatory: A Ten-Point Plan' (2018), *Journal of Intellectual Property Law & Practice* 13, 5: 377.

Anderson, R., De Carvalho, N., and Taubman, A. (eds), *Competition Policy and Intellectual Property in Today's Global Economy* (WTO Internal Only). Cambridge: Cambridge University Press, 2021.

Angeli, Michela, 'Willing to Define Willingness: The (Almost) Final Word on SEP-Based Injunctions in Light of Samsung and Motorola' (2015), *Journal of European Competition Law & Practice* 6, 4: 221–241.

Babey, Fabio and Rizvi, Salim, 'Die Frand-Verpflichtung Fair, Reasonable and Non-Discriminatory terms (FRAND) im Lichte des Kartellrechts', *Wirtschaft und Wettbewerb* 62(9) (2012), 808–818.

Baldia, Sonia, 'The Transaction Cost Problem in International Intellectual Property Exchange and Innovation Markets' (2013), *Northwestern Journal of International Law & Business* 34: 1.

Baumann, Antje, 'Einschaltung von Schiedsgerichten zur Bestimmung der FRAND-Konditionen' (2018), *GRUR*: 145.

Berman, Harold J., *Law and Revolution*, Cambridge and London: Harvard University Press, 1983.

Blackwell, Nicholas G., 'Making the Lion Gate Relief at Mycenae: Tool Marks and Foreign Influence' (2014), *American Journal of Archaeology* 118, 3: 451–488.

Botsman, Rachel, *Who Can You Trust?*, New York: PublicAffairs, 2017.

Brennan, Lorin and Dodd, Jeff C., 'A Preliminary Review of the UNIDROIT Contracts Principles as Applied to Intellectual Property', presented at UNICTRAL Annual Meeting, June 2009.

Brennan, Lorin and Dodd, Jeff C., 'A Concept Proposal for a Model Intellectual Property Law', in Jacques de Werra (ed.), *Research Handbook on Intellectual Property Licensing*, Cheltenham: Edward Elgar Publishing, 2013, p. 257.

Bresler, Judith and Lerner, Ralph E., *Art Law: The Guide for Collectors, Investors, Dealers, & Artists*, New York: Practising Law Institute, 2013.

Brooks, Roger G. and Geradin, Damien, 'Interpreting and Enforcing the Voluntary FRAND Commitment', 20 July 2010, available at: http://ssrn.com/abstract=1645878.

Caron, Christophe, 'L'efficacité des s FRAND: entre droit des brevets, droit civil et normalisation' (May 2013), *La Semaine Juridique, édition générale* 21, 20: 1006.

Carter, James H., 'FRAND Royalty Disputes: A New Challenge for International Arbitration?', in Arthur W. Rovine (ed.), *Contemporary Issues in International Arbitration and Mediation –the Fordham Papers 2013*, Leiden/Boston: Martinus Nijhoff Brill, 2013, p. 67.

Chen, Connie, Gilliland Taylor, C., Purcell, Jay and Kishore, Sandeep, 'The Silent Epidemic of Exclusive University Licensing Policies on Compounds for Neglected Diseases and Beyond' (2010), *PLoS Neglected Tropical Diseases* 4, 3: e570.

Contreras, Jorge L., 'A Market Reliance Theory for FRAND Commitments and Other Patent Pledges' (2015), *Utah Law Review*, 479–558.

Contreras, Jorge L., 'A New Perspective on FRAND Royalties: Unwired Planet v. Huawei' (2017), available at: www.ssrn.com/abstract=2949449.

Contreras, Jorge L. and Newman, David L., 'Developing a Framework for Arbitrating Standards-Essential Patent Disputes' (2014), *Journal of Dispute Resolution* 1: 23.

Dizon Michael, Anthony C., 'The Symbiotic Relationship Between Global Contracts and the International IP Regime' (2009), *Journal of Intellectual Property Law & Practice* 4: 559.

Dratler, Jay, *Licensing of Intellectual Property*, New York: Law Journals Press, 1994.

Ferro, Frodo, 'The Nature of FRAND Commitments Under French Contract and Property Law' (2018), *The Journal of Intellectual Property Law & Practice*, 980–988.

Friedl, Gunther and Ann Christoph, 'Entgeltberechnung für FRAND-Lizenzen an standardessenziellen Patenten' (2014), *GRUR*: 948.

Geradin, Damien, 'Confidentiality of FRAND Royalties in Arbitration', 2015, available at https://frandlitigationarbitration.wordpress.com/2015/02/28/confidentiality-of-frand-royalties-in-arbitration/.

Gilmore, Grant, 'On the Difficulties of Codifying Commercial Law' (1948), *Yale Law Journal* 57: 1341.

Haskel, Jonathan and Westlake, Stian, *Capitalism without Capital*, Princeton: Princeton University Press, 2018.

Hilty, Reto M. and Liu, Kung-Chung (eds), 'Compulsory Licensing: Practical Experiences and Ways Forward', *MPI Studies in Intellectual Property and Competition Law No. 22*, Munich, 2015.

Hunt, Edwin S. and Murray, James, *A History of Business, in Medieval Europe 1200–1550*, Cambridge: Cambridge University Press, 1999.

Jacob, Robin, 'Competition Authorities Support Grasshoppers: Competition Law as a Threat to Innovation' (2013), *Competition Policy International* 9, 2: 15.

Kesan, Jay P. and Hayes, Carol, 'Standard Setting Organizations and FRAND Licensing', in Robert D. Anderson, Nuni Pires de Carvalho and Antony Taubman (eds), *Competition Policy and Intellectual Property in Today's Global Economy*, Chapter 10.

Kim, Yoonhee, 'Lifting Confidentiality of FRAND Royalties in SEP Arbitration' (2014), *Columbia Science & Technology Law Review* 16: 1.

Kiriatzi, Evangelia and Knappett, Carl (eds), *Human Mobility and Technological Transfer in the Prehistoric Mediterranean*, Cambridge: Cambridge University Press, 2016.

Larsen, M. T., *Ancient Kanesh: A Merchant Colony in the Bronze Age of Anatolia*, Cambridge: Cambridge University Press, 2015.

Larouch, Pierre, Padilla, Jorge, Taffet, Richard S., 'Settling FRAND Disputes: Is Mandatory Arbitration a Reasonable and Non-Discriminatory Alternative?' (2014), *Journal of Competition Law & Economics*: 581.

Lemley, Mark A. and Shapiro, Carl, 'A Simple Approach to Setting Reasonable Royalties for Standard-Essential Patents' (2013), *Berkeley Technology Law Journal* 28: 1135.

Lichtman, Doug, 'Understanding the RAND Commitment' (2010), *Houston Law Review* 47: 1023.

Liddicoat, John, 'Standing on the Edge: What Type of "Exclusive Licensees" Should Be Able to Initiate Patent Infringement Actions?' (2017), *International Review of Intellectual Property and Competition Law* 48, 6: 626–651.

Llewellyn, K. N., 'Across Sales on Horseback' (1939), 52 *Harvard Law Review* 725, 728–729.

Llewellyn, Karl N., 'Why We Need the Uniform Commercial Code' (1957), 10 *Florida Law Review* 10: 367.

Maldonado, Kassandra, 'Breaching RAND and Reaching for Reasonable: Microsoft v. Motorola and Standard-Essential Patent Litigation' (2014), *Berkeley Technology Law Journal* 29: 419.

McGuire, Mary-Rose, 'Die FRAND-Erklärung, Anwendbares Recht, Rechtsnatur und Bindungswirkung am Beispiel eines ETSI-Standards' (2018), *GRUR*: 128.

Menell, Peter S. and Depoorter, Ben, 'Using Fee Shifting: A Proposal to Promote Fair Use and Fair Licensing' (2014), *California Law Review* 105: 53–85.

Milgrim, Roger and Bensen, Eric, *Milgrim on Licensing*, New York: Matthew Bender, 1991.

Nimmer, Raymond and Dodd, Jeff, *Modern Licensing Law, 2019–2020*, Eagan, MN: Thomson Reuters, 2020.

OECD, 'Knowledge Networks and Markets, OECD Science' (2013), *Technology and Industry Policy Papers* 7: 7–11, 29–35.

Picht, Peter, 'Unwired Planet v Huawei: A Seminal SEP/FRAND decision from the UK' (2017), *Journal of Intellectual Property Law & Practice*, 12, 10: 867–880, available at https://doi.org/10.1093/jiplp/ jpx152.

Picht, Peter, 'Post-Signing Adjustment of SEP/FRAND Licenses' (2018), *les Nouvelles*, 99.

Picht, Peter, 'Schiedsverfahren in SEP/FRAND-Streitigkeiten – Überblick und Kernprobleme, Max Planck Institute for Innovation & Competition', Discussion Paper No. 13, October 14 2018.

Rothman, Jennifer E., 'The Questionable Use of Custom in Intellectual Property' (1899), *Virginia Law Review*: 93.

Schill, Stephan, 'Lex Mercatoria', in Rüdiger Wolfrum (ed.), *Max Planck Encyclopedia of Public International Law*, Vol VI, Oxford: Oxford University Press, 2012, pp. 823–830.

Stacey, Philip D., 'Rule 44.1, Bodum USA v. La Cafetiere, and the Challenge of Determining Foreign Law' (2011), *Seventh Circuit Review* 6: 472.

Venturi, Zen-Ruffinen Marie-Noëlle, *La résiliation pour justes motifs des contrats de durée*, Zurich: Fribourg, 2007.

Weber, Rolf H. 'Competition Law versus FRAND Terms in IT Markets' (2011), *World Competition Law and Economics Review* 34, 1: 51–71.

Weber, Rolf H. and Rizvi, Salim, 'FRAND – Versuch einer Strukturierung' (2011), *RJB/ZBJV*: 433–462.

de Werra, Jacques, 'Arbitrating International Intellectual Property Disputes: Time to Think Beyond the Issue of (Non-) Arbitrability' (2012), *International Business Law Journal* 3: 299.

de Werra, Jacques (ed.), *Research Handbook on Intellectual Property Licensing*, Cheltenham: Edward Elgar Publishing, 2013.

de Werra, Jacques, 'The Need to Harmonize Intellectual Property Licensing Law: a European Perspective', in Jacques de Werra (ed.), *Research Handbook on Intellectual Property Licensing*, Cheltenham: Edward Elgar Publishing, 2013, p. 450.

de Werra, Jacques, 'New Developments of IP Arbitration and Mediation in Europe: The Patent Mediation and Arbitration Center Instituted by the Agreement on a Unified Patent Court' (2014), *Revista Brasileira de Arbitragem*: 17.

de Werra, Jacques, 'Patents and Trade Secrets in the Internet Age' (2015), *Revue de Droit Suisse II* 134: 146.

de Werra, Jacques, 'Can Exclusive Licensees Sue for Infringement of Licensed IP Rights? A Case Study Confirming the Need to Create Global IP Licensing Rules' (2017), *Harvard Journal of Law and Technology* 30: 189.

de Werra, Jacques, 'Les licences FRAND: chance ou risque pour l'harmonisation globale du droit des contrats de licence de brevets?, sic!', 2019, 77.

Wilkof, Neil, 'Will There Ever Be Clear Law About the Terminated Sublicense?', blogpost on Ipkat, 2 November 2012.

Wollgast, Heike and de Castro, Ignacio, 'WIPO Arbitration and Mediation Center: New 2014 WIPO Rules', *ASA Bulletin 2/2014*, p. 286.

Wu, Xiaoping, 'Interplay between Patents and Standards in the Information and Communication Technology (ICT) Sector and its Relevance to the Implementation of the WTO Agreements', WTO Working Paper ERSD-2017-08, 7 April 2017.

24

Fitting Machine-Generated Data into Trade Regulatory Holes

PETER K. YU*

Abstract

In an era when the Internet of Things has slowly transformed into the 'Internet of Everything', data generated or collected by networked sensors, interconnected devices, and intelligent machines have been highly valuable. In October 2017, the European Commission proposed a new sui generis *data producer's right for nonpersonal, anonymized machine-generated data. If countries began to create new rights in these data – whether based on the EU proposal or other proposals – the cross-border flow of such data would raise questions about the need for new trade standards. In view of this emerging trade policy debate, the present chapter highlights two sets of challenges concerning the development of new trade standards for regulating the cross-border flow of machine-generated data: (1) national policy development and (2) international norm setting. The chapter begins by identifying five sets of policy questions that have to be addressed before the creation of a new national regime for the protection of machine-generated data. The chapter then turns to the potential complications that would arise in the international norm-setting arena. Taken together, these two sets of challenges show how the protection, regulation, and overall governance of machine-generated data may not fit well with the existing international trade regime.*

Introduction

In an era when the Internet of Things has slowly transformed into the 'Internet of Everything',[1] data generated or collected by networked

* This chapter draws on research the author conducted for an earlier article in the *Tulane Law Review*.

[1] Mark Burdon and Mark Andrejevic, 'Big Data in the Sensor Society', in Cassidy R. Sugimoto, Hamid R. Ekbia and Michael Mattioli (eds), *Big Data Is Not a Monolith*, Cambridge, MA: MIT Press, 2016, 72; Yann Ménière and Ilja Rudyk, 'The Fourth

sensors, interconnected devices, and intelligent machines have been highly valuable.[2] As industry executives, policymakers, commentators, and pundits have excitedly declared, 'data is the new oil'.[3] The appropriateness of this analogy is certainly open to debate, but it will be difficult to overlook the enormous and ever-growing value of machine-generated data and the unlimited potential for their use and reuse, both of which were frequently done in unanticipated ways.[4] Indeed, as the world increasingly relies on machine learning and artificial intelligence, and as input data take on the additional roles of training and feedback data,[5] machine-generated data will only become more valuable.

Given this fast-growing development, it is understandable why industries and their supportive policymakers have actively pushed for greater protection of machine-generated data. In October 2017, the European Commission proposed a new *sui generis* data producer's right for non-personal, anonymized machine-generated data.[6] As the Commission defined, '[m]achine-generated data is created without the direct intervention of a human by computer processes, applications or services, or by sensors processing information received from equipment, software or machinery, whether virtual or real'.[7] This right 'aim[s] at clarifying the legal situation and giving more choice to the data producer, by opening

Industrial Revolution from the European Patent Office Perspective', in Xavier Seuba, Christophe Geiger and Julien Pénin (eds), *Intellectual Property and Digital Trade in the Age of Artificial Intelligence and Big Data*, Geneva and Strasbourg: International Centre for Trade and Sustainable Development and Center for International Intellectual Property Studies, 2018, 33; Paul Ohm and Scott Peppet, 'What if Everything Reveals Everything?', in Sugimoto, Ekbia and Mattioli (above), 46.

2 'Building a European Data Economy', COM(2017) 9 final, 2.

3 '"Data is the new oil", a phrase that is common currency among leaders in industry, commerce, and politics, is usually attributed to Clive Humby in 2006, the originator of Tesco's customer loyalty card.' Dawn E. Holmes, *Big Data: A Very Short Introduction*, Oxford: Oxford University Press, 2017, 20.

4 Burdon and Andrejevic (n. 1), 69; Margaret Foster Riley, 'Big Data, HIPAA, and the Common Rule: Time for Big Change?', in I. Glenn Cohen, Holly Fernandez Lynch, Effy Vayena and Urs Gasser (eds), *Big Data, Health Law, and Bioethics*, Cambridge: Cambridge University Press, 2018, 251; Viktor Mayer-Schönberger and Kenneth Cukier, *Big Data: A Revolution That Will Transform How We Live, Work, and Think*, Boston: Houghton Mifflin Harcourt, 2013, 153.

5 Ajay Agrawal, Joshua Gans and Avi Goldfarb (eds), *Prediction Machines: The Simple Economics of Artificial Intelligence*, Boston: Harvard Business Review Press, 2018, 43.

6 'Building a European Data Economy' (n. 2), 13.

7 Ibid., 9.

up the possibility for users to utilise their data and thereby contribute to unlocking machine-generated data'.[8]

If countries began to create new rights in machine-generated data – whether based on the EU proposal or other proposals – the cross-border flow of such data would raise questions about the need for new trade standards. Additional complications would also arise over the potential incoherency between these new trade standards and those other standards that have already been developed, or are now being developed, at bilateral, regional, multilateral, and plurilateral fora, including those explored in other chapters in this edited volume.

In view of this emerging trade policy debate, the present chapter highlights two sets of challenges concerning the development of new trade standards for regulating the cross-border flow of machine-generated data: (1) national policy development and (2) international norm setting. The chapter begins by identifying five sets of policy questions that have to be addressed before the creation of a new national regime for the protection of machine-generated data. The chapter then turns to the potential complications that would arise in the international norm-setting arena. Taken together, these two sets of challenges show how the protection, regulation, and overall governance of machine-generated data may not fit well with the existing international trade regime.

National Policy Development

As far as data governance is concerned, countries have taken very different approaches. While the European Union places high value on the protection of personal data, the United States emphasizes the need to foster the free movement of data, due in large part to the needs of its technology companies.[9] These cross-Atlantic differences have generated some notable controversies, such as the non-compliance of the US 'safe harbour' privacy framework with the 1995 EU Data Protection Directive and the cross-border ramifications of the EU General Data Protection Regulation, which took effect in May 2018.[10]

[8] Ibid., 13.

[9] Peter K. Yu, 'Data Producer's Right and the Protection of Machine-Generated Data' (2019) 93 *Tulane Law Review* 859, 889–892.

[10] Ibid., 865, 920.

As if these disagreements were not challenging enough, countries such as China have increasingly required the localization of data.[11] Such requirements are consistent with the country's decades-long information control policy.[12] Described by Mira Burri as 'new-generation barriers to digital trade',[13] data localization requirements have attracted trenchant critiques from policymakers and commentators in developed countries – most notably the United States.[14] These requirements have also sparked fears among foreign technology companies to the point that these companies have now heavily lobbied for the development of new trade standards to promote the free movement of data. Article 14.11.2 of the Trans-Pacific Partnership (TPP) Agreement, for instance, requires each signatory to 'allow the cross-border transfer of information by electronic means, including personal information, when this activity is for the conduct of the business of a covered person'.

Thus, if a new national regime is to be developed to protect machine-generated data, countries may take different approaches. In view of such divergence, this section focuses on five sets of policy questions that have to be addressed before the creation of new rights in machine-generated data. To provide a concrete example for all five sets of questions, this section draws illustrations from the proposed EU data producer's right.

Modality of Protection

The first set of policy questions concerns the modality of protection. As far as intellectual property laws are concerned, policymakers and commentators tend to create new rights utilizing the property model. Despite its many strengths, this model is not always the best for developing intellectual property protection.[15] Nor is it the only model

[11] On data localization requirements from around the world, see Anupam Chander and Uyên P. Lê, 'Data Nationalism' (2015) 64 *Emory Law Journal* 677.

[12] Henry Gao, 'Digital or Trade? The Contrasting Approaches of China and US to Digital Trade' (2018) 21 *Journal of International Economic Law* 297, 318–320.

[13] Mira Burri, *Should There Be New Multilateral Rules for Digital Trade?*, Geneva: International Centre for Trade and Sustainable Development and World Economic Forum, 2013, 7. See also Chapter 20 in this volume.

[14] Office of the United States Trade Representative, *Findings of the Investigation into China's Acts, Policies, and Practices Related to Technology Transfer, Intellectual Property, and Innovation under Section 301 of the Trade Act of 1974* (2018), 178.

[15] Peter K. Yu, 'The Political Economy of Data Protection' (2010) 84 *Chicago-Kent Law Review* 777, 792; Peter K. Yu, 'Ten Common Questions about Intellectual Property and Human Rights' (2007) 23 *Georgia State University Law Review* 709, 735.

for developing such protection. As commentators have shown, the interests of data producers could be easily protected using trade secrecy, unfair competition law, cost-sharing arrangements, private contracts or technological protection measures.[16] One should not forget that the original proposal for the EU Directive on the Legal Protection of Databases (EU Database Directive) was based on unfair competition law principles.[17]

To be sure, a data producer's right established through trade secrecy will be very different from one utilizing the property model.[18] While the latter prevents any party from using the generated data absent any permissible limitation or exception, the former requires data producers to undertake reasonable precautions to ensure that the data remain protected through secrecy.[19] Likewise, although contracts offer protection to data producers, such protection is limited to those enjoying the privity of contract.[20]

The different protections offered by these rights were indeed the focus of the European Commission. In its staff working document, the Commission stated that the proposed data producer's right 'could be envisaged as a right *in rem*' or 'as a set of purely defensive rights'.[21] As the Commission elaborated:

> [The data producer's] right could be envisaged as a *right in rem* and assign the exclusive right to utilise certain data, including the right to licence its usage. This would include a set of rights enforceable against any party

[16] Josef Drexl, 'Designing Competitive Markets for Industrial Data – Between Propertisation and Access' (2017) 8 *Journal of Intellectual Property, Information Technology and Electronic Commerce Law* 257, 292; P. Bernt Hugenholtz, 'Against "Data Property"', in Hanns Ullrich, Peter Drahos and Gustavo Ghidini (eds), *Kritika: Essays on Intellectual Property*, Vol. 3, Cheltenham: Edward Elgar Publishing, 2018, 52; Yu (n. 9), 877.

[17] J. H. Reichman and Pamela Samuelson, 'Intellectual Property Rights in Data?' (1997) 50 *Vanderbilt Law Review* 51, 81.

[18] Drexl (n. 16), 291.

[19] Robert G. Bone, 'Trade Secrecy, Innovation and the Requirement of Reasonable Secrecy Precautions', in Rochelle C. Dreyfuss and Katherine J. Strandburg (eds), *The Law and Theory of Trade Secrecy: A Handbook of Contemporary Research*, Cheltenham: Edward Elgar Publishing, 2011.

[20] National Research Council, *A Question of Balance: Private Rights and the Public Interest in Scientific and Technical Databases*, Washington, DC: National Academies Press, 1999, 61; Reichman and Samuelson (n. 17), 137; Guy A. Rub, 'Copyright Survives: Rethinking the Copyright-Contract Conflict' (2017) 103 *Virginia Law Review* 1141, 1209–1213.

[21] 'Commission Staff Working Document on the Free Flow of Data and Emerging Issues of the European Data Economy', SWD(2017) 2 final, 33.

> independent of contractual relations thus preventing further use of data by third parties who have no right to use the data, including the right to claim damages for unauthorised access to and use of data.
>
> ...
>
> Alternatively, instead of creating the data producer right as a right *in rem*, it could be conceived of as *a set of purely defensive rights*. This option would follow the choice made in the design of the protection given to know-how by the Trade Secrets Protection Directive. Its objective would be to enhance the sharing of data by giving at least the defensive elements of an *in rem* right, i.e. the capacity for the de facto data holder to sue third parties in case of illicit misappropriation of data. This approach thus equates to a protection of a de facto 'possession' rather than to the concept of 'ownership'.[22]

The Commission's explanation is particularly instructive on issues relating to the modality of protection. While the 'right *in rem*' discussion covers the strengths of the property model, the 'defensive rights' approach steers the protection toward trade secrecy or unfair competition laws.[23]

Allocation of Rights

The second set of policy questions relates to allocation of rights. If the property model is to be used, such allocation will focus on ownership interests. Thus far, three groups of players have fairly strong claims to machine-generated data, even though one could arguably include other groups in the mix.[24] In his influential proposal for a new data producer's right, Herbert Zech described a data producer as 'the economically responsible operator of equipment that generates the data'.[25] This position contrasts interestingly with extant European copyright laws that

[22] Ibid., 33–34.

[23] Reto Hilty, 'Big Data: Ownership and Use in the Digital Age', in Seuba, Geiger and Pénin (n. 1), 89.

[24] Drexl (n. 16), 277; Thomas J. Farkas, 'Data Created by the Internet of Things: The New Gold without Ownership?' (2017) 23 *Revista La Propiedad Inmaterial* 5, 6–7; Hilty (n. 23), 91; Wolfgang Kerber, 'A New (Intellectual) Property Right for Non-Personal Data? An Economic Analysis' (2016) 65 *GRUR Int* 989, 991.

[25] Herbert Zech, 'A Legal Framework for a Data Economy in the European Digital Single Market: Rights to Use Data' (2016) 11 *Journal of Intellectual Property Law and Practice* 460, 469.

consider those making necessary arrangements for the creation of computer-generated works as authors.[26]

For illustrative purposes, this section considers the data produced by the networked sensors in a smart car – an example that has been used *ad nauseum* in discussions of machine-generated data. Most certainly, the car owner has a strong claim to these data, as the owner will need them to repair the car.[27] For privacy protection, the owner may also need the ability to opt out from automatic data generation, especially if he or she does not trust the anonymization process.[28] The owner's demand for opting out is easy to understand. While the produced or collected car data may provide valuable information about traffic patterns, road conditions, and engine performance,[29] they could also reveal highly personal information about the owner's driving habits.[30]

Like the car owner, the car manufacturer also has a strong claim to these data, as the manufacturer will need them to improve car design, anticipate problems generated by design defects, and develop solutions to address those problems.[31] In recent years, some car manufacturers have suggested, somewhat counterintuitively, that car owners do not actually have ownership interests despite paying handsomely for their vehicles.[32] If these owners did not even own the cars they bought, it would be highly unlikely for them to own the data generated by the sensors in those cars.[33]

As if the fight over data control between these two parties were not complicated enough, the software developer has an equally strong claim to the data produced by these sensors. Just as the car owner and the car manufacturer need data to repair or improve the car, the software

[26] E.g. Copyright, Designs and Patents Act 1988, s 9(3) (England and Wales); Copyright and Related Rights Act 2000, s 21(f) (Ireland).

[27] Drexl (n. 16), 262; Farkas (n. 24), 6; Mayer-Schönberger and Cukier (n. 4), 133.

[28] 'Building a European Data Economy' (n. 2), 13.

[29] Hugenholtz (n. 16), 48–49.

[30] Drexl (n. 16), 262; Farkas (n. 24), 6.

[31] 'Commission Staff Working Document' (n. 21), 35–36; Michael Bailey, 'Will Big Data Diminish the Role of Humans in Decision Making?', in Sugimoto, Ekbia and Mattioli (n. 1), 166.

[32] These suggestions occurred in the United States Copyright Office's 2015 rule-making proceeding concerning the anti-circumvention provision of the Digital Millennium Copyright Act. Peter K. Yu, 'The Anatomy of the Human Rights Framework for Intellectual Property' (2016) 69 *SMU Law Review* 37, 89–90.

[33] Drexl (n. 16), 267.

designer also needs data to improve the software.[34] Moreover, the programmers hired by this developer have designed the software to enable the sensors and the car computer to produce and collect data. In cases involving copyright law and artificial intelligence, commentators have widely agreed that computer programmers should have ownership interests in computer-generated works.[35] As Annemarie Bridy observed, 'Intuition and the principle of transitivity both suggest that the programmer of generative software is the logical owner of the copyright in the works generated by his or her software. He or she is, after all, *the author of the author* of the works.'[36]

Nevertheless, if considerable progress has been made for machines to conduct 'deep learning'[37] or 'artificial general intelligence',[38] the rights of

[34] Paul R. Daugherty and H. James Wilson, *Human + Machine: Reimagining Work in the Age of AI*, Boston: Harvard Business Review Press, 2018, 114; Mayer-Schönberger and Cukier (n. 4), 105, 107; Jerome H. Reichman, Paul F. Uhlir, and Tom Dedeurwaerdere, *Governing Digitally Integrated Genetic Resources, Data, and Literature: Global Intellectual Property Strategies for a Redesigned Microbial Research Commons*, Cambridge: Cambridge University Press, 2016, 323.

[35] Arthur R. Miller, 'Copyright Protection for Computer Programs, Databases, and Computer-Generated Works: Is Anything New since CONTU?' (1993) 106 *Harvard Law Review* 977, 1049; National Commission on New Technological Uses of Copyrighted Works, *Final Report of the National Commission on New Technological Uses of Copyrighted Works* (1979) 45; Pamela Samuelson, 'Allocating Ownership Rights in Computer-Generated Works' (1986) 47 *University of Pittsburgh Law Review* 1185, 1192.

[36] Annemarie Bridy, 'Coding Creativity: Copyright and the Artificially Intelligent Author' (2012) *Stanford Technology Law Review* 5, 21.

[37] As a government report on artificial intelligence explained:

'Deep learning uses structures loosely inspired by the human brain, consisting of a set of units (or "neurons"). Each unit combines a set of input values to produce an output value, which in turn is passed on to other neurons downstream. For example, in an image recognition application, a first layer of units might combine the raw data of the image to recognize simple patterns in the image; a second layer of units might combine the results of the first layer to recognize patterns-of-patterns; a third layer might combine the results of the second layer; and so on.'

National Science and Technology Council, *Preparing for the Future of Artificial Intelligence* (2016) 9. On deep learning, see Ethem Alpaydin, *Machine Learning: The New AI*, Cambridge, MA: MIT Press, 2016, 104–109; John D. Kelleher, *Deep Learning*, Cambridge, MA: MIT Press, 2019; John D. Kelleher and Brendan Tierney, *Data Science*, Cambridge, MA: MIT Press, 2018, 121–130; Thierry Poibeau, *Machine Translation*, Cambridge, MA: MIT Press, 2017, 181–195.

[38] '[Artificial general intelligence] is said to possess "a reasonable degree of self-understanding and autonomous self-control, [has] the ability to solve a variety of complex problems in a variety of contexts, and [can] learn to solve new problems that [it] didn't know about at the time of [its] creation"'. Michael Guihot, Anne F. Matthew

the software developer may be called into question. In that scenario, the legislature or the court may take a pragmatic approach to create a legal fiction to respond to technological change. A paradigmatic example of such a legal fiction is the work-made-for-hire doctrine in US copyright law.[39] Although authors have to be humans[40] – as the United States Copyright Office recently made clear following the many interesting questions generated by the so-called 'monkey selfie'[41] – corporations are non-human, institutional authors that have enjoyed protection under the Copyright Act. Given the ready availability of this legal fiction, some commentators have suggested the use of the work-made-for-hire doctrine to address the complicated relationship between machines and authorial works.[42] Meanwhile, others have suggested that the ownership questions should be determined on a case-by-case basis.[43] Some commentators have gone even further to call for the recognition of machines as authors and inventors.[44]

In sum, in the example concerning data produced by the networked sensors in a smart car, complications will arise over who should have control over the generated data.[45] While this section has shown that car owners, car manufacturers and software manufacturers all have strong claims to machine-generated data, one should not overlook the possibility of a fourth, and highly attractive, option: the release of these data into the public domain for all to use.[46] As Josef Drexl rightly noted, before

and Nicolas P. Suzor, 'Nudging Robots: Innovative Solutions to Regulate Artificial Intelligence' (2017) 20 *Vanderbilt Journal of Entertainment and Technology Law* 385, 396. On artificial general intelligence, see Ben Goertzel and Cassio Pennachin (eds), *Artificial General Intelligence*, Berlin: Springer, 2007.

39 17 USC s 201(b).

40 United States Copyright Office, *Circular 1: Copyright Basics* (2017), 1.

41 Naruto *v.* Slater, 888 F.3d 418, 420 (9th Cir. 2018); United States Copyright Office, *Compendium of US Copyright Office Practices*, 3rd ed. (2017) s.313.2.

42 Bridy (n. 36), 26; Shlomit Yanisky-Ravid, 'Generating Rembrandt: Artificial Intelligence, Copyright, and Accountability in the 3A Era – The Human-Like Authors Are Already Here – A New Model' (2017) *Michigan State Law Review* 659, 707–718.

43 Jani McCutcheon, 'Curing the Authorless Void: Protecting Computer-Generated Works Following *IceTV* and *Phone Directories*' (2013) 37 *Melbourne University Law Review* 46, 68.

44 Ryan Abbott, 'Inventive Machines: Rethinking Invention and Patentability', in Seuba, Geiger and Pénin (n. 1), 117–118.

45 Who has initial control over the generated data may not matter as much if transaction costs are low. Nevertheless, commentators have warned about the potential holdups that may prevent effective Coasian bargaining. Kerber (n. 24), 997; Yu (n. 9), 889.

46 Hugenholtz (n. 16), 49.

deciding who owns what, we need to first determine whether data should be owned in the first place.[47] Likewise, Reto Hilty warned that asking the question 'who "owns" the data? . . . is already suggestive, because the primary question should be: can (or should) data be "owned" at all?'[48]

Indeed, even if the answers to these questions are in the affirmative, one does not always have to pick between these three groups of players. One could easily support co-ownership arrangements among some or all of these players,[49] similar to what the joint ownership of copyright works already allows. When such co-ownership arrangements occur, new questions will arise over the specific interests each player owns and what specific rights these interests entail. Co-ownership arrangements will also likely create more transaction costs than those involving sole ownership, thereby exacerbating the concern about the creation of a thicket of rights in machine-generated data.[50]

Duration of Protection

The third set of policy questions pertains to the duration of protection. Article 10(3) of the EU Database Directive offers protection for about 15 years that can be indefinitely extended based on a 'substantial change . . . to the contents of a database, including any substantial change resulting from the accumulation of successive additions, deletions or alterations'. Article 8(1) of the now-abandoned Treaty on Intellectual Property in Respect of Databases, which was proposed for the 1996 diplomatic conference of the World Intellectual Property Organization (WIPO), also included an option that would offer protection for 25 years, indefinitely extendable based on a similar 'substantial change' condition.

Given these prior developments, one may wonder whether rights in machine-generated data should last for at least 15 years. Nevertheless, if the goal of these rights is to ensure the opportunity for data producers and their collaborators to analyse the generated data, the protection may not need to last for such a long period of time.[51] For instance, the original proposal for the EU Database Directive offered protection for only

[47] Drexl (n. 16), 260.
[48] Hilty (n. 23), 88–89.
[49] Ibid., 91.
[50] Drexl (n. 16), 277.
[51] Kerber (n. 24), 991; Zech (n. 25), 469.

10 years.[52] Indeed, Jerome Reichman and Paul Uhlir have found the 15-year term under the EU Database Directive 'completely arbitrary'.[53]

Moreover, with the latest technology, data analysis can be done fairly quickly, not to mention that much of this analysis can be done in real time.[54] Even Professor Zech, the leading proponent of the data producer's right, does not believe that the right should last for too long.[55] Those European commentators in support of creating such a right also seem to have reached a consensus that the duration of protection could be as short as two to five years, with possible extension.[56]

Finally, law and economics literature has shown that a market head start could help innovators maintain a healthy competitive edge.[57] Such a head start is similar to the limited competitive advantage the United States Court of Appeals for the Second Circuit provided to sports leagues and their licensees in *NBA v. Motorola, Inc.*[58] In that case, the court created a 'hot news' doctrine to allow the 'producers' of data through professional basketball games to retain limited control over the in-progress transmission of these data. Notwithstanding the benefits provided by a head start, how much of a head start data producers should have largely depends on empirical analysis. The head start they need may also depend on the state of technology, with variations from sector to sector.[59]

Scope of Protection

The fourth set of policy questions regards the scope of protection. This question is particularly important because a carefully defined scope will

52 Reichman and Samuelson (n. 17), 81.

53 J. H. Reichman and Paul F. Uhlir, 'Database Protection at the Crossroads: Recent Developments and Their Impact on Science and Technology' (1999) 14 *Berkeley Technology Law Journal* 793, 817.

54 Drexl (n. 16), 264; Executive Office of the (US) President, *Big Data: Seizing Opportunities, Preserving Values: Interim Progress Report* (2015) 2.

55 Zech (n. 25), 469.

56 Kerber (n. 24), 991.

57 Stephen Breyer, 'The Uneasy Case for Copyright: A Study of Copyright in Books, Photocopies, and Computer Programs' (1970) 84 *Harvard Law Review* 281, 299–308; Reichman and Samuelson (n. 17), 141.

58 105 F.3d 841, 843 (2nd Cir. 1997).

59 'Building a European Data Economy' (n. 2), 17; Drexl (n. 16), 260; James Manyika et al., *Big Data: The Next Frontier for Innovation, Competition, and Productivity*, New York: McKinsey Global Institute, 2011, 8.

help prevent or address the problem of 'overlapping rights' – that is, the existence of multiple, and often competing, layers of rights covering the same subject matter.[60] As Bernt Hugenholtz observed:

> [A] film shot with a digital camera would qualify not only as a work protected by copyright, but also as machine-generated (sensor) data subject to a 'data producer's right'. Similarly, the aggregate stock market data in a financial database would be protected both by the sui generis right and the 'data producer's right', since the data are recorded automatically by the computerized stock exchange.[61]

In its staff working document, the European Commission made a distinction between semantic and syntactic information:

> An ebook or a photographic image . . . has a semantic level which is the expression of ideas or the presentation of objects or persons. Copyright covers this level of information. The data file of such an ebook or image, however, is merely a representation of signs encoding such information usually requiring tools to present the information.[62]

While the distinction between semantic and syntactic information is thought-provoking – and could help address the much-needed divide between copyright and data right – it is unclear if law-makers, policy-makers, litigants, and law enforcement personnel could easily make that distinction. As Professor Hugenholtz explained:

> [A]ny copy of the film's digital file (the syntactic data) would by necessity also reproduce the copyright protected work (the semantic layer). Thus, the new data right could be invoked against any digital copying (or streaming) of the digitized copyright work. For the same reason, the new right would broadly overlap with the database right, even if its scope were confined to the syntactic layer. The phonographic right discussed above illustrates this point. Whereas its subject matter, like the proposed 'data producer's right', is limited to the recorded signal (i.e. syntactic audio data), its scope extends into the semantic realm. Reproducing a CD recording of a musical performance will, by necessity, result in the reproduction of the underlying musical work and performance.[63]

[60] Estelle Derclaye and Matthias Leistner, *Intellectual Property Overlaps: A European Perspective*, Oxford: Hart Publishing, 2011; Neil Wilkof and Shamnad Basheer (eds), *Overlapping Intellectual Property Rights*, Oxford: Oxford University Press, 2012.

[61] Hugenholtz (n. 16), 62.

[62] 'Commission Staff Working Document' (n. 21), 34, fn. 156.

[63] Hugenholtz (n. 16), 63–64.

Consider, for example, the use of multiple camera drones to shoot a telecast of a professional basketball game, similar to the one involved in *NBA v. Motorola, Inc.* Using the definition provided by the European Commission, the telecast, which is protected by copyright law in the United States and many other jurisdictions, will fall squarely within the category of semantic information. By contrast, the statistics about the professional basketball players involved – such as minutes played, points scored, rebounds, assists, steals, blocks and turnovers – will be classified as syntactic information. As such, the data generated by the camera drones will be protected by the proposed EU data producer's right.

Yet when all of the syntactic information has been inputted into a computer that stores three-dimensional image files relating to professional basketball players, similar to those found in the video game *NBA Live*, the computer-generated telecast will bear a strong resemblance to the copyrighted telecast, blurring the distinction between semantic and syntactic information. In this instance, the interplay of these two types of information will certainly worry the NBA. If licensing arrangements are to be developed, the different types of right involved will also raise considerable complications.

At some point, policymakers and commentators will have to recognize the inability to use a simple binary to separate semantic and syntactic information. Rather, all the information will fall on a spectrum, in which syntactic information, as numbers and symbols, could be combined to form meaning and be transformed into semantic information. This spectrum is similar to the one involving unstructured, semi-structured and structured data – with semantic information on one end and unstructured data and syntactic information on the other end.[64]

To complicate matters even further, there is no hard-and-fast rule for determining whether it is more desirable to protect semantic or syntactic information. Using the example of a pothole located by car sensors, Professor Drexl explained why 'it would be better to avoid protecting the semantic information the sensors of a car collect', even though

[64] Holmes (n. 3), 5–6. Semi-structured data are defined as '[d]ata that do not conform to fixed fields but contain tags and other markers to separate data elements'. Manyika et al. (n. 59), 33. Examples of such data 'include XML or HTML-tagged text'. Ibid.

intellectual property rights generally protect this type of information.[65] As he observed:

> [T]he question of whether the law should protect the semantic or the syntactic information, or even only the integrity of the digital file, will depend on the circumstances. This analysis would seem to argue for context-specific regulation. Even a general regime on the protection of industrial data would thus appear problematic since, in some instances, protecting semantic information such as in the case of trade secrets seems the right approach, while protection of data collected through sensors in the public sphere should probably not be extended to the meaning these data are able to convey.[66]

Limitations and Exceptions

The last set of policy questions involves the creation of limitations and exceptions – or, more positively, 'the modalities of access'.[67] As Timo Minssen and Justin Pierce lamented: 'Where data are not owned or licensed, the user will need to rely on an exception to [intellectual property right] infringement to use data. This has given rise to fierce controversies between data "owners", data researchers, and entities that provide enabling technologies, large research infrastructures, and standardization platforms.'[68] Although data are often referred to as 'new oil', one cannot ignore the fact that oil is a finite resource.[69] Because of this crucial distinction, it could be quite beneficial for data to be used simultaneously by multiple parties or reused by others after their earlier use.[70]

One potential exception to rights in machine-generated data is the exception for text and data mining (TDM), which would facilitate data

[65] Drexl (n. 16), 263.

[66] Ibid.

[67] Josef Drexl et al., *Data Ownership and Access to Data*, Munich: Max Planck Institute for Innovation and Competition, 2016, 12.

[68] Timo Minssen and Justin Pierce, 'Big Data and Intellectual Property Rights in the Health and Life Sciences', in Cohen, Lynch, Vayena and Gasser (n. 4), 311.

[69] Holmes (n. 3), 20; Teresa Scassa, 'Data Ownership' (2018) *Centre for International Governance Innovation Paper* No. 187, 1; Lauren Henry Scholz, 'Big Data Is Not Big Oil: The Role of Analogy in the Law of New Technologies' (2019) 863 *Tennessee Law Review* 291.

[70] Scassa (n. 69), 1.

use and reuse.[71] A similar exception has been adopted or explored as part of the copyright law reform in Australia, the European Union, Singapore and other parts of the world.[72] In the United Kingdom, for example, such an exception can now be found in section 29A(1) of the Copyright, Designs and Patents Act 1988, which allows '[t]he making of a copy of a work by a person who has lawful access to the work' in order to 'carry out a computational analysis of anything recorded in the work for the sole purpose of research for a non-commercial purpose'. Other exceptions that could be of great public benefit are those concerning 'government access, scientific research, data portability, platform interoperability, the nonprotection of public sector information, and the need to address anticompetitive concerns'.[73]

To promote competition, the European Commission suggested the use of fair, reasonable, and non-discriminatory (FRAND) licences to facilitate the utilization and dissemination of machine-generated data.[74] As the Commission stated in its communication document, 'framework potentially based on certain key principles, such as [FRAND] terms, could be developed for data holders ... to provide access to the data they hold against remuneration after anonymisation'.[75]

Finally, to ensure the effectiveness and vitality of these limitations and exceptions, some jurisdictions may consider the adoption of 'contract override' legislation to prohibit the use of private contracts to circumvent the safeguards provided by these limitations and exceptions.[76] In August 2014, the United Kingdom adopted the Copyright and Rights in Performances (Quotation and Parody) Regulations 2014, which rendered unenforceable contractual terms that purport to prevent or restrict the newly created permitted acts, such as those relating to quotation,

[71] Michael W. Carroll, 'Copyright and the Progress of Science: Why Text and Data Mining Is Lawful' (2019) 53 *U.C. Davis Law Review* 893; Matthew Sag, 'The New Legal Landscape for Text Mining and Machine Learning' (2019) 66 *Journal of the Copyright Society of the U.S.A.*

[72] Christophe Geiger, Giancarlo Frosio and Oleksandr Bulayenko, 'Crafting a Text and Data Mining Exception for Machine Learning and Big Data in the Digital Single Market', in Seuba, Geiger and Pénin (n. 1), 97; Xavier Seuba, Christophe Geiger and Julien Pénin, 'Introduction', in Seuba, Geiger and Pénin (n. 1), 15; Yu (n. 9), 914.

[73] Yu (n. 9), 915–916.

[74] 'Building a European Data Economy' (n. 2), 13; 'Commission Staff Working Document' (n. 21), 39.

[75] 'Building a European Data Economy' (n. 2), 13.

[76] Drexl (n. 16), 276, 291.

caricature, parody and pastiche.[77] To the extent that the limitations and exceptions are highly beneficial to the public, a contract override would prevent parties with weak bargaining positions from being forced to contract away those important flexibilities and safeguards.[78]

International Norm Setting

As the previous section has noted, countries will likely adopt diverging approaches to protecting machine-generated data. What approaches they end up with will likely depend on how they address the five sets of policy questions identified in this chapter. Regardless of which approaches they ultimately choose, any effort to develop new trade standards for regulating the cross-border flow of machine-generated data will be confronted with a second set of challenges: international norm setting.

Obviously, the biggest barrier in international negotiations in this emerging area is the lack of consensus among the negotiating parties. Such a lack is unsurprising, considering that the European Union remains the only party that has advanced a proposal for protecting machine-generated data. Nevertheless, even if countries could agree to protect these data at the international level, they would still need to determine how best to incorporate such protection into the international trade regime.

Today, there are at least three dominant routes for such incorporation: (1) intellectual property; (2) electronic commerce; and (3) investment. While the first route is the most established – with carefully delineated minimum standards laid down in the Agreement on Trade-Related Aspects of Intellectual Property Rights (TRIPS Agreement) – the second route is under exploration at both the multilateral and non-multilateral levels. Although the third route remains the most far-fetched, due to the international community's continuous disagreement over investment protections,[79] this route deserves some policy and scholarly attention, as investment chapters have now become a standard feature of bilateral, regional, or plurilateral trade agreements.

[77] Copyright, Designs and Patents Act 1988, s 30A(2).

[78] 'Building a European Data Economy' (n. 2), 12.

[79] Peter K. Yu, 'Six Secret (and Now Open) Fears of ACTA' (2011) 64 *SMU Law Review* 975, 1077.

This section discusses each route in turn. The goal of this section is not to identify the different international norms that have already been developed, or are now being developed, in the areas of intellectual property, electronic commerce and investment. Instead, the section highlights the challenges of fitting machine-generated data into the existing trade regime. It further identifies the various complications that the protection of such data will generate in each individual area.

Intellectual Property

The first area in which new trade standards for regulating the cross-border flow of machine-generated data can be developed is intellectual property. As Professor Zech explained in his proposal for a new data producer's right:

> [A]s in classic intellectual property rights, one could bring forward the argument that incentives are created to generate and to reveal data (and hence, indirectly, to promote innovations that are made possible through the use of data) and that markets for information goods (that otherwise would not be tradable or would only be tradable with higher transaction costs) are created. Another important aspect seems to be that such legal regulation would clearly determine who benefits from the use of data. This would prevent that machines are designed in a way that they are difficult to be read out or that other mechanisms would be created which grant de facto exclusivity.[80]

Notwithstanding the common justifications that rights in machine-generated data share with other forms of intellectual property rights, the former could create complications with the latter. To begin with, existing international intellectual property agreements are filled with language prohibiting the protection of raw data. Article 10.2 of the TRIPS Agreement makes clear that the protection of compilations of data or other material 'shall not extend to the data or material itself'. Article 5 of the WIPO Copyright Treaty also includes a similar provision:

> Compilations of data or other material, in any form, which by reason of the selection or arrangement of their contents constitute intellectual creations, are protected as such. This protection does not extend to the data or the material itself and is without prejudice to any copyright subsisting in the data or material contained in the compilation.

[80] Zech (n. 25), 470.

In addition, the creation of new rights in machine-generated data could generate, or exacerbate, the problem of 'overlapping rights', which the previous section has briefly mentioned. For instance, such new rights could create complications with the pre-existing protections for not only databases but also data themselves. While the EU Database Directive continues to use copyright to protect databases that constitute intellectual creations, it also offers *sui generis* protection to databases that are ineligible for copyright protection.[81] If created, the proposed EU data producer's right would add a new layer of protection for uncopyrightable machine-generated data to these two layers of rights even when the invested resources were used for 'the creation of materials which make up the contents of a database',[82] as opposed to the 'obtaining, verification or presentation of the[se] contents' (as required by Article 7(1) of the EU Database Directive).

If one focuses on data instead, the creation of new rights in machine-generated data might create further complications with pre-existing laws covering trade secrets[83] and data exclusivities (such as those used to protect test or other data that have been submitted for the regulatory approval of agrochemical, pharmaceutical and biological products).[84] After all, these alternative forms of intellectual property rights have already been used to protect data. Indeed, the European Commission's staff working document suggested that the proposed data producer's right could take the form of a defensive right.[85] Such a right would likely be quite similar to the protection currently offered under trade secret or unfair competition law.[86]

When overlaps arise, the new rights in machine-generated data could lead to regime clashes and overprotection.[87] Such clashes and overlaps, in turn, would undermine the protections offered in pre-existing intellectual property regimes, especially in relation to their limitations, safeguards

[81] Council Directive 96/9, Articles 3(1), 7–11.

[82] Case C-203/02, British Horseracing Board Ltd *v.* William Hill Organisation Ltd (2004) ECLI:EU:C:2004:695 [1] (Grand Chamber).

[83] Zech (n. 25), 465.

[84] Peter K. Yu, 'Data Exclusivities and the Limits to TRIPS Harmonization' (2019) 46 *Florida State University Law Review* 641, 686–689; Peter K. Yu, 'Data Exclusivities in the Age of Big Data, Biologics, and Plurilaterals' (2018) 6 *Texas A&M Law Review Arguendo* 22, 32–33.

[85] 'Commission Staff Working Document' (n. 21), 33–34.

[86] Hilty (n. 23), 89.

[87] Derclaye and Leistner (n. 60), 318.

and flexibilities.[88] If these overlaps are to be avoided, commentators have suggested the need for pre-emption tools.[89] As Professor Hugenholtz observed, 'The only way to prevent the data right from becoming an all-encompassing "super–[intellectual property] right" would be to categorically exclude all data that (possibly) represent subject matter protected under traditional [intellectual property] regimes: not only copyright, the database right and neighboring rights, but also design right and perhaps patent law'.[90]

Electronic Commerce

The second area in which new trade standards for regulating the cross-border flow of machine-generated data can be developed is electronic commerce. The past decade has seen active discussions of digital trade and cross-border data flows at the World Trade Organization (WTO) and other international and regional fora.[91] Many of the bilateral, regional and plurilateral trade agreements that have recently been completed, or are under current negotiations, also include dedicated chapters to promote the free movement of data.[92] To some extent, the electronic commerce chapters included in these agreements 'represent . . . a distinct attempt to compensate for the lack of progress in the WTO and remedy the ensuing uncertainties'.[93]

Consider, for example, the electronic commerce chapter of the TPP Agreement, which many have considered the most comprehensive chapter in the area among all bilateral, regional, and plurilateral trade agreements.[94] This chapter has now been incorporated by reference into the Comprehensive and Progressive Agreement for Trans-Pacific

[88] Hugenholtz (n. 16), 62–63.

[89] 17 USC s 301. On pre-emption in the copyright area, see Peter K. Yu, 'Fictional Persona Test: Copyright Preemption in Human Audiovisual Characters' (1998) 20 *Cardozo Law Review* 355, 367–375.

[90] Hugenholtz (n. 16), 64.

[91] Mira Burri, 'The Governance of Data and Data Flows in Trade Agreements: The Pitfalls of Legal Adaptation' (2017) 51 *U.C. Davis Law Review* 65, 77–99; Christopher Kuner, 'Regulation of Transborder Data Flows under Data Protection and Privacy Law: Past, Present and Future' (2011) *Organisation for Economic Co-Operation and Development Digital Economy Paper* No. 187. See also Chapter 20 in this volume.

[92] Burri (n. 91), 99–125.

[93] Ibid., 101.

[94] Ibid., 113.

Partnership (CPTPP), which entered into force in December 2018.[95] Among the wide variety of issues covered in this chapter are customs duties, non-discriminatory treatment of digital products, domestic electronic transactions, electronic authentication and signatures, online consumer protection, personal information protection, paperless trading, access to and use of the Internet for electronic commerce, cross-border transfer of information by electronic means, Internet interconnection charge sharing, location of computing facilities, unsolicited commercial electronic messages, cooperation on cybersecurity matters, and the source code of computer software.

As Mira Burri explained, these issues emerge in international and regional fora in part because 'data needs to cross borders for a thriving data economy; [but] at the same time, states do exercise jurisdiction within their borders as a rule of public international law'.[96] In her view, trade rules affect data in three ways:

> (i) . . . they regulate the cross-border flow of data by regulating trade in goods and services as well as the protection of intellectual property; (ii) . . . they may install certain beyond-the-border rules that demand changes in domestic regulation – for example, with regard to intermediaries' liability; and (iii) . . . trade law can limit the policy space that regulators have at home.[97]

Among the restrictions commentators have identified in this area are 'requirements for data localisation, mandates for local processing of data . . . requiring government approval for data transfers', as well as measures 'that are discriminatory in their treatment of foreign data suppliers'.[98]

Within the TPP electronic commerce chapter, Article 14.11.2 covers the 'cross-border transfer of information by electronic means'. That provision states explicitly that '[e]ach Party shall allow the cross-border transfer of information by electronic means, including personal information, when this activity is for the conduct of the business of a covered

[95] Peter K. Yu, 'Thinking about the Trans-Pacific Partnership (and a Mega-Regional Agreement on Life Support)' (2017) 20 *SMU Science and Technology Law Review* 97, 104–106.

[96] Burri (n. 91), 68.

[97] Ibid.

[98] Keith E. Maskus, 'Fostering Innovation in Digital Trade', in Seuba, Geiger and Pénin (n. 1), 26.

person'. Article 14.13.1 turns to 'location of computing facilities'. Although the provision recognizes the discretion each signatory has in developing 'its own regulatory requirements regarding the use of computing facilities, including requirements that seek to ensure the security and confidentiality of communications', it prohibits the application of these requirements 'in a manner which would constitute a means of arbitrary or unjustifiable discrimination or a disguised restriction on trade'.

It is worth noting that any new trade standards that are developed to regulate the cross-border flow of machine-generated data will focus on non-personal, anonymized data – similar to the European Commission's proposal for a new data producer's right.[99] Nevertheless, the increased sophistication of data analytics has raised questions about the effectiveness of data anonymization. In today's 'era of runaway data',[100] it has been increasingly difficult to predict when seemingly anonymized machine-generated data would become personal or personally identifying. As one commentator observed, 'Even when aggregating non-personal data (e.g. machine data from a board computer), powerful correlation algorithms working on big data may be able to correlate such data with an individual person, thus transforming non-personal data into personal data.'[101] Likewise, Viktor Mayer-Schönberger and Kenneth Cukier lamented, 'Given enough data, perfect anonymization is impossible no matter how hard one tries.'[102]

Moreover, seemingly anonymized data may be highly personal. Consider, for instance, the data about car locations appearing on navigation apps. As Professor Hilty explained:

> The colour green [on these apps] is used for flowing traffic, orange for slow-moving traffic, and red to signal a traffic jam. This information is not collected based on hundreds of helicopters or drones flying over the country, sending pictures to traffic control centres. Instead, this information is generated by correlative movements of the mobile telephones of the car drivers passing through the same positions; Apple, Android, and

[99] 'Building a European Data Economy' (n. 2), 13.

[100] Frank Pasquale, *The Black Box Society: The Secret Algorithms That Control Money and Information*, Cambridge, MA: Harvard University Press, 2015, 19.

[101] Peter Bittner, 'Intellectual Property Management Challenges Arising from Pervasive Digitalisation: The Effect of the Digital Transformation on Daily Life', in Seuba, Geiger and Pénin (n. 1), 71.

[102] Mayer-Schönberger and Cukier (n. 4), 155.

> all other applications are based on similar technologies. It goes without saying that individual drivers could be identified; their data could for instance be connected with data produced by the car itself, or advertisements could be sent to them, for example for nearby restaurants when there is a traffic jam.[103]

In sum, given the potential, and arguably inevitable, overlap between personal and non-personal data, policymakers and commentators should develop a deeper understanding of the interplay between the protections for personal or personally identifying data and those for non-personal, anonymized machine-generated data. If policymakers are unsure how to protect the former, they should pause to think more deeply about the privacy implications of any new trade standards that are being developed to cover the latter.

Investment

The final area in which new trade standards for regulating the cross-border flow of machine-generated data can be developed is investment. Today, countries continue to disagree over the standards needed to protect cross-border investment. For instance, the Organisation for Economic Co-operation and Development's attempt to establish a Multilateral Agreement on Investment and past efforts to inject investment issues into the WTO trade negotiations have largely failed.[104]

Despite these futile endeavours, developed countries have actively negotiated bilateral, regional and plurilateral trade agreements that contain investment chapters. The recent years have also seen the multinational corporations' growing willingness to use investor-state dispute settlement (ISDS) as an alternative mechanism for resolving cross-border intellectual property disputes with host states.[105] As I noted in an earlier

[103] Hilty (n. 23), 91.

[104] Peter T. Muchlinski, 'The Rise and Fall of the Multilateral Agreement on Investment: Where Now?' (2000) 34 *International Lawyer* 1033; James Salzman, 'Labor Rights, Globalization and Institutions: The Role and Influence of the Organization for Economic Cooperation and Development' (2000) 21 *Michigan Journal of International Law* 769, 804–831.

[105] Peter K. Yu, 'The Pathways of Multinational Intellectual Property Dispute Settlement', in Christopher Heath and Anselm Kamperman Sanders (eds), *Intellectual Property and International Dispute Resolution*, Alphen aan den Rijn: Kluwer Law International, 2019; Peter K. Yu, 'State-to-State and Investor-State Copyright Dispute Settlement', in Ysolde Gendreau (ed.), *Le droit d'auteur en action: Perspectives internationales sur les recours*, Montreal: Les Éditions Thémis, 2019.

article, the growing use of this mechanism has now sparked a transformation that is similar to what we experienced three decades ago when intellectual property was married to trade through the TRIPS Agreement.[106]

At the time of writing, there is no indication that the producers of machine-generated data have plans to follow the leads of Philip Morris, Eli Lilly and Bridgestone in using ISDS to protect their data.[107] Nevertheless, because 'most international investment agreements define "investment" broadly to cover all forms of "intellectual property rights",[108] these relevant agreements will cover rights in machine-generated data. If new rights are to be created based on the property model, data producers will have rather compelling arguments for using ISDS to resolve cross-border disputes involving these rights. After all, a key attraction of this mechanism is to offer '[p]rotection against uncompensated expropriation of property'.[109] As the Office of the United States Trade Representative declared in a 2015 fact sheet, ISDS provides '[a]n assurance that the property of investors will not be seized by the government without the payment of just compensation'.[110]

When disputes over ownership of machine-generated data are tied to the right to private property in human rights law, property-based arguments will find additional support in international and regional human rights instruments.[111] In *Anheuser-Busch Inc.* v. *Portugal*, the European Court of Human Rights extended the protection of 'the peaceful enjoyment of . . . possessions' in Protocol No. 1 to the European Convention of

[106] Peter K. Yu, 'The Investment-Related Aspects of Intellectual Property Rights' (2017) 66 *American University Law Review* 829, 831.

[107] Yu (n. 9), 924.

[108] Yu (n. 106), 861.

[109] Ibid., 866, fn. 163.

[110] Office of the United States Trade Representative, *Fact Sheet: Investor-State Dispute Settlement (ISDS)* (2015).

[111] Yu (n. 32), 85–95. On the increasing focus on the assetization, or investment-related aspects, of intellectual property rights, see Rochelle Dreyfuss and Susy Frankel, 'From Incentive to Commodity to Asset: How International Law Is Reconceptualizing Intellectual Property' (2015) 36 *Michigan Journal of International Law* 557; Ole-Andreas Rognstad, *Property Aspects of Intellectual Property*, Cambridge: Cambridge University Press, 2018, 68–71, 126–199; Yu (n. 106); Peter K. Yu, 'The Second Transformation of the International Intellectual Property Regime', in Jonathan Griffiths and Tuomas Mylly (eds), *Global Intellectual Property Protection and New Constitutionalism: Hedging Exclusive Rights*, Oxford: Oxford University Press, 2021.

Human Rights to cover both registered trademarks and trademark applications of a multinational corporation.[112] Article 17(2) of the Charter of Fundamental Rights of the European Union, which focuses on the right to property, also explicitly covers intellectual property.

Conclusion

Today, it is commonplace to find data 'collected by sensors, which surround us in smartphones, tablets, laptops, wearable technologies and sensor-enabled clothing, RFID-equipped passports, cars, homes, and offices'.[113] When this sensor-pervasive environment is combined with ubiquitous communication, sophisticated correlation algorithms, powerful data analysis, drastically reduced information storage costs and the ever-increasing use of machine learning and artificial intelligence, it is foreseeable that machines will generate as many data as they could.[114] After all, governments and businesses may choose to err on the side of overgeneration. As Woodrow Hartzog wrote succinctly, 'In the world of big data, more is always better.'[115]

Nevertheless, as we start exploring ways to handle the ever-growing volume of machine-generated data, policymakers and commentators will need to pay greater attention to the complications caused by the development of new trade standards to regulate the cross-border flow of machine-generated data. As the second half of this chapter has shown, these standards do not fall squarely into the traditional trade-related areas of intellectual property, electronic commerce, and investment. Because of this mismatch, problems and complications will arise when these new standards are being retrofit to an international trade regime that was established decades ago.

Legal standards have always lagged behind technology, and language in international treaties has lagged behind even further.[116] As we

112 (2007) 45 *European Human Rights Report* 36.

113 Fred H. Cate, 'Big Data, Consent, and the Future of Data Protection', in Sugimoto, Ekbia and Mattioli (n. 1), 3.

114 Burdon and Andrejevic (n. 1), 74; Scott R. Peppet, 'Regulating the Internet of Things: First Steps toward Managing Discrimination, Privacy, Security, and Consent' (2014) 93 *Texas Law Review* 85, 93.

115 Woodrow Hartzog, *Privacy's Blueprint: The Battle to Control the Design of New Technologies*, Cambridge, MA: Harvard University Press, 2018, 51.

116 Colin B. Picker, 'A View from 40,000 Feet: International Law and the Invisible Hand of Technology' (2001) 23 *Cardozo Law Review* 149, 184; Peter K. Yu, 'Trade Agreement

continue to develop trade regulatory responses to the challenges posed by our fast-growing data-driven economy and the proliferation of networked sensors, interconnected devices, and intelligent machines, we will need to undertake a deeper interrogation of the complex relationship between trade standards and new technology. Highlighting two distinct sets of challenges confronting the creation of new trade standards for regulating the cross-border flow of machine-generated data, this chapter underscores the need for greater research and policy attention on the difficult task of fitting square pegs of machine-generated data into the round trade regulatory holes.

Bibliography

Abbott, Ryan, 'Inventive Machines: Rethinking Invention and Patentability', in Xavier Seuba, Christophe Geiger and Julien Pénin (eds), *Intellectual Property and Digital Trade in the Age of Artificial Intelligence and Big Data*, Geneva and Strasbourg: International Centre for Trade and Sustainable Development and Center for International Intellectual Property Studies, 2018.

Agrawal, Ajay, Gans, Joshua and Goldfarb, Avi (eds), *Prediction Machines: The Simple Economics of Artificial Intelligence*, Boston: Harvard Business Review Press, 2018.

Alpaydin, Ethem, *Machine Learning: The New AI*, Cambridge, MA: MIT Press, 2016.

Bailey, Michael, 'Will Big Data Diminish the Role of Humans in Decision Making?', in Cassidy R. Sugimoto, Hamid R. Ekbia and Michael Mattioli (eds), *Big Data Is Not a Monolith*, Cambridge, MA: MIT Press, 2016.

Bittner, Peter, 'Intellectual Property Management Challenges Arising from Pervasive Digitalisation: The Effect of the Digital Transformation on Daily Life', in Xavier Seuba, Christophe Geiger and Julien Pénin (eds), *Intellectual Property and Digital Trade in the Age of Artificial Intelligence and Big Data*, Geneva and Strasbourg: International Centre for Trade and Sustainable Development and Center for International Intellectual Property Studies, 2018.

Bone, Robert G., 'Trade Secrecy, Innovation and the Requirement of Reasonable Secrecy Precautions', in Rochelle C. Dreyfuss and Katherine J. Strandburg

Cats and the Digital Technology Mouse', in Bryan Mercurio and Ni Kuei-Jung (eds), *Science and Technology in International Economic Law: Balancing Competing Interests*, Abingdon: Routledge, 2014, 202.

(eds), *The Law and Theory of Trade Secrecy: A Handbook of Contemporary Research*, Cheltenham: Edward Elgar Publishing, 2011.

Breyer, Stephen, 'The Uneasy Case for Copyright: A Study of Copyright in Books, Photocopies, and Computer Programs' (1970), *Harvard Law Review* 84: 281–351.

Bridy, Annemarie, 'Coding Creativity: Copyright and the Artificially Intelligent Author' (2012), *Stanford Technology Law Review* 5: 1–28.

Burdon, Mark and Andrejevic, Mark, 'Big Data in the Sensor Society', in Cassidy R. Sugimoto, Hamid R. Ekbia and Michael Mattioli (eds), *Big Data Is Not a Monolith*, Cambridge, MA: MIT Press, 2016.

Burri, Mira, *Should There Be New Multilateral Rules for Digital Trade?*, Geneva: International Centre for Trade and Sustainable Development and World Economic Forum, 2013.

Burri, Mira, 'The Governance of Data and Data Flows in Trade Agreements: The Pitfalls of Legal Adaptation' (2017), *U.C. Davis Law Review* 51: 65–132.

Carroll, Michael W., 'Copyright and the Progress of Science: Why Text and Data Mining Is Lawful' (2019), *U.C. Davis Law Review* 53: 893–964.

Cate, Fred H., 'Big Data, Consent, and the Future of Data Protection', in Cassidy R. Sugimoto, Hamid R. Ekbia and Michael Mattioli (eds), *Big Data Is Not a Monolith*, Cambridge, MA: MIT Press, 2016.

Chander, Anupam and Lê, Uyên P., 'Data Nationalism' (2015), *Emory Law Journal* 64: 677–739.

Daugherty, Paul R. and Wilson, H. James, *Human + Machine: Reimagining Work in the Age of AI*, Boston: Harvard Business Review Press, 2018.

Derclaye, Estelle and Leistner, Matthias, *Intellectual Property Overlaps: A European Perspective*, Oxford: Hart Publishing, 2011.

Drexl, Josef et al., *Data Ownership and Access to Data*, Munich: Max Planck Institute for Innovation and Competition, 2016.

Drexl, Josef, 'Designing Competitive Markets for Industrial Data: Between Propertisation and Access' (2017), *Journal of Intellectual Property, Information Technology and Electronic Commerce Law* 8: 257–292.

Dreyfuss, Rochelle and Frankel, Susy, 'From Incentive to Commodity to Asset: How International Law Is Reconceptualizing Intellectual Property' (2015), *Michigan Journal of International Law* 36: 557–602.

European Commission, 'Building a European Data Economy', COM(17) 9 final, 2017.

European Commission, 'Commission Staff Working Document on the Free Flow of Data and Emerging Issues of the European Data Economy', SWD(2017) 2 final, 2017.

Executive Office of the (US) President, *Big Data: Seizing Opportunities, Preserving Values: Interim Progress Report*, 2015.

Farkas, Thomas J., 'Data Created by the Internet of Things: The New Gold without Ownership?' (2017), *Revista La Propiedad Inmaterial* 23: 5–17.

Gao, Henry, 'Digital or Trade? The Contrasting Approaches of China and US to Digital Trade' (2018), *Journal of International Economic Law* 21: 297–321.

Geiger, Christophe, Frosio, Giancarlo and Bulayenko, Oleksandr, 'Crafting a Text and Data Mining Exception for Machine Learning and Big Data in the Digital Single Market', in Xavier Seuba, Christophe Geiger and Julien Pénin (eds), *Intellectual Property and Digital Trade in the Age of Artificial Intelligence and Big Data*, Geneva and Strasbourg: International Centre for Trade and Sustainable Development and Center for International Intellectual Property Studies, 2018.

Goertzel, Ben, and Pennachin, Cassio (eds), *Artificial General Intelligence*, Berlin: Springer, 2007.

Guihot, Michael, Matthew Anne F. and Suzor, Nicolas P., 'Nudging Robots: Innovative Solutions to Regulate Artificial Intelligence' (2017), *Vanderbilt Journal of Entertainment and Technology Law* 20: 385–456.

Hartzog, Woodrow, *Privacy's Blueprint: The Battle to Control the Design of New Technologies*, Cambridge, MA: Harvard University Press, 2018.

Hilty, Reto, 'Big Data: Ownership and Use in the Digital Age', in Xavier Seuba, Christophe Geiger and Julien Pénin (eds), *Intellectual Property and Digital Trade in the Age of Artificial Intelligence and Big Data*, Geneva and Strasbourg: International Centre for Trade and Sustainable Development and Center for International Intellectual Property Studies, 2018.

Holmes, Dawn E., *Big Data: A Very Short Introduction*, Oxford: Oxford University Press, 2017.

Hugenholtz, P. Bernt, 'Against "Data Property"', in Hanns Ullrich, Peter Drahos and Gustavo Ghidini (eds), *Kritika: Essays on Intellectual Property*, Vol. 3, Cheltenham: Edward Elgar Publishing, 2018.

Kelleher, John D., *Deep Learning*, Cambridge, MA: MIT Press, 2019.

Kelleher, John D. and Tierney, Brendan, *Data Science*, Cambridge, MA: MIT Press, 2018.

Kerber, Wolfgang, 'A New (Intellectual) Property Right for Non-Personal Data? An Economic Analysis' (2016), *GRUR International* 65: 989–998.

Kuner, Christopher, 'Regulation of Transborder Data Flows under Data Protection and Privacy Law: Past, Present and Future' *Organisation for Economic Co-Operation and Development Digital Economy Paper* No. 187, 2011.

Manyika, James et al., *Big Data: The Next Frontier for Innovation, Competition, and Productivity*, New York: McKinsey Global Institute, 2011.

Maskus, Keith E., 'Fostering Innovation in Digital Trade', in Xavier Seuba, Christophe Geiger and Julien Pénin (eds), *Intellectual Property and Digital Trade in the Age of Artificial Intelligence and Big Data*, Geneva and

Strasbourg: International Centre for Trade and Sustainable Development and Center for International Intellectual Property Studies, 2018.

Mayer-Schönberger, Viktor and Cukier, Kenneth, *Big Data: A Revolution That Will Transform How We Live, Work, and Think*, Boston: Houghton Mifflin Harcourt, 2013.

McCutcheon, Jani, 'Curing the Authorless Void: Protecting Computer-Generated Works Following *IceTV* and *Phone Directories*' (2013), *Melbourne University Law Review* 37: 46–102.

Ménière, Yann and Rudyk, Ilja, 'The Fourth Industrial Revolution from the European Patent Office Perspective', in Xavier Seuba, Christophe Geiger and Julien Pénin (eds), *Intellectual Property and Digital Trade in the Age of Artificial Intelligence and Big Data*, Geneva and Strasbourg: International Centre for Trade and Sustainable Development and Center for International Intellectual Property Studies, 2018.

Miller, Arthur R., 'Copyright Protection for Computer Programs, Databases, and Computer-Generated Works: Is Anything New since CONTU?' (1993), *Harvard Law Review* 106: 977–1073.

Minssen, Timo and Pierce, Justin, 'Big Data and Intellectual Property Rights in the Health and Life Sciences', in I. Glenn Cohen, Holly Fernandez Lynch, Effy Vayena and Urs Gasser (eds), *Big Data, Health Law, and Bioethics*, Cambridge: Cambridge University Press, 2018.

Muchlinski, Peter T., 'The Rise and Fall of the Multilateral Agreement on Investment: Where Now?' (2000), *International Lawyer* 34: 1033–1053.

National Commission on New Technological Uses of Copyrighted Works, *Final Report of the National Commission on New Technological Uses of Copyrighted Works*, 1979.

National Research Council, *A Question of Balance: Private Rights and the Public Interest in Scientific and Technical Databases*, Washington, DC: National Academies Press, 1999.

National Science and Technology Council, *Preparing for the Future of Artificial Intelligence*, 2016.

Office of the United States Trade Representative, *Fact Sheet: Investor-State Dispute Settlement (ISDS)*, 2015.

Office of the United States Trade Representative, *Findings of the Investigation into China's Acts, Policies, and Practices Related to Technology Transfer, Intellectual Property, and Innovation under Section 301 of the Trade Act of 1974*, 2018.

Ohm, Paul and Peppet, Scott, 'What if Everything Reveals Everything?', in Cassidy R. Sugimoto, Hamid R. Ekbia and Michael Mattioli (eds), *Big Data Is Not a Monolith*, Cambridge, MA: MIT Press, 2016.

Pasquale, Frank, *The Black Box Society: The Secret Algorithms That Control Money and Information*, Cambridge, MA: Harvard University Press, 2015.

Peppet, Scott R., 'Regulating the Internet of Things: First Steps toward Managing Discrimination, Privacy, Security, and Consent' (2014), *Texas Law Review* 93: 85–178.

Picker, Colin B., 'A View from 40,000 Feet: International Law and the Invisible Hand of Technology' (2001), *Cardozo Law Review* 23: 149–219.

Poibeau, Thierry, *Machine Translation*, Cambridge, MA: MIT Press, 2017.

Reichman, J. H. and Samuelson, Pamela, 'Intellectual Property Rights in Data?' (1997), *Vanderbilt Law Review* 50: 51–166.

Reichman, J. H. and Uhlir, Paul F., 'Database Protection at the Crossroads: Recent Developments and Their Impact on Science and Technology' (1999), *Berkeley Technology Law Journal* 14: 793–838.

Reichman, Jerome H., Uhlir, Paul F. and Dedeurwaerdere, Tom, *Governing Digitally Integrated Genetic Resources, Data, and Literature: Global Intellectual Property Strategies for a Redesigned Microbial Research Commons*, Cambridge: Cambridge University Press, 2016.

Riley, Margaret Foster, 'Big Data, HIPAA, and the Common Rule: Time for Big Change?', in I. Glenn Cohen, Holly Fernandez Lynch, Effy Vayena and Urs Gasser (eds), *Big Data, Health Law, and Bioethics*, Cambridge: Cambridge University Press, 2018.

Rognstad, Ole-Andreas, *Property Aspects of Intellectual Property*, Cambridge: Cambridge University Press, 2018.

Rub, Guy A., 'Copyright Survives: Rethinking the Copyright-Contract Conflict' (2017), *Virginia Law Review* 103: 1141–1245.

Sag, Matthew, 'The New Legal Landscape for Text Mining and Machine Learning' (2019), *Journal of the Copyright Society of the U.S.A.* 66: 291.

Salzman, James, 'Labor Rights, Globalization and Institutions: The Role and Influence of the Organization for Economic Cooperation and Development' (2000), *Michigan Journal of International Law* 21: 769–848.

Samuelson, Pamela, 'Allocating Ownership Rights in Computer-Generated Works' (1986), *University of Pittsburgh Law Review* 47: 1185–1228.

Scassa, Teresa, 'Data Ownership', *Centre for International Governance Innovation Paper* No. 187, 2018.

Scholz, Lauren Henry, 'Big Data Is Not Big Oil: The Role of Analogy in the Law of New Technologies' (2019), *Tennessee Law Review* 86: 863–893.

Seuba, Xavier, Geiger, Christophe and Pénin, Julien, 'Introduction', in Xavier Seuba, Christophe Geiger and Julien Pénin (eds), *Intellectual Property and Digital Trade in the Age of Artificial Intelligence and Big Data*, Geneva and Strasbourg: International Centre for Trade and Sustainable Development and Center for International Intellectual Property Studies, 2018.

United States Copyright Office, *Circular 1: Copyright Basics*, 2017.

United States Copyright Office, *Compendium of U.S. Copyright Office Practices*, 3rd ed., 2017, chapter 300.

Wilkof, Neil and Basheer, Shamnad (eds), *Overlapping Intellectual Property Rights*, Oxford: Oxford University Press, 2012.

Yanisky-Ravid, Shlomit, 'Generating Rembrandt: Artificial Intelligence, Copyright, and Accountability in the 3A Era – The Human-Like Authors Are Already Here – A New Model' (2017), *Michigan State Law Review* 659–726.

Yu, Peter K., 'Fictional Persona Test: Copyright Preemption in Human Audiovisual Characters' (1998), *Cardozo Law Review* 20: 355–414.

Yu, Peter K., 'Ten Common Questions about Intellectual Property and Human Rights' (2007), *Georgia State University Law Review* 23: 709–753.

Yu, Peter K., 'The Political Economy of Data Protection' (2010), *Chicago-Kent Law Review* 84: 777–801.

Yu, Peter K., 'Six Secret (and Now Open) Fears of ACTA' (2011), *SMU Law Review* 64: 975–1094.

Yu, Peter K., 'Trade Agreement Cats and the Digital Technology Mouse', in Bryan Mercurio and Ni Kuei-Jung (eds), *Science and Technology in International Economic Law: Balancing Competing Interests*, Abingdon: Routledge, 2014.

Yu, Peter K., 'The Anatomy of the Human Rights Framework for Intellectual Property' (2016), *SMU Law Review* 69: 37–95.

Yu, Peter K., 'The Investment-Related Aspects of Intellectual Property Rights' (2017), *American University Law Review* 66: 829–910.

Yu, Peter K., 'Thinking about the Trans-Pacific Partnership (and a Mega-Regional Agreement on Life Support)' (2017), *SMU Science and Technology Law Review* 20: 97–133.

Yu, Peter K., 'Data Exclusivities in the Age of Big Data, Biologics, and Plurilaterals' (2018), *Texas A&M Law Review Arguendo* 6: 22–33.

Yu, Peter K., 'Data Exclusivities and the Limits to TRIPS Harmonization' (2019), *Florida State University Law Review* 46: 641–708.

Yu, Peter K., 'Data Producer's Right and the Protection of Machine-Generated Data' (2019), *Tulane Law Review* 93: 859–929.

Yu, Peter K., 'State-to-State and Investor-State Copyright Dispute Settlement', in Ysolde Gendreau (ed.), *Le droit d'auteur en action: Perspectives internationales sur les recours*, Montreal: Les Éditions Thémis, 2019.

Yu, Peter K., 'The Pathways of Multinational Intellectual Property Dispute Settlement', in Christopher Heath and Anselm Kamperman Sanders (eds), *Intellectual Property and International Dispute Resolution*, Alphen aan den Rijn: Kluwer Law International, 2019.

Yu, Peter K., 'The Second Transformation of the International Intellectual Property Regime', in Jonathan Griffiths and Tuomas Mylly (eds), *Global Intellectual Property Protection and New Constitutionalism: Hedging Exclusive Rights*, Oxford: Oxford University Press, 2021.

Zech, Herbert, 'A Legal Framework for a Data Economy in the European Digital Single Market: Rights to Use Data' (2016), *Journal of Intellectual Property Law and Practice* 11: 460–470.

PART V

Looking Forward

25

Looking Forward: Building the Foundations for Policymaking in the Knowledge Economy

ANTONY TAUBMAN

Abstract

This chapter recapitulates and puts into their broader context the contributing authors' diverse insights into trade in knowledge today, the gaps identified in conceptual understanding and empirical data, and the prospects for addressing these gaps. A stronger empirical and theoretical platform can support further policy dialogue and research, but requires improving the reach, quality and granularity of statistics, and analysing available data in more sophisticated ways, including through greater integration of different forms of data (such as measures of the value and trends of trade as a proxy for knowledge transactions, and more nuanced interpretation of IP statistics). Policy and legal analysis need to 'unbundle' the knowledge component from various proxies for it (such as trade in IP-rich goods, trade in knowledge-intensive services, and trade in IP rights for such goods as software and creative content), and distinguish the component of global value chains comprised of IP transactions. This would provide a surer foundation for policymakers to identify and implement positive opportunities to leverage indigenous knowledge resources and incoming knowledge flows for sustainable development and welfare-enhancing trade and economic policy, and address anomalies such as taxation distortion and flawed assumptions about the true economic value of knowledge-based trade in goods and services. These developments pose challenges for policy coherence and international governance, given the diversification of approaches at domestic level and in the emerging patchwork of bilateral and regional agreements, contrasting with the policy coherence and interoperability between jurisdictions that the WTO TRIPS Agreement has brought about over the past 25 years. Multilateral institutions – founded on the principle that international cooperation is positive-sum in character – may seek to update and consolidate the governance framework for knowledge flows, or at least work towards informed policy coherence and dialogue, supported by a forward-looking research agenda and guided by the inherently non-rivalrous character of technological knowledge.

> The unique characteristics of ideas make material progress possible, but that's not all. Ideas matter not just for what humans have, but also for how they are. During the Pleistocene, human nature evolved in a Malthusian world of objects. We developed an ugly tendency to split humanity into 'us' and 'them.' A world that also includes ideas justifies a new mindset that treats all humans with the dignity and respect that we offer to 'us.' It is a world in which we may derive net material benefits from the presence of others.[1]

> Hope in life comes from the interconnections among all the people in the world. We believe that if we all work for what we think individually is good, then we as a whole will achieve more power, more understanding, more harmony as we continue the journey... The experience of seeing the Web take off by the grassroots effort of thousands gives me tremendous hope that if we have the individual will, we can collectively make of the world what we want.[2]

> The protection and enforcement of intellectual property rights should contribute to the promotion of technological innovation and to the transfer and dissemination of technology, to the mutual advantage of producers and users of technological knowledge and in a manner conducive to social and economic welfare, and to a balance of rights and obligations.[3]

> [K]nowledge resources are not rivalrous, yet negotiations over the terms of trade in knowledge products retain a strong zero sum-flavour which seems to betray a lack of practical confidence in systemic benefits from strengthened intellectual property law and administration, rendering any strengthening of intellectual property standards a bare trade concession.[4]

Introduction: Trade in Knowledge Today: Towards a Positive-Sum View

Policy discussions, political discourse, trade negotiations and scholarly analysis addressing international trade in knowledge today should each –

[1] Paul Romer, Nobel Lecture: On the possibility of progress (5 February 2019), available at https://paulromer.net/prize/.

[2] Tim Berners-Lee, *Weaving the Web*, New York: Harper Collins, 1999, at 209.

[3] WTO TRIPS Agreement, Article 7.

[4] Antony Taubman, 'Cereal Offenders: Access and Equity in Trade Negotiations on Knowledge Resources', in Jay Kesan (ed.), *Agricultural Biotechnology and Intellectual Property: Seeds of Change* (2007), at 97.

ideally – aim, in their diverse modes and methods, to work towards understanding the optimal, balanced and effective, relationship between three complex and variable factors – trade settings, intellectual property (IP) systems and the dissemination of technology. The present volume aims to contribution to this work by strengthening its empirical and analytical foundation. It therefore offers a range of fresh insights into the convergence of economic insights, regulatory mechanisms and technological developments that shape prospects for the knowledge economy. A central motif is the distinctive nature of knowledge – in particular its non-rivalrous and more readily diffused characteristics – and the possibilities this offers for a positive-sum approach to promoting and regulating knowledge flows that yield social and economic welfare, and contribute to today's global policy challenges.

Thomas Jefferson's oft-quoted discussion of the diffusion of ideas for social benefit expresses the inherently non-rivalrous character of ideas in pellucid terms:

> the moment [an idea] is divulged, it forces itself into the possession of every one, and the receiver cannot dispossess himself of it. Its peculiar character, too, is that no one possesses the less, because every other possesses the whole of it. He who receives an idea from me, receives instruction himself without lessening mine; as he who lights his taper at mine, receives light without darkening me. That ideas should freely spread from one to another over the globe, for the moral and mutual instruction of man, and improvement of his condition, seems to have been peculiarly and benevolently designed by nature, when she made them, like fire, expansible over all space, without lessening their density in any point, and like the air in which we breathe, move, and have our physical being, incapable of confinement or exclusive appropriation.[5]

And in marking out the ideal contours of the regulation of knowledge, he applies a contingent, utilitarian frame to the possibility of such 'exclusive appropriation':

> Inventions then cannot, in nature, be a subject of property. Society may give an exclusive right to the profits arising from them, as an encouragement ... to pursue ideas which may produce utility, but this

[5] Thomas Jefferson to Isaac McPherson (13 August 1813), The Writings of Thomas Jefferson. Edited by Andrew A. Lipscomb and Albert Ellery Bergh. 20 vols. Washington: Thomas Jefferson Memorial Association, 1905, 13:333–35, available at https://press-pubs.uchicago.edu/founders/documents/a1_8_8s12.html.

> may or may not be done, according to the will and convenience of the society, without claim or complaint from anybody. Considering the exclusive right to invention as given not of natural right, but for the benefit of society, I know well the difficulty of drawing a line between the things which are worth to the public the embarrassment of an exclusive patent, and those which are not. As a member of the patent board for several years, while the law authorized a board to grant or refuse patents, I saw with what slow progress a system of general rules could be matured.[6]

Why open this supposedly 'forward-looking' chapter by looking back two centuries? This historic observation throws into sharp relief the continuing, essential challenge of regulating knowledge: how to reconcile its distinctive non-rivalrousness with the contingent, utilitarian character of regulation, and to resolve the apparent conflict between two normative intuitions. On the one hand, knowledge should be readily shared. On the other, originators of knowledge should be duly recognized and rewarded. Along these lines, two seeming paradoxes arise in considering the relationship in today's economy between trade, knowledge and the IP system.

- First, trade negotiations are typically structured as zero-sum trade-offs between rivalrous interests: trade opening commitments are conceived as 'concessions'[7] when it is one of the essential findings of classical trade economics that they are ostensibly welfare-enhancing; the very incorporation of the Agreement on Trade-Related Aspects of Intellectual Property Rights within the system of multilateral trade law has been construed as a concession in itself, even while the Agreement purportedly sets a benchmark for sound, flexible and balanced policy settings for the knowledge economy.
- The second paradox is that the intellectual property system, in a formal sense, is largely structured in terms of rights to exclude protected content, and yet as a policy tool is intended to bring about inclusive benefits in the form of shared social and economic welfare and benefits, in a positive-sum framework of 'mutual advantage of producers and users of technological knowledge' (in line with the objectives articulated in Article 7 of TRIPS).

[6] Ibid.

[7] Notably in Article II, General Agreement on Tariffs and Trade (GATT 1947).

Resolving these paradoxes – in particular making effective use of the IP system and international trade to catalyse the availability of the promised positive-sum benefits of the generation and dissemination of knowledge – goes to the heart of understanding the potential for enhanced and more equitable social and economic welfare resulting from knowledge flows that remains a challenge for policymakers today. This will be assisted by an holistic and cross-disciplinary approach that seeks to integrate the three interlocking developments outlined in the previous section: knowledge as integral to economic growth, the law of IP as a policy tool and the opportunities afforded by disruptive technologies.

'The Very Idea': Tracing Three Convergent Trends

The more immediate spur for the work collected in this volume – and the broader conversation it forms part of – has been the progressive convergence, over the past three decades, and the burgeoning impact of three disruptive developments, each originating around the year 1990: at that time, not immediately connected, but increasingly interconnected since then. The first concerns a fundamental rebasing of the theory of economic growth – incorporation of knowledge as an endogenous factor of growth. The second concerns a frameshift in how trade negotiators reconceived IP, exemplified by the negotiations establishing an 'adequate and effective' level of protection of IP rights as an integral element of multilateral trade law commitments. And the third development was the creation of technological possibilities for global connectivity and the sharing of knowledge – with the creation of the World Wide Web.

Knowledge, Endogenous to Growth

First, 1990 saw the publication of Paul Romer's paper, 'Endogenous Technological Change',[8] which sought to explain how technological change, as a driver of economic growth, could be incorporated within a model of economic growth and need not be treated as an external, or

[8] Paul Romer, 'Endogenous Technological Change', *Journal of Political Economy*, Vol. 98, No. 5, Part 2, pp. S71–S102 (1990).

exogenous, factor. The endeavour, as he later explained it, was 'to uncover the private and public sector choices that cause the rate of growth of the residual to vary across countries'[9] – referring to the 'Solow residual', or component of growth in economic output that couldn't be attributed to capital accumulation or increased labour output. This 1990 paper posited three premises:

(i) An emphasis on technological change – or 'improvement in the instructions for mixing together raw materials' – as a central factor in enabling economic growth.
(ii) The incorporation of technological change as an endogenous factor: 'technological change arises in large part because of intentional actions taken by people who respond to market incentives'. (He clarifies that this 'does not mean that everyone who contributes to technological change is motivated by market incentives [but] market incentives nonetheless play an essential role in the process whereby new knowledge is translated into goods with practical value'.)
(iii) Most importantly, against a notion of classical economics focused on the management of scarcity, ideas are distinctive in that they are inherently non-rivalrous: 'instructions for working with raw materials are inherently different from other economic goods. Once the cost of creating a new set of instructions has been incurred, the instructions can be used over and over again at no additional cost. Developing new and better instructions is equivalent to incurring a fixed cost. This property is taken to be the defining characteristic of technology. Discoveries differ from other inputs in the sense that many people can use them at the same time'.[10]

This analysis underpins our understanding of how technological innovation enables exponential growth, leading to vastly greater prospects, more widely dispersed, than a reliance on the inherently scarce and rivalrous factors of capital and labour. The essential shift in framing the problem was the incorporation into the model of growth a concentration on the economics of technological innovation as an activity undertaken by firms and by other actors. This can be understood in terms of the incentives offered, which rely in part on the partial

[9] Paul Romer, 'The Origins of Endogenous Growth', *The Journal of Economic Perspectives*, 8, 1 (Winter, 1994): 3–22, at 8.
[10] Ibid., at 72.

excludability of new technologies. 'The second premise implies that technological change takes place because of the actions of self-interested individuals, so improvements in the technology must confer benefits that are at least partially excludable.' And this contributes to economic growth, in line with the first premise that 'growth is driven fundamentally by the accumulation of a partially excludable, nonrival input'. A reliance on price-taking competition will not be sufficient to generate the technologies that underpin the possibilities of exponential economic growth.

Later, in 1994, coincidentally the year the first multilateral negotiations on trade-related aspects of IP concluded, Romer reflected on the possibilities for the insights of this endogenous growth theory to inform a wide range of critical policy issues:

> If macroeconomists look only at the cross-country regressions deployed in the convergence controversy, it will be easy to be satisfied with neoclassical models in which market incentives and government policies have no effect on discovery, diffusion, and technological advance. But if we make use of all of the available evidence, economists can move beyond these models and begin once again to make progress toward a complete understanding of the determinants of long-run economic success. Ultimately, this will put us in position to offer policy-makers something more insightful than the standard neoclassical prescription-more saving and more schooling. We will be able to rejoin the ongoing policy debates about tax subsidies for private research, antitrust exemptions for research joint ventures, the activities of multinational firms, the effects of government procurement, the feedback between trade policy and innovation, the scope of protection for intellectual property rights, the links between private firms and universities, the mechanisms for selecting the research areas that receive public support, and the costs and benefits of an explicit government-led technology policy. We will be able to address the most important policy questions about growth: In a developing country like the Philippines, what are the best institutional arrangements for gaining access to the knowledge that already exists in the rest of the world? In a country like the United States, what are the best institutional arrangements for encouraging the production and use of new knowledge?[11]

These insights from economic theory have continuing application today as policymakers, treaty negotiators and legislators seek to develop and

[11] 'The Origins of Endogenous Growth', 21–22.

refine a balanced and effective legal and policy framework for the knowledge economy. The international framework is, however, more complex than the conventional North–South dichotomy between knowledge producers and consumers prevalent in 1995. Many developing countries show a growing capacity to absorb, adapt and generate new technological knowledge, while also acknowledging and strengthening indigenous knowledge systems and forms of creativity, creating a richer, more diverse picture, yielding greater prospects for knowledge-driven economic social and cultural development across the globe. This more diverse and nuanced view is apparent in the evolving, less polarized diversity of attitudes towards the legal framework for knowledge creation and dissemination, exemplified by the TRIPS Agreement,[12] understood increasingly – in its applied form and in the light of experience – as capable of the positive-sum benefits it purportedly aims for.

A Positive-Sum Approach to IP Law and Policy?

Second, it was in 1990 that the substance of what emerged as the TRIPS Agreement largely took shape, resulting in the circulation of the 'Brussels text'[13] in December of that year. This version was already close to the form and content of the text subsequently adopted in 1994. The major geopolitical shifts in 1989[14] had paved the way for negotiations on TRIPS to define the notion of 'trade-related aspects' of IP rights in terms of an agreed minimum level of 'effective and adequate'[15] protection of IP in domestic legal systems. The TRIPS negotiations are generally conceived as a conventional trade negotiation defined by zero-sum trade-offs and concessions: indeed, the very existence of the Agreement, in itself, and in the form of an agreed set of minimum

[12] Peter K. Yu, 'TRIPS and Its Contents (5 September 2019)', *IDEA: The IP Law Review*, Vol. 60, 2019, Texas A&M University School of Law Legal Studies Research Paper No. 19–36, available at https://ssrn.com/abstract=3448332.

[13] Draft Final Act Embodying the Results of the Uruguay Round of Multilateral Trade Negotiations: Revision, MTN.TNC/W/35/Rev.1, 3 December 1990.

[14] Antony Taubman, 'Thematic Review: Negotiating "Trade-Related Aspects" Of Intellectual Property Rights', in Jayashree Watal and Antony Taubman (editors), *The Making of TRIPS*, Geneva: WTO, 2015.

[15] Preambular para. 1, TRIPS Agreement.

standards for their domestic laws, represented a concession by developing countries.[16] Yet, already in 1990, the negotiations had developed a substantive thread that constituted an informed debate about how to frame the optimal role and balance of an IP system as an instrument of public policy.[17] As a partially defensive move to safeguard their domestic policy space in the knowledge economy, faced with the prospect under TRIPS of considerably more excludability of knowledge goods, a coalition of developing countries tabled a paper in mid-1990 that, inter alia, phrased the policy role of intellectual property in the following, positive-sum terms:

> intellectual property rights are granted not only in acknowledgement of the contributions of inventors and creators, but also to assist in the diffusion of technological knowledge and its dissemination to those who could benefit from it in a manner conducive to social and economic welfare and agree that this balance of rights and obligations inherent in all systems of intellectual property rights should be observed ... the protection and enforcement of intellectual property rights should contribute to the promotion of technological innovation and enhance the international transfer of technology to the mutual advantage of producers and users of technological knowledge.[18]

This proposed text led, albeit in modified form, to Article 7 of the concluded TRIPS Agreement (cited as an epigraph at the opening of this chapter), expressly framing the policy objectives of the IP system for the first time within the multilateral treaty system. Since then, the Article 7 formulation has served as a foundation for a continuing, vigorous and diverse international conversation about what forms of implementation of IP law and policy both promote innovation[19] and technology diffusion[20] for social and economic welfare, and what it means to strike a balance of rights and obligations,[21] as well as providing policy

[16] Indonesian Trade Minister S.B. Joedono at the Marrakesh Conference adopting the WTO Agreement: 'Among the new obligations which we consider as a major concession is the agreement on intellectual property', MTN.TNC/MIN(94)ST/17 (12 April 1994).

[17] A view argued in Taubman, 'Thematic review: Negotiating "trade-related aspects" of intellectual property rights', pp. 22–25.

[18] MTN.TNC/W/35/Rev.1, 3 December 1990 ('Brussels draft')

[19] See, for example, extracts from successive TRIPS Council minutes concerning 'Innovation', available at www.tripsims.wto.org.

[20] See, for example, extracts from successive reports concerning implementation of Article 66.2 of TRIPS, available at www.tripsims.wto.org.

[21] See, for example, extracts from successive TRIPS Council minutes concerning 'Public Interest', available at www.tripsims.wto.org.

grounding for the legal interpretation of more specific treaty provisions in the context of dispute settlement.[22]

The debates, in effect, about what it means to attain in practice the objectives of Article 7 take up some of the policy issues adumbrated by Romer in concluding the contemporaneous 1994 article cited above. One critical element of the Article 7 formulation of the core objectives of the IP system is the expectation of 'mutual advantage' of producers and users of technological knowledge – a hint at the non-rivalrousness of knowledge, stressed at the time by Romer as its distinctive characteristic, opening up prospects for a non-zero sum approach to policymaking and trade negotiations in the information economy – a reminder, perhaps, that negotiations over trade in knowledge should expressly recognize this distinctive property of knowledge goods. And, at the same time, a short distance away in Geneva, the practical possibility of seemingly boundless non-zero-sum sharing of knowledge was taking shape.

Global Knowledge Diffusion Becomes a Practical Possibility

Third, it was also in 1990, that the World Wide Web, the first GUI hypertext browser and editor was created by Tim Berners-Lee and colleagues,[23] following his proposal for a distributed hypertext system.[24] Thus what evolved into the World Wide Web was invented at the nuclear research institution CERN, coincidentally some 30 minutes by bicycle from the TRIPS negotiations, yet at that time unbeknown to the TRIPS negotiators.[25] Tellingly, the proposal had been based on Berners-Lee's observations of actual patterns of collaborative knowledge sharing in CERN:

> CERN . . . involves several thousand people, many of them very creative, all working toward common goals. Although they are nominally organised into a hierarchical management structure, this does not constrain the

[22] See in particular WTO dispute settlement panel reports concerning the cases US – *Section 211 Appropriations Act* (8.57), Canada – *Pharmaceutical Patents* (7.26), Australia – *Tobacco Plain Packaging* (7.2402, 7.2403, 7.2411).

[23] A Little History of the World Wide Web, available at www.w3.org/History.html.

[24] Tim Berners-Lee, 'Information Management: A Proposal', CERN (March 1989, May 1990), available at www.w3.org/History/1989/proposal.html.

[25] Lars Anell, 'Keynote speech at the TRIPS Symposium, 26 February 2015', in Watal and Taubman, *The Making of TRIPS*, Geneva: WTO, 2015, pp. 285–291.

> way people will communicate, and share information, equipment and software across groups. The actual observed working structure of the organisation is a multiply connected 'web' whose interconnections evolve with time. In this environment, a new person arriving, or someone taking on a new task, is normally given a few hints as to who would be useful people to talk to. Information about what facilities exist and how to find out about them travels in the corridor gossip and occasional newsletters, and the details about what is required to be done spread in a similar way.[26]

Access to knowledge had become a practical problem:

> The technical details of past projects are sometimes lost forever, or only recovered after a detective investigation in an emergency. Often, the information has been recorded, it just cannot be found ... CERN is constantly changing as new ideas are produced, as new technology becomes available, and in order to get around unforeseen technical problems. When a change is necessary, it normally affects only a small part of the organisation. A local reason arises for changing a part of the experiment or detector. At this point, one has to dig around to find out what other parts and people will be affected.[27]

The proposal, then, was for:

> a universal linked information system, in which generality and portability are more important than fancy graphics techniques and complex extra facilities. The aim would be to allow a place to be found for any information or reference which one felt was important, and a way of finding it afterwards. The result should be sufficiently attractive to use that the information contained would grow past a critical threshold, so that the usefulness of the scheme would in turn encourage its increased use. The passing of this threshold accelerated by allowing large existing databases to be linked together and with new ones.[28]

Originally conceived for one (large) research institution, the ensuing World Wide Web was, of course, 'sufficiently attractive' to expand beyond all expectations, becoming, by the time TRIPS entered into force in 1995, a source of knowledge for some 45 million users accessing some 24,000 websites; today, more than half the world's population has access to some 1.7 billion websites.[29] The very function of the Web exemplified, in practice, the non-rivalrous characteristic of knowledge by enabling its

[26] Berners-Lee, 'Information Management: A Proposal'.
[27] Ibid.
[28] Ibid.
[29] Source of statistics: internetlivestats.com.

seemingly limitless, almost seamless sharing. The Web saw the realization, in practice, of the idea of a universal source of information conceived by such diverse visionaries as Francis Bacon,[30] Paul Otlet[31] and Vannevar Bush.[32] By 1996, the exponential growth of the Web had precipitated a major recalibration of international IP norms, in the form of the WIPO Internet Treaties,[33] which sought, in effect, to clarify or redefine the partial excludability of knowledge in a novel environment which dramatically transformed its practical availability.[34]

Building a Platform

Against this background, this volume forms part of a broader, necessary dialogue among policymakers and scholars from a range of disciplines on the contemporary facets of 'trade in knowledge'. The collection is intended to strengthen the conceptual and empirical foundation for further work, at the international policy level, in the academy, and in the planning and delivery practical programmes, to understand and unlock the development potential of trade in knowledge. The call for papers, scholarly and policy dialogues, and ultimately this collection have aspired to clarify and provide new insights into the distinctive characteristics of knowledge goods, responding to the increasing practical ease of their dissemination, their increasing integration into forms of trade and related commercial activities, and the implicit – but imperfectly understood and attained – opportunities offered by their non-rivalrous characteristics.

In the hope of its editors, and thanks to the superb contributions of the collected authors, this volume can help to inform our current understanding of knowledge flows in trade, in both conceptual and empirical terms, to map out their implications for knowledge-based development,

[30] Francis Bacon, 'The New Atlantis', available at www.gutenberg.org/files/2434/2434-h/2434-h.htm.

[31] Paul Otlet, 'Traité de documentation', Brussels: Editiones Mundaneum, 1934.

[32] Vannevar Bush, 'As We May Think', *The Atlantic*, July 1945.

[33] See Meier-Ewert and Gutierrez, Chapter 4, in this volume, p. 116.

[34] This is the normative essence of the specification of a right to authorize any communication of copyright works to the public, by wire or wireless means, including 'the making available to the public of works in a way that the members of the public may access the work from a place and at a time individually chosen by them' (Article 8, WCT); this excludability is partially offset by the recognition of the legitimate scope for limitations and exceptions, confirmed as applicable in the digital environment (Article 10 and the respective agreed statement).

and to assess options for regulation of the knowledge economy that enhance the possibilities for greater diffusion of the welfare benefits expected from technological advances. The diverse contributions demonstrate in practice how more powerful and nuanced analytical tools, and more precise and sophisticated use of data, can build a stronger empirical and theoretical platform to support further policy dialogue and research, in turn supporting domestic policy formation, capacity building and international cooperation, institutional development, and norm-setting. Even so, contributors have illustrated and charted certain gaps in the coverage and reliability of currently available data, and identified prospects for a stronger conceptual understanding of knowledge flows and their nexus with trade and transactions in IP, based on a firmer empirical foundation. And there are considerable cautions against hasty, broad-brush assumptions about the character of knowledge flows and the absorptive capacity of different economies, suggesting a continuing need for more nuanced and tailored policy analysis supported by more granular and precise empirical data.

The contributing authors have shown the way forward according to four general themes, corresponding to the four substantive sections of this volume:

Conceptual clarity: through reviewing and updating the conceptual framework, rethinking 'trade' in terms of how digital technology has reshaped the very character of trade and elicited diverse regulatory responses. Evolution and diversification in the economics, commercial models and technological possibilities of knowledge flows impel a fresh understanding of the essential nature and the practical consequences of the international transactions we choose to define, regulate and analyse as 'trade'. This necessary recalibration of 'trade' enhances the prospects for a better understanding of the significance of the knowledge components of transactions which may be overlooked purely because they are, by definition, 'invisible' or 'intangible', overcoming the intuitive preference for implicitly valuing more highly those transactions that are defined by the physical relocation of solid objects; this recalibration in turn provides the groundwork for an updated approach to measuring knowledge flows.

Better data and better use of data: rebasing and refreshing our empirical understanding by addressing the challenges of mapping, measuring and assessing the impact of IP transactions and knowledge flows associated with international trade. The significance of knowledge-based flows and transactions will inevitably be understated or misunderstood if they are undercounted, or not counted at all: the goal of objective and informed policymaking would be advanced by a systematic, and cross-cutting, programme of filling the known gaps in data coverage and by developing new metrics that capture the true exchange of value and of intangible content in the billions of daily transactions in the digital environment and in the IP licensing and transfer arrangements that constitute a significant and undervalued component of value chains.

Insights for policymakers: understanding the implications for trade and development, through innovation and knowledge diffusion, particularly in IP-intensive industries and global value chains; and developing a foundation for better-tailored, empirically-informed policy support that recognizes the diversity, and the differing technological capacities and economic situation, of distinct economies, regions and sectors. Innovation and technology policy needs to respond to the increasing mobility of knowledge and of knowledge workers, the significance of dynamic knowledge networks not defined by national boundaries or geographical distance, and the unbundling of production capacity, together with the evolution of a number of developing and transition economies as centres of knowledge production and technological inovation.

Implications for governance. Framing the regulatory response: the identifying lessons for governance and regulatory structures to enhance knowledge flows and their potential benefits, recognizing that 'ideas are economic goods which are unlike conventional private goods and that markets are inherently less successful at producing and transmitting ideas than they are with private goods'.[35] This observation underscores the strong sensitivity to regulatory structures of the dissemination of usable knowledge; to some extent, it is the regulatory system – and specifically IP laws – that enable markets in ideas to develop and that structure and define those markets. Regulatory intervention in a range of areas doubtless is a key factor determining how successfully markets function to ensure that ideas are generated and are disseminated and used effectively for the overall public benefit, and regulation can distort or inhibit knowledge flows, sometimes in unexpected ways.

However, the contributing authors have not addressed these four areas in isolation from one another. To the exact contrary, these themes form a natural line of development, linked together dynamically – building a clearer understanding of the evolving character of international knowledge flows and knowledge-based transactions, that in turn helps shape an improved empirical framework for measuring and analysing this trade in knowledge, feeding then into a more sophisticated and nuanced

[35] Paul Romer, 'Two Strategies for Economic Development: Using Ideas and Producing Ideas', *Proceedings of the World Bank Annual Conference on Development Economics 1992*, Washington, DC: The International Bank for Reconstruction and Development, 1993, pp. 63–92, at 89.

understanding of the implications for trade and development, which should then contribute ultimately to a clearer conceptual foundation for the work of international institutions and for the formulation and negotiation of new or adapted norms. On the model of this interdisciplinary, cumulative dialogue, this book above all seeks to illuminate, inform and invigorate these dynamic linkages.

Rethinking 'Trade'

The triple convergence identified above – recognition of the knowledge component of economic growth, the policy role of the IP system and the opportunities afforded by new technologies – has opened up entirely new markets (and important non-market avenues) for the dissemination of knowledge and creative content, greatly facilitating knowledge flows and creating new possibilities for economic development and more equitable access to international markets. Authors' contributions have explored the implications of trade in knowledge as integral to sustained and widely distributed economic growth, and the possibilities afforded by conceiving trade in terms of ideas ('bits') and not simply things ('atoms'), both as dispersed global value chains and of trade in 'pure' IP content as such particularly in the creative sectors. This offers a vantage point for the reconsideration of what constitutes trade, and thus how the value of international transactions can be rebased in terms of knowledge flows, legitimate returns for the use of knowledge and facilitating valuable access to knowledge, and need not be limited to or measured by the physical passage of materials across borders ('things you can drop on your foot'). Just as knowledge is now better framed as endogenous to our understanding of growth, rather than confined to a black box as an exogenous factor, the IP component of international transactions may be better understood as 'endogenous' to trade, particularly when this concerns valuable content and the knowledge transactions that partly constitute dispersed value chains.

Policy and legal analysis therefore need more systematically to 'unbundle' the knowledge component from various proxies for it (such as trade in IP-rich goods, trade in knowledge-intensive services and trade in IP rights for such goods as software and creative content), so that the knowledge dimension can be better understood. As contributors have shown, this would help address such shortcomings as the distorting effect of taxation arrangements, and the mismatch between trade statistics and the true character of cross-border commercial transactions and the related flow of valuable knowledge. There is a risk that perceptions of economic interests – and thus ensuing trade policy initiatives and development planning – may be influenced by an inherent preference for valuing the physical carrier of knowledge, rather than the content as such. The archetypal knowledge economy example is the smartphone. If conceived purely as a traded good – as a chattel – each imported smartphone may be construed as a deficit in the balance of trade in goods up to its full value; but, as the embodiment of countless knowledge transactions, IP inputs, and steps of intangible value addition, its true economic characteristics would lead to a dramatically different interpretation of its significance for trade, development, and national commercial and industrial interests. The purely trade-in-goods perception, although immediately intuitively attractive, is not merely inaccurate – it can be wildly misleading and can lead to a distorted view of policy interests. It is striking to consider even the 'known unknowns' – such as full data on international trade for consumer licences for IP content, and on the intangible components of dispersed development and production chains – that, if addressed, could significantly alter perceptions of trade balances and trade policy priorities.

A significant proportion of the trade in knowledge goods falls within the scope of trade in services. Pointing to the way we may therefore need to rethink the character of services trade, Lee Tuthill, Antonia Carzaniga and Martin Roy[36] map out how technologies are transforming the tradability of services, increasing the growth of services supplied electronically cross-border, across a wide range of sectors, from medical, to educational, financial, audiovisual, or professional services, posing challenges for governments as they seek to adapt, including on policies that could potentially disrupt the growth of cross-border digital trade such as localization of data. Equally, the commercial transactions that lead to transfer of knowledge goods, with major systemic implications for economic and development policy, include many forms of activity that transcend even the expanded or more flexible notions of 'trade' that include trade purely in IP licences or transferring ownership: thus, contributors look at the significance of knowledge flows through mergers and acquisitions[37] and through foreign direct investment,[38] as complementing different forms of trade as such.

[36] Chapter 3 in this volume, p. 84 *supra*.
[37] Chapter 12 in this volume, p. 376 *supra*.
[38] Chapter 11 in this volume, p. 352 *supra*.

A More Inclusive, Comprehensive and Granular Empirical Base

The very intangible character of knowledge flows, and of trade in a purely digital, partially borderless environment, inevitably makes them harder to track, and thus to measure, than trade in knowledge embedded in physical goods. Hence, some of the most valuable elements of international trade – those that entail transactions purely in knowledge as such – are among the most inaccurately and incompletely measured, both in terms of specific bilateral flows and general international patterns. Yet the close attention now paid to trade balances and the impact of dispersed production and value chains makes it all the more imperative to develop more inclusive, comprehensive and granular statistics, covering knowledge flows through trade and transactions over IP. If the intangible, IP-related component of trade – including the massive international trade in B2C IP licences on major content platforms – is discounted, in favour of the more readily and comprehensively counted trade in goods, this may distort policymakers' perceptions of economies' current essential interests and, worse, their future prospects for the creation of fulfilling and productive employment.

Building a clearer, more nuanced conception of the true economic and development characteristics of knowledge-based trade today will therefore require a stronger empirical and theoretical platform to support further policy dialogue and research. This includes improving the reach and quality of statistics, and improving the analysis of available data, including through greater integration of different forms of data (such as measurement of the value and trends of trade as a proxy for knowledge transactions and the consequences of mergers and acquisitions for the analysis of knowledge flows), and more nuanced and granular analysis of IP statistics (including greater attention to patent quality as measured, for instance, through citations). Policy and legal analysis ideally need to 'unbundle' the knowledge component from various proxies for it (such as trade in IP-rich goods, trade in knowledge-intensive services and trade in IP rights for such goods as software and creative content).

Measuring Trade in IP Content

What has been measured – notably, the incomplete count of licence fees for the use of IP – shows considerably faster growth since TRIPS entered into force than trade in goods and services in general and even trade in high-tech products. While these statistics provide a useful baseline, they are known to have considerable limitations and lacunae, with a relatively small number of countries providing complete statistics. Further, definitional and classification issues arise, linked in part to the changing and diversifying patterns of trade in IP rights, which limits the capacity to gauge accurately the actual pattern, direction and scale of trade particularly in IP-protected content, whether in the form of IP licences over digital products or the IP transactions that form part of the knowledge transfer taking place in dispersed production chains. Joscelyn Magdeleine and Andreas Maurer[39] propose a number of solutions to the shortcomings in the statistical coverage, including greater synergies in data collection and compilation, better understanding of emerging business models, and greater granularity according to the characteristics of the firms that trade in IP products. They discuss the need for a new international dataset covering international IP-related flows (including relevant services items as well as merchandise statistics to cover embedded IP). The existing OECD–WTO Trade in Value Added (TiVA) initiative could, for instance, be extended to better measure IP embedded in traded products.

The need for – and potential insights from – a more nuanced and broader-based methodology is well illustrated by how Thomas Neubig and Sacha Wunsch-Vincent[40] map the distortions caused by tax planning to international flows of knowledge through IP transactions, in particular the statistics collected on charges for the use of IP, in turn affecting measurement of imports and exports, as well as GDP and productivity. They point out how statisticians, tax authorities and analysts can develop more accurate and granular data, including through improved classification and greater disaggregation of IP transactions, demonstrating convincingly how improved understanding of cross-border flows of IP is essential for analysing the modern economy, and for sounder empirically-based policymaking.

The trade in digital products, such as video games, video on demand, digital music and e-publishing, is at once one of the most dynamic areas of trade in IP licences, as entire industry sectors shift from analogue and physical media to digital distribution platforms – and offers, at least in principle, significant opportunities for content creators across the globe who have had limited opportunities in the past to benefit from their works. However, this area in particular remains elusive when it comes to incorporation in official trade statistics, given that much of the essential

[39] Chapter 5 in this volume, p. 171 *supra*.
[40] Chapter 6 in this volume, p. 194 *supra*.

data is proprietary and not captured in publicly available trade statistics. Thus, Erick S. Oh[41] demonstrates the value of access to proprietary data in filling significant gaps in the official statistics, pointing the way to improved data coverage in future which would in turn strengthen policymakers' understanding of the value and potential of these sectors. Authors have also shown the way to more effective integration of data across different domains for a more holistic and better empirically grounded picture overall. Thus Vito Amendolagine, Cristina Chaminade, José Guimón and Roberta Rabellotti[42] show the importance of tracking foreign direct investments relating to research and development as a conduit for transmission of technological knowledge across borders; their insights into the uneven distribution of such investment can guide strategies for low-income countries and smaller middle-income countries to benefit more systematically for investment-led technological development.

Patent Data as a Guide for Policymakers

Technological innovation and improved connectivity has enabled the programmes of WIPO[43] in particular and other international organizations[44], national[45] and regional[46] patent offices and other platforms[47] and initiatives[48], to ensure that patent data are increasingly well ordered, accessible and harmonized, and supported by enhanced analytical and reporting tools, although considerable work still needs to be done to ensure truly inclusive global coverage and accessibility. Patent data, and the application of new analytical methodologies, provide a valuable complement to trade statistics in mapping knowledge flows. This analysis offers insights into changing patterns of innovation, R&D collaboration, technology sourcing, technology transfer and knowledge flows in general.

[41] Chapter 10 in this volume, p. 323 *supra*.
[42] Chapter 11 in this volume, p. 352 *supra*.
[43] See www3.wipo.int/ipstats/.
[44] See www.oecd-ilibrary.org/science-and-technology/data/oecd-patent-statistics_patent-data-en.
[45] E.g. IP Australia, Patent Analytics Hub, www.ipaustralia.gov.au/tools-resources/patent-analytics-hub.
[46] E.g. European Patent Office (www.epo.org/about-us/annual-reports-statistics/statistics.html).
[47] E.g. The Lens (www.lens.org/).
[48] E.g. the IP Statistics Task Force which convenes regular conferences in the series IP Statistics for Decision Makers (IPSDM). (www.oecd.org/site/stipatents/).

The overall picture is one of progressive diversification away from the conventional pattern of flows from developed to developing economies, but with significant differences across regions, and some evidence of reverse knowledge flows,[49] providing a statistical foundation for a more nuanced and differentiated understanding of the patterns of knowledge generation and transmission. Such analysis may provide greater insights into the impact of major policy developments such as the consequences of the TRIPS Agreement itself for the flow of pharmaceutical-related knowledge, and the impact of the Paris Agreement on climate change.[50]

Despite the extensive work done on patent analytics across jurisdictions, there are obstacles to more coherent and systematic use of data collected under different national systems, discussed in this volume.[51] Contributors to this volume have nonetheless convincingly demonstrated the value, and the prospects, for fresh and more finely nuanced use of patent data to understand trade and knowledge flows. Critically, these lines of analysis can include a qualitative component, and make use of a wider range of metadata, shifting the analytical frame beyond simple headcounts of patent filings. Thus, by analysing patent citations as an indicator of the value of knowledge published in patent applications, Andrew Torrance, Jevin West and Lisa Friedman[52] confirm a general assumption that knowledge flows generally run from established developed economies to developing countries, but with China a significant, and increasingly important, exception to this trend. Laurie Ciaramella, Gaétan De Rassenfosse and Florian Seliger[53] show how patent data illuminates cross-border knowledge flows through R&D collaboration, technology sourcing and technology transfer, by analysing applications sourced from parties in two different countries or applied for in one country but invented elsewhere, as well as assignments of patent ownership. In turn, this provides more robust insights into knowledge flows within and beyond critical regions such as East Asia, and important developments such as intensified knowledge flows in the ICT area and the emergence of 'reverse' knowledge flows, displaying a more

[49] Ciaramella, de Rassenfosse and Seliger, Chapter 8 in this volume.

[50] Torrence, West and Friedman, Chapter 7 in this volume.

[51] In particular by Dubbert et al., Chapter 9 in this volume, p. 293 *supra*.

[52] Chapter 7 in this volume, p. 218 *supra*.

[53] Chapter 8 in this volume, p. 265 *supra*.

diversified and complex pattern than the traditional north–south dichotomy evident, for instance, in Romer's 1994 paper cited above (p. 775).[54]

In an excellent foundation for exploring future analytical possibilities, Jacob Dubbert, Alexander Giczy, Nicholas Pairolero and Andrew Toole[55] provide a reference to help policymakers evaluate the trade in knowledge literature, particularly the interpretation of IP-based evidence for policy decisions. They review the analytical methodologies that use patent data to illuminate cross-border trade in knowledge, showing the diverse ways patent data can be used to track innovation, technology transfer and knowledge flows. Direct indicators, such as patent counts, patent citations and royalty payments, can be supplemented by indirect applications that shed light on relationships between different countries, industry sectors or firms and measure technology transfer and knowledge flows. Patent data can inform indices of patent strength, IPR intensity, technological proximity, and knowledge flow through international inventor mobility. They conclude that IP data are a valuable source of information for learning about technology transfer and knowledge flows across borders. Yet policymakers need to be guided by experts who can review empirical findings who understand the origin, nature and nuances of data, and should not overlook the limitations and variability of data. Territorial differences in patent coverage and practice can limit the value of international comparisons. Greater attention needs to be shown to patent assignments – transfer of ownership of patents, including the transfer of patent portfolios in international mergers and acquisitions – as a critical, and statistically ever more important, component of international knowledge flows.[56] Further limitations on patent counts and similar quantitative analysis arise from the difficulty in assessing the motivations and licensing strategies employed by those holding patents.[57] The authors also advocate a transparent, reliable and reproducible method for disambiguating data elements such as inventor and owner names.

[54] Note 9 *supra*.

[55] Chapter 9 in this volume, p. 293 *supra*.

[56] Ibid.

[57] In the context of public health, see for instance the diverse range of practices categorized and analysed in Antony Taubman, 'A Typology of Intellectual Property Management for Public Health Innovation and Access: Design Considerations for Policymakers', *Open AIDS J.* (2010) 4: 4–24, available at www.ncbi.nlm.nih.gov/pmc/articles/PMC2878976/.

Gaétan de Rassenfosse, Florian Seliger and Laurie Ciaramella[58] amply show the potential of more sophisticated and nuanced analysis of patent data analysis in mapping longer term trends in knowledge flow between developed and developing nations, by considering R&D collaboration evidenced by cross-border co-inventorship, cross-border technology sourcing based on patent applications on patents for inventions invented elsewhere, and the knowledge transfer tracked through assignment of patent ownership. These metrics consistently show significant interaction with East Asia, a growing concentration on information and communication technologies, growing activity between Europe and Asia, and prospects for 'reverse' knowledge flows in particular as China's technology capacity increases. Their analysis is accompanied by a valuable commentary on the limitations of using patent data: not all inventions are patented and patents are of variable utility and quality; patents are only one aspect of effective knowledge; effects observed may be a consequence of economic growth more widely; and limited data on firms' ownership structures prevents finer-grained analysis (such as distinguishing offshoring R&D from contracting).

Mergers and acquisitions have attracted considerably more attention from a policy perspective as a means of acquiring and internationally transferring technological knowledge, in particular through the transfer in ownership of entire patent portfolios. Mapping patterns of mergers and acquisitions therefore provides an additional metric for tracking cross-border knowledge flows. Holger Ernst, Carsten Guderian and Marco Richter[59] therefore explore the application of novel analytical tools making use of patent data to trace knowledge flows more accurately in this context, overcoming some of the shortcomings from conventional patent analysis. The Patent Asset Index of a patent portfolio measures the aggregate strength of a full patent portfolio, gauging each patent is measured by its competitive impact, comprising technology relevance and market coverage. They illustrate the applicability of this approach in a complex competition analysis of the impact of a merger, demonstrating the potential of new forms of patent analytics to support decision-making concerned with international trade and cross-border knowledge flows. Their work demonstrates how future-oriented, quantitative patent analytics can help improve policy choices with bearing on cross-border knowledge flows and innovation.

[58] Chapter 8 in this volume, p. 265 *supra*.
[59] Chapter 12 in this volume, p. 376 *supra*.

Insights for Policymakers: Knowledge Flows, Trade and Development Today

Against the background of radically transformed linkages between trade, IP and knowledge flows, the more nuanced, granular and sophisticated use of data described in the previous section offers invaluable guidance for policymakers seeking to understand, to respond to and ultimately to shape and secure social benefits from the shifting patterns of innovation, flows of knowledge and production capacities. The mobility of knowledge and of knowledge workers, the possibility of dynamic knowledge networks not defined by national boundaries or geographical distance, and the unbundling of production capacity, together with the evolution of a number of developing and transition economies as centres of knowledge production and technological innovation, all contribute to fast evolving and ever-diversifying ecosystems for innovation and the production and dissemination of knowledge. These factors are reshaping how, where and by whom innovation takes place, how and where the resultant new knowledge is developed, transacted and disseminated, and how countries can benefit directly and indirectly through technology spillovers.

Some of the most striking and consequential insights from the contributors concern the implications of these trends for trade and development, in an international policy context that lays considerable stress on the need to leverage new technology and information flows to support development. The contributions map change and diversity in how developing countries engage in knowledge transfers, consequently leading to more diverse policy implications for different economies. Differences – quantitative and qualitative – are clearly apparent in terms of economic scale and dynamism, engagement in international knowledge flows, and capacity for absorption and effective uptake of knowledge for their development: this provides an important corrective to assumptions that enhanced access to flows of knowledge would in itself lead naturally to gains in income and productivity. Greater granularity and nuance in empirical data and in reported practical experience must inevitably lead to greater granularity and nuance in policy prescriptions. Thus, Keith Maskus and Lee Branstetter[60] observe that our consideration of flows of knowledge needs to be complemented by attention to human capital and absorptive capacity in developing countries, given that

[60] Chapter 13 in this volume, p. 405 *supra*.

differences in those attributes go some way to explaining divergent outcomes. This will become all the more important as the transfer of manufacturing jobs to developing countries may ease, leading to increased need to focus on services and knowledge-based employment in such economies, and with it an accentuated need to develop indigenous human capital – including through the assistance of the improved access to learning that is now made feasible through new technologies which remove some of the obstacles to knowledge. In turn, strengthened human capital may enable developing countries to specialize in specific services and knowledge-based sectors.

Holger Ernst, Carsten Guderian and Marco Richter[61] draw on insights from patent analytics to map out the strategic challenges for policymakers looking to bolster national technological capabilities and the establishment of new, technology-based products and applications. As technology creation becomes increasingly globally dispersed, policymakers should encourage and support the establishment of overseas R&D activities to overcome the dominant home country orientation. Further nuance is needed to recognize the context-specific character of some technology-based innovations, which may only flourish in specific international or emerging markets and not in established (home) markets. The evolving patterns in global patenting trends may also help identify emerging competitors that are likely to disrupt established business practices that are concentrated in certain geographical areas.

Mercedes Delgado and Margaret Kyle[62] deploy data analysis to chart the effect of implementation of the TRIPS Agreement on trade in IP-intensive goods, in a diversifying global landscape for innovation and technology diffusion. To the extent that trade is linked with knowledge flows, TRIPS may have contributed to enhanced access to such goods on the part of developing countries, with the patterns in contrast with assumptions of a continuing north–south divide. Equally, the scope for policy flexibility may be signalled by their finding that TRIPS exceptions were not shown to undermine the gains realized from stronger IP protection. However, like other authors, they draw attention to the need for further analysis and a circumspect approach to drawing conclusions from existing data. They point to the essential need for further research to develop improved measures for access to the fruits of innovation

[61] Chapter 12 in this volume, p. 376 *supra*.

[62] Chapter 14 in this volume, p. 431 *supra*.

beyond the value of trade as such, given especially the potential effects of IP on prices of innovative goods.

Contributors have demonstrated the need for, and potential of, more precise analysis of knowledge flows associated with global production chains, including also the recognition of knowledge flows beyond the more readily measured use of the formal IP system. Hence Roberta Piermartini and Stela Rubínová[63] have charted the higher than expected spillovers of non-codified knowledge that have resulted from the intensified interaction between foreign firms and domestic suppliers enabled by global production chains. Significant insights for policymakers also flow from their observations that production linkages are especially conducive to knowledge spillovers when firms in the knowledge-receiving country are both sourcing from and selling to the international supply chain, and that even though knowledge spillovers naturally depend on geographical distance, knowledge diffusion has become less localized as international supply chains have become more global.

Nikolas Zolas and Travis Lybbert[64] show the way to new, more sophisticated insights into knowledge flows and development implications of global value chains by analysing the linkages between patent trends and industry and product classifications. Opening up a new vein of research on global value chains, they seek to characterize the role of patents in the organization and structure of global value chains. The results show, once again, the benefits of a more nuanced approach to drawing policy conclusions that stems from a more careful look at the data. Hence they find that international patent inflows and outflows do increase value-added trade on average, but that it is primarily industries in high-income countries that drive this trend. Middle-income countries, they find, experience greater production fragmentation and declining value-added trade as share of exports as a consequence of patent inflows. The different experiences of high- and middle-income countries may be explained by differences in compositions of patents, patenting motives or strategies, and knowledge absorption capacities (reinforcing the similar observations of Maskus and Branstetter[65]). They maintain that the way patent flows influence global value chains may offer guidance for those seeking to formulate and implement innovation policy. An improved foundation of data is needed, however, for more precise policy insights.

[63] Chapter 15 in this volume, p. 453 *supra*.
[64] Chapter 16 in this volume, p. 471 *supra*.
[65] Chapter 13 in this volume, p. 405 *supra*.

This would include better input-output data for low-income countries, improved measurements of cross-border trade in ideas (such as licensing and royalties) and more firm-level data. But even improved data analysis, they point out, is inherently backward-looking, and the patterns determined by their analysis may not carry through to global value chains currently being dramatically transformed through digital technologies. What is clear, however, is if analysis is to support more effective policymaking, including in determining how to engage in global value chains in a rapidly transforming global economy, it needs to be able to recognize and respond to the very different circumstances of different countries, regions and sectors.

Making and Remaking Rules and Institutions

The triple convergence – a focus on knowledge-based growth, recognition of trade in IP and the practical impact of diffusion of technology – outlined earlier in this chapter has fundamentally reframed the context for international rules and institutions dealing with the evolving knowledge economy, creating significant challenges for systems that have been marked by a degree of inertia and reactiveness. One essential need is for our understanding of the rules and their institutional context to be based on a sound empirical understanding of the nature, extent and development implications of knowledge flows. But it is also critical to understand the diversity of regulatory responses in other contexts. The conventional legal paradigm for IP law and related regulations governing the knowledge economy – epitomized by the TRIPS Agreement and its implementation – is of the articulation of an international, multilateral set of rules, which national legislation subsequently implements. However, the emerging international framework has become ever more complex, with overlapping and potentially conflicting rules flowing from bilateral and regional agreements, the *de facto* reach of domestic laws of the major players, and the kind of private ordering that may result in an information law merchant (as described by Jacques de Werra and Jeff Dodd[66]). Meanwhile, 25 years after the TRIPS Agreement entered into force, multilateral normsetting has been effectively inert, despite the identification of IP issues over 20 years ago in the context, for instance,

[66] Chapter 23 in this volume, p. 685 *supra*.

of the WTO e-commerce work programme[67] and in the context of the mandatory periodic reviews of the TRIPS Agreement under Article 71.[68] Even so, Holger Ernst, Carsten Guderian & Marco Richter draw on their use of patent analysis in support of policymaking to promote cross-border trade in knowledge to call for the WTO to continue its role in relation to the IP system, arguing that the TRIPS Agreement 'has been an immense success story since its introduction, enabling cross-border knowledge flows and providing cross-border trade opportunities and innovation incentives by allowing countries, firms and individuals to profit from their knowledge'.[69]

A well-calibrated, balanced and nuanced normative and institutional framework is, in any event, indispensable, given the distinctive qualities of knowledge products and the particular challenges both for overcoming market failure in their production and for ensuring equitable distribution of their benefits.[70] In 1992, Romer observed that 'we must recognize that ideas are economic goods which are unlike conventional private goods and that markets are inherently less successful at producing and transmitting ideas than they are with private goods'.[71] This observation underscores the strong sensitivity to regulatory structures of the dissemination of usable knowledge; to some extent, it is the regulatory system – and specifically IP laws – that enable markets in ideas to develop and that structure and define those markets. Regulatory intervention in a range of areas doubtless is a key factor determining how successfully markets function to ensure that ideas are generated and are disseminated and used effectively for the overall public benefit, and regulation can distort or inhibit knowledge flows, sometimes in unexpected ways.

Based on their fresh appraisal of the character of knowledge flows, Keith Maskus and Lee Branstetter lay out a set of considerations for policymakers. Against their observation that '[c]ontinued erosion of

[67] WTO Secretariat, 'Electronic Commerce and the Role of the WTO', Geneva, 1998, at 59–64, available at www.wto.org/english/res_e/booksp_e/special_study_2_e.pdf; see also 'Electronic Commerce Work Programme', WTO document IP/C/W/233 (7 December 2000).

[68] See, for example, Review of the Implementation of the Agreement under Article 71.1, WTO document IP/C/W/210 (3 October 2000).

[69] Chapter 12 in this volume, p. 376 *supra*.

[70] As outlined in Antony Taubman, 'Cereal Offenders: Access and Equity in Trade Negotiations on Knowledge Resources', in Jay Kesan (ed), *Agricultural Biotechnology and Intellectual Property: Seeds of Change* (2007).

[71] Romer, 'Two Strategies', note 35 *supra*, at 89.

pro-digital-trade norms and practices could be as injurious to global welfare as the trade wars of the 1930s',[72] they frame the role of the policymaker in terms of overcoming 'unseen barriers ... standing in the way of universal technological convergence' and observe that:

> the successful acquisition of frontier technological knowledge often requires the prior mastery of more basic knowledge and skills, a cumulative process. Finally, successful technology transfer requires coordinated capabilities among many individuals. When we consider the scale and complexity of the human capital investment required to support international 'knowledge flows', the mystery of its difficulty begins to fade.[73]

Human capital formation in developing countries is central to the goal of enabling effective use of knowledge flows, a prospect that technological advances, such as AI-driven computer-aided learning systems, may enable – a prospect that policymakers should take up. Information technology also enables growth in international trade in knowledge-intensive services, creating fresh export opportunities for advanced countries, while developing countries may overcome the 'knowledge trap' through specialization and gain from trade, 'reducing the range of capabilities required to escape that trap'. They observe how technological change opens up new prospects for technology diffusion, and see a potential role for 'a revitalized WTO, capable of coordinating policy in a digital age of expanding data flows'. With that in mind, they point to the present volume as an important step towards 'the WTO becoming more knowledgeable of these emerging technologies and international trade opportunities', and point to the need for continuing work by scholars and analysts.

Regulating Trade in Digital Content

Several contributing authors explore the regulatory implications of the continuing transition towards diffusion of knowledge products and creative content through digital means, a consequence of the triple convergence framing the present chapter. Erick Oh has mapped these developments and shown the prospects for a stronger empirical base that makes better use of the more complete data compiled by the private sector. In considering the opportunities both for access to creative

[72] Chapter 13 in this volume, p. 423 *supra*.
[73] Chapter 13 in this volume, p. 406 *supra*.

content and for infringement of the rights of its creators resulting from the transformation to digital diffusion, and illustrating how empirical analysis can flow into clearer understanding of the policy implications and in turn guide policymakers' options, Michael Smith and Rahul Telang[74] look at the available evidence to assess the losses for creative industries, and consider the impact on innovation and ultimately the wellbeing of society, in view of the significance of international trade in copyright goods. Their review addresses the empirical evidence to find that copyright piracy undermines legitimate sales, in turn reducing incentives to invest in content. They set out evidence derived from the literature as to the effectiveness of anti-piracy measures, concluding that active enforcement does influence consumer behaviour and has more effect on digital sales rather than conventional physical channels. Even so, they maintain that policymakers would be better informed on the basis of more extensive research including particularly field experiments.

Mary LaFrance[75] contrasts different regulatory responses in the key established jurisdictions of the EU and the US to the advent of streaming of creative content, demonstrating that even with the legal reforms sparked by the growth of internet trade in content, current policy challenges require further changes to copyright and neighbouring rights systems essentially designed in an analogue age. A particular policy challenge identified is the tendency to favour larger rights holders, as compared with independent artists, and to entrench existing internet service providers which are better resourced to monitor and filter unlicensed content – thus creating barriers to entry for emerging artists and competing digital platforms. Turning to the challenges for the developing world, Keith Nurse, Erica Smith, Kayla Grant and Alicia Shepherd[76] set out considerations for regulatory and institutional responses to the development opportunities offered by the growth of the digital creative economy, with particular consideration of the potential for blockchain technology. Their analysis leads to diverse institutional and legal proposals to promote wider access for creators to the digital marketplace, confirming the need for a multifaceted approach as against legal reform in isolation. Hence they propose building distribution platforms, strengthening institutional and human resources in the creative industries, targeted marketing strategies, and strengthening the

[74] Chapter 17 in this volume, p. 498 *supra*.
[75] Chapter 19 in this volume, p. 555 *supra*.
[76] Chapter 18 in this volume, p. 531 *supra*.

legal, technological and institutional infrastructure for collective management of copyright.

The contributing authors have set out a broader range of legal and regulatory issues posed by the advent of big data and enhanced cross-border data flows from the international perspective. Bilateral and regional trade agreements have reshaped the international legal and regulatory environment for trade in knowledge, and Mira Burri[77] draws on a close review of regional normsetting that are reformulating the legal framework for digital trade to raise searching questions about the optimal regulatory model for the data-driven economy. She proposes that cross-border data issues in trade agreements be addressed horizontally, and not in a manner directly related to a discrete service or a discrete transaction. And she advocates mechanisms to balance the free flow of data and the non-economic concerns raised by cross-border transfer, such as protection of personal data. Trade law has shown its capacity to provide flexible mechanisms that reconcile different values. Recent regional agreements may serve as stepping-stones, at a time when governments are under considerable pressure to respond to increasing recognition of the economic and policy significance of data and of cross-border information flows. This creates a pressing need for better understanding of the implications of the data economy for trade law, and a response to the pressure for 'digital protectionism'.

The Regulatory Challenges of Cross-Border Data Flows

The chapter by Nigel Cory[78] provides a complementary account of the overarching legal and regulatory issues raised by emerging patterns in trade in knowledge and cross-border flows of data, also framing the issue in terms of an emerging dilemma between the free flow of data and 'digital protectionism'. He identifies an overarching difficulty: the nature of trade in data and knowledge-intensive goods and services has been transformed profoundly, while policymakers lag behind in formulating responses at the domestic and international levels, and he argues that a gap is growing between the direction of technological innovation and the domestic and international policy frameworks, which he sees as enabling countries to impede the economic and social benefits these technologies offer. His analysis frames these challenges in terms of policies that can

[77] Chapter 20 in this volume, p. 591 *supra*.
[78] Chapter 21 in this volume, p. 623 *supra*.

impede cross-border data; the context for protection of copyright and trade secrets on the intersection between IP rights, data flows and digitalization; and the impact of regulation of Internet-based platforms and services that are key agents in facilitating and managing data flows, services, and digital IP. He sets the emerging task for policymakers in terms of a choice for a truly global market for digitally-enabled trade in goods and services and a reversal of an emerging threat of digital protectionism.

Lucas Spadano and Luiza Tângari Coelho[79] similarly survey the evolving regulatory environment for cross-border knowledge flows within multilateral, plurilateral and bilateral trade agreements, as the basis for an analysis of the question whether new multilateral disciplines are called for, especially in the light of recent trends in plurilateral and bilateral agreements. Strengthening an emerging theme, they observe that the law inevitably lags behind social change and is slow to respond to the impact of evolving information technology, a lag still more evident on the international plane than on the domestic level. They call for improved 'commitment to existing multilateral rules, guidelines on issues such as R&D subsidies and policies on open access to science, as well as a possible new e-commerce agreement including undertakings to keep data flows free', while cautioning against the assumption that there is an immediate need for new multilateral rules, arguing that existing WTO rules already apply to knowledge flows in several ways. Equally, they caution against linkages between the call for free flow of data, and issues such as performance requirements and protection of IP rights – suggesting they should for now remain at the level of bilateral or plurilateral negotiations. In their view, any initiative to develop new multilateral behind-the-border regulations with bearing on digital industry policies requires full understanding and measurement of their impact – this points to the need for further research so as to understand the effect of new rules (focusing on those recently established in bilateral and regional trade agreements) and the underlying policy considerations.

Looking forward to the possibility of national and international normsetting to deal with machine-generated data, Peter Yu[80] addresses the potential tensions arising from the possibility of retrofitting the 'square pegs' of rules tailored for cross-border flows of such data into the 'round holes' of the conventional trade rules regime, incorporating

[79] Chapter 22 in this volume, p. 649 *supra*.
[80] Chapter 24 in this volume, p. 738 *supra*.

also the established IP system. He sees contrast and controversy already in the approaches to data governance by the European Union and the United States, with differing emphases on protection of personal data as against the free movement of data. Drawing as a case study in normsetting for machine-generated data the 2017 European Commission proposal for a new *sui generis* data producer's right, he sets out the normative questions in terms of modality, allocation of rights, duration, scope, and limitations and exceptions. He concludes that standards for machine-generated data do not fit easily into the traditional trade-related regulatory system.

Towards Coherent Principles for Trade in IP Licences

The value of looking beyond the formal international framework of multilateral and regional agreements is emphatically confirmed by Jacques de Werra and Jeff Dodd[81] who focus on the centrality of cross-border IP licensing as the most common legal framework for international knowledge-based transactions, one that is tailored to the specific characteristics of knowledge-based intangibles. In the absence of an accepted framework of commercial legal principles governing this licensing – central to trade in knowledge – private ordering regimes have instead taken shape to frame these transactions – a body of 'information law merchant', akin to the cross-jurisdictional *lex mercatoria* developed by European traders in the medieval period. However, this favours large incumbent players, creating barriers to entry for new actors, disadvantaging smaller firms, increasing transaction and performance costs, and fostering disputes. FRAND licensing is another form of private ordering which has also failed to provide a suitable foundation for international trade in IP, in view of its piecemeal and fragmented development. Their close analysis of the complex legal and policy difficulties raised forms the foundation for a proposal for international organizations to address the general principles relating to international IP commercial contracts. Their chapter sets out a set of specific issues that a set of coherent principles could address, while distinguishing such commercially-focused work from consumer transactions, broader public policy considerations (such as competition, consumer protection or employment law), and the framing of IP regimes as such. Such a project would be as important for

[81] Chapter 23 in this volume, p. 685 *supra*.

supporting twenty-first century commerce as was the previous century's work on the recognition and validation of commercial transactions in tangible goods.

International Regulatory Responses

Wolf Meier-Ewert and Jorge Gutierrez[82] provide a broader perspective on the contemporary challenges for international norm setting for the knowledge economy by reviewing the evolution of the international dimension of IP law since the earliest multilateral instruments were drawn up in the nineteenth century. They chart growing diversity in recent years, in a period when the establishment of new multilateral rules proves elusive, with normsetting taking the form of nonbinding guidance, international non-state solutions, and numerous regional agreements. These responses to the regulatory challenges thrown up by the internet and digital trade have displaced the traditional treaty-making avenues. These diverse approaches are now helping to shape the operational context for digital business models by determining rules for such matters as Internet service provider (ISP) liability, 'safe harbour' provisions, and the issue of orphan works, in the absence of international agreement. Such responses seem also likely to apply to emerging issues such as online exhaustion of IP rights, data mining and IP questions connected with artificial intelligence.

Similarly, Lee Tuthill, Antonia Carzaniga and Martin Roy[83] illustrate how negotiators have begun to shape new legal frameworks via regional trade agreements (RTAs) that elaborate upon and, in some respects, extend beyond existing multilateral trade rules, and in doing so demonstrate the emerging complexity of the international legal framework dealing with information flows. They observe that RTAs generally contain soft provisions on cooperation or best endeavour provisions to avoid unnecessary barriers to electronic information flows, with few such agreements having binding commitments. They cite recent agreements, the CPTPP and the revised Singapore–Australia Agreement, as requiring the parties to allow the cross-border transfer of information by electronic means, including personal information, when this activity is for the conduct of the business of a covered person. However, they also allow the parties to adopt measures that are inconsistent with this obligation to

[82] Chapter 4 in this volume, p. 108 *supra*.
[83] Chapter 3 in this volume, p. 84 *supra*.

achieve a legitimate public policy objective, provided that the measures are not applied in an arbitrary or unjustifiable manner and do not impose restrictions greater than what is required to achieve the objective concerned. They observe that data localization requirements are a form of data flow restriction that may, at most, make data transfer impossible, or at the least, require duplicate facilities to be established that might not otherwise be needed from a commercial standpoint. Such requirements, depending on how they are designed and implemented, might, under some circumstances, already be disciplined by specific commitments under the GATS. Nonetheless, explicit disciplines on localization are found only in very recently negotiated agreements, which prohibit such measures. However, these agreements also recognize the rights of the parties to adopt or maintain infringing measures necessary to achieve legitimate public policy objectives, provided that they are not applied in a manner that would constitute a means of arbitrary or unjustifiable discrimination or a disguised restriction on trade.

Ultimately, we are left with the suggestion that the core principles of intellectual property law and policy, and of trade law and policy, remain appropriate for the knowledge economy, but considerable challenges attend to their effect clarification and adaptation for trade in pure content and in data as such.

Conclusion

This volume is intended to contribute to, to animate and to inform further policy dialogue, and to equip policymakers with a more sturdy empirical platform and a better adapted set of policy tools to respond to the challenges of knowledge-based development in a fluid and at times volatile policy environment. It was conceived as the foundation for a fresh set of conversations, as a spur to inquiry, rather than as a set of policy prescriptions. Hence this conclusion only encourages readers to consider and to respond to the ideas and possibilities set out in the preceding chapters and briefly recapitulated in this concluding chapter. Some essential themes, however, that may continue to guide this conversation could include:

- exploring the possibilities for regulatory settings that enable the production and dissemination of knowledge, as a nonrivalrous public good, moving beyond zero-sum assumptions to fulfil the positive-sum benefits for producers and users of knowledge identified in principle in the TRIPS Agreement;

- recognizing that the intangible knowledge component, including traded IP rights and embedded IP, should be considered 'endogenous' to trade policy, and not an extraneous or ancillary element;
- forging an empirical foundation for understanding knowledge flows that is more inclusive, granular and nuanced;
- strengthening a conception of the contemporary role and future possibilities for deploying knowledge flows for social and economic welfare; and
- recognizing and enabling the diverse regulatory responses – whether law, policy or practice, and whether national, regional, international – that provide the necessary foundation for knowledge-based human flourishing, on the basis of an informed and dynamic understanding of the kind of empirical foundation and policy understanding that the scholars and analysts contributing to this volume have so convincingly exhibited.

A COVID Epilogue

This project had already been completed when the first reports emerged of a novel coronavirus that rapidly escalated into the pandemic that has since convulsed societies across the globe, caused widespread death and suffering, and brought chaos to national economies and to international trade. No attempt is made here to assess or respond to the gravity and severity of this fundamental upheaval and its impact on and implications for the issues explored in this volume. Nonetheless, it is clear that the value of innovation systems and the equitable dissemination of the benefits of new knowledge production is more acutely understood than ever, and that the disruption of trade and potentially of established production chains is likely to accentuate the need and demand for more effective sharing and absorption of knowledge through digital platforms and through the licensing and other transmission of knowledge products as policymakers seek first to understand and then to adapt to the 'new normal'. The editors therefore express the hope that the ideas and possibilities explored in this volume will help to illuminate the difficult path ahead through a more complex policy landscape.

Bibliography

Anell, Lars, 'Keynote speech at the TRIPS Symposium, 26 February 2015', in Jayashree Watal and Antony Taubman, *The Making of TRIPS*, Geneva: WTO, 2015, 285–291.

Bacon, Francis, 'The New Atlantis', available at www.gutenberg.org/files/2434/2434-h/2434-h.htm.

Berners-Lee, Tim, 'Information Management: A Proposal', CERN (March 1989, May 1990), available at www.w3.org/History/1989/proposal.html.

Berners-Lee, Tim, *Weaving the Web*, New York: Harper Collins, 1999.

Bush, Vannevar, 'As We May Think', *The Atlantic*, July 1945.

Jefferson, Thomas, *The Writings of Thomas Jefferson.* Edited by Andrew A. Lipscomb and Albert Ellery Bergh. 20 vols, Washington, DC: Thomas Jefferson Memorial Association, 1905, 13: 333–335, available at https://press-pubs.uchicago.edu/founders/documents/a1_8_8s12.html.

Otlet, Paul, *Traité de documentation*, Brussels: Editiones Mundaneum, 1934.

Romer, Paul, 'Endogenous Technological Change', *Journal of Political Economy*, (1990), 98, 5 Part 2: S71–S102.

Romer, Paul, 'Two Strategies for Economic Development: Using Ideas and Producing Ideas', in *Proceedings of the World Bank Annual Conference on Development Economics 1992*, Washington, DC: The International Bank for Reconstruction and Development, 1993, 63–92 at 89.

Romer, Paul, 'The Origins of Endogenous Growth', *The Journal of Economic Perspectives* (Winter, 1994), 8: 3–22, at 8.

Romer, Paul, 'Nobel Lecture: On the possibility of progress' (February 5, 2019), available at https://paulromer.net/prize/.

Taubman, Antony, 'Cereal Offenders: Access and Equity in Trade Negotiations on Knowledge Resources', in Jay Kesan (ed.), *Agricultural Biotechnology and Intellectual Property: Seeds of Change*, Oxford: CABI Publishing Co., 2007.

Taubman, Antony, 'A Typology of Intellectual Property Management for Public Health Innovation and Access: Design Considerations for Policymakers', *Open AIDS Journal* (2010) 4: 4–24, available at www.ncbi.nlm.nih.gov/pmc/articles/PMC2878976/.

Taubman, Antony, 'Thematic review: Negotiating "Trade-Related Aspects" of Intellectual Property Rights', in Jayashree Watal and Antony Taubman (eds), *The Making of TRIPS*, Geneva: WTO, 2015.

World Wide Web Consortium (W3C), 'A Little History of the World Wide Web', n.d., available at www.w3.org/History.html.

WTO Secretariat, 'Electronic Commerce and the Role of the WTO', Geneva, 1998, at 59–64, available at www.wto.org/english/res_e/booksp_e/special_study_2_e.pdf.

Yu, Peter K., 'TRIPS and Its Contents', *IDEA: The IP Law Review*, (2019) 60, Texas A&M University School of Law Legal Studies Research Paper No. 19-36, available at SSRN: https://ssrn.com/abstract=3448332.

INDEX

For EU product safety concerns, contact us at Calle de José Abascal, 56–1°, 28003 Madrid, Spain or eugpsr@cambridge.org.

www.ingramcontent.com/pod-product-compliance
Lightning Source LLC
LaVergne TN
LVHW010337220926
848484LV00004BB/916
* 9 7 8 1 1 0 8 4 9 0 4 2 9 *